WHERE TO STAY ENGLAND 1997

CONTENTS

Key to Symbols

Inside back cover

Front cover:
Middle Ord Manor House,
Berwick-upon-Tweed,
Northumberland.
Back cover: (from top)
Holmfield, Kendal, Cumbria.
Shawswell Country House,
Rendcomb, Gloucestershire.
The Old Parsonage, Royal
Tunbridge Wells, Kent.

D1741097

1

WELCOME TO THE GUIDE

You may be in England for business or pleasure. Rushing around or enjoying a well-earned holiday. Wherever you're heading, at the end of the day if you're looking for accommodation, you can depend on *Where to Stay*.

Sure signs of where to stay

Many different types of accommodation are described in this guide, though they all have one thing in common. Each entry has been inspected (or applied for inspection) under the ETB's official National Quality Grading and Classification Scheme. The Scheme is your assurance of facilities and service: Crowns show you the range of facilities provided to guests; Quality Gradings indicate the overall standard of welcome, service and accommodation. To find out more, turn to page 4.

Easy to use

Whether you know exactly in which town you want to stay or have only an idea of the area you wish to visit, it couldn't be easier to find accommodation to suit you in *Where to Stay*.

For this reason, we've included a comprehensive town index and full colour location maps to help you locate your accommodation easily. We've also listed establishment entries in alphabetical order by location, region by region. In fact, you'll find all the information you need is listed in an easy-to-follow format.

Turn to the Information section beginning on page 407 for lots of useful information and advice on making a booking, as well as events and location maps. It's all there to make finding your accommodation easy and put your mind at rest - and make sure you've nothing to think about but planning what to visit when you arrive!

A SIGN OF QUALITY

Knowing what to expect is vital when choosing a place to stay whether you're taking a short break, are away on business, or visiting family or friends. Whatever type of accommodation you are looking for, you'll find that establishments in *Where to Stay* offer reassurance provided by the English Tourist Board's official National Quality Grading and Classification Scheme.

Classification of facilities

An establishment's assessment under the Scheme will usually consist of two parts: the first, using the Crown symbol, classifies the range of services and facilities provided for guests; the second, from De Luxe to Approved, indicates the overall quality standard of these services and facilities.

The range of services and facilities provided is classified under one of six bands: from **Listed** (clean and comfortable accommodation, but limited range of services and facilities) to **Five Crown** (providing a full range of services and facilities). Quite simply, the more Crowns, the wider the range

Please note that a higher number of Crowns does not necessarily imply that the quality on offer is superior to that available at an establishment with fewer Crowns.

Quality grading

A separate quality grading indicates the overall standard of services and facilities. Graded establishments are awarded one of the following quality gradings:

DE LUXE
   (excellent overall standard)

HIGHLY COMMENDED
   (very good overall standard)

COMMENDED
   (good overall standard)

APPROVED
   (acceptable overall standard)

Before awarding a quality grading, Tourist Board inspectors check in as a guest, only identifying themselves after paying the bill. They assess the warmth of the welcome and level of care and service they receive, as well as the standard and state of the decor, furnishings and fittings. Their overall assessment takes the nature and size of the establishments into account; you will therefore find that all types of accommodation have been able to achieve a Highly Commended or De Luxe quality grading.

If no quality grade appears alongside the Crown classification, it means that the proprietor has applied for but was still awaiting inspection at the time of going to press.

Range of facilities

Listed and then **One to Five Crown** tell you the range of facilities provided. The more Crowns, the wider the range. Below is an indication of some of the facilities you can expect under each classification.

Listed Clean and comfortable accommodation, but limited range of facilities and services.

♛ There will be additional facilities, including washbasin and chair in your bedroom, and you will have the use of a telephone.

♛♛ There will be a colour TV in your bedroom or in a lounge and you can enjoy morning tea/coffee in your room. At least some of the bedrooms will have private bath (or shower) and WC.

♛♛♛ At least half of the bedrooms will have private bath (or shower) en-suite. You will also be able to order a hot evening meal.

♛♛♛♛ Your bedroom will have a colour TV, radio and telephone; 90% of bedrooms will have private bath and/or shower and WC en-suite. There will be lounge service until midnight and evening meals can be ordered up to 2030 hours.

♛♛♛♛♛ Every bedroom will have private bath, fixed shower and WC en-suite. The restaurant will be open for breakfast, lunch and dinner (or you can take meals into your room from breakfast until midnight) and you will benefit from an all-night lounge service. A night porter will also be on duty.

Lodge accommodation

The Lodge classification covers purpose-built bedroom accommodation that you will find along major roads and motorways. The range of facilities is indicated by **One** to **Three Moon** symbols. A separate quality grading indicates the overall standard of these facilities.

● Your bedroom will have at least a washbasin and radio or colour TV. Tea/coffee may be from a vending machine in a public area.

●● Your room will have colour TV, tea/coffee-making facilities and en-suite bath or shower with WC.

●●● You will find colour TV and radio, tea/coffee-making facilities and comfortable seating in your bedroom and there will be a bath, shower and WC en-suite. The reception will be manned throughout the night.

Accessible Scheme

If you have difficulty walking or are a wheelchair user, it is important to be able to identify those establishments that will be able to cater for your requirements. If you book accommodation displaying an Accessible symbol, there's no longer any guesswork involved. Establishments can be awarded one of these categories of accessibility:

Category 1 accessible to all wheelchair users including those travelling independently

Category 2 accessible to a wheelchair user with assistance

Category 3 accessible to a wheelchair user able to walk short distances and up at least three steps.

See page 10 for a full list of establishments in this guide who have an Accessible symbol.

FINDING YOUR IDEAL ACCOMMODATION

Whatever your requirements, your preferences or your price range, *Where to Stay* will lead you straight to a selection of fine accommodation in England. From prices, quality and facilities on offer, you can see what's available at a glance.

Regional sections

The guide is divided into eleven regional sections. See the map on page 12. Each section contains an alphabetical listing of the region's cities, towns and villages with their accommodation establishments.

At the beginning of each section is a brief description of the area and a selection of interesting places to visit which may persuade you to stay a little longer - an illustrative map shows where they can be found.

Town index and location maps

The town index on page 431 and the colour location maps at the back of the guide show all the places featuring accommodation in this guide.

If the place you plan to visit is included in the town index, turn to the page number given for accommodation.

If, however, it is not included in the town index - or you just have a general idea of the area in which you wish to stay - use the colour location maps. You will find accommodation in all the places printed in black. Then simply refer back to the town index for the relevant page.

Service and facilities

Each accommodation listing contains detailed information to help you decide if it is right for you. This information has been provided by the proprietors themselves, and our aim has been to ensure that it is as objective and factual as possible.

Below the establishment name you will find the Crown classification, Listed or One to Five Crown, which indicates the range of services and facilities provided. The quality grading, De Luxe, Highly Commended, Commended or Approved tells you the overall standard of services and facilities. Detailed information on classification and gradings can be found on page 408.

At-a-glance symbols at the end of each entry give you additional information on services and facilities - a key to symbols can be found on the back cover flap. Keep this open to refer to as you read.

Accessibility

If you are a wheelchair user or have difficulty walking, look for the Accessible symbol. You will find a full list of entries participating in the National Accessible Scheme on page 10.

Check for changes

Please remember that changes may occur after the guide is printed. When you have found a suitable place to stay we advise you to contact the establishment to check availability, and also to confirm prices and any specific facilities which may be important to you. The coupons at the back of the guide will help you with your enquiries.

Then make your booking and, if you have time, confirm it in writing.

Further information

You may find it useful to read the information pages at the back of this guide (see page 407), particularly the section on cancellations.

Town Name ▶

Map reference ▶

Town description ▶

Establishment name ▶
National Crown classification ▶
and quality grading

Address, telephone and ▶
fax numbers

Establishment description ▶

National wheelchair access ▶
category

Accommodation, ▶
price guide and facilities

At-a-glance symbols - see ▶
flap on back cover

TAUNTON

Somerset
Map Ref 1D1

County town, well-known for its public schools, sheltered by gentle hill-ranges on the River Tone

Tower Hotel ♠♠
👑👑👑 COMMENDED

River Street, Taunton TA9 2PW
☎ (01823) 000111
Fax (01823) 000111

Charming family-run hotel with walled garden and conservatory restaurant. Ideal base for exploring.
Wheelchair access category 2 ♿
Bedrooms: 10 single, 20 twin, 13 double
Bathrooms: 43 private

Bed & breakfast

per night:	£min	£max
Double	53.00	104.00

Lunch available
Evening meal 1930 (last orders 2130)
Parking for 40
Cards accepted: Access, Visa, Amex

🔣🔣🔣🔣🔣🔣🔣🔣🔣🔣🔣🔣🔣🔣🔣
🍸10-70 ♌ ▶ 🔣🔣 SP 🔣 T

A LOOK AT SOME OF THE BEST

The award of a DE LUXE quality grade recognises an establishment's excellent overall standard of such things as warmth of welcome, general atmosphere and ambience, efficiency of service, as well as the quality of facilities and standard of fittings.

The inspector's overall assessment takes the nature and size of an establishment into account; you will therefore find all types of accommodation can achieve a DE LUXE quality grading.

This page features those establishments in *Where to Stay* that have achieved the highest quality grade of DE LUXE. Use the Town Index at the back of the guide to find page numbers for their fully detailed entries.

The Courtyard, Corbridge, Northumberland

Broadview, Crewkerne, Somerset
Causa Grange, Rosley, Cumbria
Cockford Hall, Clun, Shropshire
The Courtyard, Corbridge, Northumberland
Holmfield, Kendal, Cumbria
Hope House, Tynemouth, Tyne & Wear
Isbourne Manor House, Winchcombe, Gloucestershire
Meadowland, Bath, Bath and North East Somerset
Middle Ord Manor House, Berwick-upon-Tweed, Northumberland
The Old Parsonage, Royal Tunbridge Wells, Kent
Shawswell Country House, Rendcomb, Gloucestershire
Tavern House, Tetbury, Gloucestershire

Broadview, Crewkerne, Somerset

Meadowland, Bath, Bath and North East Somerset

USE YOUR *i*'S

When it comes to your next England break, the first stage of your journey could be closer than you think. You've probably got a Tourist Information Centre nearby which is there to serve the local community - as well as visitors.

So make us your first stop. We'll be happy to help you, wherever you're heading.

Many Tourist Information Centres can provide you with maps and guides, helping you plan well in advance. And sometimes it's even possible for us to book your accommodation, too.

A visit to your nearest Information Centre can pay off in other ways as well. We can point you in the right direction when it comes to finding out about all the special events which are happening in the local region.

In fact, we can give you details of places to visit within easy reach... and perhaps tempt you to plan a day trip or weekend away.

Across the country, there are more than 550 Tourist Information Centres so you're never far away. You'll find the address of your nearest Tourist Information Centre in your local Phone Book.

NATIONAL ACCESSIBLE SCHEME

Throughout Britain, the Tourist Boards are inspecting all types of places to stay, on holiday or business, that provide accessible accommodation for wheelchair users and others who may have difficulty walking.

The Tourist Boards recognise three categories of accessibility:

Category 1
Accessible to all wheelchair users including those travelling independently.

Category 2
Accessible to a wheelchair user with assistance.

Category 3
Accessible to a wheelchair user able to walk short distances and up at least three steps.

If you have additional needs or special requirements of any kind, we strongly recommend that you make sure these can be met by your chosen establishment before you confirm your booking.

The criteria the Tourist Boards have adopted do not, necessarily, conform to British Standards or to Building Regulations. They reflect what the Boards understand to be acceptable to meet the practical needs of wheelchair users.

The following establishments listed in this *Where to Stay* guide had been inspected and given an access category at the time of going to press. Use the Town Index at the back of the guide to find page numbers for their full entries.

Category 1

CROOKHAM, NORTHUMBERLAND
- The Coach House
DULVERTON, SOMERSET
- Scatterbrook Farm
LUDLOW, SHROPSHIRE
- Corndene
SELSEY, WEST SUSSEX
- St Andews Lodge
SHEFFIELD
- University of Sheffield
WIMBORNE MINSTER, DORSET
- Northill House

Category 2

ASHBOURNE, DERBYSHIRE
- Ilam Hall YHA
GARBOLDISHAM, NORFOLK
- Ingleneuk Lodge
LUDLOW, SHROPSHIRE
- Corndene
STRATFORD-UPON-AVON, WARWICKSHIRE
- Penshurst Guesthouse

Category 3

AMBLESIDE, CUMBRIA
- Borrans Park Hotel
- Rowanfield Country Guesthouse
ARUNDEL, WEST SUSSEX
- Mill Lane House
BAKEWELL, DERBYSHIRE
- Tannery House
BOSCASTLE, CORNWALL
- The Old Coach House
CONGLETON, CHESHIRE
- Sandhole Farm
DEVIZES, WILTSHIRE
- Pinecroft
ELLERBY, NORTH YORKSHIRE
Ellerby Hotel

ERLESTOKE, WILTSHIRE
- Longwater
FROME, SOMERSET
- Fourwinds Guest House
HADLEIGH, SUFFOLK
- Odds and Ends House
HENLEY-ON-THAMES,
OXFORDSHIRE
- Holmwood
HENSTRIDGE, SOMERSET
- Fountain Inn Motel
INGLETON, NORTH YORKSHIRE
- Riverside Lodge
LENHAM, KENT
- The Dog & Bear Hotel
NAILSWORTH,
GLOUCESTERSHIRE
- Apple Orchard House
NORTHALLERTON,
NORTH YORKSHIRE
- Lovesome Hill Farm

RICHMOND, NORTH YORKSHIRE
- Mount Pleasant Farm
SANDBACH, CHESHIRE
- Canal Centre and Village Store
SARRE, KENT
- Crown Inn (The Famous Cherry
Brandy House)
SOUTH CAVE,
EAST RIDING OF YORKSHIRE
- Rudstone Walk Farmhouse
& Country Cottages
STRATFORD-UPON-AVON,
WARWICKSHIRE
- Church Farm
THIRSK, NORTH YORKSHIRE
- Doxford House
WESTOW, NORTH YORKSHIRE
- Blacksmiths Arms Inn
WINCHESTER, HAMPSHIRE
- Shawlands
YOXALL, STAFFORDSHIRE
- The Moat

The National Accessible Scheme forms part of the Tourism for All Campaign that is being promoted by all three National Tourist Boards. Additional help and guidance on finding suitable holiday accommodation for those with special needs can be obtained from:
Holiday Care Service
2 Old Bank Chambers,
Station Road,
Horley, Surrey RH6 9HW.
Tel: (01293) 774535.
Fax: (01293) 784647.
Minicom: (01293) 776943.

KEY TO
REGIONAL SECTIONS

This *Where to Stay* guide is divided into 11 regional sections as shown on the map below. To identify each regional section and its page number, please refer to the key opposite. The index lists the counties of England and indicates under which regional section you will find them.

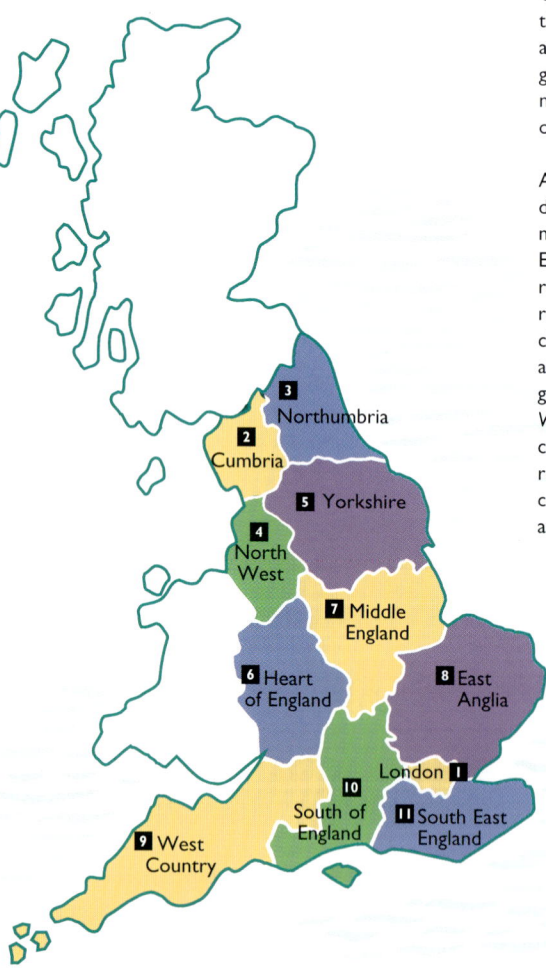

Colour location maps showing all the cities, towns and villages with accommodation listed in this guide, and an index to the place names, can be found at the back of the guide.

As you are probably aware, during 1996 the boundaries and names of a number of counties in England were changed as the result of local government reorganisation. The main county changes that had been announced at the time of compiling the 1997 guide have been reflected in *Where to Stay*, particularly in the county index opposite, the regional section maps, in the colour location maps at the back and in the town descriptions.**

If you want to find out more about what there is to see and do in a particular area, contact the appropriate Regional Tourist Board. Details are given both at the beginning and end of each regional section.

KEY TO MAP

** This is how you will find the following county changes have been reflected in *Where to Stay*:

Avon is replaced by Bath & North East Somerset, City of Bristol, North Somerset and South Gloucestershire

Cleveland is replaced by Tees Valley

Humberside is replaced by East Riding of Yorkshire, North Lincolnshire and North East Lincolnshire.

Although there have been changes to the unitary authority boundaries in the following areas, you will see that the familiar regional names have been retained for: Greater Manchester, Merseyside, South Yorkshire, Tyne & Wear, West Midlands and West Yorkshire

Please note that further changes are planned for 1997 which have yet to be confirmed.

COUNTY INDEX

Bath & North East Somerset:
West Country
Bedfordshire:
East Anglia
Berkshire:
South of England
Buckinghamshire:
South of England
Cambridgeshire:
East Anglia
Cheshire:
North West
City of Bristol:
West Country
Cornwall:
West Country
Cumbria:
Cumbria
Derbyshire:
Middle England
Derbyshire High Peak District:
North West
Devon:
West Country
Dorset (Eastern):
West Country
Dorset (Western):
South of England
Durham:
Northumbria
East Riding of Yorkshire:
Yorkshire
Essex:
East Anglia
Gloucestershire:
Heart of England
Greater London:
London
Greater Manchester:
North West
Hampshire:
South of England
Hereford & Worcester:
Heart of England
Hertfordshire:
East Anglia
Isle of Wight:
South of England
Isles of Scilly:
West Country
Kent:
South East England

Lancashire:
North West
Leicestershire:
Middle England
Lincolnshire:
Middle England
Merseyside:
North West
Norfolk:
East Anglia
North Lincolnshire:
Yorkshire
North East Lincolnshire:
Yorkshire
North Somerset:
West Country
North Yorkshire:
Yorkshire
Northamptonshire:
Middle England
Northumberland:
Northumbria
Nottinghamshire:
Middle England
Oxfordshire:
South of England
Shropshire:
Heart of England
Somerset:
West Country
South Gloucestershire:
West Country
South Yorkshire:
Yorkshire
Staffordshire:
Heart of England
Suffolk:
East Anglia
Surrey:
South East England
Tees Valley:
Northumbria
Tyne & Wear:
Northumbria
Warwickshire:
Heart of England
West Midlands:
Heart of England
West Sussex:
South East England
Wiltshire:
West Country

WHERE TO STAY

The official and best selling accommodation guides, offering the reassurance of the national quality grading and classification scheme

INSPECTED & QUALITY GRADED

Hotels & Guesthouses in England '97
£9.99

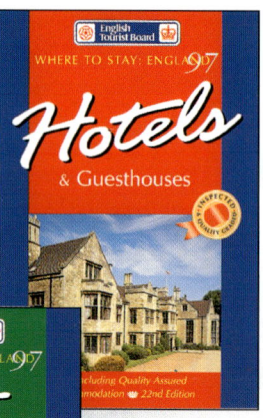

Bed & Breakfast, Farmhouses, Inns & Hostels in England '97
£8.99

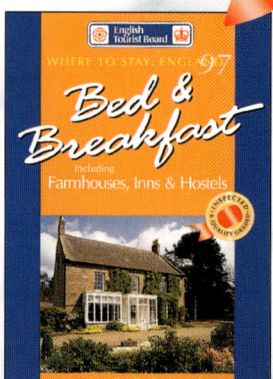

Self Catering Holiday Homes in England '97
£6.99

Camping & Caravan Parks in Britain '97
£4.99

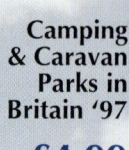

Families Welcome in England '97
£4.99

Somewhere Special in England '97
£7.99

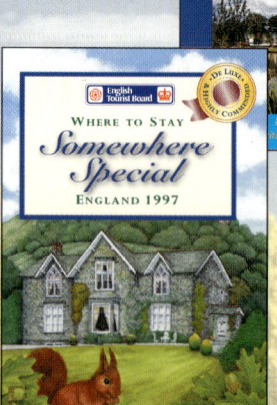

THE ENGLAND FOR EXCELLENCE AWARDS
WINNERS 1995

The England for Excellence Awards were created by the English Tourist Board to recognise and reward the highest standards of excellence and quality in all major sectors of tourism in England. The coveted Leo statuette, presented each year to winners, has become firmly established as the ultimate accolade in the English tourism industry.

Over the past eight years the Leo has been won by all types and sizes of business with one common attribute - excellence in the facilities and services they offer.

Hotel of the Year
Sponsored by Yellow Pages

The Four Seasons Hotel, London
(Five Crown, De Luxe)
London

Bed and Breakfast of the Year
Sponsored by Blackpool Pleasure Beach

Tree Tops
(Two Crown, De Luxe)
Berwick-upon-Tweed,
Northumberland

Holiday Centre of the Year
Sponsored by Senior King

Potters Leisure
Hopton on Sea, Norfolk

Self-Catering Holiday of the Year
Sponsored by Country Holidays Group

The Corbyn Holidays Suites & Villas - Brights of Nettlebe
(Five Key, De Luxe)
Torquay, Devon

Visitor Attraction of the Year
Sponsored by Hilton National

Hampton Court Palace
Surrey

Tourism Town of the Year
Sponsored by Marks & Spencer

Manchester - The City Visitor Destination

Tourism for All Award
Sponsored by Gould & Portmans

Cheshire County Council
'Tourism for All' Programme

Tourist Information Centre of the Year
Sponsored by Ordnance Survey

Sunderland Tourist Information Centre
Tyne and Wear

Outstanding Contribution to English Tourism Award
Sponsored by Hilton International

BBC TV / Pride and Prejudice

COUNTRY CODE

Always follow the Country Code

Enjoy the countryside and respect its life and work ‧ Guard against all risk of fire ‧ Fasten all gates ‧ Keep your dogs under close control ‧ Keep to public paths across farmland ‧ Use gates and stiles to cross fences, hedges and walls ‧ Leave livestock, crops and machinery alone ‧ Take your litter home ‧ Help to keep all water clean ‧ Protect wildlife, plants and trees ‧ Take special care on country roads ‧ Make no unnecessary noise

Information on accommodation listed in this guide has been supplied by the proprietors. As changes may occur you are advised to check details at the time of booking.

ACCESSIBILITY

Look for the 🚾♿🚶 symbols which indicate accessibility for wheelchair users. These are described in detail at the front of this guide.

National gradings and classifications were correct at the time of going to press but are subject to change. Please check at the time of booking.

WHERE TO STAY IN ENGLAND

Published by: English Tourist Board, Thames Tower, Black's Road, Hammersmith, London W6 9EL. ISBN 0 86143 199 5
Managing Editor: Jane Collinson
Technical Manager: Marita Sen
Compilation & Production: Guide Associates, Croydon
Design and illustrations: Jackson Lowe Marketing, Lewes, East Sussex
Colour Photography: Mike Williams (front cover)
Cartography: Colin Earl
Typesetting: Reed Technologies and Information Services, London and Jackson Lowe Marketing, Lewes
Printing and Binding: Bemrose Security Printing, Derby
Advertisement Sales: Madison Bell Ltd, 3 St. Peter's Street, Islington Green, London N1 8JD. (0171) 359 7737.

Important:
The information contained in this guide has been published in good faith on the basis of information submitted to the English Tourist Board by the proprietors of the premises listed, who have paid for their entries to appear. The English Tourist Board cannot guarantee the accuracy of the information in this guide and accepts no responsibility for any error or misrepresentation. All liability for loss, disappointment, negligence or other damage caused by reliance on the information contained in this guide, or in the event of bankruptcy, or liquidation, or cessation of trade of any company, individual or firm mentioned, is hereby excluded. Please check carefully all prices and other details before confirming a reservation.

The English Tourist Board
The Board is a statutory body created by the Development of Tourism Act 1969 to develop and market England's tourism. Its main objectives are to provide a welcome for people visiting England; to encourage people living in England to take their holidays there; and to encourage the provision and improvement of tourist amenities and facilities in England. The Board has a statutory duty to advise the Government on tourism matters relating to England and, with Government approval and support, administers the national classification and grading schemes for tourist accommodation in England.

LONDON

No one can capture the atmosphere of London in words alone. One of the eternally great cities, it remains true that 'if you're tired of London, you're tired of life'.

Buckingham Palace, the Tower and Madame Tussaud's are just the beginning... London has more than 100 museums and galleries, the finest theatres in the world and some of the most exciting shops, restaurants and markets.

Stroll through the many gracious parks, discover Jack the Ripper's East End, explore 'the City', follow in the footsteps of Dickens. Or if you prefer, hop on a red bus or catch a black cab. Whichever way you go, seeing the sights of London is an unforgettable experience.

FOR MORE INFORMATION CONTACT:
London Tourist Board
26 Grosvenor Gardens, London SW1W 0DU

Where to Go in London - see pages 18-20
Where to Stay in London - see pages 24-33

LONDON

Where to Go and What to See

You will find hundreds of interesting places to visit during your stay in London, just some of which are listed in these pages. Contact any Tourist Information Centre in the region for more ideas on days out in London.

■ **Bankside Gallery**
48 Hopton Street,
London SE1 9JH
Tel: (0171) 928 7521
Home of The Royal Watercolour Society and The Royal Society of Painter-Printmakers. Changing exhibitions of watercolours and prints.

■ **British Museum**
Great Russell Street,
London WC1B 3DG
Tel: (0171) 636 1555
One of the great museums of the world, showing the works of man from all over the world from prehistoric times to the present day.

■ **Cabinet War Rooms**
Clive Steps,
King Charles Street,
London SW1A 2AQ
Tel: (0171) 930 6961
The underground headquarters used by Winston Churchill and the British Government during World War II. Includes Cabinet Room,

transatlantic telephone room and Map Room.

■ **Design Museum**
Shad Thames,
London SE1 2YD
Tel: (0171) 403 6933
A study collection showing the development of design in mass production. Review of new products, graphics gallery, and changing programme of exhibitions.

■ **Dickens House**
48 Doughty Street,
London WC1N 2LF
Tel: (0171) 405 2127
Charles Dickens' home from 1837-1839. Collection of letters, pictures, first editions, furniture, memorabilia, restored rooms.

■ **Fan Museum**
12 Crooms Hill,
London SE10 8ER
Tel: (0181) 305 1441
The only venue in the world devoted entirely to the art and craft

of the fan. Changing exhibitions. Beautifully restored 18thC houses. Gift shop.

■ **Guards Museum**
Wellington Barracks,
Birdcage Walk,
London SW1E 6HQ
Tel: (0171) 414 3428
Collection of uniforms, colours and artefacts spanning over 300 years of history of the Foot Guards.

■ **Hampton Court Palace**
Hampton Court,
Surrey KT8 9AU
Tel: (0181) 781 9500
Oldest Tudor palace in England. Tudor kitchens, tennis courts, maze, state apartments and King's apartments.

■ **HMS Belfast**
Morgan's Lane, Tooley Street,
London SE1 2JH
Tel: (0171) 407 6434
11,500 tonne World War II cruiser moored on the Thames. Now a

floating naval museum, with seven decks to explore. Many naval exhibits on show.

■ Imperial War Museum
Lambeth Road,
London SE1 6HZ
Tel: (0171) 416 5000
The story of 20thC war from Flanders to Bosnia. Features include the Blitz Experience, Operation Jericho and the Trench Experience.

■ London Dungeon
28-34 Tooley Street,
London SE1 2SZ
Tel: (0171) 403 0606
World's first medieval horror museum. Now featuring two major shows: "The Jack the Ripper Experience" and "The Theatre of the Guillotine".

■ Madame Tussaud's
Marylebone Road,
London NW1 5LR
Tel: (0171) 935 6861
Wax figures in themed settings, including The Garden Party, 200 Years, Superstars, The Grand Hall, The Chamber of Horrors and The Spirit of London.

■ Museum of London
150 London Wall,
London EC2Y 5HN

Tel: (0171) 600 3699
Galleries illustrate over 2000 years of the capital's social history, from prehistoric times to the 20thC. Regular temporary exhibitions, lunchtime lecture programmes.

■ Museum of the Moving Image
South Bank, Waterloo,
London SE1 8XT
Tel: (0171) 928 3535
A celebration of cinema and television. 44 exhibit areas offer plenty of hands-on participation, and a cast of actors to tell visitors more.

■ National Gallery
Trafalgar Square,
London WC2N 5DN
Tel: (0171) 839 3321
Western painting from 1260-1920, including work by Van Gogh, Rembrandt, Cezanne, Turner, Gainsborough, Leonardo da Vinci, Renoir and Botticelli.

■ National Maritime Museum
Romney Road, Greenwich,
London SE10 9NF
Tel: (0181) 858 4422
Britain's maritime heritage illustrated through actual and model ships, paintings, uniforms, navigation and astronomy

instruments, archives and photographs. Queen's House.

■ National Portrait Gallery
St Martin's Place,
London WC2H 0HE
Tel: (0171) 306 0055
Permanent collection of portraits of famous men and women from the Middle Ages to the present day.

■ National Postal Museum
King Edward Building,
King Edward Street,
London EC1A 1LP
Tel: (0171) 239 5420
One of the most important and extensive collections of postage stamps in the world, including the Phillips and Berne Collections. Temporary exhibitions.

■ Natural History Museum
Cromwell Road,
London SW7 5BD
Tel: (0171) 938 9123
Home of the wonders of the natural world, one of the most popular museums in the world, and one of London's finest landmarks.

■ Old Royal Observatory
(Flamsteed House),
Greenwich Park,
London SE10 9NF
Tel: (0181) 858 4422

Museum of time and space. Greenwich Meridian, working telescopes, planetarium and timeball. Wren's Octagon Room. Intricate clocks and computer simulations. Restored in 1993.

■ Rock Circus
London Pavilion, Piccadilly Circus, London W1V 9LA
Tel: (0171) 734 7203
The exhibition is an amazing combination of stereo sound through personal headsets, audio animatronic (moving) and Madame Tussauds (wax) figures of over 50 rock stars.

■ Royal Air Force Museum
Grahame Park Way, London NW9 5LL
Tel: (0181) 205 2266
Britain's National Museum of aviation features over 70 full size aircraft, Flight Simulator, "Touch & Try" Jet Provost Trainer and Eurofighter 2000 Theatre.

■ Science Museum
Exhibition Road, London SW7 2DD
Tel: (0171) 938 8000
National Museum of Science and Industry. Full size replica of Apollo 11 Lunar Lander, launch pad, Wellcome Museum of History of Medicine, flight lab, food for thought, optics.

■ Sherlock Holmes Museum
221B Baker Street, London NW1 6XE
Tel: (0171) 935 8866
Grade 2 listed lodging house. 1st floor Holmes' apartment. Second floor Mrs Hudson's room and Doctor Watson's room. Third floor souvenir shop. Reading room and exhibition room.

■ Thames Barrier Visitors' Centre
Unity Way, London SE18 5NJ
Tel: (0181) 854 1373
Exhibition with 10-min video, a working scale model and a multimedia show. Also riverside walkways, children's play area and Thames Barrier Buffet.

■ Tower Bridge
London SE1 2UP
Tel: (0171) 403 3761
Exhibition explains the history of the bridge and how it operates. Original steam powered engines on view. Panoramic views from fully-glazed walkways. Gift shop.

■ Tower of London
Tower Hill, London EC3N 4AB
Tel: (0171) 709 0765
Building spans 900 years of British history. The nation's Crown Jewels, regalia and armoury robes on display. Home of the "Beefeaters" and ravens.

■ Victoria and Albert Museum
Cromwell Road, London SW7 2RL
Tel: (0171) 938 8500
The V & A is the world's finest museum of the decorative arts. Its collection, housed in magnificent Victorian buildings, span 2000 years including sculpture and furniture.

FIND OUT MORE
A free information pack about holidays and attractions in London is available on written request from:
London Tourist Board and Convention Bureau,
26 Grosvenor Gardens, London SW1W 0DU.

TOURIST INFORMATION

Tourist and leisure information can be obtained from Tourist Information Centres throughout England. Details of centres and other information services in Greater London are given below. The symbol 🛏 means that an accommodation booking service is provided.

Tourist Information Centres

Points of arrival
Victoria Station, Forecourt, SW1 🛏
Easter-October, daily 0800-1900.
November-Easter, reduced
opening hours.
Liverpool Street Underground Station, EC2 🛏
Monday-Friday 0800-1800.
Saturday-Sunday 0845-17.30.
Heathrow Terminals 1, 2, 3 Underground Station Concourse (Heathrow Airport) 🛏
Daily 0800-1800.
Heathrow Terminal 3 Arrivals Concourse 🛏
0600-2300.
Waterloo International Arrivals Hall 🛏
0830-2100
The above information centres provide a London and Britain tourist information service, offer a hotel accommodation booking service, stock free and saleable publications on Britain and London and sell theatre tickets, tourist tickets for bus and underground and tickets for sightseeing tours.

Inner London
British Travel Centre 🛏
12 Regent Street, Piccadilly
Circus, SW1Y 4PQ
Monday-Friday 0900-1830.
Saturday-Sunday 1000-1600
(0900-1700 Saturdays May-
September).

Tower Hamlets Tourist Information Centre
107a Commercial Street, E1 6BG
Tel: (0181) 375 2549
Monday-Friday 0930-1630.
Greenwich Tourist Information Centre 🛏
46 Greenwich Church Street,
SE10 9BL
Tel: (0181) 858 6376
April-September, daily
1015-1645. October-March,
reduced opening hours.
Hackney Museum and Tourist Information Centre
Central Hall, Mare Street, E8
Tel: (0181) 985 9055
Tuesday-Friday 1000-1700.
Saturday 1330-1700.
Islington Tourist Information Centre 🛏
44 Duncan Street, N1 8BW
Tel: (0171) 278 8787
Monday 1400-1600.
Tuesday-Saturday 1000-1700.
Lewisham Tourist Information Centre
Lewisham Library, Lewisham
High Street, SE13 6LG
Tel: (0181) 297 8317
Monday 1000-1700.
Tuesday-Friday 0900-1700
Selfridges 🛏
Oxford Street, W1. Basement
Services Arcade
Open during normal store hours.
Southwark Tourist Information Centre 🛏
Hay's Galleria,
Tooley Street, SE1 2HD
Tel: (0171) 403 8299

Monday-Friday 1030-1700.
Saturday-Sunday 1100-1700.
(Reduced winter opening).

Outer London
Bexley Tourist Information Centre
Central Library, Townley Road,
Bexleyheath DA6 7HJ
Tel: (0181) 303 9052
Monday, Tuesday, Thursday
0930-2000.
Wednesday & Friday 0930-1730.
Saturday 0930-1700.
Also at Hall Place Visitor Centre
Bourne Road, Bexley
Tel: (01322) 558676
June-September, daily 1130-1630.
Croydon Tourist Information Centre 🛏
Katharine Street,
Croydon CR9 1ET
Tel: (0181) 253 1009
Monday-Wednesday & Friday
0900-1800. Thursday 0930-1800.
Saturday 0900-1700.
Sunday 1200-1700.
Foots Cray Tourist Information Centre 🛏
Tesco Store Car Park,
Edgington Way, Sidcup DA14 5AH
Summer only, Monday-Saturday
1000-1800.
Sunday 1000-1600.
Harrow Tourist Information Centre
Civic Centre, Station Road,
Harrow HA1 2XF
Tel: (0181) 424 1103
Monday-Friday 0900-1700.

Hillingdon Tourist Information Centre

Central Library,
14 High Street,
Uxbridge UB8 1HD
Tel: Uxbridge (01895) 250706
Monday, Tuesday
& Thursday 0930-2000.
Friday & Wednesday 0930-1730.
Saturday 0930-1600.

Hounslow Tourist Information Centre

24 The Treaty Centre,
Hounslow High Street,
Hounslow TW3 1ES
Tel: (0181) 572 8279
Monday, Wednesday, Friday
& Saturday 0930-1730.
Tuesday, Thursday 0930-2000.

Kingston Tourist Information Centre

The Market House,
The Market Place,
Kingston upon Thames
KT1 1JS
Tel: (0181) 547 5592
Monday-Friday 1000-1700.
Saturday 0900-1600.

Redbridge Tourist Information Centre

Town Hall, High Road, Ilford,
Essex IG1 1DD
Tel: (0181) 478 3020
Monday-Friday 0830-1700.

Richmond Tourist Information Centre 🛏

Old Town Hall,
Whittaker Avenue,
Richmond upon Thames
TW9 1TP
Tel: (0181) 940 9125
Monday-Friday 1000-1800.
Saturday 1000-1700.
May-October,
also Sunday 1015-1615.

Twickenham Tourist Information Centre

The Altrium, Civic Centre,
York Street,
Twickenham TW1 3BZ
Tel: (0181) 891 7272
Monday-Friday 0900-1700.

Visitorcall

The London Tourist Board and Convention Bureau's 'Phone Guide to London' operates 24 hours a day. To access a full range of information call 0839 123456. To access specific lines dial 0839 123 followed by:

What's on this week - 400
What's on next 3 months - 401
Sunday in London - 407
Rock and pop concerts - 422
Popular attractions - 480
Where to take children - 424
Museums - 429
Palaces (including Buckingham Palace) - 481
Current exhibitions - 403
Changing the Guard - 411
Popular West End shows - 416
London dining - 485
Calls cost 45p per minute cheap rate, 50p per minute at all other times (as at October '96).
To order a Visitorcall card please call (0171) 971 0026. Information for callers using push-button telephones: (0171) 971 0027.

Artsline

London's information and advice service for disabled people on arts and entertainment. Call (0171) 388 2227.

Hotel Accommodation Service

The London Tourist Board and Convention Bureau helps visitors to find and book accommodation at a wide range of prices in hotels and guesthouses, including budget accommodation, throughout the Greater London area.

Reservations are made with hotels which are members of LTB, denoted in this guide with the symbol ⋀ by their name. Reservations can be made by credit card holders via the telephone accommodation reservations service on (0171) 824 8844 by simply giving the reservation clerk your card details (Access or Visa) and room requirements. LTB takes an administrative booking fee. The service operates Monday-Friday 0930-1730.

Reservations on arrival are handled at the Tourist Information Centres operated by LTB at Victoria Station, Liverpool Street Station, Waterloo International, Selfridges and Heathrow. Go to any of them on the day when you need accommodation. A communication charge and a refundable deposit are payable when making a reservation.

Which part of London?

The majority of tourist accommodation is situated in the central parts of London and is therefore very convenient for most of the city's attractions and night life.

However, there are many hotels in outer London which provide other advantages, such as easier parking. In the 'Where to Stay' pages which follow, you will find accommodation listed under INNER LONDON (covering the E1 to W14 London Postal Area) and OUTER LONDON (covering the remainder of Greater London). Colour maps 6 and 7 at the back of the guide show place names and London Postal Area codes and will help you to locate accommodation in your chosen area of London.

LONDON INDEX

If you are looking for accommodation in a particular establishment in London and you know its name, this index will give you the page number of the full entry in the guide.

ENQUIRY COUPONS

To help you obtain further information about advertisers and accommodation featured in this guide you will find enquiry coupons at the back. Send these directly to the establishments in which you are interested. Remember to complete both sides of the coupon.

WHERE TO STAY (LONDON)

Accommodation entries in this section are listed under **Inner London** (covering the postcode areas E1 to W14) and **Outer London** (covering the remainder of Greater London) - please refer to the colour location maps 6 and 7 at the back of this guide.

If you want to look up a particular establishment, use the index on the previous page which will give you the page number.

At-a-glance symbols at the end of each accommodation entry give useful information about services and facilities. A key to symbols can be found inside the back cover flap. Keep this open for easy reference.

INNER LONDON

Colour maps 6 & 7 at the back of the guide show place names and London Postal Area Codes and will help you locate accommodation in your chosen area of London

LONDON E4

Aucklands

Listed

25 Eglington Road, North Chingford, London E4 7AN
☎ (0181) 529 1140
Fax (0181) 508 3837
Comfortable Edwardian period family home with exclusive facilities in quiet suburb, easy access to City. Solar-heated swimming pool in landscaped garden. Gourmet meals on request.
Bedrooms: 1 double, 1 twin
Bathrooms: 1 public

Bed & breakfast per night:

	£min	£max
Single	30.00	
Double	60.00	

Half board per person:

	£min	£max
Daily	45.00	

Lunch available
Evening meal 1700 (last orders 2300)

LONDON E10

Sleeping Beauty Motel **M**

APPROVED

543 Lea Bridge Road, Leyton, London E10 7EB
☎ (0181) 556 8080
Fax (0181) 556 8080

All rooms en-suite with bath and shower, satellite TV, direct-dial telephone, hairdryer, hospitality tray, trouser press, mini fridge, safe. Ironing facilities, 24-hour reception, lift, free car park, bar.
Bedrooms: 16 double, 21 twin, 4 triple
Bathrooms: 40 en-suite

Bed & breakfast per night:

	£min	£max
Single	40.00	45.00
Double	45.00	50.00

Parking for 34
Cards accepted: Access, Visa, Diners, Amex, Switch/Delta

LONDON N1

Kandara Guest House **M**

Listed

68 Ockendon Road, London N1 3NW
☎ (0171) 226 5721 & 226 3379
Small family-run guesthouse near the Angel, Islington. Free street parking and good public transport to West End and City.
Bedrooms: 4 single, 2 double, 3 twin, 1 triple
Bathrooms: 3 public

Bed & breakfast per night:

	£min	£max
Single	26.00	29.00
Double	36.00	39.00

Cards accepted: Access, Visa

LONDON N7

Five Kings Guest House **M**

59 Anson Road, Tufnell Park, London N7 0AR
☎ (0171) 607 3996 & 607 6466
Privately-run guesthouse in a quiet residential area. 15 minutes to central London. Unrestricted parking in road.
Bedrooms: 6 single, 3 double, 3 twin, 2 triple, 2 family rooms
Bathrooms: 9 en-suite, 3 public, 2 private showers

Bed & breakfast per night:

	£min	£max
Single	18.00	27.00
Double	30.00	38.00

Cards accepted: Access, Visa

LONDON N13

71 Berkshire Gardens

Listed APPROVED

Palmers Green, London N13 6AA
☎ (0181) 888 5573
2-storey house with garden, 5 minutes' bus ride from Wood Green Piccadilly line underground station. Car parking available.
Bedrooms: 1 single, 1 twin
Bathrooms: 1 public

Bed & breakfast

per night:	£min	£max
Single	14.00	17.00
Double	26.00	30.00

Lunch available
Evening meal 1800 (last orders 2000)
Parking for 1

🐎10 🗶🖳📺🖵🛇👜ᵁᴸ🔌ⓈⒺ✂🎿📺🛏 🚗✳✈�🚭

LONDON N22

Pane Residence

Listed

154 Boundary Road, Wood Green,
London N22 6AE
☎ (0181) 889 3735
*In a pleasant location 6 minutes' walk
from Turnpike Lane underground
station and near Alexandra Palace.
Kitchen facilities available.*
Bedrooms: 1 single, 2 twin
Bathrooms: 1 public
Bed & breakfast

per night:	£min	£max
Single	16.00	18.00
Double	23.00	27.00

Parking for 2

🐎1 🖳👜ᵁᴸ👜🛏🚗✳✈�

LONDON NW4

Rilux House

♛♛

1 Lodge Road, London NW4 4DD
☎ (0181) 203 0933
Fax (0181) 203 6446
*High standard, all private facilities,
kitchenette and garden. Quiet. Close to
underground, buses, M1, 20 minutes
West End. Convenient for Wembley,
easy route to Heathrow, direct trains to
Gatwick and Luton airports. Close to
Middlesex University.*
Bedrooms: 1 twin
Bathrooms: 1 en-suite
Bed & breakfast

per night:	£min	£max
Single	27.50	30.00
Double	45.00	50.00

Parking for 1

🐎👜🖳🖵📺🛇👜ᵁᴸ👜✂🎿📺🛏 🚗✳✈�Ⓓᴬᴾ🚭ⓈᴾⓉ

LONDON NW10

30 All Souls Avenue

Listed

Willesden, London NW10 6AR
☎ (0181) 965 6051
Fax (0181) 965 6051
*Family-run house, 20 minutes from
Baker Street.*
Bedrooms: 1 single, 2 twin
Bathrooms: 2 public

Bed & breakfast

per night:	£min	£max
Single	15.00	18.00
Double	28.00	34.00

Half board per

person:	£min	£max
Daily	18.00	20.00
Weekly	105.00	115.00

🐎8 🖳🖵🛇👜ᵁᴸⓈ✂🎿🛏🚗✳ 🐕�

J and T Guest House

Listed

98 Park Avenue North, Willesden
Green, London NW10 1JY
☎ (0181) 452 4085
Fax (0181) 450 2503
*Small guesthouse in north west London
close to underground. Easy access to
Wembley Stadium complex. 5 minutes
from M1.*
Bedrooms: 1 single, 1 double, 3 twin,
1 triple
Bathrooms: 2 en-suite, 4 private
Bed & breakfast

per night:	£min	£max
Single	29.00	35.00
Double	42.00	52.00

Parking for 2
Cards accepted: Access, Visa,
Switch/Delta

🐎👜📞🖳🖵🛇👜ᵁᴸ🛏🚗✈� Ⓣ

LONDON SE6

41 Minard Road

Listed COMMENDED

Catford, London SE6 1NP
☎ (0181) 697 2596
*English home in quiet residential area
off A205 South Circular Road. 10
minutes' walk to Hither Green station
for 20-minute journey to central
London.*
Bedrooms: 1 single, 2 twin
Bathrooms: 1 public
Bed & breakfast

per night:	£min	£max
Single	18.00	18.00
Double	36.00	36.00

Half board per

person:	£min	£max
Daily	25.00	25.00
Weekly	157.50	

Evening meal 1700 (last orders
2000)

🐎🗶🖵🛇👜ᵁᴸ👜📺📺🛏🚗✳✈� Ⓢᴾ

LONDON SE12

Kingsland House

45 Southbrook Road, Lee, London
SE12 8LJ
☎ (0181) 318 4788
Detached house in conservation area,

---

*close to Blackheath and Greenwich
and with easy access to City and West
End. Off A205 South Circular Road and
8 minutes' walk from Lee station.
Homely atmosphere.*
Bedrooms: 1 single, 2 twin
Bathrooms: 2 public
Bed & breakfast

per night:	£min	£max
Single	22.00	25.00
Double	42.00	48.00

🐎🖵🛇👜📺🛏🚗✳�

LONDON SE21

Diana Hotel

♛♛

88 Thurlow Park Road, London
SE21 8HY
☎ (0181) 670 3250
Fax (0181) 761 9152
*Comfortable and friendly family-run
hotel near Dulwich Village, a pleasant
suburb 10 minutes by train from
central London.*
Bedrooms: 1 single, 4 double, 3 twin,
2 triple, 1 family room
Bathrooms: 4 en-suite, 2 public,
2 private showers
Bed & breakfast

per night:	£min	£max
Single	28.00	38.00
Double	38.00	48.00

Evening meal 1800 (last orders
1930)
Parking for 3
Cards accepted: Access, Visa

🐎👜🖵🛇👜📺📺🛏🚗�ⓈᴾⓉ

LONDON SE22

Bedknobs ⛰

Listed COMMENDED

58 Glengarry Road, East Dulwich,
London SE22 8QD
☎ (0181) 299 2004
Fax (0181) 693 5611
*Carefully restored Victorian family-run
house offering many home comforts,
excellent service and a warm welcome.
BTA London B&B Award 1992.*
Bedrooms: 1 double, 2 twin
Bathrooms: 2 public
Bed & breakfast

per night:	£min	£max
Single	20.00	32.00
Double	40.00	60.00

🐎🖳🖵🛇👜ᵁᴸ👜Ⓢ✂🛏🚗✈�

For further information on
accommodation establishments
use the coupons at the
back of this guide.

LONDON SW1

Brindle House Hotel ⚠

Listed

1 Warwick Place North, London
SW1V 1QW
☎ (0171) 828 0057
Fax (0171) 931 8805
*Small and quiet (off main road) bed
and breakfast ideally located for
Victoria bus, train and underground
stations. Good atmosphere.*
Bedrooms: 4 single, 4 double, 2 twin,
2 triple
Bathrooms: 2 public, 5 private
showers

**Bed & breakfast
per night:**

	£min	£max
Single	28.00	30.00
Double	38.00	44.00

Cards accepted: Access, Visa, Diners,
Amex

Caswell Hotel

Listed

25 Gloucester Street, London
SW1V 2DB
☎ (0171) 834 6345
*Pleasant, family-run hotel, near Victoria
coach and rail stations, yet in a quiet
location.*
Bedrooms: 1 single, 6 double, 6 twin,
3 triple, 2 family rooms
Bathrooms: 7 en-suite, 5 public

**Bed & breakfast
per night:**

	£min	£max
Single	28.00	52.00
Double	39.00	65.00

Central House Hotel ⚠

Listed APPROVED

39 Belgrave Road, London
SW1V 2BB
☎ (0171) 834 8036 & 828 0644
Fax (0171) 834 1854
*Situated within minutes of Victoria
coach, rail and underground stations. All*

rooms have en-suite facilities,
telephones, etc. Newly refurbished with
lift serving all floors.
Bedrooms: 4 single, 18 double,
19 twin, 6 triple, 3 family rooms
Bathrooms: 50 en-suite, 1 public

**Bed & breakfast
per night:**

	£min	£max
Single	35.00	49.00
Double	55.00	69.00

Cards accepted: Access, Visa

Elizabeth Hotel ⚠

👑

37 Eccleston Square, Victoria,
London SW1V 1PB
☎ (0171) 828 6812

*Friendly, quiet hotel overlooking
magnificent gardens of stately
residential square (circa 1835), close to
Belgravia yet within 5 minutes' walk of
Victoria. Free colour brochure.*
Bedrooms: 6 single, 5 double, 4 twin,
16 triple, 7 family rooms
Bathrooms: 26 en-suite, 8 private,
1 public, 1 private shower

**Bed & breakfast
per night:**

	£min	£max
Single	36.00	55.00
Double	62.00	84.00

Ad See display advertisement on this
page

For ideas on places to visit
refer to the introduction at
the beginning of this section.

Georgian House Hotel ⚠

Listed

35 St. George's Drive, London
SW1V 4DG
☎ (0171) 834 1438
Fax (0171) 976 6085
*Traditional B&B in a quiet residential
area of City of Westminster, within
walking distance of Victoria station,
shopping areas and important sights.
Student rooms.*
Bedrooms: 8 single, 12 double,
3 twin, 6 triple, 5 family rooms
Bathrooms: 29 en-suite, 2 public

**Bed & breakfast
per night:**

	£min	£max
Single	18.00	39.00
Double	31.00	53.00

Cards accepted: Access, Visa,
Switch/Delta

Windermere Hotel ⚠

👑👑👑 COMMENDED

142-144 Warwick Way, Victoria,
London SW1V 4JE
☎ (0171) 834 5163 & 834 5480
Fax (0171) 630 8831
*Previous winner of BTA Trophy and
Certificate of Distinction for small
hotels. A friendly, charming hotel with
well-appointed rooms and a licensed
restaurant.*
Bedrooms: 3 single, 11 double,
5 twin, 1 triple, 3 family rooms
Bathrooms: 19 en-suite, 2 public

**Bed & breakfast
per night:**

	£min	£max
Single	34.00	57.00
Double	59.00	86.00

**Half board per
person:**

	£min	£max
Daily	40.00	52.50

Evening meal 1800 (last orders
2130)
Cards accepted: Access, Visa, Amex,
Switch/Delta

LONDON SW5

Beaver Hotel

♔♔

57-59 Philbeach Gardens, London
SW5 9ED
☎ (0171) 373 4553
Fax (0171) 373 4555
*In a quiet, tree-lined crescent of late
Victorian terraced houses, close to
Earl's Court Exhibition Centre and 10
minutes from the West End.*
Bedrooms: 17 single, 6 double,
10 twin, 4 triple
Bathrooms: 24 en-suite, 5 public
Bed & breakfast

per night:	£min	£max
Single	29.00	49.00
Double	42.00	66.00

Parking for 23
Cards accepted: Access, Visa, Diners,
Amex

Merlyn Court Hotel

♔♔

2 Barkston Gardens, London
SW5 0EN
☎ (0171) 370 1640
Fax (0171) 370 4986

*Well-established, family-run, good value
hotel in quiet Edwardian square, close
to Earl's Court and Olympia. Direct
underground link to Heathrow, the
West End and rail stations. Car park
nearby.*
Bedrooms: 4 single, 4 double, 4 twin,
2 triple, 3 family rooms
Bathrooms: 8 en-suite, 3 private,
6 public, 1 private shower
Bed & breakfast

per night:	£min	£max
Single	25.00	50.00
Double	35.00	60.00

Cards accepted: Access, Visa

Swiss House Hotel

Listed COMMENDED

171 Old Brompton Road, London
SW5 0AN
☎ (0171) 373 2769 & 373 9383
Fax (0171) 373 4983

*High quality budget priced hotel,
conveniently situated near London
museums, shopping/exhibition centres.
Gloucester Road underground station is
within easy walking distance. Winner of
BTA award for best value B&B in
London.*
Bedrooms: 5 single, 5 double, 2 twin,
4 triple
Bathrooms: 15 en-suite, 1 public,
1 private shower
Bed & breakfast

per night:	£min	£max
Single	39.00	56.00
Double	72.00	72.00

Cards accepted: Access, Visa, Diners,
Amex, Switch/Delta

LONDON SW5

Continued

Windsor House

Listed

12 Penywern Road, London
SW5 9ST
☎ (0171) 373 9087
Fax (0171) 385 2417

*Budget-priced bed and breakfast
establishment in Earl's Court. Easily
reached from airports and motorway.
The West End is minutes away by
underground. NCP parking.*
Bedrooms: 2 single, 4 double, 4 twin,
1 triple, 7 family rooms
Bathrooms: 10 en-suite, 6 public,
6 private showers

Bed & breakfast

per night:	£min	£max
Single	24.00	38.00
Double	32.00	48.00

See display advertisement on
page 29

LONDON SW7

Abcone Hotel

APPROVED

10 Ashburn Gardens, London
SW7 4DG
☎ (0171) 370 3383
Fax (0171) 373 3082
*Close to Gloucester Road underground
and convenient for High Street
Kensington, Knightsbridge, Olympia,
Earl's Court, museums and Hyde Park.*
Bedrooms: 17 single, 15 double,
3 twin
Bathrooms: 28 en-suite, 4 public

Bed & breakfast

per night:	£min	£max
Single	40.00	74.00
Double	50.00	89.00

Evening meal 1900 (last orders
2130)
Cards accepted: Access, Visa, Diners,
Amex, Switch/Delta

Five Sumner Place Hotel

Listed **HIGHLY COMMENDED**

5 Sumner Place, South Kensington,
London SW7 3EE
☎ (0171) 584 7586
Fax (0171) 823 9962
*Recent winner of the Best Small Hotel
in London Award. Situated in South
Kensington, the most fashionable area.
This family owned and run hotel offers
first-class service and personal
attention.*
Bedrooms: 3 single, 10 double
Bathrooms: 13 en-suite, 1 public

Bed & breakfast

per night:	£min	£max
Single	72.00	82.00
Double	96.00	116.00

Cards accepted: Access, Visa, Amex

LONDON SW14

The Plough Inn

APPROVED

42 Christchurch Road, East Sheen,
London SW14 7AF
☎ (0181) 876 7833 & 876 4533
Fax (0181) 392 8801

Delightful old pub, part 16th C, next to

---

*Richmond Park. En-suite
accommodation, traditional ales,
home-cooked food.*
Bedrooms: 3 double, 3 twin, 1 triple
Bathrooms: 6 en-suite, 1 private

Bed & breakfast

per night:	£min	£max
Single	50.00	55.00
Double	65.00	70.00

**Half board per
person:**

	£min	£max
Daily	55.00	65.00

Lunch available
Evening meal 1930 (last orders
2130)
Parking for 4
Cards accepted: Access, Visa, Amex

LONDON SW19

Compton Guest House

Listed

65 Compton Road, Wimbledon,
London SW19 7QA
☎ (0181) 947 4488 & 879 3245
Fax (0181) 947 4488
*Family-run guesthouse in pleasant,
peaceful area, 5 minutes from
Wimbledon station (British Rail and
District Line). Easy access to the West
End, central London, M1, M2, M3, M4
and M25. Quality rooms, with excellent
service. About 12 minutes' walk to
Wimbledon tennis courts.*
Bedrooms: 2 single, 1 double, 2 twin,
1 triple, 2 family rooms
Bathrooms: 2 public

Bed & breakfast

per night:	£min	£max
Single	33.00	38.00
Double	45.00	64.00

Parking for 2

Please check prices and other
details at the time of booking.

LONDON W1

Bentinck House Hotel ⚠

Listed

20 Bentinck Street, London
W1M 5RL
☎ (0171) 935 9141
Fax (0171) 224 5903
Family-run bed and breakfast hotel in the heart of London's fashionable West End, close to Bond Street underground and Oxford Street.
Bedrooms: 8 single, 1 double, 3 twin, 5 triple
Bathrooms: 12 en-suite, 4 public
Bed & breakfast

per night:	£min	£max
Single	45.00	55.00
Double	69.00	79.00

Half board per person:

	£min	£max
Daily	45.00	65.00
Weekly	300.00	450.00

Evening meal 1800 (last orders 2200)
Cards accepted: Access, Visa, Diners, Amex, Switch/Delta

Lincoln House Hotel ⚠

COMMENDED

33 Gloucester Place, London
W1H 3PD
☎ (0171) 486 7630
Fax (0171) 486 0166
Georgian hotel of distinctive character. En-suite rooms with all modern comforts. Superb location, competitively priced, in the heart of London's West End.
Bedrooms: 6 single, 8 double, 4 twin, 3 triple, 1 family room
Bathrooms: 20 en-suite, 2 private, 1 public
Bed & breakfast

per night:	£min	£max
Single	39.00	59.00
Double	59.00	79.00

Cards accepted: Access, Visa, Diners, Amex, Switch/Delta

Wigmore Court Hotel ⚠

COMMENDED

23 Gloucester Place, Portman Square, London W1H 3PB
☎ (0171) 935 0928
Fax (0171) 487 4254
Small, clean, fully refurbished family hotel. Large en-suite rooms - ideal for families. 3 minutes' walk to Oxford Street. Competitively priced.

Bedrooms: 4 single, 6 double, 3 twin, 3 triple, 2 family rooms
Bathrooms: 16 private, 1 public
Bed & breakfast

per night:	£min	£max
Single	35.00	50.00
Double	60.00	79.00

Cards accepted: Access, Visa, Diners

Wyndham Hotel

Listed

30 Wyndham Street, London
W1H 1DD
☎ (0171) 723 7204 & 723 9400
Fax (0171) 723 7204
Small family-run B&B in a Georgian terrace, around the corner from Baker Street and a short walk from Oxford Street.
Bedrooms: 5 single, 4 double, 2 twin
Bathrooms: 1 public, 9 private showers
Bed & breakfast

per night:	£min	£max
Single	32.00	34.00
Double	42.00	44.00

ENQUIRY COUPONS

To help you obtain further information about advertisers featured in this guide you will find enquiry coupons at the back. Send these directly to the establishments in which you are interested. Remember to complete both sides of the coupon.

LONDON W2

Abbey Court Hotel ♈

Listed

174 Sussex Gardens, London
W2 1TP
☎ (0171) 402 0704
Fax (0171) 262 2055

*Central London hotel, reasonable prices.
Within walking distance of Lancaster
Gate, Paddington station and Hyde
Park. Easy access to tourist attractions
and shopping. Car parking at modest
charge.*
Bedrooms: 14 single, 24 double,
7 twin, 10 triple, 2 family rooms
Bathrooms: 57 en-suite

Bed & breakfast

per night:	£min	£max
Single	30.00	39.00
Double	38.00	58.00

Parking for 20
Cards accepted: Access, Visa, Amex

See display advertisement on
page 31

Beverley House Hotel ♈

142 Sussex Gardens, London
W2 1UB
☎ (0171) 723 3380
Fax (0171) 262 0324

*Refurbished bed and breakfast hotel,
serving traditional English breakfast
and offering high standards at low
prices. Close to Paddington station,
Hyde Park and museums.*
Bedrooms: 6 single, 5 double, 6 twin,
6 triple
Bathrooms: 23 en-suite

Bed & breakfast

per night:	£min	£max
Single	39.00	48.00
Double	44.00	66.00

Evening meal 1800 (last orders
2200)
Parking for 2
Cards accepted: Access, Visa, Diners,
Amex

Dylan Hotel ♈

Listed

14 Devonshire Terrace, Lancaster
Gate, London W2 3DW
☎ (0171) 723 3280
Fax (0171) 402 2443

*Small hotel in central location, 4
minutes from Paddington and
Lancaster Gate underground stations.
Marble Arch, Hyde Park and Oxford
Street close by. Not just a hotel, a home
from home.*
Bedrooms: 4 single, 4 double, 7 twin,
3 triple

Bathrooms: 7 en-suite, 3 public,
4 private showers

Bed & breakfast

per night:	£min	£max
Single	30.00	35.00
Double	42.00	55.00

Cards accepted: Access, Visa, Diners,
Amex, Switch/Delta

Hyde Park Rooms Hotel ♈

Listed

137 Sussex Gardens, Hyde Park,
London W2 2RX
☎ (0171) 723 0225 & 723 0965

*Small centrally located private hotel
with personal service. Clean,
comfortable and friendly. Within
walking distance of Hyde Park and
Kensington Gardens. Car parking
available.*
Bedrooms: 5 single, 6 double, 2 twin,
1 triple
Bathrooms: 7 en-suite, 2 private,
2 public

Bed & breakfast

per night:	£min	£max
Single	24.00	38.00
Double	36.00	48.00

Parking for 3
Cards accepted: Access, Visa, Diners,
Amex, Switch/Delta

Manor Court Hotel ♈

Listed

7 Clanricarde Gardens, London
W2 4JJ
☎ (0171) 727 5407 & 729 3361
Fax (0171) 229 2875

*Bed and breakfast hotel run by
management.*
Bedrooms: 5 single, 5 double, 4 twin,
5 triple, 1 family room
Bathrooms: 6 en-suite, 3 private,
4 public, 7 private showers

Bed & breakfast

per night:	£min	£max
Single	25.00	30.00
Double	40.00	50.00

Cards accepted: Access, Visa, Diners,
Amex

Nayland Hotel ♈

COMMENDED

132-134 Sussex Gardens, London
W2 1UB
☎ (0171) 723 4615
Fax (0171) 402 3292

*Centrally located, close to many
amenities and within walking distance
of Hyde Park and Oxford Street.
Quality you can afford.*

Bedrooms: 11 single, 8 double,
17 twin, 5 triple
Bathrooms: 41 en-suite

Bed & breakfast

per night:	£min	£max
Single	40.00	55.00
Double	48.00	74.00

Evening meal 1800 (last orders
2100)
Parking for 5
Cards accepted: Access, Visa, Diners,
Amex

Westpoint Hotel ♈

Listed

170-172 Sussex Gardens, London
W2 1TP
☎ (0171) 402 0281
Fax (0171) 224 9114

*Inexpensive accommodation in central
London. Close to Paddington and
Lancaster Gate underground stations.
Easy access to tourist attractions,
shopping and Hyde Park.*
Bedrooms: 12 single, 15 double,
16 twin, 14 triple, 6 family rooms
Bathrooms: 31 en-suite, 10 public,
9 private showers

Bed & breakfast

per night:	£min	£max
Single	24.00	38.00
Double	29.00	48.00

Parking for 15
Cards accepted: Access, Visa, Diners,
Amex

See display advertisement on
page 31

LONDON W5

Corfton Guest House

APPROVED

42 Corfton Road, Ealing, London
W5 2HT
☎ (0181) 998 1120

*Close to Ealing Broadway station, in a
quiet residential area of considerable
character.*
Bedrooms: 3 single, 3 double, 1 twin,
2 triple
Bathrooms: 1 en-suite, 3 private,
2 public

Bed & breakfast

per night:	£min	£max
Single	15.00	35.00
Double	23.00	35.00

Parking for 6

Please mention this guide
when making your booking.

ACCOMMODATION

Central London

Budget Prices

WESTPOINT HOTEL

170 Sussex Gardens, Hyde Park, London W2 1PT.
Tel: (0171) 402 0281 (Reservations) Fax: (0171) 224 9114.

**Most rooms with private shower & toilet, radio/intercom
& colour TV. Children welcome. TV lounge.**

This hotel has long been a popular choice amongst tourists because of its central location,
being near to Hyde Park and only 2 minutes from Paddington and Lancaster Gate tube stations.
The West End's tourist attractions, including theatres, museums and Oxford Street stores,
are within easy reach. Individuals, families and groups are all welcome.

• PRIVATE CAR PARK • DIRECT A2 BUS FROM HEATHROW •

RATES: **Low Season**
Singles from £24 per person.
Doubles from £15 per person.
Family rooms from £13 per person.

High Season
Singles from £28 per person.
Doubles from £20 per person.
Family rooms from £18 per person.

ABBEY COURT HOTEL

174 Sussex Gardens, Hyde Park, London W2 1TP.
Tel: (0171) 402 0704 Fax: (0171) 262 2055.
Open all year. Radio Intercom in every room. Children welcome.
Most rooms with private shower, toilet and colour TV.

• CAR PARKING AVAILABLE • A2 BUS FROM HEATHROW •

Central London hotel in a pleasant avenue near Hyde Park and within 2 minutes' walking distance
of Paddington main line and tube station and Lancaster Gate tube station. The tourist attractions
of the West End including theatres, museums and Oxford Street are within easy reach. Individuals,
families, school parties and groups are all welcome and group tours can be arranged.

TERMS per person:
Low Season: Single from £26, double from £16 p.p., family rooms from £14 p.p.
High Season: Single from £28, double from £23 p.p., family rooms from £18 p.p.

SASS HOUSE HOTEL

11 Craven Terrace, Hyde Park, London W2 3QD.
Tel: (0171) 262 2325 Fax: (0171) 262 0889

★ Centrally located – within easy reach of London's most famous tourist attractions.
★ Nearest underground Paddington and Lancaster Gate. ★ Served by a network of bus routes.
★ Colour television lounge. ★ Centrally heated. ★ Radio and intercom in all rooms.
★ Most rooms with showers/toilets. ★ Parking facilities available.
★ A2 bus from Heathrow.

TERMS per person:
Low season: Singles from £22, doubles from £16 p.p., family rooms from £15 p.p.
High season: Singles from £34, doubles from £19 p.p., family rooms from £18 p.p.

Creffield Lodge ♦

Listed

2-4 Creffield Road, Ealing, London
W5 3HN
☎ (0181) 993 2284
Fax (0181) 992 7082

Victorian-style property on ground and
two upper floors, located in quiet
residential road, adjacent to
150-bedroom Carnarvon Hotel.
Bedrooms: 9 single, 4 double, 4 twin,
1 triple
Bathrooms: 7 en-suite, 5 public

Bed & breakfast per night:	£min	£max
Single	35.00	55.00
Double	55.00	70.00

Half board per person:	£min	£max
Daily	50.00	70.00

Lunch available
Evening meal 1830 (last orders
2130)
Parking for 20
Cards accepted: Access, Visa, Diners,
Amex

🛏🖎👤📧🖵📶📺🗙 SP T

Grange Lodge Hotel

👑 APPROVED

48-50 Grange Road, Ealing, London
W5 5BX
☎ (0181) 567 1049
Fax (0181) 579 5350
Quiet, comfortable hotel within a few
hundred yards of the underground
station. Midway between central
London and Heathrow.
Bedrooms: 7 single, 2 double, 2 twin,
2 triple
Bathrooms: 9 en-suite, 2 public

Bed & breakfast per night:	£min	£max
Single	27.00	39.00
Double	38.00	51.00

Parking for 10
Cards accepted: Access, Visa, Diners,
Switch/Delta

🛏🖎🖵 S 🖵 📺 📶 📶 🖧❊ DAP SP T

> For further information on
> accommodation establishments
> use the coupons at the
> back of this guide.

OUTER LONDON

Colour maps 6 & 7 at the back of
the guide show place names and
London Postal Area Codes and will
help you locate accommodation in
your chosen area of London

CROYDON

Tourist Information Centre ☎ (0181) 253
1009

Iverna

Listed

1 Annandale Road, Addiscombe,
Croydon CR0 7HP
☎ (0181) 654 8639
Large house in a quiet road, close to
East Croydon station. London Victoria
15 minutes away. No smoking in public
areas.
Bedrooms: 3 single, 1 twin
Bathrooms: 1 public

Bed & breakfast per night:	£min	£max
Single	22.00	25.00
Double	40.00	42.00

Evening meal 1800 (last orders
2100)
Parking for 2

🛏🖎👤📧🖵👤🖳 UL S 🗙📶 🖧❊🚗 DAP

Markington Hotel

🛡🛡

9 Haling Park Road, South Croydon,
Surrey CR2 6NG
☎ (0181) 681 6494
Fax (0181) 688 6530
Friendly, comfortable private hotel with
fully equipped rooms, all en-suite. Free
car parking. Bar, restaurant. Close to
public transport.
Bedrooms: 10 single, 6 double,
2 twin, 2 triple
Bathrooms: 20 en-suite, 2 public

Bed & breakfast per night:	£min	£max
Single	35.00	49.50
Double	45.00	55.00

Evening meal 1830 (last orders
2030)
Parking for 17
Cards accepted: Access, Visa, Amex,
Switch/Delta

🛏🖎📧🖵👤📶 🖳 S 🗙📶 📺 ◑📶
🖧⏰30🗙🖧 SP

70 Smitham Bottom Lane

Purley, Surrey CR8 3DD
☎ (0181) 763 9288
Attractive detached family house with
large drive for off-road parking.
Bedrooms: 1 single, 3 double
Bathrooms: 2 public

Bed & breakfast per night:	£min	£max
Single	15.00	15.00
Double	30.00	30.00

🛏👤📶 UL 🗙📶 📺 📶 ⏰12❊🚗

HEATHROW AIRPORT

See under West Drayton

PURLEY

Stocks

Listed COMMENDED

51 Selcroft Road, Purley, Surrey
CR8 1AJ
☎ (0181) 660 3054
Central London 20 minutes by train.
Convenient for M25, M23 and Gatwick
Airport. Within walking distance of
Purley station.
Bedrooms: 1 single, 1 double,
1 triple
Bathrooms: 1 en-suite, 1 public

Bed & breakfast per night:	£min	£max
Single	20.00	22.00
Double	36.00	40.00

Parking for 3

🛏⏰3🖎👤🖵 UL 🗙📺📶 🖧❊🗙
🚗 DAP SP T

WEMBLEY

Elm Hotel ♦

🛡🛡 APPROVED

1-7 Elm Road, Wembley, Middlesex
HA9 7JA
☎ (0181) 902 1764
Fax (0181) 903 8365
Ten minutes' walk (1200 yards) from
Wembley Stadium and Conference
Centre. 150 yards from Wembley
Central underground and mainline
station.
Bedrooms: 6 single, 8 double, 8 twin,
4 triple, 1 family room
Suites available
Bathrooms: 24 en-suite, 2 public

Bed & breakfast per night:	£min	£max
Single	35.00	45.00
Double	45.00	55.00

Evening meal 1800 (last orders
2000)
Parking for 7
Cards accepted: Access, Visa,
Switch/Delta

🛏👤📧🖎🖵👤 S 📶 ◑📶 🖧⏰30

> All accommodation in this
> guide has been graded, or is
> awaiting a grading, by a trained
> Tourist Board inspector.

WEST DRAYTON

The Alice House

Listed APPROVED

9 Hollycroft Close, Sipson, West
Drayton, Middlesex UB7 OJJ
☎ (0181) 897 9032
*Small, clean and comfortable
guesthouse. Convenient for Heathrow
Airport, but with no noise from flight
path. Car service to airport available.
Evening meal by arrangement. Close
M4, M25. London 40 minutes. Parking.*
Bedrooms: 1 single, 1 double, 1 twin
Bathrooms: 1 public
Bed & breakfast

per night:	£min	£max
Single	32.00	34.00
Double	42.00	45.00

Evening meal 1800 (last orders
2000)
Parking for 6

AT-A-GLANCE SYMBOLS

Symbols at the end of each accommodation entry
give useful information about services
and facilities. A key to symbols can be found
inside the back cover flap.

Keep this open for easy reference.

USE YOUR *i*'s

There are more than 550 Tourist Information Centres
throughout England offering friendly help with
accommodation and holiday ideas as well as
suggestions of places to visit and things to do.
You'll find the address of your nearest Tourist
Information Centre in your local Phone Book.

USE YOUR _i_'s

There are more than 550 Tourist Information Centres throughout England offering friendly help with accommodation and holiday ideas as well as suggestions of places to visit and things to do. There may well be a centre in your home town which can help you before you set out. You'll find the address of your nearest Tourist Information Centre in your local Phone Book.

CHECK THE MAPS

The colour maps at the back of this guide show all the cities, towns and villages for which you will find accommodation entries.

Refer to the town index to find the page on which it is listed.

ENQUIRY COUPONS

To help you obtain further information about advertisers and accommodation featured in this guide you will find enquiry coupons at the back. Send these directly to the establishments in which you are interested. Remember to complete both sides of the coupon.

CUMBRIA

Cumbria is simply one of the most extraordinarily beautiful places on earth. Wordsworth lived here among its shimmering lakes and towering crags, and called it 'the loveliest spot that man hath ever found'; a 'spot' which attracts walkers, climbers and watersports enthusiasts, all year round.

But you don't have to be energetic! There are pretty villages, working farms, museums, visitors centres - plus the whole of the Lake District National Park to explore.

To the west of the Lakes lies Cumbria's unspoilt coastline. To the north you'll find the wild North Pennines and Borderlands. To the southeast, the peaceful Eden Valley. And between... paradise.

FOR MORE INFORMATION CONTACT:
Cumbria Tourist Board
Ashleigh, Holly Road, Windermere,
Cumbria LA23 2AQ
Tel: (015394) 44444 **Fax:** (015394) 44041

Where to Go in Cumbria – see pages 36-39
Where to Stay in Cumbria – see pages 40-62

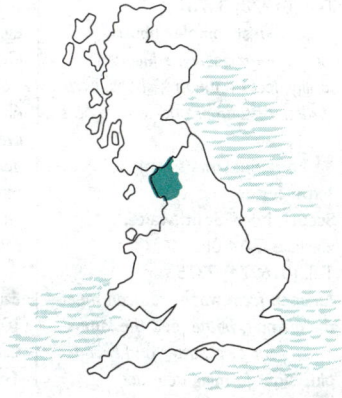

CUMBRIA

Where to Go and What to See

You will find hundreds of interesting places to visit during your stay in Cumbria, just some of which are listed in these pages. The number against each name will help you locate it on the map (page 39). Contact any Tourist Information Centre in the region for more ideas on days out in Cumbria.

1 Linton Tweeds
Shaddon Mills, Shaddon Gate,
Carlisle, Cumbria CA2 5TZ
Tel: (01228) 27569
Shows history of weaving in Carlisle up to Lintons today. Available for visitors to have hands on weaving and other activities.

2 Tullie House Museum and Art Gallery
Castle Street, Carlisle,
Cumbria CA3 8TP
Tel: (01228) 34781
Major tourist complex housing: museum, art gallery, education facility, lecture theatre, shops, herb garden, restaurant and terrace bars.

3 Four Seasons Farm Experience
Sceugh Mire, Southwaite,
Carlisle CA4 0LS
Tel: (016974) 73753
An open farm where you can meet the animals, bottle feed the lambs, make your own butter and bread, plus other farming activities.

4 Senhouse Roman Museum
The Battery, Sea Brows,
Maryport, Cumbria CA15 6JD
Tel: (01900) 816168
Once the headquarters of Hadrian's Coastal Defence system. UK's largest group of Roman altars, stones and inscriptions from a single site. Roman military equipment, stunning sculpture.

5 Lakeland Sheep and Wool Centre
Egremont Road, Cockermouth,
Cumbria CA13 0QX
Tel: (01900) 822673
An all weather attraction with live sheep shows and working dog demonstrations. Includes large screen and other tourism exhibitions on the area, a wool shop and seafood restaurant.

6 The Printing House Museum
102 Main Street, Cockermouth,
Cumbria CA13 9LX
Tel: (01900) 824984

Printing machinery and equipment. Tour of the museum follows the development of printing from the 15thC to the present day.

7 Dalemain Historic House and Gardens
Dalemain Estate Office
Penrith,
Cumbria CA11 0HB
Tel: (017684) 86450
Historic house with Georgian furniture. Westmorland and Cumberland Yeomanry Museum, agricultural bygones, adventure playground, licensed restaurant, famous gardens.

8 Mirehouse
Underskiddaw,
Cumbria CA12 4QE
Tel: (017687) 72287
17thC house with wide ranging literary and artistic connections. Grounds to Bassenthwaite Lake include playgrounds, garden, tearoom.

9 Dove Cottage & Wordsworth Museum

Town End, Grasmere,
Ambleside, Cumbria LA22 9SH
Tel: (015394) 35544
Wordsworth's home 1799-1808. Poet's possessions, museum with manuscripts, farmhouse reconstruction, paintings and drawings. Special events throughout the year.

10 Rydal Mount

Ambleside, Cumbria LA22 9LU
Tel: (015394) 33002
William Wordsworth's home for 37 years. Family portraits, furniture, first editions and personal possessions. Garden landscaped by the poet. 9thC Norse Mound, magnificent views.

11 Sellafield Visitors Centre

Sellafield, Seascale,
Cumbria CA20 1PG
Tel: (019467) 27027
Exhibition of nuclear power and the nuclear industry.

12 Eskdale Corn Mill

Boot, Holmrook,
Cumbria CA19 1TG
Tel: (019467) 23335
A historic water-powered corn mill near Dalegarth Station, approached via packhorse bridge. Early wooden machinery, milling and farming. Exhibition and waterfalls.

13 Brockhole - Lake District National Park Visitor Centre

Windermere,
Cumbria LA23 1LJ
Tel: (015394) 46601
Exhibitions include National Park Story, slide shows, films, shop, gardens, grounds, adventure playground, drystone walling area, trails, events. Gaddums restaurant, tearoom, putting.

14 Muncaster Castle, Gardens and Owl Centre

Ravenglass,
Cumbria CA18 1RQ
Tel: (01229) 717614
14thC pele tower with 15th and 19thC additions. Gardens contain an exceptional collection of rhododendrons and azaleas. Extensive collection of owls.

15 Ravenglass and Eskdale Railway

Ravenglass, Cumbria CA18 1SW
Tel: (01229) 717171
England's oldest narrow-guage railway runs for 7 miles through glorious scenery to the foot of England's highest hills. Most trains steam hauled.

16 Steam Yacht Gondola

Pier Cottage, Coniston,
Cumbria LA21 8AJ
Tel: (015394) 41288
Victorian steam powered vessel now National Trust owned and completely renovated with opulently upholstered saloon.

17 Amazonia

Glebe Road, Bowness-on-Windermere,
Cumbria LA23 3HE
Tel: (015394) 48002
Large display of exotic reptiles and insects from around the world including pythons, crocodiles and tarantula spiders! Visitors are able to handle certain animals.

18 The World of Beatrix Potter

The Old Laundry, Crag Brow,
Bowness-on-Windermere,
Windermere, Cumbria LA23 3BX
Tel: (015394) 88444
The life and works of Beatrix Potter presented on a 9 screen video wall, film on her life, and three-dimensional recreations of some of the scenes from her popular tales.

19 Levens Hall

Levens, Kendal, Cumbria LA8 0PD
Tel: (015395) 60321
Elizabethan mansion, incorporating a pele tower. Famous topiary

garden laid out in 1694, steam
collection, plant centre, shop, play
and picnic areas.

20 Sizergh Castle
Kendal, Cumbria LA8 8AE
Tel: (015395) 60070
*Strickland family home for 750
years, now National Trust owned.
With 14thC pele tower, 15thC
great hall, 16thC wings. Stuart
connections. Rock garden, rose
garden, daffodils.*

**23 Lakeside & Haverthwaite
Railway**
Haverthwaite Station,
Ulverston,
Cumbria LA12 8AL
Tel: (015395) 31594
*Standard gauge steam railway
operating a daily seasonal service
through the beautiful Leven Valley.
Steam and diesel locomotives
on display.*

**26 South Lakes
Wild Animal Park**
Crossgates,
Dalton-in-Furness,
Cumbria LA15 8JR
Tel: (01229) 466086
*Wild animal park in over 14 acres
with over 120 species of animals
from all over the world. Large
water-fowl ponds.
Miniature railway.*

**21 Heron Corn Mill
and Museum of Papermaking**
Waterhouse Mills,
Beetham, Milnthorpe,
Cumbria LA7 7AR
Tel: (015395) 63363
*Restored working corn mill featuring
14ft high waterwheel. The museum
shows paper-making both historic
and modern with artefacts, displays
and diagrams.*

22 Heron Glass
54 The Gill, Ulverston,
Cumbria LA12 7BL
Tel: (01229) 581121
*A combined visitor centre and
workshop. Traditional glassmaking
demonstrations daily.
Factory shop.*

**24 Phil Cotton's Classic Bikes
Working Museum**
Victoria Road,
Ulverston,
Cumbria LA12 0BY
Tel: (01229) 586099
*Classic motorcycle display, with
video, restoration areas and small
shop.*

25 Holker Hall and Gardens
Cark in Cartmel,
Cumbria LA11 7PL
Tel: (015395) 58328
*Victorian wing, formal and
woodland garden, deer park,
motor museum, adventure
playground and gift shop.
Exhibitions including Timeless Toys
and Teddies.*

27 The Dock Museum
North Road,
Barrow-in-Furness,
Cumbria LA14 2PW
Tel: (01229) 870871
*Presents the story of steel
shipbuilding for which
Barrow is famous.
Interactive displays, nautical
adventure playground.*

28 Furness Abbey
Barrow-in-Furness,
Cumbria LA13 0TJ
Tel: (01229) 823420
*Ruins of a 12C Cistercian abbey.
Extensive remains include
transepts, choir, west tower
of church, canopied seats
and arches.*

SCOTLAND

NORTHUMBERLAND

Longtown

Brampton

Carlisle **1** **2**

Silloth

Southwaite **3**

Maryport **4**

Bassenthwaite

DURHAM

Broughton

Cockermouth **5** **6**

CUMBRIA

Penrith **7**

Workington

Keswick **8**

Pooley Bridge

Whitehaven

Cleator Moor

Appleby-in-Westmorland

Egremont

Brough

Kirkby Stephen

Grasmere **9**

Seascale **11**

Ambleside **10**

Boot **12**

Windermere **13**

Coniston **16**

Bowness-on-Windermere **17** **18**

Ravenglass **14** **15**

Kendal **19** **20**

Sedbergh

Millom

Grange-over-Sands

Beetham

Kirkby Lonsdale

NORTH YORKSHIRE

Ulverston

22 **23** **25**

21

26 **24**

Cark in Cartmel

Barrow-in-Furness **27** **28** Dalton-in-Furness

LANCS

29

FIND OUT MORE

Further information about holidays and attractions in Cumbria is available from:
Cumbria Tourist Board,
Ashleigh,
Holly Road,
Windermere,
Cumbria LA23 2AQ.
Tel: (015394) 44444

These publications are available from the Cumbria Tourist Board:

■ **Cumbria The Lake District Touring Map** - including tourist information and touring caravan and camping parks £3.45. Laminated poster £2.95.

■ **Days Out in Cumbria** - Over 200 ideas for a great day out £1.25.

■ **Short Walks** - Good for Families - route descriptions, maps and information for 14 walks in lesser known areas of Cumbria 95p.

■ **Wordsworth's Lake District** - folded map showing major Wordsworthian sites plus biographical details 60p. Japanese language version £1. Laminated poster £1.

WHERE TO STAY (CUMBRIA)

Accommodation entries in this region are listed in alphabetical order of place name, and then in alphabetical order of establishment.

Map references refer to the colour location maps at the back of this guide.

The first number indicates the map to use; the letter and number which follow refer to the grid reference on the map.

At-a-glance symbols at the end of each accommodation entry give useful information about services and facilities. A key to symbols can be found inside the back cover flap.

Keep this open for easy reference.

AMBLESIDE

Cumbria
Map ref 5A3

Market town situated at the head of Lake Windermere and surrounded by fells. The historic town centre is now a conservation area and the country around Ambleside is rich in historic and literary associations. Good centre for touring, walking and climbing.
Tourist Information Centre
☎ (015394) 32582

Barnes Fell Guest House ⚑
Listed COMMENDED
Low Gale, Ambleside LA22 0BB
☎ Windermere (015394) 33311
Convenient yet peaceful non-smoking Victorian guesthouse, furnished with antiques. Delicious food, fine views and a warm welcome.
Bedrooms: 3 double
Bathrooms: 1 en-suite, 1 public

Bed & breakfast
per night:	£min	£max
Single	16.00	37.00
Double	30.00	54.00

Half board per
person:	£min	£max
Daily	24.00	39.00
Weekly	149.00	245.00

Evening meal 1930 (last orders 2030)

⛵ 12 🕭 🖵 🔌 ♿ 🎱 UL S ⌣ 🏧 🖭
🌺 ✕ 🚲 SP

Borrans Park Hotel ⚑
👑👑👑 HIGHLY COMMENDED
Borrans Road, Ambleside LA22 0EN
☎ (015394) 33454
Fax (015394) 33003

Peacefully situated between the village and lake. Enjoy candlelit dinners, 120 fine wines, and four-poster bedrooms with private spa baths.
Wheelchair access category 3 ♿
Bedrooms: 9 double, 1 twin, 2 triple
Bathrooms: 12 en-suite

Bed & breakfast
per night:	£min	£max
Single	29.00	49.00
Double	58.00	78.00

Half board per
person:	£min	£max
Daily	45.00	55.00
Weekly	255.00	329.00

Evening meal 1900 (last orders 1800)
Parking for 20
Cards accepted: Access, Visa, Switch/Delta

⛵ ♿ 🛏 🖵 🔌 🖭 ♿ 🎱 🛎 S ⌣ 🖭 🏧
🚲 🌺 ✕ 🚲 SP

Broadview ⚑
Listed COMMENDED
Low Fold, Lake Road, Ambleside LA22 0DN
☎ (015394) 32431
Spacious, comfortable Victorian guesthouse with some en-suite rooms and superb views. Easy walk to village and lake.
Bedrooms: 3 double, 1 twin, 1 triple, 1 family room
Bathrooms: 2 en-suite, 2 public

Bed & breakfast
per night:	£min	£max
Single	20.00	20.00
Double	35.00	42.00

Open February–November

⛵ 🎱 UL S ⌣ 🏧 🚲 ✕ 🚲

The Gables Hotel ⚑
👑👑👑 COMMENDED
Compston Road, Ambleside LA22 9DJ
☎ (015394) 33272
In a quiet residential area overlooking the park, tennis courts, bowling green and Loughrigg Fell. Convenient for shops, walking and water sports.
Bedrooms: 3 single, 5 double, 1 twin, 4 triple
Bathrooms: 13 en-suite

Bed & breakfast
per night:	£min	£max
Single	28.00	
Double	46.00	

Evening meal 1845 (last orders 1915)
Parking for 7
Open January–November
Cards accepted: Access, Visa

⛵ ♿ 🖵 🎱 🛎 S 🖭 TV 🏧 🚲 🚲 🚲

Glenside ⚑
COMMENDED
Old Lake Road, Ambleside LA22 0DP
☎ (015394) 32635
17th C farm cottage, comfortable bedrooms with original oak beams, TV lounge. Between town and lake, ideal centre for walking. Private parking.
Bedrooms: 2 double, 1 twin
Bathrooms: 1 public

Bed & breakfast
per night:	£min	£max
Single	14.00	16.00
Double	28.00	32.00

Parking for 3
Open February–November

⛵ 5 🎱 UL 🛎 ⌣ 🖭 TV 🏧 ✕ 🚲 OAP T

Greenbank ⚈

HIGHLY COMMENDED

Skelwith Bridge, Ambleside
LA22 9NW
☎ (015394) 33236
*Set in a beautiful rural location just 3
miles from Ambleside. Glorious views
from delightfully furnished, cosy rooms.
Home-made bread and cakes a
speciality.*
Bedrooms: 2 double, 1 twin
Bathrooms: 3 en-suite, 1 public

Bed & breakfast

per night:	£min	£max
Double	36.00	42.00

Parking for 6

Hideaway Cottage ⚈

McIver Lane, Ambleside LA22 ODU
☎ (015394) 34858
*Cottage/bungalow offering ground floor
only facilities. In a quiet woodland
location only 2 minutes' stroll from
Lake Windermere. Prices below are per
room.*
Bedrooms: 3 double
Bathrooms: 2 en-suite, 1 private

Bed & breakfast

per night:	£min	£max
Double	32.00	40.00

Parking for 3
Open February–December

High Wray Farm

Listed COMMENDED

High Wray, Ambleside LA22 0JE
☎ (015394) 32280

*173-acre livestock farm. Charming
17th C old world farmhouse, once
owned by Beatrix Potter, with oak
beams and log fire. In quiet location,
ideal centre for touring or walking.
Panoramic views and lake shore walks
close by.*
Bedrooms: 2 double, 1 twin
Bathrooms: 1 en-suite, 1 public

Bed & breakfast

per night:	£min	£max
Single	15.50	17.00

Parking for 7

The Howes

Listed COMMENDED

Stockghyll Brow, Ambleside
LA22 0 9Z
☎ (015394) 32444
*Private detached house near Stockghyll
Waterfalls, with 2 ground floor en-suite
bedrooms.*
Bedrooms: 1 double, 1 twin
Bathrooms: 2 en-suite

Bed & breakfast

per night:	£min	£max
Single	25.00	30.00
Double	38.00	45.00

Parking for 2

Invergowrie Guest House

COMMENDED

Lake Road, Ambleside LA22 0DB
☎ (015394) 33479

*Family-run guesthouse offering bed and
breakfast, English or Continental. Views
of fells from most bedrooms.*
Bedrooms: 2 single, 3 double
Bathrooms: 4 en-suite, 1 private,
2 public

Bed & breakfast

per night:	£min	£max
Single	15.00	20.00
Double	30.00	40.00

Parking for 7
Open February–November

Laurel Villa ⚈

HIGHLY COMMENDED

Lake Road, Ambleside LA22 0DB
☎ (015394) 33240
*Detached Victorian house, visited by
Beatrix Potter. En-suite bedrooms
overlooking the fells. Within easy reach
of Lake Windermere and the village.
Private car park.*
Bedrooms: 7 double, 1 twin
Bathrooms: 8 en-suite

Bed & breakfast

per night:	£min	£max
Single	50.00	50.00
Double	60.00	80.00

Half board per

person:	£min	£max
Daily	50.00	60.00

Evening meal 1900 (last orders
1700)
Parking for 10
Cards accepted: Access, Visa, Amex

Mill Cottage ⚈

Listed APPROVED

Rydal Road, Ambleside LA22 9AN
☎ (015394) 34830
*Grade II listed restaurant and
guesthouse in riverside location
adjacent to the famous Bridge House.*
Bedrooms: 3 double, 1 twin, 1 family
room
Bathrooms: 2 en-suite, 1 public

Bed & breakfast

per night:	£min	£max
Single	17.00	19.00
Double	19.00	21.00

Half board per

person:	£min	£max
Daily	35.00	45.00

Lunch available
Evening meal 1830 (last orders
2100)

The Old Vicarage ⚈

COMMENDED

Vicarage Road, Ambleside
LA22 9DH
☎ (015394) 33364
Fax (015394) 34734

*Quietly situated in own grounds in
heart of village. Car park, quality
en-suite accommodation, friendly
service. Family-run. Pets welcome.*
Bedrooms: 7 double, 1 twin, 1 triple,
1 family room
Bathrooms: 10 en-suite

Bed & breakfast

per night:	£min	£max
Single	28.00	
Double	46.00	

Parking for 12
Cards accepted: Access, Visa,
Switch/Delta

Park House Guest House

COMMENDED

3 Compston Villas, Compston Road,
Ambleside LA22 9DJ
☎ Windermere (015394) 31692

Continued ▶

AMBLESIDE
Continued

Quality Victorian house centrally positioned overlooking park and fells. A friendly welcome, well-appointed rooms and excellent breakfasts await all our guests.
Bedrooms: 2 single, 2 double, 2 triple
Bathrooms: 3 en-suite, 1 public, 1 private shower
Bed & breakfast

per night:	£min	£max
Single	13.75	19.00
Double	30.00	40.00

Riverside Lodge Country House ⋒

COMMENDED
Nr. Rothay Bridge, Ambleside
LA22 0EH
☎ (015394) 34208
Georgian country house of character with 2 acres of grounds through which the River Rothay flows. 500 yards from the centre of Ambleside.
Bedrooms: 1 single, 2 double, 1 twin
Bathrooms: 2 en-suite, 2 private
Bed & breakfast

per night:	£min	£max
Double	42.00	59.00

Parking for 20
Cards accepted: Access, Visa

Rowanfield Country Guesthouse ⋒

HIGHLY COMMENDED
Kirkstone Road, Ambleside
LA22 9ET
☎ (015394) 33686
Fax (015394) 31569

Idyllic setting, panoramic lake and mountain views. Laura Ashley style decor. Scrumptious food created by proprietor/chef. Superior room available at supplement.
Wheelchair access category 3⋔
Bedrooms: 5 double, 1 twin, 1 triple
Bathrooms: 7 en-suite
Bed & breakfast

per night:	£min	£max
Double	52.00	56.00

Half board per

person:	£min	£max
Daily	42.00	45.00
Weekly	255.00	271.00

Evening meal 1900 (last orders 1900)
Parking for 8
Open March–December
Cards accepted: Access, Visa, Switch/Delta

Smallwood House Hotel ⋒

COMMENDED
Compston Road, Ambleside
LA22 9DJ
☎ (015394) 32330
Family-run hotel in central position, offering warm and friendly service, good home cooking and value-for-money quality and standards.
Bedrooms: 7 double, 3 twin, 3 triple, 2 family rooms
Bathrooms: 15 private, 2 public
Bed & breakfast

per night:	£min	£max
Single	25.00	29.50
Double	34.00	43.00

Half board per

person:	£min	£max
Daily	30.00	33.50
Weekly	205.00	225.00

Lunch available
Evening meal 1800 (last orders 2000)
Parking for 11
Cards accepted: Access, Visa

APPLEBY-IN-WESTMORLAND

Cumbria
Map ref 5B3

Former county town of Westmorland, at the foot of the Pennines in the Eden Valley. The castle was rebuilt in the 17th C, except for its Norman keep, ditches and ramparts. It now houses a Rare Breeds Survival Trust Centre. Good centre for exploring the Eden Valley.
Tourist Information Centre
☎ (017683) 51177

Bongate House ⋒

COMMENDED
Appleby-in-Westmorland
CA16 6UE
☎ Appleby (017683) 51245
Family-run Georgian guesthouse on the outskirts of a small market town. Large garden. Relaxed friendly atmosphere, good home cooking.
Bedrooms: 1 single, 3 double, 2 twin, 1 triple, 1 family room
Bathrooms: 5 en-suite, 1 public

Bed & breakfast

per night:	£min	£max
Single	17.00	19.50
Double	34.00	39.00

Half board per

person:	£min	£max
Daily	25.00	27.50
Weekly	160.00	180.00

Evening meal 1900 (last orders 1800)
Parking for 10

Bridge End Farm

HIGHLY COMMENDED
Kirkby Thore, Penrith CA10 1UZ
☎ Kirkby Thore (017683) 61362
450-acre arable & dairy farm. Relax in 18th C farmhouse in Eden Valley. Spacious rooms overlooking Pennine Hills, alongside River Eden. Delicious home-made breakfast and dinners.
Bedrooms: 2 double, 1 twin
Bathrooms: 2 en-suite, 1 private, 1 public
Bed & breakfast

per night:	£min	£max
Single	20.00	22.00
Double	38.00	40.00

Half board per

person:	£min	£max
Daily	27.50	29.00
Weekly	185.50	199.50

Evening meal 1800 (last orders 1930)
Parking for 3

Dufton Hall Farm

APPROVED
Dufton, Appleby-in-Westmorland
CA16 6DD
☎ Appleby (017683) 51573
60-acre mixed farm. Spacious 18th C farmhouse offering en-suite, well-appointed rooms. Ideal walking area. Village pub close by.
Bedrooms: 2 double, 1 twin
Bathrooms: 2 en-suite, 1 private
Bed & breakfast

per night:	£min	£max
Single		18.00
Double		32.00

Parking for 3
Open April–October

Howgill House ⋒

COMMENDED
Appleby-in-Westmorland
CA16 6UW
☎ Appleby (017683) 51574 & 51240
Private family-run house standing in a

large garden. On B6542, half a mile from the town centre.
Bedrooms: 1 single, 1 twin, 2 triple
Bathrooms: 3 public

Bed & breakfast

per night:	£min	£max
Single	15.00	
Double	28.00	

Parking for 6
Open April–September

ARNSIDE

Cumbria
Map ref 5A3

Small coastal village in an Area of Outstanding Natural Beauty, with spectacular views across the Kent Estuary of the Lakeland hills. Excellent base for bird-watching. The incoming tide creates an impressive tidal bore.

Willowfield Hotel ⚑

COMMENDED

The Promenade, Arnside, Carnforth, Lancashire LA5 0AD
☎ (01524) 761354
Non-smoking, relaxed, family-run hotel with panoramic outlook over estuary to Lakeland hills. Good home cooking and quiet situation.
Bedrooms: 2 single, 3 double, 3 twin, 2 triple
Bathrooms: 6 en-suite, 2 public

Bed & breakfast

per night:	£min	£max
Single	19.00	23.00
Double	38.00	46.00

Half board per

person:	£min	£max
Daily	30.00	34.00
Weekly	196.00	224.00

Evening meal from 1830
Parking for 8
Cards accepted: Access, Visa

BORROWDALE

Cumbria
Map ref 5A3

Stretching south of Derwentwater to Seathwaite in the heart of the Lake District, the valley is walled by high fellsides. It can justly claim to be the most scenically impressive valley in the Lake District. Excellent centre for walking and climbing.

Yew Craggs

Listed COMMENDED

Rosthwaite, Keswick CA12 5XB
☎ (017687) 77260
Beside Rosthwaite Bridge in the centre

of the Borrowdale Valley. Good for walking, superb views in all directions.
Bedrooms: 3 double, 2 triple
Bathrooms: 1 public

Bed & breakfast

per night:	£min	£max
Single	16.00	19.00

Half board per

person:	£min	£max
Weekly	105.00	112.00

Parking for 6
Open February–November

BRAMPTON

Cumbria
Map ref 5B2

Excellent centre for exploring Hadrian's Wall. Wednesday is market day around the Moot Hall in this delightful sandstone-built town. Wall plaque marks the site of Bonnie Prince Charlie and his Jacobite army headquarters whilst they laid siege to Carlisle Castle in 1745.

Cracrop Farm ⚑

HIGHLY COMMENDED

Kirkcambeck, Brampton CA8 2BW
☎ Roadhead (016977) 48245
Fax (016977) 48333
425-acre mixed farm. Superior accommodation on farm which has won prizes in farming and wildlife competition. Farm trails in unspoilt, picturesque countryside. Relax in sauna and spa bath.
Bedrooms: 1 single, 2 double, 1 twin
Bathrooms: 4 en-suite, 1 public

Bed & breakfast

per night:	£min	£max
Single	25.00	
Double	50.00	50.00

Evening meal 1800 (last orders 1300)
Parking for 4

Hare & Hounds Inn

Talkin Village, Brampton CA8 1LE
☎ (016977) 3456
Typical country inn with a cosy atmosphere and real ale, only 500 yards from the golf-course and Talkin Tarn with boating, fishing, swimming, windsurfing and birdwatching.
Bedrooms: 2 double, 2 twin
Bathrooms: 2 private, 1 public

Bed & breakfast

per night:	£min	£max
Single	15.00	25.00
Double	25.00	35.00

Half board per

person:	£min	£max
Daily	20.00	32.00
Weekly	125.00	175.00

Lunch available
Evening meal 1900 (last orders 2100)
Parking for 18

High Rigg Farm

APPROVED

Walton, Brampton CA8 2AZ
☎ (016977) 2117
202-acre mixed farm. 18th C listed farmhouse on roadside, 1 mile from Walton and Roman Wall, 3.5 miles from Brampton. Family-run with pedigree cattle and sheep, farm trail to waterfall. Friendly atmosphere, delicious food. Good stopover or holiday base.
Bedrooms: 1 family room
Bathrooms: 1 public

Bed & breakfast

per night:	£min	£max
Single	15.00	16.00
Double	28.00	30.00

Half board per

person:	£min	£max
Daily	24.00	25.00
Weekly	155.00	162.00

Evening meal 1800 (last orders 1400)
Parking for 4

BROUGHTON-IN-FURNESS

Cumbria
Map ref 5A3

Old market village whose historic charter to hold fairs is still proclaimed every year on the first day of August in the market square.

Broom Hill

New Street, Broughton-in-Furness LA20 6JD
☎ (01229) 716358 & 0860 724719
Fax (01229) 716358
Manor house with large secluded gardens and fine views. All usual facilities.
Bedrooms: 3 double
Bathrooms: 2 en-suite, 1 private

Bed & breakfast

per night:	£min	£max
Single	17.50	20.00
Double	35.00	40.00

Parking for 7
Open March–October

CALDBECK

Cumbria
Map ref 5A2

Quaint limestone village lying on the northern fringe of the Lake District National Park. John Peel, the famous huntsman who is immortalised in song, is buried in the churchyard. The fells surrounding Caldbeck were once heavily mined, being rich in lead, copper and barytes.

The Briars

Caldbeck, Wigton CA7 8DS
☎ (016974) 78633
140-acre mixed farm. In the lovely village of Caldbeck overlooking Caldbeck Fells. Ideal for touring the Lakes and Scottish Borders. On Cumbria Way route.
Bedrooms: 2 double, 1 twin
Bathrooms: 1 en-suite, 2 public

Bed & breakfast

per night:	£min	£max
Single	18.00	20.00
Double	36.00	40.00

Parking for 3
Open March–October

Oddfellows Arms Inn

COMMENDED

Caldbeck CA7 8EA
☎ (016974) 78227
Fax (016974) 78530
A 200-year-old inn, full of character. Open fires, friendly locals, good ales and food. Recently refurbished en-suite bedrooms.
Bedrooms: 1 double, 1 twin, 1 family room
Bathrooms: 3 en-suite

Bed & breakfast

per night:	£min	£max
Single	25.00	35.00
Double	45.00	55.00

Half board per

person:	£min	£max
Daily	30.00	55.00
Weekly	189.00	346.00

Lunch available
Evening meal 1830 (last orders 2100)
Parking for 6
Cards accepted: Access, Visa, Switch/Delta

Swaledale Watch

HIGHLY COMMENDED

Whelpo, Caldbeck, Wigton CA7 8HQ
☎ (016974) 78409
300-acre mixed farm. Enjoy great comfort, fine food, beautiful surroundings and peaceful countryside on this working farm, central for touring or walking the rolling northern fells.
Bedrooms: 2 double, 2 triple
Bathrooms: 4 en-suite

Bed & breakfast

per night:	£min	£max
Single	17.00	20.00
Double	34.00	39.00

Half board per

person:	£min	£max
Daily	27.00	30.00
Weekly	189.00	210.00

Evening meal 1900 (last orders 1400)
Parking for 10

CARLISLE

Cumbria
Map ref 5A2

Cumbria's only city is rich in history. Attractions include the small red sandstone cathedral and 900-year-old castle with magnificent view from the keep. Award-winning Tullie House Museum and Art Gallery brings 2,000 years of Border history dramatically to life. Excellent centre for shopping.
Tourist Information Centre ☎ (01228) 512444

Albion Guest House

Listed APPROVED

32 London Road, Carlisle CA1 2EL
☎ (01228) 36694
Central Carlisle, recently refurbished small and friendly guesthouse. Helpful hosts will tailor arrangements to your requirements. Ideal for small groups.
Bedrooms: 3 single, 1 double, 4 twin, 1 triple
Bathrooms: 3 public

Bed & breakfast

per night:	£min	£max
Single	16.00	18.50
Double	27.00	30.00

Evening meal 1830 (last orders 1930)
Parking for 3

Beech Croft

COMMENDED

Aglionby, Carlisle CA4 8AQ
☎ (01228) 513762
Spacious, modern, detached house in a delightful rural setting. 1 mile on the A69 from M6 junction 43. High quality accommodation in a friendly family atmosphere.
Bedrooms: 1 single, 1 double, 1 twin
Bathrooms: 1 en-suite, 2 private

Bed & breakfast

per night:	£min	£max
Single	19.00	19.00
Double	38.00	42.00

Parking for 4

Corner House Hotel and Bar

APPROVED

4 Grey Street, Off London Road, Carlisle CA1 2JP
☎ (01228) 33239
Fax (01228) 46628
Warm welcome for short or long stay guests. Good food, bar, games room, Sky TV in lounge. All rooms en-suite, four- poster beds. Easy access bus/train and M6 junctions 42/43.
Bedrooms: 4 single, 3 double, 2 twin, 1 triple
Bathrooms: 10 en-suite, 1 public

Bed & breakfast

per night:	£min	£max
Single	20.00	25.00
Double	35.00	40.00

Half board per

person:	£min	£max
Daily	23.50	33.50
Weekly	160.00	210.00

Lunch available
Evening meal 1730 (last orders 2030)

Craighead

COMMENDED

6 Hartington Place, Carlisle CA1 1HL
☎ (01228) 596767
Grade II listed Victorian town house with spacious rooms and original features. Short walk to city centre, bus and rail stations. Friendly and comfortable. Fresh farm food.
Bedrooms: 1 single, 2 double, 1 twin, 1 family room
Bathrooms: 1 en-suite, 2 public

Please mention this guide when making your booking.

You are advised to confirm your booking in writing.

Bed & breakfast per night:	£min	£max
Single	14.00	16.50
Double	30.00	36.00

🐴🔌🖥♿⚲ ♿ UL S ⛷ TV 🚪 ♿🛥🚲
SP 🎣 T ◎

Croft End 🔺

Listed COMMENDED

Hurst, Ivegill, Carlisle CA4 0NL
☎ (017684) 84362
Rural bungalow situated midway between junction 41 and 42 of M6, 3 miles west of Southwaite service area. Ideal stopover for northbound or southbound travellers.
Bedrooms: 2 double
Bathrooms: 1 public

Bed & breakfast per night:	£min	£max
Single	15.00	16.00
Double	30.00	32.00

Half board per night:	£min	£max
Daily	17.00	19.00
Weekly	110.00	120.00

Parking for 4

🐴1🔥♿🖥⚲♿ UL ⛷ TV 🚪 ♿🛥✶
🚲

East View Guest House

♨

110 Warwick Road, Carlisle
CA1 1JU
☎ (01228) 22112
All rooms en-suite, with colour TV and hospitality tray. 10 minutes from buses, railway, city centre, restaurants, river walks.
Bedrooms: 1 single, 3 double, 1 twin, 1 triple, 2 family rooms
Bathrooms: 8 en-suite

Bed & breakfast per night:	£min	£max
Single	18.00	20.00
Double	32.00	35.00

Parking for 4

🐴🖥⚲♿ UL S 🚪 ♿🛥✶🚲 DAP SP

The Gill Farm 🔺

♨ COMMENDED

Blackford, Carlisle CA6 4EL
☎ Kirklinton (01228) 75326
124-acre arable & livestock farm. Ideal halfway stopping place or a good base for touring Cumbria's beauty spots. In peaceful countryside, 3 miles from M6 junction 44. From Carlisle go north to Blackford, fork right at sign for Longpark, Cliff and Scaleby, after 100 yards turn right, half a mile turn left, Gill Farm on left up this road.
Bedrooms: 1 double, 1 twin, 1 triple
Bathrooms: 2 public

Bed & breakfast per night:	£min	£max
Single	17.50	19.00
Double	32.00	34.00

Parking for 6
Open January–November

🐴♿ UL 🕍 TV 🚪 ♿✎✿🚲 SP 🎣 T

Howard House

♨♨♨ HIGHLY COMMENDED

27 Howard Place, Carlisle CA1 1HR
☎ (01228) 29159 & 512550
Lawrence and Sandra invite you to their spacious Victorian home in quiet location. City centre, bus/rail stations, riverside walks. Four-poster en-suite rooms. Home cooking. Family historians welcome. Come, let us spoil you.
Bedrooms: 1 single, 1 double, 1 twin, 1 triple, 1 family room
Bathrooms: 2 en-suite, 2 public

Bed & breakfast per night:	£min	£max
Single	15.00	18.00
Double	30.00	38.00

Half board per person:	£min	£max
Daily	25.00	28.00
Weekly	168.00	189.00

Evening meal 1800 (last orders 1900)
Cards accepted: Access, Visa

🐴🔌🖥♿⚲🕍 UL ♿ S ⛷🕍 TV 🚪
♿🛥✿🚲 DAP 🔺 SP T ◎

Langleigh House 🔺

♨ COMMENDED

6 Howard Place, Carlisle CA1 1HR
☎ (01228) 30440
Beautifully restored late Victorian house, 10 minutes' walk from city centre. Friendly atmosphere. All rooms en-suite. Private car park.
Bedrooms: 3 double
Bathrooms: 3 en-suite

Bed & breakfast per night:	£min	£max
Single	25.00	36.00
Double	36.00	36.00

Parking for 10

🐴♿🖥⚲🕍 UL ⛷♿ 🚪 ♿🛥✶

Metal Bridge House

♨

Metal Bridge, Rockcliffe, Carlisle
CA6 4HG
☎ Rockcliffe (0122874) 695

Just off A74 (Metal Bridge) 4 miles north of M6 junction 44 (Carlisle),

large detached house adjacent to restaurant/bar. Country setting, comfortable and spacious rooms, friendly welcome.
Bedrooms: 1 double, 2 twin
Bathrooms: 1 public

Bed & breakfast per night:	£min	£max
Single	18.00	
Double	27.00	

Parking for 5

🐴♿ UL 🕍 TV 🚪 ♿✿🚲

New Pallyards 🔺

♨♨♨ COMMENDED

Hethersgill, Carlisle CA6 6HZ
☎ Nicholforest (01228) 577 308
Fax (01228) 577 308
65-acre mixed farm. Warmth and hospitality await you in this 18th C modernised farmhouse. Country setting, easily accessible from M6, A7, M74. En-suite rooms. National award winner.
Bedrooms: 1 double, 1 twin, 1 triple
Bathrooms: 3 en-suite, 1 public

Bed & breakfast per night:	£min	£max
Single	20.00	25.00
Double	38.00	41.00

Half board per person:	£min	£max
Daily	32.00	33.00
Weekly	158.00	177.00

Evening meal 1900 (last orders 1930)
Parking for 7
Cards accepted: Access, Visa, Amex

✎✿ DAP 🔌 TV 🚪 ♿🛥🍴 ∪ ⛷
✎✿ DAP 🔺 SP T ◎

Streethead Farm 🔺

♨♨ COMMENDED

Ivegill, Carlisle CA4 0NG
☎ Southwaite (016974) 73327
230-acre mixed & dairy farm. Distant hills, log fires, en-suite bedrooms on working farm between Penrith and Carlisle (8 miles). 10 minutes from junctions 41 and 42 of M6. Ideal for Lakes or Scotland. Brochure available.
Bedrooms: 1 double, 1 triple
Bathrooms: 1 en-suite, 1 private

Bed & breakfast per night:	£min	£max
Single	16.00	18.00
Double	32.00	36.00

Parking for 2
Open March–October

🐴7♿⚲🕍 UL S TV 🚪 ♿✿✶🚲 SP 🎣

Map references apply to the colour maps at the back of this guide.

CARTMEL

Cumbria
Map ref 5A3

Picturesque conserved village based on a 12th C priory with a well-preserved church and gatehouse. Just half a mile outside the Lake District National Park, this is a peaceful base for walking and touring, with historic houses and beautiful scenery.

Bank Court Cottage

COMMENDED

The Square, Cartmel,
Grange-over-Sands LA11 6QB
☎ (015395) 36593
Character cottage in a quiet garden setting, within private courtyard. Historic village of great interest, surrounded by lovely countryside.
Bedrooms: 1 single, 1 double
Bathrooms: 1 public

Bed & breakfast

per night:	£min	£max
Single	17.50	23.00
Double	32.00	46.00

Half board per person:

	£min	£max
Daily	24.75	31.75
Weekly	171.75	206.00

CARTMEL FELL

Cumbria
Map ref 5A3

Small village set in tranquil countryside in an upland area of great beauty. Noted for its 16th C church with 3-tiered pulpit.

Lightwood Farmhouse

COMMENDED

Cartmel Fell, Bowland Bridge,
Grange-over-Sands LA11 6NP
☎ Newby Bridge (015395) 31454

17th C farmhouse with original oak beams. Extensive views, large garden with streams. Home cooking. Just off the A592 near Bowland Bridge.
Bedrooms: 3 double, 2 twin, 2 triple, 1 family room
Bathrooms: 8 en-suite

Bed & breakfast

per night:	£min	£max
Single	25.00	30.00
Double	44.00	50.00

Half board per person:

	£min	£max
Daily	36.00	
Weekly	240.00	

Evening meal from 1900
Parking for 10
Cards accepted: Access, Visa

CONISTON

Cumbria
Map ref 5A3

The 803m fell Coniston Old Man dominates the skyline to the east of this village at the northern end of Coniston Water. Arthur Ransome set his "Swallows and Amazons" stories here. Coniston's most famous resident was John Ruskin, whose home, Brantwood, is open to the public. Good centre for walking.

Arrowfield Country Guest House M

HIGHLY COMMENDED

Little Arrow, Coniston LA21 8AU
☎ (015394) 41741
Elegant Lakeland house in rural setting, offering quality accommodation. Immediate access to fells. Superb breakfasts, including home-made bread and jams.
Bedrooms: 1 single, 2 double, 2 twin
Bathrooms: 2 en-suite, 1 public

Bed & breakfast

per night:	£min	£max
Single	19.00	21.50
Double	34.00	46.00

Parking for 6
Open February–November

Brigg House M

HIGHLY COMMENDED

Torver, Coniston LA21 8AY
☎ (015394) 41592
Country house in beautiful setting at the foot of Coniston Old Man. All rooms en-suite. Varied breakfast menu. Non-smoking.
Bedrooms: 2 double, 1 twin
Bathrooms: 3 en-suite, 1 public

Bed & breakfast

per night:	£min	£max
Double	40.00	42.00

Parking for 4
Open March–November

Church House Inn

COMMENDED

Torver, Coniston LA21 8AZ
☎ (015394) 41282
Delightful unspoilt 14th C inn in the beautiful Torver Valley. Bar food, restaurant, beer garden and large car park.
Bedrooms: 4 double, 1 twin, 1 triple
Bathrooms: 4 en-suite, 2 private, 1 public

Bed & breakfast

per night:	£min	£max
Single	18.00	20.00
Double	44.00	46.00

Lunch available
Evening meal 1815 (last orders 2130)
Parking for 60
Cards accepted: Access, Visa, Diners, Amex

Crook Farm

Listed COMMENDED

Torver, Coniston LA21 8BP
☎ (015394) 41453
Farmhouse beautifully decorated and furnished to the highest standards. See your breakfast being cooked in the cosy Aga-warmed kitchen.
Bedrooms: 2 double, 1 triple
Bathrooms: 1 public

Bed & breakfast

per night:	£min	£max
Single	16.00	16.00
Double	32.00	32.00

Parking for 6

How Head Cottage

East of Lake Coniston, Coniston
LA21 8AA
☎ (015394) 41594
Fax (015394) 41594
Detached cottage in own grounds, overlooking lake and surrounding fells. Comfortable accommodation.
Bedrooms: 1 double, 1 twin, 1 triple
Bathrooms: 3 en-suite

Bed & breakfast

per night:	£min	£max
Single	25.00	25.00
Double	36.00	40.00

Parking for 9

Thwaite Cottage M

COMMENDED

Waterhead, Coniston LA21 8AJ
☎ (015394) 41367
Beautiful 17th C cottage in 2 acres of secluded garden and woodland. 5 minutes' walk from village, 200 yards from lake. Non-smoking, perfect peace.

George + Dragon = £17/person

Bedrooms: 2 double, 1 triple
Bathrooms: 1 en-suite, 2 private

Bed & breakfast per night:

	£min	£max
Double	34.00	40.00

Parking for 3

DENT

Cumbria
Map ref 5B3

Very picturesque village with narrow cobbled streets, lying within the boundaries of the Yorkshire Dales National Park.

Sun Inn ⋔

2x2x6

Listed APPROVED

Main Street, Dent, Sedbergh
LA10 5QL
☎ (01539) 625208

17th C inn with original beams, in an outstanding conservation area. Reputation for good value bar meals and serves beer from the local Dent Brewery.

Bedrooms: 2 double, 1 twin, 1 triple
Bathrooms: 1 public

Bed & breakfast per night:

	£min	£max
Single	17.50	20.00
Double	33.00	35.00

Lunch available
Evening meal 1830 (last orders 2030)
Parking for 20
Cards accepted: Access, Visa, Switch/Delta

ESKDALE

Cumbria
Map ref 5A3

Several minor roads lead to the west end of this beautiful valley, or it can be approached via the east over the Hardknott Pass, the Lake District's steepest pass. Scafell Pike and Bow Fell lie to the north and a miniature railway links the Eskdale Valley with Ravenglass on the coast.

Woolpack Inn ⋔

APPROVED

Boot, Eskdale CA19 1TH
☎ (01946) 723230
Fax (01946) 723230

Comfortable hotel serving real ale and home-cooked food, set in beautiful scenery at the head of the Eskdale Valley.

Bedrooms: 3 double, 4 twin, 1 family room

Bathrooms: 1 public, 4 private showers

Bed & breakfast per night:

	£min	£max
Single	19.50	24.50
Double	39.00	49.00

Half board per person:

	£min	£max
Daily	24.45	38.45
Weekly	175.00	270.00

Lunch available
Evening meal 1830 (last orders 2100)
Parking for 40
Cards accepted: Access, Visa

GRASMERE

Cumbria
Map ref 5A3

Described by William Wordsworth as "the loveliest spot that man hath ever found", this village, famous for its gingerbread, is in a beautiful setting overlooked by Helm Crag. Wordsworth lived at Dove Cottage. The cottage and museum are open to the public.

Beck Allans ⋔

Listed HIGHLY COMMENDED

College Street, Grasmere LA22 9SZ
☎ (015394) 35563
Fax (015394) 35563

Lakeland guesthouse hidden in the delightful well timbered grounds of Beck Allans Holiday Apartments. Centre of village, adjacent River Rothay, super views. Accommodation includes 2-bedroom family suite. Aga-cooked breakfast. Sky movies. Swimming pool and jacuzzi.

Bedrooms: 3 double, 1 twin
Bathrooms: 4 en-suite

Bed & breakfast per night:

	£min	£max
Double	43.00	51.00

Parking for 15
Open January–November
Cards accepted: Access, Visa

Craigside House ⋔

COMMENDED

Grasmere, Ambleside LA22 9SG
☎ (015394) 35292

Delightfully furnished Victorian house on the edge of the village near Dove Cottage. In a large, peaceful garden overlooking the lake and hills.

Bedrooms: 2 double, 1 twin
Bathrooms: 3 en-suite

Bed & breakfast per night:

	£min	£max
Single	29.00	53.00
Double	58.00	62.00

Parking for 6

Dunmail House ⋔

Listed APPROVED

Keswick Road, Grasmere, Ambleside
LA22 9RE
☎ (015394) 35256

Traditional stone house in lovely grounds, with friendly family atmosphere and beautiful views from all rooms.

Bedrooms: 1 single, 1 double, 1 twin, 1 triple
Bathrooms: 2 en-suite, 1 public

Bed & breakfast per night:

	£min	£max
Single	18.50	20.00
Double	35.00	50.00

Parking for 6

How Foot Lodge ⋔

♛♛

Town End, Grasmere LA22 9SQ
☎ (015394) 35366

Lovely Victorian guesthouse owned by the Wordsworth Trust, in own grounds overlooking Grasmere Lake and close to Dove Cottage.

Bedrooms: 4 double, 2 twin
Bathrooms: 4 en-suite, 2 private

Bed & breakfast per night:

	£min	£max
Single	30.00	40.00
Double	52.00	60.00

Parking for 6
Open February–December
Cards accepted: Access, Visa

GRASMERE

Continued

Kirk Allans Riverside Bed & Breakfast

COMMENDED

Church Bridge, Stock Lane,
Grasmere, Ambleside LA22 9SN
☎ (015394) 35219
Fax (015394) 35219
In village centre, incorporating attractive riverside frontage overlooking church. Comfortable en-suite rooms with colour TV, tea/coffee facilities. Private parking. Brochure available.
Bedrooms: 3 double
Bathrooms: 3 en-suite
Bed & breakfast

per night:	£min	£max
Double	40.00	46.00

Parking for 3
Open March–October

Redmayne M

HIGHLY COMMENDED

Keswick Road, Grasmere, Ambleside
LA22 9QY
☎ (015394) 35635
Superb private situation overlooking the Vale of Grasmere. Comfortable, beautifully appointed en-suite bedrooms. Non-smoking. Private parking.
Bedrooms: 1 double, 1 twin
Bathrooms: 2 en-suite
Bed & breakfast

per night:	£min	£max
Double	36.00	48.00

Parking for 2
Open February–November

Riversdale M

HIGHLY COMMENDED

Grasmere LA22 9RQ
☎ (015394) 35619
Delightful, old, tastefully furnished, 6-bedroomed Lakeland house. Riverside setting with fine views. Warm and welcoming and offering every comfort. Exceptional breakfast. Private parking.
Bedrooms: 3 double
Bathrooms: 2 en-suite, 1 private
Bed & breakfast

per night:	£min	£max
Double	42.00	54.00

Parking for 4

Travellers Rest M

Grasmere, Ambleside LA22 9RR
☎ (015394) 35604

Charming 16th C inn nestling in the heart of Lakeland and with superb views. Cumbrian hospitality includes good food, real ales, open fires and comfortable accommodation.
Bedrooms: 5 double, 3 twin
Bathrooms: 4 en-suite, 2 public
Bed & breakfast

per night:	£min	£max
Single	17.95	28.95
Double	35.90	57.90

Lunch available
Evening meal 1900 (last orders 2130)
Parking for 45
Cards accepted: Access, Visa, Switch/Delta

Woodland Crag Guest House M

HIGHLY COMMENDED

Howe Head Lane, Grasmere, Ambleside LA22 9SG
☎ (015394) 35351
Charming Victorian Lakeland-stone house with lake and fell views. Beautiful walks radiate from here. Peacefully situated in landscaped grounds on edge of village. No smoking, please.
Bedrooms: 2 single, 2 double, 1 twin
Bathrooms: 3 en-suite, 1 public
Bed & breakfast

per night:	£min	£max
Single	23.00	25.00
Double	25.00	27.00

Parking for 5

GRAYRIGG

Cumbria
Map ref 5B3

Village on the A685 north of Kendal. Important in the development of the Quaker church.

Grayrigg Hall Farm

Listed

Grayrigg, Kendal LA8 9BU
☎ (01539) 824689
1400-acre mixed farm. 18th C working farm in beautiful open countryside. Easy access to Lakes and dales. Good home cooking and a friendly welcome.
Bedrooms: 1 double, 1 triple
Bathrooms: 1 public
Bed & breakfast

per night:	£min	£max
Single	15.00	16.00
Double	29.00	30.00

Half board per person:

	£min	£max
Daily	21.00	22.00

Evening meal 2000 (last orders 2100)
Parking for 2
Open March–October

Punchbowl House

COMMENDED

Grayrigg, Kendal LA8 9BU
☎ (01539) 824345
Spacious Victorian farmhouse with log fires, in peaceful surroundings between Lakes and dales. Non-smoking.
Bedrooms: 2 double, 1 twin
Bathrooms: 1 en-suite, 1 public
Bed & breakfast

per night:	£min	£max
Single	16.00	30.00
Double	32.00	38.00

Parking for 6

HAWKSHEAD

Cumbria
Map ref 5A3

Lying near Esthwaite Water, this village has great charm and character. Its small squares are linked by flagged or cobbled alleys and the main square is dominated by the market house, or Shambles, where the butchers had their stalls in days gone by.

Red Lion Inn M

The Square, Hawkshead, Ambleside
LA22 0NS
☎ (015394) 36213
Fax (015394) 36747
14th C coaching inn in the centre of Hawkshead, a uniquely beautiful village in England's most beautiful corner.
Bedrooms: 9 double, 2 twin
Bathrooms: 11 en-suite
Bed & breakfast

per night:	£min	£max
Single	40.00	40.00
Double	60.00	60.00

Half board per person:

	£min	£max
Daily	45.00	45.00
Weekly	250.00	275.00

Lunch available
Evening meal 1900 (last orders 2130)
Parking for 12
Cards accepted: Access, Visa, Diners, Amex, Switch/Delta

The Sun Inn ▲▲

⚜⚜⚜ COMMENDED

Hawkshead, Ambleside LA22 0NT
☎ Windermere (015394) 36236
Fax (015394) 36674
16th C inn with original beams. A family-run business with friendly atmosphere, good food and wine. Very good value for money, families welcome.
Bedrooms: 6 double, 2 twin
Bathrooms: 8 en-suite

Bed & breakfast
per night:	£min	£max
Double	50.00	58.00

Lunch available
Evening meal 1800 (last orders 2130)
Parking for 8
Cards accepted: Access, Visa

⌂1🖵♨♿🗝🛏Ⓢ✂📺🗐🗜⛵🚲
♒ SP 🏠

This attractive village is set on a hill, and has a grammar school founded in 1613.

The Blue Bell at Heversham ▲▲

⚜⚜⚜⚜ HIGHLY COMMENDED

Princes Way, Heversham, Milnthorpe LA7 7EE
☎ Milnthorpe (015395) 62018
Fax (015395) 62455
Country hotel in a rural haven, an ideal touring centre. Adjacent to A6 south of Kendal.
Bedrooms: 1 single, 14 double, 6 twin, 1 triple
Bathrooms: 22 en-suite

Bed & breakfast
per night:	£min	£max
Single	37.50	49.50
Double	64.00	95.00

Half board per person:
Daily	£min	£max
	55.50	67.50

Lunch available
Evening meal 1900 (last orders 2130)
Parking for 100
Cards accepted: Access, Visa, Amex, Switch/Delta

⌂🏢📞📭🖵♨♿🗝🛏Ⓢ🖊📺Ⓘ🗐
🗜👤80♨♿❄ DAP ♒ SP 🏠 Ⓣ

A key to symbols can be found inside the back cover flap.

Overlooking the moors and close to the Lancashire border in an Area of Outstanding Natural Beauty. Holme Moss provides a particularly good scenic viewpoint.

Marwin House

Listed

Duke Street, Holme, Carnforth, Lancashire LA6 1PY
☎ Lancaster (01524) 781144 & 0378 135659
Situated in the small unspoilt village of Holme, 2 miles from M6 motorway. Gateway to Lake District and Yorkshire Dales.
Bedrooms: 1 double, 1 triple
Bathrooms: 1 public

Bed & breakfast
per night:	£min	£max
Single	16.00	16.00
Double	30.00	32.00

Parking for 2

⌂🖵♨♿ UL 🗝Ⓢ✂🖊📺🗐🗜❄
🐾🚲♒ SP

The "Auld Grey Town" lies in the valley of the River Kent with a backcloth of limestone fells. Situated just outside the Lake District National Park, it is a good centre for touring the Lakes and surrounding country. Ruined castle, reputed birthplace of Catherine Parr.
Tourist Information Centre ☎ (01539) 725758

Fairways Guest House

⚜⚜ COMMENDED

102 Windermere Road, Kendal LA9 5EZ
☎ (01539) 725564
On the main Kendal-Windermere road. Victorian guesthouse with en-suite facilities. TV, tea and coffee in all rooms. Four-poster bedrooms. Private parking.
Bedrooms: 3 double
Bathrooms: 3 en-suite, 1 public

Bed & breakfast
per night:	£min	£max
Single	18.00	20.00
Double	32.00	36.00

Parking for 4

⌂🏢📭🖵♨ UL 🗝Ⓢ✂🖊🗐🗜▶
🐾🚲

Gateside Farm

Listed COMMENDED

Windermere Road, Kendal LA9 5SE
☎ (01539) 722036

300-acre dairy & livestock farm. Traditional Lakeland farm easily accessible from the motorway and on the main tourist route through Lakeland. One night and short stays are welcome.
Bedrooms: 3 double, 1 twin, 1 family room
Bathrooms: 3 en-suite, 2 public

Bed & breakfast
per night:	£min	£max
Single	18.00	22.00
Double	33.00	38.00

Evening meal (last orders 1700)
Parking for 7

⌂🖵♨ UL 🖊🗐❄🚲 SP

Holmfield ▲▲

Listed DE LUXE

41 Kendal Green, Kendal LA9 5PP
☎ (01539) 720790
Fax (01539) 720790
Superb location. Elegant Edwardian house in large gardens. Panoramic views, swimming pool, croquet. Spacious bathrooms, lovely bedrooms, including four-poster. No smoking.
Bedrooms: 2 double, 1 twin
Bathrooms: 2 private, 2 public

Bed & breakfast
per night:	£min	£max
Single	19.00	25.00
Double	38.00	45.00

Parking for 7

⌂13🏊🏢📭🖵♨♿ UL 🗝Ⓢ✂🖊
📺🗐🗜♨❄🐾🚲 SP 🏠 Ⓣ

Newalls Farmhouse ▲▲

Listed COMMENDED

Skelsmergh, Kendal LA9 6NU
☎ (01539) 723202
500-acre dairy farm. Tastefully modernised farmhouse, with visitors' own private entrance into a large garden. Pubs and restaurants within 2 miles. Warm welcome assured.
Bedrooms: 2 double
Bathrooms: 1 en-suite, 1 public

Bed & breakfast
per night:	£min	£max
Single	15.00	16.00
Double	30.00	32.00

Continued ▶

KENDAL
Continued

Parking for 2
Open April–October

Park Lea
COMMENDED
15 Sunnyside, Kendal LA9 7DJ
☎ (01539) 740986
Fax (01539) 740986
Delightful Victorian house close to castle and river, overlooking parkland. Abbot Hall, Brewery Arts and town centre 5 minutes' walk.
Bedrooms: 2 double, 1 twin
Bathrooms: 2 en-suite, 1 private

Bed & breakfast per night:	£min	£max
Single	16.00	25.00
Double	32.00	36.00

Parking for 2

7 Thorny Hills
COMMENDED
Kendal LA9 7AL
☎ (01539) 720207
Beautiful, unspoilt Georgian town house. Peaceful, pretty location close to town centre. Good home cooking. Self-catering available. Non-smokers only, please.
Bedrooms: 2 double, 1 twin
Bathrooms: 3 private

Bed & breakfast per night:	£min	£max
Single	20.00	21.00
Double	38.00	38.00

Half board per person:	£min	£max
Daily	27.50	29.50

Evening meal from 1800
Parking for 3
Open January–November

WELCOME HOST
This is a nationally recognised customer care programme which aims to promote the highest standards of service and a warm welcome. Establishments who are taking part in this initiative are indicated by the ⊕ symbol.

KESWICK
Cumbria
Map ref 5A3

Beautifully positioned town beside Derwentwater and below the mountains of Skiddaw and Blencathra. Excellent base for walking, climbing, watersports and touring. Motor-launches operate on Derwentwater and motor boats, rowing boats and canoes can be hired.
Tourist Information Centre
☎ (017687) 72645

Acorn House Hotel
HIGHLY COMMENDED
Ambleside Road, Keswick CA12 4DL
☎ (017687) 72553
Fax (017687) 75332
Elegant Georgian house set in colourful garden. All bedrooms tastefully furnished, some four-poster beds. Cleanliness guaranteed. Close to town centre.
Bedrooms: 6 double, 1 twin, 3 triple
Bathrooms: 9 en-suite, 1 private

Bed & breakfast per night:	£min	£max
Single	25.00	35.00
Double	48.00	60.00

Parking for 10
Open February–November
Cards accepted: Access, Visa

Anworth House
Listed COMMENDED
27 Eskin Street, Keswick CA12 4DQ
☎ (017687) 72923
Small, friendly, family-run guesthouse. All rooms en-suite. Close to town centre, leisure pool, parks and lake.
Bedrooms: 1 single, 2 double, 2 triple
Bathrooms: 5 en-suite

Bed & breakfast per night:	£min	£max
Single	18.00	
Double	36.00	

Evening meal 1800 (last orders 1500)

Avondale Guest House
COMMENDED
20 Southey Street, Keswick CA12 4EF
☎ (017687) 72735
High quality, comfortable guesthouse with well-appointed en-suite rooms. Close to town centre, lake and parks. Non-smokers only, please.

Bedrooms: 1 single, 4 double, 1 twin
Bathrooms: 4 en-suite, 1 public

Bed & breakfast per night:	£min	£max
Single	18.50	19.50
Double	37.00	39.00

Cards accepted: Access, Visa, Switch/Delta

Bank Tavern
Listed
47 Main Street, Keswick CA12 5DS
☎ (017687) 72663
Fax (017687) 75168
A country pub in the town centre.
Bedrooms: 2 double, 2 twin, 1 triple
Bathrooms: 1 public

Bed & breakfast per night:	£min	£max
Single	15.00	15.00
Double	30.00	30.00

Lunch available
Evening meal 1800 (last orders 2100)
Parking for 5

Beckside
COMMENDED
5 Wordsworth Street, Keswick CA12 4HU
☎ (017687) 73093
Small, no-smoking guesthouse in a central location. Accent on home cooking. Optional evening meal.
Bedrooms: 3 double, 1 twin
Bathrooms: 4 en-suite

Bed & breakfast per night:	£min	£max
Single	18.00	18.50
Double	36.00	38.00

Half board per person:	£min	£max
Daily	29.00	29.50
Weekly	203.00	206.50

Evening meal 1830 (last orders 1300)

Birkrigg Farm
Listed APPROVED
Newlands, Keswick CA12 5TS
☎ Braithwaite (017687) 78278
250-acre mixed farm. Pleasantly and peacefully located in the lovely Newlands Valley, amongst beautiful mountain scenery. 5 miles from Keswick, between Braithwaite and Buttermere.
Bedrooms: 1 single, 2 double, 1 twin, 1 triple, 1 family room
Bathrooms: 2 public

50

Bed & breakfast

per night:	£min	£max
Single	15.00	17.00
Double	30.00	34.00

Parking for 6
Open March–November

Dancing Beck

Underskiddaw, Keswick CA12 4PZ
☎ (017687) 73800
Lakeland house, with views of Derwent Valley and Lakeland mountains, 2.5 miles from Keswick, just off A591 Keswick-Carlisle road.
Bedrooms: 1 double, 2 twin
Bathrooms: 1 en-suite, 1 private,
1 private shower
Bed & breakfast

per night:	£min	£max
Double	40.00	44.00

Parking for 3
Open March–October

Hazeldene Hotel ⚊

APPROVED

The Heads, Keswick CA12 5ER
☎ (017687) 72106
Fax (017687) 75435
Beautiful and central with open views of Skiddaw and Borrowdale and Newlands Valleys. Midway between town centre and Lake Derwentwater.
Bedrooms: 5 single, 9 double, 4 twin,
4 triple
Bathrooms: 17 en-suite, 3 private,
2 public
Bed & breakfast

per night:	£min	£max
Single	23.00	29.00
Double	46.00	58.00

Half board per

person:	£min	£max
Daily	37.00	43.00
Weekly	249.00	288.00

Evening meal 1830 (last orders 1600)
Parking for 18
Open February–November

Kings Head Hotel ⚊

APPROVED

Thirlspot, Keswick CA12 4TN
☎ (017687) 72393
Fax (017687) 72309
Situated at the foot of Helvellyn on the main A591, approximately 5 miles south of Keswick. This 17th C former coaching inn is family-run and offers a wide range of real ales and wines, with good food and comfortable accommodation.

Bedrooms: 3 single, 8 double, 3 twin,
2 triple, 1 family room
Bathrooms: 17 en-suite, 1 public
Bed & breakfast

per night:	£min	£max
Single	17.95	28.95
Double	35.90	57.90

Half board per

person:	£min	£max
Daily	27.95	38.95
Weekly	195.95	252.95

Lunch available
Evening meal 1800 (last orders 2130)
Parking for 60
Cards accepted: Access, Visa, Switch/Delta

Littletown Farm ⚊

COMMENDED

Newlands, Keswick CA12 5TU
☎ Braithwaite (017687) 78353
150-acre mixed farm. In the beautiful, unspoilt Newlands Valley. En-suite bedrooms. Comfortable residents' lounge, dining room and cosy bar. Traditional 4-course dinner 6 nights a week.
Bedrooms: 4 double, 2 twin, 2 triple,
2 family rooms
Bathrooms: 6 en-suite, 1 public
Bed & breakfast

per night:	£min	£max
Single	24.00	28.00
Double	48.00	56.00

Half board per

person:	£min	£max
Daily	35.00	39.00
Weekly	215.00	240.00

Evening meal from 1900
Parking for 10
Open March–December
Cards accepted: Access, Visa

Lonnin Garth Country Guesthouse ⚊

COMMENDED

Portinscale, Keswick CA12 5RS
☎ (017687) 74095
Country house set in own grounds overlooking the northern fells, with lovely views. A friendly base for walking, touring and relaxing.
Bedrooms: 3 double, 2 twin
Bathrooms: 4 en-suite, 1 public
Bed & breakfast

per night:	£min	£max
Single	18.50	21.00
Double	37.00	42.00

Parking for 6

Lynwood House ⚊

COMMENDED

35 Helvellyn Street, Keswick
CA12 4EP
☎ (017687) 72398

Non-smoking, Victorian, licensed guesthouse, 5 minutes from town centre. Comfortable lounge, colour TV in each room, own key. Genuine home cooking.
Bedrooms: 1 single, 3 double,
1 triple
Bathrooms: 1 public
Bed & breakfast

per night:	£min	£max
Single	15.00	15.50
Double	30.00	32.00

Half board per

person:	£min	£max
Daily	24.50	25.00
Weekly	162.00	165.00

Evening meal 1830 (last orders 1930)

Ravensworth Hotel ⚊

HIGHLY COMMENDED

29 Station Street, Keswick
CA12 5HH
☎ (017687) 72476
Small, family-run licensed hotel, decorated to a high standard of comfort, situated close to Keswick's amenities. An ideal Lake District base.
Bedrooms: 7 double, 1 twin
Bathrooms: 7 en-suite, 1 private
Bed & breakfast

per night:	£min	£max
Single	21.00	35.00
Double	30.00	50.00

Parking for 5
Open March–November
Cards accepted: Access, Visa

Richmond House ⚊

37-39 Eskin Street, Keswick
CA12 4DG
☎ (017687) 73965
Family-run guesthouse, home-from-home, easy walking distance to town centre and lake. Vegetarians catered for. Non-smokers only, please.

Continued ▶

KESWICK

Continued

Bedrooms: 3 single, 4 double, 1 twin, 1 triple
Bathrooms: 8 en-suite, 1 public

Bed & breakfast per night:

	£min	£max
Single	16.00	21.50
Double	32.00	43.00

Half board per person:

	£min	£max
Daily	25.50	31.00
Weekly	160.00	185.00

Evening meal 1900 (last orders 1700)
Cards accepted: Access, Visa, Amex

🛏4🏠💻♿🍴⑤✗🅿️📺🖥️📞
🍴20✗🚭 SP ◉

Watendlath Guest House ⋀

Listed COMMENDED

15 Acorn Street, Keswick
CA12 4EA
☎ (017687) 74165
Within easy walking distance of the lake, hills and town centre. We offer a warm and friendly welcome and traditional English breakfast.
Bedrooms: 4 double, 1 twin
Bathrooms: 2 en-suite, 1 public

Bed & breakfast per night:

	£min	£max
Double	28.00	35.00

Open February–December

🛏🏠💻♿🔌ⓊⓁⓈ🖥️🅿️✗🚭
SP

Whitehouse Guest House

COMMENDED

15 Ambleside Road, Keswick
CA12 4DL
☎ (017687) 73176
Fully refurbished, small, friendly guesthouse 5 minutes' walk from the town centre. Colour TV, electric blankets, tea/coffee. Most rooms with en-suite facilities.
Bedrooms: 4 double
Bathrooms: 3 private, 1 public, 1 private shower

Bed & breakfast per night:

	£min	£max
Double	30.00	37.00

Parking for 3
Open March–October

🛏🏠💻♿ⓊⓁ🖥️📺🖥️🅿️🚭

For further information on accommodation establishments use the coupons at the back of this guide.

KIRKBY STEPHEN

Cumbria
Map ref 5B3

Old market town close to the River Eden, with many fine Georgian buildings and an attractive market square. St Stephen's Church is known as the "Cathedral of the Dales". Good base for exploring the Eden Valley and the Dales.

Augill House Farm ⋀

👑 HIGHLY COMMENDED

Brough, Kirkby Stephen CA17 4DX
☎ Brough (017683) 41305

40-acre mixed farm. Spacious Georgian farmhouse, where the emphasis is on good food and hospitality. Enjoy super breakfasts and delicious 4-course dinners served in our lovely conservatory overlooking the garden.
Bedrooms: 2 double, 1 twin
Bathrooms: 3 en-suite

Bed & breakfast per night:

	£min	£max
Double	40.00	42.00

Half board per person:

	£min	£max
Daily	30.00	32.00
Weekly	190.00	195.00

Evening meal from 1900
Parking for 6

🛏12📞🏠💻♿🔌ⓊⓁ✗🅿️📺🖥️
🖥️✋🔆✗🚭 SP

Ing Hill Lodge ⋀

👑👑 COMMENDED

Mallerstang Dale, Mallerstang, Kirkby Stephen CA17 4JT
☎ (017683) 71153
Fax (017683) 71153
Delightful Georgian country home in Mallerstang Valley with glorious views. Peace, quiet, open fires, home cooking and a warm welcome.
Bedrooms: 2 double, 1 triple
Bathrooms: 3 en-suite, 1 public

Bed & breakfast per night:

	£min	£max
Double	40.00	50.00

Half board per person:

	£min	£max
Daily	32.50	37.50

Evening meal from 1930
Parking for 5

🏠💻♿🍴⑤✗🖥️🅿️🔆🚭 SP

The Old Rectory

Listed HIGHLY COMMENDED

Crosby Garrett, Kirkby Stephen
CA17 4PW
☎ (017683) 72074

Grade II listed 17th C rectory of immense character. Oak beams, panelled rooms and log fires. In picturesque village 4 miles from Kirkby Stephen. Home Aga cooking.*
Bedrooms: 2 double, 1 twin
Bathrooms: 2 en-suite, 1 private

Bed & breakfast per night:

	£min	£max
Single	20.00	26.00
Double	36.00	40.00

Half board per person:

	£min	£max
Daily	28.00	30.00

Evening meal 1800 (last orders 2100)
Parking for 3

🛏🏠💻♿🔌ⓊⓁⓈ✗🖥️📺🖥️🅿️🔆
🖥️ SP

KIRKBY-IN-FURNESS

Cumbria
Map ref 5A3

Commercial Inn

👑👑 APPROVED

Askew Gate Brow,
Kirkby-in-Furness LA17 7TE
☎ Kirkby in Furness (01229) 889039
En-suite accommodation with own entrance, adjoining 200-year-old licensed freehouse. Situated south of the Lake District, 12 miles from Coniston, 20 miles from Windermere.
Bedrooms: 2 double
Bathrooms: 2 en-suite

Bed & breakfast per night:

	£min	£max
Single	23.50	
Double	35.00	

Evening meal 1800 (last orders 2000)
Parking for 8

🍴🏠💻♿🔌🖥️📺🖥️🅿️🔆✻🖥️

LAMPLUGH

Cumbria
Map ref 5A3

Near the A5086 between Cockermouth and Cleator Moor, Lamplugh is a scattered village famous for its "Lamplugh Pudding". Ideal touring base for the western Lake District.

Briscoe Close Farm
Listed COMMENDED

Scalesmoor, Lamplugh, Workington CA14 4TZ
☎ (01946) 861633
Bungalow close to family-run farm. Near Loweswater and Ennerdale, half a mile from A5086. Home cooking using produce grown on farm.
Bedrooms: 2 double
Bathrooms: 1 public

Bed & breakfast per night:	£min	£max
Single	16.00	16.00
Double	32.00	32.00

Half board per person:	£min	£max
Daily	23.00	23.00
Weekly	150.00	150.00

Evening meal from 1900
Parking for 2

LAZONBY

Cumbria
Map ref 5B2

Busy, working village of stone cottages, set beside the River Eden amid sweeping pastoral landscape. Good fishing available.

Banktop House
COMMENDED

Lazonby, Penrith CA10 1AQ
☎ Penrith (01768) 898268
Listed house in garden and cobbled courtyard setting. Ideal for Eden Valley walks and attractions, central Ullswater, Pennines and Scottish borders.
Bedrooms: 1 double, 1 twin
Bathrooms: 1 en-suite, 1 private

Bed & breakfast per night:	£min	£max
Single	18.00	19.00
Double	32.00	35.00

Parking for 3
Open March–October

LEVENS

Cumbria
Map ref 5B3

Village at the southern tip of Scout Scar, overlooking the Lyth Valley. Just outside the village is Levens Hall, an Elizabethan mansion with topiary gardens open to the public.

Olde Peat Cotes
Listed

Sampool Lane, Levens, Kendal LA8 8EH
☎ Sedgwick (015395) 60096
Modern bungalow with homely atmosphere, lovely views and beautiful garden. Fishing available on River Kent. Suitable for wheelchairs.
Bedrooms: 1 double, 1 twin
Bathrooms: 1 public

Bed & breakfast per night:	£min	£max
Single	10.00	10.00
Double	20.00	20.00

Parking for 2

LONGTOWN

Cumbria
Map ref 5A2

Perfect base from which to explore the magnificent Borderlands, lying adjacent to the site of the Battle of Solway Moss fought in 1542 between the English and the Scots. Handsome bridge and England's largest sheep market.
Tourist Information Centre ☎ (01228) 791876

Craigburn
COMMENDED

Penton, Longtown, Carlisle CA6 5QP
☎ Nicholforest (01228) 577214
Fax (01228) 577214

250-acre mixed farm. One of the best farmhouses for delicious food. Beautiful bedrooms, some four-poster beds. Pets' corner.
Bedrooms: 3 double, 3 twin, 2 triple
Bathrooms: 8 en-suite

Bed & breakfast per night:	£min	£max
Single	25.00	26.00
Double	42.00	44.00

Half board per person:	£min	£max
Daily	33.00	35.00

Evening meal 1800 (last orders 1400)
Parking for 20
Cards accepted: Access, Visa

LORTON

Cumbria
Map ref 5A3

High and Low Lorton are set in a beautiful vale north of Crummock Water and at the foot of the Whinlatter Pass. Church of St Cuthbert is well worth a visit.

New House Farm
HIGHLY COMMENDED

Lorton, Cockermouth CA13 9UU
☎ (01900) 85404
Fax (01900) 85404

The very best of small country guest houses in quiet Lakeland valley. Old fashioned hospitality and traditional cuisine. Major tourism award winners 1994 and 1995.
Bedrooms: 3 double
Bathrooms: 3 en-suite

Bed & breakfast per night:	£min	£max
Single	30.00	40.00
Double	50.00	60.00

Half board per person:	£min	£max
Daily	45.00	50.00

Lunch available
Evening meal 1930 (last orders 1930)
Parking for 20

LOWESWATER

Cumbria
Map ref 5A3

Scattered village lying between Loweswater, one of the smaller lakes, and Crummock Water. Mountains surround this quiet valley of three lakes, giving some marvellous views.

Brook Farm
COMMENDED

Thackthwaite, Loweswater, Cockermouth CA13 0RP
☎ Lorton (01900) 85606
300-acre hill farm. In quiet surroundings and a good walking area, 5 miles from Cockermouth. Carrying sheep and suckler cows.
Bedrooms: 1 double, 1 twin
Bathrooms: 1 public
Bed & breakfast

per night:	£min	£max
Single	17.00	18.00
Double	34.00	36.00

Half board per

person:	£min	£max
Daily	24.00	25.00
Weekly	161.00	175.00

Evening meal from 1900
Parking for 3
Open May–October

Kirkstile Inn
Listed COMMENDED

Loweswater, Cockermouth
CA13 0RU
☎ Lorton (0190085) 219
A 16th C inn near an oak-fringed beck running between Loweswater and Crummock Water lakes, surrounded by fells.
Bedrooms: 5 double, 2 twin, 3 triple
Bathrooms: 8 en-suite, 2 public
Bed & breakfast

per night:	£min	£max
Single	20.00	45.00
Double	40.00	55.00

Lunch available
Evening meal 1830 (last orders 2100)
Parking for 40
Cards accepted: Access, Visa

> Half board prices are given per person, but in some cases these may be based on double/twin occupancy.

ORTON

Cumbria
Map ref 5B3

Small, attractive village with the background of Orton Scar, it has some old buildings and a spacious green. George Whitehead, the itinerant Quaker preacher, was born here in 1636.

Vicarage
Listed COMMENDED

Orton, Penrith CA10 3RQ
☎ (015396) 24873
Fax (015396) 24873
Warm, comfortable accommodation in a working vicarage overlooking rooftops and fells. Ideal for walkers visiting the Lakes and Yorkshire Dales. M6 junction 38.
Bedrooms: 1 double, 2 twin
Bathrooms: 1 public
Bed & breakfast

per night:	£min	£max
Single	16.00	
Double	32.00	

Half board per

person:	£min	£max
Daily	25.00	

Evening meal 1900 (last orders 2100)
Parking for 2

OXEN PARK

Cumbria
Map ref 5A3

Situated between lakes Windermere and Coniston and close to Grizedale Forest Park.

The Manor House
COMMENDED

Oxen Park, Ulverston LA12 8HG
☎ Ulverston (01229) 861345
18th C manor house between Lakes Windermere and Coniston, adjacent to Grizedale Forest. A haven of peace and comfort. Noted in "Good Beer Guide".
Bedrooms: 1 single, 3 double, 1 twin
Bathrooms: 3 en-suite, 2 private
Bed & breakfast

per night:	£min	£max
Single	19.00	25.00
Double	40.00	50.00

Lunch available
Evening meal 1830 (last orders 2130)
Parking for 25

PENRITH

Cumbria
Map ref 5B2

Ancient and historic market town, the northern gateway to the Lake District. Penrith Castle was built as a defence against the Scots. Its ruins, open to the public, stand in the public park. High above the town is the Penrith Beacon, made famous by William Wordsworth.
Tourist Information Centre ☎ (01768) 867466

Albany House
Listed COMMENDED

5 Portland Place, Penrith
CA11 7QN
☎ (01768) 863072
Large Victorian terraced house run by proprietress and providing good facilities. Ideal for Lake District and stopover to or from Scotland. Children welcome, special diets catered for on request.
Bedrooms: 1 double, 3 triple, 1 family room
Bathrooms: 1 en-suite, 2 public
Bed & breakfast

per night:	£min	£max
Double	31.00	46.00

Parking for 1

Glendale
Listed COMMENDED

4 Portland Place, Penrith
CA11 7QN
☎ (01768) 862579
Victorian town house overlooking pleasant gardens. Spacious family rooms. Children and pets welcome. Special diets catered for on request.
Bedrooms: 1 single, 1 double, 3 triple
Bathrooms: 1 public
Bed & breakfast

per night:	£min	£max
Single	18.00	19.00
Double	33.00	34.00

Parking for 1

> Map references apply to the colour maps at the back of this guide.

> For ideas on places to visit refer to the introduction at the beginning of this section.

Hornby Hall Country House M

Listed HIGHLY COMMENDED

Hornby Hall Farm, Brougham, Penrith CA10 2AR
☎ Culgaith (01768) 891114 & Vodaphone 0831 482108
Fax (01768) 88248

850-acre mixed farm. 16th C farmhouse with original dining hall. Fishing on Eamont available. Easy reach of Lakes and Yorkshire Dales. Home-cooked local produce.
Bedrooms: 2 single, 2 double, 3 twin
Suites available
Bathrooms: 2 en-suite, 3 public

Bed & breakfast

per night:	£min	£max
Single	20.00	30.00
Double	50.00	60.00

Half board per

person:	£min	£max
Daily	35.00	45.00
Weekly	210.00	270.00

Evening meal 1900 (last orders 2100)
Parking for 10
Cards accepted: Access, Visa

Newton Rigg College M

Listed

Penrith CA11 0AH
☎ (01768) 863791
Fax (01768) 867249
College in beautiful setting with standard and en-suite accommodation. Bar, dining room, shop, sporting facilities. Self-catering also available.
Bedrooms: 8 single
Bathrooms: 8 en-suite

Bed & breakfast

per night:	£min	£max
Single	16.00	19.00
Double	30.00	34.00

Half board per

person:	£min	£max
Daily	22.50	25.00

Lunch available
Evening meal 1800 (last orders 1930)
Parking for 300
Open June–August and Christmas

The White House M

COMMENDED

Clifton, Penrith CA10 2EL
☎ (01768) 865115

Situated in a rural area, an 18th C converted farmhouse where guests' comfort and enjoyment take priority. Ullswater, Haweswater, Eden Valley nearby. Fully licensed. For non-smokers only.
Bedrooms: 2 single, 1 twin, 2 triple
Bathrooms: 3 en-suite, 2 private

Bed & breakfast

per night:	£min	£max
Single	19.00	28.00
Double	42.00	42.00

Half board per

person:	£min	£max
Daily	31.50	33.50
Weekly	199.50	213.50

Evening meal 1900 (last orders 1200)
Parking for 8
Open January–October and Christmas

Causa Grange M

DE LUXE

Rosley, Wigton CA7 8DD
☎ Wigton (016973) 45358
Charming Victorian house set in the heart of the countryside yet only 8 miles from historic Carlisle. Overlooking Caldbeck Fells towards Lake District. Fine food and furnishings, log fires and a warm welcome.
Bedrooms: 1 double, 1 twin
Bathrooms: 1 en-suite, 1 private, 1 public

Bed & breakfast

per night:	£min	£max
Single	25.00	30.00
Double	45.00	52.00

Half board per

person:	£min	£max
Daily	32.00	42.00
Weekly	214.00	239.00

Evening meal 1800 (last orders 2100)
Parking for 9

Small seaside village with fine Norman church and a public school founded in the 16th C. Dramatic red sandstone cliffs make up impressive St Bees Head, parts of which are RSPB reserves and home to puffins and black guillemot. Start or finishing point of Wainwright's Coast to Coast Walk.

Stonehouse Farm

Listed APPROVED

Main Street, Next to Railway Station, St Bees CA27 0DE
☎ Whitehaven (01946) 822 224
50-acre livestock farm. Modernised Georgian listed farmhouse, conveniently and attractively situated next to station, shops and hotels. Start of Coast-to-Coast Walk. Golf-course, long-stay car park.
Bedrooms: 1 single, 2 double, 2 twin, 1 family room
Bathrooms: 1 en-suite, 3 public

Bed & breakfast

per night:	£min	£max
Single	18.00	20.00
Double	30.00	38.00

Parking for 8

Far Sawrey and Near Sawrey lie near Esthwaite Water. Both villages are small but Near Sawrey is famous for Hill Top Farm, home of Beatrix Potter, now owned by the National Trust and open to the public.

Tower Bank Arms M

Listed COMMENDED

Near Sawrey, Ambleside LA22 0LF
☎ Hawkshead (015394) 36334
Fax (015394) 36334
Next door to Hill Top, the former home of Beatrix Potter. It features in the tale of Jemima Puddleduck.
Bedrooms: 2 double, 1 twin
Bathrooms: 3 en-suite

Bed & breakfast

per night:	£min	£max
Single		33.00
Double		45.00

Lunch available
Evening meal 1830 (last orders 2100)

Continued ▶

SAWREY

Continued

Parking for 8
Cards accepted: Access, Visa, Amex, Switch/Delta

SCOTBY

Cumbria
Map ref 5A2

Oakleigh Bed and Breakfast

Listed **COMMENDED**
10 Broomfallen Road, Scotby,
Carlisle CA4 8DB
☎ Carlisle (01228) 513993
Detached Victorian house with 1 acre of garden, situated in quiet village.
Bedrooms: 1 double, 1 twin
Bathrooms: 1 en-suite, 1 public
Bed & breakfast

per night:	£min	£max
Single	16.00	18.00
Double	36.00	40.00

Evening meal 1900 (last orders 2000)
Parking for 3

SILECROFT

Cumbria
Map ref 5A3

Quiet, coastal community offering pebble and sand beaches, 9-hole golf-course, coastal walks and access to Black Combe and the Whicham Valley.

Miners Arms 𝐀

COMMENDED
Silecroft, Millom LA18 5LP
☎ Millom (01229) 772325 & 773397
Small, friendly coaching inn 5 minutes' drive from the beach and golf-course. Hospitality enjoyed by visitors and locals alike.
Bedrooms: 2 double, 2 twin
Bathrooms: 3 en-suite, 1 private, 1 public
Bed & breakfast

per night:	£min	£max
Single	20.00	20.00
Double	32.00	32.00

Half board per

person:	£min	£max
Daily	25.00	35.00
Weekly	170.00	210.00

Lunch available
Evening meal 1800 (last orders 2200)
Parking for 50

STAVELEY

Cumbria
Map ref 5A3

Large village built in slate, set between Kendal and Windermere at the entrance to the lovely Kentmere Valley.

Stock Bridge Farm 𝐀

Listed **COMMENDED**
Kendal Road, Staveley, Kendal
LA8 9LP
☎ (01539) 821580
20-acre mixed farm. Comfortable, well-appointed 17th C farmhouse on edge of bypassed village midway between Kendal and Windermere on A591. Central heating. English breakfast. Friendly, personal attention.
Bedrooms: 1 single, 4 double,
1 triple
Bathrooms: 1 public
Bed & breakfast

per night:	£min	£max
Single	15.00	
Double	30.00	

Parking for 6
Open March–October

TEBAY

Cumbria
Map ref 5B3

Village lying amongst high fells at the north end of the Lune Gorge.

Primrose Cottage

Listed **COMMENDED**
Orton Road, Tebay, Penrith
CA10 3TL
☎ Penrith (015396) 24791
Approximately 50 yards from M6, junction 38. Overnight stops/short breaks, excellent facilities. Close to Lakes and Yorkshire Dales.
Bedrooms: 2 double, 1 twin
Bathrooms: 1 private, 1 public
Bed & breakfast

per night:	£min	£max
Single	18.00	25.00
Double	32.00	40.00

Half board per

person:	£min	£max
Daily	28.00	35.00

Lunch available
Parking for 6

TROUTBECK

Cumbria
Map ref 5A3

On the Penrith to Keswick road, Troutbeck was the site of a series of Roman camps. The village now hosts a busy weekly sheep market.

Lane Head Farm Guest House 𝐀

Troutbeck, Penrith CA11 0SY
☎ Threlkeld (017687) 79220
Charming 17th C former farmhouse in quiet location, 4 miles from Ullswater lake. Good home cooking, table licence. Log fire, some en-suite and four-poster rooms.
Bedrooms: 1 single, 5 double, 2 twin,
1 family room
Bathrooms: 5 en-suite, 1 public
Bed & breakfast

per night:	£min	£max
Single	16.00	25.00
Double	32.00	44.00

Half board per

person:	£min	£max
Daily	23.95	32.95
Weekly	150.00	207.00

Evening meal 1900 (last orders 2000)
Parking for 10

Troutbeck Inn 𝐀

COMMENDED
Troutbeck, Penrith CA11 0SJ
☎ Greystoke (017684) 83635
A warm, friendly welcome awaits you in this family-run country inn. 10 minutes from M6, Ullswater and Keswick. Good bar food and personal service. Ideal for all Lakeland activities.
Bedrooms: 4 double, 1 twin, 1 triple
Bathrooms: 6 en-suite
Bed & breakfast

per night:	£min	£max
Single	22.00	25.00
Double	38.00	46.00

Evening meal 1830 (last orders 2100)
Parking for 50

Map references apply to the colour maps at the back of this guide.

ULLSWATER

Cumbria
Map ref 5A3

This beautiful lake, which is over 7 miles long, runs from Glenridding to Pooley Bridge. Lofty peaks ranging around the lake make an impressive background. A steamer service operates along the lake between Pooley Bridge, Howtown and Glenridding in the summer.

Bank House Farm

HIGHLY COMMENDED

Matterdale End, Penrith CA11 0LF
☎ Glenridding (017684) 82040 &
0831 236076
Fax (017684) 82040
Elevated former farmhouse set in 12 acres. Large garden offering peace and tranquillity in a fellside location. Extensive views of the Ullswater fells. Laura Ashley/Liberty furnishings and Aga-cooked breakfast.
Bedrooms: 2 double, 1 twin
Bathrooms: 3 en-suite

Bed & breakfast

per night:	£min	£max
Single	23.50	25.00
Double	47.00	50.00

Parking for 4

Bridge End Farm

COMMENDED

Hutton, Hutton John, Penrith CA11 0LZ
☎ Greystoke (017684) 83273
14-acre mixed farm. Warmest hospitality in 17th C farmhouse, situated in own grounds with gardens to river. Lakeland fell views. 5 miles west of M6, half a mile A66, 3 miles Ullswater.
Bedrooms: 2 double, 1 twin, 1 triple
Bathrooms: 4 en-suite

Bed & breakfast

per night:	£min	£max
Double	32.00	36.00

Half board per

person:	£min	£max
Daily	23.00	26.00
Weekly	155.00	160.00

Evening meal 1830 (last orders 1700)
Parking for 6
Open April–October

Elm House

COMMENDED

Pooley Bridge, Penrith CA10 2NH
☎ Pooley Bridge (017684) 86334
Fax (017684) 86334
Pleasant country house in unspoilt

village. Ideal base for visiting Lakes. A warm and friendly stay assured.
Bedrooms: 4 double, 1 twin
Bathrooms: 2 private, 1 public

Bed & breakfast

per night:	£min	£max
Single	18.00	20.00
Double	32.00	36.00

Parking for 5

Land Ends

COMMENDED

Watermillock, Ullswater, Penrith CA11 0NB
☎ Pooley Bridge (017684) 86438
Fax (017684) 86959
Converted farmhouse/barn set in 7 acres of grounds with two small lakes. 1.5 miles from Ullswater. En-suite accommodation. Quiet setting. Cosy lounge.
Bedrooms: 3 single, 4 double, 2 twin
Bathrooms: 9 en-suite

Bed & breakfast

per night:	£min	£max
Single	26.00	28.00
Double	48.00	52.00

Parking for 15

Netherdene Guest House

COMMENDED

Troutbeck, Penrith CA11 0SJ
☎ Greystoke (017684) 83475
Traditional country house in its own quiet grounds, with extensive mountain views, offering comfortable well-appointed rooms and personal attention. Ideal base for touring Lakeland.
Bedrooms: 1 single, 2 double, 1 twin, 1 triple
Bathrooms: 5 en-suite

Bed & breakfast

per night:	£min	£max
Single	18.00	22.00
Double	32.00	37.00

Half board per

person:	£min	£max
Daily	24.00	26.00
Weekly	160.00	170.00

Evening meal 1830 (last orders 1600)
Parking for 6

Tymparon Hall

COMMENDED

Newbiggin, Stainton, Penrith CA11 0HS
☎ Greystoke (017684) 83236

150-acre livestock farm. Delightful 18th C manor house with colourful summer garden in excellent location. Lake Ullswater a 10-minute drive.
Bedrooms: 3 double
Bathrooms: 2 en-suite, 1 public

Bed & breakfast

per night:	£min	£max
Single	20.00	20.00
Double	38.00	40.00

Half board per

person:	£min	£max
Daily	28.00	31.00
Weekly	185.00	195.00

Evening meal 1830 (last orders 1430)
Open April–October

White Lion Inn

COMMENDED

Patterdale, Penrith CA11 0NW
☎ Patterdale (017684) 82214
Old world country inn with friendly atmosphere, on Lake Ullswater near Helvellyn. An ideal centre for walking, fishing and sailing. Traditional beer.
Bedrooms: 2 single, 2 double, 3 twin
Bathrooms: 6 en-suite

Bed & breakfast

per night:	£min	£max
Single	25.00	

Lunch available
Evening meal 1830 (last orders 2145)
Parking for 50

WASDALE

Cumbria
Map ref 5A3

A very dramatic valley with England's deepest lake, Wastwater, highest mountain, Scafell Pike, and smallest church. The eastern shore of Wastwater is dominated by the 1,500 ft screes dropping steeply into the lake. A good centre for walking and climbing.

Church Stile Farm House

COMMENDED

Church Stile, Nether Wasdale, Gosforth, Seascale CA20 1ET
☎ Seascale (019467) 26028
495-acre hill farm. Traditional

Continued ▶

WASDALE

Continued

Cumbrian farmhouse in the pretty village of Nether Wasdale, with superb views, walks and climbing.
Bedrooms: 1 single, 1 double, 1 triple
Bathrooms: 3 en-suite

Bed & breakfast

per night:	£min	£max
Single	17.00	17.50
Double	38.00	40.00

Half board per person:

	£min	£max
Daily	30.00	32.00
Weekly	210.00	220.00

Evening meal 1830 (last orders 2000)
Parking for 2
Open January–November

🛇🐾🎠🖳🖵💆🖐🖩 UL 🛡 S ⚒ 🖭 🛒 ♨
♃♪✈🕊 🚐 SP

WELTON

Cumbria
Map ref 5A2

Old and new houses spread around a large village green with a tall maypole at Welton, "the place by a spring", between Caldbeck and Carlisle.

Lakelynn

Listed COMMENDED

Warnell, Welton, Carlisle CA5 7HW
☎ (016974) 76239
Tudor former farmhouse with comfortable family suite, set in pretty and unusual gardens with a panoramic view of the Eden Valley and close to the Cumbrian Way. Varied fine food menus.
Bedrooms: 1 triple
Bathrooms: 1 en-suite

Bed & breakfast

per night:	£min	£max
Single		19.50
Double		36.00

Half board per person:

	£min	£max
Daily	23.00	30.00

Evening meal 1800 (last orders 2100)
Parking for 4

🛇🐾🖳🖵💆🖐 UL 🛡 S ⚒ 🖭 🛒 ♨ 🚐
✈ 🕊 ⊚

For ideas on places to visit refer to the introduction at the beginning of this section

WINDERMERE

Cumbria
Map ref 5A3

Once a tiny hamlet before the introduction of the railway in 1847, now adjoins Bowness which is on the lakeside. Centre for sailing and boating. A good way to see the lake is a trip on a passenger steamer. Steamboat Museum has a fine collection of old boats.
Tourist Information Centre
☎ *(015394) 46499*

Aaron Slack 👭

⌂ COMMENDED

48 Ellerthwaite Road, Windermere LA23 2BS
☎ (015394) 44649 & Mobile 0374 638714
Small, friendly guesthouse for non-smokers in a quiet part of Windermere, close to all amenities and concentrating on personal service.
Bedrooms: 2 double, 1 twin
Bathrooms: 2 en-suite, 1 private

Bed & breakfast

per night:	£min	£max
Single	15.00	22.00
Double	30.00	44.00

Cards accepted: Access, Visa, Amex

🛇🐾12🖳🖵💆🖐 UL 🛡 S ⚒ 🖭 🛒 ♨ ✈
🚐 🕊 T

The Beaumont Hotel 👭

⌂⌂ HIGHLY COMMENDED

Holly Road, Windermere LA23 2AF
☎ (015394) 47075
Fax (015394) 47075

Elegant Victorian house hotel with beautiful lounge. All rooms are en-suite, with colour TV, hairdryer, tea/coffee making facilities. Some four-posters. Warm, personal service.
Bedrooms: 1 single, 7 double, 1 twin, 1 family room
Suites available
Bathrooms: 10 en-suite

Bed & breakfast

per night:	£min	£max
Single	25.00	36.00
Double	46.00	56.00

Parking for 10
Open March–October
Cards accepted: Access, Visa, Amex

🛇🐾6🖳🖵💆🖐 🛡 S ⚒ 🖭 🖩
🚐 ❋ ✈ 🚐 SP

Beckside Cottage 👭

Listed COMMENDED

4 Park Road, Windermere LA23 2AW
☎ (015394) 42069 & 88105
Comfortable cottage with en-suite bedrooms. Full central heating, colour TV, tea/coffee and clock/radio all rooms. Full English breakfast served. Ideally situated, close to Windermere village.
Bedrooms: 1 single, 2 double, 1 triple
Bathrooms: 4 en-suite

Bed & breakfast

per night:	£min	£max
Single	15.00	18.00
Double	30.00	36.00

Parking for 3

🛇🐾6🖳🖵💆🖐 UL 🛡 S 🖩 🛒 ♨ 🚐 DAP SP

Boston House 👭

⌂⌂⌂ COMMENDED

4 The Terrace, Windermere LA23 1AJ
☎ (015394) 43654
Fax (015394) 43654

Charmingly peaceful Victorian listed building within 5 minutes' walk of trains and town centre. Delicious food, panoramic views and/or four-poster beds, private parking.
Bedrooms: 3 double, 1 twin, 1 family room
Bathrooms: 4 en-suite, 2 public

Bed & breakfast

per night:	£min	£max
Double	40.00	52.00

Half board per person:

	£min	£max
Daily	30.00	37.00
Weekly	195.00	240.00

Evening meal 1900 (last orders 1900)
Parking for 6
Open February–November
Cards accepted: Access, Visa

🛇🐾🖳🖵💆🖐 🛡 S ⚒ 🖭 🖩 🛒 ♨
🚐 SP 🏠

Cambridge House 👭

Listed COMMENDED

9 Oak Street, Windermere LA23 1EN
☎ (015394) 43846
Village centre location convenient for all amenities. Modern, comfortable rooms with en-suite facilities. Full English, continental or vegetarian breakfast.

Bedrooms: 5 double, 1 triple
Bathrooms: 6 en-suite

Bed & breakfast

per night:	£min	£max
Single	15.00	18.00
Double	30.00	36.00

The Common Farm

Windermere LA23 1JQ
☎ (015394) 43433
200-acre dairy farm. Picturesque and homely 17th C farmhouse in peaceful surroundings, less than 1 mile from Windermere village.
Bedrooms: 1 double, 1 family room
Bathrooms: 1 public

Bed & breakfast

per night:	£min	£max
Double	30.00	32.00

Parking for 4
Open March–November

Fairfield Country House Hotel ▲

COMMENDED

Brantfell Road,
Bowness-on-Windermere,
Windermere LA23 3AE
☎ (015394) 46565
Fax (015394) 46565
Small, friendly 200-year-old country house with half an acre of peaceful secluded gardens. 2 minutes' walk from Lake Windermere and village. Private car park, leisure facilities.
Bedrooms: 1 single, 5 double, 1 twin, 1 triple, 1 family room
Bathrooms: 8 en-suite, 1 private, 1 public

Bed & breakfast

per night:	£min	£max
Single	24.00	28.00
Double	48.00	56.00

Half board per

person:	£min	£max
Daily	39.00	43.00
Weekly	255.00	285.00

Evening meal 1900 (last orders 1900)
Parking for 14
Cards accepted: Access, Visa

Holly Lodge ▲

COMMENDED

6 College Road, Windermere
LA23 1BX
☎ (015394) 43873
Fax (015394) 43873
Traditional Lakeland stone guesthouse,

built in 1854. In a quiet area off the main road, close to the village centre, buses, railway station and all amenities.
Bedrooms: 1 single, 5 double, 2 twin, 3 triple
Bathrooms: 6 en-suite, 2 public

Bed & breakfast

per night:	£min	£max
Single	17.00	20.00
Double	34.00	40.00

Half board per

person:	£min	£max
Daily	28.00	31.00

Evening meal from 1830
Parking for 7

Howbeck ▲

HIGHLY COMMENDED

New Road, Windermere LA23 2LA
☎ (015394) 44739

Ideally situated between Windermere and Bowness, quality bed and breakfast accommodation. Tastefully decorated and furnished, hearty breakfast and personal welcome.
Bedrooms: 6 double, 3 twin, 1 triple
Bathrooms: 10 en-suite

Bed & breakfast

per night:	£min	£max
Double	32.00	54.00

Parking for 15
Open February–October, December
Cards accepted: Access, Visa

Kirkwood Guest House ▲

COMMENDED

Prince's Road, Windermere
LA23 2DD
☎ (015394) 43907
Large Victorian house conveniently situated in a quiet location between Windermere and Bowness. En-suite rooms, honeymoon suite, four-poster beds. Tours arranged.
Bedrooms: 4 double, 2 triple, 1 family room
Bathrooms: 7 en-suite

Bed & breakfast

per night:	£min	£max
Double	38.00	60.00

Parking for 1
Cards accepted: Access, Visa

Lakes Hotel ▲

1 High Street, Windermere
LA23 1AF
☎ (015394) 42751 & 88133
Fax (015394) 46026
Attractive small Victorian bed and breakfast hotel, just 1 minute's walk from rail/bus stations and local shops. Spacious rooms, all with private facilities. Warm hospitality, excellent breakfasts. Local mini-coach tours our speciality. Los Angeles Times recommended.
Bedrooms: 1 single, 3 double, 2 twin, 1 triple, 1 family room
Bathrooms: 8 en-suite

Bed & breakfast

per night:	£min	£max
Single	20.00	25.00
Double	40.00	48.00

Half board per

person:	£min	£max
Daily	30.00	35.00
Weekly	200.00	225.00

Evening meal 1900 (last orders 2100)
Parking for 10
Open February–November
Cards accepted: Access, Visa, Switch/Delta

Laurel Cottage ▲

COMMENDED

St. Martin's Square,
Bowness-on-Windermere,
Windermere LA23 3EF
☎ (015394) 45594
Fax (015394) 45594
Charming early 17th C cottage with front garden, situated in centre of Bowness. Superb selection of restaurants within one minute's stroll.
Bedrooms: 2 single, 10 double, 1 twin, 2 triple
Bathrooms: 10 en-suite, 2 public

Bed & breakfast

per night:	£min	£max
Single	21.00	24.00
Double	34.00	56.00

Parking for 8

Lingmoor

Listed

7 High Street, Windermere
LA23 1AF
☎ (015394) 44947
Friendly homely accommodation, family-run, close to train station, buses, shops and Tourist Information Centre. Good full English breakfast guaranteed.

Continued ▶

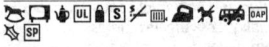

WINDERMERE

Continued

Bedrooms: 1 single, 3 double, 2 twin,
1 family room
Bathrooms: 3 en-suite, 1 public
Bed & breakfast

per night:	£min	£max
Single	13.00	17.00
Double	26.00	32.00

New Hall Bank

Listed

Fallbarrow Road,
Bowness-on-Windermere,
Windermere LA23 3AJ
☎ (015394) 43558
*In a quiet area within 2 minutes'
walking distance of town centre and
the lake. Ample parking space. Lake
views.*
Bedrooms: 2 single, 7 double,
3 triple, 2 family rooms
Bathrooms: 2 public, 1 private
shower
Bed & breakfast

per night:	£min	£max
Single	17.00	20.00
Double	32.00	40.00

Parking for 16

Oldfield House ⋀

COMMENDED

Oldfield Road, Windermere
LA23 2BY
☎ (015394) 88445
Fax (015394) 43250

*Friendly, informal atmosphere within a
traditionally-built Lakeland residence.
Quiet central location, free use of
swimming and leisure club.*
Bedrooms: 2 single, 4 double,
1 triple, 1 family room
Bathrooms: 8 en-suite, 1 public
Bed & breakfast

per night:	£min	£max
Single	21.50	32.50
Double	38.00	60.00

Parking for 7
Open February–December
Cards accepted: Access, Visa, Amex,
Switch/Delta

Osborne Guest House

⚜ ⚜

3 High Street, Windermere
LA23 1AF
☎ (015394) 46452
*Traditional Lakeland house, central for
all transport, tours and walks. Clean,
comfortable accommodation. Full
breakfast. Developed by present
owners since 1982.*
Bedrooms: 1 double, 2 triple
Bathrooms: 3 en-suite
Bed & breakfast

per night:	£min	£max
Single	14.00	18.50
Double	28.00	37.00

Cards accepted: Access, Visa

The Poplars ⋀

⚜ ⚜ COMMENDED

Lake Road, Windermere LA23 2EQ
☎ (015394) 42325 & 46690
*Small family-run guesthouse on the
main lake road, offering en-suite
accommodation coupled with fine
cuisine and homely atmosphere. Golf
and fishing can be arranged.*
Bedrooms: 1 single, 3 double, 2 twin,
1 triple
Bathrooms: 6 en-suite, 1 private,
1 public
Bed & breakfast

per night:	£min	£max
Single	17.50	20.50
Double	35.00	41.00

Half board per

person:	£min	£max
Daily	29.50	32.50
Weekly	189.00	210.50

Evening meal 1800 (last orders
1800)
Parking for 7
Open February–December

St. John's Lodge ⋀

⚜ ⚜ ⚜ COMMENDED

Lake Road, Windermere LA23 2EQ
☎ (015394) 43078
*Small private hotel midway between
Windermere and the lake, managed by
the chef/proprietor and convenient for
all amenities and services. Facilities of
local sports and leisure club available
to guests.*
Bedrooms: 1 single, 9 double, 2 twin,
2 triple
Bathrooms: 12 en-suite, 2 private
Bed & breakfast

per night:	£min	£max
Single	20.00	25.00
Double	37.00	50.00

Half board per

person:	£min	£max
Daily	30.00	35.00
Weekly	198.00	215.00

Evening meal 1900 (last orders
1800)
Parking for 11
Open February–November
Cards accepted: Access, Visa

Upper Oakmere ⋀

Listed COMMENDED

3 Upper Oak Street, Windermere
LA23 2LB
☎ (015394) 45649
*Ideal location, 100 yards from main
High Street. Friendly atmosphere, home
cooking. Single people/party bookings.
Open all year. Pets welcome.*
Bedrooms: 3 double, 1 triple,
1 family room
Bathrooms: 2 en-suite, 1 public
Bed & breakfast

per night:	£min	£max
Single	12.00	15.00
Double	22.00	31.00

Half board per

person:	£min	£max
Daily	18.95	21.95
Weekly	99.00	125.65

Lunch available
Evening meal 1730 (last orders
1830)
Parking for 2

Villa Lodge

⚜ ⚜ COMMENDED

Cross Street, Windermere
LA23 1AE
☎ (015394) 43318
Fax (015394) 43318

*Friendliness and cleanliness guaranteed.
Peacefully situated in quiet cul-de-sac
overlooking Windermere village.
Splendid views. Safe private parking.*
Bedrooms: 1 single, 4 double, 1 twin,
1 family room
Bathrooms: 3 en-suite, 4 private
Bed & breakfast

per night:	£min	£max
Single	16.00	18.00
Double	32.00	50.00

Parking for 9
Open February–December
Cards accepted: Access, Visa

Virginia Cottage

1 & 2 Crown Villas, Kendal Road,
Bowness-on-Windermere,
Windermere LA23 3EJ
☎ (015394) 44891
*Just a minute from the lake, shops
restaurants and entertainment. Wide
range of rooms, friendly atmosphere,
family run.*
Bedrooms: 1 single, 7 double,
3 triple
Bathrooms: 3 en-suite, 1 private,
3 public, 2 private showers
Bed & breakfast

per night:	£min	£max
Single	16.00	19.00
Double	36.00	54.00

Parking for 9
Cards accepted: Access, Visa

White Lodge Hotel

COMMENDED

Lake Road, Windermere LA23 2JS
☎ (015394) 43624
Fax (015394) 47000
*Victorian family-owned hotel with good
home cooking, only a short walk from
Bowness Bay. All bedrooms have
private bathroom, colour TV and tea
making facilities, some with lake views
and four-posters.*
Bedrooms: 3 single, 6 double, 2 twin,
1 triple
Bathrooms: 12 en-suite
Bed & breakfast

per night:	£min	£max
Single	22.00	29.00
Double	44.00	58.00

Half board per

person:	£min	£max
Daily	35.00	41.00
Weekly	220.00	260.00

Lunch available
Evening meal 1900 (last orders
2000)
Parking for 20
Open March–November
Cards accepted: Access, Visa

A deep-water port on the west
Cumbrian coast. There are the ruins
of the 14th C Workington Hall,
where Mary Queen of Scots stayed
in 1568.

Morven Guest House

APPROVED

Siddick Road, Siddick, Workington
CA14 1LE
☎ (01900) 602118
*Detached house north-west of town.
Ideal base for western lakes and coast.
Start of coast to coast cycleway. Car
park, cycle storage.*
Bedrooms: 3 single, 1 double, 3 twin,
1 triple
Bathrooms: 8 en-suite
Bed & breakfast

per night:	£min	£max
Single	24.00	32.00
Double	38.00	46.00

Half board per

person:	£min	£max
Daily	36.00	42.00

Lunch available
Evening meal 1800 (last orders
1600)
Parking for 20

AT-A-GLANCE SYMBOLS

Symbols at the end of each accommodation entry
give useful information about services
and facilities. A key to symbols can be found
inside the back cover flap.

Keep this open for easy reference.

COUNTRY CODE

Always follow the Country Code

Enjoy the countryside and respect its life and work Guard against all risk of fire Fasten all gates Keep your dogs under close control Keep to public paths across farmland Use gates and stiles to cross fences, hedges and walls Leave livestock, crops and machinery alone Take your litter home Help to keep all water clean Protect wildlife, plants and trees Take special care on country roads Make no unnecessary noise

USE YOUR *i*'s

There are more than 550 Tourist Information Centres throughout England offering friendly help with accommodation and holiday ideas as well as suggestions of places to visit and things to do. You'll find the address of your nearest Tourist Information Centre in your local Phone Book.

CHECK THE MAPS

The colour maps at the back of this guide show all the cities, towns and villages for which you will find accommodation entries.

Refer to the town index to find the page on which it is listed.

NORTHUMBRIA

Spectacular countryside awaits the visitor to Northumbria. The high Cheviots and the rugged Pennines leave an indelible impression while the majestic coastline offers sandy beaches, quaint fishing villages and surprisingly lively seaside resorts!

In contrast, Northumbria is also a region with vibrant industrial heritage, cosmopolitan cities and a long tradition of excellence in both the sporting and cultural arenas.

Soak up the history - don't miss Durham Cathedral - explore Catherine Cookson country and visit a traditional Northern pub. Or why not the Metro Centre, Europe's largest shopping city! Wherever you go, you'll be sure of a warm, northern welcome.

FOR MORE INFORMATION CONTACT:
Northumbria Tourist Board
Aykley Heads, Durham DH1 5UX
Tel: (0191) 375 3000 **Fax:** (0191) 386 0899

Where to Go in Northumbria - see pages 64-67
Where to Stay in Northumbria - see pages 68-82

NORTHUMBRIA

Where to Go and What to See

You will find hundreds of interesting places to visit during your stay in Northumbria, just some of which are listed in these pages. The number against each name will help you locate it on the map (page 67). Contact any Tourist Information Centre in the region for more ideas on days out in Northumbria.

1 Lindisfarne Castle

Holy Island,
Berwick-upon-Tweed
Northumberland TD15 2SH
Tel: (01289) 89244
Fort converted into a private home in 1903 for Edward Hudson by the architect Edwin Lutyens.

2 Farne Islands

Seahouses off Northumberland coast,
Northumberland
Tel: (01665) 720651
Bird reserve holding around 55,000 pairs of breeding birds of 21 species. Also home to a large colony of grey seals.

3 Bamburgh Castle

Bamburgh, Northumberland,
NE69 7DF
Tel: (01668) 214208
Magnificent coastal castle completely restored in 1900. Collections of china, porcelain, furniture, paintings, arms and armour.

4 Alnwick Castle

Alnwick,
Northumberland NE66 1NQ
Tel: (01665) 510777
Largest inhabited castle in England after Windsor Castle. Home of the Percys, Dukes of Northumberland since 1309.

5 Cragside House, Gardens and Grounds

Cragside, Rothbury,
Northumberland NE65 7PX
Tel: (01669) 620333
House built 1864-84 for the first Lord Armstrong, Tyneside Industrialist. The first house to be lit by electricity generated by water power.

6 Kielder Water Leaplish Waterside Park

Kielder,
Northumberland NE48 1BX
Tel: (01434) 240395
Largest man made lake in Western Europe. Water sports, fishing, log cabins and caravan site. Cycle hire, crazy golf and restaurant.

7 Wallington House Walled Garden and Grounds

Wallington, Cambo,
Northumberland NE61 4AR
Tel: (01670) 74283
Built 1688 on site of earlier medieval castle. Altered in 1740s. Interior has plasterwork, porcelain, furniture, pictures and needlework.

8 Morpeth Chantry Bagpipe Museum

The Chantry, Bridge Street,
Morpeth,
Northumberland NE61 1PJ
Tel: (01670) 519466
Set in a 13thC church building, this unusual museum specialises in the history and development of Northumbrian small pipes and their music.

9 Sea Life Centre

Grand Parade, Long Sands,
Tynemouth,
Tyne & Wear NE30 4JF
Tel: (0191) 257 6100
Journey beneath the North Sea and

discover thousands of amazing creatures. Over 30 hi-tech displays.

10 Wet 'N Wild
Rotary Way,
North Shields,
Tyne & Wear NE29 6DA
Tel: (0191) 296 1333
Tropical indoor waterpark. A fun water playground providing the UK's wildest and wettest indoor rapid experience.

11 Castle Keep
Saint Nicholas Street,
Castle Garth,
Newcastle upon Tyne NE1 1RQ
Tel: (0191) 232 7938
Built 1168-1178. One of the finest surviving examples of a Norman keep in the country. Panoramic views of the city from the roof. Small museum within keep.

12 Bede's World
Church Bank,
Jarrow,
Tyne & Wear NE32 3DY
Tel: (0191) 489 2106
New museum opened May 1995. Late 18thC hall, excavated finds from Anglo-Saxon and medieval monastery of St Pauls Jarrow nearby. Anglo-Saxon farm with rare breeds.

13 Metroland
Gateshead,
Tyne & Wear NE11 9YZ
Tel: (0191) 493 2048
Europe's only indooor theme park within a large shopping complex. Rollercoaster, dodgems, swinging chairs, pirate ship plus live entertainment.

14 Housesteads Roman Fort
Hadrian's Wall,
Northumberland NE47 6NN
Tel: (01434) 344363
Best preserved and most impressive of the Roman forts. Vercovicium was a 5-acre fort for extensive civil settlement. Only example of a Roman hospital.

15 Wildfowl & Wetlands Trust
Washington,
Tyne & Wear NE38 8LE
Tel: (0191) 416 5454
Collection of 1,250 wildfowl of 108 varieties. Viewing gallery, picnic areas, hides and winter wild bird feeding station. Flamingos, wild grey heron. Food available.

16 Beamish – The North of England Open Air Museum
Beamish, Co Durham DH9 0RG
Tel: (01207) 231811
Visit a town, colliery village, farm and railway station recreated to show life in the North of England early this century. Pockerley Manor illustrates life in the early 1800s.

17 Durham Castle
Palace Green,
Durham DH1 3RW
Tel: (0191) 374 3863
Fine Bailey castle founded in 1072, Norman chapel dating from 1080. Kitchens and great hall dated 1499 and 1284 respectively.

18 Durham Cathedral
Durham DH1 3EH
Tel: (0191) 386 4266
Widely considered to be the finest example of Norman church architecture in England. Has the tombs of St Cuthbert and The Venerable Bede.

19 Killhope Leadmining Centre
Cowshill,
St John's Chapel,
Co Durham DL13 1AR
Tel: (01388) 537505
Most complete lead mining site in Great Britain. Includes crushing mill with 34ft water wheel, reconstruction of Victorian machinery and miners accommodation.

20 High Force Waterfall
Forest-in-Teesdale,
Middleton-in-Teesdale,
Co Durham DL12
Tel: (01833) 640209
High Force is the most majestic of the waterfalls on the River Tees. The falls are only a short walk from a bus stop, car park and picnic area.

21 Raby Castle
Staindrop,
Co Durham DL2 3AH
Tel: (01833) 660202
Medieval castle in 200-acre park. 600-year-old kitchen and carriage collection. Walled gardens and deer park. Home of Lord Barnard's family for over 350 years.

22 Butterfly World
Preston Park, Yarm Road,
Stockton-on-Tees,
Tees Valley TS18 3RH
Tel: (01642) 791414
An indoor tropical garden populated by exotic free-flying butterflies and complemented by a display of fascinating insects and reptiles.

23 Preston Hall Museum
Yarm Road, Stockton-on-Tees,
Tees Valley TS18 3RH
Tel: (01642) 781184
A Georgian country house set in a park which is a museum of Victoriana. Return to a bygone age, stroll along a high street, explore 100 acres of parkland overlooking the Tees.

24 Captain Cook Birthplace Museum
Stewart Park,
Marton,
Middlesbrough,
Tees Valley TS7 6AS
Tel: (01642) 311211
Early life and voyages of Captain Cook and the countries he visited. Temporary exhibitions.

25 Ormesby Hall
Church Lane,
Ormesby,
Middlesbrough,
Tees Valley TS7 9AS
Tel: (01642) 324188
18thC Palladian mansion with impressive contemporary plasterwork. Magnificent stableblock attributed to Carr of York. Model railway exhibition and children's play area.

26 Hartlepool Historic Quay
Maritime Avenue,
Hartlepool,
Tees Valley TS24 0XZ
Tel: (01429) 860006
An exciting reconstruction of a seaport of the 1800s with buildings and lively quayside.

27 Saltburn Smugglers Heritage Centre
Ship Inn, Saltburn-by-the-Sea,
Tees Valley TS12 1HF
Tel: (01287) 625252
Experience the authentic sights, sounds and smells of Saltburn's smuggling heritage. Listen to tales of John Andrew, "King of the Smugglers".

FIND OUT MORE
Further information about holidays and attractions in Northumbria is available from:
Northumbria Tourist Board,
Aykley Heads,
Durham DH1 5UX.
Tel: (0191) 375 3000

SCOTLAND

Berwick-upon-Tweed

1 Holy Island

2 Farne Islands

Belford **3** Bamburgh

Wooler

Alnwick **4**

Amble

Rothbury **5**

6 Keilder

Otterburn

NORTHUMBERLAND

Cambo **7** Ashington

Bellingham Morpeth **8** Blyth

Whitley Bay

North Shields

Newcastle-upon-Tyne **10 9** Tynemouth

Haltwhistle Hexham **11 12** South Shields

Housesteads **14** Prudhoe Jarrow

Haydon Gateshead **13**

Bridge **TYNE & WEAR**

15 Sunderland

Stanley **16** Washington

Consett Beamish

Durham **17 18**

19 Peterlee

Cowshill

Crook

DURHAM **HARTLE** **26** Hartlepool

20 Bishop **POOL** **TEES VALLEY**

Forest-in-Teesdale Auckland Redcar

Staindrop **21** Middlesbrough **27** Saltburn-by-the-Sea

Stockton **22 23** Ormesby

CUMBRIA -on-Tees **24 25** Guisborough

Barnard Castle Marton **REDCAR &**

Darlington **STOCKTON** **MIDDLES** **CLEEVELAND**

-ON- TEES **BROUGH**

NORTH YORKSHIRE

0 — 20 Miles

0 — 30 Kms

These publications are available free from the Northumbria Tourist Board:
■ **Northumbria Breaks 1997**
■ **Bed & Breakfast Map - Northumbria and Cumbria**
■ **Great Days Out - regional attraction guide**

■ **Freedom Caravan and Camping Guide - Northumbria, Yorkshire, East Riding, Cumbria and North West**
■ **Schools Out - educational brochure**

Also available are (prices include postage and packaging):
■ **Northumbria Touring Map and Guide** £4.75
■ **Leisure Guide to Northumbria** £10.99
■ **Walk Northumbria** £6.

WHERE TO STAY (NORTHUMBRIA)

Accommodation entries in this region are listed in alphabetical order of place name, and then in alphabetical order of establishment.

Map references refer to the colour location maps at the back of this guide. The first number indicates the map to use; the letter and number which follow refer to the grid reference on the map.

At-a-glance symbols at the end of each accommodation entry give useful information about services and facilities. A key to symbols can be found inside the back cover flap. Keep this open for easy reference.

ALNMOUTH

Northumberland
Map ref 5C1

Quiet village with pleasant old buildings, at the mouth of the River Aln where extensive dunes and sands stretch along Alnmouth Bay. 18th C granaries, some converted to dwellings, still stand.

High Buston Hall ⋀

⚜⚜⚜ HIGHLY COMMENDED

High Buston, Alnmouth, Alnwick NE66 3QH
☎ Alnwick (01665) 830341
Fax (01665) 830341
Elegant listed Georgian house with commanding coastal views. Comfortable and stylish with traditional furnishings. Relaxed atmosphere, warm hospitality and peaceful village setting.
Bedrooms: 3 double
Bathrooms: 2 en-suite, 1 private
Bed & breakfast

per night:	£min	£max
Single	35.00	40.00
Double	50.00	65.00

Parking for 9
Open January–November

ALNWICK

Northumberland
Map ref 5C1

Ancient and historic market town, entered through the Hotspur Tower, an original gate in the town walls. The medieval castle, the second biggest in England and still the seat of the Dukes of Northumberland, was restored from ruin in the 18th C.
Tourist Information Centre ☎ (01665) 510665

Roseworth ⋀

⚜⚜ HIGHLY COMMENDED

Alnmouth Road, Alnwick NE66 2PR
☎ (01665) 603911
Mrs Anne Bowden welcomes you to "Roseworth". Semi-detached, private home set in large gardens. Ample parking in quiet residential area to the south of Alnwick on Alnmouth Road. Brochure on request. Non-smokers welcome.
Bedrooms: 2 double, 1 twin
Bathrooms: 2 en-suite, 1 public
Bed & breakfast

per night:	£min	£max
Single	18.00	20.00
Double	36.00	40.00

Parking for 6
Open March–November

BAMBURGH

Northumberland
Map ref 5C1

Village with a spectacular red sandstone castle standing 150 ft above the sea. On the village green the magnificent Norman church stands opposite a museum containing mementoes of the heroine Grace Darling.

Glenander Guest House ⋀

⚜⚜ HIGHLY COMMENDED

27 Lucker Road, Bamburgh NE69 7BS
☎ (01668) 214 336
Fax (01668) 214100
Built early this century and recently carefully and tastefully modernised, providing quality accommodation. All rooms en-suite with hospitality trays, hairdryers, colour TV. All day access.
Bedrooms: 1 double, 2 twin
Bathrooms: 3 en-suite
Bed & breakfast

per night:	£min	£max
Single	20.00	30.00
Double	39.00	55.00

Mizen Head Hotel ⋀

⚜⚜⚜ APPROVED

Lucker Road, Bamburgh NE69 7BS
☎ (01668) 214254
Privately-owned, fully licensed hotel in own grounds, with accent on good food and service. Convenient for beaches, castle and golf. 2 minutes' walk from village centre.

Information on accommodation listed in this guide has been supplied by the proprietors. As changes may occur you are advised to check details at the time of booking.

All accommodation in this guide has been graded, or is awaiting a grading, by a trained Tourist Board inspector.

Bedrooms: 2 single, 5 double, 4 twin, 4 family rooms
Bathrooms: 11 en-suite, 2 public

Bed & breakfast

per night:	£min	£max
Single	21.50	42.50
Double	43.00	74.00

Half board per person:

	£min	£max
Daily	33.50	50.00
Weekly	224.00	300.00

Lunch available
Evening meal 1830 (last orders 2000)
Parking for 30
Cards accepted: Access, Visa

BARDON MILL

Northumberland
Map ref 5B2

Small hamlet midway between Haydon Bridge and Haltwhistle, within walking distance of Vindolanda, an excavated Roman settlement, and near the best stretches of Hadrian's Wall.

Winshields Farm

COMMENDED

Bardon Mill, Hexham NE47 7AN
☎ Haltwhistle (01434) 344243
500-acre hill farm. 18th C farmhouse, situated just below highest point of Hadrian's Wall, with Pennine Way and Hadrian's Wall running through land.
Bedrooms: 1 double, 1 twin, 1 triple
Bathrooms: 2 public

Bed & breakfast

per night:	£min	£max
Single	17.00	18.00
Double	34.00	38.00

Parking for 6
Open June–September

Establishments should be open throughout the year, unless otherwise stated.

The symbols in each entry give information about services and facilities. A 'key' to these symbols appears at the back of this guide.

BARNARD CASTLE

Durham
Map ref 5B3

High over the Tees, a thriving market town with a busy market square. Bernard Baliol's 12th C castle (now ruins) stands nearby. The Bowes Museum, housed in a grand 19th C French chateau, holds fine paintings and furniture. Nearby are some magnificent buildings.
Tourist Information Centre ☎ (01833) 690909

Bowfield Farm

Listed

Scargill, Barnard Castle, County Durham DL12 9SU
☎ Teesdale (01833) 638636
127-acre mixed farm. 17th C stone-built farmhouse overlooking Stang Ridge Forest, 4 miles from Barnard Castle off the A66. Comfortable caravan also available for holiday letting.
Bedrooms: 1 single, 1 double, 1 twin
Bathrooms: 1 public

Bed & breakfast

per night:	£min	£max
Single	13.00	
Double	26.00	

Evening meal 1800 (last orders 1600)
Parking for 8

Browns Antiques

Listed COMMENDED

34 The Bank, Barnard Castle, County Durham DL12 8PN
☎ Teesdale (01833) 637891 & Mobile 0860 725589
Fax (01833) 637891
The guest suite is on the first floor behind the antique shop and dates from 1540. It has original beams and fireplace and an adjoining sitting room with fridge, TV and own bathroom. Furnished with antiques.
Bedrooms: 1 twin
Bathrooms: 1 private

Bed & breakfast

per night:	£min	£max
Single	25.00	30.00
Double	35.00	40.00

Open March–May, July–November

George & Dragon Inn

Listed APPROVED

Boldron, Barnard Castle, County Durham DL12 9RF
☎ Teesdale (01833) 638215
Attractive inn in beautiful Teesdale,

---

offering comfortable accommodation and friendly hospitality.
Bedrooms: 1 double, 1 twin
Bathrooms: 1 public

Bed & breakfast

per night:	£min	£max
Single	15.00	16.00
Double	31.00	32.00

Half board per person:

	£min	£max
Daily	20.50	21.00
Weekly	140.00	140.00

Lunch available
Evening meal 1900 (last orders 1730)
Parking for 20

Raygill Farm

Listed APPROVED

Lartington, Barnard Castle, County Durham DL12 9DG
☎ Teesdale (01833) 690118
120-acre arable farm. Warm, comfortable accommodation in recently converted barn. Home cooking. Riding for beginners to advanced. Superb countryside, woodlands and moors.
Bedrooms: 1 double, 2 twin, 1 family room
Bathrooms: 1 en-suite, 3 public

Bed & breakfast

per night:	£min	£max
Single	18.00	21.00
Double	30.00	35.00

Half board per person:

	£min	£max
Daily	24.00	30.00
Weekly	160.00	200.00

Evening meal 1700 (last orders 2100)
Parking for 20

BARNINGHAM

Durham
Map ref 5B3

Village 4 miles south-east of Barnard Castle.

Stangfoot Farm

Listed

Barningham, Richmond, North Yorkshire DL11 7EA
☎ Teesdale (01833) 621343
50-acre livestock farm. Stangfoot is a working farm on the Scargill to Reeth road at the foot of the Stang Forest. 3 miles south of A66.
Bedrooms: 1 single, 1 double, 1 twin
Bathrooms: 1 en-suite, 1 public

Continued ▶

BARNINGHAM

Continued

Bed & breakfast per night:	£min	£max
Single	15.00	
Double	30.00	

Half board per person:	£min	£max
Daily	22.00	

Evening meal 1800 (last orders 1500)
Parking for 4
Open April–October

♿ 5 🐕 ♨ 📠 ⓤⓛ 🍴 🐾 📺 ⛱ 🅿 ♨ U ✏ 🐩 ✗ ⚓ 🏵 ⒹⒶⓅ 🏠

BEAMISH

Durham
Map ref 5C2

Village made famous by the award-winning Beamish, North of England Open Air Museum, which covers every aspect of the life, buildings and artefacts of the North East of 1913. Also in the area are Causey Arch and Tanfield Railway.
Tourist Information Centre ☎ (0191) 370 2533

The Beamish Mary Inn ⚠

⚜⚜⚜ APPROVED

Beamish, Stanley, County Durham DH9 0QH
☎ (0191) 370 0237
Fax (0191) 370 0091
Traditional Victorian inn, in former mining village of No Place. Off A693, opposite Beamish Museum, between Durham and Newcastle.
Bedrooms: 2 double, 1 twin
Bathrooms: 2 en-suite, 1 public

Bed & breakfast per night:	£min	£max
Single	20.00	25.00
Double	34.00	40.00

Half board per person:	£min	£max
Daily	24.00	30.50

Lunch available
Evening meal 1900 (last orders 2130)
Parking for 12
Cards accepted: Access, Visa, Switch/Delta

🖥 ♨ Ⓢ 🏧 🖨 ♨ 🔍 U ✗ 🏵 ⚓ 🏠

BERWICK-UPON-TWEED

Northumberland
Map ref 5B1

Guarding the mouth of the Tweed, England's northernmost town with the best 16th C city walls in Europe. The handsome Guildhall and barracks date from the 18th C. Three bridges cross to Tweedmouth, the oldest built in 1634.
Tourist Information Centre ☎ (01289) 330733

Ladythorne House

Listed COMMENDED

Cheswick, Berwick-upon-Tweed TD15 2RW
☎ (01289) 387382
Grade II listed building, dated 1721, set in farmland. Only 15 minutes' walk from the beaches.
Bedrooms: 1 single, 1 double, 2 twin, 2 triple
Bathrooms: 3 public

Bed & breakfast per night:	£min	£max
Single	12.00	15.00
Double	24.00	30.00

Parking for 8

♿ ⓤⓛ 🏧 Ⓢ 🍴 🐾 📺 ♨ 🏵 ⚓ 🐾 SP 🏠

Middle Ord Manor House ⚠

⚜⚜⚜ DE LUXE

Middle Ord Farm, Berwick-upon-Tweed TD15 2XQ
☎ (01289) 306323

550-acre mixed farm. Award-winning accommodation within Georgian farmhouse - "England for Excellence" silver award 1994; "Pride of Northumbria" best B&B award 1993 and 1994. Central for touring Borders, coast and Holy Island.
Bedrooms: 2 double, 1 twin
Bathrooms: 3 en-suite, 1 public

Bed & breakfast per night:	£min	£max
Single	25.00	
Double	50.00	

Parking for 6
Open April–October

🚪 📠 ♨ ♨ ⓤⓛ 🍴 🐾 📺 ⛱ ♨ U ✗ ✗ ⚓ 🏠 🔅

The Old Vicarage Guest House ⚠

⚜⚜ HIGHLY COMMENDED

24 Church Road, Tweedmouth, Berwick-upon-Tweed TD15 2AN
☎ (01289) 306909
Spacious, detached 19th C vicarage, refurbished to a high standard. 10 minutes' walk from town centre and beautiful beaches.
Bedrooms: 1 single, 4 double, 1 twin, 1 triple
Bathrooms: 4 en-suite, 1 public

Bed & breakfast per night:	£min	£max
Single	15.00	35.00
Double	30.00	48.00

Parking for 4

♿ 🐕 ♨ 🖥 ♨ 💧 ⓤⓛ Ⓢ 🍴 🐾 🏧 🖨 ♨ ❋ ⒹⒶⓅ SP Ⓣ

BISHOP AUCKLAND

Durham
Map ref 5C2

Busy market town on the bank of the River Wear. The Bishop's Palace, a castellated Norman manor house altered in the 18th C, stands in beautiful gardens. Entered from the market square by a handsome 18th C gatehouse, the park is a peaceful retreat of trees and streams.
Tourist Information Centre ☎ (01388) 604922

Five Gables

⚜⚜ COMMENDED

Binchester, Bishop Auckland, County Durham DL14 8AT
☎ Weardale (01388) 608204
300 yards from A688 between Bishop Auckland and Spennymoor. Victorian house with views over countryside and Weardale. 15 minutes from Durham City, and within easy reach of all popular tourist attractions in the North of England.
Bedrooms: 1 single, 1 double, 1 triple
Bathrooms: 2 en-suite, 1 private

Bed & breakfast per night:	£min	£max
Single	20.00	25.00
Double	28.00	38.00

Parking for 2

♿ 5 🐕 ♨ 🖥 💧 ♨ ⓤⓛ Ⓢ 🍴 🐾 📺 🏧 🖨 ♨ ✗ ⚓ 🐾 SP

CHESTER-LE-STREET

Durham
Map ref 5C2

Originally a Roman military site, town with modern commerce and light industry on the River Wear. The ancient church replaced a wooden sanctuary which sheltered the remains of St Cuthbert for 113 years. The Anker's house beside the church is now a museum. Home of Durham County Cricket Club.

Low Urpeth Farm House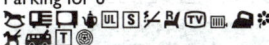

Listed HIGHLY COMMENDED

Ouston, Chester-Le-Street, County Durham DH2 1BD
☎ (0191) 410 2901
Fax (0191) 410 0081
500-acre arable & livestock farm. Leave A1(M) at Chester-le-Street. Take A693, signpost Beamish. At second roundabout turn right to Ouston. Pass garage, down hill, over roundabout and turn left into farm at "Trees Please" sign.
Bedrooms: 1 double, 2 twin
Bathrooms: 2 private, 1 public
Bed & breakfast

per night:	£min	£max
Single	22.50	
Double	35.00	

Parking for 6

Waldridge Fell House

HIGHLY COMMENDED

Waldridge Lane, Waldridge, Chester-Le-Street, County Durham DH2 3RY
☎ (0191) 389 1908
Former village chapel, stone-built in 1868. Panoramic views and country walks. Children half price. One and a half miles from cricket ground.
Bedrooms: 3 triple, 2 family rooms
Bathrooms: 1 en-suite, 1 public, 1 private shower
Bed & breakfast

per night:	£min	£max
Single	23.00	
Double	38.00	

Parking for 8

The National Grading and Classification Scheme is explained in full at the back of this guide.

CONSETT

Durham
Map ref 5B2

Former steel town on the edge of rolling moors. Modern development includes the shopping centre and a handsome Roman Catholic church, designed by a local architect. To the west, the Derwent Reservoir provides water sports and pleasant walks.

Bee Cottage Farm

HIGHLY COMMENDED

Castleside, Consett, County Durham DH8 9HW
☎ (01207) 508224

46-acre livestock farm. 1.5 miles west of the A68, between Castleside and Tow Law. Unspoilt views. Ideally located for Beamish Museum and Durham. No smoking. Tea-room open 1-6 pm.
Bedrooms: 1 single, 3 double, 2 twin, 1 triple, 2 family rooms
Bathrooms: 1 en-suite, 2 private, 5 public
Bed & breakfast

per night:	£min	£max
Single	24.00	
Double	40.00	

Half board per person:

	£min	£max
Daily	32.00	
Weekly	224.00	

Lunch available
Evening meal 1930 (last orders 2100)
Parking for 20

CORBRIDGE

Northumberland
Map ref 5B2

Small town on the River Tyne. Close by are extensive remains of the Roman military town Corstopitum, with a museum housing important discoveries from excavations. The town itself is attractive with shady trees, a 17th C bridge and interesting old buildings, notably a 14th C vicarage.

The Courtyard

DE LUXE

Mount Pleasant, Sandhoe, Corbridge NE45 4LX
☎ Hexham (01434) 606850
Fax (01434) 606632

A warm, friendly welcome greets visitors to this lovingly restored and beautifully furnished country house, dating from 1730. Surrounded by open countryside, with panoramic views over the beautiful Tyne Valley.
Bedrooms: 1 double, 1 twin, 1 triple
Bathrooms: 3 en-suite
Bed & breakfast

per night:	£min	£max
Single	40.00	50.00
Double	50.00	60.00

Parking for 6

Dilston Mill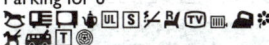

Listed COMMENDED

Corbridge NE45 5QZ
☎ Hexham (01434) 633493
Fax (01434) 633513
Somewhere special. Historic former watermill, on the banks of Devils Water. Overlooked by Dilston Castle ruins. Comfort, warm welcome, beautiful setting, excellent breakfasts. Close to amenities.
Bedrooms: 1 double, 1 twin, 1 triple
Bathrooms: 3 private
Bed & breakfast

per night:	£min	£max
Single	22.00	25.00
Double	40.00	44.00

Parking for 3

CORBRIDGE
Continued

Fellcroft
HIGHLY COMMENDED

Station Road, Corbridge NE45 5AY
☎ Hexham (01434) 632384
Well-appointed stone-built Edwardian house with full private facilities and colour TV in both bedrooms. Quiet road in country setting, half a mile south of market square. Excellent choice of eating places nearby. Non-smokers only, please. 10 per cent reduction for weekly half board stays.
Bedrooms: 2 twin
Bathrooms: 1 en-suite, 1 private

Bed & breakfast

per night:	£min	£max
Single	18.50	20.50
Double	30.00	33.00

Half board per person:	£min	£max
Daily	22.50	28.00

Parking for 3

Fox & Hounds Hotel
COMMENDED

Stagshaw Bank, Corbridge
NE45 5QW
☎ Hexham (01434) 633024
Fax (01434) 633024

400-year-old coaching inn with a 70-seat conservatory restaurant. Owners operate and live on premises.
Bedrooms: 4 double, 4 twin
Bathrooms: 8 en-suite

Bed & breakfast

per night:	£min	£max
Single	25.00	30.00
Double	40.00	40.00

Lunch available
Evening meal 1700 (last orders 2130)
Parking for 40

Riverside Guest House
COMMENDED

Main Street, Corbridge NE45 5LE
☎ Hexham (01434) 632942
Fax (01434) 633883
Well-furnished, comfortable family guesthouse run by resident owners. An ideal base for touring Hadrian's Wall and the English Border country.
Bedrooms: 2 single, 5 double, 2 twin, 1 family room
Bathrooms: 6 en-suite, 1 public

Bed & breakfast

per night	£min	£max
Single	25.00	40.00
Double	36.00	56.00

Parking for 6
Cards accepted: Access, Visa, Switch/Delta

Thornbrough High House
Listed COMMENDED

Corbridge NE45 5PR
☎ Hexham (01434) 633080
500-acre mixed farm. Stone-built, Grade II listed farmhouse and buildings with outstanding views over Tyne Valley. Surrounded by lovely gardens, quiet situation.
Bedrooms: 1 double, 2 twin
Bathrooms: 3 en-suite

Bed & breakfast

per night:	£min	£max
Single	25.00	
Double	50.00	

Half board per person:	£min	£max
Daily	40.00	

Evening meal 1830 (last orders 2000)
Parking for 11

COTHERSTONE
Durham
Map ref 5B3

Village with remains of Norman castle, 3 miles north-west of Barnard Castle. Home of Cotherstone cheese.

Glendale
HIGHLY COMMENDED

Cotherstone, Barnard Castle, County Durham DL12 9UH
☎ Teesdale (01833) 650384
Dormer bungalow with beautiful gardens and large pond, in quiet, rural surroundings. Take Briscoe road from Cotherstone for 200 yards.
Bedrooms: 3 double
Bathrooms: 3 en-suite, 1 public

Bed & breakfast

per night:	£min	£max
Single	18.00	22.00
Double	30.00	32.00

Parking for 4

COWSHILL
Durham
Map ref 5B2

Alston and Kilhope Riding Centre
COMMENDED

Low Cornriggs Farm, Cowshill, Bishop Auckland, County Durham DL13 1AQ
☎ Bishop Auckland (01388) 537600
Fax (01388) 537600
60-acre mixed farm. 200-year-old farmhouse with magnificent views, on the Weardale Way. Licensed dining room, log fires, all food fresh and home-made. Horse riding.
Bedrooms: 1 double, 2 twin
Bathrooms: 3 en-suite, 1 public

Bed & breakfast

per night:	£min	£max
Single	18.00	20.00
Double	36.00	39.00

Half board per person:	£min	£max
Daily	28.00	30.00
Weekly	190.00	200.00

Lunch available
Evening meal 1930 (last orders 2100)
Parking for 6

CRASTER
Northumberland
Map ref 5C1

Small fishing village with a fine northward view of Dunstanburgh Castle. Fishing cobles in the tiny harbour, stone cottages at the water's edge and a kippering shed where Craster's famous delicacy is produced give the village its unspoilt charm.

Cottage Inn
COMMENDED

Dunstan Village, Craster, Alnwick NE66 3ZS
☎ Embleton (01665) 576658
Family-run inn half a mile from the sea. All rooms are ground floor and have garden view. Noted for food. Special breaks available.
Bedrooms: 2 double, 8 twin
Bathrooms: 10 en-suite

Bed & breakfast

per night:	£min	£max
Single	35.00	
Double	59.00	

Half board per person:	£min	£max
Daily	40.00	
Weekly	240.00	

Lunch available
Evening meal 1800 (last orders 2130)
Parking for 30
Cards accepted: Access, Visa, Switch/Delta

🐕🐾⌨🖊👤📘S✂🏧🖊🔍♨♿

CROOKHAM

Northumberland
Map ref 5B1

Pretty hamlet taking its name from the winding course of the River Till which flows in the shape of a shepherd's crook. Three castles - Etal, Duddo and Ford - can be seen, and nearby the restored Heatherslaw Mill is of great interest.

The Coach House ♨

HIGHLY COMMENDED

Crookham, Cornhill-on-Tweed
TD12 4TD
☎ (01890) 820293 & 820284
Fax (01890) 820284
Spacious rooms, arranged around a courtyard, in rolling country near the Scottish border. Home-cooked, quality fresh food. Rooms specially equipped for disabled guests.
Wheelchair access category 1♿
Bedrooms: 2 single, 2 double, 5 twin
Bathrooms: 7 en-suite, 2 public

Bed & breakfast per night:	£min	£max
Single	23.00	34.00
Double	46.00	68.00

Half board per person:	£min	£max
Daily	38.50	49.50

Evening meal 1930 (last orders 1930)
Parking for 12
Open March–November
Cards accepted: Access, Visa

🐕♿👤📘S🖊TV🖥🚗♨🕸🐾

TOWN INDEX

This can be found at the back of the guide. If you know where you want to stay, the index will give you the page number listing all accommodation in your chosen town, city or village.

DURHAM

Durham
Map ref 5C2

Ancient city with its Norman castle and cathedral, now a World Heritage site, set on a bluff high over the Wear. A market and university town and regional centre, spreading beyond the market-place on both banks of the river.
Tourist Information Centre ☎ (0191) 384 3720

The Anchorage ♨

👑👑 **COMMENDED**

25 Langley Road, Newton Hall, Durham DH1 5LR
☎ (0191) 386 2323
Fax (0191) 384 1842
Large detached family home, 1 mile north of city, convenient for commercial, countryside, tourist areas. Spacious accommodation, en-suite bath/shower. Non-smoking.
Bedrooms: 1 triple
Bathrooms: 1 en-suite

Bed & breakfast per night:	£min	£max
Single	18.00	18.00
Double	36.00	36.00

Parking for 2

🐕⌨🖥📘👤🖊S✂🏧TV🖥🚗♨🚐

Bay Horse Inn ♨

👑👑👑 **COMMENDED**

Brandon Village, Durham, County Durham DH7 8ST
☎ (0191) 378 0498
Ten stone-built chalets 3 miles from Durham city centre. All have shower, toilet, TV, tea and coffee facilities and telephone. Ample car parking.
Bedrooms: 3 double, 6 twin, 1 family room
Bathrooms: 10 en-suite

Bed & breakfast per night:	£min	£max
Single	30.00	30.00
Double	39.00	39.00

Lunch available
Evening meal 1900 (last orders 2200)
Parking for 25
Cards accepted: Access, Visa

🐕♿🍴⌨🖥👤🍷✂🖊🖥🚗▶♨🚐T

Castledene ♨

Listed COMMENDED

37 Nevilledale Terrace, Durham, County Durham DH1 4QG
☎ (0191) 384 8386
Fax (0191) 384 8386
Edwardian end-of-terrace house half a mile west of the market place. Within

walking distance of the riverside, cathedral and castle.
Bedrooms: 2 twin
Bathrooms: 1 public

Bed & breakfast per night:	£min	£max
Single	22.00	22.00
Double	36.00	36.00

Parking for 6

🐕7♨⌨👤🖊🖊TV🖥🚗♨🚐

College of Saint Hild and Saint Bede ♨

Listed

Durham DH1 1SZ
☎ (0191) 374 3069 & 374 3064
Fax (0191) 374 4740
University accommodation set in spacious grounds, close proximity to historic city centre and cathedral.
Bedrooms: 400 single, 80 twin, 1 triple
Bathrooms: 105 public

Bed & breakfast per night:	£min	£max
Single	14.00	17.00
Double	28.00	34.00

Half board per person:	£min	£max
Daily	20.70	23.70
Weekly	144.90	165.90

Lunch available
Evening meal 1800 (last orders 1900)
Parking for 130
Open March–April, July–September

🐕1♿📘S✂🖊TV🕐🖥🚗🚐🍽400
♨🎾♀🐾🐕

Collingwood College Cumbrian Wing ♨

👑👑👑 **COMMENDED**

South Road, Durham, County Durham DH1 3LT
☎ (0191) 374 4500
Fax (0191) 374 4595
Durham's newest college, situated in woodland near the city centre. En-suite rooms coupled with unrivalled cuisine. Perfect for conferences and holidaymakers alike.
Bedrooms: 197 single, 16 twin
Bathrooms: 213 en-suite

Bed & breakfast per night:	£min	£max
Single	26.50	28.00
Double	44.00	46.00

Half board per person:	£min	£max
Daily	32.50	34.00
Weekly	180.00	238.00

Lunch available
Evening meal 1800 (last orders 1900)

Continued ▶

DURHAM

Continued

Parking for 130
Open January, March–April,
July–September, December

🛇🛅🕭🕭Ⓢ✕📺▣🖵🚗⚲175
🔍🔎❄🌼 DAP SP ⊛

Elmgarth 🅼

🕮🕮 COMMENDED

Mainsforth, Nr. Ferryhill, Durham,
County Durham DL17 9AA
☎ Ferryhill (01740) 652676
*300 year old cottage in quiet village
and conservation area. Local walks,
nature reserve. Ideal centre for dales,
coast and city. A1M, exit 60.*
Bedrooms: 1 double, 1 triple
Bathrooms: 1 en-suite, 1 private

Bed & breakfast

per night:	£min	£max
Single	18.00	20.00
Double	36.00	36.00

Parking for 3

🛇🕭🖳🕭♿🕭ⓊⓁ🗝✕📺🖵❄🌼🐾
SP

Lothlorien

🕮 COMMENDED

Front Street, Witton Gilbert,
Durham, County Durham DH7 6SY
☎ (0191) 371 0067
*Period country cottage only 5 minutes
by car from Durham City centre and
on a direct route to Hadrian's Wall. A
good centre for touring.*
Bedrooms: 1 single, 1 double, 1 twin
Bathrooms: 2 public

Bed & breakfast

per night:	£min	£max
Single	18.00	
Double	36.00	

Parking for 3

🛇🕭ⓊⓁ🕭📺🖵🚗∪✕🐾🕌

Saint Cuthberts Society 🅼

Listed

12 South Bailey, Durham, County
Durham DH1 3EE
☎ (0191) 374 3464
Fax (0191) 374 4753
*Situated at tip of the peninsula on
banks of the River Wear. Close to
cathedral and city centre.*
Bedrooms: 51 single, 28 twin,
4 triple
Bathrooms: 23 public

Bed & breakfast

per night:	£min	£max
Single	17.00	17.00
Double	34.00	34.00

Half board per

person:	£min	£max
Daily	24.20	24.20
Weekly	152.46	152.46

Lunch available
Evening meal 1800 (last orders
1900)
Open March–April, July–September

🛇🕮🛅🕭♿🕭Ⓢ✕🕭📺🖵🚗❄✕
DAP 🏇⊛

EASINGTON

Tees Valley
Map ref 5C3

The Grapes 🅼

🕮🕮🕮 COMMENDED

Scaling Dam, Saltburn-by-the-Sea,
Cleveland TS13 4TP
☎ Saltburn (01287) 640461
*Grade II listed old coaching inn in
hamlet of Scaling, 6 miles from coast.
Directly opposite leisure reservoir
(sailing and fishing) and wildlife
sanctuary. Traditional dining area with
carvery on Sunday.*
Bedrooms: 2 single, 1 double, 2 twin
Bathrooms: 5 en-suite

Bed & breakfast

per night:	£min	£max
Single	25.00	30.00
Double	44.00	50.00

Lunch available
Evening meal 1900 (last orders
2115)
Parking for 65
Cards accepted: Access, Visa,
Switch/Delta

🛇👞☎🖳🕭♿🕭Ⓢ🕭📺▣🖵✕🐾
🗞

EDMUNDBYERS

Durham
Map ref 5B2

Small village in hilly country beneath
Muggleswick Common. A winding,
man-made lake on the River
Derwent just north complements
smaller reservoirs southward across
the common, offering fishing and
picnic areas.

The Burnside 🅼

🕮 COMMENDED

Edmundbyers, Consett, County
Durham DH8 9NG
☎ (01207) 255257
*Tranquil apartments in grounds of
owner's home. 10 acres of gardens and
fields with stream, peacocks. At north
end of Pennine chain.*
Bedrooms: 2 double, 2 twin, 2 family
rooms
Bathrooms: 4 en-suite, 1 public

Bed & breakfast

per night:	£min	£max
Single	17.00	20.00
Double	33.00	40.00

Half board per

person:	£min	£max
Daily	24.00	35.00
Weekly	168.00	245.00

Lunch available
Parking for 10

🛇🕭🖳♿🕭Ⓢ✕📺🖵🐾 SP

Redwell Hall Farm

🕮 APPROVED

Shotley Bridge, Consett, County
Durham DH8 9TS
☎ Consett (01207) 55216
*Traditional stone-built farm situated in
picturesque valley and close to
beautiful Derwent Reservoir.
Accommodation is in farmhouse
annexe. Ideal for visiting Durham,
Hexham, Tynedale and the North
Pennines. Conversational German.*
Bedrooms: 1 double, 1 family room
Bathrooms: 2 public

Bed & breakfast

per night:	£min	£max
Single	19.50	23.00
Double	34.00	36.00

Half board per

person:	£min	£max
Daily	29.50	33.00

Parking for 20

🛇🕭ⓊⓁ🕭Ⓢ🕭📺🖵🚗🏷❄🐾

EGLINGHAM

Northumberland
Map ref 5B1

Small village north of Alnwick with a
medieval church which stands on
the site of a former Saxon church.
South of the village lies an ancient
earthwork called the Ringses with 3
stone and earth ramparts.

Ash Tree House 🅼

🕮 HIGHLY COMMENDED

The Terrace, Eglingham, Alnwick
NE66 2UA
☎ Powburn (01665) 578533
*A warm Northumbrian welcome with
good home cooking awaits you in this
lovely stone-built home set in the
glorious North Northumbrian
countryside. Winner of the Lion Heart
Award for Hospitality 1994.*
Bedrooms: 1 double, 1 twin
Bathrooms: 1 public

Bed & breakfast

per night:	£min	£max
Single	17.00	18.00
Double	34.00	36.00

Half board per person:

	£min	£max
Daily	27.00	28.00
Weekly	189.00	196.00

Evening meal 1900 (last orders 2000)
Parking for 3

☎10 Ⓤ🅻📞♿✕📺🖥✿✕🚐🛇 SP ◎

EMBLETON

Northumberland
Map ref 5C1

Coastal village beside a golf-course spread along the edge of Embleton Bay. The old church was extensively restored in the 19th C. The vicarage incorporates a medieval pele tower.

Doxford Farmhouse ⋀

👑 COMMENDED
Chathill NE67 5DY
☎ Charlton Mires (01665) 579235
Fax (01665) 579215

400-acre mixed farm. Listed Georgian farmhouse set in wooded grounds. Pollution-free beaches and moorland are within easy reach. Lake and woodland nature trail. Home cooking and home-made bread.
Bedrooms: 1 double, 1 twin, 1 triple, 1 family room
Suite available
Bathrooms: 1 en-suite, 1 public

Bed & breakfast per night:

	£min	£max
Single	17.00	25.00
Double	34.00	38.00

Half board per person:

	£min	£max
Daily	27.00	29.00
Weekly	170.00	183.00

Evening meal 1830 (last orders 1400)
Parking for 8
Cards accepted: Visa

☎🐎♿Ⓤ🅻🅸Ⓢ♿📺🖥💻🚐♟24 ⚓✈✿♨⌚🎣✿🚐🏛

The ⋀ symbol after an establishment name indicates that it is a Regional Tourist Board member.

GLANTON

Northumberland
Map ref 5B1

Attractive peaceful village in Northumberland National Park en route to Ingram Valley.

Northfield Farm

Listed HIGHLY COMMENDED
Glanton, Alnwick NE66 4AG
☎ Powburn (01665) 578203 & 0860 895497
15-acre smallholding. Original 18th C farmhouse with many original features remaining including beamed ceilings and fireplaces. On smallholding with various domestic animals and livestock. Near small village of Glanton, 2 miles from A697, amidst the Cheviots.
Bedrooms: 2 double, 1 twin
Bathrooms: 1 public

Bed & breakfast per night:

	£min	£max
Single	20.00	20.00
Double	34.00	34.00

Parking for 12
Open April–October

☎🐎🐾♿📞❄Ⓤ🅻🅸Ⓢ♿📺🖥💻⌚✿🚐 SP 🏛

HALTWHISTLE

Northumberland
Map ref 5B2

Small market town with interesting 12th C church, old inns and blacksmith's smithy. North of the town are several important sites and interpretation centres of Hadrian's Wall. Ideal centre for archaeology, outdoor activity or touring holidays.
Tourist Information Centre ☎ (01434) 322002

Ashcroft ⋀

👑 COMMENDED
Lantys Lonnen, Haltwhistle NE49 0DA
☎ Hexham (01434) 320213
Large, stone-built, early 19th C residence, south facing, with mature terraced gardens. Well placed for exploring the Roman Wall and Northumberland.
Bedrooms: 1 single, 3 double, 1 twin, 2 triple
Bathrooms: 1 private, 2 public

Bed & breakfast per night:

	£min	£max
Single	16.00	20.00
Double	36.00	40.00

Parking for 14

☎🐎♿📞❄Ⓤ🅻🅸Ⓢ♿♿📺🖥💻 ♟36⚓✿ SP 🏛

Broomshaw Hill Farm ⋀

👑 HIGHLY COMMENDED
Willia Road, Haltwhistle NE49 9NP
☎ Hexham (01434) 320866 & (0589) 808240
Fax (01434) 320866
5-acre livestock farm. Attractive modernised 18th C stone-built farmhouse. On conjunction of bridleway and footpath, both leading to Hadrian's Wall 1 mile away.
Bedrooms: 2 double, 1 twin
Bathrooms: 1 en-suite, 1 public

Bed & breakfast per night:

	£min	£max
Single	18.00	20.00
Double	32.00	40.00

Parking for 8
Open February–October

☎🐎🖥♿Ⓤ🅻🅸♿📺🖥💻🚐Ⓤ⌚✿🚐 SP

Hall Meadows ⋀

👑 COMMENDED
Main Street, Haltwhistle NE49 0AZ
☎ (01434) 321021
Built in 1888, a large family house with pleasant garden in the centre of town. Ideally placed for Hadrian's Wall.
Bedrooms: 1 single, 1 double, 1 twin
Bathrooms: 1 public

Bed & breakfast per night:

	£min	£max
Single	16.00	16.00
Double	32.00	32.00

Parking for 3

☎🐎♿Ⓤ🅻🅸♿📺🖥💻🚐✿🚐

Oaky Knowe Farm ⋀

Listed COMMENDED
Haltwhistle NE49 0NB
☎ Hexham (01434) 320648
300-acre livestock farm. Overlooking the Tyne Valley, within walking distance of Haltwhistle and the Roman Wall, this comfortable farmhouse offers friendly family holidays.
Bedrooms: 1 twin, 2 triple
Bathrooms: 1 public

Bed & breakfast per night:

	£min	£max
Single	14.00	16.00
Double	28.00	30.00

Half board per person:

	£min	£max
Daily	22.00	24.00
Weekly	150.00	165.00

Evening meal 1700 (last orders 1530)
Parking for 8

☎🐎♿🖥♿Ⓤ🅻🅸✳♿📺🖥💻✕✿ 🚐 OAP SP 🏛

HALTWHISTLE

Continued

The Spotted Cow Inn 🏮

⬥ COMMENDED

Castle Hill, Haltwhistle NE49 0EW
☎ (01434) 320327
*Traditional pub-restaurant with beamed
ceilings, dating from 18th C, serving
real ales and fresh food cooked to
order. En-suite bedrooms with colour
TV, tea/coffee facilities. Children
welcome.*
Bedrooms: 2 double, 1 twin
Bathrooms: 3 en-suite
Bed & breakfast

per night:	£min	£max
Single	20.00	22.50
Double	40.00	40.00

Lunch available
Evening meal 1830 (last orders
2100)
Parking for 10
Cards accepted: Access, Visa

🛇🐾🖵🌢🖳Ⓢ✂🛏🖭🕿🔍🗠

HAMSTERLEY FOREST

Durham

See under Barnard Castle, Bishop
Auckland

HEIGHINGTON

Durham
Map ref 5C3

Village 2 miles south-west of
Newton Aycliffe. Built around a
large green giving fine views of the
Tees Valley.

Eldon House 🏮

⬥⬥ HIGHLY COMMENDED

East Green, Heighington, Darlington,
County Durham DL5 6PP
☎ Aycliffe (01325) 312270
*17th C manor house with large garden
overlooking the village green. Large,
comfortable, well-appointed rooms.
Ample parking. Tennis court. Coal/wood
fire in sitting room.*
Bedrooms: 3 twin
Bathrooms: 1 en-suite, 2 private
Bed & breakfast

per night:	£min	£max
Single	27.00	32.00
Double	40.00	45.00

Parking for 6

🛇🐾🖵Ⓤ🖳🔒🖭🖭🖳🗠🔍✲🗠🗠

For ideas on places to visit
refer to the introduction at
the beginning of this section.

HEXHAM

Northumberland
Map ref 5B2

Old coaching and market town near
Hadrian's Wall. Since pre-Norman
times a weekly market has been
held in the centre with its
market-place and abbey park, and
the richly-furnished 12th C abbey
church has a superb Anglo- Saxon
crypt.
*Tourist Information Centre ☎ (01434)
605225*

Anick Grange

⬥ COMMENDED

Hexham NE46 4LP
☎ (01434) 603807
*363-acre mixed farm. 17th C
farmhouse, 1 mile from Hexham.
Superb open views. Comfortable,
informal and a warm welcome.*
Bedrooms: 1 single, 1 twin, 1 triple
Bathrooms: 1 en-suite, 1 public
Bed & breakfast

per night:	£min	£max
Single	16.00	18.00
Double	32.00	36.00

Parking for 4
Open April–September

🛇1🖵🌢Ⓤ🖭🖳Ụ🗠

Dene House 🏮

⬥⬥ HIGHLY COMMENDED

Juniper, Hexham NE46 1SJ
☎ (01434) 673413

*Stone farmhouse with beamed ceilings,
log fires and flowers everywhere. Very
quietly situated in 9 acres of farmland,
4 miles south of Hexham.*
Bedrooms: 1 single, 1 double, 1 twin
Bathrooms: 1 en-suite, 1 private,
1 public
Bed & breakfast

per night:	£min	£max
Single	18.00	20.00
Double	36.00	40.00

Half board per

person:	£min	£max
Daily	28.00	30.00

Evening meal 1800 (last orders
1900)
Parking for 3

🛇🐾🖵🌢Ⓤ🔒Ⓢ✂🛏🖭🖳🗠✲🗠

Kitty Frisk House

⬥⬥ HIGHLY COMMENDED

Corbridge Road, Hexham
NE46 1UN
☎ (01434) 601533
Fax (01434) 601533

*Large, detached elegant Edwardian
house set in mature woodland.
Comfortable, spacious bedrooms with
en-suite and private facilities.*
Bedrooms: 1 double, 2 twin
Bathrooms: 2 en-suite, 1 private
Bed & breakfast

per night:	£min	£max
Single	22.50	30.00
Double	45.00	50.00

Parking for 6

🛇🖵🌢ⓊⒶ🖳✂🛏🖭🖭🖳🗠✲🗠🗠

Peth Head Cottage 🏮

⬥⬥ HIGHLY COMMENDED

Juniper Village, Steel, Hexham
NE47 0LA
☎ (01434) 673286
Fax (01434) 673038

*Rose-covered stone cottage in quiet
hamlet. Charming bedrooms and
attractive lounge for guests. Picturesque
rural location, ideal for walking and
touring holidays.*
Bedrooms: 1 single, 1 double, 1 twin
Bathrooms: 3 en-suite
Bed & breakfast

per night:	£min	£max
Single	18.00	18.00
Double	36.00	36.00

Parking for 5

🛇🖪🌢Ⓤ🖳✂🖭🖭🖳🗠✲🗠🗠
🗠Ⓣ

Rose and Crown Inn 🏮

⬥⬥ HIGHLY COMMENDED

Main Street, Slaley, Hexham
NE47 0AA
☎ (01434) 673263
Fax (01434) 673305
*Warm, friendly, family-run business with
good wholesome home cooking and
a la carte restaurant. All bedrooms
en-suite in this 200 year old listed
village freehouse in Slaley.*

Bedrooms: 1 single, 2 twin
Bathrooms: 3 en-suite

Bed & breakfast per night:

	£min	£max
Single	20.00	25.00
Double	35.00	45.00

Half board per person:

	£min	£max
Daily	30.00	35.00

Lunch available
Evening meal 1830 (last orders 2200)
Parking for 32
Cards accepted: Access, Visa, Switch/Delta

Rye Hill Farm ⏃

ⵚⵚ COMMENDED

Slaley, Hexham NE47 0AH
☎ (01434) 673259
Fax (01434) 673608

30-acre livestock farm. Warm and comfortable barn conversion, 5 miles south of Hexham, where you can enjoy the peace of rural life. Noted for the food and the friendly atmosphere.
Bedrooms: 2 double, 2 twin, 2 family rooms
Bathrooms: 6 en-suite

Bed & breakfast per night:

	£min	£max
Single	24.00	24.00
Double	40.00	40.00

Half board per person:

	£min	£max
Daily	30.00	34.00
Weekly	189.00	214.00

Evening meal 1930 (last orders 1700)
Parking for 6

Thistlerigg Farm

Listed

High Warden, Hexham NE46 4SR
☎ (01434) 602041
630-acre mixed farm. Farmhouse built in 1908. Scenic views, within walking distance of a Roman hill fort and close to Northumberland National Park.
Bedrooms: 1 double, 1 twin, 1 triple
Bathrooms: 1 public

Bed & breakfast per night:

	£min	£max
Double	28.00	30.00

Parking for 3
Open April–October

HOLY ISLAND

Northumberland
Map ref 5B1

Still an idyllic retreat, tiny island and fishing village and cradle of northern Christianity. It is approached from the mainland at low water by a causeway. The clifftop castle (National Trust) was restored by Sir Edwin Lutyens.

Britannia

ⵚⵚ

Holy Island, Berwick-upon-Tweed TD15 2RX
☎ Berwick-upon-Tweed (01289) 389218
Comfortable, friendly bed and breakfast in centre of Holy Island. Hot and cold water, tea-making facilities in all rooms. TV lounge. En-suite available.
Bedrooms: 1 double, 1 twin, 1 triple
Bathrooms: 1 en-suite, 1 public

Bed & breakfast per night:

	£min	£max
Single	17.00	
Double	28.00	34.00

Parking for 4
Open March–October

Crown & Anchor Hotel ⏃

ⵚⵚ APPROVED

Fenkle Street, Holy Island, Berwick-upon-Tweed TD15 2RX
☎ Berwick-upon-Tweed (01289) 389215
Old-fashioned inn with public bar, no-smoking lounge bar and dining room. Bedrooms en-suite and centrally heated. Beautiful views and quietly situated.
Bedrooms: 2 double, 1 twin
Bathrooms: 3 en-suite, 1 public

Bed & breakfast per night:

	£min	£max
Single	18.00	25.00
Double	32.00	45.00

Lunch available
Parking for 5

North View ⏃

ⵚⵚⵚ HIGHLY COMMENDED

Marygate, Holy Island, Berwick-upon-Tweed TD15 2SD
☎ Berwick-upon-Tweed (01289) 389272
400-year-old listed building on historic and beautiful island. Ideally situated for visiting many of Northumberland's tourist attractions.

Bedrooms: 2 double, 1 twin
Bathrooms: 3 en-suite

Bed & breakfast per night:

	£min	£max
Single	22.50	30.00
Double	45.00	49.00

Half board per person:

	£min	£max
Daily	34.50	42.00

Lunch available
Evening meal 1900 (last orders 2100)
Parking for 6
Cards accepted: Access, Visa

KIELDER FOREST

Northumberland

See under Kielder Water, West Woodburn

KIELDER WATER

Northumberland
Map ref 5B2

A magnificent man-made lake, the largest in Northern Europe, with over 27 miles of shoreline. On the edge of the Northumberland National Park and near the Scottish border, Kielder can be explored by car, on foot or by ferry.

The Pheasant Inn (by Kielder Water) ⏃

ⵚⵚⵚ COMMENDED

Stannersburn, Falstone, Hexham NE48 1DD
☎ Hexham (01434) 240382

Historic inn with beamed ceilings and open fires. Home cooking. Fishing, riding and all water sports nearby. Close to Kielder Water, Hadrian's Wall and the Scottish border.
Bedrooms: 4 double, 3 twin, 1 family room
Bathrooms: 8 en-suite

Bed & breakfast per night:

	£min	£max
Single	30.00	35.00
Double	52.00	56.00

Half board per person:

	£min	£max
Daily	45.00	48.00

Continued ▶

KIELDER WATER

Continued

Lunch available
Evening meal 1900 (last orders 2100)
Parking for 30
Cards accepted: Access, Visa, Switch/Delta

LESBURY

Northumberland
Map ref 5C1

Village 1 mile north-west of Alnmouth near the Northumberland coast.

Dukes Ryde

HIGHLY COMMENDED

Longhoughton Road, Lesbury, Alnwick NE66 3AT
☎ Alnwick (01665) 830855
Delightful and imposing early 20th C house set in secluded gardens, on the outskirts of Lesbury village, near beaches and golf-courses.
Bedrooms: 1 double, 2 twin
Bathrooms: 2 en-suite, 1 private

Bed & breakfast per night:	£min	£max
Single	25.00	25.00
Double	40.00	40.00

Parking for 6

LOWICK

Northumberland
Map ref 5B1

Inland from Holy Island and near the A1, Lowick has a long, wide main street with a few shops and inns and is in agricultural land between the foothills of the Cheviots and the coast.

Black Bull Inn

COMMENDED

Main Street, Lowick, Berwick-upon-Tweed TD15 2UA
☎ (01289) 388228
Originally built in 1645, the inn has seen many changes, including a separate dining room in 1988, and en-suite bedrooms in 1994. Informality and comfort are the aims.
Bedrooms: 2 double, 1 twin
Bathrooms: 2 en-suite, 1 private

Bed & breakfast per night:	£min	£max
Single	20.00	26.00
Double	40.00	52.00

Lunch available
Evening meal 1830 (last orders 2100)
Parking for 40
Cards accepted: Access, Visa, Switch/Delta

MIDDLESBROUGH

Tees Valley
Map ref 5C3

Boom-town of the mid 19th C, today's Teesside industrial and conference town has a modern shopping complex and predominantly modern buildings. An engineering miracle of the early 20th C is the Transporter Bridge which replaced an old ferry.
Tourist Information Centre ☎ (01642) 243425 or 264330

Maltby Farm

APPROVED

Maltby, Middlesbrough, Cleveland TS8 0BP
☎ (01642) 590121
187-acre mixed farm. Traditional Yorkshire farmhouse, over 200 years old, looking south on to the Cleveland Hills.
Bedrooms: 1 single, 1 twin, 1 triple
Bathrooms: 1 public

Bed & breakfast per night:	£min	£max
Single	16.00	17.00
Double	32.00	34.00

Half board per person:	£min	£max
Daily	23.00	24.00
Weekly	135.00	140.00

Evening meal 1800 (last orders 2000)
Parking for 6
Open April–October

MIDDLETON-IN-TEESDALE

Durham
Map ref 5B3

Small stone town of hillside terraces overlooking the river, developed by the London Lead Company in the 18th C. Five miles up-river is the spectacular 70-ft waterfall, High Force.

Brunswick House

COMMENDED

55 Market Place, Middleton-in-Teesdale, Barnard Castle, County Durham DL12 0QH
☎ Teesdale (01833) 640393

18th C listed stone-built guesthouse retaining much character and many original features. Comfort, friendly service and outstanding home cooking are assured.
Bedrooms: 2 double, 1 twin, 1 family room
Bathrooms: 3 en-suite, 1 private

Bed & breakfast per night:	£min	£max
Single	21.00	30.00
Double	42.00	42.00

Half board per person:	£min	£max
Daily		36.00
Weekly		210.00

Evening meal 1930 (last orders 1900)
Parking for 5
Cards accepted: Access, Visa

MORPETH

Northumberland
Map ref 5C2

Market town on the River Wansbeck. There are charming gardens and parks, among them Carlisle Park which lies close to the ancient remains of Morpeth Castle. The chantry building houses the Northumbrian Craft Centre and the bagpipe museum.
Tourist Information Centre ☎ (01670) 511323

East Stobswood House

COMMENDED

Widdrington, Morpeth NE61 3AY
☎ (01670) 790468
Comfortable, well-furnished ex-farmhouse with 2-acre garden. 7 miles north-east of Morpeth, easy access A1 and A1068. 3.5 miles to golden sand and dunes of Druridge Bay and within easy reach of Warkworth and Alnwick Castles.
Bedrooms: 2 double, 1 twin
Bathrooms: 1 public

Bed & breakfast per night:	£min	£max
Single	16.00	20.00
Double	32.00	40.00

Parking for 4
Open March–November

NEWCASTLE UPON TYNE

Tyne and Wear
Map ref 5C2

Commercial and cultural centre of the North East, with a large indoor shopping centre, Quayside market, museums and theatres which offer an annual 6 week season by the Royal Shakespeare Company. Norman castle keep, medieval alleys, old Guildhall.
Tourist Information Centre ☎ (0191) 261 0610 or 230 0030

Grosvenor Hotel ⚠

⚜⚜⚜ APPROVED

Grosvenor Road, Jesmond, Newcastle upon Tyne NE2 2RR
☎ (0191) 281 0543
Fax (0191) 281 9217
Friendly hotel in quiet residential suburb, offering a wide range of facilities. Close to city centre.
Bedrooms: 17 single, 8 double, 9 twin, 6 triple
Bathrooms: 32 en-suite, 5 public

Bed & breakfast per night:	£min	£max
Single	20.00	40.00
Double	30.00	60.00

Half board per person:	£min	£max
Daily	25.00	50.00
Weekly	175.00	350.00

Lunch available
Evening meal 1830 (last orders 2100)
Parking for 30
Cards accepted: Access, Visa, Diners, Amex, Switch/Delta

🛇🛆🕭📞🖵🎄♦️🎣⑤🐾📺◑ 📻🔒🏊120 ᴏᴀᴘ 🕱 ꜱᴘ 🆃

NORHAM

Northumberland
Map ref 5B1

Border village on the salmon-rich Tweed, dominated by its dramatic castle ruin. Near Castle Street is the church, like the castle destroyed after the Battle of Flodden, but rebuilt. Norham Station Railway Museum is just outside the town.

Dromore House ⚠

Listed COMMENDED

12 Pedwell Way, Norham, Berwick-upon-Tweed TD15 2LD
☎ Berwick-upon-Tweed (01289) 382313
Guesthouse in a small village on the River Tweed, between the Cheviot and Lammermuir Hills. Quiet beaches are within easy reach.

Bedrooms: 1 double, 1 twin, 1 triple
Bathrooms: 2 private, 1 public

Bed & breakfast per night:	£min	£max
Single	16.00	19.00
Double	32.00	38.00

Half board per person:	£min	£max
Daily	24.00	27.00
Weekly	168.00	189.00

Evening meal 1700 (last orders 1900)
Parking for 3

🛇🛆🖵♦️ᵁᴸ🔒🎄📺📻🐾🏠

REDCAR

Tees Valley
Map ref 5C3

Lively holiday resort near Teesside with broad sandy beaches, a fine racecourse, a large indoor funfair at Coatham and other seaside amusements. Britain's oldest existing lifeboat can be seen at the Zetland Museum.

Waterside House

⚜

35 Newcomen Terrace, Redcar, Cleveland TS10 1DB
☎ (01642) 481062
Large terraced property overlooking the sea, close to town centre and leisure centre. Warm, friendly atmosphere with true Yorkshire hospitality.
Bedrooms: 2 single, 3 triple, 1 family room
Bathrooms: 2 public

Bed & breakfast per night:	£min	£max
Single	14.00	16.00
Double	25.00	27.00

Half board per person:	£min	£max
Daily	19.50	21.50
Weekly	136.50	150.50

Evening meal 1700 (last orders 1900)

🛇🖵♦️ᵁᴸ🔒🎄📺📻🐾ꜱᴘ

> Establishments should be open throughout the year, unless otherwise stated.

> The ⚠ symbol after an establishment name indicates that it is a Regional Tourist Board member.

ROTHBURY

Northumberland
Map ref 5B1

Old market town on the River Coquet near the Simonside Hills. It makes an ideal centre for walking and fishing or for exploring this beautiful area from the coast to the Cheviots. Cragside House and Gardens (National Trust) are open to the public.

Silverton House

Listed COMMENDED

Silverton Lane, Rothbury, Morpeth NE65 7RJ
☎ (01669) 621395
Imaginative and comfortable conversion from an old workhouse, on the outskirts of Rothbury in lovely countryside.
Bedrooms: 1 double, 1 twin
Bathrooms: 1 en-suite, 1 private

Bed & breakfast per night:	£min	£max
Single	16.00	17.00
Double	32.00	34.00

🛇🛆🕭♦️🎄🖵ᵁᴸ✂️🎣📺📻🛏🐾🏠

Thropton Demesne Farmhouse ⚠

⚜⚜ HIGHLY COMMENDED

Thropton, Rothbury, Morpeth NE65 7LT
☎ (01669) 620196
Fax (01669) 620196
24-acre mixed farm. Traditional farmhouse peacefully situated in the picturesque Coquet Valley. Spectacular views. Ideally placed for fishing, golf and walking. Home-made bread.
Bedrooms: 1 double, 1 twin, 1 triple
Bathrooms: 2 en-suite, 1 private

Bed & breakfast per night:	£min	£max
Single	25.00	38.00
Double	36.00	38.00

Parking for 6

🛇🖵♦️🎄ᵁᴸ🔒✂️🎣📻🛏🐾❄️✈️🐾 ꜱᴘ🏠

> Map references apply to the colour maps at the back of this guide.

> A key to symbols can be found inside the back cover flap.

RYTON

Tyne and Wear
Map ref 5C2

On a wooded site above the Tyne, Ryton has a 12th C church with a Jacobean screen and good 19th C oak carving. Small pit working, notable for the spectacular 1826 Stargate Explosion, ceased in 1967. Easy access to the A1, Hadrian's Wall and rural Northumbria.

Barmoor Old Manse ⚠

`Listed` `APPROVED`

The Old Manse, Barmoor, Ryton
NE40 3BD
☎ (0191) 413 2438
Large stone Victorian house, built as manse for Congregational church in 1862. Delightful garden. Near MetroCentre, Roman Wall and Beamish Museum.
Bedrooms: 1 double, 2 twin
Bathrooms: 1 public
Bed & breakfast

per night:	£min	£max
Single	16.00	17.50
Double	32.00	35.00

Parking for 2

🛇 📛 🖵 👶 🔟 ⬆ ⚡ ✕ 📺 🗔 🛋 ❋ 🚗 `SP`

SEAHOUSES

Northumberland
Map ref 5C1

Small modern resort developed around a 19th C herring port. Just offshore, and reached by boat from here, are the rocky Farne Islands (National Trust) where there is an important bird reserve. The bird observatory occupies a medieval pele tower.

'Leeholme' ⚠

`Listed` `COMMENDED`

93 Main Street, Seahouses
NE68 7TS
☎ (01665) 720230
A warm welcome awaits you at this small homely bed and breakfast. 5 minutes' walk to Seahouses harbour and shops. Hearty breakfast assured.
Bedrooms: 1 double, 1 twin
Bathrooms: 1 public
Bed & breakfast

per night:	£min	£max
Single	15.00	
Double	30.00	

Parking for 2
Open March–October

🛇 📛 🖵 👶 🔟 ⬆ ⚡ ✕ 🗔 🛋 📞 🚗

SHOTLEY BRIDGE

Durham
Map ref 5B2

Fashionable suburb of Consett where German craftsmen settled in the 17th C. In the 19th C with the coming of the railway to serve Consett Iron Works, the village found fame as a spa. The local railway line has now been developed as a walkway and the track follows the valley to Swalwell.

The Manor House Inn ⚠

`Listed` `COMMENDED`

Caterway Heads, Shotley Bridge, Consett, County Durham DH8 9LX
☎ Consett (01207) 255268
Small family-run inn, offering warm, comfortable accommodation. Delicious food, ales and wines. Overlooking an Area of Outstanding Natural Beauty and Derwent reservoir.
Bedrooms: 2 double, 1 twin, 1 family room
Bathrooms: 2 en-suite, 2 public
Bed & breakfast

per night:	£min	£max
Single	22.00	25.00
Double	38.50	45.00

Lunch available
Evening meal 1900 (last orders 2130)
Parking for 50
Cards accepted: Access, Visa, Diners, Amex, Switch/Delta

🛇 🏥 🖳 🖵 👶 `S` ✕ 🗔 🛋 ❋ 🚗 `SP`

SPENNYMOOR

Durham
Map ref 5C2

Booming coal and iron town from the 18th C until early in the present century when traditional industry gave way to lighter manufacturing and trading estates were built. On the moors south of the town there are fine views of the Wear Valley.

Idsley House ⚠

`👑👑` `HIGHLY COMMENDED`

4 Green Lane, Spennymoor, County Durham DL16 6HD
☎ Bishop Auckland (01388) 814237
Detached Victorian residence in quiet area at junction of A167/A688, opposite council offices. Just 8 minutes south of Durham City. Tastefully furnished, spacious bedrooms, safe parking on premises.
Bedrooms: 1 single, 1 double, 2 twin, 1 triple
Bathrooms: 4 private, 1 public

Bed & breakfast		
per night:	£min	£max
Double	38.00	40.00

Parking for 8
Cards accepted: Access, Visa, Switch/Delta

🛇 📛 🖵 👶 🔟 ⬆ 🔟 ⚡ ✕ 📺 🗔 🛋 ❋

STAINDROP

Durham
Map ref 5B3

Village 5 miles north-east of Barnard Castle, not far from Raby Castle, one of the most impressive castles in the north of England.

Gazebo House ⚠

`👑👑👑` `HIGHLY COMMENDED`

4 North Green, Staindrop, Darlington, County Durham DL2 3JN
☎ Teesdale (01833) 660222
Fax (01833) 660222

18th C house with listed gazebo (illustrated) in garden. Adjacent Raby Park and Castle. Ideal base for Lake District and Yorkshire Dales.
Bedrooms: 1 double, 1 twin
Bathrooms: 1 en-suite, 1 private
Bed & breakfast

per night:	£min	£max
Single	18.00	
Double	38.00	

Half board per person:	£min	£max
Daily	33.00	52.00

Evening meal 1900 (last orders 2200)

🛇 📞 📛 🖵 👶 ⚡ 🔟 📺 🗔 🛋 ❋ 🏥

SUNDERLAND

Tyne and Wear
Map ref 5C2

Ancient coal and shipbuilding port on Wearside, with important glassworks since the 17th C, although glassmaking here dates back more than 1,000 years.
Tourist Information Centre ☎ (0191) 565 0990 or 565 0960

Bed & Breakfast Stop

COMMENDED

183 Newcastle Road, Fulwell, Sunderland, Tyne & Wear SR5 1NR
☎ (0191) 548 2291
Tudor-style semi-detached house on the A1018 Newcastle to Sunderland road. 5 minutes to the railway station and 10 minutes to the seafront and city centre.
Bedrooms: 1 single, 1 twin, 1 triple
Bathrooms: 1 public

Bed & breakfast per night:	£min	£max
Single	15.00	17.00
Double	28.00	30.00

Half board per person:	£min	£max
Daily	21.00	23.00
Weekly	133.00	140.00

Evening meal 1800 (last orders 1200)
Parking for 3

TANFIELD

Durham
Map ref 5C2

Tanfield Lane Farm

Listed

Tanfield, Stanley, County Durham DH9 9QE
☎ Stanley (01207) 232739
200-acre mixed farm. Farmhouse situated 2 miles from Beamish Museum, 2 miles from Stanley and 6 miles from A1M. Close to Causey Arch and Tanfield Steam Railway. 15 minutes from Gateshead.
Bedrooms: 1 twin, 1 triple
Bathrooms: 1 public

Bed & breakfast per night:	£min	£max
Single	15.00	15.00
Double	30.00	30.00

Parking for 8

Please mention this guide when making your booking.

TYNEMOUTH

Tyne and Wear
Map ref 5C2

At the mouth of the Tyne, old Tyneside resort adjoining North Shields with its fish quay and market. The pier is overlooked by the gaunt ruins of a Benedictine priory and a castle. Splendid sands, amusement centre and park.

Hope House

DE LUXE

47 Percy Gardens, Tynemouth, North Shields NE30 4HH
☎ (0191) 257 1989
Fax (0191) 257 1989
Double-fronted Victorian house with superb coastal views from most rooms. Tastefully furnished, with large bedrooms. Fine cuisine and quality wines.
Bedrooms: 2 double, 1 twin
Bathrooms: 2 en-suite, 1 private, 1 public

Bed & breakfast per night:	£min	£max
Single	37.50	45.00
Double	42.50	57.50

Lunch available
Evening meal 1800 (last orders 2100)
Parking for 5
Cards accepted: Access, Visa, Diners, Amex

WARKWORTH

Northumberland
Map ref 5C1

A pretty village overlooked by its medieval castle. A 14th C fortified bridge across the wooded Coquet gives a superb view of 18th C terraces climbing to the castle. Upstream is a curious 14th C Hermitage and in the market square is the Norman church of St Lawrence.

Beck 'N' Call

HIGHLY COMMENDED

Birling West Cottage, Warkworth, Morpeth NE65 0XS
☎ Alnwick (01665) 711653
Country cottage set in half an acre of terraced gardens with stream. First cottage on the right entering Warkworth from Alnwick.
Bedrooms: 2 double, 1 triple
Bathrooms: 2 en-suite, 2 public

Bed & breakfast per night:	£min	£max
Single	18.00	19.00
Double	36.00	38.00

Parking for 4

Bide A While

Listed COMMENDED

4 Beal Croft, Warkworth, Morpeth NE65 0XL
☎ Alnwick (01665) 711753
Bungalow on small executive housing estate of 8 dwellings.
Bedrooms: 1 double, 1 family room
Bathrooms: 1 private, 1 public

Bed & breakfast per night:	£min	£max
Single	17.00	19.00
Double	30.00	34.00

Parking for 3

WASHINGTON

Tyne and Wear
Map ref 5C2

New Town based on an old coal-mining village. The original pit-head buildings and mining apparatus now serve as a museum. The Old Hall (National Trust), seat of George Washington's ancestors, was rescued from its dilapidated state in the 1930s, restored and furnished.

White Lodge Guest House

COMMENDED

Fatfield, Washington NE38 8AB
☎ (0191) 417 3063
Comfortable, detached guesthouse standing in half an acre of land, offering good food and friendly service. Easy access to Sunderland, Durham, Newcastle and MetroCentre. All rooms colour TV, tea/coffee making facilities.
Bedrooms: 1 family room
Bathrooms: 2 public

Bed & breakfast per night:	£min	£max
Single	15.00	20.00
Double	30.00	35.00

Parking for 4

A key to symbols can be found inside the back cover flap.

WEST WOODBURN

Northumberland
Map ref 5B2

Small hamlet on the River Rede in rolling moorland country.

Bay Horse Inn

West Woodburn, Hexham
NE48 2RX
☎ Hexham (01434) 270218
18th C coaching inn beside River Rede. On A68 between Corbridge and Otterburn and near Bellingham.
Bedrooms: 2 double, 2 twin, 1 family room
Bathrooms: 5 en-suite, 1 public
Bed & breakfast

per night:	£min	£max
Single	20.00	25.00
Double	40.00	45.00

Lunch available
Evening meal 1900 (last orders 2100)
Parking for 25
Cards accepted: Access, Visa, Switch/Delta

WYLAM

Northumberland
Map ref 5B2

Well-kept village on the River Tyne, famous as the birthplace of the railway pioneer, George Stephenson. The cottage in which he was born is open to the public, and the Wylam Railway Museum also commemorates William Hedley and Timothy Hackworth.

Wormald House

HIGHLY COMMENDED
Main Street, Wylam NE41 8DN
☎ (01661) 852529 & 852552
Pleasant country home located near centre of Wylam, George Stephenson's birthplace. House stands on site of Timothy Hackworth's birthplace (Stephenson's contemporary).
Bedrooms: 1 double, 1 twin
Bathrooms: 2 en-suite
Bed & breakfast

per night:	£min	£max
Single	17.50	18.00
Double	35.00	36.00

Parking for 4
Cards accepted: Visa

COUNTRY CODE

Always follow the Country Code

🌾 Enjoy the countryside and respect its life and work 🌾 Guard against all risk of fire 🌾 Fasten all gates 🌾 Keep your dogs under close control 🌾 Keep to public paths across farmland 🌾 Use gates and stiles to cross fences, hedges and walls 🌾 Leave livestock, crops and machinery alone 🌾 Take your litter home 🌾 Help to keep all water clean 🌾 Protect wildlife, plants and trees 🌾 Take special care on country roads 🌾 Make no unnecessary noise

NORTH WEST

The legacy of the Industrial Revolution can be seen in the North West's fine Victorian architecture, magnificent mill buildings and miles of canals - once used for transportation but today, navigated for pleasure.

Manchester and Liverpool are vibrant centres of popular and 'high' culture while stylish Lytham St Anne's, Southport or glittering Blackpool are among Britain's most famous coastal resorts.

Explore elegant Chester, the historic city of Lancaster or, in total contrast, the pretty villages of the Wirral and the unspoilt border country of Cheshire. From birdlife to nightlife, markets to music festivals, the North West has it all.

FOR MORE INFORMATION CONTACT:
North West Tourist Board
Swan House, Swan Meadow Road,
Wigan Pier, Wigan WN3 5BB
Tel: (01942) 821222 **Fax:** (01942) 820002

Where to Go in the North West -
see pages 84-87
Where to Stay in the North West -
see pages 88-96

NORTH WEST

Where to Go and What to See

You will find hundreds of interesting places to visit during your stay in the North West, just some of which are listed in these pages. The number against each name will help you locate it on the map (page 87). Contact any Tourist Information Centre in the region for more ideas on days out in the North West.

1 Frontierland Western Theme Park
Marine Road, Morecambe,
Lancashire LA4 4DG
Tel: (01524) 410024
Over 40 thrill rides and attractions including the Texas Tornado, the Polo Tower Perculator and Stampede Roller Coaster.

2 Lancaster Castle
Shire Hall, Castle Parade,
Lancaster, Lancashire
Tel: (01524) 64998
Collection of coats of arms, dungeons, crown court, Jane Scott's chair. Grand Jury Room. External tour of castle walls.

3 Blackpool Pleasure Beach
Ocean Boulevard,
Blackpool, Lancashire FY4 1EZ
Tel: (01253) 341033
Amusement park with rides including Space Invader, Big Dipper and Revolution. Funshineland for children. Summer season ice show, Mystique illusion show in Horseshoe Bar.

4 Blackpool Sea Life Centre
The Promenade,
Blackpool,
Lancashire FY1 5AA
Tel: (01253) 22445
Tropical sharks up to 8 feet in length housed in a 100,000 gallon display with underwater walk-through.

5 Blackpool Tower
Promenade,
Blackpool,
Lancashire FY1 4BJ
Tel: (01253) 22242
Tower Ballroom, Bug World, Jungle Jim's playground. Out of this World. Children's entertainment in Hornpipe Galley, Undersea World. Tower Circus, Laser fantasy and Lift Ride.

6 Ribchester Museum of Childhood
Church Street,
Ribchester,
Lancashire PR3 3YE
Tel: (01254) 878520

Large 10-room building contaning childhood toys, dolls and dolls' houses, 20-piece model fairground, Tom Thumb replica, collectors' toy shop.

7 Pleasureland Amusement Park
Marine Drive,
The Fun Coast,
Southport,
Merseyside PR8 1RX
Tel: (01704) 532717
Traditional amusement park with wide variety of thrilling and family rides.

8 Astley Hall
Astley Park,
Chorley,
Lancashire PR7 1NP
Tel: (01257) 262166
Hall dates from 1580 with subsequent additions. Unique collection of furniture including a fine Elizabethan bed and the famous shovel board table in the Long Gallery.

9 Camelot Theme Park and Rare Breeds Farm

Park Hall Road, Charnock Richard, Lancashire PR7 5LP
Tel: (01257) 453044
Magical kingdom offering over 100 thrilling rides, attractions and medieval entertainment.

10 Wildfowl and Wetland Centre

Martin Mere, Burscough, Lancashire L40 0TA
Tel: (01704) 895181
45 acres of gardens with over 1600 ducks geese and swans of 120 different kinds. Two flocks of flamingos. 300-acre wild area with 20-acre lake.

11 East Lancashire Railway

Bolton Street Station, Bury, Lancashire BL9 0EY
Tel: (0161) 764 7790
Eight-mile-long preserved railway operated principally by steam traction, transport museum nearby.

12 Rufford Old Hall

Rufford, Ormskirk, Lancashire L40 1SG
Tel: (01704) 821254
Fine 15thC building with a magnificent Great Hall, particularly noted for its immense moveable screen.

13 Wigan Pier

Wallgate, Wigan, Lancashire WN3 4EU
Tel: (01942) 323666
The Way We Were – life in Wigan in 1900. World's largest steam mill engine, cotton machinery hall, shops, picnic gardens, cafeteria, waterbuses and Victorian classroom.

14 Granada Studios Tour

Water Street, Manchester, Greater Manchester M60 9EA
Tel: (0161) 832 9090
Major television theme park providing an insight into the fascinating world behind the TV screen. Visit three of the most famous streets in Britain.

15 Museum of Science and Industry in Manchester

Liverpool Road, Castlefield, Manchester, Greater Manchester M3 4JP
Tel: (0161) 832 2244
The Museum of Science and Industry in Manchester based in the world's oldest passenger railway station, with 15 galleries that amaze, amuse and entertain.

16 Knowsley Safari Park

Prescot, Merseyside L34 4AN
Tel: (0151) 430 9009
Five-mile drive through game reserves, set in 400 acres of parkland containing lions, tigers, elephants, rhinos, etc. Large picnic areas and children's amusement park.

17 Albert Dock

The Colonnades, Albert Dock, Liverpool, L3 4AA
Tel: (0151) 708 8854
Britain's largest Grade 1 listed historic building. Restored 4-sided dock, including shops, bars, restaurants, entertainment, marina and maritime museum.

18 Croxteth Hall and Country Park

Off Muirhead Avenue East, Liverpool, Merseyside L12 0HB
Tel: (0151) 228 5311
500 acre country park and hall with displays, furnished rooms and walled garden. Farm with rare breeds, miniature railway, gift shop, picnic area, riding centre, adventure playground.

19 Tate Gallery Liverpool

Albert Dock, Liverpool L3 4BB
Tel: (0151) 709 3223
The national collection of modern art in the North of England.

20 **Dunham Massey Hall and Park**
Altrincham, Cheshire WA14 4SJ
Tel: (0161) 941 1025
Historic house, garden and park with restaurant and shop.

21 **Lyme Park**
Disley, Cheshire SK12 2NX
Tel: (01663) 762023
Country estate within 1377 acres of moorland, woodland and park. Magnificent house with 17 acres of historic gardens.

22 **Quarry Bank Mill**
Styal, Cheshire SK9 4LA
Tel: (01625) 527468
Georgian water-powerd cotton-spinning mill. Four floors of displays and demonstrations, 284 acres of parkland.

23 **Norton Priory Museum and Gardens**
Tudor Road, Runcorn,
Cheshire WA7 1SX
Tel: (01928) 569895
Excavated Augustinian priory, remains of church, cloister and chapter house. Later site of Tudor

mansion and Georgian house. Walled garden and woodland.

24 **Boat Museum**
Dock Yard Road, Ellesmere Port,
Cheshire L65 4FW
Tel: (0151) 355 5017
Over 50 historic craft, largest floating collection in the world with restored buildings, traditional cottages, workshops, steam engines, boat trips, shop and cafe.

25 **Arley Hall and Gardens**
Arley, Northwich,
Cheshire CW9 6NA
Tel: (01565) 777353
Early Victorian building set in 12 acres of magnificent gardens. 15thC Tythe barn. Unique collection of water colours of the area.

26 **Macclesfield Silk Museum**
The Heritage Centre,
Roe Street, Macclesfield,
Cheshire SK11 6UT
Tel: (01625) 613210
Information centre, town history exhibition, silk museum, Sunday school, history exhibition, guided trails.

27 **Jodrell Bank Science Centre and Arboretum**
Lower Withington,
Macclesfield, Cheshire SK11 9DL
Tel: (01477) 571339
Exhibition and interactive exhibits on astronomy, space, satellites, energy and the environment. Planetarium and the world-famous Lovell telescope and 35 acre arboretum.

28 **Cheshire Oaks Designer Outlet Village**
Ellesmere Port,
The Wirral L65 9JJ
Over 60 individual stores selling famous branded goods.

29 **Chester Zoo**
Upton-by-Chester,
Chester, Cheshire CH2 1LH
Tel: (01244) 380280
Penguin pool with underwater views, tropical house, spectacular displays of spring and summer bedding plants. Chimpanzee house and new monorail.

FIND OUT MORE

Further information about holidays and attractions in the North West is available from:
North West Tourist Board,
Swan House,
Swan Meadow Road,
Wigan Pier,
Wigan WN3 5BB.
Tel: (01942) 821222

These publications are available free from the North West Tourist Board:
■ **North West Welcome Guide**
■ **Discover England's North West**
■ **Attraction Map**
■ **Group Travel Guide**
■ **Bed & Breakfast Map**
■ **Caravan and Camping Parks Guide**

CUMBRIA

0   20 Miles

0   30 Kms

NORTH
YORKSHIRE

1 Morecambe

2 Lancaster

Fleetwood

LANCASHIRE

Clitheroe

Blackpool **3 4**   Ribchester   Nelson
5   **6**   Burnley

Lytham St Annes   Preston   Blackburn   Accrington
          Darwen   Rawtenstall

WEST
YORKSHIRE

Southport   **7**   **9** **8** Chorley
    Burscough   Charnock   Ramsbottom
    Ormskirk   **10** Richard   Bolton Bury **11** Rochdale
Formby   **12** Skelmersdale   Oldham
        13 Wigan   **GREATER**
    Kirkby   **MANCHESTER**

MERSEYSIDE St Helens   Salford **14 15** Manchester
New Brighton **17** **16** Prescot   Stockport
Hoylake **18 19** Huyton Warrington Altrincham Cheadle
Birkenhead Liverpool   **20**   **21**
          23   Styal **22** Disley
          Runcorn Arley Knutsford Wilmslow

DERBY-
SHIRE

Ellesmere **24 28**   **25**
Port   Northwich   Alderley
             Edge **26** Macclesfield
29 Chester Winsford **27** Lower Withington
             Congleton

WALES

CHESHIRE   Sandbach
          Crewe Alsager
                Kidsgrove
        Nantwich

STAFFORDSHIRE

WHERE TO STAY (NORTH WEST)

Accommodation entries in this region are listed in alphabetical order of place name, and then in alphabetical order of establishment.

Map references refer to the colour location maps at the back of this guide.

The first number indicates the map to use; the letter and number which follow refer to the grid reference on the map.

At-a-glance symbols at the end of each accommodation entry give useful information about services and facilities. A key to symbols can be found inside the back cover flap.

Keep this open for easy reference.

ALDERLEY EDGE

Cheshire
Map ref 4B2

Picturesque town taking its name from the wooded escarpment towering above the Cheshire plain, with fine views and walks. A romantic local legend tells of the Wizard and sleeping warriors who will save the country in crisis. Excellent shops. Chorley Hall, nearby, boasts a moat.

Dean Green Farm

♛ ♛ ♛ HIGHLY COMMENDED

Nusery Lane, Nether Alderley, Macclesfield SK10 4TX
☎ Chelford (01625) 861401
131-acre beef farm. Situated between A34 and A535 at Nether Alderley. Grade II oak-beamed farmhouse surrounded by pastureland looking towards Alderley Edge. Convenient for Knutsford, Wilmslow and Macclesfield.
Bedrooms: 1 double
Bathrooms: 1 en-suite
Bed & breakfast

per night:	£min	£max
Single		29.37
Double		58.75

Half board per

person:	£min	£max
Daily		44.06

Evening meal 1800 (last orders 2100)
Parking for 10

⌂🖵♿🚻🅿🍴🖨📺🛏💼🗡✒
✳🗡🎿🛒

ASHLEY

Greater Manchester
Map ref 4A2

Castle Hill Farmhouse ⚅

♛ ♛ COMMENDED

Castle Mill Lane, Ashley, Altrincham, Cheshire WA15 0RB
☎ (0161) 929 0496 & Mobile 0831 445104
Fax (0161) 929 0496
Castle Hill Farmhouse is set in 110 acres of best Cheshire countryside. The house dates back approximately 170 years and boasts a wealth of original features.
Bedrooms: 1 double, 1 triple, 1 family room
Bathrooms: 3 en-suite, 1 public
Bed & breakfast

per night:	£min	£max
Single	30.00	
Double	40.00	

Evening meal 1900 (last orders 2030)
Parking for 30

🐕🖵♿🅿🍴🗡✒🛏💼🚻✳🗡🎿🛒 T

A key to symbols can be found inside the back cover flap.

All accommodation in this guide has been graded, or is awaiting a grading, by a trained Tourist Board inspector.

BLACKPOOL

Lancashire
Map ref 4A1

Britain's largest fun resort, with Blackpool Pleasure Beach, 3 piers and the famous Tower. Host to the spectacular autumn illuminations - "the greatest free show on earth". *Tourist Information Centre ☎ (01253) 21623*

Ashbeian Hotel

♛ ♛ ♛ COMMENDED

49 High Street, Blackpool FY1 2BN
☎ (01253) 26301
All en-suite bedrooms, good public parking. Privately owned. Splendid menus. Terrific value. Just off seafront, an easy walk to everything.
Bedrooms: 1 single, 2 double, 2 triple
Bathrooms: 5 en-suite
Bed & breakfast

per night:	£min	£max
Single	11.00	22.00
Double	22.00	44.00

Half board per

person:	£min	£max
Daily	18.00	30.00
Weekly	112.00	150.00

Evening meal 1700 (last orders 1930)
Cards accepted: Access, Visa

🐕5🖵♿🚻🅿🍴📺🛏💼
DAP SP T

Sunray ⚅

♛ ♛ ♛ COMMENDED

42 Knowle Avenue, Blackpool FY2 9TQ
☎ (01253) 351937
Fax (01253) 593307

Modern semi in quiet residential part of north Blackpool. Friendly personal service and care. 1.75 miles north of tower along promenade. Turn right at Uncle Tom's Cabin. Sunray is about 300 yards on left.
Bedrooms: 3 single, 2 double, 2 twin, 2 triple
Bathrooms: 9 en-suite, 1 public

Bed & breakfast

per night:	£min	£max
Single	25.00	28.00
Double	50.00	56.00

Half board per

person:	£min	£max
Daily	37.00	40.00
Weekly	220.00	240.00

Evening meal 1750 (last orders 1500)
Parking for 6
Cards accepted: Access, Visa, Amex

BURNLEY

Lancashire
Map ref 4B1

"A town amidst the Pennines". Towneley Hall has fine period rooms and is home to Burnley's art gallery and museum. The Kay-Shuttleworth collection of lace and embroidery can be seen at Gawthorpe Hall (National Trust). Burnley Mechanics Arts Centre is a well-known jazz and blues venue.
Tourist Information Centre ☎ (01282) 455485

Ormerod Hotel
🛏🛏 HIGHLY COMMENDED
121-123 Ormerod Road, Burnley
BB11 3QW
☎ (01282) 423255
Small bed and breakfast hotel in quiet, pleasant surroundings facing local parks. Recently refurbished, all en-suite facilities. 5 minutes from town centre.
Bedrooms: 4 single, 2 double, 2 twin, 2 triple
Bathrooms: 10 en-suite

Bed & breakfast

per night:	£min	£max
Single	20.00	24.00
Double	34.00	37.00

Parking for 7

Half board prices are given per person, but in some cases these may be based on double/twin occupancy.

CHESTER

Cheshire
Map ref 4A2

Roman and medieval walled city rich in treasures. Black and white buildings are a hallmark, including "The Rows" - two-tier shopping galleries. The racecourse is the only one in the country where horses race anti-clockwise. 900-year-old cathedral, zoo.
Tourist Information Centre ☎ (01244) 317962 or 351609 or 322220

Cheyney Lodge Hotel ♙
🛏🛏🛏 COMMENDED
77-79 Cheyney Road, Chester
CH1 4BS
☎ (01244) 381925
Small, friendly hotel of unusual design, featuring indoor garden and fish pond. 10 minutes' walk from city centre and on main bus route. Personally supervised with emphasis on good food.
Bedrooms: 1 single, 4 double, 2 twin, 1 triple
Bathrooms: 8 en-suite

Bed & breakfast

per night:	£min	£max
Single	24.00	24.00
Double	39.00	44.00

Half board per

person:	£min	£max
Daily	28.95	31.95
Weekly	202.65	223.65

Lunch available
Evening meal 1800 (last orders 2000)
Parking for 12
Cards accepted: Access, Visa

Curzon Hotel ♙
🛏🛏🛏 COMMENDED
52-54 Hough Green, Chester
CH4 8JQ
☎ (01244) 678581
Fax (01244) 680866

A warm welcome awaits in this privately owned large Victorian house with beautiful gardens. Close to racecourse, River Dee and golf. Fine cuisine prepared by chef-proprietor Markus Imfeld.
Bedrooms: 4 single, 4 double, 1 twin, 4 triple, 3 family rooms

---

Bathrooms: 16 en-suite

Bed & breakfast

per night:	£min	£max
Single	35.00	40.00
Double	45.00	65.00

Half board per

person:	£min	£max
Daily	40.00	50.00
Weekly	245.00	385.00

Evening meal 1900 (last orders 2100)
Parking for 24
Cards accepted: Access, Visa, Diners, Amex

Edwards House Hotel
🛏🛏 HIGHLY COMMENDED
61-63 Hoole Road, Chester
CH2 3NJ
☎ (01244) 318055 & 319888
Victorian property with well proportioned bedrooms, all en-suite. Convenient for city centre, Chester Zoo, M53/M56 motorways and A55 North Wales trunk road.
Bedrooms: 2 single, 5 double, 3 triple
Bathrooms: 10 en-suite

Bed & breakfast

per night:	£min	£max
Single	21.00	29.00
Double	35.00	49.00

Half board per

person:	£min	£max
Daily	27.50	37.00
Weekly	192.50	259.00

Evening meal 1830 (last orders 1930)
Parking for 10
Cards accepted: Access, Visa

Grove House ♙
🛏🛏 HIGHLY COMMENDED
Holme Street, Tarvin, Chester
CH3 8EQ
☎ Tarvin (01829) 740893
Fax (01829) 741769

Warm welcome in relaxing environment. Spacious, comfortable rooms, attractive garden. Ample parking. Within easy reach of Chester (4 miles) and major North West and North Wales tourist attractions.

Continued ▶

CHESTER

Continued

Bedrooms: 1 single, 1 double, 1 twin
Bathrooms: 1 en-suite, 1 public

Bed & breakfast

per night:	£min	£max
Single	20.00	35.00
Double	46.00	56.00

Parking for 8

🐾🕿12📟🖵♿🖢🔌UL⑤⌦TV🏚🖴
🗚🅿☼✈🚲

Mitchells of Chester

👑 HIGHLY COMMENDED

Green Gables House, 28 Hough
Green, Chester CH4 8JQ
🕿 (01244) 679004
*Tastefully restored, elegant Victorian
residence, with steeply pitched slated
roofs, a sweeping staircase, antique
furniture in tall rooms with moulded
cornices. Compact landscaped gardens.
Close to city centre.*
Bedrooms: 1 single, 1 double, 1 twin,
1 family room
Bathrooms: 2 en-suite, 2 private,
1 public

Bed & breakfast

per night:	£min	£max
Single	25.00	28.00
Double	39.50	39.50

Parking for 5

🐾♿🖳📟🖢🔌UL⑤⌦TV🏚🖴☼
🚲 OAP SP

Tickeridge House

Listed

Whitchurch Road, Milton Green,
Chester CH3 9DS
🕿 Tattenhall (01829) 770443
*Chester 5 miles, off A41 at Milton
Green. Worth looking for and certainly
worth staying. Beautifully appointed
house with all rooms on ground floor.
Very warm welcome. Succulent full
English breakfast. Look forward to
meeting you, all facilities for your
comfort.*
Bedrooms: 2 double, 1 family room
Bathrooms: 1 en-suite, 1 public

Bed & breakfast

per night:	£min	£max
Single	15.00	20.00
Double	30.00	35.00

Parking for 6
Cards accepted: Visa

🐾♿🖳📟🖵♿🖢🔌UL🛈⑤⌦🏚🖴☼

🚲 OAP SP

CHORLEY

Lancashire
Map ref 4A1

Set between the Pennine moors and
the Lancashire Plain, Chorley has
been an important town since
medieval times, with its "Flat-Iron"
and covered markets. The rich
heritage includes Astley Hall and
Park, Hoghton Tower, Rivington
Country Park and the
Leeds-Liverpool Canal.

The Original Farmers Arms 🏔

Listed COMMENDED

Towngate, Eccleston, Chorley
PR7 5QS
🕿 Eccleston (01257) 451594
Fax (01257) 453329
*Village pub and restaurant with a
warm and friendly atmosphere offering
an extensive menu of home-made
dishes at reasonable prices, served all
day and every day 12 noon to 10pm.*
Bedrooms: 2 double, 2 twin
Bathrooms: 1 en-suite, 1 public

Bed & breakfast

per night:	£min	£max
Single	20.00	25.00
Double	30.00	35.00

Lunch available
Evening meal 1200 (last orders
2200)
Parking for 36
Cards accepted: Access, Visa

🐾🖳📟🖵🖢🔌⑤🏚✈🚲🎴

Parr Hall Farm

Parr Lane, Eccleston, Chorley
PR7 5SL
🕿 Eccleston (01257) 451917
Fax (01257) 451917
*15-acre mixed farm. 18th C listed
farmhouse, tastefully restored. Oak
beams, open views. Village location
within walking distance of restaurants
and pubs. Easy access to Lakes and
dales.*
Bedrooms: 2 double, 1 twin
Bathrooms: 3 en-suite

Bed & breakfast

per night:	£min	£max
Single	22.50	27.50
Double	35.00	45.00

Parking for 20
Cards accepted: Access, Visa

🖵🖢🔌UL🏚▶☼✈🚲🎴

Half board prices are given
per person, but in some cases
these may be based on
double/twin occupancy.

CLITHEROE

Lancashire
Map ref 4A1

Ancient market town with an
800-year-old castle keep and a wide
range of award-winning shops. Good
base for touring Ribble Valley,
Trough of Bowland and Pennine
moorland. Country market on
Tuesdays and Saturdays.
Tourist Information Centre 🕿 *(01200)
25566*

Brooklands

Listed COMMENDED

9 Pendle Road, Clitheroe BB7 1JQ
🕿 (01200) 22797 changing to
(01200) 422797
*Comfortable, detached Victorian home
in Ribble Valley. 5 minutes' walk
town/train. Ideal base for Lakes, dales,
West Coast and motorways. Brochure
available.*
Bedrooms: 1 double, 2 twin
Bathrooms: 1 en-suite, 2 public

Bed & breakfast

per night:	£min	£max
Single	15.00	17.50
Double	28.00	35.00

Parking for 5

🐾🖳♿🖢🔌UL🛈TV🏚🖴▶☼🚲◉

Lower Standen Farm 🏔

Whalley Road, Clitheroe BB7 1PP
🕿 (01200) 424176
*30-acre mixed farm. 17th C farmhouse.
Excellent for walking holidays.
Self-catering cottage also available.*
Bedrooms: 2 double, 1 twin
Bathrooms: 1 en-suite, 1 public,
1 private shower

Bed & breakfast

per night:	£min	£max
Single	15.00	17.00
Double	30.00	35.00

Parking for 3

🐾🖳📟🖵🖢🔌UL🛈🏚TV🏚🖴🖴☼
🚲◉

Rakefoot Farm 🏔

Listed COMMENDED

Chaigley, Clitheroe BB7 3LY
🕿 Chipping (01995) 61332 &
Mobile (0589) 279063
*100-acre dairy farm. Traditional B & B
(with optional evening meal) in
farmhouse in beautiful Forest of
Bowland. 5 miles from Clitheroe, 12
miles M6 junctions 31/32. Panoramic
views, home cooking and a warm
welcome await. Self-catering also
available in recent stone barn
conversion.*
Bedrooms: 2 double, 1 twin
Bathrooms: 3 en-suite, 1 public

For ideas on places to visit
refer to the introduction at
the beginning of this section.

Bed & breakfast

per night:	£min	£max
Single	15.00	19.00
Double	27.00	35.00

Half board per person:

	£min	£max
Daily	25.00	27.50
Weekly	164.50	175.00

Evening meal 1700 (last orders 1900)
Parking for 6

🐴🞣🕭🗏🖵🖙🖐🆙🆂✂🖪📺🅃
🖩🖧☎↻↑🗡🞕🚜♿ OAF 🚫 SP 🖐🅣

COLNE

Lancashire
Map ref 4B1

Old market town with mixed industries bordering the moorland Bronte country. Nearby are the ruins of Wycoller House, featured in Charlotte Bronte's "Jane Eyre" as Ferndean Manor.

148 Keighley Road

👑👑 HIGHLY COMMENDED

Colne BB8 0PJ
☎ (01282) 862002
Edwardian town house. Comfortable, attractive bedrooms. Friendly and helpful hosts. Close to open countryside. Non-smokers only, please.
Bedrooms: 1 single, 2 double
Bathrooms: 1 private, 1 public

Bed & breakfast

per night:	£min	£max
Single	16.00	18.00
Double	32.00	36.00

Parking for 1
Open March–December

🐴11🖵♿🖙🆙🆂✂🖪🖩🚜🞡✗
🚜

CONGLETON

Cheshire
Map ref 4B2

Important cattle market and silk town on the River Dane, now concerned with general textiles. Nearby are Little Moreton Hall, a Tudor house surrounded by a moat, the Bridestones, remains of a chambered tomb, and Mow Cop, topped by a folly.
Tourist Information Centre ☎ (01260) 271095

Sandhole Farm 🅜

👑👑 HIGHLY COMMENDED

Hulme Walfield, Congleton
CW12 2JH
☎ Marton Heath (01260) 224419
Fax (01260) 224766
200-acre arable and mixed farm.

Charming en-suite accommodation in tastefully converted stables, adjacent to attractive, traditional farmhouse. Two miles north of Congleton on A34.
Wheelchair access category 3🚶
Bedrooms: 2 single, 6 double, 8 twin, 1 triple, 1 family room
Bathrooms: 16 en-suite, 2 private

Bed & breakfast

per night:	£min	£max
Single		35.00
Double		45.00

Parking for 40
Cards accepted: Access, Visa, Diners

🐴🞣🕭☎♿🆙🆂✂🖪🖩📺🖧
🖩↻🗡🞡🞕🚜♿ SP ⊕

CREWE

Cheshire
Map ref 4A2

Famous for its railway junction, this small market town is at the heart of the beautiful south Cheshire countryside and well located for visiting local attractions. Original home of the Rolls Royce motor car.

The Hand and Trumpet Inn

👑👑 COMMENDED

Main Road, Wrinehill, Crewe
CW3 9BJ
☎ (01270) 820048
Fax (01270) 820087
Comfortable rural inn, convenient for Crewe and the Potteries. Set in landscaped gardens. Husband and wife operated.
Bedrooms: 4 double, 2 twin
Bathrooms: 6 en-suite

Bed & breakfast

per night:	£min	£max
Single	25.00	25.00
Double	30.00	35.00

Lunch available
Evening meal 1900 (last orders 2200)
Parking for 20
Cards accepted: Access, Visa, Diners

🐴🞣🕭🖵♿🆙🆂✂🖪🖩📍60♿
🗡🞕🞡🚜 SP 🅣

FARNDON

Cheshire
Map ref 4A2

Farndon Arms Inn and Restaurant

👑👑 APPROVED

High Street, Farndon, Chester
CH3 6PY
☎ (01829) 270570 & Mobile 0831 847945
Fax (01829) 270570
Pleasant 16th C family-run coaching inn on the English/Welsh border. Close to Chester and Wrexham and a short

drive from Liverpool and Manchester. Restaurant, bar and function room.
Bedrooms: 2 single, 3 double, 1 twin
Bathrooms: 3 en-suite, 1 public

Bed & breakfast

per night:	£min	£max
Single	19.50	25.00
Double	39.00	39.00

Lunch available
Evening meal 1700 (last orders 2200)
Parking for 30
Cards accepted: Access, Visa

🐴🖵♿🖙🆙🆂✂🖪🖩🚜📍40♿
🐕🚜🚫

GARSTANG

Lancashire
Map ref 4A2

Picturesque country market town. The gateway to the fells, it stands on the Lancaster Canal and is a popular cruising centre. Close by are the remains of Greenhalgh Castle (no public access) and the Bleasdale Circle. Discovery Centre shows history of Over Wyre and Bowland fringe areas.
Tourist Information Centre ☎ (01995) 602125

Ashdene 🅜

👑

Parkside Lane, Nateby, Preston
PR3 0JA
☎ (01995) 602676
Family-run bed and breakfast. All rooms en-suite and with colour TV. 5 miles junctions 32/33 of M6, 20 minutes Blackpool, 30 minutes Lake District.
Bedrooms: 1 double, 2 twin
Bathrooms: 3 en-suite, 1 public

Bed & breakfast

per night:	£min	£max
Single	19.00	19.00
Double	35.00	35.00

Parking for 6

🐴🖵♿🖙🆙🖙📺🖩🚜🚜

Guy's Thatched Hamlet 🅜

👑👑👑 COMMENDED

Canalside, St. Michael's Road, Bilsborrow, Garstang, Preston
PR3 0RS
☎ Brock (01995) 640849 & 640010
Fax (01995) 640141

Continued ▶

GARSTANG
Continued

Friendly, family-run thatched canalside tavern, restaurant, pizzeria, lodgings, craft shops, cricket ground with thatched pavilion and crown green bowling. Conference centre. Off junction 32 of M6, then 3 miles north on A6 to Garstang.
Bedrooms: 28 double, 20 twin, 5 family rooms
Bathrooms: 53 en-suite
Bed & breakfast

per night:	£min	£max
Double	44.00	59.50

Half board per person:

	£min	£max
Daily	35.00	42.00

Lunch available
Evening meal 1800 (last orders 2330)
Parking for 300
Cards accepted: Access, Visa, Amex, Switch/Delta

GREAT ECCLESTON
Lancashire
Map ref 4A1

Cartford Hotel ⚊
APPROVED
Cartford Lane, Little Eccleston, Preston PR3 0YP
☎ (01995) 670166
Country riverside pub and coaching inn, with 1.5 miles of fishing rights. Within easy reach of Blackpool and the Lake District.
Bedrooms: 5 double, 1 twin
Bathrooms: 5 en-suite, 1 private
Bed & breakfast

per night:	£min	£max
Single	30.50	35.50
Double	42.50	45.50

Lunch available
Evening meal 1900 (last orders 2130)
Parking for 100
Cards accepted: Access, Visa

HYDE
Greater Manchester
Map ref 4B2

Needhams Farm ⚊
COMMENDED
Uplands Road, Werneth Low, Gee Cross, Hyde, Cheshire SK14 3AQ
☎ (0161) 368 4610
Fax (0161) 367 9106
30-acre beef farm. 500-year-old farmhouse with exposed beams in all

rooms and an open fire in bar/dining room. Excellent views. Well placed for Manchester city and the airport.
Bedrooms: 1 single, 4 double, 1 twin, 1 triple
Bathrooms: 5 en-suite, 1 public
Bed & breakfast

per night:	£min	£max
Single	18.00	20.00
Double	30.00	34.00

Half board per person:

	£min	£max
Daily	25.00	27.00

Evening meal 1900 (last orders 2130)
Parking for 12
Cards accepted: Access, Visa

LIVERPOOL
Merseyside
Map ref 4A2

Vibrant city which became prominent in the 18th C as a result of its sugar, spice and tobacco trade with the Americas. Today the historic waterfront is a major attraction. Home to the Beatles, the Grand National and 2 20th C cathedrals, as well as many museums and galleries.
Tourist Information Centre ☎ (0151) 709 3631 or 708 8854

Anna's
COMMENDED
65 Dudlow Lane, Calderstones, Liverpool L18 2EY
☎ (0151) 722 3708
Fax (0151) 722 8699
Large family house with friendly atmosphere, in select residential area close to all amenities. Direct transport routes to city centre. 1 mile from end of M62 motorway.
Bedrooms: 1 double, 3 twin
Bathrooms: 1 public
Bed & breakfast

per night:	£min	£max
Single	18.50	22.00
Double	33.00	40.00

Parking for 6

Somersby Guest House
COMMENDED
57 Green Lane, off Menlove Avenue, Liverpool L18 2EP
☎ (0151) 722 7549
Attractive house with secure parking, delightfully situated in exclusive area with easy access to city centre, airport and M62.

Bedrooms: 2 double, 1 twin, 1 family room
Bathrooms: 2 public
Bed & breakfast

per night:	£min	£max
Single	20.00	
Double	35.00	

Parking for 6

MACCLESFIELD
Cheshire
Map ref 4B2

Cobbled streets and quaint old buildings stand side by side with modern shops and three markets. Centuries of association with the silk industry; museums feature working exhibits and social history. Stunning views of the Peak District National Park.
Tourist Information Centre ☎ (01625) 504114

Sandpit Farm
COMMENDED
Messuage Lane, Marton, Macclesfield SK11 9HS
☎ Marton Heath (01260) 224254
110-acre arable farm. Comfortable, oak-beamed house. Twin and double rooms are en-suite. Convenient for stately homes and National Trust properties. Easy access to Peak District, Chester and Manchester Airport. 4 miles north of Congleton, 1 mile west of A34.
Bedrooms: 1 single, 1 double, 1 twin
Bathrooms: 2 en-suite, 1 public
Bed & breakfast

per night:	£min	£max
Single	16.00	
Double	38.00	

Parking for 4

MALPAS
Cheshire
Map ref 4A2

Millhey Farm
⚊⚊
Barton, Malpas SY14 7HY
☎ Broxton (01829) 782431
140-acre mixed farm. Typical, lovely Cheshire black and white part-timbered farmhouse in conservation area, 9 miles from Chester, close to Welsh Border country. On A534, just off A41.
Bedrooms: 1 twin, 1 triple
Bathrooms: 2 en-suite, 1 public

Bed & breakfast

per night:	£min	£max
Single	15.00	
Double	30.00	

Parking for 2

See under Alderley Edge, Ashley, Hyde, Stockport, Styal, Wilmslow

NANTWICH

Cheshire
Map ref 4A2

Old market town on the River Weaver made prosperous in Roman times by salt springs. Fire destroyed the town in 1583 and many buildings were rebuilt in Elizabethan style. Churche's Mansion (open to the public) survived the fire.
Tourist Information Centre ☎ (01270) 610983 or 610880

Lea Farm
COMMENDED
Wrinehill Road, Wybunbury, Nantwich CW5 7NS
☎ Crewe (01270) 841429
160-acre dairy farm. Charming farmhouse in beautiful gardens where peacocks roam. Comfortable lounge, pool/snooker, fishing pool. Ideal surroundings.
Bedrooms: 1 double, 1 twin, 1 triple
Bathrooms: 2 en-suite, 1 public

Bed & breakfast

per night:	£min	£max
Single	17.00	20.00
Double	29.00	33.00

Half board per

person:	£min	£max
Daily	24.00	29.00
Weekly	145.00	175.00

Evening meal 1800 (last orders 1900)
Parking for 22

Oakland House ⋀
HIGHLY COMMENDED
252 Newcastle Road (A500), Blakelow, Shavington, Nantwich CW5 7ET
☎ Willaston (01270) 67134 &
Mobile (0589) 683418
Fax (01270) 651752
Friendly welcome, home comforts, rural views. Superior accommodation at reasonable rates. On A500 (A52) 5 miles from M6 junction 16. Within easy reach of Nantwich, Chester, Stapeley Water Gardens and Bridgemere Garden World. Winner of

1996 North West Tourism Award for Place to Stay (B&B category).
Bedrooms: 3 double, 2 twin
Bathrooms: 5 en-suite
Bed & breakfast

per night:	£min	£max
Single		27.00
Double		36.00

Parking for 10
Cards accepted: Visa

NEW BRIGHTON

Merseyside
Map ref 4A2

This resort on the Mersey Estuary has 7 miles of coastline, with fishing off the sea wall and pleasant walks along the promenade. Attractions include New Palace Amusements, Floral Pavilion Theatre, ten pin bowling and good sports facilities.

Sea Level Hotel
126 Victoria Road, New Brighton, Wallasey L45 9LD
☎ (0151) 639 3408
Fax (0151) 639 3408
Homely, family-run hotel offering a warm welcome and wholesome food. Light meals available until 11pm.
Bedrooms: 8 single, 3 double, 2 twin, 2 triple
Bathrooms: 1 en-suite, 3 public

Bed & breakfast

per night:	£min	£max
Single	16.00	21.00
Double	29.00	39.00

Evening meal 1845 (last orders 1900)
Parking for 10
Cards accepted: Access, Visa

NORTHWICH

Cheshire
Map ref 4A2

An important salt-producing town since Roman times, Northwich has been replanned with a modern shopping centre and a number of black and white buildings. Unique Anderton boat-lift on northern outskirts of town.

Manor Farm ⋀
COMMENDED
Acton Bridge, Northwich CW8 3QP
☎ Weaverham (01606) 853181
100-acre livestock farm. Secluded Georgian-style farmhouse and

traditional buildings, set in 100 acres of grassland with river frontage in the Weaver Valley.
Bedrooms: 1 single, 2 twin
Bathrooms: 1 en-suite, 2 private
Bed & breakfast

per night:	£min	£max
Single	18.00	22.00
Double	36.00	44.00

Parking for 14

Park Dale Guest House ⋀
Listed COMMENDED
140 Middlewich Road, Rudheath, Northwich CW9 7DS
☎ (01606) 45228
Fax (01606) 331770
Warm and friendly accommodation within easy reach of town centre and the tourist attractions of the north west. Convenient for motorway links and Manchester Airport.
Bedrooms: 3 single, 2 twin, 1 triple
Bathrooms: 3 en-suite, 1 public
Bed & breakfast

per night:	£min	£max
Single	16.50	22.00
Double	34.00	36.00

Lunch available
Evening meal 1730 (last orders 1930)
Parking for 7

Springfield Guest House ⋀
COMMENDED
Chester Road, Delamere, Oakmere, Northwich CW8 2HB
☎ Sandiway (01606) 882538
Family guesthouse erected in 1863. On A556 close to Delamere Forest, midway between Chester and M6 junction 19. Manchester Airport 25 minutes' drive.
Bedrooms: 4 single, 1 double, 1 twin, 1 family room
Bathrooms: 2 en-suite, 1 public
Bed & breakfast

per night:	£min	£max
Single	20.00	25.00
Double	36.00	50.00

Parking for 12
Open March–November and Christmas

Establishments should be open throughout the year, unless otherwise stated.

OLDHAM

Greater Manchester
Map ref 4B1

The magnificent mill buildings which made Oldham one of the world's leading cotton-spinning towns still dominate the landscape. Ideally situated on the edge of the Peak District, it is now a centre of culture, sport and shopping. Art gallery has fine collections.
Tourist Information Centre ☎ (0161) 627 1024

Boothstead Farm
Listed COMMENDED

Rochdale Road, Denshaw, Oldham OL3 5UE
☎ Saddleworth (01457) 878622
200-acre livestock farm. 18th C farmhouse on fringe of Saddleworth (A640) between junctions 21 and 22 of M62 motorway.
Bedrooms: 1 double, 1 twin
Bathrooms: 1 public

Bed & breakfast per night:

	£min	£max
Single	18.00	20.00
Double	34.00	36.00

Parking for 4

Globe Farm Guest House
COMMENDED

Huddersfield Road, Standedge, Delph, Oldham OL3 5LU
☎ Saddleworth (01457) 873040
18-acre mixed farm. Quarter of a mile from the Pennine Way and high walking country. Bed and breakfast accommodation, 24-bed bunkhouse (self-catering or with meals) and small campsite.
Bedrooms: 3 single, 2 double, 2 twin
Bathrooms: 7 en-suite

Bed & breakfast per night:

	£min	£max
Single	18.50	25.00
Double	36.00	

Half board per person:

	£min	£max
Daily	25.00	31.50
Weekly	125.00	

Evening meal 1830 (last orders 1900)
Parking for 30
Cards accepted: Access, Visa

Map references apply to the colour maps at the back of this guide.

PRESTON

Lancashire
Map ref 4A1

Scene of decisive Royalist defeat by Cromwell in the Civil War and later of riots in the Industrial Revolution. Local history exhibited in Harris Museum. Famous for its Guild and the celebration that takes place every 20 years.
Tourist Information Centre ☎ (01772) 253731

Smithy Farm
Listed

Huntingdonhall Lane, Dutton, Longridge, Preston PR3 2ZT
☎ Ribchester (01254) 878250
Set in the beautiful Ribble Valley, 20 minutes from the M6. Homely atmosphere, children half price.
Bedrooms: 1 double, 1 twin, 1 family room
Bathrooms: 1 public

Bed & breakfast per night:

	£min	£max
Single	16.00	16.00
Double	25.00	25.00

Half board per person:

	£min	£max
Daily	17.50	21.00
Weekly	122.50	147.00

Evening meal 1900 (last orders 2130)
Parking for 4
Open February–December

RIBBLE VALLEY

See under Clitheroe

ROCHDALE

Greater Manchester
Map ref 4B1

Pennine mill town made prosperous by wool and later cotton-spinning, famous for the Co-operative Movement started in 1844 by a group of Rochdale working men. Birthplace of John Bright (Corn Law opponent) and more recently Gracie Fields. Fine Victorian Gothic town hall.
Tourist Information Centre ☎ (01706) 356592

Leaches Farm Bed and Breakfast

Leaches Farm, Ashworth Valley, Rochdale, Lancashire OL11 5UN
☎ (01706) 41116/7 & 228520
140-acre livestock farm. 18th C

Pennine hill farmhouse with panoramic views and moorland walks. 10 minutes from M62/M66.
Bedrooms: 1 single, 1 double, 1 twin
Bathrooms: 1 public

Bed & breakfast per night:

	£min	£max
Single	18.00	20.00
Double	34.00	36.00

Parking for 6

ST MICHAEL'S ON WYRE

Lancashire
Map ref 4A1

Village near Blackpool with interesting 13th C church of St Michael containing medieval stained glass window depicting sheep shearing, and clock tower bell made in 1548.

Compton House
COMMENDED

Garstang Road, St Michael's on Wyre, Preston PR3 0TE
☎ St. Michaels (01995) 679378
Fax (01995) 679378
Well-furnished country house in own grounds in a picturesque village, near M6 and 40 minutes from Lake District. Fishing in the Wyre. "Best-Kept Guesthouse" award 1995.
Bedrooms: 1 single, 1 double, 1 twin
Bathrooms: 2 en-suite, 1 private

Bed & breakfast per night:

	£min	£max
Single	20.00	20.00
Double	40.00	40.00

Parking for 6

SANDBACH

Cheshire
Map ref 4A2

Small Cheshire town, originally important for salt production. Contains narrow, winding streets, timbered houses and a cobbled market-place. Town square has 2 Anglo-Saxon crosses to commemorate the conversion to Christianity of the King of Mercia's son.

Canal Centre and Village Store
Listed COMMENDED

Hassall Green, Sandbach CW11 4YB
☎ Crewe (01270) 762266

The house and shop, built circa 1777 at the side of Lock 57 on the Trent and Mersey Canal, have served canal users for over 200 years. Off A533 near Sandbach and junction 17 on M6 - signposted. Gift shop, tearooms, store and licensed restaurant (Tues-Sat from 7pm).
Wheelchair access category 3🚶
Bedrooms: 1 single, 3 double, 2 twin
Bathrooms: 2 en-suite, 1 private, 1 public
Bed & breakfast per night:

	£min	£max
Single	16.00	18.00
Double	32.00	36.00

Lunch available
Evening meal 1900 (last orders 2130)
Parking for 7
Cards accepted: Access, Visa, Switch/Delta

Moss Cottage Farm

⏥ HIGHLY COMMENDED

Hassall Road, Winterley, Sandbach CW11 4RU
☎ Crewe (01270) 583018
Beamed farmhouse in quiet location just off A534, with lovely walks, fishing and golf. All rooms have TV, tea-making facilities and hand basins. Evening meals by arrangement.
Bedrooms: 1 single, 1 double, 1 twin
Bathrooms: 2 public
Bed & breakfast per night:

	£min	£max
Single	17.00	18.00
Double	32.00	34.00

Evening meal 1700 (last orders 2000)
Parking for 10

The map references refer to the colour maps towards the end of the guide.
The first figure is the map number; the letter and figure which follow indicate the grid reference on the map.

SINGLETON

Lancashire
Map ref 4A1

Ancient parish dating from 1175, mentioned in Domesday Book. Chapel and day school dating back to 1865. Mainly rural area to the north of St Anne's.

Old Castle Farm 🏍

Listed APPROVED

Garstang Road, Singleton, Blackpool FY6 8ND
☎ Poulton-le-Fylde (01253) 883839
Take junction 3 off M55, follow Fleetwood sign to first traffic lights. Turn right, travel 200 yards on A586 to bungalow on the right.
Bedrooms: 1 double, 1 twin, 1 triple
Bathrooms: 1 public
Bed & breakfast per night:

	£min	£max
Single	15.00	
Double	30.00	

Parking for 20
Open April–October

SOUTHPORT

Merseyside
Map ref 4A1

Delightful Victorian resort noted for gardens, sandy beaches and 6 golf-courses, particularly Royal Birkdale. Attractions include the Atkinson Art Gallery, Southport Railway Centre, Pleasureland and the annual Southport Flower Show. Excellent shopping, particularly in Lord Street's elegant boulevard.
Tourist Information Centre ☎ (01704) 533333

Sandy Brook Farm 🏍

⏥⏥ APPROVED

52 Wyke Cop Road, Scarisbrick, Southport PR8 5LR
☎ Scarisbrick (01704) 880337
27-acre arable farm. Comfortable accommodation in converted farm buildings in rural area of Scarisbrick, offering a friendly welcome. 3.5 miles from seaside town of Southport. Special facilities for disabled guests. Silver award-winner NWTB "place to stay".
Bedrooms: 1 single, 1 double, 2 twin, 1 triple, 1 family room
Bathrooms: 6 en-suite
Bed & breakfast per night:

	£min	£max
Single	18.50	18.50
Double	32.00	32.00

Parking for 9

STOCKPORT

Greater Manchester
Map ref 4B2

Once an important cotton-spinning and manufacturing centre, Stockport has an impressive railway viaduct, a shopping precinct built over the River Mersey and a new leisure complex. Lyme Hall and Vernon Park Museum nearby.
Tourist Information Centre ☎ (0161) 474 3320 or 474 3321

Northumbria House

⏥ COMMENDED

35 Corbar Road, Stockport, Cheshire SK2 6EP
☎ (0161) 483 4000
Edwardian house set in a large garden in a quiet, residential area close to bus, rail stations and airport. Lots of tourist information. German and French spoken. Non-smokers only, please.
Bedrooms: 1 double, 1 twin
Bathrooms: 1 public
Bed & breakfast per night:

	£min	£max
Single	17.00	20.00
Double	32.00	38.00

Parking for 3

STYAL

Cheshire
Map ref 4B2

Willow Cottage 🏍

⏥ HIGHLY COMMENDED

56 Hollin Lane, Styal, Wilmslow SK9 4JH
☎ Wilmslow (01625) 523630
Comfortable modern dormer bungalow set in rural surroundings yet convenient for motorways, airport, restaurants and Styal Country Park and Mill. Free transport to and from airport.
Bedrooms: 1 single, 1 twin
Bathrooms: 1 public
Bed & breakfast per night:

	£min	£max
Single	18.00	20.00
Double	35.00	40.00

Parking for 6
Cards accepted: Access, Visa

TARPORLEY

Cheshire
Map ref 4A2

Old town with gabled houses and medieval church of St Helen containing monuments to the Done family, a historic name in this area. Spectacular ruins of 13th C Beeston Castle nearby.

Roughlow Farm

⚜ ⚜ COMMENDED

Willington, Tarporley CW6 0PG
☎ Kelsall (01829) 751199
Fax (01829) 751199
18th C sandstone farmhouse in idyllic situation with magnificent views to Shropshire and Wales. Elegant house with very comfortable en-suite bedrooms. Attractive garden with cobbled courtyard. Very peaceful situation, 15 minutes from Chester.
Bedrooms: 3 twin
Bathrooms: 3 en-suite
Bed & breakfast

per night:	£min	£max
Single	25.00	35.00
Double	50.00	60.00

Evening meal from 1930
Parking for 11

WILMSLOW

Cheshire
Map ref 4B2

Nestling in the valleys of the Rivers Bollin and Dane, Wilmslow retains an intimate village atmosphere. Easy-to-reach attractions include Quarry Bank Mill at Styal. Lindow Man was discovered on a nearby common. Romany's Caravan sits in a memorial garden.

Fern Bank Guest House

⚜ ⚜ COMMENDED

188 Wilmslow Road, Handforth, Wilmslow SK9 3JX
☎ (01625) 523729
Detached Victorian house, built 1881, standing in its own grounds. Tastefully furnished with antiques, large south-facing conservatory. Manchester Airport 10 minutes by car. Long-stay car parking next door.
Bedrooms: 2 single, 1 double, 1 twin
Bathrooms: 4 en-suite, 1 public
Bed & breakfast

per night:	£min	£max
Single	28.00	33.00
Double	39.00	44.00

Parking for 6

Rylands Farm Guest House Ⓜ

⚜ ⚜ COMMENDED

Altrincham Road, Wilmslow SK9 4LT
☎ (01625) 535646 & 548041
Fax (01625) 535646
Family-run, many exposed beams, colour co-ordinated rooms. Secure parking. Secretarial and laundry services. Free travel to airport. All rooms en-suite.
Bedrooms: 4 double, 2 twin
Bathrooms: 6 en-suite
Bed & breakfast

per night:	£min	£max
Single	33.00	33.00
Double	39.50	39.50

Half board per person:	£min	£max
Daily	45.50	45.50

Evening meal 1745 (last orders 1800)
Parking for 18
Cards accepted: Visa

WIRRAL

Merseyside

See under New Brighton

USE YOUR *i*'s

There are more than 550 Tourist Information Centres throughout England offering friendly help with accommodation and holiday ideas as well as suggestions of places to visit and things to do. There may well be a centre in your home town which can help you before you set out. You'll find the address of your nearest Tourist Information Centre in your local Phone Book.

YORKSHIRE

Yorkshire encompass an area of vastly differing landscapes and moods. The wildness of the Yorkshire Moors and 'Brontë Country' soften into the mellow valleys of the Yorkshire Dales, contrasted by the coastline of towering cliffs, lively resorts and pleasant fishing ports.

Many of the grandest gardens in Britain are here. It's also where you can taste fish and chips at their best, sample ale straight from the brewery or go down a coalmine!

Don't miss historic York with its world-famous Minster. You'll also find some of the best museums and industrial heritage sites in England.

FOR MORE INFORMATION CONTACT:
Yorkshire Tourist Board
312 Tadcaster Road, York YO2 2HF
Tel: (01904) 707961 or 707070 (24 hour brochure line)
Fax: (01904) 701414

Where to Go in Yorkshire - see pages 98-101
Where to Stay in Yorkshire - see pages 102-126

YORKSHIRE

Where to Go and What to See

You will find hundreds of interesting places to visit during your stay in Yorkshire, just some of which are listed in these pages. The number against each name will help you locate it on the map (page 101). Contact any Tourist Information Centre in the region for more ideas on days out in Yorkshire.

1 Sea Life Centre
Scalby Mills,
Scarborough,
North Yorkshire YO12 6RP
Tel: (01723) 376125
At the Sea Life Centre you have the opportunity to meet creatures that live in and around the oceans of the British Isles, ranging from starfish and crabs to rays and seals.

2 North Yorkshire Moors Railway
Pickering Station,
Pickering,
North Yorkshire YO18 7AJ
Tel: (01751) 472508
Operates the route between Grosmont and Pickering, through some of the most magnificent scenery of the North York Moors National Park.

3 Flamingo Land Theme Park, Zoo and Holiday Village
Kirby Misperton,
North Yorkshire YO17 0UX
Tel: (01653) 668287
One price family funpark with over 100 attractions, nine shows and Europe's largest privately owned zoo. Large lake, children's and thrill rides.

4 Fountains Abbey and Studley Royal
Ripon,
North Yorkshire HG4 3DZ
Tel: (01765) 608888
Largest monastic ruin in Britain, founded by Cistercian monks in 1132. Landscaped garden laid out 1720-40 with lake, formal watergarden, temples and deer park.

5 Lightwater Valley Theme Park
North Stainley, Ripon,
North Yorkshire HG4 3HT
Tel: (01765) 635321
175 acres of country park featuring range of white-knuckle rides (including the world's biggest rollercoaster), skill testing activities, leisurely pursuits, live entertainment.

6 Castle Howard
Malton,
North Yorkshire YO6 7DA
Tel: (01653) 648444
Set in 1,000 acres of magnificent parkland with nature walks, scenic lake and stunning rose gardens. Attractions include important furniture and works of art.

7 Sewerby Hall and Gardens
Sewerby, Bridlington,
East Riding of Yorkshire
YO15 1EA
Tel: (01262) 673769
Children's zoo, aviary, old English walled garden, bowls, putting, golf, children's corner, museum, art gallery, Amy Johnson collection, novel train from park to North Beach.

8 Yorkshire Dales Falconry & Conservation Centre
Crows Nest, Giggleswick,
North Yorkshire LA2 8AS
Tel: (01729) 825164
Falconry centre with many species

of birds of prey from around the world including vultures, eagles, hawks, falcons and owls. Free flying displays, lecture room and aviaries.

9 Ripley Castle
Ripley,
North Yorkshire HG3 3AY
Tel: (01423) 770152
Ingilby family home since 1345, fine armour, furniture, chandeliers, panelling, priests hiding hole. Langley Castle in Barbara Taylor Bradford's book "Voice from the Heart".

10 Beningbrough Hall
Shipton-by-Beningbrough,
York YO6 1DD
Tel: (01904) 470666
Handsome Baroque house built 1716, nearly 100 pictures from the National Portrait Gallery. Victorian laundry, potting shed, garden, adventure playground, National Trust shop.

11 Skipton Castle
Skipton,
North Yorkshire BD23 1AQ
Tel: (01756) 792442
One of the most complete and well-preserved medieval castles in England. Beautiful Conduit Court with famous yew.

12 Archaeological Resource Centre
St Saviourgate, York YO1 2NN
Tel: (01904) 654324
Visitors can "touch the past", handling ancient finds of pottery and bone, stitching Roman sandals and picking a Viking padlock. A/V display and exploration of dig by computer.

13 Jorvik Viking Centre
Coppergate, York YO1 1NT
Tel: (01904) 643211
Visitors travel back in time in a timecar to a recreation of Viking York. They will see excavated remains of Viking houses and a display of objects found.

14 National Railway Museum
Leeman Road, York YO2 4XJ
Tel: (01904) 621261
Experience nearly 200 years of technical and social history on the railways and see the way they shaped the world.

15 York Castle Museum
The Eye of York, York YO1 1RY
Tel: (01904) 653611
England's most popular museum of everyday life including reconstructed streets and period rooms, Edwardian park, costume and jewellery, arms and armour, craft workshops.

16 York Minster
Deangate, York YO1 2JA
Tel: (01904) 624426
The largest Gothic cathedral in England. Museum of Saxon and Norman remains, chapter house and crypt. Unrivalled views from Norman tower.

17 Hornsea Freeport
Hornsea,
East Riding of Yorkshire
HU18 1UT
Tel: (01964) 534211
Brand names such as Laura Ashley and Alexon all at discount prices. Birds of prey, Butterfly World, Neptunes Kingdom and more.

18 Harewood House
Harewood, Leeds LS17 9LQ
Tel: (0113) 288 6225
18thC Carr/Adam house, Capability Brown landscape, fine Sevres and Chinese porcelain, English and Italian paintings, Chippendale furniture. Exotic bird garden.

19 National Museum of Photography, Film and Television
Pictureville, Bradford,
West Yorkshire BD1 1NQ
Tel: (01274) 727488
This free museum houses the largest cinema screen (Imax) in

Britain. Fly on a magic carpet, operate a TV camera, become a newsreader for a day.

20 Transperience
Transperience Way,
Low Moor,
Bradford,
West Yorkshire BD12 7HQ
Tel: (01274) 690909
With historic vehicle rides and state of the art interactive technology. Travel on a unique journey through the past, present and future of public transport.

21 Royal Armouries Museum
Leeds LS10 1LT
Tel: (0113) 220 1999
History in action at Britain's newest museum. The thrill of jousting tournaments and terror of battlefield recaptured. See one of the world's finest collections of arms and armour.

22 Tetley's Brewery Wharf
The Waterfront,
Leeds LS1 1QG
Tel: (0113) 242 0666
A unique new development which

brings to life the story through the ages of one of the greatest British traditions – the pub.

23 Museum of Army Transport
Beverley,
East Riding of Yorkshire
HU17 0NG
Tel: (01482) 860445
Army road, rail, sea and air exhibits excitingly displayed in two huge indoor exhibition halls, plus the last remaining Blackburn Beverly aircraft. D-Day exhibition.

24 Eureka! The Museum for Children
Discovery Road, Halifax,
West Yorkshire HX1 2NE
Tel: (01422) 330069
Eureka! is the first museum of its kind designed especially for children up to the age of 12. Wherever you go in Eureka! you can touch, listen, feel and smell, as well as look.

25 Piece Hall
Halifax, West Yorkshire HX1 1RE
Tel: (01422) 358087
Historic, colonnaded cloth hall, surrounding open-air courtyard and

comprising 40 speciality shops, art gallery, Tourist Information Centre, three weekly markets and Calderdale Kaleidoscope display.

26 National Coal Mining Museum for England
Caphouse Colliery,
New Road, Overton,
Wakefield,
West Yorkshire WF4 4RH
Tel: (01924) 848806
Exciting, award-winning museum of the Yorkshire coalfield including guided underground tour in authentic old workings, surface displays, working steam winder.

27 Yorkshire Sculpture Park
Bretton, Wakefield,
West Yorkshire WF4 4LG
Tel: (01924) 830302
Beautiful parkland containing regular exhibitions of contemporary sculpture. Permanent collection includes sculpture by Barbara Hepworth and Henry Moore.

28 National Fishing Heritage Centre
Alexandra Dock, Grimsby,
North East Lincolnshire
DN31 1UZ
Tel: (01472) 344867
Spectacular 1950's steam trawler experience. See, hear, smell and touch a series of recreated environments. Museum displays, shop, aquarium and historic fishing vessels.

29 Pleasure Island Theme Park
Kings Road, Cleethorpes,
North East Lincolnshire
DN35 0PL
Tel: (01472) 211511
The East Coast's newest outdoor theme park with great rides, slides and attractions including the Big Splash, Boomerang, Giant Wheel, Mini Mine Train, Terror Rack and Octopus rides.

Map of Yorkshire and surrounding areas

DURHAM
TEES VALLEY
CUMBRIA
• Staithes
• Whitby
Richmond •
• Great Ayton
Northallerton •
Scalby **1**
Scarborough
Hawes •
• Leyburn
Helmsley •
Kirby Misperton
Pickering **2**
Filey
NORTH YORKSHIRE
3
Horton-in-Ribblesdale •
Shipton-by-Beningbrough
Malton **6**
Sewerby **7**
Giggleswick •
Ripon **4 5**
Bridlington
Settle **8**
Ripley **9**
10
Harrogate •
YORK
Pocklington •
Skipton **11**
Otley •
York **12 13**
Hornsea **17**
Ilkley •
Wetherby •
14 15 16
LANCASHIRE
18
EAST RIDING OF YORKSHIRE
WEST
Harewood
Bradford
Leeds
Beverley **23**
Withernsea
Haworth •
19 20
21 22
Selby •
Hessle • Hull
Hebden Bridge •
YORKSHIRE
Pontefract •
Todmorden •
Halifax
Wakefield •
Goole •
NORTH LINCOLNSHIRE
Huddersfield •
24 25
26 27 Bretton
Brigg •
Grimsby **28**
Overton •
N. EAST LINCOLNSHIRE
Holmfirth •
Barnsley •
Doncaster •
Scunthorpe •
Cleethorpes **29**
GREATER MANCHESTER
SOUTH YORKSHIRE
LINCOLNSHIRE
Sheffield •
Rotherham •
CHESHIRE
DERBYSHIRE
NOTTINGHAMSHIRE

0   20 Miles
0   30 Kms

FIND OUT MORE

Further information about holidays and attractions in Yorkshire, East Riding and Northern Lincolnshire is available from **Yorkshire Tourist Board**, 312 Tadcaster Road, York YO2 2HF. Tel: (01904) 707961 or 707070 (24 hour brochure line)

These publications are available free from the Yorkshire Tourist Board:

■ **Main Holidays and Shortbreaks guide** - information on the region, including hotels, self-catering and caravan and camping parks

■ **Days Out in Yorkshire** (available Easter '97) - information on attractions, major events, getting around the region, etc.

■ **Bed & Breakfast Touring Map**

■ **What's On** - 3 issues per year

■ **Overseas Brochure** - French, Dutch, German

■ **'Freedom'** - caravan and camping guide

■ **Getting Around Yorkshire** - guide to public transport

WHERE TO STAY (YORKSHIRE)

Accommodation entries in this region are listed in alphabetical order of place name, and then in alphabetical order of establishment.

Map references refer to the colour location maps at the back of this guide.
The first number indicates the map to use; the letter and number which follow refer to the grid reference on the map.

At-a-glance symbols at the end of each accommodation entry give useful information about services and facilities. A key to symbols can be found inside the back cover flap.
Keep this open for easy reference.

AMPLEFORTH

North Yorkshire
Map ref 5C3

Stone-built village in Hambleton Hills. Famous for its abbey and college, a Benedictine public school, founded in 1802, of which Cardinal Hume was once abbot.

Carr House Farm 🏔

⚜⚜ COMMENDED

Shallowdale, Ampleforth, York YO6 4ED
☎ Coxwold (01347) 868526
375-acre mixed farm. "Good food, welcome, walking" in peaceful "Herriot/Heartbeat" countryside. Romantic en-suite four-poster bedrooms. Just 30 minutes from York. Has been featured in the "Observer".
Bedrooms: 3 double
Bathrooms: 3 en-suite

Bed & breakfast
per night:	£min	£max
Single	15.00	
Double	30.00	

Half board per person:
	£min	£max
Daily	25.00	

Evening meal 1800 (last orders 1800)
Parking for 3
🐎7🛁🖭👤📶🚿📺🛏🚗🅿♨🚘
♥🖊❀✕🍴🐾🏮Ⓣ

A key to symbols can be found inside the back cover flap.

ARKENGARTHDALE

North Yorkshire
Map ref 5B3

Picturesque Yorkshire dale, once an important and prosperous lead-mining valley developed by Charles Bathurst in the 18th C.

The Ghyll 🏔

⚜⚜⚜ COMMENDED

Arkle Town, Richmond DL11 6EU
☎ Richmond (01748) 884353
Fax (01748) 884015
Set in wonderful countryside with spectacular views of Arkengarthdale. All bedrooms have en-suite facilities and colour TV. Ideal for walking and touring.
Bedrooms: 1 double, 2 twin
Bathrooms: 3 en-suite

Bed & breakfast
per night:	£min	£max
Single	17.50	
Double	35.00	

Parking for 10
Open January–November
🐎🖭👤🚿📶🅿🔌🖂✕🖭🚗♨🚘🐾

For ideas on places to visit refer to the introduction at the beginning of this section.

All accommodation in this guide has been graded, or is awaiting a grading, by a trained Tourist Board inspector.

ASKRIGG

North Yorkshire
Map ref 5B3

The name of this dales village means "ash tree ridge". It is centred on a steep main street of high, narrow 3-storey houses and thrived on cotton and later wool in 18th C. Once famous for its clock making.

Home Farm

Listed HIGHLY COMMENDED

Stalling Busk, Askrigg, Leyburn DL8 3DH
☎ Wensleydale (01969) 650360
65-acre mixed farm. Licensed 17th C beamed, dales farmhouse with log fires, beautiful Victorian and antique furnishings, brass bedsteads and patchwork quilts. Traditional cooking and home-made bread.
Bedrooms: 3 double
Bathrooms: 2 public

Bed & breakfast
per night:	£min	£max
Double	35.00	35.00

Half board per person:
	£min	£max
Daily		55.00

Evening meal 1900 (last orders 1800)
Parking for 4
🐎🖭👤🚿📶🖂✕🖭📺🛏🚗♨🚘
OAP SP

Milton House 🏔

⚜⚜ COMMENDED

Askrigg, Leyburn DL8 3HJ
☎ Wensleydale (01969) 650217
Large, comfortable, family house in a beautiful dales village, central for

touring or walking. Colour TV lounge and wholesome Yorkshire cooking. Private parking.
Bedrooms: 3 double
Bathrooms: 3 en-suite

Bed & breakfast per night:

	£min	£max
Double	37.00	

Evening meal 1900 (last orders 1900)
Parking for 3

Thornsgill Guest House ⚑

♛♛ HIGHLY COMMENDED

Moor Road, Askrigg, Leyburn DL8 3HH
☎ Wensleydale (01969) 650617
Spacious, early 20th C family house in the Yorkshire Dales National Park. En-suite bedrooms. Wholesome Yorkshire food. Relaxed, friendly atmosphere.
Bedrooms: 2 double, 1 twin
Bathrooms: 2 en-suite, 1 private

Bed & breakfast per night:

	£min	£max
Double	42.00	

Half board per person:

	£min	£max
Daily	34.00	

Evening meal from 1830
Parking for 3

BENTHAM

North Yorkshire
Map ref 5B3

Bentham is said to mean "Home on the Common". A weekly market has been held here since the 14th C. Good walking country.

Grassrigg Bed & Breakfast ⚑

Listed COMMENDED

45 Goodenber Road, Bentham, Lancaster LA2 7JD
☎ (015242) 61210
Family-run bed and breakfast offering warm, friendly service. Situated close to the centre of the quiet market town of Bentham.
Bedrooms: 1 single, 1 double
Bathrooms: 1 public

Bed & breakfast per night:

	£min	£max
Single	15.00	15.00
Double	30.00	30.00

Parking for 3

BEVERLEY

East Riding of Yorkshire
Map ref 4C1

Beverley's most famous landmark is its beautiful medieval Minster with Percy family tomb. Many attractive squares and streets, notably Wednesday and Saturday Market, North Bar Gateway and the Museum of Army Transport, Flemingate. Famous racecourse.
Tourist Information Centre ☎ (01482) 867430 or 883898

Eastgate Guest House ⚑

♛ COMMENDED

7 Eastgate, Beverley, North Humberside HU17 0DR
☎ Hull (01482) 868464
Fax (01482) 871899
Family-run Victorian guesthouse, established and run by the same proprietor for 28 years. Close to the town centre, Beverley Minster, Museum of Army Transport and railway station.
Bedrooms: 6 single, 3 double, 3 twin, 3 triple, 3 family rooms
Bathrooms: 7 en-suite, 3 public

Bed & breakfast per night:

	£min	£max
Single	18.50	32.00
Double	32.00	44.00

BINGLEY

West Yorkshire
Map ref 4B1

Bingley Five-Rise is an impressive group of locks on the Leeds and Liverpool Canal. Town claims to have first bred the Airedale terrier originally used for otter hunting. Among fine Georgian houses is Myrtle Grove where John Wesley stayed. East Riddlesden Hall is nearby.

Five Rise Locks Hotel ⚑

♛♛ HIGHLY COMMENDED

Beck Lane, Bingley BD16 4DD
☎ Bradford (01274) 565296
Fax (01274) 568828
Newly renovated Victorian mill owner's house set in a quiet position in its own grounds. Relaxed atmosphere, varied menu and wine list. Prices are per room.
Bedrooms: 7 double, 2 twin
Bathrooms: 9 en-suite

Bed & breakfast per night:

	£min	£max
Single	32.50	45.00
Double	48.00	55.00

Half board per person:

	£min	£max
Daily	36.00	57.00

Evening meal 1930 (last orders 2030)
Parking for 15
Cards accepted: Access, Visa, Switch/Delta

March Cote Farm ⚑

Listed COMMENDED

Off Woodside Avenue, Cottingley, Bingley BD16 1UB
☎ Bradford (01274) 487433 & Mobile 0831 373141
Fax (01274) 488153
230-acre mixed & livestock farm. 17th C fully modernised farmhouse, long established. Friendly atmosphere and good farmhouse cooking. Ideal for visiting the dales, moors and Bradford.
Bedrooms: 2 double, 1 twin
Bathrooms: 1 en-suite, 2 private, 1 public

Bed & breakfast per night:

	£min	£max
Single	17.00	18.00
Double	34.00	36.00

Half board per person:

	£min	£max
Daily	25.00	27.00
Weekly	175.00	189.00

Evening meal 1820 (last orders 2000)
Parking for 5

BISHOP MONKTON

North Yorkshire
Map ref 5C3

Masons Arms ⚑

♛♛

Saint Johns Road, Bishop Monkton, Harrogate HG3 3QU
☎ Ripon (01765) 677427
Cosy, country inn set in a pretty rural village 8.5 miles from Harrogate, off the main Harrogate to Ripon road, 3.5 miles south of Ripon.
Bedrooms: 2 double, 1 twin
Bathrooms: 3 en-suite

Bed & breakfast per night:

	£min	£max
Single	25.00	
Double	40.00	

Lunch available
Evening meal 1830 (last orders 2100)
Parking for 35
Cards accepted: Access, Visa

BISHOP THORNTON

North Yorkshire
Map ref 5C3

Small village in Nidderdale, near Brimham Rocks.

Hatton House Farm

Listed HIGHLY COMMENDED

Colber Lane, Bishop Thornton, Harrogate HG3 3JA
☎ Harrogate (01423) 770315
150-acre dairy & livestock farm. Farmhouse accommodation with special emphasis on well-presented, home-cooked food. Open all year round. No smoking indoors, please.
Bedrooms: 2 double, 1 twin
Bathrooms: 1 public

Bed & breakfast per night:	£min	£max
Single	18.00	25.00
Double	34.00	38.00

Half board per person:	£min	£max
Daily	25.00	28.00
Weekly	150.00	200.00

Evening meal 1830 (last orders 1800)
Parking for 10
🏃♿👁🛏🏷🅂🕮✂🐎📺🎬💷🍺⛵✿ 🍴🚐

BOROUGHBRIDGE

North Yorkshire
Map ref 5C3

On the River Ure, Boroughbridge was once an important coaching centre with 22 inns and in the 18th C a port for Knaresborough's linens. It has fine old houses, many trees and a cobbled square with market cross. Nearby stand 3 megaliths known as the Devil's Arrows.

Laurel Manor Farm 🏔

👑👑 HIGHLY COMMENDED

Brafferton, Helperby, York YO6 2NZ
☎ Harrogate (01423) 360436

28-acre livestock farm. Historic farmhouse, tranquil edge of village location, 4 excellent pubs nearby. 28 acres of grounds and gardens. En-suite bedrooms, four poster bed, antiques, tennis court. 5 miles A1(M), 12 miles York.

Bedrooms: 2 double, 1 triple
Bathrooms: 2 en-suite, 1 private, 1 public

Bed & breakfast per night:	£min	£max
Single	23.00	25.00
Double	46.00	50.00

Half board per person:	£min	£max
Daily	35.00	41.00
Weekly	210.00	250.00

Evening meal from 1930
Parking for 6
🏃♿👁🛏🏷🅂✂🐎🕮💷⛲⛵✿ 🚐🚫🆂🏠

BRADFORD

West Yorkshire
Map ref 4B1

City founded on wool, with fine Victorian and modern buildings. Attractions include the cathedral, city hall, Cartwright Hall, Lister Park, Moorside Mills Industrial Museum and National Museum of Photography, Film and Television. *Tourist Information Centre ☎ (01274) 753678*

Carlton House Guest House

Listed APPROVED

Thornton Road, Thornton, Bradford BD13 3QE
☎ (01274) 833397
Detached, Victorian house in open countryside between the Bronte villages of Thornton and Haworth.
Bedrooms: 1 single, 1 double, 2 triple
Bathrooms: 4 en-suite

Bed & breakfast per night:	£min	£max
Single	20.00	
Double	32.00	

Parking for 6
🏃♿🛏🏷🅂🕮💷⛲🚐

Ivy Guest House 🏔

Listed

3 Melbourne Place, Bradford BD5 0HZ
☎ (01274) 727060 & (0421) 509207
Fax (01274) 306347
Large, detached, listed house built of Yorkshire stone. Car park and gardens. Close to city centre, National Museum of Photography, Film and Television and Alhambra Theatre.
Bedrooms: 3 single, 2 double, 4 twin, 1 triple
Bathrooms: 3 public

Bed & breakfast per night:	£min	£max
Single	18.00	18.00
Double	30.00	30.00

Half board per person:	£min	£max
Daily	21.00	24.00
Weekly	147.00	168.00

Lunch available
Evening meal 1800 (last orders 2000)
Parking for 15
Cards accepted: Access, Visa, Diners, Amex, Switch/Delta
🏃♿🛏👁🛌🅂🕮💷⛲✿🍴🚫 🆂🏠📞◉

COXWOLD

North Yorkshire
Map ref 5C3

This well-known beauty spot in Hambleton and Howardian Hills is famous as home of Laurence Sterne, the 18th C country parson and author of "Tristram Shandy" books who, in 1760, lived at Shandy Hall, now open to the public.

Sunley Woods Farm 🏔

Listed

Husthwaite, York YO6 3TQ
☎ (01347) 868418
180-acre mixed farm. Comfortable farmhouse 18 miles north of York with glorious views overlooking the White Horse at Kilburn. Convenient for York and coast.
Bedrooms: 1 single, 1 double, 1 twin
Bathrooms: 1 public

Bed & breakfast per night:	£min	£max
Single	12.50	13.00
Double	25.00	26.00

Parking for 4
Open March–October
🏃♿📛🛏👁🛌🐎📺🕮💷⛲🍴🚐 🆂

CROPTON

North Yorkshire
Map ref 5C3

Moorland village at the top of a high ridge with stone houses, some of cruck construction, a Victorian church and the remains of a 12th C moated castle. Cropton Forest nearby.

Burr Bank Cottage 🏔

👑👑👑 HIGHLY COMMENDED

Cropton, Pickering YO18 8HL
☎ Lastingham (01751) 417777
Fax (01751) 417789
Stone cottage in 50 acres with wonderful views. Peaceful, well-appointed accommodation, a warm welcome and home cooking.
Bedrooms: 1 single, 1 double, 1 twin
Bathrooms: 3 en-suite

Bed & breakfast per night:	£min	£max
Single	21.00	21.00
Double	42.00	42.00

Half board per person:	£min	£max
Daily	33.00	33.00
Weekly	210.00	210.00

Evening meal 1900 (last orders 1900)
Parking for 10

🛇🛏♿📞🖵🖥❄🐾 UL S ✂ Ⅿ TV ▥ 🖨 🍴U❀✕🚲 SP ◉

New Inn ⋈

👑👑👑 COMMENDED

Cropton, Pickering YO18 8HH
☎ Lastingham (01751) 417330
Fax (01751) 417310
Character inn in picturesque village setting. Warm welcome, good food, comfortable en-suite accommodation. Award-winning ales from own brewery. Rural location, convenient for moors and coast.
Bedrooms: 5 double, 2 triple
Suite available
Bathrooms: 6 en-suite, 1 private

Bed & breakfast per night:	£min	£max
Single	25.00	35.00
Double	45.00	50.00

Half board per person:	£min	£max
Daily	32.50	37.50
Weekly	210.00	245.00

Lunch available
Evening meal 1800 (last orders 2100)
Parking for 30
Cards accepted: Access, Visa

🛇🖵♿S✂Ⅿ TV ▥ 🖨🍴40🔍 U❀✕🚲 SP ◉

DRIFFIELD

East Riding of Yorkshire
Map ref 4C1

Lively market town on edge of Wolds with fine Early English church, All Saints. Popular with anglers for its trout streams which flow into the River Hull. Its 18th C canal is lined with barges and houseboats.

The White Horse Inn ⋈

👑👑👑 COMMENDED

Main Street, Hutton Cranswick, Driffield, East Riding of Yorkshire YO25 9QN
☎ (01377) 270383
Fax (01377) 270383
Set beside the village green and pond.

A unique combination of village inn/hotel, restaurant, cabaret and function venue.
Bedrooms: 2 single, 3 double, 1 twin, 2 family rooms
Bathrooms: 8 en-suite

Bed & breakfast per night:	£min	£max
Single	25.00	29.50
Double	40.00	45.00

Half board per person:	£min	£max
Daily	30.00	
Weekly	210.00	

Lunch available
Evening meal 1730 (last orders 2100)
Parking for 100
Cards accepted: Access, Visa, Switch/Delta

🛇🖵♿📞S✂TV ▥ 🖨🍴350🔍U🍴❀🚲 SP

EASINGWOLD

North Yorkshire
Map ref 5C3

Market town of charm and character with a cobbled square and many fine Georgian buildings.

The George ⋈

👑👑👑 COMMENDED

Market Place, Easingwold, York YO6 3AD
☎ (01347) 821698
Fax (01347) 823448
18th C coaching inn overlooking cobbled square in delightful Georgian market town. 15 minutes York, dales, moors. Good food. Cask beers.
Bedrooms: 7 double, 4 twin, 1 triple, 1 family room
Bathrooms: 13 en-suite

Bed & breakfast per night:	£min	£max
Single	35.00	45.00
Double	50.00	60.00

Half board per person:	£min	£max
Daily	37.50	47.50
Weekly	245.00	

Lunch available
Evening meal 1900 (last orders 2130)
Parking for 8
Cards accepted: Access, Visa, Switch/Delta

🛇🖵♿📞S Ⅿ TV ▥ 🖨🍴50🍴✕🚲 SP 🎣

The Old Vicarage ⋈

👑👑👑 COMMENDED

Market Place, Easingwold, York YO6 3AL
☎ (01347) 821015
Delightful 18th C country house with

extensive lawned gardens and croquet lawn. In centre of market town, 12 miles north of York, and ideal as a touring centre for North Yorkshire.
Bedrooms: 1 single, 3 double, 2 twin
Bathrooms: 6 en-suite

Bed & breakfast per night:	£min	£max
Single	25.00	
Double	42.00	55.00

Parking for 5
Open February–November

🛇🖵🖥♿UL✂Ⅿ▥🖨❀🚲✕ 🚲🎣 T

ELLERBY

North Yorkshire
Map ref 5C3

Hamlet 3 miles south of Staithes.

Ellerby Hotel ⋈

👑👑👑 COMMENDED

Ellerby, Saltburn-by-the-Sea, Cleveland TS13 5LP
☎ Whitby (01947) 840342
Fax (01947) 841221
Residential country inn within the North York Moors National Park, 9 miles north of Whitby, 1 mile inland from Runswick Bay.
Wheelchair access category 3🚶
Bedrooms: 5 double, 4 triple
Bathrooms: 9 en-suite

Bed & breakfast per night:	£min	£max
Single	33.00	36.00
Double	50.00	56.00

Lunch available
Evening meal 1900 (last orders 2200)
Parking for 60
Cards accepted: Access, Visa, Switch/Delta

🛇🛏♿📞🖵🖥❄🐾S Ⅿ ▥ 🖨 🍴40🍴❀🚲 SP 🎣

FLAMBOROUGH

East Riding of Yorkshire
Map ref 5D3

Village with strong seafaring tradition, high on chalk headland dominated by cliffs of Flamborough Head, a fortress for over 2000 years. St Oswald's Church is in the oldest part of Flamborough.

The Grange ⋈

Listed COMMENDED

Flamborough, Bridlington, North Humberside YO15 1AS
☎ Bridlington (01262) 850207
Fax (01262) 851359
475-acre arable & livestock farm.
Continued ▶

FLAMBOROUGH

Continued

Family-run Georgian farmhouse offering a warm welcome. Half a mile from the village, close to RSPB reserve at Bempton.
Bedrooms: 1 double, 2 twin
Bathrooms: 2 public

Bed & breakfast

per night:	£min	£max
Single	14.00	15.00
Double	28.00	30.00

Parking for 6

FLAXTON

North Yorkshire
Map ref 5C3

Attractive village with broad greens, just west of the A64 York to Malton highway.

Grange Farm

APPROVED

Oak Busk Lane, Flaxton, York
YO6 7RL
☎ York (01904) 468219
130-acre arable & livestock farm. South-facing, modernised farmhouse in its own gardens. 8 miles from York, off the A64 York to Scarborough road, through Flaxton village and right down Oak Busk Lane. After half a mile turn right to farm.
Bedrooms: 2 double, 1 twin
Bathrooms: 1 en-suite, 1 public

Bed & breakfast

per night:	£min	£max
Single	15.00	17.00
Double	30.00	34.00

Parking for 10

GARFORTH

West Yorkshire
Map ref 4B1

Town 7 miles east of Leeds, between Temple Newsam Estate and Lotherton Hall.

Myrtle House

Listed

31 Wakefield Road, Garforth, Leeds
LS25 1AN
☎ Leeds (0113) 286 6445
Spacious Victorian terraced house between M62 and A1. All rooms have tea and coffee making facilities, TV and vanity basins.
Bedrooms: 1 single, 1 double, 3 twin, 1 triple
Bathrooms: 3 public

Bed & breakfast

per night:	£min	£max
Single	16.00	18.00
Double	32.00	36.00

GILLAMOOR

North Yorkshire
Map ref 5C3

Village much admired by photographers for its views of Farndale, including "Surprise View" from the churchyard.

Royal Oak Inn

COMMENDED

Gillamoor, York YO6 6HX
☎ Kirkbymoorside (01751) 431414
Old country inn on the edge of the North York Moors. Tastefully renovated, with plenty of character and charm. Open log fires.
Bedrooms: 5 double, 1 twin
Bathrooms: 6 en-suite

Bed & breakfast

per night:	£min	£max
Single	30.00	36.00
Double	40.00	50.00

Lunch available
Evening meal 1900 (last orders 2100)
Parking for 9
Cards accepted: Access, Visa

GRASSINGTON

North Yorkshire
Map ref 5B3

Tourists visit this former lead-mining village to see its "smiddy", antique and craft shops and Upper Wharfedale Museum of country trades. Popular with fishermen and walkers. Numerous prehistoric sites. Grassington Feast in October. National Park Centre.

Clarendon Hotel

COMMENDED

Hebden, Grassington, Skipton
BD23 5DE
☎ Skipton (01756) 752446
Yorkshire Dales village inn serving good food and ales. Personal supervision at all times. Steaks and fish dishes are specialities.
Bedrooms: 2 double, 1 twin
Bathrooms: 3 en-suite

Bed & breakfast

per night:	£min	£max
Single	25.00	35.00
Double	40.00	50.00

Lunch available
Evening meal 1900 (last orders 2100)
Parking for 30

Craiglands

COMMENDED

1 Brooklyn, Threshfield, Skipton
BD23 5ER
☎ (01756) 752093
Welcoming guesthouse offering comfortable accommodation, just 10 minutes' walk from Grassington centre. Ideally situated for walkers and as a dales touring base.
Bedrooms: 1 single, 2 double, 1 twin
Bathrooms: 3 en-suite, 1 private

Bed & breakfast

per night:	£min	£max
Single	18.00	22.50
Double	40.00	46.00

Parking for 3
Cards accepted: Access, Visa

Foresters Arms Hotel

Listed APPROVED

20 Main Street, Grassington, Skipton
BD23 5AA
☎ (01756) 752349
Formerly an old coaching inn, situated in picturesque village, serving lunch and evening meals and hand-pulled ales.
Bedrooms: 1 single, 4 double, 2 triple
Bathrooms: 1 en-suite, 2 public

Bed & breakfast

per night:	£min	£max
Single	16.00	20.00
Double	32.00	50.00

Lunch available
Evening meal 1800 (last orders 2030)
Parking for 2

Franor House

3 Wharfeside Avenue, Threshfield, Skipton BD23 5BS
☎ (01756) 752115
Large semi-detached house in quiet surroundings. Take B6265 from Skipton, turning right for Grassington. Wharfeside Avenue is half a mile - first turning on left.
Bedrooms: 1 single, 1 twin, 1 triple
Bathrooms: 2 en-suite, 1 private

Bed & breakfast

per night:	£min	£max
Single	18.00	20.00
Double	36.00	40.00

Parking for 4

Grange Cottage ⚠

Linton, Skipton BD23 5HH
☎ (01756) 752527
Stone-built cottage with open fires and warm hospitality. In a quiet backwater of a picture postcard village, perfect for hiking and car touring in the dales.
Bedrooms: 1 double, 1 twin
Bathrooms: 1 public, 1 private shower

Bed & breakfast per night:

	£min	£max
Single	18.50	19.00
Double	37.00	38.00

Parking for 4
Open March–October

HALIFAX

West Yorkshire
Map ref 4B1

Founded on the cloth trade, and famous for its building society, textiles, carpets and toffee. Most notable landmark is Piece Hall where wool merchants traded, now restored to house shops, museums and art gallery. Home also to Eureka! The Museum for Children.
Tourist Information Centre ☎ (01422) 368725

Beech Court

40 Prescott Street, Halifax HX1 2QW
☎ (01422) 366004
Late Victorian residence, just off the town centre. Well furnished and decorated, with emphasis on high standards and good service.
Bedrooms: 1 single, 1 twin, 1 triple
Bathrooms: 2 public

Bed & breakfast per night:

	£min	£max
Single	18.00	18.00
Double	34.00	34.00

Parking for 3

The Elms

Keighley Road, Illingworth, Halifax HX2 8HT
☎ (01422) 244430
Victorian residence with gardens and original ornate ceilings, within 3 miles of Halifax. Traditional Yorkshire family welcome.
Bedrooms: 2 single, 1 double, 1 triple
Bathrooms: 2 en-suite, 1 private, 1 public

Bed & breakfast per night:

	£min	£max
Single	19.00	20.00
Double	35.00	38.00

Half board per person:

	£min	£max
Daily	27.00	29.00

Evening meal 1800 (last orders 2000)
Parking for 14

Halifax Guest House ⚠

130 Skircoat Road, Halifax HX1 2RE
☎ (01422) 355912
Family-run bed and breakfast 5 minutes from the town centre of Halifax. Both rooms have colour TV and tea and coffee facilities. Full English breakfast. Friendly Yorkshire welcome.
Bedrooms: 1 single, 1 family room
Bathrooms: 2 public

Bed & breakfast per night:

	£min	£max
Single	17.00	19.00
Double	34.00	38.00

Half board per person:

	£min	£max
Daily	23.00	25.00

Parking for 2

HARROGATE

North Yorkshire
Map ref 4B1

A major conference, exhibition and shopping centre, renowned for its spa heritage and award winning floral displays, spacious parks and gardens. Famous for antiques, toffee, fine shopping and excellent tea shops, also its Royal Pump Rooms and Baths.
Tourist Information Centre ☎ (01423) 525666

Alamah ⚠

88 Kings Road, Harrogate HG1 5JX
☎ (01423) 502187
Fax (01423) 566175
Comfortable rooms, personal attention, friendly atmosphere and full English breakfast. 300 metres from town centre. Garages/parking.
Bedrooms: 2 single, 2 double, 2 twin, 1 family room
Bathrooms: 5 en-suite, 2 private showers

Bed & breakfast per night:

	£min	£max
Single	23.00	25.00
Double	42.00	48.00

Evening meal 1830 (last orders 1400)
Parking for 8

Crescent Lodge ⚠

20 Swan Road, Harrogate HG1 2SA
☎ (01423) 503688
Elegant and well-appointed town house, welcoming a maximum of 6 guests. Quiet, yet close to all amenities. Grade II listed.
Bedrooms: 2 single, 2 twin
Bathrooms: 2 en-suite, 1 public

Bed & breakfast per night:

	£min	£max
Single	22.00	
Double	48.00	

Parking for 2

Knabbs Ash ⚠

Skipton Road, Felliscliffe, Harrogate HG3 2LT
☎ (01423) 771040
Fax (01423) 771515

Award-winning country house, set back off the A59 Harrogate to Skipton road, 6 miles west of Harrogate. In its own grounds, in a panoramic, tranquil setting. Ideal area for walking and exploring the Yorkshire Dales.
Bedrooms: 2 double, 1 twin
Bathrooms: 3 en-suite

Bed & breakfast per night:

	£min	£max
Single	25.00	30.00
Double	40.00	42.00

Parking for 6

17 Peckfield Close ⚠

Hampsthwaite, Harrogate HG3 2ES
☎ (01423) 770765
In picturesque village 4 miles from Harrogate off A59. Large, attractive garden. At start of Nidderdale Walk.
Bedrooms: 1 single, 2 twin
Bathrooms: 1 public

Continued ▶

HARROGATE

Continued

Bed & breakfast per night:	£min	£max
Single	15.00	17.00
Double	30.00	34.00

Half board per person:	£min	£max
Daily	21.00	23.00
Weekly	126.00	138.00

Parking for 2

HAWES

North Yorkshire
Map ref 5B3

The capital of Upper Wensleydale on the famous Pennine Way, renowned for great cheeses. Popular with walkers. Dales National Park Information Centre and Folk Museum. Nearby is spectacular Hardraw Force waterfall.

East House ⚜

🏅 COMMENDED

Gayle, Hawes DL8 3RZ
☎ Wensleydale (01969) 667405
Detached house in a quiet position, overlooking the fells. Ideal centre for touring or walking the dales.
Bedrooms: 1 single, 2 triple
Bathrooms: 1 en-suite, 1 public

Bed & breakfast per night:	£min	£max
Single	16.00	17.00
Double	32.00	35.00

Parking for 3
Open March–October

Ebor Guest House ⚜

🏅

Burtersett Road, Hawes DL8 3NT
☎ Wensleydale (01969) 667337
Small, family-run guesthouse, double-glazed and centrally-heated throughout. Walkers are particularly welcome. Centrally located for touring the dales.
Bedrooms: 1 single, 2 double, 1 twin
Bathrooms: 2 en-suite, 1 public

Bed & breakfast per night:	£min	£max
Single	15.00	17.00
Double	34.00	36.00

Parking for 5

Springbank House ⚜

🏅🏅 COMMENDED

Springbank, Townfoot, Hawes DL8 3NW
☎ Wensleydale (01969) 667376
Delightful Victorian house near the centre of Hawes with superb views over the surrounding fells.
Bedrooms: 2 triple
Bathrooms: 2 en-suite

Bed & breakfast per night:	£min	£max
Double	32.00	34.00

Parking for 3
Open February–October

White Hart Inn ⚜

🏅

Main Street, Hawes DL8 3QL
☎ Wensleydale (01969) 667259
17th C coaching inn with a friendly welcome, offering traditional fare. Open fires, Yorkshire ales. Central for exploring the dales.
Bedrooms: 1 single, 4 double, 2 twin
Bathrooms: 2 public

Bed & breakfast per night:	£min	£max
Single	18.00	18.00
Double	34.00	34.00

Lunch available
Evening meal 1900 (last orders 2100)
Parking for 7
Cards accepted: Access, Visa, Amex

HAWORTH

West Yorkshire
Map ref 4B1

This Pennine town is famous as home of the Bronte family. The Parsonage is now a Bronte Museum where furniture and possessions of the family are displayed. Moors and Bronte waterfalls nearby and steam trains on the Keighley and Worth Valley Railway pass through.
Tourist Information Centre ☎ (01535) 642329

The Apothecary Guest House & Tea Rooms ⚜

Listed APPROVED

86 Main Street, Haworth, Keighley BD22 8DA
☎ Keighley (01535) 643642
Fax (01535) 643642
At the top of Haworth Main Street opposite the famous Bronte church, 1 minute from the parsonage and moors.
Bedrooms: 1 single, 4 double, 2 twin, 1 triple
Bathrooms: 7 en-suite, 1 private

Bed & breakfast per night:	£min	£max
Single	17.00	19.00
Double	32.00	38.00

Parking for 7
Cards accepted: Access, Visa

Ashmount ⚜

🏅🏅🏅 COMMENDED

Mytholmes Lane, Haworth, Keighley BD22 8EZ
☎ Keighley (01535) 645726
Victorian Gothic villa with half acre of garden. Outstanding views across Haworth and the moors. 300 yards from the village centre.
Bedrooms: 3 double, 3 twin
Suite available
Bathrooms: 5 en-suite, 1 private

Bed & breakfast per night:	£min	£max
Single	25.00	25.00
Double	35.00	35.00

Half board per person:	£min	£max
Daily	27.50	39.00
Weekly	154.00	218.00

Evening meal 1800 (last orders 2000)
Parking for 6
Cards accepted: Access, Visa, Amex

Ebor House ⚜

🏅 APPROVED

Lees Lane, Haworth, Keighley BD22 8RA
☎ Keighley (01535) 645869
Yorkshire stone-built house of character, conveniently placed for the main tourist attractions of Haworth, including the Worth Valley Railway and Bronte Parsonage and Museum.
Bedrooms: 3 twin
Bathrooms: 1 public

Bed & breakfast per night:	£min	£max
Single	16.00	16.00
Double	30.00	30.00

Parking for 2

Hole Farm ⚜

🏅🏅 HIGHLY COMMENDED

Dimples Lane, Haworth, Keighley BD22 8QS
☎ Keighley (01535) 644755
8-acre smallholding. 17th C farmhouse, 10 minutes' walk from Bronte Parsonage and 2 minutes' walk from the moors. Panoramic views of Haworth. Farm has pigs, peacocks, geese, cattle and horses.
Bedrooms: 2 double
Bathrooms: 2 en-suite

Bed & breakfast per night:	£min	£max
Single	24.99	
Double		35.00

Parking for 4

⛿🖃⌨♨⛽🆄🅻🅂✂🍴🎇⛎❄✈🚐

Old White Lion Hotel ⚠

👑👑👑 COMMENDED

Haworth, Keighley BD22 8DU
☎ Keighley (01535) 642313
Fax (01535) 646222
Family-run, centuries old coaching inn. Candlelit restaurant using local fresh produce, cooked to order and featured in good food guides. Old world bars, popular with locals, serving home-made bar meals and traditional ales.
Bedrooms: 3 single, 8 double, 1 twin, 2 triple
Bathrooms: 14 en-suite

Bed & breakfast per night:	£min	£max
Single	38.50	45.00
Double	50.00	60.00

Half board per person:	£min	£max
Daily	37.00	52.00

Lunch available
Evening meal 1900 (last orders 2150)
Parking for 8
Cards accepted: Access, Visa, Diners, Amex

⛿📞🖃⌨♨🅂🍴📺⛿🎇🍴60✈ SP 🏢◎

Originally a small town on packhorse route, Hebden Bridge grew into a booming mill town in 18th C with rows of "up-and-down" houses of several storeys built against hillsides. Ancient "pace-egg play" custom held on Good Friday. *Tourist Information Centre ☎ (01422) 843831*

Myrtle Grove ⚠

👑👑 COMMENDED

Old Lees Road, Hebden Bridge
HX7 8AL
☎ Halifax (01422) 846078
Comfortable, homely stone cottage, dating back to 1800s, at the foot of Ann Wood, overlooking Heptonstall. Perfect location for just relaxing and walking the many footpaths.
Bedrooms: 1 double
Bathrooms: 1 en-suite

Bed & breakfast per night:	£min	£max
Single	20.00	25.00
Double	35.00	40.00

Parking for 2

⛿5🖃⌨♨🆄🏧🅂✂📺🎇🍴❄🚐

Robin Hood Inn ⚠

Listed COMMENDED

Pecket Well, Hebden Bridge
HX7 8QR
☎ (01422) 842593
Traditional inn on the edge of Calderdale and Pennine Way, Bronte country, Hardcastle Crags. Near Hebden Bridge. Real ale and home-made food.
Bedrooms: 1 double, 1 twin, 1 triple, 1 family room
Bathrooms: 1 en-suite, 1 public

Bed & breakfast per night:	£min	£max
Single	17.50	25.00
Double	33.00	39.50

Half board per person:	£min	£max
Daily	22.50	30.00
Weekly	130.00	175.00

Lunch available
Evening meal 1700 (last orders 2130)
Parking for 28
Cards accepted: Visa, Switch/Delta

⛿🖃⌨♨🅂✂🎇🍴🍷🎇❄🚐 DAP 🎇 SP 🏢

Dales village on the edge of the Yorkshire Dales National Park, 5 miles south-east of Settle.

Littledale Croft

👑👑 COMMENDED

Malham Road, Hellifield, Skipton
BD23 4JH
☎ (01729) 850894
Fax (01729) 850794
New bungalow with open views, just off the A65 on the Malham Road. Within easy reach of the Yorkshire Dales, Three Peaks and the Lake District.
Bedrooms: 2 double, 1 twin
Bathrooms: 1 en-suite, 1 public

Bed & breakfast per night:	£min	£max
Single	20.00	20.00
Double	34.00	40.00

Parking for 5
Open March–October

⛿⛿♨🆄🅻🅂✂📺🎇❄✈🚐

Wenningber Farm ⚠

🖃 HIGHLY COMMENDED

Airton Road, Hellifield, Skipton
BD23 4JR
☎ (01729) 850856
120-acre mixed farm. Charming farmhouse, with log fire and oak beams, just 5 miles from Malham in the heart of the Yorkshire Dales.
Bedrooms: 1 double, 1 twin
Bathrooms: 1 public

Bed & breakfast per night:	£min	£max
Single	20.00	25.00
Double	35.00	39.00

Parking for 10

⛿⛿🖃⌨♨🆄🅻🅂✂📺🎇⛎🍴❄🚐🏢

Pretty town on the River Rye at the entrance to Ryedale and the North York Moors, with large square and remains of 12th C castle, several inns and All Saints' Church.

Stilworth House

👑👑 COMMENDED

1 Church Street, Helmsley, York
YO6 5AD
☎ (01439) 771072 & 770507
Comfortable relaxed atmosphere in elegant Georgian town house off the market square of Helmsley. Pretty en-suite rooms with colour TV, hairdryer, tea/coffee facilities. Private car park.
Bedrooms: 3 double, 1 twin, 1 triple
Bathrooms: 5 en-suite

Bed & breakfast per night:	£min	£max
Single	25.00	35.00
Double	35.00	50.00

Parking for 4

⛿⛿🖃⌨♨🆄🅂🎇📺🎇🍴🎇❄✈🚐 SP

HOLMFIRTH

West Yorkshire
Map ref 4B1

This village has become famous as the location for the filming of the TV series "Last of the Summer Wine". It has a postcard museum and is on the edge of the Peak District National Park.
Tourist Information Centre ☎ (01484) 687603

Red Lion Inn

COMMENDED

Sheffield Road, Jackson Bridge, Holmfirth, Huddersfield HD7 7HS
☎ (01484) 683499
Well-appointed, family-run inn in attractive "Summer Wine" country, close to the Peak District and Yorkshire Dales.
Bedrooms: 4 double, 2 twin
Bathrooms: 3 en-suite, 1 public

Bed & breakfast per night:

	£min	£max
Single	20.00	27.00
Double	28.00	42.00

Lunch available
Evening meal 1730 (last orders 2030)

Spring Head House Ⓜ

Listed COMMENDED

15 Holmfirth Road, Shepley, Huddersfield HD8 8BB
☎ Huddersfield (01484) 606300
Fax (01484) 608030
Large Georgian house with a garden, close to Holmfirth and "Summer Wine" country and with easy access to the M1 and M62.
Bedrooms: 1 single, 1 twin
Bathrooms: 1 en-suite, 1 public

Bed & breakfast per night:

	£min	£max
Single	17.50	25.00
Double	35.00	35.00

Parking for 3
Cards accepted: Access, Visa

29 Woodhead Road

COMMENDED

Holmfirth, Huddersfield HD7 1JU
☎ (01484) 683962
200-year-old family home, 5 minutes' walk from Holmfirth. Tea and coffee available at any time. Good walking area and pleasant countryside.
Bedrooms: 1 twin
Bathrooms: 1 private

Bed & breakfast per night:

	£min	£max
Single	14.50	15.00
Double	29.00	30.00

Parking for 2

HORNSEA

East Riding of Yorkshire
Map ref 4D1

Small holiday town situated on strip of land between beach bordering North Sea and Hornsea Mere, a large natural freshwater lake. Some sailing and fishing permitted on protected nature reserve. Hornsea Pottery and retail "freeport" attract many visitors.

Southfield Guest House Ⓜ

COMMENDED

61 Eastgate, Hornsea, North Humberside HU18 1NB
☎ (01964) 534961
Victorian house situated close to seafront. Homely and comfortable with benefit of stairlift to first floor. Good food and hospitality assured.
Bedrooms: 1 single, 2 double, 1 twin, 1 triple
Bathrooms: 1 en-suite, 1 public

Bed & breakfast per night:

	£min	£max
Single	13.00	15.00
Double	26.00	30.00

Half board per person:

	£min	£max
Daily	20.00	22.00
Weekly	120.00	140.00

Evening meal 1800 (last orders 1900)
Parking for 2

All accommodation in this guide has been graded, or is awaiting a grading, by a trained Tourist Board inspector.

Information on accommodation listed in this guide has been supplied by the proprietors. As changes may occur you are advised to check details at the time of booking.

HUDDERSFIELD

West Yorkshire
Map ref 4B1

Founded on wool and cloth, has a famous choral society. Town centre redeveloped, but several good Victorian buildings remain, including railway station, St Peter's Church, Tolson Memorial Museum, art gallery and nearby Colne Valley Museum.
Tourist Information Centre ☎ (01484) 430808

White House Ⓜ

COMMENDED

Holthead, Slaithwaite, Huddersfield HD7 5TY
☎ (01484) 842245
Fax (01484) 842245
Lovely 18th C inn with traditional ale and comfortable en-suite accommodation. Notable cuisine in warm and friendly surroundings. In the country, only 4 miles from Huddersfield on the B6107 Meltham to Marsden road.
Bedrooms: 1 single, 6 double, 1 twin
Bathrooms: 6 en-suite, 2 private, 1 public

Bed & breakfast per night:

	£min	£max
Single	28.00	35.00
Double	40.00	40.00

Half board per person:

	£min	£max
Daily	25.00	33.00

Lunch available
Evening meal 1800 (last orders 2130)
Parking for 100
Cards accepted: Access, Visa, Diners, Amex, Switch/Delta

HUNTON

North Yorkshire
Map ref 5C3

Typical dales village 5 miles east of Leyburn.

The Countryman's Inn

COMMENDED

Hunton, Bedale DL8 1PY
☎ Bedale (01677) 450554 & Mobile 0850 863153
Fax (01677) 450570
Modernised village inn and restaurant, retaining its old world charm, with log fires and beamed ceilings. Four-poster room. Just off A684 between Bedale and Leyburn, convenient for Yorkshire Dales.
Bedrooms: 6 double, 1 twin
Bathrooms: 7 en-suite

Bed & breakfast per night:	£min	£max
Single	30.00	35.00
Double	45.00	60.00

Evening meal 1900 (last orders 2130)
Parking for 20
Cards accepted: Access, Visa, Amex

INGLEBY GREENHOW

North Yorkshire
Map ref 5C3

Perched on the edge of Cleveland Hills, the village boasts the Norman church of St Andrew's with well-preserved carving and effigies of a priest and a knight. Ingleby Moor rises 1300 ft above village.

Manor House Farm

HIGHLY COMMENDED

Ingleby Greenhow, Great Ayton
TS9 6RB
☎ Great Ayton (01642) 722384

168-acre mixed farm. In a picture book setting surrounded by hills and forests, in North York Moors National Park. Ideal for nature lovers, walking, touring and relaxing. Fine food and wines.

Bedrooms: 1 double, 2 twin
Bathrooms: 1 en-suite, 2 private

Half board per person:	£min	£max
Daily	36.50	41.00
Weekly	255.50	255.50

Evening meal 1900 (last orders 1600)
Parking for 66
Cards accepted: Access, Visa, Switch/Delta
12

The map references refer to the colour maps towards the end of the guide. The first figure is the map number; the letter and figure which follow indicate the grid reference on the map.

INGLETON

North Yorkshire
Map ref 5B3

Thriving tourist centre for fell-walkers, climbers and pot-holers. Popular walks up beautiful Twiss Valley to Ingleborough Summit, Whernside, White Scar Caves and waterfalls.

Langber Country Guest House

Tatterthorne Road, Ingleton, Carnforth LA6 3DT
☎ (015242) 41587

Detached country house in hilltop position with panoramic views. Good touring centre for dales, lakes and coast. Comfortable accommodation. Friendly service - everyone welcome.

Bedrooms: 1 single, 2 double, 1 twin, 2 triple, 1 family room
Bathrooms: 4 en-suite, 1 public

Bed & breakfast per night:	£min	£max
Single	15.50	25.00
Double	29.50	43.00

Half board per person:	£min	£max
Daily	22.00	28.00
Weekly	142.00	165.00

Evening meal 1830 (last orders 1700)
Parking for 6

Riverside Lodge

COMMENDED

24 Main Street, Ingleton, Carnforth, Lancashire LA6 3HJ
☎ (015242) 41359

Victorian house with conservatory, set in the Yorkshire Dales. Wheelchair access and pets welcome. Sauna, games room, river fishing.

Wheelchair access category 3
Bedrooms: 6 double, 2 twin
Bathrooms: 8 en-suite

Bed & breakfast per night:	£min	£max
Single	33.00	39.00
Double	44.00	52.00

Evening meal 1900 (last orders 1900)
Parking for 8
Open February–November

KNARESBOROUGH

North Yorkshire
Map ref 4B1

Picturesque market town on the River Nidd, famous for its 11th C castle ruins, overlooking town and river gorge. Attractions include oldest chemist's shop in country, prophetess Mother Shipton's cave, Dropping Well and Court House Museum. Boating on river.

Newton House Hotel

COMMENDED

5-7 York Place, Knaresborough
HG5 0AD
☎ Harrogate (01423) 863539
Fax (01423) 869748

Charming, family-run, 17th C former coaching inn, situated 2 minutes' walk from the market square, castle and river. 10 minutes Harrogate, 20 minutes York, 30 minutes the dales.

Bedrooms: 1 single, 6 double, 3 twin, 2 triple
Bathrooms: 11 en-suite, 1 private

Bed & breakfast per night:	£min	£max
Single	32.50	37.50
Double	50.00	60.00

Half board per person:	£min	£max
Daily	35.00	49.50
Weekly	220.00	262.00

Evening meal 1900 (last orders 2030)
Parking for 10
Cards accepted: Access, Visa, Switch/Delta

LEEDS

West Yorkshire
Map ref 4B1

Large city with excellent modern shopping centre and splendid Victorian architecture. Museums and galleries including Temple Newsam House (the Hampton Court of the North), Tetley's Brewery Wharf and the Royal Armouries Museum; also home of Opera North.
Tourist Information Centre ☎ (0113) 242 5242

The White House

Listed APPROVED

157 Middleton Park Road, Leeds
LS10 4LZ
☎ (0113) 271 1231

Spacious, detached house. Excellent local transport from near the door.

Continued ▶

LEEDS

Continued

Convenient for M1, M62 and West Riding towns and ideal stopover for North/South travel. Non-smokers only, please.
Bedrooms: 3 twin
Bathrooms: 1 public

Bed & breakfast per night:

	£min	£max
Single	16.00	16.00
Double	32.00	32.00

Parking for 3

LEEDS/BRADFORD AIRPORT

See under Bingley, Bradford, Leeds, Otley

LEYBURN

North Yorkshire
Map ref 5B3

Attractive dales market town where Mary Queen of Scots was reputedly captured after her escape from Bolton Castle. Fine views over Wensleydale from nearby.
Tourist Information Centre ☎ (01969) 623069 or 622773

Clyde House ᛗ

Listed COMMENDED

5 Railway Street, Leyburn DL8 5AY
☎ Wensleydale (01969) 623941
17th C former coaching inn offering good homely accommodation. Close to the market square. South facing rooms overlook dale. Brochure on request.
Bedrooms: 2 double, 1 twin, 1 family room
Bathrooms: 4 en-suite

Bed & breakfast per night:

	£min	£max
Single	20.00	25.00
Double	36.00	42.00

LONG MARSTON

North Yorkshire
Map ref 4C1

Close to the site of the Battle of Marston Moor, a decisive Civil War battle of 1644. A monument commemorates the event.

Gill House Farm ᛗ

HIGHLY COMMENDED

Tockwith Road, Long Marston, York YO5 8PJ
☎ Rufforth (01904) 738379 &
Mobile 0850 511140
600-acre mixed farm. Peaceful period farmhouse set in glorious countryside

---

overlooking the Vale of York. Warm welcome. Good bus route and lots of local eating places.
Bedrooms: 2 double, 1 triple, 1 family room
Bathrooms: 4 en-suite

Bed & breakfast per night:

	£min	£max
Single	30.00	
Double	44.00	

Parking for 5
Cards accepted: Access, Visa

LUND

East Riding of Yorkshire
Map ref 4C1

Village near Beverley close to the route of "The Minster Way".

Clematis House, Farmhouse Bed & Breakfast ᛗ

COMMENDED

1 Eastgate, Lund, Driffield, North Humberside YO25 9TQ
☎ Driffield (01377) 217204
Fax (01377) 217204
389-acre arable & livestock farm. Family-run working farm in pretty, rural village. Farmhouse with character, spacious yet cosy, with en-suite rooms and tea/coffee making facilities. Secluded walled garden, TV lounge.
Bedrooms: 1 double, 1 twin
Bathrooms: 2 en-suite

Bed & breakfast per night:

	£min	£max
Single	19.00	19.00
Double	37.00	37.00

Parking for 4

MALHAM

North Yorkshire
Map ref 5B3

Hamlet of stone cottages amid magnificent rugged limestone scenery in the Yorkshire Dales National Park. Malham Cove is a curving, sheer white cliff 240 ft high. Malham Tarn, one of Yorkshire's few natural lakes, belongs to the National Trust. National Park Centre.

Beck Hall Guest House ᛗ

APPROVED

Malham, Skipton BD23 4DJ
☎ Settle (01729) 830332
Family-run guesthouse in a spacious riverside garden. Homely atmosphere, four-poster beds, log fires and home cooking.

Bedrooms: 11 double, 3 twin
Bathrooms: 9 en-suite, 2 private, 1 public

Bed & breakfast per night:

	£min	£max
Single	20.00	25.00
Double	31.00	39.00

Half board per person:

	£min	£max
Daily	22.45	26.45

Lunch available
Evening meal 1900 (last orders 2000)
Parking for 30

Miresfield Farm ᛗ

COMMENDED

Malham, Skipton BD23 4DA
☎ Airton (01729) 830414
In a beautiful garden bordering the village green and a tumbling stream. Ideal base for touring the national park.
Bedrooms: 1 single, 5 double, 4 twin, 4 triple
Bathrooms: 11 en-suite, 1 private, 1 public

Bed & breakfast per night:

	£min	£max
Single	25.00	30.00
Double	40.00	44.00

Half board per person:

	£min	£max
Daily	28.00	30.00
Weekly	196.00	210.00

Evening meal 1830 (last orders 1200)
Parking for 16

MALTON

North Yorkshire
Map ref 5D3

Thriving farming town on the River Derwent with large livestock market. Famous for racehorse training. The local museum has Roman remains and the Eden Camp Modern History Theme Museum transports visitors back to wartime Britain. Castle Howard within easy reach.
Tourist Information Centre ☎ (01653) 600048

New Globe Inn

Listed

Yorkersgate, Malton YO17 0AA
☎ (01653) 692395
Quaint old pub, right in the centre of town.
Bedrooms: 1 double, 2 twin
Bathrooms: 1 public

Bed & breakfast per night:	£min	£max
Single	16.00	18.00
Double	30.00	32.00

Parking for 22

MARKET WEIGHTON

East Riding of Yorkshire
Map ref 4C1

Small town on the western side of the Yorkshire Wolds. A tablet in the parish church records the death of William Bradley in 1820 at which time he was 7 ft 9 in tall and weighed 27 stone!

Arras Farmhouse

Listed APPROVED

Arras Farm, Market Weighton, York
YO4 3RN
☎ (01430) 872404
Fax (01430) 871500

460-acre arable farm. Large farmhouse and grounds, peaceful and comfortable, on A1079 between Market Weighton and Beverley. 3 miles from Market Weighton at crossroads.
Bedrooms: 2 double, 1 twin
Bathrooms: 2 en-suite, 1 public

Bed & breakfast per night:	£min	£max
Single	18.00	20.00
Double	30.00	34.00

Parking for 5

MIDDLEHAM

North Yorkshire
Map ref 5C3

Town famous for racehorse training, with cobbled squares and houses of local stone. Norman castle, once principal residence of Warwick the Kingmaker and later Richard III. Ruins of Jervaulx Abbey nearby.

Black Swan Hotel

COMMENDED

Market Place, Middleham DL8 4NP
☎ Wensleydale (01969) 622221
Unspoilt 17th C inn, with open fires and beamed ceilings, allied to 20th C comforts. Emphasis on food.
Bedrooms: 1 single, 4 double, 1 twin, 1 triple
Bathrooms: 7 en-suite

Bed & breakfast per night:	£min	£max
Single	26.00	30.00
Double	46.00	62.00

Half board per person:	£min	£max
Daily	32.50	38.50

Lunch available
Evening meal 1830 (last orders 2100)
Parking for 3
Cards accepted: Access, Visa

MYTON-ON-SWALE

North Yorkshire
Map ref 5C3

Small village on the mighty River Swale.

Plump House Farm

Myton-on-Swale, York YO6 2RA
☎ Boroughbridge (01423) 360650
160-acre mixed farm. A warm welcome with comfortable en-suite accommodation on a working family farm. Easy access to York and Harrogate and an ideal centre for the coast, dales and moors. Reductions for children.
Bedrooms: 1 double, 1 family room
Bathrooms: 2 en-suite

Bed & breakfast per night:	£min	£max
Single	15.00	
Double	30.00	

Half board per person:	£min	£max
Daily	21.00	

Evening meal 1800 (last orders 2000)
Parking for 4

NORTHALLERTON

North Yorkshire
Map ref 5C3

Formerly a staging post on coaching route to the North and later a railway town. Today a lively market town and administrative capital of North Yorkshire. Parish church of All Saints dates from 1200.
Tourist Information Centre ☎ (01609) 776864

Lovesome Hill Farm

COMMENDED

Lovesome Hill, Northallerton
DL6 2PB
☎ (01609) 772311
165-acre mixed farm. 19th C

farmhouse. Tastefully converted granary adjoins with spacious, quality en-suite rooms. Conversion won architectural award in 1995. 4 miles north of Northallerton on A167.
Wheelchair access category 3
Bedrooms: 1 single, 1 double, 1 twin, 1 family room
Bathrooms: 4 en-suite

Bed & breakfast per night:	£min	£max
Single	18.00	22.00
Double	36.00	44.00

Half board per person:	£min	£max
Daily	28.00	32.00
Weekly	189.00	224.00

Evening meal from 1900
Parking for 10
Open February–November

NUNNINGTON

North Yorkshire
Map ref 5C3

On the River Rye, this picturesque village has a splendid Hall which houses some magnificent 17th C tapestries.

Sunley Court

COMMENDED

Nunnington, York YO6 5XQ
☎ (01439) 748233
200-acre arable and mixed farm. Modern farmhouse in open countryside. Home cooking, log fires and emphasis on comfort. Central to York, North York Moors and coast.
Bedrooms: 2 single, 1 double, 1 twin
Bathrooms: 2 private, 1 public

Bed & breakfast per night:	£min	£max
Single	15.00	16.00
Double	30.00	32.00

Half board per person:	£min	£max
Daily	25.00	
Weekly	175.00	

Lunch available
Evening meal 1800 (last orders 2100)
Parking for 9
Open March–October

Establishments should be open throughout the year, unless otherwise stated.

113

OSMOTHERLEY

North Yorkshire
Map ref 5C3

The famous "Lyke Wake Walk", across the Cleveland Hills to Ravenscar 40 miles away, starts here in this ancient village. Attached to the village cross is a large stone table used as a "pulpit" by John Wesley.

Quintana House M

Listed COMMENDED

Back Lane, Osmotherley, Northallerton DL6 3BJ
☎ (01609) 883258
Detached, stone cottage near national park village centre, within 90 metres of the Cleveland Way, affording panoramic views of Black Hambleton. Non-smokers only, please.
Bedrooms: 1 double, 1 twin
Bathrooms: 1 public
Bed & breakfast

per night:	£min	£max
Double	34.00	37.00

Half board per person:	£min	£max
Daily	24.00	37.00
Weekly	168.00	259.00

Evening meal 1830 (last orders 2000)
Parking for 5
⌖⑤📞🗆👤🖫👜⑤🗡ʬ◨🖬🖾
☊🌣🗡🎮🏠

OTLEY

West Yorkshire
Map ref 4B1

Charming market and small manufacturing town in Lower Wharfedale, the birthplace of Thomas Chippendale, painted by Turner. Old inns, medieval 5-arched bridge, local history museum, maypole, historic All Saints' Church. Beautiful countryside. Location for "Emmerdale Farm" and "Heartbeat".
Tourist Information Centre ☎ (0113) 247 7707

Paddock Hill

APPROVED

Norwood, Otley LS21 2QU
☎ (01943) 465977
Converted farmhouse on the B6451. Open fires and lovely views. Within easy reach of Herriot, Bronte and Emmerdale country, the dales, Skipton, Harrogate and Leeds. Reservoir fishing nearby.
Bedrooms: 1 double, 2 twin
Bathrooms: 1 public, 1 private shower

Bed & breakfast per night:	£min	£max
Single	14.00	18.00
Double	28.00	36.00

Parking for 3
⌖🛁👜⑤👤🖫👜◨🖬🖾👜🌣🏠🏠

Wood Top Farm M

♕ HIGHLY COMMENDED

Off Norwood Edge, Lindley, Otley LS21 2QS
☎ (01943) 464010
Fax (01943) 464010
7-acre mixed farm. Quiet 18th C farmhouse in an Area of Outstanding Natural Beauty, half a mile off B6451. Ideal for country lovers and central for Leeds, Bradford, Harrogate, Skipton, York, Haworth and the dales. Cosy bedrooms with adjoining private bathroom/dressing room. Room service for tea and coffee, varied breakfast menu. Non-smoking. Stabling available.
Bedrooms: 1 single, 1 twin
Bathrooms: 1 en-suite, 1 private shower

Bed & breakfast per night:	£min	£max
Single	20.00	25.00
Double	40.00	44.00

Parking for 6
⌖⑩📞🗆👤⑤⌖🗡🎮🖬🖾🖁⑧
☋🎵🌣🏠🏠

PATELEY BRIDGE

North Yorkshire
Map ref 5C3

Small market town at centre of Upper Nidderdale. Flax and linen industries once flourished in this remote and beautiful setting.

North Pasture Farm

♕ HIGHLY COMMENDED

Brimham Rocks, Summer Bridge, Harrogate HG3 4DW
☎ Harrogate (01423) 711470
135-acre dairy farm. Parts of the house date back to 1400 and 1657. John Wesley preached in what is now the lounge.
Bedrooms: 2 double, 1 twin
Bathrooms: 3 en-suite

Bed & breakfast per night:	£min	£max
Single	25.00	
Double	39.00	

Half board per person:	£min	£max
Daily	29.50	

Evening meal from 1830
Parking for 6
Open April–October
👜⑤⌖🎮🖬🖾🖁☋🌣🗡🏠🏠

PENISTONE

South Yorkshire
Map ref 4B1

Busy little market town on the River Don. The church dates from the 13th C.

Aldermans Head Manor M

♕ HIGHLY COMMENDED

Hartcliffe Hill Road, Langsett, Stocksbridge, Sheffield S30 5GY
☎ Barnsley (01226) 766209
Fax (01226) 766209

Award-winning country manor house close to "Summer Wine" country. Licensed, panoramic views across Peak District, 50 acres, home cooking, non smoking.
Bedrooms: 2 double, 2 twin
Bathrooms: 3 en-suite, 1 private

Bed & breakfast per night:	£min	£max
Single	30.00	40.00
Double	45.00	60.00

Evening meal 1800 (last orders 2000)
Parking for 12
⌖⑫📞🖭🗆👤⑤⌖🗡🎮🖬
🖁🍽⑫🌣🗡🏠🏠◎

PICKERING

North Yorkshire
Map ref 5D3

Market town and tourist centre on edge of North York Moors. Parish church has complete set of 15th C wall paintings depicting lives of saints. Part of 12th C castle still stands. Beck Isle Museum. The North York Moors Railway begins here.
Tourist Information Centre ☎ (01751) 473791

Eden House M

♕ COMMENDED

120 Eastgate, Pickering YO18 7DW
☎ (01751) 472289 & 477024
Fax (01751) 477024
Delightful listed cottage situated on the A170 road to the East Coast. On the outskirts of a small market town.
Bedrooms: 2 double, 1 twin
Bathrooms: 1 en-suite, 1 public

Bed & breakfast per night:	£min	£max
Single	20.00	25.00
Double	32.00	35.00

Half board per person:	£min	£max
Daily	26.00	27.50

Evening meal 1830 (last orders 2000)
Parking for 3

♿♨✉口...

Grindale House

COMMENDED

123 Eastgate, Pickering YO18 7DW
☎ (01751) 476636
18th C stone townhouse. Lovely rooms with antique furniture, private bathrooms, TV. Car park, secure bicycle storage. Friendly informal atmosphere. Non-smoking.
Bedrooms: 2 double, 1 twin
Bathrooms: 2 en-suite, 1 private

Bed & breakfast per night:	£min	£max
Single	23.00	25.00
Double	31.00	44.00

Parking for 8

The Old Vicarage

COMMENDED

Yedingham, Malton YO17 8SL
☎ West Heslerton (01944) 728426
Delightful, Georgian former vicarage set in large gardens with panoramic views of moors and wolds. Pretty village, with local inn, approximately 7 miles from Pickering, on River Derwent in the heart of Ryedale. Dinner by arrangement.
Bedrooms: 2 double, 1 twin
Bathrooms: 1 en-suite, 1 public

Bed & breakfast per night:	£min	£max
Single	14.00	18.00
Double	28.00	36.00

Half board per person:	£min	£max
Daily	22.50	27.00

Parking for 4

Rains Farm

COMMENDED

Allerston, Pickering YO18 7PQ
☎ Scarborough (01723) 859333
6-acre livestock farm. Renovated farmhouse in peaceful, picturesque location in the Vale of Pickering. Ideal touring base for moors and coast. Good food, warm welcome.

Bedrooms: 1 single, 2 double, 2 twin
Bathrooms: 5 en-suite

Bed & breakfast per night:	£min	£max
Single	18.50	24.00
Double	37.00	40.00

Half board per person:	£min	£max
Daily	29.00	30.50
Weekly	199.00	210.00

Evening meal 1800 (last orders 1400)
Parking for 6
Cards accepted: Access, Visa, Switch/Delta

Sunnyside

HIGHLY COMMENDED

Carr Lane, Middleton, Pickering YO18 8PD
☎ (01751) 476104
Fax (01751) 476104
Large, south-facing chalet bungalow with private parking and a garden, in an open country aspect. Some ground floor rooms.
Bedrooms: 1 double, 1 twin, 1 triple
Bathrooms: 3 en-suite

Bed & breakfast per night:	£min	£max
Single	24.00	24.00
Double	36.00	36.00

Half board per person:	£min	£max
Daily	30.00	30.00
Weekly	200.00	200.00

Evening meal from 1930
Parking for 4
Open April–October
Cards accepted: Access, Visa

RAVENSCAR

North Yorkshire
Map ref 5D3

Splendidly-positioned small coastal resort with magnificent views over Robin Hood's Bay. Its Old Peak is the end of the famous Lyke Wake Walk or "corpse way".

Smugglers Rock Country Guest House

Ravenscar, Scarborough YO13 0ER
☎ Scarborough (01723) 870044
Georgian country house, reputedly a former smugglers' haunt, with panoramic views over the surrounding national park and sea. Half a mile from the village. Ideal centre for touring, walking and pony trekking.

Bedrooms: 2 single, 2 double, 2 twin, 1 triple, 1 family room
Bathrooms: 8 en-suite

Bed & breakfast per night:	£min	£max
Single	21.00	23.00
Double	42.00	46.00

Half board per person:	£min	£max
Daily	29.50	31.00
Weekly	185.00	189.00

Evening meal 1830 (last orders 1630)
Parking for 12
Open March–November

REDMIRE

North Yorkshire
Map ref 5B3

Peaceful and little-known dales village at east end of Wensleydale. Pale stone cottages scattered around a large green with ancient oak tree and pinfold where stray animals were penned.

Bolton Arms

COMMENDED

Redmire, Leyburn DL8 4EA
☎ Wensleydale (01969) 624336

An old inn - quiet and friendly atmosphere. In an unspoilt village in the heart of Wensleydale - near castles, waterfalls and market towns.
Bedrooms: 2 double, 2 twin
Bathrooms: 4 en-suite

Bed & breakfast per night:	£min	£max
Single	22.00	27.00
Double	44.00	54.00

Half board per person:	£min	£max
Daily	33.00	38.00
Weekly	231.00	266.00

Lunch available
Evening meal 1900 (last orders 2100)
Parking for 12
Cards accepted: Access, Visa

RICHMOND

North Yorkshire
Map ref 5C3

Market town on edge of Swaledale with 11th C castle, Georgian and Victorian buildings surrounding cobbled market-place. Green Howards' Museum is in the former Holy Trinity Church. Attractions include the Georgian Theatre, Richmondshire Museum and Easby Abbey.
Tourist Information Centre ☎ (01748) 850252 or 825994

Carlin House

COMMENDED

6 Frenchgate, Richmond DL10 4JG
☎ (01748) 826771
Grade II listed 18th C town house located at lower entrance to Richmond's market square. Geologists especially welcome.
Bedrooms: 1 single, 1 double
Bathrooms: 1 en-suite, 1 private
Bed & breakfast

per night:	£min	£max
Single	20.00	25.00
Double	36.00	40.00

Holmedale

COMMENDED

Dalton, Richmond DL11 7HX
☎ Teesdale (01833) 621236
Georgian house in a quiet village, midway between Richmond and Barnard Castle. Ideal for the Yorkshire and Durham dales.
Bedrooms: 1 double, 1 triple
Bathrooms: 1 public
Bed & breakfast

per night:	£min	£max
Single	15.00	
Double	26.00	

Half board per person:	£min	£max
Daily	20.00	

Evening meal 1800 (last orders 1200)
Parking for 2

The symbols in each entry give information about services and facilities. A 'key' to these symbols appears at the back of this guide.

Mount Pleasant Farm

Whashton, Richmond DL11 7JP
☎ (01748) 822784

40-acre mixed farm. Just the place for that special holiday or short break. En-suite rooms in a renovated stable. Well known for our farmer's breakfast and delicious dinners, warm welcome and personal service. Real peace and quiet in lovely countryside.
Wheelchair access category 3
Bedrooms: 2 double, 1 twin, 2 triple
Bathrooms: 3 en-suite, 2 private
Bed & breakfast

per night:	£min	£max
Single	20.00	20.00
Double	36.00	38.00

Half board per person:	£min	£max
Daily	29.50	29.50

Evening meal 1830 (last orders 1200)
Parking for 6

RIPON

North Yorkshire
Map ref 5C3

Small, ancient city with impressive cathedral containing Saxon crypt which houses church treasures from all over Yorkshire. "Setting the Watch" tradition kept nightly by horn-blower in Market Square. Fountains Abbey nearby.

The Coopers

APPROVED

36 College Road, Ripon HG4 2HA
☎ (01765) 603708
Spacious, comfortable Victorian house in quiet area. En-suite facilities available. Special rates for children. Cyclists welcome (storage for bicycles). Take-away meals acceptable in rooms.
Bedrooms: 1 single, 1 twin, 1 triple
Bathrooms: 1 private, 1 public
Bed & breakfast

per night:	£min	£max
Single	16.00	17.00
Double	28.00	34.00

Parking for 3

Lowgate Cottage

Listed COMMENDED

Lowgate Lane, Sawley, Ripon HG4 3EL
☎ Sawley (01765) 620302
Restored dwelling, peacefully located in one-third of an acre of beautiful gardens. 10 minutes' walking distance from Fountains Abbey and Studley Park.
Bedrooms: 1 double, 1 twin
Bathrooms: 1 public
Bed & breakfast

per night:	£min	£max
Double		31.00

Parking for 4
Open April–October

Mallard Grange

Listed HIGHLY COMMENDED

Aldfield, Ripon HG4 3BE
☎ Sawley (01765) 620242
460-acre mixed farm. Peaceful, welcoming 16th C farmhouse in open countryside, near Fountains Abbey. Spacious and comfortable, high quality traditionally furnished rooms. Delicious breakfast.
Bedrooms: 1 double, 1 twin
Bathrooms: 1 public
Bed & breakfast

per night:	£min	£max
Double	36.00	

Parking for 4
Open April–October

Moor End Farm

COMMENDED

Knaresborough Road, Littlethorpe, Ripon HG4 3LU
☎ (01765) 677419
41-acre livestock farm. Comfortable rooms, TV lounge with log fire. Home cooking and a warm Yorkshire welcome. Non-smokers only, please. Ideal centre for Yorkshire Dales, York and Harrogate.
Bedrooms: 2 double, 1 twin
Bathrooms: 2 en-suite, 1 public
Bed & breakfast

per night:	£min	£max
Double	32.00	

Half board per person:	£min	£max
Daily	25.00	
Weekly	168.00	

Evening meal 1830 (last orders 1600)
Parking for 7
Open January–November

St George's Court ⚑

Listed **COMMENDED**

Old Home Farm, Grantley, Ripon
HG4 3EU
☎ Sawley (01765) 620618
*Set in 20 acres of beautifully secluded
farmland. Comfortable rooms in
renovated farm buildings. Enjoy a
delicious breakfast in our listed
farmhouse.*
Bedrooms: 3 double, 1 twin, 1 family
room
Bathrooms: 5 en-suite

Bed & breakfast

per night:	£min	£max
Single	25.00	25.00
Double	36.00	40.00

Half board per

person:	£min	£max
Daily	29.00	31.00

Evening meal 1900 (last orders
2000)
Parking for 14

🐎♿⌨🖵♨🛇🅂✂🎱🗄🚗🐾✳🚌
SP

SCARBOROUGH

North Yorkshire
Map ref 5D3

Large, popular East Coast seaside
resort, formerly a spa town.
Beautiful gardens and two splendid
sandy beaches. Castle ruins date
from 1100; fine Georgian and
Victorian houses. Scarborough
Millennium depicts 1,000 years of
town's history. Sea Life Centre.
*Tourist Information Centre ☎ (01723)
373333*

Killerby Cottage Farm ⚑

COMMENDED

Killerby Lane, Cayton, Scarborough
YO11 3TP
☎ (01723) 581236
Fax (01723) 585465
*400-acre arable farm. Character
farmhouse, with stained glass craft
centre. Farm also has horses. 1.5 miles
from Cayton Bay, between Scarborough
and Filey.*
Bedrooms: 2 double, 1 twin
Bathrooms: 1 en-suite, 1 public

Bed & breakfast

per night:	£min	£max
Single	18.00	25.00
Double	36.00	40.00

Parking for 10

🐎♿⌨🖵♨🆄🅿🆃🅅🗄🚗✳🚌

*Establishments should be
open throughout the year,
unless otherwise stated.*

SELBY

North Yorkshire
Map ref 4C1

Small market town on the River
Ouse, believed to have been
birthplace of Henry I, with a
magnificent abbey containing much
fine Norman and Early English
architecture.
*Tourist Information Centre ☎ (01757)
703263*

Hazeldene Guest House ⚑

Listed **APPROVED**

34 Brook Street, Doncaster Road,
Selby YO8 0AR
☎ (01757) 704809
Fax (01757) 709300
*Situated by the A19 in pleasant market
town, only 12 miles from York. M62
and A1 are both 7 miles distant.*
Bedrooms: 3 single, 1 double, 2 twin,
3 triple, 1 family room
Bathrooms: 1 en-suite, 2 public

Bed & breakfast

per night:	£min	£max
Single	17.00	19.00
Double	30.00	38.00

Parking for 6

🐎♿2⌨♨🆄🅂✂🗄🚗✈🚌

SETTLE

North Yorkshire
Map ref 5B3

Town of narrow streets and
Georgian houses in an area of great
limestone hills and crags. Panoramic
view from Castleberg Crag which
stands 300 ft above town.
*Tourist Information Centre ☎ (01729)
825192*

Golden Lion Hotel ⚑

APPROVED

Duke Street, Settle BD24 9DY
☎ (01729) 822203
*17th C coaching inn with log fire,
offering simply furnished bedrooms and
specialising in a wide variety of English
and continental dishes.*
Bedrooms: 1 single, 5 double, 5 twin
Bathrooms: 1 en-suite, 2 public

Bed & breakfast

per night:	£min	£max
Single	22.50	28.00
Double	45.00	54.00

Lunch available
Evening meal 1800 (last orders
2200)
Parking for 9
Cards accepted: Access, Visa

🐎♿♨🛇🅿🆅🗄🖵🚗♦⛷🍴🚌

Maypole Inn ⚑

COMMENDED

Maypole Green, Main Street, Long
Preston, Skipton BD23 4PH
☎ Long Preston (01729) 840219 &
840755
*17th C inn, with open fires, on the
village green. Easy access to many
attractive walks in the surrounding
dales. 4 miles from Settle.*
Bedrooms: 1 single, 2 double, 1 twin,
1 triple, 1 family room
Bathrooms: 6 en-suite

Bed & breakfast

per night:	£min	£max
Single	24.00	26.00
Double	35.00	39.00

Lunch available
Evening meal 1830 (last orders
2100)
Parking for 25
Cards accepted: Access, Visa, Diners,
Amex

🐎♿☎⌨🖵♨🛇🅂✂🆃🖵🚗
🍴60♦🍴🗄🚗SP🏠🆃

Whitefriars Country Guest
House ⚑

APPROVED

Church Street, Settle BD24 9JD
☎ (01729) 823753
*Historic family-run guesthouse, set in
spacious gardens, in heart of Settle.
Ideal for exploring the Dales,
Settle-Carlisle Railway. Non-smokers
only, please.*
Bedrooms: 1 single, 3 double, 3 twin,
1 triple, 1 family room
Bathrooms: 3 en-suite, 2 public

Bed & breakfast

per night:	£min	£max
Single	17.00	17.50
Double	34.00	42.00

Half board per

person:	£min	£max
Daily	27.00	31.50
Weekly	167.10	195.30

Evening meal 1900 (last orders
2000)
Parking for 9

🐎♿♨🛇🅂✂🆃🖵🗄🚗✳🍴🚌SP
🏠

*The map references refer
to the colour maps towards
the end of the guide.
The first figure is the
map number; the letter and
figure which follow indicate
the grid reference
on the map.*

SHEFFIELD

South Yorkshire
Map ref 4B2

Local iron ore and coal gave Sheffield its prosperous steel and cutlery industries. The modern city centre has many interesting buildings - cathedral, Cutlers' Hall, Crucible Theatre, Graves and Mappin Art Galleries - and Meadowhall Shopping Centre nearby.
Tourist Information Centre ☎ (0114) 273 4671 or 273 4672

Holme Lane Farm Private Hotel ♔

♕ COMMENDED

38 Halifax Road, Grenoside, Sheffield S30 3PB
☎ (0114) 246 8858
15-acre arable farm. Converted barn and cottage on A61, 3 miles from motorway and Sheffield. Near Meadowhall Shopping Centre and a short run from the Peak District.
Bedrooms: 4 single, 1 double, 2 twin
Bathrooms: 7 en-suite

Bed & breakfast per night:	£min	£max
Single	26.00	26.00
Double	45.00	45.00

Parking for 10
Cards accepted: Access, Visa

SKIPTON

North Yorkshire
Map ref 4B1

Pleasant market town at gateway to dales, with farming community atmosphere.
Tourist Information Centre ☎ (01756) 792809

Ringwood House ♔

Listed COMMENDED

1 Salisbury Street, Skipton BD23 1NQ
☎ (01756) 791135 & 0385 780972
Gateway to the dales. Elegant Victorian, Yorkshire stone town house within easy walking distance of Skipton market place. Warm and friendly hospitality. En-suite facilities available.
Bedrooms: 1 single, 1 double, 1 twin
Bathrooms: 1 en-suite, 2 public

Bed & breakfast per night:	£min	£max
Single	18.00	20.00
Double	32.00	36.00

Parking for 2

SOUTH CAVE

East Riding of Yorkshire
Map ref 4C1

Lying on the famous Ermine Street, the Roman road stretching from Lincoln to York. Located only 3 miles from the River Humber, it is an ideal centre for touring the county of Humberside.

Rudstone Walk Farmhouse & Country Cottages ♔

♕♕ HIGHLY COMMENDED

South Cave, Brough, East Yorkshire HU15 2AH
☎ Howden (01430) 422230
Fax (01430) 424552
303-acre arable farm. Historic farmhouse with converted buildings around attractive courtyard provides lovely, relaxing en-suite accommodation, good food and a warm welcome.
Wheelchair access category 3 ♿
Bedrooms: 7 double, 7 twin
Bathrooms: 14 en-suite, 1 public

Bed & breakfast per night:	£min	£max
Single	35.00	65.00
Double	49.00	75.00

Half board per person:	£min	£max
Daily	50.00	80.00
Weekly	250.00	520.00

Evening meal 1900 (last orders 1600)
Parking for 50
Cards accepted: Access, Visa, Diners, Amex, Switch/Delta

STARBOTTON

North Yorkshire
Map ref 5B3

Quiet, picturesque village midway between Kettlewell and Buckden in Wharfedale. Many buildings belong to the 17th C and several have dated lintels.

Bushey Lodge Farm ♔

♕♕ HIGHLY COMMENDED

Starbotton, Skipton BD23 5HY
☎ Kettlewell (01756) 760424
2000-acre mixed farm. Traditional dales farmhouse in quiet position in Upper Wharfedale village. Extensive views along the valley. Both rooms en-suite, with TV, tea/coffee facilities.
Bedrooms: 1 double, 1 twin
Bathrooms: 2 en-suite

Bed & breakfast per night:	£min	£max
Single	20.00	
Double	40.00	

Parking for 6

SUTTON BANK

North Yorkshire
Map ref 5C3

Escarpment of the Hambleton Hills, 5 miles east of Thirsk. Spectacular views. Gliding from summit.

High House Farm ♔

♕ COMMENDED

Sutton Bank, Thirsk YO7 2HA
☎ Thirsk (01845) 597557
113-acre mixed farm. Family-run, set in open countryside and offering magnificent views. Splendid walking country, ideal for quiet relaxing holiday. Good food and hospitality. East Coast 1 hour, York and North York Moors half an hour.
Bedrooms: 2 triple
Bathrooms: 1 public

Bed & breakfast per night:	£min	£max
Single	17.00	20.00
Double	34.00	40.00

Parking for 2
Open April–October

TERRINGTON

North Yorkshire
Map ref 5C3

In the Howardian Hills, the name of this picturesque village is said to refer in Old English to the practice of sorcery. There is a church and an old rectory now known as Terrington Hall.

Gate Farm ♔

♕ COMMENDED

Ganthorpe, Terrington, York YO6 4QD
☎ Coneysthorpe (01653) 648269
150-acre dairy farm. Stone-built farmhouse offering traditional Yorkshire hospitality in a quiet village near Castle Howard. Convenient for the moors, wolds, the East Coast and York.
Bedrooms: 1 double, 1 twin, 1 family room
Bathrooms: 1 en-suite, 1 public, 1 private shower

(first listing - Bed & breakfast)

Bed & breakfast per night:	£min	£max
Single	15.00	20.00
Double	30.00	40.00

Half board per person:	£min	£max
Daily	25.00	

Evening meal 1830 (last orders 1600)
Parking for 3
Open March–October

🛇🗄🖳♿🍽�ⓊⓁ🅢📺🗄🛄⚓U
🎵✳🚗

THIRSK

North Yorkshire
Map ref 5C3

Thriving market town with cobbled square surrounded by old shops and inns and also with a local museum. St Mary's Church is probably the best example of Perpendicular work in Yorkshire.

Angel Inn 🅰

👑👑👑 COMMENDED

Long Street, Topcliffe, Thirsk
YO7 3RW
☎ (01845) 577237
Fax (01845) 578000
Well-appointed, attractive village inn, renowned for good food and traditional ales. Ideal centre for touring York and Herriot country.
Bedrooms: 2 single, 8 double, 4 twin, 1 family room
Bathrooms: 15 en-suite

Bed & breakfast per night:	£min	£max
Single	35.00	39.50
Double	50.00	55.00

Half board per person:	£min	£max
Daily	37.50	52.50

Lunch available
Evening meal 1830 (last orders 2130)
Parking for 150
Cards accepted: Access, Visa, Switch/Delta

🛇2☎🗄🖳♿🍽🅢📺📺🗄🛄
🍽150♦🎵✳✈🚗 SP T

Ashton House

👑👑 HIGHLY COMMENDED

166 Front Street, Sowerby, Thirsk
YO7 1JN
☎ (01845) 526803
Fax (01845) 524915
Superb centre for touring Yorkshire's moors and dales. Home cooking, pleasant ambience in a comfortable house beside the village green.
Bedrooms: 3 double
Bathrooms: 1 en-suite, 1 private

(second listing - Bed & breakfast)

Bed & breakfast per night:	£min	£max
Single	16.50	18.50
Double	33.00	37.00

Parking for 4

🛇👑5🖳♿🍽ⓊⓁ🅢📺📺🗄🛄⚓
U🎵✳🚗🏮

Doxford House 🅰

👑👑 APPROVED

Front Street, Sowerby, Thirsk
YO7 1JP
☎ (01845) 523238
Handsome, Georgian house with attractive garden, overlooking greens of Sowerby. Comfortable rooms, all en-suite. Ideal centre for touring moors and dales.
Wheelchair access category 3🡇
Bedrooms: 1 double, 1 twin, 2 triple
Bathrooms: 4 en-suite

Bed & breakfast per night:	£min	£max
Single	21.00	22.00
Double	32.00	34.00

Half board per person:	£min	£max
Daily	24.00	25.00

Evening meal from 1830
Parking for 4

🛇👑🗄🖳♿ⓊⓁ🅢📺📺🗄🛄⚓✳
🚗🏮

Highfield House 🅰

👑👑 HIGHLY COMMENDED

Asenby, Thirsk YO7 3QT
☎ (01845) 577857 & Mobile 0836 729702
Fax (01845) 577857
Secluded, listed Georgian house with gardens on the River Swale. Situated in a peaceful village setting, in the heart of "Herriot Country" 5 miles south-west of Thirsk. Private fishing.
Bedrooms: 1 single, 1 double, 1 twin
Bathrooms: 1 en-suite, 2 public

Bed & breakfast per night:	£min	£max
Single	20.00	26.00
Double	36.00	40.00

Half board per person:	£min	£max
Daily	28.00	36.00
Weekly	168.00	216.00

Evening meal 1900 (last orders 2000)
Parking for 8

🛇10🗄🖳♿🍽ⓊⓁ🅢📺📺🗄
🛄U🎵✳✈🚗 SP 🏮 T ◎

Map references apply to the colour maps at the back of this guide.

Lord Nelson Inn 🅰

Listed COMMENDED

40 St James Green, Thirsk
YO7 1AQ
☎ (01845) 522845
Fax (018450) 522845
Family-run freehouse overlooking St James' Green. Traditional ales and meals, 2 bars, function room and large garden.
Bedrooms: 1 double, 2 twin
Bathrooms: 1 public

Bed & breakfast per night:	£min	£max
Double		35.00

Lunch available
Evening meal 1900 (last orders 2000)
Parking for 20
Cards accepted: Access, Visa, Switch/Delta

🛇🗄🖳♿🅢🛄⚓🍽60♦🎵🕭
✳✈🚗

Plump Bank 🅰

👑👑 COMMENDED

Felixkirk Road, Thirsk YO7 2EW
☎ (01845) 522406
From Thirsk take the A170 Scarborough road. After 1 mile turn left for Felixkirk and Boltby and house is on the left after 100 yards.
Bedrooms: 1 double, 1 twin
Bathrooms: 2 en-suite

Bed & breakfast per night:	£min	£max
Double	32.00	36.00

Parking for 9
Open June–September

🖳♿ⓊⓁ📺🛄⚓U✈🚗

Thornborough House Farm

👑👑 COMMENDED

South Kilvington, Thirsk YO7 2NP
☎ (01845) 522103
Fax (01845) 522103
28-acre mixed farm. 200-year-old farmhouse in an ideal position for walking and touring in the North York Moors and Yorkshire Dales.
Bedrooms: 1 double, 1 twin, 1 family room
Bathrooms: 2 en-suite, 1 private

Bed & breakfast per night:	£min	£max
Single	14.00	18.00
Double	28.00	36.00

Half board per person:	£min	£max
Daily	22.50	27.50
Weekly	140.00	170.00

Evening meal from 1830
Parking for 6
Cards accepted: Access, Visa

🛇🗄🖳♿🍽ⓊⓁ🅢📺📺🗄🛄⚓
✳🚗 DAP 🐕 SP ◎

THIRSK

Continued

Town Pasture Farm

COMMENDED

Boltby, Thirsk YO7 2DY
☎ (01845) 537298
180-acre mixed farm. Farmhouse with views of the Hambleton Hills, in picturesque Boltby village within the boundary of the North York Moors National Park.
Bedrooms: 1 twin, 1 triple
Bathrooms: 2 en-suite
Bed & breakfast

per night:	£min	£max
Single	15.00	
Double	30.00	

Half board per person:	£min	£max
Daily	23.50	

Parking for 4

THORNTON WATLASS

North Yorkshire
Map ref 5C3

Picturesque village in Lower Wensleydale.

The Buck Inn

COMMENDED

Thornton Watlass, Ripon HG4 4AH
☎ Bedale (01677) 422461
Friendly village inn overlooking the delightful cricket green in a small village, 3 miles from Bedale on the Masham road, and close to the A1. Ideal centre for exploring both the dales and North York Moors.
Bedrooms: 1 single, 3 double, 2 twin, 1 triple
Bathrooms: 5 en-suite, 1 public
Bed & breakfast

per night:	£min	£max
Single	32.00	
Double	50.00	

Lunch available
Evening meal 1830 (last orders 2130)
Parking for 40
Cards accepted: Access, Visa, Diners, Amex

The National Grading and Classification Scheme is explained in full at the back of this guide.

TODMORDEN

West Yorkshire
Map ref 4B1

In beautiful scenery on the edge of the Pennines at junction of 3 sweeping valleys. Until 1888 the county boundary between Yorkshire and Lancashire cut this old cotton town in half, running through the middle of the Town Hall.
Tourist Information Centre ☎ (01706) 818181

Cherry Tree Cottage

COMMENDED

Woodhouse Road, Todmorden, Lancashire OL14 5RJ
☎ (01706) 817492
Sympathetically restored, part 17th C country cottage with modern amenities and lovely views. Emphasis on friendly atmosphere and fresh, home-cooked fare.
Bedrooms: 2 twin
Bathrooms: 1 en-suite, 1 private
Bed & breakfast

per night:	£min	£max
Single	16.50	23.00
Double	33.00	38.00

Half board per person:	£min	£max
Daily	23.50	30.00
Weekly	164.50	210.00

Evening meal 1800 (last orders 1900)
Parking for 2

UPPER CUMBERWORTH

West Yorkshire
Map ref 4B1

Lower Janewell Farm

7 Barnsley Road, Upper Cumberworth, Huddersfield HD8 8XG
☎ Huddersfield (01484) 606381
Dating from the early 18th C, the establishment is a beautifully renovated weaving mill with stunning views.
Bedrooms: 1 double
Suite available
Bathrooms: 1 private
Bed & breakfast

per night:	£min	£max
Single	27.00	35.00
Double	54.00	70.00

Parking for 4

WAKEFIELD

West Yorkshire
Map ref 4B1

Thriving city with cathedral church of All Saints boasting 247-ft spire. Old Bridge, a 9-arched structure, has fine medieval chantry chapels of St Mary's. Fine Georgian architecture and good shopping centre (The Ridings). National Coal Mining Museum for England nearby.
Tourist Information Centre ☎ (01924) 305000 or 305001

The Poplars

APPROVED

Bradford Road, Wrenthorpe, Wakefield WF2 0QL
☎ (01924) 375682
Tastefully restored, 200-year-old house with open beams. Country location close to Wakefield (A650), M1 exit 41 and M62 exit 29.
Bedrooms: 1 single, 3 twin
Bathrooms: 2 en-suite, 1 public
Bed & breakfast

per night:	£min	£max
Single	32.00	
Double	40.00	

Parking for 6
Cards accepted: Access, Visa

WESTOW

North Yorkshire
Map ref 5C3

The grey walls and red roofs of Westow are on a slope of the Derwent's wooded valley. The Hall, where the Idle family had their seat, stands at a corner of the village by the wayside and the solitary church stands in fields outside.

Blacksmiths Arms Inn

COMMENDED

Westow, York YO6 7NE
☎ Malton (01653) 618365 & 618343
Inn of character. Family-run establishment with very good facilities. All welcome.
Wheelchair access category 3
Bedrooms: 2 single, 2 double, 2 twin
Bathrooms: 6 en-suite
Bed & breakfast

per night:	£min	£max
Single	21.00	23.50
Double	42.00	47.00

Lunch available
Parking for 12

Woodhouse Farm

Listed **APPROVED**

Westow, York YO6 7LL
☎ Whitwell on the Hill (01653)
618378

*300-acre mixed farm. Traditional 18th
C listed farmhouse with log fires. Range
of farm buildings, pond, orchard,
garden. Animals include sheep, poultry,
goats, dogs and cats.*
Bedrooms: 1 double, 1 family room
Bathrooms: 1 en-suite, 1 public

**Bed & breakfast
per night:**

	£min	£max
Single	15.00	17.50
Double	30.00	35.00

**Half board per
person:**

	£min	£max
Daily	25.00	27.50
Weekly	150.00	170.00

Evening meal 1830 (last orders
2030)
Parking for 12
Open April–October

🛇🐾⬛🛅📞🖵👜🏧🕸💲⌀🔌📺📖🌀🚪
🛁🌸🏇🖼🏧

Map ref 4C1

Ancient walled city nearly 2000
years old containing many
well-preserved medieval buildings.
Its Minster has over 100 stained
glass windows. Attractions include
Castle Museum, National Railway
Museum, Jorvik Viking Centre and
York Dungeon.
*Tourist Information Centre ☎ (01904)
621756 or 621756 or 620557*

The Acer ⚠

52 Scarcroft Hill, The Mount, York
YO2 1DE
☎ (01904) 653839 & 637613
Fax (01904) 637613
*Small Victorian hotel in a quiet
residential area adjoining the
Knavesmire and racecourse. Half a
mile from the city centre.*
Bedrooms: 3 double, 2 twin, 1 triple
Bathrooms: 1 en-suite, 5 private

**Bed & breakfast
per night:**

	£min	£max
Single	25.00	
Double	44.00	54.00

**Half board per
person:**

	£min	£max
Daily	32.50	37.50

Lunch available
Evening meal 1800 (last orders
2000)
Parking for 4
Cards accepted: Access, Visa, Amex

🛇🐾⬛🛅🍴📞🖵👜🏧🛅💲🖼🏧🏧🚪DAP
🕸SP🏇

Arndale Hotel ⚠

👑👑👑 HIGHLY COMMENDED

290 Tadcaster Road, York YO2 2ET
☎ (01904) 702424

*Delightful Victorian house, directly
overlooking racecourse. Beautiful
enclosed walled gardens giving a
country atmosphere within the city.
Antiques, fresh flowers, four-poster
beds, whirlpool baths. Enclosed gated
car park.*
Bedrooms: 7 double, 2 twin, 1 triple
Bathrooms: 10 en-suite

**Bed & breakfast
per night:**

	£min	£max
Single	35.00	45.00
Double	45.00	59.00

Parking for 20

🛇🐾8🛅🖼🖵🖵🖵👜🏧🏧🖼🚪🌸🏇
🏇SP🖂T

Beech House ⚠

👑👑👑

6-7 Longfield Terrace, Bootham,
York YO3 7DJ
☎ (01904) 634581
*Small, family-run guesthouse with a
warm welcome and a relaxing
atmosphere, only 5 minutes' walk from
York Minster.*
Bedrooms: 1 single, 5 double, 2 twin
Bathrooms: 8 en-suite

**Bed & breakfast
per night:**

	£min	£max
Single	21.00	30.00
Double	38.00	46.00

Evening meal from 1800
Parking for 5

🛇🐾10📞🖂🖵🖵👜🏧🏧🛅💲🖼🏧🚪🏇
🏇SP🖂T🔘

Bloomsbury Hotel ⚠

127 Clifton, York YO3 6BL
☎ (01904) 634031
*An elegantly appointed large Victorian
town house, centrally situated with
large private car park. Recently totally
refurbished. Completely non-smoking.*
Bedrooms: 2 single, 8 double, 4 twin,
4 triple
Bathrooms: 18 en-suite

**Bed & breakfast
per night:**

	£min	£max
Single	36.00	50.00
Double	45.00	65.00

Parking for 8
Cards accepted: Access, Visa,
Switch/Delta

🛇🐾🖵🖵👜🏧🏧🛅💲🖼🏧🚪📺📖🚪
📍12🚪🐾🏇DAP SP

Bowen House ⚠

👑👑

4 Gladstone Street, Huntington
Road, York YO3 7RF
☎ (01904) 636881
*Within a short walk of York Minster
and city centre, this late Victorian,
family-run guesthouse combines high
quality facilities with old-style charm.
Private car park. Traditional or
vegetarian breakfasts. Non-smoking
throughout.*
Bedrooms: 1 single, 2 double, 1 twin,
1 family room
Bathrooms: 3 en-suite, 1 public,
1 private shower

**Bed & breakfast
per night:**

	£min	£max
Single	20.00	23.00
Double	32.00	45.00

Parking for 4
Cards accepted: Access, Visa

🛇🐾🖵🖵👜🏧🏧🛅💲🖼🏧🚪📺📖🚪
🏇DAP SP🏇T

Burton Villa ⚠

Listed **COMMENDED**

22 Haxby Road, York YO3 7JX
☎ (01904) 626364

*Noted for friendly atmosphere, good
breakfasts and high standards. 7
minutes' walk from York Minster.
Private parking.*
Bedrooms: 1 single, 6 double, 2 twin,
1 triple, 2 family rooms
Bathrooms: 8 en-suite, 1 public

**Bed & breakfast
per night:**

	£min	£max
Single	16.00	22.50
Double	30.00	48.00

Parking for 7
Cards accepted: Access, Visa,
Switch/Delta

🛇🐾🖵🖵👜🏧🏧🛅💲🖼🏧🚪🚪SP🖂T
🔘

City Guest House ⚠

👑

68 Monkgate, York YO3 7PF
☎ (01904) 622483
*Small, friendly, family-run B & B in
attractive Victorian town-house. Ideally*

Continued ▶

YORK
Continued

situated 5 minutes' walk to York
Minster and close to attractions. Private
parking. Cosy en-suite rooms.
Restaurants nearby. Non-smoking.
Bedrooms: 2 single, 3 double, 1 twin,
1 family room
Bathrooms: 5 en-suite, 2 private
showers

Bed & breakfast

per night:	£min	£max
Single	14.00	20.00
Double	28.00	44.00

Parking for 4
Cards accepted: Access, Visa

Cook's Guest House ♙

👑 COMMENDED

120 Bishopthorpe Road, York
YO2 1JX
☎ (01904) 652519
Featured on TV's "This Morning", small,
friendly and comfortable guesthouse
with unique decor. 10 minutes' walk to
city, railway station and racecourse.
Bedrooms: 1 double, 1 triple
Bathrooms: 1 public

Bed & breakfast

per night:	£min	£max
Single	18.00	20.00
Double	26.00	32.00

Cumbria House ♙

Listed COMMENDED

2 Vyner Street, Haxby Road, York
YO3 7HS
☎ (01904) 636817
Family-run guesthouse, 12 minutes'
walk from York Minster. En-suites
available. Easily located from ring road.
Private car park. Brochure.
Bedrooms: 1 single, 1 double, 1 twin,
1 triple, 1 family room
Bathrooms: 2 en-suite, 2 public

Bed & breakfast

per night:	£min	£max
Single	16.00	20.00
Double	30.00	40.00

Parking for 5

Curzon Lodge and Stable Cottages ♙

👑👑 HIGHLY COMMENDED

23 Tadcaster Road, Dringhouses,
York YO2 2QG
☎ (01904) 703157

Delightful 17th C listed house and
former stables in pretty conservation
area overlooking York racecourse, once
a home of the Terry "chocolate" family.
All en-suite, some four-posters. Many
antiques. Large enclosed car park.
Bedrooms: 1 single, 4 double, 3 twin,
1 triple, 1 family room
Bathrooms: 10 en-suite

Bed & breakfast

per night:	£min	£max
Single	30.00	40.00
Double	45.00	60.00

Parking for 16
Cards accepted: Access, Visa

Fairthorne ♙

👑 COMMENDED

356 Strensall Road, Earswick, York
YO3 9SW
☎ (01904) 768609
Fax (01904) 768609
Detached dormer bungalow with
spacious gardens. Four miles from York
city centre.
Bedrooms: 1 double, 1 triple
Bathrooms: 2 en-suite

Bed & breakfast

per night:	£min	£max
Single	18.00	
Double	30.00	

Parking for 6

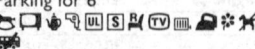

Foss Bank Guest House

👑👑 APPROVED

16 Huntington Road, York YO3 7RB
☎ (01904) 635548
Small Victorian family-run guesthouse,
comfortable and friendly, on the
north-east side of the city. 5 minutes'
walk from the city wall.
Bedrooms: 2 single, 3 double, 1 twin
Bathrooms: 2 en-suite, 4 private
showers

Bed & breakfast

per night:	£min	£max
Single	16.00	18.00
Double	32.00	38.00

Parking for 5
Open February–December

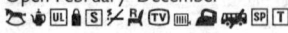

Four Seasons Hotel ♙

👑👑 COMMENDED

7 St Peter's Grove, Bootham, York
YO3 6AQ
☎ (01904) 622621
Fax (01904) 620976

Beautiful, high-quality Victorian hotel, in
quiet tree-lined grove. Only 5 minutes'
walk from city centre. All rooms
en-suite. Private car park.
Bedrooms: 2 double, 1 twin, 1 triple,
1 family room
Bathrooms: 5 en-suite

Bed & breakfast

per night:	£min	£max
Double	44.00	56.00

Parking for 8
Cards accepted: Access, Visa

Fourposter Lodge Hotel

👑👑 COMMENDED

68-70 Heslington Road, Barbican
Road, York YO1 5AU
☎ (01904) 651170

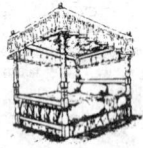

Victorian villa, lovingly restored and
furnished for your comfort. Just 10
minutes' walk from historic York with
all its fascinations.
Bedrooms: 8 double, 1 twin, 1 triple
Bathrooms: 10 en-suite

Bed & breakfast

per night:	£min	£max
Single	35.00	38.00
Double	50.00	54.00

Half board per person:	£min	£max
Daily	37.50	39.50

Evening meal 1830 (last orders
2000)
Parking for 8
Cards accepted: Access, Visa, Amex

Hillcrest Guest House ♙

👑👑 COMMENDED

110 Bishopthorpe Road, York
YO2 1JX
☎ (01904) 653160
Elegant Victorian town house, 10

minutes' walk from city centre. Private car park. Generous breakfast selection. Special diets catered for. Easy access to ring roads.

Bedrooms: 3 single, 5 double, 2 twin, 1 triple, 2 family rooms
Bathrooms: 7 en-suite, 3 public

Bed & breakfast

per night:	£min	£max
Single	14.00	19.00
Double	26.00	40.00

Half board per

person:	£min	£max
Daily	22.50	27.50
Weekly	241.50	339.50

Evening meal 1800 (last orders 1500)
Parking for 8
Cards accepted: Access, Visa

Holly Lodge

⚜️ APPROVED

206 Fulford Road, York YO1 4DD
☎ (01904) 646005
Listed Georgian building on the A19, convenient for both the north and south and within walking distance of the city centre. Close to university, golf course and Barbican centre. Quiet rooms and private car park.
Bedrooms: 3 double, 1 twin, 1 family room
Bathrooms: 5 en-suite

Bed & breakfast

per night:	£min	£max
Single	20.00	30.00
Double	30.00	50.00

Parking for 5
Cards accepted: Access, Visa

Holme Lea Manor Guest House

⚜️⚜️

18 St Peter's Grove, Bootham, York YO3 6AQ
☎ (01904) 623529
Elegant Victorian house, providing spacious accommodation with a nice garden. An easy walk away from York city centre. Family-managed. French, Spanish and Italian are spoken.
Bedrooms: 6 double, 2 twin
Bathrooms: 8 en-suite

Bed & breakfast

per night:	£min	£max
Single	25.00	25.00
Double	40.00	50.00

Parking for 8
Cards accepted: Access, Visa

Jacobean Lodge Hotel

⚜️⚜️⚜️ COMMENDED

Plainville Lane, Wigginton, York YO3 8RG
☎ (01904) 768403
Fax (01904) 768403

Converted 17th C farmhouse, 4 miles north of York. Set in picturesque gardens with ample parking. Open log fire, warm, friendly atmosphere and traditional cuisine.
Bedrooms: 2 single, 9 double, 1 twin, 2 triple
Bathrooms: 14 en-suite

Bed & breakfast

per night:	£min	£max
Single	28.00	34.00
Double	40.00	56.00

Lunch available
Evening meal 1900 (last orders 2200)
Parking for 70
Cards accepted: Access, Visa, Switch/Delta

The Lodge

⚜️⚜️ COMMENDED

302 Strensall Road, Old Earswick, York YO3 9SW
☎ (01904) 761387

Modern family house in its own grounds. Large comfortable rooms. No smoking establishment. Easy access to York. Real Yorkshire hospitality. Bargain winter breaks.
Bedrooms: 1 single, 1 double, 1 triple
Bathrooms: 2 en-suite, 1 public

Bed & breakfast

per night:	£min	£max
Single	17.00	23.00
Double	32.00	34.00

Parking for 3

Midway House Hotel

⚜️⚜️⚜️ COMMENDED

145 Fulford Road, York YO1 4HG
☎ (01904) 659272
Fax (01904) 621799
Non-smoking, family-run hotel. Spacious en-suite bedrooms with four-poster and ground floor rooms available. Close to city centre and university. Private parking.
Bedrooms: 7 double, 3 twin, 2 triple
Bathrooms: 11 en-suite, 1 private, 1 public

Bed & breakfast

per night:	£min	£max
Single	20.00	40.00
Double	36.00	50.00

Evening meal 1900 (last orders 1900)
Parking for 14
Cards accepted: Access, Visa, Diners, Amex

Newton Guest House

⚜️ APPROVED

Neville Street, Haxby Road, York YO3 7NP
☎ (01904) 635627
Family-run, friendly guesthouse, a few minutes' walk from city centre. Private car park. Non-smoking. Breakfast menu. Your comfort is first priority.
Bedrooms: 1 single, 2 double, 1 twin, 1 triple
Bathrooms: 4 en-suite, 1 private

Bed & breakfast

per night:	£min	£max
Single	18.00	20.00
Double	30.00	36.00

Parking for 5
Cards accepted: Access, Visa

Northolme Guest House

Listed APPROVED

114 Shipton Road, Rawcliffe, York YO3 6RN
☎ (01904) 639132

Detached house with private car park. Garden to front and rear. The establishment has 5 bedrooms, 3 are en-suite and 2 are standard. Situated 1.5 miles from the city centre in a semi-rural setting.
Bedrooms: 1 single, 2 double, 1 twin, 1 triple

Continued ▶

YORK
Continued

Bathrooms: 3 en-suite, 1 public

Bed & breakfast

per night:	£min	£max
Single	15.00	20.00
Double	28.00	36.00

Parking for 6

Oaklands Guest House M

COMMENDED

351 Strensall Road, Old Earswick,
York YO3 9SW
☎ (01904) 768443
*Friendly, well-furnished house, 3 miles
from the city and within easy reach of
the A64 and A1237.*
Bedrooms: 1 double, 1 twin, 1 triple
Bathrooms: 1 en-suite, 1 public

Bed & breakfast

per night:	£min	£max
Single	17.00	22.00
Double	32.00	38.00

Parking for 7

Orillia House M

89 The Village,
Stockton-on-the-Forest, York
YO3 9UP
☎ (01904) 400600 & Mobile 0850
108181

*A warm welcome awaits you in this
300-year-old house of charm and
character, opposite church. Three miles
north east of York.*
Bedrooms: 2 double, 1 twin, 2 triple
Bathrooms: 5 en-suite

Bed & breakfast

per night:	£min	£max
Single	22.00	25.00
Double	36.00	40.00

Parking for 10
Cards accepted: Access, Visa

Papillon Hotel M

Listed

43 Gillygate, York YO3 7EA
☎ (01904) 636505
*Small, friendly city centre guesthouse
with personal attention at all times.
300 yards from York Minster. En-suite*

---

*available. No smoking, please. Car
parking. Phone for details.*
Bedrooms: 2 single, 1 double, 2 twin,
3 triple
Bathrooms: 3 en-suite, 2 public

Bed & breakfast

per night:	£min	£max
Single	20.00	25.00
Double	35.00	50.00

Parking for 7

---

23 St Marys M

HIGHLY COMMENDED

Bootham, York YO3 7DD
☎ (01904) 622738
*Situated near the city in a quiet
location. Individually styled bedrooms
with embroidered linen re-creating
elegance and comfort of a bygone era.*
Bedrooms: 2 single, 6 double,
1 triple
Bathrooms: 9 en-suite

Bed & breakfast

per night:	£min	£max
Single	30.00	34.00
Double	50.00	66.00

Parking for 3

Southlands Bed & Breakfast M

COMMENDED

Huntington Road, Huntington, York
YO3 9PX
☎ (01904) 766796
Fax (01904) 764536
*Southlands stands in its own attractive
gardens in the village of Huntington,
only 1.8 miles from York city centre.*
Bedrooms: 2 double, 1 twin
Bathrooms: 3 en-suite

Bed & breakfast

per night:	£min	£max
Single	24.00	25.00
Double	32.00	38.00

Parking for 4

Stanley Guest House M

COMMENDED

Stanley Street, Haxby Road, York
YO3 7NW
☎ (01904) 637111
*Friendly, comfortable guesthouse, 10
minutes' walk to York Minster and city
and close to many attractions. All
rooms en-suite. No smoking. Warm
welcome assured.*
Bedrooms: 2 single, 2 double, 1 twin,
1 triple
Bathrooms: 6 en-suite

Bed & breakfast

per night:	£min	£max
Single	20.00	22.50
Double	35.00	40.00

Parking for 5
Cards accepted: Access, Visa

Tower Guest House M

COMMENDED

2 Feversham Crescent, Wigginton
Road, York YO3 7HQ
☎ (01904) 655571 & 635924
*Comfortable and spacious 19th C
guesthouse with friendly, informative
hosts. Strolling distance from York
Minster and city centre attractions.*
Bedrooms: 2 double, 1 twin, 2 triple
Bathrooms: 5 en-suite

Bed & breakfast

per night:	£min	£max
Single	18.00	25.00
Double	35.00	40.00

Parking for 5
Cards accepted: Access, Visa

Victoria Villa

Listed **APPROVED**

72 Heslington Road, York YO1 5AU
☎ (01904) 631647
*Victorian town house, close to city
centre. Offering clean and friendly
accommodation and a full English
breakfast.*
Bedrooms: 1 single, 2 double, 1 twin,
2 triple
Bathrooms: 2 public

Bed & breakfast

per night:	£min	£max
Single	16.00	20.00
Double	28.00	34.00

Parking for 4

Warrens Guest House M

COMMENDED

30 Scarcroft Road, York YO2 1NF
☎ (01904) 643139
*Centrally situated guesthouse. All rooms
en-suite with colour TV and
tea/coffee-making facilities. Full English
breakfast. Four-poster beds available,
also some ground-floor bedrooms. Car
park.*
Bedrooms: 1 single, 1 double, 2 twin,
1 triple, 1 family room
Bathrooms: 5 en-suite, 1 private

Bed & breakfast

per night:	£min	£max
Single	25.00	30.00
Double	35.00	42.00

Parking for 8
Open February–November

[symbols]

Wellgarth House

⬥⬥ **COMMENDED**

Wetherby Road, Rufforth, York
YO2 3QB
☎ Rufforth (01904) 738592 &
738595
Fax (01904) 738595
*Individual and attractive country
guesthouse in the delightful village of
Rufforth. Ideal touring base for York
and the Yorkshire Dales.*
Bedrooms: 1 single, 3 double, 2 twin,
1 triple
Bathrooms: 6 en-suite, 1 public
**Bed & breakfast
per night:** £min £max

	£min	£max
Single	18.00	25.00
Double	32.00	44.00

Parking for 10
Cards accepted: Access, Visa

York Lodge Guest House

Listed

64 Bootham Crescent, Bootham,
York YO3 7AH
☎ (01904) 654289
*Family-run guesthouse, within 10
minutes' walk of city centre attractions,
offering a warm, friendly and relaxing
stay.*
Bedrooms: 1 single, 3 double, 2 twin,
2 triple
Bathrooms: 4 en-suite, 2 public
**Bed & breakfast
per night:**

	£min	£max
Single	14.50	16.00
Double	30.00	38.00

Parking for 3
Cards accepted: Access, Visa

AT-A-GLANCE SYMBOLS

Symbols at the end of each accommodation entry
give useful information about services
and facilities. A key to symbols can be found
inside the back cover flap.

[symbols]

Keep this open for easy reference.

ENQUIRY COUPONS

To help you obtain further information
about advertisers and accommodation featured in
this guide you will find enquiry coupons at the back.
Send these directly to the establishments
in which you are interested.
Remember to complete both sides of the coupon.

USE YOUR *i*'s

There are more than 550 Tourist Information Centres throughout England offering friendly help with accommodation and holiday ideas as well as suggestions of places to visit and things to do. There may well be a centre in your home town which can help you before you set out. You'll find the address of your nearest Tourist Information Centre in your local Phone Book.

CHECK THE MAPS

The colour maps at the back of this guide show all the cities, towns and villages for which you will find accommodation entries.

Refer to the town index to find the page on which it is listed.

COUNTRY CODE

Always follow the Country Code ✿ Enjoy the countryside and respect its life and work ✿ Guard against all risk of fire ✿ Fasten all gates ✿ Keep your dogs under close control ✿ Keep to public paths across farmland ✿ Use gates and stiles to cross fences, hedges and walls ✿ Leave livestock, crops and machinery alone ✿ Take your litter home ✿ Help to keep all water clean ✿ Protect wildlife, plants and trees ✿ Take special care on country roads ✿ Make no unnecessary noise

HEART OF ENGLAND

The heart of England is a pot pourri of rural charm and urban vitality. From the spa town of Cheltenham to the busy streets of Birmingham, from the remote grandeur of the Western Marches to the gentle beauty of tiny Cotswold villages, the area will appeal to culture buffs and country lovers alike.

Visit Shakespeare country and Stratford with its world-famous theatre. Discover the craftsmanship of the Potteries and explore the rich industrial heritage of the Black Country. Or simply escape to the Staffordshire peaks, the Malvern Hills, or the gently meandering byways of the Severn Valley.

FOR MORE INFORMATION CONTACT:
Heart of England Tourist Board
Lark Hill Road, Worcester WR5 2EZ
Tel: (01905) 763436 or 763439
Fax: (01905) 763450

Where to Go in the Heart of England -
see pages 128-131
Where to Stay in the Heart of England -
see pages 132-190

HEART OF ENGLAND

Where to Go and What to See

You will find hundreds of interesting places to visit during your stay in the Heart of England, just some of which are listed in these pages. The number against each name will help you locate it on the map (page 131). Contact any Tourist Information Centre in the region for more ideas on days out in the Heart of England.

1 Spode
Spode Works, Church Street,
Stoke-on-Trent,
Staffordshire ST4 1BX
Tel: (01782) 744220
Visitors are shown the various processes in the making of Bone China. Samples can be bought at the Spode Shop.

2 Wedgwood Visitor Centre
Barlaston, Stoke-on-Trent,
Staffordshire ST12 9ES
Tel: (01782) 204141
Located in the Wedgwood Factory which lies within a 500 acre country estate. See potters and decorators at work. Museum and shop.

3 Alton Towers Theme Park
Alton, Staffordshire ST10 4DB
Tel: (0990) 204060
Theme Park with over 125 rides and attractions including Nemesis, Haunted House, Runaway Mine Train, Congo River Rapids, Log Flume, Thunderlooper and Toyland tours.

4 Shugborough Estate
Shugborough, Milford, Stafford,
Staffordshire ST17 0XB
Tel: (01889) 881388
18thC mansion house with fine collection of furniture. Gardens and park contain beautiful neo-classical monuments.

5 The Shrewsbury Quest
193 Abbey Foregate,
Shrewsbury,
Shropshire SY2 6AH
Tel: (01743) 243324
12thC Shrewsbury historical site. Visitors are invited to solve three mysteries, creating manuscripts and playing medieval garden games.

6 Ironbridge Gorge Museum
Ironbridge, Telford,
Shropshire TF8 7AW
Tel: (01952) 433522
Worlds first cast iron bridge, Museum of the River Visitor Centre, Tar Tunnel, Jackfield Tile Museum, Coalport China Museum, Rosehill

House, Blists Hill Museum and Museum of Iron.

7 Walsall Arboretum
Lichfield Street,
Walsall, West Midlands
Tel: (01922) 653141
Picturesque Victorian park with over 79 acres of gardens, lakes and parkland, just 5 minutes walk from Walsall town centre. The arboretum is home to the Walsall illuminations.

8 Black Country Museum
Tipton Road, Dudley,
West Midlands DY1 4SQ
Tel: (0121) 557 9643
Midlands open air museum with shops, chapel, canal trip into limestone cavern houses, underground mining display and electric tramway.

9 Birmingham Botanical Gardens and Glasshouses
Westbourne Road,
Edgbaston, Birmingham,

West Midlands B15 3TR
Tel: (0121) 454 1860
Fifteen acres of ornamental gardens and glasshouses. Tropical plants of botanical interest. Aviaries with exotic birds and children's play area.

10 National Sea Life Centre
The Water's Edge, Brindleyplace,
Birmingham B1 2HL
Tel: (0121) 633 4700
Over 55 fascinating displays. The opportunity to come face-to-face with literally 100's of fascinating sea creatures from sharks to shrimps.

11 Cadbury World
Linden Road, Bournville,
Birmingham,
West Midlands B30 2LD
Tel: (0121) 451 4180
Story of Chocolate from Aztec times to present day includes chocolate-making demonstration and children's fantasy factory.

12 National Motorcycle Museum
Coventry Road, Bickenhill,
Solihull, West Midlands B92 0EJ
Tel: (01675) 443311
Museum with a collection of 650 British machines from 1898-1993, housed in a new high architectural standard building.

13 Museum of British Road Transport
St Agnes Lane,
Hales Street, Coventry,
West Midlands CV1 1NN
Tel: (01203) 832425
Museum with a collection of over 400 cars, commercial vehicles, cycles and motorcycles from 1818 to present day.

14 Rugby School Museum
10 Little Church Street,
Rugby, Warwickshire CV21 3AW
Tel: (01788) 574117
Tells the story of the School, scene of Tom Brown's Schooldays, and contains early memorabilia of the game of rugby invented on the School Close.

15 Severn Valley Railway
The Railway Station, Bewdley,
Worcestershire DY12 1BG
Tel: (01299) 403816
Preserved standard gauge steam railway running 16 miles between Kidderminster, Bewdley and Bridgnorth. Collection of locomotives and passenger coaches.

16 Warwick Castle
Warwick,
Warwickshire CV34 4QU
Tel: (01926) 406600
Set in 60 acres of grounds with state rooms, armoury, dungeon,

torture chamber, clock tower. Exhibits include a Royal Weekend Party 1898, a preparation for battle scene and Kingmaker Feasts.

17 Ragley Hall
Alcester,
Warwickshire B49 5NJ
Tel: (01789) 762090
17thC Palladian House, home of the Earl and Countess of Yarmouth, restored with French furnishing. Also 3D maze, woodland walk and lakeside picnic area.

18 Heritage Motor Centre
Banbury Road,
Gaydon,
Warwick,
Warwickshire CV35 0BJ
Tel: (01926) 641188
Purpose-built transport museum containing collection of historic British cars. 63 acre site including 4 wheel drive circuit, playground, picnic area and nature reserve.

19 Elgar's Birthplace Museum
Crown East Lane,
Lower Broadheath,
Worcester,
Worcestershire WR2 6RH
Tel: (01905) 333224
The cottage in which Edward Elgar was born, now houses a museum of photographs, musical scores, letters and records.

20 Shakespeare's Birthplace

Henley Street,
Stratford-upon-Avon
Warwickshire CV37 6QW
Tel: (01789) 204016
Evoking the busy market town into which he was born, the exhibition covers Shakespeare's home background, schooling, marriage and theatre career in London.

21 Worcester Cathedral

10A College Green
Worcester, WR1 2LH
Tel: (01905) 611002
Norman crypt and chapter house. King John's Tomb. Prince Arthur's Chantry, medieval cloisters and buildings.

22 Malvern Hills Children's Zoo

Solitaire, Danemoor Cross,
Welland, Malvern,
Worcestershire WR13 6NJ
Tel: (01684) 310016
Tropical animals, pets corner and creepy-crawly house. Visitors can handle the animals, reptiles and see snake demonstrations daily.

23 The New Mappa Mundi & Chained Library Museum

Hereford Cathedral,
5 The Cloister, Hereford,
Herefordshire HR1 2NG
Tel: (01432) 359880
The New Library of Hereford Cathedral is open to visitors. See also the unique Mappa Mundi, the largest and most complete map in the world, drawn in 1289.

24 The National Birds of Prey Centre

Newent, Gloucestershire GL18 1JJ
Tel: (01531) 820286
Large collection of birds of prey. Flying demonstrations daily, weather permitting, with eagles, falcons, hawks, owls and vultures. Also breeding aviaries.

25 Three Choirs Vineyards

Baldwins Farm, Newent,
Gloucestershire GL18 1LS
Tel: (01531) 890555
Home of internationally awarded Three Choirs wine. Visitors are welcome to look round the vineyards and taste the wines at no charge.

26 National Waterways Museum

Llanthony Warehouse,
Gloucester Docks,
Gloucester GL1 2EH
Tel: (01452) 318054
Three floors of dockside warehouse with lively displays telling the story of Britain's canals. Outside craft area with demonstrations. Cafe and shop.

27 Soldiers of Gloucestershire Museum

Custom House,
Gloucester Docks,
Gloucester GL1 2HE
Tel: (01452) 522682
Listed Victorian building in historic docks. The story of Gloucestershire's foot and horse soldiers in the last 300 years.

FIND OUT MORE

Further information about holidays and attractions in the Heart of England is available from: **Heart of England Tourist Board,** Lark Hill Road, Worcester WR5 2EZ. Tel: (01905) 763436 (24 hours)

These publications are available free from the Heart of England Tourist Board:
- **Bed & Breakfast Touring Map**
- **Great Escapes - short breaks and leisure holidays for all seasons**
- **Events list**

Also available are:
Places to Visit in the Heart of England - a comprehensive guide to over 750 varied attractions and things to see, also great ideas for where to go in winter, (over £40 in discount vouchers included). £3.99
- **Cotswolds Map** £2.95
- **Cotswold/Wyndean Map** £3.25
- **Shropshire/Staffordshire Map** £3.25

Please add 60p postage for up to 3 items, plus 25p for each additional 3 items.

CHESHIRE

DERBYSHIRE

Leek

Newcastle-
under-Lyme

Stoke-on-Trent

1

Barlaston **2**

Alton **3**

Whitchurch

Uttoxeter

Oswestry

Market Drayton

STAFFORDSHIRE

SHROPSHIRE

Stafford **4**

Newport

Rugeley

LEICESTER-
SHIRE

Wellington

Cannock

Lichfield

Shrewsbury **5**

Telford

Wolverhampton

Tamworth

Ironbridge **6**

Walsall

**WEST
MIDLANDS**

Atherstone

Much Wenlock

7

Bridgnorth

Wombourne

Nuneaton

Bishop's Castle

Dudley **8**

Birmingham

9 **10**

Bickenhill

Coventry

Kidderminster

11

Bournville

Solihull

12

13

Ludlow

Bewdley **15**

Rugby **14**

Kenilworth

Hatton

Bromsgrove

Warwick **16**

Leamington
Royal
Spa

Stoke Heath

Redditch

17 Alcester

Droitwich

Gaydon **18**

Leominster

19 Lower Broadheath

Stratford-
upon-Avon

20

Wellesbourne

Kington

Bromyard

21

Worcester

WARWICKSHIRE

**HEREFORD
& WORCESTER**

22 Pershore

Welland

Evesham

Hereford **23**

Upton upon
Severn

Broadway

Ledbury

Tewkesbury

WALES

24 **25**

Newent

Winchcombe

Gloucester

Cheltenham

Stow on the Wold

26 **27**

Painswick

Northleach

GLOUCESTERSHIRE

OXFORDSHIRE

Coleford

Stroud

Cirencester

0 ___ 20 Miles

Berkeley

Nailsworth

0 ___ 30 Kms

Tetbury

**SOUTH
GLOUCS**

WILTSHIRE

WHERE TO STAY (HEART OF ENGLAND)

Accommodation entries in this region are listed in alphabetical order of place name, and then in alphabetical order of establishment.

Map references refer to the colour location maps at the back of this guide. The first number indicates the map to use; the letter and number which follow refer to the grid reference on the map.

At-a-glance symbols at the end of each accommodation entry give useful information about services and facilities. A key to symbols can be found inside the back cover flap. Keep this open for easy reference.

ABBOTS BROMLEY

Staffordshire
Map ref 4B3

Attractive conservation village with a green, a Butter Cross and 18th C almshouses. Well-known for the ancient Horn Dance which takes place each year in September when dancers in Tudor dress bear reindeer antlers. Nearby are Shugborough Hall (National Trust) and Alton Towers.

Crown Inn ♠♠

APPROVED

Market Place, Abbots Bromley, Rugeley WS15 3BS
☎ Burton upon Trent (01283) 840227
Fax (01283) 840227
Comfortable and friendly English country inn in centre of attractive village. Home-cooked food using local fresh produce, fully licensed.
Bedrooms: 1 single, 2 double, 2 twin, 1 triple
Bathrooms: 2 public

Bed & breakfast

per night:	£min	£max
Single	20.00	29.00
Double	40.00	

Half board per

person:	£min	£max
Daily	29.00	39.00

Lunch available
Evening meal 1800 (last orders 2100)
Parking for 30
Cards accepted: Access, Visa, Switch/Delta
🐾🖵👌🥤📷⏴🍽️👕40✿🐎DAP
🏠

ALCESTER

Warwickshire
Map ref 2B1

Town has Roman origins and many old buildings around the High Street. It is close to Ragley Hall, the 18th C Palladian mansion with its magnificent baroque Great Hall.

Orchard Lawns ♠♠

HIGHLY COMMENDED

Wixford, Alcester B49 6DA
☎ Stratford-on-Avon (01789) 772668
Charming house with character, set in delightful gardens, in small village 7 miles from Stratford-upon-Avon. Ideal touring centre.
Bedrooms: 1 single, 1 double, 1 twin
Bathrooms: 1 en-suite, 1 public

Bed & breakfast

per night:	£min	£max
Single	17.00	19.00
Double	34.00	38.00

Parking for 6
Cards accepted: Access, Visa
🐾5🖵⏴🍽️📺📷⏴🍽️🐕🐎
🏠

Sambourne Hall Farm ♠♠

HIGHLY COMMENDED

Wike Lane, Sambourne, Redditch, Worcestershire B96 6NZ
☎ Studley (01527) 852151
315-acre arable & livestock farm. Beautiful mid-17th C farmhouse in a peaceful village, close to local pub. Just off the A435 between Alcester and Studley and 9 miles from Stratford-upon-Avon.
Bedrooms: 1 double, 1 family room
Bathrooms: 1 en-suite, 1 private

Bed & breakfast

per night:	£min	£max
Single	20.00	25.00
Double	35.00	40.00

Parking for 6
🐾🖵👌🥤🖵S🍽️📷📺📷⏴✿🐎
🏠

ALDSWORTH

Gloucestershire
Map ref 2B1

Village near many interesting places such as Northleach with its beautiful church, Burford, one of the finest Cotswold towns, Chedworth Roman Villa and Bibury with its trout farm and famous row of cottages.

The Old Chapel ♠♠

Aldsworth, Cheltenham GL54 3QZ
☎ Cotswold (01451) 844547
Grade II converted chapel, with original features. In unspoilt peaceful Cotswold village. Situated off B4425 to Cirencester, giving easy access to other delightful villages.
Bedrooms: 1 double, 1 twin
Bathrooms: 2 private, 2 public

Bed & breakfast

per night:	£min	£max
Single	20.00	22.00
Double	35.00	38.00

Parking for 3
🐾5🖵🍽️📺📷🐕🐎🏠

Map references apply to the colour maps at the back of this guide.

ALTON

Staffordshire
Map ref 4B2

Alton Castle, an impressive 19th C building, dominates the village which is set in spectacular scenery. Nearby is Alton Towers, a romantic 19th C ruin with innumerable tourist attractions within one of England's largest theme parks in its 800 acres of magnificent gardens.

Bank House

APPROVED

Smithy Bank, Alton, Stoke-on-Trent ST10 4AA
☎ Oakamoor (01538) 702524
Central in Alton village, 1 mile from Alton Towers and close to Dovedale and Manifold Valley. 3 good inns serving meals within 200 metres. Family-run.
Bedrooms: 2 double, 1 twin, 3 family rooms
Bathrooms: 4 en-suite, 1 public

Bed & breakfast

per night:	£min	£max
Single	19.00	19.00
Double	38.00	38.00

Parking for 6

Bee Cottage

Listed COMMENDED

Saltersford Lane, Alton, Stoke-on-Trent ST10 4AU
☎ Oakamoor (01538) 702802
Traditional stone-built cottage, extended over a period of 200 years. In countryside, 1 mile from Alton Towers. Adjoining paddock and orchard extending to 2 acres.
Bedrooms: 2 double, 1 twin
Bathrooms: 1 en-suite, 1 public

Bed & breakfast

per night:	£min	£max
Single	20.00	25.00
Double	30.00	36.00

Parking for 5
Open March–November

Bradley Elms Farm

HIGHLY COMMENDED

Threapwood, Cheadle, Stoke-on-Trent ST10 4RA
☎ Cheadle (01538) 753135
Well-appointed farm accommodation providing a comfortable and relaxing atmosphere for that well-earned break. On the edge of the Staffordshire Moorlands. 3 miles from Alton Towers, close to the Potteries and the Peak District National Park.
Bedrooms: 3 double, 3 twin, 2 triple, 1 family room

Bathrooms: 9 en-suite, 1 public

Bed & breakfast

per night:	£min	£max
Double	39.00	43.00

Half board per

person:	£min	£max
Daily	35.50	44.50

Evening meal 1830 (last orders 2000)
Parking for 10

Bulls Head Inn

APPROVED

High Street, Alton ST10 4AQ
☎ Oakamoor (01538) 702307
Fax (01538) 702065
In the village of Alton close to Alton Towers, an 18th C inn with real ale and home cooking.
Bedrooms: 3 double, 1 twin, 2 family rooms
Bathrooms: 6 en-suite, 1 public

Bed & breakfast

per night:	£min	£max
Single	25.00	40.00
Double	45.00	55.00

Lunch available
Evening meal 1900 (last orders 2200)
Parking for 10
Cards accepted: Access, Visa, Switch/Delta

Capri Bed & Breakfast

Gallows Green, Alton, Stoke-on-Trent ST10 4BN
☎ Oakamoor (01538) 702613
Detached house set in almost 2 acres of land in Alton village. All rooms have en-suite or private facilities. One mile to Alton Towers.
Bedrooms: 2 double, 1 family room
Bathrooms: 2 en-suite, 1 private

Bed & breakfast

per night:	£min	£max
Single	25.00	25.00
Double	35.00	35.00

Parking for 6
Open March–November

The Cross Inn

APPROVED

Cauldon Low, Waterhouses, Stoke-on-Trent ST10 3EX
☎ Leek (01538) 308338 & (0585) 823108
Old country inn, set in the heart of the Staffordshire Moorlands. Alton Towers 2.5 miles, Peak Park 5 miles.
Bedrooms: 1 single, 2 double, 1 twin, 1 family room
Bathrooms: 5 en-suite

Bed & breakfast

per night:	£min	£max
Single	15.00	20.00

Lunch available
Evening meal 1900 (last orders 2200)
Parking for 50

Fields Farm

COMMENDED

Chapel Lane, Threapwood, Alton, Stoke-on-Trent ST10 4QZ
☎ Cheadle (01538) 752721 & Mobile 0850 310381
Fax (01538) 752721

Traditional farmhouse hospitality and comfort in picturesque Churnet Valley, 10 minutes from Alton Towers. Near Peak Park and within easy reach of Potteries and many stately homes. Stabling available. Ideal for walking, cycling, riding and fishing. Dogs by arrangement.
Bedrooms: 2 double, 1 twin
Bathrooms: 2 en-suite, 1 public

Bed & breakfast

per night:	£min	£max
Single	20.00	
Double	32.00	

Half board per

person:	£min	£max
Daily	25.00	
Weekly	154.00	

Evening meal 1900 (last orders 2200)
Parking for 6

Hillside Farm

Listed APPROVED

Alton Road, Denstone, Uttoxeter ST14 5HG
☎ Rocester (01889) 590760
Victorian farmhouse with extensive views to the Weaver Hills and Churnet Valley. Situated 2 miles south of Alton Towers on B5032.
Bedrooms: 1 double, 2 triple, 1 family room
Bathrooms: 1 private, 1 public

Bed & breakfast

per night:	£min	£max
Single	15.00	18.00
Double	28.00	32.00

Continued ▶

ALTON
Continued

Parking for 7
Open March–November
🐕🖥💧ᵁᴸ🅰Ⓢ TV 🖼☀✕✈🚜

AMBERLEY
Gloucestershire
Map ref 2B1

The Dial Cottage
👑 HIGHLY COMMENDED
Amberley, Stroud GL5 5AL
☎ Stroud (01453) 872563

*17th C Cotswold cottage situated in
600 acres of National Trust land,
Minchinhampton Common, within the
Royal Triangle.*
Bedrooms: 2 double, 1 twin
Bathrooms: 3 en-suite
**Bed & breakfast
per night:**

	£min	£max
Single	30.00	40.00
Double	50.00	70.00

Parking for 10
Open March–November
Cards accepted: Access, Visa, Amex
🐕7🗄🖥💧🥤ᵁᴸ🅰✕🖼🖼
⛎☀✕🚜

ARLINGHAM
Gloucestershire
Map ref 2B1

Small, quiet village in a horseshoe
bend of the River Severn. The parish
church contains medieval glass and
interesting sculptures. Berkeley
Castle and the Wildfowl Trust at
Slimbridge are nearby and there is
easy access from the M5 and A38.

Horseshoe View 🏚
Listed COMMENDED
Overton Lane, Arlingham,
Gloucester GL2 7JJ
☎ Gloucester (01452) 740293
*Ideally situated for touring. Close to the
Forest of Dean, Wildfowl Trust and the
M5, with many other places of interest
nearby.*
Bedrooms: 1 single, 2 double, 1 twin
Bathrooms: 1 en-suite, 2 public

**Bed & breakfast
per night:**

	£min	£max
Single	12.50	13.00
Double	25.00	30.00

Parking for 5
🐕5🗄ᵁᴸ🖼 TV ✕🚜 DAP SP

ARMSCOTE
Warwickshire
Map ref 2B1

Willow Corner 🏚
👑 COMMENDED
Armscote, Stratford-upon-Avon
CV37 8DE
☎ (01608) 682391 & Mobile 0836
556639

*Spacious, 300-year-old, Cotswold-stone
thatched cottage, nestled in a peaceful
hamlet with a pub. Open fireplaces,
beams throughout, cottage garden.*
Bedrooms: 1 double, 1 twin, 1 triple
Bathrooms: 1 public
**Bed & breakfast
per night:**

	£min	£max
Single	22.50	30.00
Double	50.00	60.00

Parking for 3
🐕3🖥💧ᵁᴸ TV 🖼🖼☀✕🚜

AVON DASSETT
Warwickshire
Map ref 2C1

Village on the slopes of the Dasset
Hills, with good views. The church,
with its impressive tower and spire,
dates from 1868 but incorporates a
14th C window with 15th C glass.

Crandon House 🏚
👑 HIGHLY COMMENDED
Avon Dassett, Leamington Spa
CV33 0AA
☎ Fenny Compton (01295) 770652
Fax (01295) 770652

*20-acre mixed farm. Farmhouse
offering a high standard of
accommodation with superb views over
unspoilt countryside. Quiet and
peaceful. Easy access to Warwick,*

Stratford and Cotswolds. 4 miles from
junctions 11 and 12 of M40.
Bedrooms: 1 double, 2 twin
Bathrooms: 2 en-suite, 1 private
**Bed & breakfast
per night:**

	£min	£max
Single	25.00	30.00
Double	37.00	42.00

**Half board per
person:**

	£min	£max
Daily	32.00	38.00
Weekly	200.00	250.00

Evening meal from 1900
Parking for 22
Cards accepted: Access, Visa
🐕8🖥💧🥤ᵁᴸ🅰Ⓢ✕🖼 TV 🖼🖂
✕☀🚜 SP

BACTON
Hereford and Worcester
Map ref 2A1

Village in the Golden Valley of west
Herefordshire, chiefly visited for the
monument in its church to Blanche
Parry, one of Queen Elizabeth's
maids of honour. Tradition says she
worked the embroidery now
framed there.

Pentwyn Cottage Gardens
Listed
Pentwyn Cottage, Bacton, Hereford
HR2 0AP
☎ (01981) 240508
*In the heart of the Golden Valley,
300-year-old cottage. 1.5 acre garden
and plant nursery with unusual
perennials. Home-made preserves and
cream teas a speciality.*
Bedrooms: 2 double
Bathrooms: 1 public
**Bed & breakfast
per night:**

	£min	£max
Single	14.00	16.00
Double	28.00	32.00

Parking for 12
🐕🖾🖥💧🥤ᵁᴸ🅰Ⓢ🖼🖼🖂☀🚜
SP

BALSALL COMMON
West Midlands
Map ref 4B3

Close to Kenilworth and within easy
reach of Coventry.

Avonlea 🏚
Listed APPROVED
135 Kenilworth Road, Balsall
Common, Coventry CV7 7EU
☎ Berkswell (01676) 533003 &
Mobile 0850 915611
Fax (01676) 533003
*19th C cottage extended to provide
spacious and comfortable*

accommodation, set back from main A425 road. Ample off-road parking.
Bedrooms: 1 single, 1 double, 1 twin
Bathrooms: 1 public

Bed & breakfast

per night:	£min	£max
Single	22.00	22.00
Double	44.00	44.00

Parking for 5

BARLASTON

Staffordshire
Map ref 4B2

Wedgwood Memorial College

Station Road, Barlaston,
Stoke-on-Trent ST12 9DG
☎ Stoke-on-Trent (01782) 372105 & 373427
Fax (01782) 372393
Pleasant, well-appointed adult residential college with relaxed, homely ambience. In quiet village, yet close to National Trust downs and Potteries. Convenient for Peak District, Alton Towers. Good quality, home-cooked food with an imaginative repertoire of vegetarian dishes. Limited facilities for disabled.
Bedrooms: 9 single, 7 twin, 3 triple, 2 family rooms
Bathrooms: 6 en-suite, 7 public

Bed & breakfast

per night:	£min	£max
Single	12.50	
Double	25.00	

Half board per

person:	£min	£max
Daily	18.50	
Weekly	129.50	

Lunch available
Evening meal 1830 (last orders 1830)
Parking for 40
Cards accepted: Access, Visa

A key to symbols can be found inside the back cover flap.

All accommodation in this guide has been graded, or is awaiting a grading, by a trained Tourist Board inspector.

BERKELEY

Gloucestershire
Map ref 2B1

Town dominated by the castle where Edward II was murdered. Dating from Norman times, it is still the home of the Berkeley family and is open to the public April to September and October Sundays. The Jenner Museum is here and Slimbridge Wildfowl Trust is nearby.

Pickwick Farm

Listed COMMENDED

Berkeley GL13 9EU
☎ Dursley (01453) 810241
120-acre dairy farm. A warm welcome at this easily located family farm, formerly a coaching inn used by Charles Dickens. Close to Berkeley Castle, Slimbridge Wildfowl Trust and 3 golf courses. Non-smoking establishment.
Bedrooms: 1 double, 2 twin
Bathrooms: 1 public

Bed & breakfast

per night:	£min	£max
Single	16.00	16.50
Double	32.00	33.00

Parking for 3

BERKSWELL

West Midlands
Map ref 4B3

Pretty village with an unusual set of 5-holed stocks on the green. It has some fine houses, cottages, a 16th C inn and a windmill open to the public Sunday afternoons, May to end September. The Norman church is one of the finest in the area, with many interesting features.

Elmcroft Country Guesthouse

Listed HIGHLY COMMENDED

Elmcroft, Hodgetts Lane, Berkswell, Coventry CV7 7HO
☎ (01676) 535204
Country guesthouse in close proximity to the National Exhibition Centre and ideal base for all of Warwickshire's tourist attractions.
Bedrooms: 1 single, 2 double, 2 twin
Bathrooms: 5 en-suite

Bed & breakfast

per night:	£min	£max
Single	25.00	
Double	40.00	

Parking for 8

BEWDLEY

Hereford and Worcester
Map ref 4A3

Attractive town on the River Severn, approached by a bridge designed by Telford. The town has many elegant buildings and an interesting craft and folk museum. On the Severn Valley Steam Railway. *Tourist Information Centre ☎ (01299) 404740*

Horsehill Cottage

Listed COMMENDED

Ribbesford, Bewdley, Worcestershire DY12 2TT
☎ (01299) 400793
Fax (01299) 400793
Country house set in 3 acres on Worcestershire Way. Superb views, English breakfast cooked on an Aga. Few minutes' walk for fishing and golf.
Bedrooms: 1 single, 1 double, 1 triple
Bathrooms: 1 en-suite, 1 private, 1 public

Bed & breakfast

per night:	£min	£max
Single	12.00	15.00
Double	36.00	43.00

BIBURY

Gloucestershire
Map ref 2B1

Village on the River Coln with stone houses and the famous 17th C Arlington Row, former weavers' cottages. Arlington Mill is now a folk museum. Trout farm and Bansley House Gardens nearby are open to the public.

Cotteswold House

HIGHLY COMMENDED

Arlington, Bibury, Cirencester GL7 5ND
☎ Cirencester (01285) 740609
Fax (01285) 740609
Enjoy the relaxed friendly atmosphere of this family home. Ideally situated for touring the Cotswolds. All bedrooms en-suite with TV. Guest lounge/dining room. No smoking, please. Parking.
Bedrooms: 2 double, 1 twin
Bathrooms: 3 en-suite

Bed & breakfast

per night:	£min	£max
Single	25.00	
Double	40.00	

Parking for 4

BIDFORD-ON-AVON

Warwickshire
Map ref 2B1

Attractive village with an ancient 8-arched bridge, riverside picnic area and a main street with some interesting 15th C houses.

Broom Hall Inn

APPROVED

Bidford Road, Broom, Alcester B50 4HE
☎ Stratford-upon-Avon (01789) 773757

Family-owned country inn with carvery restaurant and extensive range of bar meals. Close to Stratford-upon-Avon and Cotswolds.

Bedrooms: 4 single, 4 double, 4 twin
Bathrooms: 12 en-suite

Bed & breakfast per night:	£min	£max
Single	20.00	37.50
Double	40.00	60.00

Half board per person:	£min	£max
Daily	34.50	

Lunch available
Evening meal 1900 (last orders 2200)
Parking for 80
Cards accepted: Access, Visa, Amex

40

BIRDLIP

Gloucestershire
Map ref 2B1

Hamlet at the top of a very steep descent down to the Gloucester Vale with excellent viewpoint over Crickley Hill Country Park.

Beechmount

COMMENDED

Birdlip, Cirencester GL4 8JH
☎ Gloucester (01452) 862262

Family-run guesthouse with personal attention. Ideal centre for the Cotswolds. Choice of menu for breakfast, unrestricted access.

Bedrooms: 1 single, 2 double, 1 twin, 2 triple, 1 family room
Bathrooms: 2 en-suite, 1 public

Bed & breakfast per night:	£min	£max
Single	14.50	30.00
Double	28.00	44.00

Evening meal 1900 (last orders 1000)
Parking for 7
Cards accepted: Access, Visa, Switch/Delta

BIRMINGHAM

West Midlands
Map ref 4B3

Britain's second city, whose attractions include Centenary Square and the ICC with Symphony Hall, the NEC, the City Art Gallery, Barber Institute of Fine Arts, 17th C Aston Hall, science and railway museums, Jewellery Quarter, Cadbury World, 2 cathedrals and Botanical Gardens.
Tourist Information Centre ☎ (0121) 693 6300 or 780 4321

Heath Lodge Hotel

Coleshill Road, Marston Green, Birmingham B37 7HT
☎ (0121) 779 2218
Fax (0121) 779 2218

Licensed family-run hotel, quietly situated and less than 2 miles from the National Exhibition Centre and Birmingham Airport. Courtesy car to airport.

Bedrooms: 9 single, 3 double, 5 twin, 1 family room
Bathrooms: 13 en-suite, 1 public, 1 private shower

Bed & breakfast per night:	£min	£max
Single	28.50	39.50
Double	39.50	52.00

Evening meal 1830 (last orders 2030)
Parking for 24
Cards accepted: Access, Visa, Diners, Amex

5 TV 20 OAP SP T

Lyndhurst Hotel

APPROVED

135 Kingsbury Road, Erdington, Birmingham B24 8QT
☎ (0121) 373 5695
Fax (0121) 373 5695

Within half a mile of M6 (junction 6) and within easy reach of the city and National Exhibition Centre. Comfortable bedrooms, spacious restaurant. Personal service in a quiet friendly atmosphere.

Bedrooms: 10 single, 2 double, 2 twin
Bathrooms: 13 en-suite, 1 private

Bed & breakfast per night:	£min	£max
Single	25.00	39.50
Double	39.50	52.50

Half board per person:	£min	£max
Daily	37.00	51.50

Evening meal 1800 (last orders 2000)
Parking for 12
Cards accepted: Access, Visa, Diners, Amex

TV 30 SP T

BIRMINGHAM AIRPORT

West Midlands

See under Balsall Common, Berkswell, Birmingham, Coleshill, Coventry, Hampton in Arden, Meriden, Solihull

BISHOP'S CASTLE

Shropshire
Map ref 4A3

A 12th C Planned Town with a castle site at the top of the hill and a church at the bottom of the main street. Many interesting buildings with original timber frames hidden behind present day houses. On the Welsh border close to the Clun Forest in quiet, unspoilt countryside.

The Boars Head Hotel

COMMENDED

Church Street, Bishop's Castle SY9 5AE
☎ (01588) 638521 & Mobile 0374 201272
Fax (01588) 630126

Old world inn, with en-suite accommodation in original stables. Comfortable dining area serves wide choice of bar meals. A la carte restaurant also available.

Bedrooms: 1 double, 2 twin, 1 family room
Bathrooms: 4 en-suite

Bed & breakfast per night:	£min	£max
Single	33.00	38.00
Double	50.00	56.00

Lunch available
Evening meal 1830 (last orders 2130)
Parking for 20
Cards accepted: Access, Visa, Diners, Amex, Switch/Delta

SP

Castle Hotel

👑👑 COMMENDED

The Square, Bishop's Castle
SY9 5DG
☎ Bishops Castle (01588) 638403
300-year-old unspoilt coaching inn. Large, well-kept garden with views over the town and valley.
Bedrooms: 1 single, 4 double, 2 twin
Bathrooms: 2 en-suite, 2 public
Bed & breakfast

per night:	£min	£max
Single	25.00	30.00
Double	45.00	50.00

Lunch available
Evening meal 1830 (last orders 2100)
Parking for 40
Cards accepted: Access, Visa, Switch/Delta

Old Time

👑 APPROVED

29 High Street, Bishop's Castle
SY9 5BE
☎ (01588) 638467
Grade II listed 15th C house in town centre with shop, courtyard, garden and craft workshop. Originally a "cruck cottage".
Bedrooms: 2 double
Bathrooms: 2 en-suite
Bed & breakfast

per night:	£min	£max
Single	18.00	20.00
Double	32.00	35.00

BLEDINGTON

Gloucestershire
Map ref 2B1

Village close to the Oxfordshire border, with a pleasant green and a beautiful church.

Kings Head Inn & Restaurant 𝔸

👑👑👑 COMMENDED

The Green, Bledington, Oxford
OX7 6HD
☎ Kingham (01608) 658365
Fax (01608) 658902

15th C inn located in the heart of the Cotswolds, facing the village green. Authentic lounge bars, notable restaurant. Delightful en-suite rooms.

Bedrooms: 10 double, 2 twin
Bathrooms: 12 en-suite
Bed & breakfast

per night:	£min	£max
Single	40.00	45.00
Double	60.00	75.00

Lunch available
Evening meal 1900 (last orders 2200)
Parking for 60
Cards accepted: Access, Visa, Switch/Delta

BLOCKLEY

Gloucestershire
Map ref 2B1

This village's prosperity was founded in silk mills and other factories but now it is a quiet, unspoilt place. An excellent centre for exploring pretty Cotswold villages, especially Chipping Campden and Broadway.

21 Station Road 𝔸

👑👑 COMMENDED

Blockley, Moreton-in-Marsh
GL56 9ED
☎ (01386) 700402
Beautifully presented Cotswold-stone house on edge of delightful village. Ideal base for touring Cotswolds and Shakespeare country. Tastefully decorated, comfortable, non-smoking accommodation with full en-suite facilities. A warm welcome awaits you.
Bedrooms: 1 double, 2 twin
Bathrooms: 3 en-suite
Bed & breakfast

per night:	£min	£max
Single	20.00	20.00
Double	35.00	35.00

Parking for 9

BODENHAM

Hereford and Worcester
Map ref 2A1

Attractive village with old timbered cottages and stone houses and an interesting church. Here the River Lugg makes a loop and flows under an ancient bridge at the end of the village.

Maund Court

👑👑 HIGHLY COMMENDED

Bodenham, Hereford HR1 3JA
☎ (01568) 797282
150-acre mixed farm. Attractive 15th C farmhouse with a large garden,

swimming pool and croquet. Riding, golf and pleasant walks nearby. Ideal centre for touring.
Bedrooms: 2 double, 1 twin
Bathrooms: 3 en-suite
Bed & breakfast

per night:	£min	£max
Single	22.00	24.00
Double	36.00	38.00

Evening meal from 1900
Parking for 8
Open March–October

BOURTON-ON-THE-HILL

Gloucestershire
Map ref 2B1

Attractive village with 18th C Bourton House and impressive 16th C tithe barn. Sezincote House is nearby, built at the beginning of the 19th C in Indian style with Repton landscaped gardens which are open to the public, as is Batsford Arboretum.

Bourton Heights

👑👑 COMMENDED

Blockley Road, Bourton-on-the-Hill, Moreton-in-Marsh GL56 9AJ
☎ Cotswold (01386) 700544
Country house with a beautiful view of surrounding fields and garden. Rooms separate from owners' accommodation.
Bedrooms: 3 double
Bathrooms: 3 en-suite
Bed & breakfast

per night:	£min	£max
Single	25.00	40.00
Double	30.00	45.00

Parking for 3

Half board prices are given per person, but in some cases these may be based on double/twin occupancy.

Information on accommodation listed in this guide has been supplied by the proprietors. As changes may occur you are advised to check details at the time of booking.

BOURTON-ON-THE-WATER

Gloucestershire
Map ref 2B1

The River Windrush flows through this famous Cotswold village which has a green, and cottages and houses of Cotswold stone. Its many attractions include a model village, Birdland, a Motor Museum and the Cotswold Perfumery.

Berkeley Guesthouse

COMMENDED

Moore Road,
Bourton-on-the-Water, Cheltenham
GL54 2AZ
☎ Cotswold (01451) 810388
Detached house with a homely, relaxed atmosphere, furnished to a high standard. Personal attention. Attractive gardens, sun lounge, car park. No smoking.
Bedrooms: 2 double, 1 twin
Bathrooms: 3 en-suite

Bed & breakfast
per night:	£min	£max
Single	18.50	21.00
Double	35.00	39.00

Parking for 4

Coombe House

HIGHLY COMMENDED

Rissington Road,
Bourton-on-the-Water, Cheltenham
GL54 2DT
☎ Cotswold (01451) 821966
Fax (01451) 810477
Gentle elegance in quiet Cotswold home. Pretty, thoughtfully equipped en-suite bedrooms. Gardeners' garden. Ample parking. Non-smoking haven. Restaurants a riverside walk away.
Bedrooms: 3 double, 2 twin, 2 triple
Bathrooms: 6 en-suite, 1 private

Bed & breakfast
per night:	£min	£max
Single	40.00	48.00
Double	54.00	66.00

Parking for 10
Cards accepted: Access, Visa, Amex

Fairlie

Listed COMMENDED

Riverside, Bourton-on-the-Water,
Cheltenham GL54 2DP
☎ Cotswold (01451) 821842
Quiet character house in the heart of the village, with attractive rooms overlooking the river. Relaxed and comfortable surroundings.

Bedrooms: 2 double, 1 twin
Bathrooms: 1 public

Bed & breakfast
per night:	£min	£max
Double	32.00	33.00

Farncombe

HIGHLY COMMENDED

Clapton, Bourton-on-the-Water,
Cheltenham GL54 2LG
☎ Cotswold (01451) 820120 &
Mobile 0378 843123
Fax (01451) 820120
Quiet comfortable accommodation with superb views of the Windrush Valley. In the hamlet of Clapton, 2.5 miles from Bourton-on-the-Water. No-smoking house.
Bedrooms: 2 double, 1 twin
Bathrooms: 1 en-suite, 1 public,
2 private showers

Bed & breakfast
per night:	£min	£max
Single	18.00	28.00
Double	35.00	42.00

Parking for 3

Lamb Inn

COMMENDED

Great Rissington,
Bourton-on-the-Water, Cheltenham
GL54 2LP
☎ Cotswold (01451) 820388
Fax (01451) 820724
Country inn in rural setting, with home-cooked food, including steaks and local trout, served in attractive restaurant. Beer garden and real ale. Honeymoon suite also available.
Bedrooms: 13 double, 1 twin
Suite available
Bathrooms: 14 en-suite

Bed & breakfast
per night:	£min	£max
Single	35.00	55.00
Double	44.00	75.00

Lunch available
Evening meal 1900 (last orders 2130)
Parking for 10
Cards accepted: Access, Visa, Amex

Lansdowne House

COMMENDED

Lansdowne, Bourton-on-the-Water,
Cheltenham GL54 2AT
☎ Cotswold (01451) 820812

Large period stone family house. Tastefully furnished en-suite accommodation with a combination of old and antique furniture. Tea/coffee trays, colour TVs, parking, garden.
Bedrooms: 2 double, 1 triple
Bathrooms: 3 en-suite

Bed & breakfast
per night:	£min	£max
Single	23.00	29.00
Double	30.00	35.00

Parking for 4

Mousetrap Inn

APPROVED

Lansdowne, Bourton-on-the-Water,
Cheltenham GL54 2AR
☎ Cotswold (01451) 820579
Small homely inn with beer garden. TV and tea/coffee makers in all rooms. Bar meals, and open fires in winter.
Bedrooms: 7 double, 2 twin
Bathrooms: 9 en-suite

Bed & breakfast
per night:	£min	£max
Single	25.00	28.00
Double	40.00	45.00

Lunch available
Evening meal 1830 (last orders 2100)
Parking for 12

2 Naight Villas

Listed COMMENDED

Lansdowne, Bourton-on-the-Water,
Cheltenham GL54 2AR
☎ Cotswold (01451) 810827
Victorian villa, relaxing and comfortable, overlooking the River Windrush and within easy walking distance of the amenities of Bourton-on-the-Water.
Bedrooms: 1 double, 1 triple
Bathrooms: 2 public

Bed & breakfast
per night:	£min	£max
Single	19.00	
Double	34.00	

Parking for 2
Open March–September

Please check prices and other details at the time of booking.

The Ridge ♨

Whiteshoots Hill,
Bourton-on-the-Water, Cheltenham
GL54 2LE
☎ Cotswold (01451) 820660
*Large country house surrounded by
beautiful grounds. Central for visiting
many places of interest and close to all
amenities. Ground floor en-suite
bedrooms available.*
Bedrooms: 2 double, 2 twin, 1 triple
Bathrooms: 4 en-suite, 1 private,
1 public

Bed & breakfast per night:	£min	£max
Single	25.00	30.00
Double	33.00	38.00

Parking for 12

Rooftrees Guesthouse ♨

Rissington Road,
Bourton-on-the-Water, Cheltenham
GL54 2DX
☎ Cotswold (01451) 821943
*Detached Cotswold-stone family house,
all rooms individually decorated, 8
minutes' level walk from village centre.
Home cooking with fresh local produce.
3 en-suite bedrooms: 2 rooms are on
ground floor, 2 rooms have
four-posters. No smoking.*
Bedrooms: 3 double
Bathrooms: 3 en-suite

Bed & breakfast per night:	£min	£max
Double	38.00	42.00

Half board per person:	£min	£max
Daily	31.00	33.00
Weekly	210.00	220.00

Evening meal 1830 (last orders
1200)
Parking for 8
Cards accepted: Access, Visa,
Switch/Delta

Strathspey ♨

APPROVED

Lansdowne, Bourton-on-the-Water,
Cheltenham GL54 2AR
☎ Cotswold (01451) 820694
*Character, Cotswold-stone house 400
yards' walk from village centre. Quiet
location with pretty riverside walk.*
Bedrooms: 3 double
Bathrooms: 3 en-suite

Bed & breakfast per night:	£min	£max
Double	34.00	38.00

Parking for 4
Open April–October

BRAILES

Warwickshire
Map ref 2C1

Agdon Farm ♨

Listed APPROVED

Brailes, Banbury, Oxfordshire
OX15 5JJ
☎ (01608) 685226 & Mobile 0850
847786
*520-acre mixed farm. Old
Cotswold-stone farmhouse in a
"Designated area of Outstanding
Natural Beauty". We keep sheep,
horses, cats and dogs. Well situated for
touring the Cotswolds, Oxford, Warwick
and Stratford-upon-Avon.*
Bedrooms: 2 double, 1 twin
Bathrooms: 1 public

Bed & breakfast per night:	£min	£max
Single	20.00	
Double	35.00	

Half board per person:	£min	£max
Daily	24.50	
Weekly	140.00	

Evening meal 1800 (last orders
2100)
Parking for 8

BREDENBURY

Hereford and Worcester
Map ref 2A1

Redhill Farm

Listed

Bredenbury, Bromyard,
Herefordshire HR7 4SY
☎ Bromyard (01885) 483255 &
483535
Fax (01885) 483535
*86-acre mixed farm. 17th C farmhouse
in peaceful, unspoilt countryside with
panoramic views. Central for Malvern,
Hereford, Worcester, Ledbury and
Ludlow. Children and pets welcome. A
home-from-home on the A44 road.
Horses and gallop on farm.*
Bedrooms: 1 double, 1 twin, 1 triple
Bathrooms: 3 private, 1 public

Bed & breakfast per night:	£min	£max
Single	17.00	18.00
Double	30.00	32.00

Evening meal 1900 (last orders
2100)
Parking for 11

BRIDGNORTH

Shropshire
Map ref 4A3

Red sandstone riverside town in 2
parts - High and Low - linked by a
cliff railway. Much of interest
including a ruined Norman keep,
half-timbered 16th C houses,
Midland Motor Museum and Severn
Valley Railway.
*Tourist Information Centre ☎ (01746)
763358*

The Albynes ♨♨

Nordley, Bridgnorth WV16 4SX
☎ (01746) 762261

*263-acre mixed farm. Large country
house, peacefully set in parkland with
spectacular views of Shropshire
countryside. On B4373 - Bridgnorth 3
miles, Ironbridge 4 miles.*
Bedrooms: 1 double, 2 twin
Bathrooms: 2 en-suite, 1 private

Bed & breakfast per night:	£min	£max
Single	20.00	22.00
Double	36.00	40.00

Parking for 8

Aldenham Weir ♨

♨♨ COMMENDED

Muckley Cross, Bridgnorth
WV16 4RR
☎ Morville (01746) 714352
*Superb country house, set in 11.5
acres, with working mill race, weir and
trout stream for fishing. All rooms
en-suite. Close to Ironbridge Gorge
Museum. Quietly located off the A458,
central between Much Wenlock and
Bridgnorth.*
Bedrooms: 3 double, 2 twin, 1 triple
Bathrooms: 6 en-suite

Bed & breakfast per night:	£min	£max
Single	25.00	25.00
Double	38.00	38.00

Continued ▶

BRIDGNORTH

Continued

Parking for 7

Church House

⚜

Aston Eyre, Bridgnorth WV16 6XD
☎ Morville (01746) 714248
You are invited to a peaceful holiday in this oak-beamed cottage on a 6-acre smallholding. Overlooking Shropshire's rolling hills, it nestles behind a Norman church. Evening meals by arrangement.
Bedrooms: 1 twin, 1 family room
Bathrooms: 1 en-suite, 1 private

Bed & breakfast per night:

	£min	£max
Double	32.00	36.00

Half board per person:

	£min	£max
Daily	28.00	30.00
Weekly	182.00	196.00

Evening meal 1800 (last orders 2000)
Parking for 4
Open April–October

Middleton Lodge ⋀

⚜⚜ HIGHLY COMMENDED

Middleton Priors, Bridgnorth WV16 6UR
☎ Ditton Priors (01746) 712228
Imposing stone building in its own grounds, in a quiet hamlet in the Shropshire hills, 6 miles from Bridgnorth. Non-smokers only, please.
Bedrooms: 2 double, 1 twin
Bathrooms: 2 en-suite, 1 private

Bed & breakfast per night:

	£min	£max
Single	25.00	25.00
Double	45.00	55.00

Parking for 4

The Old Forge House

Listed

Hampton Loade, Bridgnorth WV15 6HD
☎ Quatt (01746) 780338
Fax (01746) 780338
200-year-old house in woodland setting, peaceful and homely. Pub and River Severn within 100 yards. Severn Valley railway reached by passenger ferry across river.
Bedrooms: 1 double, 1 twin, 1 triple
Bathrooms: 1 en-suite, 1 private, 1 public

Bed & breakfast per night:

	£min	£max
Single	18.00	20.00
Double	30.00	36.00

Parking for 6

BROAD CAMPDEN

Gloucestershire
Map ref 2B1

Vine Cottage

Listed COMMENDED

Broad Campden, Chipping Campden GL55 6US
☎ Evesham (01386) 840282
Idyllic Cotswold cottage in quiet no-through lane in conservation village one mile from Chipping Campden. Pretty garden and beautiful countryside.
Bedrooms: 1 single, 1 twin
Bathrooms: 1 public

Bed & breakfast per night:

	£min	£max
Single	19.00	20.00
Double	38.00	40.00

Parking for 1

BROADWAY

Hereford and Worcester
Map ref 2B1

Beautiful Cotswold village called the "Show village of England", with 16th C stone houses and cottages. Near the village is Broadway Tower with magnificent views over 12 counties and a country park with nature trails and adventure playground.

Barn House Bed & Breakfast ⋀

⚜⚜ HIGHLY COMMENDED

Barn House, 152 High Street, Broadway, Worcestershire WR12 7AJ
☎ (01386) 858633
Fax (01386) 853593

Substantial listed 17th C house in 16 acres of scenic grounds. Superb facilities include a magnificent barn room and swimming pool.
Bedrooms: 3 double, 1 twin
Bathrooms: 3 en-suite, 1 private, 2 public

Bed & breakfast per night:

	£min	£max
Single	25.00	50.00
Double	45.00	70.00

Parking for 42

Broadway Court ⋀

Listed HIGHLY COMMENDED

89 High Street, Broadway, Worcestershire WR12 7AL
☎ (01386) 852237
Fax (01386) 852237
Grade II listed barn conversion overlooking secluded, walled cottage garden with country views. Delightful and spacious en-suite bedrooms, beautiful panelled dining room. Two minutes' walk to village centre.
Bedrooms: 3 double, 1 twin
Bathrooms: 4 en-suite

Bed & breakfast per night:

	£min	£max
Double	50.00	50.00

Parking for 10

Cinnibar Cottage ⋀

Listed HIGHLY COMMENDED

45 Bury End, (Snowshill Rd.,), Broadway, Worcestershire WR12 7AF
☎ (01386) 858 623
170-year-old Cotswold-stone cottage. Quiet situation with open country views, half a mile from Broadway village green, along Snowshill Road. Non-smoking establishment.
Bedrooms: 1 double, 1 twin
Bathrooms: 1 public

Bed & breakfast per night:

	£min	£max
Double	34.00	37.00

Parking for 2

Crown and Trumpet Inn ⋀

⚜⚜⚜ APPROVED

Church Street, Broadway, Worcestershire WR12 7AE
☎ (01386) 853202
Fax (01386) 853874
Traditional English inn with log fires and oak beams, quietly located just off the village green. Home-cooked local and seasonal English food.
Bedrooms: 4 double, 1 twin
Bathrooms: 5 en-suite

Bed & breakfast per night:

	£min	£max
Single	15.00	25.00
Double	40.00	

Lunch available
Evening meal 1830 (last orders 2130)
Parking for 6

🐴🖥♿🐕🍴💺📶🏛🎨🔍⛎✿⛔SP🎫

Eastbank ♏
♕♕♕

Station Drive, Broadway,
Worcestershire WR12 7DF
☎ (01386) 852659
*Quiet location, half a mile from village.
All rooms fully en-suite (bath/shower),
with colour TV and beverage facilities.
Homely atmosphere. Free brochure.*
Bedrooms: 2 double, 2 twin, 2 triple
Bathrooms: 6 en-suite

Bed & breakfast

per night:	£min	£max
Single	15.00	
Double	32.00	50.00

Evening meal 1900 (last orders 1000)
Parking for 6

🐴2🗄📺🖥♿🐕🍴📶🏛💺✂🎨🏛🎨 ✿🚐OAP SP🎫

Leasow House ♏
♕♕ HIGHLY COMMENDED

Laverton Meadow, Broadway,
Worcestershire WR12 7NA
☎ Stanton (01386) 584526
Fax (01386) 584596

*17th C Cotswold-stone farmhouse
tranquilly set in open countryside close
to Broadway village.*
Bedrooms: 3 double, 2 twin, 2 triple
Bathrooms: 7 en-suite

Bed & breakfast

per night:	£min	£max
Double	52.00	60.00

Parking for 14
Cards accepted: Access, Visa, Amex

🐴♿🏪🗄📺🖥♿🐕🍴📶🏛💺🎨🏛🎨 ✿🚐🎪

Millhay Cottage
Listed COMMENDED

Bury End, Broadway, Worcestershire
WR12 7JS
☎ (01386) 858241
*House set in a superb garden off the
Snowshill Road and adjacent to
Cotswold Way. Accommodation is a
self-contained suite (2 bedrooms,
bathroom, wc): maximum 4 persons.*
Bedrooms: 1 family room
Bathrooms: 1 private

Bed & breakfast

per night:	£min	£max
Single	22.00	24.00
Double	42.00	46.00

Parking for 12

🐴🖥♿📶UL🏛💺📶🏛🎨✂🔍✿🚐

Mount Pleasant Farm ♏
♕♕ HIGHLY COMMENDED

Childswickham, Broadway,
Worcestershire WR12 7HZ
☎ (01386) 853424
*500-acre mixed farm. Large Victorian
farmhouse with excellent views. Very
quiet accommodation with all modern
amenities. Approximately 3 miles from
Broadway.*
Bedrooms: 2 double, 1 twin
Bathrooms: 3 en-suite

Bed & breakfast

per night:	£min	£max
Single	25.00	
Double	40.00	44.00

Parking for 8

🐴3🖥♿📶UL📺🏛💺📶🏛🎨⛎🐴🚐

Olive Branch Guest House ♏
♕♕

78 High Street, Broadway,
Worcestershire WR12 7AJ
☎ (01386) 853440
Fax (01386) 853440

*16th C house with modern amenities
close to centre of village. Traditional
English breakfast served. Reduced rates
for 3 nights or more.*
Bedrooms: 2 single, 3 double, 2 twin,
1 triple
Bathrooms: 6 en-suite, 1 private,
1 public

Bed & breakfast

per night:	£min	£max
Single	19.00	19.50
Double	40.00	56.00

Evening meal 1900 (last orders 2000)
Parking for 8
Cards accepted: Amex

🐴♿🗄📺🖥♿📶UL🏛💺📺🏛💺📶♿⛎✿ 🎨🚐SP🎪🎫

Orchard Grove ♏
♕♕ HIGHLY COMMENDED

Station Road, Broadway,
Worcestershire WR12 7DE
☎ Evesham (01386) 853834
*Attractive detached Cotswold house,
just minutes from village centre,
tastefully appointed for guests' every*

---

*comfort. Warm welcome assured.
Non-smokers only, please.*
Bedrooms: 1 double, 1 twin
Bathrooms: 1 en-suite, 1 private

Bed & breakfast

per night:	£min	£max
Single	25.00	
Double	42.00	45.00

Parking for 3

🐴10📶🗄🖥♿🐕🍴📶UL🏛💺✂🎨📺🏛 📶🐴✈🚐

Shenberrow Hill
Listed

Stanton, Broadway, Worcestershire
WR12 7NE
☎ (01386) 584468
*9-acre horses farm. Attractive country
house, quietly situated in beautiful
unspoilt Cotswold village. Heated
swimming pool. Friendly, helpful service.
Inn nearby.*
Bedrooms: 2 double, 2 twin
Bathrooms: 2 public

Bed & breakfast

per night:	£min	£max
Single	25.00	25.00
Double	39.00	42.00

Evening meal 1800 (last orders 2000)
Parking for 6

🐴3♿📶🗄🖥♿🐕🍴📶UL🏛💺🏛🎨🐴🔍 ⛎✿✈🚐

Southwold Guest House ♏
♕♕ COMMENDED

Station Road, Broadway,
Worcestershire WR12 7DE
☎ (01386) 853681 & Mobile (0589)
950833
*Warm welcome, friendly service, good
cooking at this large Edwardian house,
only 4 minutes' walk from village
centre. Reductions for 2 or more nights;
bargain winter breaks.*
Bedrooms: 1 single, 5 double, 2 twin
Bathrooms: 5 en-suite, 2 public

Bed & breakfast

per night:	£min	£max
Single	15.00	17.00
Double	30.00	40.00

Parking for 8
Cards accepted: Access, Visa, Amex,
Switch/Delta

🐴🖥♿🐕📶UL📺🏛💺✿🚐SP

COLOUR MAPS

Colour maps at the back of
this guide pinpoint all places
in which you will find
accommodation listed.

BROADWAY

Continued

Tudor Cottage

⛊

High Street, Broadway,
Worcestershire WR12 7DT
☎ (01386) 852674
*Classic 17th C Cotswold-stone Grade II
house in centre of the village. All
bedrooms en-suite. Off-street parking.*
Bedrooms: 2 double, 1 twin
Bathrooms: 3 en-suite

Bed & breakfast

per night:	£min	£max
Single	30.00	35.00
Double	45.00	50.00

Parking for 4

⛊🏠🛏🗴🛇♿🔌UL🛆S✂️🎿🖭🧺🚗🚲

White Acres Guesthouse ⛊

⛊⛊ HIGHLY COMMENDED

Station Road, Broadway,
Worcestershire WR12 7DE
☎ (01386) 852320
*Spacious Victorian house with en-suite
bedrooms, 3 with four-poster beds.
Off-road parking. 4 minutes' walk from
village centre. Reductions for 2 or more
nights. Bargain winter breaks.*
Bedrooms: 5 double, 1 twin
Bathrooms: 6 en-suite

Bed & breakfast

per night:	£min	£max
Double	38.00	42.00

Parking for 8
Open March–October

🛇🏠🔌♿UL✂️🎿🖭🧺🚗❀🐾
🚲SP T

Windrush House ⛊

⛊⛊ COMMENDED

Station Road, Broadway,
Worcestershire WR12 7DE
☎ (01386) 853577
*Edwardian guesthouse on the A44, 300
yards from the village centre, offering
personal service. Evening meals by
arrangement. 10 per cent reduction in
tariff after 2 nights. A no-smoking
establishment.*
Bedrooms: 4 double, 1 twin
Bathrooms: 5 en-suite

Bed & breakfast

per night:	£min	£max
Single	18.00	25.00
Double	36.00	44.00

Half board per

person:	£min	£max
Daily	30.00	34.00
Weekly	200.00	220.00

Parking for 5

🗴🛇♿UL🛆✂️🎿📺🖭🧺❀🚲SP

BROMSGROVE

Hereford and Worcester
Map ref 4B3

This market town near the Lickey
Hills has an interesting museum and
craft centre and 14th C church with
fine tombs and a Carillon tower.
The Avoncroft Museum of Buildings
is nearby where many old buildings
have been re-assembled, having been
saved from destruction.
*Tourist Information Centre ☎ (01527)
831809*

The Barn ⛊

⛊⛊ COMMENDED

Woodman Lane, Clent, Stourbridge,
Worcestershire DY9 9PX
☎ Hagley (01562) 885879 &
Kingswinford (01384) 401977
*Converted Georgian barn on
smallholding. At foot of Clent Hills with
access to the hills from property. Easy
access to Birmingham and National
Exhibition Centre.*
Bedrooms: 1 triple
Bathrooms: 1 en-suite

Bed & breakfast

per night:	£min	£max
Single	25.00	
Double	50.00	

Parking for 11

🛇🏠🛏🗴🛇♿UL S✂️🎿🖭🚗❀
🚲🏘

The Grahams

Listed COMMENDED

95 Old Station Road, Bromsgrove,
Worcestershire B60 2AF
☎ (01527) 874463
*Modern house in quiet, pleasant
location close to the A38, 3 miles from
the M5 and 1.5 miles from the M42.
Within easy reach of National
Exhibition Centre, Worcester and
Stratford. Car parking, TV lounge,
tea/coffee facilities.*
Bedrooms: 2 single, 1 twin
Bathrooms: 1 public

Bed & breakfast

per night:	£min	£max
Single	16.00	17.00
Double	32.00	34.00

Half board per

person:	£min	£max
Daily	22.00	23.00
Weekly	132.00	138.00

Evening meal 1800 (last orders
0900)
Parking for 2

🛇2🗴♿UL🛆✂️📺🖭🚗🚗✕🚲🏘

Hill Farm ⛊

⛊⛊ COMMENDED

Rocky Lane, Bournheath,
Bromsgrove, Worcestershire
B61 9HU
☎ (01527) 872403
*50-acre market garden. Georgian listed
farmhouse, tastefully maintained
throughout. Traditional farmhouse fare.
Families welcome.*
Bedrooms: 3 single, 2 twin
Bathrooms: 5 en-suite

Bed & breakfast

per night:	£min	£max
Single	18.50	20.00
Double	36.00	40.00

Evening meal 1800 (last orders
2000)
Parking for 6

⛊🏠🛏🗴🛇♿UL🛆S✂️🎿📺🖭🚗❀
🐾🚲🏘

Lower Bentley Farm ⛊

⛊⛊ COMMENDED

Lower Bentley Lane, Lower Bentley,
Bromsgrove, Worcestershire
B60 4JB
☎ (01527) 821286

*300-acre dairy & livestock farm.
Victorian farmhouse in picturesque,
tranquil countryside yet only 5 miles
from M5, M42. Easy access to
Midlands main attractions, including
Warwick, NEC and Black Country.*
Bedrooms: 1 double, 2 twin
Bathrooms: 2 en-suite, 1 private

Bed & breakfast

per night:	£min	£max
Single	20.00	22.50
Double	36.00	36.00

Parking for 6

⛊🏠🛏🗴🛇♿UL S🎿📺🖭🚗U❀
🚲SP ♨

For ideas on places to visit
refer to the introduction at
the beginning of this section.

Half board prices are given
per person, but in some cases
these may be based on
double/twin occupancy.

BROMYARD

Hereford and Worcester
Map ref 2B1

Market town on the River Frome surrounded by orchards, with black and white houses and a Norman church. Nearby at Lower Brockhampton is a 14th C half-timbered moated manor house owned by the National Trust. Heritage Centre.
Tourist Information Centre ☎ (01885) 482038

Park House 🅰🅰
♛♛

28 Sherford Street, Bromyard, Herefordshire HR7 4DL
☎ (01885) 482294
Close to town centre, restaurant and shops, and a desirable location for touring. Ample parking.
Bedrooms: 1 single, 1 double, 1 twin, 2 triple
Bathrooms: 3 en-suite, 1 public

Bed & breakfast

per night:	£min	£max
Single	16.00	20.00
Double	30.00	32.00

Parking for 6
🏠♿♨📺 Ⓤ Ⓛ Ⓢ ✂🕮 📺 🖼 🚘❄🦮🚂

BROSELEY

Shropshire
Map ref 4A3

Lord Hill Guest House
Listed

Duke Street, Broseley TF12 5LU
☎ Telford (01952) 884270
Former public house renovated to a high standard. Easy access to Ironbridge, Bridgnorth, Shrewsbury and Telford town centre.
Bedrooms: 1 single, 1 double, 5 twin
Bathrooms: 3 private, 2 public, 1 private shower

Bed & breakfast

per night:	£min	£max
Single	16.00	18.00
Double	30.00	34.00

Parking for 9
🏠♿8 🎿♨🖥📺🖼❄🦮 ⓄAP SP

BUCKNELL

Shropshire
Map ref 4A3

Village by the River Redlake with thatched black and white cottages, a Norman church and the remains of an Iron Age fort on a nearby hill. It is a designated Area of Outstanding Natural Beauty.

The Hall 🅰🅰
♛♛ COMMENDED

Bucknell SY7 0AA
☎ (01547) 530249
200-acre mixed farm. Georgian farmhouse in the picturesque village of Bucknell, with a peaceful and relaxed atmosphere.
Bedrooms: 2 double, 1 twin
Bathrooms: 1 en-suite, 1 public

Bed & breakfast

per night:	£min	£max
Single	17.00	
Double	34.00	

Half board per person:

	£min	£max
Daily	26.00	
Weekly	175.00	

Evening meal 1800 (last orders 1200)
Parking for 4
Open March–November
🏠🍷7🖥♿ Ⓤ Ⓛ ✂🕮 📺❄🦮🚂

BURTON UPON TRENT

Staffordshire
Map ref 4B3

An important brewing town with the Bass Museum of Brewing, where the Bass shire horses are stabled. There are 3 bridges with views over the river and some interesting public buildings including the 18th C St Modwen's Church.
Tourist Information Centre ☎ (01283) 516609 or 508589

Hayfield House
Listed

13 Ashby Road, Woodville, Swadlincote, Derbyshire DE11 7BZ
☎ Burton on Trent (01283) 225620
Victorian villa on the A50 in South Derbyshire, close to the Leicestershire/Staffordshire/Derbyshire border.
Bedrooms: 1 triple, 1 family room
Bathrooms: 1 private, 1 public

Bed & breakfast

per night:	£min	£max
Single	18.00	18.00
Double	32.00	32.00

Parking for 3
🏠🖥♨♿ Ⓤ Ⓛ Ⓢ 🕮 📺 🖼 🚘❄🚐

New Inn Farm

Listed

Needwood, Burton upon Trent DE13 9PB
☎ Burton-upon-Trent (01283) 575435 & Mobile 0831 099621
122-acre mixed farm. In the heart of Needwood Forest on the main B5234 Newborough to Burton upon Trent road. B5017 goes right past the farmhouse gate. Central for Uttoxeter, Lichfield, Derby and Burton upon Trent.
Bedrooms: 1 single, 1 double, 1 triple
Bathrooms: 1 public

Bed & breakfast

per night:	£min	£max
Single	15.00	
Double	30.00	

Parking for 6
🏠♿♨ Ⓤ Ⓛ ✂🕮 📺 🖼 🚘❄🦮🚐

BUTTERTON

Staffordshire
Map ref 4B2

Village close to Thor's Cave, Hartington and the beautiful scenery of Dovedale.

Butterton Moor House 🅰🅰
♛♛ HIGHLY COMMENDED

Parsons Lane, Butterton, Leek ST13 7PD
☎ (01538) 304506
Fax (01538) 304506

Beautiful 17th C Peak District farmhouse with beams, antiques. Superb facilities, all en-suite. Indoor swimming pool, snooker room.
Bedrooms: 2 double, 1 twin
Bathrooms: 3 en-suite, 1 public

Bed & breakfast

per night:	£min	£max
Single	35.00	
Double	45.00	50.00

Parking for 12
🏠♿8🖥♨♿ Ⓤ Ⓛ Ⓢ 🖴 ✂🕮 📺 🖼 🚘
🔍🌂♿❄🦮🚐

CALMSDEN

Gloucestershire
Map ref 2B1

The Old House

Listed **COMMENDED**

Calmsden, Cirencester GL7 5ET
☎ Cirencester (01285) 831240
*300-acre arable & livestock farm.
Attractive 15th C Cotswold stone
house, full of charm and character, in a
peaceful rural setting.*
Bedrooms: 1 double, 1 twin
Bathrooms: 2 public
Bed & breakfast

per night:	£min	£max
Single	17.50	25.00
Double	35.00	50.00

Parking for 5
Open March–October

CANON FROME

Hereford and Worcester
Map ref 2B1

This village in the Frome Valley has a
modest Victorian church within the
shadow of the 18th C Frome Court.

Mill Cottage

COMMENDED

Canon Frome, Ledbury,
Herefordshire HR8 2TD
☎ Ledbury (01531) 670506 &
Mobile 0831 762902
*Set in beautiful wooded grounds
intersected by the River Frome, two
large, comfortable en-suite rooms in
separate wing with guest lounge.*
Bedrooms: 1 double, 1 twin
Bathrooms: 2 en-suite, 1 public
Bed & breakfast

per night:	£min	£max
Single	20.00	25.00
Double	31.00	37.00

Parking for 6

CARDINGTON

Shropshire
Map ref 4A3

Grove Farm

Listed **APPROVED**

Cardington, Church Stretton
SY6 7JZ
☎ Longville (01694) 771451
*7-acre mixed farm. Oak-beamed
farmhouse built in 1667, in delightful
village 5 miles from Church Stretton.
Excellent walking country. Homely
atmosphere.*

Bedrooms: 1 twin, 1 triple
Bathrooms: 1 public
Bed & breakfast

per night:	£min	£max
Single	16.00	17.00
Double	28.00	32.00

Parking for 10

CHEADLE

Staffordshire
Map ref 4B2

Caverswall Castle ⋀

Caverswall ST11 9EA
☎ Caverswall (01782) 393239
Fax (01782) 394590
*Medieval and Jacobean castle, panelled
en-suite bedrooms, billiard room,
swimming pool and extensive grounds.
Once home to Wedgwood family. Near
Potteries, Peak District and Alton
Towers.*
Bedrooms: 3 double
Bathrooms: 3 en-suite
Bed & breakfast

per night:	£min	£max
Double	60.00	80.00

Parking for 18

CHELMARSH

Shropshire
Map ref 4A3

An unspoilt village near the River
Severn, with old timbered cottages
and an imposing 14th C church.

Bulls Head Inn ⋀

COMMENDED

Chelmarsh, Bridgnorth WV16 6BA
☎ Highley (01746) 861469
Fax (01746) 862646

*17th C village inn with warm friendly
atmosphere. All rooms en-suite. TV
lounge, jacuzzi. Magnificent views.*
Bedrooms: 1 single, 3 double, 1 twin,
1 triple
Bathrooms: 6 en-suite
Bed & breakfast

per night:	£min	£max
Single	22.50	27.00
Double	34.00	41.00

Half board per person:	£min	£max
Daily	30.50	35.00
Weekly	175.00	192.50

Lunch available
Evening meal 1900 (last orders
2130)
Parking for 50
Cards accepted: Access, Visa,
Switch/Delta

CHELTENHAM

Gloucestershire
Map ref 2B1

Cheltenham was developed as a spa
town in the 18th C and has some
beautiful Regency architecture, in
particular the Pittville Pump Room.
It holds international music and
literature festivals and is also famous
for its race meetings and cricket.
*Tourist Information Centre ☎ (01242)
522878*

Barn End

Listed

23 Cheltenham Road, Bishop's
Cleeve, Cheltenham GL52 4LU
☎ (01242) 672404
*Large, spacious and comfortable
detached house. Convenient for
Cheltenham (4 miles) and its
racecourse (2 miles), also Tewkesbury,
Stratford and Cotswolds. Horse riding,
walking and golf on Cleeve Common (1
mile).*
Bedrooms: 1 double, 2 twin
Bathrooms: 1 en-suite, 1 public
Bed & breakfast

per night:	£min	£max
Single	37.00	50.00
Double	37.00	50.00

Parking for 7

Beaumont House Hotel ⋀

HIGHLY COMMENDED

Shurdington Road, Cheltenham
GL53 0JE
☎ (01242) 245986
Fax (01242) 520044
*Ideally situated where Cheltenham
meets the Cotswolds, close to town
centre or hill walks: Relaxation, comfort
and service are our hallmarks. Private
parking, garden.*
Bedrooms: 2 single, 6 double, 5 twin,
1 triple, 1 family room
Bathrooms: 15 en-suite
Bed & breakfast

per night:	£min	£max
Single	37.00	37.00
Double	45.00	58.00

Half board per person:	£min	£max
Daily	39.00	44.00
Weekly	241.00	261.00

Evening meal 1900 (last orders 2000)
Parking for 20
Cards accepted: Access, Visa, Amex

Cleyne Hage ⚠

Southam Lane, Southam, Cheltenham GL52 3NY
☎ (01242) 518569 & Mobile 0850 285338
Fax (01242) 518569
Cotswold-stone house in secluded setting between B4632 and A435, on the Cotswold Way, 3 miles north of Cheltenham. Open view of hills and racecourse. Off-road parking. Non-smokers only, please.
Bedrooms: 1 single, 1 double, 1 twin
Bathrooms: 2 en-suite, 2 public

Bed & breakfast

per night:	£min	£max
Single	18.00	20.00
Double	35.00	45.00

Parking for 8
Open March–October
Cards accepted: Access, Visa

Elmington Bed and Breakfast ⚠

Listed HIGHLY COMMENDED

44 Leckhampton Road, Cheltenham GL53 0BB
☎ (01242) 573357
Victorian mid-terrace house on 4 levels, in wide tree-lined road leading to town centre.
Bedrooms: 1 single, 1 double, 1 twin
Bathrooms: 1 en-suite, 1 public

Bed & breakfast

per night:	£min	£max
Single	18.00	20.00
Double	36.00	45.00

Ham Hill Farm ⚠

COMMENDED

Whittington, Cheltenham GL54 4EZ
☎ (01242) 584415
160-acre mixed farm. Farmhouse, built in 1983 to a high standard, with good views of the Cotswolds. 2 miles from Cheltenham, on the Cotswold Way.
Bedrooms: 4 double, 2 twin, 1 family room
Bathrooms: 6 en-suite, 1 public

Bed & breakfast

per night:	£min	£max
Single	23.50	23.50
Double	40.00	44.00

Parking for 7

Lawn House ⚠

COMMENDED

11 London Road, Cheltenham GL52 6EX
☎ (01242) 578486
Fax (01242) 578486
Elegant Grade II listed house. Good parking and close to town centre. Friendly atmosphere, family-run. TVs, beverage trays, good food, comfortable rooms. A non-smoking establishment.
Bedrooms: 2 single, 3 double, 2 twin, 1 triple
Bathrooms: 3 en-suite, 2 public

Bed & breakfast

per night:	£min	£max
Single	22.50	29.00
Double	39.00	49.00

Half board per person:

	£min	£max
Daily	31.50	58.00
Weekly	200.00	350.00

Evening meal 1730 (last orders 1900)
Parking for 10
Cards accepted: Access, Visa, Switch/Delta

Lonsdale House ⚠

COMMENDED

Montpellier Drive, Cheltenham GL50 1TX
☎ (01242) 232379
Fax (01242) 232379
Regency house situated 5 minutes' walk from the town hall, promenade, shopping centre, parks and theatre. Easy access to all main routes.
Bedrooms: 5 single, 2 double, 1 twin, 2 triple, 1 family room
Bathrooms: 3 en-suite, 4 public

Bed & breakfast

per night:	£min	£max
Single	18.00	30.00
Double	36.00	45.00

Parking for 6
Cards accepted: Access, Visa

Information on accommodation listed in this guide has been supplied by the proprietors. As changes may occur you are advised to check details at the time of booking.

Old Rectory ⚠

COMMENDED

Woolstone, Cheltenham GL52 4RG
☎ Bishops Cleeve (01242) 673766
Beautiful Victorian rectory in peaceful hamlet, 4 miles north of the Regency town of Cheltenham. Tranquil spot with lovely views.
Bedrooms: 2 double, 1 twin
Bathrooms: 3 en-suite

Bed & breakfast

per night:	£min	£max
Single	28.00	28.00
Double	40.00	40.00

Parking for 6

St. Michaels ⚠

COMMENDED

4 Montpellier Drive, Cheltenham GL50 1TX
☎ (01242) 513587
Elegant Edwardian guesthouse offering delightful accommodation in a friendly informal atmosphere. Quiet location five minutes' walk from town hall, promenade, restaurants and theatres. Parking.
Bedrooms: 2 double, 1 twin, 2 triple
Bathrooms: 4 en-suite, 1 public

Bed & breakfast

per night:	£min	£max
Single	23.00	30.00
Double	35.00	44.00

Parking for 3
Cards accepted: Access, Visa

The Wynyards ⚠

HIGHLY COMMENDED

Butts Lane, Woodmancote, Cheltenham GL52 4QH
☎ (01242) 673876
Secluded old Cotswold-stone house in elevated position with panoramic views. Set in open countryside on outskirts of small village, 4 miles from Cheltenham.
Bedrooms: 1 double, 2 twin
Bathrooms: 2 private, 1 public

Bed & breakfast

per night:	£min	£max
Single	18.00	18.00
Double	36.00	36.00

Parking for 6

A key to symbols can be found inside the back cover flap.

CHIPPING CAMPDEN

Gloucestershire
Map ref 2B1

Outstanding Cotswold wool town with many old stone gabled houses, a splendid church and 17th C almshouses. Nearby are Kiftsgate Court Gardens and Hidcote Manor Gardens (National Trust).

Manor Farm

👑👑 COMMENDED

Weston Subedge, Chipping Campden GL55 6QH
☎ Evesham (01386) 840390 & Mobile (0589) 108812
600-acre mixed farm. Traditional 17th C farmhouse, an excellent base for touring the Cotswolds, Shakespeare country and Hidcote Gardens. Warm, friendly atmosphere. Walled garden. All rooms en-suite with tea/coffee making facilities, TV/radio. 1.5 miles from Chipping Campden.
Bedrooms: 2 double, 1 twin
Bathrooms: 3 en-suite

Bed & breakfast per night:	£min	£max
Single	25.00	25.00
Double	40.00	40.00
Parking for 8		

Nineveh Farm

👑

Campden Road, Mickleton, Chipping Campden GL55 6PS
☎ (01386) 438921 & 438923

27-acre livestock & horses farm. 18th C farmhouse with Virginia creeper, beams and flagstones. Working farm with homely accommodation and log fires. Ideal for Cotswolds, Stratford, Warwick Castle and Chipping Campden with its famous High Street.
Bedrooms: 2 double, 1 twin
Bathrooms: 2 en-suite, 1 private

Bed & breakfast per night:	£min	£max
Double	36.00	50.00

Half board per person:	£min	£max
Daily	30.00	42.00
Parking for 7		

Orchard Hill House

👑👑 HIGHLY COMMENDED

Broad Campden, Chipping Campden GL55 6UU
☎ Evesham (01386) 841473
Fax (01386) 841030

17th C Cotswold-stone restored farmhouse. Breakfast in flagstoned dining room with inglenook fireplace around 10ft elm farmhouse table.
Bedrooms: 1 double, 1 twin, 1 triple
Bathrooms: 3 en-suite

Bed & breakfast per night:	£min	£max
Single	38.00	45.00
Double	44.00	55.00
Parking for 6		

Sparlings

👑 COMMENDED

Leysbourne, High Street, Chipping Campden GL55 6HL
☎ Evesham (01386) 840505

Fully centrally heated, comfortable, attractive 18th C Cotswold house in Chipping Campden High Street. Walled garden. Easy parking. Children over 6 welcome.
Bedrooms: 1 double, 1 twin
Bathrooms: 1 en-suite, 1 private

Bed & breakfast per night:	£min	£max
Single	26.50	26.50
Double	45.00	47.00

Wyldlands

Listed COMMENDED

Broad Campden, Chipping Campden GL55 6UR
☎ Evesham (01386) 840478
Rooms with a view. Welcoming comfortable home in conservation village. "Yellow Book" garden. Ideal walking and touring. Traditional inn nearby.
Bedrooms: 2 double, 1 twin
Bathrooms: 1 en-suite, 2 public

Bed & breakfast per night:	£min	£max
Single	22.00	25.00
Double	36.00	40.00
Parking for 4		

CHURCH STRETTON

Shropshire
Map ref 4A3

Church Stretton lies under the eastern slope of the Longmynd surrounded by hills. It is ideal for walkers, with marvellous views, golf and gliding. Wenlock Edge is not far away.

Acton Scott Farm

👑 COMMENDED

Acton Scott, Church Stretton SY6 6QN
☎ Marshbrook (01694) 781260
320-acre mixed farm. Conveniently situated 17th C farmhouse of character with comfortable, spacious rooms and log fires. Beautiful countryside.
Bedrooms: 1 double, 1 twin, 1 family room
Bathrooms: 1 en-suite, 1 public

Bed & breakfast per night:	£min	£max
Double	30.00	40.00
Parking for 6		
Open March–October		

The Elms

Listed

Little Stretton, Church Stretton SY6 6RD
☎ (01694) 723084
Victorian country house in spacious grounds, decorated and furnished in Victorian style.
Bedrooms: 2 double, 1 twin
Bathrooms: 2 public

Bed & breakfast per night:	£min	£max
Single		19.00
Double		33.00
Parking for 3		

Gilberries Cottage

👑 COMMENDED

Wall-under-Heywood, Church Stretton SY6 7HZ
☎ Longville (01694) 771400
Country cottage adjoining family farm, in peaceful and beautiful countryside. Ideal for walking. Numerous places of interest nearby.

Bedrooms: 1 twin, 1 triple
Bathrooms: 1 public

Bed & breakfast

per night:	£min	£max
Single	20.00	20.00
Double	32.00	36.00

Parking for 8
Open February–November

Woolston Farm ▲

👑 COMMENDED

Church Stretton SY6 6QD
☎ Marshbrook (01694) 781201
350-acre mixed farm. Victorian farmhouse in the small hamlet of Woolston, off A49. Ideal position for touring Shropshire. Outstanding views and good farmhouse fare.
Bedrooms: 2 double, 1 twin
Bathrooms: 1 en-suite, 1 public

Bed & breakfast

per night:	£min	£max
Single		17.00
Double		34.00

Half board per

person:	£min	£max
Daily	25.50	
Weekly	164.50	

Evening meal 1850 (last orders 2000)
Parking for 2
Open January–November

CIRENCESTER

Gloucestershire
Map ref 2B1

"Capital of the Cotswolds", Cirencester was Britain's second most important Roman town with many finds housed in the Corinium Museum. It has a very fine Perpendicular church and old houses around the market place.
Tourist Information Centre ☎ (01285) 654180

Landage House

Listed COMMENDED

Rendcomb, Cirencester GL7 7HB
☎ (01285) 831250
Superb small "manor" type house. Very warm and comfortable, quiet at night. Excellent walks, glorious views.
Bedrooms: 1 double, 2 twin
Bathrooms: 1 en-suite, 1 public

Bed & breakfast

per night:	£min	£max
Single	27.50	
Double	50.00	

Parking for 4

The Masons Arms ▲

👑👑 COMMENDED

High Street, Meysey Hampton, Cirencester GL7 5JT
☎ (01285) 850164
Fax (01285) 850164

Seeking peace and tranquillity? Treat yourself to a break in this 17th C inn set beside the village green. Oak beams and log fire. A warm welcome awaits you.
Bedrooms: 6 double, 1 twin, 1 triple
Bathrooms: 8 en-suite

Bed & breakfast

per night:	£min	£max
Single	28.00	32.00
Double	44.00	49.00

Lunch available
Evening meal 1900 (last orders 2130)
Parking for 8
Cards accepted: Access, Visa

The Old Rectory ▲

👑👑 COMMENDED

Rodmarton, Cirencester GL7 6PE
☎ (01285) 841246
Fax (01285) 841246
17th C rectory set in three-quarters of an acre of gardens. Cirencester 6 miles, Tetbury 5 miles. Equidistant Swindon, Cheltenham and Gloucester.
Bedrooms: 1 double, 1 twin
Bathrooms: 2 en-suite

Bed & breakfast

per night:	£min	£max
Single	20.00	25.00
Double	35.00	40.00

Half board per

person:	£min	£max
Daily	29.50	35.00

Evening meal 1900 (last orders 2100)
Parking for 6

Smerrill Barns ▲

👑👑 COMMENDED

Kemble, Cirencester GL7 6BW
☎ (01285) 770907
Fax (01285) 770706

Accommodation in a listed barn, providing all modern facilities. Situated 3 miles from Cirencester on the A429.
Bedrooms: 1 single, 4 double, 1 twin, 1 family room
Bathrooms: 7 en-suite, 1 public

Bed & breakfast

per night:	£min	£max
Single	30.00	35.00
Double	45.00	55.00

Parking for 7
Cards accepted: Access, Visa, Switch/Delta

Sunset

Listed COMMENDED

Baunton Lane, Cirencester GL7 2NQ
☎ (01285) 654822

Small, friendly, detached house pleasantly situated close to Cirencester. Easy access to Cheltenham, Gloucester and Swindon.
Bedrooms: 2 single, 1 twin
Bathrooms: 1 public

Bed & breakfast

per night:	£min	£max
Single	13.50	15.00
Double	27.00	30.00

Parking for 4
Open April–October

The Village Pub

Listed APPROVED

Barnsley, Cirencester GL7 5EF
☎ (01285) 740421
The Village Pub has 5 rooms, all with private facilities, and is situated in a pretty Cotswold village.
Bedrooms: 4 double, 1 twin
Bathrooms: 4 en-suite, 1 private

Bed & breakfast

per night:	£min	£max
Single	32.00	
Double	47.00	

Continued ▶

CIRENCESTER

Continued

Lunch available
Evening meal 1900 (last orders 2130)
Parking for 40
Cards accepted: Access, Visa, Amex

Wimborne House 🅜

🏵🏵 COMMENDED

91 Victoria Road, Cirencester
GL7 1ES
☎ (01285) 653890

Victorian Cotswold-stone house, with a warm and friendly atmosphere and spacious rooms. Four-poster room. Non-smokers only, please.
Bedrooms: 4 double, 1 twin
Bathrooms: 5 en-suite
Bed & breakfast

per night:	£min	£max
Single	20.00	28.00
Double	30.00	40.00

Half board per

person:	£min	£max
Daily	21.50	26.50
Weekly	145.50	180.50

Evening meal 1830 (last orders 1730)
Parking for 6

CLEOBURY MORTIMER

Shropshire
Map ref 4A3

Village with attractive timbered and Georgian houses and a church with a wooden spire. It is close to the Clee Hills with marvellous views.

Kings Arms Hotel

🏵🏵🏵

Church Street, Cleobury Mortimer, Kidderminster, Worcestershire
DY14 8BS
☎ (01299) 270252
16th C coaching inn, famous for fine food, in centre of picturesque village. Close to golf, fishing, safari park and Severn Valley Railway.
Bedrooms: 2 double, 1 twin
Bathrooms: 3 en-suite, 1 public

Bed & breakfast per night:	£min	£max
Single	25.00	28.00
Double	50.00	50.00

Half board per person:	£min	£max
Daily	30.00	50.00

Lunch available
Evening meal 1900 (last orders 2100)
Parking for 4
Cards accepted: Access, Visa

The Old Bake House 🅜

🏵🏵 COMMENDED

46/47 High Street, Cleobury Mortimer, Kidderminster, Worcestershire DY14 8DQ
☎ (01299) 270193
Grade II listed townhouse, formerly both a public house and bakery, with 18th C frontage. Home cooking. Vegetarians welcome, special diets by arrangement.
Bedrooms: 1 double, 1 twin
Bathrooms: 1 en-suite, 1 private

Bed & breakfast per night:	£min	£max
Single	16.00	18.00
Double	32.00	36.00

Half board per person:	£min	£max
Daily	23.00	25.00
Weekly	155.00	170.00

Evening meal 1900 (last orders 2000)
Parking for 2

CLUN

Shropshire
Map ref 4A3

Small, ancient town on the Welsh border with flint and stone tools in its museum and Iron Age forts nearby. The impressive ruins of a Norman castle lie beside the River Clun and there are some interesting 17th C houses.

Birches Mill 🅜

🏵 HIGHLY COMMENDED

Birches Mill, Clun, Craven Arms
SY7 8NL
☎ (01588) 640409
Fax (01588) 640409
17th C farmhouse in secluded valley on river banks. Exposed beams, inglenook with open fire, traditional furnishings and pretty cottage garden.
Bedrooms: 2 double, 1 twin
Bathrooms: 1 public

Bed & breakfast per night:	£min	£max
Double	37.00	37.00

Half board per person:	£min	£max
Daily	32.50	32.50

Evening meal 1900 (last orders 2030)
Parking for 5
Open April–October

Clun Farm

Listed COMMENDED

High Street, Clun, Craven Arms
SY7 8JB
☎ (01588) 640432
200-acre mixed farm. 16th C double cruck farmhouse situated in Clun High Street, within 200 metres of 3 public houses and restaurants.
Bedrooms: 2 single, 1 triple, 1 family room
Bathrooms: 1 en-suite, 1 public

Bed & breakfast per night:	£min	£max
Single	16.00	18.00
Double	32.00	36.00

Parking for 6

Cockford Hall 🅜

🏵🏵 DE LUXE

Cockford Bank, Clun, Craven Arms
SY7 8LR
☎ Craven Arms (01588) 640327
Fax (01588) 640881
Historic Georgian house, beautifully restored, with wonderful views of the Clun Valley. House furnished with antiques. Superb bathrooms.
Bedrooms: 1 double, 1 twin
Suite available
Bathrooms: 2 en-suite

Bed & breakfast per night:	£min	£max
Single	25.00	30.00
Double	50.00	60.00

Half board per person:	£min	£max
Daily	40.00	45.00
Weekly	252.00	283.50

Evening meal 1900 (last orders 2100)
Parking for 6
Cards accepted: Access, Visa, Amex

All accommodation in this guide has been graded, or is awaiting a grading, by a trained Tourist Board inspector.

Hurst Mill Farm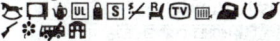

👑 COMMENDED

Clun, Craven Arms SY7 0JA
☎ (01588) 640224
100-acre mixed farm. Attractive farmhouse and old mill in the lovely Clun Valley. River and woodland trails, 2 riding ponies, pets welcome. Previous winner of "Great Shropshire Breakfast" challenge.
Bedrooms: 1 double, 2 twin
Bathrooms: 1 en-suite, 2 public

Bed & breakfast
per night:	£min	£max
Single	16.00	18.00
Double	32.00	36.00

Half board per
person:	£min	£max
Daily	25.00	25.00
Weekly	170.00	170.00

Parking for 8

CLUNGUNFORD

Shropshire
Map ref 4A3

Village near the River Clun and Stokesay Castle, a 13th C fortified manor house with an Elizabethan gatehouse.

Broadward Hall

Listed COMMENDED

Clungunford, Craven Arms SY7 0QA
☎ Bucknell (01547) 530357
176-acre mixed farm. Grade II listed, castellated building, 9 miles west of Ludlow in rural Clun Valley surroundings.
Bedrooms: 2 twin, 1 triple
Bathrooms: 2 public

Bed & breakfast
per night:	£min	£max
Single	14.00	15.00
Double	28.00	30.00

Half board per
person:	£min	£max
Daily	23.00	24.00
Weekly	148.00	

Evening meal 1900 (last orders 0900)
Parking for 15
Open March–November

A key to symbols can be found inside the back cover flap.

COLEFORD

Gloucestershire
Map ref 2A1

Small town in the Forest of Dean with the ancient iron mines at Clearwell Caves nearby, where mining equipment and geological samples are displayed. There are several forest trails in the area.
Tourist Information Centre ☎ (01594) 812388

Millend House and Garden

👑 HIGHLY COMMENDED

Newland, Coleford GL16 8NF
☎ Dean (01594) 832128
250-year-old traditional stone-built house, in 2 acres of lovely hillside gardens and woodlands. Situated at the end of a valley looking down towards Newland and the "Cathedral of the Forest".
Bedrooms: 1 double, 2 twin
Bathrooms: 1 en-suite, 1 public

Bed & breakfast
per night:	£min	£max
Single	23.00	28.00
Double	36.00	44.00

Parking for 4

Oak Farm

Listed APPROVED

Ross Road, English Bicknor, Coleford GL16 7PA
☎ Forest of Dean (01594) 860606
7-acre mixed farm. Modern farmhouse with superb views from all rooms, ideal for exploring the Forest of Dean and Wye Valley.
Bedrooms: 1 single, 1 double, 1 twin
Bathrooms: 1 en-suite, 1 private

Bed & breakfast
per night:	£min	£max
Single	14.00	16.00
Double	26.00	32.00

Evening meal from 1900
Parking for 6

For ideas on places to visit refer to the introduction at the beginning of this section.

Half board prices are given per person, but in some cases these may be based on double/twin occupancy.

COLESHILL

Warwickshire
Map ref 4B3

Close to Birmingham's many attractions including the 17th C Aston Hall with its plasterwork and furnishings, the Railway Museum and Sarehole Mill, an 18th C water-powered mill restored to working order.

Maxstoke Hall Farm

👑👑 HIGHLY COMMENDED

Maxstoke, Coleshill, Birmingham B46 2QT
☎ (01675) 463237
Fax (01675) 463237

230-acre arable farm. Elegant farmhouse, 1634, with en-suite rooms. 10 minutes from M42 and M6, 15 minutes from National Exhibition Centre and Birmingham Airport.
Bedrooms: 1 single, 2 twin
Bathrooms: 3 en-suite, 1 public

Bed & breakfast
per night:	£min	£max
Single	27.00	27.00
Double	47.00	47.00

Evening meal 1830 (last orders 2000)
Parking for 30

The Old Rectory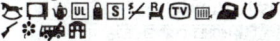

👑👑 HIGHLY COMMENDED

Church Lane, Maxstoke, Coleshill, Birmingham B46 2QW
☎ (01675) 462248
Fax (01675) 481615

Elegant Victorian rectory built from local sandstone, set in 5 acres of walled garden. Quiet and secluded situation, relaxed atmosphere.
Bedrooms: 2 double, 1 twin
Bathrooms: 3 en-suite

Continued ▶

COLESHILL
Continued

Bed & breakfast

per night:	£min	£max
Single	29.00	29.00
Double	46.00	46.00

Parking for 10

COTSWOLDS

See under Aldsworth, Berkeley, Bibury, Birdlip, Bledington, Blockley, Bourton-on-the-Water, Broad Campden, Broadway, Cheltenham, Chipping Campden, Cirencester, Donnington, Fairford, Gloucester, Great Rissington, Guiting Power, Lechlade, Moreton-in-Marsh, Nailsworth, Northleach, Nympsfield, Painswick, Rendcomb, Slimbridge, Stonehouse, Stow-on-the-Wold, Stroud, Teddington, Tetbury, Tewkesbury, Winchcombe, Wotton-under-Edge
See also Cotswolds in South of England region.

COVENTRY

West Midlands
Map ref 4B3

Modern city with a long history. It has many places of interest including the post-war and ruined medieval cathedrals, art gallery and museums, some 16th C almshouses, St Mary's Guildhall, Lunt Roman fort and the Belgrade Theatre.
Tourist Information Centre ☎ *(01203) 832303 or 832304*

Abigail Guesthouse
Listed COMMENDED
39 St. Patrick's Road, Coventry
CV1 2LP
☎ (01203) 221378
Family-run establishment in centre of city, very clean and friendly. Convenient for station, cathedral and city centre shopping, also NEC and NAC.
Bedrooms: 2 single, 1 double, 1 twin, 1 triple
Bathrooms: 2 public
Bed & breakfast

per night:	£min	£max
Single	16.00	18.00
Double	30.00	34.00

Falcon Hotel M
13-19 Manor Road, Coventry
CV1 2LH
☎ (01203) 258615
Fax (01203) 520680
Close to Coventry railway station, ideal for the travelling businessman. Ten

minutes from NEC, M6 motorway and Birmingham Airport. Large free car park. Shops, social and cultural activities readily at hand.*
Bedrooms: 6 single, 2 double, 3 twin, 3 triple, 1 family room
Bathrooms: 15 en-suite
Bed & breakfast

per night:	£min	£max
Single	35.00	45.00
Double	50.00	65.00

Half board per

person:	£min	£max
Daily	32.00	50.00

Lunch available
Evening meal 1900 (last orders 2145)
Parking for 50
Cards accepted: Access, Visa, Diners, Amex

Mill Farmhouse
Mill Lane, Fillongley, Coventry
CV7 8EE
☎ Fillongley (01676) 541898
Beautiful farmhouse set in picturesque countryside, offering peace and tranquillity. Detached bed and breakfast apartments with en-suite bathrooms and colour TV. Private car park and gardens. 15 minutes from Coventry, NEC, Birmingham Airport.
Bedrooms: 1 double, 1 twin
Bathrooms: 2 en-suite
Bed & breakfast

per night:	£min	£max
Single	25.00	
Double	40.00	45.00

Half board per

person:	£min	£max
Daily	27.00	33.00

Evening meal 1800 (last orders 2000)
Parking for 4

Westwood Cottage
79 Westwood Heath Road, Westwood Heath, Coventry
CV4 8GN
☎ (01203) 471084
Fax (01203) 471084
One of 4 sandstone farm cottages, circa 1834, in rural surroundings. Recently converted but with character maintained and offering comfortable accommodation for a small number of guests.
Bedrooms: 2 single, 1 double, 1 twin
Bathrooms: 4 en-suite

Bed & breakfast

per night:	£min	£max
Single	18.00	
Double	33.00	35.00

Parking for 5

CRAVEN ARMS

Shropshire
Map ref 4A3

Busy village on A49 renowned for its sheep markets. Close to Wenlock Edge and the Longmynd and an ideal centre for walking with many fine views. Nearby Stokesay Castle, a 13th C fortified manor house, the ruins of Hopton Castle and Ludlow.

Castle View
Listed HIGHLY COMMENDED
148 Stokesay, Craven Arms SY7 9AL
☎ (01588) 673712
Large, comfortable stone-built Victorian house. Within easy walking distance of Stokesay Castle and on route of the Shropshire Way.
Bedrooms: 1 double, 1 twin
Bathrooms: 1 en-suite, 1 private
Bed & breakfast

per night:	£min	£max
Single	16.00	
Double	32.00	34.00

Parking for 3

DEERHURST

Gloucestershire
Map ref 2B1

Deerhurst House M
HIGHLY COMMENDED
Deerhurst, Gloucester GL19 4BX
☎ Tewkesbury (01684) 292135 &
Mobile 0850 520051
Classical Georgian country house set in 3 acres on edge of ancient riverside village of Deerhurst, midway between Cheltenham, Tewkesbury and Gloucester.
Bedrooms: 1 double, 1 twin
Bathrooms: 2 private
Bed & breakfast

per night:	£min	£max
Single	25.00	25.00
Double	40.00	45.00

Parking for 10

DONNINGTON

Gloucestershire
Map ref 2B1

Holmleigh

Listed **APPROVED**

Donnington, Moreton-in-Marsh
GL56 0XX
☎ Cotswold (01451) 830792
*15-acre dairy farm. Farmhouse
accommodation with friendly welcome.
In a peaceful setting with own private
lane from the village of Donnington, 1
mile from Stow-on-the-Wold.*
Bedrooms: 2 twin
Bathrooms: 1 private, 1 public

Bed & breakfast

per night:	£min	£max
Single	12.50	14.00
Double	25.00	28.00

Parking for 3
Open April–October

🐎🖤5🕎🖃📺♿🍽📺Ⓤ🖊🖤📺📟❄🗡
🚐

DROITWICH

Hereford and Worcester
Map ref 2B1

Old town with natural brine springs,
now incorporated into the Brine
Baths Health Centre, developed as a
spa at the beginning of the 19th C.
Of particular interest is the Church
of the Sacred Heart with splendid
mosaics. Fine parks and a Heritage
Centre.
Tourist Information Centre ☎ *(01905)
774312*

Caulin Court

Listed

Ladywood, Droitwich,
Worcestershire WR9 0AL
☎ Worcester (01905) 756382 &
Mobile (0585) 246699
*Lovely old country house set in 20
acres, 2 miles from Droitwich, 3 miles
from Worcester. Easy access to
motorways.*
Bedrooms: 1 double, 1 twin
Bathrooms: 1 en-suite, 1 private

Bed & breakfast

per night:	£min	£max
Single	20.00	22.50
Double	22.50	25.00

Parking for 6

🐎🖤10🖃📺♿🕎Ⓤ🖊📟🖤🕯🔌
♿❄🚐🅿

Map references apply to
the colour maps at the
back of this guide.

Richmond Guest House 🏔

Listed

3 Ombersley St. West, Droitwich,
Worcestershire WR9 8HZ
☎ Worcester (01905) 775722
Fax (01905) 794500
*Victorian-built guesthouse in the town
centre, 5 minutes from railway station
and bus route. English breakfast. 30
minutes from National Exhibition
Centre via M5/M42.*
Bedrooms: 8 single, 1 twin, 4 triple,
2 family rooms
Bathrooms: 3 public

Bed & breakfast

per night:	£min	£max
Single	16.00	18.00
Double	28.00	30.00

Parking for 12

🐎🖤🖃📺♿🕎Ⓤ🖊🔌📺📟🖤

South Hall Farm

👑👑 COMMENDED

Doverdale, Droitwich,
Worcestershire WR9 0QB
☎ Cutnall Green (01299) 851236
Fax (01299) 851531

*Three-storey 17th C farmhouse in 3
acres of mature gardens surrounded by
open countryside. Well proportioned
comfortable rooms, log fires. Cordon
Bleu cooking. Traditional decoration.
Brass four-poster bed.*
Bedrooms: 1 double, 2 twin
Bathrooms: 1 en-suite, 1 public

Bed & breakfast

per night:	£min	£max
Single	18.00	25.00
Double	36.00	50.00

**Half board per
person:**

	£min	£max
Daily	28.00	

Evening meal 1900 (last orders
2000)
Parking for 6

🐎🖤12📺🖃📺♿🕎Ⓤ🔌🖊🔌📟
🖤🔍🔌♿🕯❄🗡🚐🏔

Temple Broughton Farm

👑👑 HIGHLY COMMENDED

Broughton Green, Droitwich,
Worcestershire WR9 7EF
☎ Himbleton (01905) 391456
*Grade II listed farmhouse in very quiet
situation. Rolling countryside, superb
views. Tennis court, animals. Evening
meal by arrangement.*
Bedrooms: 2 double, 1 twin
Bathrooms: 2 en-suite, 1 private

Bed & breakfast

per night:	£min	£max
Single	20.00	20.00
Double	40.00	45.00

Parking for 12

🖤🖃📺♿🕎Ⓤ🖊🖤📺📟🖤� 🍽16♿❄
🚐🏔

DUNCHURCH

Warwickshire
Map ref 4C3

The 14th C church has a sandstone
tower, Norman doorway and
Norman font. The northern chapel
arcade is Victorian. Nearby is a
statue of Lord John Scott, the
seafaring sportsman, dating from
1867.

Toft Hill

Listed **COMMENDED**

Dunchurch, Rugby CV22 6NR
☎ Rugby (01788) 810342
*Large country house set in mature
gardens, half a mile from the centre of
Dunchurch on Southam road.*
Bedrooms: 1 single, 1 twin, 1 triple
Bathrooms: 1 en-suite, 1 public

Bed & breakfast

per night:	£min	£max
Single	19.00	19.00
Double	38.00	38.00

Parking for 5

🐎🖤8🖤Ⓤ📺📟🖤🔌🕯❄🚐

EASTCOMBE

Gloucestershire
Map ref 2B1

Pretoria Villa

Listed

Wells Road, Eastcombe, Stroud
GL6 7EE
☎ Gloucester (01452) 770435
*Cotswold-stone double-fronted
detached house, built c1900, with
private gardens. In quiet village lane
with beautiful views.*
Bedrooms: 1 single, 1 double, 1 twin
Bathrooms: 1 en-suite, 2 private,
1 public

Bed & breakfast

per night:	£min	£max
Single	20.00	20.00
Double	40.00	40.00

**Half board per
person:**

	£min	£max
Daily	32.00	32.00
Weekly	210.00	210.00

Evening meal 1830 (last orders
2030)
Parking for 3

🐎🖤5🖤♿🔌Ⓤ🕯🖊🔌📺📟❄🐕
🚐

ECCLESHALL

Staffordshire
Map ref 4B3

Small market town has long associations with the Bishops of Lichfield, 6 of whom are buried in the large 12th C parish church. The ruined castle was formerly the residence of these bishops.

Glenwood

Croxton, Eccleshall, Stafford
ST21 6PF
☎ Wetwood (01630) 620238
16th C timber-framed cottage in an ideal position for visiting the many attractions of Staffordshire and Shropshire.
Bedrooms: 2 double, 1 twin
Bathrooms: 1 en-suite, 1 public
Bed & breakfast

per night:	£min	£max
Single	16.00	20.00
Double	30.00	38.00

Parking for 6

ECKINGTON

Hereford and Worcester
Map ref 2B1

Large and expanding village in a fruit growing and market gardening area beside the Avon, which is crossed here by a 15th C bridge. Half-timbered houses are much in evidence.

The Anchor Inn & Restaurant ♙

COMMENDED
Cotheridge Lane, Eckington, Pershore, Worcestershire
WR10 3BA
☎ Evesham (01386) 750356
Fax (01386) 750356
Traditional village inn off the main road, comfortable lounge, separate restaurant. Chef-prepared cuisine. Central for Worcester, Evesham, Cheltenham and Tewkesbury.
Bedrooms: 2 double, 3 twin
Bathrooms: 5 en-suite
Bed & breakfast

per night:	£min	£max
Single	25.00	30.00
Double	35.00	40.00

Lunch available
Evening meal 1900 (last orders 2130)
Parking for 30
Cards accepted: Access, Visa

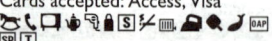

Sandrene ♙

COMMENDED
Tewkesbury Road, Eckington, Pershore, Worcestershire
WR10 3AW
☎ Evesham (01386) 750756
Relax in our small, friendly country home, overlooking Bredon Hill. Good hospitality, accommodation and food. Within walking distance of two pubs.
Bedrooms: 1 single, 1 double
Bathrooms: 2 en-suite
Bed & breakfast

per night:	£min	£max
Single	25.00	30.00
Double	40.00	45.00

Half board per person:	£min	£max
Daily	35.00	40.00
Weekly	210.00	240.00

Evening meal from 1800
Parking for 2

ELLESMERE

Shropshire
Map ref 4A2

Small market town with old streets and houses and situated close to 9 lakes. The largest, the Mere, has many waterfowl and recreational facilities and some of the other meres have sailing and fishing.

The Ellesmere Hotel ♙

High Street, Ellesmere SY12 0ES
☎ (01691) 622055
Fax (01691) 622055
17th C coaching inn with stunningly redesigned interior and en-suite bedrooms. Restaurant, lounge and bar serving wholesome, hearty food. Quality wines, spirits and cask conditioned ales.
Bedrooms: 3 single, 7 double, 2 twin
Bathrooms: 12 en-suite
Bed & breakfast

per night:	£min	£max
Single	25.00	30.00
Double	43.00	

Half board per person:	£min	£max
Daily	35.00	

Lunch available
Evening meal 1700 (last orders 2130)
Parking for 20
Cards accepted: Access, Visa

ENDON

Staffordshire
Map ref 4B2

Village between Stoke-on-Trent and Leek, noted for its well-dressing ceremony on Spring Bank Holiday.

Hollinhurst Farm

Listed COMMENDED
Park Lane, Endon, Stoke-on-Trent
ST9 9JB
☎ Stoke-on-Trent (01782) 502633
116-acre dairy farm. 17th C farmhouse within easy reach of Potteries, Peak District and Alton Towers. Panoramic views, walking and touring.
Bedrooms: 1 double, 1 twin, 1 family room
Bathrooms: 1 en-suite, 2 public
Bed & breakfast

per night:	£min	£max
Double	30.00	34.00

Parking for 10
Open January–November

EVESHAM

Hereford and Worcester
Map ref 2B1

Market town in the centre of a fruit-growing area. There are pleasant walks along the River Avon and many old houses and inns. A fine 16th C bell tower stands between 2 churches near the medieval Almonry Museum.
Tourist Information Centre ☎ (01386) 446944

Chequers Inn ♙

COMMENDED
Fladbury, Pershore, Worcestershire
WR10 2PZ
☎ (01386) 860276 & 860527
Fax (01386) 861286

14th C inn between Evesham and Pershore, on the edge of the Cotswolds. Off B4084 and A44, in a quiet village location, 17 miles from Stratford-upon-Avon.

Please check prices and other details at the time of booking.

Bedrooms: 4 double, 4 twin
Bathrooms: 8 en-suite

Bed & breakfast

per night:	£min	£max
Single	39.00	42.50
Double	55.00	65.00

Lunch available
Evening meal 1830 (last orders 2130)
Parking for 30
Cards accepted: Access, Visa, Amex, Switch/Delta

🐎📞📧🖳🖥♿🛏Ⓢ🖩🛏🍽25♪🎵
✕🚗⚓SP🎡

The Croft

👑👑 HIGHLY COMMENDED

54 Greenhill, Evesham,
Worcestershire WR11 4NF
☎ (01386) 446035

Splendid Georgian home offering comfortable overnight and holiday accommodation. Large private garden and ample parking.
Bedrooms: 1 double, 1 twin, 1 triple
Bathrooms: 2 en-suite, 1 private

Bed & breakfast

per night:	£min	£max
Single	30.00	36.00
Double	40.00	46.00

Parking for 6

🐎📧🖳🖥♿ⓊⓁⓈ🖩TV🖩🛏❋🚗

Far Horizon 🅰

👑 COMMENDED

Long Hyde Road, South Littleton,
Evesham, Worcestershire
WR11 5TH
☎ (01386) 831691
Elegant family home of character, with fine views over surrounding Cotswolds and Malvern Hills. Rural location 3 miles from Evesham.
Bedrooms: 1 single, 1 double, 1 twin
Bathrooms: 1 en-suite, 2 private

Bed & breakfast

per night:	£min	£max
Single	17.50	20.00
Double	35.00	40.00

Parking for 3

🐎10📧🖳♿🖥✕🖩🖩❋✕
🚗

Please mention this guide when making your booking.

Fircroft 🅰

👑👑 COMMENDED

84 Greenhill, Evesham,
Worcestershire WR11 4NH
☎ (01386) 45828
Comfortable B & B offering a relaxed and unobtrusive environment. Elegant house in attractive gardens, situated three quarters of a mile north of town centre. No smoking.
Bedrooms: 1 double, 1 twin, 1 triple
Bathrooms: 1 en-suite, 2 public

Bed & breakfast

per night:	£min	£max
Single	25.00	25.00
Double	35.00	42.00

Parking for 6
Open March–October

🐎🖳♿ⓊⓁⓈ🖩✕🖩🖩❋🐎🚗Ⓣ

Glencoyne

Listed APPROVED

Lenchwick, Evesham,
Worcestershire WR11 4TG
☎ (01386) 870901
Ground floor accommodation in large chalet bungalow. Beautiful gardens and conservatory overlooking a lake, available to guests. Two miles from Evesham centre.
Bedrooms: 1 twin
Bathrooms: 1 public

Bed & breakfast

per night:	£min	£max
Single	18.00	18.00
Double	36.00	36.00

Parking for 5

🐎5🚗📧🖳♿ⓊⓁⓈ🖩TV🖩🛏❋✕
🚗

Park View Hotel 🅰

👑

Waterside, Evesham,
Worcestershire WR11 6BS
☎ (01386) 442639
Family-run hotel offering comfortable accommodation in a friendly atmosphere. Riverside situation, close to town centre. Ideal base for touring the Cotswolds and Shakespeare country.
Bedrooms: 10 single, 4 double, 10 twin, 1 triple, 1 family room
Bathrooms: 7 public

Bed & breakfast

per night:	£min	£max
Single	20.50	24.00
Double	34.00	41.00

Evening meal 1800 (last orders 1900)
Parking for 50
Cards accepted: Access, Visa, Diners, Amex

🐎♿Ⓢ🖩TV🖩🛏🍽30SPⓉ

EWEN

Gloucestershire
Map ref 2B1

Village in the South Cotswolds of attractive stone cottages and houses.

Wild Duck Inn 🅰

👑👑👑 COMMENDED

Drakes Island, Ewen, Cirencester
GL7 6BY
☎ Cirencester (01285) 770310 & 770364
Fax (01285) 770924

15th C Cotswold-stone inn, set in a rural position in the village. Two four-poster rooms in the oldest part of the building. All rooms with private facilities. Delightful garden.
Bedrooms: 7 double, 3 twin
Bathrooms: 10 en-suite

Bed & breakfast

per night:	£min	£max
Single	49.50	49.50
Double	69.50	90.00

Lunch available
Evening meal 1900 (last orders 2145)
Parking for 50
Cards accepted: Access, Visa, Amex, Switch/Delta

🐎♿🚗📧🖳♿📞Ⓢ🛏TV🖩🛏❋🍽
🍽🍺 U♪❋🎡Ⓣ

The symbols in each entry give information about services and facilities. A 'key' to these symbols appears at the back of this guide.

National gradings and classifications were correct at the time of going to press but are subject to change. Please check at the time of booking.

FAIRFORD

Gloucestershire
Map ref 2B1

Small town with a 15th C wool church famous for its complete 15th C stained glass windows, interesting carvings and original wall paintings. It is an excellent touring centre and the Cotswolds Wildlife Park is nearby.

East End House

👑👑 HIGHLY COMMENDED

Fairford GL7 4AP
☎ Cirencester (01285) 713715
Fax (01285) 713505

Spacious accommodation in large Georgian family home in peaceful conservation area. Private parking, gardens, tennis court. Listed building. Family run.
Bedrooms: 1 twin, 1 family room
Bathrooms: 2 private

Bed & breakfast per night:	£min	£max
Single	25.00	27.50
Double	50.00	55.00

Half board per person:	£min	£max
Daily	40.00	42.50
Weekly	287.50	287.50

Parking for 8

Waiten Hill Farm ⚐

👑👑 APPROVED

Fairford GL7 4JG
☎ Cirencester (01285) 712652
Fax (01285) 712652
350-acre mixed farm. Imposing 19th C farmhouse, overlooking River Coln, old mill and famous church. Short walk to shops, pubs and restaurants. Ideal for touring the Cotswolds and water parks.
Bedrooms: 2 double, 1 twin
Bathrooms: 1 en-suite, 1 public

Bed & breakfast per night:	£min	£max
Single	20.00	25.00
Double	30.00	35.00

Parking for 8

FOREST OF DEAN

See under Coleford, Lydney, Newent, Newland, Parkend

FOWNHOPE

Hereford and Worcester
Map ref 2A1

Attractive village close to the River Wye with black and white cottages and other interesting houses. It has a large church with a Norman tower and a 14th C spire.

Green Man Inn ⚐

👑👑👑 COMMENDED

Fownhope, Hereford HR1 4PE
☎ Hereford (01432) 860243
Fax (01432) 860207

15th C black and white coaching inn, midway between Ross-on-Wye and Hereford, in the picturesque village of Fownhope. On B4224, close to the River Wye and set in the beautiful Wye Valley.
Bedrooms: 1 single, 13 double, 1 twin, 4 triple
Bathrooms: 19 en-suite

Bed & breakfast per night:	£min	£max
Single	31.00	32.00
Double	49.00	52.00

Half board per person:	£min	£max
Daily	37.25	39.25
Weekly	243.00	252.50

Lunch available
Evening meal 1900 (last orders 2100)
Parking for 80
Cards accepted: Access, Visa, Diners, Amex, Switch/Delta

GARWAY

Hereford and Worcester
Map ref 2A1

A small village in the delightful countryside of the Monnow Valley. There is fine Norman work in the church, which has a detached tower, and a nearby circular 14th C dovecote once belonging to the Knights Templar.

The Old Rectory

👑 HIGHLY COMMENDED

Garway, Hereford HR2 8RH
☎ (01600) 750363
Fax (01600) 750364
Victorian rectory with peaceful gardens

and beautiful views over Monnow Valley to Brecon Beacons and Black Mountains. Double four-poster available.
Bedrooms: 1 double, 1 twin
Bathrooms: 2 public

Bed & breakfast per night:	£min	£max
Double	35.00	40.00

Half board per person:	£min	£max
Daily	31.50	34.00

Parking for 4
Open March–December
Cards accepted: Access, Visa

GLOUCESTER

Gloucestershire
Map ref 2B1

A Roman city and inland port, its cathedral is one of the most beautiful in Britain. Gloucester's many attractions include museums and the restored warehouses in the Victorian docks containing the National Waterways Museum, Robert Opie Packaging Collection and other attractions.
Tourist Information Centre ☎ (01452) 421188

Merrivale ⚐

👑 COMMENDED

Tewkesbury Road, Norton, Gloucester GL2 9LQ
☎ (01452) 730412
Large private house with a pleasant garden, 3 miles north of Gloucester. TV and tea/coffee-making facilities in all bedrooms.
Bedrooms: 2 double, 3 twin, 1 triple
Bathrooms: 1 public, 2 private showers

Bed & breakfast per night:	£min	£max
Single	16.00	17.50
Double	32.00	35.00

Parking for 8

Notley House and Coach House ⚐

👑👑👑 COMMENDED

93 Hucclecote Road, Hucclecote, Gloucester GL3 3TR
☎ (01452) 611584
Fax (01452) 371229
Affordable quality accommodation. Ideal for historic Gloucester and the Cotswolds. Tastefully furnished en-suite rooms, suites with four-poster bed.
Bedrooms: 1 single, 2 double, 2 twin, 1 triple, 1 family room

Bathrooms: 5 en-suite, 2 private showers

Bed & breakfast

per night:	£min	£max
Single	23.50	41.00
Double	38.00	59.00

Half board per person:

	£min	£max
Daily	30.00	50.00
Weekly	185.00	315.00

Evening meal 1900 (last orders 2000)
Parking for 8
Cards accepted: Access, Visa

Severn Bank

COMMENDED

Minsterworth, Gloucester GL2 8JH
☎ (01452) 750357
Fax (01452) 750357
Fine riverside country house in 6 acres of grounds, 4 miles west of Gloucester. Viewpoint for Severn Bore Tidal Wave. Ideal for touring Forest of Dean and the Cotswolds.
Bedrooms: 1 single, 2 double, 3 triple
Bathrooms: 4 en-suite, 1 public

Bed & breakfast

per night:	£min	£max
Single	18.00	20.00
Double	36.00	40.00

Parking for 6

GOODRICH

Hereford and Worcester
Map ref 2A1

Village standing above the River Wye with the magnificent ruins of a red sandstone castle high above it, now in the care of English Heritage.

The Inn on the Wye

COMMENDED

Kerne Bridge, Goodrich,
Ross-on-Wye, Herefordshire
HR9 5QT
☎ Symonds Yat (01600) 890872
Fax (01600) 890594
Tastefully refurbished old coaching inn on bank of River Wye. Good food and accommodation, regular entertainment, interesting architecture. Good walking country.
Bedrooms: 10 double
Bathrooms: 10 en-suite

Bed & breakfast

per night:	£min	£max
Single	39.00	43.00
Double	43.50	43.50

Half board per person:

	£min	£max
Daily	49.00	60.00
Weekly	300.00	400.00

Lunch available
Evening meal 1900 (last orders 2200)
Parking for 65
Cards accepted: Access, Visa, Diners, Amex, Switch/Delta

GOTHERINGTON

Gloucestershire
Map ref 2B1

Pardon Hill Farm

COMMENDED

Gotherington, Cheltenham
GL52 4RD
☎ Cheltenham (01242) 672468
Fax (01242) 672468
300-acre mixed farm. Family-run. Outstanding views from all rooms. Ideal centre for walking and touring.
Bedrooms: 1 single, 1 double, 1 twin
Bathrooms: 3 en-suite

Bed & breakfast

per night:	£min	£max
Single	25.00	25.00
Double	40.00	40.00

Parking for 10

GREAT RISSINGTON

Gloucestershire
Map ref 2B1

One of two villages overlooking the River Windrush near Bourton-on-the-Water.

Lower Farmhouse

Listed APPROVED

Great Rissington, Cheltenham
GL54 2LH
☎ Cotswold (01451) 810163 & 810187
Self-contained bed and breakfast accommodation in barn conversion, adjacent to listed farmhouse. On north-west edge of Great Rissington, on road to Bourton-on-the-Water.
Bedrooms: 1 single, 1 double
Bathrooms: 1 public

Bed & breakfast

per night:	£min	£max
Single	16.00	18.00
Double	32.00	36.00

Parking for 4

GUITING POWER

Gloucestershire
Map ref 2B1

Unspoilt village with stone cottages and a green. The Cotswold Farm Park, with a collection of rare breeds, an adventure playground and farm trail, is nearby.

Farmers Arms

COMMENDED

Guiting Power, Cheltenham
GL54 5TZ
☎ Cotswold (01451) 850358

Country pub in lovely unspoilt Cotswold village, 13 miles from Cheltenham. Good access to local places of interest.
Bedrooms: 2 double
Bathrooms: 1 en-suite, 1 private, 1 public

Bed & breakfast

per night:	£min	£max
Single	20.00	25.00
Double	38.00	40.00

Half board per person:

	£min	£max
Daily	35.00	45.00
Weekly	190.00	260.00

Lunch available
Evening meal 1900 (last orders 2115)
Parking for 24

Halfway House

Kineton, Guiting Power, Cheltenham
GL54 5UG
☎ Cotswold (01451) 850344
Fax (01451) 850344
17th C inn serving good food and offering a warm welcome.
Bedrooms: 2 double, 1 twin
Bathrooms: 2 public

Bed & breakfast

per night:	£min	£max
Single	20.00	20.00
Double	30.00	30.00

Half board per person:

	£min	£max
Daily	30.00	40.00
Weekly	180.00	210.00

Continued ▶

GUITING POWER
Continued

Lunch available
Evening meal 1830 (last orders 2130)
Parking for 15
Cards accepted: Access, Visa, Switch/Delta

🛇🛆🕯🖐✕🎖⌨ ▤🚪🍷🛆⌖☀🚐🛇 SP

HAMPTON IN ARDEN
West Midlands
Map ref 4B3

Midway between Birmingham and Coventry and with the National Exhibition Centre on the doorstep.

Chelsea Lodge
👑👑 COMMENDED

48 Meriden Road, Hampton in Arden, Solihull B92 0BT
☎ (01675) 442408
Fax (01675) 442408
Comfortable, refurbished detached property with delightful gardens. Walking distance to Hampton in Arden railway station (direct NEC/Birmingham Airport) and village pubs. Village location yet 3 miles NEC, 4 miles Solihull.
Bedrooms: 3 twin
Bathrooms: 2 en-suite, 1 private
Bed & breakfast

per night:	£min	£max
Single	19.00	30.00
Double	38.00	45.00

Parking for 4

🛇🕯8⌨🍴🖐🎖 UL S✕🎵 TV ▤🛆☀🚐

The Cottage Guest House
Listed COMMENDED

Kenilworth Road, On A452 to Balsall Common, Hampton in Arden, Solihull B92 0LW
☎ Solihull (01675) 442323
Fax (01675) 443323
Charming cottage 2.5 miles from National Exhibition Centre and Birmingham Airport. All bedrooms en-suite with TV, radio alarms, tea and coffee facilities.
Bedrooms: 3 single, 3 double, 1 twin, 2 triple
Bathrooms: 7 en-suite, 1 public
Bed & breakfast

per night:	£min	£max
Single	20.00	25.00
Double	36.00	39.00

Parking for 15

🛇🕯👥⌨🍴🖐🎖 UL S✕🎵 TV ▤
🛆🍷☀ OAP SP

Pear Tree House ♨
👑👑👑

10 Station Road, Hampton in Arden, Solihull B92 0BJ
☎ (01675) 443993
Fax (01675) 443991
Comfortable Victorian house close to National Exhibition Centre and Birmingham Airport. All rooms en-suite and individually furnished. Near local railway station.
Bedrooms: 1 single, 2 twin
Bathrooms: 3 en-suite
Bed & breakfast

per night:	£min	£max
Single	20.00	35.00
Double	38.00	45.00

Parking for 4
Cards accepted: Access, Visa

🛇🕯5⌨🍴🖐🎖 UL ▤🛆☀🚐

HENLEY-IN-ARDEN
Warwickshire
Map ref 2B1

Old market town which in Tudor times stood in the Forest of Arden. It has many ancient inns, a 15th C Guildhall and parish church. Coughton Court with its Gunpowder Plot connections is nearby.

Holland Park Farm ♨
👑👑 COMMENDED

Buckley Green, Henley-in-Arden, Solihull, West Midlands B95 5QF
☎ Henley in Arden (01564) 792625
100-acre mixed farm. Georgian-style farmhouse situated off A3400 near Henley-in-Arden. Two large twin/family bedrooms en-suite. Good pubs and restaurants nearby.
Bedrooms: 2 triple
Bathrooms: 2 en-suite
Bed & breakfast

per night:	£min	£max
Single	23.00	25.00
Double	36.00	40.00

Parking for 5

🛇🕯⌨🍴🖐🎖 UL S🎵 TV ▤🛆☀
🚐

Irelands Farm ♨
👑👑 HIGHLY COMMENDED

Irelands Lane, Henley-in-Arden, Solihull, West Midlands B95 5SA
☎ (01564) 792476
220-acre arable farm. Secluded farmhouse in peaceful countryside. Close to Stratford, Warwick, National Exhibition Centre and the Cotswolds. 1 mile off A3400 between Henley and M42.
Bedrooms: 2 double, 1 twin
Bathrooms: 2 en-suite, 1 private

per night:	£min	£max
Single	20.00	22.00
Double	30.00	35.00

Parking for 6

🛇🕯⌨🖐🎖 UL S✕🎵 TV ▤🛆🍷✎☀
🚐🏠

HEREFORD
Hereford and Worcester
Map ref 2A1

Agricultural county town, its cathedral containing much Norman work and a large chained library. Among the city's varied attractions are several museums including the Cider Museum and the Old House. *Tourist Information Centre* ☎ *(01432) 268430*

Collins House ♨
👑👑 COMMENDED

19 St Owen Street, Hereford HR1 2JB
☎ (01432) 272416
Fax (01432) 357717
Fully restored early Georgian town house, c1722, combining comfort, character and convenience in historic town centre. Private parking. No smoking, please.
Bedrooms: 1 double, 2 twin
Bathrooms: 3 en-suite
Bed & breakfast

per night:	£min	£max
Single	28.00	29.50
Double	38.00	39.00

Parking for 3
Cards accepted: Access, Visa

🛇🕯5⌨🍴🖐🎖 UL ✕🎵 TV ▤🛆
🍷☀🏹🚐 SP 🏠

Cwm Craig Farm
👑👑 COMMENDED

Little Dewchurch, Hereford HR2 6PS
☎ Carey (01432) 840250
190-acre arable & livestock farm. Spacious Georgian farmhouse on edge of Wye Valley, surrounded by superb, unspoilt countryside. 5 miles south of Hereford. Easy access from M50.
Bedrooms: 1 double, 1 twin, 1 family room
Bathrooms: 1 en-suite, 2 public
Bed & breakfast

per night:	£min	£max
Single	16.00	16.00
Double	30.00	34.00

Parking for 6

🛇🕯🖐🎖✕🎵 TV ▤🛆🍷☀🏹🚐

Felton House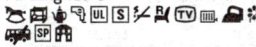

HIGHLY COMMENDED

Felton, Hereford HR1 3PH
☎ (01432) 820366
*The tranquil charm of a
Victorian/Edwardian stone rectory.
Four-poster and brass beds. Wide
breakfast choice. Modern comforts and
warm welcome. Tiny hamlet 8 miles
Hereford, Leominster, Bromyard, off
A417.*
Bedrooms: 1 single, 2 double, 1 twin
Bathrooms: 2 en-suite, 1 private,
1 public

Bed & breakfast

per night:	£min	£max
Single	18.50	21.00
Double	37.50	42.00

Parking for 6

Lower Bartestree Farm

APPROVED

Bartestree, Hereford HR1 4DT
☎ (01432) 851005
*Comfortable accommodation in a
peaceful setting with splendid views.
Home-made bread, preserves and
crafts available. Off A438, 4 miles from
city centre.*
Bedrooms: 1 twin, 1 triple
Bathrooms: 1 public

Bed & breakfast

per night:	£min	£max
Double		32.00

Parking for 5

Sink Green Farm

COMMENDED

Rotherwas, Hereford HR2 6LE
☎ Holme Lacy (01432) 870223
*170-acre livestock farm. 16th C
farmhouse on family-run farm.
Overlooking River Wye and 3 miles
from Hereford city centre.
Establishment is non-smoking.*
Bedrooms: 2 double, 1 twin
Bathrooms: 3 en-suite

Bed & breakfast

per night:	£min	£max
Single	20.00	24.00
Double	36.00	42.00

Parking for 10

Half board prices are given
per person, but in some cases
these may be based on
double/twin occupancy.

Hereford and Worcester
Map ref 2A1

Attractive village on the River Wye
which is famous for fishing. Its
church was built in the 19th C in
Italianate style with the help of
Italian workers. The interior
contains gold mosaics and marble.

Aspen House

COMMENDED

Hoarwithy, Hereford HR2 6QP
☎ Hereford (01432) 840353 &
0860 709924
Fax (01432) 840353
*Sandstone building dating back to the
1700s, set in attractive village
alongside the River Wye amidst the
beautiful countryside of the Wye Valley.*
Bedrooms: 3 double
Bathrooms: 3 en-suite

Bed & breakfast

per night:	£min	£max
Single	30.00	34.00
Double	35.00	39.00

Parking for 7

Shropshire
Map ref 4A3

Small town on the Severn where the
Industrial Revolution began. It has
the world's first iron bridge built in
1779. The Ironbridge Gorge
Museum, of exceptional interest,
comprises a rebuilt
turn-of-the-century town and sites
spread over 6 square miles.
*Tourist Information Centre ☎ (01952)
432166*

Bird in Hand Inn

COMMENDED

Waterloo Street, Ironbridge, Telford
TF8 7HG
☎ (01952) 432226
*Family-run inn, circa 1774, in the centre
of Ironbridge Gorge, with spectacular
views over the River Severn and the
gorge. En-suite rooms and extensive
menu, including traditional Sunday
roast.*
Bedrooms: 1 double, 1 twin, 1 family
room
Bathrooms: 3 en-suite

Bed & breakfast

per night:	£min	£max
Single	25.00	35.00
Double	35.00	45.00

Lunch available
Evening meal (last orders 2200)
Parking for 30
Cards accepted: Access, Visa

The Golden Ball Inn

COMMENDED

1 Newbridge Road, Ironbridge,
Telford TF8 7BA
☎ Telford (01952) 432179
*Traditional character inn, full of beams
and fireplaces. Ironbridge's oldest pub,
serving good food and traditional ales 7
days a week.*
Bedrooms: 2 double, 1 twin
Bathrooms: 3 en-suite

Bed & breakfast

per night:	£min	£max
Single	30.00	35.00
Double	40.00	45.00

Lunch available
Evening meal 1800 (last orders
2130)
Parking for 35
Cards accepted: Access, Visa

Warwickshire
Map ref 4B3

The main feature of the town is the
ruined 12th C castle. It has many
royal associations but was damaged
by Cromwell. A good base for
visiting Coventry, Leamington Spa
and Warwick.
*Tourist Information Centre ☎ (01926)
852595 or 850708*

Banner Hill Farmhouse

Rouncil Lane, Kenilworth CV8 1NN
☎ (01926) 852850
*250-acre mixed farm. Listed farmhouse
in Warwickshire countryside, also
mobile home. In middle of nowhere
and no distance from anywhere. NAC
10 minutes, NEC and
Stratford-upon-Avon 20 minutes.*
Bedrooms: 3 twin
Bathrooms: 1 en-suite, 1 public

Bed & breakfast

per night:	£min	£max
Single	15.00	22.50
Double	34.00	37.50

Half board per

person:	£min	£max
Daily	20.00	25.00
Weekly	75.00	95.00

Lunch available
Parking for 8

KIDDERMINSTER

Hereford and Worcester
Map ref 4B3

The town is the centre for carpet manufacturing. It has a medieval church with good monuments and a statue of Sir Rowland Hill, a native of the town and founder of the penny post. West Midlands Safari Park is nearby. Severn Valley Railway station.

Cedars Hotel

COMMENDED
Mason Road, Kidderminster,
Worcestershire DY11 6AG
☎ (01562) 515595
Fax (01562) 751103
Charming conversion of a Georgian building close to the River Severn, Severn Valley Railway and Worcestershire countryside. 15 minutes from M5.
Bedrooms: 2 single, 7 double, 7 twin, 4 triple, 2 family rooms
Bathrooms: 22 en-suite

Bed & breakfast per night:	£min	£max
Single	31.25	53.00
Double	43.30	65.00

Evening meal 1900 (last orders 2030)
Parking for 23
Cards accepted: Access, Visa, Diners, Amex

KINGTON

Hereford and Worcester
Map ref 2A1

Market town on the Welsh border, with Offa's Dyke close by. The Hergest Croft Gardens are well-known for their beautiful displays of azaleas and rhododendrons during May and June.

Hall's Mill House

COMMENDED
Huntington, Kington, Herefordshire
HR5 3QA
☎ Clifford (01497) 831409

Recently restored mill house in idyllic countryside overlooking River Arrow. Easy access to Offa's Dyke, Hay-on-

Wye and border market towns/churches/castles.
Bedrooms: 1 double, 1 twin
Bathrooms: 1 en-suite, 1 private

Bed & breakfast per night:	£min	£max
Single	18.00	18.00
Double	36.00	36.00

Half board per person:	£min	£max
Daily	26.00	30.00

Evening meal 1900 (last orders 2000)
Parking for 6
Open April–September

KNOCKDOWN

Gloucestershire
Map ref 2B2

Avenue Farm

Listed COMMENDED
Knockdown, Tetbury GL8 8QY
☎ Chipping Sodbury (01454) 238207
300-acre mixed farm. 300-year-old farmhouse, just off the A433, adjacent to Westonbirt Arboretum and 30 minutes' drive from Bath.
Bedrooms: 1 double, 2 twin
Bathrooms: 1 public, 3 private showers

Bed & breakfast per night:	£min	£max
Single	17.50	20.00
Double	30.00	35.00

Parking for 3

LEAMINGTON SPA

Warwickshire
Map ref 4B3

18th C spa town with many fine Georgian and Regency houses. Tea can be taken in the 19th C Pump Room. The attractive Jephson Gardens are laid out alongside the river and there is a museum and art gallery.
Tourist Information Centre ☎ (01926) 311470

8 Clarendon Crescent

Leamington Spa CV32 5NR
☎ (01926) 429840
Elegant Regency house situated in a quiet backwater of Leamington Spa, 5 minutes' walk from town centre, overlooking private dell.
Bedrooms: 2 single, 1 double, 1 twin
Bathrooms: 3 en-suite, 1 private

Bed & breakfast per night:	£min	£max
Single	25.00	30.00
Double	50.00	50.00

Parking for 1

Hill Farm

COMMENDED
Lewis Road, Radford Semele,
Leamington Spa CV31 1UX
☎ (01926) 337571
350-acre mixed farm. Farmhouse set in large attractive garden, 2 miles from Leamington town centre and close to Warwick Castle and Stratford-upon-Avon.
Bedrooms: 3 double, 2 twin
Bathrooms: 3 en-suite, 1 public

Bed & breakfast per night:	£min	£max
Single	18.00	20.00
Double	32.00	40.00

Parking for 10

27 Newbold Street

Leamington Spa CV32 4HN
☎ (01926) 336303
Fax (01926) 336303
Regency house with garden in town centre. Adjacent to Royal Spa Centre, Jephson Gardens, Newbold Comyn Park and River Leam. Close to bus, coach and railway station.
Bedrooms: 1 single, 1 double, 1 twin
Bathrooms: 3 en-suite

Bed & breakfast per night:	£min	£max
Single	18.00	25.00
Double	40.00	50.00

Parking for 1

The National Grading and Classification Scheme is explained in full at the back of this guide.

The symbols in each entry give information about services and facilities. A 'key' to these symbols appears at the back of this guide.

The Orchard

Listed APPROVED

3 Sherbourne Terrace, Clarendon
Street, Leamington Spa CV32 5SP
☎ (01926) 428198
*Victorian double-fronted terrace with
walled garden. 5 minutes' walk to town
centre. Overseas visitors and children
welcome.*
Bedrooms: 1 single, 1 twin, 1 triple
Bathrooms: 2 public

Bed & breakfast

per night:	£min	£max
Single	15.00	18.00
Double	30.00	34.00

Half board per person:	£min	£max
Daily	19.00	22.00
Weekly	105.00	120.00

Lunch available
Evening meal from 1800

135 Rugby Road

Milverton, Leamington Spa
CV32 6DJ
☎ Warwick (01926) 427224
*Large Victorian villa on the outskirts of
town, close to tennis and bowls clubs.*
Bedrooms: 1 single, 1 double, 1 twin
Bathrooms: 2 public

Bed & breakfast

per night:	£min	£max
Single	15.00	18.00
Double	30.00	30.00

Snowford Hall

COMMENDED

Snowford Hall Farm, Hunningham,
Leamington Spa CV33 9ES
☎ Marton (01926) 632297
Fax (01926) 633599
*200-acre mixed farm. 18th C
farmhouse off the Fosse Way, on the
edge of Hunningham village. On
elevated ground overlooking quiet
surrounding countryside. Self-catering
also available.*
Bedrooms: 1 double, 2 twin
Bathrooms: 1 en-suite, 1 public,
1 private shower

Bed & breakfast

per night:	£min	£max
Double	36.00	40.00

Parking for 4

Stonehouse Farm

Listed COMMENDED

Leicester Lane, Cubbington Heath,
Leamington Spa CV32 6QZ
☎ (01926) 336370
*Friendly, Grade II listed Queen Anne
farmhouse, with extensive views over
Warwickshire's beautiful countryside. A*

*mile from the Royal Showground and
close to Leamington Spa, Warwick and
Stratford.*
Bedrooms: 3 twin
Bathrooms: 1 en-suite, 1 public

Bed & breakfast

per night:	£min	£max
Single	21.00	26.50
Double	35.00	42.00

Evening meal from 1930
Parking for 6

LECHLADE

Gloucestershire
Map ref 2B1

Attractive village on the River
Thames and a popular spot for
boating. It has a number of fine
Georgian houses and a 15th C
church. Nearby is Kelmscott Manor,
with its William Morris furnishings,
and 18th C Buscot House (National
Trust).

Apple Tree House

Buscot, Faringdon, Oxfordshire
SN7 8DA
☎ Faringdon (01367) 252592
*Listed property offering comfortable
B & B in National Trust village near
Lechlade. River Thames 5 minutes'
walk through village. Large garden.*
Bedrooms: 2 double, 1 twin
Bathrooms: 1 en-suite, 1 public

Bed & breakfast

per night:	£min	£max
Single	22.00	
Double	34.00	40.00

Parking for 8

Cambrai Lodge

Listed COMMENDED

Oak Street, Lechlade GL7 3AY
☎ (01367) 253173 & Mobile 0860
150467
*Friendly, family-run guesthouse, recently
modernised, close to River Thames.
Ideal base for touring the Cotswolds.
Garden and ample parking.*
Bedrooms: 2 single, 1 double, 1 twin
Bathrooms: 2 en-suite, 1 public

Bed & breakfast

per night:	£min	£max
Single	20.00	25.00
Double	32.00	38.00

Parking for 13

LEDBURY

Hereford and Worcester
Map ref 2B1

Town with cobbled streets and
many black and white timbered
houses, including the 17th C market
house and old inns. Nearby is
Eastnor Castle with an interesting
collection of tapestries and armour.
Tourist Information Centre ☎ *(01531)
636147*

Kilmory

HIGHLY COMMENDED

Bradlow, Ledbury, Herefordshire
HR8 1JF
☎ (01531) 631951
*Detached dormer bungalow with
attractive gardens, located on the
outskirts of Ledbury and with
wonderful views of the Malverns.*
Bedrooms: 1 double, 1 twin
Bathrooms: 2 private

Bed & breakfast

per night:	£min	£max
Single	18.00	18.00
Double	33.00	36.00

Parking for 4

Mainstone House

Listed COMMENDED

Trumpet, Ledbury, Herefordshire
HR8 2RA
☎ Trumpet (01531) 670230
*Large 17th C former farmhouse with
wealth of exposed beams. Four miles
from Ledbury towards Hereford, with a
convenient "old world" pub opposite.*
Bedrooms: 1 double, 1 family room
Bathrooms: 2 private

Bed & breakfast

per night:	£min	£max
Double	32.00	32.00

Parking for 8

WELCOME HOST

This is a nationally recognised
customer care programme
which aims to promote
the highest standards of
service and a warm welcome.
Establishments who are taking
part in this initiative are
indicated by the ⊛ symbol.

LEEK

Staffordshire
Map ref 4B2

Old silk and textile town, with some interesting buildings and a number of inns dating from the 17th C. Its art gallery has displays of embroidery. Brindley Mill, designed by James Brindley, has been restored as a museum.
Tourist Information Centre ☎ (01538) 381000

Abbey Inn

⚜⚜ COMMENDED

Abbey Green Road, Leek ST13 8SA
☎ (01538) 382865
17th C inn with accommodation in a separate annexe, set in beautiful countryside, 1 mile from the town and just off the main A523.
Bedrooms: 2 single, 4 double, 1 twin
Bathrooms: 7 en-suite

Bed & breakfast per night:	£min	£max
Single	27.00	30.00
Double	42.00	46.00

Lunch available
Evening meal 1830 (last orders 2100)
Parking for 60
Cards accepted: Access, Visa, Diners, Amex, Switch/Delta

☼🏥📞▣❑🌢⌨🛡Ⓢ🏛♦❀✕ ᴤᴘ🎣

Three Horseshoes Inn & Restaurant 🅰

⚜⚜⚜ COMMENDED

Buxton Road, Blackshaw Moor, Leek ST13 8TW
☎ (01538) 300296
Fax (01538) 300320

Log fire, slate floor, oak and pine beams, good food and wines. Cottage-style rooms. Convenient for Peak District National Park and Alton Towers.
Bedrooms: 4 double, 2 twin
Bathrooms: 6 en-suite

Bed & breakfast per night:	£min	£max
Single	40.00	46.00
Double	46.00	58.00

Lunch available
Evening meal 1900 (last orders 2100)

Parking for 100
Cards accepted: Access, Visa, Amex, Switch/Delta

☼📞▣❑🌢⌨🛡Ⓢ✂📺🏛🛏⛵ ▸❀ ᴤᴘ🇹

LEOMINSTER

Hereford and Worcester
Map ref 2A1

The town owed its prosperity to wool and has many interesting buildings, notably the timber-framed Grange Court, a former town hall. The impressive Norman priory church has 3 naves and a ducking stool. Berrington Hall (National Trust) is nearby.
Tourist Information Centre ☎ (01568) 616460

Bedford House

⚜

Dilwyn, Hereford HR4 8JJ
☎ Pembridge (01544) 388260
20-acre mixed farm. Small, friendly farm offering peace and quiet, excellent accommodation, and good home cooking. In village south-west of Leominster, central for exploring Herefordshire, Worcestershire, Gloucestershire and Radnorshire. Welcome cup of tea.
Bedrooms: 1 double, 1 twin, 1 triple
Bathrooms: 1 en-suite, 1 public

Bed & breakfast per night:	£min	£max
Single	17.00	
Double	34.00	

Half board per person:	£min	£max
Daily	25.00	

Evening meal from 1830
Parking for 3
Open March–November

☼▣🌢⌨ UL Ⓢ📺🏛🛏⛵⌨ ▸❀🚌

Heath House 🅰

⚜⚜ HIGHLY COMMENDED

Stoke Prior, Leominster, Herefordshire HR6 0NF
☎ Steens Bridge (01568) 760385
Attractive stone farmhouse full of beams and history, set in peaceful countryside. Room to move and relax in comfort.
Bedrooms: 1 double, 2 twin
Bathrooms: 2 en-suite, 1 private

Bed & breakfast per night:	£min	£max
Single	22.00	24.00
Double	40.00	44.00

Half board per person:	£min	£max
Daily	32.00	39.00
Weekly	203.00	252.00

Evening meal 1900 (last orders 2000)
Parking for 6
Open March–November

☼🏥9▣🌢⌨🛡 UL Ⓢ✂📺🏛🛏 U ▸❀🚗🏍🎣🇹 ⦿

Royal Oak Hotel 🅰

⚜⚜⚜

South Street, Leominster, Herefordshire HR6 8JA
☎ (01568) 612610
Fax (01568) 612710
Grade II listed Georgian coaching house dating from 1723, with log fires in winter, real ales and an emphasis on good food and wines at reasonable prices.
Bedrooms: 2 single, 9 double, 5 twin, 2 triple
Bathrooms: 18 en-suite

Bed & breakfast per night:	£min	£max
Single	33.50	37.50
Double	45.00	55.00

Half board per person:	£min	£max
Daily	32.75	37.75
Weekly	206.33	237.83

Lunch available
Evening meal 1830 (last orders 2130)
Parking for 25
Cards accepted: Access, Visa, Diners, Amex

☼🏥♿🏥▣❑🌢⌨🛡Ⓢ✂📺🛏 🍴225 ᴏᴀᴘ ᴤᴘ🏍🇹

Tyn-Y-Coed 🅰

⚜⚜ COMMENDED

Shobdon, Leominster, Herefordshire HR6 9NY
☎ Kingsland (01568) 708277
Husband and wife team in country house with large garden, providing friendly bed & breakfast service to holidaymakers and tourists.
Bedrooms: 1 double, 1 twin
Bathrooms: 1 en-suite, 1 public

Bed & breakfast per night:	£min	£max
Single	22.00	27.50
Double	34.00	45.00

Parking for 2
Open April–October

🌢⌨ UL ✂📺🛏🚗❀✕🚌

LICHFIELD

Staffordshire
Map ref 4B3

Lichfield is Dr Samuel Johnson's
birthplace and commemorates him
with a museum and statue. The 13th
C cathedral has 3 spires and the
west front is full of statues. Among
the attractive town buildings is the
Heritage Centre. The Regimental
Museum is in Whittington Barracks.
*Tourist Information Centre ☎ (01543)
252109*

20 Beacon Street

Lichfield WS13 7AD
☎ (01543) 262338
*Spacious and elegant Georgian town
house with a welcoming atmosphere,
conveniently situated near Lichfield
Cathedral and all amenities.*
Bedrooms: 2 double
Bathrooms: 1 en-suite, 1 public,
1 private shower
**Bed & breakfast
per night:**

	£min	£max
Single	18.00	20.00
Double	34.00	38.00

Parking for 5

Coppers End

COMMENDED

Walsall Road, Muckley Corner,
Lichfield WS14 0BG
☎ (01543) 372910
Fax (01543) 372910

*Detached guesthouse of character and
charm in its own grounds. Rural
location with easy access to M6,
Birmingham, Lichfield and M1.
Residential licence. Telephone for
half-board rates.*
Bedrooms: 1 single, 2 double, 2 twin
Bathrooms: 1 en-suite, 1 public
**Bed & breakfast
per night:**

	£min	£max
Single	22.00	30.00
Double	35.00	42.00

Evening meal 1900 (last orders
2030)
Parking for 10
Cards accepted: Access, Visa, Diners,
Amex, Switch/Delta

LONGHOPE

Gloucestershire
Map ref 2B1

Village between Gloucester and
Ross-on-Wye at the foot of May
Hill, crowned with a prominent
clump of trees which can be seen
for miles around. The War
Memorial is an imposing stone lion,
based on the badge of the
Gloucestershire Regiment.

New House Farm

Barrell Lane, Longhope GL17 0LS
☎ Gloucester (01452) 830484
*80-acre livestock farm. Georgian
farmhouse, 7 miles east of
Ross-on-Wye between A40 and M50.
Public footpath leading to May Hill
(National Trust).*
Bedrooms: 1 double, 1 twin, 1 triple
Bathrooms: 1 private, 1 public
**Bed & breakfast
per night:**

	£min	£max
Single	20.00	22.00
Double	36.00	40.00

**Half board per
person:**

	£min	£max
Daily	31.00	33.00
Weekly	217.00	231.00

Lunch available
Evening meal 1800 (last orders
2000)
Parking for 10

LOXLEY

Warwickshire
Map ref 2B1

There is an attractive black and
white farmhouse and some cottages
in this pleasant village overlooking a
wooded valley, only a few miles from
Stratford-upon-Avon and close to
Warwick and Leamington Spa.

Loxley Farm

HIGHLY COMMENDED

Loxley, Warwick CV35 9JN
☎ Stratford-upon-Avon (01789)
840265
*6-acre horses farm. Picturesque,
half-timbered thatched farmhouse
dating from the late 13th C, set in 2
acres of garden. Accommodation in
converted 17th C thatched
half-timbered barn next to house.*
Bedrooms: 2 double
Bathrooms: 2 en-suite

**Bed & breakfast
per night:**

	£min	£max
Single	30.00	32.00
Double	44.00	46.00

Parking for 10

LUDLOW

Shropshire
Map ref 4A3

Outstandingly interesting border
town with a magnificent castle high
above the River Teme, 2
half-timbered old inns and an
impressive 15th C church. The
Reader's House, with its 3-storey
Jacobean porch, should also be seen.
*Tourist Information Centre ☎ (01584)
875053*

Bull Hotel

14 The Bull Ring, Ludlow SY8 1AD
☎ (01584) 873611
Fax (01584) 873666
*Oldest pub in Ludlow, earliest mention
c1343. Was known as Peter of Proctors
House and probably dates back to
c1199.*
Bedrooms: 2 double, 2 twin
Bathrooms: 4 en-suite
**Bed & breakfast
per night:**

	£min	£max
Single	30.00	30.00
Double	43.00	43.00

Lunch available
Parking for 8
Cards accepted: Access, Visa, Amex

The Church Inn

Butter Cross, Ludlow SY8 1AW
☎ (01584) 872174
Fax (01584) 877146
*Georgian inn, centrally located on one
of the most ancient sites in Ludlow.
Good food and CAMRA listed for ales.*
Bedrooms: 5 double, 2 twin, 1 triple
Bathrooms: 8 en-suite
**Bed & breakfast
per night:**

	£min	£max
Single	28.00	28.00
Double	45.00	55.00

Lunch available
Evening meal 1800 (last orders
2100)
Cards accepted: Access, Visa

LUDLOW
Continued

Corndene ⚘
⚜ COMMENDED
Coreley, Ludlow SY8 3AW
☎ (01584) 890324
Country house of character in the heart of rural Shropshire. Beautiful and secluded situation only 5 minutes off A4117 (Ludlow 7 miles). Spacious en-suite rooms, tasty home cooking and relaxing atmosphere. No smoking indoors, please.
Wheelchair access category 1 ♿
Bedrooms: 3 twin
Bathrooms: 3 en-suite

Bed & breakfast per night:

	£min	£max
Single	24.00	24.00
Double	42.00	42.00

Parking for 5
Open March–November

Longlands
⚜
Woodhouse Lane, Richards Castle, Ludlow SY8 4EU
☎ Richards Castle (01584) 831636
35-acre livestock farm. Farmhouse set in lovely rural landscape. Home-grown produce. Convenient for Ludlow, Mortimer Forest and Croft Castle. Interesting 14th C church and remains of 11th C castle in village.
Bedrooms: 1 double, 1 twin
Suite available
Bathrooms: 1 en-suite, 1 private

Bed & breakfast per night:

	£min	£max
Double	36.00	40.00

Half board per person:

	£min	£max
Daily	27.00	29.00

Evening meal 1830 (last orders 1930)
Parking for 2

The Moor Hall ⚘
⚜⚜⚜ HIGHLY COMMENDED
Cleedownton, Ludlow SY8 3EG
☎ Stoke St Millborough (01584) 823209 & 823333
Fax (01584) 823387

Built c1789, the Moor Hall is set in 5 acres of mature grounds with pools, amid unspoilt countryside, yet close to historic Ludlow. Relaxed, informal atmosphere. Fishing.
Bedrooms: 2 double, 1 twin
Bathrooms: 3 en-suite

Bed & breakfast per night:

	£min	£max
Single	25.00	35.00
Double	45.00	60.00

Half board per person:

	£min	£max
Daily	37.50	45.00
Weekly	235.00	285.00

Evening meal 1900 (last orders 2000)
Parking for 12

Number Twenty Eight ⚘
⚜⚜⚜ HIGHLY COMMENDED
28 Lower Broad Street, Ludlow SY8 1PQ
☎ (01584) 876996
Fax (01584) 876996

Listed town house of charm and character. Centrally situated. Emphasis on warm hospitality and quiet, relaxed atmosphere with good food and wines.
Bedrooms: 2 double, 1 twin, 1 triple
Bathrooms: 4 en-suite, 1 public

Bed & breakfast per night:

	£min	£max
Single	27.50	50.00
Double	40.00	60.00

Half board per person:

	£min	£max
Daily	37.50	47.50
Weekly	250.00	300.00

Evening meal 1930 (last orders 2030)
Cards accepted: Access, Visa, Amex

Seifton Court ⚘
⚜⚜ COMMENDED
Culmington, Ludlow SY8 2DG
☎ Seifton (01584) 861214
Period farmhouse, 5 miles from Ludlow on the B4365 road. Set in the beautiful Corve Dale valley. Near Longmynd, Ironbridge. Ideal for walking and visiting National Trust properties. Farmhouse fare using home-grown produce.
Bedrooms: 1 single, 1 double, 1 twin
Bathrooms: 3 en-suite, 1 public

Bed & breakfast per night:

	£min	£max
Single	20.00	25.00
Double	36.00	50.00

Half board per person:

	£min	£max
Daily	30.00	38.00
Weekly	204.00	224.00

Lunch available
Evening meal 1800 (last orders 1900)
Parking for 7

Snitton Court
Snitton, Ludlow SY8 3EZ
☎ (01584) 891066
Large country house with a wealth of exposed beams, set amidst delightful countryside and within 4 miles of Ludlow. Good walking country.
Bedrooms: 3 double
Bathrooms: 2 public

Bed & breakfast per night:

	£min	£max
Single	16.00	17.00
Double	32.00	34.00

Parking for 6

The Wheatsheaf Inn ⚘
⚜⚜⚜ COMMENDED
Lower Broad Street, Ludlow SY8 1PQ
☎ (01584) 872980
Fax (01584) 872980
Family-run mid-17th C beamed inn, 100 yards from the town centre, nestling under Ludlow's historic 13th C Broad Gate, the last remaining of 7 town gates.
Bedrooms: 4 double, 1 twin
Bathrooms: 5 en-suite, 1 public

Bed & breakfast per night:

	£min	£max
Single	25.00	25.00
Double	40.00	40.00

Half board per person:

	£min	£max
Daily	27.00	32.00

Lunch available
Evening meal 1830 (last orders 2100)
Cards accepted: Access, Visa, Switch/Delta

The ⚘ symbol after an establishment name indicates that it is a Regional Tourist Board member.

LYDNEY

Gloucestershire
Map ref 2B1

Small town in the Forest of Dean close to the River Severn, where Roman remains have been found. It has a steam centre with engines, coaches and wagons.

Treetops

HIGHLY COMMENDED

Viney Hill, Lydney GL15 4LZ
☎ Dean (01594) 516149
You'll find a warm welcome at this country home. Relax in lovely garden with ponds and waterfalls. See unspoilt Forest of Dean and the Wye and Severn Valleys.
Bedrooms: 1 single, 1 double, 1 twin
Bathrooms: 1 en-suite, 2 private
Bed & breakfast

per night:	£min	£max
Single	18.00	20.00
Double	36.00	40.00

Parking for 3

Upper Viney Farmhouse

COMMENDED

Viney Hill, Lydney GL15 4LT
☎ Dean (01594) 516672 & Mobile (0589) 079905
Stone-built house dating back to the 16th C, featuring many oak beams, inglenook fireplaces. Character bedrooms with modern facilities.
Bedrooms: 1 double, 1 twin, 1 family room
Bathrooms: 2 en-suite, 1 private
Bed & breakfast

per night:	£min	£max
Single	20.00	25.00
Double	36.00	40.00

Half board per person:	£min	£max
Daily	33.00	35.00

Evening meal (last orders 1900)
Parking for 6

Map references apply to the colour maps at the back of this guide.

A key to symbols can be found inside the back cover flap.

MALVERN

Hereford and Worcester
Map ref 2B1

Spa town in Victorian times, its water is today bottled and sold worldwide. 6 resorts, set on the slopes of the Hills, form part of Malvern. Great Malvern Priory has splendid 15th C windows. It is an excellent walking centre.
Tourist Information Centre ☎ (01684) 892289

Nags Head

APPROVED

19-21 Bank Street, Malvern, Worcestershire WR14 2JG
☎ (01684) 574373
Fax (01684) 574373
Self-contained flat with sofa bed in lounge, sleeping capacity for 4 people, private kitchen, bathroom and lounge.
Bedrooms: 1 double
Bathrooms: 1 en-suite
Bed & breakfast

per night:	£min	£max
Single	22.50	25.00
Double	42.00	50.00

Lunch available
Parking for 2

York House

COMMENDED

Walwyn Road, Colwall, Malvern, Worcestershire WR13 6QG
☎ (01684) 540449
Large Edwardian house in centre of picturesque village. Close to Malvern and the hills, in an Area of Outstanding Natural Beauty.
Bedrooms: 2 double, 1 twin
Bathrooms: 2 en-suite, 1 private
Bed & breakfast

per night:	£min	£max
Single	25.00	30.00
Double	35.00	40.00

Parking for 4

TOWN INDEX

This can be found at the back of the guide. If you know where you want to stay, the index will give you the page number listing all accommodation in your chosen town, city or village.

MARKET DRAYTON

Shropshire
Map ref 4A2

Old market town with black and white buildings and 17th C houses, also acclaimed for its gingerbread. Hodnet Hall is in the vicinity with its beautiful landscaped gardens covering 60 acres.
Tourist Information Centre ☎ (01630) 652139

Heath Farm Bed and Breakfast

Listed

Heath Farm, Hodnet, Market Drayton TF9 3JJ
☎ Hodnet (01630) 685570
Fax (01743) 249970
60-acre mixed farm. Traditional farmhouse welcome. Situated 1.5 miles south of Hodnet off the A442, approached by private drive.
Bedrooms: 1 double, 2 twin
Bathrooms: 1 public
Bed & breakfast

per night:	£min	£max
Single	15.00	15.00
Double	30.00	30.00

Parking for 5

MERIDEN

West Midlands
Map ref 4B3

Village halfway between Coventry and Birmingham. Said to be the centre of England, marked by a cross on the green.

Cooperage Farm Bed and Breakfast

APPROVED

Old Road, Meriden, Coventry CV7 7JP
☎ (01676) 523493
Fax (01676) 523876
6-acre mixed farm. 300-year-old red brick, Grade II listed farmhouse, set in beautiful countryside. Ideally situated for the National Exhibition Centre, airport and touring the centre of England.
Bedrooms: 2 double, 2 twin, 2 triple
Bathrooms: 4 en-suite, 1 public
Bed & breakfast

per night:	£min	£max
Single	25.00	30.00
Double	45.00	50.00

Continued ▶

MERIDEN
Continued

Evening meal 1800 (last orders 1900)
Parking for 6

🛏️1🚷♿🍴🖭🎣🛎️UL🔒S📺TV ◐🖭🖐️✱🚗 DAP SP 🎏

MINSTERLEY

Shropshire
Map ref 4A3

Village with a curious little church of 1692 and a fine old black and white hall. The lofty ridge known as the Stiperstones is 4 miles to the south.

Cricklewood Cottage
HIGHLY COMMENDED

Plox Green, Minsterley, Shrewsbury SY5 0HT
☎ Shrewsbury (01743) 791229
Delightful 18th C cottage with countryside views, at foot of Stiperstones Hills. Exposed beams, inglenook fireplace, traditional furnishings. Lovely cottage garden. Excellent restaurants and inns nearby.
Bedrooms: 2 double, 1 twin
Bathrooms: 3 en-suite

Bed & breakfast

per night:	£min	£max
Single	21.00	31.50
Double	38.00	42.00

Half board per

person:	£min	£max
Daily	32.50	32.50
Weekly	192.50	192.50

Evening meal 1830 (last orders 1000)
Parking for 4

🛏️8🖭♿UL🍴S🔒✂️📺TV 🖭🖐️♿U ✱🐕 SP 🎏

MORETON-IN-MARSH

Gloucestershire
Map ref 2B1

Attractive town of Cotswold stone with 17th C houses, an ideal base for touring the Cotswolds. Some of the local attractions include Batsford Park Arboretum, the Jacobean Chastleton House and Sezincote Garden.

Blue Cedar House 🏔
COMMENDED

Stow Road, Moreton-in-Marsh GL56 0DW
☎ (01608) 650299
Attractive detached residence set in half-acre garden in the Cotswolds, with pleasantly decorated, well-equipped

---

accommodation and garden room. Close to village centre.
Bedrooms: 1 single, 1 double, 1 twin, 1 family room
Bathrooms: 2 en-suite, 2 public

Bed & breakfast

per night:	£min	£max
Single	19.00	28.00
Double	34.00	44.00

Half board per

person:	£min	£max
Daily	25.00	30.00

Evening meal 1800 (last orders 1800)
Parking for 7
Open February–November

🛏️🖭♿🎣UL S📺TV 🖭 🖐️✱ 🐕🚗

Ditchford Farmhouse 🏔
COMMENDED

Stretton on Fosse, Moreton-in-Marsh GL56 9RD
☎ Shipston-on-Stour (01608) 663307
10-acre arable farm. Secluded Georgian farmhouse in lovely north Cotswold countryside. Large garden with children's corner. Home-grown produce and country cooking. Winter breaks with log fires. Private facilities available. Licensed.
Bedrooms: 3 double, 1 twin, 2 family rooms
Bathrooms: 3 en-suite, 3 private

Bed & breakfast

per night:	£min	£max
Single	17.95	25.00
Double	35.90	50.00

Half board per

person:	£min	£max
Daily	29.90	36.95
Weekly	119.00	175.00

Evening meal from 1830
Parking for 8

🛏️🚷♿🍴🎣🛎️S✂️📺TV 🖭🖐️♿✱🐕 DAP SP 🎏

Dorn Priory 🏔
COMMENDED

Dorn, Moreton-in-Marsh GL56 9NS
☎ (01608) 650152

17th C Cotswold house in peaceful surroundings. Set in a small hamlet on edge of Cotswolds, within easy reach of Stratford-upon-Avon and Oxford.
Bedrooms: 1 twin, 1 family room
Bathrooms: 1 public

Bed & breakfast

per night:	£min	£max
Single	16.00	
Double	32.00	

Parking for 10
Open April–October

🛏️🚷♿🍴🎣UL S✂️📺TV 🖭🖐️♿🐾✱ 🚗🎏

Lower Farm Barn 🏔

Great Wolford, Shipston-on-Stour, Warwickshire CV36 5NQ
☎ Barton on the Heath (01608) 674435
900-acre arable farm. 18th C converted barn combines modern comforts with exposed beams and ancient stonework. Use of attractive drawing room. Quiet village between A3400, A44 and A429.
Bedrooms: 1 double, 1 twin
Bathrooms: 1 en-suite, 1 private, 1 public

Bed & breakfast

per night:	£min	£max
Single	18.00	22.00
Double	31.00	36.00

Parking for 10

🛏️🖭♿🎣S📺TV 🖭🖐️♿🎣U✱ 🚗🎏

New Farm 🏔
COMMENDED

Dorn, Moreton-in-Marsh GL56 9NS
☎ (01608) 650782

250-acre dairy farm. Old Cotswold farmhouse. All rooms spacious, en-suite and furnished with antiques and with colour TV, coffee and tea facilities. Dining room with large impressive fireplace. Full English breakfast served with hot crispy bread.
Bedrooms: 2 double, 1 twin
Bathrooms: 2 en-suite, 1 private

Bed & breakfast

per night:	£min	£max
Single	17.00	20.00
Double	34.00	35.00

Parking for 10

🛏️3🖭♿🎣UL📺TV 🖭🖐️✱🚗 SP

Old Farm 🏔
COMMENDED

Dorn, Moreton-in-Marsh GL56 9NS
☎ (01608) 650394

250-acre mixed farm. Enjoy the delights of a 15th C farmhouse - a comfortable family home. Spacious bedrooms. Tennis and croquet. Children welcome. Surrounded by beautiful Cotswolds scenery.
Bedrooms: 2 double, 1 twin, 1 triple
Bathrooms: 1 en-suite, 1 public

Bed & breakfast

per night:	£min	£max
Single	20.00	20.00
Double	32.00	34.00

Parking for 8
Open March–October

MUCH WENLOCK

Shropshire
Map ref 4A3

Small town close to Wenlock Edge in beautiful scenery and full of interest. In particular there are the remains of an 11th C priory with fine carving and the black and white 16th C Guildhall.

The Plume of Feathers ⚑

COMMENDED

Harley, Much Wenlock, Shrewsbury SY5 6LP
☎ Telford (01952) 727360 & Mobile 0802 388866
17th C inn with newly constructed accommodation and 70-seat restaurant, noted for home cooking. Impressive rural views. Central for Shrewsbury, Bridgnorth and Ironbridge. Special rates for 5-night stays, October-March.
Bedrooms: 4 double, 2 twin, 1 triple, 2 family rooms
Bathrooms: 9 en-suite

Bed & breakfast

per night:	£min	£max
Single	28.00	
Double	38.00	44.00

Half board per

person:	£min	£max
Daily	34.00	36.00

Lunch available
Evening meal 1800 (last orders 2200)
Parking for 76
Cards accepted: Access, Visa, Switch/Delta

Walton House ⚑

Listed COMMENDED

35 Barrow Street, Much Wenlock TF13 6EP
☎ (01952) 727139
Two minutes' walk from town centre. 5 miles from Ironbridge Gorge, 13 miles from Shrewsbury, 8 miles from Bridgnorth and 10 miles from Telford town centre. Lawns and patio.
Bedrooms: 1 single, 2 twin
Bathrooms: 1 public

Bed & breakfast

per night:	£min	£max
Single	15.00	15.00
Double	30.00	30.00

Parking for 2
Open April–October

NAILSWORTH

Gloucestershire
Map ref 2B1

Ancient wool town with several elegant Jacobean and Georgian houses, surrounded by wooded hillsides with fine views.

Aaron Farm ⚑

COMMENDED

Nympsfield Road, Nailsworth, Stroud GL6 0ET
☎ Stroud (01453) 833598
Fax (01453) 836737
Former farmhouse, with large en-suite bedrooms and panoramic views of the Cotswolds. Ideal touring centre. Many walks and attractions. Home cooking. Brochure on request.
Bedrooms: 1 double, 2 twin
Bathrooms: 3 en-suite

Bed & breakfast

per night:	£min	£max
Single	22.00	28.00
Double	34.00	38.00

Half board per

person:	£min	£max
Daily	28.00	30.00
Weekly	196.00	210.00

Evening meal 1800 (last orders 2000)
Parking for 4

Apple Orchard House ⚑

COMMENDED

Orchard Close, Springhill, Nailsworth, Stroud GL6 0LX
☎ (01453) 832503
Fax (01453) 836213
Victoria Jennings has been caring for visitors for 15 years in her elegant, spacious house with pretty garden. Panoramic views of Cotswold Hills from

bedrooms and sitting room. Small, historic town, excellent touring centre, 15 minutes M4/M5. Colour brochure.
Wheelchair access category 3⟡
Bedrooms: 1 single, 1 double, 1 twin
Bathrooms: 2 en-suite, 1 private

Bed & breakfast

per night:	£min	£max
Single	18.00	28.00
Double	34.00	40.00

Half board per

person:	£min	£max
Daily	29.50	32.50
Weekly	194.50	213.50

Evening meal 1800 (last orders 1700)
Parking for 3
Cards accepted: Access, Visa, Amex

NEWENT

Gloucestershire
Map ref 2B1

Small town with the largest collection of birds of prey in Europe at the Falconry Centre. Flying demonstrations daily. Glass workshop where visitors can watch glass being blown. There is a "seconds" shop. North of the village is the Three Choirs Vineyard.
Tourist Information Centre ☎ (01531) 822145

Glendalough

Listed

Kilcot, Newent GL18 1NN
☎ Gorsley (01989) 720294
Fax (01989) 720294
Situated on the edge of the Forest of Dean, close to Ross and Gloucester. Traditional English or vegetarian breakfast.
Bedrooms: 1 single, 1 double, 1 twin
Bathrooms: 1 public

Bed & breakfast

per night:	£min	£max
Single	15.00	15.00
Double	30.00	30.00

Parking for 3

NEWLAND

Gloucestershire
Map ref 2A1

Probably the most attractive of the villages of the Forest of Dean. The church is often referred to as "the Cathedral of the Forest"; it contains a number of interesting monuments and the Forest Miner's Brass. Almshouses nearby were endowed by William Jones, founder of Monmouth School.

Scatterford Farm

HIGHLY COMMENDED

Newland, Coleford GL16 8NG
☎ Dean (01594) 836562
Fax (01594) 836323
Beautiful 15th C farmhouse with spacious rooms, good views and delicious breakfasts with home made bread. Ideal for walking, cycling and riding.
Bedrooms: 2 double, 1 twin
Bathrooms: 2 en-suite, 1 private
Bed & breakfast

per night:	£min	£max
Single	18.50	23.00
Double	37.00	46.00

Parking for 8

NEWPORT

Shropshire
Map ref 4A3

Small market town on the Shropshire Union Canal has a wide High Street and a church with some interesting monuments. Newport is close to Aqualate Mere which is the largest lake in Staffordshire.

Lane End Farm

COMMENDED

Chetwynd, Newport TF10 8BN
☎ Sambrook (01952) 550337
Delightful period farmhouse set in lovely countryside. Located on A41 near Newport. Ideal touring base and beautiful local walks.
Bedrooms: 2 double
Bathrooms: 2 en-suite
Bed & breakfast

per night:	£min	£max
Single	18.00	20.00
Double	36.00	36.00

Evening meal 1800 (last orders 2100)
Parking for 5

Sambrook Manor

Listed

Sambrook, Newport TF10 8AL
☎ Sambrook (01952) 550256
260-acre mixed farm. Old manor farmhouse built in 1702. Close to Stoke Potteries, Shrewsbury, Ironbridge, Wolverhampton and many places of historic interest.
Bedrooms: 1 single, 1 double, 1 triple
Bathrooms: 2 public
Bed & breakfast

per night:	£min	£max
Single	16.00	16.00
Double	32.00	32.00

Parking for 10

NORTHLEACH

Gloucestershire
Map ref 2B1

Village famous for its beautiful 15th C wool church with its lovely porch and interesting interior. There are also some fine houses including a 17th C wool merchant's house containing Keith Harding's World of Mechanical Music. The Cotswold Countryside Collection is in the former prison.

Bank Villas Guesthouse

COMMENDED

West-end, Northleach, Cheltenham GL54 3HG
☎ Cotswold (01451) 860464
Attractive residence with leaded windows, situated off the historic Fosse Way. An excellent base for exploring the beautiful Cotswolds and local places of interest.
Bedrooms: 2 single, 1 double, 1 twin, 1 triple
Bathrooms: 1 en-suite, 2 public
Bed & breakfast

per night:	£min	£max
Single	17.00	18.00
Double	32.00	34.00

Northfield Bed & Breakfast

COMMENDED

Cirencester Road (A429), Northleach, Cheltenham GL54 3JL
☎ Cotswold (01451) 860427
Detached family house in the country with large gardens and home-grown produce. Excellent centre for visiting the Cotswolds and close to local services.
Bedrooms: 1 double, 2 family rooms
Bathrooms: 3 en-suite

Bed & breakfast per night:	£min	£max
Single		20.00
Double	38.00	44.00

Half board per person:	£min	£max
Daily	29.00	36.00

Evening meal 1800 (last orders 1900)
Parking for 10

NYMPSFIELD

Gloucestershire
Map ref 2B1

Pretty village high up in the Cotswolds, with a simple mid-Victorian church and a prehistoric long barrow nearby.

Rose and Crown Inn

COMMENDED

Nympsfield, Stonehouse GL10 3TU
☎ Dursley (01453) 860240
Fax (01453) 860240
300-year-old inn, in quiet Cotswold village, close to Cotswold Way. Easy access to M4/M5.
Bedrooms: 1 double, 3 triple
Bathrooms: 3 en-suite, 1 private
Bed & breakfast

per night:	£min	£max
Single	27.50	29.50
Double	50.00	54.00

Half board per person:	£min	£max
Daily	35.00	49.00
Weekly	245.00	343.00

Lunch available
Evening meal 1830 (last orders 2130)
Parking for 30
Cards accepted: Access, Visa, Diners, Amex, Switch/Delta

OAKAMOOR

Staffordshire
Map ref 4B2

Small village below a steep hill amid the glorious scenery of the Churnet Valley. Its industrial links have now gone, as the site of the factory which made 20,000 miles of copper wire for the first Atlantic cable has been transformed into an attractive picnic site on the riverside.

Ribden Farm ⚠

⚜⚜ HIGHLY COMMENDED

Oakamoor, Stoke-on-Trent
ST10 3BW
☎ (01538) 702830
Fax (01538) 702830

98-acre livestock farm. Grade II listed 18th C farmhouse in open countryside, one and a half miles from Alton Towers. TV and tea/coffee in all rooms.
Bedrooms: 2 double, 1 triple, 3 family rooms
Bathrooms: 5 en-suite, 1 private

Bed & breakfast

per night:	£min	£max
Double	36.00	44.00

Parking for 3
Cards accepted: Access, Visa, Diners, Switch/Delta

⛺🖥️📬🖵♿🖐️🍴🆙⚡📺📖📠
❄️✕🚲🏕️

OMBERSLEY

Hereford and Worcester
Map ref 2B1

A particularly fine village full of black and white houses including the 17th C Dower House and some old inns. The church contains the original box pews.

The Crown and Sandys Arms ⚠

⚜⚜ COMMENDED

Ombersley, Droitwich,
Worcestershire WR9 0EW
☎ Worcester (01905) 620252
Fax (01905) 620769
Freehouse with comfortable bedrooms, draught beers and open fires. Home-cooked meals available lunchtimes and evenings, 7 days a week.
Bedrooms: 1 single, 3 double, 1 twin, 1 triple, 1 family room

Bathrooms: 6 en-suite, 1 public

Bed & breakfast

per night:	£min	£max
Single	25.00	30.00
Double	45.00	48.00

Lunch available
Evening meal 1800 (last orders 2145)
Parking for 100
Cards accepted: Access, Visa, Amex, Switch/Delta

⛺📞📬🖵♿🖐️🍴🆙✂️🐾📺📖🖐️
🍴30♿❄️✕🚲

ONNELEY

Staffordshire
Map ref 4A2

Village on the line between Shropshire and Staffordshire counties, within easy reach of Bridgemere Garden World.

The Wheatsheaf Inn at Onneley ⚠

⚜⚜ COMMENDED

Bar Hill Road, Onneley, Madeley
CW3 9QF
☎ Stoke-on-Trent (01782) 751581
Fax (01782) 751499
18th C country inn with bars, Spanish restaurant, conference and function facilities. On A525, 7 miles from Newcastle-under-Lyme. Close to Potteries, Keele University and M6. Convenient for Alton Towers and Chester.
Bedrooms: 4 double, 1 twin
Bathrooms: 5 en-suite

Bed & breakfast

per night:	£min	£max
Single	45.00	45.00
Double	50.00	60.00

Half board per person:

	£min	£max
Daily	57.00	
Weekly	309.00	

Lunch available
Evening meal 1800 (last orders 2130)
Parking for 150
Cards accepted: Access, Visa, Diners, Amex

⛺📞📬🖵♿🖐️🍴🅂📺📖📠🍴100
♿♿❄️📟 SP T

The symbols in each entry give information about services and facilities. A 'key' to these symbols appears at the back of this guide.

OSWESTRY

Shropshire
Map ref 4A3

Town close to the Welsh border, the scene of many battles. To the north are the remains of a large Iron Age hill fort. An excellent centre for exploring Shropshire and Offa's Dyke.
Tourist Information Centre ☎ (01691) 662488 or 662753

Frankton House

⚜⚜ HIGHLY COMMENDED

Welsh Frankton, Oswestry
SY11 4PA
☎ (01691) 623422

Large old farmhouse, completely refurbished as a guesthouse. In rural Shropshire, close to A5. Canal and hire boats nearby, also riding stables and golf-course.
Bedrooms: 2 double, 2 twin
Bathrooms: 2 en-suite, 2 private, 1 public

Bed & breakfast

per night:	£min	£max
Single	18.00	20.00
Double	36.00	40.00

Parking for 14

⛺♿🖵♿🖐️🍴🆙✂️🐾📺📖📠🛏️♿❄️
✕🚲◎

PAINSWICK

Gloucestershire
Map ref 2B1

Picturesque wool town with inns and houses dating from the 14th C. Painswick Rococo Garden is open to visitors from January to November, and the house is a Palladian mansion. The churchyard is famous for its yew trees.

Culvert Cottage

⚜⚜ COMMENDED

Kingsmill Lane, Painswick, Stroud
GL6 6RT
☎ (01452) 812293
Situated alongside Wash Brook on the southern edge of the village, in lovely gardens and opposite historic Kings Mill.
Bedrooms: 1 double, 1 twin
Bathrooms: 1 en-suite, 1 private

Continued ▶

PAINSWICK

Continued

Bed & breakfast

per night:	£min	£max
Single	20.00	20.00
Double	33.00	38.00

Parking for 2
Open March–November

🐴⬛♿🎗️🖭🖩💺✕🏛️❄🍴🚍 SP

Hambutts Mynd

👑👑

Edge Road, Painswick, Stroud
GL6 6UP
☎ (01452) 812352
Old corn windmill, c1700-50, with original beams. Panoramic views from all bedrooms. 200 yards from main road. Dogs accepted. Weekly rates available.
Bedrooms: 1 single, 1 double, 1 twin
Bathrooms: 1 private, 1 public

Bed & breakfast

per night:	£min	£max
Single	22.00	
Double	40.00	43.00

Parking for 3
Open March–December

🐴8⬛🎗️🖩🖭📶💺✕🖾TV🏛️❄🍴
🚍✕

PARKEND

Gloucestershire
Map ref 2A1

Village in the Forest of Dean, once an important industrial and railway centre, but now quiet and peaceful and a good base for exploring the forest.

Deanfield

Listed **COMMENDED**

Royal Forest Of Dean, Parkend,
Lydney GL15 4JF
☎ Lydney (01594) 562256

Historic 1840 quarry master's village residence set in heart of Forest of Dean. Backs on to RSPB reserve and cycle trail. Special all-year offer - 4 nights for the price of 3.
Bedrooms: 1 single, 1 twin, 1 triple
Bathrooms: 1 en-suite, 1 public

Bed & breakfast

per night:	£min	£max
Single	16.00	22.00
Double	32.00	40.00

Parking for 8

🐴♿🖭🖩💻♿🎗️🖩📶🅂💺✕🏛️🍴🖉🔌
❄✕🚍 SP🏤

PONTESBURY

Shropshire
Map ref 4A3

With views of the Rea Valley from nearby Pontesford Hill, this village is the site of a 7th C battle between a King of Mercia and a King of the West Saxons. Most of the village church was rebuilt in the last century, except for the 13th C chancel which retains its original roof.

Marehay Farm 🏔️

👑👑 **HIGHLY COMMENDED**

Ratlinghope, Pontesbury,
Shrewsbury SY5 0SJ
☎ Linley (01588) 650289
5-acre livestock farm. Splendid isolation at 1,100ft in the Long Mynd and Stiperstones environmentally sensitive area. Peace and quiet. Good walking and bird-watching.
Bedrooms: 2 twin
Bathrooms: 2 en-suite

Bed & breakfast

per night:	£min	£max
Single	16.00	20.00
Double	32.00	40.00

Parking for 4

🐴🖭♿🎗️🖩🅂💺✕🖾TV🏛️🖉🔌❄
✕🚍 SP🏤

RENDCOMB

Gloucestershire
Map ref 2B1

On the river Churn north of Cirencester. Nearby are Chedworth Roman Villa and Fosse Way.

Shawswell Country House 🏔️

👑👑 **DE LUXE**

Rendcomb, Cirencester GL7 7HD
☎ Cirencester (01285) 831779
17th C country house with quality accommodation. Idyllic setting in 25 acres offering peace, tranquillity and wonderful views. From A435 take turning to Rendcomb and follow "no-through road" to the end.
Bedrooms: 1 single, 3 double, 1 twin
Bathrooms: 5 en-suite

Bed & breakfast

per night:	£min	£max
Single	30.00	35.00
Double	40.00	55.00

Parking for 8
Open February–November

🐴10🖭🖩♿🎗️🖩✕🖾🏛️🍴🖉🔌U❄
🚍 DAP SP🏤

ROCK

Hereford and Worcester
Map ref 4A3

The Old Forge

Listed **COMMENDED**

Gorst Hill, Rock, Kidderminster,
Worcestershire DY14 9YG
☎ (01299) 266745
Recently renovated country cottage, near the Wyre Forest. Ideal for country walks and visiting local places of interest. Short and midweek breaks.
Bedrooms: 1 twin, 1 triple
Bathrooms: 1 public

Bed & breakfast

per night:	£min	£max
Single	16.00	
Double	30.00	

Parking for 5
Open January–November

🐴♿🖭🖩♿🎗️🖩✕🖾TV🏛️🍴🖉🔌❄
✕🚍

ROSS-ON-WYE

Hereford and Worcester
Map ref 2A1

Attractive market town with a 17th C market hall, set above the River Wye. There are lovely views over the surrounding countryside from the Prospect and the town is close to Goodrich Castle and the Welsh border.
Tourist Information Centre ☎ (01989) 562768

The Arches Country House

👑👑 **COMMENDED**

Walford Road, Ross-on-Wye,
Herefordshire HR9 5PT
☎ (01989) 563348
Small, family-run hotel, set in half an acre of lawned garden, 10 minutes' walk from town centre. Warm, friendly atmosphere. All rooms furnished to a high standard with views of the garden. Victorian-style conservatory to relax in.
Bedrooms: 1 single, 4 double, 1 twin, 1 triple
Bathrooms: 4 en-suite, 2 public

Bed & breakfast

per night:	£min	£max
Single	19.00	25.00
Double	36.00	44.00

Half board per

person:	£min	£max
Daily	29.00	33.00
Weekly	113.00	147.00

Evening meal from 1900
Parking for 10

🐎♿🖵♠🅟🟊🆂🗡️🎿🏛️🚗🌸🚐
🅞🅐🅟 🆂🅿

Brookfield House

👑👑 APPROVED

Over Ross, Ross-on-Wye,
Herefordshire HR9 7AT
☎ (01989) 562188
*Queen Anne/Georgian listed building
close to the town centre. Private car
park. Easy reach of M50 and A40.*
Bedrooms: 2 single, 3 double, 3 twin
Bathrooms: 3 en-suite, 3 public

Bed & breakfast

per night:	£min	£max
Single	17.50	32.00
Double	34.00	40.00

Parking for 11
Cards accepted: Access, Visa, Amex

🐎🖵♠🆂🎿🏛️🚗🌸🚐 🆂🅿 🏮🆃

Kings Head Hotel

👑👑👑

8 High Street, Ross-on-Wye,
Herefordshire HR9 5HL
☎ (01989) 763174
Fax (01989) 769578
*Family-owned and managed offering
en-suite accommodation, good food
and a safe haven for the traveller.*
Bedrooms: 10 double, 4 twin,
7 triple, 2 family rooms
Bathrooms: 23 en-suite

Bed & breakfast

per night:	£min	£max
Single	40.00	48.00
Double	65.00	65.00

Half board per

person:	£min	£max
Daily	45.00	50.00

Lunch available
Evening meal 1900 (last orders
2100)
Parking for 25
Cards accepted: Access, Visa,
Switch/Delta

🐎♿📞📧🖵♠🅟🟊🆂🎿🏛️🚗🚐
🆂🅿🏮

Lavender Cottage

Listed

Bridstow, Ross-on-Wye,
Herefordshire HR9 6QB
☎ (01989) 562836
*Part 17th C character property, 1 mile
from Ross-on-Wye. Take Hereford road,
turn right to Foy and then first turning
on left.*
Bedrooms: 1 double, 2 twin
Bathrooms: 1 public

Bed & breakfast

per night:	£min	£max
Single	15.00	15.00
Double	30.00	30.00

Half board per

person:	£min	£max
Daily	24.00	24.00
Weekly	168.00	168.00

Evening meal from 1830
Parking for 3

🐎🆔5🖵♠📶🆄🅛🎿🗡️🏛️🚗🌸🐾🚐
🏮

Merrivale Place 🏔

👑

The Avenue, Ross-on-Wye,
Herefordshire HR9 5AW
☎ (01989) 564929
*Fine Victorian house in quiet tree-lined
avenue. Large comfortable rooms and
lovely views. Home cooking. Near town
and river.*
Bedrooms: 2 double, 1 twin
Bathrooms: 2 public

Bed & breakfast

per night:	£min	£max
Single	19.00	20.00
Double	34.00	36.00

Evening meal 1830 (last orders
1600)
Parking for 6
Open March–October

🐎🐄♿🆄🅛🆂🎿🗡️🏛️🚗🌸🐾🚐🏮

The Old Rectory 🏔

👑👑 COMMENDED

Hope Mansell, Ross-on-Wye,
Herefordshire HR9 5TL
☎ (01989) 750382
Fax (01989) 750382
*Georgian house in beautiful rural
surroundings near Ross-on-Wye.
Friendly atmosphere, comfortable
rooms with period furniture. Lovely
mature gardens and all-weather tennis
court.*
Bedrooms: 2 double, 1 twin
Bathrooms: 1 private, 2 public

Bed & breakfast

per night:	£min	£max
Double	37.00	40.00

Parking for 4

🐎🖵♠🆄🅛📶🆂🗡️🏛️🚗🌸⚲
🚐🆂🅿🏮

Rudhall Farm

👑👑 HIGHLY COMMENDED

Ross-on-Wye, Herefordshire
HR9 7TL
☎ Upton Bishop (01989) 780240 &
Mobile (0585) 871379

*Savour the tranquillity of our elegant
early-Georgian farmhouse, offering*

*well-appointed accommodation, country
house hospitality and comfort with style
- "somewhere special". In picturesque
valley with lake, woodland and
millstream. Perfect for exploring Wye
Valley. Aga cooked breakfasts.*
Bedrooms: 1 single, 2 double
Bathrooms: 1 en-suite, 1 private,
1 public

Bed & breakfast

per night:	£min	£max
Single	20.00	22.00
Double	37.00	40.00

Parking for 10
Open January–November

🖵♠🅟🆄🅛🆂🎿🗡️🏛️🚗🌸🐾
🚐🏮

Thatch Close

👑👑 COMMENDED

Llangrove, Ross-on-Wye,
Herefordshire HR9 6EL
☎ Llangarron (01989) 770300
*13-acre mixed farm. Secluded Georgian
country farmhouse midway between
Ross-on-Wye and Monmouth.
Home-produced vegetables and meat.
Ideal for country lovers of any age.
Guests welcome to help with animals.
Map sent on request. Ordnance Survey:
51535196.*
Bedrooms: 2 double, 1 twin
Bathrooms: 2 en-suite, 1 private

Bed & breakfast

per night:	£min	£max
Double	30.00	36.00

Half board per

person:	£min	£max
Daily	26.00	30.00
Weekly	170.00	200.00

Lunch available
Evening meal 1830 (last orders
1800)
Parking for 7

🐎♿🅟📶🆄🅛♠🆂🗡️🏛️🚗🌸
🚐🆂🅿

Wailea

👑👑

Ballingham, Hereford HR2 6NH
☎ Carey (01432) 840255
*Modern bungalow with garden in quiet,
unspoilt village offering exceptional
views along the Wye Valley and
surrounding countryside. Ideal touring
centre.*
Bedrooms: 1 twin
Bathrooms: 1 en-suite

Bed & breakfast

per night:	£min	£max
Single	15.00	
Double	30.00	

Evening meal 1800 (last orders
2000)
Parking for 2

🐎🆔5♿📧🖵♠🆄🅛🆂🗡️📺🏛️🚗
🌸🐾🚐🆂🅿

RUGBY

Warwickshire
Map ref 4C3

Town famous for its public school which gave its name to Rugby Union football and which featured in "Tom Brown's Schooldays".
Tourist Information Centre ☎ *(01788) 535348*

Lawford Hill Farm ⚠

⚜ COMMENDED

Lawford Heath Lane, Rugby
CV23 9HG
☎ (01788) 542001
100-acre mixed farm. Bed and breakfast all the year round in this spacious Georgian farmhouse. Set in 1 acre of attractive garden with fishing available. Close to National Agricultural Centre, Stratford-upon-Avon and the Cotswolds.
Bedrooms: 2 double, 1 twin
Bathrooms: 1 public
Bed & breakfast

per night:	£min	£max
Single	18.00	20.00
Double	36.00	40.00

Parking for 6

White Lion Inn ⚠

Listed APPROVED

Coventry Road, Pailton, Rugby
CV23 0QD
☎ (01788) 832359
Fax (01788) 832359
17th C coaching inn, recently refurbished but maintaining all old world features. Close to Rugby, Coventry and Stratford. Within 2 miles of motorways.
Bedrooms: 9 twin
Bathrooms: 3 en-suite, 2 public
Bed & breakfast

per night:	£min	£max
Single	18.50	25.00
Double	32.00	45.00

Lunch available
Evening meal 1830 (last orders 2200)
Parking for 60
Cards accepted: Access, Visa

Half board prices are given per person, but in some cases these may be based on double/twin occupancy.

RUGELEY

Staffordshire
Map ref 4B3

Town close to Cannock Chase which has over 2000 acres of heath and woodlands with forest trails and picnic sites. Nearby is Shugborough Hall (National Trust) with a fine collection of 18th C furniture and interesting monuments in the grounds.

Park Farm

⚜ COMMENDED

Hawkesyard, Armitage Lane, Rugeley
WS15 1ED
☎ (01889) 583477
40-acre livestock farm. While convenient for towns and attractions in the area, Park Farm is quietly tucked away in scenic hills.
Bedrooms: 2 triple
Bathrooms: 2 en-suite
Bed & breakfast

per night:	£min	£max
Single	16.00	20.00
Double	32.00	40.00

Parking for 23

RUSHTON SPENCER

Staffordshire
Map ref 4B2

Village with an interesting church built in the 14th C of wood, some of which still remains. It is close to the pleasant Rudyard Reservoir.

Barnswood Farm

Listed

Rushton Spencer, Macclesfield, Cheshire SK11 0RA
☎ (01260) 226261
100-acre dairy farm. In a lovely setting overlooking Rudyard Lake 400 yards down the field. Alton Towers, Peak District and the Potteries all within a 15-mile radius. Homely welcome, English breakfast.
Bedrooms: 2 double, 1 triple, 1 family room
Bathrooms: 2 public
Bed & breakfast

per night:	£min	£max
Single	15.00	
Double	28.00	

Parking for 5

SEVERN STOKE

Hereford and Worcester
Map ref 2B1

Village to the south of Worcester with a picturesque group of houses surrounding the church and magnificent views across the Severn to the Malvern Hills.

Madge Hill House

⚜⚜

Severn Stoke, Worcester WR8 9JN
☎ (01905) 371362
Georgian house in peaceful country setting, between Tewkesbury and Worcester on A38. En-suite bedrooms with TV.
Bedrooms: 1 double, 1 twin
Bathrooms: 2 en-suite
Bed & breakfast

per night:	£min	£max
Single	17.00	
Double	34.00	

Parking for 2

SHIFNAL

Shropshire
Map ref 4A3

Small market town, once an important staging centre for coaches on the Holyhead road. Where industrialism has not prevailed, the predominating architectural impression is Georgian, though some timber-framed houses survived the Great Fire of 1591.

Drayton Lodge ⚠

Listed

Opposite Shifnal Golf Club, Shifnal
TF11 8QW
☎ Telford (01952) 460244
Family farmhouse where our children have grown up and left the nest. We enjoy good company. Easy reach of Weston Park, Ironbridge and Cosford. Evening meal by arrangement.
Bedrooms: 1 single, 1 double, 2 twin
Bathrooms: 1 en-suite, 1 public
Bed & breakfast

per night:	£min	£max
Single	14.00	16.00
Double	30.00	32.00

Parking for 20

For ideas on places to visit refer to the introduction at the beginning of this section.

SHREWSBURY

Shropshire
Map ref 4A3

Beautiful historic town on the River Severn retaining many fine old timber-framed houses. Its attractions include Rowley's Museum with Roman finds, remains of a castle, Clive House Museum, St Chad's 18th C round church, rowing on the river and the Shrewsbury Flower Show in August.
Tourist Information Centre ☎ (01743) 350761

Abbey Lodge Guest House M

Listed COMMENDED

68 Abbey Foregate, Shrewsbury SY2 6BG
☎ (01743) 235832 & Mobile 0860 335225
Georgian guesthouse. Friendly family-run business close to town centre. Some bedrooms en-suite. Car park at rear.
Bedrooms: 4 single, 3 double, 1 twin, 3 family rooms
Bathrooms: 4 en-suite, 3 public, 2 private showers

Bed & breakfast

per night:	£min	£max
Single	15.00	17.50
Double	30.00	36.00

Parking for 11
Cards accepted: Access, Visa

Acton Burnell Farm

Listed HIGHLY COMMENDED

Acton Burnell, Shrewsbury SY5 7PQ
☎ Acton Burnell (01694) 731207
300-acre arable farm. Newly, prettily decorated room (double or twin) with beautiful view and private sitting room overlooking garden. Peaceful village, 13th C castle. Shrewsbury, Church Stretton and Ironbridge 30 minutes' drive.
Bedrooms: 1 twin
Bathrooms: 1 private

Bed & breakfast

per night:	£min	£max
Single	15.00	16.50
Double	30.00	33.00

Parking for 4
Open April–October

Ashton Lees

HIGHLY COMMENDED

Dorrington, Shrewsbury SY5 7JW
☎ Dorrington (01743) 718378
Comfortable family home set in large secluded garden, 6 miles south of

Shrewsbury on A49. Convenient for exploring the town and surrounding countryside.
Bedrooms: 2 double, 1 twin
Bathrooms: 1 en-suite, 1 public

Bed & breakfast

per night:	£min	£max
Single	18.00	21.00
Double	36.00	42.00

Half board per

person:	£min	£max
Daily	25.50	28.50
Weekly	165.00	184.00

Evening meal 1830 (last orders 0900)
Parking for 6

The Castle Vaults Inn

Listed

16 Castle Gates, Shrewsbury SY1 2AB
☎ (01743) 358807
Family inn incorporating an open-plan Mexican eating house. Situated in the shadows of Shrewsbury Castle. Roof garden. Some rooms en-suite.
Bedrooms: 3 single, 3 double, 1 twin
Bathrooms: 4 en-suite, 1 public

Bed & breakfast

per night:	£min	£max
Single	25.00	35.00
Double	42.00	45.00

Lunch available
Evening meal 1800 (last orders 2200)

Chatford House M

Bayston Hill, Shrewsbury SY3 0AY
☎ (01743) 718301
5-acre mixed farm. Comfortable farmhouse built in 1776, 5.5 miles south of Shrewsbury off A49. Through Bayston Hill, take third right (Stapleton) then right to Chatford.
Bedrooms: 3 twin
Bathrooms: 1 public

Bed & breakfast

per night:	£min	£max
Single	15.00	
Double	30.00	

Parking for 4
Open April–October

166 Copthorne Rd

Listed

Shrewsbury SY3 8LP
☎ (01743) 353602
Situated in a quiet area of the town, within walking distance of the shops.
Bedrooms: 1 single, 1 twin
Bathrooms: 1 public

Bed & breakfast

per night:	£min	£max
Single	17.00	
Double	34.00	

Parking for 2

33 Coton Crescent

Listed APPROVED

Coton Hill, Shrewsbury SY1 2NZ
☎ (01743) 359398

Built around 1900, an Edwardian style house with 5 bedrooms, bathroom, lounge, dining room and kitchen. In a crescent of similar houses.
Bedrooms: 1 single, 2 twin
Bathrooms: 1 public, 1 private shower

Bed & breakfast

per night:	£min	£max
Single	15.00	18.00
Double	28.00	34.00

Hillsboro

Listed COMMENDED

1 Port Hill Gardens, Shrewsbury SY3 8SH
☎ (01743) 231033
Charming Edwardian private house in quiet residential area, near park, river and Shrewsbury School. 5 minutes from town centre. Traditional breakfast a speciality. Parking.
Bedrooms: 1 double, 1 twin
Bathrooms: 1 public

Bed & breakfast

per night:	£min	£max
Single	16.00	16.00
Double	32.00	32.00

Parking for 2

Lion and Pheasant Hotel M

COMMENDED

49-50 Wyle Cop, Shrewsbury SY1 1XJ
☎ (01743) 236288
Fax (01743) 244475
Ancient inn of character with many exposed beams and original fireplaces. Bars and restaurant open to non-residents.
Bedrooms: 5 single, 6 double, 8 twin, 1 family room

Continued ▶

SHREWSBURY

Continued

Bathrooms: 17 en-suite, 3 private, 2 public

Bed & breakfast per night:

	£min	£max
Single	28.50	45.00
Double	57.00	60.00

Half board per person:

	£min	£max
Daily	39.00	57.00

Lunch available
Evening meal 1900 (last orders 2130)
Parking for 20
Cards accepted: Access, Visa, Diners, Amex, Switch/Delta

Merevale House

Listed COMMENDED

66 Ellesmere Road, Shrewsbury
SY1 2QP
☎ (01743) 243677
Lovely Victorian house. Attractive bedrooms with washbasins, TV, drinks and biscuits, hairdryer and many extra home comforts. Vegetarians catered for. 10 minutes from town. Private parking. Brochure.
Bedrooms: 1 single, 3 double
Bathrooms: 1 public

Bed & breakfast per night:

	£min	£max
Single	16.00	16.00
Double	32.00	32.00

Parking for 8

Roseville

HIGHLY COMMENDED

12 Berwick Road, Shrewsbury
SY1 2LN
☎ (01743) 236470

Late Victorian detached town house, close to town centre. Comfortable, relaxed atmosphere and fine food. A no-smoking establishment.
Bedrooms: 1 single, 1 double, 1 twin
Bathrooms: 2 en-suite, 1 private

Bed & breakfast per night:

	£min	£max
Single	20.00	30.00
Double	40.00	44.00

Parking for 3
Open February–December

Shorthill Lodge

HIGHLY COMMENDED

Shorthill, Lea Cross, Shrewsbury
SY5 8JE
☎ (01743) 860864
Attractive, comfortable house in open country setting, inglenook log fire and centrally heated in winter. Five miles south of Shrewsbury, off A488. Nearby pub/restaurant and golf course. Brochure available.
Bedrooms: 1 double, 1 twin
Bathrooms: 2 en-suite, 1 public

Bed & breakfast per night:

	£min	£max
Single	21.00	25.00
Double	32.00	36.00

Parking for 3

The Stiperstones Guest House

COMMENDED

18 Coton Crescent, Coton Hill, Shrewsbury SY1 2NZ
☎ (01743) 246720 & 350303
Fax (01743) 350303
Always a warm welcome. Tastefully furnished, quality accommodation. Very comfortable and clean. Extensive facilities, off-road parking. Close to town centre and river. Special rates.
Bedrooms: 1 single, 3 double, 1 twin, 1 triple
Bathrooms: 3 public

Bed & breakfast per night:

	£min	£max
Single	18.00	20.00
Double	34.00	35.00

Half board per person:

	£min	£max
Daily	28.00	30.00
Weekly	182.00	196.00

Evening meal 1900 (last orders 1200)
Parking for 8

Please check prices and other details at the time of booking.

Establishments should be open throughout the year, unless otherwise stated.

SLIMBRIDGE

Gloucestershire
Map ref 2B1

The Wildfowl and Wetlands Trust Centre was founded by Sir Peter Scott and has the world's largest collection of wildfowl. Of special interest are the wild swans and the geese which wander around the grounds.

Tudor Arms Lodge

COMMENDED

Shepherds Patch, Slimbridge, Gloucester GL2 7BP
☎ Dursley (01453) 890306
Fax (01453) 890103
Newly-built lodge adjoining an 18th C freehouse, alongside Gloucester and Sharpness Canal. Renowned Slimbridge Wildfowl and Wetlands Trust centre only 800 yards away.
Bedrooms: 4 double, 5 twin, 2 triple, 1 family room
Bathrooms: 12 en-suite

Bed & breakfast per night:

	£min	£max
Single	29.50	32.50
Double	39.50	42.50

Half board per person:

	£min	£max
Daily	28.60	38.40
Weekly	180.00	235.00

Lunch available
Evening meal 1900 (last orders 2200)
Parking for 70
Cards accepted: Access, Visa, Amex

SOLIHULL

West Midlands
Map ref 4B3

On the outskirts of Birmingham. Some Tudor houses and a 13th C church remain amongst the new public buildings and shopping centre. The 16th C Malvern Hall is now a school and the 15th C Chester House at Knowle is now a library. *Tourist Information Centre ☎ (0121) 704 6130 or 704 6134*

The Gate House

Listed

Barston Lane, Barston, Solihull
B92 0JN
☎ Hampton in Arden (01675) 443274
Early Victorian mansion house set in beautiful countryside. Close to the National Exhibition Centre, International Convention Centre, airport and motorway.

Bedrooms: 1 single, 1 double, 2 twin
Bathrooms: 3 en-suite, 1 public
Bed & breakfast

per night:	£min	£max
Single	20.00	30.00
Double	38.00	45.00

Parking for 20

🛇🖭🖵♿🎇Ⓤ✂🅗TV🖩🖴❋🏃🚗

STAFFORD

Staffordshire
Map ref 4B3

The town has a long history and some half-timbered buildings still remain, notably the 16th C High House. There are several museums in the town and Shugborough Hall and the famous angler Izaak Walton's cottage, now a museum, are nearby.
Tourist Information Centre ☎ (01785) 240204

Littywood Farm ⋀
♛♛

Bradley, Stafford ST18 9DW
☎ (01785) 780234
Fax (01785) 780770
400-acre mixed farm. Beautiful 14th C manor offering country house accommodation, secluded yet easily accessible from the M6. Centrally heated.
Bedrooms: 1 double, 1 twin
Bathrooms: 1 en-suite, 1 public
Bed & breakfast

per night:	£min	£max
Single	20.00	25.00
Double	30.00	50.00

Parking for 6

🛇1🖵♿🅗🅐🅗TV🖩🖊✒❋🏃🚗🎏

STAUNTON

Gloucestershire
Map ref 2B1

Village in attractive countryside, midway between Gloucester, Ledbury and Tewkesbury.

Kilmorie Guest House
♛♛ APPROVED

Gloucester Road, Corse, Snigs End, Staunton, Gloucester GL19 3RQ
☎ Gloucester (01452) 840224

7-acre livestock & fruit farm. Built by

Chartists in 1847, Grade II listed smallholding in conservation area. Modernised, comfortable and friendly. TV all rooms. Ideally situated for touring Cotswolds, Forest of Dean and Malvern Hills.
Bedrooms: 1 single, 3 double, 1 twin, 1 family room
Bathrooms: 1 en-suite, 1 private, 1 public
Bed & breakfast

per night:	£min	£max
Single	14.00	
Double	28.00	

Half board per

person:	£min	£max
Daily	20.50	
Weekly	136.50	

Lunch available
Evening meal from 1800
Parking for 8

🛇5♿🖭🖵♿Ⓤ🅐🅗🆂🅗TV🖩🖴
🎇❋🎏🏠

STIPERSTONES

Shropshire
Map ref 4A3

Below the spectacular ridge of the same name, from which superb views over moorland, forest and hills may be enjoyed.

Sycamore Cottage
♛♛ COMMENDED

5 Perkins Beach, Stiperstones, Minsterley, Shrewsbury SY5 0PQ
☎ Shrewsbury (01743) 790914
Delightful accommodation in beamed cottage at foot of Stiperstones Hills. Log fire. Friendly welcome. Wonderful views. Ideal walking country.
Bedrooms: 1 twin
Bathrooms: 1 en-suite
Bed & breakfast

per night:	£min	£max
Single		18.50
Double		33.00

Half board per

person:	£min	£max
Daily		28.00
Weekly		196.00

Evening meal 1930 (last orders 2200)
Parking for 3

🖭🖵🎇Ⓤ🆂🖩🍴❋🚗

Tankerville Lodge ⋀
♛ COMMENDED

Stiperstones, Minsterley, Shrewsbury SY5 0NB
☎ Shrewsbury (01743) 791401
Country house noted for warm hospitality, set in superb landscape which offers breathtaking views. Ideal

touring base for Shropshire and Welsh borderland. Adjacent to Stiperstones Nature Reserve.
Bedrooms: 1 double, 3 twin
Bathrooms: 2 public
Bed & breakfast

per night:	£min	£max
Single	15.95	18.45
Double	31.90	31.90

Half board per

person:	£min	£max
Daily	25.45	27.95
Weekly	169.75	187.25

Evening meal 1900 (last orders 0900)
Parking for 5

🛇5♿🅐🆂🅗TV🖩🖴🚗♿❋🚜🆂🅿

STOKE LACY

Hereford and Worcester
Map ref 2A1

Small village by the River Leadon, on the cider trail, a few miles from Bromyard. The 14th C half-timbered manor house of Lower Brockhampton (National Trust) is nearby.

Nether Court ⋀
♛♛ HIGHLY COMMENDED

Stoke Lacy, Bromyard, Herefordshire HR7 4HJ
☎ Hereford (01432) 820247

300-acre mixed farm. Victorian farmhouse in peaceful village surroundings. Small lake for wildlife. Good restaurant within walking distance. Near Hereford, Ludlow, Malvern, Leominster and Worcester.
Bedrooms: 1 single, 2 double
Bathrooms: 2 en-suite, 1 private
Bed & breakfast

per night:	£min	£max
Single	22.00	22.00
Double	35.00	

Evening meal from 1800

🛇🖵♿🎇Ⓤ🅐🅗TV🚗🖊🎵✒❋
🏃🚜🎏

A key to symbols can be found inside the back cover flap.

STOKE-ON-TRENT

Staffordshire
Map ref 4B2

Famous for its pottery. Factories of several famous makers, including Josiah Wedgwood, can be visited. The City Museum has one of the finest pottery and porcelain collections in the world.
Tourist Information Centre ☎ *(01782) 284600*

The Hollies

COMMENDED

Clay Lake, Endon, Stoke-on-Trent
ST9 9DD
☎ (01782) 503252
Delightful Victorian house in a quiet country setting off B5051. Convenient for M6, the Potteries and Alton Towers. Non-smokers only, please.
Bedrooms: 2 double, 3 triple
Bathrooms: 4 en-suite, 1 private, 1 public

Bed & breakfast

per night:	£min	£max
Single	20.00	30.00
Double	32.00	40.00

Parking for 5

Reynolds Hey

COMMENDED

Park Lane, Endon, Stoke-on-Trent
ST9 9JB
☎ (01782) 502717
Restored 17th C stone farmhouse in quiet location with lovely views of open countryside. Spacious rooms with TV, tea/coffee-making. Convenient for Alton Towers, Royal Doulton and the moors and dales of Staffordshire and Derbyshire.
Bedrooms: 2 double, 1 twin
Bathrooms: 2 en-suite, 1 private

Bed & breakfast

per night:	£min	£max
Single	15.00	17.00
Double	30.00	30.00

Half board per

person:	£min	£max
Daily	23.00	23.00
Weekly	150.00	150.00

Evening meal from 1900
Parking for 3
Open January–November

Verdon Guest House

Listed APPROVED

44 Charles Street, Hanley,
Stoke-on-Trent ST1 3JY
☎ (01782) 264244
Large, friendly guesthouse almost in town centre and close to bus station. Convenient for all pottery factory visits, museum and Festival Park. Alton Towers 20 minutes, M6 10 minutes. All rooms with cable TV, some en-suite.
Bedrooms: 1 single, 3 double, 4 twin, 4 triple
Bathrooms: 4 en-suite, 3 public

Bed & breakfast

per night:	£min	£max
Single	17.00	18.00
Double	32.00	38.00

Parking for 8
Cards accepted: Access, Visa

STONE

Staffordshire
Map ref 4B2

Town on the River Trent with the remains of a 12th C Augustinian priory. It is surrounded by pleasant countryside. Trentham Gardens with 500 acres of parklands and recreational facilities is within easy reach.

Couldreys

COMMENDED

8 Airdale Road, Stone ST15 8DW
☎ (01785) 812500
Fax (01785) 811761
Edwardian house quietly situated on town outskirts, providing every comfort plus home-made bread! Excellent restaurants within walking distance. Convenient for M6, Wedgwood and Potteries. Non-smokers only, please.
Bedrooms: 1 double, 1 twin
Bathrooms: 1 en-suite, 1 private

Bed & breakfast

per night:	£min	£max
Single	20.00	
Double	32.00	36.00

Parking for 2

STONEHOUSE

Gloucestershire
Map ref 2B1

Village in the Stroud Valley with an Elizabethan Court, later restored and altered by Lutyens.

Merton Lodge

8 Ebley Road, Stonehouse
GL10 2LQ
☎ (01453) 822018
Former gentleman's residence offering a warm welcome. Cotton and linen sheets only. No smoking. Three miles from M5 junction 13, over 4 roundabouts, straight on along Old Road, under foot bridge. Located virtually opposite garden centre. Short walk from carvery/pub.
Bedrooms: 3 double
Bathrooms: 1 en-suite, 2 public

Bed & breakfast

per night:	£min	£max
Single	15.00	17.00
Double	30.00	34.00

Parking for 6

Oldends Farm Bed and Breakfast

COMMENDED

Oldends Lane, Stonehouse
GL10 3RL
☎ Stroud (01453) 822135
95-acre livestock & horses farm. 16th C farmhouse surrounded by orchards and open fields. Two miles from M5, junction 13, and within walking distance of Stonehouse. En-suite rooms. Breakfast menu. Pub food 100 yards.
Bedrooms: 1 single, 1 twin, 1 family room
Bathrooms: 2 en-suite, 1 private

Bed & breakfast

per night:	£min	£max
Single	15.50	17.50
Double	35.00	35.00

Parking for 6

STOURBRIDGE

West Midlands
Map ref 4B3

Town on the River Stour, famous for its glassworks. Several of the factories can be visited and glassware purchased at the factory shops.

St. Elizabeth's Cottage

COMMENDED

Woodman Lane, Clent, Stourbridge
DY9 9PX
☎ Hagley (01562) 883883
Beautiful country cottage with lovely gardens and interior professionally decorated throughout. 20 minutes from Birmingham and close to motorway links.
Bedrooms: 1 double, 1 twin
Bathrooms: 2 private, 1 public

Bed & breakfast

per night:	£min	£max
Single	22.00	25.00
Double	44.00	50.00

Parking for 2

STOW-ON-THE-WOLD

Gloucestershire
Map ref 2B1

Attractive Cotswold wool town with a large market-place and some fine houses, especially the old grammar school. There is an interesting church dating from Norman times. Stow-on-the-Wold is surrounded by lovely countryside and Cotswold villages.
Tourist Information Centre ☎ (01451) 831082

Aston House 🅰

Listed COMMENDED

Broadwell, Moreton-in-Marsh
GL56 0TJ
☎ Cotswold (01451) 830475
Cotswold-stone chalet-bungalow in quiet village, 1.5 miles from Stow-on-the-Wold. Central for touring Cotswolds. Pub within walking distance. Reduced rates for weekly B&B.
Bedrooms: 2 double, 1 twin
Bathrooms: 2 en-suite, 1 private
Bed & breakfast

per night:	£min	£max
Double	36.00	40.00

Parking for 3
Open February–November
🛥 10 🛁 🖵 📺 📶 🔒 Ⓢ 🍴 🖩 ☼ ✕ 🐾

Corsham Field Farmhouse 🅰

🏠🏠 APPROVED

Bledington Road, Stow-on-the-Wold,
Cheltenham GL54 1JH
☎ Cotswold (01451) 831750
100-acre mixed farm. Homely farmhouse with breathtaking views. Ideally situated for exploring the Cotswolds. En-suite and standard rooms. TVs, guest lounge, tea/coffee facilities. Good pub food 5 minutes' walk away.
Bedrooms: 1 double, 1 twin, 2 triple, 3 family rooms
Bathrooms: 5 en-suite, 1 public
Bed & breakfast

per night:	£min	£max
Single	15.00	25.00
Double	27.00	38.00

Parking for 10
🛥🛁🖵📺📶Ⓢ🍴📺🖩☎Ⓤ☼ 🐾

Cross Keys Cottage 🅰

🏠🏠 COMMENDED

Park Street, Stow-on-the-Wold,
Cheltenham GL54 1AQ
☎ Cotswold (01451) 831128
Just a few minutes' walk from Stow Square, this pretty 17th C cottage offers delightful accommodation and a warm welcome. Superb breakfasts and all facilities. Four-poster.

Bedrooms: 2 double, 1 twin
Bathrooms: 1 en-suite, 2 public
Bed & breakfast

per night:	£min	£max
Single	25.00	36.00
Double	42.00	48.00

🖵🖵🛁📶Ⓤ🍴📺🖩☎Ⓤ🐾Ⓣ

The Hollies 🅰

🏠🏠 COMMENDED

Lower Swell Road,
Stow-on-the-Wold, Cheltenham
GL54 1LD
☎ Cotswold (01451) 830577
Fax (01451) 830577
Cotswold family home, large garden with uninterrupted views across the Dikler Valley. Ample parking. Ten minutes to market square.
Bedrooms: 2 double
Bathrooms: 2 en-suite
Bed & breakfast

per night:	£min	£max
Single	20.00	25.00
Double	35.00	40.00

Parking for 3
Open February–October
🖵🖵🛁🐾📶Ⓤ✂🍴🖩☎🐾☼✕🐾

Horse and Groom Inn 🅰

🏠🏠 COMMENDED

Upper Oddington,
Moreton-in-Marsh GL56 0XH
☎ Cotswold (01451) 830584
16th C old world character inn serving lunchtime and evening meals all year round. Families welcome. En-suite rooms.
Bedrooms: 5 double, 2 twin
Bathrooms: 7 en-suite
Bed & breakfast

per night:	£min	£max
Single	27.50	32.50
Double	25.00	35.00

Lunch available
Evening meal 1830 (last orders 2130)
Parking for 40
Cards accepted: Access, Visa, Switch/Delta
🛥🛁🖵🏧🖵🖵🛁🔒Ⓢ🖩☎► ☼🐾⚲SP🐾

Journeys End 🅰

🏠🏠 COMMENDED

Evenlode, Moreton-in-Marsh
GL56 0NN
☎ Moreton-in-Marsh (01608) 650786
20-acre mixed farm. Peace, perfect peace. Gabled, Cotswold-stone farmhouse in quiet village. Approximately 3 miles from Moreton-in-Marsh and Stow-on-the-Wold. One bedroom is on ground floor.

Bedrooms: 3 double, 1 twin, 1 family room
Bathrooms: 5 en-suite
Bed & breakfast

per night:	£min	£max
Single	17.00	25.00
Double	34.00	40.00

Parking for 5
🛥🛁🖵🖵🛁📶Ⓤ🔒🍴📺🖩☎☼ 🐾

Little Spinney

🏠🏠 COMMENDED

Moreton Road, Stow-on-the-Wold,
Cheltenham GL54 1EG
☎ Cotswold (01451) 870448

Comfortable residence set in 15 acres, high on the western edge of Stow and with glorious views. Homely, relaxed atmosphere. Home cooking.
Bedrooms: 1 double, 1 twin, 1 triple
Bathrooms: 2 en-suite, 1 private
Bed & breakfast

per night:	£min	£max
Single	22.50	27.50
Double	40.00	50.00

Half board per person:	£min	£max
Daily	30.00	35.00
Weekly	200.00	230.00

Evening meal 1900 (last orders 2100)
Parking for 8
Open March–December
🛥6🛁🖵🛁📶Ⓤ🔒Ⓢ✂🍴📺🖩🛁 ☼🐾SP

Old Farmhouse Hotel 🅰

🏠🏠 COMMENDED

Lower Swell, Stow-on-the-Wold,
Cheltenham GL54 1LF
☎ Cotswold (01451) 830232 &
Freephone 0500 657842
Fax (01451) 870962

Sympathetically converted 16th C Cotswold-stone farmhouse in a quiet hamlet, 1 mile west of Stow-on-the-Wold. Offers warm and unpretentious hospitality.

Continued ►

STOW-ON-THE-WOLD
Continued

Bedrooms: 9 double, 4 twin, 1 family room
Suite available
Bathrooms: 14 en-suite, 1 public

Bed & breakfast

per night:	£min	£max
Single	21.50	58.00
Double	43.00	97.00

Half board per person:	£min	£max
Daily	35.00	65.00
Weekly	245.00	455.00

Lunch available
Evening meal 1900 (last orders 2100)
Parking for 25
Cards accepted: Access, Visa, Switch/Delta

South Hill Farmhouse ⚏

Fosseway, Stow-on-the-Wold,
Cheltenham GL54 1JU
☎ Cotswold (01451) 831219
Fax (01451) 831554

Base your touring holiday in this Victorian farmhouse. Individually furnished and spacious en-suite rooms, a hearty breakfast, lounge with open fires.
Bedrooms: 3 double, 1 twin, 1 triple
Bathrooms: 4 en-suite, 1 private, 1 public

Bed & breakfast

per night:	£min	£max
Double	38.00	40.00

Parking for 6

The map references refer to the colour maps towards the end of the guide. The first figure is the map number; the letter and figure which follow indicate the grid reference on the map.

STRATFORD-UPON-AVON
Warwickshire
Map ref 2B1

Famous as Shakespeare's home town, Stratford's many attractions include his birthplace, New Place where he died, the Royal Shakespeare Theatre and Gallery, "The World of Shakespeare" 30 minute theatre and Hall's Croft (his daughter's house).
Tourist Information Centre ☎ (01789) 293127

Abberley ⚏
COMMENDED
12 Albany Road,
Stratford-upon-Avon CV37 6PG
☎ Stratford upon Avon (01789) 295934
Comfortable home set in a quiet residential area yet within easy walking distance of theatres and town centre. Non-smokers only, please.
Bedrooms: 1 twin
Bathrooms: 1 en-suite

Bed & breakfast

per night:	£min	£max
Double	42.00	44.00

Parking for 2

Amelia Linhill Guesthouse ⚏
Listed **APPROVED**
35 Evesham Place,
Stratford-upon-Avon CV37 6HT
☎ Stratford-on-Avon (01789) 292879
Fax (01789) 414478
Comfortable Victorian guesthouse offering warm welcome and good food. 5 minutes' walk from town centre and theatres and convenient for Cotswolds. Baby sitting service.
Bedrooms: 1 single, 1 double, 3 twin, 2 triple, 1 family room
Bathrooms: 2 en-suite, 2 public

Bed & breakfast

per night:	£min	£max
Single	15.00	18.00
Double	30.00	36.00

Half board per person:	£min	£max
Daily	22.00	25.00

Lunch available
Evening meal 1700 (last orders 1930)

Braeside Guest House
COMMENDED
129 Shipston Road,
Stratford-upon-Avon CV37 7LW
☎ (01789) 261648

Attractive detached family-run guesthouse, 10 minutes' walk from Royal Shakespeare Theatre and town centre along old tramway footpath. Double/family room and twin room are en-suite, single has private bathroom. Ample parking.
Bedrooms: 1 single, 1 twin, 1 triple
Bathrooms: 2 en-suite, 1 public

Bed & breakfast

per night:	£min	£max
Single	17.00	18.00
Double	34.00	35.00

Parking for 4

Bronhill House ⚏
Listed
260 Alcester Road,
Stratford-upon-Avon CV37 9JQ
☎ (01789) 299169
Detached family house in elevated position, 1 mile from Stratford-upon-Avon. Family-run with relaxed friendly atmosphere. A non-smoking establishment.
Bedrooms: 2 double, 1 twin
Bathrooms: 1 en-suite, 2 private, 2 public

Bed & breakfast

per night:	£min	£max
Single	15.00	20.00
Double	25.00	32.00

Parking for 5

Brook Lodge ⚏
HIGHLY COMMENDED
192 Alcester Road,
Stratford-upon-Avon CV37 9DR
☎ Stratford upon Avon (01789) 295988
Fax (01789) 295988

Immaculately maintained guesthouse, convenient for all local attractions. Prettily decorated and comfortable en-suite bedrooms. Highest standards throughout. Large car park.
Bedrooms: 4 double, 1 twin, 2 triple
Bathrooms: 6 en-suite, 1 private

Bed & breakfast

per night:	£min	£max
Single	25.00	45.00
Double	38.00	50.00

Parking for 10
Cards accepted: Access, Visa, Amex, Switch/Delta

Carlton Guest House

COMMENDED

22 Evesham Place,
Stratford-upon-Avon CV37 6HT
☎ (01789) 293548
Elegantly furnished house combining Victorian origins with all modern facilities. 5 minutes' walk to the theatre and town centre. Private parking.
Bedrooms: 2 single, 2 double, 1 twin, 1 triple
Bathrooms: 3 en-suite, 1 public

Bed & breakfast per night:	£min	£max
Single	21.00	21.00
Double	42.00	48.00

Parking for 3

Chadwyns Guest House

Listed

6 Broad Walk, Stratford-upon-Avon
CV37 6HS
☎ Stratford-on-Avon (01789) 269077
Fax (01789) 269077
Traditionally furnished Victorian house, family-run, in old town near theatre. Colour TV, tea/coffee making facilities all rooms. Vegetarian alternative breakfast.

Bedrooms: 1 single, 1 double, 2 triple, 2 family rooms
Bathrooms: 2 en-suite, 2 public

Bed & breakfast per night:	£min	£max
Single	18.00	25.00
Double	32.00	40.00

Parking for 2
Cards accepted: Access, Visa, Switch/Delta

Cherangani

COMMENDED

61 Maidenhead Road,
Stratford-upon-Avon CV37 6XU
☎ (01789) 292655
Pleasant detached house in a quiet, residential area, offering warm, attractive accommodation. Within walking distance of the town and theatre.
Bedrooms: 1 twin
Bathrooms: 1 public

Bed & breakfast per night:	£min	£max
Single	16.00	18.00
Double	32.00	36.00

Parking for 3

Church Farm

COMMENDED

Dorsington, Stratford-upon-Avon
CV37 8AX
☎ (01789) 720471 & Mobile 0831 504194
Fax (01789) 720830
127-acre mixed farm. Situated in beautiful countryside, most rooms en-suite, TV, tea and coffee facilities. Close to Stratford-upon-Avon, Warwick, the Cotswolds and Evesham.
Wheelchair access category 3
Bedrooms: 3 double, 2 twin, 2 family rooms
Bathrooms: 6 en-suite, 1 public

Bed & breakfast per night:	£min	£max
Double	32.00	38.00

Parking for 12

STRATFORD-UPON-AVON
Continued

Clomendy Guest House ⚠

157 Evesham Road,
Stratford-upon-Avon CV37 9BP
☎ (01789) 266957

Small, detached, mock-Tudor family-run guesthouse, convenient for town centre, Anne Hathaway's cottage and theatres. Stratford-in-Bloom commendation winner. Rail/coach guests met and returned. No smoking, please.
Bedrooms: 1 single, 1 double, 1 twin
Bathrooms: 1 public, 1 private shower
Bed & breakfast

per night:	£min	£max
Single	15.00	18.00
Double	28.00	36.00

Parking for 5

Curtain Call ⚠
♛♛ APPROVED

142 Alcester Road,
Stratford-upon-Avon CV37 9DR
☎ (01789) 267734
Ten-minute walk from town. En-suite rooms, four-poster bed available, colour TV in all rooms, relaxed atmosphere - all at reasonable prices.
Bedrooms: 2 single, 2 double, 1 triple
Bathrooms: 3 en-suite, 1 public
Bed & breakfast

per night:	£min	£max
Single	16.00	19.00
Double	32.00	38.00

Parking for 5
Cards accepted: Access, Visa, Switch/Delta

Faviere ⚠
♛♛ COMMENDED

127 Shipston Road,
Stratford-upon-Avon CV37 7LW
☎ Stratford-on-Avon (01789) 293764
Fax (01789) 269365
Modern residential establishment with rear bedrooms overlooking river. Within 10 minutes' walk of the town centre, situated on the A3400 south of town.
Bedrooms: 1 single, 1 double, 1 family room

Bathrooms: 2 en-suite, 1 private
Bed & breakfast

per night:	£min	£max
Single	25.00	35.00
Double	35.00	40.00

Parking for 6
Open January–February, April–December

Field View ⚠
♛♛ APPROVED

35 Banbury Road,
Stratford-upon-Avon CV37 7HW
☎ (01789) 292694
10 minutes' walk from Stratford town centre, offering comfortable, family-type accommodation.
Bedrooms: 1 double
Bathrooms: 1 public
Bed & breakfast

per night:	£min	£max
Single	15.00	17.00
Double	30.00	34.00

Parking for 3

Green Gables ⚠
♛♛ COMMENDED

47 Banbury Road,
Stratford-upon-Avon CV37 7HW
☎ (01789) 205557
Edwardian house in a residential area, within 10 minutes' walk of the town centre and theatre.
Bedrooms: 1 double
Bathrooms: 1 private, 1 public
Bed & breakfast

per night:	£min	£max
Double	37.00	39.00

Parking for 3

Highcroft ⚠
♛♛ COMMENDED

Banbury Road, Stratford-upon-Avon CV37 7NF
☎ (01789) 296293

Lovely country house in 2-acre garden, only 2 miles from Stratford-upon-Avon, on A422. Families welcome. Friendly, relaxed atmosphere.
Bedrooms: 1 double, 1 family room
Bathrooms: 2 en-suite

Bed & breakfast

per night:	£min	£max
Single	18.00	20.00
Double		36.00

Parking for 3

Houndshill House ⚠
♛♛♛

Banbury Road, Ettington,
Stratford-upon-Avon CV37 7NS
☎ (01789) 740267
Fax (01789) 740075
Family-run pub with restaurant, 4 miles from Stratford-upon-Avon. Informal and friendly atmosphere.
Bedrooms: 2 single, 3 double, 2 twin, 1 triple
Bathrooms: 8 en-suite
Bed & breakfast

per night:	£min	£max
Single	30.00	
Double	50.00	

Lunch available
Evening meal 1900 (last orders 2200)
Parking for 50
Cards accepted: Access, Visa, Switch/Delta

Moonlight Bed & Breakfast ⚠
Listed COMMENDED

144 Alcester Road,
Stratford-upon-Avon CV37 9DR
☎ Stratford upon Avon (01789) 298213
Small family guesthouse near town centre, offering comfortable accommodation at reasonable prices. Tea/coffee making facilities and colour TV. En-suite rooms available.
Bedrooms: 1 single, 1 double, 1 twin, 1 triple
Bathrooms: 2 en-suite, 1 public
Bed & breakfast

per night:	£min	£max
Single	15.00	16.50
Double	28.00	33.00

Parking for 4

Moonraker House ⚠
♛♛ COMMENDED

40 Alcester Road,
Stratford-upon-Avon CV37 9DB
☎ Stratford-on-Avon (01789) 299346 & 267115
Fax (01789) 295504
Family-run, near town centre. Beautifully co-ordinated decor throughout. Some rooms with four-poster beds and garden terrace available for non-smokers.
Bedrooms: 16 double, 2 twin, 4 triple

Bathrooms: 22 en-suite

Bed & breakfast

per night:	£min	£max
Single	35.00	50.00
Double	43.00	65.00

Parking for 24
Cards accepted: Access, Visa

🐶♿️🏥🛏️🖥️🔌⚓🛎️Ⓢ⚡🚭📺📶
🚗 DAP SP T

Moss Cottage 🅰️
🏵️🏵️ COMMENDED

61 Evesham Road,
Stratford-upon-Avon CV37 9BA
☎ (01789) 294770
Pauline and Jim Rush welcome you to their charming detached cottage. Walking distance theatre/town. Spacious en-suite accommodation. Hospitality tray, TV. Parking.
Bedrooms: 2 double
Bathrooms: 2 en-suite

Bed & breakfast

per night:	£min	£max
Single	25.00	30.00
Double	34.00	42.00

Parking for 3
🐶9📶⌨️🔌🚭📺📺📶 🚗🚐 SP

Newlands 🅰️
🏵️🏵️ COMMENDED

7 Broad Walk, Stratford-upon-Avon
CV37 6HS
☎ (01789) 298449
Fax (01789) 298449
Park your car at Sue Boston's home and take a short walk to the Royal Shakespeare Theatre, town centre and Shakespeare properties.
Bedrooms: 1 single, 1 double, 2 triple
Bathrooms: 3 en-suite, 1 public

Bed & breakfast

per night:	£min	£max
Single	19.00	21.00
Double	40.00	44.00

Parking for 2
Cards accepted: Access, Visa, Switch/Delta
🐶10🖥️🔌🚭🛎️Ⓢ🚭📺📺📶
🚗✈️🚐

Parkfield 🅰️
🏵️🏵️

3 Broad Walk, Stratford-upon-Avon
CV37 6HS
☎ (01789) 293313
Fax (01789) 293313
Delightful Victorian house. Quiet location, 5 minutes' walk from theatre and town. Some rooms en-suite. Colour TV, tea and coffee facilities and parking. Choice of breakfast, including vegetarian. A non-smoking house.
Bedrooms: 1 single, 1 double, 1 twin, 4 triple
Bathrooms: 5 en-suite, 1 public

Bed & breakfast

per night:	£min	£max
Single	18.00	
Double	36.00	

Parking for 8
Cards accepted: Access, Visa, Diners
🐶🖥️🔌🚭🔌⚓🛎️Ⓢ🚭📶 🚗✈️

Penshurst Guesthouse 🅰️
Listed COMMENDED

34 Evesham Place,
Stratford-upon-Avon CV37 6HT
☎ (01789) 205259 & 295322
Fax (01789) 295322

Karen and Yannick offer an exceptionally warm welcome to their prettily refurbished Victorian townhouse 5 minutes' walk from town centre, and serve delicious breakfasts from 7am right up until 1030am. A strictly non-smoking establishment.
Wheelchair access category 2♿️
Bedrooms: 2 single, 2 double, 1 twin, 1 triple, 2 family rooms
Bathrooms: 2 en-suite, 2 public

Bed & breakfast

per night:	£min	£max
Single	15.00	19.00
Double	28.00	40.00

Half board per person:

	£min	£max
Daily	20.50	27.50
Weekly	146.50	182.50

Evening meal 1800 (last orders 1400)
🐶🏥🖥️🔌🚭🔌⚓🛎️Ⓢ🚭📶 🚗✈️ DAP
🚐 SP

The Poplars 🅰️
Listed COMMENDED

Mansell Farm, Newbold-on-Stour,
Stratford-upon-Avon CV37 8BZ
☎ Stratford upon Avon (01789) 450540
172-acre dairy farm. Modern farmhouse in picturesque surroundings offers friendly welcome. Two hostelries within walking distance serve good food. Six miles south of Stratford-upon-Avon on A3400.
Bedrooms: 1 single, 1 twin, 1 triple
Bathrooms: 2 en-suite, 1 public

Bed & breakfast

per night:	£min	£max
Single	15.00	16.50
Double	30.00	33.00

Half board per person:

	£min	£max
Daily	23.00	24.50
Weekly	140.00	168.00

Evening meal 1830 (last orders 2000)
Parking for 3
🐶🖥️🔌🚭🔌⚓🛎️Ⓢ🚭📶🌸🚐

Ravenhurst 🅰️
🏵️🏵️

2 Broad Walk, Stratford-upon-Avon
CV37 6HS
☎ Stratford-on-Avon (01789) 292515

Quietly situated, a few minutes' walk from the town centre and places of historic interest. Comfortable home, with substantial breakfast provided. Four-poster en-suite available.
Bedrooms: 4 double, 1 twin
Bathrooms: 5 en-suite

Bed & breakfast

per night:	£min	£max
Double	38.00	50.00

Parking for 4
Cards accepted: Access, Visa, Diners, Amex
🐶🏥🖥️🔌🚭🛎️Ⓢ🚭⚡📶 🚗✈️🚐
T

Sequoia House 🅰️
🏵️🏵️ COMMENDED

51-53 Shipston Road,
Stratford-upon-Avon CV37 7LN
☎ Stratford-on-Avon (01789) 268852 & 294940
Fax (01789) 414559
Beautifully-appointed private hotel with large car park and delightful garden walk to the theatre, riverside gardens and Shakespeare properties. Fully air-conditioned dining room.
Bedrooms: 2 single, 10 double, 12 twin
Bathrooms: 8 en-suite, 12 private, 3 public

Bed & breakfast

per night:	£min	£max
Single	29.00	49.00
Double	39.00	76.00

Lunch available
Parking for 33
Cards accepted: Access, Visa, Diners, Amex, Switch/Delta
🐶5🖥️📞🔌🚭🔌⚓🛎️Ⓢ🚭⚡📶 🚗
🍴60♿️🌸✈️ DAP SP T

STRATFORD-UPON-AVON

Continued

Twelfth Night

COMMENDED

Evesham Place, Stratford-upon-Avon
CV37 6HT
☎ (01789) 414595
Elegant Victorian villa once owned for almost a quarter of a century by the governors of the Royal Shakespeare Company. Delightfully refurbished for the connoisseur. Non-smokers only, please.
Bedrooms: 6 double
Bathrooms: 6 en-suite

Bed & breakfast

per night:	£min	£max
Double	46.00	58.00

Parking for 7
Cards accepted: Access, Visa

Whitchurch Farm

APPROVED

Wimpstone, Stratford-upon-Avon
CV37 8NS
☎ Alderminster (01789) 450275
260-acre mixed farm. Listed Georgian farmhouse set in park-like surroundings on the edge of the Cotswolds. Ideal for a touring holiday. Small village 4 miles south of Stratford-upon-Avon.
Bedrooms: 2 double, 1 twin
Bathrooms: 3 en-suite, 1 public

Bed & breakfast

per night:	£min	£max
Single	18.00	20.00
Double	34.00	36.00

Half board per person:

	£min	£max
Daily	26.00	28.00

Evening meal from 1830
Parking for 3

Wood View

HIGHLY COMMENDED

Pathlow, Stratford-upon-Avon
CV37 0RQ
☎ (01789) 295778
Fax (01789) 295778
Beautifully situated comfortable home, with fine views over fields and woods. Ideal for touring Stratford-upon-Avon and the Cotswolds.
Bedrooms: 2 twin
Bathrooms: 2 en-suite

Bed & breakfast

per night:	£min	£max
Double	44.00	50.00

Parking for 6

STROUD

Gloucestershire
Map ref 2B1

This old town, surrounded by attractive hilly country, has been producing broadcloth for centuries and the local museum has an interesting display on the subject. Many of the mills have been converted into craft centres and for other uses.
Tourist Information Centre ☎ (01453) 765768

Downfield Hotel

COMMENDED

134 Cainscross Road, Stroud
GL5 4HN
☎ (01453) 764496
Fax (01453) 753150

Imposing hotel in quiet location. Home cooking. 1 mile from town centre, 5 miles from M5 motorway, junction 13, on main A419 road.
Bedrooms: 4 single, 9 double, 7 twin, 1 triple
Bathrooms: 11 en-suite, 3 public

Bed & breakfast

per night:	£min	£max
Single	20.00	29.00
Double	33.00	39.00

Half board per person:

	£min	£max
Daily	28.00	35.00
Weekly	196.00	245.00

Evening meal 1830 (last orders 2000)
Parking for 23
Cards accepted: Access, Visa, Diners, Amex, Switch/Delta

The Laye-Bye

COMMENDED

7 Castlemead Road, Rodborough, Stroud GL5 3SF
☎ (01453) 751514 & 762205
Spacious elevated town house in discreet cul-de-sac. Attractive views, quiet garden, tastefully decorated. All modern facilities.
Bedrooms: 2 single, 2 double
Bathrooms: 4 en-suite, 1 public

Bed & breakfast

per night:	£min	£max
Single	12.50	17.00
Double	25.00	30.00

Half board per person:

	£min	£max
Daily	19.50	24.00
Weekly	130.00	160.00

Evening meal from 1800
Parking for 4

Whitegates Farm

COMMENDED

Cowcombe Hill, Chalford, Stroud
GL6 8HP
☎ Cirencester (01285) 760758
Peaceful hillside farmhouse with lovely views, gardens, orchards and 16 rambling acres. Good walking, central for touring. Non-smokers only, please. Spanish spoken.
Bedrooms: 1 double, 1 twin
Bathrooms: 1 en-suite, 1 private

Bed & breakfast

per night:	£min	£max
Double	36.00	44.00

Parking for 6

TEDDINGTON

Gloucestershire
Map ref 2B1

Village a few miles east of Tewkesbury and north of Cheltenham, with just a few farms and houses, but an interesting church.

Bengrove Farm

COMMENDED

Bengrove, Teddington, Tewkesbury
GL20 8JB
☎ Cheltenham (01242) 620332
Fax (01242) 620851
10-acre mixed farm. Large, interesting 14th C farmhouse with attractive rooms, timbered and beamed. 2 twin rooms, lounge and guests' bathroom. Comfortably furnished.
Bedrooms: 2 twin
Bathrooms: 1 public

Bed & breakfast

per night:	£min	£max
Single	18.00	18.00
Double	30.00	30.00

Parking for 10

TELFORD

Shropshire
Map ref 4A3

New Town named after Thomas Telford, the famous engineer who designed many of the country's canals, bridges and viaducts. It is close to Ironbridge with its monuments and museums to the Industrial Revolution, including restored 18th C buildings.
Tourist Information Centre ☎ *(01952) 291370*

Allscott Inn

☗☗☗ APPROVED

Walcot, Wellington, Telford
TF6 5EQ
☎ (01952) 248484
Homely country inn offering delicious food and comfortable accommodation. Beer garden. Easy access Shrewsbury, Ironbridge and Telford.
Bedrooms: 2 double, 2 twin
Bathrooms: 2 en-suite, 1 public

Bed & breakfast per night:

	£min	£max
Single	20.00	30.00
Double	35.00	40.00

Lunch available
Evening meal 1900 (last orders 2200)
Parking for 50
Cards accepted: Access, Visa, Amex
🛏🚵🖥🛋☎Ⓢ⊁🅜📺🗄🖐🐾❄🚐

Old Rectory

☗☗

Stirchley Village, Telford TF3 1DY
☎ (01952) 596308 & 596518
Fax (01952) 596308
Large, comfortable guesthouse dating from 1734. Set in an acre of secluded gardens, on edge of town park. Convenient for town centre and Ironbridge museums. Three miles from M54, junction 4.
Bedrooms: 2 single, 1 double, 2 twin, 1 family room
Bathrooms: 3 en-suite, 1 private, 2 public

Bed & breakfast per night:

	£min	£max
Single	22.00	30.00
Double	32.50	40.00

Half board per person:

	£min	£max
Daily	30.00	38.00
Weekly	195.00	245.00

Evening meal 1800 (last orders 2100)
Parking for 6
🛏🚵🖥🖨🛋☎🅤🅤Ⓢ⊁🅜📺🗄🖐
🕛🅟❄🚐 SP🏠Ⓣ

TETBURY

Gloucestershire
Map ref 2B2

Small market town with 18th C houses and an attractive 17th C Town Hall. It is a good touring centre with many places of interest nearby including Badminton House and Westonbirt Arboretum.

The Old Rectory

☗☗☗ HIGHLY COMMENDED

Didmarton GL9 1DS
☎ Chipping Sodbury (01454) 238233
Comfortable small former rectory, set in an attractive village on A433, south-west of Tetbury. Food within walking distance.
Bedrooms: 2 double, 1 twin
Bathrooms: 1 en-suite, 2 private

Bed & breakfast per night:

	£min	£max
Single	21.00	21.00
Double	35.00	37.00

Parking for 4
🛏9🖥🖨☎🖥🅤⊁🅜📺🗄🖐❄🖐
🚐🏠

Tavern House

☗☗ DE LUXE

Willesley, Tetbury GL8 8QU
☎ (01666) 880444
Fax (01666) 880254

Grade II listed Cotswold stone house (formerly a staging post) on the A433 Bath road, 1 mile from Westonbirt Arboretum and 4 miles from Tetbury.
Bedrooms: 3 double, 1 twin
Bathrooms: 4 en-suite

Bed & breakfast per night:

	£min	£max
Single	42.50	47.50
Double	57.00	67.00

Parking for 4
Cards accepted: Access, Visa
🛏10🖥🛋☎🖥🅤🛋🖐⊁🅜🗄🖐
🕛🅟❄🖐🚐 SP🏠Ⓣ

The 🏍 symbol after an establishment name indicates that it is a Regional Tourist Board member.

TEWKESBURY

Gloucestershire
Map ref 2B1

Tewkesbury's outstanding possession is its magnificent church, built as an abbey, with a great Norman tower and beautiful 14th C interior. The town stands at the confluence of the Severn and Avon and has many medieval houses, inns and several museums.
Tourist Information Centre ☎ *(01684) 295027*

Abbots Court Farm 🏍

☗☗ COMMENDED

Church End, Twyning, Tewkesbury
GL20 6DA
☎ (01684) 292515
Fax (01684) 292515

450-acre arable & dairy farm. Large, comfortable farmhouse in excellent touring area. Most rooms en-suite. 3 games rooms, grass tennis court, fishing available.
Bedrooms: 1 single, 1 double, 2 twin, 2 triple, 2 family rooms
Bathrooms: 6 en-suite, 1 public

Bed & breakfast per night:

	£min	£max
Single	20.50	25.00
Double	31.00	35.00

Parking for 20
🛏🚵🖥🛋☎🖥🅰Ⓢ🅜📺🗄🖐🐾🔍
🕛🌸❄🚐 DAP SP🏠

Lampitt House 🏍

☗☗ COMMENDED

Lampitt Lane, Bredon's Norton, Tewkesbury GL20 7HB
☎ Bredon (01684) 772295

Comfortable house set in 1.5 acre garden in picturesque Cotswold village at the foot of Bredon Hill. Extensive views. Tewkesbury 4 miles. Beautiful hill and riverside walks.
Bedrooms: 2 double, 1 twin
Bathrooms: 3 en-suite

Continued ▶

TEWKESBURY

Continued

Bed & breakfast per night:	£min	£max
Single	25.00	30.00
Double	36.00	40.00

Half board per person:	£min	£max
Daily	30.00	32.00
Weekly	210.00	224.00

Evening meal 1800 (last orders 2000)
Parking for 6

Personal Touch

Listed APPROVED

37 Tirle Bank Way, Tewkesbury GL20 8ES
☎ (01684) 297692
Semi-detached overlooking farmland. Leave M5 at junction 9, Tewkesbury. Second left past traffic lights, then left and immediately right, follow road round to right.
Bedrooms: 2 twin
Bathrooms: 1 public

Bed & breakfast per night:	£min	£max
Single	16.50	
Double	33.00	

Lunch available
Evening meal from 1830
Parking for 2

Town Street Farm ⋀

COMMENDED

Tirley, Gloucester GL19 4HG
☎ Gloucester (01452) 780442
Fax (01452) 780890

500-acre mixed farm. 18th C farmhouse set in beautiful surroundings and within half a mile of the River Severn.
Bedrooms: 1 double, 1 triple
Bathrooms: 2 en-suite, 1 public

Bed & breakfast per night:	£min	£max
Single	24.00	
Double	36.00	

Parking for 4

UPTON-UPON-SEVERN

Hereford and Worcester
Map ref 2B1

Attractive country town on the banks of the Severn and a good river cruising centre. It has many pleasant old houses and inns, and the pepperpot landmark is now the Heritage Centre.
Tourist Information Centre ☎ (01684) 594200

Tiltridge Farm and Vineyard ⋀

HIGHLY COMMENDED

Upper Hook Road,
Upton-upon-Severn, Worcester WR8 0SA
☎ (01684) 592906
Fax (01684) 594142

9-acre vineyard. Fully renovated period farmhouse close to Upton and Malvern showground. Warm welcome and wine from our own vineyard!
Bedrooms: 2 double, 1 triple
Bathrooms: 3 en-suite

Bed & breakfast per night:	£min	£max
Single	25.00	25.00
Double	40.00	40.00

Parking for 12

Welland Court ⋀

HIGHLY COMMENDED

Upton-upon-Severn, Worcester WR8 0ST
☎ (01684) 594426 & 594413
Fax (01684) 594426
Built c.1450 and enlarged in the 18th C. Rescued from a dilapidated state and modernised to a high standard. It lies at the foot of the Malvern Hills and is an ideal base for touring the Wye and Teme valleys.
Bedrooms: 1 double, 2 twin
Bathrooms: 3 en-suite

Bed & breakfast per night:	£min	£max
Single	40.00	40.00
Double	60.00	60.00

Half board per person:	£min	£max
Daily	55.00	65.00
Weekly	300.00	400.00

Parking for 13
Cards accepted: Access, Visa

WARWICK

Warwickshire
Map ref 2B1

Castle rising above the River Avon, 15th C Beauchamp Chapel attached to St Mary's Church, medieval Lord Leycester's Hospital almshouses and several museums. Nearby is Ashorne Hall Nickelodeon and the new National Heritage museum at Gaydon.
Tourist Information Centre ☎ (01926) 492212

Apothecary's

COMMENDED

The Old Dispensary, Stratford Road, Wellesbourne, Warwick CV35 9RN
☎ Stratford-upon-Avon (01789) 470060
Comfortable en-suite accommodation is offered in this 19th C village house, situated south of Warwick. Traditional English breakfast and optional evening meal. Please ring for brochure.
Bedrooms: 1 double, 1 twin
Bathrooms: 2 en-suite

Bed & breakfast per night:	£min	£max
Single	22.00	25.00
Double	40.00	46.00

Evening meal 1900 (last orders 2030)
Parking for 3

Austin House ⋀

96 Emscote Road, Warwick CV34 5QJ
☎ (01926) 493583
Black and white Victorian house three-quarters of a mile from Warwick Castle, 1 mile from Royal Leamington Spa and 8 miles from Stratford-upon-Avon.
Bedrooms: 1 single, 1 double, 1 twin, 4 triple
Bathrooms: 5 en-suite, 1 public

Bed & breakfast per night:	£min	£max
Single	15.50	18.50
Double	31.00	37.00

Parking for 8
Cards accepted: Access, Visa, Switch/Delta

The Croft ♨

COMMENDED

Haseley Knob, Warwick CV35 7NL
☎ Haseley Knob (01926) 484447
Fax (01926) 484447
Friendly family atmosphere in picturesque rural setting. In Haseley Knob village off the A4177 between Balsall Common and Warwick, convenient for NEC, National Agricultural Centre, Stratford and Coventry. 15 minutes from Birmingham Airport.
Bedrooms: 1 single, 1 double, 1 twin, 2 triple
Bathrooms: 5 en-suite, 2 public

Bed & breakfast per night:	£min	£max
Single	20.00	30.00
Double	39.00	42.00

Evening meal 1800 (last orders 1900)
Parking for 10
Cards accepted: Access, Visa, Switch/Delta

30 Eastley Crescent ♨

HIGHLY COMMENDED

Warwick CV34 5RX
☎ (01926) 496480
Next to A46 and 5 minutes from M40. A comfortable, non-smoking establishment.
Bedrooms: 1 single, 1 double
Bathrooms: 1 en-suite, 1 private, 1 public

Bed & breakfast per night:	£min	£max
Single	16.00	18.00
Double	34.00	34.00

Parking for 2

Forth House ♨

HIGHLY COMMENDED

44 High Street, Warwick CV34 4AX
☎ (01926) 401512
Fax (01926) 490809
Ground floor and first floor guest suites with private sitting rooms and bathrooms at the back of the house. Overlooking peaceful garden, in town centre.
Bedrooms: 1 double, 1 twin
Bathrooms: 2 en-suite

Bed & breakfast per night:	£min	£max
Single	30.00	40.00
Double	44.00	52.00

Parking for 2

Lower Rowley ♨

COMMENDED

Wasperton, Warwick CV35 8EB
☎ (01926) 624937
Fax (01926) 624937
Situated on edge of hamlet between Warwick and Stratford-upon-Avon with wonderful views from guest lounge of surrounding countryside and River Avon.
Bedrooms: 1 double, 1 twin
Bathrooms: 1 en-suite, 1 private, 1 public

Bed & breakfast per night:	£min	£max
Double	40.00	45.00

Parking for 3

Lower Watchbury Farm ♨

COMMENDED

Wasperton Lane, Barford, Warwick CV35 1DH
☎ (01926) 624772 & Mobile (0589) 478795
50-acre mixed farm. Well-appointed accommodation on working farm, in rural surroundings outside Barford. M40 2 miles, Stratford-upon-Avon 7 miles, Warwick 3 miles. All rooms en-suite, large garden. Good pubs nearby.
Bedrooms: 1 single, 1 double, 1 triple
Bathrooms: 2 en-suite, 1 private

Bed & breakfast per night:	£min	£max
Single	21.50	23.50
Double	37.00	40.00

Parking for 3

Merrywood

Listed HIGHLY COMMENDED

Hampton on the Hill, Warwick CV35 8QR
☎ (01926) 492766
Family house in small village 2 miles from Warwick, with open views from both of the rooms.
Bedrooms: 1 single, 1 twin
Bathrooms: 2 public

Bed & breakfast per night:	£min	£max
Single	17.50	18.50
Double	27.50	30.00

Parking for 3

Northleigh House ♨

HIGHLY COMMENDED

Five Ways Road, Hatton, Warwick CV35 7HZ
☎ (01926) 484203 & Mobile 0374 101894
Fax (01926) 484006

Comfortable, peaceful country house where the elegant rooms are individually designed and have en-suite bathroom, fridge, kettle and remote-control TV.
Bedrooms: 1 single, 5 double, 1 twin
Bathrooms: 7 en-suite

Bed & breakfast per night:	£min	£max
Single	30.00	38.00
Double	38.00	55.00

Parking for 8
Open February–November
Cards accepted: Access, Visa

Old Rectory ♨

COMMENDED

Vicarage Lane, Sherbourne, Warwick CV35 8AB
☎ Barford (01926) 624562
Fax (01926) 624995

Georgian country house with beams and inglenooks, furnished with antiques. En-suite bedrooms, many with brass beds, all with direct-dial telephone and colour TV. Spa bath available. A la carte restaurant, bar, hearty breakfast. Half a mile from M40, junction 15.
Bedrooms: 2 single, 6 double, 3 twin, 2 triple, 1 family room
Bathrooms: 12 en-suite, 2 private

Bed & breakfast per night:	£min	£max
Single	33.00	45.00
Double	48.00	65.00

Evening meal 1900 (last orders 2030)
Parking for 16
Cards accepted: Access, Visa, Switch/Delta

WARWICK
Continued

Shrewley House 🔺

⬛ HIGHLY COMMENDED

Hockley Road, Shrewley, Warwick
CV35 7AT
☎ Claverdon (0192684) 2549
Fax (0192684) 2216

*Listed 17th C farmhouse and home set
amidst beautiful 1.5 acre gardens.
King-sized four-poster bedrooms, all
en-suite, with many thoughtful extras.
Four miles from Warwick.*
Bedrooms: 3 double
Bathrooms: 3 en-suite

Bed & breakfast

per night:	£min	£max
Single	35.00	42.00
Double	52.00	72.00

Evening meal (last orders 1930)
Parking for 17
Cards accepted: Access, Visa

🐴🖇️📞🔌📺✕🛡️⛨🔑📺 🖩🖴🔔✿✕🐾🎁

Shrewley Pools Farm 🔺

⬛ Listed COMMENDED

Haseley, Warwick CV35 7HB
☎ (01926) 484315

*260-acre mixed farm. Traditional
mid-17th C beamed farmhouse set in
1 acre of gardens. 5 miles north of
Warwick on the A4177.*
Bedrooms: 1 twin, 1 triple
Bathrooms: 1 en-suite, 1 public

Bed & breakfast

per night:	£min	£max
Single	20.00	25.00
Double	40.00	45.00

Half board per

person:	£min	£max
Daily	29.00	35.00
Weekly	200.00	240.00

Lunch available
Evening meal 1800 (last orders
2100)
Parking for 10

🐴🔌📺🛡️⛨🔑📺📺 🖩🔔✿ ✕DAP SP🎁

Tudor House Inn 🔺

⬛⬛⬛

90-92 West Street, Warwick
CV34 6AW
☎ (01926) 495447
Fax (01926) 492948

*Inn of character dating from 1472,
with a wealth of beams. One of the few
buildings to survive the great fire of
Warwick in 1694. Opposite Warwick
Castle and close to Warwick
racecourse.*
Bedrooms: 3 single, 5 double, 2 twin,
1 family room
Bathrooms: 6 en-suite, 1 public,
2 private showers

Bed & breakfast

per night:	£min	£max
Single	25.00	39.95
Double	55.90	60.00

Lunch available
Evening meal 1800 (last orders
2300)
Parking for 6
Cards accepted: Access, Visa, Diners,
Amex, Switch/Delta

🐴🖇️📞🔌📺🔌🔔📺🛡️🖩 🖴🔔15 ✿✕DAP🔄SP🎁

WATERHOUSES

Staffordshire
Map ref 4B2

*Village in the valley of the River
Hamps, once the terminus of the
Leek and Manifold Light Railway, 8
miles of which is now a
macadamised walkers' path.*

Ye Olde Crown 🔺

⬛⬛ APPROVED

Leek Road, Waterhouses,
Stoke-on-Trent ST10 3HL
☎ (01538) 308204

*17th C coaching inn, on the edge of the
Peak District National Park and at the
start of the beautiful Manifold Valley. It
is built of natural stone and has a
wealth of original oak beams.*
Bedrooms: 2 single, 3 double, 1 twin,
1 family room
Bathrooms: 5 en-suite, 1 public

Bed & breakfast

per night:	£min	£max
Single	15.50	23.50
Double	37.00	37.00

Lunch available
Evening meal 1900 (last orders
2130)
Parking for 50
Cards accepted: Access, Visa

🐴🖇️📺🔌🛡️🖩 🖴🐾🎁

National gradings and
classifications were correct
at the time of going to press
but are subject to change.
Please check at the time
of booking.

WEM

Shropshire
Map ref 4A3

*Small town connected with Judge
Jeffreys who lived in Lowe Hall. Well
known for its ales.*

Forncet 🔺

⬛ Listed COMMENDED

Soulton Road, Wem, Shrewsbury
SY4 5HR
☎ (01939) 232996

*Spacious, centrally heated Victorian
house on the edge of this small market
town, 200 yards from British Rail
station.*
Bedrooms: 1 single, 1 twin, 1 triple
Bathrooms: 2 public

Bed & breakfast

per night:	£min	£max
Single	15.00	
Double	30.00	

Half board per

person:	£min	£max
Daily		23.00

Evening meal 1830 (last orders
1930)
Parking for 6

🐴🚫🔌⛨🛡️🔑📺📺🖩 🖴🔔✿ ✕🎁SP

Foxleigh House 🔺

⬛⬛ COMMENDED

Foxleigh Drive, Wem, Shrewsbury
SY4 5BP
☎ (01939) 233528

*Pretty bedrooms, private bathrooms in
elegant country house on Shropshire
Way. Ideal for touring. Comfort and
warm welcome.*
Bedrooms: 1 twin, 1 family room
Bathrooms: 2 private

Bed & breakfast

per night:	£min	£max
Single	20.00	22.00
Double	37.00	42.00

Half board per

person:	£min	£max
Daily	29.50	31.00

Evening meal 1830 (last orders
2000)
Parking for 7

🐴10📺🔌🔔⛨🛡️🔑🖩🖴🔔U ✿🎁SP🎁T

Lowe Hall Farm 🔺

⬛⬛ COMMENDED

Wem, Shrewsbury SY4 5UE
☎ (01939) 232236

*180-acre dairy farm. Historically
famous Grade II listed country
residence. Centrally located for
Ironbridge, Telford, Chester, Llangollen*

and Hawkstone Follies. High standard of food, decor and accommodation guaranteed.
Bedrooms: 1 twin, 2 triple
Bathrooms: 1 en-suite, 1 public

Bed & breakfast

per night:	£min	£max
Single	18.00	18.00
Double	35.00	35.00

Half board per

person:	£min	£max
Daily	24.00	24.00
Weekly	161.00	161.00

Evening meal 1830 (last orders 1930)
Parking for 8

🐎🖥♨🛴🅿ⓈⓀ📺▥🧺🛟♫✕🚐 SP 🏠

Soulton Hall ♨

👑👑👑👑 COMMENDED
Wem, Shrewsbury SY4 5RS
☎ (01939) 232786
Fax (01939) 234097

Super home cooking and en-suite rooms at this Tudor manor house ensure a relaxing holiday. Moated Domesday site in grounds, private riverside and woodland walks.
Bedrooms: 3 double, 1 twin, 1 triple
Bathrooms: 4 en-suite, 1 private

Bed & breakfast

per night:	£min	£max
Single	31.50	38.00
Double	49.00	63.00

Half board per

person:	£min	£max
Daily	41.50	48.50
Weekly	315.00	306.50

Evening meal 1900 (last orders 2030)
Parking for 23
Cards accepted: Access, Visa, Diners

🐎🖥📞🖵🛀♨🐕ⓈⓀ▥🧺🛟 🛟10🛟♫✕❀🚐 DAP 🔌 SP 🏠 Ⓣ

Village near the lovely countryside of the Long Mynd and close to the Welsh border and Offa's Dyke.

Crown Inn ♨

Listed COMMENDED
Wentnor, Bishop's Castle SY9 5EE
☎ Linley (01588) 650613
Fax (01588) 650613

Traditional 16th C country inn set in the rolling hills of South Shropshire. Easy access to Midland gliding club, several golf clubs, trout fishing, horse riding and hill walking. A warm welcome, fresh home-cooked food and real ales.
Bedrooms: 2 double, 2 twin
Bathrooms: 2 public

Bed & breakfast

per night:	£min	£max
Single	22.00	
Double	40.00	

Lunch available
Evening meal 1900 (last orders 2100)
Parking for 20
Cards accepted: Access, Visa, Switch/Delta

🐎⌦🖥🛴♨🛀ⓈⓀ▥🚐♨🛟30🛟♫► ✕❀🚐 SP 🏠 Ⓣ

One of the most beautiful Herefordshire villages, full of framed houses, at the heart of the Black and White Trail. It is dominated by the church which has a fine spire.

Hill Top Farm

👑👑 COMMENDED
Wormsley, Hereford HR4 8LZ
☎ Bridge Sollars (01981) 590246

200-acre arable & livestock farm. Comfortable stone-built farmhouse under brow of hill, deep in the Herefordshire countryside. Magnificent views over fields and woods to Black Mountains. On Black and White Trail.
Bedrooms: 1 twin, 1 triple
Bathrooms: 1 en-suite, 1 private

Bed & breakfast

per night:	£min	£max
Single		16.00
Double		36.00

Parking for 6
Open February–November

🐎♨🛴ⓊⓁ Ⓢ✕📺▥❀🚐

The Dog Inn & Restaurant ♨

👑 COMMENDED
Main Street, Whittington, Lichfield WS14 9JU
☎ Lichfield (01543) 432252
17th C inn with bar and restaurant. Open seven days a week. Bar meals, real ales. Off the A51 Lichfield to Tamworth road.
Bedrooms: 3 single, 1 double, 2 twin
Bathrooms: 6 private showers

Bed & breakfast

per night:	£min	£max
Single	28.20	
Double	39.90	

Lunch available
Evening meal 1800 (last orders 2130)
Parking for 40
Cards accepted: Access, Visa, Diners, Amex, Switch/Delta

🐎🖥🛴♨ⒾⓈ✕📺▥🧺🛟♫►❀🚐 ♨Ⓣ

Ancient town with a folk museum and railway museum. To the south lies Sudeley Castle with its fine collection of paintings and toys and an Elizabethan garden.

Almsbury Farm ♨

👑👑 HIGHLY COMMENDED
Vineyard Street, Winchcombe, Cheltenham GL54 5LP
☎ Cheltenham (01242) 602403 & 603957

286-acre arable & dairy farm. Old Cotswold stone 17th C farmhouse on the edge of Winchcombe. Only 5 minutes' walk from shops and pubs, yet in peaceful countryside. Warm welcome assured.
Bedrooms: 1 double, 1 triple
Bathrooms: 2 en-suite

Bed & breakfast

per night:	£min	£max
Single	25.00	30.00
Double	40.00	45.00

Continued ▶

WINCHCOMBE
Continued

Parking for 6
Open February–November

🚭🏛🖭□🐕🦮 UL ⅃🛏🖼☀🐾🚕 SP
🏠 T

Ireley Grounds ⚠

👑👑 HIGHLY COMMENDED

Broadway Road, Winchcombe,
Cheltenham GL54 5NY
☎ Cheltenham (01242) 603736 &
Mobile 0836 322230
*Impressive farmhouse, offering
comfortable accommodation, with
four-poster beds in double rooms.
Standing in 6 acres, with spectacular
views, 1 mile from Winchcombe.*
Bedrooms: 2 double, 1 triple
Bathrooms: 3 en-suite
Bed & breakfast

per night:	£min	£max
Single	25.00	40.00
Double	36.00	50.00

Parking for 100

🚭🏛🖭□🖐♨ S ⅃🛏🖼⏱180 U☀
🦮🚕🏝 T

Isbourne Manor House ⚠

👑👑 DE LUXE

Castle Street, Winchcombe,
Cheltenham GL54 5JA
☎ Cheltenham (01242) 602281

*Listed part-Georgian, part-Elizabethan
house overlooking grounds of Sudeley
Castle and situated within attractive
gardens bordered by the River
Isbourne. 2 minutes from both open
countryside and town centre. Spacious
rooms with en-suite facilities.*

Bedrooms: 2 double, 1 twin
Bathrooms: 2 en-suite, 1 private
Bed & breakfast

per night:	£min	£max
Single	38.00	48.00
Double	48.00	58.00

Parking for 5

🚭10🏛🖭□🖐♨⏚ UL ⅃🛏 TV 🖭
🚪 U☀🦮🚕 SP 🏠 T

Manor Farm

👑👑 HIGHLY COMMENDED

Greet, Winchcombe, Cheltenham
GL54 5BJ
☎ Cheltenham (01242) 602423
*400-acre mixed farm. Cotswolds manor
in quiet hamlet. Good views of
Cotswold Escarpment and steam
railway. Near racecourse. Picturesque,
well-equipped self-catering cottages
also available.*
Bedrooms: 2 double, 1 twin
Bathrooms: 3 en-suite
Bed & breakfast

per night:	£min	£max
Single	20.00	22.00
Double	40.00	44.00

Parking for 10
Open January–November

🚭□🖐♨ UL ⅃ TV 🖭🚪⏱10 U☀
☀🦮🚕🏠

Mercia

👑👑 HIGHLY COMMENDED

Hailes Street, Winchcombe,
Cheltenham GL54 5HU
☎ Cheltenham (01242) 602251
*Black and white Cotswold-stone Tudor
cottage with beamed walls and ceilings.
Private parking at rear. Pleasant garden
and views. 15 minutes from M5.*
Bedrooms: 2 double, 1 twin
Bathrooms: 2 en-suite, 1 private
Bed & breakfast

per night:	£min	£max
Single	19.00	22.00
Double	36.00	38.00

Parking for 3

🚭🖐♨⏚ UL ⅈ S ⅃🛏 TV 🖭🚪 U☀
🦮 SP 🏠

Parks Farm

Listed COMMENDED

Sudeley, Winchcombe, Cheltenham
GL54 5BX
☎ Cheltenham (01242) 603874
*600-acre livestock farm. Grade II listed
old farm cottages set in middle of farm
with glorious views. On Wardens Way
footpath.*
Bedrooms: 2 twin
Bathrooms: 1 public
Bed & breakfast

per night:	£min	£max
Single	17.50	17.50
Double	35.00	35.00

Parking for 2

🚭4🏛🖐 UL ⅃ TV 🖭☀🦮🚕🏠

The Plaisterers Arms ⚠

👑 COMMENDED

Abbey Terrace, Winchcombe,
Cheltenham GL54 5LL
☎ Cheltenham (01242) 602358
Fax (01242) 602358

*Old Cotswold stone inn with en-suite
bed and breakfast accommodation,
close to Sudeley Castle and town
centre. Extensive menu, pub lunches,
bar snacks and evening meals available
every day. Large garden, patio and
children's area.*
Bedrooms: 3 double, 1 twin, 1 triple
Bathrooms: 5 en-suite, 1 public
Bed & breakfast

per night:	£min	£max
Single	22.00	24.50
Double	35.00	39.50

AT-A-GLANCE SYMBOLS

Symbols at the end of each accommodation entry

give useful information about services

and facilities. A key to symbols can be found

inside the back cover flap.

Keep this open for easy reference.

Lunch available
Evening meal 1830 (last orders 2130)
Cards accepted: Access, Visa, Amex, Switch/Delta

🛇🖆🖵👁♿🅢⌇🏚🖃🔍ᑌ☼🅓🅐🅟
🗟🅢🅟🎐

WORCESTER

Hereford and Worcester
Map ref 2B1

Lovely riverside city dominated by its Norman and Early English cathedral, King John's burial place. Many old buildings including the 15th C Commandery and the 18th C Guildhall. There are several museums and the Royal Worcester porcelain factory.
Tourist Information Centre ☎ *(01905) 726311 or 723471*

Burgage House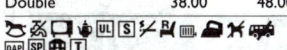

4 College Precincts, Worcester WR1 2LG
☎ (01905) 25396
Comfortable accommodation in elegant Georgian mews house in cobbled street next to cathedral. Close to River Severn, cricket ground, shops and restaurant.
Bedrooms: 1 single, 1 double, 1 twin, 1 family room
Bathrooms: 1 en-suite, 2 public

Bed & breakfast

per night:	£min	£max
Single	26.00	30.00
Double	38.00	48.00

🛇🖆🗟🖵👁♿🅤🅛🅢⌇✖🖃🔍✈🚐
🅓🅐🅟🅢🅟🎐🅣

Little Lightwood Farm

COMMENDED

Lightwood Lane, Cotheridge, Worcester WR6 5LT
☎ Cotheridge (01905) 333236
56-acre dairy farm. Farmhouse accommodation with en-suite rooms, tea-making facilities and heating in all

---

bedrooms. Delightful views of the Malvern Hills. Just off the A44 from Worcester to Leominster, 3.5 miles from Worcester.
Bedrooms: 2 double, 1 twin
Bathrooms: 3 en-suite

Bed & breakfast

per night:	£min	£max
Single	21.00	24.00
Double	35.00	38.00

Parking for 6
Open February–December

🛇🗟1🖂🖵🖵👁♿🅤🅛⌇✖🖃📺🖃🔍☼
✈🚐🎐

Loch Ryan Hotel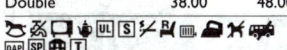

♛♛♛

119 Sidbury, Worcester WR5 2DH
☎ (01905) 351143
Fax (01905) 351143
Historic hotel, once home of Bishop Gore, close to cathedral, Royal Worcester Porcelain factory and Commandery. Attractive terraced garden. Imaginative food. Holders of Heartbeat and Worcester City clean food awards.
Bedrooms: 1 single, 3 double, 5 twin, 1 family room
Bathrooms: 10 en-suite

Bed & breakfast

per night:	£min	£max
Single	40.00	45.00
Double	55.00	65.00

Half board per

person:	£min	£max
Daily	43.50	

Evening meal 1800 (last orders 1900)
Parking for 10
Cards accepted: Access, Visa, Diners, Amex

🛇🖵👁♿🖎🅢⌇✖🖃📺🖃🔍🖃🏺☼
✈🅓🅐🗟🅢🅟🎐

The Old Smithy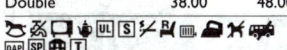

Listed HIGHLY COMMENDED

Pirton, Worcester WR8 9EJ
☎ (01905) 820482
17th C country house of historic

---

interest, in peaceful countryside, only 4.5 miles from M5 motorway (junction 7) and Worcester city. Ideal central base for touring Cotswolds, Stratford-upon-Avon, Warwick and Potteries.
Bedrooms: 1 double, 1 twin
Bathrooms: 1 private, 1 public

Bed & breakfast

per night:	£min	£max
Single	16.00	19.00
Double	32.00	40.00

Half board per

person:	£min	£max
Daily	25.00	30.00
Weekly	170.00	200.00

Evening meal from 1830
Parking for 6

🛇🖆🖂🖵👁♿🅤🅛⌇✖🖃📺🖃🔍☼✈
✈🚐🎐🅣

Retreat Farm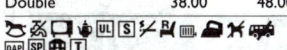

Listed HIGHLY COMMENDED

Camp Lane, Grimley, Worcester WR2 6LU
☎ (01905) 640266
60-acre arable farm. 17th C farmhouse, overlooking River Severn and Bevere Lock. Within walking distance of the Camp House Inn and Wagon Wheel Restaurant.
Bedrooms: 2 double
Bathrooms: 2 en-suite

Bed & breakfast

per night:	£min	£max
Single	20.00	
Double	38.00	

Parking for 14
Open April–October

🛇12🖵👁♿🅤🅛✖🖃🔍ᑌ🎵☼✈🚐🎐

Rose Place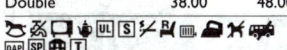

♛♛ HIGHLY COMMENDED

Hindlip Lane, Claines, Worcester WR3 8SA
☎ (01905) 451526 & 28684
Fax (01905) 27143
Grade II Georgian country house,*

Continued ▶

CHECK THE MAPS

The colour maps at the back of this guide show

all the cities, towns and villages for which you will

find accommodation entries.

Refer to the town index to find the page

on which it is listed.

WORCESTER
Continued

close to Worcester. Set in 3 acres of walled gardens and grounds.
Bedrooms: 2 double, 1 twin
Bathrooms: 2 en-suite, 1 private
Bed & breakfast

per night:	£min	£max
Single	30.00	40.00
Double	40.00	50.00

Parking for 20

Wood View

High Park, Whittington, Worcester WR5 2RS
☎ (01905) 351893
Homely 200-year-old country house close to M5 junction 7 on the A44, 4 miles from Worcester and 6 from Pershore. Large garden and paddocks. Non-smokers only, please.
Bedrooms: 2 double, 1 twin
Bathrooms: 1 en-suite, 2 public
Bed & breakfast

per night:	£min	£max
Single	19.00	25.00
Double	32.00	40.00

Parking for 4

WOTTON-UNDER-EDGE
Gloucestershire
Map ref 2B2

Small town in the southern Cotswolds. Berkeley Castle is within easy reach.

Hillesley Mill

Alderley, Wotton-under-Edge GL12 7QT
☎ Dursley (01453) 843258
Easily accessible converted cotton/woollen mill, nestling in undulating fields and prolific woodland, overlooking a mill lake and stream.
Bedrooms: 1 double, 1 twin
Bathrooms: 1 en-suite, 1 private
Bed & breakfast

per night:	£min	£max
Single	20.00	24.00
Double	36.00	42.00

Parking for 8

WYE VALLEY

See under Fownhope, Goodrich, Hereford, Ross-on-Wye

WYRE PIDDLE
Hereford and Worcester
Map ref 2B1

On the north bank of the River Avon between Pershore and Evesham, with an ancient village cross.

Arbour House Bed and Breakfast

HIGHLY COMMENDED

Main Road, Wyre Piddle, Pershore, Worcestershire WR10 2HU
☎ Evesham (01386) 555833

Formerly the George Inn and originating from the 1500s. Grade II listed Georgian building, partially timber-framed, with original beams, flagstone floors and real fires.
Bedrooms: 2 twin
Bathrooms: 2 en-suite

COUNTRY CODE

Always follow the Country Code
🌿Enjoy the countryside and respect its life and work 🌿 Guard against all risk of fire 🌿 Fasten all gates 🌿 Keep your dogs under close control 🌿 Keep to public paths across farmland 🌿 Use gates and stiles to cross fences, hedges and walls 🌿 Leave livestock, crops and machinery alone 🌿 Take your litter home 🌿 Help to keep all water clean 🌿 Protect wildlife, plants and trees 🌿 Take special care on country roads 🌿 Make no unnecessary noise

Bed & breakfast

per night:	£min	£max
Single	25.00	26.00
Double	40.00	42.00

Half board per person:

	£min	£max
Daily	32.50	
Weekly	220.00	

Evening meal 1800 (last orders 1900)
Parking for 5

☇10 ⌂⊡ ⟊ ⬚ ⓤⓁ ⌕ Ⓢ ⤬ ⊬ ⑰
⌨ ✾ ✗ ⇞ ⬆ ⒮⒫ ⌕ Ⓣ

Wheelchair access category 3♿
Bedrooms: 3 twin
Bathrooms: 3 en-suite, 1 public

Bed & breakfast

per night:	£min	£max
Single	30.00	40.00
Double	45.00	55.00

Parking for 6

☇ ⌂⊡ ⟊ ⬚ ⓤⓁ ⊬ ⑰ ⌨ ⌨ ♪ ✾
⇞

YOXALL

Staffordshire
Map ref 4B3

Small village near the Needwood Forest north of Lichfield. Once the home of Thomas Gisborne, booklover and campaigner against slavery.

The Moat ⚐

👑👑 HIGHLY COMMENDED

Town Hill, Yoxall, Burton upon Trent DE13 8NN
☎ Burton upon Trent (01543) 472210
Country house sited in 2.5 acres of garden, dry moated, of historic interest. Grounds listed Grade II.

COUNTRY CODE

Always follow the Country Code
Enjoy the countryside and respect its life and work Guard against all risk of fire Fasten all gates Keep your dogs under close control Keep to public paths across farmland Use gates and stiles to cross fences, hedges and walls Leave livestock, crops and machinery alone Take your litter home Help to keep all water clean Protect wildlife, plants and trees Take special care on country roads Make no unnecessary noise

ENQUIRY COUPONS

To help you obtain further information about advertisers and accommodation featured in this guide you will find enquiry coupons at the back. Send these directly to the establishments in which you are interested. Remember to complete both sides of the coupon.

CHECK THE MAPS

The colour maps at the back of this guide show all the cities, towns and villages for which you will find accommodation entries.

Refer to the town index to find the page on which it is listed.

MIDDLE ENGLAND

Middle England can be enjoyed on foot, by car - and in some places, by canal boat.

From the heights of the High Peaks to the tranquil shire countryside, this region is as rich in history as it is in colour and contrast.

The English Civil War began in Middle England; the tapestry of history is closely woven - with historic houses, heritage centres and museums bearing witness.

Don't miss Lincoln or the Lace-making city of Nottingham, elegant Buxton spa or Skegness by the sea! And then there's Sherwood Forest, haunt of the legendary Robin Hood...

FOR MORE INFORMATION CONTACT:
East Anglia Tourist Board *(Lincolnshire)*
Toppesfield Hall, Hadleigh, Suffolk IP7 5DN
Tel: (01473) 822922 **Fax:** (01473) 823063

Heart of England Tourist Board *(Derbyshire, Nottinghamshire, Leicestershire, Northamptonshire)*
Lark Hill Road, Worcester WR5 2EZ
Tel: (01905) 763436 or 763439
Fax: (01905) 763450

Where to Go in Middle England -
see pages 192-195

Where to Stay in Middle England -
see pages 196-214

MIDDLE ENGLAND

Where to Go and What to See

You will find hundreds of interesting places to visit during your stay in Middle England, just some of which are listed in these pages. The number against each name will help you locate it on the map (page 195). Contact any Tourist Information Centre in the region for more ideas on days out in Middle England.

1 Gainsborough Old Hall
Parnell Street, Gainsborough,
Lincolnshire DN21 2NB
Tel: (01427) 612669
Late medieval timber-framed manor house built c1460, with fine medieval kitchen. Displays on the building and its restoration.

2 World Of Robin Hood
Haughton, Retford,
Nottinghamshire DN22 8DZ
Tel: (01623) 860210
A hands-on medieval experience including The Crusaders, Medieval Market Place, Sherwood Forest, Castle Dungeons Armoury and the Great Hall.

3 Chatsworth House and Garden
Bakewell, Derbyshire DE45 1PP
Tel: (01246) 582204
Built 1687-1707. Collection of fine pictures, books, drawings, furniture. Garden laid out by Capability Brown with fountains and cascade. Farmyard and adventure playground.

4 Lincoln Cathedral
Lincoln LN2 1PZ
Tel: (01522) 544544
Medieval Gothic cathedral of outstanding historical and architectural merit.

5 Museum of Lincolnshire Life
Burton Road,
Lincoln LN1 3LY
Tel: (01522) 528448
The region's largest social history museum. Agricultural, industrial and social history of Lincolnshire from a teapot to a World War I tank. Victorian room setting.

6 The Heights of Abraham
Matlock Bath,
Matlock,
Derbyshire DE4 3PD
Tel: (01629) 582365
Cable car ride across Derwent Valley gives access to Alpine Centre with refreshments, superb views, woodland, prospect tower and two show caves.

7 The National Tramway Museum
Crich, Matlock,
Derbyshire DE4 5DP
Tel: (01773) 852565
Collection of 50 trams from Britain and overseas built 1873-1957. Tram rides on one-mile route, period street scene, depots, power station, workshops, exhibitions.

8 Midland Railway Centre
Butterley Station, Ripley,
Derby DE5 3QZ
Tel: (01773) 747674
Over 25 locomotives and 80 items of historic rolling stock of Midland and LMS origin. Steam-hauled passenger service, museum site. Country and farm parks.

9 American Adventure
Pit Lane, Ilkeston,
Derbyshire DE7 5SX
Tel: (01773) 531521
American theme park with more than 100 rides including Nightmare Niagara Log Flume, Rocky

Mountain, Rapids Ride, The Missile, Motion Master Simulator Cinema and many other attractions.

10 Southwell Minster
Bishop's Drive,
Southwell,
Nottinghamshire NG25 0JP
Tel: (01636) 812649
Building begun c1108. Saxon tympanum, Norman nave and crossing, early English choir. Outstanding foliage carving in Chapter House. Archbishop's Palace ruins.

11 The Galleries of Justice
Shire Hall,
High Pavement,
Nottingham NG1 1HN
Tel: (0115) 952 0555
Condemned! is the visitor attraction at the Galleries of Justice which offers a major crime and punishment experience. Based in and around former 19thC courthouse.

12 Newstead Abbey
Linby, Nottingham NG15 8GE
Tel: (01623) 793557
800-year-old remains of priory church, converted into country house in 16thC. Home of Lord Byron with possessions and manuscripts. Parkland, lake, gardens.

13 Nottingham Industrial Museum
Courtyard Buildings,
Wollaton Park,
Nottingham NG8 2AE
Tel: (0115) 928 4602
18thC stables presenting history of Nottingham's industries: printing, pharmacy, hosiery and lace. Victorian beam engine, horse gin, transport.

14 Belvoir Castle
Belvoir, Lincolnshire NG32 1PD
Tel: (01476) 870262
The present castle is fourth to be built on this site and dates from 1816. Art treasures including works by Poussin, Rubens, Holbein and Reynolds. Museum of Queen's Royal Lancers.

15 Belton House, Park & Gardens
Belton, Grantham,
Lincolnshire NG32 2LS
Tel: (01476) 66116
The crowning achievement of Restoration country house architecture, built in 1685-88 for Sir John Brownlow. Alterations by James Wyatt in 1777.

16 Sudbury Hall
Sudbury, Derbyshire DE6 5HT
Tel: (01283) 585305
Grand 17thC house. Plasterwork ceilings, ceiling paintings, carved staircase and overmantel. Museum of Childhood in old servants' wing.

17 Great Central Railway
Great Central Station,
Great Central Road,
Loughborough,
Leicestershire LE11 1RW
Tel: (01509) 230726
Preserved main line steam railway operating over 8.5 miles from Loughborough to Leicester North.

18 Ye Olde Pork Pie Shoppe
Dickinson & Morris Ltd,
10 Nottingham Street,
Melton Mowbray,
Leicestershire LE13 1NW
Pork pie shop and bakery in 17C building. History of shop and Melton Mowbray Pork Pie industry. Demonstrations of traditional craft of hand raising pork pies.

19 Spalding Tropical Forest
Glenside North,
Pinchbeck,
Spalding,
Lincolnshire PE11 3SD
Tel: (01775) 710882
One half-acre glass house enclosing a tropical environment. Four zones including tropical rain forest, Japanese and Australian tropical plants and Mediterranean temperate zone.

20 Oakham Castle
Market Place, Oakham,
Leicestershire
Tel: (01572) 723654
*Splendid 12thC Great Hall of
fortified manor house. Unique
horseshoe forfeits left by peers of
the realm.*

21 Newarke Houses Museum
The Newarke, Leicester LE2 7BY
Tel: (0116) 247 3222
*Local history and crafts from 1485.
Toys and games, clocks, mechanical
instruments. 19thC street scene,
early 20thC shop. Feature on 19thC
giant Daniel Lambert.*

22 Twycross Zoo
Twycross, Near Atherstone,
Warwickshire CV9 3PX
Tel: (01827) 880250
*Gorillas, orangutans, chimpanzees,
modern gibbon complex, elephants,
lions, cheetahs, giraffes, reptile
house. Pets corner. Rides.*

23 Rockingham Castle
Rockingham,
Leicestershire LE16 8TH
Tel: (01536) 770240
*Elizabethan house within walls of
Norman castle. Fine pictures.
Extensive views and gardens with
roses and ancient yew hedge.*

24 Lamport Hall
Lamport,
Northampton NN6 9HD
Tel: (01604) 686272
*17th/18thC house, home of Isham
family, mainly John Webb and
Francis Smith. Beautiful high room
(1655) fine library (1732). Garden
home to the 1st Gnome in England.*

25 Holdenby House and Gardens
Holdenby,
Northampton NN6 8DJ
Tel: (01604) 770074
*Remains of Elizabethan palace and
gardens. Fragrant border, falconry*
*centre, armoury, 17thC homestead,
tea room and shop.*

26 National Dragonfly Museum
Ashton Mill, Ashton,
Northampton PE8 5LB
Tel: (01832) 272427
*Discover the wonder and plight of
dragonflies. See also the Victorian
diesel hydro-electric generating
pumping hall and craft exhibitions.
Gift shop.*

27 Sulgrave Manor
Sulgrave, Near Banbury,
Oxfordshire OX17 2SD
Tel: (01295) 760205
*Small manor house of Shakespeare's
time, with furniture of period. Fine
kitchen. Early English home of
ancestors of George Washington.*

FIND OUT MORE

Further information about
holidays and attractions in Middle
England is available from either:
East Anglia Tourist Board,
Toppesfield Hall,
Hadleigh,
Suffolk IP7 5DN.
Tel: (01473) 822922
or **Heart of England Tourist
Board**,
Lark Hill Road,
Worcester WR5 2EZ
Tel: (01905) 763436 or 763439

These publications are available
free from the East Anglia Tourist
Board:
■ **Great Escapes** - short breaks
■ **Touring Map**

These publications are available
free from the Heart of England
Tourist Board:
■ **Places to Visit** (chargeable)
■ **Peak District and
Derbyshire Guide**
■ **Rutland, Rockingham Forest
and Stamford Guide**

WEST YORKSHIRE

EAST RIDING OF YORKSHIRE

NORTH LINCOLNSHIRE

N.E. LINCS

0 — 20 Miles
0 — 30 Kms

SOUTH YORKSHIRE

Glossop

Worksop
Retford
1 Gainsborough

Mablethorpe

Chesterfield

NOTTINGHAM-SHIRE
2

Bakewell **3**
Matlock **6**
Butterley
Crich **7**
8
Ashbourne Ripley
Ilkeston **9**

Mansfield
Ollerton

4 **5** Lincoln

Ingoldmells

Skegness

LINCOLNSHIRE

Newark

Sleaford

Boston

Southwell **10**

DERBYSHIRE
Derby
11 **12** **13**
Nottingham
14
Belvoir
15 Belton
Grantham

16 Sudbury

STAFFORD-SHIRE
Swadlincote

17 Loughborough
Bourne
19 Spalding

Ashby de la Zouch
18 Melton Mowbray
Stamford
Market Deeping

NORFOLK

LEICESTERSHIRE
22 Twycross
21 Leicester
20 Oakham

WEST MIDLANDS

Hinckley

Foxton

23 Rockingham

Corby
Oundle
Kettering

CAMBRIDGESHIRE

Market Harborough

24 Lamport

NORTHAMPTONSHIRE

Holdenby **25**
Wellingborough

WARWICKSHIRE
Daventry
Northampton
Ashton **26**
27 Sulgrave

BEDFORDSHIRE

OXFORDSHIRE
BUCKS

195

WHERE TO STAY (MIDDLE ENGLAND)

Accommodation entries in this region are listed in alphabetical order of place name, and then in alphabetical order of establishment.

Map references refer to the colour location maps at the back of this guide.

The first number indicates the map to use; the letter and number which follow refer to the grid reference on the map.

At-a-glance symbols at the end of each accommodation entry give useful information about services and facilities. A key to symbols can be found inside the back cover flap.

Keep this open for easy reference.

ABTHORPE

Northamptonshire
Map ref 2C1

Three miles south-west of Towcester, formerly owned by the Duke of Grafton.

Stone Cottage
Listed COMMENDED
Main Street, Abthorpe, Towcester
NN12 8QN
☎ Silverstone (01327) 857544
Fax (01327) 858654
Grade II listed cottage in delightful secluded position in conservation village. Convenient for Silverstone, Cotswolds, Oxford, M1 and M40 motorways.
Bedrooms: 1 single, 2 twin
Bathrooms: 2 public
Bed & breakfast

per night:	£min	£max
Single	20.00	20.00
Double	36.00	36.00

Parking for 8

ALDWARK

Derbyshire
Map ref 4B2

Tithe Farm ⋀
COMMENDED
Aldwark, Grange Mill, Matlock
DE4 4HX
☎ Carsington (01629) 540263
Peacefully situated, within 10 miles of Matlock, Bakewell, Ashbourne, the dales and historic houses. Extensive breakfast menu with home-made bread and preserves.

Bedrooms: 1 twin, 1 triple
Bathrooms: 1 en-suite, 1 private
Bed & breakfast

per night:	£min	£max
Single	24.00	25.00
Double	38.00	40.00

Parking for 6
Open April–October

ALFRETON

Derbyshire
Map ref 4B2

Ivy Beech
Listed COMMENDED
Highstairs Lane, Stretton, Alfreton, Derby DE55 6FD
☎ Chesterfield (01246) 863397
Private house in its own grounds, down a country lane but close to the main trunk road. An ideal centre for touring.
Bedrooms: 1 single, 2 twin
Bathrooms: 2 public
Bed & breakfast

per night:	£min	£max
Single	15.50	
Double	31.00	

Evening meal 1900 (last orders 2000)
Parking for 5

COLOUR MAPS

Colour maps at the back of this guide pinpoint all places in which you will find accommodation listed.

ALKMONTON

Derbyshire
Map ref 4B2

At the end of a 5-mile stretch of straight Roman road, Alkmonton has fantastic views of the surrounding countryside as far as Staffordshire.

Dairy House Farm ⋀
COMMENDED
Alkmonton, Longford, Ashbourne
DE6 3DG
☎ Ashbourne (01335) 330359
Fax (01335) 330359
82-acre livestock farm. Old red brick farmhouse with oak beams, inglenook fireplace and a comfortable atmosphere. Guests have their own lounge and dining room. Non-smokers only and no pets please. Children over 12 only.
Bedrooms: 3 single, 3 double, 1 twin
Bathrooms: 4 en-suite, 1 public
Bed & breakfast

per night:	£min	£max
Single	16.00	23.00
Double	32.00	38.00

Half board per person:	£min	£max
Daily	28.00	35.00
Weekly	196.00	245.00

Lunch available
Evening meal 1900 (last orders 1900)
Parking for 8

ASHBOURNE

Derbyshire
Map ref 4B2

Market town on the edge of the Peak District National Park and an excellent centre for walking. Its impressive church with 212-ft spire stands in an unspoilt old street. Ashbourne is well-known for gingerbread and its Shrovetide football match.
Tourist Information Centre ☎ (01335) 343666

Bentley Brook Inn ⚊

COMMENDED

Fenny Bentley, Ashbourne DE6 1LF
☎ (01335) 350278
Fax (01335) 350422

Traditional family-run country inn with large garden in Peak District National Park. Close to Dovedale, Alton Towers and Chatsworth.
Bedrooms: 1 single, 5 double, 3 twin
Suites available
Bathrooms: 6 en-suite, 1 private, 2 public

Bed & breakfast per night:

	£min	£max
Single	32.50	37.50
Double	47.50	57.50

Lunch available
Evening meal 1900 (last orders 2130)
Parking for 60
Cards accepted: Access, Visa, Diners, Amex, Switch/Delta

Collycroft Farm

Listed

Clifton, Ashbourne DE6 2GN
☎ (01335) 342187
260-acre mixed farm. A warm welcome is assured in this pleasant farmhouse. Lovely garden and excellent views across the surrounding countryside. South of Ashbourne on the A515 Lichfield road.
Bedrooms: 1 double, 1 twin, 1 triple
Bathrooms: 1 en-suite, 1 public

Bed & breakfast per night:

	£min	£max
Single	16.00	18.00
Double	32.00	36.00

Parking for 8

Jinglers Inn/Fox and Hounds

Listed

Belper Road, Bradley, Ashbourne DE6 3EN
☎ (01335) 370855

Country coaching inn with 2 names, set in 18 acres. 6 letting rooms and caravan site. Clay pigeon shooting. Just outside Ashbourne on A517.
Bedrooms: 1 single, 2 double, 3 twin
Suites available
Bathrooms: 4 en-suite, 2 private

Bed & breakfast per night:

	£min	£max
Single	15.00	17.50
Double	30.00	30.00

Lunch available
Evening meal 1800 (last orders 2200)
Parking for 100

Mercaston Hall ⚊

APPROVED

Mercaston, Brailsford, Ashbourne DE6 3BL
☎ (01335) 360263 & Mobile 0836 648102
55-acre mixed farm. Listed buildings in attractive, quiet countryside. Hard tennis court. Kedleston Hall (National Trust) 1 mile, Carsington Reservoir 5 minutes away.
Bedrooms: 2 double, 1 twin
Bathrooms: 2 en-suite, 1 private

Bed & breakfast per night:

	£min	£max
Single	21.00	23.50
Double	32.00	37.00

Parking for 16

ASHBY ST LEDGERS

Northamptonshire
Map ref 4C3

The Olde Coach House Inn ⚊

COMMENDED

Ashby St Ledgers, Rugby, Warwickshire CV23 8UN
☎ Rugby (01788) 890349
Fax (01788) 891922
18th C coaching inn in the protected village of Ashby St Ledgers. 3 miles from the M1, 4 miles south of Rugby.
Bedrooms: 4 double, 1 twin, 1 family room
Bathrooms: 6 private

Bed & breakfast per night:

	£min	£max
Single	48.00	50.00
Double	60.00	70.00

Half board per person:

	£min	£max
Daily	63.00	65.00

Lunch available
Evening meal 1800 (last orders 2130)
Parking for 60
Cards accepted: Access, Visa, Amex, Switch/Delta

ASHFORD IN THE WATER

Derbyshire
Map ref 4B2

Limestone village in attractive surroundings of the Peak District approached by 3 bridges over the River Wye. There is an annual well-dressing ceremony and the village was well-known in the 18th C for its black marble quarries.

Gritstone House ⚊

HIGHLY COMMENDED

Greaves Lane, Ashford in the Water, Bakewell DE45 1QH
☎ Bakewell (01629) 813563
Fax (01629) 813563
Charming 18th C Georgian house offering friendly service and accommodation designed with comfort and style in mind. Ideal centre for exploring the Peak District's scenery and country houses, and close to an extensive range of dining-out facilities.
Bedrooms: 2 double, 1 twin
Bathrooms: 1 en-suite, 1 public

Bed & breakfast per night:

	£min	£max
Double	36.00	45.00

ASHOVER

Derbyshire
Map ref 4B2

Unspoilt village with a 13th C church.

Old School Farm

COMMENDED

Uppertown, Ashover, Chesterfield S45 0JF
☎ Chesterfield (01246) 590813
25-acre mixed farm. A working farm welcoming children but not pets, suitable for visitors with their own transport. In a small hamlet bordering the Peak District, ideal for Chatsworth House, Chesterfield and Matlock Bath.
Bedrooms: 1 single, 1 double, 2 family rooms
Bathrooms: 2 en-suite, 1 public

Bed & breakfast

per night:	£min	£max
Single	18.00	18.00
Double	36.00	36.00

Half board per person:

	£min	£max
Daily	24.00	26.00
Weekly	168.00	182.00

Evening meal 1900 (last orders 0930)
Parking for 10
Open March–November

ASLOCKTON

Nottinghamshire
Map ref 4C2

Pretty village on the edge of the beautiful Vale of Belvoir. Racing horses are trained nearby and can often be seen around the village.

Aslockton Grange

Listed

Aslockton, Nottingham NG13 9AJ
☎ Whatton (01949) 850204 & 0860 599946
Farmhouse surrounded by fields. The driveway is off the A52 road north to Grantham, approximately 9 miles from Nottingham, Grantham and Newark.
Bedrooms: 1 single, 2 double, 1 twin
Suite available
Bathrooms: 1 private, 1 public

Bed & breakfast

per night:	£min	£max
Single	22.00	25.00
Double	35.00	35.00

Parking for 12

BAKEWELL

Derbyshire
Map ref 4B2

Pleasant market town, famous for its pudding. It is set in beautiful countryside on the River Wye and is an excellent centre for exploring the Derbyshire Dales, the Peak District National Park, Chatsworth and Haddon Hall.
Tourist Information Centre ☎ (01629) 813227

The Ashford Hotel and Restaurant

COMMENDED

Church Street, Ashford in the Water, Bakewell DE4 1QB
☎ (01629) 812725
Fax (01629) 814749
Traditional, friendly country hotel where you will receive personal attention throughout your stay. There are open fires and a wealth of oak beams. An ideal location to relax.
Bedrooms: 1 single, 5 double, 1 twin
Bathrooms: 7 private

Bed & breakfast

per night:	£min	£max
Single	45.00	50.00
Double	70.00	90.00

Half board per person:

	£min	£max
Daily	50.00	60.00
Weekly	297.50	332.50

Lunch available
Evening meal 1900 (last orders 2130)
Parking for 45
Cards accepted: Access, Visa, Diners, Amex, Switch/Delta

Castle Cliffe Private Hotel

COMMENDED

Monsal Head, Bakewell DE45 1NL
☎ Great Longstone (01629) 640258
A Victorian stone house overlooking beautiful Monsal Dale. Noted for its friendly atmosphere, good food and exceptional views.
Bedrooms: 3 double, 4 twin, 2 family rooms
Bathrooms: 6 en-suite, 2 public, 3 private showers

Bed & breakfast

per night:	£min	£max
Single	27.00	37.00
Double	46.00	54.00

Half board per person:

	£min	£max
Daily	39.00	49.00
Weekly	225.00	260.00

Evening meal 1900 (last orders 1700)
Parking for 15
Cards accepted: Access, Visa

Melbourne House

COMMENDED

Buxton Road, Bakewell DE45 1DA
☎ (01629) 815357
Listed Georgian house with character and history, spacious en-suite bedrooms, helpful tourist information, tasty breakfast menu and warm Derbyshire welcome. Non-smokers only, please.
Bedrooms: 2 double, 1 twin
Bathrooms: 3 en-suite

Bed & breakfast

per night:	£min	£max
Single	25.00	35.00
Double	36.00	44.00

Parking for 6

Sheldon House

HIGHLY COMMENDED

Chapel Street, Monyash, Bakewell DE45 1JJ
☎ (01629) 813067
Warm welcome in comfortable family home, 5 miles from Bakewell. Ideal for walking, good pub food locally, overseas visitors welcome.
Bedrooms: 3 double
Bathrooms: 3 en-suite, 1 public

Bed & breakfast

per night:	£min	£max
Single	25.00	30.00
Double	37.00	40.00

Parking for 4

Tannery House

HIGHLY COMMENDED

Matlock Street, Bakewell DE45 1EE
☎ (01629) 815011
Fax (01629) 815327
Central Bakewell: All bedrooms are en-suite with French windows opening onto the secluded gardens. The private dining room overlooks the swimming pool.
Wheelchair access category 3
Bedrooms: 2 double, 1 twin
Bathrooms: 3 en-suite

Bed & breakfast

per night:	£min	£max
Single	25.00	27.50
Double	40.00	45.00

Evening meal 1900 (last orders
2030)
Parking for 8

🏇🚳♿📞🎱⚓🖐🖊UL🕸S✂🖨🏠 🖼♿10🔍🕯❄🌸🚐SP

BAMFORD

Derbyshire
Map ref 4B2

Village in the Peak District near the
Upper Derwent Reservoirs of
Ladybower, Derwent and Howden.
An excellent centre for walking.

Pioneer House 🏍

≋≋ COMMENDED

Station Road, Bamford, Sheffield
S30 2BN
☎ Hope Valley (01433) 650638
*Comfortable, spacious rooms, all with
private facilities, in Edwardian family
home. Friendly atmosphere, hearty
breakfasts. Central location in Peak
District.*
Bedrooms: 2 double, 1 twin
Bathrooms: 2 en-suite, 1 private

Bed & breakfast

per night:	£min	£max
Double	30.00	40.00

Evening meal 1800 (last orders
1930)
Parking for 8

🏇🚳♿📠♿🖊UL🛡S✂🖨🏠♿❄🎋 🚐SP◎

BELPER

Derbyshire
Map ref 4B2

Pleasant old market town in the
valley of the River Derwent.
Attractive scenery and a wealth of
industrial history.

Chevin Green Farm 🏍

≋≋ COMMENDED

Chevin Road, Belper, Derby
DE56 2UN
☎ (01773) 822328
*38-acre mixed farm. Extended and
improved 300-year-old beamed
farmhouse accommodation with all
bedrooms en-suite, an ideal base for
exploring Derbyshire.*
Bedrooms: 3 double, 2 twin, 1 family
room
Bathrooms: 6 en-suite

Bed & breakfast

per night:	£min	£max
Single	18.00	20.00
Double	32.00	36.00

Parking for 6

🏇🚳♿♿UL✂🖼TV🖨🏠♿U🎋🚐

32 Spencer Road

Listed HIGHLY COMMENDED

Belper DE56 1JY
☎ (01773) 823877
*Large double bedroom with own
bathroom, sitting room and TV. Car
parking available.*
Bedrooms: 1 double, 1 twin
Bathrooms: 1 public

Bed & breakfast

per night:	£min	£max
Single	12.50	15.00
Double	20.00	25.00

Parking for 1

🏇🚳🚳♿♿UL S🖼TV🖨🏠♿🚐

2 Swiss Cottage

Listed

Chevin Road, The Chevin, Belper
DE56 2UN
☎ Amber Valley (01773) 825204
*Stone cottage, very quiet, surrounded
by fields with lovely walks. Well situated
for local attractions.*
Bedrooms: 2 single

Bed & breakfast

per night:	£min	£max
Single	14.00	15.00

Parking for 2

🏇🚳UL🎋🚐

BELTON

Lincolnshire
Map ref 3A1

Attractive village including 17th C
Belton House and Park, owned by
the National Trust.

Coach House

≋≋

Belton, Grantham NG32 2LS
☎ Grantham (01476) 73636

*Idyllically situated, surrounded by
National Trust land and golf-courses.
Guest lounge overlooks extensive
gardens. Antique furnishings
complement the rooms. Access at all
times.*
Bedrooms: 2 double, 2 twin
Bathrooms: 4 en-suite

Bed & breakfast

per night:	£min	£max
Single	20.00	22.00
Double	36.00	38.00

Parking for 6

🏇🚳♿🚳♿♿🛡S✂🖼TV🖨🏠♿U ☞❄🚐SP

BIGGIN-BY-HARTINGTON

Derbyshire
Map ref 4B2

September Cottage

Listed

Main Street, Biggin-by-Hartington,
Buxton SK17 0DH
☎ Hartington (01298) 84764
*Recently converted barn in the centre
of village, midway between Ashbourne
and Buxton off the A515.*
Bedrooms: 3 double
Bathrooms: 2 en-suite, 1 public

Bed & breakfast

per night:	£min	£max
Single	16.00	18.00
Double	32.00	36.00

Half board per

person:	£min	£max
Daily	24.00	26.00
Weekly	160.00	175.00

Evening meal 1830 (last orders
1900)
Parking for 6
Open March–October

🏇🚳5🖵UL🖼TV🖨🏠❄🎋🚐

BOSTON

Lincolnshire
Map ref 3A1

Historic town famous for its church
tower, the Boston Stump, 272 ft
high. Still a busy port, the town is full
of interest and has links with
Boston, Massachusetts, through the
Pilgrim Fathers. The cells where
they were imprisoned can be seen
in the medieval Guildhall.
*Tourist Information Centre ☎ (01205)
356656*

Bramley House

Listed COMMENDED

267 Sleaford Road, Boston
PE21 7PQ
☎ (01205) 354538
*Small guesthouse, charmingly
decorated, with warm and friendly
personal service. Disabled welcome.
Large car park. No smoking.*
Bedrooms: 4 single, 2 double, 2 twin
Bathrooms: 2 en-suite, 2 public

Bed & breakfast

per night:	£min	£max
Single	15.00	
Double	30.00	40.00

Parking for 20

♿🖵♿UL S✂🖨🏠♿❄🚐◎

BOSTON
Continued

Ye Olde Magnet Tavern
Listed COMMENDED

South Square, Boston PE21 6HX
☎ (01205) 369186
Traditional 17th C English pub with cask ales, serving home-cooked food in a friendly atmosphere. Opposite the historic Guildhall Museum and within easy reach of all local amenities.
Bedrooms: 1 single, 2 double, 1 twin
Bathrooms: 4 en-suite

Bed & breakfast
per night:	£min	£max
Single	31.75	34.00
Double	41.50	49.00

Lunch available
Evening meal 1800 (last orders 2000)
Parking for 3
Cards accepted: Access, Visa

BRACKLEY
Northamptonshire
Map ref 2C1

Historic market town of mellow stone, with many fine buildings lining the wide High Street and Market Place. Sulgrave Manor (George Washington's ancestral home) and Silverstone Circuit are nearby.
Tourist Information Centre ☎ (01280) 700111

Walltree House Farm 📧
COMMENDED

Steane, Brackley NN13 5NS
☎ Banbury (01295) 811235 & 0860 913399
Fax (01295) 811147
200-acre arable farm. En-suite individual ground floor rooms in courtyard adjacent to Victorian farmhouse. Gardens and woods to relax in. Near major historic sites, shopping and sporting attractions, including Silverstone. M40 junctions 10/11. Perfect base for touring 4 counties.
Bedrooms: 2 double, 3 twin, 1 triple, 2 family rooms
Bathrooms: 6 en-suite, 2 private, 1 public

Bed & breakfast
per night:	£min	£max
Single	30.00	40.00
Double	40.00	60.00

Half board per
person:	£min	£max
Daily	30.00	50.00
Weekly	180.00	300.00

Evening meal 1900 (last orders 1900)
Parking for 10
Cards accepted: Access, Visa

BROUGHTON ASTLEY
Leicestershire
Map ref 4C3

First mentioned in the Domesday Book when it was three separate villages, Broctone, Sutone and Torp.

The Old Farm House
Listed

Old Mill Road, Broughton Astley, Leicester LE9 6PQ
☎ Sutton in the Elms (01455) 282254
Recently converted Georgian farmhouse overlooking fields. Quietly situated behind the church, near village centre. Near junctions 20/21 of M1, junction 1 of M69. French spoken. Evening meal with prior notice.
Bedrooms: 1 single, 1 twin, 1 triple
Bathrooms: 2 public

Bed & breakfast
per night:	£min	£max
Single	18.00	18.00
Double	36.00	36.00

Half board per
person:	£min	£max
Daily	25.00	

Parking for 4

BRUNTINGTHORPE
Leicestershire
Map ref 4C3

Knaptoft House Farm
HIGHLY COMMENDED

Bruntingthorpe Road, Shearsby, Lutterworth LE17 6PR
☎ Leicester (0116) 247 8388
Fax (0116) 247 8388
145-acre mixed farm. Very quiet, warm, comfortable, beautifully appointed family home surrounded by farmland. Family historians welcome - many records on premises and only 4 miles from County Records Office. A14 junction 1, M1 junction 20, M6 junction 1, A50 Shearsby 1 mile. Ample parking. JCB card also accepted.
Bedrooms: 2 double, 1 twin
Bathrooms: 2 en-suite, 1 public

Bed & breakfast
per night:	£min	£max
Single	22.00	
Double	36.00	42.00

Parking for 5
Cards accepted: Access, Visa, Switch/Delta

BUXTON
Derbyshire
Map ref 4B2

The highest market town in England and one of the oldest spas, with an elegant Crescent, Poole's Cavern, Opera House and attractive Pavilion Gardens. An excellent centre for exploring the Peak District.
Tourist Information Centre ☎ (01298) 25106

Abbey Guesthouse 📧
APPROVED

43 South Avenue, Buxton SK17 6NQ
☎ (01298) 26419
Centrally located, warm and comfortable rooms. Reduced rates for 3 nights or more. Please 'phone for our special breaks tariff.
Bedrooms: 1 twin, 1 family room
Bathrooms: 1 public, 2 private showers

Bed & breakfast
per night:	£min	£max
Single	13.50	14.50
Double	27.00	29.00

Half board per
person:	£min	£max
Daily	21.00	22.00
Weekly	134.00	154.00

Lunch available
Evening meal 1830 (last orders 1930)
Parking for 1

Cotesfield Farm 📧
Listed

Parsley Hay, Buxton SK17 0BD
☎ Longnor (01298) 83256 & Mobile 0850 451148
Fax (01298) 83256
300-acre mixed farm. In the Peak District National Park on the Tissington Trail, this farmhouse offers peace and quiet. Access from the A515 Buxton to Ashbourne road.
Bedrooms: 2 double, 1 twin
Bathrooms: 1 public

Bed & breakfast
per night:	£min	£max
Single	17.00	18.00
Double	32.00	36.00

Parking for 6

Devonshire Arms ♠

Peak Forest, Buxton SK17 8EJ
☎ (01298) 23875 & 0831 707325
17th C former coaching inn located in the heart of the Peak District, close to all attractions. All rooms refurbished to a high standard, offering en-suite facilities, tea/coffee facilities and colour TV.
Bedrooms: 2 double, 1 twin
Bathrooms: 3 en-suite

Bed & breakfast

per night:	£min	£max
Single	25.00	25.00
Double	37.00	37.00

Lunch available
Evening meal 1830 (last orders 2145)
Parking for 40

Fairhaven ♠

Listed APPROVED

1 Dale Terrace, Buxton SK17 6LU
☎ (01298) 24481
Centrally placed with ample roadside parking, offering English home cooking in a warm and friendly atmosphere.
Bedrooms: 1 single, 1 double, 1 twin, 2 triple, 1 family room
Bathrooms: 1 public

Bed & breakfast

per night:	£min	£max
Single	17.00	19.00
Double	30.00	32.00

Half board per

person:	£min	£max
Daily	22.50	24.50
Weekly	150.50	157.50

Evening meal 1800 (last orders 1600)
Cards accepted: Access, Visa, Amex

Grendon ♠

COMMENDED

Bishops Lane, Buxton SK17 6UN
☎ (01298) 78831

Family-run, Edwardian, detached house set in lovely gardens with outstanding views to national park. High standard of comfort and service. Easy walk to town and countryside.
Bedrooms: 1 double, 1 twin
Bathrooms: 2 en-suite

Bed & breakfast per night:	£min	£max
Single	22.00	30.00
Double	34.00	39.00

Half board per person:	£min	£max
Daily	22.00	28.00
Weekly	150.00	200.00

Evening meal from 1830
Parking for 8

Hawthorn Farm Guesthouse

COMMENDED

Fairfield Road, Buxton SK17 7ED
☎ (01298) 23230
A 400-year-old former farmhouse which has been in the family for 10 generations. Full English breakfast.
Bedrooms: 4 single, 2 double, 2 twin, 4 triple
Bathrooms: 5 en-suite, 2 public

Bed & breakfast

per night:	£min	£max
Single	20.00	21.00
Double	40.00	46.00

Parking for 15
Open April–October

Lynstone Guesthouse

♠

3 Grange Road, Buxton SK17 6NH
☎ (01298) 77043
A spacious homely house. Home cooking, traditional and vegetarian. Ideal base for touring and walking. Children welcome, cleanliness assured. Off-street parking. No smoking and no pets, please.
Bedrooms: 1 triple, 1 family room
Bathrooms: 1 private, 2 public

Bed & breakfast

per night:	£min	£max
Double	31.00	32.00

Parking for 3
Open March–December

Oldfield House ♠

COMMENDED

8 Macclesfield Road, Buxton
SK17 9AH
☎ (01298) 24371
Attractive detached Victorian guesthouse with gardens, near the town centre and Pavilion Gardens. Spacious en-suite bedrooms. Non-smoking.
Bedrooms: 3 double
Bathrooms: 3 en-suite, 1 public

Bed & breakfast

per night:	£min	£max
Single	20.00	24.00
Double	36.00	39.00

Half board per person:	£min	£max
Daily	29.00	29.00
Weekly	190.00	190.00

Parking for 8

Pedlicote Farm

Listed

Peak Forest, Buxton SK17 8EG
☎ (01298) 22241
1681 oak-beamed farmhouse conversion in the Peak Park, full of character, with a charming atmosphere and magnificent views.
Bedrooms: 1 double, 2 twin
Bathrooms: 2 public

Bed & breakfast

per night:	£min	£max
Single	18.00	20.00
Double	28.00	30.00

Half board per

person:	£min	£max
Daily	25.00	27.00
Weekly	175.00	175.00

Lunch available
Evening meal 1830 (last orders 2030)
Parking for 9

CASTLETON

Derbyshire
Map ref 4B2

Large village in a spectacular Peak District setting with ruined Peveril Castle and 4 great show caverns, where the Blue John stone and lead were mined. One cavern offers a mile-long underground boat journey.

Ye Olde Cheshire Cheese Inn ♠

Listed

How Lane, Castleton, Sheffield
S30 2WJ
☎ Hope Valley (01433) 620330 &
Mobile 0836 369636

17th C inn in the heart of the Peak District. En-suite rooms. Restaurant with 30 home-made dishes, including roast wild boar, pheasant, game pie. Two beamed lounge bars with real ale - no pool tables or machines! Family-run.
Continued ▶

CASTLETON

Continued

Bedrooms: 1 single, 3 double, 2 twin
Bathrooms: 1 en-suite, 5 private
**Bed & breakfast
per night:**

	£min	£max
Single	22.50	27.50
Double	45.00	55.00

**Half board per
person:**

	£min	£max
Daily	28.45	45.00
Weekly	175.00	280.00

Lunch available
Evening meal 1800 (last orders
2100)
Parking for 65
Cards accepted: Access, Visa

CONINGSBY

Lincolnshire
Map ref 4D2

Large thriving village on the edge of
the Lincolnshire Fens. It is within
easy reach of main towns and has a
pleasing church with an unusual
one-handed clock.

White Bull Inn

Listed APPROVED

55 High Street, Coningsby, Lincoln
LN4 4RB
☎ (01526) 342439
*A warm welcome awaits at this friendly
pub with real ale, riverside beer garden
and large children's playground.
Children's Certificate. Traditional
home-made meals are available every
day, lunch time and evening. Half a
mile from RAF Coningsby. Family Pub of
the Year finalist, 1995.*
Bedrooms: 2 single, 1 double, 1 twin
Bathrooms: 2 en-suite, 4 public
**Bed & breakfast
per night:**

	£min	£max
Single	14.00	16.00
Double	25.00	29.00

**Half board per
person:**

	£min	£max
Daily	18.00	20.00
Weekly	105.00	120.00

Lunch available
Evening meal 1900 (last orders
2200)
Parking for 60

CORBY GLEN

Lincolnshire
Map ref 3A1

Stonepit Farmhouse

Listed COMMENDED

Swinstead Road, Corby Glen,
Grantham NG33 4NU
☎ (01476) 550614
Fax (01476) 550614
*Picturesque stone house on edge of
village. 4 miles east of A1. Separate
ground floor guest wing facing
"Mediterranean style" courtyard.*
Bedrooms: 1 single, 1 twin
Bathrooms: 1 public
**Bed & breakfast
per night:**

	£min	£max
Single	25.00	28.00
Double	40.00	50.00

Parking for 3

COTGRAVE

Nottinghamshire
Map ref 4C2

In 1934 an Anglo-Saxon burial
ground was discovered on Mill Hill,
in this interesting, historic village.

Jerico Farm

COMMENDED

Fosse Way, Cotgrave, Nottingham
NG12 3HG
☎ Kinoulton (01949) 81733
Fax (01949) 81733
*120-acre mixed farm. With lovely views
over the Nottinghamshire Wolds, an
excellent rural location for the business
or holiday visitor yet only 8 miles from
Nottingham with its universities, sports
venues and tourist sites. Brochure
available.*
Bedrooms: 2 double, 1 twin
Bathrooms: 1 en-suite, 1 public
**Bed & breakfast
per night:**

	£min	£max
Single	18.00	25.00
Double	32.00	38.00

Parking for 4

The symbols in each entry
give information about
services and facilities.
A 'key' to these symbols
appears at the back
of this guide.

CRICH

Derbyshire
Map ref 4B2

Home of the National Tramway
Museum where visitors can ride on
trams along a 1 mile scenic route
past reconstructed 19th C buildings.
There are also workshops, a power
station, an exhibition and a
lead-mining display to be seen.

Mount Tabor House

Listed

Bowns Hill, Crich, Matlock
DE4 5DG
☎ Ambergate (01773) 857008
Fax (01773) 852040
*Unique converted chapel offers quality
en-suite accommodation in Derbyshire
"Peak Practice" village. Extensive views
of wooded countryside. Good base for
exploring the area's rich cultural and
industrial heritage.*
Bedrooms: 1 double, 1 twin
Bathrooms: 2 en-suite, 1 public
**Bed & breakfast
per night:**

	£min	£max
Single	20.00	20.00
Double	38.00	38.00

**Half board per
person:**

	£min	£max
Daily	47.00	47.00
Weekly	295.00	295.00

Evening meal 1830 (last orders
1930)
Parking for 2

Penrose

HIGHLY COMMENDED

Sandy Lane, Crich DE4 5DE
☎ Ambergate (01773) 852625 &
(0589) 297608
*Stone cottage with affordable en-suite
rooms, spectacular views overlooking
Derwent Valley, delicious home-cooked
food, 2 acres secluded gardens, ample
parking.*
Bedrooms: 2 double
Suites available
Bathrooms: 2 en-suite
**Bed & breakfast
per night:**

	£min	£max
Single	20.00	28.00
Double	30.00	48.00

**Half board per
person:**

	£min	£max
Daily	22.00	38.00
Weekly	154.00	210.00

Evening meal 1800 (last orders
2100)
Parking for 7

DERBY

Derbyshire
Map ref 4B2

Modern industrial city but with ancient origins. There is a wide range of attractions including several museums (notably Royal Crown Derby), a theatre, a concert hall, and the cathedral with fine ironwork and Bess of Hardwick's tomb. *Tourist Information Centre ☎ (01332) 255802*

Bonehill Farm

COMMENDED

Etwall Road, Mickleover, Derby DE3 5DN
☎ (01332) 513553
120-acre mixed farm. Traditional farmhouse in a rural setting, 3 miles from Derby. Alton Towers, the Peak District, historic houses and the Potteries are all within easy reach.
Bedrooms: 1 double, 1 twin, 1 triple
Bathrooms: 1 en-suite, 1 public

Bed & breakfast per night:

	£min	£max
Single	16.00	20.00
Double	32.00	38.00

Parking for 6

EDWINSTOWE

Nottinghamshire
Map ref 4C2

Village close to Sherwood Forest, famous for the legend of Robin Hood.

Duncan Wood Lodge ⋒

COMMENDED

Carburton, Worksop S80 3BP
☎ Worksop (01909) 483614
Countryside lodge in the heart of Sherwood Forest. One acre of gardens and orchard in woodland setting.
Bedrooms: 2 double, 3 twin, 1 triple
Bathrooms: 4 en-suite, 1 public

Bed & breakfast per night:

	£min	£max
Single	27.00	32.00
Double	40.00	45.00

Evening meal 1830 (last orders 2030)
Parking for 9
Cards accepted: Access, Visa

Please mention this guide when making your booking

ELMESTHORPE

Leicestershire
Map ref 4C3

Silhouetted against the horizon, the picturesque church of St Mary has a 17th C tower and 12th or 13th C font and is set in a beautiful churchyard with lovely views.

Water Meadows Farm

Listed COMMENDED

22 Billington Road East, Elmesthorpe, Leicester LE9 7SB
☎ Earl Shilton (01455) 843417
Tudor-style, oak-beamed farmhouse with extensive gardens, including 15-acre private conservation area, woodland and stream. Own produce, home cooking. On a private road. Central for visiting many places of scenic and historic interest.
Bedrooms: 1 double, 1 family room
Bathrooms: 1 public

Bed & breakfast per night:

	£min	£max
Single	18.00	18.00
Double	30.00	30.00

Half board per person:

	£min	£max
Daily	23.00	26.00
Weekly	145.00	165.00

Evening meal from 1900
Parking for 10

EYAM

Derbyshire
Map ref 4B2

Attractive village famous for the courage it showed during the plague of 1665. The church has several memorials to this time and there is a well-dressing ceremony in August. The fine 17th C manor house of Eyam Hall is open in summer, and Chatsworth is nearby.

Royal Oak ⋒

APPROVED

Town Head, Eyam, Sheffield S30 1RE
☎ Hope Valley (01433) 631390
A quaint pub in the historic and picturesque "plague village" of Eyam in the Peak Park, close to Bakewell and Buxton.
Bedrooms: 1 double, 1 twin, 1 triple
Bathrooms: 3 en-suite

Bed & breakfast per night:

	£min	£max
Double	35.00	45.00

Half board per person:

	£min	£max
Daily	28.00	38.00
Weekly	175.00	245.00

Lunch available
Evening meal 1900 (last orders 2100)
Parking for 3

FILLINGHAM

Lincolnshire
Map ref 4C2

Church Farm ⋒

Listed HIGHLY COMMENDED

Fillingham, Gainsborough DN21 5BS
☎ Hemswell (01427) 668279
Fax (01427) 668025
Large, stone farmhouse. Lovely views. 15 minutes from Lincoln and Gainsborough, 5 minutes from Hemswell Antique Centre and Lincolnshire Showground.
Bedrooms: 1 single, 1 double, 1 twin
Suite available
Bathrooms: 1 en-suite, 2 public

Bed & breakfast per night:

	£min	£max
Single	20.00	25.00
Double	30.00	35.00

Half board per person:

	£min	£max
Daily	28.50	36.00
Weekly	199.50	252.00

Parking for 3

FOXTON

Leicestershire
Map ref 4C3

Attractive village established in the 8th C. The 13th C church contains part of a Saxon Cross and a "lepers window". The Grand Union Canal passes through the village. Within walking distance is historic Foxton Locks with its unique staircase flight of 10 locks, and Inclined Plane Museum.

The Old Manse

Swingbridge Street, Foxton, Market Harborough LE16 7RH
☎ Market Harborough (01858) 545456
Period house in large gardens with warm and friendly atmosphere, on edge of conservation village, 3 miles north of Market Harborough. Good food at both local inns.

Continued ▶

FOXTON

Continued

Bedrooms: 1 double, 2 twin
Bathrooms: 2 en-suite, 1 private
Bed & breakfast

per night:	£min	£max
Single	23.00	23.00
Double	39.00	39.00

Parking for 6

GRANTHAM

Lincolnshire
Map ref 3A1

On the old Great North Road (A1), Grantham's splendid parish church has a fine spire and chained library. Sir Isaac Newton was educated here and his statue stands in front of the museum which includes displays on Newton and other famous local people.
Tourist Information Centre ☎ (01476) 566444

Roberts Roost

COMMENDED

82 Harrowby Road, Grantham NG31 9DS
☎ (01476) 560719
Family-run guesthouse in a quiet, residential area close to the town centre, with easy access to the A1.
Bedrooms: 1 single, 1 twin, 1 triple
Bathrooms: 2 public
Bed & breakfast

per night:	£min	£max
Single	15.00	18.00
Double	28.00	28.00

Evening meal 1800 (last orders 1900)
Parking for 4

GUILSBOROUGH

Northamptonshire
Map ref 4C3

Lively village, situated 500 ft above sea level and close to two large reservoirs that have plenty of water activities. A very old village with much evidence of its history to be seen.

Seven Piers ♠

Listed

Coton, Northampton NN6 8RF
☎ Northampton (01604) 740322
Detached, brick house with private garden, close to Ravensthorpe Reservoir, Althorpe House and Coton Manor Gardens.

Bedrooms: 2 single, 1 twin, 1 triple, 1 family room
Bathrooms: 2 en-suite, 1 private, 1 public
Bed & breakfast

per night:	£min	£max
Single	16.00	18.00
Double	36.00	40.00

Parking for 3

HAGWORTHINGHAM

Lincolnshire
Map ref 4D2

White Oak Grange ♠

Listed HIGHLY COMMENDED

Hagworthingham, Spilsby PE23 4LX
☎ Spilsby (01507) 588376
Fax (01507) 588377
Fine house with extensive landscaped gardens, set in open countryside of the Lincolnshire Wolds. Licensed. Home-grown produce.
Bedrooms: 2 double, 1 twin
Bathrooms: 1 en-suite, 1 public
Bed & breakfast

per night:	£min	£max
Single	18.00	22.00
Double	36.00	44.00

Half board per person:	£min	£max
Daily	27.00	31.00
Weekly	160.00	196.00

Lunch available
Evening meal 1900 (last orders 2030)
Parking for 10

HATHERSAGE

Derbyshire
Map ref 4B2

Hillside village in the Peak District, dominated by the church with many good brasses and monuments to the Eyre family which provide a link with Charlotte Bronte. Little John, friend of Robin Hood, is said to be buried here.

Hillfoot Farm ♠

Listed COMMENDED

Castleton Road, Hathersage, Sheffield S30 1AH
☎ Hope Valley (01433) 651673
Recently built accommodation onto the existing farmhouse. All rooms are en-suite with colour TV, tea/coffee facilities. 2 rooms on ground floor, 2 on first floor. Large car park.
Bedrooms: 2 double, 1 twin, 1 triple
Bathrooms: 4 en-suite

Bed & breakfast

per night:	£min	£max
Single	20.00	37.00
Double	34.00	40.00

Lunch available
Evening meal 1800 (last orders 1900)
Parking for 13

HAYFIELD

Derbyshire
Map ref 4B2

Village set in spectacular scenery at the highest point of the Peak District with the best approach to the Kinder Scout plateau via the Kinder Downfall. An excellent centre for walking. Three reservoirs close by.

The Royal Hotel ♠

♛♛♛ COMMENDED

Market Street, Hayfield, Stockport, Cheshire SK12 5EP
☎ New Mills (01663) 742721
Fax (01663) 742721
Centrally located in Hayfield at the foot of Kinder Scout in the High Peak district. Built in 1755, comprises oak panelled pub and restaurant with log fires, function room and accommodation.
Bedrooms: 2 double, 1 twin
Bathrooms: 3 en-suite, 1 public
Bed & breakfast

per night:	£min	£max
Single	29.50	35.00
Double	45.00	50.00

Half board per person:	£min	£max
Daily	38.00	44.00
Weekly	250.00	300.00

Lunch available
Evening meal 1900 (last orders 2145)
Parking for 100
Cards accepted: Access, Visa, Switch/Delta

HUSBANDS BOSWORTH

Leicestershire
Map ref 4C3

Mrs Armitage's

♛ APPROVED

31-33 High Street, Husbands Bosworth, Lutterworth LE17 6LJ
☎ Market Harborough (01858) 880066
Village centre home of character on A4304/A427, with wholesome cooking

and warm welcome. Good choice of reasonably-priced evening meals at nearby inn.
Bedrooms: 3 twin
Bathrooms: 1 public

Bed & breakfast

per night:	£min	£max
Single	15.00	17.00
Double	30.00	34.00

Parking for 6

🛌🚗♿🐕🔌Ⅶ🅰S🎫TV🖥✕🚲Ⓣ

KETTERING

Northamptonshire
Map ref 3A2

Ancient industrial town based on shoe-making. Wicksteed Park to the south has many children's amusements. The splendid 17th C ducal mansion of Boughton House is to the north.
Tourist Information Centre ☎ (01536) 410266 or 534212

Dairy Farm

👑👑👑 COMMENDED

Cranford St Andrew, Kettering NN14 4AQ
☎ Cranford (01536) 330273
350-acre mixed farm. 17th C thatched house with inglenook fireplaces and a garden with an ancient circular dovecote and mature trees. Good food.
Bedrooms: 2 double, 1 twin
Bathrooms: 2 en-suite, 1 public

Bed & breakfast

per night:	£min	£max
Single	22.00	30.00
Double	44.00	60.00

Half board per

person:	£min	£max
Daily	32.50	42.50

Evening meal 1900 (last orders 1200)
Parking for 5

🛌🚗♿🐕🔌Ⅶ🅰S🎫TV🖥🚲U✕🚲🏕

KEXBY

Lincolnshire
Map ref 4C2

Kexby Grange

Listed

Kexby, Gainsborough DN21 5PJ
☎ Gainsborough (01427) 788265
300-acre mixed farm. Pleasant, Victorian farmhouse offering a warm welcome. In rural surroundings, 4 miles from Gainsborough. Convenient for Lincoln and Hemswell Antique Centre.
Bedrooms: 1 single, 1 double
Bathrooms: 1 private, 1 public

Bed & breakfast

per night:	£min	£max
Single	14.00	14.00
Double	28.00	28.00

Half board per

person:	£min	£max
Daily	20.00	

Lunch available
Evening meal 1700 (last orders 2100)
Parking for 4

♿🔌Ⅶ🅰🎫🖥🚲♨✕🚲◎

KIRTON

Nottinghamshire
Map ref 4C2

Pasture Farm 🏔

👑👑 COMMENDED

Main Street, Kirton, Newark NG22 9LP
☎ Mansfield (01623) 836291 & 0860 431135
12-acre livestock & horses farm. Period farmhouse of immense character, dating back to c1800. Working carriage horses, farm animals and tea rooms.
Bedrooms: 1 double, 2 twin
Bathrooms: 1 en-suite, 1 public

Bed & breakfast

per night:	£min	£max
Single	28.00	35.00
Double	35.00	40.00

Lunch available
Parking for 30

🛌🚗🖥♿🐕🔌Ⅶ🅰S✕🎫🖥🚲U♨✕🚲🏕◎

LAMBLEY

Nottinghamshire
Map ref 4C2

Magnolia House 🏔

Listed COMMENDED

22 Spring Lane, Lambley, Nottingham NG4 4PH
☎ (0115) 9314404
Family home in pretty village, close to Nottingham Castle and Robin Hood country. 3 pleasant pubs in village, all serving food.
Bedrooms: 2 single, 1 double
Bathrooms: 3 private, 1 public

Bed & breakfast

per night:	£min	£max
Single	15.00	17.00
Double	30.00	34.00

Parking for 12

🛌🚗🖥♿🐕🔌Ⅶ S✕🎫TV🖥🚲U♨✕🚲

LINCOLN

Lincolnshire
Map ref 4C2

Ancient city dominated by the magnificent 11th C cathedral with its triple towers. A Roman gateway is still used and there are medieval houses lining narrow, cobbled streets. Other attractions include the Norman castle, several museums and the Usher Gallery.
Tourist Information Centre ☎ (01522) 529828

New Farm

👑👑

Burton, Lincoln LN1 2RD
☎ (01522) 527326
360-acre arable & dairy farm. Twin-bedded room with private bathroom. Use of lounge with colour TV. 2 miles north of Lincoln. Evening meal by prior arrangement. Coarse fishing in private lakes. Nature reserve close by.
Bedrooms: 1 twin
Bathrooms: 1 private

Bed & breakfast

per night:	£min	£max
Single	21.00	21.00
Double	34.00	34.00

Half board per

person:	£min	£max
Daily	26.00	30.00
Weekly	177.00	205.00

Parking for 3
Open March–November

🛌5🖥♿🔌Ⅶ🅰S✕🎫TV🖥🚲U♨✕🚲

Winnowsty House

Listed

Winnowsty Lane, Lincoln LN2 5RZ
☎ (01522) 528600
A pretty, Victorian family house in the shadow of the cathedral, 2 minutes' walk from the historic city centre.
Bedrooms: 1 triple
Bathrooms: 1 private, 1 public

Bed & breakfast

per night:	£min	£max
Single	20.00	
Double	33.00	

Parking for 2

🛌🚗Ⅶ🅰S🖥🚲🚲

LITTON

Derbyshire
Map ref 4B2

Hall Farm House

👑👑 COMMENDED

Litton, Buxton SK17 8QP
☎ (01298) 872172
Friendly family home with spacious accommodation. Ideal base for touring by car or foot around the Peak District area.
Bedrooms: 1 double, 1 twin
Bathrooms: 1 en-suite, 1 private, 1 public

Bed & breakfast

per night:	£min	£max
Single	20.00	
Double	32.00	40.00

Open January–November

🛏️2🛋️📞♿🖥️🖩✑🧺📺💻🍴🌺🎭🍴 🚗 SP

LONG BUCKBY

Northamptonshire
Map ref 4C3

Stretching for one and a half miles, this is a village with individuality and character.

Murcott Mill

👑👑 COMMENDED

Murcott, Long Buckby, Northampton NN6 7QR
☎ (01327) 842236
100-acre livestock farm. Imposing Georgian mill house overlooking open countryside. Recently renovated to a high standard, with open fires and en-suite bedrooms. Ideal stopover for M1 travellers.
Bedrooms: 1 double, 2 twin
Bathrooms: 3 en-suite, 1 public

Bed & breakfast

per night:	£min	£max
Double	35.00	40.00

Half board per

person:	£min	£max
Daily	41.50	

Evening meal 1900 (last orders 2030)
Parking for 12

🛏️🖥️📞♿🖩🛡️🖩📺💻🍴🌺🚗💻

LOUTH

Lincolnshire
Map ref 4D2

Attractive old market town set on the eastern edge of the Lincolnshire Wolds. St James's Church has an impressive tower and spire and there are the remains of a Cistercian abbey. The museum contains an interesting collection of local material.
Tourist Information Centre ☎ (01507) 609289

Plough Inn 🏔️

Listed APPROVED

Upgate, Louth LN11 9HG
☎ (01507) 603551
19th C Tudor-style coaching inn, on the A16 in the attractive market town of Louth.
Bedrooms: 2 single, 1 double, 2 twin, 1 triple, 1 family room
Bathrooms: 2 public, 1 private shower

Bed & breakfast

per night:	£min	£max
Single	18.00	20.00
Double	36.00	40.00

Half board per

person:	£min	£max
Daily	23.00	28.00

Lunch available
Evening meal 1700 (last orders 2100)
Parking for 9

🛏️🖥️♿🛡️🖩📺💻🍴🍴🐾🌺

Wickham House

👑👑 HIGHLY COMMENDED

Church Lane, Conisholme, Louth LN11 7LX
☎ North Somercotes (01507) 358465
Attractive 18th C cottage in country lane. En-suite bedrooms. Beamed sitting and dining room, separate tables, library. No smoking in cottage please.
Bedrooms: 1 single, 1 double, 1 twin
Bathrooms: 3 en-suite

Bed & breakfast

per night:	£min	£max
Double	40.00	

Parking for 4

🛏️8🖥️🛋️🖥️♿🖩🖩✑🖩💻🌺 🍴🚗 SP 🏕️

LUDFORD

Lincolnshire
Map ref 4D2

The hamlets of Ludford Magna and Ludford Parva combine to form Ludford, situated on the busy road from Market Rasen to Louth.

Hainton Walk Farm

Listed COMMENDED

Ludford, Lincoln LN3 6AP
☎ Burgh on Bain (01507) 313242
4-acre smallholding. Very peaceful and beautiful area on Lincolnshire Wolds. Outstanding views. Good food and homely atmosphere. Small pets welcome.
Bedrooms: 1 single, 1 double, 1 triple
Bathrooms: 1 public

Bed & breakfast

per night:	£min	£max
Single	15.00	15.00
Double	28.00	30.00

Half board per

person:	£min	£max
Daily	22.50	23.50
Weekly	125.00	132.00

Lunch available
Evening meal 1900 (last orders 2130)
Parking for 7

🛏️🖥️🛋️🖥️♿🖩🛡️🖩✑🖩📺💻 🍴🌺🚗 OAP SP

MARKET HARBOROUGH

Leicestershire
Map ref 4C3

There have been markets here since the early 13th C, and the town was also an important coaching centre, with several ancient hostelries. The early 17th C grammar school was once the butter market.
Tourist Information Centre ☎ (01858) 468106

The Fox Inn 🏔️

👑👑 COMMENDED

Church Street, Wilbarston, Market Harborough LE16 8QG
☎ Rockingham (01536) 771270
Old ironstone village inn offering home-cooked food, real ales and traditional pub games. Near Rockingham Castle and East Carlton Country Park.
Bedrooms: 2 double, 1 twin, 1 family room
Bathrooms: 4 en-suite

Bed & breakfast

per night:	£min	£max
Single	20.00	25.00
Double	30.00	40.00

Lunch available
Evening meal 1830 (last orders 2145)
Parking for 10
Cards accepted: Access, Visa

🛏🕮🛆🕿🛏🖵♿🗫🛈🅂🔌🏧 🚗🔍❄🐾

The George at Great Oxendon 🛦

🛏🛏🛏 COMMENDED

Great Oxendon, Market Harborough LE16 8NA
☎ (01858) 465205
Fax (01858) 465205
Bedroom accommodation and restaurant with bars and conservatory, all with views of the garden. Ex-QE2 chef/proprietor.
Bedrooms: 2 double, 1 twin
Bathrooms: 3 en-suite
Bed & breakfast

per night:	£min	£max
Single	49.50	53.00
Double	59.50	

Lunch available
Evening meal 1900 (last orders 2200)
Parking for 36
Cards accepted: Access, Visa, Amex

🛏🕮🛆🕿🛏🖵♿🗫🛈🅂🔌🏧🖹10❄🚗🅂🅿🇹◉

MATLOCK

Derbyshire
Map ref 4B2

The town lies beside the narrow valley of the River Derwent surrounded by steep wooded hills. Good centre for exploring Derbyshire's best scenery.

Farley Farm

🛏🛏

Farley, Matlock DE4 5LR
☎ (01629) 582533 & 0860 625004
250-acre mixed farm. Built in 1610 of natural stone, set in open countryside close to Peak District and many places of interest.
Bedrooms: 1 double, 1 twin, 1 family room
Bathrooms: 1 en-suite, 2 public
Bed & breakfast

per night:	£min	£max
Single	17.00	18.00
Double	32.00	36.00

Half board per

person:	£min	£max
Daily	22.50	24.50
Weekly	157.50	171.50

Evening meal 1700 (last orders 1900)
Parking for 10

🛏♿🛈🔌🅂🖵🔌📺🏧🚗∪✓❄ 🚗🅓🅐🅿🏠

Home Farm 🛦

🛏🛏 COMMENDED

Ible, Grange Mill, Matlock DE4 4HS
☎ (01629) 650349
A "retired farm", still retaining some small animals which guests are encouraged to feed.
Bedrooms: 1 double, 1 family room
Bathrooms: 2 en-suite
Bed & breakfast

per night:	£min	£max
Single	16.00	
Double	32.00	

Half board per

person:	£min	£max
Daily	23.00	
Weekly	150.00	

Evening meal 1800 (last orders 2000)
Parking for 4

🛏🖵♿🔌🅄🅻🛈🅂🔌📺🏧🚗❄✗🚗

MEDBOURNE

Leicestershire
Map ref 4C3

Picturesque village with medieval bridge.

Homestead House

🛏🛏 HIGHLY COMMENDED

5 Ashley Road, Medbourne, Market Harborough LE16 8DL
☎ Medbourne Green (01858) 565724
Fax (01858) 565324
In an elevated position overlooking the Welland Valley on the outskirts of Medbourne, a picturesque village dating back to Roman times.
Bedrooms: 3 twin
Bathrooms: 3 en-suite
Bed & breakfast

per night:	£min	£max
Single	22.00	24.00
Double	38.00	40.00

Half board per

person:	£min	£max
Daily	29.00	32.00

Evening meal 1800 (last orders 2000)
Parking for 6
Cards accepted: Access, Visa

🛏🕿🛏🖵♿🔌🅄🅻🛈🅂🔌📺🏧🚗🚗

The **🛦** symbol after an establishment name indicates that it is a Regional Tourist Board member.

MELTON MOWBRAY

Leicestershire
Map ref 4C3

Close to the attractive Vale of Belvoir and famous for its pork pies and Stilton cheese which are the subjects of special displays in the museum. It has a beautiful church with a tower 100 ft high.
Tourist Information Centre ☎ *(01664) 480992*

Manor House 🛦

🛏🛏 HIGHLY COMMENDED

Church Lane, Saxelby, Melton Mowbray LE14 3PA
☎ (01664) 812269
125-acre livestock farm. Home cooking and a warm welcome in this oak-beamed farmhouse. Parts date back several hundred years including a unique 400-year-old staircase.
Bedrooms: 2 double, 1 twin, 1 family room
Bathrooms: 1 private, 1 public
Bed & breakfast

per night:	£min	£max
Single	25.00	
Double	37.00	

Half board per

person:	£min	£max
Daily	29.00	
Weekly	185.00	

Evening meal 1900 (last orders 1200)
Parking for 6
Open April–October

🛏🖵♿🔌🅂🛈🅂🔌📺🏧🚗❄✗🚗🏠

MIDDLETON

Northamptonshire
Map ref 4C3

Valley View

🛏 COMMENDED

3 Camsdale Walk, Middleton, Market Harborough, Leicestershire LE16 8YR
☎ Rockingham (01536) 770874
Elevated, stone-built house with panoramic views of the Welland Valley. Within easy distance of Market Harborough and Corby.
Bedrooms: 1 double, 1 twin
Bathrooms: 1 public
Bed & breakfast

per night:	£min	£max
Single	15.00	15.00
Double	30.00	30.00

Parking for 2

🛏♿🅄🅻🔌📺🏧🚗❄🚗

MORETON PINKNEY

Northamptonshire
Map ref 2C1

Thriving village in the south west of the county. The annual summer fete is a major attraction.

Barewell Fields

`Listed` **HIGHLY COMMENDED**

Prestidge Row, Moreton Pinkney, Daventry NN11 3NJ
☎ Sulgrave (01295) 760754
200-acre mixed farm. In a peaceful corner of the conservation village of Moreton Pinkney, convenient for many National Trust properties, Stratford and Silverstone, M1 and M40.
Bedrooms: 1 single, 1 double, 1 twin
Bathrooms: 1 public
Bed & breakfast

per night:	£min	£max
Single	16.00	20.00
Double	32.00	40.00

Parking for 4

🛏10 🏊 📺 ♿ ⚓ ⛱ 🅿 🍴 📺 ▭ ♨ ❄ ✈ 🚐

MOUNTSORREL

Leicestershire
Map ref 4C3

The Swan Inn

APPROVED

10 Loughborough Road, Mountsorrel, Loughborough LE12 7AT
☎ (0116) 230 2340
Fax (0116) 237 6115
Traditional 17th C coaching inn in the heart of historic Mountsorrel, on the banks of the River Soar.
Bedrooms: 1 single, 1 double, 1 twin
Bathrooms: 1 public
Bed & breakfast

per night:	£min	£max
Single	20.00	20.00
Double	32.00	32.00

Lunch available
Evening meal 1900 (last orders 2130)
Parking for 12
Cards accepted: Access, Visa, Amex

🛏14 🖵 ♿ ▮ S 🅿 ▭ ♨ 🍴 ❄ 🚐 🏕

For farm holidays and accommodation suitable for young people and organised groups, please refer to the special sections at the back of this guide.

NOTTINGHAM

Nottinghamshire
Map ref 4C2

Attractive modern city with a rich history. Outside its castle, now a museum, is Robin Hood's statue. Attractions include "The Tales of Robin Hood"; the Lace Hall; Wollaton Hall; museums and excellent facilities for shopping, sports and entertainment.
Tourist Information Centre ☎ (0115) 947 0661

Adams Castle View Guesthouse

`Listed`

85 Castle Boulevard, Nottingham NG7 1FE
☎ (0115) 950 0022
Late-Victorian private dwelling, completely refurbished to accommodate guests. Close to city centre and railway station.
Bedrooms: 3 single, 1 twin
Bathrooms: 1 public
Bed & breakfast

per night:	£min	£max
Single	16.00	17.00
Double	32.00	34.00

🏊 ♿ ⚓ ⛱ S 🍴 🅿 📺 ▭ 🍴 🚐 SP

Grantham Hotel ♠

COMMENDED

24-26 Radcliffe Road, West Bridgford, Nottingham NG2 5FW
☎ (0115) 981 1373
Fax (0115) 981 8567
Family-run licensed hotel offering modern accommodation in a comfortable atmosphere. Convenient for the centre of Nottingham, Trent Bridge and the National Water Sports Centre.
Bedrooms: 13 single, 2 double, 4 twin, 2 triple, 1 family room
Bathrooms: 13 en-suite, 3 public
Bed & breakfast

per night:	£min	£max
Single	19.95	27.00
Double	36.00	39.00

Half board per person:	£min	£max
Daily	26.00	34.00
Weekly	158.00	198.00

Evening meal 1800 (last orders 1900)
Parking for 20
Cards accepted: Access, Visa, Amex, Switch/Delta

🛏3 🖵 ♿ ⛱ ▮ S 🅿 🍴 📺 ▭ ♨ 🍴 T

OAKHAM

Leicestershire
Map ref 4C3

Pleasant former county town of Rutland. Fine 12th C Great Hall, part of its castle, with a historic collection of horseshoes. An octagonal Butter Cross stands in the market-place and Rutland County Museum, Rutland Farm Park and Rutland Water are of interest.
Tourist Information Centre ☎ (01572) 724329

Hall Farm ♠

APPROVED

Cottesmore Road, Exton, Oakham, Rutland LE15 8AN
☎ (01572) 812271 & 0385 915564
25-acre arable & horses farm. Early 19th C Grade II listed stone farmhouse in open countryside. Approximately 2 miles from Rutland Water north shore. TV, hairdryer, hot drinks in all rooms.
Bedrooms: 1 single, 1 twin, 1 triple
Bathrooms: 1 public
Bed & breakfast

per night:	£min	£max
Single		15.50
Double		28.00

Parking for 6

🛏 🖵 ♿ ⛱ ⚓ ▭ ♨ ❄ 🚐 🏕

OUNDLE

Northamptonshire
Map ref 3A1

Historic town situated on the River Nene with narrow alleys and courtyards and many stone buildings, including a fine church and historic inns.
Tourist Information Centre ☎ (01832) 274333

Lilford Lodge Farm

COMMENDED

Barnwell, Peterborough PE8 5SA
☎ (01832) 272230
Fax (01832) 272230

305-acre mixed farm. 19th C farmhouse, recently converted, in the Nene Valley. On the A605, 3 miles south of Oundle, 5 miles north of A14.
Bedrooms: 1 single, 1 double, 1 twin
Bathrooms: 3 en-suite

Bed & breakfast per night:	£min	£max
Single	18.00	
Double	36.00	

Parking for 13

🏇 🖳 ♿ UL S ⚡ 🅜 TV ▥ 🖊 ✿
🦮 🚃 SP

PEAK DISTRICT

See under Aldwark, Ashbourne, Ashford in the Water, Bakewell, Bamford, Biggin-by-Hartington, Buxton, Castleton, Eyam, Hathersage, Hayfield, Litton, Tideswell, Winster

POINTON

Lincolnshire
Map ref 3A1

Greenoaks ᛗ

HIGHLY COMMENDED

Pinfold Lane, Pointon, Sleaford
NG34 0NB
☎ Sleaford (01529) 240193
Fax (01529) 240612
Georgian farmhouse with spacious, well-furnished, comfortable rooms. Centrally situated for Lincoln and Peterborough cathedrals, Georgian Stamford, stately homes and wildlife sanctuaries.
Bedrooms: 1 single, 2 twin
Bathrooms: 1 en-suite, 1 private, 1 public

Bed & breakfast per night:	£min	£max
Single	25.00	25.00
Double	40.00	45.00

Half board per person:	£min	£max
Daily	32.50	35.00
Weekly	200.00	220.00

Evening meal 1830 (last orders 2000)
Parking for 7

🏇 ♿ UL S ⚡ 🅜 TV ▥ 🖊 ✿ 🚃 🎣

RAGNALL

Nottinghamshire
Map ref 4C2

Lying 4 miles north-east of Tuxford, close to the Trent. Pretty and interesting church.

Ragnall House ᛗ

COMMENDED

Ragnall, Newark NG22 0UR
☎ Dunham-on-Trent (01777)
228575 & Mobile 0374 455792
Large listed Georgian family house in over an acre of grounds in a small village close to the River Trent. Good local inns and restaurants nearby.

Bedrooms: 1 single, 2 twin, 1 triple
Bathrooms: 1 en-suite, 1 public, 1 private shower

Bed & breakfast per night:	£min	£max
Single	15.00	17.00
Double	30.00	34.00

Parking for 8

🏇 ♿ ⬜ UL 🅐 🅜 TV ▥ 🖊 ☂ ✿ SP 🎣 T

RAITHBY

Lincolnshire
Map ref 4D2

Red Lion Inn/Le Baron Restaurant

Main Road, Raithby, Spilsby
PE23 4DS
☎ Spilsby (01790) 753727

16th C listed country inn providing comfortable accommodation. Restaurant with traditional and continental cuisine.
Bedrooms: 2 double, 1 twin
Bathrooms: 2 en-suite, 1 private, 1 public

Bed & breakfast per night:	£min	£max
Single	19.00	30.00
Double	26.00	37.00

Lunch available
Evening meal 1900 (last orders 2130)
Parking for 20
Cards accepted: Access, Visa, Amex, Switch/Delta

🏇 ⬜ ♿ 🍴 🅐 S 🅜 TV ▥ 🖊 🍷 🚃 🎣

SAXILBY

Lincolnshire
Map ref 4C2

A picturesque village offering easy access to Lincoln and Gainsborough. The "Sun Inn" is said to be haunted by a former local murderer.

Orchard Cottage

COMMENDED

3 Orchard Lane, Saxilby, Lincoln
LN1 2HT
☎ Lincoln (01522) 703192

Cottage-style house, with a guest annexe in a pleasant garden, 6 miles from Lincoln. Non-smokers only, please.
Bedrooms: 1 double, 1 twin, 1 triple
Bathrooms: 2 en-suite, 1 private, 1 public

Bed & breakfast per night:	£min	£max
Single	18.00	22.00
Double	36.00	36.00

Parking for 2

🏇 ♿ 🖳 ♿ ⬜ UL 🅐 S ⚡ 🅜 TV ▥ 🖊
☂ ✿ 🚃 🎣

SHERWOOD FOREST

See under Edwinstowe, Kirton, Ragnall, Southwell

SHIRLEY

Derbyshire
Map ref 4B2

Village in a pretty setting among little hills, with a tiny 14th C church.

The Old Byre

Listed

Hollington Lane, Shirley DE6 3AS
☎ Ashbourne (01335) 360054 &
mobile 0378 914377

18th C converted barn in quiet village, in the heart of the Derbyshire countryside. Four-poster room, inglenook fireplace, beams and log fires. Traditional English breakfast. Convenient for Alton Towers and Peak District.
Bedrooms: 2 single, 2 double
Bathrooms: 2 public

Bed & breakfast per night:	£min	£max
Single	17.50	
Double	35.00	

Parking for 3

🏇 🖳 ♿ ⬜ ♿ UL 🅐 S ⚡ 🅜 TV ▥
🖊 🎣 ✿ SP 🎣

SILVERSTONE

Northamptonshire
Map ref 2C1

Old village with a lot of history to tell, including many stories of ghosts in the local buildings. Home of the world famous Silverstone Racing Circuit.

Silverthorpe Farm

Listed **COMMENDED**

Abthorpe Road, Silverstone, Towcester NN12 8TW
☎ Towcester (01327) 858020
Large, spacious, modern bungalow with a warm and friendly atmosphere, standing in its own quiet, rural surroundings. 1.5 miles north of Silverstone.
Bedrooms: 2 twin, 1 family room
Bathrooms: 2 private, 2 public

Bed & breakfast per night:	£min	£max
Single	18.00	20.00
Double	38.00	40.00

Parking for 4

Whitley House

Listed **APPROVED**

7 Murswell Lane, Silverstone, Towcester NN12 8UT
☎ Towcester (01327) 857161
Modern house in the village of Silverstone. Central area for touring or motor race meetings. Friendly atmosphere, full English breakfast.
Bedrooms: 2 twin
Bathrooms: 1 public

Bed & breakfast per night:	£min	£max
Single	15.00	15.00
Double	30.00	30.00

Parking for 1
Open March–November and Christmas

WELCOME HOST

This is a nationally recognised customer care programme which aims to promote the highest standards of service and a warm welcome. Establishments who are taking part in this initiative are indicated by the ❀ symbol.

SKEGNESS

Lincolnshire
Map ref 4D2

Famous seaside resort with 6 miles of sandy beaches and bracing air. Attractions include swimming pools, bowling greens, gardens, Natureland Marine Zoo, golf-courses and a wide range of entertainment at the Embassy Centre. Nearby is Gibraltar Point Nature Reserve.
Tourist Information Centre ☎ *(01754) 764821*

Victoria Inn ⚊

Wainfleet Road, Skegness PE25 3RG
☎ (01754) 767333
Friendly, traditional inn with hotel annexe, providing home-cooked food. Central for town and beach facilities.
Bedrooms: 1 single, 3 double, 1 twin, 2 family rooms
Bathrooms: 4 en-suite, 1 public

Bed & breakfast per night:	£min	£max
Single	13.00	15.00
Double	24.00	30.00

Half board per person:	£min	£max
Weekly	96.00	102.00

Lunch available
Evening meal 1800 (last orders 2200)
Parking for 20
Cards accepted: Access, Visa

SKILLINGTON

Lincolnshire
Map ref 3A1

Hidden away on the edge of the Leicestershire border, still with a fragment of the old cross on its green. The pretty abbey is a small 17th C stone manor house.

Sproxton Lodge Farm

Listed

Skillington, Grantham NG33 5HJ
☎ Grantham (01476) 860307
230-acre arable farm. Quiet family farmhouse. Large lawns. Good breakfast, large TV lounge with open fire. Located about 3 miles off the A1.
Bedrooms: 1 single, 1 double, 1 triple
Bathrooms: 1 public

Bed & breakfast per night:	£min	£max
Single	15.00	15.00
Double	30.00	30.00

Parking for 4

SLEAFORD

Lincolnshire
Map ref 3A1

Market town whose parish church has one of the oldest stone spires in England and particularly fine tracery round the windows.
Tourist Information Centre ☎ *(01529) 414294*

The Tally Ho Inn

⚊ COMMENDED

Aswarby, Sleaford NG34 8SA
☎ Culverthorpe (01529) 455205
Traditional, friendly 17th C listed country inn. En-suite rooms in carefully converted stables, a la carte restaurant and bar meals. Plenty of welcoming atmosphere and character.
Bedrooms: 2 double, 4 twin
Bathrooms: 6 en-suite

Bed & breakfast per night:	£min	£max
Single	30.00	32.00
Double	45.00	48.00

Lunch available
Evening meal 1900 (last orders 2200)
Parking for 50
Cards accepted: Access, Visa, Switch/Delta

SOUTH WITHAM

Lincolnshire
Map ref 3A1

The Blue Cow Inn ⚊

Listed

29 High Street, South Witham, Grantham NG33 5QB
☎ Grantham (01572) 768432
Fax (01572) 768432
13th C beamed freehouse with log fires, real ales and home-cooked meals. Restaurant and bar meals 7 days a week. Convenient for A1, Grantham, Oakham, Stamford and Melton Mowbray.
Bedrooms: 1 single, 1 double, 2 twin
Suite available
Bathrooms: 1 en-suite, 2 public

Bed & breakfast per night:	£min	£max
Single	17.50	22.50
Double	35.00	45.00

Half board per person:	£min	£max
Daily	22.50	32.50
Weekly	150.00	200.00

Lunch available
Evening meal 1800 (last orders 2130)
Parking for 45
Cards accepted: Access, Visa

🐎🛝💺🐾♿🛈Ⓢ✖️📺🕐🛗🖨💺🍴50
🔌🅿️❄️🚲🅣

SOUTHWELL

Nottinghamshire
Map ref 4C2

Town dominated by the Norman minster which has some beautiful 13th C stone carvings in the Chapter House. Charles I spent his last night of freedom in one of the inns. The original Bramley apple tree can still be seen.

Barn Lodge 🅜

Listed COMMENDED

Duckers Cottage, Brinkley, Southwell NG25 0TP
☎ (01636) 813435
Smallholding with panoramic views, 1 mile from the centre of Southwell and close to the racecourse, railway station and River Trent.
Bedrooms: 1 double, 1 twin, 1 triple
Bathrooms: 3 en-suite
Bed & breakfast

per night:	£min	£max
Single	20.00	20.00
Double	40.00	40.00

Parking for 3

🐎🛝💺🐾♿Ⓤ🅛Ⓢ🛗❄️🚲🅓🅐🅟 SP
🅣

SPALDING

Lincolnshire
Map ref 3A1

Fenland town famous for its bulbfields. A spectacular Flower Parade takes place at the beginning of May each year and the tulips at Springfields show gardens are followed by displays of roses and bedding plants in summer. Interesting local museum.
Tourist Information Centre ☎ (01775) 725468 or 761161

Travel Stop 🅜

Ⓞ🄴 APPROVED

Locks Mill Farm, 50 Cowbit Road, Spalding PE11 2RJ
☎ (01775) 767290 & 767716
Fax (01775) 767716
Converted from farm buildings, the motel complements the 17th C farmhouse. Three-quarters of a mile from centre of Spalding on A1073 Peterborough road. Most units are on

ground floor with own porches and all are equipped with refrigerator and colour TV.
Bedrooms: 3 single, 5 double, 2 twin
Bathrooms: 10 en-suite, 2 public
Bed & breakfast

per night:	£min	£max
Single	25.00	45.00
Double	35.00	70.00

Parking for 25
Cards accepted: Access, Visa, Amex

🐎🛝💺🐾🛈Ⓢ✖️🅜📺🛗💺
Ⓤ🅿️❄️ DAP SP 🅣

STAMFORD

Lincolnshire
Map ref 3A1

Exceptionally beautiful and historic town with many houses of architectural interest, several notable churches and other public buildings all in the local stone. Burghley House, built by William Cecil, is a magnificent Tudor mansion on the edge of the town.
Tourist Information Centre ☎ (01780) 55611

Birch House 🅜

Listed COMMENDED

4 Lonsdale Road, Stamford PE9 2RW
☎ (01780) 54876 changing to 754876 & 0850 185759
Comfortable, family-run detached house on the outskirts of Stamford. All rooms have TV and tea/coffee-making facilities. Non-smokers only, please.
Bedrooms: 2 single, 1 double, 1 twin
Bathrooms: 1 public
Bed & breakfast

per night:	£min	£max
Single	16.00	
Double	32.00	

Parking for 3

🐎🛝5🐾🛗🐾♿Ⓤ🅛Ⓢ✖️🛗💺🍴🚲 SP

The Manor Cottage

Listed HIGHLY COMMENDED

Stamford Road, Collyweston, Stamford PE9 3PN
☎ (01780) 444209
Large stone-built Georgian house, set in 2 acres of grounds, with panoramic views, in the picturesque village of Collyweston, just 3 miles from historic Stamford.
Bedrooms: 1 single, 1 double, 1 twin, 1 triple
Bathrooms: 1 private, 2 public
Bed & breakfast

per night:	£min	£max
Single	15.00	30.00
Double	30.00	65.00

Parking for 10

🛝🗄️🐾♿Ⓤ🅛🛈🐾✖️🛗💺🍴🚲 SP
🅐🅣

Martins

Listed HIGHLY COMMENDED

20 High Street, Saint Martin's, Stamford PE9 2LF
☎ (01780) 52106 changing to 752106
Elegant, 17th C listed house near the town centre. Large rooms furnished with antiques. Walled garden and croquet. Street parking.
Bedrooms: 3 twin
Bathrooms: 2 public
Bed & breakfast

per night:	£min	£max
Single	30.00	30.00
Double	45.00	50.00

Half board per person:	£min	£max
Daily	40.00	45.00
Weekly	280.00	315.00

Evening meal 1930 (last orders 2030)
Parking for 3

🛝🐎♿🐾Ⓤ🅛Ⓢ🅜📺🛗💺❄️🚲 SP
🅐

Rock Lodge 🅜

👑👑

1 Empingham Road, Stamford PE9 2RH
☎ (01780) 64211 changing to 764211
Fax (01780) 482442
Victorian stone "hunting lodge" style mansion, set within huge walled gardens, close to heart of Stamford.
Bedrooms: 2 double, 1 twin
Bathrooms: 2 en-suite, 1 private
Bed & breakfast

per night:	£min	£max
Single	25.00	35.00
Double	40.00	50.00

Parking for 3

🛝10🐾♿Ⓤ🅛✖️🅜📺🛗💺❄️
🚲 SP 🅐🅣 ⊚

A key to symbols can be found inside the back cover flap.

All accommodation in this guide has been graded, or is awaiting a grading, by a trained Tourist Board inspector.

STOKE BRUERNE

Northamptonshire
Map ref 2C1

Village on the Grand Union Canal at the southern end of the long Blisworth Tunnel. The Waterways Museum traces the history of the waterways and canals over the last 200 years and there are trips on the canal in summer.

Beam End ⚹

Listed **COMMENDED**

Stoke Park, Stoke Bruerne, Towcester NN12 7RZ
☎ Roade (01604) 864638 & 864802
Fax (01604) 864638
Originally a stable for working horses on the Stoke Park Estate, now converted to provide secluded accommodation in a family home. On a private road.
Bedrooms: 1 double, 1 twin
Bathrooms: 2 private, 1 public
Bed & breakfast

per night:	£min	£max
Single	18.00	25.00
Double	38.00	45.00

Half board per

person:	£min	£max
Daily	24.00	31.00

Evening meal 1800 (last orders 2030)
Parking for 6

⛵🏠5🖳🗄👄🍷🍽📶🛏🗑📺�📺🖳🔺🛢
❀🐏SP🏠T

SWAYFIELD

Lincolnshire
Map ref 3A1

The Royal Oak Inn ⚹

Listed **COMMENDED**

High Street, Swayfield, Grantham NG33 4LL
☎ Corby Glen (01476) 550247
Fax (01476) 550996
Old world inn in country setting, 3.5 miles from A1. Well-appointed 1650 property with chalet accommodation. Separate restaurant.
Bedrooms: 2 double, 2 twin, 1 family room
Bathrooms: 5 en-suite
Bed & breakfast

per night:	£min	£max
Single	30.00	30.00
Double	40.00	40.00

Half board per

person:	£min	£max
Weekly	182.00	245.00

Lunch available
Evening meal 1830 (last orders 2230)
Parking for 40
Cards accepted: Access, Visa, Amex

⛵🏠🖳👄🍷🍽🛏📶🖳🔺🛢🔍🚬⌒📮
❀DAP🔀SP

TIDESWELL

Derbyshire
Map ref 4B2

Small town with a large 14th C church known as the "Cathedral of the Peak". There is a well-dressing ceremony each June with Morris dancing, and many choral events throughout the year.

Poppies ⚹

Listed **APPROVED**

Bank Square, Tideswell, Buxton SK17 8LA
☎ (01298) 871083
Poppies offers a warm welcome, comfortable accommodation and good vegetarian and traditional home cooking in a small restaurant, at the centre of this picturesque mid Peak District village.
Bedrooms: 1 double, 1 twin, 1 triple
Bathrooms: 1 en-suite, 1 public
Bed & breakfast

per night:	£min	£max
Single	14.50	19.00
Double	29.00	38.00

Half board per

person:	£min	£max
Daily	24.50	40.00
Weekly	157.00	230.00

Lunch available
Evening meal 1900 (last orders 2130)
Open February–December
Cards accepted: Access, Visa, Diners, Amex

⛵🏠👄🍷🛏📶🍽🖳🔺🛢📮

TOWCESTER

Northamptonshire
Map ref 2C1

Town built on the site of a Roman settlement. It has some interesting old buildings, including an inn featured in one of Dickens' novels. The racecourse lies alongside the A5 Watling Street, and motor racing takes place at nearby Silverstone.

Cutchems End ⚹

👑 **HIGHLY COMMENDED**

Yorks Farm, Watling Street, Towcester NN12 8EU
☎ Pattishall (01327) 830640 & 830645
Fax (01327) 830645

Convertd 19th C barn, retaining interesting features and utilising old materials. Delightful rural setting with extensive views over open countryside.
Bedrooms: 2 double
Bathrooms: 2 en-suite
Bed & breakfast

per night:	£min	£max
Single	21.00	21.00
Double	36.00	36.00

Half board per

person:	£min	£max
Daily	31.00	31.00
Weekly	190.00	190.00

Lunch available
Evening meal 1900 (last orders 2100)
Parking for 12

⛵🏠10 UL👄🔀📺🖳🔺❀🐏🏠

TWO DALES

Derbyshire
Map ref 4B2

Village set in beautiful Derbyshire scenery and with easy access to the country houses of Haddon and Chatsworth.

Top 'O The Hill ⚹

Listed **COMMENDED**

Sydnope Hill, Two Dales, Matlock DE4 2FN
☎ Matlock (01629) 734548
A modern, country residence overlooking the Peak Park border with superb views. On the B5057, Darley Dale to Chesterfield road.
Bedrooms: 2 double, 1 twin
Bathrooms: 1 public
Bed & breakfast

per night:	£min	£max
Single	20.00	23.00
Double	30.00	34.00

Half board per

person:	£min	£max
Daily	25.00	27.00
Weekly	161.00	167.00

Evening meal 1800 (last orders 2000)
Parking for 4

⛵🏠👄🍷UL🛏🔀📺🖳🔺❀🍽🐏

The map references refer to the colour maps towards the end of the guide. The first figure is the map number; the letter and figure which follow indicate the grid reference on the map.

UPPER BROUGHTON

Nottinghamshire
Map ref 4C3

Nestling attractively into the steep hillside with extensive views of the Vale of Belvoir, this village has two greens with beautiful flowers and ornaments.

Swan Lodge ⚔
Station Road, Upper Broughton, Melton Mowbray, Leicestershire
LE14 3BH
☎ Melton Mowbray (01664) 823686 & 822346
Fax (01664) 823860
200-acre mixed farm. 19th C farmhouse, 2 miles from the nearest village. Horse riding, fishing and miles of walking available.
Bedrooms: 1 triple
Bathrooms: 1 en-suite
Bed & breakfast
per night:

	£min	£max
Single	20.00	25.00
Double	35.00	50.00

Lunch available
Evening meal 1730 (last orders 1900)
Parking for 20
Cards accepted: Access, Visa

UPPINGHAM

Leicestershire
Map ref 4C3

Quiet market town dominated by its famous public school which was founded in 1584. It has many stone houses and is surrounded by attractive countryside.

Rutland House ⚔

61 High Street East, Uppingham
LE15 9PY
☎ (01572) 822497
Fax (01572) 822497
Family-run B & B. All rooms en-suite. Close to Rutland Water. Full English or continental breakfast. Well-placed for exploring Rutland's villages and countryside.
Bedrooms: 2 single, 1 double, 1 twin, 1 triple
Bathrooms: 5 en-suite
Bed & breakfast
per night:

	£min	£max
Single	29.00	29.00
Double	39.00	39.00

Parking for 3
Cards accepted: Access, Visa

WEEDON

Northamptonshire
Map ref 2C1

Old village steeped in history, with thatched cottages and several antique shops.

Globe Hotel ⚔
COMMENDED
High Street, Weedon, Northampton
NN7 4QD
☎ (01327) 340336
Fax (01327) 349058
19th C countryside inn. Old world atmosphere and freehouse hospitality with good English cooking, available all day. Meeting rooms. Close to M1, Stratford and many tourist spots. Send for information pack.
Bedrooms: 4 single, 6 double, 5 twin, 3 triple
Bathrooms: 18 en-suite
Bed & breakfast
per night:

	£min	£max
Single	29.50	42.50
Double	42.50	50.00

Lunch available
Evening meal (last orders 2200)
Parking for 40
Cards accepted: Access, Visa, Diners, Amex

COUNTRY CODE

Always follow the Country Code ❧ Enjoy the countryside and respect its life and work ❧ Guard against all risk of fire ❧ Fasten all gates ❧ Keep your dogs under close control ❧ Keep to public paths across farmland ❧ Use gates and stiles to cross fences, hedges and walls ❧ Leave livestock, crops and machinery alone ❧ Take your litter home ❧ Help to keep all water clean ❧ Protect wildlife, plants and trees ❧ Take special care on country roads ❧ Make no unnecessary noise

WEST HADDON

Northamptonshire
Map ref 4C3

A once rural community with the historic and attractive All Saints Church.

Pear Trees

🏰🏰 APPROVED

31 Station Road, West Haddon, Northampton NN6 7AU
☎ (01788) 510389
Attractive 18th C Northamptonshire-stone detached house in village, with good pubs/restaurants within walking distance. Four miles junction 18 M1/M6. Rugby 10 miles, Daventry 7 miles, Northampton 13 miles, nearest main line station 2 miles.
Bedrooms: 1 double, 1 twin, 1 triple
Bathrooms: 1 en-suite, 2 private, 1 public

Bed & breakfast per night:	£min	£max
Single	20.00	23.00
Double	38.00	40.00

Half board per person:	£min	£max
Daily	27.00	29.00
Weekly	180.00	190.00

Evening meal 1900 (last orders 2030)

WHALEY BRIDGE

Derbyshire
Map ref 4B2

Old textile town, whose canal warehouses are a reminder of its former importance, at the junction of the Peak Forest Canal and the Cromford and High Peak Railway. Surrounded by hills and with splendid views.

Cote Bank Farm ₥

🏰🏰 HIGHLY COMMENDED

Buxworth, Whaley Bridge, Stockport, Cheshire SK12 7NP
☎ Chinley (01663) 750566
Fax (01663) 750566
100-acre hill farm. A warm and welcoming home from home for holiday makers or business travellers. Stunning views, wonderful walks and rural tranquillity. One mile from Chinley village.
Bedrooms: 1 double, 1 twin
Bathrooms: 2 en-suite, 1 public

Bed & breakfast per night:	£min	£max
Single	20.00	25.00
Double	40.00	44.00

Parking for 2
Open March–November

WINSTER

Derbyshire
Map ref 4B2

Village with some interesting old gritstone houses and cottages, including the 17th C stone market hall now owned by the National Trust. It is a former lead mining centre.

Brae Cottage ₥

🏰

East Bank, Winster, Matlock DE4 2DT
☎ (01629) 650375
Spacious, self-contained cottage annexe on ground level, with en-suite bathroom. Garage, patio and picturesque garden. Suitable for couple or small family/group.
Bedrooms: 1 family room
Bathrooms: 1 en-suite

Bed & breakfast per night:	£min	£max
Double	30.00	32.00

Parking for 2

ENQUIRY COUPONS

To help you obtain further information

about advertisers and accommodation featured in

this guide you will find enquiry coupons at the back.

Send these directly to the establishments

in which you are interested.

Remember to complete both sides of the coupon.

EAST ANGLIA

East Anglia is the ideal 'get away from it all' destination. Here you can play golf, go fishing, follow the region's nature trails or discover the pastoral beauty of Constable country.

Pretty Hertfordshire villages await you, along with the sleepy charms of the Broads, England's newest National Park.

The untamed coastline boasts a number of much-loved seaside resorts like Great Yarmouth, Clacton and Southend-on-Sea while inland, Aldeburgh hosts a famous music festival.

Discover markets, vineyards and the gourmet delights of Cromer crab, Suffolk ham and Colchester oysters, as memorable as the surroundings in which you'll savour them.

FOR MORE INFORMATION CONTACT:
East Anglia Tourist Board
Toppesfield Hall, Hadleigh, Suffolk IP7 5DN
Tel: (01473) 822922 **Fax:** (01473) 823063

Where to Go in East Anglia - see pages 216-219
Where to Stay in East Anglia - see pages 220-248

EAST ANGLIA

Where to Go and What to See

You will find hundreds of interesting places to visit during your stay in East Anglia, just some of which are listed in these pages. The number against each name will help you locate it on the map (page 219). Contact any Tourist Information Centre in the region for more ideas on days out in East Anglia.

1 Wells Walsingham Railway
Stiffkey Road,
Wells-next-the-Sea,
Norfolk NR23 1QB
Tel: (01328) 856506
Four miles of railway. The longest 10¼ railway in the World. New locomotive Norfolk Hero now in service, largest of its kind ever built.

2 Thursford Collection
Thursford Green,
Thursford, Fakenham,
Norfolk NR21 0AS
Tel: (01328) 878477
Live musical shows, nine mechanical organs and Wurlitzer show starring Robert Wolfe.

3 Pensthorpe Waterfowl Park
Pensthorpe, Fakenham,
Norfolk NR21 0LN
Tel: (01328) 851465
Large waterfowl and wildfowl collection. Information centre, conservation shop, adventure play area, walks and nature trails. Licensed restaurant.

4 Norfolk Lavender
Caley Mill, Heacham,
King's Lynn, Norfolk PE31 7JE
Tel: (01485) 570384
Lavender is distilled from the flowers and the oil made in to a wide range of gifts. Slide show when distillery not working.

5 Sandringham
Sandringham, King's Lynn,
Norfolk PE35 6EN
Tel: (01553) 772675
Country retreat of HM The Queen. Delightful house and 60-acres of grounds and lakes. Museum of vehicles and royal memorabilia.

6 Banham Zoo
The Grove, Banham,
Norwich, Norfolk NR16 2HE
Tel: (01953) 887771
See some of the world's rare and endangered species.

7 Sainsbury Centre for Visual Arts
University of East Anglia,
Norwich, Norfolk NR4 7TJ
Tel: (01603) 456060
The Robert and Lisa Sainsbury Collection of modern and non modern art is wide-ranging and of international importance. Housed in a building purpose designed by N Foster.

8 Sea Life Centre
Marine Parade, Great Yarmouth,
Norfolk NR30 3AH
Tel: (01493) 330631
Walk under a tropical reef. Shark tank, Ray fish and British sharks, plus 25 themed displays depicting British marine life and local settings.

9 Somerleyton Hall and Gardens
Somerleyton, Lowestoft,
Suffolk NR32 5QQ
Tel: (01502) 730224
Anglo-Italian-style building with state rooms, maze. Garden with azaleas and rhododendrons. Miniature railway, shop, light luncheons and teas.

10 East Anglia Transport Museum

Chapel Road, Carlton Colville, Lowestoft, Suffolk NR33 8BL
Tel: (01502) 518459
A working museum with one of the widest ranges of street transport vehicles on display - and in action!

11 Pleasurewood Hills

Corton, Lowestoft, Suffolk NR32 5DZ
Tel: (01502) 508200
Log flume, chair lift, cine 180, two railways, pirate ship, fort, Aladdin's cave, parrot and sealion shows, roller coasters, waveswinger, Eye in the Sky, Star Ride Enterprise.

12 Otter Trust

Earsham, Bungay, Suffolk NR35 2AF
Tel: (01986) 893470
A breeding and conservation headquarters with the largest collection of otters in the world. Also lakes with collection of waterfowl and deer.

13 Bressingham Steam Museum and Gardens

Bressingham, Diss, Norfolk IP22 2AB
Tel: (01379) 687386
Steam rides through five miles of woodland, garden and nursery.

Mainline locomotives and over 50 steam engines. Alan Bloom's Dell Garden.

14 Sacrewell Farm and Country Centre

Sacrewell, Thornhaugh, Peterborough, Cambridgeshire PE8 6HJ
Tel: (01780) 782222
500-acre farm, with working watermill, farmhouse gardens, shrubberies, nature and general interest trails, 18C buildings, displays of farm, rural and domestic bygones.

15 Ely Cathedral

Chapter House, The College, Ely, Cambridgeshire CB7 4DN
Tel: (01353) 667735
One of England's finest cathedrals. Fine out buildings. Guided tours and tours of Octagon and West Tower. Brass rubbing and stained glass museum.

16 Pakenham Water Mill

Mill Road, Grimestone End, Pakenham, Bury St Edmunds, Suffolk IP3 2NB
Tel: (01787) 247179
18C working water mill on Domesday site, with oil engine and other subsidiary machinery.

17 Framlingham Castle

Framlingham, Woodbridge, Suffolk IP13 9BP
Tel: (01728) 724189
12C curtain walls with 13 towers and Tudor brick chimneys. Built by Bigod family, Earls of Norfolk. Wall walk. 17C almshouses. Home of Mary Tudor in 1553.

18 Imperial War Museum

Duxford Airfield, Duxford, Cambridgeshire CB2 4QR
Tel: (01223) 835000
Over 120 aircraft on display, tanks, vehicles, guns. Ride simulator, adventure playground, shops and restaurant.

19 National Horseracing Museum

99 High Street, Newmarket, Suffolk CB8 8JL
Tel: (01638) 667333
Five permanent galleries telling the story of horseracing. Opened by the Queen in 1983. British sporting art. Temporary Exhibition Gallery.

20 Ickworth House, Park and Gardens

Ickworth, Bury St Edmunds, Suffolk IP29 5QE
Tel: (01284) 735270
Extraordinary oval house with flanking wings begun in 1795. Fine paintings and beautiful collection of Georgian silver. Italian garden and park designed by Capability Brown.

21 Helmingham Hall Gardens

Helmingham,
Suffolk IP14 6EF
Tel: (01473) 890363
*Moated and walled garden with
many rare roses and possibly the
best kitchen garden in Britain. Also
highland cattle and safari rides in
park to view red and fallow deer.*

22 Shuttleworth Collection

Old Warden Aerodrome,
Biggleswade,
Bedfordshire SG18 9ER
Tel: (01767) 627288
*Unique historic collection of aircraft
from 1909 Bleriot to 1942 Spitfire
in flying condition. Cars dating from
1898 Panhard.*

23 Audley End House and Park

Saffron Walden,
Essex CB11 4JF
Tel: (01799) 522842
*Palatial Jacobean house remodelled
in the 18-19C. Magnificent Great
Hall. Rooms and furniture by
Robert Adam. Park by Capability
Brown.*

24 Woburn Abbey

Woburn,
Milton Keynes,
Bedfordshire MK43 0TP
Tel: (01525) 290666
*18C Palladian mansion altered by
Henry Holland, the Prince Regent's
architect. Contains a collection of
English silver, French and English
furniture and an important art
collection.*

25 Mountfitchet Castle

Stansted Mountfitchet,
Essex CM24 8SP
Tel: (01279) 813237
*Reconstructed Norman motte-and-
bailey castle and village of
Domesday period. Grand Hall,
church, prison, seige tower and
weapons.*

26 Colchester Castle

Colchester,
Essex CO1 1TJ
Tel: (01206) 282931
*Norman Keep on foundations of
Roman Temple, archaeological
material includes much on Roman
Colchester.*

27 Whipsnade Wild Animal Park

Zoological Society of London,
Dunstable,
Bedfordshire LU6 2LF
Tel: (01582) 872171
*Over 2,500 animals set in 600
acres of beautiful parkland. Great
Whipsnade Railway. Free animal
demonstrations.*

28 Hatfield House

Hatfield Park, Hatfield,
Hertfordshire AL9 5NQ
Tel: (01707) 262823
*Jacobean house built in 1611 and
Old Palace built in 1497. Contains
famous paintings, fine furniture and
possessions of Queen Elizabeth I.
Extensive park and gardens.*

29 The Gardens of the Rose

The Royal National Rose Society,
Chiswell Green,
St Albans,
Hertfordshire AL2 3NR
Tel: (01727) 850461
The Royal National Rose
Society's Garden, 20 acres of
showground and trial grounds for
new varieties of rose. 30,000
roses of all types with 1,700
different varieties.

Map of East Anglia

- LINCOLNSHIRE
- LEICESTERSHIRE
- NORTHANTS
- Thornhaugh
- **14** Peterborough
- Yaxley
- Whittlesey
- March
- Huntingdon
- St Ives
- Chatteris
- Ely **15**
- CAMBRIDGESHIRE
- St Neots
- Cambridge
- Bedford Sandy
- Great Shelford
- BEDFORD-SHIRE **22**
- Biggleswade
- Duxford **18**
- **24** Woburn
- Leighton Buzzard
- **23** Saffron Walden
- Letchworth
- Stansted Mountfitchet
- Hitchin
- Dunstable
- Luton
- **27**
- HERTFORD-SHIRE
- **25**
- Bishop's Stortford
- Hertford
- Harlow
- Hemel Hempstead
- **29** Hatfield **28**
- St Albans
- Chipping Ongar
- BUCKS Watford
- Brentwood
- Ingatestone
- BERKS
- GREATER LONDON
- SURREY
- KENT
- Wells-next-the-Sea **1**
- Sherringham
- Cromer
- Thursford
- Fakenham **2**
- North Walsham
- Pensthorpe **3**
- NORFOLK
- King's Lynn **4** **5**
- Caister-on-Sea
- Wisbech
- Swaffham
- East Dareham
- Oxborough
- **6** **7** Norwich
- **8** Great Yarmouth
- Wymondham
- Attleborough
- Somerleyton **9**
- Earsham **12**
- **10** **11** Lowestoft
- Lakenheath
- Bungay
- Mildenhall
- **13** Diss
- Bressingham
- Southwold
- Pakenham
- Halesworth
- Bury St Edmunds **16**
- SUFFOLK
- Stowmarket
- **17** Framlingham
- **19** **20**
- Newmarket Ickworth
- Aldeburgh
- **21** Helmingham
- Haverhill
- Ipswich
- Sudbury
- Hadleigh
- Harwich
- ESSEX
- **26** Colchester
- Braintree
- Coggeshall
- Clacton-on-Sea
- Chelmsford Witham
- Maldon
- West Mersea
- Burnham-on-Crouch
- Basildon
- Stanford-le-Hope
- Grays
- Southend-on-Sea
- Tilbury

0 ——— 20 Miles
0 ——— 30 Kms

FIND OUT MORE

Further information about holidays and attractions in East Anglia is available from:
East Anglia Tourist Board,
Toppesfield Hall,
Hadleigh,
Suffolk IP7 5DN.
Tel: (01473) 822922

These publications are available from the East Anglia Tourist Board (post free):

- **Great Escapes** - short breaks
- **Touring Map** - bed & breakfast and camping
- **Freedom Holiday Parks in Eastern England**

Also available are (prices include postage and packaging):

- **East Anglia Guide** £4.50
- **Gardens to Visit in East Anglia** £1.99

WHERE TO STAY (EAST ANGLIA)

Accommodation entries in this region are listed in alphabetical order of place name, and then in alphabetical order of establishment.

Map references refer to the colour location maps at the back of this guide. The first number indicates the map to use; the letter and number which follow refer to the grid reference on the map.

At-a-glance symbols at the end of each accommodation entry give useful information about services and facilities. A key to symbols can be found inside the back cover flap. Keep this open for easy reference.

ALDEBURGH

Suffolk
Map ref 3C2

A prosperous port in the 16th C, now famous for the Aldeburgh Music Festival held annually in June.

Faraway

Listed

28 Linden Close, Aldeburgh IP15 5JL
☎ (01728) 452571
Bungalow with CH, garden and car parking. Quiet, being off the main road. TV in all rooms, full English breakfast.
Bedrooms: 1 single, 1 twin, 1 triple
Bathrooms: 2 public

Bed & breakfast

per night:	£min	£max
Single	15.00	15.50
Double	30.00	31.00

Parking for 4

AMPTHILL

Bedfordshire
Map ref 2D1

Busy market town with houses of distinctive Georgian character.

Pond Farm ⋀

Listed

7 High Street, Pulloxhill, Bedford MK45 5HA
☎ Flitwick (01525) 712316
70-acre arable & horses farm. Listed building, an ideal base for touring. Close to Woburn Abbey, Whipsnade Zoo, the Shuttleworth Collection of old aircraft and Luton Airport. Resident Great Dane. Tea/coffee and colour TV all rooms.

Bedrooms: 1 double, 1 twin, 1 triple
Bathrooms: 1 public

Bed & breakfast

per night:	£min	£max
Single	16.00	20.00
Double	30.00	

Parking for 6

ATTLEBOROUGH

Norfolk
Map ref 3B1

Market town, mostly destroyed in 1559 by fire, now a cider-making centre. Church with fine Norman tower.

Hill House Farm

Listed COMMENDED

Deopham Road, Great Ellingham, Attleborough NR17 1AQ
☎ (01953) 453113
100-acre mixed farm. Friendly and comfortable accommodation. Leave the A11 and take the B1077 to Great Ellingham, take turn at bus shelter to Deopham. Farm is half a mile on, second farm on the left.
Bedrooms: 1 single, 1 double, 1 twin, 1 triple
Bathrooms: 1 public

Bed & breakfast

per night:	£min	£max
Single	15.00	
Double	30.00	

Parking for 5

AYLSHAM

Norfolk
Map ref 3B1

Small town on the River Bure with an attractive market place and interesting church. Nearby is Blickling Hall (National Trust). Also the terminal of the Bure Valley narrow gauge steam railway which runs on 9 miles of the old Great Eastern trackbed, between Wroxham and Aylsham.

The Old Bank House ⋀

HIGHLY COMMENDED

3 Norwich Road, Aylsham, Norwich NR11 6BN
☎ (01263) 733843

Relax in the comfort and traditional Victorian atmosphere of Aylsham's former private bank. We offer guests a friendly break, spacious welcoming bedrooms with TV and home-cooked meals. Lovely countryside nearby.
Bedrooms: 1 double, 1 twin, 1 triple
Bathrooms: 1 en-suite, 2 public

Bed & breakfast

per night:	£min	£max
Single	20.00	20.00
Double	34.00	36.00

Half board per person:

	£min	£max
Daily	26.50	29.50
Weekly	156.00	174.00

Evening meal 1800 (last orders
2000)
Parking for 3

🛞🍽🖵♿📞♒ⓊⓁ🛄Ⓢ⌦✂🍴TV🖨🖊🖨
🏧✕🔍🐾🚗🏛

The Old Pump House 🏔

Holman Road, Aylsham, Norwich
NR11 6BY
☎ (01263) 733789

Creature comforts, steps everywhere,
home cooking. Rambling 1750s house
beside the thatched pump, a minute
from church and marketplace. Pine
shuttered breakfast room overlooks
peaceful garden. Non-smoking.
Bedrooms: 3 double, 2 twin
Bathrooms: 3 en-suite, 2 public
Bed & breakfast

per night:	£min	£max
Single	18.00	25.00
Double	36.00	42.00

Half board per person:	£min	£max
Daily	28.00	35.00
Weekly	148.00	165.00

Evening meal from 1800
Parking for 7

🛞🖵♿📞♒ⓊⓁ🛄Ⓢ⌦✂🍴TV🖨🖊🖨❄
🚗SP🏛

Brickwall Farm

Broad Road, Bacton, Stowmarket
IP14 4HP
☎ (01449) 780197
17th C listed farmhouse which has
been sympathetically restored. Centrally
situated for exploring Mid-Suffolk and
the Heritage Coast.
Bedrooms: 3 double
Bathrooms: 3 en-suite
Bed & breakfast

per night:	£min	£max
Single	20.00	24.00
Double	35.00	35.00

Half board per person:	£min	£max
Daily	27.50	30.00
Weekly	150.00	150.00

Evening meal 1900 (last orders
2100)
Parking for 5

🍽🖵ⓊⓁ✂🍴TV🖨🖊🖨❄✕🚗🏛

Rymer Farm 🏔

Barnham, Thetford, Norfolk
IP24 2PP
☎ Elveden (01842) 890233
Fax (01842) 890653

550-acre arable farm. 17th C
farmhouse welcomes guests with tea
and log fire or summer garden room.
Enjoy real "farmer's breakfast". Farm
walks with wildlife, carp lake and
gardens. 8 miles north of historic Bury
St Edmunds.
Bedrooms: 1 twin, 1 triple
Bathrooms: 1 en-suite, 1 private
Bed & breakfast

per night:	£min	£max
Single	19.00	22.00
Double	36.00	40.00

Parking for 10

🛞♿ⓊⓁ✂🍴TV🖨🖊🚗∪🌙❄✕🚗

Busy county town with interesting
buildings and churches near the
River Ouse which has pleasant
riverside walks. Many associations
with John Bunyan including Bunyan
Meeting House, museum and statue.
The Bedford Museum and Cecil
Higgins Art Gallery are of interest.
*Tourist Information Centre ☎ (01234)
215226*

Firs Farm 🏔

Stagsden, Bedford MK43 8TB
☎ (01234) 822344
504-acre arable farm. Family-run, set in
quiet surroundings quarter-of-a-mile
south of A422, midway between
Bedford and Milton Keynes (M1
junction 14).
Bedrooms: 2 double, 1 twin
Bathrooms: 1 en-suite, 1 public
Bed & breakfast

per night:	£min	£max
Single	16.00	22.50
Double	32.00	40.00

Parking for 4

🛞♒5♿📞♒ⓊⓁ🛄♿🍴TV🖨🖨🌙❄🚗
◎

Jays End Guest House

13 Putnoe Heights, Bedford
MK41 8EB
☎ (01234) 359537
Semi-detached house, within walking
distance of the town centre. Both
rooms en-suite. Small and friendly.
Ample parking.
Bedrooms: 1 double, 1 twin
Bathrooms: 2 en-suite
Bed & breakfast

per night:	£min	£max
Single	12.50	15.00
Double	25.00	30.00

Parking for 2

🛞♒6♿📞♒ⓊⓁ🖨🖨❄✕🚗

Peacock House 🏔

Peacock Lane, Old Beetley, Dereham
NR20 4DG
☎ Dereham (01362) 860371
Beautiful period farmhouse with lovely
garden in rural setting, 3.5 miles from
Dereham. Ideal for Norwich,
Sandringham and coast. Good home
cooking and a warm welcome.
Bedrooms: 2 double, 1 twin
Bathrooms: 3 en-suite
Bed & breakfast

per night:	£min	£max
Single	17.00	20.00
Double	34.00	36.00

Parking for 4

🛞🍽♿ⓊⓁⓈ✂🍴TV🖨🖨❄🚗
🏛

Busy centre for market gardening
set on the River Ivel spanned by a
14th C bridge. Some interesting old
buildings in the market-place.
Nearby are the Shuttleworth
collection of historic aeroplanes and
Jordan's Mill.

Old Warden Guest House

Shop and Post Office, Old Warden,
Biggleswade SG18 9HQ
☎ Northill (01767) 627201
Listed, 19th C building, adjacent to
Continued ▶

BIGGLESWADE

Continued

shop and post office. Between
Biggleswade and Bedford.
Bedrooms: 1 double, 2 twin
Bathrooms: 3 en-suite

Bed & breakfast

per night:	£min	£max
Single	21.00	25.00
Double	35.00	35.00

Parking for 5

BISHOP'S STORTFORD

Hertfordshire
Map ref 2D1

Fine old town on the River Stort
with many interesting buildings,
particularly Victorian, and an
imposing parish church. The vicarage
where Cecil Rhodes was born is
now a museum.
Tourist Information Centre ☎ *(01279)
655831*

The Thatch

Listed | **HIGHLY COMMENDED**

Cambridge Road, Ugley, Bishop's
Stortford CM22 6HZ
☎ Saffron Walden (01799) 543440
Fax (01799) 543440
*Situated in hamlet just north of
Bishop's Stortford. Set in lovely
countryside, with warm and friendly
atmosphere. Convenient for Stansted
Airport and M11. Airport parking
available.*
Bedrooms: 2 double, 1 twin
Bathrooms: 1 en-suite, 1 public

Bed & breakfast

per night:	£min	£max
Single	20.00	28.00
Double	36.00	45.00

Parking for 7

BLAKENEY

Norfolk
Map ref 3B1

Picturesque village on the north
coast of Norfolk and a former port
and fishing village. 15th C Guildhall.
Marshy creeks extend towards
Blakeney Point (National Trust) and
are a paradise for naturalists, with
trips to the reserve and to see the
seals from Blakeney Quay.

Flintstones Guest House

Listed | **COMMENDED**

Wiveton, Holt NR25 7TL
☎ Cley (01263) 740337

---

*Attractive licensed guesthouse in
picturesque rural surroundings near
village green. 1 mile from Cley and
Blakeney with good sailing and
bird-watching. All rooms with private
facilities. Non-smokers only, please.*
Bedrooms: 1 single, 1 double,
3 triple
Bathrooms: 3 en-suite, 2 private

Bed & breakfast

per night:	£min	£max
Single	20.00	22.00
Double		37.00

**Half board per
person:**

	£min	£max
Daily		29.50
Weekly		192.50

Evening meal 1900 (last orders
1700)
Parking for 5

BLYTHBURGH

Suffolk
Map ref 3C2

Little Thorbyns

COMMENDED

The Street, Blythburgh, Halesworth
IP19 9LS
☎ (01502) 478664
*Good, comfortable accommodation and
a warm welcome. Close to Minsmere
RSPB sanctuary and Southwold,
Walberswick and Dunwich beaches.
Three-night mini-break from £70 per
person.*
Bedrooms: 1 single, 1 double, 1 twin
Bathrooms: 2 en-suite, 1 public

Bed & breakfast

per night:	£min	£max
Single	17.50	17.50
Double	35.00	37.00

**Half board per
person:**

	£min	£max
Daily	25.00	26.00
Weekly	165.00	165.00

Parking for 4

BOURN

Cambridgeshire
Map ref 2D1

The Bungalow

5 Gills Hill, Bourn, Cambridge
CB3 7TS
☎ Elsworth (01954) 719463
*Spacious modern bungalow overlooking
golf-course at rear. Facilities suitable for
disabled. Pleasant rural setting.*
Bedrooms: 1 double, 1 triple
Bathrooms: 2 en-suite, 1 public

Bed & breakfast

per night:	£min	£max
Single	16.50	19.00
Double	32.00	38.00

Parking for 2

BRACON ASH

Norfolk
Map ref 3B1

The Old Bakery

The Street, Bracon Ash, Norwich
NR14 8EL
☎ Mulbarton (01508) 570360
Fax (01508) 570360
*Former village bakery, dating from
1725, set in centre of pretty village, 5
miles from Norwich. All rooms en-suite.
Hearty farmhouse-style breakfasts.*
Bedrooms: 1 double, 1 twin, 1 triple
Bathrooms: 3 en-suite

Bed & breakfast

per night:	£min	£max
Single	18.00	20.00
Double	33.00	35.00

Parking for 8

BRADWELL

Essex
Map ref 3B2

Park Farmhouse

Listed | **COMMENDED**

Church Road, Bradwell, Braintree
CM7 8EP
☎ Coggeshall (01376) 563584
*16th C timber-framed farmhouse with
four-poster bed. Large garden, tranquil
setting, Blackwater Valley. Constable
country, historic centres, coast and
Stansted Airport all accessible. Parking.*
Bedrooms: 1 double, 1 twin
Bathrooms: 2 public

Bed & breakfast

per night:	£min	£max
Single	16.00	
Double	32.00	34.00

Parking for 4

Information on
accommodation listed in this
guide has been supplied by the
proprietors. As changes may
occur you are advised to check
details at the time of booking.

BRAINTREE

Essex
Map ref 3B2

The Heritage Centre in the Town Hall describes Braintree's former international importance in wool, silk and engineering. St Michael's parish church includes some Roman bricks.
Tourist Information Centre ☎ (01376) 550066

Spicers Farm

👑👑 HIGHLY COMMENDED

Rotten End, Wethersfield, Braintree CM7 4AL
☎ Great Dunmow (01371) 851021
70-acre arable farm. Attractive farmhouse set in delightful, peaceful position overlooking beautiful countryside. Comfortable and welcoming, all rooms en-suite. North-west of Braintree, convenient for Harwich, Stansted and Cambridge.
Bedrooms: 1 double, 2 twin
Bathrooms: 3 en-suite
Bed & breakfast

per night:	£min	£max
Single	20.00	20.00
Double	30.00	34.00

Parking for 10

BRECKLES

Norfolk
Map ref 3B1

Church Cottage

👑 COMMENDED

Breckles, Attleborough NR17 1EW
☎ Great Hockham (01953) 498286
Fax (01953) 498320

Charming 18th C home in beautiful Breckland. Ideal for touring East Anglia. Own coarse fishing. Heated outdoor swimming pool. Home-made bread. On B1111, 9 miles north-east of Thetford.
Bedrooms: 2 double, 1 twin
Bathrooms: 2 public
Bed & breakfast

per night:	£min	£max
Single	17.00	18.00
Double	34.00	36.00

Parking for 10

BULPHAN

Essex
Map ref 3B3

Bonny Downs Farm

Listed APPROVED

Doesgate Lane, Bulphan, Upminster RM14 3TB
☎ Basildon (01268) 542129
60-acre mixed farm. Large comfortable farmhouse offering home-cooked food. Conveniently placed for road links: M25, A13 and A127 to London and south-east England.
Bedrooms: 2 twin, 1 triple
Bathrooms: 1 private, 2 public
Bed & breakfast

per night:	£min	£max
Single	20.00	20.00
Double	30.00	30.00

Half board per

person:	£min	£max
Daily	28.00	28.00
Weekly	196.00	196.00

Evening meal 1800 (last orders 2000)
Parking for 4

BUNTINGFORD

Hertfordshire
Map ref 2D1

Southfields Farm

Listed

Throcking, Buntingford SG9 9RD
☎ Royston (01763) 281224 & (0589) 646759
Fax (01763) 281224
Warm, comfortable farmhouse 1.5 miles off A10 midway between London and Cambridge. TV, tea and coffee facilities. Closed at Christmas. No smoking in bedrooms.
Bedrooms: 1 single, 1 twin
Bathrooms: 1 public
Bed & breakfast

per night:	£min	£max
Single	18.00	
Double	36.00	

Parking for 5

The symbols in each entry give information about services and facilities. A 'key' to these symbols appears at the back of this guide.

BURNHAM OVERY STAITHE

Norfolk
Map ref 3B1

Unspoilt scenic village, steeped in naval history, Lord Nelson's playground as a boy. Captain Woodgett of the Cutty Sark once lived here and cargo ships visited the harbour. Wonderful tidal inlet with great variety of natural history. Close to Roman fort at Brancaster and famous Peddars Way.

Domville Guest House ⋀

👑 COMMENDED

Glebe Lane, Burnham Overy Staithe, King's Lynn PE31 8JQ
☎ Fakenham (01328) 738298
Standing in own grounds in a quiet lane, close to the sea. Closed for Christmas.
Bedrooms: 3 single, 2 double, 2 twin
Bathrooms: 2 en-suite, 2 public
Bed & breakfast

per night:	£min	£max
Single	17.00	18.00
Double	34.00	40.00

Half board per

person:	£min	£max
Daily	24.00	29.25

Evening meal 1900 (last orders 1200)
Parking for 10

BURY ST EDMUNDS

Suffolk
Map ref 3B2

Ancient market and cathedral town which takes its name from the martyred Saxon King, St Edmund. Bury St Edmunds has many fine buildings including the Athenaeum and Moyses Hall, reputed to be the oldest Norman house in the county.
Tourist Information Centre ☎ (01284) 764667

Craufurd House

👑👑

Howe Lane, Cockfield, Bury St Edmunds IP30 0HA
☎ (01284) 828216
Self-contained unit comprising bedroom, sitting-room and bathroom in detached country house. TV and tea/coffee facilities. In pleasant countryside overlooking fields. Easy drive from Bury St Edmunds. Lavenham 4 miles.
Bedrooms: 1 twin
Bathrooms: 1 private

Continued ▶

BURY ST EDMUNDS
Continued

Bed & breakfast per night:	£min	£max
Single	17.50	
Double	35.00	

Parking for 4
Open April–October

The Gables

107 Fornham Road, Bury St
Edmunds IP32 6AS
☎ (01284) 754257
Warm and cosy atmosphere. Situated within 5 minutes' walking distance of station and 10 minutes from town centre.
Bedrooms: 1 single, 1 double,
1 triple
Bathrooms: 1 public

Bed & breakfast per night:	£min	£max
Single	17.00	
Double	34.00	

Half board per person:	£min	£max
Daily	17.00	

Parking for 3

The Leys

Listed COMMENDED

113 Fornham Road, Bury St
Edmunds IP32 6AT
☎ (01284) 760225
Lovely, spacious Victorian house in own grounds, close to the A45 and railway station. Payphone, home-made bread and preserves.
Bedrooms: 1 double, 1 twin, 1 triple
Bathrooms: 1 en-suite, 1 public

Bed & breakfast per night:	£min	£max
Single	20.00	30.00
Double	34.00	40.00

Parking for 6

Maundrell House

Listed COMMENDED

109 Fornham Road, Bury St
Edmunds IP32 6AS
☎ (01284) 705884
Fax (01284) 705884
Large Edwardian semi-detached town house. Twin rooms overlook garden. Close to town centre, station and A45. Guests are assured of a warm welcome and good food. Meeting from coach or train by arrangement.

Bedrooms: 1 single, 2 twin
Bathrooms: 1 en-suite, 2 public

Bed & breakfast per night:	£min	£max
Single	16.00	23.00
Double	32.00	38.00

Half board per person:	£min	£max
Daily	25.00	32.00

Parking for 2

South Hill House

Listed COMMENDED

43 Southgate Street, Bury St
Edmunds IP33 2AZ
☎ (01284) 755650
Fax (01284) 752718
Grade II listed townhouse, reputed to be the school mentioned in Charles Dickens' "Pickwick Papers". 10 minutes' walk from town centre, 2 minutes' drive from A14.*
Bedrooms: 1 twin, 1 family room
Bathrooms: 2 en-suite

Bed & breakfast per night:	£min	£max
Single	25.00	30.00
Double	35.00	40.00

Parking for 4

39 Well Street

Listed APPROVED

Bury St Edmunds IP33 1EQ
☎ (01284) 768986
Elegant 19th C town house within 100 yards of all amenities. Friendly atmosphere, comfortable and well-furnished rooms.
Bedrooms: 1 single, 2 double
Bathrooms: 1 public

Bed & breakfast per night:	£min	£max
Single	18.00	20.00
Double	34.00	36.00

Parking for 2

BUXTON
Norfolk
Map ref 3C1

Belair

Listed

Crown Road, Buxton, Norwich
NR10 5EN
☎ Norwich (01603) 279637
Central for Broads and Norfolk coast, close to Buxton Mill/Restaurant. Steam railway runs from Buxton to Aylsham, where Blickling Hall can be visited, and on to Wroxham where one can have a trip on a cruiser or shop at the store.

Bedrooms: 2 double, 1 twin
Bathrooms: 1 en-suite, 2 private,
2 public

Bed & breakfast per night:	£min	£max
Single	16.00	16.00
Double	32.00	36.00

Parking for 3

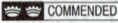
CAMBRIDGE
Cambridgeshire
Map ref 2D1

A most important and beautiful city on the River Cam with 31 colleges forming one of the oldest universities in the world. Numerous museums, good shopping centre, restaurants, theatres, cinema and fine bookshops.
Tourist Information Centre ☎ (01223) 322640

Antwerp Guest House

36 Brookfields, Mill Road,
Cambridge CB1 3NW
☎ (01223) 247690
On A1134 ring road between Addenbrookes Hospital and Cambridge Airport. Near the city's amenities and bus and railway stations. Pleasant gardens.
Bedrooms: 4 double, 4 twin
Bathrooms: 2 en-suite, 2 public

Bed & breakfast per night:	£min	£max
Single	20.00	30.00
Double	34.00	40.00

Parking for 8
Open February–November

Carlton Lodge

Listed

245 Chesterton Road, Cambridge
CB4 1AS
☎ (01223) 367792 & 566877
Small family-run business within 1 mile of the city centre and with easy access from M11 and A14.
Bedrooms: 1 double, 1 twin, 1 triple
Bathrooms: 3 en-suite, 1 public

Bed & breakfast per night:	£min	£max
Single	17.50	30.00
Double	40.00	46.00

Parking for 6

Cristinas

🏆🏆🏆

47 St. Andrews Road, Cambridge
CB4 1DL
☎ (01223) 365855 & 327700
Fax (01223) 365855
*Small family-run business in quiet
location, a short walk from city centre
and colleges.*
Bedrooms: 5 double, 3 twin, 1 triple
Bathrooms: 7 en-suite, 1 public
Bed & breakfast

per night:	£min	£max
Single	26.00	38.00
Double	39.00	47.00

Parking for 8

🚼🖵👃🆙📺📖🚗✈

Dykelands Guest House 🏔

🏆

157 Mowbray Road, Cambridge
CB1 4SP
☎ (01223) 244300
Fax (01223) 566746
*Detached guesthouse offering modern
accommodation. On south side of city.
Ideally located for city centre and for
touring the secrets of the
Cambridgeshire countryside. Children
welcome.*
Bedrooms: 1 single, 2 double, 2 twin,
2 triple, 1 family room
Bathrooms: 3 en-suite, 1 public,
2 private showers
Bed & breakfast

per night:	£min	£max
Single	19.75	25.00
Double	33.00	39.00

Parking for 7
Cards accepted: Access, Visa, Diners,
Amex, Switch/Delta

🚼🖖📭🖵👃🔒🆂✂🏴📺📖🚗✳
🆂🅿🆃

Foxhounds

Listed

71 Cambridge Road, New
Wimpole/Orwell, Royston,
Hertfordshire SG8 5QD
☎ (01223) 207344
*Former pub, part 17th C, now a family
home. On A603, 9 miles from
Cambridge and within easy reach of
Wimpole Hall (National Trust). Sitting
room for guests, large garden.*
Bedrooms: 1 single, 2 twin
Bathrooms: 2 public
Bed & breakfast

per night:	£min	£max
Single	17.00	18.00
Double	34.00	34.00

Evening meal 1930 (last orders
1930)
Parking for 3

🚼🖏👃🆙🆂✂🏴📺📖🚗▶✳
🚜

264 Hills Road

🏅 **HIGHLY COMMENDED**

Cambridge CB2 2QE
☎ (01223) 248369
Fax (01223) 441276
*Elegant 1920s detached house on
main bus route, 1 mile from city centre
and 2 miles from M11.*
Bedrooms: 1 double
Bathrooms: 1 en-suite
Bed & breakfast

per night:	£min	£max
Single	40.00	
Double	60.00	

Parking for 4
Cards accepted: Visa

🖵🖵👃🔍🆙🔒✂📖🚗✳🚜

Home From Home

🏆

39 Milton Road, Cambridge
CB4 1XA
☎ (01223) 323555 & Mobile 0850
538712
Fax (01223) 565660
*Small, friendly B & B, with spacious
rooms, 10 minutes' walk from bus
station and city centre.*
Bedrooms: 2 double, 1 twin
Bathrooms: 1 private, 2 private
showers
Bed & breakfast

per night:	£min	£max
Single	18.00	28.00
Double	35.00	40.00

Parking for 3

🚼🖵👃🔍🆙🔒✂📺📖🚗✳🗡🚜
🆂🅿

King's Tithe

🏅 **HIGHLY COMMENDED**

13a Comberton Road, Barton,
Cambridge CB3 7BA
☎ (01223) 263610
Fax (01223) 263610
*Guest often return to this up-market,
very quiet, private homely house. Two
twin bedrooms with adjacent bathroom
and separate toilet. Good bar food
available at local village pub. On
B1046 off A603 (exit junction 12 of
M11).*
Bedrooms: 2 twin
Bathrooms: 1 public
Bed & breakfast

per night:	£min	£max
Single	26.00	29.00
Double	38.00	43.00

Parking for 3
Open February–December

🚼🎱📭🖵👃🔍🆙🔒✂📺📖🚗
✳🚜

Leys Cottage 🏔

🏆 **APPROVED**

56 Wimpole Road, Barton,
Cambridge CB3 7AB
☎ (01223) 262482
Fax (01223) 264166
*Part 17th C house with modern
extension in a quiet and secluded spot
but within easy reach of Cambridge,
M11 and A14. On A603
Cambridge-Sandy road.*
Bedrooms: 1 single, 1 double, 1 twin
Bathrooms: 2 en-suite, 1 public
Bed & breakfast

per night:	£min	£max
Single	20.00	25.00
Double	32.00	38.00

Half board per person:	£min	£max
Daily	32.00	37.00

Evening meal 1900 (last orders
2030)
Parking for 4

🚼🖏📭🖵👃🔍🔒🆂✂🏴📺📖🚗⛵
✳🚜

Manor Farm

🏆🏆

Landbeach, Cambridge CB4 4ED
☎ (01223) 860165
*620-acre mixed farm. Grade II listed,
double-fronted, Georgian farmhouse,
surrounded by enclosed garden, in
centre of village next to church.*
Bedrooms: 1 double, 1 triple
Bathrooms: 2 en-suite
Bed & breakfast

per night:	£min	£max
Single	22.00	30.00
Double	35.00	40.00

Parking for 4

🚼📭🖵👃🆙🏴📖🚗🖊✳🗡🚜
🏠🆃

The Old Rectory

Listed

Green End, Landbeach, Cambridge
CB4 4ED
☎ (01223) 861507
Fax (01223) 441276
*Only 10 minutes from Cambridge
centre, historic spacious former rectory
in secluded grounds. Donkeys and rare
breed sheep. Antique furniture
throughout. All rooms en-suite. Aga
home cooking. Families welcome.*
Bedrooms: 2 double, 1 twin
Bathrooms: 3 en-suite, 1 public
Bed & breakfast

per night:	£min	£max
Single	22.00	25.00
Double	36.00	38.00

Parking for 11

🚼📭🖵👃🆙🔒🆂✂📺📖🚗✳🗡
🚜📭🆂🅿🏠

CAMBRIDGE
Continued

The Old Rectory
COMMENDED

High Street, Swaffham Bulbeck,
Cambridge CB5 OLX
☎ (01223) 811986 & 812009
*Georgian former vicarage set in own
grounds. Located 6 miles from
Cambridge and 4 miles from
Newmarket.*
Bedrooms: 1 double, 1 twin, 1 triple
Bathrooms: 1 en-suite, 1 public
Bed & breakfast

per night:	£min	£max
Single	20.00	30.00
Double	38.00	48.00

Parking for 10
🐾10⛺🖥️♨️UL♿S🍴🖾⛱️🏡🧺⚡🌳🚗
🏠

Segovia Lodge
⚜️

2 Barton Road, Newnham,
Cambridge CB3 9JZ
☎ (01223) 354105 & 323011
Fax (01223) 323011
*Within walking distance of the city
centre and colleges. Next to cricket and
tennis fields. Warm welcome, personal
service and both rooms with private
facilities. Non-smokers only, please.*
Bedrooms: 1 double, 1 twin
Bathrooms: 2 private, 1 public
Bed & breakfast

per night:	£min	£max
Double	40.00	45.00

Parking for 4
🐾10🖥️♨️🕯️🔌UL♿S✂️🖾TV🖾
🏡🌸🎯🍴🚗

CASTLE HEDINGHAM
Essex
Map ref 3B2

The Old School House
Listed

St Jame's Street, Castle Hedingham,
Halstead CO9 3EW
☎ Hedingham (01787) 461629
*Very comfortable self-contained
converted coachhouse, set in delightful
walled garden, with en-suite facilities
and private sitting room, offering a little
extra peace and privacy.*
Bedrooms: 2 twin
Bathrooms: 1 en-suite, 1 private
Bed & breakfast

per night:	£min	£max
Single	18.50	25.00
Double	37.00	40.00

Parking for 1
🐾8🖥️♨️🕯️🔌UL♿✂️🖾🏡🌸🚗
SP

CAWSTON
Norfolk
Map ref 3B1

*Village with one of the finest
churches in the country. St Agnes,
built in the Perpendicular style, was
much patronised by Michael de la
Pole, Earl of Suffolk (1414), and has a
magnificent hammer-beam roof and
numerous carved angels.*

Grey Gables Country House Hotel & Restaurant
⚜️⚜️

Norwich Road, Cawston, Norwich
NR10 4EY
☎ Norwich (01603) 871259

*Former rectory in pleasant, rural
setting, 10 miles from Norwich, coast
and Broads. Wine cellar, emphasis on
food. Comfortably furnished with many
antiques.*
Bedrooms: 2 single, 5 double, 1 twin
Bathrooms: 6 en-suite, 1 public
Bed & breakfast

per night:	£min	£max
Single	20.00	40.00
Double	40.00	60.00

Half board per person:	£min	£max
Daily	35.00	46.00
Weekly	235.00	246.00

Lunch available
Evening meal 1900 (last orders
2100)
Parking for 15
Cards accepted: Access, Visa
🐾10📞🖥️♨️🕯️🔌S✂️🖾🏡🧺🍴12
🔍🍷🌸🚗 SP 🏠 T

CHATTERIS
Cambridgeshire
Map ref 3A2

Cross Keys Inn Hotel
⚜️⚜️⚜️ **COMMENDED**

12-16 Market Hill, Chatteris
PE16 6BA
☎ March (01354) 693036 & 692644
Fax (01354) 693036

Map references apply to
the colour maps at the
back of this guide.

*Elizabethan coaching inn built around
1540, Grade II listed. A la carte menu
and bar meals. Friendly atmosphere,
oak-beamed lounge with log fires.
Ideally placed in the heart of the Fens.*
Bedrooms: 2 double, 4 twin, 1 triple
Bathrooms: 5 en-suite, 1 public
Bed & breakfast

per night:	£min	£max
Single	21.00	32.50
Double	32.50	55.00

Lunch available
Evening meal 1900 (last orders
2200)
Parking for 10
Cards accepted: Access, Visa, Diners,
Amex, Switch/Delta
🐾🍴📞🖥️♨️🕯️🔌S✂️🖾TV🖾
🏡🍷U🌸🚗 DAP SP 🏠 T

CHELMSFORD
Essex
Map ref 3B3

*The county town of Essex, originally
a Roman settlement, Caesaromagus,
thought to have been destroyed by
Boudicca. Growth of the town's
industry can be traced in the
excellent museum in Oaklands Park.
15th C parish church has been
Chelmsford Cathedral since 1914.*
*Tourist Information Centre ☎ (01245)
283400*

Neptune Cafe Motel
Listed APPROVED

Burnham Road, Latchingdon,
Chelmsford CM3 6EX
☎ Maldon (01621) 740770
*Cafe with adjoining chalet block, which
includes 2 units suitable for physically
disabled. Village location between
Maldon and Burnham-on-Crouch.*
Bedrooms: 4 double, 2 twin, 4 triple
Bathrooms: 10 en-suite
Bed & breakfast

per night:	£min	£max
Single	20.00	20.00
Double	30.00	30.00

Half board per person:	£min	£max
Daily	25.00	25.00

Lunch available
Parking for 40
🐾🔥🖥️♨️🕯️UL♿🍴🖾🌸🚗

CHOSELEY

Norfolk
Map ref 3B1

Choseley Farmhouse

Listed

Choseley, Docking, King's Lynn
PE31 8PQ
☎ Thornham (01485) 512331
17th C Norfolk farmhouse with Tudor chimneys. Foundations are thought to date back to original abbey of 1250.
Bedrooms: 1 double, 1 twin
Bathrooms: 1 public

Bed & breakfast

per night:	£min	£max
Single	15.00	
Double	30.00	

Parking for 10
Open July–September

🛏🎿🏃✕🐾🏠

COLCHESTER

Essex
Map ref 3B2

Britain's oldest recorded town standing on the River Colne and famous for its oysters. Numerous historic buildings, ancient remains and museums. Plenty of parks and gardens, extensive shopping centre, theatre and zoo.
Tourist Information Centre ☎ (01206) 282920

Darcy House

😑😑 **COMMENDED**

3-5 Culver Street East, Colchester
CO1 1LD
☎ (01206) 763938 & 768111
Georgian townhouse, built 1743, in town centre. Recently refurbished. En-suite first floor bedrooms, with colour TV and CH. Cafe and antiques room on ground floor.
Bedrooms: 3 double
Bathrooms: 3 en-suite

Bed & breakfast

per night:	£min	£max
Single	25.00	28.00
Double	45.00	50.00

Half board per

person:	£min	£max
Daily	35.00	40.00
Weekly	220.00	255.00

Lunch available
Evening meal 1730 (last orders 1930)
Cards accepted: Access, Visa, Switch/Delta

🛏12🖥🛆🏠💺🔲⬛🏠✕🐾🏠

The Maltings

Mersea Road, Abberton, Colchester
CO5 7NR
☎ (01206) 735780
Attractive period house with a wealth of beams and an open log fire, in walled garden with swimming pool.
Bedrooms: 1 single, 1 twin, 1 triple
Bathrooms: 2 public

Bed & breakfast

per night:	£min	£max
Single	15.00	20.00
Double	30.00	35.00

Parking for 8

🛏🎿🛆⬛🔲🏠💺🔲⬛🏠➰🐾🏠

Old House 🏨

COMMENDED

Ford Street, Aldham, Colchester
CO6 3PH
☎ (01206) 240456
Bed and breakfast in 14th C family home, listed as historic building, with friendly atmosphere, oak beams, log fires, large garden and ample parking. Between Harwich and Cambridge, Felixstowe and London. On A604, 5 miles west of Colchester.
Bedrooms: 1 single, 1 twin, 1 triple
Bathrooms: 1 en-suite, 2 private, 1 public

Bed & breakfast

per night:	£min	£max
Single	25.00	30.00
Double	35.00	45.00

Parking for 8
Cards accepted: Access, Visa, Switch/Delta

🛏🖥🔲🛆🛏💺🔲⬛🏠➰✕🐾🏠

Rose & Crown 🏨

😑😑😑 **COMMENDED**

East Street, Colchester CO1 2TZ
☎ (01206) 866677
Fax (01206) 866616

The oldest inn in the oldest recorded town in England. Early 15th C inn with charming en-suite bedrooms, log fire bar and noted restaurant. On Ipswich road 2 miles off A12 and half a mile from town centre.
Bedrooms: 1 single, 23 double, 2 twin, 4 triple
Bathrooms: 30 en-suite

Bed & breakfast

per night:	£min	£max
Single	49.00	58.00
Double	49.00	58.00

Half board per

person:	£min	£max
Daily	36.00	40.00

Lunch available
Evening meal 1900 (last orders 2200)
Parking for 60
Cards accepted: Access, Visa, Diners, Amex, Switch/Delta

🛏🎿🏠📞🔲🛆🛏💺🔲🏨📺🌑⬛🏠🏠🍴120🏷❄✕🐾🏠 SP 🏠 T

Silver Springs Restaurant and Motel 🏨

😑😑😑

Tenpenny Hill, Thorrington, Colchester CO7 8JG
☎ (01206) 250366
Fax (01206) 250700
A country motel set in acres of landscaped grounds with separate timbered restaurant, bar and conference facilities. On B1027, between Colchester and Clacton-on-Sea.
Bedrooms: 6 double, 6 twin, 7 triple, 2 family rooms
Suite available
Bathrooms: 21 en-suite

Bed & breakfast

per night:	£min	£max
Single	29.95	34.95
Double	39.95	49.95

Lunch available
Evening meal 1830 (last orders 2100)
Parking for 50
Cards accepted: Access, Visa, Diners, Amex, Switch/Delta

🛏🎿🔲🛆🛏💺✕🔲⬛🏠➰🍴60🐾❄✕ SP T

COMBERTON

Cambridgeshire
Map ref 2D1

The White House

😑 **COMMENDED**

196 Barton Road, Comberton, Cambridge CB3 7BU
☎ Cambridge (01223) 262886
5-acre dairy farm. Comfortable family home, warm and inviting. Cheesemaking demonstrations on Saturdays.
Bedrooms: 1 double, 1 twin
Bathrooms: 2 private showers

Bed & breakfast

per night:	£min	£max
Single	20.00	28.00
Double	35.00	48.00

Evening meal from 1830
Parking for 6

🛏4🔲🛆🛏⬛🛆🛏💺✕⬛🏠❄🐾 SP

COTTON

Suffolk
Map ref 3B2

Hill Farm

HIGHLY COMMENDED

Stonham Road, Cotton, Stowmarket
IP14 4RQ
☎ Bacton (01449) 780345
Fax (01449) 780345
*In tranquil open countryside, 16th C
moated country house set in 11 acres.
Spacious, beautifully furnished rooms,
fine food and wines.*
Bedrooms: 2 double
Suites available
Bathrooms: 1 en-suite, 1 private
Bed & breakfast

per night:	£min	£max
Single	31.00	36.00
Double	45.00	55.00

Half board per person:	£min	£max
Daily	44.50	52.50
Weekly	280.00	331.00

Evening meal 1800 (last orders
2100)
Parking for 20

CROMER

Norfolk
Map ref 3C1

Once a small fishing village and now
famous for its fishing boats that still
work off the beach and offer freshly
caught crabs. Excellent bathing on
sandy beaches fringed by cliffs. The
town boasts a fine pier, theatre,
museum and a lifeboat station.
*Tourist Information Centre ☎ (01263)
512497*

The Crowmere

Listed COMMENDED

4 Vicarage Road, Cromer
NR27 9DQ
☎ (01263) 513056
*Charming Victorian residence in quiet
road close to beach/town centre and all
amenities. Tea/coffee making facilities
and TV in all rooms. Most rooms are
en-suite. Family suites available.*
Bedrooms: 1 single, 4 double, 2 twin,
1 triple
Bathrooms: 6 en-suite, 1 public
Bed & breakfast

per night:	£min	£max
Single	18.00	28.00
Double	28.00	38.00

Parking for 6

DANBURY

Essex
Map ref 3B3

Southways

Listed

Copt Hill, Danbury, Chelmsford
CM3 4NN
☎ Chelmsford (01245) 223428
*Pleasant country house with large
garden adjoining an area of National
Trust common land.*
Bedrooms: 2 twin
Bathrooms: 1 public
Bed & breakfast

per night:	£min	£max
Single	18.00	18.00
Double	32.00	32.00

Parking for 2

DARSHAM

Suffolk
Map ref 3C2

Moate Hall

Listed

Darsham, Saxmundham IP17 3PP
☎ Saxmundham (01728) 668177
Fax (01728) 668177
*Attractive half-timbered house, ideally
situated between Aldeburgh and
Southwold and 3 miles from Heritage
Coast. Four poster bed, log fire, snooker
room, large garden, open views.*
Bedrooms: 2 double, 1 triple
Bathrooms: 2 en-suite, 1 private,
1 public
Bed & breakfast

per night:	£min	£max
Single	20.00	25.00
Double	40.00	50.00

Half board per person:	£min	£max
Daily	32.00	40.00
Weekly	200.00	250.00

Evening meal 1930 (last orders
2030)
Parking for 7

DEBDEN GREEN

Essex
Map ref 2D1

Wigmores Farm

Listed COMMENDED

Debden Green, Saffron Walden
CB11 3LX
☎ Thaxted (01371) 830050
*1000-acre arable farm. 16th C
thatched farmhouse in open
countryside, 1.5 miles from Thaxted,
just off the Thaxted to Debden road.*

Bedrooms: 1 double, 1 twin
Bathrooms: 2 public
Bed & breakfast

per night:	£min	£max
Single	20.00	20.00
Double	36.00	36.00

Half board per person:	£min	£max
Daily	31.00	33.00
Weekly	217.00	231.00

Lunch available
Evening meal 1900 (last orders
2100)
Parking for 12

DEDHAM

Essex
Map ref 3B2

A former wool town. Dedham Vale
is an Area of Outstanding Natural
Beauty and there is a countryside
centre in the village. This is John
Constable country and Sir Alfred
Munnings lived at Castle House
which is open to the public.

May's Barn Farm

HIGHLY COMMENDED

May's Lane, Off Long Road West,
Dedham, Colchester CO7 6EW
☎ Colchester (01206) 323191
*300-acre arable farm. Tranquil old
farmhouse with outstanding views over
Dedham Vale in Constable country.
Quarter mile down private lane.
Comfortable, spacious rooms, with
private facilities.*
Bedrooms: 1 double, 1 twin
Bathrooms: 1 en-suite, 1 private
Bed & breakfast

per night:	£min	£max
Single	22.00	25.00
Double	38.00	40.00

Parking for 5

WELCOME HOST

This is a nationally recognised
customer care programme
which aims to promote
the highest standards of
service and a warm welcome.
Establishments who are taking
part in this initiative are
indicated by the ⊚ symbol.

DEREHAM

Norfolk
Map ref 3B1

East Dereham is famous for its associations with the poet William Cowper and also Bishop Bonner, chaplain to Cardinal Wolsey. His home is now a museum. Around the charming market-place are many notable buildings.

Chapel Farm

Dereham Road, Whinburgh,
Dereham NR19 1AA
☎ (01362) 698433
Farmhouse B & B with full facilities, including CH, outdoor heated swimming pool, international standard snooker table. En-suite rooms. Pub close by.
Bedrooms: 3 double
Bathrooms: 3 en-suite, 1 public
Bed & breakfast

per night:	£min	£max
Single	17.00	17.00
Double	34.00	34.00

Parking for 10

Clinton House

Listed   HIGHLY COMMENDED

Well Hill, Clint Green, Yaxham,
Dereham NR19 1RX
☎ (01362) 692079
Charming 18th C country house, full of character, in peaceful location. Tennis/croquet. Good touring centre. Breakfast served in beautiful conservatory.
Bedrooms: 1 double, 1 twin, 1 triple
Bathrooms: 1 private, 2 public
Bed & breakfast

per night:	£min	£max
Single	18.00	22.00
Double	30.00	34.00

Parking for 10

Shilling Stone

Church Road, Old Beetley, Dereham
NR20 4AB
☎ (01362) 861099 & (0421) 306190
Country house 3 miles from Dereham. Rural outlook, convenient for Norfolk Broads, coast, Sandringham. Large, sunny rooms, home cooking, warm welcome. Children welcome.
Bedrooms: 1 single, 1 double, 1 twin
Bathrooms: 1 public

Bed & breakfast

per night:	£min	£max
Single	15.00	16.00
Double	30.00	30.00

Half board per person:	£min	£max
Daily	22.50	
Weekly	150.00	

Evening meal from 1830
Parking for 8

DISS

Norfolk
Map ref 3B2

Old market town built around 3 sides of the Mere, a placid water of 6 acres. Although modernised, some interesting Tudor, Georgian and Victorian buildings around the market-place remain. St Mary's church has a fine knapped flint chancel.
Tourist Information Centre ☎ (01379) 650523

Oxfootstone Granary

Low Common, South Lopham, Diss
IP22 2JS
☎ (01379) 687490
Converted barn in open countryside, erected in 1822. Guest rooms are situated in a single-storey wing, formerly cart-sheds, overlooking a large pond with waterfowl.
Bedrooms: 1 double, 1 twin
Suites available
Bathrooms: 2 en-suite
Bed & breakfast

per night:	£min	£max
Single	20.00	
Double	36.00	

Parking for 5

Rose Cottage

COMMENDED

Diss Road, Burston, Diss IP22 3TP
☎ (01379) 740602
Fax (01379) 740602

Delightful timber-framed 18th C house, situated on Church Green, opposite famous Burston Strike School. Parking and garden.
Bedrooms: 2 single, 1 double
Bathrooms: 3 private, 1 public

Bed & breakfast per night:	£min	£max
Single	20.00	
Double	38.00	

Parking for 3
Open April–September

Strenneth

COMMENDED

Airfield Road, Fersfield, Diss
IP22 2BP
☎ Bressingham (01379) 688182
Fax (01379) 688260
Family-run, 17th C period property. Log fires, oak beams. Executive and four-poster, all en-suite, some ground floor. Licensed. Pets most welcome. Close Bressingham Gardens.
Bedrooms: 4 double, 2 twin
Bathrooms: 6 en-suite, 1 public
Bed & breakfast

per night:	£min	£max
Single	25.00	
Double	36.00	

Parking for 10
Cards accepted: Access, Visa, Diners, Amex

EARLS COLNE

Essex
Map ref 3B2

Drum Inn

COMMENDED

21 High Street, Earls Colne,
Colchester CO6 2PA
☎ Bures (01787) 222368 & 222213
Traditional family-owned inn, on the A604 between Colchester and Halstead.
Bedrooms: 1 single, 2 double, 3 twin
Bathrooms: 3 en-suite, 1 private, 1 public
Bed & breakfast

per night:	£min	£max
Single		22.00

Lunch available
Evening meal 1900 (last orders 2200)
Parking for 6
Cards accepted: Access, Visa, Diners, Switch/Delta

A key to symbols can be found inside the back cover flap.

EAST BERGHOLT

Suffolk
Map ref 3B2

John Constable, the famous East Anglian artist, was born here in 1776 and at the church of St Mary are reminders of his family's associations with the area. 1 mile south of the village are Flatford Mill and Willy Lott's cottage, both made famous by Constable in his paintings.

Rosemary

Listed

Rectory Hill, East Bergholt, Colchester CO7 6TH
☎ Colchester (01206) 298241
Pleasant family house in lovely 1-acre garden in the National Garden Scheme. Wide variety of plants and old-fashioned roses. In centre of Constable country. A non-smoking establishment.
Bedrooms: 1 single, 2 twin
Bathrooms: 1 public

Bed & breakfast

per night:	£min	£max
Single	18.00	18.00
Double	36.00	36.00

Parking for 2

ELMSWELL

Suffolk
Map ref 3B2

Elmswell Hall Bed & Breakfast

Listed APPROVED

Elmswell Hall, Elmswell, Bury St Edmunds IP30 9EN
☎ (01359) 240215
Georgian house with large heated rooms, hearty breakfasts. Easy access A14. Good reasonably priced meals available locally. Ideal base for touring East Anglia.
Bedrooms: 1 double, 1 triple
Bathrooms: 1 public

Bed & breakfast

per night:	£min	£max
Single	17.50	17.50
Double	35.00	35.00

Evening meal 1930 (last orders 2030)
Parking for 6

Please mention this guide when making your booking.

ELY

Cambridgeshire
Map ref 3A2

Until the 17th C, when the Fens were drained, Ely was an island. The cathedral, completed in 1189, dominates the surrounding area. One particular feature is the central octagonal tower with a fan-vaulted timber roof and wooden lantern. *Tourist Information Centre ☎ (01353) 662062*

Hill House Farm ⚐

HIGHLY COMMENDED

9 Main Street, Coveney, Ely CB6 2DJ
☎ (01353) 778369
240-acre arable farm. High quality en-suite accommodation and food, in fine Victorian farmhouse. Situated in unspoilt Fenland village 3 miles west of Ely, with open views of the surrounding countryside and easy access to Cambridge. No smoking and no pets, please.
Bedrooms: 2 double, 1 twin
Bathrooms: 3 en-suite

Bed & breakfast

per night:	£min	£max
Single	25.00	34.00
Double	38.00	40.00

Parking for 4

Quarterway House ⚐

Ely Road, Little Thetford, Ely CB6 3HP
☎ (01353) 648964
Traditional-style CH house set in open countryside 2 miles from Ely. Relaxed, friendly atmosphere. Log fires, books, conservatory and garden. Private parking. Evening meals and special diets available.
Bedrooms: 1 double, 1 twin, 1 family room
Suites available
Bathrooms: 2 en-suite, 1 private, 1 public

Bed & breakfast

per night:	£min	£max
Single	20.00	20.00
Double	35.00	35.00

Half board per

person:	£min	£max
Daily	22.50	28.50
Weekly	155.00	214.50

Parking for 7
Cards accepted: Visa

Spinney Abbey ⚐

COMMENDED

Stretham Road, Wicken, Ely CB7 5XQ
☎ (01353) 720971

150-acre dairy farm. Spacious Georgian farmhouse set in 1 acre of garden. All rooms with private facilities. Farm borders Wicken Fen Nature Reserve.
Bedrooms: 1 double, 1 twin, 1 triple
Bathrooms: 2 en-suite, 1 private

Bed & breakfast

per night:	£min	£max
Double	38.00	38.00

Parking for 4

EPPING

Essex
Map ref 2D1

Epping retains its identity as a small market town despite its nearness to London. Epping Forest covers 2000 acres and at Chingford Queen Elizabeth I's Hunting Lodge houses a display on the forest's history and wildlife.

Uplands

Listed APPROVED

181a Lindsey Street, Epping CM16 6RF
☎ Waltham Cross (01992) 573733
Private house with rural views. Close to M25, M11 for Stansted Airport and Central Line underground for London. Payphone available.
Bedrooms: 2 single, 1 triple, 1 family room
Bathrooms: 2 public

Bed & breakfast

per night:	£min	£max
Single	16.00	16.00
Double	32.00	32.00

Parking for 6

EYKE

Suffolk
Map ref 3C2

The Old House

HIGHLY COMMENDED

Eyke, Woodbridge IP12 2QW
☎ (01394) 460213

Lovely Grade II listed house, c1600. Comfortable and friendly, with beams, open fires, large, interesting garden and views over Deben Valley. Centre of village and edge of heritage coast. Good choice of food. All rooms also let as singles.
Bedrooms: 1 double, 2 twin
Bathrooms: 3 en-suite
Bed & breakfast

per night:	£min	£max
Single	24.00	26.00
Double	38.00	42.00

Evening meal 1800 (last orders 1000)
Parking for 8

FELIXSTOWE

Suffolk
Map ref 3C2

Seaside resort that developed at the end of the 19th C. Lying in a gently curving bay with a 2-mile-long beach and backed by a wide promenade of lawns and floral gardens. Ferry links to the continent.
Tourist Information Centre ☎ (01394) 276770

Fludyer Arms Hotel ⚠

⚜⚜⚜ APPROVED
Undercliff Rd. East, Felixstowe
IP11 7LU
☎ (01394) 283279
Fax (01394) 670754
Closest hotel to the sea in Felixstowe. Two fully licensed bars and family room overlooking the sea. All rooms have superb sea views. Colour TV. Specialises in home-cooked food, with children's and vegetarian menus available.
Bedrooms: 3 single, 4 double, 1 twin
Bathrooms: 6 en-suite, 1 public
Bed & breakfast

per night:	£min	£max
Single	18.00	26.00
Double	32.00	40.00

Lunch available
Evening meal 1900 (last orders 2100)
Parking for 14
Cards accepted: Access, Visa, Amex

Sandlings

Listed
107 Cliff Road, Felixstowe IP11 9SA
☎ (01394) 672036
Modern detached house with ground floor bedrooms and 1st floor lounge with balcony giving panoramic sea views. Felixstowe Golf Club 100 yards, sailing and fishing close by. Ideal for exploring Suffolk coast and East Anglia generally.

Bedrooms: 1 single, 2 twin
Bathrooms: 1 en-suite, 1 public
Bed & breakfast

per night:	£min	£max
Single	20.00	20.00
Double	35.00	40.00

Parking for 5

FELSTED

Essex
Map ref 3B2

Potash Farm

⚜ COMMENDED
Cobblers Green, Causeway End Road, Felsted, Dunmow CM6 3LX
☎ Great Dunmow (01371) 820510
160-acre arable farm. Lovely old 15th C listed farmhouse set in a large half-moated garden, within walking distance of Felsted centre. Convenient for Stansted and London.
Bedrooms: 1 double, 2 twin
Bathrooms: 1 public
Bed & breakfast

per night:	£min	£max
Single	16.00	17.00
Double	30.00	32.00

Parking for 6

FRAMLINGHAM

Suffolk
Map ref 3C2

Pleasant old market town with an interesting church, impressive castle and some attractive houses round Market Hill. The town's history can be traced at the Lanman Museum.

Shimmens Pightle ⚠

Listed COMMENDED
Dennington Road, Framlingham, Woodbridge IP13 9JT
☎ (01728) 724036
Brian and Phyllis Collett's home is set in an acre of landscaped garden overlooking fields, on outskirts of Framlingham. Ground floor rooms with washbasins. Locally-cured bacon and home-made marmalade.
Bedrooms: 1 double, 2 twin
Bathrooms: 1 public
Bed & breakfast

per night:	£min	£max
Single	20.00	
Double	35.00	39.00

Parking for 5

FRESSINGFIELD

Suffolk
Map ref 3C2

Chippenhall Hall ⚠

⚜⚜⚜ HIGHLY COMMENDED
Fressingfield, Eye IP21 5TD
☎ Diss (01379) 586733 & 588180
Fax (01379) 586272
Listed Tudor manor, film location, heavily beamed and with inglenook fireplaces, in 7 secluded acres. Fine food and wines. 1 mile south of Fressingfield on B1116.
Bedrooms: 5 double
Bathrooms: 5 en-suite
Bed & breakfast

per night:	£min	£max
Single	49.00	58.00
Double	57.00	65.00

Half board per

person:	£min	£max
Daily	52.00	56.00
Weekly	348.00	377.00

Lunch available
Evening meal 1930 (last orders 1600)
Parking for 12
Cards accepted: Access, Visa

FRINTON-ON-SEA

Essex
Map ref 3C2

Sedate town that developed as a resort at the end of the 19th C and still retains an air of Victorian gentility. Fine sandy beaches, good fishing and golf.

Hodgenolls Farmhouse

⚜⚜ COMMENDED
Pork Lane, Great Holland, Frinton-on-Sea CO13 0ES
☎ Clacton (01255) 672054
Early 17th C timber-framed farmhouse in rural setting close to sandy beaches, Constable country, historic Colchester and Harwich. Non-smoking establishment.
Bedrooms: 2 double, 1 twin
Bathrooms: 1 en-suite, 1 public
Bed & breakfast

per night:	£min	£max
Single	25.00	25.00
Double	40.00	44.00

Parking for 5
Open March–October

GARBOLDISHAM

Norfolk
Map ref 3B2

Ingleneuk Lodge ♨

COMMENDED

Hopton Road, Garboldisham, Diss
IP22 2RQ
☎ (01953) 681541
Fax (01953) 681633

*Modern single-level home, family-run.
South-facing patio, riverside walk. Very
friendly atmosphere. On B1111, 1 mile
south of village.*
Wheelchair access category 2 ♿
Bedrooms: 2 single, 3 double, 2 twin
Bathrooms: 6 en-suite, 1 private,
1 public

**Bed & breakfast
per night:**

	£min	£max
Single	23.00	33.00
Double	37.50	51.00

**Half board per
person:**

	£min	£max
Daily	33.25	40.00
Weekly	199.00	306.00

Evening meal 1830 (last orders
1300)
Parking for 20
Cards accepted: Access, Visa, Amex,
Switch/Delta

GREAT BIRCHAM

Norfolk
Map ref 3B1

King's Head Hotel ♨

Great Bircham, King's Lynn PE31 6RJ
☎ Syderstone (01485) 578265
*Country inn with 3 bars, Italian
restaurant and beer gardens, near
Sandringham, King's Lynn and the
coast. English and Italian cuisine, fresh
Norfolk seafood and produce,
traditional Sunday lunch. Two-night
breaks available or longer.*
Bedrooms: 2 double, 3 twin
Bathrooms: 5 en-suite

**Bed & breakfast
per night:**

	£min	£max
Single	33.00	35.00
Double	53.00	58.00

**Half board per
person:**

	£min	£max
Daily	30.00	32.50
Weekly	210.00	227.50

Lunch available
Evening meal 1900 (last orders
2200)
Parking for 80
Cards accepted: Access, Visa

GREAT DUNMOW

Essex
Map ref 3B2

On the main Roman road from
Bishop's Stortford to Braintree.
Doctor's Pond near the square was
where the first lifeboat was tested
in 1785. Home of the Dunmow
Flitch trials held every 4 years on
Whit Monday.

Cowels Cottage

Cowels Farm Lane, Lindsell,
Dunmow CM6 3QG
☎ (01371) 870454
*Pink cottage, overlooking farmland in
tranquil, secluded garden. Centrally
heated, private sitting room and
bathrooms, TV. No traffic noise. 9 miles
Stansted Airport but not on a
flightpath.*
Bedrooms: 2 single, 1 family room
Bathrooms: 3 private

**Bed & breakfast
per night:**

	£min	£max
Single		20.00
Double		40.00

Parking for 4

Yarrow

COMMENDED

27 Station Road, Felsted, Great
Dunmow CM6 3HD
☎ (01371) 820878
*Edwardian house with south-facing
bedrooms, large garden and country
views. Ample parking. Quarter of a mile
to pubs and restaurants in lovely village.
20 minutes from Stansted/M11.*
Bedrooms: 2 double, 1 twin
Bathrooms: 1 en-suite, 1 private,
2 public

**Bed & breakfast
per night:**

	£min	£max
Single	16.00	18.00
Double	30.00	34.00

Parking for 6

GREAT RYBURGH

Norfolk
Map ref 3B1

The Boar Inn ♨

Listed

Great Ryburgh, Fakenham
NR21 0DX
☎ Fakenham (01328) 829212
*Village inn opposite Saxon church.
Beamed dining room and bar with
inglenook. Log fire in winter. En-suite
rooms available early 1997.*
Bedrooms: 1 single, 1 double, 1 twin
Bathrooms: 2 public

**Bed & breakfast
per night:**

	£min	£max
Single	17.00	22.00
Double	27.00	35.00

Lunch available
Evening meal 1900 (last orders
2130)
Parking for 20
Cards accepted: Access, Visa

GREAT YARMOUTH

Norfolk
Map ref 3C1

One of Britain's major seaside
resorts with 5 miles of seafront and
every possible amenity including an
award winning leisure complex
offering a huge variety of
all-weather facilities. Busy harbour
and fishing centre.

Spindrift Private Hotel ♨

APPROVED

36 Wellesley Road, Great Yarmouth
NR30 1EU
☎ (01493) 858674
Fax (01493) 858674
*Attractively situated small private hotel,
close to all amenities and with Beach
Coach Station and car park at rear.
Front bedrooms overlook gardens and
sea.*
Bedrooms: 2 single, 2 double, 1 twin,
1 triple, 1 family room
Bathrooms: 5 private, 1 public

**Bed & breakfast
per night:**

	£min	£max
Single	16.00	26.00
Double	28.00	40.00

Cards accepted: Access, Visa, Amex

Please check prices and other
details at the time of booking.

HADLEIGH

Suffolk
Map ref 3B2

Former wool town, lying on a tributary of the River Stour. The church of St Mary stands among a remarkable cluster of medieval buildings.
Tourist Information Centre ☎ (01473) 823824

The Marquis of Cornwallis ⚤

👑👑 COMMENDED

Upper Layham, Hadleigh, Ipswich IP7 5JZ
☎ (01473) 822051
Fax (01473) 822051
Large public house in 2 acres of grounds leading down to River Brett, between Constable country and Lavenham.
Bedrooms: 2 double, 1 twin
Bathrooms: 2 en-suite, 1 private, 1 public

Bed & breakfast

per night:	£min	£max
Single	29.00	29.00
Double	41.00	41.00

Lunch available
Evening meal 1900 (last orders 2130)
Parking for 22
Cards accepted: Access, Visa, Diners, Amex, Switch/Delta

Odds and Ends House ⚤

👑👑

131 High Street, Hadleigh, Ipswich IP7 5EG
☎ Ipswich (01473) 822032
Fax (01473) 822032
Comfortable house within walking distance of shops, pubs, restaurants and swimming pool. Ground floor rooms with wheelchair facilities available in recently converted garden annexe.
Wheelchair access category 3🕪
Bedrooms: 1 single, 3 double, 4 twin
Bathrooms: 6 en-suite, 1 public

Bed & breakfast

per night:	£min	£max
Single	20.00	30.00
Double	40.00	48.00

Parking for 3

Spider Hall

Listed

Lower Raydon, Ipswich IP7 5QN
☎ Ipswich (01473) 822585
Fax (01473) 824820
Charming 15th C farmhouse, Grade II listed, in rural setting with lovely views.

Convenient for many places of historic interest, ideal touring area.
Bedrooms: 1 double, 1 twin
Bathrooms: 1 public

Bed & breakfast

per night:	£min	£max
Single	18.00	20.00
Double	36.00	40.00

Parking for 6

HALESWORTH

Suffolk
Map ref 3C2

Small market town which grew firstly with navigation on the Blyth in the 18th C and then with the coming of the railways in the 19th C. Opposite the church in a beautiful 14th C building is the Halesworth Gallery.

Wissett Vineyards ⚤

👑 COMMENDED

Valley Farm, Wissett, Halesworth IP19 0JJ
☎ Linstead (01986) 785216 & mobile (0421) 625286
Fax (01986) 785443
14-acre vineyard. 16th C farmhouse, fully-modernised, standing in mature gardens of great interest. Set in one of the best known East Anglian vineyards.
Bedrooms: 2 double
Bathrooms: 1 en-suite, 1 private

Bed & breakfast

per night:	£min	£max
Single	23.00	25.00
Double	42.00	46.00

Parking for 10

HARWICH

Essex
Map ref 3C2

Port where the Rivers Orwell and Stour converge and enter the North Sea. The old town still has a medieval atmosphere with its narrow streets. To the south is the seaside resort of Dovercourt with long sandy beaches.
Tourist Information Centre ☎ (01255) 506139

Una House

👑

1 Una Road, Parkeston, Harwich CO12 4PP
☎ (01255) 551390
Three storey end-of-terrace Victorian house within walking distance of ferries. Comfortable and friendly atmosphere.

From A120 follow Parkeston Quay ferry terminal sign. First house on left from roundabout.
Bedrooms: 1 single, 2 twin
Bathrooms: 1 en-suite, 2 private

Bed & breakfast

per night:	£min	£max
Single	20.00	25.00
Double	35.00	45.00

Half board per

person:	£min	£max
Daily	30.00	35.00

Evening meal 1930 (last orders 2130)
Parking for 3

HATFIELD PEVEREL

Essex
Map ref 3B3

The Wick

Listed COMMENDED

Terling Hall Road, Hatfield Peverel, Chelmsford CM3 2EZ
☎ Chelmsford (01245) 380705
Grade II listed 16th C farmhouse in rural setting. Large garden. Easy access to London, Suffolk and East Coast ports.
Bedrooms: 1 single, 1 twin
Bathrooms: 1 private, 2 public

Bed & breakfast

per night:	£min	£max
Single	18.50	20.00
Double	38.00	40.00

Half board per

person:	£min	£max
Daily	28.50	31.00

Evening meal 1830 (last orders 1930)
Parking for 4

HEMINGFORD GREY

Cambridgeshire
Map ref 3A2

38 High Street

👑 COMMENDED

Hemingford Grey, Huntingdon PE18 9BJ
☎ St Ives (01480) 301203
Private detached house in centre of village, with large garden and quiet surroundings. Warm welcome, hearty breakfasts. 1 mile from the A14. Sorry, no smoking or pets.
Bedrooms: 2 single, 2 double
Bathrooms: 1 public

Continued ▶

HEMINGFORD GREY

Continued

Bed & breakfast per night:	£min	£max
Single	19.00	19.00
Double	38.00	38.00

Parking for 4
Open January–November

🏇🔟🦮♿🍴🖤UL🔒S✂📺🎥💼🅿❄✕🚁

HETHERSETT

Norfolk
Map ref 3B1

Magnolia House

Listed APPROVED

Cromwell Close, Hethersett
NR9 3HD
☎ Norwich (01603) 810749
Fax (01603) 810749
Family-run B & B. All rooms centrally heated, colour TV, hot and cold water, tea/coffee making facilities, own key. Laundry, public telephone and fax available. Private car park.
Bedrooms: 3 single, 1 double, 1 twin
Bathrooms: 4 public

Bed & breakfast per night:	£min	£max
Single	16.00	20.00
Double	30.00	34.00

Parking for 7
Cards accepted: Diners

🏇6♿🖥🍴🖤UL✂🎥📺💼🅿❄ ✕🚁 DAP SP

HEVINGHAM

Norfolk
Map ref 3B1

Marsham Arms Inn ⚠

⚜⚜⚜ COMMENDED

Holt Road, Hevingham, Norwich
NR10 5NP
☎ (01603) 754268
Fax (01603) 754839
Set in peaceful Norfolk countryside within reach of Norwich, the Broads and the coast. Comfortable and spacious accommodation, good food and a fine selection of ales.
Bedrooms: 3 double, 5 twin
Suites available
Bathrooms: 8 en-suite

Bed & breakfast per night:	£min	£max
Single	40.00	45.00
Double	45.00	55.00

Lunch available
Evening meal 1800 (last orders 2200)

Parking for 100
Cards accepted: Access, Visa, Amex, Switch/Delta

🏇🛃📞🖥🍴♿🖤🔒S✂📺💼🅿 🍴50🏴❄🚁 SP 🎹

HIGHAM

Suffolk
Map ref 3B2

Bauble ⚠

⚜⚜ HIGHLY COMMENDED

Higham, Colchester, Essex CO7 6LA
☎ (01206) 337254
Fax (01206) 337263
Modernised country house in mature gardens adjacent to the Rivers Brett and Stour. Ideal for touring Constable country and wool industry villages. Will accept children over 12 years old.
Bedrooms: 1 single, 2 twin
Bathrooms: 2 en-suite, 1 private

Bed & breakfast per night:	£min	£max
Single	22.00	25.00
Double	40.00	45.00

Parking for 5

🏇12🖥🍴♿🖤UL🔒🛄✂🎥💼🅿🚗 🔍❄✕🚁

HOVETON

Norfolk
Map ref 3C1

The Beehive

Listed COMMENDED

Riverside Road, Hoveton, Wroxham, Norwich NR12 8UD
☎ Norwich (01603) 784107
Large thatched riverside residence situated in a picturesque position on the Broads. Idyllic views from every aspect.
Bedrooms: 1 double, 2 twin
Bathrooms: 1 public

Bed & breakfast per night:	£min	£max
Single	25.00	
Double	39.00	

Parking for 6
Open April–October

🖥🖤♿🖤UL🔒S✂💼🅿🚗♪✕🚁

The symbols in each entry give information about services and facilities. A 'key' to these symbols appears at the back of this guide.

HUNTINGDON

Cambridgeshire
Map ref 3A2

Attractive, interesting town which abounds in associations with the Cromwell family. The town is connected to Godmanchester by a beautiful 14th C bridge over the River Great Ouse.
Tourist Information Centre ☎ (01480) 388588

Prince of Wales ⚠

⚜⚜ COMMENDED

Potton Road, Hilton, Huntingdon
PE18 9NG
☎ (01480) 830257
Fax (01480) 830257
Traditional village inn renowned for its traditional ales and good value food. Convenient for St Ives, Huntingdon, St Neots and Cambridge. On B1040, south-east of Huntingdon.
Bedrooms: 2 single, 1 double, 1 twin
Bathrooms: 4 en-suite

Bed & breakfast per night:	£min	£max
Single	20.00	35.00
Double	40.00	50.00

Lunch available
Evening meal 1900 (last orders 2115)
Parking for 9
Cards accepted: Access, Visa, Amex, Switch/Delta

🏇5📞🖥🍴♿🖤🎥💼🅿🚗🔍U❄ 🚁 SP T

INGATESTONE

Essex
Map ref 3B3

Eibiswald

Listed HIGHLY COMMENDED

85 Mill Road, Stock, Ingatestone
CM4 9LR
☎ Stock (01277) 840631
Fax (01277) 840631
Anglo-Austrian hospitality. Comfortable, modern house in quiet, pleasant rural surroundings. Close to village centre. Railway 4 miles. Convenient for Chelmsford, Brentwood, Basildon. 5 minutes from A12 on B1007, signposted Billericay.
Bedrooms: 3 double
Bathrooms: 1 en-suite, 1 public

Bed & breakfast per night:	£min	£max
Single	25.00	32.00
Double	37.00	44.00

Parking for 7

🏇12🖥🍴♿🖤UL🔒S✂📺💼🅿U ❄✕🚁 T

KELVEDON

Essex
Map ref 3B3

Village on the old Roman road from Colchester to London. Many of the buildings are 18th C but there is much of earlier date. The famous preacher Charles Spurgeon was born here in 1834.

Highfields Farm
COMMENDED

Kelvedon, Colchester CO5 9BJ
☎ (01376) 570334
Fax (01376) 570334
700-acre arable & horses farm. Farmhouse in quiet location in open countryside. Easy access to A12. Heating in all rooms.
Bedrooms: 2 twin, 1 triple
Bathrooms: 2 en-suite, 1 private

Bed & breakfast per night:

	£min	£max
Single		20.00
Double	34.00	36.00

Parking for 6

KERSEY

Suffolk
Map ref 3B2

A most picturesque village, which was famous for cloth-making, set in a valley with a water-splash. The church of St Mary is an impressive building at the top of the hill.

Fair View
HIGHLY COMMENDED

Priory Hill, Kersey, Ipswich IP7 6DU
☎ Ipswich (01473) 828606
Converted 17th C cottages with beams and inglenooks. Village location, stunning views of church. Convenient for Constable country and coast.
Bedrooms: 1 twin
Bathrooms: 1 en-suite

Bed & breakfast per night:

	£min	£max
Single	24.00	36.00
Double	36.00	42.00

Parking for 1

Red House Farm
Listed COMMENDED

Kersey, Ipswich IP7 6EY
☎ Boxford (01787) 210245
Listed farmhouse between Kersey and Boxford, central for Constable country. Rooms have TV and tea-making facilities. Swimming pool.
Bedrooms: 1 single, 1 double, 1 twin
Bathrooms: 2 en-suite, 1 public

Bed & breakfast per night:

	£min	£max
Single	20.00	22.00
Double	36.00	40.00

Half board per person:

	£min	£max
Daily	28.00	30.00
Weekly	196.00	210.00

Evening meal 1900 (last orders 1000)
Parking for 5
Cards accepted: Diners

KING'S LYNN

Norfolk
Map ref 3B1

A busy town with many outstanding buildings. The Guildhall and Town Hall are both built of flint in a striking chequer design. Behind the Guildhall in the Old Gaol House the sounds and smells of prison life 2 centuries ago are recreated.
Tourist Information Centre ☎ (01553) 763044

Maranatha Guest House
APPROVED

115 Gaywood Road, Gaywood, King's Lynn PE30 2PU
☎ (01553) 774596
Large carrstone and brick residence with gardens front and rear, 10 minutes' walk from town centre, Lynnsport and Queen Elizabeth Hospital. Direct road to Sandringham and the coast.
Bedrooms: 2 single, 2 double, 3 twin
Bathrooms: 2 en-suite, 1 private, 1 public

Bed & breakfast per night:

	£min	£max
Single	17.00	20.00
Double	28.00	32.00

Half board per person:

	£min	£max
Daily	22.00	
Weekly	154.00	

Lunch available
Evening meal 1800 (last orders 1800)
Parking for 9

Marsh Farm
COMMENDED

Wolferton, King's Lynn PE31 6HB
☎ Dersingham (01485) 540265
Fax (01485) 543143
755-acre arable farm. Farmhouse on working farm in quiet village of Wolferton, on the Norfolk coast, close to Sandringham. Links and inland golf-courses nearby. Coastal and rural walks.
Bedrooms: 2 double
Bathrooms: 1 en-suite, 1 private

Bed & breakfast per night:

	£min	£max
Single	20.00	20.00
Double	40.00	40.00

Parking for 5

KINGS LANGLEY

Hertfordshire
Map ref 2D1

Woodcote House
COMMENDED

7 The Grove, Chipperfield Road, Kings Langley WD4 9JF
☎ (01923) 262077
Fax (01923) 266198
Timber-framed house, sitting in 1 acre of landscaped gardens with quiet rural aspect. Convenient for M1 and M25 and close to Watford and Hemel Hempstead.
Bedrooms: 2 single, 1 double, 1 twin
Bathrooms: 4 en-suite

Half board per person:

	£min	£max
Daily	20.00	24.00

Evening meal 1800 (last orders 2100)
Parking for 8

LAVENHAM

Suffolk
Map ref 3B2

A former prosperous wool town of timber-framed buildings with the cathedral-like church and its tall tower. The market-place is 13th C and the Guildhall now houses a museum.

The Red House
COMMENDED

29 Bolton Street, Lavenham, Sudbury CO10 9RG
☎ (01787) 248074 & (0585) 536148
Attractive Victorian house, recently renovated. Comfortable en-suite bedrooms, pretty sitting room. Country garden. Evening meal by prior arrangement. Only a step from pubs.
Bedrooms: 2 double, 1 twin
Bathrooms: 3 en-suite

Bed & breakfast per night:

	£min	£max
Single	30.00	45.00
Double	45.00	45.00

Continued ▶

235

LAVENHAM

Continued

Parking for 8
Open February–December
🐎3 ⚲ ⓤⓁ ✠ 🅿 TV ▥ ➷ ✿ 🐎

LITTLE WENHAM

Suffolk
Map ref 3B2

Grove Farm House ⚠

🏵 COMMENDED

Little Wenham, Colchester
CO7 6QB
☎ Great Wenham (01473) 310341
190-acre arable farm. Comfortable
listed farmhouse in quiet rural setting,
15 minutes from Ipswich. Convenient
for Constable country and the coast.
Bedrooms: 1 single, 1 double, 1 twin
Bathrooms: 1 public

Bed & breakfast

per night:	£min	£max
Single	16.00	
Double	32.00	

Half board per

person:	£min	£max
Daily	23.50	28.00

Evening meal 1830 (last orders
2000)
Parking for 5
📧▤☐ ⚲ ⓤⓁ 🛈 ✠ 🅿 TV ▥ ➷ ✿ 🐎

LONG MELFORD

Suffolk
Map ref 3B2

One of Suffolk's loveliest villages,
remarkable for the length of its
main street. Holy Trinity Church is
considered to be the finest village
church in England. The National
Trust own the Elizabethan Melford
Hall and nearby Kentwell Hall is also
open to the public.

The George & Dragon ⚠

🏵 COMMENDED

Long Melford, Sudbury CO10 9JB
☎ Sudbury (01787) 371285
Fax (01787) 312428
English country inn offering traditional
service and hospitality. The best in both
beer and food.
Bedrooms: 2 double, 3 twin, 1 triple
Bathrooms: 5 en-suite, 1 private
shower

Bed & breakfast

per night:	£min	£max
Single	30.00	30.00
Double	50.00	50.00

Half board per

person:	£min	£max
Daily	40.00	50.00

Lunch available
Evening meal 1800 (last orders
2200)
Parking for 20
Cards accepted: Access, Visa,
Switch/Delta
📧 ⚲ ▤☐ ☎ ☐ 🛈 ✠ 🅿 TV ▥ ➷
📺30 🖐 ↻ ✿ DAP ✎ SP 🏠

LOWESTOFT

Suffolk
Map ref 3C1

Seaside town with wide sandy
beaches. Important fishing port with
picturesque fishing quarter. Home of
the famous Lowestoft porcelain and
birthplace of Benjamin Britten. East
Point Pavilion's exhibition describes
the Lowestoft story.
*Tourist Information Centre ☎ (01502)
523000 or 523057*

Church Farm ⚠

Listed HIGHLY COMMENDED

Corton, Lowestoft NR32 5HX
☎ (01502) 730359
Fax (01502) 730359

220-acre arable farm. Victorian
farmhouse with clean and comfortable
accommodation of high standard and a
warm, welcoming atmosphere. Situated
3 miles north of Lowestoft near quiet,
rural coastline and within easy reach of
beautiful Broadland and many local
attractions. Traditional English
breakfast. Non-smoking establishment.
Bedrooms: 3 double
Bathrooms: 3 en-suite

Bed & breakfast

per night:	£min	£max
Single	25.00	25.00
Double	36.00	38.00

Parking for 4
Open March–October
♿ 📧▤☐ ⚲ ⓤⓁ 🛈 ✠ ▥ ➷ ✿ ✕ 🐎

Hall Farm ⚠

Listed COMMENDED

Jay Lane, Church Lane, Lound,
Lowestoft NR32 5LJ
☎ (01502) 730415
101-acre arable farm. Traditional 16th
C Suffolk farmhouse within 2 miles of
the sea. Clean, comfortable
accommodation with generous English

breakfast. Farm down a quiet, private
lane half-a-mile from A12.
Bedrooms: 1 single, 1 double,
1 triple
Bathrooms: 2 private, 1 public

Bed & breakfast

per night:	£min	£max
Single	16.00	18.00
Double	34.00	36.00

Parking for 6
Open March–September
🐎 ⚲ ⓤⓁ 🛈 ✠ 🅿 TV ▥ ➷ 🐎 DAP 🏠

MANNINGTREE

Essex
Map ref 3B2

On the estuary of the River Stour.
The village has many interesting
Georgian and Victorian buildings
and the Strand attracts swans in
great numbers.

Aldhams

🏵🏵 COMMENDED

Bromley Road, Lawford,
Manningtree CO11 2NE
☎ Colchester (01206) 393210
Fax (01255) 870722

Lutyens style converted farmhouse
stands elegantly down a lime avenue, in
a beautiful garden. Large sitting room
with fire where refreshments are
served. Wonderfully peaceful.
Bedrooms: 1 single, 1 double, 1 twin
Bathrooms: 2 private, 1 public

Bed & breakfast

per night:	£min	£max
Single	25.00	30.00
Double	40.00	45.00

Parking for 10
🐎✕📧▤☐ ⚲ ⓤⓁ 🛈 ✠ 🅿 TV ▥ ➷ ✿
🐕 🐎

MARGARET RODING

Essex
Map ref 2D1

Greys

Listed COMMENDED

Ongar Road, Margaret Roding,
Dunmow CM6 1QR
☎ Good Easter (01245) 231509
340-acre arable and mixed farm.
Formerly 2 cottages pleasantly situated
on family farm just off A1060 at
telephone kiosk. Beamed throughout,

large garden. Tea/coffee available.
Charge for single occupancy by
arrangement.
Bedrooms: 2 double, 1 twin
Bathrooms: 1 public
Bed & breakfast

per night:	£min	£max
Double	36.00	40.00

Parking for 6

MUNDESLEY

Norfolk
Map ref 3C1

Small seaside resort with a superb
sandy beach and excellent bathing.
Nearby is a smock-mill still with cap
and sails.

The Grange

COMMENDED

High Street, Mundesley, Norwich
NR11 8JL
☎ (01263) 721556
Beautiful, well-furnished house with
friendly atmosphere, in attractive
garden. Ideal for the Broads and
Norwich, bird-watching, fishing and
beach.
Bedrooms: 2 double, 1 twin, 1 triple
Bathrooms: 2 public
Bed & breakfast

per night:	£min	£max
Single	17.00	18.00
Double	34.00	36.00

Parking for 10

NAYLAND

Suffolk
Map ref 3B2

Charmingly located village on the
River Stour owing its former
prosperity to the cloth trade. The
hub of the village is 15th C Alston
Court. The altar-piece of St James
Church was painted by John
Constable.

Leavenheath Farm

Listed HIGHLY COMMENDED

Locks Lane, Leavenheath, Colchester
CO6 4PF
☎ Colchester (01206) 262322 &
262938
Fax (01206) 262322

30-acre mixed farm. Small fruit farm

---

with pedigree sheep, free-range
chickens, geese and ancient bluebell
wood in Stour Valley. Lovely refurbished
oak-beamed Suffolk farmhouse
offering peace and tranquillity with
home cooking. Winter log fires and a
warm welcome.
Bedrooms: 2 double, 2 twin
Bathrooms: 3 en-suite, 1 public
Bed & breakfast

per night:	£min	£max
Single	20.00	25.00
Double	36.00	45.00

Half board per person:	£min	£max
Daily	32.00	35.00

Lunch available
Evening meal 1900 (last orders
2100)
Parking for 26

NEWMARKET

Suffolk
Map ref 3B2

Centre of the English horse-racing
world and the headquarters of the
Jockey Club and National Stud.
Racecourse and horse sales. The
National Horse Racing Museum
traces the history and development
of the Sport of Kings.
Tourist Information Centre ☎ (01638)
667200

Westley House

Listed

Westley Waterless, Newmarket
CB8 0RQ
☎ (01638) 508112
Fax (01638) 508113
Spacious Georgian-style former rectory
in quiet rural area 5 miles south of
Newmarket and convenient for
Cambridge. Large comfortable
bedrooms and drawing room opening
on to 5 acres of garden, trees and
paddocks. Visitors are our guests.
Advance bookings only, please.
Bedrooms: 1 single, 2 twin
Bathrooms: 1 private, 1 public
Bed & breakfast

per night:	£min	£max
Single	18.50	20.00
Double	37.00	40.00

Half board per person:	£min	£max
Daily	30.00	32.00
Weekly	180.00	200.00

Evening meal 1930 (last orders
2100)
Parking for 6

NORFOLK BROADS

See under Aylsham, Cawston, Great
Yarmouth, Hevingham, Hoveton,
North Walsham, Norwich, Rackheath,
Rollesby, South Walsham, Wroxham

NORTH WALSHAM

Norfolk
Map ref 3C1

Weekly market has been held here
for 700 years. 1 mile south of town
is a cross commemorating the
Peasants' Revolt of 1381. Nelson
attended the local Paston Grammar
School, founded in 1606 and still
flourishing.

Geoffrey the Dyer House

Church Plain, Worstead, North
Walsham NR28 9AL
☎ Smallburgh (01692) 536562
Carefully restored 17th C weaver's
residence, full of character and
comfort, close to beach, Broads and
Norwich. In centre of conservation
village.
Bedrooms: 2 double, 1 twin
Bathrooms: 3 en-suite
Bed & breakfast

per night:	£min	£max
Single	16.50	24.00
Double	33.00	40.00

Half board per person:	£min	£max
Daily	25.00	28.50

Lunch available
Evening meal 1830 (last orders
2200)
Parking for 4
Cards accepted: Diners

NORWICH

Norfolk
Map ref 3C1

Beautiful cathedral city and county
town on the River Wensum with
many fine museums and medieval
churches. Norman castle, Guildhall
and interesting medieval streets.
Good shopping centre and market.
Tourist Information Centre ☎ (01603)
666071

Cavell House

Listed

Swardeston, Norwich NR14 8D2
☎ Mulbarton (01508) 578195
Birthplace of nurse Edith Cavell.
Georgian farmhouse on edge of
Swardeston village. Off B1113 south of
Continued ▶

NORWICH

Continued

Norwich, 5 miles from centre. Rural setting. Close to university.
Bedrooms: 1 single, 1 double, 1 twin
Bathrooms: 2 public
Bed & breakfast

per night:	£min	£max
Single	10.00	18.00
Double	30.00	35.00

Lunch available
Parking for 10

Kingsley Lodge

COMMENDED

3 Kingsley Road, Norwich NR1 3RB
☎ (01603) 615819
Fax (01603) 615819

Quiet, friendly Edwardian house near bus station, under 10 minutes' walk to city centre. Spacious bedrooms with en-suite bathrooms, TV, tea/coffee making facilities. No smoking.
Bedrooms: 1 single, 1 double, 1 twin
Bathrooms: 3 en-suite
Bed & breakfast

per night:	£min	£max
Single	23.00	25.00
Double	36.00	38.00

Open February–December

Oakfield

HIGHLY COMMENDED

Yelverton Road, Framingham Earl,
Norwich NR14 7SD
☎ Framingham Earl (01508) 492605
Superior accommodation in beautiful, quiet setting on edge of village 4 miles south-east of Norwich. Splendid breakfasts. Local pubs serve good evening meals.
Bedrooms: 1 single, 1 double, 1 twin
Bathrooms: 1 en-suite, 1 public
Bed & breakfast

per night:	£min	£max
Single	20.00	24.00
Double	39.00	44.00

Parking for 6

The Old Rectory

Listed

Hall Road, Framingham Earl,
Norwich NR14 7SB
☎ Framingham Earl (01508) 493590
Beautifully renovated and extended 17th C family house set in 2 acres of country garden. Wealth of beams in lounge and dining room. Village 5 miles south-east of Norwich.
Bedrooms: 1 double, 1 twin
Bathrooms: 1 public
Bed & breakfast

per night:	£min	£max
Single	21.00	24.00
Double	38.00	38.00

Parking for 6

Rosedale

Listed

145 Earlham Road, Norwich
NR2 3RG
☎ (01603) 453743
Friendly, family-run Victorian guesthouse and restaurant on main B1108, 1 mile from city centre. Shopping centre, restaurants and university nearby.
Bedrooms: 3 single, 1 double, 2 twin, 2 triple
Bathrooms: 2 public
Bed & breakfast

per night:	£min	£max
Single	15.00	20.00
Double	30.00	34.00

Parking for 2

Witton Hall Farm

COMMENDED

Witton, Norwich NR13 5DN
☎ (01603) 714580
500-acre dairy farm. Elegant Georgian farmhouse in the heart of Norfolk. Peaceful, mature grounds. Swimming pool in walled garden.
Bedrooms: 2 double, 1 twin
Bathrooms: 3 en-suite
Bed & breakfast

per night:	£min	£max
Single	20.00	34.00
Double	32.00	34.00

Parking for 4
Cards accepted: Diners

ONGAR

Essex
Map ref 2D1

Bumbles

Listed COMMENDED

Moreton Road, Ongar CM5 OEZ
☎ (01277) 362695
Fax (01277) 365245
2-acre smallholding. 200-year-old cottage with beams and inglenook fireplace. Easy access to London, M11, M25 and main towns in area.
Bedrooms: 3 twin
Bathrooms: 2 public
Bed & breakfast

per night:	£min	£max
Single	17.00	20.00
Double	34.00	36.00

Parking for 6

PEASENHALL

Suffolk
Map ref 3C2

Sibton White Horse

Listed

Halesworth Road, Sibton, Peasenhall,
Saxmundham IP17 2JJ
☎ (01728) 660337
Quiet 16th C inn on the outskirts of Peasenhall, set in 3 secluded acres. Accommodation is modern and separate. Restaurant, bar meals. Play area.
Bedrooms: 2 single, 3 double, 3 twin, 1 family room
Bathrooms: 7 en-suite, 2 private
Bed & breakfast

per night:	£min	£max
Single	18.00	19.00
Double	32.00	36.00

Lunch available
Evening meal 1900 (last orders 2100)
Parking for 50

For ideas on places to visit refer to the introduction at the beginning of this section.

All accommodation in this guide has been graded, or is awaiting a grading, by a trained Tourist Board inspector.

Half board prices are given per person, but in some cases these may be based on double/twin occupancy.

PETERBOROUGH

Cambridgeshire
Map ref 3A1

Prosperous and rapidly expanding cathedral city on the edge of the Fens on the River Nene. Catherine of Aragon is buried in the cathedral. City Museum and Art Gallery. Ferry Meadows Country Park has numerous leisure facilities.
Tourist Information Centre ☎ (01733) 317336

Stoneacre 🅜
🏵🏵 COMMENDED
Elton Road, Wansford, Peterborough PE8 6JT
☎ Stamford (01780) 783283
Modern country house in rural and secluded position with delightful views across the Nene Valley. Half a mile from A1, 10 minutes from Peterborough and Stamford. Large grounds with mini golf-course.
Bedrooms: 4 double, 1 twin
Bathrooms: 3 en-suite, 1 public

Bed & breakfast per night:	£min	£max
Single	22.00	38.00
Double	28.00	44.00

Parking for 24
🛇🖙5🖧🖛🎛🛒⬜🖵📵🖼⬜🚼💈⬝⛔📺🖭
🖺🕯🛇20🕿🔱🌼🐎 SP 🎏 T

POTTER HEIGHAM

Norfolk
Map ref 3C1

On the River Thurne, the village is one of the most popular of the Broadland centres and is well known for its 13th C bridge and boatyard. The thatched church has a rare octagonal font made of brick.

Falgate Inn
🏵🏵 COMMENDED
Main Road, Potter Heigham, Great Yarmouth NR29 5HZ
☎ (01692) 670003 & mobile (0585) 735068
Bed and breakfast, with restaurant, bar snacks and beer garden. Open 7 days a week, full on-licence.
Bedrooms: 1 single, 1 double, 2 twin, 1 triple
Bathrooms: 2 en-suite, 1 public

Bed & breakfast per night:	£min	£max
Single	17.00	21.00
Double	34.00	42.00

Lunch available
Evening meal 1900 (last orders 2130)
Cards accepted: Access, Visa, Switch/Delta
🛇🖙⬝🛒S🖭⬝🌼🚐

RACKHEATH

Norfolk
Map ref 3C1

Barn Court 🅜
Listed APPROVED
6 Back Lane, Rackheath, Norwich NR13 6NN
☎ Norwich (01603) 782536
Fax (01603) 782536
Spacious accommodation in a traditional Norfolk barn conversion, built around a courtyard. Ideal base for exploring Norfolk - 3 miles Norwich. Friendly atmosphere with good home cooking.
Bedrooms: 2 double, 1 twin
Bathrooms: 1 en-suite, 1 private, 1 public

Bed & breakfast per night:	£min	£max
Single	17.00	20.00
Double	34.00	40.00

Parking for 4
🛇🛇🖧🖙🎛🖵⬝🖼⬜🖭⬝🛒S🖭⬝⛔🖼🖭
🖺🌼🎏🎏

REEDHAM

Norfolk
Map ref 3C1

This pleasant riverside village is one of the few places to get beside the water in southern Broadland. A vehicle chain ferry crosses the River Yare here.

Briars 🅜
🏵🏵🏵
10 Riverside, Reedham, Norwich NR13 3TF
☎ Great Yarmouth (01493) 700054
Fax (01493) 700054
This welcoming home has a wonderful location with comfortable pine furnished accommodation over a traditional tea room and hair salon. A 1st floor lounge, conservatory and balcony have fabulous views of a Broadland river and marshland. Station close by.
Bedrooms: 3 double
Bathrooms: 3 en-suite

Bed & breakfast per night:	£min	£max
Single	30.00	30.00
Double	45.00	45.00

Lunch available
Evening meal 1800 (last orders 2100)

Parking for 6
Cards accepted: Access, Visa, Switch/Delta
🛇🖙⬜🖵⬝🖼⬝🛒UL🖭⬜🛒S🖭⛔🖼📺🖭⬝🖺
🎵🌼🎮🛇T

RICKMANSWORTH

Hertfordshire
Map ref 2D2

Old town, where 3 rivers meet, now mainly residential. The High Street is full of interesting buildings, including the home of William Penn. Moor Park Mansion, a fine 18th C house, is now a golf clubhouse.

6 Swallow Close
Listed
Nightingale Road, Rickmansworth WD3 2DZ
☎ (01923) 720069
In a quiet cul-de-sac, 5 minutes' walk from underground station, 30 minutes to London. Convenient for M25 and Watford. All food home-made. Non-smokers only, please.
Bedrooms: 2 single, 1 double
Bathrooms: 1 public

Bed & breakfast per night:	£min	£max
Single	19.00	20.00
Double	38.00	40.00

Parking for 3
🛇🖙5🖙⬝🖵🎛UL⬝💈🖭🖺🌼🎏🍴🚐

ROLLESBY

Norfolk
Map ref 3C1

Rollesby Broad forms part of the Ormesby Broad complex and fine views can be seen from the road which runs through the middle.

The Old Court House 🅜
🏵🏵 COMMENDED
Court Road, Rollesby, Great Yarmouth NR29 5HG
☎ Great Yarmouth (01493) 369665

18th C workhouse set in 4 acres in a peaceful, rural location near the Broads. Family-run with private bar and home cooking. Large games area. Bicycles for hire. Tennis, fishing and riding nearby.
Bedrooms: 2 double, 1 twin, 1 triple, 3 family rooms

Continued ▶

ROLLESBY

Continued

Bathrooms: 5 en-suite, 2 public

Bed & breakfast

per night:	£min	£max
Single	20.00	37.00
Double	30.00	46.00

Half board per person:	£min	£max
Daily	27.00	49.00
Weekly	174.00	306.00

Evening meal 1830 (last orders 1900)
Parking for 20
Open February–October

ROYSTON

Hertfordshire
Map ref 2D1

Old town lying at the crossing of the Roman road Ermine Street and the Icknield Way. It has many interesting old houses and inns.

Hall Farm

Listed COMMENDED

Great Chishill, Royston SG8 8SH
☎ (01763) 838263
Fax (01763) 838263
805-acre arable farm. Homely accommodation on working farm, in secluded gardens on the highest point in Cambridgeshire. Royston 5 miles, Duxford Museum 4 miles, Cambridge 11 miles.
Bedrooms: 2 double, 1 twin
Bathrooms: 1 public

Bed & breakfast

per night:	£min	£max
Single	20.00	20.00
Double	35.00	35.00

Parking for 8

WELCOME HOST

This is a nationally recognised customer care programme which aims to promote the highest standards of service and a warm welcome. Establishments who are taking part in this initiative are indicated by the ⊕ symbol.

SAFFRON WALDEN

Essex
Map ref 2D1

Takes its name from the saffron crocus once grown around the town. The church of St Mary has superb carvings, magnificent roofs and brasses. A town maze can be seen on the common. Two miles south-west is Audley End, a magnificent Jacobean mansion owned by English Heritage.
Tourist Information Centre ☎ (01799) 510444

Pond Mead

⊕⊕ APPROVED

Widdington, Saffron Walden
CB11 3SB
☎ (01799) 540201
Comfortable old house on the edge of Widdington village, with its ancient tithe barn and wildlife park. Easy access to Stansted Airport, Cambridge and M11.
Bedrooms: 1 triple
Bathrooms: 1 en-suite

Bed & breakfast

per night:	£min	£max
Single	16.00	19.00
Double	32.00	

Parking for 5

Rowley Hill Lodge

⊕⊕ COMMENDED

Little Walden, Saffron Walden
CB10 1UZ
☎ (01799) 525975
Fax (01799) 516622
Quiet farm lodge with large garden, 1 mile from centre of Saffron Walden. Stansted Airport, Cambridge and Duxford 20 minutes.
Bedrooms: 1 double, 1 twin
Bathrooms: 2 en-suite

Bed & breakfast

per night:	£min	£max
Single	22.00	22.00
Double	39.00	39.00

Parking for 4

Saxons

⊕ COMMENDED

Water Lane, Radwinter, Saffron Walden CB10 2TX
☎ (01799) 599565
Charming and comfortable modernised 16th C thatched house. Large garden, covered swimming pool - very peaceful countryside. Ideal base for exploring

---

East Anglia. 30 minutes to Stansted Airport, 1 hour to London via M11 or train.
Bedrooms: 1 single, 1 twin
Bathrooms: 2 private, 2 public

Bed & breakfast

per night:	£min	£max
Single	19.50	19.50
Double	39.00	39.00

Parking for 5

ST ALBANS

Hertfordshire
Map ref 2D1

As Verulamium this was one of the largest towns in Roman Britain and its remains can be seen in the museum. The Norman cathedral was built from Roman materials to commemorate Alban, the first British Christian martyr.
Tourist Information Centre ☎ (01727) 864511

Amaryllis

Listed

25 Ridgmont Road, St Albans
AL1 3AG
☎ St Albans (01727) 862755 &
Mobile (0589) 542126

Friendly, informal family home close to city centre. Convenient for M1 and M25. Central London 20 minutes by train. Non-smokers only, please.
Bedrooms: 1 single, 1 twin, 1 triple
Bathrooms: 1 public

Bed & breakfast

per night:	£min	£max
Single	16.00	25.00
Double	32.00	36.00

Parking for 1

Care Inns

⊕⊕

29 Alma Road, St Albans AL1 3AT
☎ St Albans (01727) 867310
Comfortable family atmosphere. Ideally located close to station, city centre and cathedral. All rooms have en-suite bath/shower and toilet.
Bedrooms: 1 single, 1 double, 1 twin
Bathrooms: 3 en-suite

Bed & breakfast

per night:	£min	£max
Single		25.00
Double		40.00

Parking for 5

🐎🚪⌂🖵 ♨ UL S ▥ ◼ ⬛ SP

---

76 Clarence Road

Listed

St Albans AL1 4NG
☎ St Albans (01727) 864880
Spacious Edwardian house with comfortable rooms and pleasant conservatory. Park nearby. Seven minutes' walk to station.
Bedrooms: 1 single, 1 twin
Bathrooms: 1 public

Bed & breakfast

per night:	£min	£max
Single	18.00	22.00
Double	36.00	40.00

Parking for 2

⌂🖵 ♨ ⌁ UL ⊁ ▥ ❋ ✗ ⬛

---

2 The Limes

Listed APPROVED

Spencer Gate, St Albans AL1 4AT
☎ St Albans (01727) 831080
Modern, detached house in a quiet cul-de-sac, within 10 minutes' walk of the city centre. Home-baked bread. Friendly atmosphere.
Bedrooms: 1 single, 1 twin
Bathrooms: 1 public

Bed & breakfast

per night:	£min	£max
Single	15.00	17.00
Double	30.00	34.00

Parking for 2

🐎🛆⌂🖵 ♨ UL ⊁ TV ▥ ✗ ⬛

The Lower Red Lion

34-36 Fishpool Street, St Albans
AL3 4RX
☎ St Albans (01727) 855669
Situated in conservation area near cathedral. The last true freehouse left in St Albans.
Bedrooms: 2 single, 2 double, 2 twin, 1 triple
Bathrooms: 4 en-suite, 2 private, 2 public

Bed & breakfast

per night:	£min	£max
Single	30.00	40.00
Double	40.00	50.00

Parking for 14

🐎⌂🖵 ♨ ▥ ✗ ⬛ 🏵

The Old School House

Listed

1 Branch Road, Park Street, St Albans AL2 2LU
☎ Park Street (01727) 874239
Fax (01727) 874275
Comfortable recently converted

---

en-suite rooms in the old village school. Close to amenities and open countryside. 5 minutes' walk from local station.
Bedrooms: 1 single, 1 double, 1 twin
Bathrooms: 3 en-suite, 1 public

Bed & breakfast

per night:	£min	£max
Single	25.00	25.00
Double	40.00	40.00

Parking for 3
Cards accepted: Access, Visa

🐎⌂🖵 ♨ ⌁ UL ⛉ ⊁ ▥ ◼ ⬛ OAP
SP 🏵 T

The Squirrels

Listed APPROVED

74 Sandridge Road, St Albans
AL1 4AR
☎ St Albans (01727) 840497
Edwardian terraced house, 10 minutes' walk from town centre.
Bedrooms: 1 twin
Bathrooms: 1 private

Bed & breakfast

per night:	£min	£max
Single	17.50	20.00
Double	27.50	30.00

Parking for 7

🐎7⌂ ♨ ⌁ UL S ⊁ ▥ ◼ ⬛ T

Famous as the country retreat of Her Majesty the Queen. The house and grounds are open to the public at certain times.

Jersey House

APPROVED

1 Senters Road, Dersingham, King's Lynn PE31 6LJ
☎ Dersingham (01485) 540035
Bright, modernised house with pleasant garden. Within walking distance of Sandringham estate, near junction of Heath and Manor roads. Catholic household.
Bedrooms: 2 twin
Bathrooms: 1 en-suite, 1 private

Bed & breakfast

per night:	£min	£max
Single	15.00	25.00
Double	30.00	34.00

Parking for 3

🐎⌂ ♨ ⌁ UL S ⊁ ◼ TV ▥ ◼ ❋ ⬛
OAP SP

> The ⚘ symbol after an establishment name indicates that it is a Regional Tourist Board member.

Mill Cottage

👑👑 HIGHLY COMMENDED

Mill Cottage, Mill Road, Dersingham, King's Lynn PE31 6HY
☎ Dersingham (01485) 544411

"Seek peace and pursue it" - Psalm 34:14. By Sandringham, set amidst picturesque countryside with distant sea views, a Georgian cottage with lawned gardens, paddock and barn.
Bedrooms: 1 double, 1 twin
Bathrooms: 1 en-suite, 1 private

Bed & breakfast

per night:	£min	£max
Single	19.00	40.00
Double	34.00	62.00

Parking for 4

🐎☎⌂🖵 ♨ ⌁ UL ◼ S ⊁ ◼ TV ▥
◼ ⌕ ∪ ∩ ❋ ⬛ OAP ⬛ SP 🏵

Small town on the River Ivel on the site of a Roman settlement.
Tourist Information Centre ☎ (01767) 682728

Highfield Farm ⚘

👑👑 HIGHLY COMMENDED

Great North Road, Sandy
SG19 2AQ
☎ (01767) 682332
Fax (01767) 692503

300-acre arable farm. Beautifully peaceful, comfortable farmhouse. Most rooms en-suite. Cambridge, the Shuttleworth Collection, RSPB and London all within easy reach. Most guests return.
Bedrooms: 1 double, 3 twin, 2 family rooms
Bathrooms: 4 en-suite, 1 private, 1 public

Bed & breakfast

per night:	£min	£max
Single	20.00	27.50
Double	35.00	40.00

Parking for 14

🐎🚪 ♨ ⌁ UL S ⊁ ◼ TV ▥ ◼ ❋ ⬛

SAXMUNDHAM

Suffolk
Map ref 3C2

The church of St John the Baptist
has a hammer-beam roof and
contains a number of good
monuments.

Little Orchard

Listed | HIGHLY COMMENDED

Middleton, Saxmundham IP17 3NT
☎ Westleton (01728) 648385
*Charming early 18th C house with
open views all around. Ideally situated
for sea and countryside, Snape
Maltings and Concert Hall and
Minsmere nature reserve. First house
on left on B1125 coming from
Theberton off the B1122.*
Bedrooms: 2 double
Bathrooms: 2 en-suite
Bed & breakfast

per night:	£min	£max
Single	17.50	
Double	35.00	

Parking for 3

SOUTH LOPHAM

Norfolk
Map ref 3B2

Malting Farm

COMMENDED

Blo Norton Road, South Lopham,
Diss IP22 2HT
☎ Bressingham (01379) 687201
*70-acre dairy farm. Recently renovated,
timber-framed farmhouse with
inglenook fireplaces and four-poster
beds. Crafts, including embroidery,
patchwork, spinning. See the cows
being milked.*
Bedrooms: 2 double, 1 twin
Bathrooms: 1 private, 1 public
Bed & breakfast

per night:	£min	£max
Single	25.00	25.00
Double	38.00	40.00

Parking for 10
Cards accepted: Diners

National gradings and
classifications were correct
at the time of going to press
but are subject to change.
Please check at the time
of booking.

SOUTH MIMMS

Hertfordshire
Map ref 2D1

Best known today for its location at
the junction of the M25 and the
A1M.
Tourist Information Centre ☎ (01707)
643233

The Black Swan

Listed

62-64 Blanche Lane, South Mimms,
Potters Bar EN6 3PD
☎ Potters Bar (01707) 644180
*Comfortable accommodation in
oak-beamed bedrooms or
self-contained flats in quietly located
listed building. Breakfast provided.*
Bedrooms: 1 triple
Suite available
Bathrooms: 1 private, 1 public
Bed & breakfast

per night:	£min	£max
Single	25.00	25.00
Double	35.00	35.00

Parking for 7

SOUTH WALSHAM

Norfolk
Map ref 3C1

Village famous for having 2 churches
in adjoining churchyards. South
Walsham Broad consists of an inner
and outer section, the former being
private. Alongside, the Fairhaven
Garden Trust has woodland and
water-gardens open to the public.

Old Hall Farm

APPROVED

South Walsham, Norwich
NR13 6DT
☎ Norwich (01603) 270271
*82-acre arable farm. Thatched
farmhouse dating from 17th C on edge
of Broadland village. Good centre for
Norwich, Broads and coast.*
Bedrooms: 2 double, 1 twin
Suite available
Bathrooms: 1 private, 2 public
Bed & breakfast

per night:	£min	£max
Single	15.00	20.00
Double	30.00	40.00

Parking for 5
Open April–October

SOUTHWOLD

Suffolk
Map ref 3C2

Pleasant and attractive seaside town
with a triangular market square and
spacious greens around which stand
flint, brick and colour-washed
cottages. The parish church of St
Edmund is one of the greatest
churches in Suffolk.

No 3 Cautley Road

COMMENDED

Southwold IP18 6DD
☎ (01502) 723611
*No 3 is an elegant, Edwardian family
town house. All en-suite rooms with
colour TV. 5 minutes' walk to sea and
shops.*
Bedrooms: 2 double, 1 twin
Bathrooms: 3 private
Bed & breakfast

per night:	£min	£max
Single	30.00	35.00
Double	40.00	50.00

STEEPLE BUMPSTEAD

Essex
Map ref 3B2

An interesting building in the village
is the Moot Hall, which in the 17th
C served as a village school and was
restored as part of the 1977 Jubilee
celebrations.

Yew Tree House

COMMENDED

15 Chapel Street, Steeple
Bumpstead, Haverhill, Suffolk
CB9 7DQ
☎ (01440) 730364
Fax (01440) 730364
*Charming Victorian house, with many
period features, and comfortable
accommodation, in the centre of
Steeple Bumpstead. Breakfast menu.*
Bedrooms: 1 double, 1 twin
Bathrooms: 1 en-suite, 1 public
Bed & breakfast

per night:	£min	£max
Single	17.00	26.00
Double	29.00	34.00

Half board per person:	£min	£max
Daily	25.00	27.50
Weekly	170.00	190.00

Evening meal 1800 (last orders
2000)
Parking for 3

STOKE HOLY CROSS

Norfolk
Map ref 3C1

Salamanca Farm ⋀

👑 COMMENDED

Stoke Holy Cross, Norwich
NR14 8QJ
☎ Framingham Earl (01508) 492322
175-acre mixed farm. Picturesque
village near Norwich. Comfortable
Victorian farmhouse in a flower
arranger's garden. Guests have been
welcomed for 20 years.
Bedrooms: 3 double, 1 twin
Bathrooms: 3 en-suite, 1 private,
1 public

**Bed & breakfast
per night:**

	£min	£max
Single	18.00	22.00
Double	36.00	44.00

Parking for 8
Cards accepted: Diners

⌂6 ♿🈺S✂🅿TV▥ 🅿❢16❄ 🎿🚗◉

STOKE-BY-NAYLAND

Suffolk
Map ref 3B2

Picturesque village with a fine group
of half-timbered cottages near the
church of St Mary, the tower of
which was one of Constable's
favourite subjects. In School Street
are the Guildhall and the Maltings,
both 16th C timber-framed
buildings.

Nether Hall

Listed COMMENDED

Thorington Street,
Stoke-by-Nayland, Colchester, Essex
CO6 4ST
☎ Higham (01206) 337373

Charming Grade II listed 15th C
country house with grounds adjoining
the River Box and in the heart of
Constable country. On B1068, 3 miles
from A12. One double/twin room is on
ground floor with private external
access.
Bedrooms: 1 single, 2 double
Bathrooms: 2 en-suite, 1 private

**Bed & breakfast
per night:**

	£min	£max
Single	25.00	25.00
Double	44.00	44.00

Parking for 6

⌂10♿🈺🅿⛱UL S▥ 🅿◽Q❄ 🚗T

Ryegate House ⋀

👑👑 HIGHLY COMMENDED

Stoke-by-Nayland, Colchester
CO6 4RA
☎ Nayland (01206) 263679
Comfortable friendly house in Suffolk
village within Dedham Vale. On the
B1068, 5.5 miles from A12 and 2.5
miles from A134. All rooms en-suite.
Bedrooms: 2 double, 1 twin
Bathrooms: 3 en-suite

**Bed & breakfast
per night:**

	£min	£max
Single	23.00	26.00
Double	34.00	39.00

Parking for 6

⌂10🈺🅿⛱ UL TV▥❄🚗SP

SUTTON

Cambridgeshire
Map ref 3A2

Anchor Inn ⋀

👑👑 HIGHLY COMMENDED

Sutton Gault, Sutton, Ely CB6 2BD
☎ Ely (01353) 778537
Fax (01353) 776180
350-year-old riverside inn, gaslit and
with antique furnishings. Close to Ely
and Cambridge. Country Dining Pub of
the Year 1996.
Bedrooms: 1 twin, 1 triple
Suite available
Bathrooms: 2 en-suite

**Bed & breakfast
per night:**

	£min	£max
Single	46.00	56.00
Double	57.50	77.50

Lunch available
Evening meal 1900 (last orders
2100)
Parking for 16
Cards accepted: Access, Visa, Amex,
Switch/Delta

📞🈺🅿 🍽S✂🅿▥ 🅿❄🍴🚗SP🏠

Establishments should be
open throughout the year,
unless otherwise stated.

The ⋀ symbol after an
establishment name indicates
that it is a Regional
Tourist Board member.

SWAFFHAM

Norfolk
Map ref 3B1

Busy market town with a triangular
market-place, a domed rotunda built
in 1783 and a number of Georgian
houses. The 15th C church
possesses a large library of ancient
books.

Lodge Farm

Listed COMMENDED

Castle Acre, King's Lynn PE32 2BS
☎ Swaffham (01760) 755506
Fax (01760) 755103
Spacious country farmhouse with
garden and paddocks, 1 mile north of
historic Castle Acre. Peddars Way,
Sandringham, walking country nearby.
Bedrooms: 3 twin
Bathrooms: 1 en-suite, 1 public

**Bed & breakfast
per night:**

	£min	£max
Single	18.50	21.00
Double	21.00	23.00

Parking for 7

⌂7🈺🅿♿🈺🅿◽✂▥ 🅿❄🚗

SWAFFHAM BULBECK

Cambridgeshire
Map ref 2D1

The Black Horse Village Inn
and Restaurant

👑👑 APPROVED

35 High Street, Swaffham Bulbeck,
Cambridge CB5 0HP
☎ Cambridge (01223) 811366
Picturesque inn overlooking the village
green offering accommodation in
recently built stable block.
Bedrooms: 6 twin, 1 family room
Bathrooms: 7 private

**Bed & breakfast
per night:**

	£min	£max
Single	35.00	45.00
Double	45.00	55.00

**Half board per
person:**

	£min	£max
Daily	45.00	65.00

Lunch available
Evening meal 1900 (last orders
2100)
Parking for 16
Cards accepted: Access, Visa

⌂♿🈺🅿⛱▥🅿Q❄

A key to symbols can be
found inside the back
cover flap.

THAXTED

Essex
Map ref 3B2

Small town rich in outstanding buildings and dominated by its hilltop medieval church. The magnificent Guildhall was built by the Cutlers' Guild in the late 14th C. A windmill built in 1804 has been restored and houses a rural museum.

Piggots Mill

HIGHLY COMMENDED

Watling Lane, Thaxted, Dunmow CM6 2QY
☎ (01371) 830379
850-acre arable farm. Traditional Essex barn, now a secluded farmhouse offering excellent accommodation in the centre of Thaxted. Garden leads into meadow giving access to attractive walks.
Bedrooms: 1 double, 1 twin
Bathrooms: 2 en-suite
Bed & breakfast

per night:	£min	£max
Single	31.00	33.00
Double	46.00	49.00

Parking for 10

THOMPSON

Norfolk
Map ref 3B1

College Farm ⋀

Listed

Thompson, Thetford IP24 1QG
☎ Caston (01953) 483318
14th C farmhouse, formerly a college of priests. In quiet village away from main road. Meals available at nearby inns.
Bedrooms: 1 double, 2 twin
Bathrooms: 2 en-suite, 1 private, 1 public
Bed & breakfast

per night:	£min	£max
Single	18.00	19.00
Double	36.00	38.00

Parking for 10

COLOUR MAPS

Colour maps at the back of this guide pinpoint all places in which you will find accommodation listed.

THORNHAM

Norfolk
Map ref 3B1

The Lifeboat Inn

COMMENDED

Ship Lane, Thornham, Hunstanton PE36 6LT
☎ (01485) 512236
Fax (01485) 512323
16th C smugglers' alehouse with views across Thornham harbour to the sea.
Bedrooms: 3 double, 7 twin, 3 triple
Bathrooms: 13 en-suite
Bed & breakfast

per night:	£min	£max
Single	40.00	60.00
Double	60.00	75.00

Lunch available
Evening meal 1900 (last orders 2200)
Parking for 80
Cards accepted: Access, Visa, Diners, Switch/Delta

THURSFORD

Norfolk
Map ref 3B1

Noted for its collection of steam locomotives, mechanical musical organs and fairground engines.

The Old Forge Bistro and Fish Restaurant

Fakenham Road, Thursford, Fakenham NR21 0BD
☎ Fakenham (01328) 878345
A 14th C forge with original beams and ironwork for tethering horses. All rooms and restaurant have been fully refurbished.
Bedrooms: 2 double, 1 twin
Suite available
Bathrooms: 1 en-suite, 2 private showers
Bed & breakfast

per night:	£min	£max
Single	15.00	20.00
Double	35.00	40.00

Half board per person:	£min	£max
Daily	25.00	40.00
Weekly	150.00	200.00

Lunch available
Evening meal 1900 (last orders 2200)
Parking for 10
Open February–December
Cards accepted: Access, Visa, Switch/Delta

TIPTREE

Essex
Map ref 3B3

Linden

Listed HIGHLY COMMENDED

8 Clarkesmead, Maldon Road, Tiptree, Colchester CO5 OBX
☎ (01621) 819737 & (0585) 243425
Fax (01621) 819737
Modern architect-designed house in quiet cul-de-sac, off Maldon Road on edge of Tiptree, near A12.
Bedrooms: 1 single, 1 double, 1 twin, 1 family room
Suite available
Bathrooms: 1 private, 1 public, 1 private shower
Bed & breakfast

per night:	£min	£max
Single	20.00	22.00
Double	38.00	40.00

Parking for 6
Cards accepted: Access, Visa

WARE

Hertfordshire
Map ref 2D1

Interesting riverside town with picturesque summer-houses lining the tow-path of the River Lea. The town has many timber-framed and Georgian houses and the famous Great Bed of Ware is now in the Victoria and Albert Museum.

Ashridge

COMMENDED

3 Belle Vue Road, Ware SG12 7BD
☎ (01920) 463895
Comfortable, Edwardian residence in quiet cul-de-sac. 10 minutes' walk from Ware and station. Non-smokers only, please.
Bedrooms: 2 single, 1 double, 1 twin
Bathrooms: 2 public
Bed & breakfast

per night:	£min	£max
Single	17.50	20.00
Double	35.00	40.00

Parking for 4

All accommodation in this guide has been graded, or is awaiting a grading, by a trained Tourist Board inspector.

WELLS-NEXT-THE-SEA

Norfolk
Map ref 3B1

Seaside resort and small port on the north coast. The Buttlands is a large tree-lined green surrounded by Georgian houses and from here narrow streets lead to the quay.

Hideaway

♨♨ COMMENDED

Red Lion Yard, Wells-next-the-Sea
NR23 1AX
☎ Fakenham (01328) 710524
Single-storey extension built on to house. Own entrance and garden for guests with 24-hour access. All en-suite. Spa and sauna available.
Bedrooms: 1 double, 2 twin
Bathrooms: 3 en-suite
Bed & breakfast

per night:	£min	£max
Double	30.00	38.00

Half board per

person:	£min	£max
Daily	23.50	27.50
Weekly	155.00	183.00

Evening meal 1830 (last orders 1930)
Parking for 4

♨🖥🖵♿🍴🔌📺⅏🛏🚗 DAP SP

Scarborough House Hotel 🅜

♨♨ COMMENDED

Clubbs Lane, Wells-next-the-Sea
NR23 1DP
☎ Fakenham (01328) 710309 & 711661
Licensed hotel with restaurant, log fires, four-poster beds, private parking. Perfect for bird-watchers and ramblers. Dogs welcome.
Bedrooms: 10 double, 4 twin, 1 family room
Bathrooms: 15 en-suite
Bed & breakfast

per night:	£min	£max
Single	29.00	34.00
Double	48.00	68.00

Half board per

person:	£min	£max
Daily	37.95	47.95
Weekly	235.00	270.00

Evening meal 1930 (last orders 2100)
Parking for 15
Cards accepted: Access, Visa, Diners, Amex, Switch/Delta

♨🖥🖵♿📶S🍴⅏🛏🚗🍴 SP

> Half board prices are given per person, but in some cases these may be based on double/twin occupancy.

WITNESHAM

Suffolk
Map ref 3B2

Burnbank House

Listed COMMENDED

Church Lane, Witnesham, Ipswich
IP6 9JD
☎ Ipswich (01473) 785854
Fax (01473) 785021
Large 17th C converted barn with gardens, set in 13 acres.
Bedrooms: 1 double, 1 twin
Bathrooms: 1 en-suite, 1 private
Bed & breakfast

per night:	£min	£max
Single	20.00	
Double	35.00	

Parking for 4

♨5🖵🖥♿🖐UL S⅏📺⅏🛏🚗 🌸🚐

> Please check prices and other details at the time of booking.

> A key to symbols can be found inside the back cover flap.

COUNTRY CODE

Always follow the Country Code

🍀 Enjoy the countryside and respect its life and work 🍀 Guard against all risk of fire 🍀 Fasten all gates 🍀 Keep your dogs under close control 🍀 Keep to public paths across farmland 🍀 Use gates and stiles to cross fences, hedges and walls 🍀 Leave livestock, crops and machinery alone 🍀 Take your litter home 🍀 Help to keep all water clean 🍀 Protect wildlife, plants and trees 🍀 Take special care on country roads 🍀 Make no unnecessary noise

WIX

Essex
Map ref 3B2

New Farm House
♛♛♛ COMMENDED

Spinnell's Lane, Wix, Manningtree
CO11 2UJ
☎ Clacton (01255) 870365
Fax (01255) 870837

Modern comfortable farmhouse in large garden, 10 minutes' drive to Harwich and convenient for Constable country. From Wix village crossroads, take Bradfield Road, turn right at top of hill; first house on left.
Bedrooms: 3 single, 1 double, 3 twin, 5 family rooms
Bathrooms: 7 en-suite, 2 public

Bed & breakfast
per night:	£min	£max
Single	21.50	25.00
Double	40.00	46.00

Half board per
person:	£min	£max
Daily	34.50	38.00
Weekly	308.35	330.40

Evening meal 1830 (last orders 1730)
Parking for 18
Cards accepted: Access, Visa, Diners, Amex

🏠♿🖳♤🕭⚲⑤🏊🅿🎇🐕

WOODBRIDGE

Suffolk
Map ref 3C2

Once a busy seaport, the town is now a sailing centre on the River Deben. There are many buildings of architectural merit including the Bell and Angel Inns. The 18th C Tide Mill is now restored and open to the public.

Horse and Groom
Listed

Yarmouth Road, Melton,
Woodbridge IP12 1QB
☎ (01394) 383566
Fax (01394) 383566
Beamed coaching inn in village location, 1 mile from Woodbridge. Ideal centre for Heritage coast, Minsmere and Aldeburgh Festival.
Bedrooms: 1 single, 1 double, 2 twin, 1 triple

Bathrooms: 1 public

Bed & breakfast
per night	£min	£max
Single	18.50	20.00
Double	37.00	40.00

Half board per
person:	£min	£max
Daily	21.50	23.00

Lunch available
Evening meal 1800 (last orders 2100)
Parking for 20

🏠🖳♤🕭⑤🏊🅿🍽15🐾🎇🚗

Moat Farmhouse
Listed

Dallinghoo Road, Bredfield,
Woodbridge IP13 6BD
☎ Charsfield (01473) 737475
Converted farm building with self-contained accommodation and breakfast room, attached to farmhouse. Large garden. Three miles north of Woodbridge, 1.5 miles from A12. Brochure on request.
Bedrooms: 1 double, 1 twin
Bathrooms: 1 public

Bed & breakfast
per night	£min	£max
Single	15.00	
Double	30.00	

Parking for 3
Open February–November

🏠♿♤Ⓤ🖊🎇📺🅿🎇🐕🚗

WOODHAM FERRERS

Essex
Map ref 3B3

Woolfe's Cottage
Listed

The Street, Woodham Ferrers,
Chelmsford CM3 8RG
☎ Chelmsford (01245) 320037
Large converted Victorian cottage in historic village, 12 miles from Chelmsford on the B1418. Many excellent walking trails for ramblers.
Bedrooms: 1 double, 2 twin
Bathrooms: 1 public

Bed & breakfast
per night:	£min	£max
Single	16.00	17.00
Double	30.00	32.00

Parking for 2

🏠🖳🖳♤Ⓤ🕭🖊🎇📺🏊🅿
🕂🎇🐕🚗

The National Grading and Classification Scheme is explained in full at the back of this guide.

WOOLPIT

Suffolk
Map ref 3B2

Village with a number of attractive timber-framed Tudor and Georgian houses. St Mary's Church is one of the most beautiful churches in Suffolk and has a fine porch. The brass eagle lectern is said to have been donated by Elizabeth I.

The Bull Inn & Restaurant
♛♛ COMMENDED

The Street, Woolpit, Bury St Edmunds IP30 9SA
☎ Elmswell (01359) 240393
Public house and restaurant offering good accommodation in centre of pretty village. Large garden, ample parking. Ideal base for touring Suffolk.
Bedrooms: 1 single, 2 double
Suites available
Bathrooms: 3 en-suite

Bed & breakfast
per night:	£min	£max
Single	20.00	
Double	36.00	

Half board per
person:	£min	£max
Daily		30.00

Lunch available
Evening meal 1800 (last orders 2130)
Parking for 50
Cards accepted: Access, Visa, Diners, Amex, Switch/Delta

🏠2🖳♤🕭⑤🖊🎇🏊🍽🐾⚬🎇🎇
🚗🅿🏛

WROXHAM

Norfolk
Map ref 3C1

Yachting centre on the River Bure which houses the headquarters of the Norfolk Broads Yacht Club. The church of St Mary has a famous doorway and the manor house nearby dates back to 1623.

Garden Cottage
♛♛ HIGHLY COMMENDED

The Limes, 96 Norwich Road,
Wroxham, Norwich NR12 8RY
☎ Norwich (01603) 784376 &
783192
Beautifully converted and furnished 18th C barn; own entrance, sitting, dining rooms and patio; private parking. 150 yards to Broads, good base for North Norfolk coast and only 7 miles from Norwich.
Bedrooms: 1 double, 2 twin
Bathrooms: 3 en-suite

Bed & breakfast per night:	£min	£max
Single	25.00	35.00
Double	35.00	45.00

Half board per person:	£min	£max
Daily	35.00	45.00
Weekly	200.00	300.00

Evening meal 1900 (last orders 2100)
Parking for 3
Cards accepted: Access, Visa, Amex, Switch/Delta

🛇🛥👪🖵👜🐾👜✂🕮🛏☀🚜 SP /none;float

Manor Barn House

😃😃 COMMENDED

Back Lane, Rackheath, Wroxham, Norwich NR13 6NN
☎ Norwich (01603) 783543

Traditional Norfolk barn conversion with exposed beams, in quiet setting with pleasant gardens. Just off the A1151, 2 miles from Wroxham.

Bedrooms: 3 double, 2 twin
Bathrooms: 4 en-suite, 1 private

Bed & breakfast per night:	£min	£max
Single	18.00	25.00
Double	34.00	38.00

Parking for 8

🛇3👪🖵👜 UL🐾✂🕮 TV🛏🔌♨ 🏳☀🚜🦯 SP 🏮

WYMONDHAM

Norfolk
Map ref 3B1

Thriving historic market town of charm and architectural interest. The octagonal market cross, 12th C abbey and 15th C Green Dragon inn blend with streetscapes spanning three centuries. An excellent touring base.

Rose Farm

Listed APPROVED

School Lane, Suton, Wymondham NR18 9JN
☎ (01953) 603512
2-acre poultry farm. Homely farmhouse accommodation within easy reach of Norwich, Broads and Breckland. Quiet, rural location, but only three-quarters of a mile from A11 London/Norwich trunk road.

Bedrooms: 2 single, 1 double,
1 triple
Bathrooms: 2 public

Bed & breakfast per night:	£min	£max
Single	19.00	22.00
Double	38.00	44.00

Parking for 4
Cards accepted: Diners

🛇🦯👪🖵👜 UL👜S✂🕮 TV🛏🔌 U🎵☀🚜 T

Turret House

Listed APPROVED

27 Middleton Street, Wymondham NR18 0AB
☎ (01953) 603462
Fax (01953) 603462
Large Victorian house in centre of Wymondham within walking distance of shops, restaurants and historic abbey. Convenient for Norwich. No smoking throughout.
Bedrooms: 1 double, 1 twin
Bathrooms: 1 public

Bed & breakfast per night:	£min	£max
Single	15.00	15.00
Double	30.00	30.00

Parking for 2

🛇🦯📧🖵👜 UL✂🕮🍴🚜

COUNTRY CODE

Always follow the Country Code

🌿 Enjoy the countryside and respect its life and work 🌿 Guard against all risk of fire 🌿 Fasten all gates 🌿 Keep your dogs under close control 🌿 Keep to public paths across farmland 🌿 Use gates and stiles to cross fences, hedges and walls 🌿 Leave livestock, crops and machinery alone 🌿 Take your litter home 🌿 Help to keep all water clean 🌿 Protect wildlife, plants and trees 🌿 Take special care on country roads 🌿 Make no unnecessary noise

CHECK THE MAPS

The colour maps at the back of this guide show all the cities, towns and villages for which you will find accommodation entries.

Refer to the town index to find the page on which it is listed.

AT-A-GLANCE SYMBOLS

Symbols at the end of each accommodation entry give useful information about services and facilities. A key to symbols can be found inside the back cover flap.

Keep this open for easy reference.

WEST COUNTRY

The West Country is famous for its wildness and beauty, legends and magic... but mostly for the breathtaking variety of its scenery.

From titanic cliffs overlooking sparkling beaches to the vastness of Dartmoor and Exmoor, then on to cosy villages nestling in verdant countryside, this most compelling of regions has inspired generations of writers and artists.

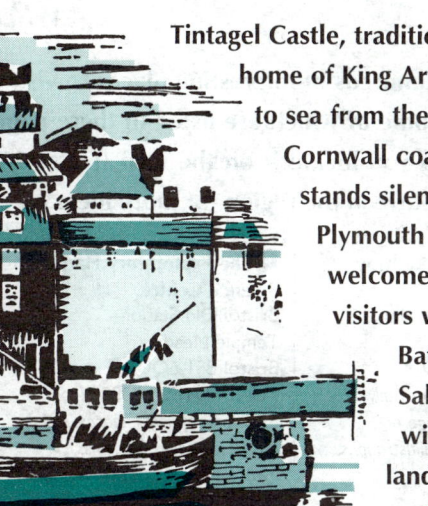

Tintagel Castle, traditionally the home of King Arthur, stares out to sea from the rugged North Cornwall coast. Stonehenge stands silent. Maritime Plymouth waits to welcome its next tide of visitors while elegant Bath and lively Salisbury bustle with life in this land of many mysteries.

FOR MORE INFORMATION CONTACT:
West Country Tourist Board
60 St Davids Hill, Exeter EX4 4SY
Tel: (01392) 425426 **Fax:** (01392) 420891

Where to Go in the West Country -
see pages 250-254
Where to Stay in the West Country -
see pages 255-309

WEST COUNTRY

Where to Go and What to See

You will find hundreds of interesting places to visit during your stay in the West Country, just some of which are listed in these pages. The number against each name will help you locate it on the map (pages 252-253). Contact any Tourist Information Centre in the region for more ideas on days out in the West Country.

1 Great Western Railway Museum
Faringdon Road, Swindon,
Wiltshire SN1 5BJ
Tel: (01793) 493189
Historic Great Western Railway locomotives, wide range of nameplates, models, illustrations, posters and tickets.

2 Dyrham Park
Dyrham,
Chippenham,
Wiltshire SN14 8ER
Tel: (0117) 937 2501
Mansion built between 1691 and 1710 for William Blathwayt. Rooms have been little changed. A herd of deer roams the 263-acre parkland.

3 Bristol Zoo Gardens
Clifton, Bristol BS8 3HA
Tel: (0117) 973 8951
Set in beautiful gardens, the zoo provides a haven for some of the world's most endangered wildlife. Plenty of activities and special events throughout the year.

4 The Exploratory Hands-on Science Centre
Bristol Old Station,
Temple Meads,
Bristol BS1 6QU
Tel: (0117) 925 2008
Exhibition of lights, lenses, lasers, bubbles, bridges, illusions, gyroscopes and much more all housed in Brunel's original engine shed and drawing office.

5 Harveys Wine Museum
12 Denmark Street,
Bristol BS1 5DQ
Tel: (0117) 927 5036
Wine museum in original 13thC cellars displaying artefacts connected with production and enjoyment of wines, especially glass, silver and corkscrews.

6 Bowood House and Gardens
Bowood Estate,
Calne, Wiltshire SN11 0LZ
Tel: (01249) 812102
18thC house by Robert Adam, collections of paintings, watercolours, Victoriana, Indiana and porcelain. Landscaped park with lake, terraces, waterfall and grottos.

7 Weston-super-Mare Sea Life Centre
Marine Parade,
Weston-super-Mare,
North Somerset BS23 1BE
Tel: (01934) 641603
All aspects of British marine life housed on Britain's first pier for 85 years.

8 Museum of Costume
Assembly Rooms, Bennett Street,
Bath BA1 2QH
Tel: (01225) 477789
Designed by John Wood the Younger in 1769. One of Bath's finest Georgian buildings. Museum of Costume housed in basement.

9 Cheddar Showcaves and Gorge
Cheddar, Somerset BS27 3QF
Tel: (01934) 742343
Beautiful caves located in Cheddar

Gorge. Gough's Cave with its cathedral-like caverns and Cox's Cave with stalagmites and stalactites. Also "The Crystal Quest" fantasy adventure.

10 Secret World
New Road Farm, East Huntspill, Highbridge, Somerset TA9 3PZ
Tel: (01278) 783250
300-year-old farm, many breeds of animals including rare breeds. Old and modern farm machinery on display. Play areas, gardens. Somerset Levels Visitor Centre.

11 Wookey Hole Caves and Papermill
Wookey Hole,
Wells,
Somerset BA5 1BB
Tel: (01749) 672243
Spectacular caves and legendary home of the Witch of Wookey. Working Victorian papermill including Fairground Memories, Old Penny Arcade, Magical Mirror Maze and Cave Diving Museum.

12 Longleat
Warminster,
Wiltshire BA12 7NW
Tel: (01985) 844400
Great Elizabethan house with lived-in atmosphere. Important libraries and Italian ceilings. Capability Brown designed parkland. Safari Park.

13 Stourhead House and Garden
Stourton, Warminster, Wiltshire BA12 6QH
Tel: (01747) 840348
Landscaped garden laid out in 1741-80, with lakes and temples, rare trees and plants. House begun in 1721 by Colen Campbell contains fine paintings and Chippendale furniture.

14 Wilton House
Wilton, Wiltshire SP2 0BJ
Tel: (01722) 743115
Home of the Earls of Pembroke for nearly 450 years. Famous Double and Single Cube rooms. Art collection. Adventure playground. Woodland walk. Wareham Bears.

15 Salisbury and South Wiltshire Museum
The King's House, 65 The Close, Salisbury, Wiltshire SP1 2EN
Tel: (01722) 332151
Grade 1 listed building. Stonehenge collection, Salisbury Giant, Early man. History of Old Sarum, Salisbury, Romans to Saxons, ceramics, Wedgwood, pictures, costume exhibitions.

16 West Somerset Railway
The Railway Station, Minehead, Somerset TA24 5BG
Tel: (01643) 704996
Preserved steam railway operating between Minehead and Bishops Lydeard, near Taunton. Longest independent railway in Britain (20 miles).

17 Clovelly Village
Clovelly, Bideford, Devon EX39 5SY
Tel: (01237) 431200
Unspoilt fishing village on North Devon coast with steep cobbled street and no vehicular access. Donkeys and sledges only means of transport. Visitor centre.

18 Dartington Crystal
Linden Close, Torrington, Devon EX38 7AN
Tel: (01805) 622321
Manufacture of hand-made crystal table glassware by skilled craftsmen. Glass centre and glassware exhibition. Visitors can watch glass blowers "hand blowing" glassware.

19 Rosemoor Garden - Royal Horticultural Society's Garden
Rosemoor, Great Torrington, Devon EX38 8PH
Tel: (01805) 624067
Garden of rare horticultural interest. Trees, shrubs, roses, alpines and arboretum. Nursery of uncommon and rare plants. 8 acres being expanded to 40 acres.

20 Haynes Motor Museum
Sparkford, Yeovil,
Somerset BA22 7LH
Tel: (01963) 440804
*Motor vehicles and memorabilia
covering the years from the turn of
the century to the present day.
Video cinema, exhibition track.*

21 Montacute House
Montacute, Yeovil,
Somerset TA15 6XP
Tel: (01935) 823289
*Late 16thC house built of local
golden Ham stone, by Sir Edward
Phelips. The Long Gallery houses
a collection of Tudor and
Jacobean portraits. Formal gardens
and park.*

22 Sherborne Castle
Sherborne, Dorset
Tel: (01935) 813182
*Built by Sir Walter Raleigh in 1594
to replace the old castle. The
Elizabethan Hall and Jacobean Oak
Room show two of the many styles
of architecture.*

24 The Dinosaur Museum
Icen Way,
Dorchester,
Dorset DT1 1EW
Tel: (01305) 269880
*Only museum in Britain devoted
exclusively to dinosaurs. Fossils,
actual-size dinosaur reconstructions,
audio-visual, "hands on".
Video gallery and computerised
displays.*

26 Weymouth Sea Life Park
Lodmoor Country Park,
Weymouth, Dorset DT4 7SX
Tel: (01305) 761070
*Spectacular displays of British
marine life where visitors come face
to face with a wide variety of
creatures. Also an exciting tropical
jungle full of birds.*

23 Athelhampton House and Gardens
Athelhampton, Dorset DT2 7LG
Tel: (01305) 848363
*Legendary site of King Athelstan's
Palace. Family home for five
centuries. Fine example of 15thC
architecture. Gardens with
fountains, pools and waterfalls.*

25 Brewers' Quay and Timewalk
Hope Square, Weymouth,
Dorset DT4 8TR
Tel: (01305) 777622
*Former brewery now housing The
Timewalk, depicting 600 years of
Weymouth's history, also The
Brewer's Tale exhibition and
shopping village with restaurants.*

27 Abbotsbury Swannery
New Barn Road, Abbotsbury
Weymouth, Dorset DT3 4JG
Tel: (01305) 871684
*The only place in the world where
over 600 swans can be visited
during the nesting and hatching
time (end May-end June). Audio-
visual presentation. Ugly duckling
trail.*

The map shows the following labeled locations:

GLOUCESTERSHIRE, **OXFORDSHIRE**, **BERKSHIRE**, **HAMPSHIRE**, **WILTSHIRE**, **SOMERSET**, **DORSET (western)**, **DORSET (eastern)**, **ISLE OF WIGHT**, **SOUTH GLOUCESTERSHIRE**, **BRISTOL**, **NORTH SOMERSET**, **BATH & NORTH EAST SOMERSET**

Chipping Sodbury, Malmesbury, Portishead, Wootton Bassett, **1** Swindon, Kingswood, **2** Chippenham, **3 4 5** Bristol, **6** Calne, Avebury, Western-super-Mare, **7** Banwell, Bath **8**, Lacock, Bradford on Avon, Devizes, Burnham-on-Sea, Cheddar **9** Midsomer, Rode, **WILTSHIRE**, Wookey Hole **11**, Frome, Trowbridge, Highbridge, Norton Wells, **10**, Shepton Mallet, Bridgwater, **12** Warminster, Amesbury, **13** Stourton, Wilton, **14**, Taunton, Wincanton, Salisbury **15**, Wellington, Yeovil, **20 21**, **22** Sherborne, Ilminster, Crewkerne, Beaminster, Honiton, Axminster, Athelhampton, Ottery St Mary, Bridport, Kingston **23**, Seaton, Maurward, **24**, Lyme Regis, **27** Dorchester, Sidmouth, Abbotsbury, **25 26** Weymouth, Fortuneswell

0 ——— 20 Miles
0 ——— 30 Kms

---

28 Killerton House
Broadclyst, Exeter,
Devon EX5 3LE
Tel: (01392) 881345
18thC house built for the Acland family. Now houses a collection of costumes shown in various room settings. 15 acres of hillside garden with rare trees and shrubs.

29 Babbacombe Model Village
Hampton Avenue, Babbacombe,
Torquay, Devon TQ1 3LA
Tel: (01803) 328669
Hundreds of models and figures laid out in 4 acres of beautiful gardens to represent a model English countryside with modern town, villages and rural areas. Scale to 1/12th.

30 Woodlands Leisure Park
Blackawton, Totnes,
Devon TQ9 7DQ
Tel: (01803) 712598
A full day of variety set in 60 acres of countryside. 12 venture playzones including 500-metre toboggan run, commando course. 34000 sq ft indoor play area, toddlers' areas and animals.

31 Plymouth Dome
The Hoe, Plymouth,
Devon PL1 2NZ
Tel: (01752) 603300
Purpose-built visitor interpretation centre showing the history of Plymouth and its people from Stone Age beginnings to satellite technology. Situated on Plymouth Hoe.

32 Cotehele
St Dominick,
Saltash,
Cornwall PL12 6TA
Tel: (01579) 351346
Medieval granite house. Working watermill. Quay on River Tamar with small shipping museum. Sailing barge "Shamrock". Formal and valley gardens, pools, dovecote. Woodland walks.

33 Newquay Pearl
Southway,
Quintrell Downs,
Newquay,
Cornwall TR8 4LE
Tel: (01637) 872991
*A large showroom with every range
of pearl and semi-precious stone,
with workshops and staff actively
working. Pick your own pearl from
our oyster tanks.*

34 Royal Cornwall Museum
River Street,
Truro,
Cornwall TR1 2SJ
Tel: (01872) 72205
*World famous mineral collection,
Old Master drawings, ceramics, oil
paintings by the Newlyn School and
others, including John Opie and
Hogarth. Geneaology library.*

35 Tate Gallery St Ives
Porthmeor Beach,
St Ives,
Cornwall TR26 1TG
Tel: (01736) 796226
*A major new gallery showing
changing groups of work from the
Tate Gallery's pre-eminent collection
of St Ives painting and sculpture.*

36 The Minack Theatre and Exhibition Centre
Porthcurno,
Penzance,
Cornwall
Tel: (01736) 810694
*Open-air cliffside theatre with
breathtaking views, presenting a
16 week season of plays and
musicals. Exhibition centre telling
the theatre's story.*

37 Flambards Village Theme Park
Culdrose Manor,
Helston,
Cornwall TR13 0GA
Tel: (01326) 574549
*Life-sized Victorian village with fully
stocked shops, carriages and
fashions. 'Britain in the Blitz' life-
sized wartime street, historic
aircraft. Exploratorium.*

FIND OUT MORE
Further information about
holidays and attractions in the
West Country is available from:
**West Country Tourist
Board,**
60 St Davids Hill,
Exeter EX4 4SY.
Tel: (01392) 425426
Fax: (01392) 420891

These publications are available
free from the West Country
Tourist Board:
- **Great Escapes in England's West Country**
- **Bed & Breakfast Touring Map**
- **West Country Inspected Holiday Homes**
- **Commended Hotels and Guesthouses**
- **Glorious Gardens of the West Country**
- **Camping and Caravan Touring Map**

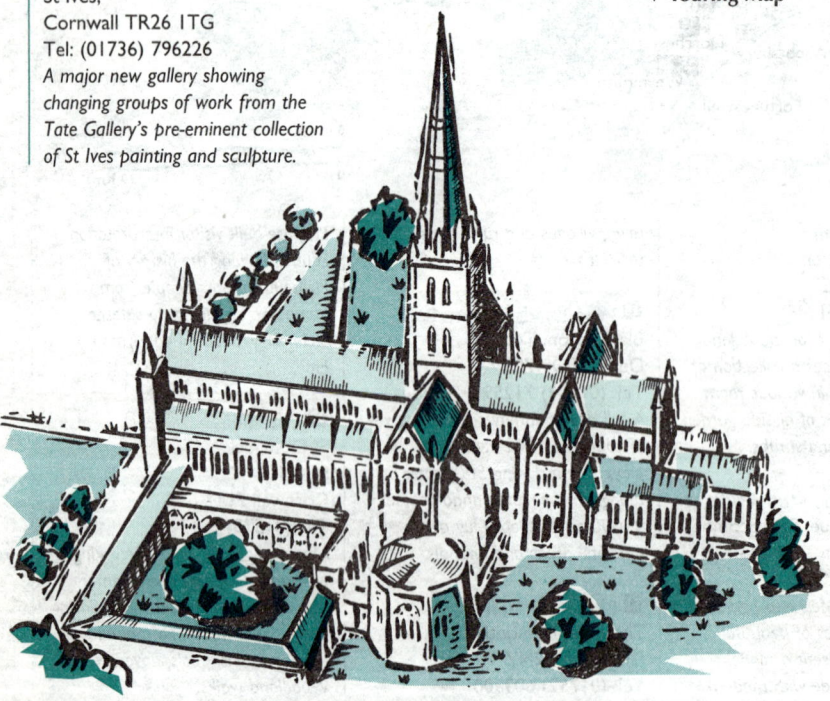

WHERE TO STAY (WEST COUNTRY)

Accommodation entries in this region are listed in alphabetical order of place name, and then in alphabetical order of establishment.

Map references refer to the colour location maps at the back of this guide. The first number indicates the map to use; the letter and number which follow refer to the grid reference on the map.

At-a-glance symbols at the end of each accommodation entry give useful information about services and facilities. A key to symbols can be found inside the back cover flap. Keep this open for easy reference.

ABBOTSBURY

Dorset
Map ref 2A3

Beautiful village near Chesil Beach, with a long main street of mellow stone and thatched cottages and the ruins of a Benedictine monastery. High above the village on a hill is a prominent 15th C chapel. Abbotsbury's famous swannery and sub-tropical gardens lie just outside the village.

Linton Cottage
Listed COMMENDED

Abbotsbury, Weymouth DT3 4JL
☎ (01305) 871339
Victorian cottage in picturesque setting. Our own honey on the breakfast table, and dinners just that extra bit special.
Bedrooms: 2 double, 1 twin
Bathrooms: 1 en-suite, 1 public

Bed & breakfast

per night:	£min	£max
Single	28.00	31.00
Double	36.00	40.00

Half board per

person:	£min	£max
Daily	30.50	32.50
Weekly	195.00	207.50

Evening meal from 1830
Parking for 4
⚒ ⛴ ♦ ⒰ ⒤ S ⅍ ⅀ TV ▥ ♫ ✕ 🚑

Swan Lodge ⚍
⬙ COMMENDED

Rodden Row, Abbotsbury,
Weymouth DT3 4JL
☎ (01305) 871249
Fax (01305) 871249
Situated on the B3157 coastal road

between Weymouth and Bridport. Swan Inn public house opposite, where food is served all day, is under the same ownership.
Bedrooms: 2 double, 2 twin, 1 triple
Bathrooms: 4 en-suite, 1 public
Bed & breakfast

per night:	£min	£max
Single	28.00	36.00
Double	42.00	52.00

Lunch available
Evening meal 1800 (last orders 2200)
Parking for 10
Cards accepted: Access, Visa
⛴ ♣ ♦ ⒤ S ⅍ ⅀ TV ▥ ♫ ⌂ ⏧80 ♦ U ✿ 🚑 DAP ⅍ SP

ALLERFORD

Somerset
Map ref 1D1

Village with picturesque stone and thatch cottages and a packhorse bridge, set in the beautiful Vale of Porlock.

Bossington Farm Park
Listed

Allerford, Minehead TA24 8HJ
☎ Porlock (01643) 862816
6-acre livestock farm. 15th C farmhouse offering homely accommodation. Lounge, TV, off-road parking. Pets welcome. Farm park and birds of prey centre.
Bedrooms: 1 twin, 1 triple
Bathrooms: 1 public
Bed & breakfast

per night:	£min	£max
Single	15.00	18.00
Double	30.00	35.00

Half board per

person:	£min	£max
Daily	25.00	
Weekly	150.00	

Lunch available
Parking for 100
⚒ ⛴ ♦ ⒰ ⒤ S ⅍ TV ▥ ♫ ⌂ U ✿ 🚑 ⛷ T

AMESBURY

Wiltshire
Map ref 2B2

Standing on the banks of the River Avon, this is the nearest town to Stonehenge on Salisbury Plain. The area is rich in prehistoric sites. *Tourist Information Centre ☎ (01980) 622833*

Church Cottage
⬙ HIGHLY COMMENDED

Church Street, Amesbury, Salisbury SP4 7EY
☎ (01980) 624650 & mobile 0585 633245
Your own bathroom, beautiful quiet bedrooms spotlessly clean, excellent 3-course breakfasts, Stonehenge 2 miles, restaurants only 2 minutes. In short, superb value.
Bedrooms: 3 double
Suite available
Bathrooms: 2 en-suite, 1 private
Bed & breakfast

per night:	£min	£max
Single	25.00	29.00
Double	35.00	40.00

⛴ ⏰10 ▤ ⌂ ♦ ⒰ ⒳ ⒰ ⒤ S ⅍ ▥ ♫ ✿ ✕ 🚑 SP ⛷ T

AMESBURY
Continued

Epworth House Bed and Breakfast ⚐
👑 COMMENDED

21 Edwards Road, Amesbury,
Salisbury SP4 7LT
☎ (01980) 624242 & Mobile 0850
452829
Fax (01980) 624242
*Restful detached house in quiet
cul-de-sac, two minutes' level walk from
Amesbury centre. Lovely enclosed
garden, excellent breakfasts.
Stonehenge nearby.*
Bedrooms: 3 double, 1 twin
Bathrooms: 1 en-suite, 2 private

Bed & breakfast
per night:	£min	£max
Single	25.00	27.50
Double	36.00	40.00

Parking for 4

⏳10 ⛽🖥🕯♿⛔️UL✂🅿TV▭🛍
❀🐾🐕

ASHBURTON
Devon
Map ref 1C2

Formerly a thriving wool centre and
important as one of Dartmoor's
four stannary towns. Today's busy
market town has many period
buildings. Ancient tradition is
maintained in the annual ale-tasting
and bread-weighing ceremony. Good
centre for exploring Dartmoor or
the south Devon coast.

New Cott Farm ⚐
👑 COMMENDED

Poundsgate, Newton Abbot
TQ13 7PD
☎ Poundsgate (01364) 631421
Fax (01364) 631338
*130-acre mixed farm. Enjoy the
freedom, peace and tranquillity of
moorland and valleys in the Dartmoor
National Park. A warm welcome and
lots of lovely home-made food to
complete your stay.*
Bedrooms: 2 double, 1 twin, 1 triple
Bathrooms: 4 en-suite

Bed & breakfast
per night:	£min	£max
Double	34.00	36.00

Half board per
person:	£min	£max
Daily	27.00	28.00
Weekly	175.00	

Evening meal 1830 (last orders
1700)
Parking for 4

⏳3 ⛽🖥🕯♿⛔️UL🅿S✂🅿TV▭🛍
🛥♪✈❀🐾

Wellpritton Farm
👑👑 HIGHLY COMMENDED

Holne, Newton Abbot TQ13 7RX
☎ Poundsgate (01364) 631273
*15-acre mixed farm. Plenty of
mouthwatering farm-produced food in
a tastefully modernised farmhouse on
the edge of Dartmoor. Special diets
catered for by arrangement. A warm
welcome and caring personal attention.*
Bedrooms: 2 double, 2 twin
Bathrooms: 3 en-suite, 1 public

Bed & breakfast
per night:	£min	£max
Single	18.00	19.00
Double	36.00	38.00

Half board per
person:	£min	£max
Daily	26.00	26.00
Weekly	175.00	175.00

Evening meal from 1900
Parking for 4

⏳⛽🖥♿⛔️UL🅿S✂TV▭🛍🛥🏹
🐾❀✈🐕

ASHTON KEYNES
Wiltshire
Map ref 2B2

Village beside the River Thames,
with houses standing along the edge
of the stream reached by bridges
from the road on the opposite bank.
Nearby stands the manor, Ashton
House.

Corner Cottage
👑👑 COMMENDED

Fore Street, Ashton Keynes,
Swindon SN6 6NP
☎ Cirencester (01285) 861454
*Homely 17th C Cotswold-stone cottage
in centre of best kept village within the
Cotswold Water Park. Ideal for water
sports and touring Cotswolds.*
Bedrooms: 1 double, 1 family room
Suite available
Bathrooms: 2 en-suite

Bed & breakfast
per night:	£min	£max
Single	22.00	24.00
Double	37.00	45.00

Parking for 4

⏳♿⛔️UL🅿S🅿TV▭🛍❀✈🐾

Map references apply to
the colour maps at the
back of this guide.

Grove Farmhouse
👑👑

Ashton Road, Leigh, Swindon
SN6 6RF
☎ Cirencester (01285) 860964
Fax (01285) 862441
*Traditional 17th C farmhouse with
stableyard, paddocks, ponds and
gardens. Quiet rural location near
water parks, riding and Cotswolds.*
Bedrooms: 1 double, 1 twin, 1 triple
Bathrooms: 3 en-suite

Bed & breakfast
per night:	£min	£max
Single	27.00	28.00
Double	40.00	40.00

Parking for 4

⏳⛽🖥♿⛔️🕯UL S✂🅿▭U❀✈🐾 SP

ASHWATER
Devon
Map ref 1C2

Village 6 miles south-east of
Holsworthy, with a pleasant village
green dominated by its church.

Renson Mill
👑👑 HIGHLY COMMENDED

Ashwater EX21 5ER
☎ Beaworthy (01409) 211665
Fax (01409) 211665
*Fabulous view in the heart of West
Devon countryside. Your welcome is
second to none by your hosts, Sonia
and Geoffrey Archer. Brochure
available.*
Bedrooms: 1 twin
Suite available
Bathrooms: 1 en-suite

Bed & breakfast
per night:	£min	£max
Single	22.00	27.00
Double	44.00	52.00

Half board per
person:	£min	£max
Daily	34.00	39.00
Weekly	210.00	

Lunch available
Evening meal 1830 (last orders
2130)
Parking for 12

⏳⛽🖥🕯♿⛔️🕯UL🅿S✂🅿TV▭
🛥U✈❀✈🐾🖥 T

AVEBURY

Wiltshire
Map ref 2B2

Set in a landscape of earthworks and megalithic standing stones, Avebury has a fine church and an Elizabethan manor. Remains from excavations may be seen in the museum. The area abounds in important prehistoric sites, among them Silbury Hill. Stonehenge stands about 20 miles due south.

New Inn
Listed APPROVED

Winterbourne Monkton, Swindon
SN4 9NW
☎ (01672) 539240
Small and friendly country pub only 1 mile from Avebury. Good, central touring position.
Bedrooms: 2 double, 3 twin
Bathrooms: 5 en-suite
Bed & breakfast

per night:	£min	£max
Double	35.00	40.00

Lunch available
Evening meal 1830 (last orders 2130)
Parking for 20
Cards accepted: Access, Visa, Switch/Delta

BARNSTAPLE

Devon
Map ref 1C1

At the head of the Taw Estuary, once a ship-building and textile town, now an agricultural centre with attractive period buildings, a modern civic centre and leisure centre. Attractions include Queen Anne's Walk, a charming colonnaded arcade and Pannier Market.
Tourist Information Centre ☎ (01271) 388583 or 388584

Bradiford Cottage ♔
COMMENDED

Bradiford, Barnstaple EX31 4DP
☎ (01271) 45039
Fax (01271) 45039
17th C cottage in quiet, rural setting. Own garden and car parking. Well placed for exploring the Atlantic coast and the moors of North Devon.
Bedrooms: 1 single, 1 double, 1 twin
Bathrooms: 2 public
Bed & breakfast

per night:	£min	£max
Single	15.00	17.00
Double	30.00	34.00

Half board per

person:	£min	£max
Daily	25.00	27.00
Weekly	106.00	174.00

Evening meal 1800 (last orders 1900)
Parking for 3

Cedars Lodge Inn
COMMENDED

Bickington Road, Barnstaple
EX31 2HP
☎ (01271) 71784
Fax (01271) 25733
Country house with lodges in 3 acres. All en-suite, satellite TV. Pub and restaurant. Just off North Devon link road.
Bedrooms: 10 double, 12 twin, 6 family rooms
Bathrooms: 28 en-suite
Bed & breakfast

per night:	£min	£max
Single	36.00	46.00
Double	56.00	66.00

Lunch available
Evening meal 1830 (last orders 2200)
Parking for 120
Cards accepted: Access, Visa, Amex, Switch/Delta

Home Park Farm Accommodation
COMMENDED

Lower Blakewell, Muddiford, Barnstaple EX31 4ET
☎ (01271) 42955

70-acre livestock farm. Panoramic scenic views combined with warm hospitality, a relaxing tranquil atmosphere and genuine farmhouse cooking await you. All rooms en-suite with TV, hairdryer, hospitality tray. Two miles north of Barnstaple and convenient for Exmoor and North Devon coast.
Bedrooms: 1 double, 2 triple
Bathrooms: 3 en-suite
Bed & breakfast

per night:	£min	£max
Single	15.00	20.00
Double	30.00	40.00

Half board per

person:	£min	£max
Daily	22.50	27.50
Weekly	150.00	160.00

Lunch available
Evening meal 1800 (last orders 1800)
Parking for 3

The Red House
HIGHLY COMMENDED

Brynsworthy, Roundswell, Barnstaple
EX31 3NP
☎ (01271) 45966
Country house, panoramic views. Both rooms colour TV, shower, hairdryer, tea/coffee facilities, central heating. Good pub food nearby.
Bedrooms: 1 double, 1 twin
Bathrooms: 1 public, 2 private showers
Bed & breakfast

per night:	£min	£max
Single	15.00	18.00
Double	30.00	36.00

Parking for 7
Open February–November

The Spinney ♔
COMMENDED

Shirwell, Barnstaple EX31 4JR
☎ Shirwell (01271) 850282
Regency former rectory with spacious accommodation, set in over an acre of grounds with views of Exmoor. Meals made from local market-day produce.
Bedrooms: 1 single, 1 double, 1 twin, 2 triple
Bathrooms: 1 en-suite, 2 public
Bed & breakfast

per night:	£min	£max
Single	16.50	16.50
Double	33.00	39.00

Half board per

person:	£min	£max
Daily	24.00	27.00
Weekly	138.00	156.00

Evening meal 1900 (last orders 1700)
Parking for 7

Waytown Farm
COMMENDED

Shirwell, Barnstaple EX31 4JN
☎ Shirwell (01271) 850396
240-acre mixed farm. Pleasantly situated 17th C farmhouse, 3 miles from Barnstaple. Exmoor and beaches
Continued ▶

BARNSTAPLE

Continued

within easy reach. Home cooking, comfortable accommodation. Access at all times.
Bedrooms: 1 single, 1 twin, 1 triple, 1 family room
Suites available
Bathrooms: 2 en-suite, 1 public

Bed & breakfast per night:

	£min	£max
Single	18.00	20.00
Double	33.00	38.00

Half board per person:

	£min	£max
Daily	25.00	28.00
Weekly	155.00	170.00

Evening meal 1830 (last orders 1600)
Parking for 6

BATH

Bath & North East Somerset Map ref 2B2

Georgian spa city beside the River Avon. Important Roman site with impressive reconstructed baths, uncovered in 19th C. Bath Abbey built on site of monastery where first king of England was crowned (AD 973). Fine architecture in mellow local stone. Pump Room and museums.
Tourist Information Centre ☎ (01225) 462831

Astor House

⚜ ⚜ COMMENDED
14 Oldfield Road, Bath BA2 3ND
☎ (01225) 429134
Fax (01225) 429134
Comfortable, spacious Victorian home with lovely views of the city and countryside yet only a short walk to the centre. Friendly welcome, varied delicious breakfasts.
Bedrooms: 4 double, 2 twin
Bathrooms: 4 en-suite, 2 public

Bed & breakfast per night:

	£min	£max
Single	22.00	40.00
Double	32.00	44.00

Parking for 6
Open February–December
Cards accepted: Access, Visa

Bailbrook Lodge Hotel

⚜ ⚜ ⚜ COMMENDED
35/37 London Road West, Bath BA1 7HZ
☎ (01225) 859090
Fax (01225) 859090

Fine Georgian house with many original features - ceilings, staircase and fireplaces. All rooms en-suite, some with four-posters. Close to centre of Bath, M4 and many historic attractions.
Bedrooms: 4 double, 4 twin, 4 family rooms
Suites available
Bathrooms: 12 en-suite

Bed & breakfast per night:

	£min	£max
Single	32.00	46.00
Double	48.00	70.00

Half board per person:

	£min	£max
Daily	33.00	40.00
Weekly	200.00	230.00

Evening meal 1930 (last orders 2130)
Parking for 20
Cards accepted: Access, Visa, Diners, Amex

Church Farm

⚜
Monkton Farleigh,
Bradford-on-Avon, Wiltshire
BA15 2QJ
☎ Batheaston (01225) 858583 & Mobile (0589) 596929
52-acre mixed farm. Sympathetically converted barn. Horses, golf and swimming. Ideal base for walking, or touring south-west England, 10 minutes from Bath.
Bedrooms: 3 double
Bathrooms: 2 en-suite, 1 private, 1 public

Bed & breakfast per night:

	£min	£max
Single	22.50	22.50
Double	35.00	40.00

Parking for 5

Dorset Villa

⚜ ⚜ APPROVED
14 Newbridge Road, Bath BA1 3JX
☎ (01225) 425975

Victorian house half a mile from Royal Crescent. En-suite rooms available. TV and coffee/tea facilities in all rooms.
Bedrooms: 5 double, 1 twin, 1 family room
Bathrooms: 5 en-suite, 1 public

Bed & breakfast per night:

	£min	£max
Single	26.00	36.00
Double	38.00	46.00

Parking for 6
Cards accepted: Access, Visa

Fern Cottage

⚜ ⚜ HIGHLY COMMENDED
74 Monkton Farleigh,
Bradford-on-Avon, Wiltshire
BA15 2QJ
☎ (01225) 859412
Fax (01225) 859018

Delightful stone-built 17th C cottage, set in fine gardens in peaceful conservation village between Bath and Bradford-on-Avon. Well-appointed rooms.
Bedrooms: 3 double
Suites available
Bathrooms: 2 en-suite, 1 private, 1 public

Bed & breakfast per night:

	£min	£max
Single	28.00	30.00
Double	45.00	50.00

Parking for 5

Flaxley Villa

⚜
9 Newbridge Hill, Bath BA1 3PW
☎ (01225) 313237
Comfortable Victorian house, just a few minutes by car to city centre and within easy reach of Royal Crescent and main attractions.
Bedrooms: 2 double, 1 twin
Bathrooms: 1 en-suite, 1 private, 1 public, 1 private shower

Bed & breakfast

Bed & breakfast per night:	£min	£max
Single	18.00	20.00
Double	36.00	42.00

Parking for 3

🛏 3 🕭 🖵 💺 🎖 ⓤⓛ ⅄ TV 🛏 🚗 🛳 SP

Gainsborough Hotel ⋀

♚♚♚

Weston Lane, Bath BA1 4AB
☎ (01225) 311380
Fax (01225) 447411

Spacious and comfortable country house hotel in own lovely grounds near the botanical gardens, and within easy walking distance of the city. High ground, nice views, own large car park. 5-course breakfast, friendly staff, warm welcome.
Bedrooms: 2 single, 6 double, 6 twin, 1 triple, 1 family room
Bathrooms: 16 en-suite

Bed & breakfast

per night:	£min	£max
Single	28.00	40.00
Double	48.00	68.00

Evening meal 1900 (last orders 2000)
Parking for 18
Cards accepted: Access, Visa, Amex

🛏 🕭 👤 🕭 🖵 💺 🎖 S 🕮 🛏 🚗 🌼 ✗ 🛳 SP T

Haute Combe Hotel

♚♚♚ COMMENDED

174/176 Newbridge Road, Bath BA1 3LE
☎ (01225) 420061 & 339064
Fax (01225) 420061
Fully-equipped en-suite rooms in comfortable, period surroundings. Easy access to city attractions. Special off-season rates. Telephone for brochure.
Bedrooms: 2 single, 3 double, 2 twin, 3 triple, 2 family rooms
Bathrooms: 11 en-suite, 1 private

Bed & breakfast

per night:	£min	£max
Single	42.00	49.00
Double	49.00	69.00

Evening meal 1900 (last orders 1800)
Parking for 12
Cards accepted: Access, Visa, Diners, Amex, Switch/Delta

🛏 🕭 👤 🕭 🖵 💺 🎖 S 🕮 TV 🛏
🚗 🎖 🌼 🛳 SP T

Kennard Hotel ⋀

♚♚ COMMENDED

11 Henrietta Street, Bath BA2 6LL
☎ (01225) 310472
Fax (01225) 460054
Georgian town house hotel of charm and character in a quiet street. A few minutes' level walk to the Abbey and Roman Baths.
Bedrooms: 2 single, 9 double, 1 twin, 1 family room
Bathrooms: 11 en-suite, 1 public

Bed & breakfast

per night:	£min	£max
Single	35.00	38.00
Double	58.00	68.00

Cards accepted: Access, Visa, Diners, Amex, Switch/Delta

🕭 📞 🕭 🖵 💺 🎖 ⓤⓛ ⅄ 🕮 🚗 ✗ 🛳
SP ★ T ◎

Kinlet Villa Guest House

♚

99 Wellsway, Bath BA2 4RX
☎ (01225) 420268
Edwardian villa retaining original features and antiques. Walking distance from city centre, good bus service, unrestricted parking. Non-smokers only, please.
Bedrooms: 1 double, 1 triple
Bathrooms: 2 public

Bed & breakfast

per night:	£min	£max
Single	17.00	18.00
Double	34.00	36.00

🛏 🖵 💺 ⓤⓛ S ⅄ 🕮 TV 🛏 🚗 ✗ 🛳
SP

Leighton House ⋀

139 Wells Road, Bath BA2 3AL
☎ (01225) 314769
Fax (01225) 443079

Enjoy a haven of friendliness in this elegant and spacious Victorian guesthouse with own car park, 10 minutes' walk from city centre.
Bedrooms: 3 double, 4 twin, 1 family room
Bathrooms: 8 en-suite

Bed & breakfast

per night:	£min	£max
Single	45.00	50.00
Double	62.00	68.00

Parking for 8
Cards accepted: Access, Visa, Switch/Delta

🛏 🕭 📞 🕭 🖵 💺 🎖 ⓤⓛ ⅄ 🕮 🛏 🚗
🌼 ✗ 🛳 SP ★ T

The Manor House

♚♚ COMMENDED

Mill Lane, Monkton Combe, Bath BA2 7HD
☎ (01225) 723128
Fax (01225) 723128

Restful, rambling 16th C manor beside mill stream in wooded valley designated as an Area of Outstanding Natural Beauty, just 2 miles south of city. Inglenook fires, Victorian conservatory, spacious bedrooms. Fine breakfasts served until noon.
Bedrooms: 2 double, 1 family room
Bathrooms: 2 en-suite, 1 private, 1 public

Bed & breakfast

per night:	£min	£max
Single	25.00	25.00
Double	45.00	45.00

Parking for 6

🛏 🕭 ⓤⓛ ⅄ 🎖 TV 🛏 🚗 🍽 10 🍷 U
🏳 🌼 🛳 OAP SP ★

Marlborough House

♚♚ COMMENDED

1 Marlborough Lane, Bath BA1 2NQ
☎ (01225) 318175 & 466127
Fax (01225) 466127
Recently renovated Victorian house 5 minutes' level walk from city centre and 2 minutes from Royal Crescent. Light and airy rooms, four-posters. Non-smoking, private parking. Discount for 3 nights or more. Minimum 2-night stay at weekends.
Bedrooms: 2 single, 2 double, 1 twin
Bathrooms: 3 en-suite, 1 public, 1 private shower

Bed & breakfast

per night:	£min	£max
Single	20.00	35.00
Double	40.00	60.00

Parking for 3
Cards accepted: Access, Visa, Amex

🛏 🕭 🕭 🖵 💺 🎖 🎖 ⓤⓛ S ⅄ 🎖 TV 🕮
🛏 ✗ 🛳 📵 SP T

Meadowland

♚♚ DE LUXE

36 Bloomfield Park, Bath BA2 2BX
☎ (01225) 311079
Set in quiet, secluded grounds and offering the highest standard in de-luxe en-suite accommodation, Meadowland is elegantly furnished and decorated. Private parking, lovely gardens,
Continued ▶

BATH
Continued

non-smoking only. A peaceful retreat for discerning travellers.
Bedrooms: 2 double, 1 twin
Bathrooms: 3 en-suite
Bed & breakfast

per night:	£min	£max
Single	40.00	45.00
Double	52.00	60.00

Parking for 6
Cards accepted: Access, Visa

Midway Cottage
COMMENDED

10 Farleigh Wick, Bradford-on-Avon, Wiltshire BA15 2PU
☎ Bradford-on-Avon (01225) 863932
Friendly, relaxed cottage with high standards of comfort and service. On A363 between Bath and Bradford-on-Avon, next door to a country inn serving excellent food.
Bedrooms: 2 double, 1 twin
Bathrooms: 3 en-suite, 1 public
Bed & breakfast

per night:	£min	£max
Single	25.00	30.00
Double	35.00	40.00

Parking for 5

Poplar Farm
Listed COMMENDED

Stanton Prior, Bath BA2 9HX
☎ Mendip (01761) 470382
Fax (01761) 470382

350-acre mixed farm. 17th C farmhouse, 5 miles west of Bath and within easy reach of park-and-ride for Bristol and Bath. Idyllic village beneath Iron Age fort. Peace and quiet. Under-cover parking.
Bedrooms: 1 double, 1 twin, 1 family room
Bathrooms: 2 en-suite, 1 public
Bed & breakfast

per night:	£min	£max
Single	18.00	24.00
Double	34.00	46.00

Parking for 10

The Priory Wing
COMMENDED

54 Lyncombe Hill, Bath BA2 4PJ
☎ (01225) 336395 & Mobile 0374 406786
Peaceful Georgian listed building bordering meadowland yet only 10 minutes' walk from city centre and railway/bus stations. Original fireplaces. Splendid organic breakfasts. Non-smokers only, please.
Bedrooms: 1 double, 1 triple
Bathrooms: 2 en-suite
Bed & breakfast

per night:	£min	£max
Single	20.00	25.00
Double	40.00	45.00

Parking for 3

The Quarrymans Arms

Box Hill, Box, Corsham, Wiltshire SN13 8HN
☎ (01225) 743569 & 742610
Fax (01225) 742610
300-year-old miners' pub, off the beaten track. Beautiful views of Colerene Valley, with a high quality imaginative menu. Only 4 miles from Bath.
Bedrooms: 1 double, 1 family room
Suite available
Bathrooms: 1 public
Bed & breakfast

per night:	£min	£max
Single	20.00	30.00
Double	35.00	45.00

Lunch available
Evening meal 1900 (last orders 2215)
Parking for 20
Cards accepted: Access, Visa, Amex, Switch/Delta

Hotel Saint Clair
COMMENDED

1 Crescent Gardens, Upper Bristol Road, Bath BA1 2NA
☎ (01225) 425543 & Mobile (01378) 834592
Fax (01225) 425543
Small family hotel 5 minutes' walk from city, 2 minutes from Royal Crescent. Large public car park 1 minute away. One-night stays welcome.
Bedrooms: 4 double, 2 twin, 2 triple, 1 family room
Bathrooms: 7 en-suite, 1 public
Bed & breakfast

per night:	£min	£max
Single	22.00	38.00
Double	32.00	50.00

Cards accepted: Access, Visa

Sampford
APPROVED

11 Oldfield Road, Bath BA2 3ND
☎ (01225) 310053
In a quiet residential area half a mile south of city centre off the A367 Exeter road.
Bedrooms: 1 double, 1 twin, 1 triple
Bathrooms: 1 public, 3 private showers
Bed & breakfast

per night:	£min	£max
Double	32.00	32.00

Parking for 2

Serendipity
Listed

19f Bradford Road, Winsley, Bradford-on-Avon, Wiltshire BA15 2HW
☎ Limpley Stoke (01225) 722380
Bungalow with beautiful gardens, 5 miles Bath, 2 miles Bradford-on-Avon. Good walking area, central for touring Cotswolds, Somerset, Wiltshire.
Bedrooms: 2 double, 1 twin
Bathrooms: 2 en-suite, 1 private, 2 public
Bed & breakfast

per night:	£min	£max
Single	18.00	22.00
Double	29.00	38.00

Parking for 5

Seven Springs
Listed COMMENDED

4 High Street, Woolley, Bath BA1 8AR
☎ (01225) 858001

In small country hamlet of Woolley, 3 miles from Bath city centre and 4 miles from M4. Lovely walks on public footpaths. Ideal for touring West Country. Bedrooms can be let as twins, doubles or family rooms. Payphone available.
Bedrooms: 1 double, 2 family rooms
Bathrooms: 3 en-suite
Bed & breakfast

per night:	£min	£max
Double	35.00	40.00

Parking for 8

Sheridan

95 Wellsway, Bearflat, Bath BA2 4RU
☎ (01225) 429562
Quiet, comfortable family guesthouse. A few minutes' drive from city centre and on main bus route to city and railway station. A non-smoking house.
Bedrooms: 1 double, 1 twin, 1 triple
Bathrooms: 1 en-suite, 1 private, 1 public

Bed & breakfast per night:	£min	£max
Single	20.00	35.00
Double	34.00	44.00

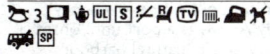

Toghill House Farm ⋔

Listed **COMMENDED**

Doynton, Bristol BS15 5RT
☎ (01225) 891261

50-acre mixed farm. Bath 5 minutes. Warm and cosy 17th C farmhouse, formerly a resting home for monks travelling from Malmesbury to Glastonbury. Views over historic Bath, Bristol and Welsh hills.
Bedrooms: 1 double, 1 triple, 1 family room
Bathrooms: 3 en-suite

Bed & breakfast per night:	£min	£max
Single	25.00	25.00
Double	40.00	44.00

Parking for 50

Wansdyke Cottage

Listed **COMMENDED**

Marksbury Gate, Bath BA2 9HE
☎ (01225) 873674 & Mobile (0589) 901571
Fax (01225) 873674

Grade II Georgian house in gardens with country views. 5 miles west of Bath on A39. Convenient for park and ride for Bristol and Bath.
Bedrooms: 2 double, 1 twin
Bathrooms: 1 private, 2 public

Bed & breakfast per night:	£min	£max
Single	15.00	18.00

Half board per person:	£min	£max
Daily	22.00	25.00

Evening meal 1900 (last orders 1700)
Parking for 4

Wellsway Guest House

51 Wellsway, Bath BA2 4RS
☎ (01225) 423434
Comfortable, clean, warm, small guesthouse on bus route. Colour TV in bedrooms. Close to local shops and only a few minutes' walk to city centre.
Bedrooms: 1 single, 1 double, 1 twin, 1 triple
Bathrooms: 1 public

Bed & breakfast per night:	£min	£max
Single	18.00	18.00
Double	28.00	36.00

Parking for 3

Wheelwrights Arms ⋔

Listed **APPROVED**

Monkton Combe, Bath BA2 7HD
☎ Limpley Stoke (01225) 722287
Ideal centre for sightseeing, a short distance from Bath. Guest rooms are in converted 17th C stables and barn.
Bedrooms: 6 double, 2 twin
Bathrooms: 8 en-suite

Bed & breakfast per night:	£min	£max
Single	30.00	35.00
Double	45.00	48.00

Half board per person:	£min	£max
Daily	35.00	38.00

Lunch available
Evening meal 1930 (last orders 2130)
Parking for 30
Cards accepted: Access, Visa

Whittington Farmhouse

HIGHLY COMMENDED

Cold Ashton, Chippenham, Wiltshire SN14 8JS
☎ Marshfield (01225) 891628
18th C farmhouse in a peaceful setting on the Cotswold Way, 5 miles north of Bath. Convenient also for Bristol and Chippenham.
Bedrooms: 2 double
Bathrooms: 2 private

Bed & breakfast per night:	£min	£max
Single	30.00	30.00
Double	38.00	40.00

Parking for 6
Open February–November

BEAMINSTER

Dorset
Map ref 2A3

Old country town of mellow local stone set amid hills and rural vales. Mainly Georgian buildings; attractive almshouses date from 1603. The 17th C church with its ornate, pinnacled tower was restored inside by the Victorians. Parnham, a Tudor manor house, lies 1 mile south.

Beam Cottage ⋔

16 North Street, Beaminster DT8 3DZ
☎ (01308) 863639
Attractive, Grade II listed cottage in centre of Beaminster, with secluded and pretty garden.
Bedrooms: 1 double, 1 twin
Bathrooms: 2 private

Bed & breakfast per night:	£min	£max
Single	18.00	20.00
Double	36.00	40.00

Half board per person:	£min	£max
Daily	28.00	30.00

Evening meal 1900 (last orders 2100)
Parking for 2
Cards accepted: Switch/Delta

BIDEFORD

Devon
Map ref 1C1

The home port of Sir Richard Grenville, the town with its 17th C merchants' houses flourished as a shipbuilding and cloth town. The bridge of 24 arches was built about 1460. Charles Kingsley stayed here while writing Westward Ho!
Tourist Information Centre ☎ (01237) 477676 or 421853

Sunset Hotel ⋔

Landcross, Bideford EX39 5JA
☎ (01237) 472962

Continued ▶

BIDEFORD

Continued

Small, elegant country hotel in peaceful, picturesque location, specialising in home cooking. Delightful en-suite bedrooms with beverages and colour TV. Book with confidence. A non-smoking establishment.
Bedrooms: 1 double, 1 twin, 1 triple, 1 family room
Bathrooms: 4 en-suite

Bed & breakfast

per night:	£min	£max
Single	25.00	30.00
Double	46.00	47.50

Half board per person:

	£min	£max
Daily	36.00	38.00
Weekly	217.50	222.50

Evening meal 1900 (last orders 1900)
Parking for 10
Open February–November
Cards accepted: Access, Visa

🐾 ☐ 🛏 💷 S ⅓ 🅿 TV ◐ ▦ ☕ ▶
❀ 🚐 OAP SP 🎣

BISHOP'S LYDEARD

Somerset
Map ref 1D1

Village 5 miles north-west of Taunton, the county town. Terminus for the West Somerset steam railway.

Slimbridge Station Farm

😃 COMMENDED

Bishop's Lydeard, Taunton TA4 3BX
☎ Bishops Lydeard (01823) 432223
Fax (01823) 432223
120-acre mixed farm. Delightful Victorian house next to the privately-owned West Somerset Steam Railway, with a limited number of trains running in the summer.
Bedrooms: 1 single, 1 double, 1 twin
Bathrooms: 1 public

Bed & breakfast

per night:	£min	£max
Single	16.50	18.00
Double	33.00	36.00

Parking for 4

🐾 🛏 ☐ 💷 UL S ⅓ 🅿 TV ▦ ❀ 🎣

BISHOPSWOOD

Somerset
Map ref 1D2

Hawthorne House 🅰

😃 COMMENDED

Bishopswood, Chard TA20 3RS
☎ Buckland St Mary (01460) 234482

19th C house in hamlet of Bishopswood in the Blackdown Hills. 5 miles north-west of Chard and 1 mile from A303. Home cooking.
Bedrooms: 2 double, 1 twin
Bathrooms: 2 en-suite, 1 private

Bed & breakfast

per night:	£min	£max
Single	22.50	24.50
Double	36.00	39.00

Half board per person:

	£min	£max
Daily	26.00	29.50
Weekly	179.50	190.00

Evening meal 1830 (last orders 1930)
Parking for 4

🐾 12 🛏 UL S ⅓ 🅿 TV ▦ ☕ ❀ 🚐
🚭 SP T

BODMIN

Cornwall
Map ref 1B2

County town south-west of Bodmin Moor with a ruined priory and church dedicated to St Petroc. Nearby are Lanhydrock House and Pencarrow House.
Tourist Information Centre ☎ (01208) 76616

Treffry Farm 🅰

😃 HIGHLY COMMENDED

Lanhydrock, Bodmin PL30 5AF
☎ (01208) 74405
Fax (01208) 74405

200-acre dairy farm. Lovely Georgian farmhouse in beautiful countryside adjoining National Trust Lanhydrock. Central for coast, moors and walks.

Bedrooms: 1 double, 2 twin
Bathrooms: 2 en-suite, 1 public, 1 private shower

Bed & breakfast

per night:	£min	£max
Double	38.00	40.00

Parking for 3

🐾 6 🛏 💷 🛏 ⅓ UL ⅓ 🅿 TV ▦
🚐 U 🎣 ❀ 🍴 🚐 🎣

BOSCASTLE

Cornwall
Map ref 1B2

Small, unspoilt village in Valency Valley. Active as a port until onset of railway era, its natural harbour affords rare shelter on this wild coast. Attractions include spectacular blow-hole, Celtic field strips, part-Norman church. Nearby St Juliot Church was restored by Thomas Hardy.

The Old Coach House 🅰

😃

Tintagel Road, Boscastle PL35 0AS
☎ (01840) 250398
Fax (01840) 250346
Relax in beautiful 300-year-old former coach house. All rooms en-suite with colour TV, teamaker, hairdryer, etc. Friendly and helpful owners. Good parking.
Wheelchair access category 3♿
Bedrooms: 1 single, 3 double, 3 twin, 1 triple
Bathrooms: 8 en-suite

Bed & breakfast

per night:	£min	£max
Single	17.00	25.00
Double	34.00	50.00

Parking for 9
Open February–November
Cards accepted: Access, Visa, Amex

🐾 6 🛏 💷 🛏 ◐ 🅿 UL S ⅓ 🅿 ▦
🚐 U 🎣 ❀ 🚐 SP 🎣 T

Tolcarne House Hotel and Restaurant 🅰

😃 COMMENDED

Tintagel Road, Boscastle PL35 0AS
☎ (01840) 250654
Delightful late Victorian house in spacious grounds with lovely views to the dramatic Cornish coastline. All rooms en-suite. Restaurant and bar. Warm welcome.
Bedrooms: 1 single, 5 double, 2 twin
Bathrooms: 8 en-suite

Bed & breakfast

per night:	£min	£max
Single	25.00	30.00
Double	40.00	56.00

Half board per person:	£min	£max
Daily	37.00	42.00
Weekly	195.00	270.00

Evening meal 1900 (last orders 2100)
Parking for 15
Open January–October and Christmas
Cards accepted: Access, Visa

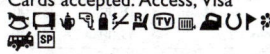

The Wellington Hotel 🏨

👑👑👑 COMMENDED

The Harbour, Boscastle PL35 0AQ
☎ (01840) 250202
Fax (01840) 250621

Historic 16th C coaching inn by Elizabethan harbour and National Trust countryside. Fine Anglo-French restaurant, specialising in regional cuisine and seafood. Freehouse with real ales, pub-grub, open fires and beams. 10 acres of private woodland walks. Pets welcome.
Bedrooms: 7 single, 11 double, 2 twin
Bathrooms: 16 en-suite, 2 public

Bed & breakfast per night:	£min	£max
Single	14.00	33.00
Double	44.00	62.00

Half board per person:	£min	£max
Daily	26.00	48.00
Weekly	171.00	305.00

Lunch available
Evening meal 1900 (last orders 2130)
Parking for 20
Cards accepted: Access, Visa, Diners, Amex, Switch/Delta

BOX

Wiltshire
Map ref 2B2

Village in an Area of Outstanding Natural Beauty, 7 miles south-west of Chippenham. It is famed for Box ground stone, used for centuries on buildings of national importance.

Hermitage

👑👑

Bath Road, Box, Corsham SN13 8DT
☎ Bath (01225) 744187 & Mobile (0585) 963952
Fax (01225) 744187
Six miles from Bath on A4 to Chippenham, 1st drive on left by 30 mph sign. 16th C house with heated pool in summer. Dining room with vaulted ceiling.
Bedrooms: 4 double, 1 triple
Bathrooms: 5 en-suite

Bed & breakfast per night:	£min	£max
Single	35.00	40.00
Double	45.00	50.00

Parking for 9

Lorne House

👑👑 COMMENDED

London Road, Box, Corsham SN14 9NA
☎ Bath (01225) 742597
Fax (01225) 742597
Victorian property, recently refurbished, on main A4 road opposite Brunel's famous Box tunnel between Bath and Chippenham. Warm and welcoming.
Bedrooms: 1 double, 3 triple
Bathrooms: 4 en-suite

Bed & breakfast per night:	£min	£max
Single	20.00	
Double	35.00	

Parking for 6
Cards accepted: Access, Visa

The map references refer to the colour maps towards the end of the guide. The first figure is the map number; the letter and figure which follow indicate the grid reference on the map.

Please check prices and other details at the time of booking.

A key to symbols can be found inside the back cover flap.

BRADFORD-ON-AVON

Wiltshire
Map ref 2B2

Huddled beside the river, the buildings of this former cloth-weaving town reflect continuing prosperity from the Middle Ages. There is a tiny Anglo-Saxon church, part of a monastery. The part-14th C bridge carries a medieval chapel, later used as a gaol.
Tourist Information Centre ☎ *(01225) 865797*

Brookfield House

👑👑 HIGHLY COMMENDED

Vaggs Hill, Southwick, Trowbridge BA14 9NA
☎ Frome (01373) 830615
150-acre dairy farm. Delightful converted country barn in quiet rural setting. Relaxed, warm and friendly atmosphere. Dairy farm 100 yards away.
Bedrooms: 2 double, 1 twin
Bathrooms: 1 en-suite, 2 public

Bed & breakfast per night:	£min	£max
Single	15.00	30.00
Double	36.00	40.00

Parking for 10

BRADWORTHY

Devon
Map ref 1C2

This ancient Saxon village has a large square bordered by shops, church and inn. Set in peaceful countryside, it is close to the coast and the Tamar Lakes.

South Worden Farm

Listed COMMENDED

Bradworthy, Holsworthy EX22 7TW
☎ (01409) 241827
20-acre mixed farm. Smallholding using principles of conservation, preservation of rare breeds and organic gardening. Excellent home cooking. No smoking, please.
Bedrooms: 1 single, 1 double, 1 twin
Bathrooms: 2 public

Bed & breakfast per night:	£min	£max
Single	13.50	
Double	27.00	

Half board per person:	£min	£max
Daily	22.00	
Weekly	140.00	

Continued ▶

BRADWORTHY

Continued

Evening meal from 1930
Parking for 3

BRIDESTOWE

Devon
Map ref 1C2

Small Dartmoor village with a much restored 15th C church, and Great Links Tor rising to the south-east.

White Hart Inn

Fore Street, Bridestowe,
Okehampton EX20 4EL
☎ (01837) 861318
17th C inn, family-run for 35 years, primarily noted for good food. En-suite accommodation. Close to Dartmoor National Park, Lydford Gorge and fishing at Roadford Lake.
Bedrooms: 2 double
Bathrooms: 2 en-suite
Bed & breakfast

per night:	£min	£max
Single	26.00	
Double	44.00	

Lunch available
Evening meal 1900 (last orders 2130)
Parking for 20
Cards accepted: Access, Visa, Diners, Amex

BRIDGERULE

Devon
Map ref 1C2

Village on the Devon/Cornwall border, cut in two by the River Tamar. Within easy reach of the North Cornwall coast.

Lodgeworthy Farm

COMMENDED
Bridgerule, Holsworthy EX22 7EH
☎ (01288) 381351
210-acre dairy farm. Old Devon longhouse in centre of village, offering a warm welcome and every comfort. Ideal touring centre, good local amenities.
Bedrooms: 1 single, 1 double, 1 family room
Bathrooms: 2 en-suite, 1 public
Bed & breakfast

per night:	£min	£max
Single	18.00	
Double	36.00	

Half board per

person:	£min	£max
Daily	25.00	
Weekly	160.00	

Evening meal 1830 (last orders 1830)
Parking for 5
Open April–September

BRIDGWATER

Somerset
Map ref 1D1

Former medieval port on the River Parrett, now small industrial town with mostly 19th C or modern architecture. Georgian Castle Street leads to West Quay and site of 13th C castle razed to the ground by Cromwell. Birthplace of Cromwellian Admiral Robert Blake is now museum. Arts centre.

Manor Farmhouse

Listed
Wembdon, Bridgwater TA5 2BB
☎ (01278) 427913 & Mobile 0831 483013
East wing of a traditional manor farmhouse set in the heart of Somerset. Ideal base for those wishing to enjoy well known beauty spots.
Bedrooms: 2 single, 1 family room
Suite available
Bathrooms: 1 en-suite, 1 public
Bed & breakfast

per night:	£min	£max
Single	15.00	18.00
Double	30.00	36.00

Half board per

person:	£min	£max
Daily	22.00	25.00
Weekly	150.00	180.00

Evening meal 1830 (last orders 2100)
Parking for 3
Open February–November

Woodlands

HIGHLY COMMENDED
35 Durleigh Road, Bridgwater TA6 7HX
☎ (01278) 423442

Beautiful listed house in 2 acres of landscaped gardens, in convenient location for exploring Quantocks and

north Somerset coastline. Tranquillity and seclusion yet close to town centre, only 3 miles from junction 24 of M5. Country house hotel quality at B & B prices.
Bedrooms: 1 single, 2 double, 1 twin
Bathrooms: 3 en-suite, 1 private, 1 public
Bed & breakfast

per night:	£min	£max
Single	18.00	30.00
Double	39.00	45.00

Half board per

person:	£min	£max
Daily	28.00	42.00
Weekly	180.00	245.00

Evening meal 1830 (last orders 1400)
Parking for 4
Cards accepted: Mastercard, Visa

BRIDPORT

Dorset
Map ref 2A3

Market town and chief producer of nets and ropes just inland of dramatic Dorset coast. Old, broad streets built for drying and twisting and long gardens for rope-walks. Grand arcaded Town Hall and Georgian buildings. Local history museum has Roman relics.
Tourist Information Centre ☎ (01308) 424901

Britmead House

HIGHLY COMMENDED
West Bay Road, Bridport DT6 4EG
☎ (01308) 422941
Fax (01308) 422516

Elegant, spacious, tastefully decorated house. Lounge and dining room overlooking garden. West Bay Harbour/Coastal Path, 10 minutes' walk away. Renowned for hospitality, delicious meals and comfort.
Bedrooms: 4 double, 3 twin
Bathrooms: 6 en-suite, 1 private
Bed & breakfast

per night:	£min	£max
Single	25.00	35.00
Double	40.00	56.00

Half board per

person:	£min	£max
Daily	33.00	41.00
Weekly	203.00	238.00

Evening meal 1900 (last orders 1700)
Parking for 8
Cards accepted: Access, Visa, Diners, Amex

⛷ 5 ♿ 🖂 🖵 📖 👤 🍽 🅂 ✂ 🅿 🎱 ⚑ ❄ 🚐 SP T

New House Farm

👑 APPROVED

Mangerton Lane, Bradpole, Bridport
DT6 3SF
☎ (01308) 422884
Mixed farm. Modern, comfortable, peaceful farmhouse set in rural Dorset hills, close to the sea. Historic Area of Outstanding Natural Beauty.
Bedrooms: 1 double, 1 family room
Bathrooms: 2 en-suite

Bed & breakfast per night:

	£min	£max
Single	16.00	18.00
Double	32.00	36.00

Half board per person:

	£min	£max
Daily	25.00	35.00

Lunch available
Evening meal 1800 (last orders 2000)
Parking for 10
Open March–November

⛷ 🖵 👤 UL 🅂 TV 🎱 🖂 ↺ ♪ ⚑ ❄ 🚐 ◎

Urella

👑👑 COMMENDED

65 Burton Road, Bridport DT6 4JE
☎ (01308) 422450
Family home in Hardy country. Ramblers' delight - or relax in our garden. Golf course nearby, West Bay 15 minutes.
Bedrooms: 1 double, 1 twin, 1 family room
Suites available
Bathrooms: 3 en-suite

Bed & breakfast per night:

	£min	£max
Single	24.00	
Double	34.00	

Half board per person:

	£min	£max
Daily	26.00	
Weekly	168.00	

Lunch available
Evening meal 1900 (last orders 2100)
Parking for 5

⛷ 🐾 🖂 🖵 👤 🍽 UL 🖀 🅂 ✂ 🅿 TV 🎱 🖂 ⚑ ❄ 🚐 SP

For ideas on places to visit refer to the introduction at the beginning of this section.

Famous for maritime links, historic harbour, Georgian terraces and Brunel's Clifton suspension bridge. Many attractions including SS Great Britain, Bristol Zoo, museums and art galleries and top name entertainments. Events include Balloon Fiesta and Regatta.
Tourist Information Centre ☎ *(0117) 926 0767*

Cully Hall Farm

👑👑 COMMENDED

Ryedown Lane, Bitton, Bristol
BS15 6JG
☎ (0117) 9323177
105-acre mixed farm. Early 17th C manor house of historic interest in peaceful setting, exactly 6 miles from Bristol and Bath. Elizabeth I is reputed to have slept here. Avon Valley Railway and Cycleway within walking distance.
Bedrooms: 3 double
Bathrooms: 1 en-suite, 1 public

Bed & breakfast per night:

	£min	£max
Single	20.00	25.00
Double	36.00	42.00

Parking for 6

⛷ 🖂 👤 🍽 UL 🖀 ✂ TV 🎱 🖂 ↺ ⚑ ❄ 🚐

The Paddock 🅜

👑 APPROVED

Hung Road, Shirehampton, Bristol
BS11 9XJ
☎ (0117) 9235140 & 9829748
Modern detached house, set in approximately 1 acre of grounds, offering quality accommodation.
Bedrooms: 4 single
Bathrooms: 4 en-suite

Bed & breakfast per night:

	£min	£max
Single	20.00	25.00
Double	40.00	50.00

Parking for 6

⛷ 👤 UL 🖀 TV 🎱 🖂 ❄ 🐾 🚐

Thornbury House

👑 COMMENDED

80 Chesterfield Road, St Andrews, Bristol BS6 5DR
☎ (0117) 9245654
Large Victorian house 1 mile from city centre, linked by frequent bus. Warm hospitality, en-suite rooms. 5 minutes from M32 and ideal for Cotswolds, West Country. Aromatherapy, Reflexology and Shiatsu available.
Bedrooms: 1 double, 1 twin
Bathrooms: 2 en-suite

Bed & breakfast per night:

	£min	£max
Single	22.00	25.00
Double	44.00	46.00

Parking for 2

⛷ 10 ♿ 🖂 🖵 👤 🍽 UL 🅂 ✂ 🎱 🖂 ❄ 🐾 🚐

Westbury Park Hotel

👑👑 HIGHLY COMMENDED

37 Westbury Road, Bristol BS9 3AU
☎ (0117) 9620465
Fax (0117) 9628607
Friendly, family-run hotel on Durdham Downs, close to city centre and M5, junction 17.
Bedrooms: 1 single, 5 double, 2 twin
Bathrooms: 8 en-suite

Bed & breakfast per night:

	£min	£max
Single	28.00	39.00
Double	44.00	49.00

Parking for 5
Cards accepted: Access, Visa, Diners, Amex

⛷ 🐾 🖂 🖵 👤 🍽 🖀 🅂 TV 🎱 🖂 ♟ 20 ❄ 🚐 T

Famous for its trawling fleet in the 19th C, a steeply-built fishing port overlooking the harbour and fish market. A statue of William of Orange recalls his landing here before deposing James II. There is an aquarium and museum. Good cliff views and walks.
Tourist Information Centre ☎ *(01803) 852861*

Richmond House Hotel 🅜

👑👑 COMMENDED

Higher Manor Road, Brixham
TQ5 8HA
☎ (01803) 882391
Detached Victorian house with well-appointed accommodation, sun-trap garden and adjacent car park. En-suite available. Convenient for shops and harbour, yet quiet location. First left after Golden Lion.
Bedrooms: 1 single, 4 double, 1 triple, 1 family room
Bathrooms: 4 en-suite, 1 private, 1 public

Bed & breakfast per night:

	£min	£max
Single	16.00	18.00
Double	32.00	40.00

Continued ▶

BRIXHAM

Continued

Parking for 5
Cards accepted: Access, Visa

🛁♿🕯♨ UL S ✗ 📺 ▥ ▸ 🚶🚐
🏠 T

BUCKFASTLEIGH

Devon
Map ref 1C2

Small manufacturing and market town just south of Buckfast Abbey on the fringe of Dartmoor. Return trips can be taken by steam train on a reopened line along the beautiful Dart Valley.

Wellpark Farm

Listed HIGHLY COMMENDED

Dean Prior, Buckfastleigh TQ11 0LY
☎ (01364) 643775
Fax (01364) 643775
500-acre arable & dairy farm. Set on the edge of Dartmoor near Buckfast Abbey. Very comfortable rooms with colour TV and tea/coffee facilities. Relaxing lounge with log fire, delicious farmhouse breakfasts, enclosed garden. A warm and friendly welcome assured. Excellent local 11th C inn. Reductions for children and weekly bookings.
Bedrooms: 1 double, 1 family room
Bathrooms: 1 public

Bed & breakfast per night:

	£min	£max
Single	15.00	18.00
Double	30.00	35.00

Parking for 3

🛁♿🕯📺▥♨ UL ✗ 📺 ▥ ▸ 🚜❋✗
🚐 SP

BUCKLAND NEWTON

Dorset
Map ref 2B3

Village midway between Sherborne and Puddletown and within easy reach of Dorchester.

Holyleas House

Listed HIGHLY COMMENDED

Buckland Newton, Dorchester DT2 7DP
☎ (01300) 345214 & Dorchester (01305) 264488
Charming, period country house, set in walled gardens. Peaceful village within easy reach of Sherborne, Dorchester and coast. Pretty rooms, glorious views and walks.
Bedrooms: 1 single, 1 double, 1 twin
Bathrooms: 3 private

Bed & breakfast per night:

	£min	£max
Single	18.00	20.00
Double	36.00	40.00

Parking for 12

🛁♿🕯📺♨ 🕯 UL ✗ 📺 ▥ 🚪🔍❋
🚐

BUDE

Cornwall
Map ref 1C2

Resort on dramatic Atlantic coast. High cliffs give spectacular sea and inland views. Golf-course, cricket pitch, folly, surfing, coarse-fishing and boating. Mother-town Stratton was base of Royalist Sir Bevil Grenville.
Tourist Information Centre ☎ (01288) 354240

Cliff Hotel ♨

♨♨♨ HIGHLY COMMENDED

Crooklets Beach, Bude EX23 8NG
☎ (01288) 353110
Fax (01288) 353110

Indoor pool and spa, solarium, putting, tennis court, bowling green, 5 acres next to National Trust cliffs, 200 yards from the beach. Chef/proprietor.
Bedrooms: 2 single, 3 double, 1 twin, 9 triple
Bathrooms: 15 en-suite

Bed & breakfast per night:

	£min	£max
Single	25.00	30.00
Double	50.00	60.00

Half board per person:

	£min	£max
Daily	30.00	38.00
Weekly	210.00	260.00

Lunch available
Evening meal 1830 (last orders 1930)
Parking for 15
Open April–September
Cards accepted: Access, Visa, Switch/Delta

🛁♿🕯📞📺♨🕯 S 📺 💿🚪
🍴🔍❋♨ 🕻↻ SP T

Clovelly House

♨♨ COMMENDED

4 Burn View, Bude EX23 8BY
☎ (01288) 352761
In a level location, opposite golf club and close to all amenities. All rooms with tea/coffee facilities, satellite TV, some en-suite.

Bedrooms: 2 single, 2 double, 1 twin, 1 triple
Bathrooms: 3 en-suite, 1 public

Bed & breakfast per night:

	£min	£max
Single	14.50	19.00
Double	29.00	40.00

Parking for 2

🛁♿3 📺♨ UL 📺 ▥ ▸ 🍴 🚐 DAP

Lower Northcott Farm

♨♨ COMMENDED

Poughill, Bude EX23 9EL
☎ (01288) 352350
Fax (01288) 352350
400-acre mixed farm. Georgian farmhouse in secluded grounds with children's safe play area. Visitors welcome to wander around and meet the animals.
Bedrooms: 1 single, 1 twin, 3 family rooms
Bathrooms: 4 en-suite, 1 public

Bed & breakfast per night:

	£min	£max
Single	17.00	
Double	34.00	

Half board per person:

	£min	£max
Daily	25.00	
Weekly	165.00	

Evening meal 1830 (last orders 1830)
Parking for 4

🛁♿📺🕯📺♨ UL S ✗ 📺 ▥ 🚪🔍
↻❋🚐 DAP SP 🐾

BURTON BRADSTOCK

Dorset
Map ref 2A3

Lying amid fields beside the River Bride, a village of old stone houses, a 14th C church and a village green. The beautiful coast road from Abbotsbury to Bridport passes by and Iron Age forts top the surrounding hills. The sheltered river valley makes a staging post for migrating birds.

Bridge Cottage Stores

Listed COMMENDED

87 High Street, Burton Bradstock, Bridport DT6 4RA
☎ Bridport (01308) 897222
Self-contained en-suite accommodation in rooms above village shop and tea room. Close to beach, on Bridport to Weymouth road.
Bedrooms: 2 double, 1 twin
Bathrooms: 3 en-suite

Bed & breakfast per night:

	£min	£max
Single	17.50	19.50
Double	35.00	39.00

Lunch available
Parking for 8

Three Horseshoes

[COMMENDED]

Mill Street, Burton Bradstock,
Bridport DT6 4QZ
☎ (01308) 897259
*Thatched inn with car park and garden
on the B3157 Bridport to Weymouth
road. Menu available AM/PM daily. Log
fire in winter.*
Bedrooms: 2 double, 1 twin
Suites available
Bathrooms: 3 en-suite
Bed & breakfast

per night:	£min	£max
Single	25.00	30.00
Double	36.00	39.00

Lunch available
Evening meal 1830 (last orders
2115)
Parking for 14
Cards accepted: Access, Visa,
Switch/Delta

CASTLE COMBE

Wiltshire
Map ref 2B2

One of England's prettiest villages, in
a steep woodland valley by a brook.
The Perpendicular church recalls
the village's prosperous times as a
cloth-weaving centre. No trace
remains of the castle, but the 13th C
effigy of its founder Walter de
Dunstanville lies in the church.

Goulters Mill Farm

[APPROVED]

Goulters Mill, Nettleton,
Chippenham SN14 7LL
☎ (01249) 782555

*Secluded 17th C mill cottage in garden
and woodland open to public. On
B4039 2 miles west of Castle Combe
down track opposite turning to Littleton
Drew.*
Bedrooms: 1 single, 1 double,
1 triple
Suites available
Bathrooms: 2 en-suite, 1 public

Bed & breakfast

per night:	£min	£max
Single	17.50	20.00
Double	40.00	60.00

Evening meal 1830 (last orders
2000)
Parking for 4
Open February–October

CHALLACOMBE

Devon
Map ref 1C1

Small, attractive village surrounded
by the stunning countryside of the
Exmoor National Park. Close to the
North Devon coast, a number of
National Trust properties and family
attractions.

Twitchen Farm

[COMMENDED]

Challacombe, Barnstaple EX31 4TT
☎ (01598) 763568
Fax (01598) 763310

*18th C stone-built courtyard farm with
unusual arched windows, characteristic
of the Fortescue Estate. Enjoy the
peace and panoramic views whilst
staying in our newly converted
accommodation. Web site address
http://bigweb.castlelink.co.uk/
north_devon/group/twitchen.ht ml*
Bedrooms: 3 double, 2 twin, 2 triple,
1 family room
Bathrooms: 8 en-suite
Bed & breakfast

per night:	£min	£max
Single	19.00	25.00
Double	38.00	50.00

Half board per person:	£min	£max
Daily	31.50	37.50
Weekly	201.50	237.50

Evening meal 1900 (last orders
1930)

Half board prices are given
per person, but in some cases
these may be based on
double/twin occupancy.

CHARD

Somerset
Map ref 1D2

Market town in hilly countryside.
The wide main street has some
handsome buildings, among them
the Guildhall, court house and
almshouses. Modern light industry
and dairy produce have replaced
19th C lace making which came at
decline of cloth trade.
Tourist Information Centre ☎ *(01460)
67463*

Wambrook Farm

[Listed]

Wambrook, Chard TA20 3DF
☎ (01460) 62371

*300-acre mixed farm. Attractive listed
farmhouse, 2 miles from Chard in
beautiful rural village. Children
welcome. From Chard take A30
towards Honiton, follow signs.*
Bedrooms: 1 double, 1 triple
Bathrooms: 1 en-suite, 1 public
Bed & breakfast

per night:	£min	£max
Single	19.00	24.00
Double	31.00	38.00

Parking for 8
Open April–October
Cards accepted: Visa

CHARMINSTER

Dorset
Map ref 2B3

Three Compasses Inn

[COMMENDED]

Charminster, Dorchester DT2 9QT
☎ Dorchester (01305) 263618

*Traditional village public house/inn with
skittle alley, set in village square.*
Bedrooms: 1 single, 1 double, 1 twin,
1 triple
Bathrooms: 2 en-suite, 3 public

Continued ▶

CHARMINSTER
Continued

Bed & breakfast per night:

	£min	£max
Single	16.00	17.50
Double	37.50	50.00

Lunch available
Evening meal 1900 (last orders 2200)
Parking for 50

🖙🖵💧🖾📺▥🖴🍴15🚐🌡

CHEDDAR

Somerset
Map ref 1D1

Large village at foot of Mendips just south of the spectacular Cheddar Gorge. Close by are Roman and Saxon sites and famous show caves. Traditional Cheddar cheese is still made here.

Tor Farm

🖤 HIGHLY COMMENDED

Nyland, Cheddar BS27 3UD
☎ (01934) 743710
33-acre mixed farm. On A371 between Cheddar and Draycott (take the road signposted Nyland). Quiet and peaceful on Somerset Levels. Ideally situated for visiting Cheddar, Bath, Wookey Hole, Glastonbury, Wells and coast.
Bedrooms: 1 single, 5 double, 1 twin, 1 family room
Bathrooms: 5 en-suite, 2 public

Bed & breakfast per night:

	£min	£max
Single	19.00	25.00
Double	33.00	46.00

Evening meal from 1800
Parking for 10
Cards accepted: Access, Visa

🖙🖾🚗🖤💧✂🖾📺▥🖴🍴20🐾✿🗡 SP T

Establishments should be open throughout the year, unless otherwise stated.

The symbols in each entry give information about services and facilities. A 'key' to these symbols appears at the back of this guide.

CHIPPENHAM

Wiltshire
Map ref 2B2

Ancient market town with modern industry. Notable early buildings include the medieval Town Hall and the gabled 15th C Yelde Hall, now a local history museum. On the outskirts Hardenhuish has a charming hilltop church by the Georgian architect John Wood of Bath.
Tourist Information Centre ☎ (01249) 657733

Frogwell House

🖤🖤

132 Hungerdown Lane, Chippenham SN14 0BD
☎ (01249) 650328
Fax (01249) 650328
Imposing late 19th C house built of local stone, modernised to provide comfortable and appealing accommodation.
Bedrooms: 1 single, 1 double, 2 twin
Bathrooms: 2 en-suite, 2 private

Bed & breakfast per night:

	£min	£max
Single	16.00	22.00
Double	32.00	40.00

Half board per person:

	£min	£max
Daily	22.00	28.00

Evening meal from 1800
Parking for 6

🖙🖵💧✂✣🖾📺▥🖴✿🚐

75 Rowden Hill

🖤

Chippenham SN15 2AL
☎ (01249) 652981
Near National Trust village of Lacock and attractive Castle Combe. Corsham Court also nearby. Friendly welcome assured.
Bedrooms: 2 double, 1 twin
Bathrooms: 1 public

Bed & breakfast per night:

	£min	£max
Single	15.00	
Double	26.00	

Parking for 5
Open April–October

🖙5🖵▥📺▥🖴🚐

Half board prices are given per person, but in some cases these may be based on double/twin occupancy.

CHULMLEIGH

Devon
Map ref 1C2

Small, hilly town above the Little Dart River, long since by-passed by the main road. The large 15th C church is noted for its splendid rood screen and 38 carved wooden angels on the roof.

The Old Bakehouse

🖤🖤 HIGHLY COMMENDED

South Molton Street, Chulmleigh EX18 7BW
☎ (01769) 580074

16th C merchant's house with licensed restaurant. En-suite bedrooms in converted bakehouse. Situated in beautiful Taw Valley between Dartmoor and Exmoor. Cosy wood burning stoves, unique atmosphere. Ideal centre for touring Devon.
Bedrooms: 1 double, 2 twin
Bathrooms: 3 en-suite

Bed & breakfast per night:

	£min	£max
Single	24.00	24.00
Double	48.00	48.00

Half board per person:

	£min	£max
Daily	38.00	38.00
Weekly	238.00	238.00

Lunch available
Evening meal 1930 (last orders 2100)
Cards accepted: Access, Visa, Switch/Delta

🖙🖾2🖾🖷🖵💧🖙🖾S✂🖾▥🖴🖴 U🍴✿🗡🚐 SP 📞 T ⊚

CHURCHILL

North Somerset
Map ref 1D1

Village of stone houses, just off the A38, dominated by Churchill Court, seat of some of the ancestors of the first Duke of Marlborough and Sir Winston Churchill.

The Mendip Gate Guest House

🖤 APPROVED

Bristol Road (A38), Churchill, Bristol BS19 5NL
☎ (01934) 852333
Comfortable family-run house on A38

between Bristol and Weston-super-Mare. Handy for airport, touring Mendips. Good local sports facilities.
Bedrooms: 2 double, 1 twin
Bathrooms: 1 en-suite, 1 private, 1 public, 1 private shower

Bed & breakfast

per night:	£min	£max
Single	18.50	20.00
Double	32.00	35.00

Half board per person:

	£min	£max
Daily	23.50	25.00

Evening meal 1800 (last orders 1900)
Parking for 8

CLAWTON

Devon
Map ref 1C2

Small village on the road between Holsworthy and Launceston.

Claw House

Listed COMMENDED

Clawton, Holsworthy EX22 6QJ
☎ Holsworthy (01409) 253930
Georgian farmhouse in pretty village. Spacious and comfortable. Lovely views. Ideal for touring Devon and Cornwall. Home cooking. Off-road parking.
Bedrooms: 1 single, 1 double, 1 triple
Bathrooms: 2 public

Bed & breakfast

per night:	£min	£max
Single	14.00	15.00
Double	28.00	30.00

Half board per person:

	£min	£max
Daily	21.00	22.00

Evening meal 1800 (last orders 2000)
Parking for 8

CLOVELLY

Devon
Map ref 1C1

Clinging to wooded cliffs, fishing village with steep cobbled street zigzagging, or cut in steps, to harbour. Carrying sledges stand beside whitewashed flower-decked cottages. Charles Kingsley's father was rector of the church set high up near the Hamlyn family's Clovelly Court.

Fuchsia Cottage

Listed COMMENDED

Burscott, Clovelly, Bideford EX39 5RR
☎ (01237) 431398
Private house with comfortable ground and first floor en-suite accommodation. Surrounded by beautiful views of sea and country. Good walking area. Ample parking.
Bedrooms: 1 single, 1 double, 1 triple
Bathrooms: 2 en-suite, 1 public

Bed & breakfast

per night:	£min	£max
Single		13.00
Double		33.00

Half board per person:

	£min	£max
Daily	19.50	23.00
Weekly	136.50	161.00

Evening meal from 1830
Parking for 3
Open April–October

COLYTON

Devon
Map ref 1D2

Surrounded by fertile farmland, this small riverside town was an early Saxon settlement. Medieval prosperity from the wool trade built the grand church tower with its octagonal lantern and the church's fine west window.

Smallicombe Farm

COMMENDED

Northleigh, Colyton EX13 6BU
☎ Wilmington (01404) 831310
25-acre mixed farm. Relax watching cows and sheep graze in glorious rural setting. Meet our prize-winning rare breed pigs. Convenient for coast from Lyme Regis to Sidmouth. Reductions for children and weekly bookings.
Bedrooms: 1 double, 1 family room
Suite available
Bathrooms: 2 en-suite

Bed & breakfast

per night:	£min	£max
Single	18.50	20.50
Double	37.00	41.00

Parking for 10

COMBWICH

Somerset
Map ref 1D1

Moxhill Farmhouse

HIGHLY COMMENDED

Moxhill Farm, Combwich, Bridgwater TA5 2PN
☎ Bridgwater (01278) 652285
Fax (01278) 652285
136-acre dairy farm. Spacious 17th C farmhouse in peaceful countryside setting near Quantock Hills and sea.
Bedrooms: 1 double, 2 family rooms
Bathrooms: 2 en-suite, 1 public

Bed & breakfast

per night:	£min	£max
Single	17.00	21.00
Double	30.00	36.00

Half board per person:

	£min	£max
Daily	29.00	33.00
Weekly	174.00	198.00

Evening meal 1930 (last orders 2030)
Parking for 3

CORSHAM

Wiltshire
Map ref 2B2

Growing town with old centre showing Flemish influence, legacy of former prosperity from weaving. The church, restored last century, retains Norman features. The Elizabethan Corsham Court, with additions by Capability Brown, has fine furniture.

Boyds Farm

HIGHLY COMMENDED

Gastard, Corsham SN13 9PT
☎ (01249) 713146
211-acre arable farm. Attractive 16th C listed farmhouse in the peaceful village of Gastard. Bath, Lacock, Castle Combe and numerous attractions are close by.
Bedrooms: 2 double, 1 twin
Bathrooms: 1 en-suite, 2 private, 1 public

Continued ▶

CORSHAM

Continued

Bed & breakfast per night:

	£min	£max
Single	20.00	20.00
Double	35.00	37.00

Parking for 6

Heatherly Cottage M

COMMENDED

Ladbrook Lane, Gastard, Corsham
SN13 9PE
☎ (01249) 701402
Fax (01249) 701412
Delightful 17th C cottage in 1.5 acres with views over open countryside. Rooms with TV and hospitality trays. Many pubs serving food nearby. Bath 9 miles. Ample parking.
Bedrooms: 2 double, 1 twin
Bathrooms: 2 en-suite, 1 private

Bed & breakfast per night:

	£min	£max
Single	20.00	20.00
Double	34.00	36.00

Parking for 10

CRACKINGTON HAVEN

Cornwall
Map ref 1C2

Tiny village on the North Cornwall coast, with a small sandy beach and surf bathing. The highest cliffs in Cornwall lie to the south.

Hallagather Farmhouse M

COMMENDED

Crackington Haven, Bude EX23 0LA
☎ St Gennys (01840) 230276
184-acre livestock farm. Ancient farmhouse, 4 miles north of Boscastle and one and a quarter miles from beach, spectacular heritage coast scenery and footpaths. Substantial Cornish breakfasts, informality, warmth and individual attention.
Bedrooms: 1 single, 1 double, 1 triple
Bathrooms: 2 en-suite, 1 private

Bed & breakfast per night:

	£min	£max
Single	13.00	17.50
Double	25.00	34.00

Parking for 6
Open February–November

CREDITON

Devon
Map ref 1D2

Ancient town in fertile valley, once prosperous from wool, now active in cider-making. Said to be the birthplace of St Boniface. The 13th C Chapter House, the church governors' meeting place, holds a collection of armour from the Civil War.

Birchmans Farm M

COMMENDED

Colebrooke, Crediton EX17 5AD
☎ Bow (01363) 82393
200-acre mixed farm. In the centre of Devon within easy reach of Exeter and Dartmoor. Home produce. All rooms en-suite with tea and coffee-making facilities.
Bedrooms: 2 double, 1 twin
Bathrooms: 3 en-suite

Bed & breakfast per night:

	£min	£max
Single	16.00	17.00
Double	30.00	32.00

Half board per person:

	£min	£max
Daily	24.00	26.00
Weekly	154.00	161.00

Evening meal (last orders 1830)
Parking for 6

CREWKERNE

Somerset
Map ref 1D2

This charming little market town on the Dorset border nestles in undulating farmland and orchards in a conservation area. Built of local sandstone with Roman and Saxon origins. The magnificent St Bartholomew's Church dates from 15th C; St Bartholomew's Fair is held in September.

Broadview Gardens M

DE LUXE

East Crewkerne, Crewkerne
TA18 7AG
☎ (01460) 73424
Fax (01460) 73424
Unusual colonial bungalow with en-suite rooms overlooking beautiful gardens. Carefully furnished with antiques. Friendly and relaxing. Quality traditional English home cooking. Truly perfect touring base, 20 minutes from coast.
Bedrooms: 1 double, 2 twin
Bathrooms: 2 en-suite, 1 private

Bed & breakfast per night:

	£min	£max
Single	25.00	35.00
Double	46.00	54.00

Half board per person:

	£min	£max
Daily	35.50	39.50
Weekly	248.50	276.50

Evening meal 1830 (last orders 1200)
Parking for 6
Cards accepted: Access, Visa

CROYDE

Devon
Map ref 1C1

Pretty village with thatched cottages near Croyde Bay. To the south stretch Saunton Sands and their dunelands Braunton Burrows with interesting flowers and plants, nature reserve and golf-course. Cliff walks and bird-watching at Baggy Point, west of the village.

Denham Farm and Country House M

COMMENDED

North Buckland, Braunton
EX33 1HY
☎ (01271) 890297
Fax (01271) 890297

160-acre mixed farm. Sample home cooking in this delightful country house, a "little gem" off the beaten track. Enjoy peace and tranquillity amid beautiful unspoilt countryside, near miles of golden sands.
Bedrooms: 6 double, 1 twin, 1 triple, 2 family rooms
Bathrooms: 10 en-suite, 1 public

Bed & breakfast per night:

	£min	£max
Double	50.00	

Half board per person:

	£min	£max
Daily	37.00	
Weekly	205.00	225.00

Evening meal 1900 (last orders 1900)
Parking for 8
Cards accepted: Access, Visa

Fig Tree Farmhouse

⌘ COMMENDED

St Mary's Road, Croyde, Braunton
EX33 1PJ
☎ (01271) 890204
Fax (01271) 890204
*400-year-old thatched Devon
longhouse, fully restored yet retaining
charm and character. On the edge of
Croyde village.*
Bedrooms: 2 double, 1 twin
Suite available
Bathrooms: 1 en-suite, 2 public
Bed & breakfast

per night:	£min	£max
Single	18.00	20.00
Double	36.00	40.00

Parking for 6
Cards accepted: Access, Visa

CROYDE BAY

Devon
Map ref 1C1

Hamlet on the North Devon coast,
west of Croyde village, with fine
surfing beaches and magnificent cliff
scenery.

West Winds 🏔

⌘⌘⌘ COMMENDED

Moor Lane, Croyde Bay, Braunton
EX33 1PA
☎ Croyde (01271) 890489 &
Mobile 0831 211247
Fax (01271) 890489

*Picturesque water's edge location,
private access to Croyde beach. Ideal
for walking, touring and golf.
Comfortable and relaxing atmosphere.*
Bedrooms: 3 double, 1 twin
Bathrooms: 3 en-suite, 1 public
Bed & breakfast

per night:	£min	£max
Single	31.00	35.00
Double	42.00	50.00

Evening meal 1830 (last orders
1800)
Parking for 6
Open March–November
Cards accepted: Access, Visa

CULLOMPTON

Devon
Map ref 1D2

Market town on former coaching
routes, with pleasant tree-shaded
cobbled pavements and some
handsome 17th C houses. Earlier
prosperity from the wool industry is
reflected in the grandness of the
church with its fan-vaulted aisle built
by a wool-stapler in 1526.

Weir Mill Farm 🏔

⌘⌘ HIGHLY COMMENDED

Jaycroft, Willand, Cullompton
EX15 2RE
☎ Tiverton (01884) 820803
Fax (01884) 820973

*105-acre livestock farm. Farmhouse
accommodation in the beautiful Culm
Valley. Only 3 miles from junction 27 of
M5, giving easy access to coast, moors
and National Trust properties.*
Bedrooms: 2 double, 1 family room
Bathrooms: 1 private, 1 public
Bed & breakfast

per night:	£min	£max
Single	18.00	20.00
Double	32.00	36.00

Half board per person:	£min	£max
Daily	26.00	30.00
Weekly	167.00	180.00

Evening meal 1830 (last orders
0900)
Parking for 5

DARTMOOR

*See under Ashburton, Bridestowe,
Buckfastleigh, Holne, Lustleigh,
Moretonhampstead, Okehampton, Peter
Tavy, Tavistock, Widecombe-in-the-Moor,
Yelverton*

Map references apply to
the colour maps at the
back of this guide.

A key to symbols can be
found inside the back
cover flap.

DARTMOUTH

Devon
Map ref 1D3

Ancient port at mouth of Dart. Has
fine period buildings, notably town
houses near Quay and Butterwalk of
1635. Harbour castle ruin. In 12th C
Crusader fleets assembled here.
Royal Naval College dominates from
Hill. Carnival, June; Regatta, August.
Tourist Information Centre ☎ *(01803)
834224*

Boringdon House

⌘⌘ HIGHLY COMMENDED

1 Church Road, Dartmouth
TQ6 9HQ
☎ (01803) 832235
*Welcoming Georgian house in large
secluded garden overlooking
Dartmouth town and harbour.
Spacious, attractive rooms. Courtyard
parking. Short walk to town centre. No
smoking.*
Bedrooms: 1 double, 2 twin
Bathrooms: 3 private
Bed & breakfast

per night:	£min	£max
Single	39.00	45.00
Double	45.00	55.00

Parking for 3

The Captains House

⌘⌘ HIGHLY COMMENDED

18 Clarence Street, Dartmouth
TQ6 9NW
☎ Torquay (01803) 832133
*18th C listed house. Tasteful decor and
personal service. Close to river and
shops.*
Bedrooms: 1 single, 3 double, 1 twin
Bathrooms: 4 en-suite, 1 private
Bed & breakfast

per night:	£min	£max
Single	25.00	30.00
Double	40.00	50.00

Cards accepted: Amex

TOWN INDEX

This can be found at the back
of the guide. If you know
where you want to stay, the
index will give you the page
number listing all
accommodation in your
chosen town, city or village.

DEVIZES

Wiltshire
Map ref 2B2

Old market town standing on the Kennet and Avon Canal. Rebuilt Norman castle, good 18th C buildings. St John's church has 12th C work and Norman tower. Museum of Wiltshire's archaeology and natural history reflects wealth of prehistoric sites in the county.
Tourist Information Centre ☎ (01380) 729408

The Gate House

Listed

Wick Lane, Devizes SN10 5DW
☎ (01380) 725283
Fax (01380) 725283
Family home, comfortable and clean. Log fire in winter. Short walk to town. Friendly welcome. No dogs and no smoking please.
Bedrooms: 1 single, 1 double, 1 twin
Suite available
Bathrooms: 1 en-suite, 1 public

Bed & breakfast

per night:	£min	£max
Single	14.50	25.00
Double	28.50	35.00

Parking for 8
Open January–November

Pinecroft

Potterne Road (A360), Devizes SN10 5DA
☎ (01380) 721433
Fax (01380) 721229
Comfortable Georgian family house with spacious rooms, exquisite garden and private parking. Only 3 minutes' walk from town centre.
Wheelchair access category 3
Bedrooms: 2 double, 2 twin, 1 family room
Suite available
Bathrooms: 4 en-suite, 1 private

Bed & breakfast

per night:	£min	£max
Single	20.00	25.00
Double	32.00	40.00

Parking for 7
Cards accepted: Access, Visa, Amex

For ideas on places to visit refer to the introduction at the beginning of this section.

DODDISCOMBSLEIGH

Devon
Map ref 1D2

Riverside village amid hilly countryside just east of Dartmoor. Former manor house stands beside granite church. Spared from the Roundheads by its remoteness, the church's chief interest lies in glowing 15th C windows said to contain Devon's finest collection of medieval glass.

Whitemoor Farm

APPROVED

Doddiscombsleigh, Exeter EX6 7PU
☎ Christow (01647) 252423
284-acre mixed farm. Homely 16th C thatched farmhouse, surrounded by garden and own farmland. Within easy reach of Dartmoor, the coast, Exeter, forest walks, birdwatching and Haldon Racecourse. Evening meal on request with good local inn nearby. Swimming pool available.
Bedrooms: 2 single, 1 double, 1 twin
Bathrooms: 1 public

Bed & breakfast

per night:	£min	£max
Single	17.00	17.50
Double	34.00	35.00

Half board per

person:	£min	£max
Daily	25.00	26.00
Weekly	169.00	172.50

Evening meal 1900 (last orders 2000)
Parking for 5
Cards accepted: Visa

DORCHESTER

Dorset
Map ref 2B3

Busy medieval county town destroyed by fires in 17th and 18th C. Cromwellian stronghold and scene of Judge Jeffreys' Bloody Assize after Monmouth Rebellion of 1685. Tolpuddle Martyrs were tried in Shire Hall. Museum has Roman and earlier exhibits and Hardy relics.
Tourist Information Centre ☎ (01305) 267992

Maumbury Cottage

Listed **COMMENDED**

9 Maumbury Road, Dorchester DT1 1QW
☎ (01305) 266726
Homely, non-smoking town centre Victorian house, convenient for all

public transport. Dorset owner has intimate local knowledge.
Bedrooms: 1 single, 1 double, 1 twin
Bathrooms: 1 public

Bed & breakfast

per night:	£min	£max
Single	15.00	16.00
Double	30.00	32.00

Parking for 2

Mountain Ash

APPROVED

30 Mountain Ash Road, Dorchester DT1 2PB
☎ (01305) 264811
Comfortable accommodation close to transport, Records Office and museums. Washbasins, TV, beverage facilities in bedrooms. Owner knowledgeable about Dorset.
Bedrooms: 1 single, 1 double, 1 twin
Bathrooms: 1 public

Bed & breakfast

per night:	£min	£max
Single	15.00	18.00
Double	30.00	36.00

Parking for 5

The Old Farmhouse

COMMENDED

Buckland Newton, Dorchester DT2 7DJ
☎ Buckland Newton (01300) 345549
200-year-old longhouse, with its own spring water, noted for warm welcome and comfort, set in the heart of the county.
Bedrooms: 2 double, 1 twin
Bathrooms: 3 en-suite

Bed & breakfast

per night:	£min	£max
Double	40.00	44.00

Parking for 10

The Old Rectory

HIGHLY COMMENDED

Winterbourne Steepleton, Dorchester DT2 9LG
☎ Martinstown (01305) 889468
Fax (01305) 889468

Built 1850 - 8 miles from beaches, 6 miles from historic Dorchester.

Surrounded by spectacular walks.
Excellent local pubs. French spoken.
Bedrooms: 2 double, 1 twin, 1 triple,
1 family room
Bathrooms: 4 en-suite, 1 private

Bed & breakfast

per night:	£min	£max
Single	30.00	40.00
Double	38.00	80.00

Evening meal 1930 (last orders
2100)
Parking for 14

Tarkaville

☻ COMMENDED

30 Shaston Crescent, Manor Park,
Dorchester DT1 2EB
☎ (01305) 266253
Attractive, modern house on edge of
town. Comfortable and friendly
atmosphere. Many facilities and ample
parking.
Bedrooms: 1 double, 1 twin
Bathrooms: 1 public

Bed & breakfast

per night:	£min	£max
Single	20.00	
Double	32.00	

Parking for 2

Yalbury Park

☻ HIGHLY COMMENDED

Frome Whitfield Farm, Frome
Whitfield, Dorchester DT2 7SE
☎ (01305) 250336
Fax (01305) 260070

170-acre mixed farm. Stone farmhouse
with large garden in parkland to River
Frome. Warm welcome for all country
lovers. 1 mile north of Dorchester.
Bedrooms: 1 double, 1 family room
Bathrooms: 2 en-suite

Bed & breakfast

per night:	£min	£max
Single	20.00	22.00
Double	40.00	44.00

Parking for 6
Open February–December

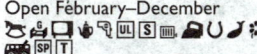
Please check prices and other
details at the time of booking.

Set among woods and hills of
south-west Exmoor, a busy riverside
town with a 13th C church. The
Rivers Barle and Exe are rich in
salmon and trout. The information
centre at the Exmoor National Park
Headquarters at Dulverton is open
throughout the year.

Dassels Country House

☻☻☻ COMMENDED

Dassels, Dulverton TA22 9RZ
☎ Anstey Mills (01398) 341203
Fax (01398) 341203

Georgian style country guesthouse,
magnificently situated on the
Devon/Somerset border, with
panoramic views.
Bedrooms: 1 single, 3 double, 3 twin,
3 triple
Bathrooms: 10 en-suite

Bed & breakfast

per night:	£min	£max
Single	27.00	30.00
Double	40.00	54.00

Half board per

person:	£min	£max
Daily	30.00	40.00
Weekly	190.00	230.00

Evening meal 1900 (last orders
2100)
Parking for 16
Cards accepted: Access, Visa, Amex,
Switch/Delta

Newhouse Farm

☻ COMMENDED

Oakford, Tiverton, Devon EX16 9JE
☎ Oakford (01398) 351347

42-acre livestock farm. Charming 16th
C farmhouse featuring oak beams and
inglenook fireplace. Pretty en-suite
bedrooms with colour TV. Home-baked
bread, delicious country cooking, warm
hospitality.

Bedrooms: 3 double
Bathrooms: 3 en-suite

Bed & breakfast

per night:	£min	£max
Single	18.00	22.00
Double	32.00	40.00

Half board per

person:	£min	£max
Daily	29.00	30.00
Weekly	175.00	180.00

Evening meal 1930 (last orders
1700)
Parking for 3

Scatterbrook Farm

Listed APPROVED

Hinam Cross, Dulverton TA22 9QQ
☎ (01398) 323857
42-acre mixed farm. Small working
farm in Exmoor National Park. Ideal
walking, riding (stabling available). Dogs
welcome and, of course, children.
Beautiful scenery.
Wheelchair access category 1 ♿
Bedrooms: 1 single, 2 double
Bathrooms: 2 en-suite, 1 public

Bed & breakfast

per night:	£min	£max
Single	15.00	20.00
Double	25.00	30.00

Half board per

person:	£min	£max
Daily	20.50	23.00
Weekly	143.50	161.00

Evening meal 1800 (last orders
1900)
Parking for 6

Ancient town with views of Exmoor.
The hilltop castle has been
continuously occupied since 1070.
Medieval prosperity from cloth built
16th C octagonal Yarn Market and the
church. A riverside mill,
packhorse bridge and 18th C hilltop
folly occupy other interesting
corners in the town.

Woodville House

Listed COMMENDED

25 West Street, Dunster, Minehead
TA24 6SN
☎ (01643) 821228
Georgian house in the residential end
of the village. Warm welcome,
comfortable accommodation, good
Continued ▶

DUNSTER

Continued

breakfast, homely relaxing atmosphere assured. Parking available in courtyard.
Bedrooms: 1 single, 1 double, 1 twin
Bathrooms: 1 public

Bed & breakfast

per night:	£min	£max
Single	16.00	19.00
Double	36.00	40.00

Parking for 4
Open March–November

Yarn Market Hotel (Exmoor) M

25 High Street, Dunster, Minehead
TA24 6SF
☎ (01643) 821425
Fax (01643) 821475
Central and accessible hotel in quaint English village, an ideal location from which to explore the Exmoor National Park.
Bedrooms: 2 double, 1 twin, 1 family room
Bathrooms: 4 en-suite

Bed & breakfast

per night:	£min	£max
Single	22.50	30.00
Double	45.00	60.00

Half board per

person:	£min	£max
Daily	34.00	41.50
Weekly	215.50	260.50

Evening meal 1800 (last orders 2000)
Parking for 3
Cards accepted: Access, Visa, Amex, Switch/Delta

EAST ALLINGTON

Devon
Map ref 1C3

Village 3 miles north-east of Kingsbridge and within easy reach of the South Devon coast.

Cuttery House

Listed

East Allington, Totnes TQ9 7QN
☎ (01548) 521259
200-year-old farmhouse refurbished to a high standard. In a charming rural setting, offering a quiet comfortable base from which to explore the beautiful South Hams.
Bedrooms: 1 single, 1 double, 1 twin, 1 triple
Bathrooms: 4 en-suite

Bed & breakfast

per night:	£min	£max
Single	17.50	20.00
Double	35.00	40.00

Evening meal 1800 (last orders 2000)
Parking for 10

EASTERTON

Wiltshire
Map ref 2B2

Village 4 miles south of Devizes, on the northern edge of Salisbury Plain.

Eastcott Manor

APPROVED

Easterton, Devizes SN10 4PL
☎ Devizes (01380) 813313
20-acre mixed farm. Grade II listed Elizabethan manor house in own 20-acre grounds. Tranquil situation on edge of Salisbury Plain. Nearest road B3098.*
Bedrooms: 2 single, 2 double
Bathrooms: 2 en-suite, 2 private

Bed & breakfast

per night:	£min	£max
Single	18.00	25.00
Double	40.00	42.00

Half board per

person:	£min	£max
Daily	33.00	40.00
Weekly	210.00	250.00

Evening meal from 1930
Parking for 20

ENFORD

Wiltshire
Map ref 2B2

Village beside the River Avon, on Salisbury Plain, 2 miles south of Upavon. Stonehenge 9 miles south.

Enford House

Enford, Pewsey SN9 6DJ
☎ Stonehenge (01980) 670414
Listed country house with pretty garden. In attractive village 7 miles from Stonehenge. Ideal centre for walking and cycling. Good food at local village pub.
Bedrooms: 1 double, 2 twin
Bathrooms: 3 public

Bed & breakfast

per night:	£min	£max
Single	17.00	17.00
Double	30.00	30.00

Evening meal 1830 (last orders 1300)
Parking for 8
Cards accepted: Amex

ERLESTOKE

Wiltshire
Map ref 2B2

Village on Salisbury Plain, 6 miles east of Westbury.

Longwater M

COMMENDED

Lower Road, Erlestoke, Devizes SN10 5UE
☎ Devizes (01380) 830095
Fax (01380) 830095

160-acre beef farm. Lakes, woods, coarse fishing and adjacent to golf-course. Traditional farm fare, with local produce and wines. Wheelchair friendly.
Wheelchair access category 3
Bedrooms: 2 double, 2 twin, 1 triple
Bathrooms: 5 en-suite

Bed & breakfast

per night:	£min	£max
Single	25.00	28.00
Double	42.00	42.00

Half board per

person:	£min	£max
Daily	33.00	40.00
Weekly	206.00	220.00

Lunch available
Evening meal 1900 (last orders 1000)
Parking for 8

WELCOME HOST

This is a nationally recognised customer care programme which aims to promote the highest standards of service and a warm welcome. Establishments who are taking part in this initiative are indicated by the ✿ symbol.

EXETER

Devon
Map ref 1D2

University city rebuilt after the 1940s around its cathedral. Attractions include 13th C cathedral with fine west front; notable waterfront buildings; Maritime Museum; Guildhall; Royal Albert Memorial Museum; underground passages; Northcott Theatre. *Tourist Information Centre ☎ (01392) 265700*

Culm Vale Country House

 APPROVED

Stoke Canon, Exeter EX5 4EG
☎ (01392) 841615 & Mobile 0374 980951
Comfortable accommodation in beautiful old country house 4 miles north east of Exeter. Friendly relaxed atmosphere, lovely gardens, ample free parking. Ideal touring centre.
Bedrooms: 2 double, 1 twin
Bathrooms: 1 en-suite, 1 public

Bed & breakfast

per night:	£min	£max
Single	20.00	
Double	30.00	35.00

Evening meal from 1830
Parking for 6

Danson House Ⅿ

COMMENDED

Marsh Green, Exeter EX5 2ES
☎ Whimple (01404) 823260

Large country house in rural location. Excellent award-winning en-suite accommodation. 2 miles from A30 and with easy access from M5.
Bedrooms: 1 single, 1 double, 1 triple
Bathrooms: 3 en-suite

Bed & breakfast

per night:	£min	£max
Single	18.00	20.00
Double	32.00	36.00

Half board per person:

	£min	£max
Daily	25.00	28.00
Weekly	150.00	165.00

Evening meal 1900 (last orders 2000)
Parking for 4

The Grange

COMMENDED

Stoke Hill, Exeter EX4 7JH
☎ (01392) 259723
Country house set in 3 acres of woodlands. 1.5 miles from the city centre. Ideal for holidays and off-season breaks. En-suite rooms.
Bedrooms: 2 double, 1 twin
Bathrooms: 3 en-suite

Bed & breakfast

per night:	£min	£max
Single	20.00	22.00
Double	30.00	37.00

Parking for 11

Hayne Barton

COMMENDED

Whitestone, Exeter EX4 2JN
☎ Longdown (01392) 811268
16-acre mixed farm. Listed farmhouse dating from 1086 (Domesday Book), set in gardens, woodland and fields overlooking Alphinbrook Valley. 4 miles from Exeter Cathedral and convenient for Dartmoor and Torquay.
Bedrooms: 2 double, 1 twin
Bathrooms: 3 en-suite

Bed & breakfast

per night:	£min	£max
Single	25.00	27.00
Double	42.00	46.00

Half board per person:

	£min	£max
Daily	34.00	36.00
Weekly	180.00	200.00

Evening meal 1930 (last orders 2030)
Parking for 10

Lochinvar Ⅿ

COMMENDED

Shepherds Park Farm, Woodbury, Exeter EX5 1LA
☎ Woodbury (01395) 232185

250-acre dairy farm. Near Woodbury village, in beautiful countryside. Spacious rooms, furnished to a high standard, with colour TV, tea/coffee facilities. Off-road parking.
Bedrooms: 1 double, 1 twin, 1 triple
Bathrooms: 2 en-suite, 1 private

Bed & breakfast

per night:	£min	£max
Single	18.00	20.00
Double	32.00	36.00

Parking for 4

EXMOOR

See under Allerford, Challacombe, Dulverton, Dunster, Lynton, West Anstey, Winsford

EXMOUTH

Devon
Map ref 1D2

Developed as a seaside resort in George III's reign, set against the woods of the Exe Estuary and red cliffs of Orcombe Point. Extensive sands, small harbour, chapel and almshouses, a model railway and A la Ronde, a 16-sided house. *Tourist Information Centre ☎ (01395) 222299*

The Mews

COMMENDED

Knappe Cross, Brixington Lane, Exmouth EX8 5DL
☎ (01395) 272198
Large part of a delightfully secluded mews building in a country setting. Midway between Exmouth and Woodbury Common. We ask that guests refrain from smoking.
Bedrooms: 1 single, 1 double, 1 twin
Bathrooms: 1 public

Bed & breakfast

per night:	£min	£max
Single	14.50	16.00
Double	29.00	32.00

Parking for 10

Establishments should be open throughout the year, unless otherwise stated.

The Ⅿ symbol after an establishment name indicates that it is a Regional Tourist Board member.

FALMOUTH

Cornwall
Map ref 1B3

Busy port and fishing harbour, popular resort on the balmy Cornish Riviera. Henry VIII's Pendennis Castle faces St Mawes Castle across the broad natural harbour and yacht basin Carrick Roads, which receives 7 rivers.
Tourist Information Centre ☎ (01326) 312300

Ivanhoe Guest House M

⚜⚜ COMMENDED

7 Melvill Road, Falmouth TR11 4AS
☎ (01326) 319083
Charming Edwardian town house situated minutes from the beaches and town centre. Most rooms are en-suite with colour TV and all amenities.
Bedrooms: 2 single, 2 double, 2 twin, 1 family room
Bathrooms: 4 en-suite, 2 public, 1 private shower

Bed & breakfast

per night:	£min	£max
Single	16.00	18.00
Double	32.00	36.00

Parking for 4
Cards accepted: Access, Visa, Diners, Amex, Switch/Delta

FENNY BRIDGES

Devon
Map ref 1D2

Village on the River Otter, 2 miles north-east of Ottery St Mary.

Skinners Ash Farm M

Listed COMMENDED

Fenny Bridges, Honiton EX14 0BH
☎ Honiton (01404) 850231
127-acre mixed farm. Family-run rare breeds farm on A30, 3 miles from Honiton and close to beaches. Home cooking, pony rides. Brochure available.
Bedrooms: 1 twin, 1 family room
Bathrooms: 2 public

Bed & breakfast

per night:	£min	£max
Single	15.50	
Double	31.00	

Half board per

person:	£min	£max
Daily	22.50	
Weekly	154.00	

Lunch available
Evening meal 1900 (last orders 2100)
Parking for 7

FIGHELDEAN

Wiltshire
Map ref 2B2

Village on the River Avon, 4 miles north of Amesbury. Stonehenge 6 miles south west.

Vale House

⚜⚜ COMMENDED

Figheldean, Salisbury SP4 8JJ
☎ Stonehenge (01980) 670713
Secluded house in centre of picturesque village, 4 miles north of Amesbury on A345. Pub food nearby. Stonehenge 2 miles.
Bedrooms: 1 single, 2 twin
Bathrooms: 1 en-suite, 1 private, 1 public

Bed & breakfast

per night:	£min	£max
Single	14.50	16.50
Double	28.50	32.50

Parking for 3

FROME

Somerset
Map ref 2B2

Old market town with modern light industry, its medieval centre watered by the River Frome. Above Cheap Street with its flagstones and watercourse is the church showing work of varying periods. Interesting buildings include 18th C wool merchants' houses.
Tourist Information Centre ☎ (01373) 467271

Fourwinds Guest House

⚜⚜ COMMENDED

19 Bath Road, Frome BA11 2HJ
☎ (01373) 462618
Fax (01373) 453029
Comfortable and friendly guesthouse with all the amenities of a small hotel. Half a mile north of town centre.
Wheelchair access category 3
Bedrooms: 1 single, 2 double, 2 twin, 1 family room
Bathrooms: 4 en-suite, 2 public

Bed & breakfast

per night:	£min	£max
Single	25.00	30.00
Double	40.00	45.00

Half board per

person:	£min	£max
Daily		40.00
Weekly		245.00

Evening meal 1800 (last orders 1900)
Parking for 12
Cards accepted: Access, Visa

GLASTONBURY

Somerset
Map ref 2A2

Market town associated with Joseph of Arimathea and the birth of English Christianity. Built around its 7th C abbey said to be the site of King Arthur's burial. Glastonbury Tor with its ancient tower gives panoramic views over flat country and the Mendip Hills.
Tourist Information Centre ☎ (01458) 832954

Meadow Barn M

⚜⚜

Middlewick Farm, Wick Lane, Glastonbury BA6 8JW
☎ (01458) 832351
20-acre beef farm. Idyllically situated amidst apple orchards and gardens, Meadow Barn has country-style ground-floor accommodation with indoor heated swimming pool. From Glastonbury take A361 Shepton Mallet road for 1.5 miles, take left turn signposted Wick, continue for 1.5 miles.
Bedrooms: 2 double, 1 twin
Bathrooms: 3 en-suite

Bed & breakfast

per night:	£min	£max
Single	20.00	23.00
Double	35.00	36.00

Half board per

person:	£min	£max
Daily	27.50	33.00
Weekly	192.50	231.00

Evening meal 1900 (last orders 2030)
Parking for 20

Pippin

Listed APPROVED

4 Ridgeway Gardens, Glastonbury BA6 8ER
☎ (01458) 834262
Peaceful location within a short walk of town centre and the Tor. Superb views over Chalice Hill. Every comfort.
Bedrooms: 1 single, 1 double, 1 twin
Bathrooms: 1 public

Bed & breakfast

per night:	£min	£max
Single	12.50	14.50
Double	27.00	31.00

Parking for 2

Wick Hollow House

8 Wick Hollow, Glastonbury
BA6 8JJ
☎ (01458) 833595
*Peaceful, self-contained accommodation
with private sitting room, on ground
floor of lovely house overlooking
Chalice Hill and the Tor. Special rates
for stays of more than 3 nights.
Children half price.*
Bedrooms: 1 family room
Suite available
Bathrooms: 1 en-suite

Bed & breakfast

per night:	£min	£max
Single	28.00	30.00
Double	38.00	43.00

Parking for 2

GOONHAVERN

Cornwall
Map ref 1B3

September Lodge

COMMENDED

Wheal Hope, Goonhavern, Truro
TR4 9QJ
☎ Perranporth (01872) 571435
*Warm relaxed atmosphere. Spacious
rooms in lovely setting, close to
beautiful beaches, golf courses and
coarse fishing lakes. Breakfasts at
flexible times.*
Bedrooms: 1 double, 1 family room
Bathrooms: 2 en-suite

Bed & breakfast

per night:	£min	£max
Single	20.00	24.00
Double	36.00	36.00

Parking for 4
Cards accepted: Access

GRAMPOUND

Cornwall
Map ref 1B3

Village on the River Fal, 6 miles
south-west of St Austell. Probus
Gardens 3 miles south-west.

Perran House

APPROVED

Fore Street, Grampound, Truro
TR2 4RS
☎ St. Austell (01726) 882066

*Delightful listed cottage in the pretty
village of Grampound, between St
Austell and Truro. Central for touring.*
Bedrooms: 2 single, 3 double, 1 twin
Bathrooms: 3 en-suite, 1 public

Bed & breakfast

per night:	£min	£max
Single	15.00	16.00
Double	34.00	36.00

Parking for 6
Cards accepted: Access, Visa

GREINTON

Somerset
Map ref 1D1

Village on the southern slopes of
the Polden Hills, within easy reach
of Bridgwater and the historic town
of Glastonbury.

West Town Farm

COMMENDED

Greinton, Bridgwater TA7 9BW
☎ Ashcott (01458) 210277

*Original part of house is over 200
years old, with large inglenook fire and
bread oven, flagstone floors and
Georgian front. Listed building.
Non-smoking establishment.*
Bedrooms: 1 double, 1 twin
Bathrooms: 2 en-suite

Bed & breakfast

per night:	£min	£max
Single	20.00	24.00
Double	36.00	40.00

Parking for 2
Open March–September

HARTLAND

Devon
Map ref 1C1

Hamlet on high, wild country near
Hartland Point. Just west, the parish
church tower makes a magnificent
landmark; the light, unrestored
interior holds one of Devon's finest
rood screens. There are spectacular
cliffs around Hartland Point and the
lighthouse.

Elmscott Farm

HIGHLY COMMENDED

Hartland, Bideford EX39 6ES
☎ (01237) 441276

*650-acre mixed farm. In a coastal
setting, quietly situated near the
Devon/Cornwall border. Signposted
from the main A39, about 4 miles
away.*
Bedrooms: 2 double, 1 twin
Bathrooms: 2 en-suite, 1 public

Bed & breakfast

per night:	£min	£max
Single	20.00	
Double	40.00	

Evening meal 1800 (last orders
2000)
Parking for 8
Open January–October

HELSTON

Cornwall
Map ref 1B3

Handsome town with steep, main
street and narrow alleys. In medieval
times it was a major port and
stannary town. Most buildings date
from Regency and Victorian periods.
The famous May dance, the Furry, is
thought to have pre-Christian
origins. A museum occupies the old
Butter Market.
*Tourist Information Centre ☎ (01326)
565431*

Longstone Farm

COMMENDED

Trenear, Helston TR13 0HG
☎ (01326) 572483
*57-acre beef farm. In peaceful
countryside in west Cornwall. Ideal for
touring and beaches. Flambards, horse
riding and swimming pool nearby.
B3297 to Redruth, left for Coverack
Bridges. Right at bottom of hill, continue
left for about 1.5 miles to Longstone
Farm.*
Bedrooms: 1 double, 1 twin, 2 triple,
1 family room
Bathrooms: 3 en-suite, 2 private

Bed & breakfast

per night:	£min	£max
Single	16.00	19.00
Double	32.00	38.00

Half board per

person:	£min	£max
Daily	24.00	
Weekly	145.00	

Continued ▶

HELSTON

Continued

Evening meal 1800 (last orders 0900)
Parking for 6
Open February–October

🛇🚱💷♿🖭Ⓢ🅟📺🖥📞🛍❋🚲
🄳🄰🄿⊚

HEMYOCK

Devon
Map ref 1D2

Celtic name for summer springs (which never run dry), set in peaceful and beautiful Blackdown Hills only 5 miles from M5 junction 26.

Orchard Lea

♿

Culmstock Road, Hemyock,
Cullompton EX15 3RN
☎ (01823) 680057
Small guesthouse with panoramic views. Good touring centre, offering peace and quiet. On B3391, 6 miles from M5 junction 27 and near A38. Ground floor accommodation for guests with mobility difficulties. Guests with learning difficulties welcomed.
Bedrooms: 1 double, 1 twin
Bathrooms: 1 public
Bed & breakfast

per night:	£min	£max
Single	13.00	15.00
Double	26.00	30.00

Half board per person:	£min	£max
Daily	18.00	20.00

Evening meal 1900 (last orders 2000)
Parking for 3
Open March–November

🛇🚱💷♿🖭Ⓢ🅟📺🖥🖥📞
🕭❋🗡🚲

HENSTRIDGE

Somerset
Map ref 2B3

Village with a rebuilt church containing the Tudor Carent tomb.

Fountain Inn Motel ⋀⋀

♿♿

High Street, Henstridge,
Templecombe BA8 0RA
☎ Stalbridge (01963) 362722
Just off the A30 on the A357 Henstridge to Stalbridge road. Country inn (1700) with modern en-suite motel-type accommodation.
Wheelchair access category 3☀
Bedrooms: 6 double

Bathrooms: 6 en-suite
Bed & breakfast

per night:	£min	£max
Single	16.00	22.00
Double	22.00	34.00

Lunch available
Evening meal 1800 (last orders 2230)
Parking for 28
Cards accepted: Access, Visa, Diners, Amex, Switch/Delta

🛇🚱♿📞💷🖥♿Ⓢ🖥🖥📞🛍❋
🚲🅢🄿

Quiet Corner Farm ⋀⋀

♿♿ COMMENDED

Henstridge BA8 0RA
☎ Stalbridge (01963) 363045
Fax (01963) 363400
5-acre livestock & fruit farm. Comfortable, welcoming 18th C farmhouse and lovely old barns, some converted to holiday cottages. In conservation village with excellent eating places and shops. Beautiful gardens and orchards. Miniature Shetland pony stud.
Bedrooms: 2 double, 1 triple
Bathrooms: 1 en-suite, 1 private, 1 public, 1 private shower
Bed & breakfast

per night:	£min	£max
Single	22.00	25.00
Double	38.00	42.00

Parking for 8

🛇💷♿🖭🖥Ⓢ🖥🖥📺🖥📞🛍❋
🗡🚲🅢🄿🎾⊚

HIGHWORTH

Wiltshire
Map ref 2B2

Small town 6 miles north-east of Swindon with square of 17th C and 18th C buildings close to the church.

Roves Farm ⋀⋀

♿♿ COMMENDED

Sevenhampton, Highworth, Swindon SN6 7QG
☎ Swindon (01793) 763939
Fax (01793) 763939
450-acre arable & livestock farm. Spacious, comfortable, quiet accommodation surrounded by beautiful countryside. Panoramic views, farm trail to woods, ponds and river. Signposted in Sevenhampton village.
Bedrooms: 1 twin, 1 triple
Bathrooms: 2 private
Bed & breakfast

per night:	£min	£max
Single	21.00	22.00
Double	34.00	35.00

Parking for 5

🛇💷♿🖭♿Ⓢ🖥🖥📺🖥📞🛍❋
❋🐕🚲🏠

HOLNE

Devon
Map ref 1C2

Woodland village on south-east edge of Dartmoor. Its 15th C church has a painted medieval screen. Charles Kingsley was born at the vicarage. Holne Woods slope to the River Dart.

Dodbrooke Farm ⋀⋀

Listed APPROVED

Michelcombe, Holne, Newton Abbot TQ13 7SP
☎ Poundsgate (01364) 631461
23-acre livestock farm. Listed 17th C longhouse in idyllic setting at foot of Dartmoor, on farm with animals and large gardens. From Ashburton on A38 take road to Two Bridges, fork left for Holne then follow signs to Michelcombe.
Bedrooms: 2 single, 2 twin
Bathrooms: 1 public
Bed & breakfast

per night:	£min	£max
Single	15.00	15.50
Double	31.00	32.00

Half board per person:	£min	£max
Daily	21.00	24.50

Evening meal from 1930
Parking for 3
Open January–November

🛇♿💷Ⓢ🖥🖥📺🖥📞🛍🕭❋🚲🏠

HOLNEST

Dorset
Map ref 2B3

Village 5 miles south-east of Sherborne.

Bookham Stud and Ryewater Farm

Listed COMMENDED

Holnest, Sherborne DT9 5PL
☎ (01963) 210248
80-acre horses farm. Delightful period stone farmhouse in idyllic setting in the centre of a small thoroughbred stud. Easy access to historic town of Sherborne.
Bedrooms: 1 single, 2 twin
Suite available
Bathrooms: 1 en-suite, 1 private, 1 public
Bed & breakfast

per night:	£min	£max
Single	15.00	25.00
Double	40.00	50.00

Parking for 6
Open March–October

HOLSWORTHY

Devon
Map ref 1C2

Busy rural town and centre of a large farming community. Market day attracts many visitors.

The Barton

COMMENDED

Pancrasweek, Holsworthy EX22 7JT
☎ Bridgerule (01288) 381315
200-acre dairy farm. At the Devon/Cornwall border on the A3072, 3.5 miles from Holsworthy and 6 miles from the Cornish coast. Friendly atmosphere and home cooking with home-produced vegetables.
Bedrooms: 2 double, 1 twin
Bathrooms: 3 en-suite

Bed & breakfast per night:	£min	£max
Single	14.00	16.00
Double	28.00	32.00

Evening meal 1800 (last orders 1600)
Parking for 5
Open April–September

Whitecroft Farm

COMMENDED

Clawton, Holsworthy EX22 6PW
☎ (01409) 254623

159-acre mixed farm. Set in rolling countryside. Relax and enjoy this character farmhouse, where comfortable, friendly service awaits. Garden and swimming pool available.
Bedrooms: 2 double, 1 twin
Bathrooms: 3 en-suite

Bed & breakfast per night:	£min	£max
Single	15.00	15.00
Double	30.00	30.00

Half board per person:	£min	£max
Daily	19.25	19.25
Weekly	115.00	115.00

Evening meal 1900 (last orders 2000)

HONITON

Devon
Map ref 1D2

Old coaching town in undulating farmland. Formerly famous for lace-making, it is now an antiques trade centre and market town. Small museum.
Tourist Information Centre ☎ (01404) 43716

Barn Park Farm

COMMENDED

Stockland Hill, Nr Cotleigh, Honiton EX14 9JA
☎ Upottery (01404) 861297
140-acre dairy farm. Barn Park farmhouse is full of character. Sloping floors, exposed beams all add to the homely atmosphere. Farm walks.
Bedrooms: 1 double, 1 twin, 1 triple
Bathrooms: 1 public, 1 private shower

Bed & breakfast per night:	£min	£max
Single	16.00	16.00
Double	30.00	32.00

Half board per person:	£min	£max
Daily	23.00	24.00
Weekly	160.00	168.00

Lunch available
Evening meal 1800 (last orders 2100)
Parking for 20

ISLES OF SCILLY

Map ref 1A3

Picturesque group of islands and granitic rocks south-west of Land's End. Peaceful and unspoilt, they are noted for natural beauty, romantic maritime history, silver sands, early flowers and sub-tropical gardens on Tresco. Main island is St Mary's.
Tourist Information Centre ☎ (01720) 422536

The Parsonage

Listed

St Agnes, Isles of Scilly TR22 0PL
☎ Scillonia (01720) 422370
Fax (01720) 422370
Old parsonage set in 1 acre of secluded, wooded grounds. Five minutes' walk from superb beaches, costal walks and island pub.
Bedrooms: 1 double, 1 triple
Bathrooms: 1 public

Bed & breakfast per night:	£min	£max
Single	17.50	22.00
Double	35.00	44.00

Evening meal 1800 (last orders 2000)

IVYBRIDGE

Devon
Map ref 1C2

Town set in delightful woodlands on the River Erme. Brunel designed the local railway viaduct. South Dartmoor Leisure Centre.
Tourist Information Centre ☎ (01752) 897035

Hillhead Farm

COMMENDED

Ugborough, Ivybridge PL21 0HQ
☎ Plymouth (01752) 892674
77-acre mixed farm. Spacious family farmhouse, surrounded by fields. All home-cooked and largely home-grown food. From A38 turn off at Wrangton Cross, turn left, take third right over crossroads, after half a mile go straight over next crossroads, after three-quarters of a mile turn left, farm is 75 yards on left.
Bedrooms: 2 double, 1 twin
Bathrooms: 1 public

Bed & breakfast per night:	£min	£max
Single	17.00	
Double	34.00	

Half board per person:	£min	£max
Daily	27.00	
Weekly	165.00	

Evening meal 1900 (last orders 2100)
Parking for 5

Strashleigh Farmhouse Bed and Breakfast

Listed COMMENDED

Ivybridge PL21 9JP
☎ Plymouth (01752) 892226
Fax (01752) 892226
420-acre dairy & livestock farm. 13th C house with high ceilings and well-appointed rooms. On a working farm, situated between Dartmoor and Bigbury Bay. Perfect base, near A38.
Bedrooms: 2 double, 1 twin
Bathrooms: 1 public

Bed & breakfast per night:	£min	£max
Single	17.00	17.00
Double	34.00	34.00

Continued ▶

IVYBRIDGE

Continued

Parking for 5
Open April–September

KILVE

Somerset
Map ref 1D1

Old village, once a smugglers' haunt, set between gentle slopes of the Quantocks and the sea.

Kilve Stores

Listed

Kilve, Bridgwater TA5 1EA
☎ Holford (01278) 741214
Very close to the sea and also ideally situated for walking on the Quantock Hills.
Bedrooms: 2 triple
Bathrooms: 1 public
Bed & breakfast

per night:	£min	£max
Single	13.50	13.50
Double	27.00	27.00

Parking for 2

KINGSBRIDGE

Devon
Map ref 1C3

Formerly important as a port, now a market town overlooking head of beautiful, wooded estuary winding deep into rural countryside. Summer art exhibitions; Cookworthy Museum.
Tourist Information Centre ☎ (01548) 853195

Court Barton

COMMENDED

Aveton Gifford, Kingsbridge TQ7 4LE
☎ (01548) 550312 & Mobile (0468) 428299
Fax (01548) 550312

40-acre mixed farm. Beautiful 16th C manor farmhouse, below the church, 100 yards from A379. Splendid hospitality guaranteed.
Bedrooms: 1 single, 2 double, 2 twin, 2 family rooms

Bathrooms: 6 en-suite, 1 public, 1 private shower
Bed & breakfast

per night:	£min	£max
Single	18.00	25.00
Double	36.00	50.00

Parking for 10
Cards accepted: Access, Visa, Switch/Delta

KINGSHEANTON

Devon
Map ref 1C1

Heanton House

Listed COMMENDED

Kingsheanton, Barnstaple EX31 4ED
☎ Barnstaple (01271) 46342
Fax (01271) 46342
Quiet, comfortable North Devon country family house. Spacious garden, guest lounge, TV, fine home cooking. Local walks near coast and Exmoor.
Bedrooms: 2 single, 2 double, 1 twin
Bathrooms: 3 public
Bed & breakfast

per night:	£min	£max
Single	17.00	20.00
Double	34.00	40.00

Lunch available
Evening meal 1900 (last orders 2000)
Parking for 7

LACOCK

Wiltshire
Map ref 2B2

Village of great charm. Medieval buildings of stone, brick or timber-frame have jutting storeys, gables, oriel windows. Magnificent church has perpendicular fan-vaulted chapel with grand tomb to benefactor who, after Dissolution, bought Augustinian nunnery, Lacock Abbey.

Old Rectory

COMMENDED

Cantax Hill, Lacock, Chippenham SN15 2JZ
☎ (01249) 730335

11-acre mixed farm. As the name implies, shares in the history of Lacock.

Located at the approach to the village and set in grounds complete with croquet. Elegant accommodation with private facilities.
Bedrooms: 2 double, 1 twin
Bathrooms: 3 en-suite
Bed & breakfast

per night:	£min	£max
Single	45.00	45.00
Double	45.00	45.00

Parking for 10
Open February–December

LAUNCESTON

Cornwall
Map ref 1C2

Medieval "Gateway to Cornwall", county town until 1838, founded by the Normans under their hilltop castle near the original monastic settlement. This market town, overlooked by its castle ruin, has a square with Georgian houses and an elaborately-carved granite church.
Tourist Information Centre ☎ (01566) 772321 or 772333

The Old Vicarage

HIGHLY COMMENDED

Treneglos, Launceston PL15 8UQ
☎ Canworthy Water (01566) 781351
Elegant Georgian vicarage set in peaceful hamlet near spectacular North Cornwall coast. Renowned for hospitality and good food. High standard of furnishings and personal attention. Non-smoking.
Bedrooms: 2 double
Bathrooms: 2 en-suite
Bed & breakfast

per night:	£min	£max
Double	41.00	44.00

Half board per

person:	£min	£max
Daily	33.00	35.00
Weekly	231.00	231.00

Evening meal 1800 (last orders 2130)
Parking for 10
Open April–October

COLOUR MAPS

Colour maps at the back of this guide pinpoint all places in which you will find accommodation listed.

Trethorne Leisure Farm

Kennards House, Launceston
PL15 8QE
☎ Pipers Pool (01566) 86324 &
86992
Fax (01566) 89903

140-acre dairy farm. You can have the
unique experience of staying on a
working leisure farm, with golf-course.
Comfortable, centrally heated rooms,
plenty of farm food and personal
attention.
Bedrooms: 2 double, 1 twin, 3 family
rooms
Bathrooms: 6 en-suite, 1 public
Bed & breakfast

per night:	£min	£max
Single	19.00	20.00
Double	36.00	38.00

Half board per person:	£min	£max
Daily	28.00	29.00
Weekly	189.00	189.00

Lunch available
Evening meal 1900 (last orders
1900)
Parking for 12

🐎🐂🕯️⚓️⑤✂️🅿️📺🛏️🔌🚗🔍✿🚐☺

LEIGH

Wiltshire
Map ref 2A3

Leighfield Lodge Farm
⚜️ COMMENDED

Leigh, Swindon SN6 6RH
☎ Malmesbury (01666) 860241 &
(01378) 521154
Fax (01666) 860241
104-acre mixed farm. Relaxed,
comfortable farmhouse
accommodation, peacefully situated.
Convenient for Cotswolds and Wiltshire
Downs. Near junction 16 of M4.
Bedrooms: 1 double, 1 family room
Suites available
Bathrooms: 2 en-suite
Bed & breakfast

per night:	£min	£max
Single	20.00	
Double	35.00	40.00

Evening meal 1800 (last orders
2000)
Parking for 12

🐎🐂🖥️⚓️⑤🏷️📺🛏️✿🚐

LEWDOWN

Devon
Map ref 1C2

Small village on the very edge of
Dartmoor. Lydford Castle is 4 miles
to the east.

Stowford Grange Farm
Listed APPROVED

Stowford, Lewdown, Okehampton
EX20 4BZ
☎ (01566) 783298
240-acre mixed farm. Listed building,
quiet village. Home-cooked food, fresh
vegetables and poultry. 10 miles from
Okehampton and 7 miles from
Launceston. Half a mile from old A30,
turn right at Royal Exchange.
Bedrooms: 3 double
Bathrooms: 2 public
Bed & breakfast

per night:	£min	£max
Single	16.00	17.00
Double	32.00	33.00

Half board per person:	£min	£max
Daily	18.00	20.00
Weekly	120.00	122.00

Evening meal from 1900
Parking for 5
Open January–November

🐎🕯️⚓️⑤🏷️📺🛏️♪🔌🔍✿🚐

LISKEARD

Cornwall
Map ref 1C2

Former stannary town with a
livestock market and light industry,
at the head of a valley running to
the coast. Handsome Georgian and
Victorian residences and a Victorian
Guildhall reflect the prosperity of
the mining boom. The large church
has an early 20th C tower and a
Norman font.

Tregondale Farm
⚜️ HIGHLY COMMENDED

Menheniot, Liskeard PL14 3RG
☎ (01579) 342407
Fax (01579) 342407
200-acre mixed farm. Characteristic
farmhouse in beautiful countryside.
En-suite bedrooms with TV and
tea/coffee. Home-produced food our
speciality. Log fires, tennis court. North
east of Menheniot, between A38 and
A390.
Bedrooms: 1 double, 1 twin, 1 triple
Bathrooms: 2 en-suite, 1 private

Bed & breakfast per night:	£min	£max
Single	18.00	20.00
Double	35.00	38.00

Half board per person:	£min	£max
Daily	26.50	29.00
Weekly	182.50	189.00

Evening meal 1900 (last orders
1800)
Parking for 3

🐎🖥️⚓️🕯️🔌⑤✂️🛏️📺🚗🔍
🐴✿🐕🚐SP◉

Tresulgan Farm
⚜️⚜️ HIGHLY COMMENDED

Menheniot, Liskeard PL14 3PU
☎ Widegates (01503) 240268
Fax (01503) 240268

145-acre mixed farm. Picturesque views
from modernised 17th C farmhouse
which has retained its character. Lots to
do in this beautiful area and a warm
and friendly welcome awaits you.
Bedrooms: 1 double, 1 triple,
1 family room
Bathrooms: 3 private
Bed & breakfast

per night:	£min	£max
Single	20.00	21.00
Double	36.00	38.00

Half board per person:	£min	£max
Daily	25.00	27.00
Weekly	175.00	189.00

Evening meal 1830 (last orders
1900)
Parking for 3

🐎🖥️⚓️🔌⑤🏷️📺🛏️🚗🔍✿
🚐DAP SP

Trewint Farm
⚜️⚜️ COMMENDED

Menheniot, Liskeard PL14 3RE
☎ (01579) 347155
Fax (01579) 347155

200-acre mixed farm. Set in peaceful,
rural surroundings with cattle and
sheep. Pony and play area for children.

Continued ▶

LISKEARD
Continued

Ideal base for touring Devon and Cornwall, 1.5 miles off A38.
Bedrooms: 1 single, 1 double, 1 family room
Bathrooms: 3 en-suite

Bed & breakfast

per night:	£min	£max
Single	20.00	25.00
Double	30.00	34.00

Half board per person:

	£min	£max
Daily	22.00	24.00
Weekly	154.00	168.00

Evening meal 1800 (last orders 1900)
Parking for 6

LONGDOWN
Devon
Map ref 1D2

Willhayes Farm ⋀

▦▦ COMMENDED

Longdown, Exeter EX6 7BN
☎ Exeter (01392) 832636
45-acre mixed farm. Mainly sheep grazing. Carp and trout ponds. Wild flowers and butterflies abound and birds of prey are often seen.
Bedrooms: 1 double, 2 twin
Bathrooms: 3 en-suite

Bed & breakfast

per night:	£min	£max
Single	16.50	20.00
Double	33.00	40.00

Evening meal 1900 (last orders 1600)
Open February–November

LOOE
Cornwall
Map ref 1C2

Small resort developed around former fishing and smuggling ports occupying the deep estuary of the East and West Looe Rivers. Narrow winding streets, with old inns; museum and art gallery are housed in interesting old buildings. Shark fishing centre, boat trips; busy harbour.

Bucklawren Farm ⋀

▦▦▦ HIGHLY COMMENDED

St Martin-by-Looe, Looe PL13 1NZ
☎ Widegates (01503) 240738
Fax (01503) 240481

534-acre arable & dairy farm. Set in glorious countryside with beautiful sea views. Only 1.5 miles from beach. Family and en-suite accommodation with colour TV. Delicious farmhouse cooking.
Bedrooms: 2 double, 2 triple, 1 family room
Bathrooms: 5 en-suite, 1 public

Bed & breakfast

per night:	£min	£max
Single	18.00	25.00
Double	36.00	40.00

Half board per person:

	£min	£max
Daily	27.50	30.00
Weekly	178.50	192.50

Evening meal 1800 (last orders 1800)
Parking for 10
Open March–October
Cards accepted: Access, Visa

Coombe Farm ⋀

▦▦ HIGHLY COMMENDED

Widegates, Looe PL13 1QN
☎ Widegates (01503) 240223
Fax (01503) 240895

Charming country house in wonderful, tranquil setting with superb views to the sea. Warm, friendly, relaxing atmosphere. Log fires. Delicious food, candlelit dining. 3.5 miles east of Looe on B3253.
Bedrooms: 3 double, 3 twin, 2 triple, 2 family rooms
Bathrooms: 10 en-suite

Bed & breakfast

per night:	£min	£max
Single	20.00	26.00
Double	40.00	52.00

Half board per person:

	£min	£max
Daily	34.00	40.00
Weekly	224.00	266.00

Evening meal 1900 (last orders 1900)
Parking for 12
Open March–October

Cards accepted: Access, Visa, Diners, Amex, Switch/Delta

Hall Barton Farm

▦▦ COMMENDED

Pelynt, Looe PL13 2LG
☎ Lanreath (01503) 220203

275-acre arable & livestock farm. Grade II listed farmhouse overlooking fields in village of Pelynt on B3359. 3 miles from Looe and Polperro. Close to coarse fishing. Pony trekking, woodland walks.
Bedrooms: 2 double, 1 twin
Bathrooms: 2 private, 1 public, 1 private shower

Bed & breakfast

per night:	£min	£max
Single	14.00	22.00
Double	28.00	40.00

Parking for 10
Open March–December

Kantara Guest House ⋀

▦ COMMENDED

7 Trelawney Terrace, Looe PL13 2AG
☎ (01503) 262093
Licensed guesthouse close to beach and shops. Informal, friendly atmosphere. Ideal family holiday setting and touring base. Satellite TV in all rooms.
Bedrooms: 1 single, 1 double, 1 twin, 1 triple, 1 family room
Bathrooms: 2 public

Bed & breakfast

per night:	£min	£max
Single	13.00	15.50
Double	26.00	31.00

Half board per person:

	£min	£max
Daily	23.00	25.50
Weekly	157.00	174.00

Evening meal 1800 (last orders 1900)
Parking for 1
Cards accepted: Access, Visa, Amex

Please mention this guide when making your booking.

Little Larnick Farm

COMMENDED

Pelynt, Looe PL13 2NB
☎ (01503) 262837
*200-acre mixed & dairy farm.
Spacious, character en-suite
accommodation in the beautiful West
Looe River Valley. Peaceful and relaxing.
Superb farmhouse breakfast.*
Bedrooms: 1 double, 1 twin, 1 triple
Bathrooms: 3 en-suite
Bed & breakfast

per night:	£min	£max
Double	34.00	38.00

Parking for 3
Open February–November

Stonerock Cottage

COMMENDED

Portuan Road, Hannafore, Looe
PL13 2DN
☎ (01503) 263651
*Modernised, old world cottage facing
south to the Channel. Ample free
parking. 2 minutes from the beach,
shops, tennis and other amenities.*
Bedrooms: 1 single, 2 double,
1 triple
Bathrooms: 1 private, 2 public
Bed & breakfast

per night:	£min	£max
Single	16.00	17.00
Double	32.00	40.00

Parking for 4
Open February–October

Trenake Farm

COMMENDED

Pelynt, Looe PL13 2LT
☎ Lanreath (01503) 220216
Fax (01503) 220216
*286-acre mixed farm. 14th C
farmhouse, 5 miles from Looe and 3
miles from Polperro. Ideal for touring
Devon and Cornwall.*
Bedrooms: 1 single, 1 double,
1 triple
Bathrooms: 1 private, 1 public
Bed & breakfast

per night:	£min	£max
Single	16.00	
Double	32.00	

Parking for 6
Open April–October

*A key to symbols can be
found inside the back
cover flap.*

Riverside village of pretty thatched
cottages gathered around its 15th C
church. The traditional Mayday
festival has dancing round the
maypole. Just west is Lustleigh
Cleave, where Dartmoor is
breached by the River Bovey which
flows through a deep valley of
boulders and trees.

The Mill

Listed

Lustleigh, Newton Abbot TQ13 9SS
☎ (01647) 277357
*12-acre smallholding. Historic riverside
millhouse on edge of beautiful
Dartmoor village. Exposed beams,
antique furniture, home-grown produce.*
Bedrooms: 1 single, 2 double
Suite available
Bathrooms: 1 en-suite, 1 public
Bed & breakfast

per night:	£min	£max
Single	19.50	19.50
Double	37.00	37.00

Parking for 3

Royal Oak of Luxborough

COMMENDED

Luxborough, Watchet TA23 0SH
☎ Washford (01984) 640319
*14th C unspoilt country inn, with
flagstone floors, low beams and
inglenook fireplaces. Fresh fish and
game specialities.*
Bedrooms: 2 double, 1 twin
Bathrooms: 2 en-suite, 1 private,
1 public
Bed & breakfast

per night:	£min	£max
Double	35.00	45.00

Lunch available
Evening meal 1900 (last orders
2200)
Parking for 8

*All accommodation in this
guide has been graded, or is
awaiting a grading, by a trained
Tourist Board inspector.*

Pretty, historic fishing town and
resort set against the fossil-rich cliffs
of Lyme Bay. In medieval times it
was an important port and cloth
centre. The Cobb, a massive stone
breakwater, shelters the ancient
harbour which is still lively with
boats.
*Tourist Information Centre ☎ (01297)
442138*

Coverdale Guest House

COMMENDED

Woodmead Road, Lyme Regis
DT7 3AB
☎ (01297) 442882
*Bright, spacious, non-smoking house.
Well furnished, comfortable bedrooms
with sea or pretty garden/country
views. Short walk to town, restaurants
and beach. Parking.*
Bedrooms: 2 single, 2 double, 1 twin,
3 triple
Bathrooms: 6 en-suite, 1 public
Bed & breakfast

per night:	£min	£max
Single	15.00	20.00
Double	30.00	40.00

Half board per person:	£min	£max
Daily	24.00	29.00

Evening meal 1830 (last orders
1630)
Parking for 12
Open March–October

Higher Spence

Wootton Fitzpaine, Bridport
DT6 6DF
☎ Charmouth (01297) 560556
*Rural farm cottage with country and
sea views. 3 miles Charmouth, 5 miles
Lyme Regis.*
Bedrooms: 1 double, 1 triple
Bathrooms: 1 public
Bed & breakfast

per night:	£min	£max
Single	12.00	14.00
Double	24.00	28.00

Parking for 3

Lydwell House

COMMENDED

Lyme Road, Uplyme, Lyme Regis
DT7 3TJ
☎ (01297) 443522
Fax (01297) 445897

Continued ▶

LYME REGIS
Continued

Delightful Edwardian house in attractive gardens, ideally located for coast and country walking. Short distance to Lyme Regis town centre and beaches.
Bedrooms: 1 single, 1 double, 1 twin, 2 family rooms
Bathrooms: 2 en-suite, 1 public

Bed & breakfast

per night:	£min	£max
Single	17.50	22.00
Double	33.00	38.00

Parking for 7

The Red House

HIGHLY COMMENDED

Sidmouth Road, Lyme Regis
DT7 3ES
☎ (01297) 442055
Superb coastal views, large garden, parking.
Bedrooms: 2 twin, 1 triple
Bathrooms: 3 en-suite

Bed & breakfast

per night:	£min	£max
Single	30.00	36.00
Double	40.00	48.00

Parking for 4
Open March–November
Cards accepted: Access, Visa, Switch/Delta

Rotherfield

COMMENDED

View Road, Lyme Regis DT7 3AA
☎ (01297) 445585
Exceptionally spacious, comfortable accommodation, own car park, home cooking, panoramic sea and countryside views. Warm welcome assured. Completely refurbished.
Bedrooms: 1 single, 3 double, 2 twin, 1 family room
Bathrooms: 4 en-suite, 2 public

Bed & breakfast

per night:	£min	£max
Single	16.50	18.50
Double	33.00	37.00

Half board per

person:	£min	£max
Daily	27.00	29.00
Weekly	177.50	197.45

Evening meal 1850 (last orders 1950)
Parking for 7

Southernhaye

COMMENDED

Pound Road, Lyme Regis DT7 3HX
☎ (01297) 443077
Fax (01297) 443077
Distinctive Edwardian house in quiet location with panoramic views over Lyme Bay, about 10 minutes' walk from town and beach.
Bedrooms: 1 single, 1 double, 1 twin
Bathrooms: 1 public

Bed & breakfast

per night:	£min	£max
Single	18.00	18.00
Double	32.00	34.00

Parking for 2

Springfield

COMMENDED

Woodmead Road, Lyme Regis
DT7 3LJ
☎ (01297) 443409

Elegant Georgian house and conservatory in partly walled garden, with well-proportioned rooms, many enjoying views over the sea. Close to major footpaths.
Bedrooms: 1 single, 2 double, 2 twin, 1 triple, 1 family room
Bathrooms: 3 en-suite, 2 public

Bed & breakfast

per night:	£min	£max
Single	15.00	18.00
Double	28.00	38.00

Parking for 9
Open February–November

White House

COMMENDED

47 Silver Street, Lyme Regis
DT7 3HR
☎ (01297) 443420
Fine views of Dorset coastline from rear of this 18th C guesthouse. A short walk from beach, gardens and shops.
Bedrooms: 5 double, 2 twin
Bathrooms: 7 en-suite

Bed & breakfast

per night:	£min	£max
Double	34.00	42.00

Parking for 6
Open April–October

LYNTON

Devon
Map ref 1C1

Hilltop resort on Exmoor coast linked to its seaside twin, Lynmouth, by a water-operated cliff railway which descends from the town hall. Spectacular surroundings of moorland cliffs with steep chasms of conifer and rocks through which rivers cascade.
Tourist Information Centre ☎ (01598) 752225

Ingleside Hotel

COMMENDED

Lynton EX35 6HW
☎ (01598) 752223
Family-run hotel with high standards in elevated position overlooking village. Ideal centre for exploring Exmoor.
Bedrooms: 4 double, 1 twin, 2 triple
Bathrooms: 7 en-suite

Bed & breakfast

per night:	£min	£max
Single	27.00	29.00
Double	46.00	50.00

Half board per

person:	£min	£max
Daily	36.00	38.00
Weekly	238.00	252.00

Evening meal 1900 (last orders 1800)
Parking for 10
Open March–October
Cards accepted: Access, Visa

South Cheriton Farm

COMMENDED

Barbrook, Lynton EX35 6LJ
☎ (01598) 753280
9-acre mixed farm. 17th C farmhouse with inglenook fireplaces and extensive exposed beams. Set high up in the beautiful Exmoor countryside and offering a traditional welcome.
Bedrooms: 2 double, 1 twin
Bathrooms: 3 en-suite

Bed & breakfast

per night:	£min	£max
Single	20.00	22.00
Double	36.00	40.00

Half board per

person:	£min	£max
Daily	28.00	30.00

Evening meal from 1900
Parking for 6
Open April–October

South View Guest House

⚜️⚜️ COMMENDED

23 Lee Road, Lynton EX35 6BP
☎ (01598) 752289
Friendly village centre guesthouse offering comfortable bed and breakfast accommodation. All rooms en-suite, overnight guests welcome, private parking. Open all year.
Bedrooms: 3 double, 2 triple
Bathrooms: 5 en-suite

Bed & breakfast per night:	£min	£max
Single	15.50	18.50
Double	25.00	35.00

Parking for 5

MALMESBURY

Wiltshire
Map ref 2B2

Overlooking the River Avon, an old town dominated by its great church, once a Benedictine abbey. The surviving Norman nave and porch are noted for fine sculptures, 12th C arches and musicians' gallery.
Tourist Information Centre ☎ (01666) 823748

Manor Farm

⚜️⚜️ COMMENDED

Corston, Malmesbury SN16 0HF
☎ (01666) 822148 & Mobile 0374 675783
Fax (01666) 822148

436-acre mixed farm. Relax and unwind in this award-winning 17th C Cotswold farmhouse. Ideally situated for visiting Cotswolds, Bath and Stonehenge. Just 3 miles from junction 17 of M4.
Bedrooms: 1 single, 2 double, 1 twin, 1 triple, 1 family room
Bathrooms: 3 en-suite, 1 public, 2 private showers

Bed & breakfast per night:	£min	£max
Single	16.00	24.00
Double	32.00	40.00

Parking for 12
Cards accepted: Access, Visa

Weavers

Listed

Worthy's Lane, Gloucester Road, Malmesbury SN16 9JS
☎ (01666) 822589
Modern split-level bungalow in private road leading to cricket club. View of abbey across River Avon. Close to town centre. Non-smokers only. Hot drinks provided.
Bedrooms: 2 single, 1 double, 1 twin
Bathrooms: 2 public

Bed & breakfast per night:	£min	£max
Single	18.00	18.50
Double	36.00	37.00

Parking for 4

Winkworth Farm

Listed COMMENDED

Lea, Malmesbury SN16 9NH
☎ (01666) 823267

230-acre beef farm. Enjoy the warm, friendly atmosphere of this 17th C Cotswold-stone farmhouse set in a secluded walled garden. Comfortable rooms, oak beams, log fires. Ideal for a quiet holiday or as a touring base, just 3 miles from Malmesbury. No smoking, please.
Bedrooms: 1 single, 2 double
Bathrooms: 1 en-suite, 1 public

Bed & breakfast per night:	£min	£max
Single	20.00	25.00
Double	36.00	40.00

Half board per person:	£min	£max
Daily	32.50	32.50

Parking for 10

MARK

Somerset
Map ref 1D1

Laurel Farm 🅜

⚜️ APPROVED

The Causeway, Mark, Highbridge TA9 4PZ
☎ Mark Moor (01278) 641216
150-acre dairy farm. 300-year-old farmhouse with beamed sitting room, log fire, colour TV. Home-produced vegetables, cream and eggs served.

Ideal touring centre on the B3139 road between Wells and Burnham-on-Sea.
Bedrooms: 1 single, 1 double, 1 family room
Bathrooms: 2 public

Bed & breakfast per night:	£min	£max
Single	14.00	16.00
Double	27.00	32.00

Evening meal 1800 (last orders 1800)
Parking for 4

MARLBOROUGH

Wiltshire
Map ref 2B2

Important market town, in a river valley cutting through chalk downlands. The broad main street, with colonnaded shops on one side, shows a medley of building styles, mainly from the Georgian period. Lanes wind away on either side and a church stands at each end.
Tourist Information Centre ☎ (01672) 513989

Laurel Cottage Guest House

⚜️⚜️ HIGHLY COMMENDED

Southend, Ogbourne St George, Marlborough SN8 1SG
☎ Ogbourne St George (01672) 841288

16th C thatched cottage, in a delightful rural setting. Low beamed ceilings and inglenook fireplace. Non-smokers only, please.
Bedrooms: 2 double, 1 twin
Bathrooms: 2 en-suite, 1 private

Bed & breakfast per night:	£min	£max
Single		35.00
Double	42.00	50.00

Parking for 5
Open April–October

The Old Vicarage 🅜

⚜️⚜️⚜️ HIGHLY COMMENDED

Burbage, Marlborough SN8 3AG
☎ (01672) 810495
Fax (01672) 810663
Victorian country house in 2-acre garden, offering peace, comfort and delicious food. South of Marlborough

Continued ▶

MARLBOROUGH

Continued

and within easy reach of Avebury, Bath, Oxford and Salisbury.
Bedrooms: 1 single, 1 double, 1 twin
Bathrooms: 3 en-suite

Bed & breakfast

per night:	£min	£max
Single	30.00	40.00
Double	60.00	80.00

Parking for 10
Cards accepted: Access, Visa

MARTINSTOWN

Dorset
Map ref 2B3

Village 3 miles west of Dorchester. Maiden Castle Iron Age fort lies to the east of the village and the Hardy Monument stands on Black Down to the south west.

Old Post Office

Listed APPROVED

Martinstown, Dorchester DT2 9LF
☎ (01305) 889254
Grade II listed Georgian cottage tastefully modernised throughout. Large garden with many small animals. Good rural base, children and pets welcome.
Bedrooms: 1 double, 2 twin
Bathrooms: 1 public

Bed & breakfast

per night:	£min	£max
Single	20.00	20.00
Double	35.00	35.00

Half board per

person:	£min	£max
Daily		27.50

Evening meal 1900 (last orders 1630)
Parking for 3

MARTOCK

Somerset
Map ref 2A3

Small town with many handsome buildings of Ham stone and a beautiful old church with tie-beam roof. Medieval treasurer's house, Georgian market house, 17th C manor.

Wychwood

HIGHLY COMMENDED

7 Bearley Road, Martock TA12 6PG
☎ (01935) 825601
Small, quality B & B in quiet position just off A303 between Montacute and

---

Tintinhull. Ideal for visiting the ten "Classic" gardens of South Somerset. Near Glastonbury and Wells. Brochure.
Bedrooms: 2 double, 1 twin
Bathrooms: 2 en-suite, 1 private, 3 public

Bed & breakfast

per night:	£min	£max
Single	26.00	30.00
Double	36.00	40.00

Half board per

person:	£min	£max
Daily		32.50

Evening meal 1900 (last orders 2000)
Parking for 3
Cards accepted: Access, Visa

MEVAGISSEY

Cornwall
Map ref 1B3

Small fishing town, a favourite with holidaymakers. Earlier prosperity came from pilchard fisheries, boat-building and smuggling. By the harbour are fish cellars, some converted, and a local history museum is housed in an old boat-building shed. Handsome Methodist chapel; shark fishing, sailing.

Kerry Anna Country House

HIGHLY COMMENDED

Treleaven Farm, Mevagissey, St Austell PL26 6RZ
☎ (01726) 843558
Fax (01726) 843558
200-acre arable farm. Country house overlooking village, surrounded by rambling farmland, wild flowers and wildlife. Outdoor swimming pool, games barn, putting green. Farm cooking.
Bedrooms: 4 double, 1 twin, 1 family room
Bathrooms: 6 en-suite

Bed & breakfast

per night:	£min	£max
Double	40.00	50.00

Half board per

person:	£min	£max
Daily	30.50	35.50
Weekly	203.00	238.00

Evening meal 1900 (last orders 1200)
Parking for 6
Open April–October

Steep House

Portmellon Cove, Mevagissey, St Austell PL26 2PH
☎ (01726) 843732

Refreshingly clean and comfortable house with large garden and covered (summertime) pool. Superb seaside views, licensed, free off-road parking.
Bedrooms: 1 single, 5 double, 1 twin, 1 triple
Bathrooms: 2 en-suite, 1 private, 2 public

Bed & breakfast

per night:	£min	£max
Single	17.00	20.00
Double	36.00	54.00

Parking for 12
Cards accepted: Access, Visa, Amex

MINEHEAD

Somerset
Map ref 1D1

Victorian resort with spreading sands developed around old fishing port on the coast below Exmoor. Former fishermen's cottages stand beside the 17th C harbour; cobbled streets climb the hill in steps to the church. Boat trips, steam railway. Hobby Horse festival 1 May.
Tourist Information Centre ☎ (01643) 702624

Hillside

HIGHLY COMMENDED

Higher Allerford, Minehead TA24 8HS
☎ Porlock (01643) 862831

Thatched cottage owned by the National Trust. Wonderful views overlooking the picturesque village of Allerford. Ideally situated for exploring Exmoor.
Bedrooms: 1 double, 1 twin
Bathrooms: 1 public

Bed & breakfast per night:	£min	£max
Single	18.00	19.00
Double	36.00	38.00

Parking for 4

🐎2🖳🛏️⬚♿🧺ⓤⓛ🔒ⓢ✂️🅜🆃🆅🌖 ▥🚗⛵☼🐾🎣🏠

Kildare Lodge 𝓜

👑 COMMENDED

Townsend Road, Minehead
TA24 5RQ
☎ (01643) 702009
Fax (01643) 706516
Family-run, Edwin Lutyens designed, Grade II listed building. Elegant a la carte restaurant; character-filled licensed bar; bar meals; well appointed en-suite accommodation, including family rooms.
Bedrooms: 1 single, 4 double, 2 twin, 2 family rooms
Suite available
Bathrooms: 9 en-suite, 1 public

Bed & breakfast per night:	£min	£max
Single	25.00	37.50
Double	44.00	68.00

Half board per person:	£min	£max
Daily	29.00	37.50
Weekly	185.00	240.00

Lunch available
Evening meal 1900 (last orders 2100)
Parking for 28
Cards accepted: Access, Visa, Diners, Amex

🐎🦽📞🖳🛏️♿🧺ⓢ🅜🆃🆅▥🚗
🍴50🚻☼❋DAP🐾SP🏠🆃

MORETONHAMPSTEAD
Devon
Map ref 1C2

Small market town with a row of 17th C almshouses standing on the Exeter road. Surrounding moorland is scattered with ancient farmhouses, prehistoric sites.

Great Doccombe Farm

👑 COMMENDED

Doccombe, Moretonhampstead, Newton Abbot TQ13 8SS
☎ (01647) 440694
8-acre mixed farm. 300-year-old farmhouse in Dartmoor National Park. Comfortable rooms, farmhouse cooking. Ideal for walking the Teign Valley and Dartmoor.
Bedrooms: 1 double, 1 triple
Bathrooms: 2 private, 2 public

Bed & breakfast per night:	£min	£max
Double	34.00	36.00

Parking for 6

🐎🦽📞🖳🛏️♿🧺ⓤⓛ🔒ⓢ✂️🅜🚗❋ SP🏠🆃

Great Sloncombe Farm 𝓜

👑👑👑 HIGHLY COMMENDED

Moretonhampstead, Newton Abbot
TQ13 8QF
☎ (01647) 440595

170-acre dairy farm. 13th C Dartmoor farmhouse. Comfortable rooms, central heating, en-suite. Large wholesome farmhouse breakfasts and delicious dinners. Friendly Devonshire welcome.
Bedrooms: 2 double, 1 twin
Bathrooms: 3 en-suite

Bed & breakfast per night:	£min	£max
Single	19.00	21.00
Double	38.00	42.00

Half board per person:	£min	£max
Daily	30.00	42.00

Evening meal 1830 (last orders 1000)
Parking for 3

🐎8🖳🛏️♿🧺ⓤⓛ🔒ⓢ✂️🅜🆃🆅▥ 🚗🚻☼🐾🎣🏠

White Hart Hotel 𝓜

👑👑👑 COMMENDED

The Square, Moretonhampstead, Newton Abbot TQ13 8NF
☎ (01647) 440406
Fax (01647) 440565
Historic inn, centre of Dartmoor town. Antiques, log fires, cosy bar. Fine restaurant and bar meals. Comfortable bedrooms with courtesy trays.
Bedrooms: 1 single, 9 double, 10 twin
Bathrooms: 20 en-suite, 1 public

Bed & breakfast per night:	£min	£max
Single	40.00	45.00
Double	55.00	73.00

Lunch available
Evening meal 1800 (last orders 2030)
Parking for 12
Cards accepted: Access, Visa, Diners, Amex, Switch/Delta

🐎10📞🖳🛏️♿🧺ⓢ🅜🆅▥🚗 🍴80🐾SP🏠🆃

Wooston Farm

👑👑 HIGHLY COMMENDED

Moretonhampstead, Newton Abbot
TQ13 8QA
☎ (01647) 440367
Fax (01647) 440367
280-acre mixed farm. Situated within Dartmoor National Park above the Teign Valley, with scenic views and walks. Two rooms are en-suite, one with four-poster bed.
Bedrooms: 2 double, 1 twin
Bathrooms: 2 en-suite, 1 private

Bed & breakfast per night:	£min	£max
Double	36.00	42.00

Half board per person:	£min	£max
Daily	29.00	32.00

Evening meal 1800 (last orders 1830)
Parking for 3

🐎8🖳🛏️♿🧺ⓤⓛ🔒ⓢ✂️🅜🆅 ▥🚗🚻☼🎣🐾

Wray Barton Manor 𝓜

👑👑 COMMENDED

Moretonhampstead, Newton Abbot
TQ13 8SE
☎ (01647) 440467
Fax (01647) 440628
Superbly appointed manor house in 3.75 acres of peaceful gardens on edge of Dartmoor. On A382, 5 miles from Bovey Tracey, 1.5 miles Moretonhampstead.
Bedrooms: 3 double, 3 twin
Bathrooms: 3 en-suite, 2 public

Bed & breakfast per night:	£min	£max
Single	18.00	24.00
Double	36.00	48.00

Parking for 20
Open April–October

🐎🖳🛏️♿🧺ⓢ✂️🅜▥☼❋🐾🏠

For farm holidays and accommodation suitable for young people and organised groups, please refer to the special sections at the back of this guide.

MORTEHOE

Devon
Map ref 1C1

Old coastal village with small, basically Norman church. Wild cliffs, inland combes; sand and surf at Woolacombe.

Sunnycliffe Hotel M

COMMENDED

Mortehoe, Woolacombe EX34 7EB
☎ Woolacombe (01271) 870597
Fax (01271) 870597

Small, select hotel beautifully situated above sandy cove overlooking beach. Traditional English food cooked by qualified chef/proprietor. Sorry, no children or pets.
Bedrooms: 6 double, 2 twin
Bathrooms: 8 en-suite, 2 public
Bed & breakfast

per night:	£min	£max
Single	25.00	28.00
Double	50.00	56.00

Half board per

person:	£min	£max
Daily	39.00	44.00
Weekly	240.00	275.00

Evening meal 1900 (last orders 1900)
Parking for 11
Open February–October

MORWENSTOW

Cornwall
Map ref 1C2

Scattered parish on the wild north Cornish coast. The church, beautifully situated in a deep combe by the sea, has a fine Norman doorway and 15th C bench-ends. Its unique vicarage was built by the 19th C poet-priest Robert Hawker. Nearby are Cornwall's highest cliffs.

Cornakey Farm

Listed COMMENDED

Morwenstow, Bude EX23 9SS
☎ (01288) 331260
220-acre mixed farm. Convenient coastal walking area with extensive views of sea and cliffs from bedrooms. Home cooking, games room. Reduced rates for children. Good touring centre.

Bedrooms: 1 double, 2 triple
Bathrooms: 1 en-suite, 2 private, 1 public
Bed & breakfast

per night:	£min	£max
Single	15.00	17.00
Double	30.00	34.00

Half board per

person:	£min	£max
Daily	22.00	24.00
Weekly	154.00	

Evening meal 1830 (last orders 1730)
Parking for 2

MYLOR BRIDGE

Cornwall
Map ref 1B3

Penmere Guest House

COMMENDED

Rosehill, Mylor Bridge, Falmouth TR11 5LZ
☎ Falmouth (01326) 374470
Fax (01326) 378828
Beautifully restored Victorian property enjoying splendid creek views, close to yachting centres. Lovely garden, perfect for a relaxing stay.
Bedrooms: 3 double, 2 twin, 1 triple
Bathrooms: 4 en-suite, 2 private
Bed & breakfast

per night:	£min	£max
Single	25.00	28.00
Double	44.00	50.00

Parking for 6

NEWQUAY

Cornwall
Map ref 1B2

Popular resort spread over dramatic cliffs around its old fishing port. Many beaches with abundant sands, caves and rock pools; excellent surf. Pilots' gigs are still raced from the harbour and on the headland stands the stone Huer's House from the pilchard-fishing days.
Tourist Information Centre ☎ *(01637) 871345*

Degembris Farmhouse M

HIGHLY COMMENDED

St Newlyn East, Newquay TR8 5HY
☎ Mitchell (01872) 510555
Fax (01872) 510230
165-acre arable farm. Cosy south-facing farmhouse offering welcoming log fires in winter, comfortable en-suite bedrooms and delicious home cooking. "A wonderful oasis from 23 million cars".

Bedrooms: 1 single, 1 double, 1 twin, 1 triple, 1 family room
Bathrooms: 3 en-suite, 1 public
Bed & breakfast

per night:	£min	£max
Single	18.00	20.00
Double	36.00	40.00

Half board per

person:	£min	£max
Daily	28.00	30.00
Weekly	196.00	210.00

Evening meal from 1830
Parking for 8

Manuels Farm M

HIGHLY COMMENDED

Quintrell Downs, Newquay TR8 4NY
☎ (01637) 873577
44-acre mixed farm. In a sheltered valley 2 miles inland from Newquay, offering the peace of the countryside with the charm of a traditional 17th C farmhouse. Beautifully furnished, log fires and delicious country cooking.
Bedrooms: 1 double, 1 triple, 1 family room
Bathrooms: 1 en-suite, 2 public
Bed & breakfast

per night:	£min	£max
Single	18.50	20.00
Double	37.00	40.00

Half board per

person:	£min	£max
Daily	30.00	
Weekly	210.00	

Evening meal 1830 (last orders 1630)
Parking for 6

Rose Cottage

HIGHLY COMMENDED

Shepherds Farm, St Newlyn East, Newquay TR8 5NW
☎ Zelah (01872) 540502
600-acre mixed farm. Come and share our warm and friendly atmosphere, with first class service in affordable quality accommodation. Cleanliness guaranteed. All rooms en-suite, colour TV and tea-making facilities. Ideal touring and beaches, 1 mile from A30 in little hamlet of Fiddlers Green.
Bedrooms: 2 double, 1 twin
Bathrooms: 3 en-suite
Bed & breakfast

per night:	£min	£max
Single	15.00	17.00
Double	30.00	34.00

Parking for 3

NEWTON FERRERS

Devon
Map ref 1C3

Hillside village overlooking wooded estuary of the River Yealm, with attractive waterside cottages and yacht anchorage.

Maywood Cottage

COMMENDED

Bridgend, Newton Ferrers, Plymouth PL8 1AW
☎ Plymouth (01752) 872372
Cottage on 3 levels, close to River Yealm estuary. Part old, all modernised. Friendly welcome, choice of breakfast and evening meal. Wonderful position for exploring West Devon and Cornwall.
Bedrooms: 2 twin
Bathrooms: 1 en-suite, 1 private

Bed & breakfast per night:	£min	£max
Single	17.50	22.50
Double	35.00	40.00

Half board per person:	£min	£max
Daily	26.00	31.00
Weekly	179.50	194.50

Evening meal 1800 (last orders 2030)
Parking for 3

NORTH CADBURY

Somerset
Map ref 2B3

Hill Ash Farm

COMMENDED

Woolston, North Cadbury, Yeovil BA22 7BL
☎ (01963) 440332
30-acre hill farm. 1766 Grade II listed thatched farmhouse. Beautiful rural setting in peaceful hamlet. 1.5 miles from A303.
Bedrooms: 2 single, 2 double
Bathrooms: 2 en-suite, 1 public

Bed & breakfast per night:	£min	£max
Single	18.00	22.00
Double	36.00	44.00

Parking for 4
Open March–October

Map references apply to the colour maps at the back of this guide.

NOSS MAYO

Devon
Map ref 1C3

Slade Barn

Listed COMMENDED

Netton Farm, Noss Mayo, Plymouth PL8 1HA
☎ Plymouth (01752) 872235
Fax (01752) 872235
50-acre arable farm. Attractive coastal barn conversion. Indoor pool, games room, tennis court, gardens. Fabulous National Trust walks. Up-market B & B and self-catering. Ideal family holiday.
Bedrooms: 2 double, 1 twin
Bathrooms: 2 public, 1 private shower

Bed & breakfast per night:	£min	£max
Single	18.00	20.00
Double	36.00	40.00

Half board per person:	£min	£max
Daily	28.00	30.00
Weekly	172.00	184.00

Parking for 6

OKEHAMPTON

Devon
Map ref 1C2

Busy market town near the high tors of northern Dartmoor. The Victorian church, with William Morris windows and a 15th C tower, stands on the site of a Saxon church. A Norman castle ruin overlooks the river to the west of the town. Museum of Dartmoor Life in a restored mill.

Higher Cadham Farm

COMMENDED

Jacobstowe, Okehampton EX20 3RB
☎ (01837) 851647
Fax (01837) 851410

139-acre mixed farm. 16th C farmhouse on a traditional Devon farm, 5 miles from Dartmoor and within easy reach of coast. On the Tarka trail.
Bedrooms: 1 single, 3 double, 2 twin, 3 family rooms
Bathrooms: 6 en-suite, 1 public

Bed & breakfast per night:	£min	£max
Single	17.00	23.00
Double	34.00	46.00

Half board per person:	£min	£max
Daily	25.00	31.00
Weekly	158.00	198.00

Lunch available
Evening meal 1900 (last orders 2000)
Parking for 6
Cards accepted: Access, Visa, Switch/Delta

Oxenham Arms

COMMENDED

South Zeal, Okehampton EX20 2JT
☎ (01837) 840244
Fax (01837) 840791
In the centre of Dartmoor village, originally built in the 12th C. Wealth of granite fireplaces, oak beams, mullion windows. Various diets available on request.
Bedrooms: 3 double, 2 twin, 3 triple
Bathrooms: 8 en-suite

Bed & breakfast per night:	£min	£max
Single	40.00	45.00
Double	50.00	60.00

Half board per person:	£min	£max
Daily	55.00	60.00
Weekly	227.50	245.00

Lunch available
Evening meal 1930 (last orders 2100)
Parking for 8
Cards accepted: Access, Visa, Diners, Amex

Week Farm

COMMENDED

Bridestowe, Okehampton EX20 4HZ
☎ Bridestowe (01837) 861221
Fax (01837) 861221

180-acre dairy & livestock farm. A warm welcome awaits you at this homely 17th C farmhouse, three-quarters of a mile from the old A30 and 6 miles from Okehampton.
Continued ▶

OKEHAMPTON

Continued

Home cooking and every comfort.
Come and spoil yourselves.
Bedrooms: 3 double, 1 triple,
1 family room
Bathrooms: 5 en-suite
Bed & breakfast
per night:

	£min	£max
Single	21.00	23.00
Double	42.00	46.00

Half board per
person:

	£min	£max
Daily	31.00	33.00

Evening meal 1900 (last orders
1700)
Parking for 10

🐎🖑⌂🖐♿ UL S ⚲✂🅟 TV ▥ 🖪
🔍↻♉♪❄🈲 DAP ⌦ SP 🏠 T

OTTERY ST MARY

Devon
Map ref 1D2

Former wool town with modern
light industry set in countryside on
the River Otter. The Cromwellian
commander, Fairfax, made his
headquarters here briefly during the
Civil War. The interesting church,
dating from the 14th C, is built to
cathedral plan.

Pitt Farm ⋔

⬥⬥⬥ COMMENDED

Fairmile, Ottery St Mary EX11 1NL
☎ (01404) 812439
190-acre mixed farm. 16th C thatched
farmhouse. En-suite rooms available,
log fires in season. Half-a-mile off A30
on B3176.
Bedrooms: 2 double, 2 twin, 2 family
rooms
Suites available
Bathrooms: 2 en-suite, 2 private,
2 public
Bed & breakfast
per night:

	£min	£max
Single	17.00	20.00
Double	34.00	40.00

Half board per
person:

	£min	£max
Daily	26.00	30.00

Evening meal 1900 (last orders
1700)
Parking for 6
Cards accepted: Amex

🐎🖑♿ S 🄻 TV ▥ 🖪 ♉✕🚲 SP 🏠

Please check prices and other
details at the time of booking.

PAIGNTON

Devon
Map ref 1D2

Lively seaside resort with a pretty
harbour on Torbay. Bronze Age and
Saxon sites are occupied by the
15th C church, which has a Norman
door and font. The beautiful
Chantry Chapel was built by local
landowners, the Kirkhams.
Tourist Information Centre ☎ (01803)
558383

South Sands Hotel ⋔

⬥⬥⬥ COMMENDED

12 Alta Vista Road, Paignton
TQ4 6BZ
☎ (01803) 557231 & Freephone
0500 432153
Fax (01803) 529947
Family-run, wonderful fresh food.
Superb, peaceful location overlooking
sea, beach, park and close to harbour.
Large car park. Dogs and children very
welcome.
Bedrooms: 2 single, 3 double, 1 twin,
5 triple, 8 family rooms
Bathrooms: 17 en-suite, 2 private
Bed & breakfast
per night:

	£min	£max
Single	20.00	28.00
Double	40.00	56.00

Half board per
person:

	£min	£max
Daily	28.00	35.00
Weekly	165.00	220.00

Evening meal 1800 (last orders
1900)
Parking for 17
Open April–October and Christmas
Cards accepted: Access, Visa

🐎🖑♿📟⌂ 🖐♿ S ⚲✂ TV ▥ 🖪
🔍♉❄ DAP ⌦ SP T

PENSFORD

Bath & North East Somerset
Map ref 2A2

Green Acres

Listed APPROVED

Stanton Wick, Pensford BS18 4BX
☎ Mendip (01761) 490397
A friendly welcome awaits you in
peaceful setting, off A37/A368. Relax
and enjoy panoramic views across
Chew Valley to Dundry Hills.
Bedrooms: 2 single, 1 double, 1 twin
Bathrooms: 1 en-suite, 4 public
Bed & breakfast
per night:

	£min	£max
Single	16.00	18.00
Double	32.00	36.00

Parking for 22

🐎🖑⚒♿⌂ 🖐♿ UL S 🄻✂ TV ▥
🖪♉🐕❄🔍🈲🚲

PENZANCE

Cornwall
Map ref 1A3

Resort and fishing port on Mount's
Bay with mainly Victorian
promenade and some fine Regency
terraces. Former prosperity came
from tin trade and pilchard fishing.
Grand Georgian style church by
harbour. Georgian Egyptian building
at head of Chapel Street and
Morrab Gardens.
Tourist Information Centre ☎ (01736)
62207

Menwidden Farm ⋔

Listed APPROVED

Ludgvan, Penzance TR20 8BN
☎ (01736) 740415
40-acre mixed farm. Centrally situated
in west Cornwall. Warm family
atmosphere and home cooking. Turn
right at Crowlas crossroads on the A30
from Hayle, signpost Vellanoweth on
right turn. Last farm on left.
Bedrooms: 1 single, 2 double, 1 twin,
1 family room
Bathrooms: 2 public
Bed & breakfast
per night:

	£min	£max
Single	15.00	
Double	30.00	

Half board per
person:

	£min	£max
Daily	23.00	
Weekly	135.00	

Evening meal 1800 (last orders
1800)
Parking for 8
Open February–November

🐎🖑 UL 🄻 TV ↻❄🚲◎

Relubbus House

Listed

Relubbus, Penzance TR20 9EL
☎ (01736) 762929
17th C barn converted into a large
house in the late 70s.
Bedrooms: 2 double, 1 twin
Bathrooms: 2 en-suite, 1 private,
1 public
Bed & breakfast
per night:

	£min	£max
Single	25.00	30.00
Double	40.00	50.00

Parking for 6
Open March–November

🐎🖑♿ UL S 🄻✂ TV ▥ 🖪♉❄🚲
🚲 SP

Map references apply to
the colour maps at the
back of this guide.

Rose Farm

⚜⚜ COMMENDED

Chyanhal, Buryas Bridge, Penzance
TR19 6AN
☎ (01736) 731808
Fax (01736) 731808
*25-acre livestock & horses farm. Small
farm with many animals. Near beaches
and shops. Land's End 7 miles,
Mousehole 2 miles. Lovely walks.
Four-poster bed available. Cosy and
relaxing.*
Bedrooms: 2 double, 1 family room
Bathrooms: 3 en-suite
**Bed & breakfast
per night:**

	£min	£max
Double	35.00	39.00

Parking for 10

Tregoddick House

Listed

Madron, Penzance TR20 8SS
☎ (01736) 62643
*Detached period house with walled
gardens. Interior has many original
fittings, granite fireplaces, etc. Located
in attractive village close to West
Penwith moors. Secure parking.*
Bedrooms: 2 twin
Bathrooms: 2 private
**Bed & breakfast
per night:**

	£min	£max
Single	17.00	20.00
Double	34.00	40.00

Parking for 2
Open January–November

PERRANUTHNOE

Cornwall
Map ref 1B3

Small village on Mount's Bay, with
lovely cliff walks.

Ednovean House

⚜⚜⚜

Perranuthnoe, Penzance TR20 9LZ
☎ Penzance (01736) 711071

*Stands in 1 acre of gardens, with
superb views of St Michael's Mount
and Mount's Bay. Ideal centre for
touring and walking.*
Bedrooms: 2 single, 4 double, 2 twin,
1 triple
Bathrooms: 6 en-suite, 1 public

**Bed & breakfast
per night:**

	£min	£max
Single	20.00	24.00
Double	38.00	48.00

**Half board per
person:**

	£min	£max
Daily	33.00	38.00
Weekly	208.00	240.00

Lunch available
Evening meal 1900 (last orders
2000)
Parking for 12
Cards accepted: Access, Visa, Amex

PETER TAVY

Devon
Map ref 1C2

Churchtown

Listed

Peter Tavy, Tavistock PL19 9NN
☎ Mary Tavy (01822) 810477
*Peaceful Victorian house in own
grounds on edge of village. Beautiful
moorland views. 5 minutes' walk to
excellent pub food.*
Bedrooms: 2 single, 2 double
Bathrooms: 2 public, 3 private
showers
**Bed & breakfast
per night:**

	£min	£max
Single	13.00	15.00
Double	26.00	30.00

Parking for 6

PIDDLETRENTHIDE

Dorset
Map ref 2B3

The Poachers Inn ⚜

⚜⚜⚜ COMMENDED

Piddletrenthide, Dorchester
DT2 7QX
☎ (01300) 348358

*Inn situated in lovely Piddle Valley on
B3143. En-suite rooms with colour TV,
telephone, tea/coffee. Restaurant. Stay
2 nights half board October–March, get
third night free.*
Bedrooms: 8 double, 1 twin, 2 family
rooms
Bathrooms: 11 en-suite

**Bed & breakfast
per night:**

	£min	£max
Double	46.00	50.00

**Half board per
person:**

	£min	£max
Daily	33.00	35.00
Weekly	230.00	245.00

Lunch available
Evening meal 1700 (last orders
2130)
Parking for 30
Cards accepted: Access, Visa

PILLATON

Cornwall
Map ref 1C2

Peaceful village on the slopes of the
River Lynher in steeply-wooded
country near the Devon border.
Within easy reach of the coast and
rugged walking country on Bodmin
Moor.

The Weary Friar Inn ⚜

⚜⚜⚜ COMMENDED

Pillaton, Saltash PL12 6QS
☎ Liskeard (01579) 350238
*Charming country inn noted for its
quality food and interesting
combination of modern comforts with
12th C character. Ideally placed for
exploring inland and coastal areas.*
Bedrooms: 2 single, 7 double, 2 twin,
1 triple
Bathrooms: 12 en-suite
**Bed & breakfast
per night:**

	£min	£max
Single	30.00	35.00
Double	40.00	50.00

Lunch available
Evening meal 1900 (last orders
2130)
Parking for 30
Cards accepted: Access, Visa

WELCOME HOST

This is a nationally recognised
customer care programme
which aims to promote
the highest standards of
service and a warm welcome.
Establishments who are taking
part in this initiative are
indicated by the ⊚ symbol.

PLYMOUTH

Devon
Map ref 1C2

Devon's largest city, major port and naval base. Old houses on the Barbican and ambitious architecture in modern centre, with aquarium, museum and art gallery, the Dome - a heritage centre on the Hoe. Superb coastal views over Plymouth Sound from the Hoe.
Tourist Information Centre ☎ (01752) 264849 or 266031 or 266030

Bowling Green Hotel ⋔
HIGHLY COMMENDED

9-10 Osborne Place, Lockyer Street, Plymouth PL1 2PU
☎ (01752) 667485
Fax (01752) 255150

Rebuilt Victorian property with views of Dartmoor. Overlooking Sir Francis Drake's bowling green on beautiful Plymouth Hoe. Centrally situated for the Barbican, Theatre Royal and leisure/conference centre.
Bedrooms: 1 single, 7 double, 2 twin, 2 triple
Bathrooms: 8 private, 4 private showers

Bed & breakfast per night:	£min	£max
Single	30.00	36.00
Double	38.00	48.00

Parking for 4
Cards accepted: Access, Visa, Diners, Amex, Switch/Delta

Gabber Farm
COMMENDED

Down Thomas, Plymouth PL9 0AW
☎ (01752) 862269
120-acre mixed & dairy farm. On the south Devon coast, near Bovisand and Wembury. Lovely walks in the area. Near diving centre. Directions are provided. Friendly welcome assured. Special weekly rates, especially for OAPs and children.
Bedrooms: 1 double, 2 twin, 1 triple, 1 family room
Bathrooms: 2 en-suite, 1 public

Bed & breakfast per night:	£min	£max
Single	16.00	18.00
Double	32.00	36.00

Half board per person:	£min	£max
Daily	24.00	26.00
Weekly	150.00	160.00

Evening meal 1900 (last orders 1800)
Parking for 4

Phantele Guest House ⋔
COMMENDED

176 Devonport Road, Stoke, Plymouth PL1 5RD
☎ (01752) 561506
Small family-run guesthouse about 2 miles from city centre. Convenient base for touring. Close to continental and Torpoint ferries.
Bedrooms: 2 single, 1 double, 1 twin, 2 triple
Bathrooms: 2 en-suite, 2 public

Bed & breakfast per night:	£min	£max
Single	15.50	25.85
Double	29.00	41.80

Half board per person:	£min	£max
Daily	21.50	33.55
Weekly	135.00	203.10

Evening meal 1830 (last orders 1700)

PORTLAND

Dorset
Map ref 2B3

Joined by a narrow isthmus to the coast, a stony promontory sloping from the lofty landward side to a lighthouse on Portland Bill at its southern tip. Villages are built of the white limestone for which the "isle" is famous.

Alessandria Hotel and Italian Restaurant ⋔
APPROVED

71 Wakeham Easton, Portland, Weymouth DT5 1HW
☎ (01305) 822270 & 820108
Fax (01305) 820561
Italy on Portland. Warm and friendly Italian hospitality from chef/proprietor Giovanni. Spacious en-suite bedrooms with all facilities. Food prepared and cooked to order. Three bedrooms on ground floor.
Bedrooms: 6 single, 3 double, 3 twin, 2 triple, 1 family room
Suite available
Bathrooms: 10 en-suite, 1 private, 3 public, 1 private shower

Bed & breakfast per night:	£min	£max
Single	26.00	46.00
Double	42.00	55.00

Half board per person:	£min	£max
Daily	35.00	45.00
Weekly	225.00	275.00

Evening meal 1900 (last orders 2100)
Parking for 19
Cards accepted: Access, Visa, Diners, Amex, Switch/Delta

PRIDDY

Somerset
Map ref 2A2

Village in the Mendips, formerly a lead-mining centre, with old inns dating from the mining era. The area is rich in Bronze Age remains, among them the Priddy nine barrows. There is a sheep fair in the village every August.

Highcroft
COMMENDED

Wells Road, Priddy, Wells BA5 3AU
☎ Wells (01749) 673446
A natural stone country house with large lawns. From Wells take A39 to Bristol for 3 miles, turn left to Priddy and Highcroft is on right after about 2 miles.
Bedrooms: 1 single, 1 double, 1 twin, 1 triple
Bathrooms: 2 en-suite, 1 public

Bed & breakfast per night:	£min	£max
Single	18.00	
Double	34.00	36.00

Parking for 5
Open February–November

ST AGNES

Cornwall
Map ref 1B3

Small town in a once-rich mining area on the north coast. Terraced cottages and granite houses slope to the church. Some old mine workings remain, but the attraction must be the magnificent coastal scenery and superb coastal walks. St Agnes Beacon offers one of Cornwall's most extensive views.

Penkerris ⋔
APPROVED

Penwinnick Road, St Agnes TR5 0PA
☎ St Agnes (01872) 552262

Enchanting Edwardian residence with own grounds in unspoilt Cornish village. Beautiful rooms, log fires in winter, good home cooking. Dramatic cliff walks and beaches nearby.
Bedrooms: 1 single, 5 double, 3 twin, 3 triple
Bathrooms: 8 en-suite, 3 public
Bed & breakfast

per night:	£min	£max
Single	15.00	30.00
Double	27.00	35.00

Half board per

person:	£min	£max
Daily	22.50	26.00
Weekly	135.00	175.00

Lunch available
Evening meal from 1830
Parking for 9
Cards accepted: Access, Visa, Diners, Amex, Switch/Delta

ST AUSTELL

Cornwall
Map ref 1B3

Leading market town, the meeting point of old and new Cornwall. One mile from St Austell Bay with its sandy beaches, old fishing villages and attractive countryside. Ancient narrow streets, pedestrian shopping precincts. Fine church of Pentewan stone and Italianate Town Hall.

Hembal Manor ♔

HIGHLY COMMENDED

Hembal Lane, Trewoon, St Austell PL25 5TD
☎ St Austell (01726) 72144
Fax (01726) 72144

Dating from the 16th C, Hembal Manor is set in 6 acres of gardens. Ideally situated for beaches and places of interest and easy travelling distance of main Cornish towns. All rooms tastefully decorated and furnished.
Bedrooms: 2 double, 1 twin
Bathrooms: 2 en-suite, 1 private, 1 public

Bed & breakfast

per night:	£min	£max
Single	23.00	26.00
Double	46.00	52.00

Parking for 6

Poltarrow Farm ♔

HIGHLY COMMENDED

St Mewan, St Austell PL26 7DR
☎ St Austell (01726) 67111
45-acre mixed farm. Beautiful farmhouse in quiet position. Ideal central base for touring coast and countryside. We aim to provide comfort, quality and personal attention.
Bedrooms: 3 double, 1 twin, 1 family room
Bathrooms: 4 en-suite, 1 private

Bed & breakfast

per night:	£min	£max
Single		20.00
Double	38.00	40.00

Parking for 5
Cards accepted: Access, Visa

ST KEW

Cornwall
Map ref 1B2

Old village sheltered by trees standing beside a stream. The church is noted for its medieval glass showing the Passion and the remains of a scene of the Tree of Jesse.

Tregellist Farm ♔

COMMENDED

Tregellist, St Kew, Bodmin PL30 3HG
☎ Bodmin (01208) 880537
130-acre mixed farm. Farmhouse, built in 1989, offering old-fashioned hospitality. Set in tiny hamlet with lovely views and pleasant walks. Central for coast and moors. Children welcome. 1.5 miles from A39.
Bedrooms: 1 double, 1 twin, 1 family room
Bathrooms: 3 en-suite

Bed & breakfast

per night:	£min	£max
Single	20.00	22.00
Double	38.00	44.00

Half board per

person:	£min	£max
Daily	30.00	30.00
Weekly	210.00	210.00

Evening meal from 1800
Parking for 6
Open February–October

ST NEOT

Cornwall
Map ref 1C2

Colliford Tavern ♔

COMMENDED

Colliford Lake, St Neot, Liskeard PL14 6PZ
☎ Cardinham (01208) 821335
Fax (01208) 821335
"An oasis on Bodmin Moor". Friendly country pub, ideally situated for exploring Cornwall. Immaculate facilities. Good home-cooked meals and fine traditional ales. Colour brochure available.
Bedrooms: 3 double, 2 twin
Bathrooms: 5 en-suite

Bed & breakfast

per night:	£min	£max
Double	29.00	50.00

Lunch available
Evening meal 1900 (last orders 2130)
Parking for 50
Open April–September
Cards accepted: Access, Visa, Amex, Switch/Delta

SALCOMBE

Devon
Map ref 1C3

Sheltered yachting resort of whitewashed houses and narrow streets in a balmy setting on the Salcombe Estuary. Palm, myrtle and other Mediterranean plants flourish. There are sandy bays and creeks for boating.
Tourist Information Centre ☎ (01548) 843927

Torre View Hotel ♔

COMMENDED

Devon Road, Salcombe TQ8 8HJ
☎ (01548) 842633
Fax (01548) 842633
Detached Victorian residence with every modern comfort, commanding extensive views of the estuary and surrounding countryside. Congenial atmosphere. No smoking, please.
Bedrooms: 6 double, 2 twin
Suites available
Bathrooms: 5 en-suite, 3 private

Bed & breakfast

per night:	£min	£max
Single	22.50	29.00
Double	45.00	52.00

Half board per

person:	£min	£max
Daily	33.00	39.00
Weekly	220.00	245.00

Continued ▶

SALCOMBE

Continued

Evening meal 1900 (last orders 1800)
Parking for 5
Open February–October
Cards accepted: Access, Visa

SALISBURY

Wiltshire
Map ref 2B3

Beautiful city and ancient regional capital set amid water meadows. Buildings of all periods are dominated by the cathedral whose spire is the tallest in England. Built between 1220 and 1258, it is one of the purest examples of Early English architecture.
Tourist Information Centre ☎ (01722) 334956

The Bell Inn

Warminster Road, South Newton, Salisbury SP2 OQD
☎ (01722) 743336
300-year-old roadside inn offering full en-suite facilities. Extensive range of bar meals. 6 miles north-west of Salisbury.
Bedrooms: 1 single, 1 double, 1 twin
Bathrooms: 3 en-suite

Bed & breakfast per night:	£min	£max
Single	20.00	
Double	34.00	36.00

Lunch available
Evening meal 1900 (last orders 2100)
Parking for 60

Beulah

Listed

144 Britford Lane, Salisbury SP2 8AL
☎ (01722) 333517
Bungalow in quiet road, 1.25 miles from city centre and overlooking meadows. Tea/coffee making facilities in bedrooms. No-smoking establishment.
Bedrooms: 1 single, 1 family room
Bathrooms: 1 public

Bed & breakfast per night:	£min	£max
Single	16.00	17.00
Double	32.00	34.00

Parking for 4

Brickworth Farmhouse

Listed COMMENDED

Brickworth Lane, Whiteparish, Salisbury SP5 2QE
☎ Whiteparish (01794) 884663
Fax (01794) 884581
Charming 18th C listed farmhouse, featured in "Ideal Home": perfect location off A36 south-east of Salisbury. Ideal for visiting Wiltshire, Hampshire and Dorset.
Bedrooms: 1 single, 2 double, 1 family room
Bathrooms: 3 en-suite, 1 private

Bed & breakfast per night:	£min	£max
Single	22.00	25.00
Double	32.00	38.00

Parking for 20

Byways House

31 Fowlers Road, City Centre, Salisbury SP1 2QP
☎ (01722) 328364
Fax (01722) 322146
Attractive family-run Victorian house close to cathedral in quiet area of city centre. Car park. Bedrooms with private bathrooms and colour satellite TV. Traditional English and vegetarian breakfasts.
Bedrooms: 4 single, 8 double, 5 twin, 2 triple, 1 family room
Bathrooms: 17 en-suite, 1 public

Bed & breakfast per night:	£min	£max
Single	24.00	32.50
Double	39.00	51.50

Parking for 15
Cards accepted: Access, Visa

Castleavon

COMMENDED

15 Wyndham Road, Salisbury SP1 3AA
☎ (01722) 339087
Large, comfortable Victorian house, furnished with antiques. Close to city centre and cathedral. Traditional breakfasts, evening meals provided to Cordon Bleu trained standard. Smoking permitted in lounge.
Bedrooms: 1 double, 1 twin
Bathrooms: 1 private, 1 public

Bed & breakfast per night:	£min	£max
Single	16.00	20.00
Double	28.00	30.00

Half board per person:	£min	£max
Daily	21.50	27.50
Weekly	135.00	170.00

Evening meal from 1800

Castlewood

45 Castle Road, Salisbury SP1 3RH
☎ (01722) 421494 & 324809
Large Edwardian house, tastefully restored throughout. Pleasant 10 minutes' riverside walk to city centre and cathedral.
Bedrooms: 2 single, 1 double, 1 twin, 1 family room
Suites available
Bathrooms: 3 en-suite, 1 public

Bed & breakfast per night:	£min	£max
Single	20.00	25.00
Double	32.00	37.00

Evening meal 1800 (last orders 2030)
Parking for 4

Cranston Guest House

APPROVED

5 Wain-a-Long Road, Salisbury SP1 1LJ
☎ (01722) 336776
Large detached town house covered in Virginia creeper. 10 minutes' walk from town centre and cathedral.
Bedrooms: 2 single, 1 double, 2 twin, 2 family rooms
Bathrooms: 5 en-suite, 1 public

Bed & breakfast per night:	£min	£max
Single	17.00	18.00
Double	32.00	35.00

Half board per person:	£min	£max
Daily	25.00	

Evening meal 1800 (last orders 1900)
Parking for 4

2 The Farriers

Middleton, Middle Winterslow, Salisbury SP5 1QS
☎ Winterslow (01980) 862881
New but traditionally built large family house, situated in a peaceful village, providing accommodation in a relaxed atmosphere.
Bedrooms: 1 double, 1 twin
Suite available
Bathrooms: 1 en-suite, 1 private

Bed & breakfast per night:	£min	£max
Single	23.00	27.00
Double	44.00	48.00

Parking for 4

The Gallery

Listed COMMENDED

36 Wyndham Road, Salisbury
SP1 3AB
☎ (01722) 324586
Fax (01722) 324586
Experience our warm hospitality and delicious breakfasts in a non-smoking environment. Well situated for exploring Salisbury and the many attractions in the area.
Bedrooms: 1 double, 2 twin
Bathrooms: 2 en-suite, 1 private
Bed & breakfast

per night:	£min	£max
Double	30.00	34.00

Hayburn Wyke Guest House

72 Castle Road, Salisbury SP1 3RL
☎ (01722) 412627
Family-run spacious guesthouse adjacent to Victoria Park. A short riverside walk from the cathedral and city centre. Old Sarum 1 mile, Stonehenge 9 miles.
Bedrooms: 2 double, 2 twin, 2 triple
Bathrooms: 2 en-suite, 1 public
Bed & breakfast

per night:	£min	£max
Single	21.00	36.00
Double	32.00	41.00

Parking for 6

Holmhurst Guest House

Listed

Downton Road, Salisbury SP2 8AR
☎ (01722) 410407
Fax (01722) 323164
Edwardian town house, a short walk from cathedral. Riverside and country walks. Easy access to coastal resorts and New Forest. Parking.
Bedrooms: 1 single, 2 double, 1 twin, 2 triple
Suites available
Bathrooms: 4 en-suite, 1 public
Bed & breakfast

per night:	£min	£max
Single	20.00	25.00
Double	34.00	38.00

Parking for 9

Kelebrae

COMMENDED

101 Castle Road, Salisbury SP1 3RP
☎ (01722) 333628
Family home, opposite Victoria Park and within walking distance of city centre. Convenient for Stonehenge. Parking.

Bedrooms: 3 double
Suite available
Bathrooms: 1 en-suite, 2 private, 1 public
Bed & breakfast

per night:	£min	£max
Double	37.00	38.00

Parking for 4

Leena's Guest House

50 Castle Road, Salisbury SP1 3RL
☎ (01722) 335419
Friendly, family-run guesthouse with pretty bedrooms and delightful public areas. Close to riverside walk to city centre and cathedral.
Bedrooms: 1 single, 2 double, 2 twin, 1 family room
Bathrooms: 5 en-suite, 1 public, 1 private shower
Bed & breakfast

per night:	£min	£max
Single	17.50	
Double	24.50	39.50

Parking for 7

The Old Bakery

35 Bedwin Street, Salisbury SP1 3UT
☎ (01722) 320100
15th C city centre cottage with interesting medieval features and cosy oak-beamed rooms. We operate an enviromentally friendly policy. Careful smokers welcome.
Bedrooms: 1 single, 1 double, 1 twin, 1 triple
Bathrooms: 3 en-suite, 2 public
Bed & breakfast

per night:	£min	£max
Single	17.00	22.00
Double	30.00	44.00

Richburn Guest House

APPROVED

23 and 25 Estcourt Road, Salisbury SP1 3AP
☎ (01722) 325189
Large, tastefully renovated Victorian house with homely family atmosphere. All modern amenities and large car park. Close to city centre and parks.
Bedrooms: 2 single, 4 double, 2 twin, 1 triple, 1 family room
Bathrooms: 2 en-suite, 2 public
Bed & breakfast

per night:	£min	£max
Single	17.50	18.00
Double	30.00	39.00

Parking for 10

Swaynes Firs Farm

APPROVED

Grimsdyke, Coombe Bissett, Salisbury SP5 5RF
☎ Martin Cross (01725) 519240

15-acre mixed farm. Country farmhouse in pleasant position with good views. Ancient Roman ditch on farm. Peacocks, ducks, chickens and horses are reared on the farm.
Bedrooms: 2 twin, 1 family room
Bathrooms: 1 en-suite, 2 private
Bed & breakfast

per night:	£min	£max
Single	20.00	20.00
Double	40.00	40.00

Parking for 9

Torrisholme

Listed COMMENDED

Stratford Sub Castle, Salisbury SP1 3LQ
☎ (01722) 329089
Village location, 1 mile from city centre, rural views, off-road parking. Convenient for Bath, Stonehenge, New Forest and South Coast.
Bedrooms: 1 single, 2 double, 2 triple
Bathrooms: 1 public
Bed & breakfast

per night:	£min	£max
Single	15.00	17.00
Double	30.00	32.00

48 Wyndham Road

Listed COMMENDED

Salisbury SP1 3AB
☎ (01722) 327757
Large comfortable Edwardian house within easy reach of city centre. En-suite facilities available. On-street parking.
Bedrooms: 2 double, 1 twin
Bathrooms: 1 en-suite, 1 public
Bed & breakfast

per night:	£min	£max
Double	30.00	35.00

Please check prices and other details at the time of booking.

SALISBURY

Continued

53 Wyndham Road

Listed COMMENDED

Salisbury SP1 3AH
☎ (01722) 322955
*Detached family home offering a warm
welcome. Surrounded by large garden.
In quiet area, 8 minutes' walk from city
centre. Private parking. Completely
non-smoking.*
Bedrooms: 1 double, 1 twin
Bathrooms: 1 public

Bed & breakfast

per night:	£min	£max
Double	30.00	32.00

Parking for 2

SALISBURY PLAIN

*See under Amesbury, Figheldean, Salisbury,
Shrewton, Warminster, Winterbourne
Stoke*

SENNEN COVE

Cornwall
Map ref 1A3

The Old Success Inn ⚠

COMMENDED

Sennen Cove, Lands End TR19 7DG
☎ Sennen (01736) 871232
Fax (01736) 871457
*Attractively modernised fisherman's inn,
nestling in a beautiful bay. Restaurant
and bar well known for meals, snacks
and seafood specialities. Friendly staff.
Small, well-behaved dogs welcome. Bay
ideal for swimmers, surfers. Great cliff
walks, golf-course nearby.*
Bedrooms: 2 single, 8 double, 2 twin
Bathrooms: 8 en-suite, 2 private,
1 public

Bed & breakfast

per night:	£min	£max
Single	19.00	37.50
Double	38.00	81.50

Half board per

person:	£min	£max
Daily	32.00	50.50
Weekly	205.00	353.50

Lunch available
Evening meal 1900 (last orders
2130)
Parking for 14
Cards accepted: Access, Visa

SHEPTON MALLET

Somerset
Map ref 2A2

Important, stone-built market town
beneath the south-west slopes of
the Mendips. Thriving rural
industries include glove and shoe
making, dairying and cider making;
the remains of a medieval
"shambles" in the square date from
the town's prosperity as a wool
centre.

Hurlingpot Farm

COMMENDED

Chelynch, Doulting, Shepton Mallet
BA4 4PY
☎ (01749) 880256
Fax (01749) 880256
*Lovely 300-year-old farmhouse in a
peaceful country setting, 2 miles east
of Shepton Mallet. A361 to Doulting,
then take Chelynch road. Turn left past
Poachers Pocket pub and left again
into farm entrance.*
Bedrooms: 1 double, 1 twin, 1 triple
Suites available
Bathrooms: 3 en-suite

Bed & breakfast

per night:	£min	£max
Single	20.00	25.00
Double	35.00	40.00

Parking for 6

Temple House Farm ⚠

COMMENDED

Doulting, Shepton Mallet BA4 4RQ
☎ (01749) 880294
Fax (01749) 880688
*200-acre dairy farm. 400-year-old
listed farmhouse with all facilities. In
rural area within easy reach of Wells,
Bath, Shepton Mallet, the walking
delights of the Mendips and plenty of
tourist attractions.*
Bedrooms: 2 triple
Bathrooms: 2 en-suite

Bed & breakfast

per night:	£min	£max
Single	18.00	20.00
Double	32.00	36.00

Half board per

person:	£min	£max
Daily	25.50	27.50

SHERBORNE

Dorset
Map ref 2B3

Dorset's "Cathedral City" of
medieval streets, golden Hamstone
buildings and great abbey church,
resting place of Saxon kings.
Formidable 12th C castle ruins and
Sir Walter Raleigh's splendid Tudor
mansion and deer park. Street
markets, leisure centre, many
cultural activities.
*Tourist Information Centre ☎ (01935)
815341*

The Alders

COMMENDED

Sandford Orcas, Sherborne
DT9 4SB
☎ (01963) 220666
*Secluded stone house set in old walled
garden, in picturesque conservation
village near Sherborne. Excellent food
available in friendly village pub.*
Bedrooms: 1 double, 1 twin
Bathrooms: 2 en-suite

Bed & breakfast

per night:	£min	£max
Single	20.00	25.00
Double	37.00	40.00

Parking for 6

The Carpenters Arms

Listed COMMENDED

Leigh, Sherborne DT9 6HJ
☎ (01935) 872438
Fax (01935) 872438
*18th C building, 3 en-suite rooms,
restaurant, bars. In beautiful
countryside, ideal for walking and close
to riding and fishing. 7 miles from
Yeovil and Sherborne, 11 miles from
Dorchester.*
Bedrooms: 2 double, 1 twin
Bathrooms: 3 en-suite

Bed & breakfast

per night:	£min	£max
Single	25.00	30.00
Double	37.00	45.00

Half board per

person:	£min	£max
Weekly	111.00	150.00

Lunch available
Evening meal 1900 (last orders
2130)

The ⚠ symbol after an
establishment name indicates
that it is a Regional
Tourist Board member.

Please mention this guide
when making your booking.

A key to symbols can be
found inside the back
cover flap.

The Queens Head

High Street, Milborne Port,
Sherborne DT9 5DQ
☎ Milborne Port (01963) 250314
Grade II listed village inn with 2 bars,
separate restaurant and comfortable
accommodation. 7 real ales and log
fires.
Bedrooms: 1 single, 2 double
Bathrooms: 1 public, 1 private
shower

Bed & breakfast

per night:	£min	£max
Single		21.00
Double		35.00

Lunch available
Evening meal 1900 (last orders
2130)
Parking for 10
Cards accepted: Access, Visa, Diners,
Amex
🛏🖵♿🛡⑤🛏⚟40🔌🦽🅿

SHREWTON

Wiltshire
Map ref 2B2

Ashwick House ⋔

🏰🏰 COMMENDED

Upper Backway, Shrewton, Salisbury
SP3 4DE
☎ (01980) 621138
Fax (01980) 620152
Large village house in quiet position.
Ideal touring centre for Salisbury, Bath,
New Forest, Stonehenge (2 miles).
Walking distance of 2 pubs. Parking in
driveway.
Bedrooms: 1 single, 2 twin
Bathrooms: 1 private, 1 public

Bed & breakfast

per night:	£min	£max
Single	14.00	16.00
Double	32.00	36.00

Half board per

person:	£min	£max
Daily	20.00	25.00
Weekly	120.00	140.00

Evening meal 1900 (last orders
2030)
Parking for 5
🛏📧🖵♿🦑Ⓤ🛡⑤✂🅿🆃🖵🔌☼
✕🦽SP🆃

ACCESSIBILITY

Look for the ♿&♿ symbols
which indicate accessibility for
wheelchair users. These are
described in detail at the
front of this guide.

SIDMOUTH

Devon
Map ref 1D2

Charming resort set amid lofty red
cliffs where the River Sid meets the
sea. The wealth of ornate Regency
and Victorian villas recalls the time
when this was one of the south
coast's most exclusive resorts.
Museum; August International
Festival of Folk Arts.
Tourist Information Centre ☎ (01395)
516441

Broad Oak

🏰🏰 HIGHLY COMMENDED

Sid Road, Sidmouth EX10 8QP
☎ (01395) 513713

Listed Victorian villa in delightful
gardens overlooking "The Byes". A
peaceful location, only a short stroll
from the town centre and Esplanade.
Bedrooms: 1 single, 1 double, 1 twin
Bathrooms: 2 en-suite, 1 public

Bed & breakfast

per night:	£min	£max
Single	22.00	22.00
Double	48.00	52.00

Parking for 4
Open February–November
📧🖵♿🦑Ⓤ⑤✂🅿🖵☼✕🦽🆃

Lower Pinn Farm

🏰🏰 COMMENDED

Pinn, Sidmouth EX10 0NN
☎ (01395) 513733 & Mobile 0374
694776
220-acre mixed farm. Situated 2 miles
west of Sidmouth, comfortable
accommodation with substantial
breakfast. Bedrooms have TV,
tea/coffee facilities, central heating.
Access at all times.
Bedrooms: 2 double, 1 twin
Bathrooms: 2 en-suite, 1 public

Bed & breakfast

per night:	£min	£max
Double	32.00	40.00

Parking for 3
🛏📧🖵♿Ⓤ⑤🅿🔌🦽SP
◉

For ideas on places to visit
refer to the introduction at
the beginning of this section.

SILVERTON

Devon
Map ref 1D2

Hayne House

🏰🏰 APPROVED

Silverton, Exeter EX5 4HE
☎ Exeter (01392) 860725
286-acre arable and mixed farm.
Detached Georgian house near
National Trust property. Situated in the
Culm Valley with views of Killerton.
Bedrooms: 1 twin, 1 family room
Bathrooms: 2 private

Bed & breakfast

per night:	£min	£max
Single	15.00	18.00
Double	30.00	36.00

Parking for 3
Open March–October
🐎♿Ⓤ🆃🖵🔌☼✕🦽SP🆃

SOUTH MOLTON

Devon
Map ref 1C1

Busy market town at the mouth of
the Yeo Valley near southern
Exmoor. Wool, mining and coaching
brought prosperity between the
Middle Ages and the 19th C and the
fine square with Georgian buildings,
a Guildhall and Assembly Rooms
reflect this former affluence.

Kerscott Farm ⋔

🏰🏰 HIGHLY COMMENDED

Ash Mill, South Molton EX36 4QG
☎ Bishops Nympton (01769)
550262
70-acre livestock farm. Peaceful,
welcoming working farm mentioned in
Domesday Book, overlooking Exmoor.
Superb views. Beautiful old world
antique interior. Excellent home farm
cooking. Non-smokers only.
Bedrooms: 2 double, 1 twin
Bathrooms: 3 en-suite

Bed & breakfast

per night:	£min	£max
Double	34.00	36.00

Half board per

person:	£min	£max
Daily	25.00	27.50

Evening meal 1830 (last orders
1400)
Parking for 8
🛏8📧♿🦑Ⓤ⑤✂🅿🆃🖵🔌☼
✕🦽🆃

You are advised to confirm
your booking in writing.

SOUTH PETHERTON

Somerset
Map ref 1D2

Small town with a restored 15th C house, King Ina's Palace. The Roman Fosse Way crosses the River Parrett to the east by way of an old bridge on which there are 2 curious carved figures.

September House

Listed COMMENDED

Lopen, South Petherton TA13 5JU
☎ (01460) 240647

Hamstone house in rural village, 18 miles from Dorset coast. Ideal touring centre. Beverage facilities in all rooms. TV lounge. Substantial English breakfast.
Bedrooms: 2 double, 1 twin
Bathrooms: 1 en-suite, 1 public
Bed & breakfast

per night:	£min	£max
Single	15.00	19.00
Double	30.00	38.00

Parking for 3

SUTTON MANDEVILLE

Wiltshire
Map ref 2B3

The Lancers Inn ⓜ

COMMENDED

Sutton Mandeville, Salisbury
SP3 5NG
☎ Salisbury (01722) 714220 & 714374
Built in 1933 to cater for trade/travel on main A30 road to West Country. Large, imposing 2-storey building in open country with views.
Bedrooms: 3 double, 1 triple
Bathrooms: 4 en-suite
Bed & breakfast

per night:	£min	£max
Single	20.00	22.00
Double	35.00	40.00

Lunch available
Evening meal 1800 (last orders 2130)
Parking for 30
Cards accepted: Access, Visa, Amex, Switch/Delta

SWINDON

Wiltshire
Map ref 2B2

Wiltshire's industrial and commercial centre, an important railway town in the 19th C, situated just north of the Marlborough Downs. The railway village created in the mid-19th C has been preserved. Railway museum, art gallery, theatre and leisure centre.
Tourist Information Centre ☎ (01793) 530328 or 493007

Courtleigh House

COMMENDED

40 Draycott Road, Chiseldon,
Swindon SN4 OLS
☎ (01793) 740246
Large detached village house with downland views, ample parking, tennis court and gardens. Easy access to Marlborough, Swindon and M4.
Bedrooms: 2 twin
Bathrooms: 1 en-suite, 1 private, 2 public
Bed & breakfast

per night:	£min	£max
Single	18.00	22.00
Double	30.00	35.00

Parking for 3

Internos

▱

3 Turnpike Road, Blunsdon, Swindon,
Wilshire SN2 4EA
☎ (01793) 721496
Fax (01793) 721496
Detached red brick house off A419, 4 miles north of Swindon and 6 miles from M4 junction 15.
Bedrooms: 1 single, 1 twin, 1 triple
Bathrooms: 2 public
Bed & breakfast

per night:	£min	£max
Single	19.00	23.00
Double	32.00	32.00

Parking for 6

The Live and Let Live

HIGHLY COMMENDED

Upper Pavenhill, Purton, Swindon
SN5 9DQ
☎ (01793) 770627
Converted stable, 5 miles west of Swindon, north of M4 (junction 16) and Wootton Bassett. At "one stop" shop turn into Pavenhill. Proceed for half a mile to right turning - Upper Pavenhill. House is 200 yards on left. Non-smokers preferred.

Bedrooms: 1 twin, 1 triple
Bathrooms: 1 public
Bed & breakfast

per night:	£min	£max
Single	20.00	20.00
Double	35.00	35.00

Parking for 3

Relian Guest House

▱▱

151-153 County Road, Swindon
SN1 2EB
☎ (01793) 521416
Quiet house adjacent to Swindon Town Football Club and short distance from town centre. Close to bus and rail stations, and A345. Free car park at rear.
Bedrooms: 4 single, 2 double, 2 twin
Suites available
Bathrooms: 3 en-suite, 2 public, 3 private showers
Bed & breakfast

per night:	£min	£max
Single	17.00	
Double	32.00	

The School House Hotel and Restaurant ⓜ

▱▱▱▱ COMMENDED

Hook Street, Hook, Swindon
SN4 8EF
☎ (01793) 851198
Fax (01793) 851025

Charming country house hotel in a converted 1860 school house. Combining modern facilities and Victorian decor. In rural hamlet but close to M4, Swindon and Cotswolds.
Bedrooms: 1 single, 8 double, 1 twin
Bathrooms: 10 en-suite
Bed & breakfast

per night:	£min	£max
Single	59.50	72.50
Double	69.50	79.95

Half board per person:	£min	£max
Daily	79.95	92.50

Lunch available
Evening meal 1800 (last orders 2200)
Parking for 40
Cards accepted: Access, Visa, Diners, Amex, Switch/Delta

TAUNTON

Somerset
Map ref 1D1

County town, well-known for its public schools, sheltered by gentle hill-ranges on the River Tone. Medieval prosperity from wool has continued in marketing and manufacturing and the town retains many fine period buildings. *Tourist Information Centre ☎ (01823) 336344*

Higher Dipford Farm

COMMENDED

Dipford, Trull, Taunton TA3 7NU
☎ (01823) 275770 & 257916
120-acre dairy farm. 14th C listed Somerset longhouse with magnificent walks and views. Antique furniture, log fires and spacious en-suite rooms. Renowned for high class cuisine using fresh dairy produce.
Bedrooms: 1 double, 1 triple, 1 family room
Bathrooms: 3 en-suite

Bed & breakfast

per night:	£min	£max
Single	27.00	32.00
Double	46.00	54.00

Half board per

person:	£min	£max
Daily	40.00	47.00
Weekly	259.00	313.00

Lunch available
Evening meal 1900 (last orders 2130)
Parking for 6
Open January, March–December
Cards accepted: Amex

Prockters Farm

West Monkton, Taunton TA2 8QN
☎ West Monkton (01823) 412269
Fax (01823) 412269
300-acre mixed farm. 300-year-old farmhouse, 3 miles from M5. Inglenook fireplaces, brass beds, collection of farm antiques. Large garden. Ground floor en-suite bedrooms. Tea and cake on arrival.
Bedrooms: 2 double, 2 twin, 1 triple
Bathrooms: 2 en-suite, 2 public

Bed & breakfast

per night:	£min	£max
Single	18.00	21.00
Double	36.00	42.00

Parking for 6
Cards accepted: Amex

The Spinney

HIGHLY COMMENDED

Curland, Taunton TA3 5SE
☎ Buckland St Mary (01460) 234362
Fax (01460) 234362
Modern detached house in quiet countryside. Lovely garden with panoramic views from slopes of Blackdown Hills.
Bedrooms: 1 twin, 2 triple
Bathrooms: 3 en-suite, 1 public

Bed & breakfast

per night:	£min	£max
Single		25.00
Double	39.00	39.00

Half board per

person:	£min	£max
Daily	28.00	36.00
Weekly	189.50	242.00

Lunch available
Evening meal 1900 (last orders 2000)
Parking for 6

TAVISTOCK

Devon
Map ref 1C2

Old market town beside the River Tavy on the western edge of Dartmoor. Developed around its 10th C abbey, of which some fragments remain, it became a stannary town in 1305 when tin-streaming thrived on the moors. Tavistock Goose Fair, October. *Tourist Information Centre ☎ (01822) 612938*

April Cottage ⚐

HIGHLY COMMENDED

Mount Tavy Road, Tavistock PL19 9JB
☎ (01822) 613280
Victorian riverside character cottage in pretty garden. Dining-room overlooks river. 5 minutes' level walk from town centre and excellent local inns. All rooms en-suite.
Bedrooms: 2 double, 1 twin
Bathrooms: 3 en-suite

Bed & breakfast

per night:	£min	£max
Double	30.00	34.00

Parking for 4

Kingfisher Cottage

COMMENDED

Mount Tavy Road, Vigo Bridge, Tavistock PL19 9JB
☎ (01822) 613801
Riverside accommodation in newly built stone cottage, comfortable and convenient. Close to town centre and Dartmoor. Ideal base for touring.
Bedrooms: 2 double, 1 twin
Bathrooms: 1 en-suite, 2 private, 1 public

Bed & breakfast

per night:	£min	£max
Single	13.00	30.00
Double	26.00	36.00

Parking for 5

TINTAGEL

Cornwall
Map ref 1B2

Coastal village near the legendary home of King Arthur. There is a lofty headland with the ruin of a Norman castle and traces of a Celtic monastery are still visible in the turf.

Castle Villa

COMMENDED

Molesworth Street, Tintagel PL34 0BZ
☎ Camelford (01840) 770373 & 770203
Over 160 years old, Castle Villa is within easy walking distance of the 11th C church, post office and King Arthur's castle.
Bedrooms: 1 single, 3 double, 1 twin
Bathrooms: 1 en-suite, 2 public

Bed & breakfast

per night:	£min	£max
Single	14.50	16.50
Double	29.00	38.00

Evening meal 1900 (last orders 2100)
Parking for 6
Cards accepted: Access, Visa, Switch/Delta

TIVERTON

Devon
Map ref 1D2

Busy market and textile town, settled since the 9th C, at the meeting of 2 rivers. Town houses, Tudor almshouses and parts of the fine church were built by wealthy cloth merchants; a medieval castle is incorporated into a private house; Blundells School.
Tourist Information Centre ☎ *(01884) 255827*

Great Bradley Farm

👑👑 HIGHLY COMMENDED

Withleigh, Tiverton EX16 8JL
☎ (01884) 256946
155-acre dairy farm. Enjoy peaceful, beautiful countryside, 20 minutes from M5. Lovely, historic farmhouse offering comfortable, attractive bedrooms and delicious food. Non-smokers only, please.
Bedrooms: 1 double, 1 twin
Bathrooms: 2 private

Bed & breakfast per night:	£min	£max
Single	17.50	19.50
Double	35.00	39.00

Half board per person:	£min	£max
Daily	28.00	30.00
Weekly	175.00	180.00

Parking for 2
Open March–October

🛇🔟💷🗝️♿💂📺▥❄🐾🚃⌂

Hornhill 🅜

👑👑 HIGHLY COMMENDED

Exeter Hill, Tiverton EX16 4PL
☎ (01884) 253352

75-acre mixed farm. Country house with superb views. Home cooking using local produce. Comfortable bedrooms, one with Victorian four-poster. 1 ground floor room. Peaceful relaxed atmosphere. Ten minutes from M5.
Bedrooms: 2 double, 1 twin
Bathrooms: 1 en-suite, 2 private

Bed & breakfast per night:	£min	£max
Single	18.50	20.50
Double	35.00	39.00

Half board per person:	£min	£max
Daily	28.50	30.00
Weekly	185.00	190.00

Evening meal 1830 (last orders 1930)
Parking for 4

🛇🔟💷🗝️♿💂📺▥❄🐾🚃⌂
🍴🔟❄🚃⌂💷

Lodge Hill Farm Guesthouse 🅜

👑👑 COMMENDED

Tiverton EX16 5PA
☎ (01884) 252907
Fax (01884) 242090
Ideally situated in a peaceful rural setting in the beautiful Exe Valley. Perfect base for exploring Devon. Easily accessible on A396, 1 mile south of Tiverton.
Bedrooms: 2 single, 2 double, 2 twin, 2 family rooms
Bathrooms: 8 en-suite, 1 public

Bed & breakfast per night:	£min	£max
Single	18.00	
Double	36.00	

Half board per person:	£min	£max
Daily	28.00	
Weekly	178.00	

Lunch available
Evening meal 1730 (last orders 2000)
Parking for 10
Cards accepted: Access, Visa, Amex, Switch/Delta

🛇📞🖵♿📶📺▥🛏️🔟▶❄🚃📵 SP ⊙

Lower Collipriest Farm

👑👑 HIGHLY COMMENDED

Tiverton EX16 4PT
☎ (01884) 252321
221-acre dairy & livestock farm. Thatched farmhouse built around courtyard garden. All rooms en-suite. Super fresh home cooking using local produce. Walks on farm by pond and river. Brochure.
Bedrooms: 1 single, 2 twin
Bathrooms: 3 en-suite

Bed & breakfast per night:	£min	£max
Single	19.50	20.00
Double	39.00	40.00

Half board per person:	£min	£max
Daily	28.00	30.00
Weekly		196.00

Evening meal 1900 (last orders 1200)
Parking for 4
Open February–November

🖵♿💷📶S🗝️💂📺▥🛏️⌂∪⌂🌸🐾🚃⌂⊙

TORQUAY

Devon
Map ref 1D2

Devon's grandest resort, developed from a fishing village. Smart apartments and terraces rise from the seafront and Marine Drive along the headland gives views of beaches and colourful cliffs.
Tourist Information Centre ☎ *(01803) 297428*

Barn Hayes Country Hotel 🅜

👑👑👑 HIGHLY COMMENDED

Brim Hill, Maidencombe, Torquay TQ1 4TR
☎ (01803) 327980
Fax (01803) 327980

Warm, friendly and comfortable country house hotel in an Area of Outstanding Natural Beauty overlooking countryside and sea. Relaxation is guaranteed in these lovely surroundings by personal service, good food and fine wines.
Bedrooms: 2 single, 4 double, 2 twin, 2 triple, 2 family rooms
Bathrooms: 10 en-suite, 2 private

Bed & breakfast per night:	£min	£max
Single	25.00	28.00
Double	50.00	56.00

Half board per person:	£min	£max
Daily	38.00	41.00
Weekly	230.00	259.00

Lunch available
Evening meal 1830 (last orders 1900)
Parking for 16
Open February–December
Cards accepted: Access, Visa

🛇🖵💷♿📶S🗝️💂📺▥🛏️▶🌸🐾 DAP 🚃 SP T ⊙

Gainsboro Hotel

👑👑 COMMENDED

22 Rathmore Road, Torquay TQ2 6NY
☎ (01803) 292032
Fax (01803) 292032

Family-run hotel providing friendly atmosphere. Close to station, seafront and amenities.
Bedrooms: 5 double, 1 twin
Bathrooms: 3 private, 1 public

Bed & breakfast

per night:	£min	£max
Single	12.00	14.00
Double	24.00	32.00

Parking for 5
Open March–September
Cards accepted: Access, Visa

[symbols]

Kingston House

⌖⌖

75 Avenue Road, Torquay TQ2 5LL
☎ (01803) 212760

Elegant Victorian building, tastefully modernised. Conveniently situated for the town and seafront. Family-run, offering traditional home cooking, with a choice of daily menu.
Bedrooms: 1 single, 2 double, 1 twin, 1 triple, 1 family room
Bathrooms: 6 en-suite

Bed & breakfast

per night:	£min	£max
Single	17.50	19.50
Double	29.00	37.00

Half board per person:

	£min	£max
Daily	22.00	26.00
Weekly	139.00	169.00

Evening meal 1800 (last orders 1630)
Parking for 6
Open March–October
Cards accepted: Access, Visa, Diners

[symbols]

Maple Lodge

⌖⌖ COMMENDED

36 Ash Hill Road, Torquay TQ1 3JD
☎ (01803) 297391
Detached guesthouse with beautiful views. Relaxed atmosphere, home cooking, en-suite rooms. Centrally situated for town and beaches.
Bedrooms: 1 single, 2 double, 1 twin, 2 triple, 1 family room
Bathrooms: 6 en-suite, 1 private, 1 public

Bed & breakfast

per night:	£min	£max
Single	15.00	18.00

Evening meal from 1800
Parking for 5
Open March–October

[symbols]

TOTNES

Devon
Map ref 1D2

Old market town steeply built near the head of the Dart Estuary. Remains of medieval gateways, a noble church, 16th C Guildhall and medley of period houses recall former wealth from cloth and shipping, continued in rural and water industries.
Tourist Information Centre ☎ (01803) 863168

Buckyette Farm ⋀

⌖⌖

Buckyette, Totnes TQ9 6ND
☎ Staverton (01803) 762638
51-acre arable farm. Victorian farmhouse in large garden in Devon valley. Children welcome. Central heating.
Bedrooms: 1 double, 2 twin, 3 triple
Bathrooms: 4 en-suite, 2 private

Bed & breakfast

per night:	£min	£max
Single	21.50	22.50
Double	35.00	37.00

Parking for 8
Open March–October

[symbols]

Old Church House Inn ⋀

⌖⌖⌖⌖ COMMENDED

Torbryan, Newton Abbot TQ12 5UR
☎ Ipplepen (01803) 812372 & 812180
Fax (01803) 812180
13th C coaching house of immense character and old world charm with inglenook fireplaces, stone walls and oak beamed ceilings. Situated in a beautiful valley between Dartmoor and Torquay.
Bedrooms: 1 single, 6 double, 2 twin, 2 triple, 1 family room
Bathrooms: 12 en-suite

Bed & breakfast

per night:	£min	£max
Single	35.00	50.00
Double	35.00	55.00

Half board per person:

	£min	£max
Daily	30.00	40.00
Weekly	210.00	280.00

Lunch available
Evening meal 1800 (last orders 2130)

Parking for 30
Cards accepted: Access, Visa

[symbols]

The Old Forge at Totnes ⋀

⌖⌖ HIGHLY COMMENDED

Seymour Place, Totnes TQ9 5AY
☎ (01803) 862174
Delightful 600-year-old stone building, with walled garden and working smithy. Cottage suite suitable for family or disabled guests. No smoking indoors. Extensive breakfast menu including traditional, vegetarian, fish and continental. Whirlpool spa, leisure lounge.
Bedrooms: 2 single, 4 double, 2 twin, 2 family rooms
Suites available
Bathrooms: 9 en-suite, 1 private, 1 public

Bed & breakfast

per night:	£min	£max
Single	35.00	55.00
Double	48.00	66.00

Parking for 10
Cards accepted: Access, Visa, Switch/Delta

[symbols]

Post Cottage

Listed

Littlehempston, Totnes TQ9 6LU
☎ (01803) 868192
Unspoilt thatched cottage, 2 miles from Totnes. Gardens, stream, parking. Guest bathroom, sitting room, TV.
Bedrooms: 1 single, 1 double, 1 twin
Bathrooms: 1 public

Bed & breakfast

per night:	£min	£max
Single	17.00	17.00
Double	34.00	34.00

Parking for 4

[symbols]

Sea Trout Inn

⌖⌖⌖ COMMENDED

Staverton, Totnes TQ9 6PA
☎ (01803) 762274
Fax (01803) 762506
Delightful beamed country inn, in attractive village by the River Dart, offering good food and friendly atmosphere. Good base for walking and touring Dartmoor and South Devon.
Bedrooms: 6 double, 3 twin, 1 triple
Bathrooms: 10 en-suite

Bed & breakfast

per night:	£min	£max
Single	39.50	42.50
Double	48.00	62.00

Continued ▶

TOTNES

Continued

Half board per person:

	£min	£max
Daily	38.00	42.00
Weekly	245.00	275.00

Lunch available
Evening meal 1900 (last orders 2145)
Parking for 50
Cards accepted: Access, Visa, Amex

🖥️🛁📞💻♿🔥Ⓢ✂️🔲🚗🍸35🔍❀
🚲🅿️SP🎡Ⓣ

The Watermans Arms ⚠

☰☰☰ HIGHLY COMMENDED

Bow Bridge, Ashprington, Totnes
TQ9 7EG
☎ (01803) 732214
Fax (01803) 732214

Famous riverside inn noted for award-winning accommodation and beautiful location in a sheltered valley at the head of Bow Creek on the River Dart.
Bedrooms: 10 double, 3 twin, 2 triple
Bathrooms: 15 en-suite
Bed & breakfast per night:

	£min	£max
Single	32.00	38.00
Double	46.00	66.00

Half board per person:

	£min	£max
Daily	42.00	50.00
Weekly	260.00	330.00

Lunch available
Evening meal 1830 (last orders 2130)
Parking for 60
Cards accepted: Access, Visa, Switch/Delta

🖥️🛁📞💻📺🔲♿🅿️🍸Ⓢ🔥🔲🚗
🚗🍸30🎵🕯️❀🚲🔦SP

TROWBRIDGE

Wiltshire
Map ref 2B2

Wiltshire's administrative centre, a handsome market and manufacturing town with a wealth of merchants' houses and other Georgian buildings.
Tourist Information Centre ☎ (01225) 777054

Welam House

☰☰☰ COMMENDED

Bratton Road, West Ashton,
Trowbridge BA14 6AZ
☎ (01225) 755908
Located in quiet village, garden with trees and lawn with a view of Westbury White Horse. Ideally situated for touring. Bowls and mini-golf for guests.
Bedrooms: 1 double, 1 twin, 1 triple
Bathrooms: 3 en-suite, 1 public
Bed & breakfast per night:

	£min	£max
Double	32.00	32.00

Parking for 6
Open March–November

🐴🕯️♿📺Ⓢ🔥📺🔲🚗🍴❀✂️🚲🎡

TRURO

Cornwall
Map ref 1B3

Cornwall's administrative centre and cathedral city, set at the head of Truro River on the Fal Estuary. A medieval stannary town, it handled mineral ore from west Cornwall; fine Georgian buildings recall its heyday as a society haunt in the second mining boom.
Tourist Information Centre ☎ (01872) 74555

Arrallas ⚠

☰☰☰ HIGHLY COMMENDED

Ladock, Truro TR2 4NP
☎ Mitchell (01872) 510379
Fax (01872) 510200
320-acre arable farm. Signed from opposite the Clock Garage, Summercourt. Farmhouse accommodation set in truly rural situation. Good food, warm welcome, attention to detail. Listed building.
Bedrooms: 2 double, 1 twin
Bathrooms: 3 en-suite
Bed & breakfast per night:

	£min	£max
Double	38.00	46.00

Half board per person:

	£min	£max
Daily	31.00	35.00
Weekly	207.50	220.50

Evening meal from 1900
Parking for 8
Open February–November

🐴🍴♿🔥ⓊⓁⓈ✂️🔲📺🔲🚗
❀🐕🚲SP🎡◎

Marcorrie Hotel ⚠

☰☰☰ APPROVED

20 Falmouth Road, Truro TR1 2HX
☎ (01872) 77374
Fax (01872) 41666

Family-run hotel 5 minutes' walk from city centre and cathedral. Ideal for business or holiday, central for visiting the country houses and gardens of Cornwall.
Bedrooms: 3 single, 3 double, 2 twin, 1 triple, 3 family rooms
Bathrooms: 9 en-suite, 1 public, 1 private shower
Bed & breakfast per night:

	£min	£max
Single	21.50	32.50
Double	42.00	46.00

Half board per person:

	£min	£max
Daily	30.00	41.00
Weekly	200.00	260.00

Evening meal 1900 (last orders 1600)
Parking for 16
Cards accepted: Access, Visa, Diners, Amex, Switch/Delta

🖥️🛁📞💻♿Ⓢ✂️📺🔲🚗
🍸20❀🚲SP🎡Ⓣ

Rock Cottage ⚠

☰☰☰ HIGHLY COMMENDED

Blackwater, Truro TR4 8EU
☎ (01872) 560252
Fax (01872) 560252

18th C beamed cottage, old world charm. Formerly village schoolmaster's home. Haven for non-smokers. Comfort, hospitality, friendly service, a la carte menu.
Bedrooms: 2 double, 1 twin
Bathrooms: 3 en-suite
Bed & breakfast per night:

	£min	£max
Single	24.50	
Double	41.00	

Evening meal 1900 (last orders 1500)
Parking for 4

[icons]

Trevispian-Vean Farm Guest House

COMMENDED

St Erme, Truro TR4 9BL
☎ (01872) 79514
300-acre mixed farm. Beautifully situated 7 miles from the coast in the heart of the countryside, the farmhouse combines modern comforts with all the charm of a 300-year-old farm. Ideal for touring Cornwall. Non-smokers only, please.
Bedrooms: 4 double, 2 twin, 4 triple, 2 family rooms
Bathrooms: 12 en-suite, 2 public

Bed & breakfast

per night:	£min	£max
Single	19.00	21.00
Double	34.00	38.00

Half board per

person:	£min	£max
Daily	25.00	27.00

Evening meal 1830 (last orders 1600)
Parking for 15
Open April–October

[icons]

WARMINSTER

Wiltshire
Map ref 2B2

Attractive stone-built town high up to the west of Salisbury Plain. A market town, it originally thrived on cloth and wheat. Many prehistoric camps and barrows nearby, along with Longleat House and Safari Park.
Tourist Information Centre ☎ (01985) 218548

Belmont Bed & Breakfast

Listed

9 Boreham Road, Warminster BA12 9JP
☎ (01985) 212799 & Mobile 0378 391188
Enjoy a friendly welcome in comfortable, spacious and well-appointed accommodation. Ideal for Stonehenge, Longleat and Stourhead. Centrally placed for the historic towns of Bath and Salisbury. Non-smoking.
Bedrooms: 2 double, 1 twin
Bathrooms: 1 public

Bed & breakfast

per night:	£min	£max
Single	25.00	30.00
Double	30.00	32.00

Parking for 4

[icons]

WELLINGTON

Somerset
Map ref 1D1

Hangeridge Farm

Wrangway, Wellington TA21 9QG
☎ (01823) 662339
55-acre mixed farm. Personal service and home cooking. Scenic walk and lovely gardens. 1 hour's drive to West Country coast.
Bedrooms: 2 double, 1 twin
Bathrooms: 2 private

Bed & breakfast

per night:	£min	£max
Single	15.00	
Double	30.00	

Parking for 4

[icons]

WELLS

Somerset
Map ref 2A2

Small city set beneath the southern slopes of the Mendips. Built between 1180 and 1424, the magnificent cathedral is preserved in much of its original glory and with its ancient precincts forms one of our loveliest and most unified groups of medieval buildings.
Tourist Information Centre ☎ (01749) 672552

Beaconsfield Farm

HIGHLY COMMENDED

Easton, Wells BA5 1DU
☎ (01749) 870308
Period character farmhouse in 4 acres of gardens and grounds with magnificent views. Beautifully decorated rooms, en-suite bathrooms. Village pub/restaurant 100 yards.
Bedrooms: 3 double
Bathrooms: 2 en-suite, 1 private

Bed & breakfast

per night:	£min	£max
Double	34.00	40.00

Parking for 10
Open April–October

[icons]

Bekynton House

COMMENDED

7 St Thomas Street, Wells BA5 2UU
☎ (01749) 672222
Fax (01749) 672222

This attractive period house with cathedral views is well appointed with charming antique furniture and comfortable en-suite rooms. Desmond and Rosaleen Gripper offer a warm welcome and delicious breakfasts. Excellent location close to cathedral and Bishop's Palace.
Bedrooms: 1 single, 4 double, 2 twin, 1 triple
Bathrooms: 5 en-suite, 1 private, 2 public

Bed & breakfast

per night:	£min	£max
Single	23.00	32.00
Double	40.00	49.00

Parking for 6
Cards accepted: Access, Visa

[icons]

Home Farm

Stoppers Lane, Coxley, Wells BA5 1QS
☎ (01749) 672434
1.5 miles from Wells, in a quiet spot just off A39. Extensive views of Mendip Hills. Pleasant rooms.
Bedrooms: 1 single, 3 double, 2 twin, 1 triple
Bathrooms: 2 en-suite, 1 private, 2 public

Bed & breakfast

per night:	£min	£max
Single	17.50	24.00
Double	35.00	48.00

Parking for 12

[icons]

Littlewell Farm Guest House

HIGHLY COMMENDED

Coxley, Wells BA5 1QP
☎ (01749) 677914
Converted 200-year-old farmhouse enjoying extensive rural views of beautiful countryside. All bedrooms have shower or bathroom en-suite. Located 1 mile south-west of Wells.
Bedrooms: 1 single, 2 double, 2 twin
Bathrooms: 4 en-suite, 1 private
Continued ▶

WELLS

Continued

Bed & breakfast

per night:	£min	£max
Single	21.00	24.00
Double	37.00	44.00

Half board per

person:	£min	£max
Daily	35.00	39.00

Evening meal 1900 (last orders 2000)

Parking for 12

⌂ 10 🐾 🖭 ◻ ♨ 🍴 🛏 💻 ♨ ∪ ↑ ❀ ✕ 🚲 🛇 SP

Milton Manor Farm

👑

Old Bristol Road, Upper Milton, Wells BA5 3AH

☎ (01749) 673394

130-acre beef farm. Elizabethan manor house, Grade II* listed, on the southern slopes of the Mendips, 1 mile north of Wells. Superb view.
Bedrooms: 1 double, 1 twin, 1 triple
Bathrooms: 1 public
Bed & breakfast

per night:	£min	£max
Single	17.00	18.00
Double	30.00	32.00

Parking for 6

⌂ 🐾 UL 🍴 🛏 TV 💻 ♨ ∪ ↑ ❀ ✕ 🚲 SP 🎏

Tor House

👑👑 HIGHLY COMMENDED

20 Tor Street, Wells BA5 2US

☎ (01749) 672322 & 672084

Fax (01749) 672322

Historic, sympathetically restored 17th C building in delightful grounds overlooking the cathedral and Bishop's Palace. Attractive, comfortable and tastefully furnished throughout. 3 minutes' walk to town centre. Ample parking.
Bedrooms: 1 single, 3 double, 1 twin, 3 family rooms
Bathrooms: 5 en-suite, 2 public
Bed & breakfast

per night:	£min	£max
Single	26.00	40.00
Double	38.00	54.00

Evening meal 1830 (last orders 1000)

Parking for 12

Cards accepted: Access, Visa, Switch/Delta

⌂ 3 🖭 🗄 ♨ 🌙 UL 🍴 S 🍴 🛏 TV 💻 ♨ 🛏 18 ↑ ❀ ✕ 🚲 DAP SP 🎏

WEST ANSTEY

Devon
Map ref 1D1

Partridge Arms Farm

👑👑 COMMENDED

Yeo Mill, West Anstey, South Molton EX36 3NU

☎ Anstey Mills (01398) 341217

Fax (01398) 341217

200-acre mixed farm. Old world farmhouse set within established family farm, offering genuine hospitality and traditional farmhouse fare. Ideal for touring, outdoor pursuits and coastal resorts.
Bedrooms: 3 double, 2 twin, 2 family rooms
Bathrooms: 4 en-suite, 1 public
Bed & breakfast

per night:	£min	£max
Single	19.00	23.50
Double	38.00	47.00

Half board per

person:	£min	£max
Daily	28.50	33.00
Weekly	192.50	224.00

Evening meal 1930 (last orders 1600)

Parking for 10

⌂ 🐾 🗄 🖭 ◻ ♨ S 🛏 TV 💻 ♨ ∪ ∫ ❀ ✕ 🚲

WESTON-SUPER-MARE

North Somerset
Map ref 1D1

Large, friendly resort developed in the 19th C. Traditional seaside attractions include theatres and a dance hall. The museum shows a Victorian seaside gallery and has Iron Age finds from a hill fort on Worlebury Hill in Weston Woods.
Tourist Information Centre ☎ *(01934) 888800*

Braeside Hotel

👑👑 COMMENDED

2 Victoria Park, Weston-super-Mare BS23 2HZ

☎ (01934) 626642

Fax (01934) 626642

Delightful, family-run hotel, ideally situated near seafront. All rooms en-suite. Single rooms always available. Unrestricted on-street parking.
Bedrooms: 2 single, 4 double, 1 twin, 1 triple, 1 family room
Bathrooms: 9 en-suite
Bed & breakfast

per night:	£min	£max
Single	22.50	22.50
Double	45.00	45.00

Half board per

person:	£min	£max
Daily	32.00	32.00
Weekly	186.00	186.00

Lunch available

Evening meal 1830 (last orders 1800)

🐾 ◻ ♨ S 🍴 🛏 💻 ♨ 🚲 SP T

Conifers

👑👑 COMMENDED

63 Milton Road, Weston-super-Mare BS23 2SP

☎ (01934) 624404

Semi-detached corner guesthouse standing back in a large garden. Completely refurbished for bed and breakfast use. 25 years' experience.
Bedrooms: 2 double, 1 twin
Bathrooms: 1 en-suite, 1 public
Bed & breakfast

per night:	£min	£max
Single	16.00	21.00
Double	32.00	38.00

Parking for 4

Open January–November

◻ ♨ UL 💻 ♨ ✕ 🚲 SP ⊛

Purn House Farm

👑👑 COMMENDED

Bleadon, Weston-super-Mare BS24 0QE

☎ (01934) 812324

Fax (01934) 811029

700-acre mixed farm. Comfortable 17th C farmhouse only 3 miles from Weston-super-Mare. En-suite available with TV. 1 ground floor room. Peaceful yet not isolated, on bus route to town centre and station.
Bedrooms: 1 twin, 2 triple, 3 family rooms
Bathrooms: 2 en-suite, 2 private, 1 public
Bed & breakfast

per night:	£min	£max
Single	16.00	24.00
Double	32.00	40.00

Parking for 10

Open February–November

⌂ 🐾 🖭 UL S 🍴 🛏 TV 💻 ♨ ∪ ∫ ❀ ✕ 🚲 SP 🎏

WHIMPLE

Devon
Map ref 1D2

Down House

👑👑 COMMENDED

Whimple, Exeter EX5 2QR

☎ (01404) 822860

Elegant and comfortable Edwardian country house in the style of Charles Rennie Mackintosh. Five acres of gardens and orchard. Splendid views. Exeter, Honiton and Sidmouth 7 miles.

Bedrooms: 1 single, 3 double, 2 twin
Bathrooms: 2 en-suite, 4 private,
3 public
Bed & breakfast

per night:	£min	£max
Single	18.00	25.00
Double	36.00	44.00

Parking for 8

WIDECOMBE-IN-THE-MOOR

Devon
Map ref 1C2

Old village in pastoral country
under the high tors of East
Dartmoor. The "Cathedral of the
Moor" stands near a tiny square,
once used for archery practice,
which has a 16th C Church House
among other old buildings.

Buzzards Reach

Listed COMMENDED

Widecombe Hill,
Widecombe-in-the-Moor, Newton
Abbot TQ13 7TE
☎ (01364) 621205
*For non-smokers only. Extensive views
from comfortable en-suite
accommodation adjoining moorland
house, overlooking the Widecombe
Valley. Private parking and access to
open moorland. Ideal for touring
Dartmoor, Devon and Cornwall.*
Bedrooms: 3 double
Suites available
Bathrooms: 3 en-suite
Bed & breakfast

per night:	£min	£max
Double	30.00	

Parking for 20

Higher Venton Farm

Listed APPROVED

Widecombe-in-the-Moor, Newton
Abbot TQ13 7TF
☎ (01364) 631235
*40-acre beef farm. 17th C thatched
farmhouse with a homely atmosphere
and farmhouse cooking. Ideal for
touring Dartmoor. 16 miles from the
coast.*
Bedrooms: 2 double, 1 twin
Bathrooms: 1 en-suite, 1 public
Bed & breakfast

per night:	£min	£max
Single	19.00	21.00
Double	32.00	39.00

Parking for 5

Sheena Tower

Widecombe-in-the-Moor, Newton
Abbot TQ13 7TE
☎ (01364) 621308
*Comfortable moorland guesthouse
overlooking Widecombe village, offering
a relaxed holiday in picturesque
surroundings. Well placed for
discovering Dartmoor.*
Bedrooms: 1 single, 2 double, 1 twin,
1 triple, 1 family room
Bathrooms: 2 en-suite, 2 public
Bed & breakfast

per night:	£min	£max
Single	16.00	18.00
Double	32.00	36.00

Half board per

person:	£min	£max
Daily	24.50	26.50

Evening meal 1900 (last orders
1200)
Parking for 6
Open February–October

WINSFORD

Somerset
Map ref 1D1

Small village on the River Exe in
splendid walking country under
Winsford Hill. On the other side of
the hill is a Celtic standing stone,
the Caratacus Stone, and nearby
across the River Barle stretches an
ancient packhorse bridge, Tarr Steps,
built of great stone slabs.

Larcombe Foot

HIGHLY COMMENDED

Winsford, Minehead TA24 7HS
☎ (01643) 851306
*Comfortable country house in tranquil,
beautiful setting, overlooking River Exe.
Lovely walks on doorstep. Ideal for
touring Exmoor and north Devon
coast.*
Bedrooms: 1 double, 1 twin
Bathrooms: 2 private
Bed & breakfast

per night:	£min	£max
Single	18.00	18.00
Double	36.00	36.00

Half board per

person:	£min	£max
Daily	28.00	28.00

Evening meal (last orders 1930)
Parking for 3
Open April–October

Please mention this guide
when making your booking.

WINTERBOURNE ABBAS

Dorset
Map ref 2A3

Main road village with numerous
prehistoric remains nearby. Maiden
Castle 3 miles south-east.

Valley House

Higher Kingston Russell,
Winterbourne Abbas, Dorchester
DT2 9EE
☎ Long Bredy (01308) 482646
Fax (01308) 482647
*Listed stone farmhouse in peaceful
West Dorset countryside, halfway
between Dorchester and Bridport.*
Bedrooms: 1 family room
Bathrooms: 1 en-suite
Bed & breakfast

per night:	£min	£max
Single	18.00	22.00
Double	36.00	44.00

Parking for 8
Open April–October

WINTERBOURNE STOKE

Wiltshire
Map ref 2B2

Scotland Lodge

COMMENDED

Winterbourne Stoke, Salisbury
SP3 4TF
☎ Shrewton (01980) 620943 &
Mobile 0860 272599
Fax (01980) 620943
*Historic, comfortable country house
with private bathrooms. Helpful service,
delicious breakfasts. Ideal touring base.
French and some German spoken.
Self-contained unit also available for
self-catering.*
Bedrooms: 1 double, 1 twin, 1 triple
Bathrooms: 3 en-suite
Bed & breakfast

per night:	£min	£max
Single	25.00	35.00
Double	35.00	45.00

Parking for 5

The National Grading and
Classification Scheme is
explained in full at the
back of this guide.

WOOTTON BASSETT

Wiltshire
Map ref 2B2

Small hillside town with attractive old buildings and a 13th C church. The church and the half-timbered town hall were both restored in the 19th C and the stocks and ducking pool are preserved.

Tockenham Court Farm

Listed HIGHLY COMMENDED

Tockenham, Wootton Bassett, Swindon SN4 7PH
☎ Swindon (01793) 852315 & Mobile 0836 241686
Fax (01793) 852315

250-acre dairy farm. 16th C listed building. Visitors are welcome to walk the fields.
Bedrooms: 2 double, 1 twin
Bathrooms: 1 private, 2 public, 1 private shower
Bed & breakfast

per night:	£min	£max
Single	18.00	20.00
Double	36.00	40.00

Parking for 4

YARCOMBE

Devon
Map ref 1D2

Tiny village between Honiton and Chard.

Crawley Farm 🏚

👑 COMMENDED

Yarcombe, Honiton EX14 9AX
☎ Chard (01460) 64760
Fax (01460) 64760

200-acre mixed farm. 17th C thatched farmhouse in Blackdown Hills. Tea-making, TV, hot and cold in bedrooms. En-suite available. Excellent pub food locally.
Bedrooms: 1 double, 1 twin, 1 triple
Bathrooms: 1 en-suite, 2 public
Bed & breakfast

per night:	£min	£max
Double	28.00	32.00

Parking for 6
Open March–November

YELVERTON

Devon
Map ref 1C2

Village on the edge of Dartmoor, where ponies wander over the flat common. Buckland Abbey is 2 miles south-west, while Burrator Reservoir is 2 miles to the east.

Greenwell Farm 🏚

👑 👑 COMMENDED

Meavy, Yelverton PL20 6PY
☎ (01822) 853563
Fax (01822) 853563
220-acre livestock farm. Fresh country air, breathtaking views and scrumptious farmhouse cuisine. This busy family farm welcomes you to share our countryside and wildlife.
Bedrooms: 2 double, 1 twin
Bathrooms: 3 en-suite
Bed & breakfast

per night:	£min	£max
Double	39.00	44.00

Half board per person:

	£min	£max
Daily	41.00	44.50
Weekly	200.00	215.00

Evening meal 1830 (last orders 1200)
Parking for 8

Peek Hill Farm

⌂⌂ COMMENDED

Dousland, Yelverton PL20 6PD
☎ (01822) 852908

300-acre livestock farm. Relax on an antique brass bed, experience a proper farmhouse breakfast, then wander down mossy moorland ways.
Bedrooms: 1 double, 1 family room
Bathrooms: 2 en-suite, 1 public

Bed & breakfast per night:

	£min	£max
Double	34.00	40.00

Half board per person:

	£min	£max
Daily	27.00	30.00
Weekly	175.00	195.00

Evening meal from 1800
Parking for 4

⌖⌂▢♿♨Ⓤ️Ⓢ✂️🎿📺▥🖥✿🚗

YEOVIL

Somerset
Map ref 2A3

Lively market town, famous for glove making, set in dairying country beside the River Yeo. Interesting parish church. Museum of South Somerset at Hendford Manor. *Tourist Information Centre ☎ (01935) 71279*

Holywell House

⌂⌂⌂ HIGHLY COMMENDED

Holywell, East Coker, Yeovil
BA22 9NQ
☎ West Coker (01935) 862612
Fax (01935) 863035

Delightful country home with fine amenities. Three acres of gardens (National Gardens Scheme), tennis court. Idyllic rural setting in quiet location off A30, 2 miles west of Yeovil.
Bedrooms: 2 double, 1 twin
Suite available
Bathrooms: 3 en-suite

Bed & breakfast per night:

	£min	£max
Single	35.00	40.00
Double	60.00	65.00

Half board per person:

	£min	£max
Daily	52.00	57.00
Weekly	330.00	360.00

Evening meal 1900 (last orders 2030)
Parking for 15

⌖⌂▢♿▢Ⓤ️Ⓢ✂️🖥▥🖥❤️♿🎯12
🔍Ⓤ🏃✿✈️🚗 SP 🏠 Ⓣ

Jessops

Listed COMMENDED

Vagg Lane, Chilthorne Domer, Yeovil
BA22 8RY
☎ (01935) 841097

New bungalow with 4 double bedrooms, 1 en-suite with four- poster bed. Panoramic views over Yeovilton - super on air display day.
Bedrooms: 4 double
Suite available
Bathrooms: 1 en-suite, 2 public

Bed & breakfast per night:

	£min	£max
Double	26.00	32.00

Half board per person:

	£min	£max
Daily	40.00	46.00

Evening meal from 1800
Parking for 7
Open January–November

⌖🐾♿🐕Ⓤ️❤️●🚗

YEOVILTON

Somerset
Map ref 2A3

Cary Fitzpaine

⌂⌂

Yeovilton, Yeovil BA22 8JB
☎ Charlton Mackerell (01458) 223250
Fax (01458) 223250

600-acre mixed farm. Elegant Georgian manor farmhouse in idyllic setting. Large gardens. High standard of accommodation, all bedrooms with en-suite bath. Four-poster bed.
Bedrooms: 1 double, 1 twin, 1 triple
Bathrooms: 2 en-suite, 1 private, 1 public

Bed & breakfast per night:

	£min	£max
Single	18.00	23.00
Double	36.00	42.00

Parking for 14

⌖🐾▢♿🐕Ⓤ️Ⓢ🖥📺▥🖥♿Ⓤ
✿🚗 SP

Information on accommodation listed in this guide has been supplied by the proprietors. As changes may occur you are advised to check details at the time of booking.

Courtry Farm

Listed

Bridgehampton, Yeovil BA22 8HF
☎ Ilchester (01935) 840327

590-acre mixed farm. Farmhouse with ground floor rooms, en-suite, TV, tea-making facilities. Tennis court. Fleet Air Arm Museum half a mile.
Bedrooms: 1 twin, 1 triple
Bathrooms: 2 en-suite

Bed & breakfast per night:

	£min	£max
Single	20.00	
Double	35.00	

Parking for 20

⌖♿⁶▢♿Ⓤ️✂️▥🔍✿🚗🏠

YETMINSTER

Dorset
Map ref 2A3

Alton Tower Farm

Listed HIGHLY COMMENDED

Yetminster, Sherborne DT9 6NN
☎ (01935) 872555

Set in glorious Dorset countryside, an ideal base for visiting places of interest. Quiet position on edge of village.
Bedrooms: 2 double, 1 twin
Bathrooms: 1 en-suite, 2 public

Bed & breakfast per night:

	£min	£max
Single	16.00	18.00
Double	32.00	40.00

Parking for 10

⌖8▢♿Ⓤ️🐕🚗 SP

The 🅜 symbol after an establishment name indicates that it is a Regional Tourist Board member.

The symbols in each entry give information about services and facilities. A 'key' to these symbols appears at the back of this guide.

ZEALS

Wiltshire
Map ref 2B2

Pretty village of thatched cottages set high over the Dorset border. Zeals House dates from the medieval period and has some 19th C work. The Palladian Stourhead House (National Trust), in its magnificent gardens, lies further north.

Cornerways Cottage

COMMENDED

Longcross, Zeals, Warminster
BA12 6LL
☎ Bourton (01747) 840477
Fax (01747) 840477

18th C cottage with original beams. Ideal position for touring Stourhead, Stonehenge, Shaftesbury and other local attractions. Riding, fishing, golf and walking locally. Close to A303, midway for London or Devon and Cornwall. Two miles from Stourhead House and Gardens, 4 miles from Longleat.

Bedrooms: 3 double
Suites available
Bathrooms: 2 en-suite, 3 public

Bed & breakfast per night:

	£min	£max
Single	19.00	20.00
Double	35.00	36.00

Half board per person:

	£min	£max
Daily	26.00	

Evening meal 1830 (last orders 1930)
Parking for 6

CHECK THE MAPS

The colour maps at the back of this guide show all the cities, towns and villages for which you will find accommodation entries.

Refer to the town index to find the page on which it is listed.

AT-A-GLANCE SYMBOLS

Symbols at the end of each accommodation entry give useful information about services and facilities. A key to symbols can be found inside the back cover flap.

Keep this open for easy reference.

USE YOUR *i*'s

There are more than 550 Tourist Information Centres throughout England offering friendly help with accommodation and holiday ideas as well as suggestions of places to visit and things to do. There may well be a centre in your home town which can help you before you set out. You'll find the address of your nearest Tourist Information Centre in your local Phone Book.

COUNTRY CODE

Always follow the Country Code ✿ Enjoy the countryside and respect its life and work ✿ Guard against all risk of fire ✿ Fasten all gates ✿ Keep your dogs under close control ✿ Keep to public paths across farmland ✿ Use gates and stiles to cross fences, hedges and walls ✿ Leave livestock, crops and machinery alone ✿ Take your litter home ✿ Help to keep all water clean ✿ Protect wildlife, plants and trees ✿ Take special care on country roads ✿ Make no unnecessary noise

ENQUIRY COUPONS

To help you obtain further information about advertisers and accommodation featured in this guide you will find enquiry coupons at the back. Send these directly to the establishments in which you are interested. Remember to complete both sides of the coupon.

COUNTRY CODE

Always follow the Country Code 🍀 Enjoy the countryside and respect its life and work 🍀 Guard against all risk of fire 🍀 Fasten all gates 🍀 Keep your dogs under close control 🍀 Keep to public paths across farmland 🍀 Use gates and stiles to cross fences, hedges and walls 🍀 Leave livestock, crops and machinery alone 🍀 Take your litter home 🍀 Help to keep all water clean 🍀 Protect wildlife, plants and trees 🍀 Take special care on country roads 🍀 Make no unnecessary noise

USE YOUR *i*'s

There are more than 550 Tourist Information Centres throughout England offering friendly help with accommodation and holiday ideas as well as suggestions of places to visit and things to do. You'll find the address of your nearest Tourist Information Centre in your local Phone Book.

CHECK THE MAPS

The colour maps at the back of this guide show all the cities, towns and villages for which you will find accommodation entries.

Refer to the town index to find the page on which it is listed.

SOUTH OF ENGLAND

The South of England is a region of contrast and fascination. While the New Forest and Chiltern Hills offer mile upon mile of unspoilt countryside, there is much to please those who prefer town life - not to mention smart little Thameside villages crammed with antiques shops, quaint tea shops and exclusive boutiques.

Historic Oxford, Winchester and Windsor fall within the region, as does Henley, home of the famous Regatta.

The bucolic charms of Dorset await - along with the delightful seaside resorts of Poole, Weymouth and Bournemouth. And don't overlook the pretty Isle of Wight, just a ferry ride away.

FOR MORE INFORMATION CONTACT:
Southern Tourist Board
40 Chamberlayne Road, Eastleigh,
Hampshire SO50 5JH
Tel: (01703) 620555 **Fax:** (01703) 620010

Where to Go in the South of England -
see pages 312-315
Where to Stay in the South of England -
see pages 316-348

SOUTH OF ENGLAND

Where to Go and What to See

You will find hundreds of interesting places to visit during your stay in the South of England, just some of which are listed in these pages. The number against each name will help you locate it on the map (page 315). Contact any Tourist Information Centre in the region for more ideas on days out in the South of England.

1 Broughton Castle
Banbury, Oxfordshire OX15 5EB
Tel: (01295) 262624
Medieval moated house built in 1300 and enlarged between 1550-1600. The home of Lord and Lady Saye and Sele and family home for 600 years. Civil War connections.

2 Blenheim Palace
Woodstock,
Oxfordshire OX20 1PX
Tel: (01993) 811091
Birthplace of Sir Winston Churchill, designed by Vanbrugh. Park designed by Capability Brown. Adventure play area, maze, butterfly house and Churchill exhibition.

3 The Oxford Story
6 Broad Street, Oxford OX1 3AJ
Tel: (01865) 728822
Heritage centre depicting eight centuries of history in sights, sounds, personalities and smells. Visitors are transported in moving desks with commentary of their choice.

4 Didcot Railway Centre
Great Western Society, Didcot, Oxfordshire OX11 7NJ
Tel: (01235) 817200
Living museum recreating the golden age of the Great Western Railway. Steam locomotives and trains, engine shed and small relics museum.

5 Bekonscot Model Village
Warwick Road, Beaconsfield, Buckinghamshire HP9 2PL
Tel: (01494) 672919
A complete model village of the 1930's, with outdoor gauge 1 model railway. Zoo, cinema, minster, cricket match and 1,400 inhabitants.

6 Beale Park
The Child-Beale Wildlife Trust
Lower Basildon,
Berkshire RG8 9NH
Tel: (01734) 845172
Established 38 years ago, the park features wildfowl, pheasants,

highland cattle, rare sheep, llamas, narrow guage railway and pet corner.

7 Windsor Castle
Windsor, Berkshire SL4 1NJ
Tel: (01753) 868286
Official residence of HM The Queen and royal residence for nine centuries. State apartments, Queen Mary's Dolls' House, exhibition of The Queen's presents and carriages.

8 Legoland Windsor
Winkfield Road, Windsor,
Berkshire SL4 4AY
Tel: (0990) 626375
A unique family park with hands-on activities, rides, themed playscapes and more Lego bricks than you ever dreamed possible.

9 Museum of Army Flying
Middle Wallop,
Hampshire SO20 8DY
Tel: (01980) 674421
Award-winning and unique collection of flying machines and

displays depicting the role of army flying since the late 19thC.

10 Jane Austen's House
Chawton, Hampshire GU34 1SD
Tel: (01420) 83262
17thC house where Jane Austen lived from 1809-1817, and wrote or revised her six great novels. Letters, pictures, memorabilia, garden.

11 Winchester Cathedral
5 The Close, Winchester,
Hampshire SO23 9LS
Tel: (01962) 853137
Originally Norman with 16thC additions. Old Saxon site adjacent. Tombs, library and medieval wall paintings.

12 The Sir Harold Hillier Gardens and Arboretum
Jermyns Lane, Ampfield,
Hampshire SO51 0QA
Tel: (01794) 368787
The largest collection of trees and shrubs of its kind in the British Isles planted within an attractive landscape of over 166 acres.

13 Marwell Zoological Park
Colden Common, Winchester,
Hampshire SO21 1JH
Tel: (01962) 777407
Set in 100 acres of parkland

surrounding Marwell Hall. Venue suitable for all age groups including disabled.

14 Broadlands
Romsey, Hampshire SO51 9ZD
Tel: (01794) 517888
Home of the late Lord Mountbatten. Magnificent 18thC house and contents. Superb views across River Test. Mountbatten exhibition and audio-visual presentation.

15 Paultons Park
Ower, Romsey,
Hampshire SO51 6AL
Tel: (01703) 814442
A whole day out for all the family in beautiful surroundings. Over 40 different attractions including rides, museums, birds, animals and entertainment.

16 Exbury Gardens
Exbury, Southampton SO4 1AZ
Tel: (01703) 891203
Over 200 acres of woodland garden, including the Rothschild collection of rhododendrons, azaleas, camellias and magnolias.

17 Tudor House Museum
St. Michael's Square, Bugle Street,
Southampton SO14 2AD
Tel: (01703) 332513

Large half-timbered Tudor house with exhibitions on Tudor, Georgian, and Victorian domestic and local history. Unique Tudor garden.

18 Royal Signals Museum
Blandford Camp,
Blandford Forum,
Dorset DT11 8RH
Tel: (01258) 482248
History of Army communication from Crimean War to Gulf War. Vehicles, uniforms, medals and badges on display.

19 The New Forest Owl Sanctuary
Crow Lane, Crow,
Ringwood,
Hampshire BH24 1EA
Tel: (01425) 476487
All the barn owls are destined to be released into the wild. The sanctuary includes an incubation room, hospital unit and 100 aviaries of various size.

20 National Motor Museum
Beaulieu,
Hampshire SO42 7ZN
Tel: (01590) 612345
Motor museum with over 200 exhibits showing history of motoring from 1895. Palace House, Wheels Experience, abbey ruins with a display of monastic life.

Collection of paintings. 250 acres wooded park, herd of Devon cattle.

26 Brownsea Island
Poole Harbour, Poole,
Dorset BH15 1EE
Tel: (01202) 707744
An island of 500 acres of woodland with beaches, glades and nature reserve. Site of Lord Baden Powell's first scout camp.

27 Compton Acres
Canford Cliffs Road,
Canford Cliffs, Poole,
Dorset BH13 7ES
Tel: (01202) 700778
Nine separate and distinct gardens of the world. The gardens include Italian, Japanese, sub tropical glen, rock, water and heather garden. Collection of statues.

28 Poole Pottery
The Quay, Poole,
Dorset BH15 1RF
Tel: (01202) 666200
Factory tour, self-guided commentary includes museum, cinema, factory and craft area. 'Have-a-go area', craft village, throwing, painting, plus craft demonstrations.

29 Corfe Castle
Corfe Castle, Wareham,
Dorset BH20 5EZ
Tel: (01929) 481294
Ruins of former Royal Castle sieged and "slighted" in 1646 by Parliamentary forces.

30 The Tank Museum
Bovington Camp, Wareham,
Dorset BH20 6JG
Tel: (01929) 405096
Largest and most comprehensive museum collection of armoured fighting vehicles in the world. Over 300 vehicles on show with supporting displays and video theatres.

21 HMS Victory
Portsmouth Historic Ships,
HM Naval Base,
Portsmouth PO1 3LJ
Tel: (01705) 839766
Vice Admiral Lord Nelson's flagship at Trafalgar. See his cabin, the "cockpit," where he died. Memorable tours of the sombre gun decks where men lived.

22 Osborne House
East Cowes,
Isle of Wight PO32 6JY
Tel: (01983) 200022
Queen Victoria and Prince Albert's seaside holiday home. Swiss Cottage where royal children learnt cooking and gardening. Victorian carriage service to Swiss Cottage.

23 Carisbrooke Castle
Newport,
Isle of Wight PO30 1XY
Tel: (01983) 522107

A splendid Norman castle, where Charles I was imprisoned. Governors' lodge houses the county museum, wheelhouse operated by donkeys.

24 Alice in Wonderland Maze and Family Park
Merritown Farm, Hurn,
Christchurch, Dorset BH23 6BA
Tel: (01202) 483444
Hedge maze, Mad Hatter's tea garden, Queen of Heart's croquet lawn, Cheshire Cat's adventure playground, Duchess' rose and herb garden, rare breeds farmyard and bouncy colour maze.

25 Kingston Lacy
Wimborne Minster,
Dorset BH21 4EA
Tel: (01202) 883402
17thC house designed for Sir Ralph Bankes by Sir Roger Pratt, altered by Sir Charles Barry in the 19thC.

HEREFORD & WORCESTER

WARWICKSHIRE

NORTHANTS

GLOUCESTERSHIRE

Cropredy

Newport Pagnell
Wolverton
Milton Keynes
Buckingham
Bletchley

[1] Banbury

Chipping Norton

Bicester

[2] Woodstock

BUCKINGHAM-
SHIRE

BEDS

Witney

Oxford **[3]**

Thame

Aylesbury
Wendover
Chesham

OXFORDSHIRE

Abingdon
Wallingford

Princes Risborough
High Wycombe

Faringdon

Wantage

[4] Didcot

Henley
on-Thames

Beaconsfield **[5]**

Marlow

Slough

Lower Basildon **[6]**

Maidenhead

Twyford

[7] **[8]**
Windsor

BERKSHIRE

Reading

Hungerford

Newbury

Wokingham

Bracknell

WILTSHIRE

Stratfield Saye

Farnborough

Fleet
Aldershot

Basingstoke

HAMPSHIRE

Alton

SURREY

[9] Middle Wallop

Chawton **[10]**

[11] Winchester

Liss

Ampfield

Colden Common

WEST
SUSSEX

[14] [15] **[12]**
Romsey

[13]
Eastleigh

Petersfield

Totton

[16] Southampton
[17]

Gillingham

Shaftesbury

Fordingbridge

Lyndhurst

Waterlooville

DORSET
(eastern)

Ringwood **[19]**

Brockenhurst

Fawley

Locks Heath
Lee-on-the-Solent

Blandford
Forum **[18]**

Wimborne
Minster **[25]**

West
Moors

[20]

Beaulieu

East
Cowes

Gosport

[21]

Portsmouth

Poole **[26] [27] [28]**

[24]

Lymington

[22]

Ryde

[29] [30]
Wareham

Bournemouth

Christchurch

Yarmouth

Newport **[23]**

ISLE OF
WIGHT

Sandown
Shanklin
Ventnor

Swanage

Freshwater

0   20 Miles

0   30 Kms

FIND OUT MORE

Further information about
holidays and attractions in the
South of England is available
from:

Southern Tourist Board,
40 Chamberlayne Road,
Eastleigh,
Hampshire SO50 5JH.
Tel: (01703) 620555

WHERE TO STAY (SOUTH OF ENGLAND)

Accommodation entries in this region are listed in alphabetical order of place name, and then in alphabetical order of establishment.

Map references refer to the colour location maps at the back of this guide. The first number indicates the map to use; the letter and number which follow refer to the grid reference on the map.

At-a-glance symbols at the end of each accommodation entry give useful information about services and facilities. A key to symbols can be found inside the back cover flap.

Keep this open for easy reference.

ABINGDON

Oxfordshire
Map ref 2C1

Attractive former county town on River Thames with many interesting buildings, including 17th C County Hall, now a museum, in the market-place and the remains of an abbey.
Tourist Information Centre ☎ (01235) 522711

1 Long Barn

Listed

Sutton Courtenay, Abingdon OX14 4BQ
☎ (01235) 848251
17th C village house 8 miles from Oxford, 2 miles from Abingdon. Easy access to Henley and the Cotswolds.
Bedrooms: 1 twin
Bathrooms: 1 private
Bed & breakfast

per night:	£min	£max
Single	15.00	15.00
Double	30.00	30.00

Parking for 3

🛏️🕗Ⓤ📺💻🖨️❄️🐾🏕️

The map references refer to the colour maps towards the end of the guide. The first figure is the map number; the letter and figure which follow indicate the grid reference on the map.

ALTON

Hampshire
Map ref 2C2

Pleasant old market town standing on the Pilgrim's Way, with some attractive Georgian buildings. The parish church still bears the scars of bullet marks, evidence of a bitter struggle between the Roundheads and the Royalists.
Tourist Information Centre ☎ (01420) 88448

Glen Derry

Listed COMMENDED

52 Wellhouse Road, Beech, Alton GU34 4AG
☎ (01420) 83235
Peaceful, secluded family home set in 3.5 acres of garden. Warm welcome assured. Ideal base for Watercress Steam Railway, Winchester and Portsmouth.
Bedrooms: 1 twin, 1 family room
Bathrooms: 1 en-suite, 1 public
Bed & breakfast

per night:	£min	£max
Single	20.00	26.00
Double	30.00	36.00

Parking for 13

🛏️👶📺💻Ⓤ✏️✂️📺💻🖨️❄️🐾

Information on accommodation listed in this guide has been supplied by the proprietors. As changes may occur you are advised to check details at the time of booking.

AMERSHAM

Buckinghamshire
Map ref 2D1

Old town with many fine buildings, particularly in the High Street. There are several interesting old inns.

The Barn

Listed HIGHLY COMMENDED

Rectory Hill, Old Amersham, Amersham HP7 0BT
☎ (01494) 722701
Fax (01494) 728826
Restored 17th C heavily beamed tithe barns with warm and friendly atmosphere. Short walk from Amersham station, excellent pubs and restaurants. Easy access to M25 and M40.
Bedrooms: 1 double, 2 twin
Bathrooms: 1 public
Bed & breakfast

per night:	£min	£max
Single	32.00	35.00
Double	50.00	53.00

Parking for 8

🛏️🕗📺🖥️👶Ⓤ✂️📺💻🖨️❄️
✖️🐾🏕️

AMPORT

Hampshire
Map ref 2C2

Broadwater ♨

👑👑 COMMENDED

Amport, Andover SP11 8AY
☎ Andover (01264) 772240
Fax (01264) 772240

Grade II listed thatched cottage. From A303 (from Andover) take turn off to Hawk Conservancy/Amport. At T-junction, turn right, take first road right (East Cholderton). Broadwater is first cottage on the right.
Bedrooms: 2 twin
Bathrooms: 2 en-suite, 1 public
Bed & breakfast

per night:	£min	£max
Single	21.00	25.00
Double	40.00	40.00

Parking for 3

ANDOVER
Hampshire
Map ref 2C2

Town that achieved importance from the wool trade and now has much modern development. A good centre for visiting places of interest. *Tourist Information Centre ☎ (01264) 324320*

The Old Barn M
Listed HIGHLY COMMENDED
Amport, Andover SP11 8AE
☎ (01264) 710410 & Mobile 0860 844772
Fax (01264) 710410
Converted old barn, in small village approximately 3 miles south west of Andover. Secluded, but only three-quarters of a mile from A303.
Bedrooms: 1 double, 1 triple
Bathrooms: 2 en-suite
Bed & breakfast

per night:	£min	£max
Single	23.00	24.00
Double	37.00	39.00

Parking for 4

The symbols in each entry give information about services and facilities. A 'key' to these symbols appears at the back of this guide.

ASCOT
Berkshire
Map ref 2C2

Small country town famous for its racecourse which was founded by Queen Anne. The race meeting each June is attended by the Royal Family.

Birchcroft House M
HIGHLY COMMENDED
Birchcroft, Brockenhurst Road, South Ascot, Ascot SL5 9HA
☎ (01344) 20574
Charming Edwardian country house in beautiful, peaceful wooded gardens. Ample parking. Warm welcome. Superb quality en-suite bedrooms. Ideal touring base, including London, (40 minutes by train), Windsor (6 miles), Heathrow (25 minutes). Golf at Wentworth, Sunningdale and Berkshire.
Bedrooms: 1 double, 2 twin
Bathrooms: 3 en-suite
Bed & breakfast

per night:	£min	£max
Single	34.00	38.00
Double	44.00	50.00

Parking for 6

Tanglewood M

Birch Lane, off Longhill Road, Chavey Down, Ascot SL5 8RF
☎ Bracknell (01344) 882528
Spacious, modern bungalow. Quiet, secluded location, large wooded garden, safe parking. 4 miles Windsor, 15 miles Heathrow. Easy access M4, M40, M3, M25. Convenient for Wentworth, Sunningdale, Ascot, Bracknell, Thames Valley and London. Telephone for directions/map as hidden away.
Bedrooms: 1 single, 2 twin
Bathrooms: 3 en-suite, 1 public
Bed & breakfast

per night:	£min	£max
Single	20.00	35.00
Double	40.00	60.00

Evening meal 1900 (last orders 2000)
Parking for 6

COLOUR MAPS

Colour maps at the back of this guide pinpoint all places in which you will find accommodation listed.

ASHURST
Hampshire
Map ref 2C3

Small village on the A35, on the edge of the New Forest and three miles north-east of Lyndhurst. Easy access to beautiful forest lawns.

Forest Gate Lodge M
Listed COMMENDED
161 Lyndhurst Road, Ashurst, Lyndhurst SO40 7AW
☎ Southampton (01703) 293026
Large, comfortable house, with direct access to New Forest. Restaurants and public houses nearby. Central to all New Forest attractions.
Bedrooms: 2 double
Bathrooms: 2 en-suite, 1 public
Bed & breakfast

per night:	£min	£max
Double	34.00	38.00

Parking for 8

AYLESBURY
Buckinghamshire
Map ref 2C1

Historic county town in the Vale of Aylesbury. The cobbled market square has a Victorian clock tower and the 15th C King's Head Inn (National Trust). Interesting county museum and 13th C parish church. Twice-weekly livestock market. *Tourist Information Centre ☎ (01296) 330559*

Longmoor Farm
HIGHLY COMMENDED
Cublington Road, Aston Abbotts, Aylesbury HP22 4ND
☎ (01296) 681010
Fax (01296) 688594
Spacious, Victorian country house, completely refurbished, built around handsome enclosed courtyard. Four acres of lovely gardens including 2 giant cedar trees.
Bedrooms: 2 double, 1 twin
Bathrooms: 1 public
Bed & breakfast

per night:	£min	£max
Single	22.00	
Double	40.00	

Parking for 10

AYLESBURY

Continued

The Seasons

👑 HIGHLY COMMENDED

9 Ballard Close, Aylesbury
HP21 9UY
☎ (01296) 84465
*Comfortable, friendly, quality
accommodation in quiet close. Good
centre for Chilterns, London, Oxford
and National Trust properties. Ideal for
business or holiday.*
Bedrooms: 1 single, 1 double, 1 twin
Bathrooms: 1 public
Bed & breakfast

per night:	£min	£max
Single	18.00	
Double	35.00	

Parking for 8

🐎10🖻♿🛏️🕅S☒📺🛍️🎇🌸✕
🚗T

BAMPTON

Oxfordshire
Map ref 2C1

Small market town, well known for
its Spring Bank Holiday Monday Fete
with Morris Dance Festival.

Cedars

👑

Mill Lane, Black Bourton, Bampton
OX18 2PJ
☎ Carterton (01993) 841368
*Large, comfortable village house in
secluded position on edge of Cotswolds.
Located between Burford and Witney,
2 miles outside Bampton.*
Bedrooms: 2 double
Bathrooms: 2 en-suite
Bed & breakfast

per night:	£min	£max
Double	30.00	42.00

Parking for 6
Open March–October

♿🖻🗖🛏️🕅🛍️🎇🌸🚗
DAP SP

> A key to symbols can be
> found inside the back
> cover flap.

> All accommodation in this
> guide has been graded, or is
> awaiting a grading, by a trained
> Tourist Board inspector.

BANBURY

Oxfordshire
Map ref 2C1

Famous for its cattle market, cakes
and nursery rhyme Cross. Founded
in Saxon times, it has some fine
houses and interesting old inns. A
good centre for touring
Warwickshire and the Cotswolds.
*Tourist Information Centre ☎ (01295)
259855*

The Lodge

👑 👑 HIGHLY COMMENDED

Main Road, Middleton Cheney,
Banbury OX17 2PP
☎ (01295) 710355
*200-year-old lodge in lovely countryside,
on outskirts of historic village, 3 miles
east of Banbury on A422 and 1 mile
from M40.*
Bedrooms: 1 double, 1 twin
Bathrooms: 2 en-suite
Bed & breakfast

per night:	£min	£max
Double	48.00	48.00

Parking for 5

🐎3♿🕅📺①🛍️🌸✕🚗🛏️

Mine Hill House

Lower Brailes, Banbury OX15 5BJ
☎ (01608) 685594

*Lovely Cotswold farmhouse, built in
1733, situated on top of a hill, with
stunning views over surrounding
countryside. Oak beams, flagstone
floors, super food.*
Bedrooms: 1 double, 1 twin, 1 triple
Bathrooms: 1 en-suite, 2 private,
1 public
Bed & breakfast

per night:	£min	£max
Single	15.50	22.00
Double	31.00	44.00

Lunch available
Evening meal 1800 (last orders
2100)
Parking for 8

🐎5🦌♿🛏️🕅S☒📺🛍️🖂∪↾
🌸🚗🛏️

Roxtones

Listed COMMENDED

Malthouse Lane, Shutford, Banbury
OX15 6PB
☎ (01295) 788240
*Stone-fronted semi-bungalow with
garden surrounds, orchard and lawns. 6*

miles from Banbury, 16 miles from
Stratford-upon-Avon and 2 miles from
Broughton Castle.
Bedrooms: 2 single, 1 double
Bathrooms: 1 public
Bed & breakfast

per night:	£min	£max
Single		15.00
Double		25.00

Half board per

person:	£min	£max
Daily		21.00
Weekly		140.00

Evening meal 1900 (last orders
2100)
Parking for 3
Open April–September

🐎🦌♿🛏️🕅S☒📺🛍️✕🚗

BARTON ON SEA

Hampshire
Map ref 2B3

Seaside village with views of the Isle
of Wight. Within easy driving
distance of the New Forest.

Bank Cottage

👑 👑 COMMENDED

Grove Road, Barton on Sea, New
Milton BH25 7DN
☎ New Milton (01425) 613677
Fax (01425) 613677

*Spacious en-suite rooms with every
comfort and facility. Very warm
welcome. Secure parking. Close to pub
and beach. Fresh sea air. Peace and
quiet.*
Bedrooms: 2 double, 1 twin
Bathrooms: 3 en-suite, 1 public
Bed & breakfast

per night:	£min	£max
Single	20.00	25.00
Double	35.00	39.00

Half board per

person:	£min	£max
Daily	27.00	32.00
Weekly	154.00	220.00

Evening meal from 1900
Parking for 6

🐎5🖻♿🛏️🕅S☒📺🛍️
🖂∪↾🌸✕🚗SP

> Map references apply to
> the colour maps at the
> back of this guide.

BEACONSFIELD

Buckinghamshire
Map ref 2C2

Former coaching town with several inns still surviving. The old town has many fine houses and an interesting church. Beautiful countryside and beech woods nearby.

Beacon House

113 Maxwell Road, Beaconsfield
HP9 1RF
☎ (01494) 672923
Extended, semi-detached house, with gardens front and back and use of patio. On Heathrow bus route and close to railway station.
Bedrooms: 1 single, 1 twin, 1 triple
Bathrooms: 2 en-suite, 1 public
Bed & breakfast

per night:	£min	£max
Single	15.00	18.00
Double	25.00	30.00

Half board per person

	£min	£max
Daily	20.00	23.00
Weekly	140.00	161.00

Evening meal 1830 (last orders 1930)
Parking for 3

⛷6🏠🛎️🖪🕯🛁ⓊⓁ✂️📺🖭📖🅿️🏵✈️
🚐

BEAULIEU

Hampshire
Map ref 2C3

Beautifully situated among woods and hills on the Beaulieu river, the village is both charming and unspoilt. The 13th C ruined Cistercian abbey and 14th C Palace House stand close to the National Motor Museum. There is a maritime museum at Bucklers Hard.

Leygreen Farm House 🐾

☖☖ COMMENDED

Lyndhurst Road, Beaulieu,
Brockenhurst SO42 7YP
☎ Lymington (01590) 612355
Comfortable Victorian farmhouse with large garden. Convenient for Beaulieu, Bucklers Hard museums and Exbury Gardens. Reductions for 3 days or more.
Bedrooms: 2 double, 1 twin
Bathrooms: 3 en-suite, 1 public
Bed & breakfast

per night:	£min	£max
Single	15.00	20.00
Double	30.00	40.00

Parking for 6

⛷🖪🛎️🖪ⓊⓁⓈ📖📺🖭📖🅿️🏵🚐📖
🆂🅿️

BICESTER

Oxfordshire
Map ref 2C1

Market town with large army depot and well-known hunting centre with hunt established in the late 18th C. The ancient parish church displays work of many periods. Nearby is the Jacobean mansion of Rousham House.
Tourist Information Centre ☎ (01869) 369055

Manor Farm 🐾

☖

Poundon, Bicester OX6 0BB
☎ (01869) 277212
Fax (01869) 277166
300-acre arable and mixed farm. 400-year-old farmhouse, tranquil, spacious and comfortable, a warm welcome to all. Take A421 Bicester to Buckingham road. Poundon turn is 3 miles along on right.
Bedrooms: 1 single, 1 double, 1 triple
Bathrooms: 2 public
Bed & breakfast

per night:	£min	£max
Single	17.00	20.00
Double	34.00	40.00

Parking for 12

⛷🖪🛎️ⓊⓁ✂️🖭📖🅿️🏵🚐 DAP 🆂🅿️

BLANDFORD FORUM

Dorset
Map ref 2B3

Almost completely destroyed by fire in 1731, the town was rebuilt in a handsome Georgian style. The church is large and grand and the town is the hub of a rich farming area.
Tourist Information Centre ☎ (01258) 454770

Farnham Farm House

Listed COMMENDED

Farnham, Blandford Forum
DT11 8DG
☎ Tollard Royal (01725) 516254
Fax (01725) 516254
350-acre arable farm. 19th C farmhouse in the Cranborne Chase with extensive views to the south. Within easy reach of the coast.
Bedrooms: 2 double, 1 twin
Bathrooms: 1 en-suite, 1 public
Bed & breakfast

per night:	£min	£max
Single	20.00	20.00
Double	40.00	40.00

Parking for 7

⛷🖪🛎️ⓊⓁⓈ📖📺🅿️🐾🏵🚐

Home Farm

☖☖ HIGHLY COMMENDED

Bryanston, Blandford Forum
DT11 0PR
☎ Blandford (01258) 452919
800-acre arable & dairy farm. Attractive Georgian farmhouse with walled garden in quiet hamlet. Area of Outstanding Natural Beauty. 1.5 miles from Blandford.
Bedrooms: 1 double, 2 twin
Bathrooms: 2 en-suite, 1 private, 2 public
Bed & breakfast

per night:	£min	£max
Single	19.00	
Double	38.00	

Parking for 10

⛷🖪🛎️🕯ⓊⓁⓈ📖📺🖭📖🅿️Ư🏵
🚐📞

Meadow House

☖

Tarrant Hinton, Blandford Forum
DT11 8JG
☎ Tarrant Hinton (01258) 830498
17th-18th C brick and flint farmhouse set in 4.5 acres. Warm welcome in peaceful, clean and comfortable family home. Noted for delicious home-produced English breakfast. Excellent base for touring.
Bedrooms: 1 single, 1 double, 1 triple
Bathrooms: 3 public
Bed & breakfast

per night:	£min	£max
Single	17.00	25.00
Double	34.00	50.00

Parking for 6

⛷🖪🛎️🖪🕯ⓊⓁⓈ✂️📖📺🖭📖🅿️
🐾🏵✈️🚐

National gradings and classifications were correct at the time of going to press but are subject to change. Please check at the time of booking.

For farm holidays and accommodation suitable for young people and organised groups, please refer to the special sections at the back of this guide.

BOURNEMOUTH

Dorset
Map ref 2B3

Seaside town set among the pines with a mild climate, sandy beaches and fine coastal views. The town has wide streets with excellent shops, a pier, a pavilion, museums and conference centre.
Tourist Information Centre ☎ *(01202) 451700*

Bay View Hotel ⚑

👑👑👑 COMMENDED

Southbourne Overcliff Drive, Bournemouth BH6 3QB
☎ (01202) 429315 & Mobile (01585) 488150
Fax (01202) 424385

Clifftop location on more relaxing side of Bournemouth. Scrumptious home-cooked food. Panoramic sea views from most rooms. Special Christmas programme.
Bedrooms: 2 single, 9 double, 3 twin
Bathrooms: 12 en-suite, 1 public

Bed & breakfast per night:

	£min	£max
Single	16.00	26.00
Double	32.00	52.00

Half board per person:

	£min	£max
Daily	23.50	33.50
Weekly	148.50	208.50

Evening meal 1830 (last orders 1930)
Parking for 12
Cards accepted: Access, Visa, Switch/Delta

🛏🕕🍴🖥🖵🛜♿🅟🛎Ⓢ⚡📺🖵
🖨♨⚘ DAP 🐾 SP

The Cottage ⚑

👑👑👑 COMMENDED

12 Southern Road, Southbourne, Bournemouth BH6 3SR
☎ (01202) 422764
Charming character family-run hotel. Restful location. Noted for home-prepared fresh cooking, cleanliness and tastefully furnished accommodation. Ample parking. Non-smoking.
Bedrooms: 1 single, 1 double, 2 twin, 1 triple, 2 family rooms
Bathrooms: 4 en-suite, 2 public, 1 private shower

Bed & breakfast per night:

	£min	£max
Single	17.50	19.00
Double	35.00	42.00

Half board per person:

	£min	£max
Daily	25.50	27.00
Weekly	165.00	175.00

Evening meal 1800 (last orders 1800)
Parking for 8
Open February–November

🛏4🍴🖥🕅♿🅟🛎Ⓢ⚡📺🖵🖨
🐾🚲 DAP SP

The Garthlyn Hotel ⚑

👑👑👑 COMMENDED

6 Sandbourne Road, Alum Chine, Westbourne, Bournemouth BH4 8JH
☎ (01202) 761016
Hotel of character with award-winning gardens. Good quality beds. 4 minutes' walk to beaches (hut available). Car park in grounds.
Bedrooms: 1 single, 5 double, 1 twin, 1 triple, 2 family rooms
Bathrooms: 9 en-suite, 1 public

Bed & breakfast per night:

	£min	£max
Single	21.00	33.00
Double	40.00	60.00

Half board per person:

	£min	£max
Daily	28.50	41.00
Weekly	171.50	230.00

Evening meal 1800 (last orders 1900)
Parking for 9
Cards accepted: Access, Visa, Switch/Delta

🛏4🍴♿🛎Ⓢ⚡📺🖵🖨🔍⚘
🐾🚲 DAP 🐾 SP

The Golden Sovereigns Hotel ⚑

👑👑👑

97 Alumhurst Road, Alum Chine, Bournemouth BH4 8HR
☎ (01202) 762088
Attractively decorated Victorian character hotel. Quiet, convenient location; beach 4 minutes' walk. Comfortable rooms, traditional home-cooking. Early booking special discounts.
Bedrooms: 1 single, 2 double, 1 twin, 2 triple, 2 family rooms
Bathrooms: 5 en-suite, 1 private, 2 public

Bed & breakfast per night:

	£min	£max
Single	15.00	30.00
Double	30.00	50.00

Half board per person:

	£min	£max
Daily	22.50	32.50
Weekly	140.00	200.00

Lunch available
Evening meal 1800 (last orders 1600)
Parking for 9
Cards accepted: Access, Visa

🛏🖥🕕♿🅟Ⓢ⚡📺🖵🖨🚲 DAP ♿
SP

Mayfield Private Hotel ⚑

👑👑

46 Frances Road, Bournemouth BH1 3SA
☎ (01202) 551839
Overlooking public gardens with tennis, bowling greens, crazy-golf. Central for sea, shops and main rail/coach stations. Some rooms have shower or toilet/shower. Licensed.
Bedrooms: 1 single, 4 double, 2 twin, 1 family room
Bathrooms: 5 en-suite, 2 public, 2 private showers

Bed & breakfast per night:

	£min	£max
Single	13.00	16.00
Double	26.00	32.00

Half board per person:

	£min	£max
Daily	19.00	22.00
Weekly	110.00	130.00

Evening meal from 1800
Parking for 5
Open January–November

🛏6🖥♿🅟🛎Ⓢ⚡📺🖵🖨⚘
🚲 DAP SP

Pinewood ⚑

Listed COMMENDED

197 Holdenhurst Road, Bournemouth BH8 8DG
☎ (01202) 292684
Friendly guesthouse, close to rail, coach stations and all amenities. Tea, coffee and satellite TV in all rooms.
Bedrooms: 1 single, 3 double, 1 twin, 3 triple
Bathrooms: 2 public

Bed & breakfast per night:

	£min	£max
Single	15.00	17.00
Double	30.00	34.00

Parking for 8

🛏5🖥♿Ⓤ🛎Ⓢ🖵🖨🚲🍴🚲

The National Grading and Classification Scheme is explained in full at the back of this guide.

Rosedene Cottage Hotel

Listed

St Peter's Road, Bournemouth
BH1 2LA
☎ (01202) 554102

Old world cottage hotel, quiet, yet in the heart of Bournemouth. A short stroll to pier, shops, gardens, Bournemouth International Centre, theatres and beaches. 20 minutes from Bournemouth International Airport.
Bedrooms: 3 single, 5 double, 1 twin, 1 triple
Bathrooms: 7 en-suite, 1 public
Bed & breakfast

per night:	£min	£max
Single	17.00	21.00
Double	30.00	42.00

Parking for 8
Cards accepted: Access, Visa, Diners, Amex

⊗≈2🛌☎📺▢♿🅜🛡Ⓢ⊁📺
🎬📧.🚗▶ DAP SP T

BRAMDEAN

Hampshire
Map ref 2C3

Village astride the A272, 1 mile west of the site of a Roman villa.

Dean Farm

Listed

Kilmeston, Alresford SO24 0NL
☎ (01962) 771286
200-acre mixed farm. Comfortable, 18th C farmhouse in Kilmeston, a small and peaceful village 1.5 miles off the A272 between Petersfield and Winchester.
Bedrooms: 3 double
Bathrooms: 1 public
Bed & breakfast

per night:	£min	£max
Single	18.00	20.00
Double	36.00	36.00

Parking for 3

⊗🐎10🗝♿🅜🛡Ⓢ⊁📺.📧🚗✱🐴
🚗

BRANSGORE

Hampshire
Map ref 2B3

Situated in extensive woodlands. In the church of St Mary is a lovely Perpendicular font which is said to have come from Christchurch.

Wiltshire House 𝗠

⚘⚘ HIGHLY COMMENDED

West Road, Bransgore, Christchurch, Dorset BH23 8BD
☎ (01425) 672450
Friendly, informal accommodation including 1 four-poster bedroom. Early Victorian residence set in large secluded garden with easy access to forest and beach.
Bedrooms: 1 double, 1 twin, 1 family room
Bathrooms: 3 en-suite, 1 public
Bed & breakfast

per night:	£min	£max
Single	16.00	20.00
Double	29.00	40.00

Parking for 4

⊗🐎🖥🛌☎♿🐕🅜Ⓢ⊁📺.📧
Ს✱🐴🚗 DAP SP T

BRIGHSTONE

Isle of Wight
Map ref 2C3

Excellent centre for visitors who want somewhere quiet. Calbourne nearby is ideal for picnics and the sea at Chilton Chine has safe bathing at high tide.

The Lodge 𝗠

Main Road, Brighstone, Newport
PO30 4DJ
☎ Isle of Wight (01983) 741272

Beautiful Victorian, family-run manor house, set in large gardens. Offering quality bed and breakfast accommodation and service. Delightful village location.
Bedrooms: 7 double, 2 triple
Bathrooms: 5 en-suite, 2 public
Bed & breakfast

per night:	£min	£max
Single	20.00	25.00
Double	40.00	50.00

Parking for 9

⊗🛌♿🐕🅜🛡⊁🐴.📧🚗Ს✱🐴
🚗

BROCKENHURST

Hampshire
Map ref 2C3

Attractive village with thatched cottages and a ford in its main street. Well placed for visiting the New Forest.

Evergreen 𝗠

⚘⚘ HIGHLY COMMENDED

Sway Road, Brockenhurst
SO42 7RX
☎ (01590) 623411
Fax (01590) 623411
Lovely house, 10 minutes' walk from village centre/station. Two friendly ponies and donkey. Beautiful rooms, all en-suite. Safe, off-road parking.
Bedrooms: 3 double
Bathrooms: 3 en-suite
Bed & breakfast

per night:	£min	£max
Double	36.00	

Parking for 3

⊗📪🖥🛌♿🅜🛡⊁🎬.📧✱🐴🚗

BUCKINGHAM

Buckinghamshire
Map ref 2C1

Interesting old market town surrounded by rich farmland. It has many Georgian buildings, including the Town Hall and Old Jail and many old almshouses and inns. Stowe School nearby has magnificent 18th C landscaped gardens.
Tourist Information Centre ☎ (01280) 823020

Folly Farm 𝗠

⚘ COMMENDED

Padbury, Buckingham MK18 2HS
☎ Winslow (01296) 712413
500-acre arable farm. On A413 between Winslow and Padbury, 2 miles south of Buckingham. Substantial farmhouse opposite Folly Inn. Convenient for Stowe Landscape Gardens, Silverstone circuit, Addington Equestrian Centre, Waddesdon Manor and Claydon House. Evening meals by arrangement.
Bedrooms: 3 double
Bathrooms: 3 en-suite
Bed & breakfast

per night:	£min	£max
Single	20.00	20.00
Double	32.00	34.00

Half board per person:	£min	£max
Daily	28.00	30.00
Weekly	189.00	189.00

Continued ▶

BUCKINGHAM
Continued

Evening meal 1830 (last orders 1200)
Parking for 10

⌨ ♿ 🛏 🅿 UL 🔒 S ⚲ ⵗ TV ▥ ❄ ✕ 🐕 🚗
OAP

BURFORD
Oxfordshire
Map ref 2B1

One of the most beautiful Cotswold wool towns with Georgian and Tudor houses, many antique shops and a picturesque High Street sloping to the River Windrush. *Tourist Information Centre ☎ (01993) 823558*

Hillborough House
⚜⚜

The Green,
Milton-under-Wychwood, Oxford
OX7 6JH
☎ Shipton-under-Wychwood
(01993) 830501
Fax (01993) 832005
Facing village green in delightful Cotswold village. Warm, spacious en-suite accommodation, cosy residents' lounge, gardens. Dinner arranged in adjoining Willows Restaurant.
Bedrooms: 4 double, 3 twin, 3 triple
Bathrooms: 10 en-suite

Bed & breakfast per night:

	£min	£max
Single	34.00	38.00
Double	50.00	54.00

Lunch available
Evening meal 1900 (last orders 2130)
Parking for 15
Cards accepted: Access, Visa, Amex

🐎 ♿ 📞 ♿ 🍴 🛏 🔒 S ⚲ ⵗ TV ▥ 🖙
🕯 ❄ 🐕 SP

Romany Inn
⚜⚜ APPROVED

Bridge Street, Bampton, Oxford
OX18 2HA
☎ Bampton Castle (01993) 850237
17th C listed Georgian building, recently refurbished, at nearby Bampton. Lounge bar, separate restaurant, chef/proprietor. Noted in pub and beer guides. Brochure available.
Bedrooms: 3 double, 2 twin, 3 triple
Bathrooms: 8 en-suite

Bed & breakfast per night:

	£min	£max
Single	21.00	25.00
Double	30.00	35.00

Half board per person:

	£min	£max
Daily	30.00	35.00
Weekly	180.00	210.00

Lunch available
Evening meal 1830 (last orders 2200)
Parking for 6
Cards accepted: Access, Visa

🐎 ♿ 🖙 ♿ 🛏 ⵗ ⚲ ⵗ TV ▥ ♿ ❄ 🐕 🏠

St Winnow
⚜ COMMENDED

160 The Hill, Burford OX18 4QY
☎ (01993) 823843

Comfortable 16th C Cotswold house, in conservation area on hill above the high street. Garden, garage and parking at rear.
Bedrooms: 1 single, 1 double, 1 twin
Bathrooms: 1 public

Bed & breakfast per night:

	£min	£max
Single	20.00	27.00
Double	36.00	45.00

Parking for 2

⌨ ♿ UL S ⚲ ⵗ TV ▥ ♿ ❄ ✕ 🐕 🏠

BURLEY
Hampshire
Map ref 2B3

Attractive centre from which to explore the south-west part of the New Forest. There is an ancient earthwork on Castle Hill nearby, which also offers good views.

Holmans 🅼
⚜⚜ HIGHLY COMMENDED

Bisterne Close, Burley, Ringwood
BH24 4AZ
☎ (01425) 402307
Charming family house in 4 acres, overlooking New Forest and near golf-course. Marvellous horseriding and stabling available. Before White Buck Inn, turn right into Bisterne Close, fourth house on right.
Bedrooms: 2 double, 1 twin
Suites available
Bathrooms: 3 en-suite

Bed & breakfast per night:

	£min	£max
Single	20.00	25.00
Double	40.00	44.00

Parking for 10

🐎 ♿🍴 ♿ 🍴 UL S ⚲ ⵗ TV ▥ ♿ U ❄
🐕

Pikes Post 🅼
⚜ HIGHLY COMMENDED

Chapel Lane, Burley, Ringwood
BH24 4DJ
☎ (01425) 402285
Pretty bungalow, quietly situated, offering high quality accommodation. Ideally placed for forest walks, country activities and South Coast beaches.
Bedrooms: 2 double, 1 twin
Bathrooms: 3 en-suite

Bed & breakfast per night:

	£min	£max
Single	27.50	30.00
Double	36.00	40.00

Parking for 5
Open February–October

♿ ⌨ ♿ UL S ⚲ ⵗ TV ▥ ♿ ❄ ✕ 🐕 T

BURSLEDON
Hampshire
Map ref 2C3

Dodwell Cottage 🅼
⚜ HIGHLY COMMENDED

Dodwell Lane, Bursledon,
Southampton SO31 1AD
☎ Southampton (01703) 406074
Fax (01703) 406074
Comfortable, beamed 18th C country cottage, close to River Hamble and country park. Ample parking. Restaurants nearby. Easy access Portsmouth/Southampton ferries.
Bedrooms: 2 double, 1 twin
Bathrooms: 3 en-suite

Bed & breakfast per night:

	£min	£max
Single	26.00	28.00
Double	39.00	42.00

Half board per person:

	£min	£max
Daily	36.00	38.00
Weekly	216.00	228.00

Evening meal 1800 (last orders 1900)
Parking for 10
Open February–December

🐎 4 ♿ UL S 🛏 ⚲ ⵗ TV ▥ ♿ 🖙 12 U
❄ ✕ 🐕 OAP ◉

CADNAM
Hampshire
Map ref 2C3

Village with numerous attractive cottages and an inn close to the entrance of the M27.

The Old Well Restaurant
⚜⚜

Copythorne, Southampton
SO40 2PE
☎ Southampton (01703) 812321 & 812700
Family-owned business for over 30

years. Spacious accommodation and friendly service, with good access to New Forest and Southampton ferries.
Bedrooms: 4 double, 2 triple
Bathrooms: 3 en-suite, 2 public

Bed & breakfast

per night:	£min	£max
Single	22.00	32.00
Double	34.00	44.00

Lunch available
Evening meal 1900 (last orders 2200)
Parking for 50
Cards accepted: Access, Visa, Switch/Delta

🐾❤️⬜♿🛈Ⓢ🏬Ⓣⓥ🏬🍴✕🚐

CHALFONT ST GILES

Buckinghamshire
Map ref 2D2

Pretty, old village in wooded Chiltern Hills yet only 20 miles from London and a good base for visiting the city. Excellent base for Windsor, Henley, the Thames Valley, Oxford and the Cotswolds.

Gorelands Corner
Listed COMMENDED

Gorelands Lane, Chalfont St Giles HP8 4HQ
☎ (01494) 872689
Fax (01494) 872689
Family home set in large garden. Easy access to M25, M40, M4 and London underground.
Bedrooms: 1 triple
Bathrooms: 1 en-suite

Bed & breakfast

per night:	£min	£max
Single	18.50	20.00
Double	37.50	40.00

Parking for 3

🐾🚂⬜♿🛈ⓤⓛ🍴🏬✿✕🚐

CHALGROVE

Oxfordshire
Map ref 2C1

Cornerstones ⋀
Listed

1 Cromwell Close, Chalgrove OX44 7SE
☎ Stadhampton (01865) 890298
Bungalow in pretty village with thatched cottages. The Red Lion (half a mile away) serves good and reasonably priced food.
Bedrooms: 2 twin
Bathrooms: 1 public

Bed & breakfast

per night:	£min	£max
Single	23.00	23.00
Double	35.00	35.00

Parking for 2

🐾5🦮♿⬜♿🛈ⓥ🏬ⓤⓛ🍴🏬✿✕🚐

CHANDLERS FORD

Hampshire
Map ref 2C3

St Lucia
Listed

68 Shaftesbury Avenue, Chandlers Ford, Eastleigh SO53 3BP
☎ (01703) 262995 & Mobile (0589) 392765
Fax (01703) 262995

Homely accommodation well placed for touring, near Winchester, South Coast and New Forest. Evening meals, home-grown produce in season. Non-smokers only, please.
Bedrooms: 2 single, 1 double, 1 twin
Bathrooms: 1 public

Bed & breakfast

per night:	£min	£max
Single	15.00	17.50
Double	30.00	30.00

Half board per

person:	£min	£max
Daily	22.50	24.00
Weekly	145.00	145.00

Evening meal 1830 (last orders 1830)
Parking for 5

🐾10⬜♿🛈ⓤⓛ🛈Ⓢ🍴🏬🚗✿✕🚐

CHARLBURY

Oxfordshire
Map ref 2C1

Large Cotswold village with beautiful views of the Evenlode Valley just outside the village and close to the ancient Forest of Wychwood.

Banbury Hill Farm ⋀
👻👻 COMMENDED

Enstone Road, Charlbury, Oxford OX7 3JH
☎ (01608) 810314
Fax (01608) 811891
54-acre mixed farm. Cotswold-stone farmhouse with extensive views across Evenlode Valley. Ideal touring centre for Blenheim Palace, Oxford and the Cotswolds.
Bedrooms: 1 single, 2 double, 1 twin, 1 triple

Bathrooms: 3 en-suite, 1 public

Bed & breakfast

per night:	£min	£max
Single	16.00	25.00
Double	32.00	40.00

Parking for 6

🐾⬜♿Ⓢ🏬🍴🏬Ⓣⓥ🏬🍴🚗✿✕🚐

CHIPPING NORTON

Oxfordshire
Map ref 2C1

Old market town set high in the Cotswolds and an ideal touring centre. The wide market-place contains many 16th C and 17th C stone houses and the Town Hall and Tudor Guildhall.
Tourist Information Centre ☎ (01608) 644379

Oak House ⋀

Chalford Park, Old Chalford, Chipping Norton OX7 5QR
☎ (01608) 641435
Fax (01608) 641435
Converted Cotswold-stone farmhouse of character, set in courtyard. Decorated and furnished to high standard. Bridleway walks in open country.
Bedrooms: 1 double, 1 twin
Bathrooms: 1 en-suite, 1 private

Bed & breakfast

per night:	£min	£max
Single	30.00	35.00
Double	40.00	40.00

Parking for 4
Open March–November

🐾8🦮⬜♿ⓤⓛ🛈🍴🏬🚂✿🚐

For farm holidays and accommodation suitable for young people and organised groups, please refer to the special sections at the back of this guide.

ACCESSIBILITY

Look for the 🦽🦽🦽 symbols which indicate accessibility for wheelchair users. These are described in detail at the front of this guide.

CHRISTCHURCH

Dorset
Map ref 2B3

Tranquil town lying between the Avon and Stour just before they converge and flow into Christchurch Harbour. Fine 11th C church.
Tourist Information Centre ☎ (01202) 471780

The Beech Tree
≋≋≋ HIGHLY COMMENDED
2 Stuart Road, Highcliffe, Christchurch BH23 5JS
☎ Highcliffe (01425) 272038

Above average standards. Superb fresh food. Ground floor rooms. Walk to beach, shops and restaurants. Luxury suite available.
Bedrooms: 5 double, 1 twin
Bathrooms: 6 en-suite
Bed & breakfast

per night:	£min	£max
Single	17.00	20.00
Double	34.00	40.00

Half board per person:

	£min	£max
Daily	25.50	28.50
Weekly	178.50	199.50

Evening meal 1800 (last orders 1800)
Parking for 7

☐♜10♿⬛▭◻↻🅿🆄🅂✂🅼TV
🖮♨🚗

COMPTON

Hampshire
Map ref 2C3

Manor House
Listed
Place Lane, Compton, Winchester SO21 2BA
☎ Twyford (01962) 712162
Comfortable country house, 8 minutes from Shawford railway station and 2 miles from city of Winchester. Non-smokers preferred.
Bedrooms: 1 double
Bathrooms: 1 public
Bed & breakfast

per night:	£min	£max
Single	12.00	12.00
Double	24.00	24.00

Parking for 1

▭◻↻🅄✂▣🖮♨❋🚗♿

CORFE CASTLE

Dorset
Map ref 2B3

One of the most spectacular ruined castles in Britain. Norman in origin, the castle was a Royalist stronghold during the Civil War and held out until 1645. The village had a considerable marble-carving industry in the Middle Ages.

Bradle Farmhouse
≋≋ COMMENDED
Bradle Farm, Church Knowle, Wareham BH20 5NU
☎ (01929) 480712
Fax (01929) 481144

550-acre mixed farm. Picturesque farmhouse in the heart of Purbeck. Superb views of castle and surrounding countryside, beach 2 miles. Warm family atmosphere with evening meals arranged at local inn.
Bedrooms: 2 double, 1 twin
Bathrooms: 2 en-suite, 1 private
Bed & breakfast

per night:	£min	£max
Double	37.00	40.00

Parking for 3

☐♜⬛▭◻↻🅄🅸🅂🅼TV🖮♨▣❋🚗
🚗🆂🅿❋🅂🅿

COTSWOLDS

See under Bampton, Burford, Charlbury, Chipping Norton, Deddington, Idbury, Minster Lovell, Shipton-under-Wychwood, Witney, Woodstock
See also Cotswolds in Heart of England region

COWES

Isle of Wight
Map ref 2C3

Regular ferry and hydrofoil services cross the Solent to Cowes. The town is the headquarters of the Royal Yacht Squadron and Cowes Week is held every August.
Tourist Information Centre ☎ (01983) 291914

Sunnymead 🅼
Listed COMMENDED
19 Worsley Road, Gurnard, Cowes PO31 8JW
☎ Isle of Wight (01983) 291093
Village location, a few minutes' walk

from beach, coastal walks, local amenities and bus route. One and a half miles from Cowes.
Bedrooms: 2 twin
Bathrooms: 2 en-suite
Bed & breakfast

per night:	£min	£max
Single	15.00	
Double	30.00	

☐♜5♿⬛▭◻↻🅄🅂🖮♨🚗❌
🚗

CRANBORNE

Dorset
Map ref 2B3

Village with an interesting Jacobean manor house. Lies south-east of Cranborne Chase, formerly a forest and hunting preserve.

The Fleur de Lys 🅼
≋≋≋
5 Wimborne Street, Cranborne, Wimborne Minster BH21 5PP
☎ (01725) 517282
Fax (01725) 517631
Charming old-world coaching inn, close to the New Forest. Cosy atmosphere, friendly hospitality. Restaurant, bar, en-suite accommodation.
Bedrooms: 1 single, 4 double, 3 twin
Bathrooms: 7 en-suite, 1 private shower
Bed & breakfast

per night:	£min	£max
Single	20.00	38.00
Double	38.00	55.00

Half board per person:

	£min	£max
Daily	38.00	50.00
Weekly	190.00	300.00

Lunch available
Evening meal 1900 (last orders 2145)
Parking for 35
Cards accepted: Access, Visa, Amex, Switch/Delta

☐♜📞▭◻↻🅸⬛♨▣🍴🚗🆂🅿🅼
🆃

DEDDINGTON

Oxfordshire
Map ref 2C1

On the edge of the Cotswolds and settled since the Stone Age, this is the only village in England to have been granted a full Coat of Arms, displayed on the 16th C Town Hall in the picturesque market square. Many places of interest include the Church of St Peter and St Paul.

The Deddington Arms
COMMENDED

Horsefair, Deddington, Banbury OX15 0SH
☎ (01869) 338364
Fax (01869) 337010

16th C coaching inn, tastefully refurbishd to provide air- conditioned restaurant and en-suite bedrooms whilst retaining the village inn atmosphere. Ideal base for Banbury, Oxford, Stratford, Warwick, Blenheim Palace and the Cotswolds.
Bedrooms: 2 double, 3 twin, 1 triple, 1 family room
Bathrooms: 7 en-suite

Bed & breakfast per night:

	£min	£max
Single	49.50	75.00
Double	59.50	75.00

Lunch available
Evening meal 1830 (last orders 2130)
Parking for 24
Cards accepted: Access, Visa, Switch/Delta

Hill Barn
Listed

Milton Gated Road, Deddington, Banbury OX15 0TS
☎ (01869) 338631
Converted barn set in open countryside with views overlooking valley and hills. Banbury-Oxford road, half a mile before Deddington, turn right to Milton Gated Road. Hill Barn is 100 yards on the right.
Bedrooms: 1 double, 2 twin
Bathrooms: 1 public

Bed & breakfast per night:

	£min	£max
Single	20.00	20.00
Double	32.00	36.00

Parking for 6

DENMEAD

Hampshire
Map ref 2C3

Comparatively modern town, south-west of the original settlement.

Forest Gate
Listed COMMENDED

Hambledon Road, Denmead, Waterlooville PO7 6EX
☎ Waterlooville (01705) 255901
Listed Georgian house in large garden, on outskirts of village. Within easy reach of maritime Portsmouth and continental ferries. Dinner by arrangement.
Bedrooms: 2 twin
Bathrooms: 2 en-suite

Bed & breakfast per night:

	£min	£max
Single	22.00	24.00
Double	36.00	40.00

Half board per person:

	£min	£max
Daily	32.00	35.50
Weekly	202.00	224.00

Evening meal from 1930
Parking for 4

DIBDEN

Hampshire
Map ref 2C3

Small village on the edge of the New Forest with a full recreation centre. Picturesque 13th C church overlooks Southampton Water.

Dale Farm House

Manor Road, Applemore Hill, Dibden, Southampton SO45 5TJ
☎ Southampton (01703) 849632
Friendly, family-run 18th C converted farmhouse in wooded setting. Large garden with play area. 250 yards from A326, adjacent to riding stables and 15 minutes from beach. Children welcome.
Bedrooms: 1 single, 3 double, 1 twin, 1 triple, 1 family room
Bathrooms: 2 en-suite, 1 public

Bed & breakfast per night:

	£min	£max
Single	19.00	
Double	34.00	

Half board per person:

	£min	£max
Daily	28.50	
Weekly	175.00	

Evening meal 1800 (last orders 1100)
Parking for 20

DOWNTON

Hampshire
Map ref 2B3

Hamlet on the A337, 4 miles south-west of Lymington.

Barlings
COMMENDED

41 Gravel Close, Downton, Salisbury, Wiltshire SP5 3JQ
☎ (01725) 510310
Well-appointed bungalow, in quiet lane, with fine views overlooking water meadows towards church. All en-suite. Old world village with good local inns.
Bedrooms: 2 double, 1 twin
Bathrooms: 3 en-suite

Bed & breakfast per night:

	£min	£max
Single		25.00
Double		35.00

Parking for 12

EDGCOTT

Buckinghamshire
Map ref 2C1

Perry Manor Farm
Listed

Buckingham Road, Edgcott, Aylesbury HP18 0TR
☎ Aylesbury (01296) 770257
200-acre livestock farm. Working sheep farm, offering peaceful and comfortable accommodation, with en-suite toilet and basin. Extensive views over Aylesbury Vale. Walkers welcome. Non-smokers only, please.
Bedrooms: 1 single, 1 double, 1 twin
Bathrooms: 1 public

Bed & breakfast per night:

	£min	£max
Single	18.00	18.00
Double	32.00	32.00

Parking for 10

Please mention this guide when making your booking.

FARINGDON

Oxfordshire
Map ref 2B2

Ancient stone-built market town in the Vale of the White Horse. The 17th C market hall stands on pillars and the 13th C church has some fine monuments. A great monastic tithe barn is nearby at Great Coxwell.

White Horse Inn

⚜⚜ **COMMENDED**

Woolstone, Faringdon SN7 7QL
☎ Uffington (01367) 820566 &
820726
Fax (01367) 820566

16th C inn 10 miles from M4 and close to White Horse Hill. Log fires, oak beams. Real ales, a la carte restaurant and bar snacks.
Bedrooms: 3 double, 2 twin, 1 triple
Bathrooms: 6 en-suite

Bed & breakfast per night:

	£min	£max
Single	35.00	40.00
Double	55.00	60.00

Half board per person:

	£min	£max
Daily	51.00	56.00

Lunch available
Evening meal 1900 (last orders 2200)
Parking for 80
Cards accepted: Access, Visa, Diners, Amex, Switch/Delta

FORDINGBRIDGE

Hampshire
Map ref 2B3

On the north-west edge of the New Forest. A medieval bridge crosses the Avon at this point and gave the town its name. A good centre for walking, exploring and fishing.

Hillbury

Listed **COMMENDED**

2 Fir Tree Hill, Camel Green Road, Alderholt, Fordingbridge SP6 3AY
☎ (01425) 652582
Fax (01425) 657587
Bungalow in quiet situation with easy access to M27. Ideal touring base for New Forest and South Coast. Riding,

swimming, golf and fishing nearby. Sorry, no pets or smokers.
Bedrooms: 1 single, 1 twin, 1 triple
Bathrooms: 1 public

Bed & breakfast per night:

	£min	£max
Single	16.00	18.00
Double	32.00	34.00

Parking for 5

HAMBLE

Hampshire
Map ref 2C3

Set almost at the mouth of the River Hamble, this quiet fishing village has become a major yachting centre.

Braymar

Listed

35 Westfield Close, Hamble, Southampton SO30 5LG
☎ Southampton (01703) 453831
Private house, in peaceful position, 5 minutes from quiet beach and pretty, sailing village of Hamble, where "Howards' Way" was filmed. 15 minutes' drive from Southampton and Portsmouth. Near M27.
Bedrooms: 1 single, 1 double, 2 twin
Bathrooms: 1 public

Bed & breakfast per night:

	£min	£max
Single	14.00	
Double	28.00	28.00

Parking for 3

HAMBLEDON

Hampshire
Map ref 2C3

In a valley, surrounded by wooded downland and marked by an air of Georgian prosperity. It was here that cricket was given its first proper rules. The Bat and Ball Inn at Broadhalfpenny Down is the cradle of cricket.

Cams

⚜⚜ **COMMENDED**

Hambledon, Waterlooville PO7 4SP
☎ Portsmouth (01705) 632865
Fax (01705) 632691
Comfortable, listed family house in beautiful setting with large garden on the edge of Hambledon village. Two pubs within walking distance. Evening meal by arrangement.
Bedrooms: 1 double, 2 twin
Bathrooms: 1 en-suite, 1 public, 1 private shower

Bed & breakfast per night:

	£min	£max
Single	17.00	19.00
Double	32.00	38.00

Half board per person:

	£min	£max
Daily	25.00	28.00

Evening meal from 1900
Parking for 6

Mornington House

Listed

Speltham Hill, Hambledon, Waterlooville PO7 4RU
☎ Portsmouth (01705) 632704
18th C private house with 2 acres of garden and paddock, in the centre of Hambledon behind the George Inn, 2 miles from famous Bat and Ball Inn.
Bedrooms: 2 twin
Bathrooms: 1 public

Bed & breakfast per night:

	£min	£max
Single	16.00	20.00
Double	30.00	30.00

Parking for 6

HAVANT

Hampshire
Map ref 2C3

Once a market town famous for making parchment. Nearby at Leigh Park extensive early 19th C landscape gardens and parklands are open to the public. Right in the centre of the town stands the interesting 13th C church of St Faith.
Tourist Information Centre ☎ (01705) 480024

High Towers ⚑

⚜⚜ **COMMENDED**

14 Portsdown Hill Road, Bedhampton, Havant PO9 3JY
☎ Portsmouth (01705) 471748
Modern residence near A3M/A27, with superb views overlooking Portsmouth, countryside and sea. Portsmouth centre and ferries 15 minutes, Havant 5 minutes. Non-smokers only, please.
Bedrooms: 2 single, 2 double
Bathrooms: 3 en-suite, 1 private, 1 public

Bed & breakfast per night:

	£min	£max
Single	20.00	26.00
Double	36.00	40.00

Parking for 6

HAYLING ISLAND

Hampshire
Map ref 2C3

Small island of historic interest, surrounded by natural harbours and with fine sandy beaches, linked to the mainland by an attractive bridge under which boats sail. Birthplace of windsurfing and home to many international sailing events.

Cockle Warren Cottage Hotel ⋔

☺☺☺ HIGHLY COMMENDED

36 Seafront, Hayling Island
PO11 9HL
☎ (01705) 464961
Fax (01705) 464838

Lovely seaside farmhouse-style hotel with large garden and heated swimming pool. French and English country cooking, home-made bread, four-poster and Victorian beds, log fires in winter.
Bedrooms: 4 double, 1 triple
Bathrooms: 5 en-suite
Bed & breakfast

per night:	£min	£max
Single	45.00	65.00
Double	54.00	88.00

Evening meal 2000 (last orders 1600)
Parking for 11
Cards accepted: Access, Visa, Amex

Newtown House Hotel ⋔

☺☺☺☺ APPROVED

Manor Road, Hayling Island
PO11 0QR
☎ Portsmouth (01705) 466131
Fax (01705) 461366
18th C converted farmhouse, set in own grounds a quarter of a mile from seafront. Indoor leisure complex with heated pool, gym, steamroom, jacuzzi and sauna. Tennis.
Bedrooms: 9 single, 9 double, 4 twin, 3 triple
Bathrooms: 25 en-suite, 1 public
Bed & breakfast

per night:	£min	£max
Single	35.00	
Double	55.00	

Half board per person:	£min	£max
Daily	48.00	
Weekly	290.00	

Lunch available
Evening meal 1900 (last orders 2130)
Parking for 45
Cards accepted: Access, Visa, Diners, Amex, Switch/Delta

HENLEY-ON-THAMES

Oxfordshire
Map ref 2C2

The famous Thames Regatta is held in this prosperous and attractive town at the beginning of July each year. The town has many Georgian buildings and old coaching inns and the parish church has some fine monuments.
Tourist Information Centre ☎ (01491) 578034

Alftrudis

☺ HIGHLY COMMENDED

8 Norman Avenue,
Henley-on-Thames RG9 1SG
☎ (01491) 573099 & Mobile 0802 408643
Fax (01494) 573099
Friendly detached Victorian house in quiet, private road, centrally situated two minutes' walk from the station, town centre and the river. Easy parking.
Bedrooms: 2 double, 1 twin
Bathrooms: 2 en-suite, 1 public
Bed & breakfast

per night:	£min	£max
Single	25.00	35.00
Double	34.00	45.00

Parking for 2

Avalon

Listed

36 Queen Street,
Henley-on-Thames RG9 1AP
☎ (01491) 577829
Spacious Victorian terrace in a quiet, central location. 2 minutes' walk from river, station and town centre.
Bedrooms: 1 single, 1 double, 1 twin
Bathrooms: 2 en-suite, 1 private shower
Bed & breakfast

per night:	£min	£max
Single	18.00	28.00
Double	36.00	40.00

Parking for 2

Crowsley House

Crowsley Road, Shiplake,
Henley-on-Thames RG9 3JT
☎ (0118) 940 3197
Attractive house in quiet riverside village, close to Henley-on-Thames. Convenient for Oxford, London, Windsor and Heathrow.
Bedrooms: 1 double, 2 twin
Bathrooms: 2 public
Bed & breakfast

per night:	£min	£max
Single	19.00	
Double	38.00	

Parking for 4

Holmwood ⋔

☺☺ HIGHLY COMMENDED

Shiplake Row, Binfield Heath,
Henley-on-Thames RG9 4DP
☎ (0118) 947 8747
Fax (0118) 947 8637
Large Georgian country house in beautiful surroundings. In Binfield Heath, equidistant from Henley and Reading, off A4155. Binfield Heath is signposted.
Wheelchair access category 3⋔
Bedrooms: 1 single, 2 double, 2 twin
Bathrooms: 5 en-suite
Bed & breakfast

per night:	£min	£max
Single	30.00	30.00
Double	50.00	50.00

Parking for 8

Lenwade

☺ HIGHLY COMMENDED

3 Western Road, Henley-on-Thames RG9 1JL
☎ (01491) 573468 & Mobile 0374 941629
Victorian house in quiet surroundings, within walking distance of the River Thames and town centre. Children welcome. Parking available.
Bedrooms: 2 double, 1 twin
Bathrooms: 2 en-suite, 2 public
Bed & breakfast

per night:	£min	£max
Single	25.00	35.00
Double	35.00	45.00

Parking for 2

New Lodge ⋔

☺ COMMENDED

Henley Park, Henley-on-Thames RG9 6HU
☎ (01491) 576340
Victorian lodge in parkland in Area of Outstanding Natural Beauty. Lovely

Continued ▶

HENLEY-ON-THAMES

Continued

walks and views. Only 1 mile from
Henley, 45 minutes from Heathrow.
Bedrooms: 2 double
Bathrooms: 1 en-suite, 1 private

Bed & breakfast

per night:	£min	£max
Single	22.00	26.00
Double	32.00	39.00

Parking for 7

HILTON

Dorset
Map ref 2B3

Village with thatched cottages
grouped against a background of
woods and downs. The church is a
blend of Decorated and
Perpendicular styles.

Stocklands House

HIGHLY COMMENDED

Hilton, Blandford Forum DT11 0DE
☎ Blandford (01258) 880580 &
881188
Fax (01258) 881188
*In secluded position with stunning
views. Log fires. Heated pool
(May-October). Professional chef. Well
situated for sightseeing.*
Bedrooms: 1 single, 1 double
Bathrooms: 2 en-suite

Half board per

person:	£min	£max
Daily	28.50	41.00
Weekly	186.00	273.00

Lunch available
Evening meal 1930 (last orders
2100)
Parking for 15

HOOK NORTON

Oxfordshire
Map ref 2C1

Quiet town with a history dating
back 1000 years when the Normans
built and buttressed its chancel walls
against attack from the invading
Danes.

Pear Tree Inn

COMMENDED

Scotland End, Hook Norton,
Banbury OX15 5NU
☎ (01608) 737482
Old beamed pub, near famous Hook

Norton brewery. 5 miles from Chipping
Norton, close to Banbury and the
Cotswolds.
Bedrooms: 1 double
Bathrooms: 1 en-suite

Bed & breakfast

per night:	£min	£max
Single	20.00	20.00
Double	35.00	35.00

Lunch available
Evening meal 1900 (last orders
2100)
Parking for 11
Cards accepted: Amex

HUNGERFORD

Berkshire
Map ref 2C2

Attractive town on the Avon Canal
and the River Kennet, famous for its
fishing. It has a wide High Street and
many antique shops. Nearby is the
Tudor manor of Littlecote with its
large Roman mosaic.

Marshgate Cottage Hotel

COMMENDED

Marsh Lane, Hungerford
RG17 0QX
☎ (01488) 682307
Fax (01488) 685475
*Family-run canalside hotel ranged
around south-facing courtyard, linked to
350-year-old thatched cottage.
Overlooks marshland and trout
streams. Lovely walks, bike hire, bird
watching. Important antiques centre. 1
hour from Heathrow.*
Bedrooms: 2 double, 1 twin, 3 triple
Bathrooms: 6 en-suite, 1 public

Bed & breakfast

per night:	£min	£max
Single	35.50	
Double	48.50	

Evening meal 1900 (last orders
2100)
Parking for 9
Cards accepted: Access, Visa, Amex

HYTHE

Hampshire
Map ref 2C3

Changri-La

HIGHLY COMMENDED

12 Ashleigh Close, Hythe,
Southampton SO45 3QP
☎ Southampton (01703) 846664
*Spacious comfortable home, in unique
position on edge of New Forest, a few
minutes' drive from Beaulieu and other
places of interest. Golf-course, pony
trekking and sports complex nearby.*

Bedrooms: 1 double, 1 twin
Bathrooms: 2 public

Bed & breakfast

per night:	£min	£max
Single	15.00	16.00
Double	30.00	32.00

Parking for 3

IDBURY

Oxfordshire
Map ref 2B1

Bould Farmhouse

HIGHLY COMMENDED

Bould, Nr Idbury, Chipping Norton
OX7 6RT
☎ Chipping Norton (01608)
658850
*300-acre mixed farm. Listed Cotswold
farmhouse, 10 minutes' drive to
Stow-on-the-Wold,
Bourton-on-the-Water and Burford.
Nature trails adjoining wood.*
Bedrooms: 1 double, 1 family room
Bathrooms: 2 en-suite, 2 public

Bed & breakfast

per night:	£min	£max
Single		25.00
Double		40.00

Parking for 6
Open February–November

Old Forge

Church Street, Idbury, Oxford
OX7 6RU
☎ Shipton-under-Wychwood
(01993) 831354
Fax (01993) 832068
*Elizabethan stone cottage/house in
Cotswolds. Massive fireplaces, oak
beams, walled garden. In quiet hamlet.
Happy family atmosphere. Children
welcome.*
Bedrooms: 1 single, 1 double, 1 twin
Bathrooms: 1 public

Bed & breakfast

per night:	£min	£max
Single	20.00	20.00
Double	30.00	30.00

Parking for 6

ISLE OF WIGHT

See under Brighstone, Cowes, Newport,
Ryde, Sandown, Shanklin

A key to symbols can be
found inside the back
cover flap.

KIDLINGTON

Oxfordshire
Map ref 2C1

Village with a beautiful old church
flanked by a row of gabled
almshouses. Has now become
dormitory satellite of Oxford.

Breffni House
Listed

9 Lovelace Drive, Kidlington
OX5 2LY
☎ Oxford (01865) 372569
*Detached property, very homely, close
to Woodstock and 2.5 miles from M40.
Sports facilities close by. Lovely gardens
and ample off-road parking.*
Bedrooms: 1 single, 1 double
Bathrooms: 1 public
Bed & breakfast

per night:	£min	£max
Single	20.00	20.00
Double	36.00	36.00

Half board per person:	£min	£max
Daily	25.00	30.00
Weekly	150.00	175.00

Evening meal 1800 (last orders
2000)
Parking for 6

KIMMERIDGE

Dorset
Map ref 2B3

Kimmeridge Farmhouse ♨
Listed

Kimmeridge, Wareham BH20 5PE
☎ Corfe Castle (01929) 480990

*750-acre mixed farm. Farmhouse built
in the 16th C, with lovely views of
surrounding countryside and the sea
within short walking distance. Warm
family atmosphere and spacious
facilities. Evening meals by
arrangement with local inn.*
Bedrooms: 2 double, 1 twin
Bathrooms: 1 en-suite, 1 public
Bed & breakfast

per night:	£min	£max
Single	20.00	25.00
Double	34.00	38.00

Parking for 3

KINGSCLERE

Hampshire
Map ref 2C2

Cleremede ♨
HIGHLY COMMENDED

Fox's Lane, Kingsclere, Newbury,
Berkshire RG20 5SL
☎ (01635) 297298 & Mobile 0374
280716
*Near Watership Down and Wayfarers
Walk. Breakfast in conservatory in
summer overlooking large garden.*
Bedrooms: 1 single, 2 twin
Suites available
Bathrooms: 2 en-suite, 1 private
Bed & breakfast

per night:	£min	£max
Single	21.00	25.00
Double	40.00	44.00

Parking for 6

11 Hook Road
Listed COMMENDED

Kingsclere, Newbury, Berkshire
RG20 5PD
☎ (01635) 298861
Fax (01635) 298861
*Comfortable, modern house in historic
Kingsclere at the foot of the beautiful
Hampshire Downs. Convenient for M3,
M4 and A34 and all local amenities.
Hook Road is off Basingstoke Road,
half a mile east of Kingsclere village
square.*
Bedrooms: 1 single, 2 twin
Suite available
Bathrooms: 1 public
Bed & breakfast

per night:	£min	£max
Single	19.00	19.00
Double	31.00	31.00

Half board per person:	£min	£max
Daily	27.00	30.00

Lunch available
Evening meal 1900 (last orders
2100)
Parking for 6

The map references refer
to the colour maps towards
the end of the guide.
The first figure is the
map number; the letter and
figure which follow indicate
the grid reference
on the map.

LAMBOURN

Berkshire
Map ref 2C2

Attractive village among the Downs
on the River Lambourn. Famous for
its racing stables.

Lodge Down ♨
COMMENDED

The Woodlands, Lambourn,
Hungerford RG17 7BJ
☎ Marlborough (01672) 540304
Fax (01672) 540304

*70-acre arable farm. Country house
with quality accommodation and
en-suite bathrooms, set in lovely
grounds. Exit junction 14 of M4, take
B4000 and follow signs to Baydon.
Lodge Down is 1 mile before Baydon
(300 metres down drive).*
Bedrooms: 1 double, 2 twin
Bathrooms: 3 en-suite, 1 public
Bed & breakfast

per night:	£min	£max
Single	18.00	25.00
Double	36.00	45.00

Parking for 11

LANE END

Buckinghamshire
Map ref 2C2

Orchid House ♨

Spring Coppice, Lane End, High
Wycombe HP14 3NU
☎ High Wycombe (01494) 881032
& Mobile 0860 314438
Fax (01494) 882100
*Set in three-quarters of an acre of
landscaped gardens, completely
surrounded by woodland plentiful in
wildlife. 5 minutes from M40
motorway, close to Marlow-on-Thames,
the Chiltern Hills and within 30
minutes of Windsor and Oxford.*
Bedrooms: 2 double
Bathrooms: 2 private, 1 public
Bed & breakfast

per night:	£min	£max
Single	20.00	30.00
Double	35.00	45.00

Parking for 6

LITTLE WITTENHAM

Oxfordshire
Map ref 2C2

Rooks Orchard

HIGHLY COMMENDED

Little Wittenham, Abingdon
OX14 4QY
☎ (01865) 407765

Attractive, peaceful and welcoming listed 17th C family house and garden, in pretty Thameside village next to nature reserve and Wittenham Clumps. "Splendid breakfasts". Abingdon, Didcot and Wallingford approximately 4 miles, Oxford 9 miles.

Bedrooms: 2 double
Bathrooms: 1 en-suite, 1 private, 1 public

Bed & breakfast per night:	£min	£max
Single	24.00	28.00
Double	38.00	45.00

Evening meal from 1900
Parking for 6

LYMINGTON

Hampshire
Map ref 2C3

Small, pleasant town with bright cottages and attractive Georgian houses, lying on the edge of the New Forest with a ferry service to the Isle of Wight. A sheltered harbour makes it a busy yachting centre.

Admiral House

Listed

5 Stanley Road, Lymington SO41 3SJ
☎ (01590) 674339

House exclusively for guests, with the owner next door. 200 yards from countryside conservation area and marinas. Many pubs and restaurants nearby.

Bedrooms: 1 single, 1 twin, 1 triple
Bathrooms: 1 public

Bed & breakfast per night:	£min	£max
Single	11.00	13.00
Double	22.00	26.00

Parking for 3

Altworth

Listed APPROVED

12 North Close, Lymington
SO41 9BT
☎ (01590) 674082

Near centre of town in quiet residential street, 5 minutes from bus/railway stations and Isle of Wight ferry. Within 30 minutes of Southampton and Bournemouth, with Brockenhurst and New Forest area only 10 minutes away.

Bedrooms: 1 single, 1 double, 1 triple
Bathrooms: 1 public

Bed & breakfast per night:	£min	£max
Single	15.00	15.00
Double	27.00	27.00

Open April–October

Efford Cottage

COMMENDED

Everton, Lymington SO41 0JD
☎ (01590) 642315 & Mobile 0374 703075
Fax (01590) 642315

Friendly, spacious, part-Georgian family home. Four course (multi-choice) breakfast, home-made bread and preserves. Traditional country cooking by qualified chef using home-grown produce when available. Parking.

Bedrooms: 3 double
Bathrooms: 3 en-suite

Bed & breakfast per night:	£min	£max
Single	20.00	30.00
Double	40.00	42.00

Half board per person:	£min	£max
Daily	30.00	45.00
Weekly	203.00	305.00

Lunch available
Evening meal 1800 (last orders 1900)
Parking for 4
12

Hideaway

Listed

Middle Common Road, Pennington, Lymington SO41 8LE
☎ (01590) 676974

Family chalet house. Pretty rooms all en-suite, some beamed and overlooking open fields. TV and tea/coffee facilities.

Bedrooms: 1 double, 1 twin, 1 triple
Bathrooms: 3 en-suite

Bed & breakfast per night:	£min	£max
Single	20.00	
Double	34.00	38.00

Parking for 5

The Hillsman House

HIGHLY COMMENDED

74 Milford Road, Lymington
SO41 8DP
☎ (01590) 674737

Splendid en-suite guestrooms enjoying views of the surrounding countryside. A full English breakfast will enhance your day whilst visiting this delightful area.

Bedrooms: 2 double, 1 twin
Bathrooms: 3 en-suite

Bed & breakfast per night:	£min	£max
Single	25.00	26.00
Double	42.00	48.00

Parking for 4
14

Our Bench

COMMENDED

9 Lodge Road, Pennington, Lymington SO41 8HH
☎ (01590) 673141
Fax (01590) 673141

All en-suite bedrooms, separate TV lounge, indoor heated pool, jacuzzi and sauna. Non-smokers only, please. Sorry, no children. Large quiet garden.

Bedrooms: 2 double, 1 twin
Bathrooms: 3 en-suite

Bed & breakfast per night:	£min	£max
Single	20.00	26.00
Double	38.00	48.00

Half board per person:	£min	£max
Daily	25.50	30.50
Weekly	175.00	210.00

Evening meal 1800 (last orders 2000)
Parking for 5

The map references refer to the colour maps towards the end of the guide. The first figure is the map number; the letter and figure which follow indicate the grid reference on the map.

LYNDHURST

Hampshire
Map ref 2C3

The "capital" of the New Forest, surrounded by attractive woodland scenery and delightful villages. The town is dominated by the Victorian Gothic-style church where the original Alice in Wonderland is buried.
Tourist Information Centre ☎ (01703) 282269

Burwood Lodge ♠
ww
Romsey Road, Lyndhurst SO43 7AA
☎ Southampton (01703) 282445
Lovely house in half-acre garden, near the village centre. All rooms with en-suite shower, WC and washbasin. Parking in grounds.
Bedrooms: 1 single, 4 double, 1 triple, 1 family room
Bathrooms: 6 en-suite, 1 private
Bed & breakfast

per night:	£min	£max
Single	20.00	25.00
Double	40.00	50.00

Parking for 8

Forest Cottage
Listed COMMENDED
High Street, Lyndhurst SO43 7BH
☎ Southampton (01703) 283461
Charming 300-year-old cottage with welcoming atmosphere, in the village, yet open forest only yards away. Guest lounge with open fire and TV.
Bedrooms: 1 single, 1 double, 1 twin
Bathrooms: 2 public
Bed & breakfast

per night:	£min	£max
Single	18.00	
Double	34.00	

Parking for 3

Little Hayes ♠
ww HIGHLY COMMENDED
43 Romsey Road, Lyndhurst SO43 7AR
☎ Southampton (01703) 283000

Lovely Victorian home, beautifully restored and furnished. Spacious rooms, friendly atmosphere and wonderful breakfast. Close to village centre and forest walks.
Bedrooms: 2 double, 1 twin
Bathrooms: 1 private, 1 public
Bed & breakfast

per night:	£min	£max
Double	34.00	42.00

Parking for 4
Open March–October
Cards accepted: Access, Visa, Switch/Delta

The Penny Farthing Hotel ♠
ww COMMENDED
Romsey Road, Lyndhurst SO43 7AA
☎ Southampton (01703) 284422
Fax (01703) 284488
Perfectly situated, friendly small hotel, 1 minute's walk from village centre, shops, restaurants, 2 minutes from open forest. Tastefully furnished rooms ensure a comfortable stay.
Bedrooms: 3 single, 5 double, 1 twin, 1 triple
Bathrooms: 10 en-suite
Bed & breakfast

per night:	£min	£max
Single	25.00	35.00
Double	45.00	70.00

Parking for 15
Cards accepted: Access, Visa

Ad See display advertisement on this page

MAIDENHEAD

Berkshire
Map ref 2C2

Attractive town on the River Thames which is crossed by an elegant 18th C bridge and by Brunel's well-known railway bridge. It is a popular place for boating with delightful riverside walks. The Courage Shire Horse Centre is nearby.
Tourist Information Centre ☎ (01628) 781110

Antonio Guest House ♠
Listed
41 Switchback Road North, Maidenhead SL6 7UF
☎ (01628) 70537 & Mobile 0378 709207
Single room, twin room and family room, all with TV. English breakfast. Parking and garage. Near local shops.
Bedrooms: 1 single, 1 double, 1 twin
Bathrooms: 1 public
Bed & breakfast

per night:	£min	£max
Single	22.50	25.00
Double	36.00	40.00

Parking for 4

The National Grading and Classification Scheme is explained in full at the back of this guide.

MAIDENHEAD

Continued

Cartlands Cottage

APPROVED

Kings Lane, Cookham Dean,
Cookham, Maidenhead SL6 9AY
☎ Marlow (01628) 482116
*Family room in self-contained garden
studio. Meals in delightful timbered
character cottage with exposed beams.
Traditional cottage garden. National
Trust common land. Very quiet.*
Bedrooms: 1 triple
Bathrooms: 1 en-suite, 1 public
Bed & breakfast

per night:	£min	£max
Single	17.00	20.00
Double	32.00	40.00

Parking for 4

Moor Farm 🅰

HIGHLY COMMENDED

Ascot Road, Holyport, Maidenhead
SL6 2HY
☎ (01628) 33761
Fax (01628) 33761
*100-acre mixed farm. 700-year-old
medieval manor in picturesque
Holyport village. 4 miles from Windsor.*
Bedrooms: 1 double, 2 twin
Bathrooms: 3 en-suite
Bed & breakfast

per night:	£min	£max
Double	39.00	49.00

Parking for 4

Sheephouse Manor 🅰

COMMENDED

Sheephouse Road, Maidenhead
SL6 8HJ
☎ (01628) 776902
Fax (01628) 25138
*Charming 16th C farmhouse in tranquil
setting yet with easy access to M4 and
M40. En-suite rooms, health suite. River
Thames nearby.*
Bedrooms: 2 single, 2 double, 1 twin
Bathrooms: 4 en-suite, 1 private
Bed & breakfast

per night:	£min	£max
Single	30.00	35.00
Double	43.00	49.00

Parking for 12
Cards accepted: Access, Visa, Amex,
Switch/Delta

MARLOW

**Buckinghamshire
Map ref 2C2**

Attractive Georgian town on the
River Thames, famous for its 19th C
suspension bridge. The High Street
contains many old houses and there
are connections with writers
including Shelley and T S Eliot.

Acha Pani 🅰

Listed COMMENDED

Bovingdon Green, Marlow SL7 2JL
☎ (01628) 483435
Fax (01628) 483435
*Modern house with large garden, in
quiet location 1 mile north of Marlow.
No children or dogs please.*
Bedrooms: 1 double, 1 twin
Bathrooms: 1 en-suite, 1 public
Bed & breakfast

per night:	£min	£max
Single	17.00	18.00
Double	32.00	35.00

Parking for 3

Acorn Lodge 🅰

Listed

79 Marlow Bottom Road, Marlow
Bottom, Marlow SL7 3NA
☎ (01628) 472197 & Mobile 0850
818458
*House with outdoor swimming pool,
backing on to woodland. Large en-suite
bedrooms with TV. Children welcome.
Within easy reach of M40, M4. London
30 miles, Heathrow/Windsor 30
minutes.*
Bedrooms: 2 single, 1 twin
Bathrooms: 1 en-suite, 1 private,
2 public
Bed & breakfast

per night:	£min	£max
Single	30.00	35.00
Double	35.00	45.00

Half board per

person:	£min	£max
Daily	18.50	22.50
Weekly	128.00	175.00

Parking for 6

Beltons

Listed

3 Davis Close, Marlow SL7 1SY
☎ (01628) 475481
*Georgian house in quiet situation,
within walking distance of town, railway
station and River Thames.*
Bedrooms: 2 single, 1 twin
Bathrooms: 1 public

Bed & breakfast

per night:	£min	£max
Single	22.50	25.00
Double	36.00	38.00

Parking for 4

Chipps Manor

Chipps Hill, Lane End, High
Wycombe HP14 3NF
☎ High Wycombe (01494) 881250
& Mobile 0378 356178
Fax (01494) 881250
*Queen Anne manor house in delightful
gardens, surrounded by fields.*
Bedrooms: 2 double, 1 twin
Bathrooms: 2 private
Bed & breakfast

per night:	£min	£max
Single	25.00	35.00
Double	50.00	70.00

Half board per

person:	£min	£max
Daily	35.00	50.00
Weekly	200.00	300.00

Parking for 4

2 Hyde Green

Listed

Marlow SL7 1QL
☎ (01628) 483526 & Mobile 0378
178802
*Comfortable family home. Quietly
situated yet only a few minutes' level
walk from town centre, River Thames
and station (Paddington 1 hour).*
Bedrooms: 1 double, 1 twin
Bathrooms: 2 en-suite, 1 public
Bed & breakfast

per night:	£min	£max
Single	23.00	26.00
Double	34.00	36.00

Parking for 2

Monkton Farmhouse

Listed COMMENDED

Monkton Farm, Little Marlow,
Marlow SL7 3RF
☎ High Wycombe (01494) 521082
Fax (01494) 443905
*150-acre dairy farm. 14th C
cruckhouse set in beautiful countryside.
Easily reached by motorway and close
to shopping and sporting facilities.*
Bedrooms: 1 single, 1 twin, 1 triple
Bathrooms: 1 public
Bed & breakfast

per night:	£min	£max
Single	20.00	25.00
Double	40.00	42.00

Parking for 6

5 Pound Lane

Listed **COMMENDED**

Marlow SL7 2AE
☎ (01628) 482649
Older style house, just off town centre, 2 minutes from River Thames and leisure complex. Double room has own balcony with delightful view.
Bedrooms: 1 double, 1 twin
Bathrooms: 1 public
Bed & breakfast

per night:	£min	£max
Single	25.00	28.00
Double	36.00	40.00

Parking for 2

MARNHULL

Dorset
Map ref 2B3

Has a fine church and numerous attractive houses.

Yew House Farm

Marnhull, Sturminster Newton
DT10 1PD
☎ (01258) 820412
Fax (01258) 821044
10-acre farm. Spacious, family farmhouse of character, in very quiet location. Superb views over open countryside.
Bedrooms: 2 double, 1 twin
Bathrooms: 3 en-suite
Bed & breakfast

per night:	£min	£max
Single	20.00	22.00
Double	40.00	44.00

Half board per person:	£min	£max
Daily	30.00	34.00
Weekly	290.00	300.00

Evening meal 1900 (last orders 2000)
Parking for 3
Open March–October

MILTON ABBAS

Dorset
Map ref 2B3

Sloping village street of thatched houses. A boys' school lies in Capability Brown's landscaped gardens amid hills and woods where the town once stood. The school chapel, former abbey church, can be visited.

Dunbury Heights

HIGHLY COMMENDED

Winterborne Stickland, Blandford Forum DT11 0DH
☎ (01258) 880445

Always a friendly welcome at this brick and flint cottage. Outstanding views to Poole and Isle of Wight. 6 miles from Blandford Forum and 1 mile from the picturesque village of Milton Abbas.
Bedrooms: 1 double, 1 twin
Bathrooms: 1 en-suite, 1 public
Bed & breakfast

per night:	£min	£max
Single	15.00	20.00
Double	35.00	35.00

Parking for 10

MILTON KEYNES

Buckinghamshire
Map ref 2C1

Designated a New Town in 1967, Milton Keynes offers a wide range of housing and is abundantly planted with trees. It has excellent shopping facilities and 3 centres for leisure and sporting activities. The Open University is based here.
Tourist Information Centre ☎ (01908) 232525 or 231742

Chantry Farm

COMMENDED

Pindon End, Hanslope, Milton Keynes MK19 7HL
☎ (01908) 510269 & Mobile 0850 166122
600-acre mixed farm. Stone farmhouse, built in 1650, with inglenook fireplaces. Surrounded by open countryside yet only 15 minutes to city centre. Swimming pool, trout lake, table tennis, clay pigeon shooting.
Bedrooms: 1 double, 2 twin
Bathrooms: 1 private, 1 public
Bed & breakfast

per night:	£min	£max
Single	18.00	20.00
Double	35.00	40.00

Parking for 7

The Croft

COMMENDED

Little Crawley, Newport Pagnell MK16 9LT
☎ North Crawley (01234) 391296
Spacious bungalow in open countryside, 15 minutes' drive from city centre. Nearby inns serve evening meals. Convenient for Bedford or Northampton.
Bedrooms: 1 single, 2 double, 1 twin
Bathrooms: 2 en-suite, 1 public
Bed & breakfast

per night:	£min	£max
Single	15.00	16.00
Double	29.00	30.00

Parking for 6

Haversham Grange

COMMENDED

Haversham, Milton Keynes MK19 7DX
☎ (01908) 312389
Fax (01908) 312389
Large 14th C stone house with many interesting features. Set in own gardens backing on to lakes.
Bedrooms: 3 twin
Bathrooms: 2 en-suite, 1 private, 1 public
Bed & breakfast

per night:	£min	£max
Single	20.00	25.00
Double	40.00	46.00

Parking for 4

Michelville House

Newton Road, Bletchley, Milton Keynes MK3 5BN
☎ (01908) 371578
Clean, compact establishment within easy reach of railway station, M1, shopping and sporting facilities. 10 minutes from Milton Keynes shopping centre.
Bedrooms: 10 single, 6 twin
Bathrooms: 4 public
Bed & breakfast

per night:	£min	£max
Single	15.00	22.00
Double	30.00	40.00

Parking for 16

Mill Farm

COMMENDED

Gayhurst, Newport Pagnell MK16 8LT
☎ Newport Pagnell (01908) 611489
Fax (01908) 611489
505-acre mixed farm. 17th C farmhouse. Hard tennis court, riding, fishing on River Ouse, which flows through farm. Good touring centre.
Bedrooms: 1 single, 1 twin, 1 family room
Bathrooms: 3 private, 2 public
Bed & breakfast

per night:	£min	£max
Single	15.00	20.00
Double	30.00	40.00

Parking for 12

MILTON KEYNES
Continued

The Old Rectory

Drayton Road, Newton Longville,
Milton Keynes MK17 0BH
☎ (01908) 375794

*Brick-built, listed Georgian house
(1769), in village setting to the south of
Milton Keynes.*
Bedrooms: 2 single, 1 double, 1 twin
Bathrooms: 1 en-suite, 2 public,
3 private showers

Bed & breakfast

per night:	£min	£max
Single	17.00	18.00
Double	40.00	44.00

Half board per person:

	£min	£max
Daily	24.00	29.00
Weekly	145.00	182.00

Evening meal 1800 (last orders
2000)
Parking for 6

MINSTEAD
Hampshire
Map ref 2B3

Cluster of thatched cottages and
detached period houses. The church,
listed in the Domesday Book, has
private boxes - one with its own
fireplace.

Grove House
Listed COMMENDED

Newtown, Minstead, Lyndhurst
SO43 7GG
☎ Southampton (01703) 813211
*9-acre smallholding. Attractive family
home, set in quiet, rural position 3
miles from Lyndhurst, with superb
walking, birdwatching and riding
(stabling available).*
Bedrooms: 1 triple
Bathrooms: 1 private

Bed & breakfast

per night:	£min	£max
Double	32.00	36.00

Parking for 1

MINSTER LOVELL
Oxfordshire
Map ref 2C1

Picturesque village on the River
Windrush with thatched cottages
and 19th C houses. Minster Lovell
Hall, built in the 15th C by the
Lovell family, is the subject of several
legends and now stands in ruins in a
beautiful riverside setting.

Hill Grove Farm
HIGHLY COMMENDED

Crawley Road, Minster Lovell,
Oxford OX8 5NA
☎ Witney (01993) 703120
Fax (01993) 700528
*300-acre mixed farm. Cotswold
farmhouse run on a family basis, in an
attractive rural setting overlooking the
River Windrush. Pleasant country
walks.*
Bedrooms: 1 double, 1 twin
Bathrooms: 1 en-suite, 1 private

Bed & breakfast

per night:	£min	£max
Double	39.00	42.00

Parking for 4

NEW FOREST

*See under Ashurst, Barton on Sea,
Beaulieu, Bransgore, Brockenhurst, Burley,
Cadnam, Dibden, Fordingbridge, Hythe,
Lymington, Lyndhurst, Minstead, New
Milton, Ringwood, Sway*

NEW MILTON
Hampshire
Map ref 2B3

New Forest residential town on the
mainline railway.

Wayward Cottage
HIGHLY COMMENDED

New Lane, Bashley, New Milton,
Hamphire BH25 5TD
☎ (01425) 611500
Fax (01425) 611500

*Comfortable, friendly forest cottage
down country lane, run by local family.
Delightful secluded garden. Forest
walks 1 mile, sea 3 miles. En-suite
rooms. Good food nearby.*
Bedrooms: 1 double, 1 twin
Bathrooms: 2 en-suite

Bed & breakfast

per night:	£min	£max
Double	32.00	40.00

Parking for 3
Open February–November

NEWBURY
Berkshire
Map ref 2C2

Ancient town surrounded by the
Downs and on the Kennet and Avon
Canal. It has many buildings of
interest, including the 17th C Cloth
Hall, which is now a museum. The
famous racecourse is nearby.
Tourist Information Centre ☎ *(01635)
30267*

The Old Farmhouse

Downend Lane, Chieveley, Newbury
RG20 8TN
☎ Chieveley (01635) 248361
*Small country farmhouse on edge of
village. Within 1 mile of M4/A34
(junction 13) and close to Newbury.
Accommodation in self-contained
annexe.*
Bedrooms: 1 family room
Suite available
Bathrooms: 1 private

Bed & breakfast

per night:	£min	£max
Single	20.00	22.00
Double	40.00	42.00

Parking for 5

Rookwood Farmhouse
HIGHLY COMMENDED

Stockcross, Newbury RG20 8JX
☎ (01488) 608676
Fax (01488) 608676
*Newly converted self-contained coach
house with period furniture. Beautifully
decorated, conservatory overlooking
outdoor heated swimming pool and
large garden. Easy access to M4 and
A4. No smoking and no pets, please.*
Bedrooms: 1 double, 1 twin
Suites available
Bathrooms: 2 en-suite

Bed & breakfast

per night:	£min	£max
Single	30.00	35.00
Double	50.00	55.00

Evening meal 1830 (last orders
2030)
Parking for 3

White Cottage

Listed **COMMENDED**

Newtown, Newbury RG20 9AP
☎ (01635) 43097
*Delightful cottage in semi-rural position,
just 2 miles south of Newbury.
Comfortable, quiet accommodation.
Children and dogs welcome.*
Bedrooms: 1 double, 1 twin
Bathrooms: 1 public

Bed & breakfast

per night:	£min	£max
Single	18.50	
Double	37.00	

Parking for 2

NEWPORT

Isle of Wight
Map ref 2C3

Commercial capital of the island,
lying on the River Medina. Vessels
sail into the harbour from Cowes.
The town has many historic
buildings including the Old
Grammar School which was a
lodging for Charles II.
Tourist Information Centre ☎ *(01983)
525450*

Magnolia House

COMMENDED

6 Cypress Road, Newport
PO30 1EY
☎ Isle of Wight (01983) 529489
*Comfortable, picturesque house, set in
peaceful gardens. Private parking. A
short walk to town centre, bus routes,
footpaths and cycleways to all parts of
the island.*
Bedrooms: 1 single, 1 double
Bathrooms: 1 en-suite, 1 private

Bed & breakfast

per night:	£min	£max
Single	25.00	25.00
Double	35.00	35.00

Parking for 2

WELCOME HOST

This is a nationally recognised
customer care programme
which aims to promote
the highest standards of
service and a warm welcome.
Establishments who are taking
part in this initiative are
indicated by the ⊚ symbol.

OXFORD

Oxfordshire
Map ref 2C1

Beautiful university town with many
ancient colleges, some dating from
the 13th C, and numerous buildings
of historic and architectural interest.
The Ashmolean Museum has
outstanding collections. Lovely
gardens and meadows with punting
on the Cherwell.
Tourist Information Centre ☎ *(01865)
726871*

Acorn Guest House

Listed

260 Iffley Road, Oxford OX4 1SE
☎ (01865) 247998
*Victorian house situated midway
between the city centre and the
ring-road. Convenient for all local
amenities and more distant attractions.*
Bedrooms: 2 single, 1 twin, 3 triple
Bathrooms: 2 public

Bed & breakfast

per night:	£min	£max
Single	20.00	26.00
Double	34.00	40.00

Parking for 5
Cards accepted: Access, Visa, Diners

Arden Lodge

Listed

34 Sunderland Avenue, off Banbury
Road, Oxford OX2 8DX
☎ (01865) 552076 & Mobile (0402)
068697
*Modern detached house in select part
of Oxford. Within easy reach of country
inns, river, city centre and meadows.
Excellent position for Blenheim,
Stratford-upon-Avon, Cotswolds,
London.*
Bedrooms: 1 single, 1 double, 1 twin
Bathrooms: 3 en-suite

Bed & breakfast

per night:	£min	£max
Single	25.00	30.00
Double	40.00	45.00

Parking for 6

Becket House

Listed

5 Becket Street, Oxford OX1 7PP
☎ (01865) 724675
Fax (01865) 513045
*Friendly guesthouse convenient for rail
and bus station, within walking distance
of city centre and colleges. Good, clean
accommodation, en-suite rooms.*
Bedrooms: 4 single, 1 double, 3 twin,
1 triple
Bathrooms: 6 en-suite, 3 private

Bed & breakfast

per night:	£min	£max
Single	25.00	35.00
Double	36.00	60.00

Cards accepted: Access, Visa,
Switch/Delta

The Bungalow

Listed

Cherwell Farm, Mill Lane, Old
Marston, Oxford OX3 0QF
☎ (01865) 557171
*Modern bungalow set in 5 acres, in
quiet location with views over open
countryside, but within 3 miles of city
centre. No smoking.*
Bedrooms: 2 double, 2 twin
Bathrooms: 1 en-suite, 1 public

Bed & breakfast

per night:	£min	£max
Single	22.00	30.00
Double	36.00	46.00

Parking for 4
Open April–October

Cherwell Croft

COMMENDED

72 Church Street, Kidlington
OX5 2BB
☎ Kidlington (01865) 373371
*Georgian stone-built house in its own
grounds. Quiet and attractive part of
Kidlington by St Mary's Church. 4 miles
from Oxford and 2 miles from
Blenheim.*
Bedrooms: 1 single, 1 double, 1 twin
Bathrooms: 1 en-suite, 1 public

Bed & breakfast

per night:	£min	£max
Single	16.00	18.00
Double	30.00	35.00

Parking for 3

College Guest House

103-105 Woodstock Road, Oxford
OX2 6HL
☎ (01865) 552579
Fax (01865) 311244
*Early Victorian residence, north of the
city in residential area. Within walking
distance of colleges, restaurants and
shops. Children welcome.*
Bedrooms: 4 single, 4 double, 4 twin
Bathrooms: 2 en-suite, 2 private,
2 public

Bed & breakfast

per night:	£min	£max
Single	20.00	30.00
Double	35.00	50.00

Continued ▶

OXFORD
Continued

Half board per
person:	£min	£max
Daily	20.00	30.00

Parking for 10
Cards accepted: Access, Visa, Amex,
Switch/Delta

Cumnor Village B & B 🅰

Listed COMMENDED

Beinn Bheag, 96 Oxford Road,
Cumnor, Oxford OX2 9PQ
☎ (01865) 864020 & 241381
Fax (01865) 247928
*Detached bungalow with large garden
in quiet village just outside the city.
Comfortable accommodation, warm
welcome. Wide choice of breakfasts.
Non-smoking.*
Bedrooms: 1 single, 1 double,
1 family room
Bathrooms: 2 en-suite, 1 public
Bed & breakfast
per night:	£min	£max
Single	19.00	27.00
Double	39.00	45.00

Parking for 4
Open January–November

Gables

HIGHLY COMMENDED

6 Cumnor Hill, Oxford OX2 9HA
☎ (01865) 862153
Fax (01865) 864054
*Relax in a friendly homely atmosphere
combined with a high standard of
comfort and service. Easy access to bus
and railway stations and 5 minutes'
drive to city centre.*
Bedrooms: 2 single, 2 double, 1 twin,
1 triple
Bathrooms: 5 en-suite, 1 private,
1 public
Bed & breakfast
per night:	£min	£max
Single	20.00	26.00
Double	40.00	46.00

Parking for 8
Cards accepted: Access, Visa

The National Grading and
Classification Scheme is
explained in full at the
back of this guide.

High Hedges

COMMENDED

8 Cumnor Hill, Oxford OX2 9HA
☎ (01865) 863395
*Close to city centre, offering a high
standard of accommodation for a
comfortable and happy stay in Oxford.*
Bedrooms: 2 double, 1 twin
Bathrooms: 3 en-suite, 1 public
Bed & breakfast
per night:	£min	£max
Single	20.00	22.00
Double	40.00	45.00

Parking for 6

Highfield West 🅰

HIGHLY COMMENDED

188 Cumnor Hill, Oxford OX2 9PJ
☎ (01865) 863007
*Comfortable home in residential
location. Good access to city centre and
ring road. Large outdoor pool, heated in
summer.*
Bedrooms: 2 single, 1 double, 1 twin,
1 family room
Bathrooms: 3 en-suite, 1 public
Bed & breakfast
per night:	£min	£max
Single	20.00	26.00
Double	39.00	50.00

Parking for 6

Mount Pleasant 🅰

APPROVED

76 London Road, Headington,
Oxford OX3 9AJ
☎ (01865) 62749 changing to
762749
Fax (01865) 62749 changing to
762749
*Small, family-run hotel offering full
facilities. On the A40 and convenient
for Oxford shopping, hospitals, colleges,
visiting the Chilterns and the
Cotswolds.*
Bedrooms: 2 double, 5 twin, 1 triple
Bathrooms: 8 en-suite
Bed & breakfast
per night:	£min	£max
Single	37.50	45.00
Double	48.00	65.00

Half board per
person:	£min	£max
Daily	52.50	60.00

Lunch available
Evening meal 1800 (last orders
2130)
Parking for 6
Cards accepted: Access, Visa, Diners,
Amex

Newton House 🅰

👑

82-84 Abingdon Road, Oxford
OX1 4PL
☎ (01865) 240561 & Mobile (0585)
485656
Fax (01865) 244647
*Centrally located, Victorian townhouse
with comfortable homely
accommodation, warm welcome and
friendly atmosphere. Special diets
catered for on request.*
Bedrooms: 7 double, 4 twin, 2 family
rooms
Bathrooms: 5 private, 3 public
Bed & breakfast
per night:	£min	£max
Single	22.00	38.00
Double	34.00	48.00

Parking for 8
Cards accepted: Access, Visa, Amex,
Switch/Delta

7 Princes Street 🅰

Listed

Oxford OX4 1DD
☎ (01865) 726755
*Restored Victorian artisan's cottage,
furnished with many antiques. Short
walk from Magdalen Bridge and
central Oxford.*
Bedrooms: 2 single, 1 double
Bathrooms: 1 public
Bed & breakfast
per night:	£min	£max
Single	16.00	20.00
Double	32.00	34.00

Parking for 2

Stonehouse Farm

Weston Road, Bletchingdon, Oxford
OX5 3EA
☎ Bletchingdon (01869) 350585
*560-acre arable farm. 17th C Cotswold
farmhouse. Ideal touring centre. 15
minutes north of Oxford, 20 minutes
south of Banbury and 10 minutes from
Blenheim Palace. Between the A4260
and A34, junction 9 of M40. 1 hour
from Heathrow.*
Bedrooms: 1 single, 1 double, 1 twin,
1 family room
Bathrooms: 2 public
Bed & breakfast
per night:	£min	£max
Single	18.00	25.00
Double	35.00	40.00

Parking for 11

West Farm

Listed

Eaton, Appleton, Abingdon
OX13 5PR
☎ (01865) 862908

1100-acre arable & livestock farm. Comfortable, centrally heated farmhouse on working farm, 5 miles west of Oxford. Children welcome (equipment, toys, etc). Tennis court. Excellent centre for touring.
Bedrooms: 1 single, 1 double, 1 triple
Bathrooms: 1 private, 1 public
Bed & breakfast

per night:	£min	£max
Single	20.00	25.00
Double	40.00	50.00

Parking for 6
Open April–December

PETERSFIELD

Hampshire
Map ref 2C3

Grew prosperous from the wool trade and was famous as a coaching centre.
Tourist Information Centre ☎ (01730) 268829

The Butts

Steep, Petersfield GU32 1AA
☎ (01730) 263878
Fax (01730) 263878
Interesting, architect-designed house in a rural setting with 10 acres of grounds and magnificent downland views. Good walking territory. Very quiet.
Bedrooms: 1 single, 1 double
Bathrooms: 1 en-suite, 1 private
Bed & breakfast

per night:	£min	£max
Single	20.00	20.00
Double	40.00	40.00

Parking for 3

Heath Farmhouse ♈

COMMENDED

Heath Road East, Petersfield
GU31 4HU
☎ (01730) 264709
4-acre horses & poultry farm. Georgian farmhouse with lovely views, set in large garden. Surrounded by quiet farmland yet only three-quarters of a mile from

town centre. Within easy reach of Portsmouth, Chichester, Winchester.
Bedrooms: 1 double, 1 twin, 1 family room
Bathrooms: 2 en-suite, 1 private, 1 public
Bed & breakfast

per night:	£min	£max
Single	20.00	20.00
Double	34.00	36.00

Parking for 5

POOLE

Dorset
Map ref 2B3

Tremendous natural harbour makes Poole a superb boating centre. The harbour area is crowded with historic buildings including the 15th C Town Cellars housing a maritime museum.
Tourist Information Centre ☎ (01202) 673322

Homeleigh

COMMENDED

105 Wimborne Road, Poole
BH15 2BP
☎ (01202) 777075
Small, friendly, non-smoking establishment, near town centre, harbour, beaches and bus/rail stations. Within easy reach of coast and New Forest.
Bedrooms: 2 twin
Bathrooms: 1 public
Bed & breakfast

per night:	£min	£max
Single	14.00	16.00
Double	28.00	32.00

Parking for 2

The Inn in the Park

26 Pinewood Road, Branksome Park, Poole BH13 6JS
☎ Bournemouth (01202) 761318
Small, friendly, family-owned pub and restaurant with sun terrace, log fire and easy access to the beach. Recommended in all leading pub guides.
Bedrooms: 3 double, 1 twin, 1 triple
Bathrooms: 5 en-suite
Bed & breakfast

per night:	£min	£max
Single	30.00	40.00
Double	40.00	50.00

Lunch available
Evening meal 1900 (last orders 2130)
Parking for 15
Cards accepted: Access, Visa

PORTSMOUTH & SOUTHSEA

Hampshire
Map ref 2C3

The first dock was built in 1194. HMS Victory, Nelson's flagship, is here and Charles Dickens' former home is open to the public. Neighbouring Southsea has a promenade with magnificent views of Spithead.
Tourist Information Centre ☎ (01705) 838635 or 826722

Ashby's Hotel ♈

4 Auckland Road West, Southsea, Portsmouth, Hampshire PO5 3NY
☎ Portsmouth (01705) 823497 &
Mobile 0802 604353
Fax (01705) 823497

Public house with various entertainments, in conservation area. Building dates back over 100 years.
Bedrooms: 2 single, 6 double, 1 twin
Bathrooms: 7 en-suite, 2 private, 1 public
Bed & breakfast

per night:	£min	£max
Single	15.00	25.00
Double	30.00	36.00

Half board per person:	£min	£max
Daily	26.00	30.00
Weekly	120.00	180.00

Lunch available
Evening meal (last orders 2000)
Parking for 100
Cards accepted: Access, Visa, Diners, Amex

The ♈ symbol after an establishment name indicates that it is a Regional Tourist Board member.

PORTSMOUTH & SOUTHSEA
Continued

Hamilton House ♠
👑👑 COMMENDED

95 Victoria Road North, Southsea,
Portsmouth, Hampshire PO5 1PS
☎ Portsmouth (01705) 823502
Fax (01705) 823502
*Delightful family-run guesthouse, 5
minutes by car to ferry terminals and
tourist attractions. Some en-suite rooms
are also available. Breakfast served
from 6am.*
Bedrooms: 1 single, 2 double, 2 twin,
1 triple, 2 family rooms
Suites available
Bathrooms: 4 en-suite, 2 public
Bed & breakfast

per night:	£min	£max
Single	17.00	19.00
Double	34.00	38.00

Half board per

person:	£min	£max
Daily	23.00	25.00
Weekly	151.00	165.00

Evening meal from 1800

READING
Berkshire
Map ref 2C2

Busy, modern county town with
large shopping centre and many
leisure and recreation facilities.
There are several interesting
museums and the Duke of
Wellington's Stratfield Saye is
nearby.
*Tourist Information Centre ☎ (0118)
956 6226*

Belstone
Listed HIGHLY COMMENDED

36 Upper Warren Avenue,
Caversham, Reading RG4 7EB
☎ (0118) 947 7435
*Friendly welcome in elegant Victorian
family house. Quiet tree-lined avenue
near river and farmland. Convenient for
town centre by car. Non-smokers only,
please.*
Bedrooms: 1 double, 1 twin
Bathrooms: 1 public
Bed & breakfast

per night:	£min	£max
Single	26.00	28.50
Double	40.00	44.00

Parking for 2

The Elms ♠
👑👑 COMMENDED

Gallowstree Road, Rotherfield
Peppard, Henley-on-Thames,
Oxfordshire RG9 5HT
☎ (0118) 972 3164
*Bed and breakfast near Reading.
Heated swimming pool. All normal
services, large garden, good parking.
Excellent pub close by.*
Bedrooms: 1 single, 1 double, 1 twin
Bathrooms: 2 en-suite, 1 public
Bed & breakfast

per night:	£min	£max
Single	15.00	25.00
Double	35.00	40.00

Evening meal 1930 (last orders
2000)
Parking for 13

10 Greystoke Road
Listed COMMENDED

Caversham, Reading RG4 0EL
☎ (0118) 947 5784
*Private home in quiet, residential area.
TV lounge, tea and coffee-making
facilities. Non-smokers only, please.*
Bedrooms: 2 single, 1 double
Bathrooms: 2 public
Bed & breakfast

per night:	£min	£max
Single	18.00	21.00
Double	30.00	35.00

Parking for 2

The Six Bells ♠
👑👑 COMMENDED

Beenham Village, Beenham, Reading
RG7 5NX
☎ (0118) 971 3368
*Village pub, overlooking farmland. Four
miles from Theale M4 junction 12, 1
mile off A4. Newly-built bedrooms.
Home cooking always available - varied
menu.*
Bedrooms: 1 single, 2 double, 1 twin
Bathrooms: 4 en-suite
Bed & breakfast

per night:	£min	£max
Single		36.00
Double		49.00

Lunch available
Evening meal 1830 (last orders
2130)
Parking for 35
Cards accepted: Access, Visa,
Switch/Delta

You are advised to confirm
your booking in writing.

RINGWOOD
Hampshire
Map ref 2B3

Market town by the River Avon
comprising old cottages, many of
them thatched. Although just
outside the New Forest, there is
heath and woodland nearby and it is
a good centre for horse-riding and
walking.

Lochend
Listed COMMENDED

Hurst Corner, Salisbury Road,
Ringwood BH24 1AX
☎ (01425) 473836
*50-year-old chalet bungalow in
one-third of an acre plot on main
Salisbury Road, 10 minutes' walk from
Ringwood centre. Easy access to New
Forest, South Coast and Salisbury.*
Bedrooms: 1 double, 1 triple
Suites available
Bathrooms: 1 en-suite, 1 private
shower
Bed & breakfast

per night:	£min	£max
Single	18.00	20.00
Double	32.00	36.00

Parking for 4

Old Stacks ♠
👑👑 HIGHLY COMMENDED

154 Hightown Road, Ringwood
BH24 1NP
☎ (01425) 473840
*Home from home hospitality in
delightful spacious bungalow set in
lovely garden. Wonderful breakfast.
Cosy log fires in winter. Close to country
inn and New Forest. Ideal base for
touring south coast.*
Bedrooms: 1 double, 1 twin
Bathrooms: 1 en-suite, 1 private
Bed & breakfast

per night:	£min	£max
Single	20.00	25.00
Double	34.00	40.00

Parking for 4

ACCESSIBILITY
Look for the ♿ symbols
which indicate accessibility for
wheelchair users. These are
described in detail at the
front of this guide.

ROMSEY

Hampshire
Map ref 2C3

Town grew up around the important abbey and lies on the banks of the River Test, famous for trout and salmon. Broadlands House, home of the late Lord Mountbatten, is open to the public.
Tourist Information Centre ☎ (01794) 512987

Country Accommodation ♪

🏆🏆 COMMENDED

The Old Post Office, New Road, Michelmersh, Romsey SO51 0NL
☎ (01794) 368739 & Mobile 0374 734478

Character rooms in ground floor independent annexe. Quiet village, 3 miles from Romsey. All en-suite, tea/coffee, TV. Good local pubs and restaurants.
Bedrooms: 2 double, 1 twin
Bathrooms: 3 en-suite

Bed & breakfast per night:

	£min	£max
Single	25.00	25.00
Double	40.00	40.00

Parking for 10
Cards accepted: Access, Visa

Highfield House

🏆🏆🏆 HIGHLY COMMENDED

Newtown Road, Awbridge, Romsey SO51 0GG
☎ (01794) 340727
Fax (01794) 341450
In unspoilt rural village, overlooking golf-course. Delightful setting and charming gardens. Home cooking a speciality. Close to Mottisfont Abbey National Trust and Hillier Arboretum.
Bedrooms: 1 double, 2 twin
Bathrooms: 3 en-suite, 1 public

Bed & breakfast per night:

	£min	£max
Double	40.00	45.00

Evening meal from 1900
Parking for 10

8 The Meads ♪

Listed APPROVED

Romsey SO51 8HB
☎ (01794) 512049
Small, friendly home in pleasant, quiet location in town centre. Comfortable rooms, great breakfast. Parking. No smoking, please.
Bedrooms: 1 double, 1 twin
Bathrooms: 1 public

Bed & breakfast per night:

	£min	£max
Single	18.00	20.00
Double	30.00	32.00

Parking for 1
Open April–October

Stoneymarsh Cottage ♪

Listed

Stoneymarsh, Romsey SO51 0LB
☎ Braishfield (01794) 368867
Fax (01794) 368786
Old dairy farmhouse, retaining much of its character. Warm welcome, good English breakfast. Set in open countryside yet central for Winchester, Salisbury and New Forest. Ample parking.
Bedrooms: 1 twin, 1 triple
Bathrooms: 2 private, 1 public

Bed & breakfast per night:

	£min	£max
Single	18.00	
Double	32.00	35.00

Parking for 20

ROWLAND'S CASTLE

Hampshire
Map ref 2C3

The Fountain Inn ♪

Listed APPROVED

34 The Green, Rowland's Castle, Havant PO9 6AB
☎ Portsmouth (01705) 412291
Fax (01705) 412291
Small, but comfortable, village pub on the green. Our food is good and home cooked, our welcome big and our prices reasonable. All the accommodation is non-smoking (smoking only in bar).
Bedrooms: 1 single, 4 double, 2 triple
Bathrooms: 4 en-suite, 1 public

Bed & breakfast per night:

	£min	£max
Single	24.00	36.00
Double	36.00	56.00

Half board per person:

	£min	£max
Daily	30.00	42.00
Weekly	189.00	265.00

Lunch available
Evening meal 1900 (last orders 2130)
Parking for 20
Cards accepted: Access, Visa, Amex

RYDE

Isle of Wight
Map ref 2C3

The island's chief entry port, connected to Portsmouth by ferries and hovercraft. 7 miles of sandy beaches with a half-mile pier, esplanade and gardens.
Tourist Information Centre ☎ (01983) 562905

Sillwood Acre ♪

🏆🏆 HIGHLY COMMENDED

Church Road, Binstead, Ryde PO33 3TB
☎ Isle of Wight (01983) 563553
Large Victorian house near Ryde, convenient for the ferry and hovercraft terminals. Two spacious en-suite rooms. Non-smoking.
Bedrooms: 1 double, 1 triple
Bathrooms: 2 en-suite

Bed & breakfast per night:

	£min	£max
Single	16.00	18.00
Double	32.00	36.00

Parking for 3

SANDOWN

Isle of Wight
Map ref 2C3

The 6-mile sweep of Sandown Bay is one of the island's finest stretches, with excellent sands. The pier has a pavilion and sun terrace; the esplanade has amusements, bars, eating-places and gardens.
Tourist Information Centre ☎ (01983) 403886

Annandale Guest House ♪

Listed COMMENDED

30 St John's Road, Sandown PO36 8HA
☎ Isle of Wight (01983) 402955
Small, comfortable, family-run guesthouse, 2 to 3 minutes' walk from the shops, beach, pier and theatre.
Bedrooms: 1 double, 1 twin, 1 triple, 1 family room
Bathrooms: 1 public

Bed & breakfast per night:

	£min	£max
Single	13.50	15.50
Double	27.00	31.00

Continued ▶

SANDOWN

Continued

Evening meal 1800 (last orders 1800)
Open April–September
🐎🖵♿ⓤⓛⓈ🚲

SAUNDERTON

Buckinghamshire
Map ref 2C1

Small village close to the Ridgeway long distance footpath. The site of a Roman villa is near the church.

Hunter's Gate

Listed

Deanfield, Saunderton, High Wycombe HP14 4JR
☎ High Wycombe (01494) 481446
6-acre smallholding. 4-bedroomed house with a 1-bedroomed flat above garage, in a valley overlooked by Bledlow Ridge, half-a-mile from Wycombe/Princes Risborough road. Set in 5 acres in a quiet area but only half-a-mile to BR station for London.
Bedrooms: 1 double, 1 twin
Bathrooms: 1 en-suite, 1 private, 1 public

Bed & breakfast per night:	£min	£max
Single	15.00	17.50
Double	30.00	35.00

Parking for 4
🐎🖵♿ⓤⓛ🅸Ⓢ📺🚗♿🚲

SELBORNE

Hampshire
Map ref 2C2

Village made famous by Gilbert White, who was a curate here and is remembered for his classic book "The Natural History of Selborne", published in 1788.

8 Goslings Croft

Listed HIGHLY COMMENDED

Selborne, Alton GU34 3HZ
☎ (01420) 511285
Fax (01420) 587451
Family home, set on edge of historic village, adjacent to National Trust land. Ideal base for walking and touring. Non-smokers only, please.
Bedrooms: 1 twin
Bathrooms: 1 en-suite

Bed & breakfast per night:	£min	£max
Single	19.50	19.50
Double	32.50	32.50

Parking for 1
🐎🕼🖵♿ⓤⓛ🅸Ⓢ✂🚗✕🚲

SHAFTESBURY

Dorset
Map ref 2B3

Hilltop town with a long history. The ancient and cobbled Gold Hill is one of the most attractive in Dorset. There is an excellent small museum containing a collection of buttons for which the town is famous.
Tourist Information Centre ☎ (01747) 853514

The Knoll

♛

Bleke Street, Shaftesbury SP7 8AH
☎ (01747) 855243
Spacious Victorian family house with outstanding views, set in large garden, but within level walking distance of town centre and famous Gold Hill. Ideal centre for artists. Non-smoking.
Bedrooms: 1 single, 2 double
Bathrooms: 2 en-suite, 1 private, 1 public

Bed & breakfast per night:	£min	£max
Single	21.00	26.00
Double	42.00	42.00

Half board per person:	£min	£max
Daily	32.00	37.00

Evening meal 1930 (last orders 2030)
Parking for 4
🐎🕼🖵♿🔌ⓤⓛⓈ✂🚗♿✕🚲

SHANKLIN

Isle of Wight
Map ref 2C3

Set on a cliff with gentle slopes leading down to the beach, esplanade and marine gardens. The picturesque, old thatched village nestles at the end of the wooded chine.
Tourist Information Centre ☎ (01983) 862942

Hazelwood Hotel ♛

♛♛♛ COMMENDED

14 Clarence Road, Shanklin PO37 7BH
☎ Isle of Wight (01983) 862824
Fax (01983) 862824
Detached, friendly, comfortable hotel in a quiet tree-lined road, close to all amenities. Daily bookings taken. Parking available.
Bedrooms: 2 single, 4 double, 2 twin, 1 triple, 1 family room
Bathrooms: 8 en-suite, 1 public

Bed & breakfast per night:	£min	£max
Single	16.00	19.50
Double	32.00	39.00

Half board per person:	£min	£max
Daily	23.00	26.50
Weekly	146.00	173.50

Evening meal 1800 (last orders 1600)
Parking for 5
Cards accepted: Access, Visa, Diners, Amex
🐎2♿🖵♿🔌🍴ⓤⓛ🅸Ⓢ♿📺🚗🖥✿🚗ⓄⒶⓅ🅂P🅣

SHIPTON BELLINGER

Hampshire
Map ref 2B2

Parsonage Farm

♛ COMMENDED

Shipton Bellinger, Tidworth SP9 7UF
☎ Stonehenge (01980) 842404
Former farmhouse of 16th/17th C origins in quiet village. Walled garden, stables, paddocks. Situated off A338 opposite parish church and Boot Inn. Convenient for Stonehenge.
Bedrooms: 1 single, 1 twin, 1 triple
Bathrooms: 1 private, 2 public

Bed & breakfast per night:	£min	£max
Single	20.00	30.00
Double	35.00	50.00

Parking for 6
🐎10🖵♿ⓤⓛ✂📺🚗✿✕🚗🏠

SHIPTON-UNDER-WYCHWOOD

Oxfordshire
Map ref 2B1

Situated in the ancient Forest of Wychwood with many fine old houses and an interesting parish church. Nearby is Shipton Court, a gabled Elizabethan house set in beautiful grounds that include an ornamental lake and a tree-lined avenue approach.

Courtlands

Listed COMMENDED

6 Courtlands Road, Shipton-under-Wychwood, Oxford OX7 6DF
☎ (01993) 830551
Relaxed, friendly house in centre of unspoilt village. Ideal for Cotswolds touring. Oxfordshire cycleway close by. Tea/coffee, TV, guest lounge.
Bedrooms: 1 single, 2 double, 1 twin
Suites available
Bathrooms: 2 en-suite, 1 private, 1 public

Bed & breakfast per night:	£min	£max
Single	20.00	20.00
Double	35.00	38.00

🛏️🚫⛽️🖥️♿🍴UL S ⚰️🛏️📺📠💻🅿️❄️🐾🚗

SIXPENNY HANDLEY

Dorset
Map ref 2B3

The Barleycorn House

👑👑 COMMENDED

Deanland, Sixpenny Handley,
Salisbury, Wiltshire SP5 5PD
☎ Handley (01725) 552583
Fax (01725) 552090
*Converted 17th C inn retaining original
period features, in peaceful
surroundings with many nearby walks.
Relaxed atmosphere and home
cooking.*
Bedrooms: 1 single, 1 double, 1 twin
Bathrooms: 2 en-suite, 1 public

Bed & breakfast per night:	£min	£max
Single	18.50	18.50
Double	37.00	37.00

Half board per person:	£min	£max
Daily	27.50	27.50
Weekly	179.50	179.50

Evening meal from 1830
Parking for 5

🛏️🍴⛽️♿UL🔒⚰️🛏️📺📠💻🐾🚗

SOULDERN

Oxfordshire
Map ref 2C1

Tower Fields

👑👑 COMMENDED

Tusmore Road, Souldern, Bicester
OX6 9HY
☎ Bicester (01869) 346554
Fax (01869) 345157
*Converted 18th C cottages and 14
acre smallholding with rare breeds of
poultry, sheep and cattle. Small
collection of vintage cars.*
Bedrooms: 1 double, 1 twin
Bathrooms: 2 private

Bed & breakfast per night:	£min	£max
Single	22.00	24.00
Double	44.00	44.00

Half board per person:	£min	£max
Daily	30.50	30.50

Parking for 4

🛏️🔥🍴⛽️🖥️♿UL🔒⚰️🛏️📺💻📠
🔔☀️🚗🚙

SOUTHAMPTON

Hampshire
Map ref 2C3

One of Britain's leading seaports
with a long history, now a major
container port. In the 18th C it
became a fashionable resort with
the assembly rooms and theatre.
The old Guildhall and the Wool
House are now museums. Sections
of the medieval wall can still be
seen.
*Tourist Information Centre ☎ (01703)
221106*

Ashelee Lodge 🏔️

Listed COMMENDED

36 Atherley Road, Shirley,
Southampton SO15 5DQ
☎ (01703) 222095
*Homely guesthouse, garden with pool.
Half a mile from city centre, near
station, M27 and Sealink ferryport.
Good touring base for New Forest,
Salisbury and Winchester.*
Bedrooms: 1 single, 1 double, 1 twin,
1 triple
Bathrooms: 1 public

Bed & breakfast per night:	£min	£max
Single	15.00	16.00
Double	30.00	32.00

Half board per person:	£min	£max
Weekly	145.00	155.00

Evening meal from 1800
Parking for 2
Cards accepted: Access, Visa

🛏️🍴⛽️♿🖥️🔒 S ⚰️🛏️📺💻🐾🚗❄️
🍴🚙◎

Beacon Guest House

Listed

49 Archers Road, Southampton
SO15 2NF
☎ (01703) 225910 & Mobile 0860
224625
*Friendly, comfortable accommodation,
commercial and private. Close to city
centre, restaurants, docks and county
cricket ground, with easy access to the
New Forest and Winchester.*
Bedrooms: 1 single, 2 double, 1 twin,
2 family rooms
Bathrooms: 2 public

Bed & breakfast per night:	£min	£max
Single	14.50	16.00
Double	27.00	32.00

Parking for 4

🛏️🍴♿UL S ⚰️💻📠🍴🚗 SP T

SOUTHSEA

Hampshire

See under Portsmouth & Southsea

STOCKBRIDGE

Hampshire
Map ref 2C2

Set in the Test Valley which has
some of the best fishing in England.
The wide main street has houses of
all styles, mainly Tudor and
Georgian.

Carbery Guest House 🏔️

👑👑👑 COMMENDED

Salisbury Hill, Stockbridge
SO20 6EZ
☎ Andover (01264) 810771
Fax (01264) 811022

*Fine old Georgian house in an acre of
landscaped gardens and lawns,
overlooking the River Test. Games and
swimming facilities, riding and fishing
can be arranged. Ideal for touring the
south coast and the New Forest.*
Bedrooms: 4 single, 3 double, 2 twin,
1 triple, 1 family room
Bathrooms: 8 en-suite, 1 public

Bed & breakfast per night:	£min	£max
Single	24.00	31.00
Double	46.00	50.00

Half board per person:	£min	£max
Daily	36.00	43.00
Weekly	248.00	297.00

Evening meal 1900 (last orders
1800)
Parking for 12

🛏️🍴⛽️🖥️♿🔒 S ⚰️💻📠🔍❄️
🍴🚙

The map references refer
to the colour maps towards
the end of the guide.
The first figure is the
map number; the letter and
figure which follow indicate
the grid reference
on the map.

STURMINSTER NEWTON

Dorset
Map ref 2B3

Every Monday this small town holds a livestock market. One of the bridges over the River Stour is a fine medieval example and bears a plaque declaring that anyone "injuring" it will be deported.

Holebrook Farm

Listed HIGHLY COMMENDED

Lydlinch, Sturminster Newton DT10 2JB
☎ Hazelbury Bryan (01258) 817348
126-acre mixed farm. Georgian stone farmhouse with a warm welcome and friendly atmosphere. Also 3 delightful stable annexes with own sitting rooms and shower units. Swimming pool, clay pigeon shooting and fishing available.
Bedrooms: 1 single, 4 twin
Bathrooms: 3 private, 1 public

Bed & breakfast per night:	£min	£max
Single	27.00	34.00
Double	42.00	50.00

Half board per person:	£min	£max
Daily	34.50	37.00

Evening meal 1900 (last orders 1500)
Parking for 10

Newton House

Listed COMMENDED

Newton, Sturminster Newton DT10 2DQ
☎ (01258) 472783
Georgian Grade II listed village home, owned by the Pitt-Rivers family until 1987. Patio and formal garden. Family atmosphere.
Bedrooms: 2 single, 2 double, 1 twin
Bathrooms: 1 en-suite, 1 private, 2 public

Bed & breakfast per night:	£min	£max
Single	20.00	20.00
Double	40.00	40.00

Parking for 6

Half board prices are given per person, but in some cases these may be based on double/twin occupancy.

SWAY

Hampshire
Map ref 2C3

Small village on the south-western edge of the New Forest. It is noted for its 220-ft tower, Peterson's Folly, built in the 1870s by a retired Indian judge to demonstrate the value of concrete as a building material.

Manor Farm

Listed COMMENDED

Coombe Lane, Sway, Lymington SO41 6BP
☎ Lymington (01590) 683542
30-acre beef farm. 18th C, Grade II listed farmhouse, surrounded by open fields and forest. Off B3055 Sway-Brockenhurst road.
Bedrooms: 1 double, 1 family room
Bathrooms: 2 en-suite, 1 public

Bed & breakfast per night:	£min	£max
Single	15.00	20.00
Double	34.00	38.00

Parking for 20

WARNFORD

Hampshire
Map ref 2C3

Paper Mill

Listed COMMENDED

Peake Lane, Warnford, Southampton SO32 3LA
☎ West Meon (01730) 829387

Self-contained mill house in unique setting on River Meon. Take A272 from Petersfield or Winchester to West Meon Hut traffic lights, turn south on A32, follow road to Warnford, past George and Falcon and turn left into Peake Lane.
Bedrooms: 1 double
Bathrooms: 1 en-suite

Bed & breakfast per night:	£min	£max
Single	25.00	
Double	45.00	

Parking for 1
Open April–September

WENDOVER

Buckinghamshire
Map ref 2C1

Historic town on the Icknield Way set amid beautiful scenery and spectacular views of the Chilterns. There are many old timbered cottages and inns, one visited by Oliver Cromwell. The church has some interesting carving.
Tourist Information Centre ☎ (01296) 696759

The Red Lion Hotel

COMMENDED

9 High Street, Wendover, Aylesbury HP22 6DU
☎ (01296) 622266
Fax (01296) 625077

17th C coaching inn. Great location for walking in Chilterns. Excellent reputation for food and drink. Popular with locals.
Bedrooms: 3 single, 10 double, 4 twin, 4 triple
Bathrooms: 21 en-suite

Bed & breakfast per night:	£min	£max
Single	44.95	48.95
Double	54.95	59.95

Half board per person:	£min	£max
Daily	54.95	58.95
Weekly	350.00	395.00

Lunch available
Evening meal 1800 (last orders 2200)
Parking for 60
Cards accepted: Access, Visa, Diners, Amex, Switch/Delta

WEST LULWORTH

Dorset
Map ref 2B3

Well-known for Lulworth Cove, the almost landlocked circular bay of chalk and limestone cliffs.

Graybank Guest House

Listed

Main Road, West Lulworth, Wareham BH20 5RL
☎ (01929) 400256
Victorian guesthouse in beautiful

countryside, 5 minutes' walk from
Lulworth Cove and the coastal path.
Ideal base for walking, touring or just
unwinding.
Bedrooms: 1 single, 2 double, 1 twin,
1 triple, 2 family rooms
Bathrooms: 3 public

Bed & breakfast

per night:	£min	£max
Single	15.00	19.00
Double	30.00	38.00

Parking for 7
Open February–November

Newlands Farm

▥ COMMENDED

West Lulworth, Wareham
BH20 5PU
☎ (01929) 400376
Fax (01929) 400536
*750-acre arable & livestock farm. 19th
C farmhouse, with outstanding views to
sea and distant Purbeck Hills. At
Durdle Door, 1 mile west of Lulworth
Cove.*
Bedrooms: 1 double, 1 triple
Bathrooms: 1 public, 2 private
showers

Bed & breakfast

per night:	£min	£max
Double	40.00	44.00

Parking for 10
Open March–November

The Old Barn Ⓜ

Listed

Lulworth Cove, West Lulworth,
Wareham BH20 5RL
☎ (01929) 400305

*Converted barn in peaceful, picturesque
coastal village. Choice of rooms with
continental breakfast or
please-yourself-rooms with light
self-catering facilities. Large gardens.
Ideal base for touring Dorset.
Restaurants nearby.*
Bedrooms: 2 single, 2 double, 1 twin,
1 triple, 1 family room
Bathrooms: 3 public

Bed & breakfast

per night:	£min	£max
Single	16.00	20.00
Double	32.00	40.00

Parking for 9
Cards accepted: Access, Visa

WEST STOUR

Dorset
Map ref 2B3

The Ship Inn

▥▥▥ COMMENDED

West Stour, Gillingham SP8 5RP
☎ East Stour (01747) 838640
*18th C mail coach inn with fine views
over the Dorset countryside. Log fires
during winter and traditional
hand-pumped ales throughout the year.
Central for touring the West Country.
Good home-cooked food served 7 days
a week.*
Bedrooms: 1 single, 2 double, 1 twin,
2 triple
Bathrooms: 6 en-suite, 1 public

Bed & breakfast

per night:	£min	£max
Single	28.00	30.00
Double	38.00	45.00

Lunch available
Evening meal 1900 (last orders
2130)
Parking for 50
Cards accepted: Access, Visa

WESTBURY

Buckinghamshire
Map ref 2C1

Mill Farm House

Westbury, Brackley,
Northamptonshire NN13 5JS
☎ Brackley (01280) 704843
*1000-acre mixed farm. Grade II listed
farmhouse, overlooking a colourful
garden including a covered heated
swimming pool. Situated in the centre
of Westbury village.*
Bedrooms: 1 single, 1 double,
1 triple
Bathrooms: 1 en-suite, 2 private,
1 public

Bed & breakfast

per night:	£min	£max
Single	20.00	25.00
Double	38.00	45.00

Half board per

person:	£min	£max
Daily	30.00	40.00

Evening meal 1930 (last orders
2130)
Parking for 6

A key to symbols can be
found inside the back
cover flap.

WICKHAM

Hampshire
Map ref 2C3

Lying in the Meon Valley, this market
town is built around the Square and
in Bridge Street can be seen some
timber-framed cottages. Still the site
of an annual horse fair.

Chiphall Acre Ⓜ

▥▥ COMMENDED

Droxford Road, Wickham, Fareham
PO17 5AY
☎ (01329) 833188 & 662182
Fax (01329) 664680

*Ancient market village, in unspoilt
Meon Valley. Delightful house with
beautiful gardens. (Gravel
Drive-Wickham side of Roebuck Inn on
A32).*
Bedrooms: 1 double, 1 twin, 1 triple
Bathrooms: 3 en-suite, 1 public

Bed & breakfast

per night:	£min	£max
Single	20.00	30.00
Double	40.00	45.00

Evening meal 1800 (last orders
2000)
Parking for 3

Montrose Ⓜ

▥▥ HIGHLY COMMENDED

Solomons Lane, Shirrell Heath,
Southampton SO32 2HU
☎ (01329) 833345
*Attractive, comfortable accommodation
in lovely Meon Valley, offering personal
attention. Equidistant from main towns
and convenient for continental ferries
and motorway links.*
Bedrooms: 2 double, 1 twin
Bathrooms: 1 en-suite, 1 public

Bed & breakfast

per night:	£min	£max
Single	23.00	28.00
Double	42.00	48.00

Parking for 6
Cards accepted: Access, Visa

WIMBORNE MINSTER

Dorset
Map ref 2B3

Market town centred on the twin-towered Minster Church of St Cuthberga which gave the town the second part of its name. Good touring base for the surrounding countryside, depicted in the writings of Thomas Hardy.
Tourist Information Centre ☎ (01202) 886116

Acacia House

👑👑 HIGHLY COMMENDED

2 Oakley Road, Wimborne Minster
BH21 1QJ
☎ Bournemouth (01202) 883958
Fax (01202) 881943

Beautifully decorated rooms are what the discerning traveller expects. What comes as a surprise is Eveline Stimpson's tea and cake welcome.
Bedrooms: 1 single, 1 double, 1 twin, 1 triple
Bathrooms: 2 en-suite, 1 private, 1 public

Bed & breakfast per night:	£min	£max
Single	17.00	25.00
Double	38.00	40.00

Parking for 3

🎠🖥️📞📺♿🆔🛏️🔒✂️🛏️🖊️❄️✗🐾

Ashton Lodge

👑👑 COMMENDED

10 Oakley Hill, Wimborne Minster
BH21 1QH
☎ Bournemouth (01202) 883423
Fax (01202) 886180
Large, detached, family house, with attractive gardens and relaxed, friendly atmosphere. Off-street parking available. Payphone. Children welcome.
Bedrooms: 1 single, 1 twin, 2 triple
Bathrooms: 2 en-suite, 2 public

Bed & breakfast per night:	£min	£max
Single	18.50	
Double	40.00	

Parking for 4

🎠🖥️📞♿🆔🛏️🔒✂️🛏️📺🖊️♨️❄️✗🐾

Northill House 🏔️

👑👑👑 COMMENDED

Horton, Wimborne Minster
BH21 7HL
☎ Witchampton (01258) 840407

Mid-Victorian former farmhouse, modernised to provide comfortable bedrooms, all en-suite. Log fires and cooking using fresh produce. Ideal touring centre.
Wheelchair access category 1♿
Bedrooms: 5 double, 3 twin, 1 triple
Bathrooms: 9 en-suite

Bed & breakfast per night:	£min	£max
Single	39.00	39.00
Double	69.00	69.00

Half board per person:	£min	£max
Daily	48.50	48.50
Weekly	305.55	305.55

Evening meal 1930 (last orders 1830)
Parking for 12
Open February–December
Cards accepted: Access, Visa, Amex

🎠🖥️8♿📞📼🖥️♿🆔🔒🛏️♨️🛏️📧✂️❄️✗🐾 SP T

Twynham

Listed

67 Poole Road, Wimborne Minster
BH21 1QB
☎ Wimborne (01202) 887310
Friendly, family home, recently refurbished, with vanity unit, TV and beverages in rooms. Within walking distance of town centre.
Bedrooms: 2 double
Bathrooms: 2 public

Bed & breakfast per night:	£min	£max
Single	15.00	18.00
Double	30.00	34.00

Parking for 2

🎠🖥️📞♿📼🆔✂️🛏️❄️✗🐾

WINCHESTER

Hampshire
Map ref 2C3

King Alfred the Great made Winchester the capital of Saxon England. A magnificent Norman cathedral, with one of the longest naves in Europe, dominates the city. Home of Winchester College founded in 1382.
Tourist Information Centre ☎ (01962) 840500 or 848180

Cathedral View 🏔️

👑👑 COMMENDED

9A Magdalen Hill, Winchester
SO23 0HJ
☎ (01962) 863802
Guesthouse with views across historic city and cathedral. 5 minutes' walk from city centre. En-suite facilities, TV, parking.
Bedrooms: 3 double, 1 twin, 1 family room
Bathrooms: 3 en-suite, 2 private

Bed & breakfast per night:	£min	£max
Single	30.00	35.00
Double	40.00	45.00

Parking for 4

🎠🖥️♿🖐️🆔🔒✂️🛏️📺🖊️♨️❄️✗🐾

85 Christchurch Road 🏔️

👑👑 COMMENDED

Winchester SO23 9QY
☎ (01962) 868661
Fax (01962) 868661
Comfortable, friendly Victorian family house in St Cross, Winchester. Ideal for exploring city and Hampshire. Off-street parking. Non-smokers only, please.
Bedrooms: 1 single, 1 double, 1 twin
Bathrooms: 2 en-suite, 2 public

Bed & breakfast per night:	£min	£max
Single	19.00	22.00
Double	36.00	42.00

Parking for 3

🎠🖥️♿🆔🔒✂️🛏️🖊️♨️✗🐾

The Farrells 🏔️

👑👑 COMMENDED

5 Ranelagh Road, St Cross, Winchester SO23 9TA
☎ (01962) 869555
A warm welcome awaits you at this comfortable Victorian house close to city centre, St Cross Hospital and water meadows.
Bedrooms: 2 double, 1 twin
Bathrooms: 1 en-suite, 1 private, 2 public

Bed & breakfast per night:	£min	£max
Single	18.00	24.00
Double	34.00	40.00

Parking for 2

🐎⛔📺♿🔌🔒⬇📺📺💻✕🐾

32 Hyde Street

APPROVED

Winchester SO23 7DX
☎ (01962) 851621
Attractive 18th C town house close to city centre and recreational amenities.
Bedrooms: 1 double, 1 triple
Bathrooms: 1 public

Bed & breakfast per night:	£min	£max
Single	18.00	20.00
Double	30.00	32.00

🐎3⛔📺♿🔌✕📺💻✕🐾

Ivy House

Listed HIGHLY COMMENDED

45 Vernham Road, Greenacres,
Winchester SO22 6BS
☎ (01962) 855512
Situated in quiet residential road, 5 minutes' drive from city centre. Family-run house, decorated and furnished to a high standard. Two-night weekend break available at £55 per person.
Bedrooms: 1 single, 1 double, 1 twin
Bathrooms: 1 public

Bed & breakfast per night:	£min	£max
Single	17.50	
Double	35.00	

Parking for 3

🐎12⛔📺♿🔌📺📺✕📺💻❋✕🐾

44 Kilham Lane **A**

COMMENDED

Winchester SO22 5PT
☎ (01962) 852259 & Mobile (0585) 462993

Detached property in quiet and peaceful area, three-quarters of a mile from city centre. Close to Farley Mount country walking park.
Bedrooms: 1 double, 2 twin
Bathrooms: 2 en-suite, 1 private, 1 public

Bed & breakfast per night:	£min	£max
Single	20.00	25.00
Double	34.00	40.00

Parking for 4
Open March–October

🐎10♿🔌📺📺📺✕📺💻📺🐾✕🐾🐴

54 St Cross Road

Listed COMMENDED

Winchester SO23 9PS
☎ (01962) 852073
Fax (01962) 852073
Victorian family house, with warm, welcoming atmosphere. Close to water meadows and 10 minutes' walk from city centre.
Bedrooms: 1 single, 1 double, 1 twin
Bathrooms: 1 public

Bed & breakfast per night:	£min	£max
Single	18.00	20.00
Double	34.00	36.00

Parking for 2

🐎2⛔📺♿🔌📺📺✕💻📺✕🐾 SP

67 St Cross Road

COMMENDED

Winchester SO23 9RE
☎ (01962) 863002
Fax (01962) 863002
Large, terraced town house, with comfortable rooms, good food and a friendly atmosphere.
Bedrooms: 1 double, 1 family room
Bathrooms: 1 public

Bed & breakfast per night:	£min	£max
Double	32.00	34.00

🐎4⛔📺♿🔌📺📺💻✕🐾

St Margaret's

Listed COMMENDED

3 St Michael's Road, Winchester
SO23 9JE
☎ (01962) 861450
Light and comfortable rooms in Victorian house, conveniently situated near city centre and cathedral.
Bedrooms: 1 double, 1 twin
Bathrooms: 2 public

Bed & breakfast per night:	£min	£max
Double	36.00	36.00

Parking for 2

🐎4⛔📺♿📺✕💻✕🐾

> The symbols in each entry give information about services and facilities. A 'key' to these symbols appears at the back of this guide.

Shawlands **A**

COMMENDED

46 Kilham Lane, Winchester
SO22 5QD
☎ (01962) 861166
Fax (01962) 861166

Attractive, modern house, situated in a quiet, elevated position overlooking open countryside. Delightful garden. 1.5 miles from city centre.
Wheelchair access category 3🚶
Bedrooms: 2 double, 2 twin, 1 triple
Bathrooms: 1 private, 3 public

Bed & breakfast per night:	£min	£max
Single	22.00	25.00
Double	35.00	40.00

Parking for 4

🐎♿📺♿🔌📺📺📺✕💻📺✕🐾

Stratton House **A**

Stratton Road, St Giles Hill,
Winchester SO23 0JQ
☎ (01962) 863919 & 864529
Fax (01962) 842095
Lovely old Victorian house with an acre of grounds, in an elevated position on St Giles Hill.
Bedrooms: 1 single, 3 double, 2 twin, 1 triple
Bathrooms: 6 en-suite, 1 private

Bed & breakfast per night:	£min	£max
Single	22.00	30.00
Double	44.00	50.00

Half board per person:	£min	£max
Daily	29.00	37.00
Weekly	199.00	249.00

Evening meal 1800 (last orders 1600)
Parking for 8
Cards accepted: Access, Visa, Switch/Delta

🐎⛔📺♿📺📺✕📺💻✕📺💻❋✕🐾 DAP SP 🏠 T

> The **A** symbol after an establishment name indicates that it is a Regional Tourist Board member.

WINDSOR

Berkshire
Map ref 2D2

Town dominated by the spectacular castle, home of the Royal Family for over 900 years. Parts are open to the public. There are many attractions including the Great Park, Eton and trips on the river.
Tourist Information Centre ☎ (01753) 852010

Alma House

Listed

56 Alma Road, Windsor SL4 3HA
☎ (01753) 862983 & 855620
Fax (01753) 855620
Elegant, family-run Victorian house within 5 minutes' walk of castle, town centre, river and parks. Internationally known.
Bedrooms: 1 single, 1 triple, 2 family rooms
Bathrooms: 1 en-suite, 1 public
Bed & breakfast

per night:	£min	£max
Single	27.00	40.00
Double	36.00	47.00

Parking for 5

Chasela

Listed

30 Convent Road, Windsor SL4 3RB
☎ (01753) 860410
Warm, modern house 1 mile from the castle. Easy access M4, M40, M25, M3, Heathrow. TV, tea/coffee facilities in rooms. Breakfast room overlooks lovely garden. Payphone.
Bedrooms: 1 single, 1 twin
Bathrooms: 1 public
Bed & breakfast

per night:	£min	£max
Single	16.00	20.00
Double	32.00	40.00

Parking for 5

Clarence Hotel

Listed **COMMENDED**

9 Clarence Road, Windsor SL4 5AE
☎ (01753) 864436
Fax (01753) 857060
Comfortable hotel with licensed bar and steam room, near town centre, castle and Eton. All rooms en-suite, TV, hairdryer, radio and tea-maker. Convenient for Heathrow Airport.
Bedrooms: 4 single, 4 double, 7 twin, 4 triple, 2 family rooms
Bathrooms: 21 en-suite, 1 public

Bed & breakfast

per night:	£min	£max
Single	35.00	40.00
Double	39.00	52.00

Parking for 4
Cards accepted: Access, Visa, Diners, Amex, Switch/Delta

Halcyon House

COMMENDED

131 Clarence Road, Windsor
SL4 5AR
☎ (01753) 863262
Fax (01753) 863262
A warm welcome at a family-run guesthouse, 10 minutes' walk from the town centre and river. Ideal base for London. Off-street parking.
Bedrooms: 2 double, 2 twin
Bathrooms: 3 en-suite, 1 private, 1 public
Bed & breakfast

per night:	£min	£max
Single	29.00	39.00
Double	39.00	45.00

Parking for 6

Tanglewood

Listed **HIGHLY COMMENDED**

Oakley Green, Windsor SL4 4PZ
☎ (01753) 860034
Picturesque chalet-style guesthouse in beautiful garden. Rural area overlooking open fields on B3024. Windsor 10 minutes' drive, Heathrow 15 miles. Excellent meals at nearby pub.
Bedrooms: 2 twin
Bathrooms: 1 public
Bed & breakfast

per night:	£min	£max
Double	38.00	38.00

Parking for 2
Open May–September

WITNEY

Oxfordshire
Map ref 2C1

Town famous for its blanket-making and mentioned in the Domesday Book. The market-place contains the Butter Cross, a medieval meeting place, and there is a green with merchants' houses.
Tourist Information Centre ☎ (01993) 775802

Field View

HIGHLY COMMENDED

Wood Green, Witney OX8 6DE
☎ (01993) 705485 & Mobile (0468) 614347
Situated in 2 acres on edge of the bustling market town of Witney. Ideal for Oxford University and the Cotswolds.
Bedrooms: 1 double, 2 twin
Bathrooms: 3 en-suite
Bed & breakfast

per night:	£min	£max
Single	25.00	25.00
Double	40.00	44.00

Parking for 10

Quarrydene

17 Dene Rise, Witney OX8 5LU
☎ (01993) 772152 & Mobile 0850 054786
My 1930s detached home will give you a friendly welcome. A few minutes' walk from town centre, but in a very quiet cul de sac. Good location for Oxford/Cotswolds/Stratford.
Bedrooms: 2 single, 1 double, 1 twin
Bathrooms: 1 en-suite, 2 public
Bed & breakfast

per night:	£min	£max
Single	16.00	19.00
Double	32.00	36.00

Half board per person:	£min	£max
Daily	20.00	24.00
Weekly	140.00	168.00

Parking for 2

WOODCOTE

Oxfordshire
Map ref 2C2

Hedges

COMMENDED

South Stoke Road, Woodcote, Reading, Berkshire RG8 0PL
☎ Checkendon (01491) 680461
Comfortable family house in rural situation on edge of village. Area of

Outstanding Natural Beauty. Reading 10 miles, Oxford 18 miles. Easy access to London and M4.
Bedrooms: 2 single, 2 twin
Bathrooms: 1 private, 2 public
Bed & breakfast

per night:	£min	£max
Single	15.00	17.50
Double	30.00	35.00

Parking for 3
🛞🖵🖤ⓊⓁ🏵🖩🖵☀🚐

WOODSTOCK

Oxfordshire
Map ref 2C1

Small country town clustered around the park gates of Blenheim Palace, the superb 18th C home of the Duke of Marlborough. The town has well-known inns and an interesting museum. Sir Winston Churchill was born and buried nearby.
Tourist Information Centre ☎ (01993) 811038

Gorselands Farmhouse Auberge ᐱ
⌃
Boddington Lane, Long Hanborough, Witney OX8 6PU
☎ Freeland (01993) 881895
Fax (01993) 882799

Stone country farmhouse with exposed beams, snooker room, conservatory. Convenient for Blenheim Palace, Oxford and Cotswold villages. Evening meals available. Licensed for wine and beer. Grass tennis court.
Bedrooms: 1 single, 2 double, 1 twin, 2 family rooms
Suite available
Bathrooms: 6 en-suite
Bed & breakfast

per night:	£min	£max
Single	21.00	29.00
Double	35.00	42.00

Half board per

person:	£min	£max
Daily	27.45	38.95
Weekly	179.00	250.00

Evening meal 1900 (last orders 2100)
Parking for 7
Cards accepted: Access, Visa, Amex
🛞🖧🖵🖤🅢🖅🏵ⓉⓋ◐🖩🖵🔍
🔍☀🚐🆂🅿🏵Ⓣ

The Kings Head Inn
👑👑👑 COMMENDED
Chapel Hill, Wootton, Woodstock, Oxford OX20 1DX
☎ Witney (01993) 811340
Fax (01993) 811340
15th C Cotswold village inn with individually appointed cottage style rooms and acclaimed restaurant and bar serving freshly prepared food with fish specialities. Two miles north of Woodstock.
Bedrooms: 3 double
Suites available
Bathrooms: 3 en-suite
Bed & breakfast

per night:	£min	£max
Single	30.00	49.95
Double	50.00	80.00

Half board per

person:	£min	£max
Daily	40.00	58.00
Weekly	250.00	385.00

Lunch available
Evening meal 1900 (last orders 2200)
Parking for 8
Cards accepted: Access, Visa, Switch/Delta
🛞10🖧🗖🍴🖵🖤🅹🖩🖵🔍☀
🐾🚐ᴰᴬᴾ🏵🆂🅿Ⓣ

The Laurels
👑👑 HIGHLY COMMENDED
Hensington Road, Woodstock OX20 1JL
☎ (01993) 812583
Fax (01993) 812583
Fine Victorian house, charmingly furnished with an emphasis on comfort and quality. Just off town centre and a short walk from Blenheim Palace.
Bedrooms: 2 double, 1 twin
Bathrooms: 2 en-suite, 1 private
Bed & breakfast

per night:	£min	£max
Single	30.00	40.00
Double	36.00	46.00

Parking for 3
Cards accepted: Access, Visa, Switch/Delta
🛞7🖵🖤ⓊⓁ🅢🖅🖹🖩🐾🚐ᴰᴬᴾⓉ

Plane Tree House
👑
15 High Street, Woodstock, Oxford OX20 1TE
☎ (01993) 813075
Located in Woodstock town centre, 2 minutes' from Blenheim Palace. Ideal base for touring the Cotswolds.
Bedrooms: 1 double, 1 twin, 1 triple
Bathrooms: 1 public
Bed & breakfast

per night:	£min	£max
Double		35.00

🛞🖵🖤ⓊⓁ🅢🖅🖹ⓉⓋ🖩🐾🚐

Punch Bowl Inn ᐱ
Listed APPROVED
12 Oxford Street, Woodstock, Oxford OX20 1TR
☎ (01993) 811218
Fax (01993) 811393
Family-run pub in the centre of Woodstock, close to Blenheim Palace. A good touring centre for Oxford and the Cotswolds.
Bedrooms: 2 single, 5 double, 2 twin, 2 family rooms
Bathrooms: 3 en-suite, 3 public
Bed & breakfast

per night:	£min	£max
Single	28.00	32.00
Double	38.00	42.00

Lunch available
Evening meal 1800 (last orders 2130)
Parking for 20
Cards accepted: Access, Visa, Amex, Switch/Delta
🛞🖧🖵🖤🅸🅢🖅🖩🖵🖤🏵🖦Ⓣ

The Ridings
👑👑 COMMENDED
32 Banbury Road, Woodstock OX20 1LQ
☎ (01993) 811269
Detached house in a quiet, rural setting. 10 minutes' walk to town centre and Blenheim Palace. Go past the Tourist Information Centre for 300 yards then take left fork.
Bedrooms: 1 double, 2 twin
Bathrooms: 1 en-suite, 1 public
Bed & breakfast

per night:	£min	£max
Single	30.00	30.00
Double	38.00	42.00

Parking for 4
🛞🗖🖵🖤ⓊⓁ🖅🖹ⓉⓋ🖩☀🐾🚐

Shepherds Hall Inn
👑👑
Witney Road, Freeland, Witney OX8 8HQ
☎ Freeland (01993) 881256
Well-appointed inn offering good accommodation. All rooms en-suite. Ideally situated for Oxford, Woodstock and the Cotswolds, on the A4095 Woodstock to Witney road.
Bedrooms: 1 single, 1 double, 2 twin, 1 triple
Bathrooms: 5 en-suite
Bed & breakfast

per night:	£min	£max
Single	25.00	30.00
Double	38.50	45.00

Lunch available
Evening meal 1900 (last orders 2200)
Parking for 50
Cards accepted: Access, Visa
🛞📞🗖🖵🖤🍴🅸🖩🔍☀🚐

COUNTRY CODE

Always follow the Country Code
🌱 Enjoy the countryside and respect its life and work 🌱 Guard against all risk of fire 🌱 Fasten all gates 🌱 Keep your dogs under close control 🌱 Keep to public paths across farmland 🌱 Use gates and stiles to cross fences, hedges and walls 🌱 Leave livestock, crops and machinery alone 🌱 Take your litter home 🌱 Help to keep all water clean 🌱 Protect wildlife, plants and trees 🌱 Take special care on country roads 🌱 Make no unnecessary noise

CHECK THE MAPS

The colour maps at the back of this guide show all the cities, towns and villages for which you will find accommodation entries.

Refer to the town index to find the page on which it is listed.

USE YOUR *i*'s

There are more than 550 Tourist Information Centres throughout England offering friendly help with accommodation and holiday ideas as well as suggestions of places to visit and things to do. You'll find the address of your nearest Tourist Information Centre in your local Phone Book.

SOUTH EAST ENGLAND

South East England conjures up images of cricket on the village green, traditional village pubs and Sussex cream teas with lashings of home-made jam!

The beauty is, the fantasy is reality. South East England truly is unspoilt.

Visit Kent, the Garden of England, with its oasthouses, abundant vineyards, fruitful orchards and pretty weatherboard cottages.

Wander across the glorious South Downs, the heathland of Surrey, or head for Dover's white cliffs or the buzz of Regency Brighton.

Explore the medieval Cinque Ports and the region's churches, castles, manor houses and gardens. It's all here. As it has been for centuries.

FOR MORE INFORMATION CONTACT:
South East England Tourist Board,
The Old Brew House, Warwick Park,
Tunbridge Wells, Kent TN2 5TU
Tel: (01892) 540766 **Fax:** (01892) 511008

Where to Go in South East England -
see pages 350-353
Where to Stay in South East England -
see pages 354-380

SOUTH EAST ENGLAND

Where to Go and What to See

You will find hundreds of interesting places to visit during your stay in South East England, just some of which are listed in these pages. The number against each name will help you locate it on the map (page 353). Contact any Tourist Information Centre in the region for more ideas on days out in South East England.

1 Royal Engineers Museum
Prince Arthur Road,
Gillingham,
Kent ME4 4UG
Tel: (01634) 406397
The characters, lives and work of Britain's soldier-engineers 1066-1945. Medals, uniforms, scientific and technical equipement. Collection of ethnography and decorative arts.

2 The Historic Dockyard
Chatham, Kent ME4 4TE
Tel: (01634) 812551
Historic 18thC 80 acre dockyard. Museum with seven major attractions including the award-winning 'Wooden Walls' gallery, sail and colour loft, working ropery.

3 Brogdale Horticultural Trust
Brogdale Farm,
Brogdale Road,
Faversham, Kent ME13 8XZ
Tel: (01795) 535286
National Fruit Collection with 4,000

varieties of fruit in 30 acres of orchards: apples, pears, cherries, plums, currants, quinces, medlars and other fruits.

4 Belmont
Belmont Park,
Throwley,
Kent ME13 0HH
Tel: (01795) 890202
Late 18thC country mansion designed by Samuel Wyatt, seat of the Harris family since 1801. Harris clock collection, mementoes of connections with India. Gardens and pinetum.

5 Leeds Castle
Leeds, Maidstone,
Kent ME17 1PL
Tel: (01622) 765400
Castle on two islands in lake dating from 12thC. Furniture, tapestries, art treasures. Dog Collar Museum. Gardens, parkland, duckery, aviaries, maze, grotto, small vineyard, greenhouses.

6 The Royal Horticultural Society's Garden
Wisley, Surrey GU23 6QB
Tel: (01483) 224234
World famous RHS garden covering 250 acres of vegetable, fruit and ornamental gardening. Trial grounds, glasshouses, rock garden, ponds. Rose, model and specialist gardens.

7 Guildford Boat House River Trips
Millbrook, Guildford,
Surrey GU1 3XJ
Tel: (01483) 504494
Regular trips from Guildford to St. Catherine's Lock and Farncombe along River Wey. Also 'Alfred Leroy' cruising restaurant. Rowing boats and canoes.

8 Guildford Cathedral
Stag Hill, Guildford,
Surrey GU2 5UP
Tel: (01483) 565287
New Anglican cathedral, foundation

stone laid 1936 and consecrated 1961. Notable glass engravings, embroidered kneelers. Modern furnishings. Brass Rubbing Centre.

9 Loseley House and Park Farm
Loseley Park,
Guildford,
Surrey GU3 1HS
Tel: (01483) 304440
Elizabethan mansion with decorated ceilings, unusual chalk fireplace, period furniture and paintings. Parkland and farm with famous Jersey cows, rare breeds and trailer tours.

10 Denbies Wine Estate
London Road, Dorking,
Surrey RH5 6AA
Tel: (01306) 876616
England's largest wine estate, 250 acres in beautiful countryside. Winery and visitor centre featuring 3-D time-lapse film of vine growing. Viewing and picture galleries.

11 Birdworld and Underwaterworld
Holt Pound, Farnham,
Surrey GU10 4LD
Tel: (01420) 22140
20 acres of garden and parkland with ostriches, flamingoes, hornbills, parrots, emus, pelicans etc. Penguin island, tropical and marine fish. Plant area, seashore walk.

12 Hever Castle and Gardens
Hever, Edenbridge,
Kent TN8 7NG
Tel: (01732) 865224
Moated castle, family home of Anne Boleyn. Restored by Astor family. Fine interior, furniture, paintings and panelling. Gardens, lake, topiary, maze, miniature model houses exhibition.

13 Headcorn Flower Centre and Vineyard
Grigg Lane, Headcorn,
Ashford, Kent TN27 9LX
Tel: (01622) 890250
Walk around 6 acres of vines. Reservoir with wildlife. Weekend and group tours visit flowerhouses with chrysanthemums and orchid lilies flowering all year.

14 Dover Castle and Hellfire Corner
Dover, Kent CT16 1HU
Tel: (01304) 201628
One of the most powerful medieval fortresses in Western Europe. St Mary-in-Castro Saxon church. Roman lighthouse, Hellfire Corner, 'All The Queen's Men' exhibition.

15 Groombridge Place Gardens
Groombridge,
Royal Tunbridge Wells,
Kent TN3 9QG
Tel: (01892) 863999

Grade I listed 17thC restored walled gardens. Drunken topiary garden, oriental and sculpture gardens, ancient and mystical woodland with spring-fed pools.

16 Bedgebury National Pinetum
Goudhurst, Kent TN17 2SL
Tel: (01580) 211044
The Forestry Commission's superb collection of specimen conifers in 150 acres with lake and streams. Plus many rhododendrons and azaleas.

17 Leonardslee Gardens
Lower Beeding,
West Sussex RH13 6PP
Tel: (01403) 891212
Rhododendrons and azaleas in a peaceful 240-acre valley garden with seven beautiful lakes. Rock garden, Bonsai exhibition and wallabies.

18 The Bluebell Railway
Sheffield Park,
East Sussex TN22 3QL
Tel: (01825) 722370
9 miles of vintage steam and train railway from Sheffield Park to Horsted Keynes and extension to Kingscote. Largest collection of engines in the south. Victorian stations and museum.

19 Brickwall House and Gardens
Northiam,
East Sussex TN31 6NL
Tel: (01797) 223329
Formal gardens with terracotta entrance gates, 18thC bowling alley, sunken topiary garden, yew hedges, chess garden, arboretum. Jacobean house with 17thC plaster ceilings.

20 Great Dixter House and Gardens
Northiam,
East Sussex TN31 6PH
Tel: (01797) 253107
Fine example of 15thC manor house with antique furniture and needlework. Unique great hall restored by Lutyens who also designed garden – topiary, meadow garden, flower beds.

21 Buckleys Yesterday's World
89-90 High Street, Battle,
East Sussex TN33 0AQ
Tel: (01424) 775378
Over 100,000 exhibits in a Wealden hall house recall shopping and domestic life from 1850 to 1950 with smells and commentaries. Railway station, play village, garden.

22 A Smugglers Adventure At St. Clements Caves
West Hill, Hastings,
East Sussex TN34 3HY
Tel: (01424) 422964
An extensive exhibition of 18thC smuggling, housed in 2000 sq m of caves. Exhibition, museum, video theatre, extensive Adventure Walk incorporating dramatic special effects.

23 Brighton Sea Life Centre
Marine Parade,
Brighton,
East Sussex BN2 1TB
Tel: (01273) 604234
Discover the thrilling world beneath the waves as the Brighton Sea Life Centre takes you on an unforgettable voyage of discovery.

24 Foredown Tower Countryside Centre
Foredown Road, Portslade,
East Sussex BN41 2EW
Tel: (01273) 422540
Water tower housing a camera obscura, an unusual viewing device used by artists and astronomers since the 17thC. Popular entertainment in Victorian times.

25 Charleston Farmhouse
Firle, Lewes, East Sussex BN8 6LL
Tel: (01323) 811265
A 17-18thC farmhouse, home of Vanessa and Clive Bell and Duncan Grant. House and contents decorated by the artists. Restored garden room. Traditional flint-walled garden.

26 Amberley Museum
Houghton Bridge, Amberley,
Arundel, West Sussex BN18 9LT
Tel: (01798) 831370
Open-air industrial history centre in chalk quarry. Working craftsmen, narrow gauge railway, early buses, working machines and many other exhibits. Nature trail and visitor centre.

27 The Wildfowl and Wetlands Centre
Mill Road, Arundel,
West Sussex BN18 9PB
Tel: (01903) 883355
Reserve in 60 acres of watermeadows. Tame swans, ducks, geese and many wild birds. Film theatre and visitor centre with gallery.

28 Weald and Downland Open Air Museum
Singleton,
West Sussex PO18 0EU
Tel: (01243) 811348
Open-air museum of rescued historic buildings from South East England reconstructed on downland. 35 buildings include medieval farmstead and watermill.

29 Pallant House
9 North Pallant, Chichester,
West Sussex PO19 1TJ
Tel: (01243) 774557
Queen Anne townhouse with important works by British and European masters of the 20thC. Antiques include the world's greatest collection of Bow porcelain.

A map of South East England showing the counties of Bucks, Berks, Greater London, Essex, Surrey, Kent, West Sussex and East Sussex, with numbered attraction locations and town names.

Town and place names shown on the map include:

ESSEX · **BUCKS** · **GREATER LONDON** · **BERKS**

Gravesend · Gillingham · Herne Bay · Margate · Dartford · Rochester · Whitstable · Broadstairs · Ramsgate · Chatham · Sittingbourne · Faversham · Sandwich · Walton-on-Thames · Sevenoaks · Canterbury · Deal · Weybridge · Epsom · Maidstone · Throwley · Woking · Leatherhead · Wisley · Warlingham · Oxted · **KENT** · Reigate · Paddock Wood · Headcorn · Guildford · Dorking · Horley · Edenbridge · Ashford · Farnham · **SURREY** · Royal Tunbridge Wells · Cranbrook · Dover · Cranleigh · Crawley · Groombridge · Goudhurst · Tenterden · Folkestone · Haslemere · Horsham · Crowborough · Northiam · Hythe · **WEST SUSSEX** · Lower Beeding · **EAST SUSSEX** · New Romney · Midhurst · Haywards Heath · Sheffield Park · Heathfield · Singleton · Storrington · Cuckfield · Uckfield · Battle · Burgess Hill · Firle · Hailsham · Hastings · Arundel · Portslade · Bexhill-on-Sea · Shoreham · Brighton · Pevensey · Chichester · Worthing · Newhaven · Eastbourne · Birdham · Bognor Regis · Seaford · Earnley

0 ——— 20 Miles
0 ——— 30 Kms

---

30 Earnley Butterflies and Gardens

133 Almodington Lane, Earnley,
West Sussex PO20 7JR
Tel: (01243) 512637
*Ornamental butterfly house,
covered theme gardens from
around the world, exotic bird
garden, children's play area, small
animal farm and pottery.*

31 Sussex Falconry Centre

Locksacre Aquatic Nursery,
Wophams Lane, Birdham,
West Sussex PO20 7BS
Tel: (01243) 512472
*Aviaries containing birds of prey
including hawks, falcons and owls.
Flying displays of birds throughout
the day, weather permitting.*

FIND OUT MORE

Further information about
holidays and attractions in South
East England is available from:
**South East England
Tourist Board,**
The Old Brew House,
Warwick Park,
Tunbridge Wells,
Kent TN2 5TU.
Tel: (01892) 540766

These publications are available
free from the South East England
Tourist Board:

■ **Great Escapes**
■ **Accommodation Guide**
■ **Events South East**
■ **Bed and Breakfast Touring
Map**

■ **Outstanding Churches and
Cathedrals**

Also available is (price includes
postage and packaging):
■ **South East England Leisure
Map** *£4*
■ **Hundreds of Place to Visit
in the South East** *£2.80*
■ **Villages to Visit** *£2.50*

WHERE TO STAY (SOUTH EAST ENGLAND)

Accommodation entries in this region are listed in alphabetical order of place name, and then in alphabetical order of establishment.

Map references refer to the colour location maps at the back of this guide. The first number indicates the map to use; the letter and number which follow refer to the grid reference on the map.

At-a-glance symbols at the end of each accommodation entry give useful information about services and facilities. A key to symbols can be found inside the back cover flap. Keep this open for easy reference.

ALDINGTON

Kent
Map ref 3B4

Once the home of Elizabeth Barton, the "Holy Maid" or "Nun of Kent".

Hogben Farm

Listed COMMENDED

Church Lane, Aldington, Ashford
TN25 7EH
☎ (01233) 720219
Small 16th C country house, surrounded by pretty garden and 17 acres of farmland. Convenient for Channel ports, Channel Tunnel, Canterbury, Rye, Tenterden and Romney Marsh. Evening meals by prior arrangement.
Bedrooms: 1 double, 2 twin
Bathrooms: 1 en-suite, 1 private, 1 public, 1 private shower

Bed & breakfast

per night:	£min	£max
Single	19.50	21.50
Double	39.00	43.00

Half board per person:	£min	£max
Daily	29.50	31.50
Weekly	177.00	189.00

Evening meal 1800 (last orders 2000)
Parking for 6

A key to symbols can be found inside the back cover flap.

ARDINGLY

West Sussex
Map ref 2D3

Famous for the South of England Agricultural Showground with its famous antique fairs and the public school. Nearby is Wakehurst Place (National Trust), the gardens of which are administered by the Royal Botanic Gardens, Kew.

Jordans

COMMENDED

Church Lane, Ardingly, Haywards Heath RH17 6UP
☎ (01444) 892681
Fax (01444) 414269
Victorian country house set in beautiful gardens opposite medieval village church. Behind South of England Showground, close to many facilities and 20 minutes from Gatwick.
Bedrooms: 1 single, 1 twin
Bathrooms: 1 public

Bed & breakfast

per night:	£min	£max
Single	23.00	25.00
Double	38.00	40.00

Parking for 5

Information on accommodation listed in this guide has been supplied by the proprietors. As changes may occur you are advised to check details at the time of booking.

ARUNDEL

West Sussex
Map ref 2D3

Picturesque, historic town on the River Arun, dominated by Arundel Castle, home of the Dukes of Norfolk. There are many 18th C houses, the Toy and Military Museum, Wildfowl and Wetlands Centre and Museum and Heritage Centre.
Tourist Information Centre ☎ (01903) 882268

Arundel Vineyards

COMMENDED

The Vineyard, Church Lane, Lyminster, Arundel BN17 7QF
☎ (01903) 883393
3-acre vineyard & grazing farm. Modern farmhouse in English vineyard in beautiful countryside. From Arundel, turn south on to A284 Littlehampton/Lyminster road (new split junction). Signposted 1 mile on right.
Bedrooms: 1 double, 1 twin
Bathrooms: 2 en-suite

Bed & breakfast

per night:	£min	£max
Single	24.00	
Double	36.00	38.00

Parking for 15

Mill Lane House

COMMENDED

Slindon, Arundel BN18 0RP
☎ Slindon (01243) 814440
17th C house in beautiful National Trust village. Magnificent views to coast.

Pubs within easy walking distance. One mile from A29/A27 junction.
Wheelchair access category 3
Bedrooms: 1 single, 3 double, 2 twin, 1 triple
Suite available
Bathrooms: 7 en-suite, 1 public

Bed & breakfast per night:	£min	£max
Single	25.00	25.00
Double	38.50	38.50

Half board per person:	£min	£max
Daily	29.10	34.85
Weekly	189.45	228.95

Evening meal 1900 (last orders 1000)
Parking for 7

Pindars

HIGHLY COMMENDED
Lyminster, Arundel BN17 7QF
☎ (01903) 882628
Charming country house in small village offers comfortable bedrooms, good food and warm hospitality. Beautiful garden. Non-smoking. On A284 off A27.
Bedrooms: 2 double, 1 twin
Bathrooms: 1 en-suite, 1 public

Bed & breakfast per night:	£min	£max
Single	22.00	22.00
Double	32.00	42.00

Half board per person:	£min	£max
Daily	26.50	31.50

Evening meal from 1900
Parking for 7
Cards accepted: Access, Visa
10

ASHFORD

Kent
Map ref 3B4

Once a market centre for the farmers of the Weald of Kent and Romney Marsh. The town centre has a number of Tudor and Georgian houses.
Tourist Information Centre ☎ (01233) 629165

Fishponds Farm

Pilgrims Way, Brook, Ashford TN25 5PP
☎ (01233) 812398
Rural farmhouse with lake in Wye Downs Nature Reserve, 3 miles south-east of Wye on lane to Brabourne.
Bedrooms: 1 double, 1 twin
Bathrooms: 2 en-suite

Bed & breakfast per night:	£min	£max
Single	20.00	20.00
Double	32.00	32.00

Parking for 10

Goldwell Manor

Listed APPROVED
Great Chart, Ashford TN23 3BY
☎ (01233) 631495
Fax (01233) 631495
11th C manor house, listed in Domesday Book (1066), in countryside with exceptional views. 3 miles Ashford, 3 miles M20 junction 9. Short/long stay reductions available.
Bedrooms: 1 double, 1 twin, 1 triple
Bathrooms: 1 public

Bed & breakfast per night:	£min	£max
Single	16.00	20.00
Double	38.00	50.00

Parking for 14
1

Warren Cottage

APPROVED
136 The Street, Willesborough, Ashford TN24 0NB
☎ (01233) 621905 & 632929
Fax (01233) 623400

300-year-old guesthouse with oak beams, open fireplaces and a cosy atmosphere. On old coaching route with easy access to M20 and a short drive from many places of interest.
Email:
101666.571@compuserve.com.
Bedrooms: 2 single, 2 double
Bathrooms: 4 en-suite, 1 public

Bed & breakfast per night:	£min	£max
Single	25.00	29.90
Double	42.00	59.80

Half board per person:	£min	£max
Daily	35.00	39.90
Weekly	245.00	275.00

Lunch available
Evening meal 1830 (last orders 2130)
Parking for 13
Cards accepted: Access, Visa, Switch/Delta
20

AYLESFORD

Kent
Map ref 3B3

Wickham Lodge

COMMENDED
73 High Street, Aylesford ME20 7AY
☎ Maidstone (01622) 717267
Fax (01622) 718791
Period house fronting river by Aylesford Bridge. Lawns to river bank in front, walled garden to rear. Quiet position close to M2/M20 motorways. French spoken.
Bedrooms: 1 single, 1 double, 1 triple
Bathrooms: 2 en-suite, 1 private

Bed & breakfast per night:	£min	£max
Single	25.00	40.00
Double	45.00	50.00

Half board per person:	£min	£max
Daily	33.50	48.50
Weekly	234.50	339.50

Evening meal from 2000
Parking for 4
Cards accepted: Access, Visa

BATTLE

East Sussex
Map ref 3B4

The Abbey at Battle was built on the site of the Battle of Hastings, when William defeated Harold II and so became the Conqueror in 1066. The museum has a fine collection relating to the Sussex iron industry.
Tourist Information Centre ☎ (01424) 773721

Moons Hill Farm

COMMENDED
The Green, Ninfield, Battle TN33 9LH
☎ Ninfield (01424) 892645
10-acre mixed farm. Modernised farmhouse in Ninfield village centre, in the heart of "1066" country. A warm welcome and Sussex home cooking. Pub opposite.
Bedrooms: 1 double, 2 twin
Bathrooms: 3 en-suite, 1 public

Continued ▶

BATTLE
Continued

Bed & breakfast
per night:

	£min	£max
Single	15.00	20.00
Double	30.00	35.00

Parking for 12
Open January–November

Netherfield Hall M
COMMENDED

Netherfield, Battle TN33 9PQ
☎ (01424) 774450
Comfortable, spacious, character building in quiet, rural surroundings in historic area. Take A2100 from Battle to London. First turning on left to Netherfield. After 2 miles there is a church on the right and Netherfield Hall is opposite.
Bedrooms: 3 double
Bathrooms: 2 en-suite, 1 public, 1 private shower
Bed & breakfast
per night:

	£min	£max
Single	30.00	40.00
Double	40.00	50.00

Parking for 7
Open January, March–December

BIDDENDEN
Kent
Map ref 3B4

Perfect village with black and white houses, a tithe barn and a pond. Part of the village is grouped around a green with a village sign depicting the famous Biddenden Maids. It was an important centre of the Flemish weaving industry, hence the beautiful Old Cloth Hall.

Bettmans Oast M
HIGHLY COMMENDED

Hareplain Road, Biddenden, Ashford TN27 8LJ
☎ (01580) 291463
Grade II listed oast house and converted barn set in 10 acres near Sissinghurst Castle, a quarter of a mile from Three Chimneys pub. Lovely gardens and log fires in winter.
Bedrooms: 1 single, 1 twin, 1 family room
Bathrooms: 1 en-suite, 1 public
Bed & breakfast
per night:

	£min	£max
Single	20.00	20.00
Double	35.00	40.00

Half board per
person:

	£min	£max
Daily	27.50	30.00
Weekly	192.50	210.00

Evening meal 1900 (last orders 2100)
Parking for 4

BIRCHINGTON
Kent
Map ref 3C3

Town on the north coast of Kent with sandy beaches and rock pools. Powell Cotton Museum is in nearby Quex Park.

Elmstead M
HIGHLY COMMENDED

2 Kings Avenue, Minnis Bay, Birchington CT7 9QL
☎ Thanet (01843) 847407
Attractive accommodation overlooking Minnis Bay. Close to the ancient City of Canterbury, interesting towns, villages and coastlines. 2-night breaks available.
Bedrooms: 1 double, 1 twin
Bathrooms: 1 en-suite, 1 private
Bed & breakfast
per night:

	£min	£max
Single	15.00	18.00
Double	34.00	40.00

Evening meal 1830 (last orders 2030)
Parking for 2

Woodchurch Farmhouse
Listed COMMENDED

Woodchurch, Birchington CT7 0HE
☎ Thanet (01843) 832468
6-acre farm. This Elizabethan farmhouse provides a warm welcome and ensures a comfortable stay. An excellent base for exploring south-east Kent.
Bedrooms: 1 double, 2 twin
Bathrooms: 1 public
Bed & breakfast
per night:

	£min	£max
Single	15.00	15.00
Double	30.00	30.00

Parking for 6

All accommodation in this guide has been graded, or is awaiting a grading, by a trained Tourist Board inspector.

BIRLING GAP
East Sussex
Map ref 2D3

Birling Gap Hotel M
APPROVED

Birling Gap, Seven Sisters Cliffs, East Dean, Eastbourne, East Sussex BN20 0AB
☎ Eastbourne (01323) 423197
Fax (01323) 423030

Magnificent Seven Sisters clifftop position, with views of country, sea, beach. Superb downland and beach walks. Old world "Thatched Bar" and "Oak Room Restaurant". Coffee shop and games room, function and conference suite. Off A259 coast road at East Dean, 1.5 miles west of Beachy Head.
Bedrooms: 1 single, 2 double, 3 twin, 3 triple
Bathrooms: 9 en-suite, 1 public
Bed & breakfast
per night:

	£min	£max
Single	20.00	50.00
Double	30.00	60.00

Half board per
person:

	£min	£max
Daily	29.00	38.00
Weekly	183.00	245.00

Lunch available
Evening meal 1830 (last orders 2115)
Parking for 100
Cards accepted: Access, Visa, Diners, Amex, Switch/Delta

BOSHAM
West Sussex
Map ref 2C3

Village built on a piece of land jutting out into an inlet of Chichester Harbour, with Bosham Walk craft centre. A yachtsman's delight and the place where King Canute staged his confrontation with the tide.

Critchfield House
Listed HIGHLY COMMENDED

Bosham Lane, Bosham, Chichester PO18 8HG
☎ (01243) 572370

Charming period house in picturesque sailing village, within easy walking distance of harbour. Pretty bedrooms, beamed dining room with log fire.
Bedrooms: 1 double, 2 twin
Bathrooms: 2 en-suite, 1 private

Bed & breakfast

per night:	£min	£max
Single	25.00	35.00
Double	45.00	

Parking for 3
Open March–October
⌾8♨♿⌷□♨♒∪∟Ⓢ✂⊞🔥🐾
🐎🏠

White Barn 🅼
HIGHLY COMMENDED
Crede Lane, Bosham, Chichester
PO18 8NX
☎ (01243) 573113
Fax (01243) 573113
Architecturally outstanding single-storey house of character, in quiet cul-de-sac, with en-suite rooms and offering fine food to discerning guests.
Bedrooms: 1 double, 2 twin
Bathrooms: 3 en-suite

Bed & breakfast

per night:	£min	£max
Single	32.00	60.00
Double	50.00	65.00

Half board per person:

	£min	£max
Daily	41.00	50.00
Weekly	275.00	330.00

Evening meal from 1915
Parking for 4
Cards accepted: Access, Visa
♿⌷□♨∪∟Ⓢ✂📺⊞🔥🐾
🐎SP🏠

BOXGROVE
West Sussex
Map ref 2C3

Village at the foot of the Downs. Boxgrove Priory is probably the loveliest group of monastic ruins in England. To the north is Halnaker Mill, an 18th C tower mill celebrated by Hillaire Belloc.

The Brufords 🅼
Listed COMMENDED
66 The Street, Boxgrove, Chichester
PO18 0EE
☎ Chichester (01243) 774085
Large village house with quiet annexe

accommodation. Situated opposite Boxgrove Priory (1105AD) and 1 mile from Goodwood.
Bedrooms: 1 double, 1 twin
Bathrooms: 2 en-suite

Bed & breakfast

per night:	£min	£max
Single	25.00	30.00
Double	40.00	45.00

Parking for 3
🖐♿⌷□♨♒∪∟⊞🔥🐾🐎🏠

BRASTED
Kent
Map ref 2D2

Standing in a park adjoining the village is 18th C Brasted Place. The work of Robert Adam, this fine house was once the home of Napoleon III.

The Mount House 🅼
Listed COMMENDED
Brasted, Westerham TN16 1JB
☎ Westerham (01959) 563617
Fax (01959) 561296
Large early Georgian family residence in centre of village. Listed Grade II.
Bedrooms: 1 single, 1 double, 1 twin
Bathrooms: 1 en-suite, 1 public

Bed & breakfast

per night:	£min	£max
Single	20.00	25.00
Double	40.00	50.00

Parking for 3
⌾10♨□♨∪∟📺⊞🔥🐾
🐾🐎🏠

BRENCHLEY
Kent
Map ref 3B4

In the centre of this village is a small green, around which stand half-timbered, tile-hung and weatherboarded houses.

Rose and Crown Inn 🅼
Listed APPROVED
High Street, Brenchley, Tonbridge
TN12 7NQ
☎ (01892) 722107

Converted 14th C stables and stores opposite palace of Duke of St Albans, son of Charles II and Nell Gwyn.
Bedrooms: 4 double, 1 twin, 1 triple
Suite available

Bathrooms: 6 en-suite

Bed & breakfast

per night:	£min	£max
Single	30.00	39.00
Double	40.00	59.00

Lunch available
Evening meal 1900 (last orders 2130)
Parking for 20
Cards accepted: Access, Visa
⌾♨♿⌷□♨♒Ⓢ⊞🔥🐾🔻
∪🖐🐾🏠T

BRIGHTON & HOVE
East Sussex
Map ref 2D3

Brighton's attractions include the Royal Pavilion, Volks Electric Railway, Sea Life Centre and Marina Village, Conference Centre and "The Lanes" and several theatres. Neighbouring Hove is a resort in its own right. *Tourist Information Centre ☎ (01273) 323755; for Hove (01273) 746100 or 778087*

Aegean Hotel 🅼
APPROVED
5 New Steine, Brighton, East Sussex
BN2 1PB
☎ Brighton (01273) 686547
Family-run hotel where you can be sure of a warm welcome and satisfaction for your long or short stay.
Bedrooms: 4 single, 1 double, 1 twin, 4 triple
Bathrooms: 7 en-suite, 1 public, 1 private shower

Bed & breakfast

per night:	£min	£max
Single	18.00	28.00
Double	36.00	52.00

Half board per person:

	£min	£max
Daily	29.00	39.00
Weekly	190.00	260.00

Evening meal 1830 (last orders 1930)
Cards accepted: Access, Visa, Diners, Amex
⌾□♨🖐Ⓞ⊞🔥🐾🏠T

Map references apply to the colour maps at the back of this guide.

For ideas on places to visit refer to the introduction at the beginning of this section.

BRIGHTON & HOVE
Continued

'Brighton' Marina House Hotel ♨

8 Charlotte Street, Marine Parade, Brighton, East Sussex BN2 1AG
☎ Brighton (01273) 605349 &
Freephone 0500 099989
Fax (01273) 605349

Cosy, elegantly furnished, well-equipped, clean, comfortable, caring, family-run. Near sea, central for Palace Pier, Royal Pavilion, conference and exhibition halls, the famous Lanes, tourist attractions. Flexible breakfast, check-in/out times. Offering all facilities. Free street parking. Best in price range.
Bedrooms: 3 single, 2 double, 2 twin, 3 triple
Bathrooms: 7 en-suite, 1 public

Bed & breakfast per night:	£min	£max
Single	15.00	39.00
Double	35.00	59.00

Half board per person:	£min	£max
Daily	25.00	49.00
Weekly	160.00	304.00

Lunch available
Evening meal 1830 (last orders 1700)
Cards accepted: Access, Visa, Diners, Amex

[symbols]

The Brighton Twenty One Hotel ♨

21 Charlotte Street, Marine Parade, Brighton, East Sussex BN2 1AG
☎ Brighton (01273) 686450
Fax (01273) 695560

Early Victorian town house with elegantly furnished bedrooms. Exquisite Victorian room features a grand brass

bed. Discounts: 10% 2 nights, 20% 4 nights, 30% 7 nights.
Bedrooms: 4 double, 2 twin
Suite available
Bathrooms: 6 en-suite, 1 public

Bed & breakfast per night:	£min	£max
Single	25.00	50.00
Double	35.00	80.00

Half board per person:	£min	£max
Daily	35.00	45.00
Weekly	171.00	220.00

Evening meal 1830 (last orders 2000)
Cards accepted: Access, Visa, Diners, Amex

[symbols]

[Ad] See display advertisement on this page

Cavalaire House ♨
COMMENDED

34 Upper Rock Gardens, Brighton, East Sussex BN2 1QF
☎ Brighton (01273) 696899
Fax (01273) 600504
Victorian townhouse, close to sea and town centre. Resident proprietors offer comfortably furnished rooms with or without private facilities. Book 7 nights and get 1 night free.

Bedrooms: 1 single, 3 double, 3 twin,
2 triple
Bathrooms: 1 en-suite, 2 private,
1 public, 3 private showers

Bed & breakfast

per night:	£min	£max
Single	18.00	19.00
Double	42.00	48.00

Cards accepted: Access, Visa, Amex

Diana House 🏔

Listed **APPROVED**

25 St Georges Terrace, Brighton,
East Sussex BN2 1JJ
☎ Brighton (01273) 605797
*Large, friendly guesthouse close to sea,
town and conference centre. All rooms
have TV, hospitality tray, clock/radio,
shaver point. Some rooms en-suite.
24-hour access.*
Bedrooms: 4 double, 2 twin, 2 triple,
1 family room
Bathrooms: 3 private, 1 public,
5 private showers

Bed & breakfast

per night:	£min	£max
Single	16.00	19.00
Double	32.00	38.00

Evening meal 1800 (last orders
2000)
Cards accepted: Access, Visa

BURWASH

East Sussex
Map ref 3B4

Village of old houses, many from the
Tudor and Stuart periods. One of
the old ironmasters' houses is
Bateman's (National Trust) which
was the home of Rudyard Kipling.

Church House 🏔

Listed **COMMENDED**

High Street, Burwash, Etchingham
TN19 7EH
☎ (01435) 883282

*Listed Georgian family home in centre
of village, close to Batemans.
Surrounded by beautiful countryside.
Friendly atmosphere. Walking distance
of inns.*
Bedrooms: 1 double
Bathrooms: 1 private

---

per night:	£min	£max
Single	25.00	
Double	40.00	

Parking for 2

Glydwish Place 🏔

Listed **HIGHLY COMMENDED**

Fontridge Lane, Burwash
TN19 7DG
☎ (01435) 882869 & Mobile 0850
421732
Fax (01435) 882749
*Tranquil setting with beautiful views.
Numerous interesting places to visit.
Excellent pubs in surrounding villages.
Lovely walks. All bedrooms overlooking
gardens. Sauna, solarium, gym.*
Bedrooms: 3 double
Suite available
Bathrooms: 1 en-suite, 3 public

Bed & breakfast

per night:	£min	£max
Single	20.00	30.00
Double	45.00	55.00

Parking for 14

CANTERBURY

Kent
Map ref 3B3

Place of pilgrimage since the
martyrdom of Becket in 1170 and
the site of Canterbury Cathedral.
Visit St Augustine's Abbey, St
Martin's (the oldest church in
England), Royal Museum and Art
Gallery and the Canterbury Tales.
Nearby is Howletts Wild Animal
Park. Good shopping centre.
*Tourist Information Centre ☎ (01227)
766567*

Abberley House 🏔

Listed

115 Whitstable Road, Canterbury
CT2 8EF
☎ (01227) 450265
*Family-run guesthouse within easy
walking distance of the city and
university. Tea/coffee-making facilities,
wash-basins. Non-smokers only, please.*
Bedrooms: 2 double, 1 twin
Bathrooms: 1 public, 1 private
shower

Bed & breakfast

per night:	£min	£max
Single	22.00	25.00
Double	35.00	40.00

Parking for 3

Bower Farm House

HIGHLY COMMENDED

Stelling Minnis, Canterbury
CT4 6BB
☎ Stelling Minnis (01227) 709430
*Delightful heavily beamed 17th C
farmhouse between the villages of
Stelling Minnis and Bossingham.
Canterbury and Hythe are
approximately 7 miles away.*
Bedrooms: 1 double, 1 twin
Bathrooms: 1 en-suite, 1 private

Bed & breakfast

per night:	£min	£max
Single	18.00	18.00
Double	36.00	36.00

Parking for 8

Castle Court Guest House 🏔

Listed

8 Castle Street, Canterbury
CT1 2QF
☎ (01227) 463441
Fax (01227) 463441
*Friendly family-run guesthouse in listed
Georgian building, close to cathedral,
parks, restaurants and bus/railway
station. Full English breakfast. En-suite
rooms available. TV in all rooms.*
Bedrooms: 1 single, 3 double, 2 twin,
2 triple
Bathrooms: 8 en-suite, 3 public

Bed & breakfast

per night:	£min	£max
Single	18.00	25.00
Double	30.00	45.00

Parking for 4
Cards accepted: Access, Visa

Cathedral Gate Hotel 🏔

36 Burgate, Canterbury CT1 2HA
☎ (01227) 464381
Fax (01227) 462800
*Central position at main entrance to
the cathedral. Car parking nearby. Baby
listening service. Old world charm at
reasonable prices. English breakfast
extra.*
Bedrooms: 5 single, 7 double, 7 twin,
3 triple, 2 family rooms
Bathrooms: 12 en-suite, 3 public,
2 private showers

Bed & breakfast

per night:	£min	£max
Single	21.00	47.50
Double	40.00	72.00

Evening meal 1900 (last orders
2100)

Continued ▶

CANTERBURY
Continued

Parking for 12
Cards accepted: Access, Visa, Diners, Amex, Switch/Delta

Clare-Ellen Guest House ▲▲
☺ HIGHLY COMMENDED

9 Victoria Road, Wincheap, Canterbury CT1 3SG
☎ (01227) 760205
Fax (01227) 784482

Victorian house with large, elegant en-suite rooms, 6 minutes' walk to town centre. 5 minutes to Canterbury East train station. Car park and garage available.
Bedrooms: 1 single, 1 double, 1 twin, 1 triple, 1 family room
Bathrooms: 4 en-suite, 1 private, 1 public

Bed & breakfast

per night:	£min	£max
Single	22.00	28.00
Double	42.00	48.00

Parking for 9
Cards accepted: Access, Visa, Switch/Delta

The Corner House ▲▲
Listed

113 Whitstable Road, Canterbury CT2 8EF
☎ (01227) 761352
Fax (01227) 761065
Just a few minutes' walking distance from city, university, shops and restaurants. Spacious family house with friendly hospitality.
Bedrooms: 1 double, 2 twin
Bathrooms: 2 public

Bed & breakfast

per night:	£min	£max
Single	20.00	24.00
Double	30.00	38.00

Parking for 4

The Farmhouse Park Farm
☺ HIGHLY COMMENDED

Upper Mystole Park Farm, Pennypot Lane, Mystole, Canterbury CT4 7BT
☎ (01227) 730589

90-acre fruit farm. Modern farmhouse in the heart of Kent and with magnificent views. Set between historic Canterbury and beautiful Chilham (A28). Dover 25 minutes. Good home cooking.
Bedrooms: 2 double, 1 twin
Bathrooms: 2 en-suite, 1 private

Bed & breakfast

per night	£min	£max
Single	18.00	20.00
Double	35.00	38.00

Half board per person:

	£min	£max
Daily	26.00	27.50
Weekly	170.00	180.00

Evening meal 1830 (last orders 2000)
Parking for 6

Magnolia House ▲▲
☺ HIGHLY COMMENDED

36 St Dunstans Terrace, Canterbury CT2 8AX
☎ (01227) 765121 & Mobile (0585) 595970
Fax (01227) 765121

Quiet Georgian house in attractive city street. Close to university, gardens, river and city centre. Walled garden, ideal for guests to relax in. Winner 1995 "Welcome to Kent Hospitality Award".
Bedrooms: 1 single, 4 double, 2 twin
Bathrooms: 7 en-suite

Bed & breakfast

per night:	£min	£max
Single	36.00	45.00
Double	58.00	80.00

Evening meal 1800 (last orders 1900)
Parking for 4
Cards accepted: Access, Visa, Amex, Switch/Delta

Old Stone House ▲▲
Listed COMMENDED

The Green, Wickhambreaux, Canterbury CT3 1RQ
☎ (01227) 728591

Map references apply to the colour maps at the back of this guide.

One of the oldest houses in Kent, parts dating from 12th C. Once the home of Joan Plantagenet, wife of the Black Prince. Ten minutes east of Canterbury, 30 minutes from Folkestone and Dover.
Bedrooms: 1 single, 2 double, 1 twin
Bathrooms: 2 en-suite, 1 public

Bed & breakfast

per night	£min	£max
Single	20.00	25.00
Double	40.00	45.00

Parking for 4

Oriel Lodge ▲▲
☺ HIGHLY COMMENDED

3 Queens Avenue, Canterbury CT2 8AY
☎ (01227) 462845
Edwardian house in residential area near city centre and restaurants. Clean, well-furnished rooms, lounge, log fire. Private parking. Smoking in lounge area only.
Bedrooms: 1 single, 3 double, 1 twin, 1 triple
Bathrooms: 2 en-suite, 2 public

Bed & breakfast

per night:	£min	£max
Single	20.00	27.00
Double	36.00	57.00

Parking for 6
Cards accepted: Access, Visa

Pointers Hotel ▲▲
☺☺☺ COMMENDED

1 London Road, Canterbury CT2 8LR
☎ (01227) 456846
Fax (01227) 831131

Family-run Georgian hotel close to city centre, cathedral and university. Licensed restaurant.
Bedrooms: 1 single, 6 double, 2 twin, 3 family rooms
Bathrooms: 11 en-suite, 1 private

Bed & breakfast

per night:	£min	£max
Single	38.00	40.00
Double	50.00	60.00

Half board per person:	£min	£max
Daily	39.00	54.00
Weekly	273.00	378.00

Evening meal 1930 (last orders 2030)
Parking for 10
Cards accepted: Access, Visa, Diners, Amex, Switch/Delta

The Willows

HIGHLY COMMENDED

Howfield Lane, Chartham Hatch,
Canterbury CT4 7HG
☎ (01227) 738442
Fax (01227) 738442
Dr and Mrs Gough welcome you to The Willows, situated in a quiet country lane, 2 miles from Canterbury Cathedral. A garden for enthusiasts. No smoking.
Bedrooms: 1 double, 1 twin
Bathrooms: 1 en-suite, 1 private

Bed & breakfast

per night:	£min	£max
Single	18.00	20.00
Double	42.00	42.00

Half board per person:	£min	£max
Daily	28.00	30.00

Evening meal 1900 (last orders 2000)
Parking for 8

CHICHESTER

West Sussex
Map ref 2C3

The county town of West Sussex with a beautiful Norman cathedral. Noted for its Georgian architecture but also has modern buildings like the Festival Theatre. Surrounded by places of interest, including Fishbourne Roman Palace and Weald and Downland Open-Air Museum.
Tourist Information Centre ☎ (01243) 775888

Abelands Barn

HIGHLY COMMENDED

Bognor Road, Merston, Chichester
PO20 6DY
☎ (01243) 533826
Fax (01243) 555533
Listed converted agricultural barns on A259 just 2 miles outside Chichester on coast road to Bognor Regis. Close to Festival Theatre and Goodwood.
Bedrooms: 2 double, 1 twin
Bathrooms: 3 en-suite

Bed & breakfast per night:	£min	£max
Single	22.50	25.00
Double	45.00	50.00

Parking for 5
Cards accepted: Access, Visa

Annas

COMMENDED

27 Westhampnett Road, Chichester
PO19 4HW
☎ (01243) 788522 & Mobile (0585) 446077
Fax (01243) 788522
Tastefully furnished, ideally situated for Goodwood, city centre and Festival Theatre.
Bedrooms: 1 single, 2 double, 1 twin
Bathrooms: 2 en-suite, 1 public

Bed & breakfast

per night:	£min	£max
Double	45.00	50.00

Parking for 2

Hedgehogs

Listed COMMENDED

45 Whyke Lane, Chichester
PO19 2JT
☎ (01243) 780022
About half-a-mile from city centre, bus/railway stations and theatre. Secluded garden, TV lounge. Parking. Weekly terms available. Cyclists and hikers welcome. No smoking.
Bedrooms: 2 double, 1 twin
Bathrooms: 2 public

Bed & breakfast

per night:	£min	£max
Single	21.00	24.00
Double	32.00	38.00

Parking for 4

Home Farm House

Listed HIGHLY COMMENDED

Elms Lane, West Wittering,
Chichester PO20 8LW
☎ West Wittering (01243) 514252
Spacious modern house with pretty garden, in peaceful lane. Splendid en-suite double with sitting area. Excellent walks, birds, beaches and theatre.
Bedrooms: 2 double
Bathrooms: 1 en-suite, 1 private

Bed & breakfast

per night:	£min	£max
Single	25.00	30.00
Double	44.00	50.00

Parking for 3
Open April–October

CHIDDINGSTONE

Kent
Map ref 2D2

Pleasant village of 16th and 17th C, preserved by the National Trust, with an 18th C "castle" and attractive Tudor inn.

Hoath Holidays

Listed APPROVED

Hoath House, Chiddingstone Hoath, Edenbridge TN8 7DB
☎ Cowden (01342) 850362
Tudor family house with beamed and panelled rooms and extensive gardens. Convenient for Chartwell, Hever, Penshurst, Gatwick and London.
Bedrooms: 2 twin
Bathrooms: 1 public

Bed & breakfast

per night:	£min	£max
Single	21.00	21.00
Double	42.00	42.00

Parking for 8

CHILHAM

Kent
Map ref 3B3

Extremely pretty village of mostly Tudor and Jacobean houses. The village rises to the spacious square with the castle and the 15th C church.

Jullieberrie House

COMMENDED

Canterbury Road, Chilham,
Canterbury CT4 8DX
☎ Canterbury (01227) 730488
Modern house with lovely views over lake and woodland. On the A28 Ashford to Canterbury road, close to Chilham village.
Bedrooms: 2 double, 2 twin
Bathrooms: 2 en-suite, 1 public

Bed & breakfast

per night:	£min	£max
Single	20.00	25.00
Double	32.00	38.00

Parking for 5

Half board prices are given per person, but in some cases these may be based on double/twin occupancy.

CHILHAM
Continued

Woodchip House ⚐

Listed

Maidstone Road, Chilham,
Canterbury CT4 8DD
☎ Canterbury (01227) 730386

*A large family house set in an acre of
mature gardens in Chilham, close to
Canterbury and Leeds Castle.*
Bedrooms: 2 double, 2 twin
Bathrooms: 2 public
**Bed & breakfast
per night:**

	£min	£max
Single	15.00	20.00
Double	40.00	45.00

Parking for 3
Open February–November

The Woolpack Inn ⚐

COMMENDED

High Street, Chilham, Canterbury
CT4 8DL
☎ Canterbury (01227) 730208 &
730351
Fax (01227) 731053

*Ancient inn, c 1422, with inglenook
fireplaces and oak-beamed restaurant,
in picturesque Chilham. Regional
specialities, locally brewed ales.
Half-board daily prices are for a
minimum 2-night stay.*
Bedrooms: 7 double, 3 twin, 1 triple,
2 family rooms
Suites available
Bathrooms: 13 en-suite
**Bed & breakfast
per night:**

	£min	£max
Single	37.50	40.00
Double	47.50	50.00

**Half board per
person:**

	£min	£max
Daily	37.50	40.00
Weekly	262.50	280.00

Lunch available
Evening meal 1900 (last orders
2130)

Parking for 30
Cards accepted: Access, Visa, Amex,
Switch/Delta

CLIFTONVILLE
Kent

See under Margate

CRANBROOK
Kent
Map ref 3B4

Old town, a centre for the weaving
industry in the 15th C. The 72-ft
high Union Mill is a 3-storey
windmill, still in working order.

Tolehurst Barn ⚐

COMMENDED

Cranbrook Road, Frittenden,
Cranbrook TN17 2BP
☎ (01580) 714385

*Converted 17th C beamed barn in
farmland - quiet and rural, all modern
conveniences. On A229, convenient for
the heart of Kent and places of historic
interest. Only 5 minutes from
Sissinghurst. Languages spoken.*
Bedrooms: 2 double, 1 twin
Bathrooms: 3 en-suite
**Bed & breakfast
per night:**

	£min	£max
Single	17.50	17.50
Double	35.00	35.00

**Half board per
person:**

	£min	£max
Daily	27.50	27.50

Evening meal 1900 (last orders
2100)
Parking for 6

The White Horse Inn ⚐

⚐

High Street, Cranbrook TN17 3EX
☎ (01580) 712615
*Victorian public house and restaurant
in the centre of the smallest town in
Kent, once the "capital" of the Weald.*
Bedrooms: 1 single, 1 twin, 1 triple
Bathrooms: 1 public
**Bed & breakfast
per night:**

	£min	£max
Single	26.00	
Double	36.00	

**Half board per
person:**

	£min	£max
Daily	25.00	
Weekly	150.00	

Lunch available
Evening meal 1830 (last orders
2130)
Parking for 12
Cards accepted: Access, Visa

CRAWLEY
West Sussex
Map ref 2D2

One of the first New Towns built
after World War II, but it also has
some old buildings. Set in
magnificent wooded countryside.

The Manor House ⚐

COMMENDED

Bonnetts Lane, Ifield, Crawley
RH11 0NY
☎ (01293) 510000 & 512298
*100-year-old manor house in pleasant
rural surroundings on Gatwick's
doorstep. Family-run establishment
offering comfortable and spacious
accommodation.*
Bedrooms: 1 single, 2 double, 2 twin,
1 family room
Bathrooms: 4 en-suite, 2 private,
1 public
**Bed & breakfast
per night:**

	£min	£max
Single	25.00	35.00
Double	35.00	40.00

Parking for 25
Cards accepted: Access, Visa

Waterhall Country House ⚐

COMMENDED

Prestwood Lane, Tfield Wood,
Crawley RH11 0LA
☎ (01293) 520002
Fax (01293) 539905
*Attractive country house in open
countryside, 5 minutes from Gatwick.
Warm and friendly welcome. Off-road
parking. Guest lounge/conservatory.*
Bedrooms: 1 single, 1 double, 2 twin,
1 family room
Bathrooms: 4 en-suite, 1 private,
1 public
**Bed & breakfast
per night:**

	£min	£max
Single	25.00	25.00
Double	40.00	40.00

Parking for 25

DEAL

Kent
Map ref 3C4

Coastal town and popular holiday resort. Deal Castle was built by Henry VIII as a fort and the museum is devoted to finds excavated in the area. Also the Time-Ball Tower museum. Angling available from both beach and pier.
Tourist Information Centre ☎ (01304) 369576

Sondes Lodge Guesthouse ⋒

Listed COMMENDED

14 Sondes Road, Deal CT14 7BW
☎ (01304) 368741
Four-bedroomed restored Victorian home. Close to Deal town, pier, castles and golf courses. Friendly, relaxed atmosphere.
Bedrooms: 2 double, 1 twin, 1 family room
Bathrooms: 4 private showers
Bed & breakfast

per night:	£min	£max
Single	20.00	30.00
Double	35.00	45.00

Cards accepted: Access, Visa
🛏🖵♿ⓤ🛍📠✈🚕 ᴅᴀᴘ 🐾 SP

DORKING

Surrey
Map ref 2D2

Ancient market town and a good centre for walking, delightfully set between Box Hill and the Downs.

Bulmer Farm

⚜⚜ COMMENDED

Holmbury St Mary, Dorking
RH5 6LG
☎ (01306) 730210
30-acre beef farm. 17th C character farmhouse with beams and inglenook fireplace, in the Surrey hills. Choice of twin rooms in the house or double/twin en-suite rooms in tastefully converted barn adjoining the house. Village is 5 miles from Dorking.
Bedrooms: 3 double, 5 twin
Bathrooms: 5 en-suite, 2 public
Bed & breakfast

per night:	£min	£max
Single	18.00	30.00
Double	36.00	40.00

Parking for 12
🛏12♿♿ⓤⓈ🛍✂📺🛍📠🛎12✿ ✈🚕🏕

Mark Ash

Listed

Abinger Common, Dorking
RH5 6JA
☎ (01306) 731326
Victorian house in lovely garden opposite village green. Area of Outstanding Natural Beauty. One mile off A25. Dorking 4 miles, Guildford 8 miles. Convenient for Gatwick Airport.
Bedrooms: 1 single, 1 double, 1 twin
Bathrooms: 2 public
Bed & breakfast

per night:	£min	£max
Single	25.00	
Double	40.00	

Parking for 4
Open March–November
🛏🖵🚃♿ⓤ🎱✂📺📺🛍📠🔍 🚃✿✈🚕🏕

Steyning Cottage

Listed

Horsham Road, South Holmwood, Dorking RH5 4NE
☎ (01306) 888481
Detached tile-hung house adjacent to A24 and within walking distance of Leith Hill. Gatwick Airport approximately 20 minutes away, Heathrow 45 minutes. French spoken.
Bedrooms: 1 single, 1 twin
Bathrooms: 1 public
Bed & breakfast

per night:	£min	£max
Single	16.00	20.00
Double	32.00	34.00

Half board per person:

	£min	£max
Daily	24.00	28.00
Weekly	115.00	205.00

Evening meal 1900 (last orders 2000)
Parking for 4
🛏🖵ⓤ🎱📺🛍📠✿🚕

Sturtwood Farm

⚜⚜ COMMENDED

Partridge Lane, Newdigate, Dorking RH5 5EE
☎ (01306) 631308
Fax (01306) 631908
140-acre mixed farm. Attractive 18th C farmhouse, 5 miles south of Dorking, where you are assured of a warm welcome. 12 minutes from Gatwick. Many National Trust properties in the area.
Bedrooms: 1 single, 2 twin
Bathrooms: 1 en-suite, 2 private, 1 public
Bed & breakfast

per night:	£min	£max
Single	20.00	25.00
Double	35.00	40.00

Evening meal from 1900
Parking for 6
🛏🖵♿ⓤⓁⓈ✂🛍📠✿🚕🏕

DOVER

Kent
Map ref 3C4

A Cinque Port and busiest passenger port in the world. Still a historic town and seaside resort beside the famous White Cliffs. The White Cliffs Experience attraction traces the town's history through the Roman, Saxon, Norman and Victorian periods.
Tourist Information Centre ☎ (01304) 205108

Coldred Court Farm ⋒

⚜⚜ HIGHLY COMMENDED

Church Road, Coldred, Dover CT15 5AQ
☎ (01304) 830816
Fax (01304) 830816
7-acre mixed farm. 1620 farmhouse full of old world charm, with modern facilities. Situated 1 mile from the A2, 10 minutes from Dover.
Bedrooms: 2 double, 1 twin
Bathrooms: 3 en-suite
Bed & breakfast

per night:	£min	£max
Single	30.00	40.00
Double	40.00	45.00

Half board per person:

	£min	£max
Daily	42.50	52.50
Weekly	262.50	367.50

Evening meal 1800 (last orders 2030)
Parking for 13
🛏♿🚃🖵♿ⓤⓁ🔒Ⓢ✂📺🛍 📠🛎🔍✿✈🚕🏕 SP 🏕 Ⓣ

Dover Hotel

⚜⚜ APPROVED

122-124 Folkestone Road, Dover CT17 9SP
☎ (01304) 206559 & 208109
Fax (01304) 203936
Family-run business, 200 yards from the railway station and minutes away from the docks. Bar, restaurant and pool table facilities.
Bedrooms: 2 single, 6 double, 4 twin, 3 triple, 3 family rooms
Bathrooms: 12 en-suite, 6 private
Bed & breakfast

per night:	£min	£max
Single	25.00	30.00
Double	40.00	45.00

Half board per person:

	£min	£max
Daily	31.50	
Weekly	264.60	

Continued ▶

DOVER
Continued

Lunch available
Evening meal (last orders 2030)
Parking for 50
Cards accepted: Access, Visa, Diners, Amex

Elmo Guest House ⚑

120 Folkestone Road, Dover
CT17 9SP
☎ (01304) 206236
Conveniently situated for ferries and Hoverport terminals and 10 minutes' drive to Channel Tunnel. Within easy reach of town centre and railway station. Overnight stops our speciality.
Bedrooms: 1 single, 2 double,
1 triple, 1 family room
Bathrooms: 2 public
Bed & breakfast

per night:	£min	£max
Single	12.00	17.00
Double	22.00	32.00
Parking for 7		

Esther House

Listed COMMENDED

55 Barton Road, Dover CT16 2NF
☎ (01304) 241332
Fax (01304) 241332
Non-smoking B and B with warm Christian atmosphere. Close to ferries and town centre. Ideal base for touring and 15 minutes from Channel Tunnel. Early breakfasts. Evening meals by arrangement. Special and weekend breaks from £11.00 per person per night.
Bedrooms: 1 single, 1 twin, 1 triple
Bathrooms: 1 public
Bed & breakfast

per night:	£min	£max
Single	13.00	18.00
Double	26.00	34.00

Evening meal 1830 (last orders 1930)

Owler Lodge

HIGHLY COMMENDED

Alkham Valley Road, Alkham, Dover
CT15 7DF
☎ (01304) 826375
Small family-run guesthouse with inglenook and beams. In centre of village of Alkham on B2060 between Dover and Folkestone. 3 miles from Channel Tunnel, 4 miles from Dover Docks.

Bedrooms: 2 double, 1 twin
Bathrooms: 3 en-suite
Bed & breakfast

per night:	£min	£max
Single	30.00	32.00
Double	42.00	44.00

Half board per person:

	£min	£max
Daily	32.00	33.00

Evening meal 1800 (last orders 2100)
Parking for 6

EAST GRINSTEAD

West Sussex
Map ref 2D2

A number of fine old houses stand in the High Street, one of which is Sackville College, founded in 1609.

Middle House Cookhams ⚑

⚜ COMMENDED

Sharpthorne, East Grinstead
RH19 4HU
☎ (01342) 810566
Fax (01342) 810566
Central portion of large 100-year-old country house, with open southerly aspect. In village south of East Grinstead.
Bedrooms: 1 single, 1 double, 1 twin
Bathrooms: 1 en-suite, 1 public
Bed & breakfast

per night:	£min	£max
Single	20.00	25.00
Double	40.00	50.00

Parking for 4

EASTBOURNE

East Sussex
Map ref 3B4

One of the finest, most elegant resorts on the south-east coast situated beside Beachy Head. Long promenade, plenty of gardens, theatres, Towner Art Gallery, "How We Lived Then" museum of shops and social history.
Tourist Information Centre ☎ (01323) 411400

Bay Lodge Hotel

⚜⚜ COMMENDED

61-62 Royal Parade, Eastbourne
BN22 7AQ
☎ (01323) 732515
Fax (01323) 735009

Small seafront hotel opposite Pavilion Gardens, close to bowling greens and marina. Large sun-lounge. All double/twin bedrooms have en-suite or private facilities. Non-smokers' lounge.
Bedrooms: 3 single, 5 double, 4 twin
Bathrooms: 4 en-suite, 5 private,
2 public
Bed & breakfast

per night:	£min	£max
Single	19.00	25.00
Double	38.00	48.00

Half board per person:

	£min	£max
Daily	27.00	33.00
Weekly	179.00	222.00

Evening meal 1800 (last orders 1800)
Open March–October and Christmas
Cards accepted: Access, Visa

Black Robin Farm ⚑

Listed COMMENDED

Beachy Head, Eastbourne
BN20 7XX
☎ (01323) 643357 & Mobile 0973 418654
Fax (01323) 643357
1000-acre livestock farm. Farmhouse B&B at Beachy Head. Peaceful location with excellent views. Full English or vegetarian breakfast. Close to town, beach and South Downs Way.
Bedrooms: 1 double, 2 twin
Bathrooms: 1 public
Bed & breakfast

per night:	£min	£max
Double		36.00

Parking for 4

ENGLEFIELD GREEN

Surrey
Map ref 2D2

Suburban village 3 miles west of Staines.

4 Fircroft ⚑

Listed

Bagshot Road, Englefield Green,
Egham TW20 0RS
☎ Egham (01784) 432893
Detached house, 10 minutes from Windsor, 15 minutes from M25, near Wentworth Golf Club. Convenient for

trains to Waterloo. Also near Ascot, Saville Gardens and Legoland.
Bedrooms: 1 single, 1 twin
Bathrooms: 1 public

Bed & breakfast

per night:	£min	£max
Single	17.00	17.00
Double	34.00	34.00

Parking for 3

FARNHAM

Surrey
Map ref 2C2

Town noted for its Georgian houses. Willmer House (now a museum) has a facade of cut and moulded brick with fine carving and panelling in the interior. The 12th C castle has been occupied by Bishops of both Winchester and Guildford.
Tourist Information Centre ☎ (01252) 715109

Heathfield

🏠 COMMENDED

44 Sandrock Hill Road, Boundstone, Farnham GU10 4RS
☎ (01252) 793200
Fax (01252) 793200
Semi-rural Victorian family house.
Bedrooms: 1 single, 1 twin
Bathrooms: 2 public

Bed & breakfast

per night:	£min	£max
Single	17.50	
Double	33.00	

Parking for 2

High Wray ♙

Listed COMMENDED

73 Lodge Hill Road, Farnham GU10 3RB
☎ (01252) 715589 & 724386
Visitors welcome as family guests. Gracious house with interesting garden. Wing purpose-built for disabled guests. Home-grown vegetables and eggs.
Bedrooms: 1 single, 1 twin
Bathrooms: 2 private, 1 public

Bed & breakfast

per night:	£min	£max
Single	16.00	16.00
Double	40.00	40.00

Half board per

person:	£min	£max
Daily	22.00	26.00
Weekly	142.80	168.00

Evening meal 1830 (last orders 2000)
Parking for 7

FAVERSHAM

Kent
Map ref 3B3

Historic town, once a port, dating back to prehistoric times. Abbey Street has more than 50 listed buildings. Roman and Anglo-Saxon finds and other exhibits can be seen in a museum in the Maison Dieu at Ospringe. Fleur de Lis Heritage Centre.
Tourist Information Centre ☎ (01795) 534542

Barnsfield ♙

Listed

Hernhill, Faversham ME13 9JH
☎ Canterbury (01227) 750973 & Deal (01304) 368550
Listed Grade II country cottages, just off A299, set in 3 acres of orchards, 6 miles from Canterbury.
Bedrooms: 2 double, 1 twin
Bathrooms: 1 en-suite, 1 public

Bed & breakfast

per night:	£min	£max
Single	16.00	24.00
Double	30.00	44.00

Half board per

person:	£min	£max
Daily	22.00	32.00

Parking for 10
Cards accepted: Access, Visa

The Granary ♙

🏠🏠 HIGHLY COMMENDED

Plumford Lane, Ospringe, Faversham ME13 0DS
☎ (01795) 538416 & Mobile 0860 817713
Fax (01795) 538416
Delightfully converted granary in peaceful setting with large garden. Own lounge with colour TV. Close to M2 and Canterbury. Friendly welcome.
Bedrooms: 1 double, 1 twin, 1 triple
Bathrooms: 2 en-suite, 1 private

Bed & breakfast

per night:	£min	£max
Single	25.00	30.00
Double	42.00	42.00

Parking for 8
Cards accepted: Access, Visa, Switch/Delta

Leaveland Court ♙

🏠🏠 HIGHLY COMMENDED

Leaveland, Faversham ME13 0NP
☎ Challock (01233) 740596
300-acre arable farm. Enchanting Grade II listed 15th C timbered farmhouse in quiet rural setting*

---

adjacent to Leaveland church. 5 minutes from M2 Faversham, 20 minutes from Canterbury.
Bedrooms: 2 double, 1 twin
Bathrooms: 3 en-suite, 1 public

Bed & breakfast

per night:	£min	£max
Single	22.50	25.00
Double	40.00	45.00

Parking for 6
Open February–November
Cards accepted: Access, Visa

Owens Court Farm

🏠 COMMENDED

Selling, Faversham ME13 9QN
☎ Canterbury (01227) 752247
Fax (01227) 752247

265-acre fruit farm. Comfortable Georgian farmhouse in quiet lane, 1 mile off A2. 3 miles from Faversham, 9 miles from Canterbury.
Bedrooms: 1 single, 1 twin, 1 triple
Bathrooms: 1 public

Bed & breakfast

per night:	£min	£max
Single	17.00	17.00
Double	34.00	34.00

Parking for 4

Preston Lea ♙

🏠🏠 HIGHLY COMMENDED

Canterbury Road, Faversham ME13 8XA
☎ (01795) 535266
Fax (01795) 533388

Beautiful, imposing Victorian house with turrets and other interesting features, set in large secluded grounds. Only 15 minutes from Canterbury and 30 minutes from Channel ports and Eurotunnel.
Bedrooms: 2 double, 1 twin
Bathrooms: 2 en-suite, 1 private

Continued ▶

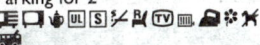

FAVERSHAM
Continued

Bed & breakfast per night:

	£min	£max
Single	30.00	35.00
Double	40.00	45.00

Parking for 11
Cards accepted: Access, Visa

White Horse Inn Ⱥ
♛♛♛ COMMENDED

Boughton, Faversham ME13 9AX
☎ Canterbury (01227) 751700 & 751343
Fax (01227) 751090

15th C coaching inn with oak beams and inglenook fireplaces. Freshly prepared regional specialities, locally brewed award-winning ales. Half board daily prices are for a minimum 2-night stay.
Bedrooms: 7 double, 4 twin, 2 triple
Suites available
Bathrooms: 13 en-suite

Bed & breakfast per night:

	£min	£max
Single	37.50	40.00
Double	47.50	50.00

Half board per person:

	£min	£max
Daily	37.50	40.00
Weekly	262.50	280.00

Lunch available
Evening meal 1900 (last orders 2130)
Parking for 50
Cards accepted: Access, Visa, Amex, Switch/Delta

TOWN INDEX

This can be found at the back of the guide. If you know where you want to stay, the index will give you the page number listing all accommodation in your chosen town, city or village.

FINDON

West Sussex
Map ref 2D3

Downland village well-known for its annual sheep fair and its racing stables. The ancient landmarks, Cissbury Ring and Chanctonbury Ring, found on the South Downs Way, are nearby.

Findon Tower
♛ COMMENDED

Cross Lane, Findon, Worthing
BN14 0UG
☎ (01903) 873870
Elegant Edwardian country house in large secluded garden. Spacious accommodation with en-suite facilities. Warm, friendly welcome, relaxed and peaceful atmosphere. Rural views, snooker room. Excellent food in village restaurants and pubs.
Bedrooms: 2 double, 1 twin
Bathrooms: 2 en-suite, 1 private

Bed & breakfast per night:

	£min	£max
Single	25.00	35.00
Double	35.00	45.00

Parking for 10

FOLKESTONE

Kent
Map ref 3C4

Popular resort and important cross-channel port. The town has a fine promenade, the Leas, from where orchestral concerts and other entertainments are presented. Horse-racing at Westenhanger Racecourse nearby.
Tourist Information Centre ☎ *(01303) 258594*

Abbey House Hotel Ⱥ
♛

5-6 Westbourne Gardens, off Sandgate Road, Folkestone
CT20 2JA
☎ (01303) 255514
Fax (01303) 245098
Pleasant garden square location in residential West End, close to Leas Cliff Hall and bandstand. Easy access to ferry and Channel Tunnel. Unlimited street parking.
Bedrooms: 3 single, 2 double, 5 twin, 4 family rooms
Bathrooms: 3 en-suite, 4 public

Bed & breakfast per night:

	£min	£max
Single	19.00	26.00
Double	35.00	45.00

Half board per person:

	£min	£max
Daily	29.00	36.00
Weekly	177.00	199.00

Evening meal 1830 (last orders 1930)
Cards accepted: Visa

Beachborough Park Ⱥ
♛♛♛ APPROVED

Newington, Folkestone CT18 8BW
☎ (01303) 275432
Fax (01843) 845131
Beautiful setting, ideal for sightseeing and very convenient for tunnel and ferries. Very comfortable for both active people and those just seeking peace and quiet.
Bedrooms: 4 double, 2 twin, 2 family rooms
Bathrooms: 8 en-suite

Bed & breakfast per night:

	£min	£max
Single	25.00	45.00
Double	41.00	50.00

Half board per person:

	£min	£max
Daily	30.00	45.00
Weekly	175.00	245.00

Lunch available
Evening meal 1900 (last orders 2100)
Parking for 30
Cards accepted: Access, Visa, Switch/Delta

FULKING

West Sussex
Map ref 2D3

Downers Vineyard Ⱥ
Listed APPROVED

Clappers Lane, Fulking, Henfield
BN5 9NH
☎ Brighton (01273) 857484 & Mobile 0378 392367
Fax (01273) 857068
18-acre vineyard & grazing farm. Quiet rural position, 1 mile north of the South Downs and Devil's Dyke, 8 miles from Brighton.
Bedrooms: 2 triple
Bathrooms: 2 public

Bed & breakfast per night:

	£min	£max
Single	19.00	21.00
Double	33.00	35.00

Parking for 6

GATWICK AIRPORT

West Sussex

See under Crawley, East Grinstead, Horley, Smallfield

GUILDFORD

Surrey
Map ref 2D2

Bustling town with many historic monuments, one of which is the Guildhall clock jutting out over the old High Street. The modern cathedral occupies a commanding position on Stag Hill.
Tourist Information Centre ☎ (01483) 444333

Beevers Farm

Listed

Chinthurst Lane, Bramley, Guildford GU5 0DR
☎ (01483) 898764
In peaceful surroundings 2 miles from Guildford, near villages with pubs and restaurants. Convenient for Heathrow and Gatwick. Friendly atmosphere. Non-smokers only.
Bedrooms: 3 twin
Bathrooms: 1 en-suite, 1 public
Bed & breakfast

per night:	£min	£max
Double	28.00	39.00

Parking for 10
Open February–November
🛏🍴🗄📶♿🛄💷🔥☀🕐🛏🚭✕🐾Ⓣ

High Edser ⚠

Listed **COMMENDED**

Shere Road, Ewhurst, Cranleigh, Guildford GU6 7PQ
☎ (01483) 278214 & (01585) 379136
Fax (01483) 278200
14th-15th C family home set in Area of Outstanding Natural Beauty. 6 miles from Guildford and Dorking, within easy reach of airports and many tourist attractions. Non-smokers only, please.
Bedrooms: 2 double, 1 twin
Bathrooms: 1 public
Bed & breakfast

per night:	£min	£max
Single	20.00	25.00
Double	40.00	40.00

Parking for 7
🛏🍴🗄📶♿🛄💷💰✕📺🛄🚗🔍☀🐾

Map references apply to the colour maps at the back of this guide.

Littlefield Manor ⚠

👑👑

Littlefield Common, Guildford GU3 3HJ
☎ Worplesdon (01483) 233068 & 232687
Fax (01483) 233686
120-acre mixed farm. 17th C listed manor house with Tudor origins, set in large walled garden surrounded by farmland.
Bedrooms: 1 double, 1 twin
Bathrooms: 2 en-suite
Bed & breakfast

per night:	£min	£max
Single	30.00	35.00
Double	50.00	55.00

Evening meal 1900 (last orders 2130)
Parking for 10
Cards accepted: Access, Visa
🛏10🍴♿📶Ⓤ🛄📺🛄🚗☀✕🐾Ⓣ

HAILSHAM

East Sussex
Map ref 2D3

An important market town since Norman times and still one of the largest markets in Sussex. Two miles west, at Upper Dicker, is Michelham Priory, an Augustinian house founded in 1229.
Tourist Information Centre ☎ (01323) 844426

Sandy Bank ⚠

👑👑 **COMMENDED**

Old Road, Magham Down, Hailsham BN27 1PW
☎ (01323) 842488
Fax (01323) 842488
Well-appointed en-suite rooms in recent development adjacent to cottage, plus one en-suite in cottage. In attractive Sussex countryside with easy access to Downs and sea. Ideal base for touring Sussex. Friendly atmosphere. Evening meals by prior arrangement.
Bedrooms: 3 twin
Bathrooms: 3 en-suite
Bed & breakfast

per night:	£min	£max
Single	22.00	
Double	40.00	

Evening meal 1900 (last orders 2030)
Parking for 3
🛏🍴🗄♿🛄🚗☀✕🐾

Establishments should be open throughout the year, unless otherwise stated.

HARTFIELD

East Sussex
Map ref 2D2

Pleasant village in Ashdown Forest, the setting for A A Milne's "Winnie the Pooh" stories.

Stairs Farmhouse and Tea Room ⚠

Listed **COMMENDED**

High Street, Hartfield TN7 4AB
☎ (01892) 770793
Fax (01892) 770793
17th C modernised farmhouse with various period features, in picturesque village. Close to Pooh Bridge and Hever Castle. Views over open countryside. Home produced additive-free meals provided. Tea room and farm shop.
Bedrooms: 1 double, 2 twin
Bathrooms: 1 private, 2 public
Bed & breakfast

per night:	£min	£max
Single	20.00	35.00
Double	40.00	45.00

Half board per person:

	£min	£max
Daily	30.00	45.00

Lunch available
Evening meal 1800 (last orders 1930)
Parking for 16
Cards accepted: Access, Visa
🛏🗄🍴♿📶💷🔥✕📺🛄🚗🛏6☀🅿🐾

HASLEMERE

Surrey
Map ref 2C2

Town set in hilly, wooded countryside, much of it in the keeping of the National Trust.

Town House

Listed **HIGHLY COMMENDED**

High Street, Haslemere GU27 2JY
☎ (01428) 643310
Fax (01428) 641080
Period house in centre of quiet town. Panelled reception rooms, period furniture throughout. Easy walking to restaurants and pubs.
Bedrooms: 2 double, 1 twin
Bathrooms: 2 en-suite, 1 private
Bed & breakfast

per night:	£min	£max
Single	25.00	25.00
Double	38.00	40.00

Parking for 3
Open February–December
🛏4♿📶Ⓤ✕🔥📺🛄🚗☀✕🐾🐾

HASTINGS

East Sussex
Map ref 3B4

Ancient town which became famous as the base from which William the Conqueror set out to fight the Battle of Hastings. Later became one of the Cinque Ports, now a leading resort. Castle, Hastings Embroidery inspired by the Bayeux Tapestry and Sea Life Centre.
Tourist Information Centre ☎ (01424) 781111

Eagle House Hotel M

👑👑👑

12 Pevensey Road, St. Leonards-on-Sea, Hastings TN38 0JZ
☎ (01424) 430535 & 441273
Fax (01424) 437771
Large Victorian residence in its own grounds. Well placed for most local amenities and for visiting "1066" country.
Bedrooms: 14 double, 4 twin
Bathrooms: 18 en-suite, 2 public

Bed & breakfast

per night:	£min	£max
Single	31.60	31.60
Double	49.00	49.00

Half board per person:

	£min	£max
Daily	43.45	43.45
Weekly	282.15	282.15

Lunch available
Evening meal 1830 (last orders 2030)
Parking for 14
Cards accepted: Access, Visa, Diners, Amex

🛏5🏨📞🖥📺🛋🍴❄✈🚗

HAWKHURST

Kent
Map ref 3B4

Village in 3 parts: Gill's Green, Highgate and the Moor. There is a colonnaded shopping centre, large village green, church and inn which is associated with the Hawkhurst smuggling gang.

Southgate Little Fowlers

👑👑 COMMENDED

Rye Road, Hawkhurst, Cranbrook TN18 5DA
☎ (01580) 752526

17th C former dower house amidst many National Trust attractions - Sissinghurst, Scotney, Dixter, Batemans, Bodiam. Period bedrooms with beautiful views. Superb breakfast in flower-filled original Victorian conservatory. Few minutes' walk for evening meals.
Bedrooms: 1 double, 1 triple
Bathrooms: 2 en-suite

Bed & breakfast

per night:	£min	£max
Double	40.00	46.00

Parking for 5
Open March–October

🛏🖥♿🗝📺🛋🍴❄🚗⊗

HAYWARDS HEATH

West Sussex
Map ref 2D3

Busy market town and administrative centre of mid-Sussex, with interesting old buildings and a modern shopping centre.

The Anchorhold M

Listed APPROVED

35 Paddock Hall Road, Haywards Heath RH16 1HN
☎ (01444) 452468
Fax (01444) 453350
Bed and breakfast in a peaceful, detached cottage situated in a large garden. Close to town centre and British Rail station.
Bedrooms: 2 single, 2 twin
Bathrooms: 1 public

Bed & breakfast

per night:	£min	£max
Single	16.00	
Double	32.00	

Parking for 3

🛏🖥📺🛋🍴🚗
SP 🏘

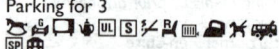

The map references refer to the colour maps towards the end of the guide. The first figure is the map number; the letter and figure which follow indicate the grid reference on the map.

HERSTMONCEUX

East Sussex
Map ref 3B4

Pleasant village noted for its woodcrafts and the beautiful 15th C moated Herstmonceux Castle (gardens only open to visitors).

Conquerors M

👑👑 HIGHLY COMMENDED

Stunts Green, Herstmonceux, Hailsham BN27 4PR
☎ (01323) 832446
Fax (01323) 832446
13-acre mixed farm. Charming single-storey home set in own farmland with spectacular views over 1066 country to Eastbourne and the sea. Total tranquillity in complete comfort.
Bedrooms: 1 double, 2 twin
Bathrooms: 2 en-suite, 1 private

Bed & breakfast

per night:	£min	£max
Single	20.00	25.00
Double	40.00	48.00

Parking for 25

🛏10🏨♿🗝📺🛋🚗❄🏘 T

The Stud Farm

👑👑 COMMENDED

Bodle Street Green, Herstmonceux, Hailsham BN27 4RJ
☎ (01323) 833201
Fax (01323) 833201
70-acre mixed farm. Upstairs, 2 bedrooms and bathroom let as one unit to party of 2, 3 or 4. Downstairs, twin-bedded en-suite room. Guests' sitting room and sunroom.
Bedrooms: 1 double, 2 twin
Bathrooms: 1 en-suite, 1 public

Bed & breakfast

per night:	£min	£max
Single	22.00	25.00
Double	34.00	38.00

Half board per person:

	£min	£max
Daily	27.50	33.50
Weekly	178.50	213.50

Evening meal from 1830
Parking for 3

🛏🏨📞🖥♿📺🛋✈🚗

The symbols in each entry give information about services and facilities. A 'key' to these symbols appears at the back of this guide.

HOLLINGBOURNE

Kent
Map ref 3B3

Pleasant village near romantic Leeds Castle in the heart of orchard country at the foot of the North Downs. Some fine half-timbered houses and a flint and ragstone church.

Woodhouses M

Listed | APPROVED

49 Eyhorne Street, Hollingbourne, Maidstone ME17 1TR
☎ Maidstone (01622) 880594
Fax (01622) 880594
Interconnected listed cottages dating from 17th C, with inglenook fireplace and exposed wooden beams. Well-stocked cottage garden.
Bedrooms: 1 double, 2 twin
Bathrooms: 3 en-suite

Bed & breakfast per night:	£min	£max
Single	17.50	18.50
Double	34.00	35.00

Parking for 4

HOLMBURY ST MARY

Surrey
Map ref 2D2

Pleasant valley village with a church which was established in the 1870s when the railway came to Dorking. Magnificent views from Holmbury Hill.

Royal Oak M

Listed | APPROVED

Holmbury St Mary, Dorking RH5 6PF
☎ Dorking (01306) 730120
Attractive country pub set on the village green in Surrey hills. Many lovely walks, convenient for railway stations, London, Gatwick and South Coast.
Bedrooms: 1 single, 1 double
Bathrooms: 2 en-suite

Bed & breakfast per night:	£min	£max
Single	25.00	
Double	38.00	

Lunch available
Evening meal 1800 (last orders 2130)
Parking for 16
Cards accepted: Access, Visa, Switch/Delta

HORLEY

Surrey
Map ref 2D2

Town on the London to Brighton road, just north of Gatwick Airport, with an ancient parish church and 15th C inn.

Belmont House M

COMMENDED

46 Massetts Road, Horley RH6 7DS
☎ (01293) 820500 & 775341
Fax (01293) 783812
Friendly family guesthouse in pleasant, quiet and green residential area, 2 minutes from shops, restaurants and railway station. 1.5 miles from Gatwick Airport.
Bedrooms: 2 double, 2 twin, 3 triple
Bathrooms: 4 en-suite, 1 public

Bed & breakfast per night:	£min	£max
Single	26.00	35.00
Double	36.00	45.00

Parking for 22
Cards accepted: Access, Visa, Amex

Chalet Guest House M

COMMENDED

77 Massetts Road, Horley RH6 7EB
☎ (01293) 821666
Fax (01293) 821619
Comfortable modern guesthouse. Convenient for Gatwick Airport, motorways, railway station, local bus, shops, pubs and restaurants.
Bedrooms: 3 single, 1 double, 1 twin, 1 triple
Bathrooms: 5 en-suite, 1 public

Bed & breakfast per night:	£min	£max
Single	26.00	34.00
Double	44.00	44.00

Parking for 14
Cards accepted: Access, Visa

The Lawn Guest House M

HIGHLY COMMENDED

30 Massetts Road, Horley RH6 7DE
☎ (01293) 775751
Fax (01293) 821803
Classic Victorian house with mature garden, 2 minutes from Horley centre, restaurants, pubs and main rail station to London/Brighton. 5 minutes' drive to Gatwick, long-term parking. Non-smoking.
Bedrooms: 1 double, 4 twin, 2 triple
Bathrooms: 7 en-suite

Bed & breakfast per night:	£min	£max
Double	42.00	45.00

Parking for 10
Cards accepted: Access, Visa, Amex

Woodlands Guest House

COMMENDED

42 Massetts Road, Horley RH6 7DS
☎ (01293) 782994
Fax (01293) 776358
1 mile from Gatwick airport. All rooms en-suite with colour TV, tea/coffee facilities. Residents' lounge. Car parking. Courtesy car by arrangement. Non-smoking.
Bedrooms: 1 single, 2 double, 2 twin
Bathrooms: 5 en-suite, 1 public

Bed & breakfast per night:	£min	£max
Single	27.50	30.00
Double	38.00	40.00

Parking for 32

HOVE

East Sussex

See under Brighton & Hove

LEATHERHEAD

Surrey
Map ref 2D2

Old county town in the Green Belt, with the modern Thorndike Theatre.

Bronwen

Listed

Crabtree Drive, Givons Grove, Leatherhead KT22 8LJ
☎ (01372) 372515
Large family house in the Green Belt at Leatherhead. Adjoins open farmland and is close to National Trust areas of Headley Heath and Box Hill. 20 minutes from Gatwick, 30 minutes from Heathrow, 40 minutes from central London.
Bedrooms: 1 single, 1 double, 1 triple
Bathrooms: 1 en-suite, 1 public

Bed & breakfast per night:	£min	£max
Single	21.00	25.00
Double	42.00	50.00

Half board per person:	£min	£max
Daily	30.00	35.00
Weekly	200.00	250.00

Continued ▶

LEATHERHEAD

Continued

Lunch available
Evening meal 1900 (last orders 2100)
Parking for 4

🛇🔥🏠🖨👤♿Ⓤ🔒Ⓢ✕🐾TV🖿🎦
🍴❋✕🚗SP

LENHAM

Kent
Map ref 3B4

Shops, inns and houses, many displaying timber-work of the late Middle Ages, surround a square which is the centre of the village. The 14th C parish church has one of the best examples of a Kentish tower.

The Dog & Bear Hotel ⋒

👑👑👑 COMMENDED

The Square, Lenham, Maidstone ME17 2PG
☎ Maidstone (01622) 858219
Fax (01622) 859415

15th C coaching inn retaining its old world character and serving good Kent ale, lagers and fine wines with home cooking. En-suite rooms. 5 minutes' drive from Leeds Castle. Half board daily prices are for a minimum 2-night stay.
Wheelchair access category 3☆
Bedrooms: 3 single, 13 double, 5 twin, 2 triple, 1 family room
Suites available
Bathrooms: 24 en-suite

Bed & breakfast
per night:	£min	£max
Single	37.50	40.00
Double	47.50	50.00

Half board per
person:	£min	£max
Daily	37.50	40.00
Weekly	262.50	280.00

Lunch available
Evening meal 1900 (last orders 2130)
Parking for 26
Cards accepted: Access, Visa, Amex, Switch/Delta

🛇🔥🏠🍷🖨🏠👤♿Ⓢ✕🖿🖿🗲
🍴50🔔SP🎦Ⓣ

LEWES

East Sussex
Map ref 2D3

Historic county town with Norman castle. The steep High Street has mainly Georgian buildings. There is a folk museum at Anne of Cleves House and the archaeological museum is in Barbican House. *Tourist Information Centre ☎ (01273) 483448*

Ousedale House ⋒

👑👑👑 HIGHLY COMMENDED

Offham, Lewes BN7 3QF
☎ (01273) 478680
Fax (01273) 486510
Victorian country house with 3.5 acres of garden and woodland. Panoramic view of Ouse Valley. Convenient Glyndebourne (hampers provided) and National Trust properties.
Bedrooms: 1 double, 2 twin
Bathrooms: 2 en-suite, 1 private

Bed & breakfast
per night:	£min	£max
Single	22.00	25.00
Double	48.00	50.00

Half board per
person:	£min	£max
Daily	34.00	39.00

Evening meal 1800 (last orders 1830)
Parking for 17
Cards accepted: Access, Visa, Amex

🛇12🏠🖨🏠👤♿Ⓢ✕🐾TV🖿
🖿🍴25❋✕🚗🚭SP🎦◎

LIMPSFIELD

Surrey
Map ref 2D2

Arawa ⋒

Listed

58 Granville Road, Limpsfield, Oxted RH8 0BZ
☎ Oxted (01883) 714104
Family home near North Downs Way, Chartwell and Hever. Near rail service to London and 30 minutes to Gatwick by car. Friendly and comfortable.
Bedrooms: 2 twin
Bathrooms: 2 public

Bed & breakfast
per night:	£min	£max
Single	18.00	27.00
Double	32.00	50.00

Parking for 1

🛇🔥🏠🖨👤♿🦮Ⓤ Ⓢ✕TV🖿🏠
❋🚗Ⓣ

LYMINSTER

West Sussex
Map ref 2D3

Links up with Littlehampton looking inland, and across the watermeadows to the churches and towers of Arundel.

Sandfield House ⋒

👑👑 COMMENDED

Lyminster, Littlehampton BN17 7PG
☎ Littlehampton (01903) 724129
Fax (01903) 859986
Spacious country-style family house in 2 acres. Between Arundel and sea, in area of great natural beauty.
Bedrooms: 1 double
Bathrooms: 1 public

Bed & breakfast
per night:	£min	£max
Double	34.00	38.00

Parking for 4

🛇🖨🏠👤♿ⓊⓈ🐾TV🖿🏠❋✕
🚗

MAIDSTONE

Kent
Map ref 3B3

Busy county town of Kent on the River Medway has many interesting features and is an excellent centre for excursions. Museum of Carriages, Museum and Art Gallery, Archbishop's Palace, Mote Park. *Tourist Information Centre ☎ (01622) 673581 or 602169*

Grove House ⋒

Listed HIGHLY COMMENDED

Grove Green Road, Weavering Street, Maidstone ME14 5JT
☎ (01622) 738441

Attractive comfortable home in pleasant surroundings.
Bedrooms: 2 double, 1 twin
Bathrooms: 2 en-suite, 1 private

Bed & breakfast
per night:	£min	£max
Single	20.00	25.00
Double	40.00	45.00

Parking for 6

🖨👤♿Ⓤ✕🖿❋✕🚗

Willington Court ♙

[HIGHLY COMMENDED]

Willington Street, Maidstone
ME15 8JW
☎ (01622) 738885
Fax (01622) 631790
Charming Grade II listed building. Antiques, four-poster bed. Friendly and relaxed atmosphere. Adjacent to Mote Park and near Leeds Castle.
Bedrooms: 2 double, 1 twin
Bathrooms: 2 en-suite, 1 private
Bed & breakfast

per night:	£min	£max
Single	26.00	34.00
Double	40.00	48.00

Parking for 6
Cards accepted: Access, Visa, Diners, Amex

Oldest and most famous resort in Kent. Many Regency and Victorian buildings survive from the town's early days. There are 9 miles of sandy beach. "Dreamland" is a 20-acre amusement park and the Winter Gardens offers concert hall entertainment.
Tourist Information Centre ☎ (01843) 220241

The Malvern Hotel ♙

[COMMENDED]

29 Eastern Esplanade, Cliftonville, Margate CT9 2HL
☎ Thanet (01843) 290192
Overlooking the sea, promenade and lawns. Close indoor/outdoor bowls complex, Margate Winter Gardens, amenities and Channel ports. Parking (unrestricted) outside and opposite hotel. TV and tea-making facilities - most rooms en-suite with shower and toilet (no baths).
Bedrooms: 1 single, 6 double, 2 twin, 1 family room
Bathrooms: 8 en-suite, 1 public
Bed & breakfast

per night:	£min	£max
Single	20.00	30.00
Double	36.00	42.00

Cards accepted: Access, Visa, Diners, Amex

Establishments should be open throughout the year, unless otherwise stated.

Historic, picturesque town just north of the South Downs, with the ruins of Cowdray House, medieval castle and 15th C parish church. Polo at Cowdray Park. Excellent base for Chichester, Petworth, Glorious Goodwood and the South Downs Way.
Tourist Information Centre ☎ (01730) 817322

Crown Inn ♙

[Listed]

Edinburgh Square, Midhurst
GU29 9NL
☎ (01730) 813462
16th C freehouse behind and below the church. Large selection of real ales, good wine list, open fires. TV and central heating.
Bedrooms: 1 single, 1 double, 1 twin
Bathrooms: 1 public
Bed & breakfast

per night:	£min	£max
Single	15.00	20.00
Double	25.00	30.00

Lunch available
Evening meal 1900 (last orders 2000)

Lies on one of the pilgrims' ways to Canterbury. There are some good period houses, a well-restored church, a village pump of wrought-iron and a village green.

Fairseat House ♙

[Listed] [HIGHLY COMMENDED]

Newick, Lewes BN8 4PJ
☎ (01825) 722263
Edwardian period house set in 5 acres with heated pool. Comfortable, prettily decorated rooms, including four-poster. Convenient for Newhaven, Bluebell Railway and Glyndebourne.
Bedrooms: 2 double, 1 twin
Bathrooms: 2 en-suite, 1 private
Bed & breakfast

per night:	£min	£max
Single	27.00	42.00
Double	42.00	60.00

Half board per person:	£min	£max
Daily	31.75	52.50

Lunch available
Evening meal 1930 (last orders 2030)
Parking for 6
Cards accepted: Access, Visa

Village on the Romney Marsh with a 13th C church, 2 miles from the Cinque Port of New Romney.

Rose & Crown Inn ♙

[Listed]

Old Romney, Romney Marsh
TN29 9SQ
☎ New Romney (01797) 367500
17th C traditional country inn with modern chalet accommodation, 100 yards south of A259 at Old Romney crossroad (2.25 miles west of New Romney).
Bedrooms: 5 twin
Bathrooms: 5 en-suite
Bed & breakfast

per night:	£min	£max
Single	23.00	28.00
Double	38.00	44.00

Lunch available
Evening meal 1900 (last orders 2100)
Parking for 20

Pleasant town on the edge of National Trust woodland and at the foot of the North Downs. Chartwell (National Trust), the former home of Sir Winston Churchill, is close by.

The New Bungalow ♙

[Listed] [APPROVED]

Old Hall Farm, Tandridge Lane, Oxted RH8 9NS
☎ South Godstone (01342) 892508
Fax (01342) 892508
40-acre livestock farm. Spacious, modern bungalow set in green fields and reached by a private drive. 5 minutes' drive from M25.
Bedrooms: 1 twin, 1 family room
Bathrooms: 1 public
Bed & breakfast

per night:	£min	£max
Single	22.00	25.00
Double	32.00	35.00

Parking for 5

PARTRIDGE GREEN

West Sussex
Map ref 2D3

Small village between Henfield and Billingshurst.

Pound Cottage Bed and Breakfast ⚊

COMMENDED

Mill lane, Littleworth, Partridge Green, Horsham RH13 8JU
☎ (01403) 710218 & 711285
Pleasant country house in quiet surroundings. 8 miles from Horsham, 25 minutes from Gatwick. Just off the B2135 West Grinstead to Steyning road.
Bedrooms: 1 single, 1 double, 1 twin
Bathrooms: 1 public

Bed & breakfast per night:	£min	£max
Single	16.00	16.00
Double	32.00	32.00

Half board per person:	£min	£max
Daily	22.00	22.00
Weekly	154.00	154.00

Evening meal from 1830
Parking for 8
🐎 ⬚ ♨ ⓤ 🅟 ✻ 📺 🏛 ❊ ✕ 🚐

PENSHURST

Kent
Map ref 2D2

Pretty village in a hilly wooded setting with Penshurst Place, the ancestral home of the Sidney family since 1552, standing in delightful grounds with a formal Tudor garden.

Finch Green ⚊

Listed COMMENDED

Chiddingstone Hoath, Edenbridge TN8 7DJ
☎ (01892) 870648
Fax (01892) 870648
Delightful period cottage in quiet rural location with pretty views. Comfortable rooms and friendly atmosphere. Close to Penshurst and Hever. Three excellent pubs nearby.
Bedrooms: 2 single, 1 double, 1 twin
Bathrooms: 2 en-suite, 2 private

Bed & breakfast per night:	£min	£max
Single	25.00	30.00
Double	40.00	44.00

Parking for 4
🐎 10 🖃 ♨ ⓤ ✻ 🔏 🏛 🔌 ❊ ✕ 🚐

PETWORTH

West Sussex
Map ref 2D3

Town dominated by Petworth House (National Trust), the great 17th C mansion, set in 2000 acres of parkland laid out by Capability Brown. The house contains wood-carvings by Grinling Gibbons. *Tourist Information Centre* ☎ *(01798) 343523*

White Horse Inn ⚊

⚊ ⚊ HIGHLY COMMENDED

The Street, Sutton, Pulborough RH20 1PS
☎ Sutton (01798) 869221
Fax (01798) 869291

Pretty Georgian village inn close to South Downs Way. Roman villa 1 mile. Garden, log fires. 4 miles Petworth, 5 miles Pulborough.
Bedrooms: 4 double, 2 twin
Bathrooms: 5 en-suite, 1 private shower

Bed & breakfast per night:	£min	£max
Single	48.00	48.00
Double	58.00	68.00

Half board per person:	£min	£max
Daily	43.00	62.00
Weekly	218.00	302.00

Lunch available
Evening meal 1900 (last orders 2145)
Parking for 10
Cards accepted: Access, Visa, Diners, Amex
🐎 📞 ⬚ ♨ 🅢 ✻ 🔌 ❊ ✕ 🚐 ⚟
SP 🎏 T

WELCOME HOST

This is a nationally recognised customer care programme which aims to promote the highest standards of service and a warm welcome. Establishments who are taking part in this initiative are indicated by the ⚘ symbol.

POYNINGS

West Sussex
Map ref 2D3

Set in the South Downs behind Brighton, with Dyke Hill above, on which there was an Iron Age camp, and the Devil's Dyke along the southern side.

Poynings Manor Farm ⚊

COMMENDED

Poynings, Brighton BN45 7AG
☎ Brighton (01273) 857371
Fax (01273) 857371
260-acre mixed farm. Charming old farmhouse in quiet scenic surroundings. Ideal for walkers, riders and country lovers. Coast 15 minutes, Gatwick 30 minutes.
Bedrooms: 1 double, 2 twin
Bathrooms: 2 public

Bed & breakfast per night:	£min	£max
Single	25.00	
Double	38.00	40.00

Evening meal from 1900
Parking for 6
🐎 📞 🖃 ♨ ⓤ 🅢 🅟 ✻ 🏛 🔌 ⊃ ∪ ↑ ❊ 🐎 🚐

RAMSGATE

Kent
Map ref 3C3

Popular holiday resort with good sandy beaches. At Pegwell Bay is replica of a Viking longship. Terminal for car-ferry service to Dunkirk and Ostend. *Tourist Information Centre* ☎ *(01843) 583333*

Eastwood Guest House ⚊

Listed COMMENDED

28 Augusta Road, Ramsgate CT11 8JS
☎ Thanet (01843) 591505
Fax (01843) 591505

Pretty Victorian villa, close to ferry port and amenities. Comfortable rooms, mostly en-suite. Lock-up garages available. Breakfast served from 6.45 am, dinner available.
Bedrooms: 1 single, 4 double, 4 twin, 6 family rooms
Bathrooms: 10 en-suite, 3 public

Bed & breakfast per night:	£min	£max
Single	15.00	25.00
Double	30.00	35.00

Half board per person:	£min	£max
Daily	20.00	25.00
Weekly	140.00	175.00

Evening meal 1830 (last orders 1930)
Parking for 20

ROGATE

West Sussex
Map ref 2C3

On the main road between Midhurst and Petersfield, Rogate probably gets its name from its position as gateway to wooded hill slopes, the habitat of deer.

Trotton Farm

COMMENDED

Trotton, Petersfield, Hampshire
GU31 5EN
☎ Midhurst (01730) 813618
Fax (01730) 816093
Farmhouse just off the A272, access through yard. Accommodation and lounge/games room in a converted cartshed adjoining farmhouse. All rooms with en-suite shower.
Bedrooms: 1 double, 2 twin
Bathrooms: 3 en-suite

Bed & breakfast per night:	£min	£max
Single	25.00	30.00
Double	35.00	40.00

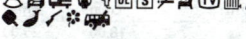

ROTTINGDEAN

East Sussex
Map ref 2D3

The quiet High Street contains a number of fine old buildings and the village pond and green are close by.

Braemar Guest House

Steyning Road, Rottingdean,
Brighton BN2 7GA
☎ Brighton (01273) 304263
Family-run guesthouse, proud of its cheerful atmosphere, in an old world village where Rudyard Kipling once lived.
Bedrooms: 5 single, 5 double, 2 twin, 2 triple
Bathrooms: 3 public, 2 private showers

Bed & breakfast per night:	£min	£max
Single	15.00	17.50
Double	30.00	35.00

ROYAL TUNBRIDGE WELLS

Kent
Map ref 2D2

This "Royal" town became famous as a spa in the 17th C and much of its charm is retained, as in the Pantiles, a shaded walk lined with elegant shops. Heritage attraction "A Day at the Wells". Rich in parks and gardens and a good centre for walks. Excellent shopping centre.
Tourist Information Centre ☎ (01892) 515675

Chequers

HIGHLY COMMENDED

Camden Park, Royal Tunbridge Wells TN2 5AD
☎ Tunbridge Wells (01892) 532299
Friendly family house, origins 1840. Part-walled garden. Unique private location, 10 minutes from Pantiles, high street, railway station. Peaceful, comfortable, central base. Non-smokers only, please.
Bedrooms: 1 single, 1 twin
Bathrooms: 1 en-suite, 1 private

Bed & breakfast per night:	£min	£max
Single	18.00	20.00
Double	35.00	38.00

Parking for 5

Cheviots

COMMENDED

Cousley Wood, Wadhurst, East Sussex TN5 6HD
☎ Wadhurst (01892) 782952
On B2100 between Lamberhurst and Wadhurst. Comfortable bed and breakfast in modern country house with extensive garden. Home cooking. Convenient base for walking and motoring. Close to Bewl Water.
Bedrooms: 2 single, 2 twin
Bathrooms: 2 en-suite, 1 public

Bed & breakfast per night:	£min	£max
Single	17.00	25.00
Double	34.00	50.00

Half board per person:	£min	£max
Daily	32.00	40.00
Weekly	213.00	266.00

Evening meal from 1800
Parking for 4
Cards accepted: Access, Visa, Switch/Delta

Hawkenbury Farm

Hawkenbury Road, Royal Tunbridge Wells TN3 9AD
☎ Tunbridge Wells (01892) 536977
Fax (01892) 536200
Comfortable accommodation on small working farm in quiet location one and a half miles south-east of Tunbridge Wells. Unlimited parking, views and walks. Many National Trust properties nearby.
Bedrooms: 1 double, 1 twin
Bathrooms: 1 en-suite, 1 private

Bed & breakfast per night:	£min	£max
Double	36.00	40.00

Parking for 7

Manor Court Farm

Ashurst, Royal Tunbridge Wells TN3 9TB
☎ Fordcombe (01892) 740279
350-acre mixed farm. Georgian farmhouse with friendly atmosphere. Spacious rooms and lovely views overlooking Medway Valley. Good base for walking and touring. Weekend cream teas. On A264, half a mile east of Ashurst village (Tunbridge Wells to East Grinstead road).
Bedrooms: 1 double, 2 twin
Bathrooms: 1 private, 2 public

Bed & breakfast per night:	£min	£max
Single	19.00	29.00
Double	38.00	40.00

Parking for 19

Nellington Mead

Nellington Road, Royal Tunbridge Wells TN4 8SQ
☎ Tunbridge Wells (01892) 545037
Comfortable modern house with extensive garden. Easy access to Kent/Sussex countryside, historic houses and gardens, London and coast.
Bedrooms: 1 twin
Bathrooms: 1 en-suite

Bed & breakfast per night:	£min	£max
Single	20.00	20.00
Double	39.00	39.00

Continued ▶

ROYAL TUNBRIDGE WELLS
Continued

Half board per person:

	£min	£max
Daily	30.00	30.00
Weekly	210.00	210.00

Evening meal from 1900
Parking for 5
Open January–November

🐎🖵📺📖♨🈂✂🐎🖩🖳🛏🎁🚲🐕🐾

The Old Parsonage ♏
👑👑👑 DE LUXE

Church Lane, Frant, Royal Tunbridge Wells TN3 9DX
☎ Frant (01892) 750773
Fax (01892) 750773
Peacefully situated by the village church (2 pubs and restaurant nearby), this classic Georgian country house provides superior accommodation: en-suite bedrooms, antique-furnished reception rooms, spacious conservatory and ballustraded terrace overlooking the secluded walled garden. SEETB 1995 "Bed and Breakfast of the Year" Award winner.
Bedrooms: 2 double, 1 twin
Bathrooms: 3 en-suite
Bed & breakfast per night:

	£min	£max
Single	34.00	44.00
Double	54.00	64.00

Parking for 12
Cards accepted: Access, Visa

🐎🖵📖♨🈂🔍S📺🖩🛏❄🎁🚲🐾🏠T

RYE
East Sussex
Map ref 3B4

Cobbled, hilly streets and fine old buildings make Rye, once a Cinque Port, a most picturesque town. Noted for its church with ancient clock, potteries and antique shops. Town Model Sound and Light Show gives a good introduction to the town.
Tourist Information Centre ☎ (01797) 226696

Aviemore Guest House ♏
👑 APPROVED

28/30 Fishmarket Road, Rye TN31 7LP
☎ (01797) 223052
Fax (01797) 223052

Owner-run, friendly guesthouse offering a warm welcome and hearty breakfast. Overlooking "Town Salts" and the River Rother. 2 minutes from town centre.
Bedrooms: 1 single, 4 double, 3 twin
Bathrooms: 4 en-suite, 2 public
Bed & breakfast per night:

	£min	£max
Single	17.00	22.00
Double	30.00	42.00

Half board per person:

	£min	£max
Daily	23.00	28.00
Weekly	151.00	179.00

Evening meal 1800 (last orders 2200)
Cards accepted: Access, Visa, Amex

🐎🖵♨🈂S🛏📺🖩🚲🐾 DAP 🚲 SP T

Green Hedges ♏
👑👑👑 HIGHLY COMMENDED

Hillyfields, Rye Hill, Rye TN31 7NH
☎ (01797) 222185
Country house in a private road. 1.5 acres of landscaped gardens with heated swimming pool. Short stroll to town centre. Ample parking. Home-grown organic produce.
Bedrooms: 2 double, 1 twin
Bathrooms: 3 en-suite, 1 public
Bed & breakfast per night:

	£min	£max
Single	40.00	60.00
Double	50.00	60.00

Parking for 7
Cards accepted: Access, Visa

🐎12🖵♨🈂🔍U📖S✂🛏🖩🚲
🏊❄🎁🐾🖳SP

Jeake's House ♏
👑👑👑 HIGHLY COMMENDED

Mermaid Street, Rye TN31 7ET
☎ (01797) 222828
Fax (01797) 222623

Recapture the past in this historic building, in a cobblestoned street at the heart of the old town. Honeymoon suite available.
Bedrooms: 1 single, 7 double, 1 twin, 2 triple, 1 family room

Bathrooms: 7 en-suite, 1 private, 2 public, 2 private showers
Bed & breakfast per night:

	£min	£max
Single	22.50	54.00
Double	41.00	59.00

Cards accepted: Access, Visa, Amex

🐎🖵📖♨🈂S🛏🖩🚲🐾
SP🏠T❄

Kimblee ♏
👑👑 COMMENDED

Main Street, Peasmarsh, Rye TN31 6UL
☎ Peasmarsh (01797) 230514 &
Mobile 0831 841004
Country house with views from all aspects, 250 metres from pub/restaurant and 5 minutes' drive on the A268 from Rye. Warm welcome.
Bedrooms: 3 double
Bathrooms: 3 en-suite
Bed & breakfast per night:

	£min	£max
Single	18.00	20.00
Double	36.00	38.00

Parking for 4
Cards accepted: Access, Visa

🐎🖵♨🔍U🈂S🛏🖩🚲🐾
🖳 DAP SP T

The Old Vicarage
Listed COMMENDED

Rye Harbour, Rye TN31 7TT
☎ (01797) 222088
Imposing Victorian former vicarage, quietly situated close to sea and nature reserve. Antique furniture and open fires. Good English breakfast.
Bedrooms: 1 double, 1 twin
Bathrooms: 1 public
Bed & breakfast per night:

	£min	£max
Single	18.00	25.00
Double	36.00	39.00

Parking for 4

🐎🖵♨U🈂S✂🖩🚲🐾SP

Playden Cottage Guesthouse ♏
👑👑👑 HIGHLY COMMENDED

Military Road, Rye TN31 7NY
☎ (01797) 222234

Large character cottage, said to be "Grebe" from E. F. Benson's Mapp and Lucia novels. Personal service in a comfortable family home. Pretty gardens, rural aspect, peaceful.

Bedrooms: 1 double, 2 twin
Bathrooms: 3 en-suite, 1 public

Bed & breakfast

per night:	£min	£max
Single	37.50	60.00
Double	50.00	60.00

Half board per

person:	£min	£max
Daily	37.00	72.00
Weekly	241.50	273.00

Evening meal 1800 (last orders
2030)
Parking for 7
Cards accepted: Access, Visa

⌖12▯♿🅿♨️🛡ⓢ🅿📺📻🖊☀️
🚐🚭 SP 🏠 Ⓣ ◎

Saint Margarets 🔔

Listed COMMENDED

Dumbwomans Lane, Udimore, Rye
TN31 6AD
☎ (01797) 222586
*Comfortable, friendly chalet bungalow
with sea views. Car parking.
Shower/WC en-suite. On B2089, 2
miles west of Rye.*
Bedrooms: 2 double, 1 twin
Suites available
Bathrooms: 3 en-suite

Bed & breakfast

per night:	£min	£max
Double	29.00	30.00

Parking for 3
Open February–November

⌖♿▯♨️🛡🅿🖊🖥🚐

Strand House 🔔

COMMENDED

Winchelsea TN36 4JT
☎ (01797) 226276
Fax (01797) 224806

*The old-world charm of one of
Winchelsea's oldest houses, dating
from the 15th C, with oak beams and
inglenooks. Overlooking National Trust
pastureland. Four-poster bedroom.
Residents' licence.*
Bedrooms: 8 double, 1 twin, 1 triple
Bathrooms: 8 en-suite, 1 public

Bed & breakfast

per night:	£min	£max
Single	28.00	34.00
Double	40.00	60.00

Evening meal 1800 (last orders
1900)
Parking for 12
Cards accepted: Access, Visa

⌖5♿🏠▯♨️🛡ⓢ🖊📺
🖥🖊☀️🚐🚭 SP 🏠

Top o'The Hill at Rye 🔔

COMMENDED

Rye Hill, Rye TN31 7NH
☎ (01797) 223284
Fax (01797) 227030
*Small, friendly inn offering fine
traditional food and cottage-style
accommodation. Central for touring
Kent and Sussex, Channel ports nearby.
Large car park, garden.*
Bedrooms: 5 double, 2 twin, 1 triple
Bathrooms: 8 en-suite

Bed & breakfast

per night:	£min	£max
Single	25.00	26.00
Double	42.00	48.00

Lunch available
Evening meal 1900 (last orders
2100)
Parking for 32
Cards accepted: Access, Visa

⌖♿▯▯♨️🛡📺🖥🖊12Ⓤ
☀️🚭 SP 🏠 ◎

ST NICHOLAS AT WADE

Kent
Map ref 3C3

Village in the Isle of Thanet with
ancient church built of knapped flint.

Streete Farm House

Listed

Court Road, St Nicholas at Wade,
Birchington CT7 0NH
☎ Thanet (01843) 847245
*50-acre arable and mixed farm. 16th C
farmhouse on the outskirts of the
village, with original oak-panelled dining
room.*
Bedrooms: 1 single, 2 double
Bathrooms: 1 public

Bed & breakfast

per night:	£min	£max
Single	16.00	17.50
Double	32.00	35.00

Parking for 4

⌖3▯♨️🅾️🛡📺🖥☀️🚶🚐🏠

SANDWICH

Kent
Map ref 3C3

Delightful old market town, once a
Cinque Port, now 2 miles from the
sea. Many interesting old buildings
including the 16th C Barbican and
the Guildhall which contains the
town's treasures. Several excellent
golf-courses.

St Crispin Inn 🔔

Listed COMMENDED

The Street, Worth, Deal CT14 0DF
☎ (01304) 612081
Old country inn, heavily beamed bars,

*log fires, antique furniture in bedrooms.
Good home-cooked food, real ales. Best
village pub in Kent (awarded 1988 and
1994). Large pretty garden. Good
location for golf-courses and ferries.*
Bedrooms: 4 twin, 2 triple
Bathrooms: 6 en-suite

Bed & breakfast

per night:	£min	£max
Single		35.00
Double		50.00

Lunch available
Evening meal 1800 (last orders
2130)
Parking for 30
Cards accepted: Access, Visa, Amex,
Switch/Delta

⌖♿🏠▯♨️🛡ⓢ🖥🖊🅿☀️🏠

SARRE

Kent
Map ref 3C3

Attractive Dutch-gabled houses can
be seen in this Thanet village.
Names of many famous people are
inscribed on the walls of the 16th C
Crown Inn, noted for the
manufacture of cherry brandy.

Crown Inn (The Famous Cherry Brandy House) 🔔

COMMENDED

Ramsgate Road, Sarre, Birchington
CT7 0LF
☎ Birchington (01843) 847808
Fax (01843) 847914

*Ancient traditional inn, convenient for
Canterbury. Inglenook fireplaces,
gleaming brasses, freshly prepared
regional specialities. Excellent locally
brewed ales. Half board daily prices
are for a minimum 2-night stay.*
Wheelchair access category 3🚶
Bedrooms: 9 double, 2 twin, 1 triple
Bathrooms: 12 en-suite

Bed & breakfast

per night:	£min	£max
Single	43.50	
Double	56.50	

Half board per

person:	£min	£max
Daily	37.50	40.00
Weekly	262.50	280.00

Lunch available
Evening meal 1900 (last orders
2200)
Parking for 40

Continued ▶

SARRE

Continued

Cards accepted: Access, Visa, Amex, Switch/Delta

🐾♿🛇📞🖥️□♨🛎️Ⓢ✕🏛️🖥️
🍴10✿🚐🛇SP🎣T

SEAFORD

East Sussex
Map ref 2D3

The town was a bustling port until 1579 when the course of the River Ouse was diverted. The downlands around the town make good walking country, with fine views of the Seven Sisters cliffs.
Tourist Information Centre ☎ (01323) 897426

Rowans ♏

Listed HIGHLY COMMENDED

5 Grove Road, Seaford BN25 1TP
☎ (01323) 896883
Early 1930s character home. Many original features, set in pleasant garden of 0.75 acre. Peaceful, yet close to town centre.
Bedrooms: 1 single, 1 double, 1 twin
Bathrooms: 1 public

Bed & breakfast per night:

	£min	£max
Single	18.00	18.00
Double	36.00	36.00

Evening meal 1800 (last orders 1900)
Parking for 2

🐾🍴12🛇♨Ⓢ✕🏛️🖥️🔥🎣✿✕🚐

SELSEY

West Sussex
Map ref 2C3

Almost surrounded by water, with the English Channel on two sides and an inland lake, once Pagham Harbour, and the Brook on the other two. Ideal for yachting, swimming, fishing and wildlife.

St Andrews Lodge ♏

👑👑👑 COMMENDED

Chichester Road, Selsey, Chichester PO20 0LX
☎ Chichester (01243) 606899
Fax (01243) 607826
Family-run, friendly relaxed atmosphere, licensed, en-suite bedrooms, cosy lounge, log fire. Peaceful sun trap garden. Close to natural beaches and countryside, south of Chichester.
Wheelchair access category 1♿
Bedrooms: 1 single, 3 double, 3 twin, 2 family rooms
Bathrooms: 9 en-suite

Bed & breakfast per night:

	£min	£max
Single	25.00	40.00
Double	40.00	55.00

Half board per person:

	£min	£max
Daily	29.50	37.50

Evening meal 1800 (last orders 1930)
Parking for 15
Cards accepted: Access, Visa, Amex, Switch/Delta

🐾♿📞🖥️□♨🛎️Ⓢ✕🏛️ⓉⓋ🏛️🔥
🍴♨Ⓟ✿🚐 DAP SP

SEVENOAKS

Kent
Map ref 2D2

Set in pleasant wooded country, with a distinctive character and charm. Nearby is Knole (National Trust), home of the Sackville family and one of the largest houses in England, set in a vast deer park.
Tourist Information Centre ☎ (01732) 450305

The Bull Hotel ♏

👑👑👑 APPROVED

Wrotham, Sevenoaks TN15 7RF
☎ (01732) 885522 & 883092
Fax (01732) 886288

Privately-run 14th C coaching inn, in secluded historic village 15 minutes from Sevenoaks. Just off M20 and M25/26, 30 minutes from Gatwick and London, 1 hour from Dover. Oak beams and inglenook fireplaces. Ideal for local places of interest.
Bedrooms: 1 single, 3 double, 6 twin
Bathrooms: 6 en-suite, 4 private, 1 public

Bed & breakfast per night:

	£min	£max
Single	35.00	40.00
Double	45.00	50.00

Lunch available
Evening meal 1900 (last orders 2200)
Parking for 50
Cards accepted: Access, Visa, Diners, Amex

🐾♿🛎️□♨🛎️Ⓢ🏛️🏛️🔥🍴50✿
🚐🛇 SP 🎣 T

The Moorings Hotel ♏

👑👑 APPROVED

97 Hitchen Hatch Lane, Sevenoaks TN13 3BE
☎ (01732) 452589 & 742323
Fax (01732) 456462
Friendly family hotel offering high standard accommodation for tourists and business travellers. 30 minutes from London. Close to BR station.
Bedrooms: 5 single, 5 double, 9 twin, 2 triple
Bathrooms: 21 en-suite, 1 public

Bed & breakfast per night:

	£min	£max
Single	25.00	42.00
Double	35.00	59.00

Half board per person:

	£min	£max
Daily	35.00	52.00
Weekly	245.00	364.00

Lunch available
Evening meal 1900 (last orders 2130)
Parking for 24
Cards accepted: Access, Visa, Amex, Switch/Delta

🐾♿🛎️□♨🛎️Ⓢ✕🏛️ⓉⓋ🏛️🔥
🍴45Ⓤ✿✕🚐 DAP SP T

SISSINGHURST

Kent
Map ref 3B4

1 Hillview Cottage ♏

Listed APPROVED

Starvenden Lane, Sissinghurst, Cranbrook TN17 2AN
☎ Cranbrook (01580) 712823 & Mobile 0850 909383
Total peace, Kentish countryside. Wonderful views. Tennis court. Riding close by. Minutes from Sissinghurst Castle and close to National Trust properties.
Bedrooms: 2 double
Bathrooms: 1 en-suite, 2 public

Bed & breakfast per night:

	£min	£max
Single	17.00	17.00
Double	34.00	34.00

Half board per person:

	£min	£max
Daily	29.00	29.00
Weekly	190.00	190.00

Evening meal 1800 (last orders 2000)
Parking for 6

□🎣♨✕🏛️🔥🚐🔍♿Ⓤ✿🚐

A key to symbols can be found inside the back cover flap.

SMALLFIELD

Surrey
Map ref 2D2

Small village between Horley and Lingfield, named after local estate.

Chithurst Farm

Listed COMMENDED

Chithurst Lane, Horne, Smallfield, Horley RH6 9JU
☎ (01342) 842487
92-acre dairy farm. Recently renovated 16th C listed farmhouse, with genuine beamed rooms, inglenook fireplaces and attractive garden. Set in a quiet country lane, yet convenient for Gatwick and motorways.
Bedrooms: 1 single, 1 double, 1 triple
Bathrooms: 1 public
Bed & breakfast

per night:	£min	£max
Single	15.00	19.50
Double	30.00	33.00

Parking for 3
Open February–November

SMARDEN

Kent
Map ref 3B4

Pretty village with a number of old, well-presented buildings. The 14th C St Michael's Church is sometimes known as the "Barn of Kent" because of its 36-ft roof span.

Chequers Inn ♠

COMMENDED

Smarden, Ashford TN27 8QA
☎ Ashford (01233) 770217
Fax (01233) 770623
Listed 14th C inn, wealth of oak beams, in heart of the Weald. Ideal for touring and visiting many places of historic interest. 5 golf-courses nearby. Good food always available - fresh fish a speciality.
Bedrooms: 1 single, 2 double, 2 twin
Bathrooms: 3 en-suite, 2 private, 1 public
Bed & breakfast

per night:	£min	£max
Single	23.00	23.00
Double	38.00	50.00

Lunch available
Evening meal 1800 (last orders 2200)
Parking for 18
Cards accepted: Access, Visa, Switch/Delta

SOUTHBOROUGH

Kent
Map ref 2D2

Small town between Royal Tunbridge Wells and Tonbridge with an attractive common and cricket pitch where matches can be seen regularly.

Nightingales

Listed COMMENDED

London Road, Southborough, Royal Tunbridge Wells TN4 0UJ
☎ Tunbridge Wells (01892) 528443
Fax (01892) 511376
Georgian house with lovely views over Kent countryside. Attractive, spacious bedrooms, good breakfasts, English or Continental. Families welcome, discounts for long stays. Garden, parking.
Bedrooms: 1 single, 1 double, 1 triple
Bathrooms: 1 public
Bed & breakfast

per night:	£min	£max
Single	16.00	18.00
Double	32.00	36.00

Parking for 3

STELLING MINNIS

Kent
Map ref 3B4

Off the Roman Stone Street, this quiet, picturesque village lies deep in the Lyminge Forest, south of Canterbury.

Great Field Farm ♠

Listed HIGHLY COMMENDED

Misling Lane, Stelling Minnis, Canterbury CT4 6DE
☎ (01227) 709223
42-acre mixed farm. Lovely spacious farmhouse with wealth of old pine, fine furnishings, pleasant gardens, paddocks with friendly ponies. Self-contained flat available for B&B or self catering. Quiet location midway Canterbury/Folkestone, adjacent B2068.
Bedrooms: 2 double, 1 twin
Bathrooms: 3 en-suite
Bed & breakfast

per night:	£min	£max
Single	20.00	25.00
Double	36.00	40.00

Parking for 6

SWANLEY

Kent
Map ref 2D2

West of Farningham off the A20, Swanley village consists of a narrow street of old houses and an odd little Victorian church down a by-road.

The Dees ♠

Listed COMMENDED

56 Old Chapel Road, Crockenhill, Swanley BR8 8LJ
☎ (01322) 667645
Crockenhill is 2 miles from M25 and M20. Easy access to Brands Hatch, London, Kent and Sussex coast and country. Nice double room with full private facilities plus single rooms.
Bedrooms: 2 single, 1 double
Bathrooms: 1 en-suite, 2 private, 1 public
Bed & breakfast

per night:	£min	£max
Single	12.50	20.00
Double	30.00	38.00

Parking for 2

TENTERDEN

Kent
Map ref 3B4

Most attractive market town with a broad main street full of 16th C houses and shops. The tower of the 15th C parish church is the finest in Kent. Fine antiques centre.

Finchden Manor

HIGHLY COMMENDED

Appledore Road, Tenterden TN30 7DD
☎ (01580) 764719
Early 15th C manor house, Grade II listed, with inglenook fireplaces, panelled rooms and beams. Set in 4 acres of gardens and grounds.*
Bedrooms: 1 single, 2 double
Bathrooms: 1 en-suite, 2 private, 3 public
Bed & breakfast

per night:	£min	£max
Single	26.00	28.00
Double	52.00	56.00

Parking for 3

TUNBRIDGE WELLS

See under Royal Tunbridge Wells

UCKFIELD

East Sussex
Map ref 2D3

Once a medieval market town and centre of the iron industry, Uckfield is now a busy country town on the edge of the Ashdown Forest.

Dale Hamme M

Listed **APPROVED**

Piltdown, Uckfield TN22 3XY
☎ Nutley (01825) 712422

15th C hall house with oak beams and inglenook fireplaces in idyllic rural location. On A272 going east, take second left after Piltdown Man pub into Down Street. After 1 mile turn left, house on left hand side.
Bedrooms: 2 single, 1 twin
Bathrooms: 1 private, 1 public

Bed & breakfast

per night:	£min	£max
Single	15.00	15.00
Double	34.00	34.00

Parking for 14

Old Mill Farm M

COMMENDED

High Hurstwood, Uckfield
TN22 4AD
☎ Buxted (01825) 732279
Fax (01825) 732279

50-acre beef farm. Situated in picturesque valley, off A26. Gatwick, Crowborough, Uckfield and Ashdown Forest nearby. All rooms have private facilities.
Bedrooms: 1 single, 1 twin, 1 triple
Bathrooms: 2 en-suite, 1 private

Bed & breakfast

per night:	£min	£max
Single	18.00	20.00
Double	36.00	36.00

Parking for 6

South Paddock M

HIGHLY COMMENDED

Maresfield Park, Uckfield TN22 2HA
☎ (01825) 762335

Comfortable quiet country house accommodation set in 3.5 acres of landscaped gardens. Home-made preserves and log fires. Within easy reach of Gatwick, Brighton, Glyndebourne, Hever Castle.
Bedrooms: 1 double, 2 twin
Bathrooms: 1 private, 1 public

Bed & breakfast

per night:	£min	£max
Single	32.00	36.00
Double	52.00	55.00

Parking for 6

WADHURST

East Sussex
Map ref 3B4

Village in the Sussex Weald. The village sign depicts an anvil, recalling the iron industry, and also an oasthouse, showing that this is hop country.

Best Beech Inn M

COMMENDED

Best Beech, Wadhurst TN5 6JH
☎ (01892) 782046
Fax (01892) 785092

Quiet, rural public house set in pretty Sussex countryside and surrounded by beech trees.
Bedrooms: 1 single, 3 double, 2 twin, 1 family room
Bathrooms: 3 en-suite, 1 public, 1 private shower

Bed & breakfast

per night:	£min	£max
Single	25.00	25.00
Double	35.00	40.00

Half board per

person:	£min	£max
Daily	30.00	40.00
Weekly	200.00	250.00

Lunch available
Evening meal 1900 (last orders 2130)
Parking for 30
Cards accepted: Access, Visa

WALTON-ON-THAMES

Surrey
Map ref 2D2

Busy town beside the Thames, retaining a distinctive atmosphere despite being only 12 miles from central London. Close to Hampton Court Palace, Sandown Park racecourse and Claremont Landscape Garden (National Trust), Esher.

Beech Tree Lodge M

Listed

7 Rydens Avenue,
Walton-on-Thames KT12 3JB
☎ (01932) 242738

Edwardian house in tree-lined avenue near buses, trains, shops, pubs. Handy for London, Hampton Court, Kingston and country theme parks and museums.
Bedrooms: 2 twin, 1 triple
Bathrooms: 2 public

Bed & breakfast

per night:	£min	£max
Single	17.00	25.00
Double	34.00	36.00

Parking for 8

WEST CHILTINGTON

West Sussex
Map ref 2D3

Well-kept village caught in the maze of lanes leading to and from the South Downs.

New House Farm M

COMMENDED

Broadford Bridge Road, West Chiltington, Pulborough RH20 2LA
☎ (01798) 812215
Fax (01798) 813209

50-acre mixed farm. 15th C farmhouse with oak beams and inglenook for log fires. 35 minutes' drive from Gatwick. Within easy reach of local inns and golf course.
Bedrooms: 1 double, 2 twin
Bathrooms: 2 en-suite, 1 private

Bed & breakfast

per night:	£min	£max
Single	25.00	35.00
Double	40.00	50.00

Parking for 6

WEST CLANDON	WEST MALLING	WOKING

| Surrey
Map ref 2D2 | Kent
Map ref 3B3 | Surrey
Map ref 2D2 |

Home of Clandon Park (National Trust), the Palladian mansion built in the early 1730s and home of the Queen's Royal Surrey Regiment Museum.

Became prominent in Norman times when an abbey was established here.

One of the largest towns in Surrey, which developed with the coming of the railway in the 1830s. Old Woking was a market town in the 17th C and still retains several interesting buildings. Large arts and entertainment centre.

Ways Cottage

Listed **COMMENDED**

Lime Grove, West Clandon, Guildford GU4 7UT
☎ Guildford (01483) 222454
Rural detached house in quiet location, 5 miles from Guildford. Easy reach of A3 and M25. Close to station on Waterloo/Guildford line.
Bedrooms: 1 single, 2 twin
Bathrooms: 1 en-suite, 1 public

Bed & breakfast per night:

	£min	£max
Single	17.00	19.00
Double	30.00	33.00

Half board per person:

	£min	£max
Daily	27.00	29.00
Weekly	189.00	203.00

Evening meal 1800 (last orders 2100)
Parking for 2

Westfields Farm

St. Vincents Lane, Addington, West Malling ME19 5BW
☎ (01732) 843209
Farmhouse of character, approximately 500 years old, in rural setting. Within easy reach of London, Canterbury, Tunbridge Wells and the coast. Reductions for children. Golf nearby.
Bedrooms: 1 single, 1 twin, 1 triple
Bathrooms: 2 public

Bed & breakfast per night:

	£min	£max
Single	18.00	
Double	36.00	

COLOUR MAPS

Colour maps at the back of this guide pinpoint all places in which you will find accommodation listed.

East House

Listed **APPROVED**

Beech Hill, Mayford, Woking GU22 0SB
☎ (01483) 763218
Fax (01483) 763218
Quiet, picturesque old manor house with beautiful garden.
Bedrooms: 1 single, 1 twin
Bathrooms: 1 public

Bed & breakfast per night:

	£min	£max
Single	18.00	
Double	30.00	

Parking for 6

Please check prices and other details at the time of booking.

COUNTRY CODE

Always follow the Country Code

🌾 Enjoy the countryside and respect its life and work 🌾 Guard against all risk of fire 🌾 Fasten all gates 🌾 Keep your dogs under close control 🌾 Keep to public paths across farmland 🌾 Use gates and stiles to cross fences, hedges and walls 🌾 Leave livestock, crops and machinery alone 🌾 Take your litter home 🌾 Help to keep all water clean 🌾 Protect wildlife, plants and trees 🌾 Take special care on country roads 🌾 Make no unnecessary noise

WOKING
Continued

Elm Lodge

Listed

Elm Road, Horsell, Woking
GU21 4DY
☎ (01483) 763323
Fax (01344) 845656

Comfortable Victorian home in a quiet location overlooking woodland, yet just a few minutes from town centre and British Rail main line station.
Bedrooms: 3 twin
Bathrooms: 2 public
Bed & breakfast

per night:	£min	£max
Single	28.00	28.00
Double	40.00	40.00

Parking for 6

WORTHING

West Sussex
Map ref 2D3

Largest town in West Sussex, a popular seaside resort with extensive sand and shingle beaches. Seafishing is excellent here. The museum contains finds from Cissbury Ring.
Tourist Information Centre ☎ *(01903) 210022*

Tudor Guest House

5 Windsor Road, Worthing
BN11 2LU
☎ (01903) 210265 & 202042

Ideally situated! 1 minute from seafront, restaurants, pubs, entertainment, etc. Very friendly atmosphere, top class service. Comfortable bedrooms with free trays tea/coffee/chocolate. 3 satellite channels in all rooms. Parking on premises. En-suite rooms available. English or continental breakfast.
Bedrooms: 5 single, 3 double, 1 twin
Bathrooms: 3 en-suite, 1 public, 1 private shower
Bed & breakfast

per night:	£min	£max
Single	13.50	17.50
Double	26.00	40.00

Parking for 5

WYE

Kent
Map ref 3B4

Well known for its agricultural and horticultural college. The Olantigh Tower, with its imposing front portico, is used as a setting for part of the Stour Music Festival held annually in June.

New Flying Horse Inn

COMMENDED

Upper Bridge Street, Wye, Ashford
TN25 5AN
☎ (01233) 812297
Fax (01233) 813487

17th C former coaching inn with oak beams and gleaming brasses. Ideal for touring and walking the Kent countryside and coast. Half board daily prices are for a minimum 2-night stay.

Bedrooms: 1 single, 5 double, 3 twin, 1 triple
Bathrooms: 10 en-suite
Bed & breakfast

per night:	£min	£max
Single	37.50	40.00
Double	47.50	50.00

Half board per person:

	£min	£max
Daily	37.50	40.00
Weekly	262.50	280.00

Lunch available
Evening meal 1830 (last orders 2130)
Parking for 30
Cards accepted: Access, Visa, Amex, Switch/Delta

FARM HOLIDAY GROUPS

This section of the guide lists groups specialising in farm and country-based holidays. Most offer bed and breakfast accommodation (some with evening meal) and self-catering accommodation.

To obtain further details of individual properties please contact the group(s) direct, indicating the time of year when the accommodation is required and the number of people to be accommodated. You may find the Accommodation Coupons towards the back of this Guide helpful when making contact.

The cost of sending out brochures is high, and the groups would appreciate written enquiries being accompanied by a stamped and addressed envelope (at least 228mm x 127mm).

The 'b&b' prices shown are per person per night; the self-catering prices are weekly terms per unit.

The symbol 🏠 before the name of a group indicates that it is a member of the Farm Holiday Bureau, set up by the Royal Agricultural Society of England in conjunction with the English Tourist Board.

Bed & Breakfast (GB)
Contact: Reservation service,
94 Bell Street,
Henley-on-Thames,
Oxon RG9 1XS
Tel: Henley (01491) 578803
Fax: (01491) 410806
National reservations service for hundreds of B&B's and farmhouses throughout Britain (London, England, Scotland, Wales and Ireland).
500 properties offering bed and breakfast: £15-£46 b&b.
Short breaks also available.

🏠 **Kent Country Accommodation**
Mrs R. Bannock,
Court Lodge,
Court Lodge Farm,
The Street,
Teston,
Maidstone,
Kent ME18 5AQ
Tel: (01622) 812570
Fax: (01622) 814200
Wide selection, from traditional and historical farmhouses and cottages to modern farm-building conversions. Many with interesting architectural features and leisure facilities, many welcome non-smokers. Peaceful touring caravan and camping park. Also one bunk barn sleeping 24.
18 properties offering bed and breakfast: £18-£36 per person b&b.
28 self-catering units:
low season (October-April) from £95;
high season (April-September) £150-£750.
Discounted short breaks available in low season.

🏠 **Let Devon Farms Accommodate You**
c/o Court Barton,
Aveton Gifford,
Kingsbridge
Devon TQ7 4LE
Tel: Kingsbridge (01548) 550055
Fax: (01548) 550312
Small and friendly places. Great hospitality. Self-catering, bed & breakfast or half board in quality assured accommodation on working farms. Many historic houses. Variety of rural locations from sandy beaches to moorland or gently rolling countryside. Free

colour brochure, over 100 choices.
74 properties offering bed and
breakfast: £14-£25 b&b.
41 self-catering units:
low season (October-March)
£100-£200;
high season (April-September)
£240-£600.
Short breaks also available.

 Norfolk & Suffolk Farm Holiday Group

Mrs R Bryce,
College Farm,
Hintlesham,
Ipswich,
Suffolk IP8 3NT
Tel: Hintlesham (01473) 652253
Fax: (01473) 652253
*Come to Norfolk & Suffolk and
experience farmhouse hospitality on
a working farm. We offer quality
accommodation in a friendly
atmosphere. Enjoy exploring
picturesque market towns, heritage
coastline and 'Constable country'.
Caravan and tent pitches also*

available.
34 properties offering bed and
breakfast: £15-£22 b&b.
36 self-catering units:
low season (October-March)
£100-£195;
high season (April-September)
£180-£400.
Short breaks also available.

South Pennine Farm Holiday Group

Mrs C. Walsh,
Needhams Farm,
Uplands Road,
Werneth Low,
Gee Cross,
Nr Hyde,
Cheshire SK14 3AQ
Tel: (0161) 368 4610
Fax: (0161) 367 9106
*All our properties are located in
scenic rural areas within easy reach
of Manchester, Sheffield and
Stockport. Warm welcomes await
all guests.*
5 properties offering bed and

breakfast: £17-£20 b&b.
2 self-catering units: £150-£300
depending on season.

Warwickshire Farm Holidays

The Secretary,
Crandon House,
Avon Dassett,
Leamington Spa,
Warwickshire CV33 0AA
Tel: (01295) 770652
Fax: (01295) 770652
*A warm welcome at farmhouses
offering serviced and self-catering
accommodation in comfortable and
homely surroundings, situated in
historic and picturesque
'Shakespeare country'. Caravan and
tent pitches also available.*
24 properties offering bed and
breakfast: £12-£27 b&b.
25 self-catering units:
low season (October-April)
£70-£350;
high season (May-September)
£80-£450.

COUNTRY CODE

Always follow the Country Code
Enjoy the countryside and respect
its life and work Guard against all
risk of fire Fasten all gates Keep
your dogs under close control Keep
to public paths across farmland Use
gates and stiles to cross fences, hedges
and walls Leave livestock, crops and
machinery alone Take your litter home
Help to keep all water clean
Protect wildlife, plants and trees
Take special care on country roads
Make no unnecessary noise

GROUP AND YOUTH SECTION

Most of the accommodation establishments listed in this guide are particularly suitable for people looking for relatively low-cost places to stay in England. Some establishments make a special point of providing safe, budget-priced accommodation for young people, for families or for large groups. These places, ranging from Youth Hostels, YMCA and YWCA residences and budget and student hotels to the seasonally available campuses of universities and colleges, are listed individually in the pages which follow.

Information on organisations which specialise in accommodation for young people, families and groups is given below - please contact them direct for further details.

Youth Hostels

The Youth Hostels Association (England and Wales) provides basic accommodation, usually in single-sex bunk-bedded rooms or dormitories, with self-catering facilities. Most hostels also provide low-cost meals or snacks. At the time of going to press, a night's stay at a Youth Hostel will cost between £3.85 and £17.20 (under 18) and between £5.65 and £20.50 (over 18).

In spite of the word 'youth' in the name, there is in fact no upper age limit. Indeed, many Youth Hostels also offer family accommodation, either in self-contained annexes (with kitchen, living room and bathroom) or by letting the smaller, four-to-six bed dormitories as private units. Groups are very welcome at Youth Hostels, whether for educational or leisure pursuits: some hostels offer field study facilities and many more have classrooms. The YHA also offers a wide range of adventure holidays and special interest breaks.

Youth Hostels - from medieval castles to shepherds' huts - can be found all over the country, both in countryside and coastal locations and in towns and cities. You need to be a member of the YHA in order to take advantage of the facilities. Membership entitles you to use not only the 240 hostels in England and Wales but also the thousands of Youth Hostels in other parts of the British Isles and around the world. Membership costs £3.20 (under 18) or £9.30 (over 18). Family membership is available at £9.30 (single-parent family) or £18.60 (two parent family).

Further information from:
Youth Hostels Association
Trevelyan House,
8 St Stephen's Hill, St Albans,
Hertfordshire AL1 2DY
Tel: (01727) 855215
Fax: (01727) 844126

YWCA and YMCA

The Young Womens' Christian Association, founded in 1855, has grown into the world's largest women's organisation. Among its many activities is the running of over 60 houses in Britain which offer safe, reasonably priced self-catering accommodation, mostly in single rooms, either on a permanent or temporary basis.

Most houses take short-stay visitors only during the summer months. However, some of the houses do accept short-stay visitors all the year round. Although the word 'women' appears in the name of the organisation, many of the residences now take men and boys as well as mothers and girls.

The Young Men's Christian Association (YMCA), founded in

1844, operates on much the same basis as the YWCA, taking people of both sexes at its more than 70 residences around the country either on a permanent or short-stay basis.

Further information from:
YWCA HQ
Clarendon House,
52 Cornmarket Street,
Oxford OX1 3EJ
Tel: (01865) 726110
YMCA
National Council,
640 Forest Road,
Walthamstow,
London E17 3DZ
Tel: (0181) 520 5599

Universities and Colleges

Accommodation in universities and colleges offer excellent value for money at dozens of city centre, seaside and countryside campus locations around England. This type of accommodation is particularly suitable for groups, whether on a leisure trip or participating in a conference or seminar. Beds available on campus vary from 30 to 3,000. There is a wide selection of meeting room facilities to choose from, with a maximum capacity of 2,000 people, and banqueting facilities for up to 1,500.

Most accommodation is in single 'study bedrooms', with a limited number of twin and family rooms. Availability is mainly during the academic vacation periods (usually July to September and for four week periods at Christmas and Easter), with some venues offering short-stay accommodation throughout the year.

For relaxation, there is a wide choice of recreational facilities, with most venues providing TV rooms, bars and restaurants and a variety of sporting activities, ranging from tennis, squash and swimming to team sports. Activity and special interest holidays are also on offer as are many self-catering flats and houses.

Further information from:
British Universities Accommodation Consortium (BUCA)
Box No 1150, University Park,
Nottingham NG7 2RD
Tel: (0115) 950 4571
Fax: (0115) 942 2505
Connect Venues
The Workstation,
Paternoster Row,
Sheffield S1 2BX
Tel: (0114) 249 3090
Fax: (0114) 249 3091

Other Accommodation

In addition to the above main providers on a countrywide basis of budget accommodation for young people and groups, there are, of course, the many individual student and budget hotels around England and also such places as outdoor and field study centres. Some of these feature in the following pages but for more information on what is available in a particular area, please contact a local Tourist Information Centre.

CHECK THE MAPS

The colour maps at the back of this guide show all the cities, towns and villages for which you will find accommodation entries.

Refer to the town index to find the page on which it is listed.

WHERE TO STAY (GROUP & YOUTH)

Accommodation entries in this section are listed in alphabetical order of place name, and then in alphabetical order of establishment.

Map references refer to the colour location maps at the back of this guide. The first number indicates the map to use; the letter and number which follow refer to the grid reference on the map.

At-a-glance symbols at the end of each accommodation entry give useful information about services and facilities. A key to symbols can be found inside the back cover flap. Keep this open for easy reference.

AMBLESIDE

Cumbria
Map ref 5A3

Market town situated at the head of Lake Windermere and surrounded by fells. The historic town centre is now a conservation area and the country around Ambleside is rich in historic and literary associations. Good centre for touring, walking and climbing.
Tourist Information Centre
☎ *(015394) 32582*

Ambleside Youth Hostel
Waterhead, Ambleside LA22 0EU
☎ (015394) 32304
Fax (015394) 34408
Contact: Mr Simon Ainley
Situated on the shores of Windermere, with own waterfront and jetty. Panoramic views of Lakeland fells. Family rooms, friendly atmosphere, dining room overlooking lake.
Minimum age 5
Bedrooms: 18 double/twin, 9 triple, 14 quadruple, 22 dormitories. Total number of beds: 286
Bathrooms: 20 public

Bed only

per person:	£min	£max
Daily	6.35	9.45

Bed & breakfast

per person:	£min	£max
Daily	9.25	12.35

Evening meal 1730 (last orders 1930)
Parking for 40
Cards accepted: Access, Visa, Switch/Delta

ASHBOURNE

Derbyshire
Map ref 4B2

Market town on the edge of the Peak District National Park and an excellent centre for walking. Its impressive church with 212-ft spire stands in an unspoilt old street.
Tourist Information Centre ☎ *(01335) 343666*

Ilam Hall YHA
Ilam, Ashbourne DE6 2AZ
☎ Thorpe Cloud (01335) 350212
Fax (01335) 350350
Contact: Mr K Rome
Large country mansion built in Gothic Revival style between 1820 and 1840 in the Peak District National Park, within a park administered by the National Trust.
Wheelchair access category 2
Bedrooms: 24 dormitories. Total number of beds: 148
Bathrooms: 4 en-suite, 12 public

Bed only

per person:	£min	£max
Daily	6.35	9.45

Bed & breakfast

per person:	£min	£max
Daily	9.25	12.35

Lunch available
Evening meal 1830 (last orders 1930)
Parking for 60
Open January–November and Christmas
Cards accepted: Access, Visa, Switch/Delta

ASHFORD

Kent
Map ref 3B4

Once a market centre for the farmers of the Weald of Kent and Romney Marsh. The town centre has a number of Tudor and Georgian houses.
Tourist Information Centre ☎ *(01233) 629165*

Wye College (University of London)
Wye, Ashford TN25 5AH
☎ Wye (01233) 812401
Fax (01233) 813759
Contact: Mr David Traske
Close to the A28 between Ashford and Canterbury, Wye College offers excellent conference facilities and friendly service in picturesque surroundings.
Minimum age 16
Bedrooms: 189 single, 11 double/twin. Total number of beds: 211
Bathrooms: 55 en-suite, 24 public

Bed only

per person:	£min	£max
Daily	17.63	23.50

Bed & breakfast

per person:	£min	£max
Daily	23.50	29.38

Full board

per person:	£min	£max
Weekly	325.71	366.87

Lunch available
Parking for 382
Cards accepted: Access, Visa, Switch/Delta

BASSENTHWAITE

Cumbria
Map ref 5A2

Standing in an idyllic setting, nestled at the foot of Skiddaw and Ullock Pike, this village is just a mile from Bassenthwaite Lake, the one true "lake" in the Lake District. The area is visited by many varieties of migrating birds.

Bassenthwaite Parish Rooms
Bassenthwaite, Keswick
Contact: Miss Helen Reb, Bassenthwaite Parish Rooms, Management Committee, 1 The Avenue, Bassenthwaite, Keswick, Cumbria CA12 4QJ
☎ Bassenthwaite Lake (017687) 76222
Village hall. School Road off A591. Minimum booking is for 12 people, 3 nights.
For groups only
Bedrooms: Total number of beds: 50
Bathrooms: 1 en-suite, 3 public

Bed only

per person:	£min	£max
Daily	2.00	

Parking for 10

Kiln Hill Barn
Bassenthwaite, Keswick CA12 4RG
☎ Bassenthwaite Lake (017687) 76454
Contact: Mr J K Armstrong
Farmhouse and converted barn in the country. Owned and run by the Armstrongs. Ideal for leisure and activity holidays.
Bedrooms: 1 single, 2 double/twin, 2 dormitories. Total number of beds: 39
Bathrooms: 4 public

Bed only

per person:	£min	£max
Daily		19.00

Bed & breakfast

per person:	£min	£max
Daily	19.00	19.00

Full board

per person:	£min	£max
Weekly	175.00	175.00

Evening meal 1830 (last orders 1830)
Parking for 15
Open February–November

A key to symbols can be found inside the back cover flap.

BATH

Bath & North East Somerset
Map ref 2B2

Georgian spa city beside the River Avon. Important Roman site with impressive reconstructed baths, uncovered in 19th C. Bath Abbey built on site of monastery where first king of England was crowned (AD 973). Fine architecture in mellow local stone. Pump Room and museums.
Tourist Information Centre ☎ (01225) 462831

The City of Bath YMCA
International House, Broad Street Place, Bath BA1 5LN
☎ (01225) 460471
Fax (01225) 462065
Contact: Mr A Teasdale
Open to those of both sexes and all ages. Centrally located and only minutes away from Bath's major attractions. A convenient base for city and West Country tours. Half board weekly rates available for individuals and groups.
Minimum age 17
Bedrooms: 38 single, 36 double/twin, 8 triple, 3 dormitories. Total number of beds: 190
Bathrooms: 30 public

Bed & breakfast

per person:	£min	£max
Daily	10.00	12.50

Lunch available
Evening meal 1700 (last orders 1900)

BEER

Devon
Map ref 1D2

Formerly noted for lace-making and smuggling, this picturesque fishing village lies close to some of Devon's most striking cliff scenery at Beer Head. Smugglers' caves. Quarries to west of village were worked in Roman times.

The Youth Hostel - Beer
Bovey Combe, Townsend, Beer, Seaton EX12 3LL
☎ Seaton (01297) 20296
Fax (01297) 23690
Large house standing in landscaped grounds, on hillside to the west of a picturesque fishing village.
Minimum age 7
Bedrooms: 5 quadruple, 3 dormitories. Total number of beds: 40
Bathrooms: 4 public

Bed only

per person:	£min	£max
Daily	5.20	7.75

Lunch available
Evening meal 1900 (last orders 1815)
Parking for 15
Open April–October
Cards accepted: Access, Visa

BIRMINGHAM

West Midlands
Map ref 4B3

Britain's second city, whose attractions include Centenary Square and the ICC with Symphony Hall, the NEC, the City Art Gallery, Barber Institute of Fine Arts, 17th C Aston Hall, science and railway museums, Jewellery Quarter, Cadbury World, 2 cathedrals and Botanical Gardens.
Tourist Information Centre ☎ (0121) 643 2514 or 780 4321

The University of Birmingham
Edgbaston, Birmingham
Contact: Mr E Farrar, Residences and Conferences, University of Birmingham, Edgbaston, Birmingham B15 2TT
☎ Birmingham (0121) 454 6022
Fax (0121) 456 2415
Accommodation is provided in single and twin study bedrooms with washbasins, in parkland area in the attractive suburb of Edgbaston.
Bedrooms: 1050 single, 300 double/twin. Total number of beds: 1650
Bathrooms: 160 en-suite, 100 public

Bed & breakfast

per person:	£min	£max
Daily	26.00	

Lunch available
Evening meal 1800 (last orders 2000)
Parking for 1000
Open January, March–April, June–September, December

Information on accommodation listed in this guide has been supplied by the proprietors. As changes may occur you are advised to check details at the time of booking.

BOLTON

Greater Manchester
Map ref 4A1

On the edge of the West Pennine Moors and renowned for its outstanding town centre architecture and fine shopping facilities. The Octagon Theatre has national recognition for its "theatre in the round". Samuel Crompton, inventor of the "spinning mule", is buried here.
Tourist Information Centre ☎ (01204) 364333

Bolton Institute of Higher Education

Deane Road, Bolton BL2 3BS
☎ (01204) 528851
Fax (01204) 399074
Contact: Mrs Joyce Proia
Purpose-built self-catering apartments with wash handbasin in each room. Catering is also available upon request.
For groups only
Minimum age 6
Bedrooms: 792 single. Total number of beds: 792
Bathrooms: 108 public

Bed only

per person:	£min	£max
Daily	12.00	12.00

Bed & breakfast

per person:	£min	£max
Daily	15.00	18.00

Full board

per person:	£min	£max
Weekly	140.00	175.00

Lunch available
Parking for 30
Open April, July–September
Cards accepted: Access, Visa
🛏6👪♿️ UL 🔒 S 🍴 🐾 TV 🛗 🛋☂
🔍🎣▶🏫 DAP SP

BOSCASTLE

Cornwall
Map ref 1B2

Small, unspoilt village in Valency Valley. Active as a port until onset of railway era, its natural harbour affords rare shelter on this wild coast. Attractions include spectacular blow-hole, Celtic field strips, part-Norman church. Nearby St Juliot Church was restored by Thomas Hardy.

The Youth Hostel- Boscastle Harbour

Palace Stables, Boscastle PL35 0HD
☎ (01840) 250287
Fax (01840) 250615
In superb position on harbour edge

where Valency River enters National Trust preserved fishing harbour.
Minimum age 5
Bedrooms: 4 dormitories. Total number of beds: 25
Bathrooms: 2 public

Bed only

per person:	£min	£max
Daily	5.20	8.55

Evening meal 1900 (last orders 1800)
Open March–October
Cards accepted: Access, Visa
🛏 UL 🔒 S 🐾 🍴 🐕 🚲 SP 🏫 ◎

BRIGHTON & HOVE

East Sussex
Map ref 2D3

Brighton's attractions include the Royal Pavilion, Volks Electric Railway, Sea Life Centre and Marina Village, Conference Centre and "The Lanes" and several theatres. Neighbouring Hove is a resort in its own right.
Tourist Information Centre ☎ (01273) 323755; for Hove (01273) 746100 or 778087

University of Brighton 🅼

Circus Street, Brighton
Contact: Mrs Evelyn Mohan, University of Brighton, Conference Office, Circus Street, Brighton, East Sussex BN2 2QF
☎ Brighton (01273) 643167 & 643168
Fax (01273) 643149
The university has a variety of residential accommodation in Brighton and Eastbourne available to groups, conference organisers and self-catering visitors in July, August and September.
For groups only
Bedrooms: 1000 single
Bathrooms: 298 en-suite

Bed only

per person:	£min	£max
Daily	7.50	13.50

Bed & breakfast

per person:	£min	£max
Daily	16.50	23.00

Full board

per person:	£min	£max
Weekly	189.00	287.00

Lunch available
Evening meal 1800 (last orders 1900)
Parking for 230
Open July–September
Cards accepted: Access, Visa
🛏14👪♿️🔒 S 🍴 🐾 TV 🛗 🛋🛁🐕☂
🔍🏫

CANTERBURY

Kent
Map ref 3B3

Place of pilgrimage since the martyrdom of Becket in 1170 and the site of Canterbury Cathedral. Visit St Augustine's Abbey, St Martin's (the oldest church in England), Royal Museum and Art Gallery and the Canterbury Tales. Nearby is Howletts Wild Animal Park. Good shopping centre.
Tourist Information Centre ☎ (01227) 766567

Focus Canterbury

Tanglewood, The University, Canterbury
Contact: Mr I M Sheridan, Focus Canterbury, The University, Canterbury, Kent CT2 7LX
☎ Canterbury (01227) 828000
Fax (01227) 828019
Flexible and comfortable accommodation in one of 4 colleges in attractively situated parkland campus overlooking the cathedral. Value-for-money self-catering in 5/6-bedded houses is also available - ideal for families. Sports facilities.
Minimum age 10
Bedrooms: 1490 single, 31 double/twin. Total number of beds: 1552
Bathrooms: 268 en-suite, 160 public

Bed & breakfast

per person:	£min	£max
Daily	17.90	29.90

Full board

per person:	£min	£max
Weekly	237.30	321.30

Lunch available
Evening meal 1800 (last orders 1900)
Parking for 1200
Open March–April, July–September
Cards accepted: Access, Visa
🛏10♿️🔒 S 🍴 🐾 TV 🛗 🛋🛁🐕☂🔍
🎣🍴 ∪🌛🐕 DAP SP T ◎

Kipps 🅼

40 Nunnery Fields, Canterbury CT1 3JT
☎ (01227) 786121
Fax (01227) 766992
Contact: Mr David Harman

Family-run Edwardian town house, ideal

Continued ▶

CANTERBURY

Continued

base for cathedral, coast and countryside. Fully equipped kitchen for self-catering. Discounts available.
Bedrooms: 3 single, 2 double/twin, 1 quadruple, 1 dormitories. Total number of beds: 36
Bathrooms: 3 en-suite, 3 public

Bed only

per person:	£min	£max
Daily	9.95	12.95

Bed & breakfast

per person:	£min	£max
Daily	11.40	14.40

Parking for 3
Cards accepted: Access, Visa, Switch/Delta

CARNFORTH

Lancashire
Map ref 5B3

Carnforth station was the setting for the film "Brief Encounter". Nearby are Borwick Hall, an Elizabethan manor house, and Leighton Hall which has good paintings and Gillow furniture and is open to the public.

Borwick Hall Residential Centre

Borwick, Carnforth LA6 1JU
☎ (01524) 732508
Fax (01524) 732590
Contact: Mrs Foster
Residential centre for groups with own training programmes. Two buildings, 45 places in each. Self-catering accommodation for 20. Exit 35 of M6, then A6 to Milnthorpe, first right, one mile.
For groups only
Bedrooms: 5 single, 24 double/twin, 5 triple, 2 quadruple, 4 dormitories. Total number of beds: 98
Bathrooms: 13 public

Bed only

per person:	£min	£max
Daily	9.45	13.00

Bed & breakfast

per person:	£min	£max
Daily	11.60	15.60

Full board

per person:	£min	£max
Weekly	153.65	198.80

Lunch available
Evening meal 1700 (last orders 1900)
Parking for 60

CASTLETON

Derbyshire
Map ref 4B2

Large village in a spectacular Peak District setting with ruined Peveril Castle and 4 great show caverns, where the Blue John stone and lead were mined. One cavern offers a mile-long underground boat journey.

Castleton YHA

Castleton Hall, Castle Street, Castleton, Sheffield S30 2WG
☎ Hope Valley (01433) 620235
Fax (01433) 621767
Contact: Mr A Bond
Situated in the heart of the village, offering good quality, low cost accommodation with family rooms and good meals.
Minimum age 5
Bedrooms: 1 single, 5 double/twin, 14 quadruple, 9 dormitories. Total number of beds: 148
Bathrooms: 7 en-suite, 7 public

Bed only

per person:	£min	£max
Daily	5.75	11.30

Bed & breakfast

per person:	£min	£max
Daily	8.65	14.20

Lunch available
Evening meal 1800 (last orders 2000)
Parking for 15
Open February–December
Cards accepted: Access, Visa, Switch/Delta

CHORLEY

Lancashire
Map ref 4A1

Set between the Pennine moors and the Lancashire Plain, Chorley has been an important town since medieval times, with its "Flat-Iron" and covered markets. The rich heritage includes Astley Hall and Park, Hoghton Tower, Rivington Country Park and the Leeds-Liverpool Canal.

Lancashire College

Southport Road, Chorley PR7 1NB
☎ (01257) 276719
Fax (01257) 241370
Contact: Mrs A Bithell
Purpose-built adult residential college. Lounge/bar, well designed and equipped teaching suite and conference accommmodation.
For groups only
Minimum age 18

Bedrooms: 45 single. Total number of beds: 52
Bathrooms: 9 en-suite, 12 public

Bed & breakfast

per person:	£min	£max
Daily	16.45	35.85

Lunch available
Evening meal from 1830
Parking for 100
Cards accepted: Access, Visa, Switch/Delta

COALBROOKDALE

Shropshire
Map ref 4A3

Ironbridge Gorge YHA

Coalbrookdale Institute, Paradise, Coalbrookdale, Telford
Contact: Mr & Mrs A Dyde, Ironbridge Gorge Youth Hostel, Coalbrookdale Institute, Paradise, Coalbrookdale, Telford, Shropshire TF8 7NR
☎ Telford (01952) 433281
Fax (01952) 433166
Two sites in the Gorge offer budget accommodation for groups, families and individuals. Meeting rooms available with full catering service.
Minimum age 5
Bedrooms: 21 dormitories. Total number of beds: 97
Bathrooms: 10 public

Bed only

per person:	£min	£max
Daily	6.35	9.45

Bed & breakfast

per person:	£min	£max
Daily	9.25	12.35

Lunch available
Evening meal from 1900
Parking for 6
Open February–November
Cards accepted: Access, Visa, Switch/Delta

WELCOME HOST

This is a nationally recognised customer care programme which aims to promote the highest standards of service and a warm welcome. Establishments who are taking part in this initiative are indicated by the ✿ symbol.

CONSETT

Durham
Map ref 5B2

Former steel town on the edge of rolling moors. Modern development includes the shopping centre and a handsome Roman Catholic church, designed by a local architect. To the west, the Derwent Reservoir provides water sports and pleasant walks.

Consett Y.M.C.A. ⚠

Parliament Street, Consett, County Durham DH8 5DH
☎ (01207) 502680 & 501852
Fax (01207) 501578
Contact: Mr A Forsyth

Leisure holiday facility providing easy access to the Lake District, Weardale, Scotland and Northumbria. Full programme of outdoor activities. Courses for Y.T.S., T.V.E.I., school, college, youth groups, etc, designed. Individuals welcome.
Minimum age 9
Bedrooms: 2 double/twin, 8 dormitories. Total number of beds: 65
Bathrooms: 5 en-suite, 3 public

Bed & breakfast

per person:	£min	£max
Daily	12.50	12.50

Full board

per person:	£min	£max
Weekly	111.62	111.62

Lunch available
🛏🦮🏧Ⓢ🎿📺💻🖥🛗🔌🔍🎿♿🚶🚹 SP
🏨

For ideas on places to visit refer to the introduction at the beginning of this section.

The symbols in each entry give information about services and facilities. A 'key' to these symbols appears at the back of this guide.

DARLINGTON

Durham
Map ref 5C3

Largest town in County Durham, standing on the River Skerne and home of the earliest passenger railway which first ran to Stockton in 1825. Now the home of a railway museum. Originally a prosperous market town occupying the site of an Anglo-Saxon settlement, it still holds an open market.
Tourist Information Centre ☎ *(01325) 382698*

The Arts Centre

Vane Terrace, Darlington, County Durham DL3 7AX
☎ (01325) 483271
Contact: Mr D Bould
Hostel style accommodation housed in one of the country's largest art centres. Offers a wide range of activities.
Bedrooms: 11 single, 9 double/twin. Total number of beds: 29
Bathrooms: 6 public

Bed only

per person:	£min	£max
Daily	10.00	11.00

Bed & breakfast

per person:	£min	£max
Daily	13.50	14.50

Lunch available
Parking for 20
Cards accepted: Access, Visa
🛏🦮Ⓢ🛗🍴🏨

DURHAM

Durham
Map ref 5C2

Ancient city with its Norman castle and cathedral, now a World Heritage site, set on a bluff high over the Wear. A market and university town and regional centre, spreading beyond the market-place on both banks of the river.
Tourist Information Centre ☎ *(0191) 384 3720*

College of St Hild and St Bede ⚠

University of Durham, Leazes Road, Durham, County Durham
Contact: Mrs A Hodgson, College of St Hild and, St Bede, University of Durham, Leazes Road, Durham, County Durham DH1 1SZ
☎ (0191) 374 3069 & 374 3064
Fax (0191) 374 4740
College set in spacious grounds in the medieval City of Durham, providing a splendid base for exploring Northumbria.

Minimum age 10
Bedrooms: 370 single, 45 double/twin, 1 triple. Total number of beds: 463
Bathrooms: 53 public
Bed & breakfast

per person:	£min	£max
Daily	14.00	17.00

Full board

per person:	£min	£max
Weekly	184.45	205.45

Lunch available
Evening meal 1800 (last orders 1900)
Parking for 200
Open March–April, July–September
🛏🦮🅿Ⓢ📺💻🛗🔌🔍🎿♿🍴🏨

St John's College ⚠

University of Durham, 3 South Bailey, Durham, County Durham DH1 3RJ
☎ (0191) 374 3566
Fax (0191) 374 3573
Contact: Mr Martin Clemmett
In the heart of the city, alongside Durham Cathedral and Castle. Offering good quality student accommodation to individuals, families and groups.
Bedrooms: 100 single, 13 double/twin, 1 triple. Total number of beds: 129
Bathrooms: 42 public

Bed only

per person:	£min	£max
Daily	13.75	13.75

Bed & breakfast

per person:	£min	£max
Daily	15.75	16.75

Full board

per person:	£min	£max
Weekly	175.35	182.35

Evening meal 1800 (last orders 1930)
Open March–April, July–September, December
🛏🦮Ⓢ📺💻🛗🔌🔍 DAP 🏨◎

Trevelyan College ⚠

Elvet Hill Road, Durham, County Durham DH1 3LN
☎ (0191) 374 3765 & 374 3768
Fax (0191) 374 3789
Contact: Mr J Wright
Set in parkland, within 1 mile of the city centre. Full conference facilities.
Bedrooms: 253 single, 35 double/twin. Total number of beds: 307
Bathrooms: 50 en-suite, 47 public
Bed & breakfast

per person:	£min	£max
Daily	16.95	27.50

Lunch available
Evening meal 1800 (last orders 1930)

Continued ▶

DURHAM

Continued

Parking for 100
Open January, March–April,
July–September

Van Mildert College

University of Durham, Mill Hill Lane,
Durham, County Durham
Contact: Mr J Hirst, Van Mildert
College, University of Durham,
Durham, County Durham DH1 3LH
☎ (0191) 374 3900
Fax (0191) 374 3974
*College and conference centre in
beautiful lakeside surroundings,
adjacent to golf course, opposite
Botanical Gardens. Half a mile from
Durham Cathedral and Castle World
Heritage Site. Families and small
groups welcome.*
Minimum age 17
Bedrooms: 380 single,
21 double/twin. Total number of
beds: 422
Bathrooms: 30 en-suite, 68 public

Bed & breakfast

per person:	£min	£max
Daily	16.00	17.25

Full board

per person:	£min	£max
Weekly	96.00	103.50

Lunch available
Evening meal from 1800
Parking for 100
Open March–April, July–September

EDALE

Derbyshire
Map ref 4B2

Deep, 1,250 ft valley, a mecca for
walkers. The Pennine Way starts
here, also the easiest way on to
Kinder via Jacobs Ladder. Most of
the buildings and walls are
traditionally made of stone in this
picturesque village.

Edale YHA and Activity Centre

Rowland Cote, Nether Booth, Edale,
Sheffield S30 2ZH
☎ Hope Valley (01433) 670302
Fax (01433) 670243
Contact: Mr Joe Hardy
*Large former private house in extensive
grounds. Edale YHA offers a full range
of programmes.*
Minimum age 5
Bedrooms: 28 dormitories. Total
number of beds: 140
Bathrooms: 2 en-suite, 13 public

Bed only

per person:	£min	£max
Daily	6.35	9.45

Bed & breakfast

per person:	£min	£max
Daily	9.25	12.35

Lunch available
Evening meal 1730 (last orders
1915)
Parking for 50
Cards accepted: Access, Visa,
Switch/Delta

EXFORD

Somerset
Map ref 1D1

Sheltered village on the River Exe
close to Exmoor. Attractive old
houses, shops and inns face the
village green and the Methodist
chapel has 2 windows by
Burne-Jones. A footpath
north-eastward leads to Dunkery
Beacon, Exmoor's highest point.

The Youth Hostel - Exford

Exe Mead, Exford, Minehead
TA24 7PU
☎ (01643) 831288
Fax (01643) 831650
*Situated in the centre of Exmoor, with
the River Exe flowing through the
hostel grounds.*
Minimum age 5
Bedrooms: 2 double/twin,
6 quadruple, 4 dormitories. Total
number of beds: 51
Bathrooms: 3 en-suite, 3 public

Bed only

per person:	£min	£max
Daily	5.75	8.55

Evening meal from 1900
Parking for 12
Open March–October
Cards accepted: Access, Visa

FYLINGTHORPE

North Yorkshire
Map ref 5D3

Within a stone's throw of Robin
Hood's Bay and the north east
coast.

Boggle Hole YHA

Boggle Hole, Mill Beck, Fylingthorpe,
Whitby
Contact: Ms P Saunders, Boggle
Hole Youth Hostel, Boggle Hole, Mill
Beck, Fylingthorpe, Whitby, North
Yorkshire YO22 4UQ
☎ Whitby (01947) 880352
Fax (01947) 880987
Converted mill of considerable charm

and character, in a delightful coastal
setting in the North York Moors
National Park. Field study and family
facilities.
Minimum age 5
Bedrooms: 16 dormitories. Total
number of beds: 80
Bathrooms: 8 public

Bed only

per person:	£min	£max
Daily	5.75	8.55

Bed & breakfast

per person:	£min	£max
Daily	8.65	11.45

Evening meal from 1800
Open February–November
Cards accepted: Access, Visa,
Switch/Delta

GIGGLESWICK

North Yorkshire
Map ref 5B3

Picturesque Pennine village of
period stone cottages with ancient
market cross, stocks and tithe barn.
Parish church is dedicated to St
Alkeda, an Anglo-Saxon saint. During
restoration work the tomb of a
15th C knight with his horse was
discovered.

Yorkshire Dales Field Centre

Square House, 17 Church Street,
Giggleswick, Settle BD24 0BE
☎ Settle (01729) 822965 &
(bookings) 824180
Fax (01729) 824180
Contact: Mr Peter Fish & Mrs A
Barbour
*Comfortable dales barn in quiet corner
of renowned village, Three Peaks area
of Yorkshire Dales. Any group of 12
people-plus. Good food provided on
self-catering basis.*
For groups only
Bedrooms: 2 single, 2 quadruple,
4 dormitories. Total number of
beds: 35
Bathrooms: 4 public

Bed only

per person:	£min	£max
Daily	9.00	9.00

Bed & breakfast

per person:	£min	£max
Daily	13.00	15.00

Full board

per person:	£min	£max
Weekly	133.00	147.00

Lunch available
Evening meal 1730 (last orders
1930)
Parking for 8

GOLANT

Cornwall
Map ref 1B2

The Youth Hostel and Field Study Centre

Penquite House, Golant, Fowey
PL23 1LA
☎ Fowey (01726) 833507
Fax (01726) 832947
Contact: Mr and Mrs Mike
Freemantle
Large Georgian house overlooking River Fowey, surrounded by farmland and woods. Family rooms.
Minimum age 7
Bedrooms: 1 double/twin, 1 triple,
4 quadruple, 9 dormitories. Total number of beds: 94
Bathrooms: 7 public

Bed only

per person:	£min	£max
Daily	6.35	9.45

Evening meal 1900 (last orders 2130)
Parking for 30
Open February–October
Cards accepted: Access, Visa, Switch/Delta

GRANTHAM

Lincolnshire
Map ref 3A1

On the old Great North Road (A1), Grantham's splendid parish church has a fine spire and chained library. Sir Isaac Newton was educated here and his statue stands in front of the museum which includes displays on Newton and other famous local people.
Tourist Information Centre ☎ (01476) 566444

Sedgwick Hall

Grantham College, Stonebridge Road, Grantham
Contact: M Cann, Grantham College, Stonebridge Road, Grantham, Lincolnshire NG31 9AP
☎ Grantham (01476) 63141
Student accommodation comprising single/double rooms, en-suite with communal sitting room/kitchen area. Disabled facilities. Riverside location, 5 minutes from town centre.
Bedrooms: 37 single, 6 double/twin.
Total number of beds: 49
Bathrooms: 43 en-suite

Bed only

per person:	£min	£max
Daily	18.00	22.00

Parking for 12
Open July–September
Cards accepted: Access, Visa, Amex, Switch/Delta

GREAT YARMOUTH

Norfolk
Map ref 3C1

One of Britain's major seaside resorts with 5 miles of seafront and every possible amenity including an award winning leisure complex offering a huge variety of all-weather facilities. Busy harbour and fishing centre.

Great Yarmouth Youth Hostel ⚑

2 Sandown Road, Great Yarmouth NR30 1EY
☎ (01493) 843991 & Salisbury (01722) 337494
Ideal for recreational breaks and family holidays, and with easy access to many study topics. Use first telephone number April–August, second September–March.
Bedrooms: 1 double/twin,
6 dormitories. Total number of beds: 40
Bathrooms: 2 public

Bed only

per person:	£min	£max
Daily	5.75	8.55

Evening meal from 1900
Open April–August
Cards accepted: Access, Visa

HARROGATE

North Yorkshire
Map ref 4B1

A major conference, exhibition and shopping centre, renowned for its spa heritage and award winning floral displays, spacious parks and gardens. Famous for antiques, toffee, fine shopping and excellent tea shops, also its Royal Pump Rooms and Baths.
Tourist Information Centre ☎ (01423) 525666

West End Outdoor Centre ⚑

West End, Summerbridge, Harrogate
Contact: Mrs M Verity, West End Outdoor Centre, Whitmoor Farm, West End, Summerbridge, Harrogate
HG3 4BA
☎ Blubberhouses (01943) 880207
Self-catering bunkhouse with panoramic views over Thruscross

reservoir. Well-appointed facilities, 12 miles from Harrogate and Skipton, 30 miles from York.
Bedrooms: 4 double/twin,
4 quadruple, 1 dormitory. Total number of beds: 30
Bathrooms: 1 en-suite, 4 public

Bed only

per person:	£min	£max
Daily	5.00	7.00

Parking for 15

HATFIELD

Hertfordshire
Map ref 2D1

The old town is dominated by the great Jacobean Hatfield House, built for Robert Cecil and still in the Cecil family. It has many interesting exhibits and extensive gardens open to the public.

University of Hertfordshire

College Lane, Hatfield
Contact: Mrs Tracey Thrower, University of Hertfordshire, College Lane, Hatfield, Hertfordshire
AL10 9AB
☎ Hatfield (01707) 284007
Fax (01707) 284057
Campus holiday accommodation in 3 and 5-person flats and 7 bedroom houses. All are self-contained units with fully-equipped kitchen and private bathroom. Hatfield is only 22 miles from London.
Minimum age 18
Bedrooms: 800 single,
40 double/twin. Total number of beds: 880
Bathrooms: 90 en-suite, 2 public

Bed only

per person:	£min	£max
Daily	12.36	17.04

Bed & breakfast

per person:	£min	£max
Daily	19.36	22.91

Full board

per person:	£min	£max
Weekly	232.00	360.00

Lunch available
Evening meal 1800 (last orders 2030)
Parking for 100
Open July–September
Cards accepted: Access, Visa, Switch/Delta

Please mention this guide when making your booking.

HECKFIELD

Hampshire
Map ref 2C2

Wellington Riding Ltd ⚑

Basingstoke Road, Heckfield,
Basingstoke RG27 OLJ
☎ (01734) 326308
Fax (01734) 326661
Contact: Mr John Goodman & Miss
Linda Sawyer
*Equestrian centre. Accommodation only
for unaccompanied juniors taking
riding holidays and for adults on
equestrian courses.*
Minimum age 8
Bedrooms: 5 double/twin,
4 dormitories. Total number of
beds: 49
Bathrooms: 4 public
Full board

per person:	£min	£max
Weekly	241.00	

Lunch available
Parking for 40
Cards accepted: Access, Visa,
Switch/Delta

ILKLEY

West Yorkshire
Map ref 4B1

This moorland town is famous for
its ballad. The 16th C manor house,
now a museum, displays local
prehistoric and Roman relics.
Popular walk leads up Heber's Ghyll
to Ilkley Moor, with the mysterious
Swastika Stone and White Wells,
18th C plunge baths.
Tourist Information Centre ☎ (01943)
602319

Glenmoor Centre/City of Bradford Metropolitan Council ⚑

Wells Road, Ilkley LS29 9JF
☎ (01943) 436270
Fax (01943) 436273
Contact: Mrs M Cairns
*Attractive accommodation for
residential and day conferences in a
beautiful setting, just on the edge of
Ilkley Moor. Special rates for voluntary
organisations and registered charities.
Tariffs shown based on minimum 10
delegates.*
For groups only
Bedrooms: 8 single, 12 double/twin.
Total number of beds: 32
Bathrooms: 6 en-suite, 7 public
Bed only

per person:	£min	£max
Daily	12.50	20.00

Bed & breakfast

per person:	£min	£max
Daily	12.50	20.00

Lunch available
Evening meal 1700 (last orders
1900)
Parking for 14

IVINGHOE

Buckinghamshire
Map ref 2D1

Youth Hostel, The Old Brewery House

High Street, Ivinghoe, Leighton
Buzzard, Bedfordshire LU7 9EP
☎ Cheddington (01296) 668251
Fax (01296) 662903
Contact: Andy & Gill Fortune
*Attractive Georgian building opposite
the delightful village green.*
Minimum age 5
Bedrooms: 1 double/twin,
2 quadruple, 4 dormitories. Total
number of beds: 50
Bathrooms: 3 public
Bed only

per person:	£min	£max
Daily	5.20	7.75

Evening meal from 1900
Parking for 8
Open February–November
Cards accepted: Access, Visa

KEMSING

Kent
Map ref 2D2

Youth Hostel - Kemsing Cleves ⚑

Church Lane, Kemsing, Sevenoaks
TN15 6LU
☎ Sevenoaks (01732) 761341
Fax (01732) 763044
Contact: The Warden
*19th C vicarage close to Kemsing
church, in very attractive and extensive
grounds.*
Minimum age 5
Bedrooms: 8 dormitories. Total
number of beds: 50
Bathrooms: 4 public
Bed only

per person:	£min	£max
Daily	5.75	8.55

Evening meal 1900 (last orders
1900)
Parking for 10
Open February–December
Cards accepted: Access, Visa

KIELDER FOREST

Northumberland
Map ref 5B1

City of Newcastle Outdoor Education Service ⚑

"Kielder Log Cabins', Little
Whickhope, Kielder Forest,
Northumberland
Contact: Mr G Little, City of
Newcastle Outdoor, Education
Centre, 121 Trewhitt Road, Heaton,
Newcastle upon Tyne, NE6 5DY
NE6 5DY
☎ (0191) 265 1311
*2 x 16 berth Scandinavian log chalets,
full double glazing, tumble dryer in
each chalet. Separate male and female
toilet facilities and showers. Chalets are
on our own private site with jetty
overlooking the reservoir.*
For groups only
Bedrooms: 2 double/twin,
4 quadruple, 2 dormitories. Total
number of beds: 32
Bathrooms: 4 public
Bed only

per person:	£min	£max
Daily	6.58	8.34

Parking for 10

KING'S LYNN

Norfolk
Map ref 3B1

A busy town with many outstanding
buildings. The Guildhall and Town
Hall are both built of flint in a
striking chequer design.
Tourist Information Centre ☎ (01553)
763044

Youth Hostel Association ⚑

Thoresby College, College Lane,
King's Lynn PE30 1JB
☎ Kings Lynn (01553) 772461
Contact: Ms S Walters
*16th C wing of larger medieval building
in historic centre of town, adjacent to
the River Ouse and Tourist Information
Centre. November-February -
"Rent-a-Hostel" - self-catering from
£230 for 2 nights.*
Bedrooms: 1 single, 1 triple,
2 quadruple, 2 dormitories. Total
number of beds: 36
Bathrooms: 3 public
Bed only

per person:	£min	£max
Daily	5.20	7.75

Lunch available
Evening meal 1800 (last orders
1900)
Open April–October and Christmas
Cards accepted: Access, Visa

LIVERPOOL

Merseyside
Map ref 4A2

Vibrant city which became prominent in the 18th C as a result of its sugar, spice and tobacco trade with the Americas. Today the historic waterfront is a major attraction. Home to the Beatles, the Grand National and 2 20th C cathedrals, as well as many museums and galleries.
Tourist Information Centre ☎ (0151) 709 3631 or 708 8854

City of Liverpool Y.M.C.A. (Inc.)

56 Mount Pleasant, Liverpool
L3 5SH
☎ (0151) 709 9516
Fax (0151) 708 0141
City centre hostel catering for all ages. Basic accommodation and services at a reasonable cost. Singles, twins and triples. Restaurant open 5-6.30pm.
Bedrooms: 99 single, 6 double/twin, 3 triple. Total number of beds: 124
Bathrooms: 12 public
Bed & breakfast

per person:	£min	£max
Daily	10.00	12.50

Evening meal 1700 (last orders 1830)
🛏🚶♿🕭📶Ⓢ🅿📺🖥🚗🔍✕🐕

LONDON

Map 6 & 7 at the back of the guide show place names and London Postal Area codes and will help you to locate accommodation.

Aedis Accommodation

86 Balham Park Road, London
SW12 8EA
☎ (0181) 672 7656
Contact: Mr K F Munn
Furnished bed/sitting rooms, own kitchenettes. Quiet street with no parking restrictions. 5 minutes from shops, 10 minutes from central London. Minimum age 5
Bedrooms: 4 single, 2 double/twin. Total number of beds: 8
Bathrooms: 1 public
Bed only

per person:	£min	£max
Daily	5.00	25.00

🛏8Ⓜ🚶♿☐🅿Ⓤ🚗✕🐎👟SP🅣

Establishments should be open throughout the year, unless otherwise stated.

Binnie Court

40 Greenwich High Road, Greenwich, London
Contact: Mr Paul Turton, Beaver Housing Society, Beaver House, Kivas Hall Mews, London SE13 5JQ
☎ (0181) 297 7030
Fax (0181) 297 7012
University of Greenwich self-catering, close to Greenwich town centre.
Bedrooms: 80 single, 38 double/twin
Bed only

per person:	£min	£max
Daily	10.00	10.00

Parking for 23
Open July–September
🛏♿Ⓤ🖥🚗

Campbell House

Taviton Street, London WC1H 0BX
☎ (0171) 391 1479
Fax (0171) 388 0060
Contact: Mr R L Sparvell
Specially reconstructed Georgian housing providing self-catering accommodation in a peaceful, central London location.
Minimum age 10
Bedrooms: 60 single, 40 double/twin. Total number of beds: 140
Bathrooms: 25 public
Bed only

per person:	£min	£max
Daily	14.00	16.50

Open June–September
🛏🚷🚶♿Ⓤ🍴🅿📺🖥🚗🔍🐕

Central University of Iowa Hostel

7 Bedford Place, London WC1B 5JA
☎ (0171) 580 1121
Contact: Mr Roy Oliver
Old Georgian house near the British Museum. Closest underground stations are Russell Square and Holborn.
Bedrooms: 1 single, 6 double/twin, 2 triple, 3 quadruple. Total number of beds: 31
Bathrooms: 7 public
Bed & breakfast

per person:	£min	£max
Daily	18.00	

Open May–August
Cards accepted: Access, Visa, Switch/Delta
🛏Ⓤ📺🖥🚗✕🐎🏥

City of London YHA 🅐🅐

36 Carter Lane, London EC4V 5AD
☎ (0171) 236 4965
Fax (0171) 236 7681
Contact: Mr J Piggott
In the centre of the City of London, in an area of narrow, winding streets. Former school for choirboys of St Paul's Cathedral. Other hostels throughout London - central reservations (0171) 248 6547.

Driscoll House Hotel

172 New Kent Road, London
SE1 4YT
☎ (0171) 703 4175
Fax (0171) 703 8013
Contact: Mr. T Driscoll
Long or short term accommodation offered to teachers, students and tourists. Weekly full-board price below excludes weekday lunch. During the past 80 years we have accommodated more than 50,000 people from 200 different countries.
Bedrooms: 200 single, 6 double/twin. Total number of beds: 200
Bathrooms: 14 public
Bed & breakfast

per person:	£min	£max
Daily	27.00	27.00

Full board

per person:	£min	£max
Weekly	150.00	150.00

Lunch available
Evening meal 1730 (last orders 1900)
Parking for 10
🎱Ⓤ♿Ⓢ🍴🅿📺🖥🚗🛎🍴🔍✕🅣

Bedrooms: 2 single, 5 double/twin, 7 triple, 10 quadruple, 16 dormitories. Total number of beds: 191
Bathrooms: 2 en-suite, 10 public
Bed & breakfast

per person:	£min	£max
Daily	11.80	23.55

Full board

per person:	£min	£max
Weekly	128.10	215.60

Lunch available
Evening meal 1700 (last orders 2000)
Cards accepted: Access, Visa, Switch/Delta
🛏🚶♿🕭🍴✕🅿📺🖥🚗🔍✕🐎👟SP🏥🅣◎

Ealing YMCA

25 St Marys Road, Ealing, London
W5 5RE
☎ (0181) 579 6946
Fax (0181) 579 1129
Contact: Judith Birch
Residential centre, each room with colour TV. Le Jardin restaurant on premises. Weekly prices shown below are for half board only.
Bedrooms: 129 single, 13 double/twin, 13 triple. Total number of beds: 155
Bathrooms: 13 en-suite, 30 public
Bed & breakfast

per person:	£min	£max
Daily	16.42	24.40

Full board

per person:	£min	£max
Weekly	83.69	105.27

Continued ▶

393

LONDON
Continued

Lunch available
Evening meal 1745 (last orders 1855)
Parking for 26
Cards accepted: Access, Visa, Switch/Delta

🐕♿️🖥♿️ⓈⓃ✂🏠🛏☎️🛎3🎿
🎭🔍🐾

Elizabeth House Hotel Ⓜ
118 Warwick Way, London
SW1V 1SD
☎ (0171) 630 0741
Fax (0171) 630 0740
Contact: Ms. F McGinlay
Clean and secure basic bed and breakfast accommodation in central London for men, women and families. Garden available for guests. Recently refurbished with improved facilities.
Bedrooms: 10 single, 13 double/twin, 1 triple, 3 quadruple. Total number of beds: 51
Bathrooms: 9 en-suite, 8 public
Bed only

per person:	£min	£max
Daily	15.00	22.50

Bed & breakfast

per person:	£min	£max
Daily	15.00	22.50

Cards accepted: Access, Visa, Switch/Delta

🐕♿️Ⓤ✂🖥📺🛏🛏🎿Ⓢ🅿

Imperial College Ⓜ
Vacation Accommodation Centre, Watts Way, Prince's Gardens, London
Contact: Ms Annette de Lima, Imperial College, Sales Office, Watts Way, Prince's Gardens, London
SW7 1LU
☎ (0171) 594 9494 & 594 9507
Fax (0171) 594 9505
Single and twin study bedrooms available, Easter and summer. Situated near Harrods and Hyde Park and next to South Kensington museums.
Minimum age 7
Bedrooms: 600 single, 24 double/twin. Total number of beds: 648
Bathrooms: 140 public
Bed & breakfast

per person:	£min	£max
Daily	25.00	

Lunch available
Evening meal 1600 (last orders 2130)
Open March–April, June–September
Cards accepted: Access, Visa, Switch/Delta

🐕7♿️Ⓢ🅗✂🅗📺🛏🛏🎿🎭🔍
🐾🛝🐾🅣

International House Woolwich
109 Brookhill Road, London
SE18 6RZ
☎ (0181) 854 1418
Fax (0181) 855 9257
Contact: Mr B Siderman
Purpose-built student hostel. Self-contained flats for married couples and children. Full en-suite facilities also available. Short-term visitor accommodation available July–September.
Bedrooms: 85 single, 21 double/twin. Total number of beds: 127
Bathrooms: 21 en-suite, 18 public
Bed & breakfast

per person:	£min	£max
Daily	9.00	13.30

Parking for 21
Open April, July–September, December

🐕🛝Ⓤ🅗Ⓢ🅗📺🛏🛏🔍🅧🅣

International Students Hostel Frognal House
99 Frognal, Hampstead, London
NW3 6XR
☎ (0171) 794 6893 & 794 8095
Fax (0171) 435 0724
Contact: Sr. P S Taylor
Historic, listed building in attractive grounds. Family atmosphere. Five minutes Hampstead Heath and underground, 15 minutes central London. Budget rates for long-term students.
For females only
Minimum age 16
Bedrooms: 17 single, 2 double/twin, 4 dormitories. Total number of beds: 40
Bathrooms: 15 public
Bed & breakfast

per person:	£min	£max
Daily	10.00	16.50

Evening meal from 1845

🐕Ⓤ🅗Ⓢ🅗📺🛏🛏🅧🅗🅣

International Students House Ⓜ
229 Great Portland Street, London
W1N 5HD
☎ (0171) 631 8300
Fax (0171) 631 8315
Contact: Ms Martina Downes
Comfortable accommodation, centrally located in West End. Easy access to all London's tourist attractions. Close to underground and other public transport. Restaurant, bar and fitness centre on premises.
Minimum age 16
Bedrooms: 159 single, 107 double/twin, 3 triple, 5 quadruple, 2 dormitories. Total number of beds: 421
Bathrooms: 4 en-suite, 95 public

Bed & breakfast

per person:	£min	£max
Daily	10.00	27.00

Lunch available
Evening meal 1730 (last orders 1930)
Parking for 10
Cards accepted: Access, Visa, Switch/Delta

🐕📞Ⓢ🅗📺🛏🛏🔔7🎿🎭🔍🐾
🅧🐾Ⓢ🅗🅣

John Adams Hall (Institute of Education) Ⓜ
15-23 Endsleigh Street, London
WC1H 0DH
☎ (0171) 387 4086
Fax (0171) 383 0164
Contact: Mr M Lam-Hing
An assembly of Georgian houses, the hall retains its old glory. Close to Euston, King's Cross and St Pancras stations.
Bedrooms: 127 single, 22 double/twin. Total number of beds: 171
Bathrooms: 1 en-suite, 26 public
Bed & breakfast

per person:	£min	£max
Daily	17.00	21.40

Evening meal 1730 (last orders 1830)
Open January, March–April, July–September, December
Cards accepted: Access, Visa

🐕🛝♿️Ⓢ✂🅗📺🛏🛏🔍🎭🅗🅣

Kent House Ⓜ
325 Green Lanes, London N4 2ES
☎ (0181) 802 0800 & 802 5100
Fax (0181) 802 9070
Special off-season and weekly rates for young tourists. Facilities for self-catering. Adjacent to Manor House underground station and 10 minutes from central London.
Minimum age 16
Bedrooms: 3 single, 13 double/twin, 3 dormitories. Total number of beds: 34
Bathrooms: 6 public
Bed only

per person:	£min	£max
Daily	14.00	23.00

Bed & breakfast

per person:	£min	£max
Daily	15.00	25.00

Parking for 4

🐕🦮Ⓤ🅗📺🛏🛏🔔🎭🅧🚗🐾Ⓢ
🅣

A key to symbols can be found inside the back cover flap.

Kirness House ⚑

29 Belgrave Road, Victoria, London
SW1V 1RB
☎ (0171) 834 0030
Contact: Mrs M Walker
*Small hostel very close to Victoria
station. Many European languages
spoken.
For individuals only*
Bedrooms: 6 single. Total number of
beds: 10
Bathrooms: 3 public
Bed only

per person:	£min	£max
Daily	25.00	45.00

Bed & breakfast

per person:	£min	£max
Daily	25.00	45.00

Cards accepted: Amex

Lancaster Hall Hotel (Youth Annexe)

35 Craven Terrace, Lancaster Gate,
London W2 3EL
☎ (0171) 723 9276
Fax (0171) 706 2870
Contact: Mr U Maynard
*Within easy walking distance of Hyde
Park, Kensington Gardens and Marble
Arch. Close to public transport.*
Bedrooms: 3 single, 7 double/twin,
4 triple, 3 quadruple. Total number
of beds: 41
Bathrooms: 4 public
Bed & breakfast

per person:	£min	£max
Daily	19.00	21.00

Evening meal 1800 (last orders
2100)
Parking for 13
Cards accepted: Access, Visa,
Switch/Delta

Lightfoot Hall ⚑

King's College London, Manresa
Road, London
Contact: King's Campus Vacation
Bureau, 127 Stamford Street,
London SE1 9NQ
☎ (0171) 928 3777
Fax (0171) 928 5777
*Modern 10-storey building in the
famous King's Road, Chelsea. Other
Halls of Residence in Westminster,
Wandsworth, Denmark Hill,
Hampstead and Kensington. Also
brand-new hall in Stamford Street on
the south bank of the Thames close to
Waterloo station and Eurostar terminal.
Use the above telephone and fax
numbers for central reservations.*
Bedrooms: 174 single,
24 double/twin. Total number of
beds: 222
Bathrooms: 30 public

Bed & breakfast

per person:	£min	£max
Daily	16.50	21.00

Lunch available
Evening meal 1800 (last orders
1900)
Open June–September
Cards accepted: Access, Visa,
Switch/Delta

The Lodge (Pall Mall Services)

Ledrington Road, London SE19 2BB
☎ (0181) 778 0131
Fax (0181) 676 0056
Contact: Mrs Gene Gilmour
*Set in 200 acres of parkland, 6 miles
from central London. Railway station on
site (line to London Victoria). Ample
coach and car parking. Major sporting
facilities.*
Bedrooms: 37 single, 37 double/twin,
9 triple. Total number of beds: 144
Bathrooms: 9 en-suite, 87 public
Bed only

per person:	£min	£max
Daily	16.50	22.50

Bed & breakfast

per person:	£min	£max
Daily	22.00	28.00

Lunch available
Evening meal 1700 (last orders
2100)
Parking for 200
Cards accepted: Access, Visa, Diners

London House Hotel ⚑

81 Kensington Gardens Square,
London
Contact: Miss Jackie Boughton, 16
Leinster Square, London W2 4DJ
☎ (0171) 221 1400
Fax (0171) 243 8626
*Friendly, comfortable budget hotel,
convenient for shops, theatres and
sightseeing.*
Bedrooms: 3 single, 40 double/twin,
6 triple, 16 quadruple,
11 dormitories. Total number of
beds: 220
Bathrooms: 41 en-suite, 14 public
Bed & breakfast

per person:	£min	£max
Daily	19.00	39.50

Full board

per person:	£min	£max
Weekly		73.50

Cards accepted: Access, Visa, Diners,
Amex, Switch/Delta

You are advised to confirm
your booking in writing.

Lords Hotel ⚑

20-22 Leinster Square, London
W2 4PR
☎ (0171) 229 8877
Fax (0171) 229 8377
Contact: Mr. N G Ladas
*Bed and breakfast accommodation in
central London. Direct-dial telephone,
TV. Most rooms with private facilities.*
Bedrooms: 9 single, 26 double/twin,
11 triple, 17 quadruple,
3 dormitories. Total number of
beds: 175
Bathrooms: 52 en-suite, 7 public
Bed & breakfast

per person:	£min	£max
Daily	15.00	40.00

Cards accepted: Access, Visa, Diners,
Amex, Switch/Delta

New Atlantic Hotel ⚑

1 Queen's Gardens, London
Contact: Ms J Boughton, 16 Leinster
Square, London W2 4PR
☎ (0171) 221 1400
Fax (0171) 229 3917
*Ideal for youth groups. Budget hotel in
Bayswater.*
Bedrooms: 35 single, 93 double/twin,
10 triple, 37 quadruple,
39 dormitories. Total number of
beds: 417
Bathrooms: 95 en-suite, 34 public
Bed & breakfast

per person:	£min	£max
Daily	19.00	39.50

Full board

per person:	£min	£max
Weekly		73.50

Cards accepted: Access, Visa, Diners,
Amex, Switch/Delta

O'Callaghan's

205 Earl's Court Road, London
Contact: Mr P J O'Connor,
O'Callaghan's, 205 Earls Court
Road, London SW5 9AN
☎ (0171) 370 3000 & 603 0743
Fax (0171) 370 2623
*Central London low-budget guesthouse
for tourists and students. Open all year
round.*
Bedrooms: 4 double/twin, 3 triple,
3 quadruple. Total number of
beds: 26
Bathrooms: 3 public
Bed only

per person:	£min	£max
Daily	10.00	12.00

Bed & breakfast

per person:	£min	£max
Daily	10.00	12.00

Passfield Hall ⚲

1 Endsleigh Place, London
WC1H 0PW
☎ (0171) 387 7743 & 387 3584
Fax (0171) 387 0419
*University hall of residence with
washbasin in all rooms, suitable for
individuals and families. Central for
Oxford Street and the West End.*
Bedrooms: 100 single,
34 double/twin, 10 triple. Total
number of beds: 198
Bathrooms: 36 public
Bed & breakfast

per person:	£min	£max
Daily	18.00	20.50

Open March–April, July–September
Cards accepted: Access, Visa,
Switch/Delta

🛏🕮Ⓤ🅂🎿📺💻🖪🍴

The Porchester Hotel ⚲

33 Princes Square, London
Contact: Miss Jackie Boughton, 16
Leinster Square, London W2 4DJ
☎ (0171) 221 1400
Fax (0171) 727 9976
*Ideal for youth groups, the Porchester
has its own passenger lift and offers
half the rooms with private facilities.
Value for money, affordable
accommodation.*
Bedrooms: 6 single, 17 double/twin,
12 triple, 21 quadruple,
3 dormitories. Total number of
beds: 182
Bathrooms: 33 en-suite, 10 public
Bed & breakfast

per person:	£min	£max
Daily	19.00	39.50

Full board

per person:	£min	£max
Weekly	73.50	

Evening meal 1700 (last orders
2200)
Cards accepted: Access, Visa, Amex,
Switch/Delta

🛏🕮🖳🗂🅂🎿📺💻🖪Ⓣ

Queen Alexandra's House ⚲

Bremner Road, Kensington Gore,
London SW7 2QT
☎ (0171) 589 3635
Fax (0171) 589 3177
Contact: Mrs C J Raymond
*Fine example of Victorian architecture
and a long established hostel for
women students of all ages in South
Kensington.*
For females only
Minimum age 17
Bedrooms: 75 single, 2 double/twin.
Total number of beds: 81
Bathrooms: 20 public

Bed & breakfast

per person:	£min	£max
Daily	23.00	25.00

Open May–August

🛏🕮Ⓤ🎿📺💻🖪🍴🚲🏠

Regency Court Hotel

14 Penywern Road, London
SW5 9ST
☎ (0171) 244 6615
Fax (0171) 357 8279
Contact: Mr Rajiv Awasti
*Small budget hotel close to Earl's Court
underground station. Tourists and
travellers welcome.*
Bedrooms: 5 single, 8 double/twin,
1 quadruple. Total number of
beds: 27
Bathrooms: 1 en-suite, 5 public
Bed & breakfast

per person:	£min	£max
Daily	15.00	25.00

Cards accepted: Access, Visa, Amex

🛏🖳🗂Ⓤ🎿📺💻🖪🍴🚲
🅂🄣

Hotel Saint Simeon ⚲

38 Harrington Gardens, London
SW7 4LT
☎ (0171) 373 0505 & 370 4708
Fax (0171) 589 6412
Contact: Mr. J Gojkovic
*Rooms for one, two or three people in
central London. Nearest underground
station is Gloucester Road.*
Bedrooms: 6 single, 10 double/twin,
5 dormitories. Total number of
beds: 41
Bathrooms: 4 en-suite, 6 public
Bed only

per person:	£min	£max
Daily	10.00	29.00

Bed & breakfast

per person:	£min	£max
Daily	10.00	29.00

Cards accepted: Access, Visa, Amex

🛏🖳🖳Ⓤ🎿📺💻🖪🍴🚲🅂
🄣

Tent City - Acton ⚲

Old Oak Common Lane, East Acton,
London W3 7DP
☎ (0181) 743 5708
Fax (0181) 749 9074
Contact: Ms Maxine Lambert
*"Tented" hostel and campsite close to
East Acton tube. On-site snackbar, free
baggage and valuables store. Young
and fun!*
Bedrooms: 14 dormitories. Total
number of beds: 448
Bathrooms: 24 public
Bed only

per person:	£min	£max
Daily	11.00	11.00

Lunch available
Parking for 30
Open June–September

🛏Ⓤ🅂🎿📺💻🖪🍴🚲Ⓓ🅂🄿

University of North London

Tufnell Park Hall, Huddleston Road,
London
Contact: Ms Rachel Sosville,
University of North London, Tufnell
Park Hall, Huddleston Road, London,
N7 0EG
☎ (0171) 272 4649
Fax (0171) 281 1236
*All single study rooms in a modern
building, within easy reach of central
London via public transport.*
Bedrooms: 207 single. Total number
of beds: 207
Bathrooms: 34 public
Bed only

per person:	£min	£max
Daily	14.00	14.00

Bed & breakfast

per person:	£min	£max
Daily	17.00	19.50

Full board

per person:	£min	£max
Weekly	98.00	206.50

Lunch available
Parking for 40
Open March–April, June–September
Cards accepted: Access, Visa,
Switch/Delta

🛏🍽🅂🎿📺💻🖪🍴

University of North London

James Leicester Hall, Market Road,
London
Contact: Ms Rachel Sosville,
University of North London, Tufnell
Park Hall, Huddleston Road, London,
N7 0EG
☎ (0171) 272 4649
Fax (0171) 281 1236
*Modern hostel built around a pleasant
courtyard. Easy access to the West End,
close to Piccadilly Line underground.*
Bedrooms: 216 single. Total number
of beds: 216
Bathrooms: 36 public
Bed only

per person:	£min	£max
Daily	14.00	14.00

Bed & breakfast

per person:	£min	£max
Daily	17.00	19.50

Full board

per person:	£min	£max
Weekly	98.00	206.50

Lunch available
Parking for 15
Open April, June–September
Cards accepted: Access, Visa,
Switch/Delta

🛏🅂🎿📺💻🖪🍴

University of North London

Arcade, 385-401 Holloway Road, London
Contact: Ms Rachel Sosville, University of North London, Tufnell Park Hall, Huddleston Road, London, N7 0EG
☎ (0171) 272 4649
Fax (0171) 281 1236
Single study bedrooms within 4, 5 and 6 bedroomed self-contained flats. Within easy access of West End and underground.
For groups only
Bedrooms: 374 single. Total number of beds: 374
Bathrooms: 136 public

Bed only per person:	£min	£max
Daily	14.00	14.00

Bed & breakfast per person:	£min	£max
Daily	17.00	19.50

Full board per person:	£min	£max
Weekly	98.00	206.50

Parking for 15
Open June–September
Cards accepted: Access, Visa, Switch/Delta

University of Westminster 🜨

International House, 1-5 Lambeth Road, London
Contact: Ms Nicole Chanson, University of Westminster, Commercial Services, Luxborough Suite, 35 Marylebone Road, London NW1 5LS
☎ (0171) 911 5000
Fax (0171) 911 5141
Hall of Residence offering good quality accommodation in single and twin rooms on a self-catering or B&B basis. Four tube stops away from Piccadilly Circus and within a few minutes' walk of River Thames, Houses of Parliament and Westminster Abbey. Ideal for sightseeing and for London's theatreland.
Minimum age 7
Bedrooms: 63 single, 9 double/twin. Total number of beds: 81
Bathrooms: 18 public

Bed only per person:	£min	£max
Daily	15.70	21.50

Bed & breakfast per person:	£min	£max
Daily	17.15	24.00

Lunch available
Evening meal 1730 (last orders 1930)
Parking for 2
Open April, July–September
Cards accepted: Access, Visa, Switch/Delta

University of Westminster 🜨

Furnival House, Chomeley Park, Highgate, London
Contact: Ms Nicole Chanson, University of Westminster, Commercial Services, Luxborough Suite, 35 Marylebone Road, London NW1 5LS
☎ (0171) 911 5000
Fax (0171) 911 5141
Refurbished Edwardian Hall of Residence in Highgate village, in own grounds. Good quality accommodation on self-catering or B&B basis. Within easy walking distance of Waterlow Park and Hampstead Heath and only half-an-hour from West End. Some rooms offer panoramic views of London.
Minimum age 7
Bedrooms: 85 single, 28 double/twin. Total number of beds: 113
Bathrooms: 16 public

Bed only per person:	£min	£max
Daily	15.70	21.50

Bed & breakfast per person:	£min	£max
Daily	17.15	24.00

Lunch available
Evening meal 1730 (last orders 1930)
Parking for 6
Open April, July–September
Cards accepted: Access, Visa, Switch/Delta

Urban Learning Foundation 🜨

56 East India Dock Road, London E14 6JE
☎ (0171) 987 0033
Fax (0171) 538 2620
Contact: Ms Jacqui Duggan
Purpose-built residential training centre, close to central London. Single study bedrooms arranged in 4-7 bedded apartments.
Minimum age 12
Bedrooms: 47 single. Total number of beds: 47
Bathrooms: 1 en-suite, 18 public

Bed only per person:	£min	£max
Daily	12.00	22.00

Bed & breakfast per person:	£min	£max
Daily	15.00	25.00

Lunch available
Cards accepted: Access, Visa, Amex

Y.M.C.A.

Rush Green Road, Romford RM7 0PH
☎ Romford (01708) 766211
Fax (01708) 754211
Contact: Mr Dave Ball
8 minutes' walk from Romford British Rail station, 25 minutes from Liverpool Street station. Easy access to M25 and south coast. Easy travel into London by underground (Elm Park). International hostel with many sports facilities.
Minimum age 18
Bedrooms: 148 single, 2 double/twin. Total number of beds: 150
Bathrooms: 4 en-suite, 24 public

Bed & breakfast per person:	£min	£max
Daily	16.50	19.50

Full board per person:	£min	£max
Weekly	60.28	128.65

Lunch available
Evening meal 1730 (last orders 1845)
Parking for 120
Cards accepted: Access, Visa

MATFIELD

Kent
Map ref 3B4

Village with Georgian houses, green and pond.

Old Cryals

Cryals Road, Matfield, Tonbridge TN12 7HN
☎ Brenchley (0189272) 2372
Fax (0189272) 3311
Contact: Mr C Charrington
Hostel-type accommodation for 12, in two rooms for 4 and 8. Comfortable sitting/dining room with microwave oven, TV, freezer, dishwasher. Self-catering only.
Bedrooms: 2 dormitories. Total number of beds: 12
Bathrooms: 2 public

Bed only per person:	£min	£max
Daily	6.50	7.50

Parking for 12
Open March–November

The 🜨 symbol after an establishment name indicates that it is a Regional Tourist Board member.

MATLOCK

Derbyshire
Map ref 4B2

The town lies beside the narrow valley of the River Derwent surrounded by steep wooded hills. Good centre for exploring Derbyshire's best scenery.

Matlock Youth Hostel

40 Bank Road, Matlock DE4 3NF
☎ (01629) 582983
Fax (01629) 583484
Contact: Mr & Mrs C Back
Recently refurbished well-equipped hostel offering comfortable low cost accommodation. Close to the town centre.
Minimum age 5
Bedrooms: 6 double/twin, 2 triple, 4 quadruple, 2 dormitories. Total number of beds: 49
Bathrooms: 2 en-suite, 3 public

Bed only

per person:	£min	£max
Daily	6.25	9.20

Bed & breakfast

per person:	£min	£max
Daily	9.15	12.10

Full board

per person:	£min	£max
Weekly	115.85	136.50

Lunch available
Evening meal from 1900
Parking for 6
Cards accepted: Access, Visa, Switch/Delta

MIDDLESBROUGH

Tees Valley
Map ref 5C3

Boom-town of the mid 19th C, today's Teesside industrial and conference town has a modern shopping complex and predominantly modern buildings. An engineering miracle of the early 20th C is the Transporter Bridge which replaced an old ferry.
Tourist Information Centre ☎ *(01642) 243425 or 264330*

T A D Centre

Ormesby Road, Middlesbrough, Cleveland TS3 7SF
☎ (01642) 203000
Fax (01642) 244006
Contact: Mrs K MacNaught
Modern purpose built training and conference centre. Spacious accommodation furnished to a comfortable standard, with bar and restaurant facilities for delegates.

Minimum age 18
Bedrooms: 40 single. Total number of beds: 40
Bathrooms: 40 en-suite

Bed & breakfast

per person:	£min	£max
Daily	45.00	45.00

Lunch available
Evening meal 1800 (last orders 2130)
Parking for 102
Cards accepted: Access, Visa, Switch/Delta

MOULTON

Northamptonshire
Map ref 2C1

Moulton College

West Street, Moulton, Northampton NN3 7RR
☎ Northampton (01604) 491131
Fax (01604) 491127
Contact: Mrs Margaret Lewis
Set in countryside, yet 5 miles from Northampton, Moulton College offers conference, boardroom, seminar, dining and bar facilities and accommodation.
Bedrooms: 54 single, 48 double/twin. Total number of beds: 150
Bathrooms: 24 public

Bed & breakfast

per person:	£min	£max
Daily	11.75	14.10

Full board

per person:	£min	£max
Weekly	125.00	139.00

Lunch available
Evening meal 1730 (last orders 1830)
Parking for 280
Cards accepted: Access, Visa

The ⚠ symbol after an establishment name indicates that it is a Regional Tourist Board member.

ACCESSIBILITY

Look for the symbols which indicate accessibility for wheelchair users. These are described in detail at the front of this guide.

NEWCASTLE UPON TYNE

Tyne and Wear
Map ref 5C2

Commercial and cultural centre of the North East, with a large indoor shopping centre, Quayside market, museums and theatres which offer an annual 6 week season by the Royal Shakespeare Company. Norman castle keep, medieval alleys, old Guildhall.
Tourist Information Centre ☎ *(0191) 261 0610 or 230 0030*

Leazes Terrace Student Houses

10 Leazes Terrace, Newcastle upon Tyne NE1 4LY
☎ (0191) 222 8150 & 222 7565
Fax (0191) 222 8150
Contact: Miss G McNaughton
Good value university accommodation in a late Georgian terrace in the city centre with easy access to shops and transport.
Minimum age 18
Bedrooms: 72 single, 26 double/twin, 2 triple, 2 dormitories. Total number of beds: 134
Bathrooms: 17 public

Bed only

per person:	£min	£max
Daily	12.40	12.40

Bed & breakfast

per person:	£min	£max
Daily	16.32	16.32

Full board

per person:	£min	£max
Weekly	102.00	102.00

Open July–September

University of Northumbria Newcastle ⚠

Coach Lane Campus Halls of Residence, Coach Lane, Newcastle upon Tyne, Tyne & Wear
Contact: Mrs S Cowell, University of Northumbria, Newcastle, Ellison Place, Newcastle upon Tyne, Tyne & Wear NE1 8ST
☎ (0191) 227 4024
Fax (0191) 227 3197
Accommodation in modern halls of residence, set in pleasant grounds, 3 miles from the city centre. Bed and breakfast with or without evening meal for groups or parties.
Minimum age 16
Bedrooms: 186 single, 50 double/twin. Total number of beds: 286
Bathrooms: 44 public

Bed only per person:	£min	£max
Daily	10.50	13.70

Bed & breakfast per person:	£min	£max
Daily	15.45	19.50

Full board per person:	£min	£max
Weekly	150.00	272.50

Lunch available
Evening meal 1730 (last orders 1930)
Parking for 100
Open April, July–September

NORWICH

Norfolk
Map ref 3C1

Beautiful cathedral city and county town on the River Wensum with many fine museums and medieval churches. Norman castle, Guildhall and interesting medieval streets. Good shopping centre and market.
Tourist Information Centre ☎ *(01603) 666071*

City College Norwich
Southwell Lodge, Ipswich Road, Norwich NR2 2LL
☎ (01603) 618327 & 660011
Fax (01603) 760326
Contact: Mr John Wheeler
College halls of residence set in a rural tree-screened setting within 10 minutes' walk of Norwich city centre. Lunch and supper available.
Bedrooms: 270 single, 8 double/twin.
Total number of beds: 286
Bathrooms: 13 en-suite, 32 public

Bed only per person:	£min	£max
Daily	13.00	18.00

Bed & breakfast per person:	£min	£max
Daily	16.50	21.00

Lunch available
Evening meal 1730 (last orders 1900)
Parking for 500
Cards accepted: Access, Visa, Switch/Delta

University of East Anglia 𝔐
Norwich NR4 7TJ
☎ (01603) 593277
Fax (01603) 250585
Contact: Ms J Court
Modern university in parkland, 2 miles from the centre of Norwich. Comfortable, convenient and compact. En-suite and family accommodation available.

Minimum age 14
Bedrooms: 1300 single, 50 double/twin. Total number of beds: 1300
Bathrooms: 600 en-suite, 70 public

Bed only per person:	£min	£max
Daily	11.75	19.70

Bed & breakfast per person:	£min	£max
Daily	16.75	24.65

Lunch available
Evening meal 1700 (last orders 1915)
Parking for 700
Open March–April, June–September
Cards accepted: Access, Visa, Diners, Switch/Delta

NOTTINGHAM

Nottinghamshire
Map ref 4C2

Attractive modern city with a rich history. Outside its castle, now a museum, is Robin Hood's statue. Attractions include "The Tales of Robin Hood"; the Lace Hall; Wollaton Hall; museums and excellent facilities for shopping, sports and entertainment.
Tourist Information Centre ☎ *(0115) 947 0661*

The Igloo Tourist Hostel
110 Mansfield Road, Nottingham NG1 3HL
☎ (0115) 947 5250
Contact: Mr Steve Maxwell
Dormitory accommodation for backpackers and activity groups with use of hot showers, TV lounge and kitchen. Open all day all year. No chores.
Minimum age 8
Bedrooms: 2 dormitories. Total number of beds: 16
Bathrooms: 2 public

Bed only per person:	£min	£max
Daily	8.00	8.00

Bed & breakfast per person:	£min	£max
Daily	10.00	10.00

OTTERBURN

Northumberland
Map ref 5B1

Small village set at the meeting of the River Rede with Otter Burn, the site of the Battle of Otterburn in 1388. A peaceful tradition continues in the sale of Otterburn tweeds in this beautiful region, which is ideal for exploring the Border country and the Cheviots.

Otterburn Hall
Otterburn NE19 1HE
☎ Freephone 0800 591527
Fax (0191) 385 2267
Contact: Mrs V Connell
Family holiday hotel, conference venue and training establishment in 100 acres. Offering special interest holidays. Prices quoted include dinner.
Minimum age 8
Bedrooms: 7 single, 50 double/twin, 3 triple, 5 quadruple. Total number of beds: 132
Bathrooms: 60 en-suite

Bed only per person:	£min	£max
Daily	24.00	26.00

Bed & breakfast per person:	£min	£max
Daily	30.00	37.00

Full board per person:	£min	£max
Weekly	200.00	210.00

Lunch available
Evening meal 1900 (last orders 1900)
Parking for 100
Cards accepted: Access, Visa, Amex

OXFORD

Oxfordshire
Map ref 2C1

Beautiful university town with many ancient colleges, some dating from the 13th C, and numerous buildings of historic and architectural interest. The Ashmolean Museum has outstanding collections. Lovely gardens and meadows with punting on the Cherwell.
Tourist Information Centre ☎ *(01865) 726871*

Oxford Backpackers Hostel ⋈

9a Hythe Bridge Street, Oxford OX1 2EW
☎ (01865) 721761 & 721987
Fax (01865) 721761
Contact: Mr Brent Smith
Centrally located in the heart of historic Oxford, 2 minutes' walk from bus, coach and train stations. Fully serviced, premium hostel.
Minimum age 12
Bedrooms: 1 single, 2 double/twin, 12 dormitories. Total number of beds: 90
Bathrooms: 6 public

Bed only

per person:	£min	£max
Daily	9.00	10.50

Full board

per person:	£min	£max
Weekly	54.00	60.00

Cards accepted: Access, Visa, Diners, Switch/Delta

🛏12🗗🕭UL✂🐾TV🖥🖴🛆🍴🔍✕Ⓣ

PORTSMOUTH & SOUTHSEA

Hampshire
Map ref 2C3

The first dock was built in 1194. HMS Victory, Nelson's flagship, is here and Charles Dickens' former home is open to the public. Neighbouring Southsea has a promenade with magnificent views of Spithead.
Tourist Information Centre ☎ *(01705) 833635 or 826722*

Portsmouth Y M C A ⋈

Penny Street, Portsmouth, Hampshire PO1 2NN
☎ Portsmouth (01705) 864341
Fax (01705) 293276
Contact: Mr Rob Finn
Comfortable, inexpensive accommodation right by the sea - just a few minutes from road/rail interchanges. Families and groups welcome. Brochure available.

Bedrooms: 80 single, 20 double/twin, 5 dormitories. Total number of beds: 130
Bathrooms: 15 public

Bed & breakfast

per person:	£min	£max
Daily	13.50	

Evening meal 1715 (last orders 1800)

🛏🕭UL🔒🕭S🐾TV🖥🖴🛆✕✕🐕SP🏧

University of Portsmouth Central Reservations ⋈

Nuffield Centre, St Michaels Road, Portsmouth, Hampshire PO1 2ED
☎ Portsmouth (01705) 843178
Fax (01705) 843182
Contact: Ms Elizabeth Jackson
Conference and holiday venue in self-catering flats or serviced accommodation, with sport and lecture facilities.
Bedrooms: 1510 single, 124 double/twin, 12 triple. Total number of beds: 1794
Bathrooms: 774 en-suite, 164 public

Bed only

per person:	£min	£max
Daily	11.20	11.20

Bed & breakfast

per person:	£min	£max
Daily	14.45	14.45

Full board

per person:	£min	£max
Weekly	157.65	157.65

Lunch available
Evening meal 1800 (last orders 2130)
Open March–April, June–September
Cards accepted: Access, Visa

🛏3🕭🔑🕭S🐾TV🖥🖴🍴✕🔍✕ ⚲DAP SP

POSTBRIDGE

Devon
Map ref 1C2

Tiny village in the centre of Dartmoor National Park, famous for its stone clapper bridge, probably medieval, over the East Dart River. Broadun Ring and Broadun Pound are 2 sets of prehistoric remains nearby.

The Youth Hostel - Bellever

Bellever, Postbridge, Yelverton PL20 6TU
☎ Tavistock (01822) 880227
Fax (01822) 880302
Contact: Mr Ian Harris
Hostel in the heart of Dartmoor, a good base for walking, moorland studies and adventure training.

Minimum age 5
Bedrooms: 5 quadruple, 2 dormitories. Total number of beds: 36
Bathrooms: 3 public

Bed only

per person:	£min	£max
Daily	5.75	8.55

Evening meal 1900 (last orders 1800)
Parking for 6
Open April–October
Cards accepted: Access, Visa

🛏UL🕭S✂🐾🖥◡🐾⚲

ROCHESTER

Kent
Map ref 3B3

Ancient cathedral city on the River Medway. Has many places of interest connected with Charles Dickens (who lived nearby) including the fascinating Dickens Centre. Also massive castle overlooking the river and Guildhall Museum.
Tourist Information Centre ☎ *(01634) 843666*

Capstone Farm

377 Capstone Road, Gillingham ME7 3JE
☎ Gillingham (01634) 400788
Fax (01634) 400794
Contact: Mr Chris Browne
This brand new hostel is formed from a restored oast house and farm buildings, and has excellent facilities for families and individuals.
Minimum age 5
Bedrooms: 4 double/twin, 4 quadruple, 2 dormitories. Total number of beds: 42
Bathrooms: 6 public

Bed only

per person:	£min	£max
Daily	5.55	8.25

Evening meal from 1900
Parking for 20
Open February–November
Cards accepted: Access, Visa, Switch/Delta

🛏UL🔒S✂TV🖥🐾SP⚲

TOWN INDEX

This can be found at the back of the guide. If you know where you want to stay, the index will give you the page number listing all accommodation in your chosen town, city or village.

ROSS-ON-WYE

Hereford and Worcester
Map ref 2A1

Attractive market town with a 17th C market hall, set above the River Wye. There are lovely views over the surrounding countryside from the Prospect and the town is close to Goodrich Castle and the Welsh border.
Tourist Information Centre ☎ (01989) 562768

Welsh Bicknor Youth Hostel
Welsh Bicknor Rectory,
Ross-on-Wye, Herefordshire
HR6 9JJ
☎ Dean (01594) 860300
Fax (01594) 861276
Contact: Mr C E Hawkins
Early Victorian rectory in 25 acres, on the banks of the River Wye close to the Forest of Dean.
Minimum age 5
Bedrooms: 2 double/twin,
6 quadruple, 7 dormitories. Total number of beds: 80
Bathrooms: 7 public
Bed only

per person:	£min	£max
Daily	8.55	8.55

Evening meal 1900 (last orders 1800)
Parking for 40
Open February–December
Cards accepted: Access, Visa, Switch/Delta

SAFFRON WALDEN

Essex
Map ref 2D1

Takes its name from the saffron crocus once grown around the town. The church of St Mary has superb carvings, magnificent roofs and brasses. A town maze can be seen on the common. Two miles south-west is Audley End, a magnificent Jacobean mansion owned by English Heritage.
Tourist Information Centre ☎ (01799) 510444

Youth Hostel Association ⋀
1 Myddylton Place, Saffron Walden
CB10 1BB
☎ (01799) 523117
Contact: Miss D Standing
Fine 14th C building in market town. Oak panelled room and staircase.
Bedrooms: 5 dormitories. Total number of beds: 38
Bathrooms: 3 public

Bed only

per person:	£min	£max
Daily	5.20	7.75

Evening meal 1900 (last orders 1800)
Open March–December
Cards accepted: Access, Visa, Switch/Delta

ST BRIAVELS

Gloucestershire
Map ref 2A1

Village with remains of a 13th C castle, set above the Wye Valley in the Forest of Dean. Tintern, with its magnificent abbey ruins, is nearby.

St Briavels Castle Youth Hostel
The Castle, St Briavels, Lydney
GL15 6RG
☎ Dean (01594) 530272
Fax (01594) 530849
Contact: Mr J Cotterill
13th C castle with interesting features, in centre of pleasant village. Ideal for Forest of Dean and Wye Valley.
Minimum age 4
Bedrooms: 9 dormitories. Total number of beds: 70
Bathrooms: 5 public
Bed only

per person:	£min	£max
Daily	8.55	8.55

Evening meal 1900 (last orders 1800)
Parking for 15
Open February–October and Christmas
Cards accepted: Access, Visa

ST JOHN'S CHAPEL

Durham
Map ref 5B2

Peaceful village in Upper Weardale. Pubs, village shops and cottages are set around a small market square. Nearby Harthope Burn has an attractive waterfall.

Weardale House ⋀
Ireshopeburn, Bishop Auckland,
County Durham
Contact: Mr C Jones, Y.M.C.A.
Residential Office, Herrington Burn,
Houghton-le-Spring, Tyne and Wear
DH4 4JW
☎ (0191) 385 2822 & 385 3085
Fax (0191) 385 2267
Multi-activity outdoor centre. Price quoted below is for full board Monday-Friday. Three-day (Monday-Wednesday or Wednesday-Friday) available at £83;

three-day weekend (Friday-Sunday) available at £54. All rates include catering, accommodation and multi-activity course.
For groups only
Minimum age 7
Bedrooms: 3 single, 8 dormitories. Total number of beds: 60
Bathrooms: 12 public
Full board

per person:	£min	£max
Weekly	134.00	

Lunch available
Parking for 10

ST JUST-IN-PENWITH

Cornwall
Map ref 1A3

Coastal parish of craggy moorland scattered with engine houses and chimney stacks of disused mines. The old mining town of St Just has handsome late 19th C granite buildings. North of the town are the dramatic ruined tin mines at Botallack.

The Youth Hostel - Lands End
Letcha Vean, St Just-in-Penwith
TR19 7NT
☎ Penzance (01736) 788437
Fax (01736) 787337
House in large grounds in secluded Cot Valley, with views out to sea and footpath to beach and Cornwall coastal path.
Minimum age 5
Bedrooms: 4 dormitories. Total number of beds: 44
Bathrooms: 4 public
Bed only

per person:	£min	£max
Daily	5.20	8.55

Evening meal 1800 (last orders 2000)
Parking for 10
Open March–October
Cards accepted: Access, Visa, Switch/Delta

SCARBOROUGH

North Yorkshire
Map ref 5D3

Large, popular East Coast seaside resort, formerly a spa town. Beautiful gardens and two splendid sandy beaches. Castle ruins date from 1100; fine Georgian and Victorian houses. Scarborough Millennium depicts 1,000 years of town's history. Sea Life Centre.
Tourist Information Centre ☎ *(01723) 373333*

University College Scarborough ⋀

Filey Road, Scarborough YO11 3AZ
☎ (01723) 362392
Fax (01723) 370815
Contact: Mrs E McAdam
Small, friendly college which has now completed a major refurbishment to provide you with the very best facilities.
Bedrooms: 292 single,
12 double/twin, 2 triple. Total number of beds: 322
Bathrooms: 214 en-suite, 37 public
Bed only

per person:	£min	£max
Daily	13.75	15.50

Bed & breakfast

per person:	£min	£max
Daily	19.25	21.00

Lunch available
Evening meal 1800 (last orders 2000)
Parking for 97
Open January, March–April, July–September, December

SHEFFIELD

South Yorkshire
Map ref 4B2

Local iron ore and coal gave Sheffield its prosperous steel and cutlery industries. The modern city centre has many interesting buildings - cathedral, Cutlers' Hall, Crucible Theatre, Graves and Mappin Art Galleries - and Meadowhall Shopping Centre nearby.
Tourist Information Centre ☎ *(0114) 273 4671 or 273 4672*

Sheffield YMCA Residential Centre

20 Victoria Road, Sheffield S10 2DL
☎ (0114) 268 4807
Fax (0114) 268 3472
A large sports, social and residential centre with facilities for weddings, functions and conferences.

For individuals only
Minimum age 18
Bedrooms: 81 single, 9 double/twin.
Total number of beds: 99
Bathrooms: 12 public
Bed & breakfast

per person:	£min	£max
Daily	13.00	17.00

Lunch available
Evening meal 1700 (last orders 1800)
Parking for 30

University of Sheffield ⋀

Halifax Hall of Residence, Endcliffe Vale Road, Sheffield
Contact: Ms C Davies, University of Sheffield, Conference Office, Octagon Centre, Western Bank, Sheffield, South Yorkshire S10 2TQ
☎ Sheffield (0114) 266 4196 & 282 4080
Fax (0114) 272 9097
Six comfortable halls of residence in a quiet suburb near the city centre and close to the Peak District National Park. Tapton hall of residence has been awarded National Accessible Scheme Category 1.
Wheelchair access category 1
Bedrooms: 1886 single,
106 double/twin. Total number of beds: 2311
Bathrooms: 213 en-suite, 300 public
Bed & breakfast

per person:	£min	£max
Daily	20.00	

Full board

per person:	£min	£max
Weekly	200.00	

Lunch available
Evening meal 1730 (last orders 1830)
Parking for 600
Open January, March–April, June–August

WELCOME HOST

This is a nationally recognised customer care programme which aims to promote the highest standards of service and a warm welcome. Establishments who are taking part in this initiative are indicated by the ⊛ symbol.

SHERINGHAM

Norfolk
Map ref 3B1

Holiday resort with Victorian and Edwardian hotels and a sand and shingle beach where the fishing boats are hauled up. The North Norfolk Railway operates from Sheringham station during the summer. Other attractions include museums, theatre and Splash Fun Pool.

YHA Centre ⋀

1 Cremers Drift, Sheringham NR26 8HX
☎ (01263) 823215
Fax (01263) 823215
Contact: Miss J S Cooper
Extensively renovated and modernised late Victorian building with modern additions, including facilities for disabled.
Bedrooms: 1 single, 8 double/twin, 6 triple, 11 quadruple, 6 dormitories. Total number of beds: 120
Bathrooms: 3 en-suite, 9 public
Bed only

per person:	£min	£max
Daily	5.75	8.55

Bed & breakfast

per person:	£min	£max
Daily	8.65	11.45

Evening meal 1800 (last orders 1930)
Parking for 20
Cards accepted: Access, Visa, Switch/Delta

SILSOE

Bedfordshire
Map ref 2D1

Silsoe College

Silsoe, Bedford MK45 3DT
☎ Leighton Buzzard (01525) 863000
Fax (01525) 863001
Contact: Mrs Sue Whittaker
We have an all-year-round residential facility offering a high standard of accommodation. There is excellent on-site catering available and the college has a licensed bar.
Minimum age 8
Bedrooms: 37 single
Bathrooms: 6 en-suite, 16 public
Bed only

per person:	£min	£max
Daily	19.00	25.00

Bed & breakfast

per person:	£min	£max
Daily	23.00	29.00

Lunch available
Evening meal 1700 (last orders 1830)

🐎 8 ♿ 🏠 📶 🛏 ⓢ 🏥 📺 🚿 🚗 ⚑ 20 ✗ 🎯 🎿 🐕

SLIMBRIDGE

Gloucestershire
Map ref 2B1

The Wildfowl and Wetlands Trust Centre was founded by Sir Peter Scott and has the world's largest collection of wildfowl. Of special interest are the wild swans and the geese which wander around the grounds.

Slimbridge Y.H.A. Centre

Shepherd's Patch, Slimbridge, Gloucester GL2 7BP
☎ Dursley (01453) 890275
Fax (01453) 890625
Contact: Mr J Parsons
Purpose built with its own pond and wildfowl collection. Delightful modern hostel.
Minimum age 5
Bedrooms: 11 dormitories. Total number of beds: 56
Bathrooms: 5 public

Bed only

per person:	£min	£max
Daily	6.35	9.45

Lunch available
Evening meal from 1900
Parking for 25
Open January–November
Cards accepted: Access, Visa, Switch/Delta

🐎 🖐 UL 🏠 ⓢ 🍴 🏥 📺 🚿 🚗 🕊 ✗ 🐾 SP ◎

SOWERBY BRIDGE

West Yorkshire
Map ref 4B1

Busy little town in the Calder Valley near the Calder Hebble Canal.

Mill Bank Centre

AMIT (Personal and Training Services), Mill Bank, Sowerby Bridge HX6 3DY
☎ Halifax (01422) 824388 & 824189
Contact: Mr J Haymer
Well-equipped residential centre with conference facilities, in a converted chapel overlooking a Pennine conservation village. Centrally heated, with carpets and Continental quilts. Prices vary according to number in group - please ask for details.
For groups only
Minimum age 10
Bedrooms: 1 single, 3 double/twin, 3 dormitories. Total number of beds: 22

Bathrooms: 6 public

Bed only

per person:	£min	£max
Daily	17.00	20.00

Lunch available
Parking for 10

🐎 🖐 UL 🏠 ⓢ 🍴 🏥 📺 🚿 🚗 U ✓ 🕊 DAP SP 🔭

STREATLEY

Berkshire
Map ref 2C2

Pretty village on the River Thames, linked to Goring by an attractive bridge. It has Georgian houses and cottages and beautiful views over the countryside and the Goring Gap.

Youth Hostel

Hill House, Reading Road, Streatley, Reading RG8 9JJ
☎ Goring (01491) 872278
Fax (01491) 873056
Contact: The. Warden
Victorian family house in beautiful village.
Minimum age 5
Bedrooms: 1 double/twin, 1 quadruple, 9 dormitories. Total number of beds: 51
Bathrooms: 4 public

Bed only

per person:	£min	£max
Daily	5.75	8.55

Evening meal 1900 (last orders 1900)
Parking for 6
Cards accepted: Access, Visa

🐎 🖐 UL 🏠 ⓢ 🍴 🏥 📺 🚿 🚗 ✗ 🐾 T ◎

SWANAGE

Dorset
Map ref 2B3

Began life as an Anglo-Saxon port, then a quarrying centre of Purbeck marble. Now the safe, sandy beach set in a sweeping bay and flanked by downs is good walking country, making it an ideal resort.
Tourist Information Centre ☎ (01929) 422885

The Youth Hostel

Cluny Crescent, Swanage
Contact: Mr D Pearson, Swanage YHA, Cluny Crescent, Swanage, Dorset BH19 2BS
☎ Swanage (01929) 422113
Fax (01929) 426327
Elegant Victorian house overlooking Swanage Bay. Built on site of a monastery of the Cluny Order. Four meeting/seminar rooms.

Bedrooms: 3 double/twin, 2 triple, 1 quadruple, 12 dormitories. Total number of beds: 107
Bathrooms: 11 public

Bed only

per person:	£min	£max
Daily	6.35	9.45

Bed & breakfast

per person:	£min	£max
Daily	9.25	12.35

Evening meal 1830 (last orders 1800)
Parking for 15
Open February–November and Christmas
Cards accepted: Access, Visa, Switch/Delta

🐎 3 ⛷ UL 🏠 ⓢ 🍴 🏥 📺 🚿 ✗ 🐾 ◎

TODMORDEN

West Yorkshire
Map ref 4B1

In beautiful scenery on the edge of the Pennines at junction of 3 sweeping valleys. Until 1888 the county boundary between Yorkshire and Lancashire cut this old cotton town in half, running through the middle of the Town Hall.
Tourist Information Centre ☎ (01706) 818181

The Lumbutts Centre ⚑

Lumbutts House, Lumbutts, Todmorden, Lancashire OL14 6JE
☎ (01706) 814536
Fax (01706) 819391
Contact: Mrs S Schofield
Purpose-built outdoor activity centre. Own lakes, beautiful countryside. Catered and self-catering programmes. Groups of 15-36, all ages, including disabled.
For groups only
Minimum age 7
Bedrooms: 3 double/twin, 2 triple, 4 dormitories. Total number of beds: 36
Bathrooms: 3 en-suite, 11 public

Bed only

per person:	£min	£max
Daily	13.50	18.50

Bed & breakfast

per person:	£min	£max
Daily	16.00	22.50

Full board

per person:	£min	£max
Weekly	122.50	201.50

Lunch available
Parking for 10

🐎 🖐 🏠 ⓢ 🍴 🏥 📺 🚿 U 🎣 ✗ 🐎 🐾 🔭

TOTLAND BAY

Isle of Wight
Map ref 2C3

On the Freshwater Peninsula. It is possible to walk from here around to Alum Bay.

The Youth Hostel

Hurst Hill, Totland Bay PO39 0HD
☎ Isle of Wight (01983) 752165
Fax (01983) 756443
Contact: Mr & Mrs John Ledwood
Former private home and hotel, on west side of island, near cliff top walks and beaches.
Minimum age 5
Bedrooms: 10 dormitories. Total number of beds: 78
Bathrooms: 4 public
Bed only

per person:	£min	£max
Daily	5.75	9.45

Lunch available
Evening meal 1830 (last orders 1800)
Parking for 7
Open March–November
Cards accepted: Access, Visa, Switch/Delta

TROUTBECK

Cumbria
Map ref 5A3

Most of the houses in this picturesque village are 17th C, some retain their spinning galleries and oak-mullioned windows. At the south end of the village is Townend, owned by the National Trust and open to the public, an excellently preserved example of a yeoman farmer's or statesman's house.

Windermere Youth Hostel

High Cross, Troutbeck, Windermere LA23 1LA
☎ Windermere (015394) 43543
Fax (015394) 47165
Situated in 13 acres of woodland overlooking Lake Windermere, with superb views.
Bedrooms: 1 triple, 10 quadruple, 3 dormitories. Total number of beds: 73
Bathrooms: 7 public
Bed only

per person:	£min	£max
Daily	5.50	7.95

Bed & breakfast

per person:	£min	£max
Daily	8.40	10.85

Full board

per person:	£min	£max
Weekly	110.60	127.75

Evening meal 1900 (last orders 1900)
Parking for 12
Open January–November and Christmas
Cards accepted: Access, Visa, Switch/Delta

ULLSWATER

Cumbria
Map ref 5A3

This beautiful lake, which is over 7 miles long, runs from Glenridding to Pooley Bridge. Lofty peaks ranging around the lake make an impressive background. A steamer service operates along the lake between Pooley Bridge, Howtown and Glenridding in the summer.

Patterdale Hall

Glenridding, Penrith CA11 0PT
☎ Glenridding (017684) 82233
Fax (017684) 82233
Contact: Mr Ian Ray

Hostel with Victorian features, run as residential centre for groups. Recently refurbished. Outdoor pursuit packages available or self-programming. 60 beds, small dormitories. Open all year.
Minimum age 8
Bedrooms: 10 dormitories. Total number of beds: 62
Bathrooms: 7 public
Bed & breakfast

per person:	£min	£max
Daily	16.50	19.50

Full board

per person:	£min	£max
Weekly	110.00	130.00

Lunch available
Evening meal from 1800
Parking for 30

The map references refer to the colour maps towards the end of the guide.
The first figure is the map number; the letter and figure which follow indicate the grid reference on the map.

WANTAGE

Oxfordshire
Map ref 2C2

Market town in the Vale of the White Horse where King Alfred was born. His statue stands in the town square.
Tourist Information Centre ☎ (01235) 760176

Court Hill Ridgeway Centre

Court Hill, Wantage OX12 9NE
☎ (01235) 760253
Fax (01235) 768865
Contact: Mr S Bunyard
Modern hostel with 4 barns, close to Ridgeway Path. Panoramic views across woodland.
Bedrooms: 7 quadruple, 2 dormitories. Total number of beds: 59
Bathrooms: 5 public
Bed only

per person:	£min	£max
Daily	5.20	7.75

Lunch available
Evening meal 1800 (last orders 1900)
Parking for 20
Open February–December
Cards accepted: Access, Visa, Switch/Delta

WEST LULWORTH

Dorset
Map ref 2B3

Well-known for Lulworth Cove, the almost landlocked circular bay of chalk and limestone cliffs.

The Youth Hostel - Lulworth Cove

School Lane, West Lulworth, Wareham BH20 5SA
☎ (01929) 400564
Fax (01929) 400640
Contact: The Warden
Purpose-built hostel of cedarwood, with comfortable facilities.
Minimum age 5
Bedrooms: 7 dormitories. Total number of beds: 34
Bathrooms: 2 public
Bed only

per person:	£min	£max
Daily	5.20	7.75

Evening meal 1900 (last orders 1800)
Parking for 9
Open February–November
Cards accepted: Access, Visa

WINCHESTER

Hampshire
Map ref 2C3

King Alfred the Great made Winchester the capital of Saxon England. A magnificent Norman cathedral, with one of the longest naves in Europe, dominates the city. Home of Winchester College founded in 1382.
Tourist Information Centre ☎ *(01962) 840500 or 848180*

King Alfred's College Conferences

Sparkford Road, Winchester
SO22 4NR
☎ (01962) 827200
Fax (01962) 842280
Contact: Mrs C Troth or Mrs W Truscott
Twelve residential and teaching buildings grouped compactly on a pleasant hillside site, 10 minutes' walk from Winchester city centre.
Bedrooms: 600 single,
26 double/twin, 14 triple. Total number of beds: 694
Bathrooms: 80 public

Bed only
per person:	£min	£max
Daily	12.10	12.71

Bed & breakfast
per person:	£min	£max
Daily	14.60	15.33

Full board
per person:	£min	£max
Weekly	192.50	202.13

Lunch available
Evening meal 1830 (last orders 1930)
Parking for 200
Open March–April, July–September

YORK

Map ref 4C1

Ancient walled city nearly 2000 years old containing many well-preserved medieval buildings. Its Minster has over 100 stained glass windows. Attractions include Castle Museum, National Railway Museum, Jorvik Viking Centre and York Dungeon.
Tourist Information Centre ☎ *(01904) 621756 or 621756 or 620557*

Fairfax House

99 Heslington Road, York YO1 5BJ
☎ (01904) 432095
Contact: Mrs. A E Glover
Student residence in quiet spacious grounds, within walking distance of town centre. Reduced rates for children under 12 and senior citizens.
Bedrooms: 85 single. Total number of beds: 85
Bathrooms: 14 public

Bed & breakfast
per person:	£min	£max
Daily	16.00	18.00

Open March–April, July–September

York Youth Hotel

11-13 Bishophill Senior, York
YO1 1EF
☎ (01904) 625904 & 630613
Fax (01904) 612494
Contact: Ms Maureen Sellers
Dormitory-style accommodation in the city centre. Private rooms, TV lounge, snack shop, evening meals, packed lunches, games room, residential licence. Families welcome.
Minimum age 2
Bedrooms: 7 single, 14 double/twin, 1 triple, 4 quadruple, 5 dormitories.
Total number of beds: 120
Bathrooms: 8 public

Bed only
per person:	£min	£max
Daily	9.00	14.00

Lunch available
Evening meal 1700 (last orders 1900)
Cards accepted: Access, Visa, Switch/Delta

USE YOUR *i*'s

There are more than 550 Tourist Information Centres throughout England offering friendly help with accommodation and holiday ideas as well as suggestions of places to visit and things to do. There may well be a centre in your home town which can help you before you set out. You'll find the address of your nearest Tourist Information Centre in your local Phone Book.

ENQUIRY COUPONS

To help you obtain further information about advertisers and accommodation featured in this guide you will find enquiry coupons at the back. Send these directly to the establishments in which you are interested. Remember to complete both sides of the coupon.

CHECK THE MAPS

The colour maps at the back of this guide show all the cities, towns and villages for which you will find accommodation entries.

Refer to the town index to find the page on which it is listed.

INFORMATION PAGES

NATIONAL GRADING AND CLASSIFICATION SCHEME

Sure Signs

The Tourist Boards in Britain operate a National Quality Grading and Classification Scheme for all types of accommodation. The purpose of the scheme is to identify and promote those establishments that the public can use with confidence. The system of facility classification and quality grading also acknowledges those that provide a wider range of facilities and services and higher quality standards. Over 30,000 places to stay are inspected under the scheme and offer the reassurance of a national grading and classification.

For 'serviced' accommodation (which includes hotels, motels, guesthouses, inns, B&B's and farmhouses) there are six classification bands, starting with LISTED and then from ONE to FIVE CROWN. For the new generation of 'lodges', offering budget accommodation along major roads and motorways, there are three classification bands, from ONE to THREE MOON.

Quite simply, the more Crowns or Moons, the wider the range of facilities and services offered.

Quality Grading

To help you find accommodation that offers even higher standards than those required for a Crown or Moon rating, there are four levels of quality grading, using the terms DE LUXE, HIGHLY COMMENDED, COMMENDED

and APPROVED. Wherever you see a national grading and classification sign, you can be sure that a Tourist Board inspector has been there before you, checking the place on your behalf - and will be there again, because every place with a national rating is inspected annually.

Establishments are subject to a detailed inspection that assesses the quality standard of the facilities and services provided. The initial inspection invariably involves the Tourist Board inspector staying overnight, as a normal guest, until the bill is paid the following morning. This quality assessment includes such aspects as warmth of welcome and efficiency of service, as well as the standard of furnishing, fittings and decor. The standard of meals and their presentation is also taken into account. Everything that impinges on the experience of a guest is included in the assessment. Tourist Board inspectors receive careful training to enable them to apply the quality standards consistently and fairly. Only those facilities and services provided are assessed, and due consideration is given to the style and nature of the establishment. B&B's, farmhouses and guesthouses are not expected to operate in the style of large city centre hotels, and vice versa. This means that all types of establishment, whatever their Crown or Moon classification, can achieve a high quality grade if the facilities and services they provide, however

limited in range, are to a high quality standard.

The quality grade that is awarded to an establishment is a reflection of the overall standard, taking everything into account. It is a balanced view of what is provided and, as such, cannot acknowledge individual areas of excellence. Quality grades are not intended to indicate value for money. A high quality product can be over-priced; a product of modest quality, if offered at a low price, can represent good value. The information provided by the combination of the classification and quality grade will enable you to determine for yourself what represents good value for money.

All Inspected

All establishments listed in this guide have been inspected or are awaiting inspection under the National Grading and Classification Scheme. The ratings that appear in the accommodation entries were correct at the time of going to press but are subject to change. If no rating appears in that entry it means that the inspection had not been carried out by the time of going to press. An information leaflet giving full details of the National Grading and Classification Scheme - which also covers self-catering holiday homes and caravan, chalet and camping parks - is available from any Tourist Information Centre.

GENERAL ADVICE AND INFORMATION

Making a Booking

When enquiring about accommodation, make sure you check prices and other important details. You will also need to state your requirements, clearly and precisely - for example:
• **Arrival and departure dates**, with acceptable alternatives if appropriate.
• **The type of accommodation** you need; for example, room with twin beds, private bathroom.
• **The terms**, you want; for example, room only, bed and breakfast, half board, full board.
• **If you have children** with you; their ages, whether you want them to share your room or be next door, any other special requirements, such as a cot.
• **Particular requirements** you may have, such as a special diet.

Booking by letter

Misunderstandings can easily happen over the telephone, so we strongly advise you to confirm your booking in writing if there is time.

If you decide to enquire in writing in the first place, you might find it helpful to use the Accommodation Coupons on pages 421-426, which can be cut out and posted to the places of your choice.

Remember to include your name and address, and a stamped self-addressed envelope, or an international reply coupon if you are writing from outside Britain.

Please note that the English Tourist Board does not make reservations - you should write direct to the accommodation.

Deposits

If you make you reservation weeks or months in advance, you will probably be asked for a deposit. The amount will vary according to the time of year, the number of people in your party and how long you plan to stay. The deposit will then be deducted from the final bill when you leave.

Payment on Arrival

Some establishments, especially large hotels in big towns ask you to pay for you room on arrival if you have not booked it in advance. This is especially likely to happen if you arrive late and have little or no luggage.

If you are asked to pay on arrival, it is a good idea to see your room first, to make sure it meets your requirements.

Cancellations

Legal contract

When you accept accommodation that is offered to you, by telephone or in writing, you enter a legally binding contract with the proprietor.

This means that if you cancel your booking, fail to take up the accommodation or leave early, the proprietor may be entitled

to compensation if he cannot re-let for all or a good part of the booked period. You will probably forfeit any deposit you have paid, and may well be asked for an additional payment.

The proprietor cannot make a claim until after the booked period, however, and during that time every effort should be made by the proprietor to re-let the accommodation.

If there is a dispute it is sensible for both sides to seek legal advice on the matter.

If you do have to change your travel plans, it is in your own interests to let the proprietors know in writing as soon as possible, to give them a chance to re-let your accommodation.

And remember, if you book by telephone and are asked for your credit card number, you should check whether the proprietor intends charging your credit card account should you later cancel your reservation. A proprietor should not be able to charge your credit card account with a cancellation unless he or she has made this clear at the time of your booking and you have agreed. However, to avoid later disputes, we suggest you check with the proprietor whether he or she intends to charge you credit card account if you cancel.

Insurance

A travel or holiday insurance policy will safeguard you if you have to cancel or change your holiday plans. You can arrange a policy quite cheaply through your insurance company or travel agent. Some hotels also offer their own insurance schemes.

Arriving Late

If you know you will be arriving late in the evening, it is a good idea to say so when you book. If you are delayed on your way, a telephone call to say that you will be late will help prevent any problems when you arrive.

Service Charges and Tipping

These days many places levy service charges automatically. If they do, they must clearly say so in their offer of accommodation, at the time of booking. Then the service charge becomes part of the legal contract when you accept the offer of accommodation.

If a service charge is levied automatically, there is no need to tip the staff, unless they provide some exceptional service. The usual tip for meals is ten per cent of the total bill.

Telephone Charges

Hotels can set their own charges for telephone calls made through their switchboard or from direct-dial telephones in bedrooms. These charges are often much higher than telephone companies' standard charges (to defray the cost of providing the service).

Comparing costs

It is a condition of the National Grading and Classification Scheme, that hotel's unit charges are on display, by the telephones or with the room information. But in practice it is not always easy to compare these charges with standard telephone rates. Before using a hotel telephone for long-distance calls, you may decide to ask how the charges compare.

Security of Valuables

You can deposit your valuables with the proprietor or manager during your stay, and we recommend you do this as a sensible precaution. Make sure you obtain a receipt for them.

Some places do not accept articles for safe custody, and in that case it is wisest to keep your valuables with you.

Disclaimer

Some proprietors put up a notice which disclaims liability for property brought on to their premises by a guest. In fact, they can only restrict their liability to a minimum laid down by law (The Hotel Proprietors Act 1956).

Under that Act, a proprietor is liable for the value of the loss or damage to any property (except a motor car or its contents) of a guest who has engaged overnight accommodation, but if the proprietor has the prescribed notice on display as prescribed under that Act, liability is limited to £50 for one article and a total of £100 for any one guest. The notice must be prominently displayed in the reception area or main entrance. These limits

do not apply to valuables you have deposited with the proprietor for safe-keeping, or to property lost through the default, neglect of wilful act of the proprietor or his staff.

Code of Conduct

All the places featured in this guide have agreed to observe the following Codes of Conduct:

1 To ensure high standards of courtesy and cleanliness, catering and service appropriate to the type of establishment.

2 To describe fairly to all visitors and prospective visitors the amenities, facilities and services provided by the establishment, whether by advertisement, brochure, word of mouth or any other means. To allow visitors to see accommodation, if requested, before booking.

3 To make clear to visitors exactly what is included in all prices quoted for accommodation, meals and refreshments, including service charges, taxes and other surcharges. Details of charges, if any, for heating or additional service of facilities should also be made clear.

4 To adhere to, and not to exceed, prices current at time of occupation for accommodation or other services.

5 To advise visitors at the time of booking, and subsequently of any change, if the accommodation offered is in an unconnected annexe, or similar, or by boarding out; and to indicate the location of such accommodation and any difference in comfort or amenities from accommodation in the main establishment.

6 To give each visitor, on request, details of payments due and a receipt if required.

7 To deal promptly and courteously with all enquiries, requests, reservations, correspondence and complaints from visitors.

8 To allow an English Tourist Board representative reasonable access to the establishment, on request, to confirm that the Code of Conduct is being observed.

Comments and Complaints

Hotels and the law
Places that offer accommodation have legal and statutory responsibilities to their customers, such as providing information about prices, providing adequate fire precautions and safeguarding valuables. Like other businesses, they must also abide by the Trades Description Acts 1968 and 1972 when they describe their accommodation and facilities.

All the places featured in this guide have declared that they do fulfil all applicable statutory obligations.

Information
The proprietors themselves supply the descriptions of their establishments and other information for the listings, and they pay to have their entries included in the guide. All the places featured in the guide have also been inspected or have applied for inspection under the National Grading and Classification Scheme.

The English Tourist Board cannot guarantee accuracy of information in this guide, and accepts no responsibility for any error or misrepresentation. All liability for loss, disappointment, negligence or other damage caused by reliance on the information contained in this guide, or in the event of bankruptcy or liquidation or cessation of trade of any company, individual or firm mentioned, is hereby excluded.

We strongly recommend that you carefully check prices and other details when you book your accommodation.

Problems
Of course, we hope you will not have cause for complaint, but problems do occur from time to time.

If you are dissatisfied with anything, make your complaint to the management immediately. Then the management can take action at once to investigate the matter and put things right. The longer you leave a complaint, the harder it is to deal with it effectively.

In certain circumstances, the English Tourist Board may look into complaints. However, the Board has no statutory control over establishments or their methods of operating. The Board cannot become involved in legal or contractual matters.

Feedback Questionnaire
We find it very helpful to receive your comments about the places featured in *Where to Stay* and your suggestions on how to improve the guide. Please send us your views using the Customer Feedback Questionnaire on pages 439-440 - we would like to hear from you.

Return it to:

Department AS,
English Tourist Board,
Thames Tower,
Black's Road,
Hammersmith,
London W6 9EL.

ENQUIRY COUPONS

To help you obtain further information

about advertisers and accommodation featured in

this guide you will find enquiry coupons at the back.

Send these directly to the establishments

in which you are interested.

Remember to complete both sides of the coupon.

ABOUT THE GUIDE ENTRIES

Locations

Places to stay are listed under the town, city or village where they are located. If a place is out in the countryside, you will find it listed under the nearest village or town.

Town names are listed alphabetically within each regional section of the guide, along with the name of the county they fall under, and their map reference.

Map references
These refer to the colour location maps at the back of the guide. The first figure shown is the map number, the following letter and figure indicate the grid reference on the map.

Some entries were included just before the guide went to press, so they do not appear on the maps.

Addresses
County names, which appear in the town headings, are not repeated in the entries. When you are writing, you should of course make sure you use the full address and postcode.

Telephone numbers
Telephone numbers are listed below the accommodation address for each entry. Area codes are shown in brackets, and the exchange name is also included (before the code) if it differs from that of the town under which a place is listed.

Price

The prices shown in *Where to Stay 1997* are only a general guide; they were supplied to us by proprietors in summer 1996. Remember, changes may occur after the guide goes to press, so we strongly advise you to check prices when you book your accommodation.

Prices are shown in pounds sterling and include VAT where applicable. Some places also include a service charge in their standard tariff so check this when you book.

Standardised method
There are many different ways of quoting prices for accommodation. We use a standardised method in the guide to allow you to compare prices. For example when we show:
Bed and breakfast, the prices shown are for overnight accommodation with breakfast, for single and double rooms.
The double-room price is for two people. If a double room is occupied by one person there is sometimes a reduction in price.
Halfboard, the prices shown are for room, breakfast and evening meal, per person per day and per person per week.

Some places provide only a continental breakfast in the set price, and you may have to pay extra if you want a full English breakfast.

Checking prices
According to the law, hotels with at least four bedrooms or eight beds must display their overnight accommodation charges in the reception area or entrance. In your own interests, do make sure you check prices and what they include.

Children's rates
You will find that many places charge a reduced rate for children especially if they share a room with their parents. Some places charge the full rate, however, when a child occupies a room which might otherwise have been let to an adult.

The upper age limit for reductions for children varies from one hotel to another, so check this when you book.

Seasonal packages
Prices often vary through the year, and may be significantly lower outside peak holiday weeks. Many places offer special package rates - fully inclusive weekend breaks, for example - in the autumn, winter and spring.

You can get details of bargain packages from the establishment themselves, the Regional Tourist Boards or your local Tourist Information Centre (TIC). Your local travel agent may also have information, and can help you make bookings.

Bathrooms

Each accommodation entry shows you the number of private bathrooms available, the number of private showers, and the number of public bathrooms.

'Private bathroom' means a bath and/or shower with a WC en-suite with the bedroom, or a separate bathroom with a bath plus a WC solely for the occupants of that bedroom; 'private shower' means a shower en-suite but no WC.

Public bathrooms normally have a bath, sometimes with a shower attachment. If the availability of a bath is important to you, remember to check when you book.

Meals

If an establishment serves evening meals, you will find the starting time and the last order times shown in the listing; some smaller places may ask you at breakfast or at midday whether you want an evening meal.

The prices shown in each entry are for bed and breakfast or half board, but many places also offer lunch, as you will see indicated on the listing.

Opening Period

All places are open all year, except where a specific opening period is indicated.

Symbols

The at-a-glance symbols included at the end of each entry show many of the services and facilities available at each place.

You will find the key to these symbols on the back cover flap. Open out the flap and you can check the meanings of the symbols as you go.

Alcoholic Drinks

All the places listed in the guide are licensed to serve alcohol, unless the symbol ⊞ appears. The license may be restricted - to diners only, for example - so you may want to check this when you book.

Smoking

Many places provide non-smoking areas - from no-smoking bedrooms and lounges to no-smoking sections of the restaurant. Some places prefer not to accommodate smokers, and in such cases the listing information makes this clear.

Pets

Many places accept guests with pets, but we do advise you to check this when you book, and ask about any extra charges or any rules about exactly where your pet is allowed.

Some establishments do not accept dogs at all, and these places are marked with the symbol ✕.

Visitors from overseas must not bring pets of any kind into Britain, unless they are prepared for the animals to go into lengthy quarantine. Because of the continuing threat of rabies, the penalties for ignoring these regulations are extremely severe.

Credit and Charge Cards

The credit and charge cards accepted by a place are listed immediately above the line of symbols at the end of each entry. The abbreviations used are:
Access - Access/Eurocard/Mastercard
Visa - Visa/Barclaycard
Diners - Diners
Amex - American Express
Switch/Delta - Direct debit cards

If you do plan to pay by card, check that the establishment will take your card before you book.

Some proprietors will charge you a higher rate if you pay by credit card rather than cash or cheque. The difference is to cover the percentage paid by the proprietor to the credit card company.

If you are planning to pay by credit card, you may want to ask whether it would, in fact, be cheaper to pay by cheque or cash. When you book by telephone, you may be asked for your credit card number as 'confirmation'. But remember, the proprietor may then charge your credit card account if you cancel your booking. See under Cancellations on page 409.

Conferences and Groups

Places which cater for conferences and meetings are marked with the symbol ⟟ (the number that follows the symbol shows the capacity). Rates are often negotiable, depending on the time of year, numbers of people involved and any special requirements you may have.

EVENTS FOR 1997

This is a selection of the many cultural, sporting and other events that will be taking place throughout England during 1997. Dates marked with an asterisk* were provisional at the time of going to press.

January 1997

2-13 January*
43rd London International Boat Show
Earls Court Exhibition Centre,
Warwick Road, London SW5
Contact: (01784) 473377

6 January
Old Custom: Haxey Hood Game
The Village, Haxey,
North East Lincolnshire
Contact: (01427) 752845

9-12 January
Autosports International
National Exhibition Centre,
Birmingham, West Midlands
Contact: (0171) 402 2555

February 1997

7-16 February
Great St Valentine's Fair
City Centre,
Leeds, West Yorkshire
Contact: (0113) 247 4293

9 February*
Chinese New Year Celebrations: Year of the Ox
Centered on Gerrard Street
and Leicester Square,
London WC2
Contact: (0171) 734 5161

9 February-16 March
Wildlife Photographer of the Year 1995
Lancaster City Museum,
Market Square,
Lancaster, Lancashire
Contact: (01524) 841692

9-14 February*
The Wordsworth Winter School
Dove Cottage & Wordsworth Museum, Town End,
Grasmere, Cumbria
Contact: (015394) 35544

20-23 February
Harrogate Antique and Fine Art Fair
Royal Baths Assembly Rooms,
Crescent Road, Harrogate,
North Yorkshire
Contact: (01823) 323363

March 1997

6-9 March
Crufts Dog Show
National Exhibition Centre,
Birmingham, West Midlands
Contact: (0171) 4936651

7-9 March
Working Days
Abbeydale Industrial Hamlet,
Abbeydale Road South,
Sheffield, South Yorkshire
Contact: (0114) 236 7731

11-13 March
Cheltenham Gold Cup National Hunt Racing Festival
Cheltenham Racecourse,
Cheltenham, Gloucestershire
Contact: (01242) 513014

13 March-6 April
Daily Mail Ideal Home Exhibition
Earls Court Exhibition Centre,
Warwick Road,
London SW5
Contact: (01895) 677677

22 March-6 April
Easter Activities
Salford Museum & Art Gallery,
Peel Park, The Crescent,
Salford, Greater Manchester
Contact: (0161) 736 2649

28 March
Old Custom: Pace Egg Plays
Various venues in and around
Hebden Bridge,
West Yorkshire
Contact: (01422) 843831

29 March*
Oxford and Cambridge Boat Race
River Thames, London

April 1997

3-5 April
Grand National Meeting
Aintree Racecourse,
Ormskirk Road,
Aintree, Merseyside
Contact: (0151) 523 2600

4 April
Birkenhead Park 150th Anniversary
Birkenhead Park, Merseyside

8 April
Old Custom: World Coal Carrying Championship
Royal Oak Public House,
Owl Lane, Ossett,
West Yorkshire

11-13 April
2nd North East Knitting and Needlecraft Exhibition
Leeds University Exhibition
& Conference Centre,
Willow Terrace Road,
Leeds, West Yorkshire
Contact: (0117) 970 1370

11-13 April
County Spring Flower Show - 100th Anniversary
The Lost Gardens of Heligan,
Heligan, Pentewan, Cornwall
Contact: (01872) 74057

13 April*
London Marathon
Greenwich Park,
London SE10
Contact: (0171) 620 4117

19-20 April
Bike Expo 97
Sheffield Arena,
Broughton Lane,
Sheffield, South Yorkshire
Contact: (01484) 605555

26-27 April
Centennial Orchid Society
The Floral Halls,
Marine Parade, Southport,
Merseyside

26-27 April
Rainbow Craft Fair
Meols Hall, Churchtown,
Southport, Merseyside
Contact: (01704) 28326

27 April
Three Peaks Race
Playing Field,
Horton-in-Ribblesdale,
North Yorkshire
Contact: (0113) 258 5586

May 1997

2-3 May
Nottinghamshire County Show
Newark and Notts Show Ground,
Winthorpe, Nottinghamshire
Contact: (01636) 610642

2-4 May
Cleethorpes Beer Festival
Winter Gardens, Kingsway,
Cleethorpes,
North East Lincolnshire
Contact: (01472) 692925

3 May
Gawthorpe Maypole Procession
High Street, Gawthorpe,
Ossett, West Yorkshire

3-5 May*
Rochester Sweeps Festival
Various venues,
Rochester, Kent
Contact: (01634) 843666

3-5 May*
Spalding Flower Parade and Springfields Country Fair
Springfields Show Gardens,
Spalding, Lincolnshire
Contact: (01775) 724843

3-25 May
Brighton International Festival
Various venues,
Brighton, East Sussex
Contact: (01273) 676926

4-5 May
Kids International
Telford Town Park,

Telford, Shropshire
Contact: (01952) 203009

8-11 May
Living Crafts Exhibition
Hatfield House, Hatfield,
Hertfordshire
Contact: (01582) 761235

10-25 May
Bournemouth International Festival
Various venues,
Bournemouth, Dorset
Contact: (01202) 297327

16-18 May
Keswick Jazz Festival
Keswick, Cumbria
Contact: (01900) 602122

17 May
Football: FA Challenge Cup Final
Wembley Stadium, London
Contact: (0171) 402 7151

20-23 May
Chelsea Flower Show
Royal Hospital Chelsea,
Royal Hospital Road,
London SW3

24-25 May
Air Fete 97
RAF Mildenhall, Suffolk

24 May-9 June
Salisbury Festival
Various venues,
Salisbury, Wiltshire
Contact: (01722) 323883

25-26 May
Southend Air Show
Western Esplanade,
Southend-on-Sea, Essex

25-26 May*
**North Shields Fishquay
Festival**
North Shields, Tyne and Wear
Contact: (0191) 257 5544

26 May
**Northumberland County
Show**
Tynedale Park Rugby Ground,
Corbridge, Northumberland
Contact: (01434) 344443

26 May
Surrey County Show
Stoke Park, Guildford, Surrey
Contact: (01483) 414651

28-29 May
**Corpus Christi Carpet of
Flowers and Floral Festival**
Cathedral of Our Lady
and St Philip Howard,
Cathedral House,
Arundel, West Sussex
Contact: (01903) 882297

28-31 May
**The Royal Bath
and West Show**
The Royal Bath & West
Showground,
Shepton Mallet, Somerset
Contact: (01749) 822200

29-31 May*
Dickens Festival
Various venues,
Rochester, Kent
Contact: (01634) 843666

30 May-1 June
**Great Garden and
Countryside Festival**
Holker Hall and Gardens,
Cark in Cartmel, Cumbria
Contact: (015395) 58838

June 1997

1 June*
**229th Royal Academy
Summer Exhibition**
Royal Academy of Arts,
Burlington House, Piccadilly,
London W1
Contact: (0171) 494 5615

5-7 June
**South of England
Agricultural Show**
South of England Showground,
Ardingly, West Sussex,
Contact: (01444) 892048

8 June
Open Day
Myerscough College,
Bilsborrow, Lancashire
Contact: (01995) 640611

13-29 June
**50th Aldeburgh Foundation
of Music and the Arts**
Snape Maltings Concert Hall,
Snape, Suffolk
Contact: (01728) 452935

14 June*
Durham Regatta
River Wear, Durham
Contact: (0191) 383 1594

14 June*
**Trooping the Colour - The
Queen's Birthday Parade**
Horse Guards Parade,
London SW1
Contact: (0171) 414 2479

25-26 June
Royal Norfolk Show 97
The Showground, Dereham Road,
Norwich, Norfolk
Contact: (01603) 748931

28-29 June
Middlesex Show
Uxbridge Showground,
Park Road, Uxbridge, London
Contact: (01895) 252131

28-29 June
**Royal Air Force Waddington
Air Show**
RAF Waddington, Lincolnshire
Contact: (01522) 726100

28-29 June
Vintage Vehicle Rally
Meols Hall, Churchtown,
Southport, Merseyside
Contact: (01704) 28326

30 June-3 July
The Royal Show
National Agricultural Centre,
Stoneleigh Park, Warwickshire
Contact: (01203) 696969

July 1997

1-31 July*
Hull International Festival
Various venues, Hull,
Kingston-upon-Hull
Contact: (01482) 615623

2-6 July
Henley Royal Regatta
Henley-on-Thames, Oxfordshire
Contact: (01491) 572153/4

3-20 July
The Exeter Festival
Various venues, Exeter, Devon
Contact: (01392) 265118

5-6 July
International Kite Festival
Northern Playing Fields,
Washington, Tyne and Wear
Contact: (0191) 514235

6-22 July
Chichester Festivities
Various venues,
Chichester, West Sussex
Contact: (01243) 785718

8-10 July
Great Yorkshire Show
Great Yorkshire Showground,
Harrogate, North Yorkshire
Contact: (01423) 561536

9-12 July
Claremont Fete Champetre
Claremont Landscape Garden,
Portsmouth Road,
Esher, Surrey
Contact: (01372) 453401

11-13 July*
British Grand Prix 97
Silverstone,
Northamptonshire,
Contact: (01327) 857271

11, 12, 13 July
Swanage Jazz Festival
Various venues,
Swanage, Dorset
Contact: (01929) 422885

11-20 July
"Ways with Words"
Literature Festival
Dartington Hall,
Dartington, Devon
Contact: (01803) 867311

12-13 July
Durham County Show
Clondyke Garden Centre,
Lambton Park,
Chester-Le-Street, Durham
Contact: (0191) 3885459

15-26 July
The Royal Tournament
Earls Court Exhibition Centre,
Warwick Road,
London SW5
Contact: (0171) 370 8202

19 July
Cumberland County Show
Rickerby Park,
Carlisle, Cumbria
Contact: (01228) 560364

19-20 July
Holkham Country Fair
Holkham Hall,
Wells-next-the-Sea, Norfolk
Contact: (01328) 830367

19-27 July
Whitstable Oyster Festival
Whitstable Harbour, Kent
Contact: (01227) 273570

19 July-2 August
King's Lynn Festival 97
King's Lynn Arts Centre,
King Street,
King's Lynn, Norfolk
Contact: (01553) 774725

25 July
Horse Racing: Glorious
Goodwood
Goodwood Racecourse,
Goodwood, West Sussex
Contact: (01243) 774107

26-27 July
Cumbria Steam Gathering
Cark Airfield, Flookburgh,
Cumbria
Contact: (015242) 71584

26-31 July*
Teesside International
Eisteddfod
Middlesbrough Festival Town
Centre,
Middlesbrough,
Tees Valley
Contact: (01642) 327088

1-8 August
43rd Sidmouth International
Festival of Folk Arts
The Arena and other Venues,
Sidmouth, Devon

2-9 August
Cowes Week
Cowes, Isle of Wight
Contact: (01983) 293303

2-17 August
International Gilbert and
Sullivan Festival
Buxton Opera House,
Water Street,
Buxton, Derbyshire
Contact: (01422) 359161

6-7 August
167th Bakewell Show
The Showground, Coombs Road,
Bakewell, Derbyshire
Contact: (01629) 812736

8-10 August
Bristol International Balloon
Fiesta
Ashton Court Estate,
Long Ashton, Bristol
Contact: (0117) 953 5884

8-10 August
Lowther Horse Driving
Trials and Country Fair
Lowther Castle,
Lowther, Cumbria
Contact: (01931) 712378

417

9-16 August*
Billingham International Folklore Festival
Queensway, Billingham,
Tees Valley
Contact: (01642) 558212

15-16 August
Shrewsbury Flower Show
Quarry Park, Shrewsbury,
Shropshire
Contact: (01743) 364051

15-17 August
International Birdwatching Fair
Egleton Reserve, Rutland Water,
Oakham, Leicestershire
Contact: (01572) 770651

15-17 August
Northampton Hot Air Balloon Festival
Northampton Racecourse,
St. George's Avenue,
Northampton, Northamptonshire
Contact: (01604) 233500

16-22 August
Whitby Folk Week
Various venues,
Whitby, North Yorkshire
Contact: (01757) 708424

20 August
Weymouth Carnival
The Seafront, Weymouth, Dorset
Contact: (01305) 772444

20-22 August
Ladies British Amateur Stroke Play Championships
Silloth-on-Solway Golf Club,
The Clubhouse, Silloth, Cumbria
Contact: (016973) 31304

21-26 August
International Beatles Festival
Various venues,
Liverpool, Merseyside
Contact: (0151) 236 9091

22-25 August
Clacton Jazz Festival
Various venues,
Clacton-on-Sea, Essex
Contact: (01255) 425501

23-30 August
Bude Jazz Festival
Various venues, Bude, Cornwall
Contact: (01684) 566956

24 August
Leicester International Air Display
Leicester Airport, Gartree Road,
Leicester, Leicestershire
Contact: (0116) 259 2360

24-25 August
Eye Show
Eye Show Ground, Dragon Hill,
Eye, Suffolk
Contact: (01379) 870224

25 August
Mathew Street Festival
Cavern Quarter,
Liverpool City Centre,
Mathew Street,
Liverpool
Contact: (0151) 236 9091

27-31 August
Great Dorset Steam Fair
South Down,
Tarrant Hinton, Dorset
Contact: (01258) 860361

28 August
Buckinghamshire County Show
Weedon Park, Weedon,
Aylesbury, Buckinghamshire
Contact: (01296) 83734

28 August
Muncaster Country Fair and Sheepdog Trials
Muncaster, Ravenglass,
Cumbria
Contact: (01229) 717608

29-31 August
Shepway Festival
The Leas, Folkestone, Kent
Contact: (01303) 852321

30 August
Hesket Newmarket Agricultural Show
Hog House Field, Hudscales,
Hesket Newmarket, Cumbria
Contact: (016974) 78663

September 1997

4 September
The Blenheim International Horse Trials
Blenheim Palace,
Woodstock, Oxfordshire
Contact: (01993) 813335

5-7 September
Swanage Folk Festival
Various venues,
Swanage, Dorset
Contact: (01929) 427490

6-7 September
Chatsworth Country Fair
Chatsworth House and Garden,
Bakewell, Derbyshire
Contact: (01328) 830367

6-7 September
Kirby Lonsdale Victorian Fair
Kirkby Lonsdale,
Cumbria
Contact: (015242) 71237

13 September
Romsey Show
Broadlands Park,
Romsey, Hampshire
Contact: (01794) 517521

13-14 September
Essex Steam Rally and Craft Fair
Barleylands Farm Museum,
Billericay, Essex
Contact: (01268) 532253

13-15 September*
Stanhope Agricultural Show
Unthank Park,
Stanhope, Durham
Contact: (01833) 650879

13-21 September
Southampton International Boat Show
Western Esplanade,
Southampton, Hampshire
Contact: (01784) 473377

14-20 September
Egremont Crab Fair and Sports
Baybarrow, Egremont, Cumbria
Contact: (01946) 821554

20-21 September
Newbury and Royal County of Berkshire Show
Newbury Showground,
Chieveley, Berkshire
Contact: (01635) 247111

28 September
Urswick Rushbearing
Urswick Church, Urswick,
Ulverston, Cumbria

October 1997

1-5 October
Horse of the Year Show
Wembley Arena, Empire Way,
Wembley, London
Contact: (01203) 693088

9-19 October
Norfolk and Norwich Festival 97
Various venues,
Norwich, Norfolk
Contact: (01603) 614921

10-18 October*
Hull Fair
Walton Street Fairground, Hull,
Kingston-upon-Hull
Contact: (01482) 615623

10-19 October
Cheltenham Festival of Literature
Town Hall, Imperial Square,
Cheltenham, Gloucestershire
Contact: (01242) 521621

11-25 October
Canterbury Festival
Various venues,
Canterbury, Kent
Contact: (01227) 455600

12 October
World Conker Championships
The Village Green,
Ashton, Northamptonshire

16-26 October
The London Motor Show
Earls Court Exhibition Centre,
Warwick Road, London SW5

19 October
Trafalgar Day Parade - The Sea Cadet Corps
Trafalgar Square, London WC2
Contact: (0171) 928 8978

November 1997

1 November
Grand Firework Spectacular
Leeds Castle, Leeds, Kent
Contact: (01622) 765400

1 November
Firework Displays
Christchurch Park,
Ipswich, Suffolk

1 November
Bonfire and Firework Display
Meols Hall, Churchtown,
Southport, Merseyside
Contact: (01704) 28326

6 November
Bridgwater Guy Fawkes Carnival
Town Centre,
Bridgwater, Somerset
Contact: (01278) 425344

8 November
Lord Mayor's Show
City of London,
Contact: (01992) 505306

20 November
Biggest Liar in the World Competition
Bridge Inn, Wasdale,
Santon Bridge, Cumbria
Contact: (01946) 67575

December 1997

18-22 December
Olympia International Showjumping Championships
Olympia, Hammersmith Road,
London W14
Contact: (0171) 370 8202

30 December*
Carlisle Races Christmas Meet
Carlisle Racecourse,
Durdar, Cumbria
Contact: (016973) 42634

31 December
Allendale Baal Festival
Market Square, Allendale,
Northumberland
Contact: (01434) 683763

CHECK THE MAPS

The colour maps at the back of this guide show
all the cities, towns and villages for which you will
find accommodation entries.

Refer to the town index to find the page
on which it is listed.

USE YOUR *i*'s

There are more than 550 Tourist Information Centres
throughout England offering friendly help with
accommodation and holiday ideas as well as
suggestions of places to visit and things to do.
You'll find the address of your nearest Tourist
Information Centre in your local Phone Book.

IS IT ACCESSIBLE?

If you are a wheelchair user or someone who has difficulty walking,
look for the national 'Accessible' symbol when choosing where to stay.

All the places that display a symbol have been checked by a Tourist Board inspector
against standard criteria that reflect the practical needs of wheelchair users.

There are three categories of accessibility:

Category 1 Accessible to all wheelchair users including those travelling independently

Category 2 Accessible to a wheelchair user with assistance

Category 3 Accessible to a wheelchair user able to walk short distances
and up at least three steps

Establishments in this guide which have a wheelchair access category
are listed on pages 10 and 11.

ACCOMMODATION COUPONS

▶ *Complete this coupon and mail it direct to the establishment in which you are interested. Do not send it to the English Tourist Board. Remember to enclose a stamped addressed envelope (or international reply coupon).*

▶ *Tick as appropriate and complete the reverse side if you are interested in making a booking.*

❑ *Please send me a brochure or further information, and details of prices charged.*

❑ *Please advise me, as soon as possible, if accommodation is available as detailed overleaf.*

Name: _____ (BLOCK CAPITALS)

Address: _____

_____

Postcode: _____

Telephone number: _____ Date: _____

Where to Stay 1997
Bed & Breakfast, Farmhouses, Inns & Hostels

English Tourist Board

▶ *Complete this coupon and mail it direct to the establishment in which you are interested. Do not send it to the English Tourist Board. Remember to enclose a stamped addressed envelope (or international reply coupon).*

▶ *Tick as appropriate and complete the reverse side if you are interested in making a booking.*

❑ *Please send me a brochure or further information, and details of prices charged.*

❑ *Please advise me, as soon as possible, if accommodation is available as detailed overleaf.*

Name: _____ (BLOCK CAPITALS)

Address: _____

_____

Postcode: _____

Telephone number: _____ Date: _____

Where to Stay 1997
Bed & Breakfast, Farmhouses, Inns & Hostels

English Tourist Board

ACCOMMODATION COUPONS

▶ **Complete this side if you are interested in making a booking.**

▶ **Please read the information on pages 409-413 before confirming any booking.**

Please advise me if accommodation is available as detailed below.

From (date of arrival): _____ To (date of departure): _____

or alternatively from: _____ To: _____

Adults _____ Children _____ (ages _____)
Please give the number of people and ages of children

Accommodation required: _____

_____

_____

Meals required: _____

Other/special requirements: _____

▶ **Please enclose a stamped addressed envelope (or international reply coupon).**

▶ **Complete this side if you are interested in making a booking.**

▶ **Please read the information on pages 409-413 before confirming any booking.**

Please advise me if accommodation is available as detailed below.

From (date of arrival): _____ To (date of departure): _____

or alternatively from: _____ To: _____

Adults _____ Children _____ (ages _____)
Please give the number of people and ages of children

Accommodation required: _____

_____

_____

Meals required: _____

Other/special requirements: _____

▶ **Please enclose a stamped addressed envelope (or international reply coupon).**

ACCOMMODATION COUPONS

► *Complete this coupon and mail it direct to the establishment in which you are interested. Do not send it to the English Tourist Board. Remember to enclose a stamped addressed envelope (or international reply coupon).*

► *Tick as appropriate and complete the reverse side if you are interested in making a booking.*

❑ *Please send me a brochure or further information, and details of prices charged.*
❑ *Please advise me, as soon as possible, if accommodation is available as detailed overleaf.*

Name: _____ *(BLOCK CAPITALS)*

Address: _____

_____

_____ *Postcode:* _____

Telephone number: _____ *Date:* _____

Where to Stay 1997
Bed & Breakfast, Farmhouses, Inns & Hostels

English Tourist Board

► *Complete this coupon and mail it direct to the establishment in which you are interested. Do not send it to the English Tourist Board. Remember to enclose a stamped addressed envelope (or international reply coupon).*

► *Tick as appropriate and complete the reverse side if you are interested in making a booking.*

❑ *Please send me a brochure or further information, and details of prices charged.*
❑ *Please advise me, as soon as possible, if accommodation is available as detailed overleaf.*

Name: _____ *(BLOCK CAPITALS)*

Address: _____

_____

_____ *Postcode:* _____

Telephone number: _____ *Date:* _____

Where to Stay 1997
Bed & Breakfast, Farmhouses, Inns & Hostels

English Tourist Board

ACCOMMODATION COUPONS

▶ **Complete this side if you are interested in making a booking.**

▶ **Please read the information on pages 409-413 before confirming any booking.**

Please advise me if accommodation is available as detailed below.

From (date of arrival): _____ To (date of departure): _____

or alternatively from: _____ To: _____

Adults _____ Children _____ (ages _____)
Please give the number of people and ages of children

Accommodation required: _____

_____

_____

Meals required: _____

Other/special requirements: _____

▶ **Please enclose a stamped addressed envelope (or international reply coupon).**

▶ **Complete this side if you are interested in making a booking.**

▶ **Please read the information on pages 409-413 before confirming any booking.**

Please advise me if accommodation is available as detailed below.

From (date of arrival): _____ To (date of departure): _____

or alternatively from: _____ To: _____

Adults _____ Children _____ (ages _____)
Please give the number of people and ages of children

Accommodation required: _____

_____

_____

Meals required: _____

Other/special requirements: _____

▶ **Please enclose a stamped addressed envelope (or international reply coupon).**

ACCOMMODATION COUPONS

▶ **Complete this coupon and mail it direct to the establishment in which you are interested. Do not send it to the English Tourist Board. Remember to enclose a stamped addressed envelope (or international reply coupon).**

▶ **Tick as appropriate and complete the reverse side if you are interested in making a booking.**

❑ *Please send me a brochure or further information, and details of prices charged.*
❑ *Please advise me, as soon as possible, if accommodation is available as detailed overleaf.*

Name: _____ (BLOCK CAPITALS)

Address: _____

_____

_____ Postcode: _____

Telephone number: _____ Date: _____

Where to Stay 1997
Bed & Breakfast, Farmhouses, Inns & Hostels

English Tourist Board

▶ **Complete this coupon and mail it direct to the establishment in which you are interested. Do not send it to the English Tourist Board. Remember to enclose a stamped addressed envelope (or international reply coupon).**

▶ **Tick as appropriate and complete the reverse side if you are interested in making a booking.**

❑ *Please send me a brochure or further information, and details of prices charged.*
❑ *Please advise me, as soon as possible, if accommodation is available as detailed overleaf.*

Name: _____ (BLOCK CAPITALS)

Address: _____

_____

_____ Postcode: _____

Telephone number: _____ Date: _____

Where to Stay 1997
Bed & Breakfast, Farmhouses, Inns & Hostels

English Tourist Board

ACCOMMODATION COUPONS

▶ **Complete this side if you are interested in making a booking.**

▶ **Please read the information on pages 409–413 before confirming any booking.**

Please advise me if accommodation is available as detailed below.

From (date of arrival): _____   To (date of departure): _____

or alternatively from: _____   To: _____

Adults _____ Children _____   (ages _____)
Please give the number of people and ages of children

Accommodation required: _____

_____

_____

Meals required: _____

Other/special requirements: _____

▶ **Please enclose a stamped addressed envelope (or international reply coupon).**

▶ **Complete this side if you are interested in making a booking.**

▶ **Please read the information on pages 409–413 before confirming any booking.**

Please advise me if accommodation is available as detailed below.

From (date of arrival): _____   To (date of departure): _____

or alternatively from: _____   To: _____

Adults _____ Children _____   (ages _____)
Please give the number of people and ages of children

Accommodation required: _____

_____

_____

Meals required: _____

Other/special requirements: _____

▶ **Please enclose a stamped addressed envelope (or international reply coupon).**

ADVERTISEMENT COUPONS

► *Complete this coupon and mail it direct to the advertiser from whom you would like to receive further information. Do not send it to the English Tourist Board.*

To (advertiser's name):

_____

Please send me a brochure or further information on the following, as advertised by you in the English Tourist Board's **Where to Stay 1997** *Guide:*

_____

_____

► *Complete this coupon and mail it direct to the advertiser from whom you would like to receive further information. Do not send it to the English Tourist Board.*

To (advertiser's name):

_____

Please send me a brochure or further information on the following, as advertised by you in the English Tourist Board's **Where to Stay 1997** *Guide:*

_____

_____

► *Complete this coupon and mail it direct to the advertiser from whom you would like to receive further information. Do not send it to the English Tourist Board.*

To (advertiser's name):

_____

Please send me a brochure or further information on the following, as advertised by you in the English Tourist Board's **Where to Stay 1997** *Guide:*

_____

_____

ADVERTISEMENT COUPONS

Name: _____ (BLOCK CAPITALS)

Address: _____

_____

_____ Postcode: _____

Telephone Number: _____ Date: _____

Where to Stay 1997
Bed & Breakfast, Farmhouses, Inns & Hostels

English Tourist Board

Name: _____ (BLOCK CAPITALS)

Address: _____

_____

_____ Postcode: _____

Telephone Number: _____ Date: _____

Where to Stay 1997
Bed & Breakfast, Farmhouses, Inns & Hostels

English Tourist Board

Name: _____ (BLOCK CAPITALS)

Address: _____

_____

_____ Postcode: _____

Telephone Number: _____ Date: _____

Where to Stay 1997
Bed & Breakfast, Farmhouses, Inns & Hostels

English Tourist Board

ADVERTISEMENT COUPONS

▶ **Complete this coupon and mail it direct to the advertiser from whom you would like to receive further information. Do not send it to the English Tourist Board.**

To (advertiser's name): _____

Please send me a brochure or further information on the following, as advertised by you in the English Tourist Board's **Where to Stay 1997** Guide:

_____

_____

▶ **Complete this coupon and mail it direct to the advertiser from whom you would like to receive further information. Do not send it to the English Tourist Board.**

To (advertiser's name): _____

Please send me a brochure or further information on the following, as advertised by you in the English Tourist Board's **Where to Stay 1997** Guide:

_____

_____

▶ **Complete this coupon and mail it direct to the advertiser from whom you would like to receive further information. Do not send it to the English Tourist Board.**

To (advertiser's name): _____

Please send me a brochure or further information on the following, as advertised by you in the English Tourist Board's **Where to Stay 1997** Guide:

_____

_____

ADVERTISEMENT COUPONS

Name: _____ (BLOCK CAPITALS)

Address: _____

_____

_____ Postcode: _____

Telephone Number: _____ Date: _____

Where to Stay 1997
Bed & Breakfast, Farmhouses, Inns & Hostels

English Tourist Board

Name: _____ (BLOCK CAPITALS)

Address: _____

_____

_____ Postcode: _____

Telephone Number: _____ Date: _____

Where to Stay 1997
Bed & Breakfast, Farmhouses, Inns & Hostels

English Tourist Board

Name: _____ (BLOCK CAPITALS)

Address: _____

_____

_____ Postcode: _____

Telephone Number: _____ Date: _____

Where to Stay 1997
Bed & Breakfast, Farmhouses, Inns & Hostels

English Tourist Board

COUNTRY CODE

Always follow the Country Code ❧ Enjoy the countryside and respect its life and work ❧ Guard against all risk of fire ❧ Fasten all gates ❧ Keep your dogs under close control ❧ Keep to public paths across farmland ❧ Use gates and stiles to cross fences, hedges and walls ❧ Leave livestock, crops and machinery alone ❧ Take your litter home ❧ Help to keep all water clean ❧ Protect wildlife, plants and trees ❧ Take special care on country roads ❧ Make no unnecessary noise

USE YOUR *i*'s

There are more than 550 Tourist Information Centres
throughout England offering friendly help with
accommodation and holiday ideas as well as
suggestions of places to visit and things to do.
You'll find the address of your nearest Tourist
Information Centre in your local Phone Book.

CHECK THE MAPS

The colour maps at the back of this guide show

all the cities, towns and villages for which you will

find accommodation entries.

Refer to the town index to find the page

on which it is listed.

MILEAGE CHART

The distances between towns on the mileage chart are given to the nearest mile, and are measured along routes based on the quickest travelling time, making maximum use of motorways or dual-carriageway roads. The chart is based upon information supplied by the Automobile Association.

Cities (diagonal labels, in order): Aberdeen, Aberystwyth, Barnstaple, Birmingham, Brighton, Bristol, Cambridge, Cardiff, Carlisle, Carmarthen, Colchester, Dorchester, Dover, Edinburgh, Exeter, Fort William, Glasgow, Gloucester, Guildford, Holyhead, Hull, Inverness, Kendal, Leeds, Lincoln, Liverpool, Maidstone, Manchester, Middlesbrough, Newcastle, Norwich, Nottingham, Oxford, Penzance, Perth, Plymouth, Sheffield, Southampton, Stranraer, Taunton, York, London

To	Distances
Aberystwyth	468
Barnstaple	603 211
Birmingham	431 123 178
Brighton	606 285 206 171
Bristol	514 128 100 88 169
Cambridge	462 214 267 97 120 171
Cardiff	534 117 129 108 203 46 205
Carlisle	232 236 372 196 375 282 257 302
Carmarthen	517 50 190 169 264 107 266 67 285
Colchester	515 289 291 171 112 195 48 229 310 290
Dorchester	596 203 94 170 121 62 180 121 364 182 208
Dover	586 325 272 207 81 206 124 239 401 300 116 201
Edinburgh	125 335 471 296 474 382 334 401 99 384 387 463 458
Exeter	587 195 55 161 176 84 251 113 356 174 276 54 244 455
Fort William	156 446 582 406 584 492 467 511 209 495 520 574 611 133 566
Glasgow	147 332 468 293 471 379 354 398 96 381 407 461 498 47 452 102
Gloucester	479 111 126 53 155 36 150 66 247 127 170 118 292 346 110 457 343
Guildford	564 222 174 128 44 106 91 139 332 200 103 98 97 431 147 541 428 100
Holyhead	460 105 341 165 344 251 260 206 228 155 334 333 370 327 325 438 324 216 301
Hull	361 227 321 134 260 231 139 251 170 312 192 313 264 232 305 380 266 196 239 218
Inverness	106 494 630 455 633 540 516 560 258 543 569 622 659 157 614 65 173 505 591 485 428
Kendal	279 190 326 150 329 236 245 256 47 239 319 318 355 146 310 257 143 201 286 181 164 305
Leeds	328 173 309 115 262 220 148 253 122 222 199 302 271 199 293 332 219 185 220 165 59 318 72
Lincoln	387 201 276 99 208 187 88 206 182 267 141 245 212 258 260 392 278 152 166 204 47 440 176 72
Liverpool	358 111 274 99 277 184 193 204 126 167 267 266 303 225 258 335 222 149 234 103 128 384 79 74 140
Maidstone	547 283 233 168 50 167 85 200 362 261 77 162 41 419 206 572 458 153 58 330 225 620 316 233 173 264
Manchester	352 131 262 86 264 172 160 191 120 180 213 254 291 220 246 330 216 137 222 122 98 378 74 44 85 35 249
Middlesbrough	276 244 359 172 319 269 199 288 95 293 352 351 322 148 343 281 191 234 277 235 89 308 84 64 123 144 281 114
Newcastle	234 284 389 202 350 300 229 319 59 323 282 381 354 105 373 238 153 265 307 265 142 266 101 95 154 175 311 145 39
Norwich	487 276 329 159 169 233 63 267 282 328 59 242 173 359 313 492 378 212 161 321 150 540 276 172 103 240 131 185 223 264
Nottingham	393 160 235 53 195 145 86 164 188 226 124 219 198 284 110 153 74 198 176 71 160 118 103
Oxford	503 159 170 68 109 74 81 107 271 168 124 115 146 370 154 481 367 48 67 239 189 529 225 171 130 173 106 161 227 257 161 103
Penzance	697 305 110 271 288 194 361 223 466 284 386 166 356 565 110 675 561 219 259 433 414 724 419 403 369 367 317 355 451 482 423 328 264
Perth	86 382 518 343 521 428 379 448 146 431 432 510 504 42 502 102 61 393 479 373 277 441 235 89 308 84 64 311 418 612
Plymouth	628 236 61 202 219 125 292 154 397 214 317 97 287 496 45 606 492 150 190 364 345 655 350 334 300 298 248 286 382 413 354 259 195 78 543
Sheffield	366 167 272 86 233 183 122 202 162 263 175 265 247 238 257 371 258 148 191 158 65 420 125 36 47 79 204 38 103 133 147 44 141 366 283 297
Southampton	570 221 140 137 23 130 158 86 338 188 118 71 160 484 152 207 240 293 324 193 170 66 221 237 196 118 ...
Stranraer	342 478 303 481 388 363 408 106 391 417 470 507 133 462 186 84 353 438 333 276 265 153 229 288 232 465 226 201 163 389 295 378 572 153 503 268 444
Taunton	555 162 50 129 158 51 218 80 323 141 243 45 224 422 34 533 419 77 126 291 272 581 277 260 227 225 184 212 309 340 280 186 121 144 469 75 223 91 429
York	321 201 316 129 276 156 245 117 250 209 308 280 193 300 326 213 191 234 192 38 375 91 25 81 102 238 72 50 88 181 87 184 410 238 341 60 251 223 267
London	545 238 216 120 59 120 60 153 314 221 34 62 129 417 162 523 409 102 30 281 187 572 267 199 136 215 38 203 254 285 115 36 310 460 241 168 80 419 167 211

CUSTOMER FEEDBACK QUESTIONNAIRE

We hope you have found this guide useful in selecting accommodation in England which suits your needs.

It is very helpful to the English Tourist Board to receive comments about establishments in *Where to Stay* and suggestions on how to improve the guide, and also on the National Grading and Classification Schemes.

We would like to hear from you. If you wish to do so, you can send us your views using this questionnaire. You need not name the establishment concerned.

Q1 Did you use the *Where to Stay* guide to find:

Holiday accommodation ☐

Business accommodation ☐

Both ☐

Q2 Did you use the establishment's Quality Grading/Crown or Key Classification to help you in making your choice?

Yes ☐

No ☐

Q3 If you did, was it the Quality Grading (Approved, Commended, Highly Commended or De Luxe) or the number of Crowns or Keys for facilities that influenced you most?

The Quality Grading ☐

The number of Crowns/Keys ☐

Both ☐

Q4 What was the Quality Grading and Crown or Key Classification of the establishment you chose?

....

Q5 Do you find the National Grades and Classifications:

Very easy to understand ☐

Fairly easy to understand ☐

Difficult to understand ☐

If you find them difficult to understand, please specify why:

....

....

Q6 Was the accommodation you used:

Hotel ☐

Guesthouse ☐

Farmhouse ☐

Bed & Breakfast ☐

Self-Catering Holiday Home ☐

Q7 Did the establishment chosen:

Exceed your expectations ☐

Meet your expectations ☐

Fail to meet your expectations ☐

If it failed to meet your expectations, please specify how:

....

....

Q8 Would you say the establishment offered good value for money?

Yes ☐

No ☐

Q9 Was there any feature of your stay that you would particularly praise or criticise (please specify):

....

....

....

Q10 Have you bought a *Where to Stay* guide before?

Yes ☐

No ☐

If yes, how long ago:

Last year ☐

2 years ago ☐

More than 2 years ago ☐

Q11 Did you find the *Where to Stay* guide:

Very easy to use ☐

Fairly easy to use ☐

Difficult to use ☐

Q12 Are there any aspects of the *Where to Stay* guide that you would particularly praise or criticise (please specify):

....

....

....

Q13 Is there any additional information not already featured in this guide that you would find helpful (please specify):

....

....

....

Please would you give us a few details about yourself:

Q14 Are you:

Married ☐

Single ☐

Q15 Do you have dependent children?

Yes ☐

No ☐

If yes, how many ☐

Q16 Into which age group do you fall?

17-24 ☐

25-34 ☐

35-44 ☐

45-54 ☐

55+ ☐

Q17 Are you an overseas visitor (i.e. from outside the UK visiting this country)?

Yes ☐

No ☐

Q18 Did you travel alone or with a party?

Alone ☐

Party of people ☐

of which   were adults

and   children

Q19 How long did you stay in the establishment?

                                        nights

Q20 Do you plan to use the guide to book any further stays this year?

Yes ☐

No ☐

If yes, how many ☐

Q21 What other sources of information did you use in selecting your accommodation (please specify):

....

....

Q22 Did you obtain your copy of *Where to Stay* from

Bookshop ☐

Tourist Information Centre ☐

Other (please specify) ☐

Thank you for giving us your views. Please return this questionnaire to: Department AS, English Tourist Board, Thames Tower, Black's Road, Hammersmith, London W6 9EL.

LOCATION MAPS

Every place name featured in the accommodation listings pages of this *Where to Stay* guide has a map reference to help you locate it on the maps which follow. For example, to find Colchester, Essex, which has 'Map ref 3B2', turn to Map 3 and refer to grid square B2.

All place names in the listings pages are shown in black type on the maps. This enables you to find other places in your chosen area which may have suitable accommodation - the Town Index (preceding pages) gives page numbers.

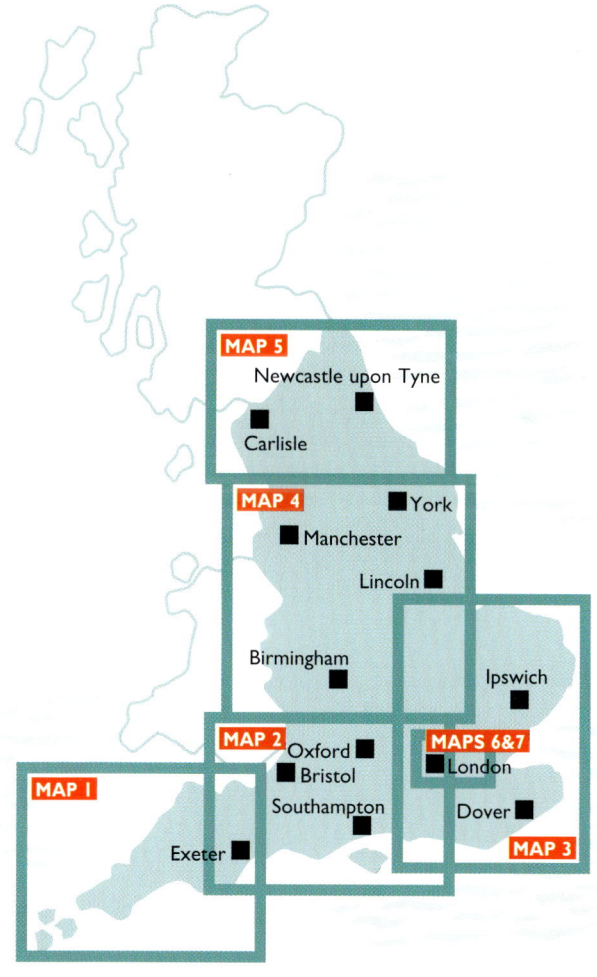

MAP I

A

B

I

2

3

Boscastle
Tintagel
St Kew
A39
A30
Bodmin
Newquay
Newquay
A392
A30
A390
A391
Golant
St Austell
Goonhavern
St Agnes
A39
Grampound
Mevagissey
Truro
A390
Mylor
Bridge
A30
A39
St Just-
in-Penwith
Perranuthnoe
A394
Falmouth
Penzance
Sennen Cove
Helston

Isles of Scilly
Isles of Scilly
(St. Mary's)

MAP I

C **D**

M4

Clevedon
NORTH SOMERSET
Weston-super-Mare
Churchill
A370
A38
Cheddar
Mark
Burnham-on-Sea
A370
M5
Greinton
A361

Ilfracombe
Lynton
Allerford
Minehead
Mortehoe
Challacombe
EXMOOR
Dunster
Kilve
Combwich
Croyde
Kingsheanton
EXFORD
Exford
Luxborough
A39
Bridgwater
Croyde Bay
A39
NATIONAL PARK
Winsford
SOMERSET
Barnstaple
A399
Dulverton
A308
Bishop's Lydeard
Hartland
Clovelly
Bideford
South Molton
West Anstey
Taunton
Morwenstow
A39
Chulmleigh
A361
Wellington
A358
Bradworthy
A377
Tiverton
Hemyock
A303
South Petherton
Bude
A39
DEVON
Cullompton
Bishopswood
Crewkerne
A386
Holsworthy
Crediton
M5
Yarcombe
Chard
A30
Bridgerule
A386
Clawton
Silverton
A373
A35
Crackington Haven
Ashwater
Okehampton
Longdown
Whimple
Fenny Bridges
Honiton
A335
Bridestowe
A30
Exeter
Ottery St Mary
Colyton
Launceston
Lewdown
Doddiscombsleigh
Exeter
A30
Lyme Regis
CORNWALL
Moretonhampstead
DARTMOOR
Lustleigh
A376
Beer
Postbridge
NATIONAL PARK
Sidmouth
St Neot
A390
Peter Tavy
Widecombe-in-the-Moor
A360
Exmouth
Liskeard
Tavistock
Holne
Ashburton
A38
Pillaton
A386
Yelverton
Buckfastleigh
A38
Plymouth City
Torquay
PLYMOUTH
Ivybridge
Totnes
Paignton
Looe
A38
Newton Ferrers
A379
East Allington
Brixham
Noss Mayo
A381
Dartmouth
Kingsbridge
Salcombe

Roscoff

Santander

N

0   25 Miles
0   40 Kilometres

Produced by COLIN EARL Cartography

443

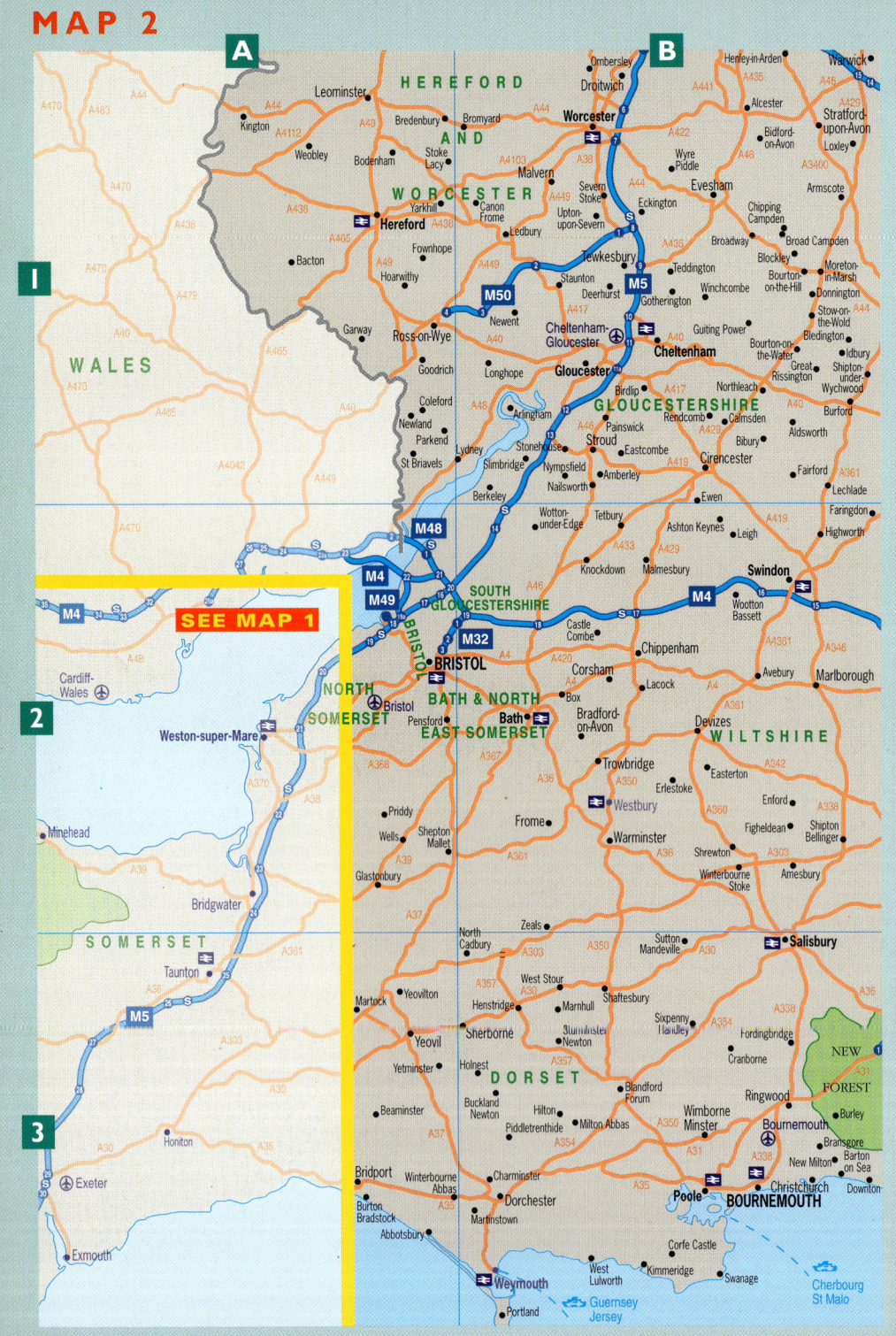

MAP 2

MAP 2

Produced by COLIN EARL Cartography

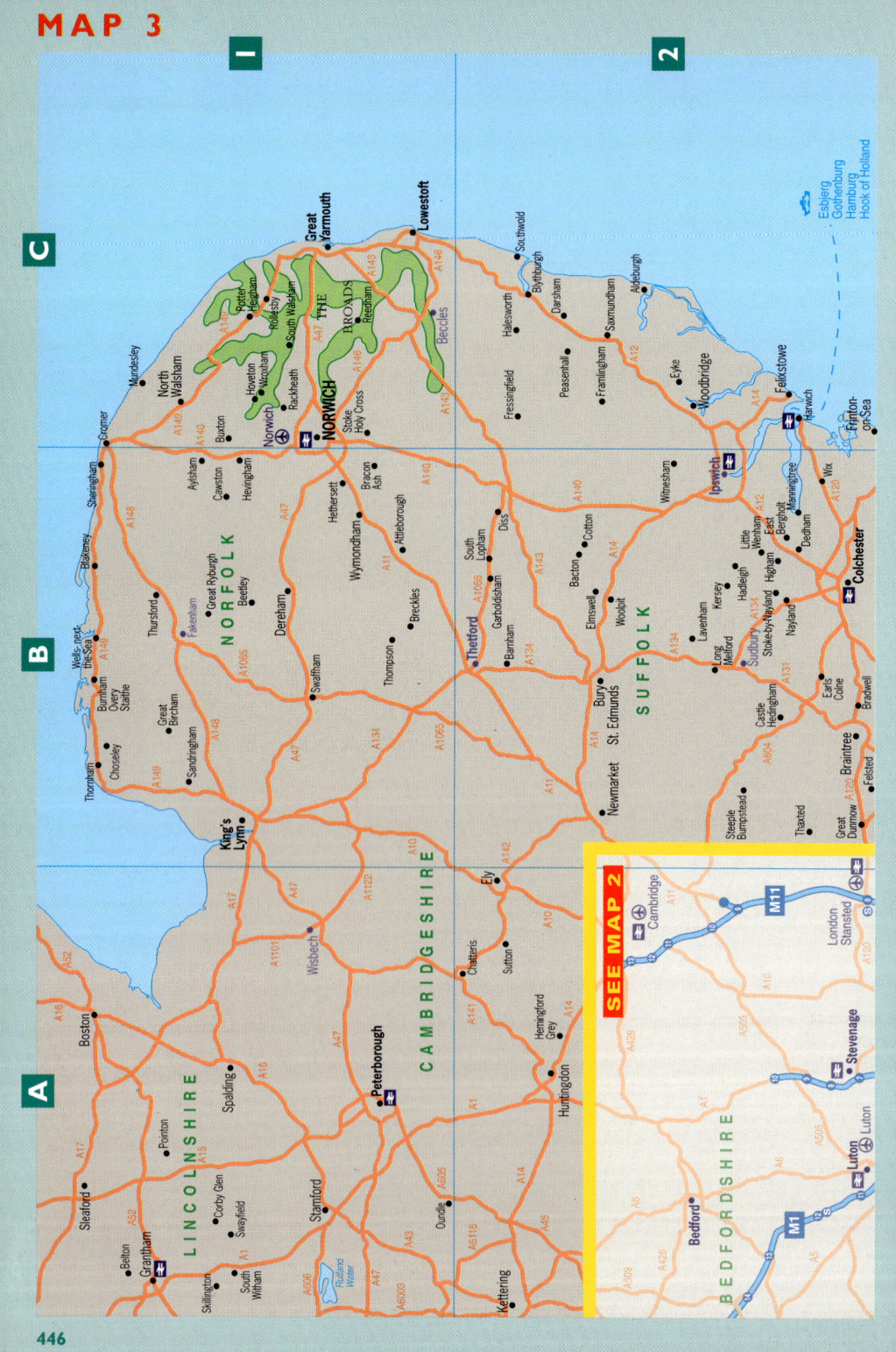

MAP 3

MAP 3

MAP 4

MAP 4

C · D

YORK

EAST RIDING OF YORKSHIRE

KINGSTON UPON HULL · **HULL**

NORTH LINCOLNSHIRE

M62 · **M180**

Humberside · **Grimsby** · Cleethorpes

NORTH EAST LINCOLNSHIRE

Rotterdam Zeebrugge

25 Miles
40 Kilometres

N

YORKSHIRE · **A1(M)**

Doncaster

Gainsborough · Fillingham · Kexby · Ludford · **Louth**

Worksop

Saxilby · Ragnall · **Lincoln** · Hagworthingham · Raithby

LINCOLNSHIRE

Edwinstowe · Kirton · Coningsby · **Skegness**

M1 · **Mansfield**

NOTTINGHAMSHIRE

Southwell · **Newark** · Lambley · Aslockton

NOTTINGHAM

Cotgrave

East Midlands · Upper Broughton · Melton Mowbray

Loughborough · Mountsorrel

LEICESTERSHIRE · Oakham

LEICESTER · Uppingham

M69 · Elmesthorpe · Broughton Astley · Medbourne · Middleton · Foxton

M1 · Bruntingthorpe · Husbands Bosworth · Market Harborough

M6 · **Rugby** · Dunchurch · Guilsborough

M45 · West Haddon · Long Buckby · Ashby St Ledgers

NORTHAMPTONSHIRE

SEE MAP 3

Boston · Grantham · King's Lynn

Stamford · Peterborough

CAMBRIDGESHIRE

Kettering · Ely · Huntingdon

Produced by COLIN EARL Cartography

449

MAP 5

A   **B**

I

2

3

SCOTLAND

M74

A74(M)

A721
A703
A702
A72
A7
A697
A58
A7
A58
A701
A74
A76
A74(M)
A75

Berwick-upon-Tweed
Norham
Holy Island
Crookham
Lowick
A1
Eglingham
Glanton
A697

NORTHUMBERLAND
NATIONAL PARK
Rothbury
Otterburn

NORTHUMBERLAND

Kielder Forest
Kielder Water
West Woodburn
A696
A68

Longtown
A6071
Carlisle
Brampton
Haltwhistle
Bardon Mill
Hexham
Corbridge
Wylam
A69
A7
Scotby
A683
A686
Shotley Bridge
Consett

Carlisle
M6
A596
Rosley
Welton
A6
A686
Edmundbyers
A68

Caldbeck
Cowshill
A689
A68
Lazonby
St John's Chapel

Bassenthwaite
Penrith
DURHAM

Workington
A66
A66
Appleby-in-Westmorland
A66
Middleton-in-Teesdale
Staindrop
Lorton
Troutbeck
Cotherstone
A688
Loweswater
Keswick
Ullswater
Barnard Castle
A66
Borrowdale
A591
A592
St Bees
Kirkby Stephen
Rannington
Lamplugh
A685
Arkengarthdale
A595
Grasmere
Orton
A6
Tebay
Wasdale
LAKE DISTRICT
Ambleside
Troutbeck
A685
CUMBRIA
NATIONAL PARK
Staveley
Hawkshead
Eskdale
Coniston
Windermere
Grayrigg
Askrigg
Redmire
Leyburn
Sawrey
Hawes
A684
Broughton-in-Furness
Kendal
Oxenholme
M6
Dent
YORKSHIRE DALES
Oxen Park
Cartmel Fell
Levens
Starbotton
Silecroft
Kirkby-in-Furness
Heversham
Holme
NATIONAL PARK
Cartmel
Arnside
A590
A6
Ireleton
Barrow-in-Furness
A590
Carnforth
Bentham
Giggleswick
Grassington
Morecambe
A683
A65
Settle
Malham
Lancaster

450

MAP 5

C

D

25 Miles
0
40 Kilometres
0

N

Amsterdam
Bergen
Esbjerg
Gothenburg
Hamburg
Haugesund
Stavanger

Bamburgh
Seahouses
A1
Embleton
Craster
Alnwick
Lesbury
Alnmouth
Warkworth
A1068
A697
Morpeth
A1
A189
A696
Whitley Bay
A19
Newcastle
NEWCASTLE
UPON TYNE
Tynemouth
Ryton
Gateshead
TYNE
AND WEAR
A692
A602
Tanfield
65
SUNDERLAND
64
Stanley
Beamish
Washington
63
Chester-
le-Street
A690
A691
Durham
62
A19
A167
61
Spennymoor
A688
A68
Bishop
Auckland
A1(M)
60
A689
A689
Hartlepool
Heighington
Stockton-
on-Tees
TEES VALLEY
Redcar
59
Easington
A171
Darlington
58
MIDDLESBROUGH
Ellerby
Whitby
A66
57
A66
Tees-side
A172
Fylingthorpe
Richmond
Ingleby
Greenhow
Ravenscar
A1
A684
Osmotherley
NORTH YORK MOORS
A169
A171
Hunton
Northallerton
NATIONAL PARK
Middleham
Gillamoor
A66
Thornton
Watlass
Scarborough
Thirsk
Helmsley
Cropton
A170
Pickering
Sutton Bank
A120
NORTH YORKSHIRE
Ampleforth
Nunnington
Coxwold
A188
Ripon
A19
A61
A1(M)
Boroughbridge
Easingwold
Terrington
Malton
A64
Flamborough
Pateley
Bridge
Bishop
Monkton
Myton-
on-Swale
A165
Bishop
Thornton
Flaxton
Westow
A614

MAP 6

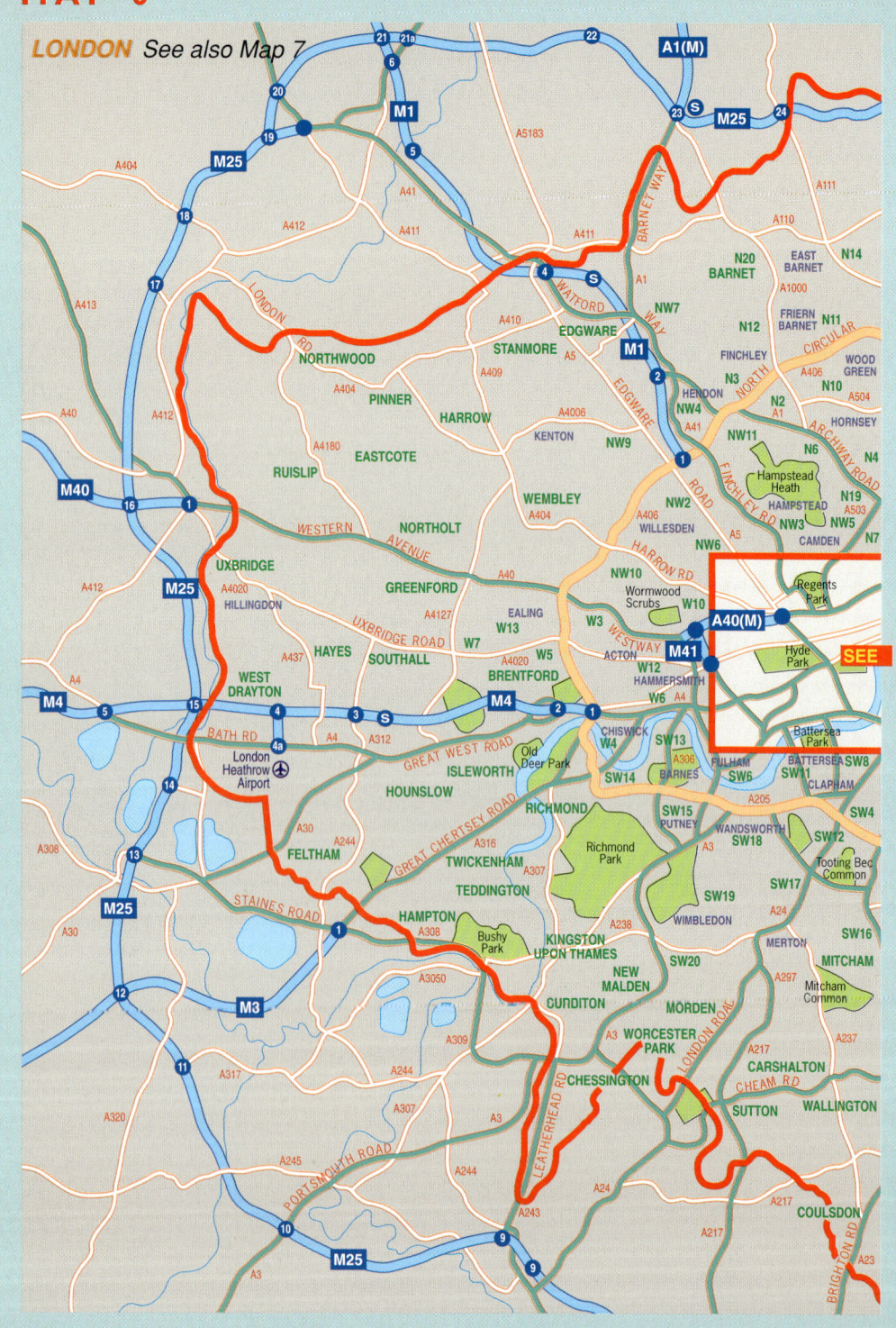

SEE

452

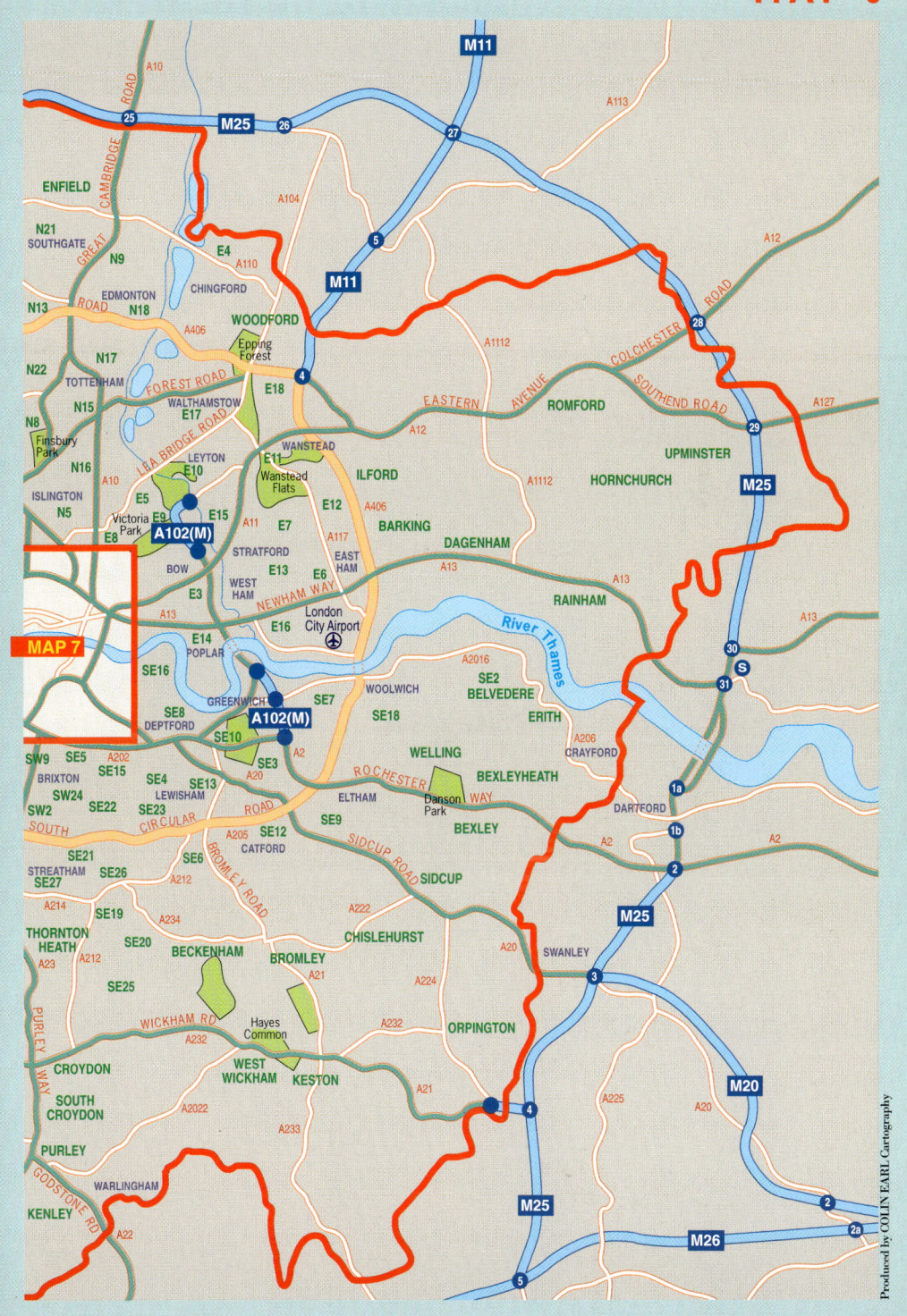

MAP 7

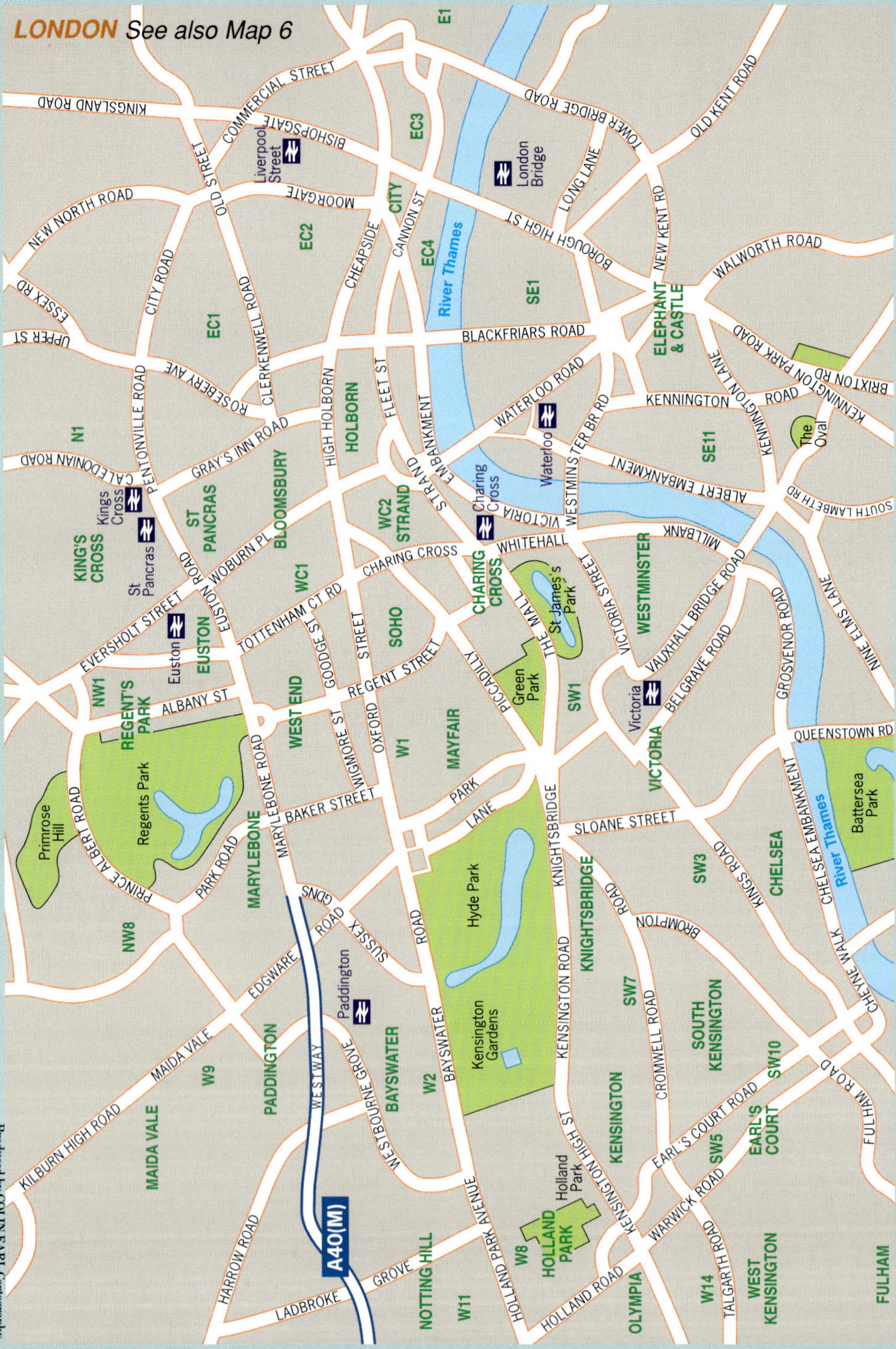
LONDON See also Map 6
KINGSLAND ROAD
COMMERCIAL STREET
BISHOPSGATE
Liverpool Street
EC3
E1
TOWER BRIDGE ROAD
London Bridge
OLD KENT ROAD
LONG LANE
OLD STREET
NEW NORTH ROAD
MOORGATE
CITY
CANNON ST
BOROUGH HIGH ST
NEW KENT RD
EC2
CHEAPSIDE
EC4
River Thames
SE1
WALWORTH ROAD
ESSEX RD
CITY ROAD
EC1
CLERKENWELL ROAD
ELEPHANT & CASTLE
UPPER ST
BLACKFRIARS ROAD
ROSEBERY AVE
HIGH HOLBORN
FLEET ST
WATERLOO ROAD
KENNINGTON LANE
KENNINGTON PARK ROAD
BRIXTON RD
PENTONVILLE ROAD
HOLBORN
EMBANKMENT
KENNINGTON ROAD
N1
GRAY'S INN ROAD
Waterloo
WESTMINSTER BR RD
SE11
The Oval
CALEDONIAN ROAD
BLOOMSBURY
STRAND
Charing Cross
ALBERT EMBANKMENT
Kings Cross
ST PANCRAS
WC2
STRAND
VICTORIA
SOUTH LAMBETH RD
St Pancras
KING'S CROSS
WOBURN PL
CHARING CROSS
WHITEHALL
MILLBANK
EUSTON ROAD
WC1
CHARING CROSS
St James's Park
VICTORIA STREET
WESTMINSTER
EVERSHOLT STREET
TOTTENHAM CT RD
SOHO
THE MALL
VAUXHALL BRIDGE ROAD
GROSVENOR ROAD
NINE ELMS LANE
Euston
EUSTON
GOODGE ST
STREET
PICCADILLY
NW1
REGENT STREET
Green Park
BELGRAVE ROAD
ALBANY ST
REGENT'S PARK
WEST END
Victoria
SW1
QUEENSTOWN RD
MARYLEBONE ROAD
WIGMORE ST
OXFORD
W1
MAYFAIR
VICTORIA
Regents Park
BAKER STREET
PARK
LANE
KNIGHTSBRIDGE
CHELSEA EMBANKMENT
Battersea Park
Primrose Hill
PRINCE ALBERT ROAD
MARYLEBONE
SLOANE STREET
River Thames
PARK ROAD
SW3
KINGS ROAD
CHELSEA
Hyde Park
KNIGHTSBRIDGE
GDNS
SUSSEX
ROAD
BROMPTON ROAD
NW8
EDGWARE ROAD
Paddington
KENSINGTON ROAD
SW7
SOUTH KENSINGTON
CHEYNE WALK
MAIDA VALE
PADDINGTON
BAYSWATER
Kensington Gardens
CROMWELL ROAD
W9
WESTWAY
WESTBOURNE GROVE
W2
BAYSWATER
KENSINGTON
SW10
FULHAM ROAD
KILBURN HIGH ROAD
MAIDA VALE
KENSINGTON HIGH ST
EARL'S COURT ROAD
EARL'S COURT
SW5
Holland Park
HARROW ROAD
A40(M)
HOLLAND PARK AVENUE
HOLLAND PARK
W8
WARWICK ROAD
LADBROKE GROVE
NOTTING HILL
W11
HOLLAND ROAD
OLYMPIA
W14
TALGARTH ROAD
WEST KENSINGTON
FULHAM

Produced by COLIN EARL Cartography

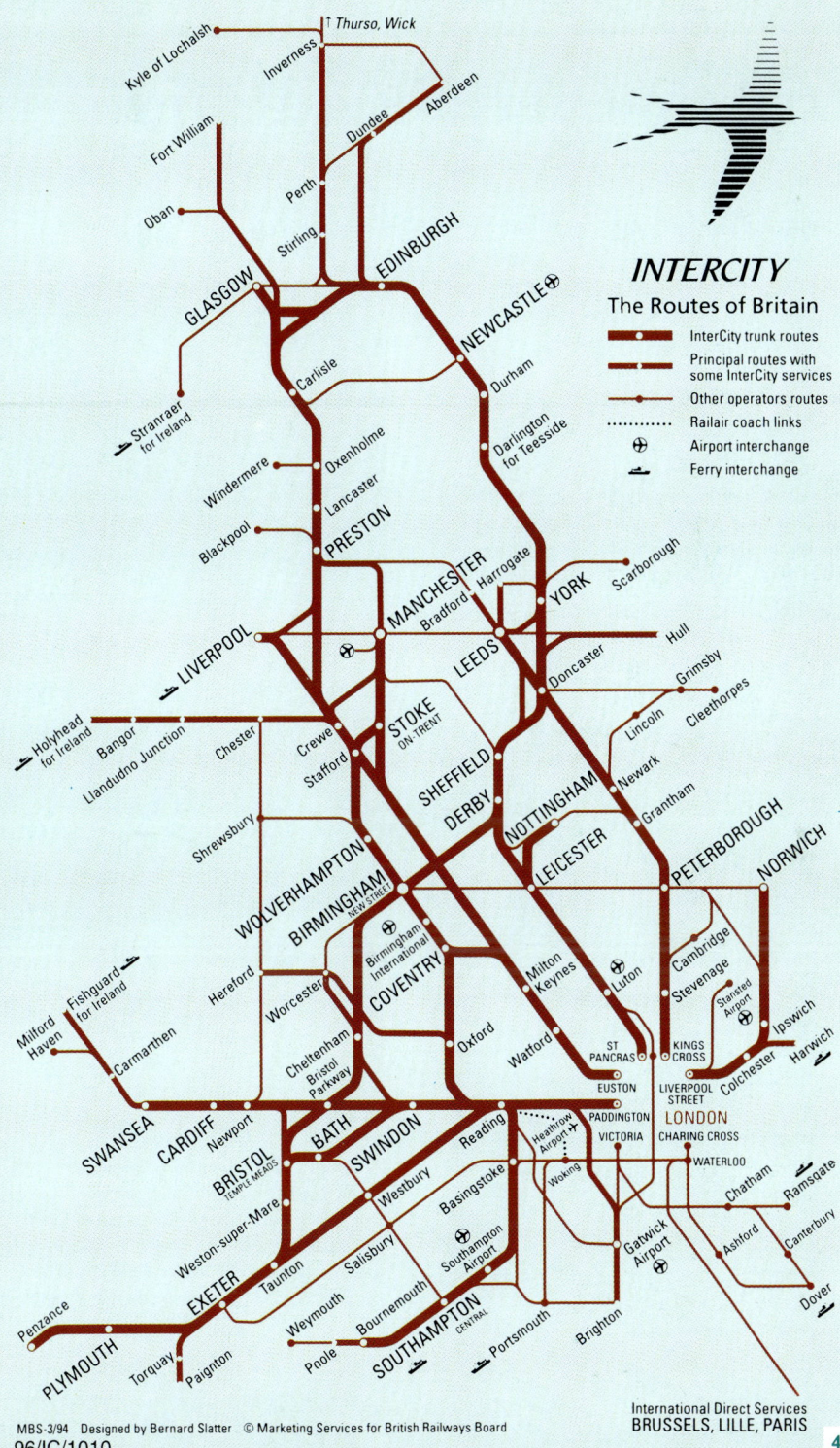

INTERCITY
The Routes of Britain

●━━●	InterCity trunk routes
┿┿┿	Principal routes with some InterCity services
●───	Other operators routes
·······	Railair coach links
✈	Airport interchange
⛴	Ferry interchange

↑ Thurso, Wick

Kyle of Lochalsh
Inverness
Fort William
Dundee
Aberdeen
Oban
Perth
Stirling
GLASGOW
EDINBURGH
NEWCASTLE ✈
Carlisle
Durham
Stranraer for Ireland
Oxenholme
Darlington for Teesside
Windermere
Lancaster
Blackpool
PRESTON
Scarborough
MANCHESTER
Harrogate
Bradford
YORK
LIVERPOOL
LEEDS
Hull
Doncaster
Grimsby
Holyhead for Ireland
Bangor
Chester
Crewe
STOKE ON-TRENT
Lincoln
Cleethorpes
Llandudno Junction
Stafford
SHEFFIELD
Newark
Shrewsbury
DERBY
NOTTINGHAM
Grantham
WOLVERHAMPTON
LEICESTER
PETERBOROUGH
NORWICH
BIRMINGHAM NEW STREET
Hereford
Birmingham International
Cambridge
Worcester
COVENTRY
Stevenage
Milford Haven
Fishguard for Ireland
Milton Keynes
Luton
Stansted Airport
Ipswich
Carmarthen
Cheltenham
Bristol Parkway
Oxford
Watford
ST PANCRAS
KINGS CROSS
Colchester
Harwich
SWANSEA
CARDIFF
Newport
BATH
SWINDON
Reading
EUSTON
LIVERPOOL STREET
LONDON
BRISTOL TEMPLE MEADS
Weston-super-Mare
Westbury
Basingstoke
Heathrow Airport ✈
PADDINGTON
VICTORIA
CHARING CROSS
WATERLOO
Chatham
Ramsgate
Woking
Gatwick Airport ✈
Ashford
Canterbury
Penzance
EXETER
Taunton
Salisbury
Southampton Airport
Weymouth
Bournemouth
Poole
SOUTHAMPTON CENTRAL
Portsmouth
Brighton
Dover
PLYMOUTH
Torquay
Paignton

International Direct Services
BRUSSELS, LILLE, PARIS

YOUR QUICK GUIDE

Where to Stay makes it quick and easy to find a place to stay that offers the standard of quality and facilities you're looking for.

The TOWN INDEX (starting on page 431) and the LOCATION MAPS (starting on page 441) show all cities, towns and villages with accommodation listings in this guide.

1 Town Index

If the place you plan to visit is included in the town index, turn to the page number given to find accommodation available there. Also check that location on the colour maps to find other places nearby which also have accommodation listings in this guide.

1	
Batley West Yorkshire	158
Battlesbridge Essex	317
Beadnell Northumberland	100
Bedale North Yorkshire	158
Bedford Bedfordshire	317
Belford Northumberland	100
Bellingham Northumberland	100
Belper Derbyshire	285
Belton Leicestershire	286
Berkhamsted Hertfordshire	318
Berrynarbor Devon	372
Berwick-upon-Tweed Northumberland	100
Bexhill-on-Sea East Sussex	509
Bexleyheath Greater London	43
Bibury Gloucestershire	217

2 Location Maps

If the place you want is not in the town index - or you only have a general idea of the area in which you wish to stay - use the colour location maps to find places in the area which have accommodation listings in this guide.

When you have found suitable accommodation, check its availability with the establishment and also confirm any other information in the published entry which may be important to you (price, whether bath and/or shower available, children/dogs/credit cards welcome, months open, etc).

If you are happy with everything, make your booking and, if time permits, confirm it in writing.